NUCLEAR WEAPONS AND INTERNATIONAL LAW IN THE POST COLD WAR WORLD

Charles J. Moxley, Jr.

With Forewords by

Robert S. McNamara
David W. Leebron
Kosta Tsipis

Austin & Winfield
Lanham • New York • Oxford

Library of Congress Cataloging-in-Publication Data

Moxley, Charles J.
Nuclear weapons and international law in the post Cold War world /
Charles J. Moxley, J.
p.   cm.
Includes index.
1.   Nuclear weapons (International law) 2. Nuclear nonproliferation. 3.
Nuclear arms control—United States. I. Title.
KZ5665. M69   2000   341.7'34—dc21   00-029866 CIP

ISBN 1-57292-152-8 (cloth: alk: ppr.)

To my Children,
Alicia, Charlie, Katrina and Lenny

TABLE OF CONTENTS

Foreword

by

Robert S. McNamara

In my 1995 book, In *Retrospect: The Tragedy and Lessons of Vietnam*, I spoke of the numerous U.S. government civilian and military leaders who were willing to risk nuclear war during the Cuban Missile Crisis and of the almost cavalier ways in which the possible use of nuclear weapons was spoken of during the Vietnam War. In that book and in *Argument Without End, In Search of Answers to the Vietnam Tragedy* (1999), I also wrote of the extraordinary extent of misinformation, misjudgment, and miscalculation affecting the decisions of the parties to those two confrontations, and how close such failings brought us to disaster. And in *Blundering into Disaster* (1986), I stated that it is inconceivable to me, as it has been to others who have studied the matter, that "limited" nuclear war would remain limited—any decision to initiate the use of nuclear weapons would imply a high probability of the same cataclysmic consequences as a total nuclear exchange. I continue to believe this to be the case. Scenarios of "surgical" use of nuclear weapons in remote areas are unrealistic. Professor Moxley is right, therefore, in his central point that any intentional use of nuclear weapons against a nuclear power, in the types of circumstances in which such weapons might be resorted to, would carry a high risk of escalation to catastrophic levels.

I have for years believed that the use of nuclear weapons on any basis would be immoral and unlawful in the broad sense in which I as a non-lawyer conceive of the matter. Professor Moxley in this book, addressing the technical and policy as well as legal issues, has given us the best exposition that I have seen of the irrationality of the U.S. policy in this area, the irrationality of the policies of the other nuclear weapons states, and the irrationality of the human race in permitting the potential use of these weapons to continue.

I am convinced the American people do not understand the reality of the nuclear weapons policies our leaders are following and that, if they did, they would broadly repudiate them. Our policy of nuclear deterrence effectively puts in the hands of the American President—acting alone, without public debate—the ability to destroy an enemy state and, if that state is a nuclear power, the initiation of action which would lead to suicide for our country. And the nuclear exchange, because of fallout, would cause heavy damage to non-belligerent nations as well.

The United States' refusal to rule out First Use, the Senate's recent rejection of the Comprehensive Test Ban Treaty, the extension of U.S. nuclear deterrent theory to counter chemical and biological weapons threats, the failure to fulfill our obligations under Article VI of the Non-Proliferation Treaty, and the threat to abrogate the Anti-Ballistic Missile Defense Treaty are all disturbing developments begging to be addressed by thoughtful members of our society and leadership.

As I have noted, human beings are fallible. Even with the best of efforts and intentions, we make mistakes. In our daily lives, they are costly but we try to learn from them. In conventional war, they cost lives, sometimes thousands of lives. But if mistakes were to affect decisions relating to the use of nuclear forces, they would result in the destruction of nations. Thus, the indefinite combination of human fallibility and nuclear weapons carries a high risk of a potential catastrophe. There is no military or policy justification for our continuing to accept such risk.

I urge the President and the Congress to investigate the claim Professor Moxley makes that, given all of the risk factors, the use of nuclear weapons is *per se* unlawful under rules of law long recognized by the United States. This is an issue that affects the whole human race and it is incumbent upon us to address it.

Professor Moxley has done us a great service by inviting us to engage this historic opportunity. *Nuclear Weapons and International Law in the Post Cold War World* will be an indispensable reference work for all who wish to debate the issue.

Robert S. McNamara   Washington, D.C.
Secretary of Defense,   March 2000
Johnson and Kennedy Administrations
President of World Bank, 1968-1981

Foreword

by

David W. Leebron

We are undoubtedly at an important time in history. With the end of the Cold War, the end of Apartheid in South Africa, and perhaps soon even a comprehensive formal peace in the Middle East, the threat of the use of nuclear weapons involving the United States seems less likely than at any time in the last fifty years. Yet at the same time, the risks of proliferation and use by others have dramatically escalated, including the possibility that such weapons may come into the hands of those other than governments, such as international terrorists. The science of nuclear weapons production is no longer within the reach of only the most scientifically sophisticated and wealthy nations.

This is a good point in history, then, to reassess the status and legality of nuclear weapons and their use. Four years ago, the International Court of Justice had that opportunity in advisory opinions issued in cases initiated by the United Nations General Assembly and the World Health Organization. Although it can be argued that these opinions substantially advanced the state of international law regarding the use of nuclear weapons, they stopped short of concluding that all such use was contrary to international law. Such an opinion, of course, would have had irresistible implications for the legality of possession of nuclear weapons.

Charles Moxley picks up where the ICJ left off. As he himself says in his Preface, Professor Moxley brings the approach of a litigator to this work. It is not a balanced presentation, but that is not a fault here, for it is not his aim. Rather, Professor Moxley seeks to set forth, as a partisan litigator, the strongest, most comprehensive case for the complete illegality of the use of nuclear weapons. He crafts a relentless brief, interspersing law with scientific analysis of the effect of nuclear weapons and military analysis of their potential use. Most important, he adopts the effective litigating tactic of using the adversary's (in this context the Government of the United States) own words to make the case. Most telling, Professor Moxley masterfully uses documents of the various branches of American armed forces to bolster the argument that international law, and in particular, the law of war, prohibits the use of nuclear weapons.

This is a bold and provocative work, and will be controversial. Not all (including me) will agree with all the arguments made or the conclusions Professor Moxley draws from those arguments and the evidence he marshals. But this comprehensive and ambitious work must undoubtedly figure in the future debates on this most important of subjects. Nuclear weapons remain unique in the world today. It is a world that has changed greatly since their first use, and arguably in ways that makes the military use of such weapons harder to justify than ever. Professor Moxley seizes this moment to set forth the arguments that require a response.

David W. Leebron
Dean and Lucy G. Moses Professor of Law
Columbia University

Foreword

by

Kosta Tsipis

The very term "nuclear weapons" turns out to be an oxymoron. A weapon is a device, a tool used in combat, the commonest method for resolving conflict. More or better weapons possession by one of the combatants allows him to create an asymmetrical final state: a winner and a loser. The conflict is resolved, for a while anyway, by the winner imposing his will on the loser. But combat with nuclear weapons cannot lead to an asymmetrical outcome: both combatants are equally destroyed. The final state is symmetrical; there is no winner and loser. So nuclear weapons cannot resolve conflict. Therefore, they are not weapons.

Neither is it possible to generate a final asymmetry by limited use, or gradual escalation of nuclear combat. One party in conflict wins once it has inflicted enough damage or pain beyond the threshold of tolerance of the opponent, at which point the opponent capitulates. So whoever reaches the threshold of tolerance of the opponent first wins. This indicates that in nuclear combat each combatant will strive to reach the threshold of pain of the opponent as swiftly as possible by making massive and immediate use of his nuclear arsenal. So, contrary to what the United States had claimed in the International Court of Justice, use of nuclear weapons cannot be limited or controlled if the goal is victory. Because if use of small tactical nuclear weapons on the battlefield does not escalate into generalized nuclear exchange that ends in symmetric destruction of the two combatants' countries, and cease-fire is agreed upon, again the outcome is symmetric: no party is defeated. Conclusion: nuclear weapons are not weapons, since they cannot generate asymmetry in nuclear combat.

This infrequently mentioned realization derives from the very nature of the nuclear force that powers these explosives. It releases gram for gram of explosive material a million times more energy than the electromagnetic force that powers ordinary explosives like TNT or

xix

dynamite. Thus, a nuclear warhead the size of an ordinary refrigerator can release the energy equivalent of an explosion of a million tons of TNT that would fill a freight train 150 miles long. One such device can destroy an entire large city, and since there is no such thing as perfect defenses, the symmetrical outcome of nuclear combat is guaranteed.

But because so much energy is released in such a small-size object in a tenth of a millionth of a second, the effects of a nuclear detonation are qualitatively completely different than those of an explosion of ordinary explosives of the same energy yield. A nuclear detonation generates temperatures of a 100 million degrees while a dynamite explosive about 3000 degrees. So while the ordinary explosive emits light and heat, the nuclear detonation emits copious amounts of γ-rays (gamma rays) and x-rays, together with light and heat. In addition, the nuclear process that releases the energy generates large amounts of radioactive nuclei that can travel around the globe emitting nuclear radiation.   The x-rays and γ-rays travel large distances in the atmosphere and cause radiation sickness among living creatures. In the case of an exo-atmospheric nuclear detonation, the γ-rays cause a giant electromagnetic pulse that can burn out electronic and electrical devices a thousand miles around. The heat from a single one megaton (one million tons) nuclear detonation creates a million-billion-billion-billion molecules of nitric oxides that destroy the fragile ozone layer in the stratosphere that protects us from harmful ultraviolet rays of the sun. All these in addition to the blast and heat effects of a nuclear detonation that caused the spectacular and ominous destruction of Hiroshima and Nagasaki at the end of World War II.

Over the centuries of evolution of the human species and human societies the value of war as a means of resolving conflict was understood and accepted. But over these centuries a set of generally accepted laws of war evolved that safeguarded human dignity and survival. Damage in the course of war had to be proportional, moderate, discriminating, and necessary in the pursuit of the goal of combat, the generation of an asymmetrical final state. The target areas had to be limited; the civilian non-combatants were to enjoy immunity from the vagaries of combat; neutrality had to be observed. Little of that ever took hold. The Acheans destroyed Troy, the Turks sacked Constantinople, the federal cavalry gave Navahoes blankets contaminated with smallpox virus, Guernica was bombed, Dresden and Tokyo were incinerated (yet neither Sir Arnold (Bomber) Harris, nor Curtis Lemay were tried Nuremberg-style and convicted). Combat has violated legal norms despite all good-will efforts of decent men. Nuclear weapons are not illegal just because they violate these laws of war, as exhaustively proven in this volume. They are illegal because they cause widespread and indiscriminate destruction *without promoting the purpose of war:* resolving conflict by creating an asymmetrical final state. They are not weapons but only wanton machines of symmetric destruction.

But what if an asymmetrical result were possible? Their use would still be illegal for all the reasons this volume explains, but the fear of such asymmetrical outcome has animated the ominous proliferation of these weapons. The Soviet Union developed them to restore nuclear symmetry with the United States. China worried about the Soviet Union; India about China, and Pakistan followed suit. Weaker nations, Iran, Iraq, N. Korea, may have attempted to develop them not to attack the United States or any other nuclear powers but in order to deter coercion or attacks against themselves. Nuclear explosives have become the "great equalizer" since they are relatively cheap to develop and stockpile. As Secretary of Defense Cohen said recently in a speech in Munich: "Would our allies have agreed to oppose Iraq's invasion of Kuwait if Iraq threatened to send a nuclear missile to London or Berlin ….?" This statement assumed that Iraq is suicidal, but it reveals the true concerns of the United States: The West won't be able to maintain a free hand to coerce and impose its will globally; ergo the decision to construct a National Missile Defense system that could intercept nuclear-tipped ballistic missiles, thereby restoring the state of nuclear asymmetry between the United States and smaller nuclear powers. But the West is merely postponing the inevitable: establishment of world-wide nuclear symmetry. International relations are simply too unstable otherwise. Eventually either most nations will have nuclear explosives in self-defense, or no one will.

Although the legal standing of pan-nuclear possession for self-protection may be debatable, when I asked a lawyer friend of mine for his opinion on this question, he reminded me that in a famous case on obscenity Justice Potter Stewart opined that while he could not frame a definition of obscenity he knew when he saw it. So with nuclear weapons. Even though under current circumstances it may be difficult to define under what circumstances their possession and use would be legal and when not, the colossal threat they present to the integrity of creation clearly exceeds the bounds of acceptability.

The conceptual basis for knowing it when I see it will be far clearer now, with Professor Moxley's extensive and probing treatment of the matter. It is truly startling to see the extent to which the United States has itself recognized the principles of international law from which the unlawfulness of the use of nuclear weapons is evident based on the inevitable effects of such weapons. Moxley literally shows the unlawfulness of these weapons out of the United States' own mouth.

Professor Moxley is right on target in his essential technical and nuclear policy points 1) that the effects of nuclear weapons are uncontrollable; 2) that virtually any use of nuclear weapons, even of the most-low yield ones, in the types of circumstances in which such use would likely take place, would carry with it a risk of precipitating the retaliatory use by the adversary of nuclear weapons; 3) that the current military mindset under U.S. policy of presumptive lawfulness serves to raise the risk of potential use in circumstances of crisis; and 4) that modern conventional weapons are reaching the point of being so effective as to be able to achieve practically any mission for which nuclear weapons might previously have been considered.

Nuclear weapons would presumably only be intentionally used in the most extreme of circumstances—circumstances that would, by their nature, likely carry with them a high risk of precipitating serious escalation, potentially with catastrophic effects. This is true even of such scenarios as the use of a low-yield nuclear weapon against warships on the High Seas or troops in sparsely populated areas–the kinds of situations relied on by the defenders of nuclear weapons before the International Court of Justice.

As to the military mindset, as long as nuclear weapons are deemed lawful by the United States and military training and operational planning proceed on that basis, the risk of use of such weapons in a crisis situation is ever present.

Hence, I welcome Professor Moxley's exhaustive and erudite examination of the legality of nuclear weapons. It is essential that our understanding of the law catch up with our understanding of the technical and policy forces. We should not squander the present historic opportunity to come to grips with the legal restraints on these weapons rather than continuing to legitimize them.

Kosta Tsipis   Cambridge, Massachusetts
(Retired) Director of the Program in   March 2000
Science and Technology for
International Security of the
Massachusetts Institute of Technology

Preface

Whether we as a nation are committed to the rule of law is, by any light, a big question, central to our national character. We pride ourselves on being so founded. The most minor of grievances is subject to legal redress. Yet there is serious question as to our submission to the rule of law with respect to perhaps the gravest threat to human life and welfare, nuclear weapons.

I would rather know the truth, whether for the assurance it gives–or the call to action. Hence this book, which examines the validity, the very *bona fides*, of the U.S. position on the issue.

With the end of the Cold War and of U.S. dependency on nuclear weapons, the political climate is such that this issue can now be addressed. This may indeed be, as they say, a time of historic opportunity. And of need. With the proliferation of these and other weapons of mass destruction and the threat of terrorism, the weapons have themselves become the main enemy, more threatening than any hostile power.

The 1998 detonation of nuclear devices by India and Pakistan, the continuing specter of nuclear trafficking from the disintegrated Soviet Union, and the increasing availability of long-range missiles capable of carrying nuclear weapons to the United States only highlight the practical immediacy of the issue. As does the fact that several of the missiles launched by the United States in August 1998 against targets in Afghanistan and Sudan reportedly landed in Pakistan, and similar supposedly highly accurate modern missiles launched by the United States in the 1991 Gulf War and the 1999 Kosovo operation ended up hitting the wrong targets.

The U.S. Senate's 1999 rejection of the Comprehensive Test Ban Treaty confirmed that this issue is still with us, and will remain so until we do something about it. Further confirmation is provided by the U.S. military's ongoing plans of record, which I review in detail, for the ready use of nuclear weapons even in the post Cold War strategic environment.

Ironically, the international law approach, rather than being utopian, may offer the best prospect for a breakthrough in our nation's dealing with these weapons. The delegitimization of nuclear weapons and perhaps eventually substantial denuclearization and regulation, as with chemical and biological weapons, ostensibly offer the prospect of greater security than the continuation of the regime of nuclear deterrence.

It is beyond question that international law, including the rules of the law of armed conflict applicable to the use of nuclear and other weapons, are the law of the land. The United States has long recognized this. Political though the area of potential use of nuclear weapons may be and central to national defense policy, it is subject to established rules of law.

With the Nuremberg prosecutions and the subsequent executions of convicted Nazi war criminals, the United States committed itself to the enforcement of international law applicable to the conducting of armed conflict. With its more recent support in 1996 of the war crime proceedings against Serbian leaders for genocide and other crimes against humanity committed against Bosnians, and with its 1999 support of international prosecution of Serbian leaders for actions against the Kosovars, the United States has reaffirmed this commitment. With the present issue of the lawfulness of the use of nuclear weapons, the chickens may have come home to roost. No nation, however great or well-intentioned, gets a free pass.

As we shall see, the proponents and opponents alike of the nuclear weapons regime generally agree on the substance of the rules of law applicable to this matter. The facts are also generally open and known and ostensibly beyond reasonable dispute. Where disagreement arises, it appears to result primarily from the distortion, ostensibly for political or strategic reasons, of facts and law otherwise acknowledged, and from the refusal to accept the implications of the application of the law to the facts.

In 1994 the United Nations General Assembly voted to submit to the International Court of Justice, the judicial branch of the United Nations, for advisory opinion the question of whether the threat or use of nuclear weapons could ever be lawful. The World Health Organization submitted a similar request. Representatives of nations from throughout the world appeared and argued the matter.

Among the States appearing was the United States, which took the position it has maintained throughout the nuclear era: that the use of nuclear weapons is subject to the rule of law but cannot be evaluated in the abstract; rather, that each particular use must be examined individually.

The U.S. position as it emerged before the Court was startling. Without even asserting the lawfulness of its high yield nuclear weapons making up the vast bulk of its arsenal, the United States drew the line of defense essentially at its relatively small number of low-yield precision nuclear weapons—weapons that, according to Presidential statements, have been substantially de-emphasized as a matter of national policy. And the United States was able to defend such low-yield weapons only through what appear to have been substantial distortions of the facts and law.

The thesis of this book is that the use of nuclear weapons is *per se* unlawful based upon rules of international law recognized by the United States and facts beyond reasonable dispute.

My professional experience has centered around litigating complex securities and commercial disputes in federal and state courts throughout the country, in serving as an arbitrator deciding such disputes in matters before the American Arbitration Association, and in teaching litigation related subjects at St. John's University School of Law and New York Law School. I have also been active over the years in lawyers groups in the arms control area.

This book grew out of such interests. It represents my effort to apply tough litigative as opposed to political or philosophical analysis to the issue of the lawfulness of the use of nuclear weapons.

I have established a web site at http://www.nuclearweaponslaw.org to facilitate communication among lawyers, public policy specialists, academics and other interested persons on the issues addressed in this book, and invite your feedback and input.

Charles J. Moxley, Jr.   New York, New York
                                                          March 2000

Acknowledgements

I am indebted to the faculty, administration and staff of St. John's University School of Law for their support of this effort over many years, including Deans Rudolph C. Hasl, Daniel A. Furlong, and Vincent C. Alexander and faculty members Nicholas R. Weiskopf, Kevin C. Fogarty, Jeff Sovern, and many others.

I am also indebted to whole generations of research assistants at St. John's for their substantial assistance, researching and drafting riders on innumerable subjects that at one time or another seemed relevant to this effort.

Among such students were Christopher Carolyn on generally accepted principles of law, Wayne Chan on nuclear policy, Christopher E. Dean on principles of foreign law, Rafael Declet, Jr., on principles of domestic tort liability, Mary Etheridge on the prerequisites for a *per se* rule and on principles of civil and criminal liability, Matthew Matera on landmines, Donna Y. Nadel on domestic law principles, Andrei Rado on *mens rea*, Joe Romero on the accuracy of nuclear weapons and the effects of the Chernobyl incident and the Hiroshima and Nagasaki bombings, Alicia Samios on statements by civilian and military leaders throughout the nuclear era as to nuclear weapons risks, and Andrea Wienert for her assistance in fine-tuning the manuscript and researching a wide range of international law issues. Aru Satkalmi of the St. John's law library was also of help far beyond the call of duty.

Most of all, Brian J. McBreen, first as a student at St. John's and then as a recent graduate and now a member of the bar, has been of immeasurable assistance to me in helping pull the book together, in performing extraordinary feats of locating and analyzing information and drafting riders on such subjects as nuclear, chemical, and biological weapons and policy issues, catastrophe theory, and *mens rea*, and in assisting in finalizing the manuscript and preparing the index. In addition to his legal talents, Brian is a genius on the internet; if it exists in cyberspace, he can find it. I think this book would have taken me another ten years without him.

To my father Charles Moxley, long gone, I owe a debt beyond description. My mother Kathryn I thank for her unending love and support.

My brother Joe Moxley, an extraordinarily gifted and prolific writer, has been of great assistance to me in conceptualizing this book and bringing it to press. Without him, I would not have gotten here. My brother Paul and my sister Peggi, both attorneys, and my sister Mona, a psychologist, also provided much support. I also thank Norma Fox Moxley for encouraging and believing in this book from the beginning.

Most immediately, I thank University Press of America editors Peter Cooper and Helen Hudson for their support and encouragement, and their patience, as this book extended itself in time and space.

No one but me is responsible for the positions taken or the conclusions reached, but I could not have completed this book without the substantial help of all of these people and many more. I have been blessed by my family, friends, and professional colleagues, and am grateful; I hope the final product is worthy of their support.

I further acknowledge the authors and publishers who granted permission to quote from the following copyrighted materials:

Briefing Book on Nuclear War © 1992 by the International Physicians for the Prevention of Nuclear War.

LaFave, Wayne R., and Scott, Austin W., Criminal Law (2nd Ed. 1986), with permission of the West Group.

Model Penal Code © 1985 by the American Law Institute.

Shroeder, Christopher H., Rights Against Risks, originally appearing at 86 Colum. L. Rev. 495 (1986).

Introduction

U.S. Position

The U.S. position is that there is no conventional or customary rule of law specifically prohibiting the use of nuclear weapons and hence that the use of such weapons is presumptively lawful. The United States recognizes, however, that the law of armed conflict, including the established rules of necessity, proportionality, discrimination, civilian immunity, neutrality, moderation, and humanity, apply to the use of any weapon, including any nuclear weapon—and acknowledges that the use of a nuclear weapon would be unlawful if, in the circumstances, it would violate any of these rules.

The United States asserts that nuclear weapons, for this purpose, are indistinguishable from conventional weapons: The legality of their use must be determined on a case-by-case basis based on the particular circumstances of each possible use.

In taking this position, the United States recognizes that, under these rules, the lawfulness of the use of nuclear weapons turns largely on the likely effects of such use. The U.S. defense before the International Court of Justice (ICJ) of the potential lawfulness of use of nuclear weapons was premised in major part on the United States' asserted ability to use certain such weapons (ostensibly, precision low-yield tactical ones) in such a way and in such circumstances as to limit and control their effects, including their radiation and, ostensibly, their escalation effects.

The United States recognizes that the use of nuclear weapons would be unlawful under the rules of necessity, proportionality and discrimination if the effects of the use would not be controllable and actually controlled during the strike.

The United States further recognizes that the strike would be unlawful under the rule of necessity if it was not actually necessary to use the nuclear weapon to achieve the particular mission, *i.e.*, if conventional weapons would suffice.

The United States similarly recognizes that the strike would be unlawful under the rule of proportionality if its effects on protected persons would likely be disproportionate to the concrete and direct military benefits of the strike.

Likewise it recognizes that the strike would be unlawful under the rule of discrimination if its effects could not discriminate military from

non-military targets so as to avoid disproportionate collateral injury to
protected persons.

The United States' defense of the lawfulness of these weapons
before the ICJ was thus specifically based on its contention that it is
able to deliver nuclear weapons (ostensibly, a small number of
precision low-yield tactical devices) accurately and directly against
discrete military targets in remote areas, and of doing so in such a way
as to control and limit resultant nuclear radiation and not endanger
substantial numbers of noncombatants. The United States further told
the Court that the potential effects of using nuclear weapons are not
materially different from using modern conventional weapons and
disputed that the limited use of low-yield nuclear weapons would
necessarily escalate into a strategic nuclear exchange.

The Existence of Binding Legal Standards

The striking point is that, notwithstanding the obvious political and
national security issues that are present, there is law in this area, and
that the United States recognizes such law,[1] and indeed, as we shall see,
has integrated it into its military training and contingency planning.
Perhaps even more striking is that the proponents and opponents alike
of the nuclear weapons regime generally agree on the substance of such
governing rules of law.

The ICJ's Nuclear Weapons Advisory Opinion

The ICJ, in its 1996 advisory opinion as to nuclear weapons,
mirrored the United States' non-defense of the lawfulness of the use of
large scale nuclear weapons, but found itself unable to decide whether a
more limited use of nuclear weapons could ever be lawful.

Specifically, the Court determined that, because of the potential of
nuclear weapons to destroy civilization and the entire ecosystem of the
planet, the use of nuclear weapons would generally be unlawful, but
that it was not in possession of sufficient facts to evaluate whether use
of nuclear weapons (ostensibly, precision low-yield tactical ones) could
be lawful in extreme circumstances of self-defense when a State's
survival was at stake.

The Court stated that it did not have sufficient facts to determine the
validity of the argument of the United States and other nuclear weapons
States to the effect that highly accurate low-yield tactical nuclear

---

[1] There are additional points of international law that are, in fact, in
contention.

weapons could be used in such a way as to limit and control their effects.

Approach

The U.S. position and the ICJ decision constitute the starting point of my analysis: The Court may not have had the facts, or even fully recognized the scope of the potentially relevant facts, but the facts exist, and are generally unclassified and openly available. We need to identify them, put them on the table and examine them in the light of the applicable law.

My analysis proceeds on two levels. First, I develop the applicable law as articulated by the United States and apply it to widely recognized and ostensibly incontrovertible facts as to nuclear weapons. Secondly, I develop certain additional principles of law which appear to be so widely recognized as to constitute binding principles of international law, and similarly apply them to the facts as to nuclear weapons.

The U.S. position and the ICJ decision are covered in Part I (Chapters 1–3); additional principles of law are covered in Parts II and III (Chapters 4–14); and the facts are covered in Part IV (Chapters 15–28). My conclusions are set forth in Part V (Chapters 29–30).

Analysis Based on U.S. Statements of the Law

Under this approach, I base the analysis upon the United States' own statements of the applicable law and upon statements of the facts so widely recognized as to be essentially incontrovertible.

The law of armed conflict is communicated to the U.S. military through military manuals setting forth such law for training and planning purposes and directing the military as to the legal restrains within which they operate. In Chapter 1, I review descriptions from U.S. military manuals of the rules of armed conflict applicable to the lawfulness or unlawfulness of the use of any weapon.

In Chapter 2, I review statements from the military manuals and from arguments of the United States before the ICJ setting forth the United States' position as to the application of such rules of law to the use of nuclear weapons. Here, we see some retrenchment from the generic statements of the applicable rules, as described in Chapter 1, but the United States' defense of these weapons is still largely on a factual level: that it can use the weapons in such a way as to keep their effects within legal limits.

Applicable Factual and Legal Questions

The U.S. focus, in its defense of nuclear weapons before the ICJ, on the asserted lawfulness of the surgical use of precision low-yield nuclear weapons against remote targets staked out not only a factual position as to the characteristics and effects of nuclear weapons and their delivery systems, but also an implicit legal position as to the scope of the facts relevant to the analysis.

Specifically, the U.S. position implies that, in evaluating the lawfulness of the limited use of precision low-yield tactical nuclear weapons, one should look at the matter in the abstract, in a hypothetical test tube type fashion, without reference to the risk factors that will inevitably be present, even with the most limited of uses, including such risks as those of hitting the wrong target or of precipitating a nuclear, chemical or biological weapons response and resultant escalation to more widespread use of such weapons.

The extent of such risk factors is only heightened by the fact that the circumstances in which the United States might actually consider the use of nuclear weapons would by definition be ones of extreme military challenge and hence of volatility, with considerable pressures of all kinds upon people and equipment.

Need for Evaluation Based on Probabilities

If it were possible to wait and see what happened, with at least the theoretical prospect of a war crimes prosecution if the strike turned out to exceed permissible limits, the integrity of the legal safeguards (and deterrent) could be preserved. But with nuclear weapons, of course, there may be no such luxury of hindsight. If the law is to be applied at all, it must be in advance, when only estimates of probabilities can be known (Chapters 1, 15, 29, 30). That limitation is inescapable, yet our thinking, as manifest by the treatment of the matter before the ICJ (Chapters 2, 3), has yet to come to grips with this aspect of the matter.

The issues as to the scope of the relevant facts and the appropriate treatment of probabilities were not focused on by the United States in its arguments to the ICJ or addressed in any depth by the ICJ in its decision, and appear not to have been much focused on at all in the literature on this subject (Chapters 2, 3). Yet they seem to be the heart of the matter.

Nor are they beyond the ability of legal systems to address. The imposition of civil and criminal liability based upon unjustifiable risk creation is a central function of law throughout the world.

The applicable rules of law, as described by the United States (Chapters 1 and 2) and as reviewed by the ICJ in its decision (Chapter 3), provide guidance as to the scope of relevant facts, and, hence, as to the consideration that must be given to probabilities in conducting the legal analysis: The rules of necessity, proportionality, and discrimination, and even those of civilian immunity and neutrality, are rules of reason (Chapter 1). Compliance is to be evaluated in light of all of the reasonably available facts, including particularly those bearing on the likely effects of the use of nuclear weapons.

Range of Factual Issues

This brings into the analysis a far wide range of facts, including such matters as the following:

- The characteristics, capabilities, and effects of nuclear weapons and their delivery systems (Chapter 15);
- U.S. declaratory and operational policy as to the circumstances in which it might use nuclear weapons and its assumptions as to how other States might act (Chapters 16-18);
- the U.S. nuclear force structure, consisting of the nuclear weapons available for use and whose potential use is the subject of U.S. military training and contingency planning (Chapter 19);
- the practical experience as to the times the United States has threatened or considered the use of nuclear weapons, reflecting the types of nuclear risks the United States has been willing to take and hence potential risk factors in the event of major confrontation in the future (Chapter 20);
- probabilities of as to the accuracy with which the United States could likely deliver nuclear weapons to designated targets (Chapter 21);
- risks inherent in the nuclear weapons regime, including the risks of inadvertent use and of precipitating undesired intentional use (Chapter 22);
- the nuclear arsenals of other States, reflecting the scope of volatility as to weapons that might be brought into play in the event of a major international confrontation (Chapter 23);
- the risks of escalation and other excessive effects (Chapters 24–26);

- the risks that even a limited use of nuclear weapons would precipitate use of chemical or biological weapons, and *vice versa* (Chapter 27); and
- the potential of today's high tech conventional weapons to accomplish missions for which nuclear weapons might previously have been considered (Chapter 28).

Potential *Per Se* Unlawfulness Based on Overall Facts

The question is whether such risk factors are so inherent in the use of nuclear weapons, in the types of circumstances in which such weapons might be used, and so serious, as to render even the most limited use of nuclear weapons unlawful. This is the central theme of the fact chapters (Chapters 15–28), and I attempt to pull it all together in Chapters 29 and 30.

Application of Established Principles of Law

The United States further argued to the ICJ there can be no *per se* rule prohibiting the use of nuclear weapons unless the United States has specifically agreed to such a rule. This raises legal issues as to the nature and sources of international law, and specifically as to the role of general principles of the law of armed conflict, such as those referred to above: Are such principles binding no matter how they cut, or is their application subject to the consent of the individual State against which they are being applied. I address this issue in Chapters 1 and 29.

Requisite Mental State for War Crimes Liability

One way of approaching the question of potential culpability for risk creation is through the required mental state for the violation in question. Is it required, for example, as the United States has at times ostensibly contended, that, to be unlawful, a particular use of nuclear weapons would have to necessarily involve the deliberate causing of impermissible effects, or are recklessness, wantonness, gross negligence or even simple negligence sufficient? I address the U.S. position on the issue in Chapters 1, 2 and 29, and analyze the issue more broadly in Chapters 6–9, and 30.

Interpretation of Law in Light of Its Purpose

As addressed in Chapter 5, it is a fundamental principle of construction that international law, like law generally, is to be interpreted and applied in light of its purposes. In Chapter 1, I address

U.S. statements as to the purposes of the law of armed conflict, and in Chapter 29 I examine the implications of such purposes.

Analysis Based on Generally Recognized Principles of Law

Where my first approach is based on U.S. statements of the applicable law, this second approach arguably involves an extension of the law, or at least a new focus, namely the recognition that certain rules of law as to the prerequisites for a *per se* rule and as to civil and criminal liability for risk creation are so widely recognized as to constitute binding principles of international law.

Prerequisites for a *Per Se* Rule

For a *per se* rule to arise, is it necessary that every single imaginable use be unlawful, or is it sufficient if most, but not necessarily all, such uses would be unlawful, or if the vast majority of the likely uses, in the circumstances in which such uses would likely take place, would be unlawful. I address this issue in Chapters 1, 2, 4 and 30.

Weighing of Probabilities

A further issue is that of the level of risk of impermissible effects that must be present for unlawfulness to incept. How are risks to be weighted, including particularly small risks of extremely severe, even apocalyptic effects? Such matters can be conceptualized as presenting *mens rea* issues as to the mental state necessary for war crimes liability or substantive issues as to limits on permissible risk creation. I address such matters in Chapters 6–8, and then, in Chapter 9, propose various formulaic approaches for evaluating probabilities as to nuclear weapons risks. I present my overall analysis in Chapter 30.

The "So What" Question

What difference would unlawfulness make, since the weapons cannot be uninvented? This is the inevitable question—the one I have been most asked from all types of audience, as I have been working on this book. The matter must be addressed if we are to substantiate the practicality of concerning ourselves with this issue.

Effects of the U.S. Position of Presumptive Lawfulness

The United States' position as to the lawfulness of the use of nuclear weapons has significant effects. It means that military training and planning—the whole military mindset—proceed on the assumption that nuclear weapons can be used (Chapters 2, 16–18). Nuclear weapons are a working part of the national arsenal and the military are charged with being prepared to use them, and in fact maintain detailed contingency plans to do so (Chapters 2, 16–19, 26).

In the extreme circumstances in which the President or the military might turn to these weapons, there would likely be little inclination or opportunity to focus on the requirements of international law. Advance planning might have covered some of the ground, but a decision would need be made, probably quickly (as we shall see, likely within minutes or even seconds) and not very clearheadedly, from a mindset of presumptive lawfulness (Chapters 2, 25–26).

The upshot is a substantial likelihood that a possible launch would not be subjected to serious consideration as to the legalities. As reflected in one of the more recent U.S. joint military manuals (applicable to all the services), the U.S. position is functionally equivalent to one of unqualified lawfulness; presumptive lawfulness becomes *per se* lawfulness as far as the constraints of the law are concerned (Chapter 2).

This serves various purposes. Some of the U.S. political and military leadership might contemplate the actual use of these weapons in extreme circumstances, notwithstanding the widescale recognition by the U.S. leadership throughout the nuclear era that nuclear weapons are so destructive and provocative as to make their actual use extremely dangerous (Chapters 24–25).

Most centrally, presumptive lawfulness serves the purpose of legitimizing nuclear deterrence, a policy which, in the contemporary strategic environment, with the end of the Cold War and demise of the Soviet Union, is substantially outmoded, to the extent that, paradoxically, the United States has formally recognized that its greatest security threat is not any enemy needing to be deterred but rather nuclear weapons themselves (Chapters 18, 23, 22, 30).

Significance of Presumed Lawfulness to Deterrence

Military response by the United States in a particular situation will likely be the product not of what the civilian or military decision-makers independently decide to do in the throes of battle, but rather of years of the United States' training of its armed forces, conceptualization and implementation of its force structure, development of contingency and target planning, and the like (Chapters 15–19, 26).

The United States acknowledged as much before the ICJ, in arguing that the credibility of nuclear deterrence depends upon the legality of the use of such weapons. If the use of nuclear weapons were determined to be unlawful, the United States would be required to revise its training, planning, equipment procurement and force structures.

One of the lead U.S. lawyers argued to the ICJ:

[E]ach of the Permanent Members of the Security Council has made an immense commitment of human and material resources to acquire and maintain stocks of nuclear weapons and their delivery systems, and many other States have decided to rely for their security on these nuclear capabilities. If these weapons could not lawfully be used in individual or collective self-defense under any circumstances, there would be no credible threat of such use in response to aggression and deterrent policies would be futile and meaningless. In this sense, it is impossible to separate the policy of deterrence from the legality of the use of the means of deterrence. Accordingly, any affirmation of a general prohibition on the use of nuclear weapons would be directly contrary to one of the fundamental premises of the national security policy of each of these many States.

The United States further stated in its memorandum to the ICJ:

It is well known that the Permanent Members of the Security Council possess nuclear weapons and have developed and deployed systems for their use in armed conflict. These States would not have borne the expense and effort of acquiring and maintaining these weapons and delivery systems if they believed that the use of nuclear weapons was generally prohibited.

Perspective of the United States

I have written this book from the perspective of the United States to highlight the extent to which the unlawfulness of the use of nuclear weapons is evident from statements of the applicable law by the United States and essentially incontrovertible facts. Yet the U.S. statements of the law are not gratuitous; they accurately describe rules of law equally binding on other States.

Time of Opportunity

The Cold War developed so quickly upon the heels of the invention of these weapons and the weapons at first appeared to be such a military panacea that there was limited political opportunity or inclination to develop a legal regime limiting their development and potential use. The U.S. position as to the lawfulness of the use of nuclear weapons has its roots in outmoded realities: (1) the existence of a limited nuclear club of which the United States was the charter member; (2) the sense, at least in the beginning, that these are just another weapon; (3) feelings of vulnerability and ideological fervor fueled by the perceived threat from the Soviet Union; and (4) the reigning strategic regime of deterrence.

The current environment presents a realistic opportunity, perhaps the first since the dawn of the nuclear age, to come to grips with the reality that nuclear weapons are so destructive, their effects so unpredictable and potentially apocalyptic (Chapter 15), the likelihood of escalation to a broader nuclear exchange from even a "low-level" launch so great (Chapters 25–26), that denuclearization is a practical and legal as well as moral imperative.

The Cold War taught us that these weapons could end up being used; they were seriously threatened on numerous occasions (Chapter 20). The nuclear club has expanded, as has the potential over time for break-out by other States (Chapter 23). While nuclear weapons previously represented, at least ostensibly, an economic way to deter the Soviet Union from exploiting its conventional weapons superiority (Chapters 18, 22), now it is the United States that has a conventional weapons superiority threatened by the actual or potential nuclear capability of other nations and terrorist forces (Chapters 18, 22).

The recognition of the unlawfulness of the use of nuclear weapons would not necessarily bar possession, and obviously, on some level, at least pending some idealized denuclearized future, deterrence would be implicit and ever present, but, as acknowledged by the United States before the ICJ, the whole mindset as to planning, training, and even thinking, would be radically altered.

Contemporary Role of Nuclear Weapons

The Nuclear Posture Review, a widescale evaluation of U.S. nuclear policy conducted at the highest levels of the civilian and military leadership and adopted by the Clinton Administration, has resulted in a substantial withdrawal from reliance on nuclear weapons, and particularly from tactical nuclear weapons. Nuclear stockpiles have been substantially cut; entire weapons systems, eliminated. MIRVing is in the process of being discontinued; nuclear testing has been stopped; and nuclear weapons budgets have been truncated. Tactical nuclear weapons are no longer placed in the hands of any U.S. ground or naval surface forces. The Army and the Marines have been de-nuclearized; the Navy no longer deploys non-strategic nuclear weapons, and the Air Force has dramatically cut its tactical nuclear stockpile. (Chapter 18).

Even as tactical nuclear weapons have been withdrawn from service and nuclear weapons generally de-emphasized, the mission, for planning purposes, of such weapons has been expanded to include widescale chemical and biological weapons targets (Chapter 27), notwithstanding pledges by the United States at the highest level of government that it would not use nuclear weapons against a non-nuclear State (Chapters 3, 30).

In addition, in the post Cold War era, the U.S. military has emphasized its continued commitment to the integration of such weapons into its active operational planning, as reflected in military manuals, such as the Chairman of the Joint Chiefs of Staff's *Joint Pub 3-12, Doctrine for Joint Nuclear Operations* (Dec. 15, 1995) and *Joint Pub 3-12.1 Doctrine for Joint Theater Nuclear Operations* (Feb. 9, 1996) (Chapters 2, 25-26, 30).

The one area the Nuclear Posture Review notably did not encompass was the legal area. This book represents an effort to foster the United States' coming to grips with this remaining area.

The Uncertain Continuation of the Luck of the Cold War

The stakes are high. On one level, deterrence may have worked, and indeed may have contributed to the demise of the Soviet venture. With its military force checked and the potential for economic and social transformation circumscribed by its inherent limitations and the costs of maintaining the military balance, the Soviet system was unable to survive. On the other hand, human life is long and empire, however brutal and entrenched, short.

However one comes out on the question of whether deterrence worked, we were lucky during the Cold War. Nuclear weapons had just been invented, and this was the first test of our civilization's ability to handle them. Risks were taken that threatened everything. But such luck cannot be counted on; human experience is to the contrary.

Thesis

We are essentially talking about Phase II—in effect, the second historical period—in the effort by our civilization and international legal system to address the challenge of nuclear weapons. My thesis is that the existing rules of law, as recognized by the United States, are adequate to the task, if we face up to the application of these rules to the full panoply of essentially indisputable facts (Chapters 29, 30).

PART I

The Law

Chapter 1: The Law as Seen by the United States

Introduction

The lawfulness of the use of nuclear weapons, like most other legality issues, turns on the interplay of the facts and the law. The two are functionally interrelated: The more we learn as to each, the more insight we gain as to what we need to learn as to the other. We can only reach a final evaluation when we have frozen in relief our determinations as to the applicable facts and law at their points of intersection.

I start, somewhat atypically, with an analysis of the law. Here's why. We all have a general sense about nuclear weapons: They cause huge explosions and release lethal radiation that can spread great distances in time and space. Nuclear war would be a disaster for everyone, but, in the meantime, nuclear deterrence, the threat of the use of these weapons, ostensibly has kept the peace during the Cold War and may continue to restrain potential adversaries. Nuclear weapons cannot be uninvented and hence are here to stay.

At first blush, this would seem to be substantially all we need to know. If my analysis is correct, however, reality is quite different: The legal analysis hinges on very specific and detailed facts as to nuclear weapons and policy and the practices of the nuclear powers. Like a litigator handling a case, to perform this analysis we must become experts in the factual areas at hand. Precisely because the indispensability of the detailed probing of such factual areas is not self-evident, and the consequent danger that the level of necessary detail would seem just a jumble of arbitrary information, I first develop the principles of law generally applicable to this area. This will enable us to see firsthand what facts we need for the analysis.

Because of the conclusions I reach, this book becomes a criticism of the U.S. position as to nuclear weapons and a suggestion for change. For that reason, I develop my analysis, to the extent possible, from the United States' own mouth, the statements of its authorized representatives. Let's maximize the areas of commonality so we can concentrate our efforts on analyzing and hopefully laying a basis for a clear distillation, if not resolution, of the areas of disagreement.

Stating the law in the first instance from the mouth of the United States graphically illustrates one key and to me startling point—the extent to which the United States and the critics of the nuclear weapons regime agree on what the law is. To an extraordinary extent, both sides rely on the same sources of the law and state it in substantially the same terms. Indeed, as we shall see, in a number of instances, the United States, at least when addressing the matter in the abstract, sees the law as more demanding than do the traditional sources.

The United States is a big country, with many mouths. To what source should we go for the authoritative statement of the U.S. position? I use, in the first instance, the military manuals[1] of the armed forces of the United States, documents used for the training of U.S. military personnel and the planning and conducting of military operations, and hence ostensibly the most direct and cogent evidence of what the United States believes the law to be.[2] I also rely heavily upon

---

[1] UNITED STATES DEPARTMENT OF THE NAVY ANNOTATED SUPPLEMENT TO THE COMMANDER'S HANDBOOK ON THE LAW OF NAVAL OPERATIONS (Naval Warfare Publication 9, 1987) (With Revision A (5 October 1989), this handbook was adopted by the U.S. Marine Corps as FLEET MARINE FORCE MANUAL (FM FM) 1-10) [hereinafter THE NAVAL/MARINE COMMANDER'S HANDBOOK]; UNITED STATES DEPARTMENT OF THE AIR FORCE, COMMANDER'S HANDBOOK ON THE LAW OF ARMED CONFLICT (Air Force Pamphlet 110-34, 25 July 1980) [hereinafter THE AIR FORCE COMMANDER'S HANDBOOK]; THE UNITED STATES DEPARTMENT OF THE AIR FORCE, INTERNATIONAL LAW—THE CONDUCT OF ARMED CONFLICT AND AIR OPERATIONS (Air Force Pamphlet 110-31, 19 November 1976) [hereinafter THE AIR FORCE MANUAL ON INTERNATIONAL LAW]; and UNITED STATES DEPARTMENT OF THE ARMY, THE LAW OF LAND WARFARE (FM27-10/18 July 1956) with Change No. 1 (15 July 1976) [hereinafter THE LAW OF LAND WARFARE].

THE NAVAL/MARINE COMMANDER'S HANDBOOK comes in two versions, the unannotated and the annotated. The unannotated version is a statement of the law without citations. The annotated version bears very extensive citations and discussion of the law and its rationale. The Introductory Note states that the unannotated version is intended for the "operational commander and his staff" and the annotated version for the "more in-depth requirements of Navy and Marine Corps judge advocates." My references are to the annotated version.

The manuals, in setting forth the applicable provisions of the law of armed conflict, generally cite to extensive treaty provisions and other recognized sources of international law. In quoting from the manuals, I do not generally include such citations or note their exclusion, although, where the underlying sources seem of particular importance to the discussion, I do refer to them.

[2] As to the legal effect of military manuals, THE LAW OF LAND WARFARE states that it is an "official publication" of the Army, but that those of its provisions which are not statutes or the text of treaties to which the United States is a party should be considered not as "binding" but as having "evidentiary value" as to custom and practice. *Id.* at 3.

The manual further states: "The purpose of this Manual is to provide authoritative guidance to military personnel on the customary and treaty law

applicable the conduct of warfare on land and to relationships between belligerents and neutral States." *Id.* at 3.

THE NAVAL/MARINE COMMANDER'S HANDBOOK is to the same effect, stating that it has been held that military manuals, while not "legislative instruments" possessing "formal binding power," are "persuasive statements of the law" ultimately to be recognized or not depending upon how accurately they reflect the law. *Id.* at 1-2 n.2 (citing THE HOSTAGES TRIAL (Wilhelm List et al), 11 TWC 1237-38, 8 LRTWC 51-52 (U.S. Military Tribunal, Nuremberg, July 8, 1947–Feb. 19, 1948)); The Peleus Trial, 1 LRTWC 19 (British Military Ct., Hamburg, 1945); The Belsen Trial, 2 LRTWC 148–49 (British Military Ct., Luneburg, 1945); The Abbage Ardenne Case (Trial of Brigadefurher Kurt Meyer), 4 LRTWC 110 (Canadian Military Ct., Ausrich, Germany, 1945); NWIP 10-2 ¶ 100 n.1; FM 27-10 ¶ 1; 15 LRTWC, DIGEST OF LAW AND CASES 21–22).

THE NAVAL/MARINE COMMANDER'S HANDBOOK indicates that it is intended to be used by military personnel in the performance of their military duties:

> This publication ... is intended for the use of operational commanders and supporting staff elements at all levels of command. It is designed to provide officers in command and their staffs with an overview of the rules of law governing naval operations in peacetime and during armed conflict. The explanations and descriptions in this publication are intended to enable the naval commander and his staff to comprehend more fully the legal foundations upon which the orders issued to them by higher authority are premised and to understand better the commander's responsibilities under international domestic law to execute his mission within that law. This publication sets forth general guidance. It is not a comprehensive treatment of the law nor is it a substitute for the definitive legal guidance provided by judge advocates and others responsible for advising commanders on the law.

Id. at 1-2.

The handbook goes on to emphasize the extent to which it should be used in operational training of naval personnel: "Officers in command of operational units are encouraged to utilize this publication as a training aid for assigned personnel." *Id.* at 2.

The handbook states that its provisions as to the law of armed conflict apply "to the conduct of U.S. naval forces during armed conflict." *Id.* at 2. It states that the law of armed conflict set forth in the document are "of special concern to the naval commander during any period in which U.S. naval forces are engaged in armed conflict." *Id.* at 1.

After stating that it sets forth the applicable international law, the handbook goes on to note the binding nature of international law on naval personnel: "At all times a commander shall observe, and require his command to observe, the principles of international law." *Id.* at 4. The handbook further notes that this

the United States' oral and written statements of the law to the ICJ in arguing the case before that Court as to the lawfulness of the use of nuclear weapons.

In this chapter I develop the law which the United States recognizes as generally applicable to the use of weapons. Then, in the next chapter, I analyze the United States' application of this law to nuclear weapons. In the ensuing chapter, I address the ICJ decision, analyzing the extent to which the Court accepted the U.S. position.

In developing the law as the United States sees it, I focus on the areas which are key to the analysis, identifying the points which are in controversy, including situations where there is disagreement as to what the law is or as to its application. I also identify certain key statements of the law that the United States appears to back away from when it comes to application of such law to nuclear weapons. Finally, I highlight the factual areas that the applicable law makes relevant,

---

obligation overrides other naval regulations: "Where necessary to fulfillment of this responsibility, a departure from other provisions of Naval Regulations is authorized." *Id.* at 4. A footnote to the foregoing emphasizes that violation of international law by naval personnel is punishable by court-martial. *See id.* at 4 n.8.

The Air Force has made similar statements as to the purpose and effects of military manuals. THE AIR FORCE COMMANDER'S HANDBOOK states, "This pamphlet informs commanders and staff members of their rights and duties under the law of armed conflict. It applies to all Air Force activities worldwide, and implements DOD Directives 5100.77, 10 July 1979"; *Id.* at i. THE AIR FORCE MANUAL ON INTERNATIONAL LAW similarly states, "This pamphlet is for the information and guidance of judge advocates and others particularly concerned with international law requirements applicable during armed conflict. It furnishes references and suggests solutions to a variety of legal problems but is not directive in nature. As an Air Force pamphlet, it does not promulgate official U.S. Government policy although it does refer to US, DOD and Air Force policies." *Id.* at i.

The United States, in its presentation to the ICJ, relied on provisions contained in its military manuals. *See, e.g.,* Conrad K. Harper, Michael J. Matheson, Bruce C. Rashkow, John H. McNeill, *Written Statement of the Government of the United States of America* (June 20, 1995), submitted to the International Court of Justice, (The Hague, The Netherlands), in connection with the Request by the United Nations General Assembly for an Advisory Opinion on the Legality of the Threat or Use of Nuclear Weapons (the "U.S. ICJ Memorandum/GA App."), *reprinted as Written Observations on the Request by the General Assembly for an Advisory Opinion,* 7 CRIM. L.F. 401, 416 n.49 (1996) (citing U.S. Army Field Manual 27-10, Change No. 1, THE LAW OF LAND WARFARE ¶ 40(a)).

setting forth the legal bases for the factual analysis I develop in later chapters.

Sources of International Law

The most basic of questions will be central to our analysis: What is international law? What are its sources? How binding is it? In the absence of an international enforcement body, can it truly be said there is a body of law regulating the use of force in war? To what extent is international law dependent upon the specific agreement of States, or of States particularly affected by the point of law at issue?

Most to the point: If a State has agreed to a principle of law or that principle is established as part of international customary law, is the State bound by all the implications and applications of that principle, even ones which it disputes? Or does its specific disputation negate or limit its subjugation to that principle of law? If my analysis is correct, this becomes one of several core issues upon which the legality of the use of nuclear weapons turns. As we shall see, the United States— regrettably to the integrity of the rule of law—is on both sides of this issue.

The complexity of this issue is reflected in the statement in the Army's *Law of Land Warfare* that "[t]he conduct of armed hostilities on land is regulated by the law of land warfare which is both written and unwritten."[3] Difficult as it can be determining the substance and application of written law, the complexities in determining the unwritten law can be even more challenging. *The Air Force Manual on International Law* quotes Article 38 of the ICJ Statute as the "most frequently cited authoritative reference" in its articulation of the following sources of international law:

> a. international conventions, whether general or particular, establishing rules expressly recognized by the contesting states;
> b. international custom, as evidence of a general practice accepted as law;
> c. the general principles of law recognized by civilized nations;
> d. subject to the provisions of Article 59, judicial decisions and the teachings of the most highly qualified

---

[3] THE LAW OF LAND WARFARE at 3.

publicists of the various nations, as subsidiary means for the determination of rules of law.[4]

These are the generally recognized sources of international law, including of that subcategory of international law known as the law of war or, more contemporaneously, the law of armed conflict. Each of these sources will be integral to our analysis, supplying portions of the overall body of law applicable to the issue at hand.[5]

Summary as to Applicable Sources

There are numerous international conventions—primarily the Hague and Geneva law, as we shall see—setting forth provisions of law limiting the levels of force permissible in armed conflict. So also, many rules of customary law containing such limitations are firmly established in the law of armed conflict and recognized by the United States. Much of the conventional law in this area has either ripened into customary law or from its inception reflected underlying customary rules, so that it is binding even upon non-signatories or States that might now seek to withdraw or condition their consent. The scope of generally accepted principles of law as a source of international law is potentially as expansive as the world's legal systems. In a broad sense, such principles as a source can be conceptualized as the "least common denominator" of the world's legal systems, principles essentially recognized across the spectrum of the world's major legal systems. So too, judicial decisions and academic and other professional writings from throughout the world constitute a broad sources of international law, and one whose significance has not fully been realized in analyzing the matter at hand.

Conventions

International conventions are ostensibly the most concrete of these sources of law. We have the convention, the agreed-to text, before us and can read and interpret it. To a considerable extent, the rules of law applicable to nuclear weapons are set forth in conventions and, as noted, the disagreement between the proponents and opponents of the

---

[4] THE AIR FORCE MANUAL ON INTERNATIONAL LAW at 1-13 n.8 (quoting Article 38 of The Statute of the International Court of Justice (Annex to UN Charter), 59 Stat 1031; TS 993).

[5] THE NAVAL/MARINE COMMANDER'S HANDBOOK states, "The rules governing the actual conduct of armed conflict are variously known as the *jus in bello*, the law of armed conflict, or international humanitarian law." *Id.* at 5-3 n.3.

current nuclear weapons regime is essentially on the application of such law to the facts as to nuclear weapons. This is true generally as to the rules of necessity, proportionality, moderation, discrimination, civilian immunity, humanity, and of neutrality, upon which we will focus.

There are some areas of disagreement as to the reach of certain conventional law. For example, the 1925 Geneva Gas Protocol, ratified by the United States in 1975, prohibits "the use in war of asphyxiating, poisonous or other gases, and of all analogous liquids, materials or devices."[6] It is recognized that rules applied by convention can apply to subsequently introduced technology, but the proponents and opponents of the nuclear weapons regime disagree on whether this particular language applies to nuclear weapons.

There are also numerous conventions in the environmental protection and human and political rights areas, which the opponents of the nuclear weapons regime claim to be applicable to nuclear weapons. Situations such as these present the familiar legal challenge of how to interpret a document, aided in this instance by the existence of an international convention setting forth modes of interpretation of international treaties and conventions.

Customary Law

Customary law is more amorphous. We do not necessarily have a specifically agreed-to text before us, but rather have to read the tea leaves of State practice and of perceptions and expressions of such practice by available sources, official and unofficial. *The Naval/Marine Commander's Handbook* defines the development of customary law: "When [State military practice] attains a degree of regularity and is accompanied by the general conviction among nations that behavior in conformity with that practice is obligatory, it can be said to have become a rule of customary law binding upon all nations."[7]

The Air Force Manual on International Law quotes Whiteman's "excellent discussion," *inter alia,* that over time certain international practices "have been found to be reasonable and wise in the conduct of foreign relations, in considerable measure the result of a balancing of interest," and have thereby "attained the stature of accepted principles

---

[6] Protocol for the Prohibition of the Use of War in Asphixiating, Poisonous or Other Gases, and of Bacteriological Methods of Warfare, June 17, 1925. 26 U.S.T. 571, 94 L.N.T.S. 65, 67, 69 (entered into force on Feb. 8, 1928) (ratified by the United States on Jan. 22, 1975, subject to certain reservations discussed hereinafter).

[7] THE NAVAL/MARINE COMMANDER'S HANDBOOK at 5-10.

or norms, and are recognized as international law or practice."[8] The manual recognizes that, in finding this and other sources of international law, resort may be had, *inter alia*, to "accepted standards as revealed in agreements or in practice or in authoritative pronouncements."[9]

The general statements of customary law are widely recognized by practitioners in the field and are not controversial. Widely recognized texts and commentaries organize, analyze and serve as the vehicle for the development of this body of law. Indeed, the U.S. military manuals and the U.S. written and oral presentations to the ICJ rely upon generally the same legal texts and commentaries as the opponents of nuclear weapons. The substance of customary international law applicable to the issue at hand is generally not in contention, the disputes having more to do, as noted, with the application of the law to such facts. Not that there are no disputes: The scope of the principles of neutrality and of environmental security, for example, are particularly in contention, but, as an overall matter, the substance of the law which we need apply is generally non-controversial.

One complicating factor in defining international law results from the overlap of conventional and customary law. As noted, conventional law can both ripen into customary law and generally accepted principles of law, and can also, in the first instance, express already existent customary law or general accepted principles.[10] In either case, we now have several bodies of law to look to, each potentially expressed in different mediums.

An example is that presented by Additional Protocol I to the 1949 Geneva Convention, which expresses anew, in the nuclear era, earlier conventional and customary rules on such subjects as the principles of proportionality, necessity, discrimination, civilian immunity, humanitarian law, prohibition on terrorist attacks, and limits on reprisals. It also prohibits any methods or means of warfare that "are

---

[8] THE AIR FORCE MANUAL ON INTERNATIONAL LAW at 1-3 (citing 1 WHITEMAN, DIGEST OF INTERNATIONAL LAW 1-2 (1963–1973)).

[9] *Id.* (citing 1 WHITEMAN, DIGEST OF INTERNATIONAL LAW 1-2 (1963–1973)).

[10] *See* THE LAW OF LAND WARFARE at 6 (stating that the provisions of conventional law "are in large part but formal and specific applications of general principles of law").

THE NAVAL/MARINE COMMANDER'S HANDBOOK states that the "lack of precision in the definition and interpretation of rules of customary law has been a principal motivation behind efforts to codify the law of armed conflict through written agreements (treaties and conventions.)" *Id.* at 5-10.

intended, or may be expected, to cause widespread, long-term and severe damage to the natural environment."[11] The United States has signed but not ratified this Protocol.[12] In signing this protocol, the United States, along with other nuclear powers, interposed a formal understanding "that the rules established by this Protocol were not intended to have any effect on and do not regulate or prohibit the use of nuclear weapons."[13]

This situation raises questions as to how we sort out such considerations as the following: the continuing requirements of the

---

[11] Protocol Additional to the Geneva Conventions of August 12, 1949, and Relating to the Protection of Victims of International Armed Conflicts (Protocol I), opened for signature Dec. 12, 1977, 1125 U.N.T.S. 4, 16 I.L.M. 1391.

[12] *See* THE NAVAL/MARINE COMMANDER'S HANDBOOK, at 5-16 to 5-17 n.30. *See also* M.J. BOWMAN & D.J. HARRIS, MULTILATERAL TREATIES: INDEX AND CURRENT STATUS: TENTH CUMULATIVE SUPPLEMENT 419 (1984); M.J. BOWMAN & D.J. HARRIS, MULTILATERAL TREATIES: INDEX AND CURRENT STATUS 260–61 (1993).

The President's stated reasons for not submitting Additional Protocol I to the Senate for ratification are set forth in Senate Treaty Doc. No. 100-2, *reprinted in* 26 I.L.M. 561 (1987) and in Annex AS5-1 to THE NAVAL/MARINE COMMANDER'S HANDBOOK at AS5-1 (primarily the judgment that Protocol I extends unacceptable rights to terrorist organizations in attacks on non-combatants). *See also* THE NAVAL/MARINE COMMANDER'S HANDBOOK at 5-16 to 5-17 n.30 and authorities cited, including the trauvaux preparatoires of Protocol, *reprinted in* LEVIE, PROTECTION OF WAR VICTIMS: PROTOCOL I TO THE 1949 GENEVA CONVENTIONS (4 v. 1979–81); BOTHE, PARTSCH & SOLF 1-603; and ICRC, COMMENTARY 19-1304.

[13] U.S. ICJ Memorandum/GA App., at 26–27 (citing International Committee of the Red Cross, Public Information Division, *CD-ROM on International Humanitarian Law* (September 1993), containing up-to-date list of signatures, ratifications, accessions and successions relating to international humanitarian law treaties, as well as the full text of reservations, declarations and objections thereto). *See also* DIGEST OF UNITED STATES PRACTICE IN INTERNATIONAL LAW 920 (J. Boyd ed., 1977), *quoted and discussed in* Peter Weiss, Burns H. Weston, Richard A. Falk, & Saul H. Mendlovitz, Draft Memorial in Support of the Application of the World Health Organization for an Advisory Opinion by the International Court of Justice on the Legality of the Use of Nuclear Weapons Under International Law, Including the W.H.O. Constitution, 4 TRANSNAT'L L. & CONTEMP. PROBS. 721, 781 (1994).

Great Britain, France and other States took this same position. *See* U.S. ICJ Memorandum/GA App. at 27. *See also* Rostow, *The World Health Organization, the International Court of Justice, and Nuclear Weapons*, 20 YALE J. INT'L L. 151, 162 (1995); THE LAW OF LAND WARFARE at 1–2.

underlying customary law and the impact, if any, upon such law of the Protocol; the scope of applicability of the newly introduced provisions of the Protocol, facially and based upon the drafting history; and the effect of the "understanding" by the United States and other nuclear powers as to non-applicability of the Protocol to nuclear weapons.

Generally Accepted Principles of Law

Generally accepted principles of law, as a source of international law, are both more and less amorphous than customary law. More amorphous in the sense that, unlike customary law, they are not so readily available in standard research materials; indeed one must make a special effort to find them and the effort can be quite challenging. Less amorphous in that lawyers as a whole know how to deal with this kind of law, at least from within their own individual legal systems.

Generally recognized principles of law are a primary source of international law. *The Naval/Marine Commander's Handbook* states: "In recent years there has been a marked tendency to include among the sources of the rules of warfare certain principles of law adopted by many nations in their domestic legislation."[14] The handbook quotes the decision of the United States Military Tribunal in *The Hostage Case*:

> The tendency has been to apply the term "customs and practices accepted by civilized nations generally" as it is used in international law, to the laws of war only. But the principle has no such restricted meaning. It applies as well to fundamental principles of justice which have been accepted and adopted by civilized nations generally. In determining whether such a fundamental rule of justice is entitled to be declared a principle of international law, an examination of the municipal laws of states in the family of nations will reveal the answer. If it is found to have been accepted generally as a fundamental rule of justice by most nations in their municipal law, its declaration as a rule of international law would seem to be fully justified.[15]

"General principles" appear to be the great unexplored and under-utilized source of the law of war. Everyone recognizes this source; it is entirely non-controversial, but its potential impact upon the issue we are examining has remained largely unexplored. In later chapters I review a number of rules of law which are generally recognized by the United States and other States throughout the world and which I conclude bear heavily upon the lawfulness of the use of nuclear

---

[14] THE NAVAL/MARINE COMMANDER'S HANDBOOK at 5-11.
[15] *Id.* at 5-11 to 5-12 (quoting *The Hostage Case*).

weapons in ways which have not been generally recognized. I focus particularly on general principles having to do with the legal significance of various levels of probability that a State's actions will result in unnecessary, disproportionate or indiscriminate injury to noncombatants, neutrals or others and upon principles having to do with the nature of a *per se* rule.

Consent lies at the basis, at least initially, of international law. Recognizing "general principles of law recognized by civilized nations" as a primary source of international law,[16] *The Air Force Manual on International Law* emphasizes that this source, like others, is based on consent, stating that international law "derives its basis primarily from State practice and State consent represented in the form of treaties, custom or general principles of law acknowledged by all States or by all principal legal systems."[17] The element of consent with respect to generally accepted principles is inherent in their wide acceptance by States. Indeed, such wide acceptance may result in the formation of customary international law as well.[18]

It will become relevant to note that consent in this latter sense is more of a constructive than a real nature. The adoption by "all principal legal systems" of a principle of law as itself constituting the establishment of that principle as a new rule of international law is conceptually different from the more familiar notion of States formulating international law through negotiating and subscribing to treaties and multinational conventions or engaging in specific State practices in the international arena over extended periods of time. This involves a form of conscious parallelism in the formation of law. The important thing to note is that the United States unequivocally recognizes such general principles as binding international law.

Subsidiary Sources of International Law

In language that will bear upon our analysis, and particularly upon my reliance upon the decisions of a number of U.S. and other domestic courts, *The Air Force Manual on International Law* refers to decisions of "national and international courts and tribunals and writings of qualified authorities" as subsidiary sources of international law[19] and cites with approval Whiteman's statement that "authoritative pronouncements" as to international law may include "[d]ecisions of

---

[16] *See* THE AIR FORCE MANUAL ON INTERNATIONAL LAW at 1-2 to 1-3.

[17] *Id.* at 1-3.

[18] *See* THE LAW OF LAND WARFARE at 6.

[19] THE AIR FORCE MANUAL ON INTERNATIONAL LAW at 1-3.

local courts and tribunals" as well as "international judicial tribunals and international arbitral bodies, according to their competence," and "teachings of universities and the writings of publicists, depending upon their merit."[20]

The Naval/Marine Commander's Handbook states that evidence of the law of armed conflict "may also be found in national military manuals, judicial decisions, the writings of publicists, and the work of various international bodies."[21]

The Air Force Manual on International Law states that the subsidiary category of judicial decisions and scholarly and professional writings exists not only as a reflection of existent law but also as an expression of it.[22] The manual quotes the U.S. Supreme Court decision in *The Paquete Habana*:

> [The works of jurists and commentators on the subject of International Law] are resorted to by judicial tribunals, not for the speculations of their authors concerning what the law ought to be, but for trustworthy evidence of what the law really is.[23]

U.S. Recognition of General Principles as Binding

The United States has recognized that generally accepted principles of law could be a sufficient basis for the unlawfulness of the use of a particular weapon or type of weapon. *The Air Force Manual on International Law* states that the use of a weapon may be unlawful based not only on "expressed prohibitions contained in specific rules of custom and convention," but also on "those prohibitions laid down in the general principles of the law of war."[24] Similarly, in discussing how the lawfulness of new weapons and methods of warfare is determined, the manual states that such determination is made based on international treaty or custom, upon analogy to weapons or methods previously determined to be lawful or unlawful, and upon the evaluation of the compliance of such new weapons or methods with established principles of law, such as the rules of necessity, discrimination and proportionality.[25]

---

[20] *Id.* at 1-3 (citing 1 WHITEMAN).

[21] THE NAVAL/MARINE COMMANDER'S HANDBOOK at 5-10 n.12.

[22] THE AIR FORCE MANUAL ON INTERNATIONAL LAW at 1-3.

[23] *Id.* at 1-13 n.9 (quoting *The Paquete Habana*, 175 U.S. 677, 700 (1900)).

[24] *Id.* at 6-1, 6-9 n.3 (quoting US Navy War College, 1955 INTERNATIONAL LAW STUDIES 45, 48, 50 (Tucker ed., 1957)).

[25] *See id.* at 6-7.

The Air Force Manual on International Law notes that the International Military Tribunal at Nuremberg in the case of the *Major War Criminals* found that international law is contained not only in treaties and custom but also in the "general principles of justice applied by jurists and practiced by military courts."[26]

This point as to the sufficiency of general principles as basis for determining the unlawfulness of military actions becomes a key acknowledgment by the United States—and one, as we shall see, which the United States backed away from before the ICJ in arguing that the use of a weapon by the United States cannot be prohibited unless the United States has specifically agreed to such a prohibition.

Contrary State Practice as Not Vitiating Treaty Obligations

There is also no doubt that treaty obligations are applicable even in the face of contrary State practice. *The Air Force Manual on International Law* states that the practice of States "does not modify" the legal obligation to comply with treaty obligations since such obligations are "contractual in nature."[27]

This rule—akin to the proposition that a high crime rate does not vitiate the criminal laws—makes perfect sense. But the United States overrode it in its arguments before the ICJ, essentially arguing, at least implicitly, that the United States is not bound by a treaty obligation affecting the use of nuclear weapons if the United States' own practice and that of other States has been inconsistent with such obligation.

Specifically, the United States argued that the superpowers' practice of deterrence—involving, as it does, the overt threat of the use of nuclear weapons—precluded the application to such weapons of treaty obligations and commitments inconsistent with the use of nuclear weapons.

Relevant Sources of Law

All four traditional sources of international law—treaties and conventions, custom, generally accepted principles, and judicial decisions and writings of qualified experts—will be relevant to our analysis. The principles of law upon which I primarily rely, those of

---

[26] *Id.* at 1-6 (citing I TRIAL OF THE MAJOR WAR CRIMINALS BEFORE THE INTERNATIONAL MILITARY TRIBUNAL 221 (1947)).

[27] *Id.* at 1-15 n.35 (citing 1 TRIAL OF THE MAJOR WAR CRIMINALS BEFORE THE INTERNATIONAL TRIBUNAL 221 (1947); Vienna Convention on the Law of Treaties, Articles 26, 27, 31 (May 23, 1969); O'CONNELL, INTERNATIONAL LAW 261–262 (1970)).

necessity, proportionality, discrimination, and neutrality, are widely embodied and reflected in each of these sources.

Nature and Purpose of the Law of Armed Conflict

The foregoing tells us where international law is located, how we can find it. But once we find it, we are going to have to interpret it in order to be able to apply it. Inevitably, there will be ambiguities as to the text of conventional and the content of customary and other law. How do we then proceed?

It is a fundamental insight and indeed rule of law, implicit in the limits of human expression, that law—be it statute, case precedent, international treaty, general principle—is to be interpreted in light of its purpose. This is fundamentally a question of ascertaining intent, either specific or constructive: What was intended by this "law," or, if the makers did not focus on this particular application, what would they have intended if they had so focused?

For this reason, our notions of the purposes of the law of armed conflict become integral to our interpretation and application of this law to the issue at hand.

The purpose of the law of armed conflict is to temper the violence of war, both for idealistic and pragmatic reasons. Idealistically, to minimize death and destruction out of compassion. Pragmatically, to protect one's own military and civilian personnel and objects from the acts of violence which one is prohibited from inflicting upon enemy persons and objects. Underlying is a core idea as to the nature of international political relations: that war exists not in isolation but in relation to peace, and that the two, war and peace, represent the human political condition. War is by nature limited not total; in the fullness of time, it will give way to peace. Life will prevail over death, reason over the dark potential of human nature. The purpose of war is to create an acceptable peace. The purpose of the law of war is to impose rationality on war so that the peace can be restored.

The Naval/Marine Commander's Handbook states that the "essential" purpose of the law of war is to provide "common ground of rationality between enemies," adding that: "The law of armed conflict is intended to preclude purposeless, unnecessary destruction of life and property and to ensure that violence is used only to defeat the enemy's military forces."[28]

The handbook goes on to describe the objective:

---

[28] THE NAVAL/MARINE COMMANDER'S HANDBOOK at 5-7 n.7.

If followed by all participants, the law of armed conflict will inhibit warfare from needlessly affecting persons or things of little military value. By preventing needless cruelty, the bitterness and hatred arising from armed conflict is lessened, and thus it is easier to restore an enduring peace. The legal and military experts who attempted to codify the laws of war more than a hundred years ago reflected this reality when they declared that the final object of an armed conflict is the "re-establishment of good relations and a more solid and lasting peace between the belligerent States."[29]

The Air Force Manual on International Law states that the law of armed conflict is "inspired by the humanitarian desire of civilized nations to diminish the effects of conflicts" and represents an attempt to prevent "degeneration of conflicts into savagery and brutality, thereby facilitating the restoration of peace and the friendly relations which must, at some point, inevitably accompany or follow the conclusion of hostilities."[30]

The manual adds that the law of armed conflict "has been said to represent in some measure minimum standards of civilization."[31] Noting that the law of armed conflict developed from "an amalgam of social, political and military considerations," the manual adds that "the primary basis for the law, and the principal reason for its respect, is that it generally serves the self-interest of everyone subject to its commands."[32] The manual further notes the principle set forth in the "Lieber Code" (discussed below) that military necessity does not justify "any act of hostility which makes the return to peace unnecessarily difficult."[33]

The manual quotes the Chairman of the Joint Chiefs of Staff:

> The Armed Forces of the United States have benefited from, and highly value, the humanitarianism encompassed by the laws of war. Many are alive today only because of the mutual restraint imposed by these rules, notwithstanding the fact that the rules have been applied imperfectly.[34]

---

[29] *Id.* at 5-7 n.7 (citing Final Protocol of the Brussels Conference of 27 August 1874, Schindler & Toman 26).

[30] THE AIR FORCE MANUAL ON INTERNATIONAL LAW at 1-5.

[31] *Id.* at 1-5, 1-15 n.30.

[32] *Id.* at 1-11.

[33] *Id.* at 1-15 n.33.

[34] *Id.* at 1-9 (citing Address by General George S. Brown, Chairman of the Joint Chiefs of Staff, DOD News Release No. 479-74 (10 Oct 1974)).

The Army's *Law of Land Warfare* states that the law of armed conflict is inspired by the desire to "diminish the evils of war" by:

> a. Protecting both combatants and noncombatants from unnecessary suffering;
> b. Safeguarding certain fundamental human rights of persons who fall into the hands of the enemy, particularly prisoners of war, the wounded and sick, and civilians; and
> c. Facilitating the restoration of peace.[35]

The severe limits implicit in these concepts as to the nature of war and the purpose of the law of armed conflict were portrayed most forcefully by the United States Military Tribunal in the *Krupp* trial:

> It is an essence of war that one or the other side must lose and the experienced generals and statesmen knew this when they drafted the rules and customs of land warfare. In short, these rules and customs of warfare are designed specifically for all phases of war. They comprise the law for such emergency. To claim that they can be wantonly—and at the sole discretion of any one belligerent— disregarded when he considers his own situation to be critical, means nothing more or less than to abrogate the laws and customs of war entirely.[36]

Emphasizing the broad scope of international law, *The Air Force Manual on International Law* adopts language of Whiteman to the effect that international law is evidenced by the "general norms of civilization."[37]

It is also in the nature of the law of war that it be dynamic, evolving out of human experience and necessity and advancing with the progress of civilization. *The Air Force Manual on International Law* recognizes as one of "the most descriptive definitions of international law" Hackworth's statement:

> International law ... is a system of jurisprudence which, for the most part, has evolved out of the experiences and the necessities of situations that have arisen from time to time. It has developed with the progress of civilization with the increasing realization by nations that their relations *inter se*, if not their existence, must be

---

[35] THE LAW OF LAND WARFARE at 3.

[36] *The Krupp Trial* (Trial of Alfred Felix Alwyn Krupp Von Bohlen und Halbach and Eleven Others), 10 LRTWC 139 (1949), *quoted in* THE NAVAL/MARINE COMMANDER'S HANDBOOK at 5-6.

[37] THE AIR FORCE MANUAL ON INTERNATIONAL LAW at 1-3 (quoting 1 WHITEMAN, DIGEST OF INTERNATIONAL LAW 1-2).

governed by and dependent upon rules of law fairly certain and generally reasonable ... .[38]

The manual similarly relies upon Whiteman's definition, which also emphasizes the dynamic nature of international law:

> International law is the standard of conduct, at a given time, for states and other entities subject thereto. It comprises the rights, privileges, powers, and immunities of states and entities invoking its provisions, as well as the correlative fundamental duties, absence of rights, liabilities and disabilities. International law is, more or less, in a continual state of change and development.[39]

Political Nature of the Law of Armed Conflict

Observing a point that has salience to this issue, *The Air Force Manual on International Law* states that international law "like domestic law, is the product of political process."[40] Relatedly, I argue that, with the demise of the Cold War, the breakup of the Soviet Union, and the emergence of a discordant multi-polar world with numerous "rogue" nations and terrorist groups, the current nuclear weapons regime—with its legitimization of nuclear weapons to support deterrence—is no longer in the political interest of the United States.

Binding Nature of International Law

The U.S. Constitution provides that treaties entered into by the United States are "the supreme Law of the Land."[41] *The Air Force Manual on International Law* notes that "state and federal courts have declared international law to be part of the law of the land."[42] The manual states that the United States is bound to follow customary international law "not because a treaty requires it, but because international law imposes the obligation on all states."[43]

The military manuals of the U.S. armed forces reiterate the U.S. commitment to observance of international law—and also the belief

---

[38] *Id.* at 1-2; 1-13 nn.5–6 (quoting 1 HACKWORTH, DIGEST OF INTERNATIONAL LAW at 1, 7 vols. (1940–43)).

[39] *Id.* at 1-2; 1-13 nn.6–7 (quoting 1 WHITEMAN, DIGEST OF INTERNATIONAL LAW 1, 15 vols. with index (1963–1973)).

[40] *Id.* at 1-3.

[41] THE LAW OF LAND WARFARE at 7 (quoting U.S. CONST. Art VI, cl. 2).

[42] THE AIR FORCE MANUAL ON INTERNATIONAL LAW at 1-5, n.26 (citing Ware v. Hylton, 3 U.S. (3 Dall.) 199 (1796); Foster v. Neilson, 27 U.S. (2 Pet.) 252, 314 (1829); and Asakura v. City of Seattle, 265 U.S. 332, 341 (1924)).

[43] *Id.* at 1-7.

that this body of law, and the restraints it imposes, are in the interests of the United States. *The Air Force Manual on International Law* states, "The primary basis for the law, and the principal reason for its respect, is that it generally serves the self-interest of everyone subject to its commands."[44] *The Navy/Marine Commander's Handbook* states, "At all times a commander shall observe and require his command to observe the principles of international law."[45]

The Air Force Manual on International Law further notes that nations have "many of the same reasons to obey international law as individuals do to follow domestic law," including "foreseeability, reciprocity, approbation and efficiency."[46] The manual states that the Air Force recognizes "the inestimable value of international law, which introduces norms of behavior and establishes identifiable parameters of acceptable actions; and we must continue to strive to substitute the rule of law for the rule of force in international law."[47]

The manual states that the United States has "always viewed the law of armed conflict as important" and notes that the United States "issued the first comprehensive code regulating armed conflict in modern times"—the "Lieber Code."[48] The manual also cites the United States' central role in the War Crime trials after the Second World War.[49]

The Lieber Code was promulgated by the United States during the Civil War and has heavily influenced the development of the law of war. *The Naval/Marine Commander's Handbook* summarizes its significance:

> In the United States, President Lincoln commissioned Dr. Francis Lieber, then a professor at Columbia College, New York City, to draft a code for the use of the Union Army during the Civil War. His code was revised by a board of Army officers, and promulgated by President Lincoln as General Orders No. 100, on 24 April 1863, as the Instructions for the Government of Armies of the United States in the Field. The Lieber Code strongly influenced the further codification of the law of armed conflict and the adoption of similar regulations by other nations, including The United States Naval War Code of 1900, and had a great influence on the drafters of

---

[44] *Id.* at 1-11.

[45] THE NAVAL/MARINE COMMANDER'S HANDBOOK at 4.

[46] THE AIR FORCE MANUAL ON INTERNATIONAL LAW at 1-3.

[47] *Id.* at 1-4 n.19 (quoting from Air Force News Release, Tuesday, November 4, 1975, Speech by The Honorable John L. McLucas, Secretary of the Air Force.).

[48] *Id.* at 1-8.

[49] *Id.*

Hague Convention No. IV regarding the Laws and Customs of War on Land.[50]

Main Corpus of the Law of Armed Conflict

As noted, proponents and opponents alike of today's nuclear weapons regime generally rely upon the same core body of law, the same conventions, customs, principles and other sources.[51]   As described by the ICJ in its recent decision, this "body of legal prescriptions,"[52] the "laws and customs of war," are largely set forth in

---

[50] THE NAVAL/MARINE COMMANDER'S HANDBOOK at 5-11 n.13.

[51] *E.g.*, HACKWORTH, DIGEST OF INTERNATIONAL LAW, 7 vols. (1940–1943); WHITEMAN, DIGEST OF INTERNATIONAL LAW, 15 vols with index (1963–1973); STONE, LEGAL CONTROLS OF INTERNATIONAL CONFLICT (1973); MCDOUGAL & FELICIANO, LAW AND MINIMUM PUBLIC ORDER (1961); SCHWARZENBERG, INTERNATIONAL LAW, INTERNATIONAL COURTS, THE LAW OF ARMED CONFLICT (1968); FALK ET AL., THE INTERNATIONAL LAW OF CIVIL WAR (1971); BISHOP, INTERNATIONAL LAW, CASES AND MATERIALS (3rd ed. 1971); BROWNLIE, PRINCIPLES OF PUBLIC INTERNATIONAL LAW (1973); FRIEDMAN, LISSITZYN, & PUGH, INTERNATIONAL LAW (1969); O'CONNELL, INTERNATIONAL LAW, 2 vols. (1970)—to name just a few, all of which are cited THE AIR FORCE MANUAL ON INTERNATIONAL LAW 1-13 n.1, 5 and relied upon in the text. Any one of these sources (and updated versions of same) would be equally likely to be relied upon by opponents of the nuclear weapons regime.

There is a considerable body of academic and other professional writing on the subject. A leading article developing the arguments as to the unlawfulness of the use of nuclear weapons is Peter Weiss, Burns H. Weston, Richard A. Falk, & Saul H. Mendlovitz, Draft Memorial in support of the Application of the World Health Organization for an Advisory Opinion by the International Court of Justice, *supra* note 13, which sets forth an extensive survey of the literature on both sides of the issue.   Another detailed exposition of the arguments against the lawfulness of the use of these weapons is in Government of the Solomon Islands, *Written Observations on the Request by the General Assembly for an Advisory Opinion, reprinted in* 7 CRIM. L.F. 299 (No. 2/1996). Arguments for the lawfulness of the use of nuclear weapons are addressed in Rostow, *The World Health Organization, the International Court of Justice, and Nuclear Weapons*, 20 YALE J. INT'L L. 151 (1995).

[52] *Legality of the Threat or Use of Nuclear Weapons*, International Court of Justice, Advisory Opinion, General List at pt. VI, 35–36, No. 95 (July 8, 1996) [hereinafter Nuclear Weapons Advisory Opinion] ¶ 75, at 27.

All but five of the fifteen ICJ opinions are available at 35 I.L.M. 809 (1996). The remaining five, the declarations of Judges Bedjaoui, Herczegh and Bravo and the individual opinions of Judges Guillaume and Ranjeva, appear at 35 I.L.M. 1343 (1996). The opinions and various of the submissions to the Court are also available at the Court's own website at <http://www.icj-cij.

"one single complex system" known as "international humanitarian law," a body of customary rules—many of which have been codified in the "Hague Law" and the "Geneva Law."[53]

The Hague Law consists of codifications undertaken in The Hague (including the Conventions of 1899 and 1907) which were based partly upon the St. Petersburg Declaration of 1868 and the results of the Brussels Conference of 1874.[54] The ICJ noted that this Hague Law, particularly the Regulations Respecting the Laws and Customs of War on Land ("Hague Regulations"), "fixed the rights and duties of belligerents in their conduct of operations and limited the choice of methods of means of injuring the enemy in an international armed conflict."[55]

The ICJ further stated that the Geneva Law, consisting of codifications undertaken in Geneva (the Conventions of 1864, 1906, 1929 and 1949), protect "the victims of war" and aim "to provide safeguards for disabled armed forces personnel and persons not taking part in the hostilities."[56] The ICJ noted that the more recent provisions of the Additional Protocols I and II of 1977 to the Geneva Conventions "give expression and attest to the unity and complexity" of international humanitarian law.[57]

---

org/>, and at <http://www.law.cornell.edu/world/>. Some of the same materials are also available in THE CASE AGAINST THE Bomb (Roger S. Clark & Madeleine Sanns eds., 1996). *See also* Roger S. Clark, *The Laws of Armed Conflict and the Use or Threat of Use of Nuclear Weapons*, 7 CRIM. L.F. 265, 266 (No. 2/1996).

[53] Nuclear Weapons Advisory Opinion ¶ 75, at 27, 35 I.L.M at 827. *See also* THE NAVAL/MARINE COMMANDER'S HANDBOOK at 5-10 to 5-12 (summarizing in detail the development of the law of armed conflict).

[54] Nuclear Weapons Advisory Opinion ¶ 75, at 27, 35 I.L.M. at 827.

[55] *Id.*

[56] *See id.* at ¶ 76, at 27.

[57] *Id.*, referring to Protocol Additional to the Geneva Conventions of 12 August 1949, and Relating to the Protection of Victims of International Armed Conflicts ("Protocol I"), 12 December 1977, 1125 U.N.T.S. 3. For related explanatory materials, *see* M. BOTHE, K. PARTSCH & W. SOLF, NEW RULES FOR VICTIMS OF ARMED CONFLICTS (1982), pp. 312, 317; and INTERNATIONAL COMMITTEE OF THE RED CROSS, COMMENTARY ON THE ADDITIONAL PROTOCOLS OF 8 JUNE 1977 662 (1987).

The ICJ further noted that since the turn of the century, the development of new means of combat—"without calling into question the longstanding principles and rules of international law"—made necessary specific prohibitions of the use of certain weapons, including explosive projectiles

As will be clear from the ensuing discussion, this body of international humanitarian law is recognized by the United States, including in its military manuals and its briefs before the ICJ.

As to the question of whether Additional Protocol I, which, as noted above, the United States has signed but not ratified, is applicable to nuclear weapons, the ICJ, in language which is instructive in several respects, stated:

> 84. Nor is there any need for the Court to elaborate on the question of the applicability of Additional Protocol I of 1977 to nuclear weapons. It need only observe that while, at the Diplomatic Conference of 1974-1977, there was no substantive debate on the nuclear issue and no specific solution concerning this question was put forward, Additional Protocol I in no way replaced the general customary rules applicable to all means and methods of combat including nuclear weapons. In particular, the Court recalls that all States are bound by those rules in Additional Protocol I which, when adopted, were merely the expression of the pre-existing customary law, such as the Martens Clause, reaffirmed in the first article of Additional Protocol I. The fact that certain types of weapons were not specifically dealt with by the 1974-1977 Conference does not permit the drawing of any legal conclusions relating to the substantive issues which the use of such weapons would raise.[58]

The Court also recognized the Martens Clause as a broad source of international law in emerging areas:

> The Court would likewise refer, in relation to [the principles of humanitarian law] to the Martens Clause, which was first included in the Hague Convention II with Respect to the Laws and Customs

---

under 400 grammes, dum-dum bullets and asphyxiating gases. Nuclear Weapons Advisory Opinion ¶76, at 27.

The Court noted that chemical and bacteriological weapons were prohibited by the 1925 Geneva Protocol and that, more recently, the use of weapons producing "non-detectable fragments," of other types of "mines, booby traps and other devices," and of "incendiary weapons," was "either prohibited or limited, depending on the case, by the Convention of 10 October 1980 on Prohibitions or Restrictions on the Use of Certain Conventional Weapons Which May Be Deemed to Be Excessively Injurious or to Have Indiscriminate Effects." *Id.* at ¶ 76, at 27, 35 I.L.M. at 827.

The Court further noted that the provisions of the Convention on "mines, booby traps and other devices" were amended on May 3, 1996 to "regulate in greater detail, for example, the use of anti-personnel land mines." *Id.*

[58] Nuclear Weapons Advisory Opinion ¶ 84, at 29, 35 I.L.M. at 828.

of War on Land of 1899 and which has proved to be an effective means of addressing the rapid evolution of military technology. A modern version of that clause is to be found in Article 1, paragraph 2, of Additional Protocol I of 1977, which reads as follows:

"In cases not covered by this Protocol or by other international agreements, civilians and combatants remain under the protection and authority of the principles of international law derived from established custom, from the principles of humanity and from the dictates of public conscience."[59]

As to the binding nature of the laws of armed conflict, the Court stated:

79. It is undoubtedly because a great many rules of humanitarian law applicable in armed conflict are so fundamental to the respect of the human person and "elementary considerations of humanity" as the Court put it in its Judgment of 9 April 1949 in the *Corfu Channel* case (I.C.J. Reports 1949, p. 22), that the Hague and Geneva Conventions have enjoyed a broad accession. Further these fundamental rules are to be observed by all States whether or not they have ratified the conventions that contain them, because they constitute intransgressible principles of international customary law.[60]

The Court added that the Nuremberg Tribunal had found the Hague Regulations to be customary law:

80. The Nuremberg International Military Tribunal had already found in 1945 that the humanitarian rules included in the Regulations annexed to the Hague Convention IV of 1907 "were recognized by all civilized nations and were regarded as being declaratory of the laws and customs of war" (International Military Tribunal, Trial of the *Major War Criminals*, 14 November 1945–1 October 1946, Nuremberg, 1947, Vol. 1, p. 254).[61]

Of the foregoing materials making up the "one single complex system" of "international humanitarian law," the Hague Regulations, Additional Protocol I and the Martens Clause are of a particularly comprehensive nature and hence, as we shall see, of particular importance to the matter of hand.

---

[59] *Id.* ¶ 78, at 28, 35 I.L.M. at 827.

[60] *Id.* ¶ 79, at 28.

[61] *Id.* ¶ 80, at 28.

Jus ad Bellum and *Jus in Bello*

A distinction is made between the bases upon which a State may lawfully resort to force and the level of force that may be used upon such resort. These have traditionally been referred to as *jus ad bellum* and *jus in bello*, respectively.

Jus ad Bellum

Historically, States were deemed generally to have the right to resort to war. This right was implicit in sovereignty. The U.N. Charter changed this, prohibiting the use of force except in individual or collective self-defense or in U.N. enforcement actions.[62] Wars started in violation of these rules are "aggressive" or "illegal" wars.[63]

The Naval/Marine Commander's Handbook states:

> 4.3.2 The Right of Self-Defense. The Charter of the United Nations recognizes that all nations enjoy the inherent right of individual and collective self-defense against armed attack. U.S. doctrine on self-defense, set forth in the JCS Peacetime Rules of Engagement for U.S. Forces provides that the use of force in self-defense against armed attack or the threat of imminent armed attack, rests upon two elements:
>
> 1. Necessity—The requirements that a use of force be in response to a hostile act or hostile intent.
>
> 2. Proportionality—The requirement that the use of force be in all circumstances limited in intensity, duration, and scope to that which is reasonably required to counter the attack or threat of attack and to ensure the continued safety of U.S. forces.[64]

---

[62] *See* THE NAVAL/MARINE COMMANDER'S HANDBOOK at 4-9 to 4-12, 5-1, for a detailed discussion of the scope of the right to self-defense under the Charter, including such matters as armed aggression short of armed attack and anticipatory self-defense, and the applicability of the requirements of necessity and proportionality to the exercise of this right. (citing the *Caroline Case*, 2 Moore 409-14, the handbook states that "anticipatory self-defense involves the use of armed force where there is a clear necessity that is instant, overwhelming, and leaving no reasonable choice of peaceful means"). *Id.* at 4-12 to 4-13. *See also* THE AIR FORCE MANUAL ON INTERNATIONAL LAW at 1-10 and 1-16 to 1-17 (quoting, *inter alia*, U.N. CHARTER arts. 2(3), 2(4), and 51).

[63] THE AIR FORCE COMMANDER'S HANDBOOK at 1-10.

[64] THE NAVAL/MARINE COMMANDER'S HANDBOOK at 4-9 to 4-10 (citations omitted).

Jus in Bello

Thus, whether a particular use of force was lawful in the first instance thus turns upon the U.N. Charter requirements. *Jus in bello*, in contrast, invokes the entire body of the law of armed conflict. *The Naval/Marine Commander's Handbook* explains:

> It is important to distinguish between resort to war, or armed conflict, and the conduct of armed conflict. "Whether or not resort to armed conflict in a particular circumstance is prohibited by the United Nations Charter (and therefore unlawful), the manner in which that armed conflict is conducted continues to be regulated by the law of armed conflict. (For purposes of this publication, the term "law of armed conflict" is synonymous with "law of war.")[65]

As to nomenclature, the manual further states, "The rules governing the actual conduct of armed conflict are variously known as the *jus in bello*, the law of armed conflict, or international humanitarian law."[66]

So also, *The Air Force Manual on International Law* states that the law of armed conflict "represents standards applicable whether or not the use of force was prohibited, permissible or unascertainable" and "neither authorizes nor prohibits the basic decision to use force."[67] "[T]he law of armed conflict does not authorize aggression—nor does it condemn aggression—it exists independently of the causes of the conflict and applies regardless of the causes."[68]

The question can be asked, does the law of armed conflict authorize the taking of military steps not prohibited—or does it only prohibit what it prohibits, without containing any authorizations? *The Air Force Manual on International Law* states:

> The law of armed conflict contains both affirmative obligations and prohibitions. Yet this body of law neither authorizes nor prohibits the basic decision to use force. That issue is related back to the concept of self defense–aggression ... . The law of armed conflict represents "standards of civilization" which have been shaped by the concepts of military necessity, humanity and chivalry. ... For these reasons, the law of armed conflict cannot be argued to authorize the use of force since the legal regulation of that issue is by a separate and distinct legal regime. The law of armed conflict

---

[65] *Id.* at 5-1 to 5-2 (citations omitted). A somewhat different analysis is applicable to so-called "reprisals," as discussed hereinafter.

[66] THE NAVAL/MARINE COMMANDER'S HANDBOOK at 5-3 n.3.

[67] THE AIR FORCE MANUAL ON INTERNATIONAL LAW at 1-15 n.30 (emphasis omitted).

[68] *Id.* at 1-14 n.24.

represents standards applicable whether or not the use of force was prohibited, permissible or unascertainable.[69]

General Rules of the Law of Armed Conflict

There are a number of rules of the law of armed conflict recognized by the United States as generally applicable to the use of force. *The Naval/Marine Commander's Handbook* identifies the "three fundamental principles" of such law:[70]

> 1. The right of belligerents to adopt means of injuring the enemy is not unlimited.[71]
> 2. It is prohibited to launch attacks against the civilian population as such.[72]
> 3. Distinctions must be made between combatants and noncombatants, to the effect that noncombatants be spared as much as possible.[73]

The handbook states that the United States considers these three fundamental principles as customary international law.[74] These principles underlie and are fleshed out in a number of overlapping rules, including those of necessity, proportionality, discrimination, moderation, humanity civilian immunity and neutrality.

Because of their centrality to our analysis, we will review the U.S. position as to the scope of each of these rules.

Rule of Proportionality

The rule of proportionality—one of the key rules upon which our analysis of this issue rests—prohibits the use of a weapon if its probable effects upon combatant or non-combatant persons or objects

---

[69] *Id.* at 1-15 n.30

[70] THE NAVAL/MARINE COMMANDER'S HANDBOOK at 8-1 (citations omitted).

[71] *Id.* at 8-1 n.3. The handbook states that this rule is based, inter alia, on Article 22 of the Hague Regulations and Article 35(1) of Additional Protocol I, and adds that the United States regards both of these provisions as customary international law. *Id.* at 8-1 n.2.

[72] *Id.* at 8-1 n.3. The handbook states that this "customary rule of international law" was codified for the first time in Additional Protocol I.

[73] *Id.* at 8-1 n.4. The handbook states that this "customary rule of international law" was similarly codified for the first time in Additional Protocol I.

[74] *Id.* at 8-1 n.1.

would likely be disproportionate to the value of the anticipated military objective.

The Naval/Marine Commander's Handbook recognizes the proportionality requirement as a customary rule of international law and describes the requirement as codified in the prohibition by Additional Protocol I of attacks "which may be expected to cause incidental loss of civilian life, injury to civilians, damage to civilian objects ... which would be excessive in relation to the concrete and direct military advantage anticipated."[75] The handbook states that it is not unlawful to cause "incidental injury or death to civilian objects, during an attack upon a legitimate military objective," but that such effects "should not ... be excessive in light of the military advantage anticipated by the attack."[76]

The Air Force Manual on International Law sets forth the effect of this rule: An attack "must be canceled or suspended" if it becomes apparent that it "may be expected" to cause excessive incidental injury to civilians and civilian objects.[77] The manual also makes it clear that the level of incidental civilian injury must be balanced not against some vague sense of the respective military advantage but rather, in the words of Additional Protocol I, against the anticipated "concrete and

---

[75] *Id.* at 5-7 and at 8-5 n.17. *See also* THE AIR FORCE MANUAL ON INTERNATIONAL LAW at 5-9.

[76] THE NAVAL/MARINE COMMANDER'S HANDBOOK at 8-5. *See also* THE AIR FORCE MANUAL ON INTERNATIONAL LAW at 3-3.

THE NAVAL/MARINE COMMANDER'S HANDBOOK elaborates that the law "recognizes that a certain number of noncombatants may become *inadvertent* victims" and permits this *unavoidable* destruction "when not disproportionate to the military advantage to be gained." *Id* at 6-42 (citing STONE, LEGAL CONTROLS OF INTERNATIONAL CONFLICT 352 (1973); MCDOUGAL & FELICIANO, LAW AND MINIMUM PUBLIC ORDER 72, 528 (1961); FM 27-10 at 3; Note, *Military Necessity in War Crimes Trials*, 29 BRIT. Y.B. INT'L L. 442 (1953); GREENSPAN, THE MODERN LAW OF LAND WARFARE 279 (1959); and 3 HYDE, INTERNATIONAL LAW 1801 (1945)).

THE NAVAL/MARINE COMMANDER'S HANDBOOK further states that the use of force in self-defense against armed attack or the threat of imminent armed attack rests upon the elements of necessity and proportionality. *Id.* at 4-9 (citing RESTATEMENT (THIRD) §2, sec. 905(1)(a), cmt. 3, at 387; sec. 905(1)(b) & Reporters' Note 3, at 388–89; U.S. Navy Reg. 1973, art. 0915. 1973).

THE AIR FORCE COMMANDER'S HANDBOOK adds that "every feasible precaution should be taken to keep civilian casualties and damage to a minimum." THE AIR FORCE COMMANDER'S HANDBOOK at 3-3.

[77] THE AIR FORCE MANUAL ON INTERNATIONAL LAW at 5-9.

direct" military advantage.[78] The manual adds, "Careful balancing of interests is required between the potential military advantage and the degree of incidental injury or damage in order to preclude situations raising issues of indiscriminate attacks violating general civilian protections."[79]

While the rule of proportionality is perhaps most typically stated in terms of protection of civilian persons and objects, the manual notes that the rule also regulates permissible injury to combatants (one's own forces as well as the enemy's). The manual states that "protected values subject to measurement" include:

> (1) The nature, degree, extent and duration of individual injuries involved in the prohibition against unnecessary suffering;
> (2) Excessive incidental injury to protected civilian persons or damage to civilian objects; and
> (3) Uncontrollable effects against one's own combatants, civilians or property.[80]

In an observation that is helpful in distinguishing the focus of various interrelated principles, the manual states that the principle of proportionality protects combatants in connection with the rule against unnecessary suffering and civilians in connection with the requirement of discrimination.[81] The anticipated injuries must be necessary vis-a-vis enemy combatants and not disproportionate to the specific value of the specific military objective. As we shall see, the force must also be used in such a way as to distinguish noncombatant persons and objects from combatant ones, not causing disproportionate injury to the former.

Most importantly, for the acting State to be able to comply with either requirement, the likely effects of the use must be controllable: If they are not, the State will not be able to make the necessary judgment that the effects will be necessary and proportionate. This will become a

---

[78] *Id.* The Air Force manual also notes that the requirement of proportionality is consistent with traditional military doctrines, such as economy of force, concentration of effort, target selection for maximization of military advantage, avoidance of excessive collateral damage, accuracy of targeting, and conservation of resources. *Id.* at 5-11.

[79] *Id.* at 5-10.

[80] *Id.* at 6-2. *See also id.* at 5-10. The manual states, "The principle of proportionality is a well recognized legal limitation on weapons or methods of warfare which requires that injury or damage to legally protected interests must not be disproportionate to the legitimate military advantages secured by the weapons." *Id.* at 6-1 to 6-2.

[81] *Id.*

key point in the analysis. It also highlights the significance of the facts as to nuclear weapons, particularly the centrality of the question as to whether, or the extent to which, their effects can be controlled. We will examine the applicable facts in detail.

The Air Force Manual on International Law states that the proportionality balancing to be conducted is between the "foreseeable injury and suffering" caused by the weapon and such factors as "effectiveness against particular targets and available alternative weapons."[82] The manual adds: "All weapons cause suffering. The critical factor in the prohibition against unnecessary suffering is whether the suffering is needless or disproportionate to the military advantages secured by the weapon, not the degree of suffering itself."[83]

Method of Performance of the Proportionality Evaluation

The Naval/Marine Commander's Handbook addresses how the proportionality evaluation is to be made. The commander "must determine whether incidental injuries and collateral damage would be excessive, on the basis of an honest and reasonable estimate of the facts available to him."[84] "[T]he commander must decide, in light of all the facts known or reasonably available to him ... whether to adopt an alternate method of attack, if reasonably available, to reduce civilian casualties and damage."[85]

The handbook states that naval commanders must take "all practicable precautions, taking into account military and humanitarian considerations, to keep civilian casualties and damage to the absolute minimum consistent with mission accomplishment and the security of the force."[86]

The Air Force Commander's Handbook clarifies that there are two proportionality analyses to be performed in each instance: "A similar reasoning process should be used to decide whether excessive damage to [noncombatant persons and objects] would be caused by a particular attack, and whether some alternative form of attack would lessen damage and casualties."[87] Thus, in analyzing the lawfulness of the use

---

[82] *Id.* at 6-2.

[83] *Id.*

[84] THE NAVAL/MARINE COMMANDER'S HANDBOOK at 8-5 (citations omitted).

[85] *Id.* at 8-5 to 8-6 (citations omitted).

[86] *Id.* at 8-5 (citations omitted).

[87] THE AIR FORCE COMMANDER'S HANDBOOK at 3-3.

of nuclear weapons, one must also consider the effects of conducting the mission through the use of conventional weapons.

The handbook further states: "The commander ... must make an honest and reasonable decision, based on all the facts known at the time, as to whether the military advantage from a particular attack is worth the expected civilian casualties,"[88] adding that the commander must go through this process "even if the enemy has deliberately used civilians to shield military objectives."[89]

The Army's *Law of Land Warfare* states the rule as follows with respect to treatment of property during combat: "There must be some reasonably close connection between the destruction of property and the overcoming of the enemy's army."[90]

Summary of Elements in the Proportionality Evaluation

There are a number of key elements here, including: (1) the nature of the proportionality test as one based on reason; (2) the objective nature of the test as one based on the full range of information reasonably available to the decision-maker; (3) the fixing of the point in time at which this cost/benefit evaluation is to be made; (4) the question of who the appropriate decision-maker is; (5) questions as to how to value the various factors in the equation, including such fundamental matters as the survival of the State and the potential destruction of substantial human life and of the human environment and preconditions to life and civilization; (6) questions as to the weight to be ascribed to the range of probabilities as to the potential effects from the strike; (7) the question of the "burden of proof" applicable to the evaluation; and (8) considerations as to alternate conventional weapons which might be used. These same or similar considerations are also applicable to the other rules we will discuss.

Proportionality as a Rule of Reason

It is evident from the above that the proportionality requirement is a rule of reason, a rational balancing of legitimate military against collateral effects. This character of the test revolutionizes the analysis. It not only opens up the law's vast experience with rules of reason, giving wing to the full potential of human wisdom, it transforms the nature of this portion of international law. Taking this approach is a jurisprudential election, with the most portentous implications.

---

[88] *Id.*
[89] *Id.*
[90] THE LAW OF LAND WARFARE at 23–24.

Analytically, there would appear to be no more potent engine of legal development than reason, which has played such a role in the development of the common law.

The question becomes whether, with reason as law, a State retains the prerogative of withholding consent to particular dictates of reason. Whether a State retains the option of saying, "The use of nuclear weapons is lawful because I do not agree to their illegality."

This implicates the most fundamental of questions, some alluded to above, as to the nature of international law: Is such law purely consensual or does it include requirements overriding a State's lack of or refusal to consent? Questions of law and fact are also raised as to the extent to which there can be a *per se* rule with respect to such a quintessentially factual matter as the determination of proportionality.

This nature of the test also complicates the analysis because of reason's inherently expansive nature. The most unlikely of seemingly incidental facts may suddenly assume decisive importance. Hence, the extensive factual analysis upon which I embark in later chapters, pulling together from numerous disciplines what appear to be the central facts relevant to rational analysis of the application of the proportionality and other rules of law to the issue at hand. Like the litigator presenting his case and the judge or jury deciding it, we must, at least in the first instance, descend into the deep and messy pit of the facts. Analysis from the law library is insufficient; the input of the military strategist, the scientist, the psychologist and many other types of expert becomes indispensable to the development of a meaningful answer.

Objective Nature of the Proportionality Determination

Does the requirement of proportionality involve a subjective or objective standard of reasonableness? *The Naval/Marine Commander's Handbook*, in the language quoted above, provides an answer: The commander must perform this proportionality balancing in light not only of the available facts but also those reasonably available. A good heart and an empty head are not enough. The decision must satisfy Socrates as well as Napoleon.

The importance of the effort upon which we are embarked is suggested by the obvious fact that a requirement of objective reasonableness hinges upon the facts reasonably available at the time the determination is being made—our next question.

The Appropriate Time to Apply the Proportionality Test

The manuals, and the very nature of the venture, make it clear that the determination of the lawfulness of the strike must be made in advance of the strike. This is not a wait-and-see situation. The eggs of Armageddon could not be unscrambled.

How far in advance?—that becomes the question. The manuals generally talk in terms of the commander's making the judgment in advance of the strike, but—given the confusion, misinformation and other distortions of decision-making which can and typically do exist in combat situations—what is sometimes referred to as the "fog of war"— sound reason would seem to require that these determinations be made on a contingency basis as much in advance of actual combat exigencies as possible.

The United States generally recognizes the need to evaluate the lawfulness of use of particular weapons during the weapons acquisition, procurement and planning process. *The Air Force Manual on International Law* states:

> Department of Defense policy requires that all actions of the Department of Defense with respect to the acquisition and procurement of weapons, and their intended use in armed conflict, shall be consistent with the obligations assumed by the United States Government under all applicable treaties, with customary international law, and, in particular, with the laws of war.[91]

Of course, not all legality issues as to the use of particular weapons are susceptible of being answered in the abstract and in advance, but public policy and the dictates of reason seem clear that, to the extent such evaluation is possible, it should be performed earlier rather than later.

The Air Force Commander's Handbook is to the same effect:

> DOD policy states that all weapons purchased by the US armed forces must be reviewed for consistency with international law. These reviews are carried out by the Judge Advocate General of the service concerned before the engineering development stage of the acquisition.[92]

The Air Force Manual on International Law further recognizes the legal obligation of the United States to conduct its training of military

---

[91] THE AIR FORCE MANUAL ON INTERNATIONAL LAW at 6-7.
[92] THE AIR FORCE COMMANDER'S HANDBOOK at 6-1.

personnel and planning of potential military operations in light of the requirements of the law of armed conflict:

> V. POLICY
>
> A. The Armed Forces of the United States will comply with the law of war in the conduct of military operations and related activities in armed conflict however such conflicts are characterized.
>
> B. The Armed Forces of the United States will insure that programs to prevent violations of the law of war to include training and dissemination as required by the Geneva Conventions ... are instituted and implemented.
>
> ***
>
> VI. RESPONSIBILITIES
>
> E. The Secretaries of the Military Departments will develop internal policies and procedures consistent with this Directive in support of the DOD law of war program in order to:
>
> 1. Provide publications, instructions, and training so that the principles and rules of the law of war will be known to members of their respective departments, the extent of such knowledge to be commensurate with each individual's duties and responsibilities.[93]

The Naval/Marine Commander's Handbook states, "The law of armed conflict has long recognized that knowledge of the requirements of the law is a prerequisite to compliance with the law and to prevention of violations of its rules, and has therefore required training of the armed forces in this body of law."[94]

These policies of early evaluation of lawfulness of weapons and training further highlight the importance to U.S. policy of whether the potential use of nuclear weapons is characterized as lawful or unlawful, and, to some extent, imply the answer to the "so what" retort to the statement of this issue. As the United States noted in its arguments before the ICJ, if the use of these weapons is unlawful, the policy of deterrence, the central defense policy of the United States developed during the Cold War and still adhered to notwithstanding the passing of its seminal *raison d'être*, becomes legally untenable:[95] Generally one cannot threaten to do that which one is not legally permitted to do.[96] Such unlawfulness would seem similarly to bear upon the legitimacy of the United States' overall nuclear weapons acquisition and

---

[93] THE AIR FORCE MANUAL ON INTERNATIONAL LAW at 1-8 to 1-9 (citations omitted).

[94] THE NAVAL/MARINE COMMANDER'S HANDBOOK at 6-4 n.9.

[95] *See infra* Chapter 3, at note 142–164 and accompanying text.

[96] *See infra* Chapter 3, at note 2 and accompanying text.

development programs, subject to distinctions between the use or threatened use and mere possession of such weapons.

The extent to which the proportionality analysis is subject to being made in advance will abide our review of the applicable factual considerations and of the specifics as to how the proportionality weighing should be performed. Obviously, to the extent a *per se* analysis is applicable, the determination is made in advance. To extent that each situation must be evaluated based on its particular facts, questions are presented as to how much of the matter can be evaluated in advance, and, perhaps even more importantly, as to the extent to which the applicable standard and the process of evaluation can be developed and refined in advance.

This question as to the point in time at which the proportionality and other such legality determinations should be made as a matter of law is also addressed in terms of the obligations of a State to take adequate precautions and preventive measures to assure that its military and other representatives observe the law. *The Air Force Manual on International Law* puts it this way: "States ... have important customary and treaty obligations to follow the law not only as national policy but to ensure its implementation, observance and enforcement by its own combatant personnel."[97] The manual notes that a State's violation of the law of war can occur through deliberate State policy or "failure to take adequate preventive measures."[98] The manual states that all States are required "through their respective Commanders-in-Chief to ensure the detailed implementation of the Conventions," adding that all states "must include the text of the Conventions in programs of military, and if possible, civil instruction."[99]

The manual notes that under Hague IV States are obligated to issue appropriate instructions to their personnel and to pay compensation for violations, and that, under the 1949 Geneva Conventions, States are "required to enact domestic legislation necessary to provide effective penal sanctions for persons who commit or order any grave breach" of the Convention, including such breaches as the following: "willful killing, ... willfully causing great suffering or serious injury to body or health, and extensive destruction and appropriation of property, not justified by military necessity and carried out unlawfully and wantonly."[100] The Army's *Law of Land Warfare* states that States are

---

[97] THE AIR FORCE MANUAL ON INTERNATIONAL LAW at 15-1.
[98] *Id.*
[99] *Id.* at 15-2.
[100] *Id.* at 15-1.

obligated under the Geneva Conference of 1949 to take preventive measures as to not only grave breaches but also other breaches.[101]

The Appropriate Decision-Maker

The limitations on the use of force that make up the law of armed conflict are primarily restrictions on the State. We understand that the State can only act through individuals and that this body of law also imposes obligations on individuals, but the primary focus, at least in the first instance, is on the State.

So the question becomes, who within the State is responsible for performing the proportionality analysis. The U.S. military manuals, as seen above, talk in terms of the military commander but also assume a higher level of review. Objective reasonableness would seem to dictate that such decisions, particularly ones involving nuclear and other weapons of mass destruction, should be made at as high a level as feasible in the circumstances. The requirement for Judge Advocate General review of the legality issues during the weapons procurement and contingency planning stages suggests that such decisions are to be made, to the extent feasible, at responsible levels of government. There are also Constitutional arguments that the decision to use nuclear weapons could properly only be made at the highest level of the civilian leadership of the United States.

Precautions have long been taken by the United States to limit nuclear decision-making and the physical ability of military personnel to release nuclear weapons. The legendary nuclear control box maintained always within the President's reach, the complex security systems whereby even those in physical control of at least some of these weapons ostensibly do not have the physical capability of firing them, the elaborate multiple key/code precautions so dramatized by Hollywood—all illustrate the seriousness with which the use of nuclear weapons has generally been taken during the nuclear era and suggest that the proportionality analysis should be made at as high a level as possible.

Obviously, the participants in this decision must include those with the applicable information, judgment and perspective. If my analysis is correct as to the wide range of relevant considerations, the decision-making process will need to call upon an equally wide range of senior experts, presumably persons at the highest levels of government and the military with at least the greatest prospect of having a full perspective on the applicable considerations.

---

[101] THE LAW OF LAND WARFARE at 181.

The Air Force Manual on International Law states:

> [D]ecisions to employ nuclear weapons emanate from a nation's
> highest level of government. The authority of United States forces
> to employ nuclear weapons resides solely with the President.[102]

The Naval/Marine Commander's Handbook is to the same effect:
"The decision to authorize employment of nuclear weapons must
emanate from the highest level of government. For the United States,
that authority resides solely in the President."[103]

The Air Force Manual on International Law similarly notes that
reprisals "must be authorized by national authorities at the highest
political level and [entail] full state responsibility."[104]

The Air Force Manual on International Law, addressing the risks of
attacks on works and installations containing "'dangerous forces,' such
as water held by a dam or radioactive material from a nuclear
generating station, if the attack would release such dangerous forces,"
notes that the decision should be made at responsible levels of
government:

> [T]here are clearly special concerns that destruction of such objects
> may unleash forces causing widespread havoc and injury far
> beyond any military advantage secured or anticipated. Target
> selection of such objects is accordingly a matter of national
> decision at appropriate high policy levels.[105]

Overriding Questions of Valuation

Saying that the level of force and attendant destructiveness may not
be disproportionate to the value of the specific military objective raises
perplexingly difficult questions of valuation. How does one determine
the value of the deaths of 100 or 1000 or 1,000,000, or even 10 or 20 or
a 100 million civilians or the destruction of sizable segments of the
human environment? Or the value of the particular military objective,
particularly if it is integral to the very survival of the State against a
dread enemy?

These are questions to which ostensibly many reasonable answers
might be posed. Even if, applying impeccable logic, one were to

---

[102] THE AIR FORCE MANUAL ON INTERNATIONAL LAW at 6-5.

[103] THE NAVAL/MARINE COMMANDER'S HANDBOOK at 10-1.

[104] THE AIR FORCE MANUAL ON INTERNATIONAL LAW at 10-5. *See also* THE
AIR FORCE COMMANDER'S HANDBOOK at 1-1; THE NAVAL/MARINE
COMMANDER'S HANDBOOK at 6-18, 6-25.

[105] THE AIR FORCE MANUAL ON INTERNATIONAL LAW at 5-11.

formulate answers to such questions, systematically ranking relative values, it would seem that someone else might readily come along, equally rationally, and put it together differently. These questions are so quintessentially subjective, so bound up in our deepest instincts, drives and values, so affected by the mythic undercurrents of our nature and inculcated attitudes and beliefs as to almost guarantee an extremely broad range of deeply held opinions and valuations.

Is there a way out? The question presents itself as to whether international law imposes or recognizes overriding values offering the potential to cut through these complexities. The above considerations as to the purpose of the law of armed conflict come to mind, and obviously there are other possibilities, which we will address.

The Weighting of Likelihoods of Lawful/Unlawful Effects

The fact that this weighing must be made in advance of the use of the weapon imposes upon us the necessity of dealing in probabilities. Again, we can mouth the rule: The principle of proportionality outlaws the use of any weapon whose effects upon combatant or non-combatant persons or objects would be disproportionate to the specific value of the specific military objective. However, at the time this evaluation must be made, it is impossible to know what the actual effects of the strike will be, even assuming we had a foolproof method for valuing such matters. Perforce, we can deal only in probabilities.

This is more than a key insight; it is a definition of the nature of the undertaking. How does one go about performing this probability analysis? How are the various levels of likelihood to be fixed? Once fixed, what weights are to be ascribed to them? Are there any governing principles on these matters? The military manuals talk in such terms as the effects "which may be expected," the military advantage "anticipated" or "secured" or "to be gained," and "foreseeable injury and suffering," but such formulations provide scant practical guidance to the decision-makers or assurance of consistency of approach.

On what will become a key consideration, should the decision-makers limit their evaluation to weighing the various probabilities with respect to what they determine to be the most likely effects or should they also consider the implications of other possible but less likely effects?

The thinking on these subjects does not appear to have been much refined, but that does not mean the law is silent. Dealing with probabilities is something legal systems across the world must do on a day-to-day basis, particularly in their tort and criminal law. In the absence of explicit guidance in international customary or conventional law, we may look to other sources, the most obvious of which are generally accepted principles of law applied to these matters by a wide range of legal systems. Based on such principles, I propose various approaches to this process.

Burden of Proof Applicable to the Proportionality Analysis

This is another aspect of the probability analysis. Once we establish what levels of probability are present as to the different relevant factors and fix the values as to such probabilities, we come to the question: What, if any, burden of proof requirement does the law throw into the mix to build in an advantage to one side or the other of the equation? To justify the military strike, must the State simply find equal balance as between the effects of the strike and the concrete and direct military benefit or is some greater showing required? What level of likelihood must be found as to the existence of proportionality itself? The military manuals do not appear to address this subject, except implicitly, insofar as they address the subjects of individual and State responsibility.

Significance of Alternate Methods of Attack

The proportionality determination must be made in light of the available alternative weapons and methods of attack. *The Air Force Commander's Handbook* states that, in making this determination, the commander must decide, "in the light of all the facts known ... whether to adopt any alternative method of attack to further reduce civilian casualties and damage."[106] *The Air Force Manual on International Law* states that application of the proportionality test requires consideration "whether some alternative form of attack would lessen collateral damage and casualties."[107] The manual adds that "those who plan or decide upon an attack" must "[t]ake all feasible precautions in the choice of means and methods of attack with a view to avoiding, and in any event to minimizing, incidental loss of civilian life, injury to civilians, and damage to civilian objects."[108]

---

[106] THE AIR FORCE COMMANDER'S HANDBOOK at 3-3.

[107] THE AIR FORCE MANUAL ON INTERNATIONAL LAW, at 5-9.

[108] *Id.* The manual adds, "When a choice is possible between several military objectives for obtaining a similar military advantage, the objective to be selected shall be that which may be expected to cause the least danger to civilian lives and to civilian objects." *Id.* at 5-10.

THE AIR FORCE COMMANDER'S HANDBOOK states that:

This requirement reveals the expansive scope of the relevant facts. It means that in making the proportionality analysis as to a putative use of a nuclear weapon, the decision-makers generally must perform detailed cost/benefit analysis as to the likely effects of use of conventional as well as nuclear weapons. This obviously raises a broad range of factual questions as to the characteristics and capabilities of today's conventional weapons. It also raises legal questions as to whether this situation implies some obligation on the State, at the planning, training and operational phases of military policy and practice, to develop and maintain a reasonably sufficient conventional weapons capability so as to maximize the extent to which conventional weapons will be available for missions potentially subject to being handled by such weapons.

Rule of Necessity

The rule of necessity provides that, in conducting a military operation, a State, even as against its adversary's forces and property, may use only such a level of force as is "necessary" or "imperatively necessary" to achieve its military objective, and that any additional level of force is prohibited as unlawful. The State must have an explicit military objective justifying each particular use of force in armed conflict and there must a reasonable connection between that objective and the use of the particular force in question. If a military operation cannot satisfy this requirement, the State must use a lower level of force or refrain from the operation altogether.

This is a rule of customary international law memorialized in numerous conventions. Violations of this rule served as the basis of convictions at Nuremberg. It is a rule of reason, requiring that a judgment be made as much in advance as possible by appropriately responsible decision-makers in light of the reasonably available facts. The State, in planning its military operations, is required to exercise all reasonable precautions to assure that the level of force to be used is within the scope of this rule. The protection of the rule runs to combatant as well as non-combatant persons and objects.

The rule precludes the use of a particular weapon if a less destructive weapon could reasonably be expected to achieve the

---

collateral damage should not ... be excessive in light of the military advantage anticipated from the attack, and in all operations, every feasible precaution should be taken to keep civilian casualties and damage to a minimum.

Id. at 3-3.

objective, and outlaws the use of a weapon not capable of being regulated or not in fact regulated by the user. If the military objective is to take out a particular bridge and this can be accomplished through a direct attack on the bridge, it is unlawful to launch a massive attack against the entire county to take out the bridge. If the military objective could be achieved with conventional weapons, the use of nuclear weapons, with the appreciably higher likely levels of destruction, would generally be unlawful. If, on the other hand, it were necessary to destroy the county to take out the bridge, the necessity requirement would ostensibly be met if the other prerequisites were present, but, even then, if taking out the bridge had minor military value compared to the level of resultant devastation, the proportionality requirement would not be met and the strike would be prohibited.

The United States recognizes this rule. *The Naval/Marine Commander's Handbook* states that the law of war seeks to prevent "unnecessary suffering and destruction" and thereby permits "only that degree and kind of force ... required for the partial or complete submission of the enemy with a minimum expenditure of time, life and physical resources."[109] The handbook repeats that the employment of "any kind or degree of force not required" for that purpose "is prohibited"[110] and quotes with approval the statement in *The Hostage Case*[111] that the destruction of property in war "to be lawful must be imperatively demanded by the necessities of war" and that there must be some "reasonable connection between the destruction of property and the overcoming of the enemy forces."[112] The handbook

---

[109] THE NAVAL/MARINE COMMANDER'S HANDBOOK. at 5-2 to 5-4 (citing *The Hostage Case* (United States v. List), 11 TWC 1253–54 (1950); MCDOUGAL & FELICIANO, LAW AND MINIMUM WORLD PUBLIC ORDER (1961) 525; *Statement of General Eisenhower*, Historical Research Center, Maxwell Air Force Base, AL, File 622.610-2, Folder 2, 1944–45, *reprinted in* SCHAFFER, WINGS OF JUDGMENT: AMERICAN BOMBING IN WORLD WAR II, at 50 (1985); RICHARDSON, MONTE CASSINO 158 (1984)). *See also* THE NAVAL/MARINE COMMANDER'S HANDBOOK at S6.2.5.6.2; THE AIR FORCE MANUAL ON INTERNATIONAL LAW at 6-1.

As to the demanding nature of the necessity requirement in the *jus ad bellum* context of self-defense, THE NAVAL/MARINE COMMANDER'S HANDBOOK quotes the requirement of U.S. Navy Regulations, 1973, article 0915, that the right of self-defense must be exercised only "as a last resort" and then only "to the extent *absolutely necessary* to accomplish the end required." *Id.* at 4-10.

[110] THE NAVAL/MARINE COMMANDER'S HANDBOOK at 5-6.

[111] *Id.* at 5-5 (citing United States v. List, 11 TWC 1253–54 (1950)).

[112] THE NAVAL/MARINE COMMANDER'S HANDBOOK at 5-4 to 5-5 n.5.

emphasizes that the protection of this rule extends to both combatants and noncombatants.[113]

This principle, while a restraint, leaves considerable leeway for the exigencies of war. *The Naval/Marine Commander's Handbook* states that, while the "wanton or deliberate destruction of areas of concentrated civilian habitation, including cities, towns and villages is prohibited,"[114] a military objective within such an area may be "bombarded if required for the submission of the enemy with the minimum expenditure of time, life, and physical resources."[115] Subject to other principles such as those of proportionality and discrimination, the principle permits the destruction of life of armed enemies and other persons whose destruction is incidentally unavoidable.[116]

But the rule does impose an affirmative obligation upon the State to be aware and control what it is doing. *The Air Force Manual on International Law* states that, while a certain level of incidental injury to civilians and civilian objects accompanying military attacks is permitted, there is an affirmative obligation to keep such effects to a "bare minimum."[117] The manual further states that a combatant is required to take "all feasible precautions in the choice of means and methods of attack with a view to avoiding, and in any event to minimizing, incidental loss of civilian life, injury to civilians, and damage to civilians objects ... ."[118]

---

[113] *Id.* at 5-4. THE AIR FORCE MANUAL ON INTERNATIONAL LAW relies upon this same statement of the rule by the U.S. Military Tribunal in The Hostage Case:

> The destruction of property to be lawful must be imperatively demanded by the necessities of war. Destruction as an end in itself is a violation of international law. There must be some reasonable connection between the destruction of property and the overcoming of the enemy forces.

Id. at 15-5; 15-10 n.40 (citing *The Hostage Case*, United States v. List, 11 TRIALS OF WAR CRIMINALS BEFORE THE NUREMBERG MILITARY TRIBUNALS 1253–54 (1950)).

[114] THE NAVAL/MARINE COMMANDER'S HANDBOOK at 8-25.

[115] *Id.* at 8-25 n.91 (citing H.R., art. 23(g); Draft Hague Rules of Air Warfare, art. 24(4); GP I, art. 51(5)(b); Conventional Weapons Convention, Protocol III, art. 3). *See also* THE AIR FORCE MANUAL ON INTERNATIONAL LAW at 6-2.

[116] *Id.* at 5-5 n.5 (quoting *The Hostage Case*, United States v. List, 11 TWC 1253–54 (1950)).

[117] THE AIR FORCE MANUAL ON INTERNATIONAL LAW at 6-2.

[118] *Id.* at 5-9, 6-2.

The Naval/Marine Commander's Handbook similarly emphasizes this positive duty imposed upon the military to "take all practicable precautions, taking into account military and humanitarian considerations, to keep civilian casualties and damage to the absolute minimum consistent with mission accomplishment and the security of the force."[119] The handbook states:

> [U]nnecessary and wasteful collateral destruction must be avoided to the extent possible and, consistent with mission accomplishment and the security of the force, unnecessary human suffering prevented. The law of naval targeting, therefore, requires that all reasonable precautions must be taken to ensure that only military objectives are targeted so that civilians and civilian objects are spared as much as possible from the ravages of war.[120]

The Necessity Principle as Deeply Entrenched

Stating that the principle of necessity is "one of the most important limitations implicit in the words of Article 22 of the Hague Regulations [that the] 'means of injuring the enemy is not unlimited,'"[121] *The Air Force Manual on International Law* quotes provisions of the Hague Regulations, *inter alia*, prohibiting the employment of arms, projectiles, or material calculated to cause unnecessary suffering (Article 23(e)) and the destruction or seizing of the enemy's property unless such destruction or seizure be imperatively demanded by the necessities of war (Article 23(g)).[122]

Another seminal source of the law of armed conflict articulating the rule of necessity is the Lieber Code, described above, promulgated by President Lincoln during the Civil War.[123] *The Air Force Manual on International Law* recognizes the Lieber Code as serving as a model for Hague IV[124] and sets forth at length the principles articulated in the Lieber Code that necessity does not justify, *inter alia*, "cruelty ..., the infliction of suffering for the sake of suffering," the "wanton

---

[119] THE NAVAL/MARINE COMMANDER'S HANDBOOK at 8-5 (footnotes omitted).

[120] *Id.* at 8-2 (footnotes omitted).

[121] THE AIR FORCE MANUAL ON INTERNATIONAL LAW at 6-1.

[122] *Id.* at 1-6 and 6-2.

[123] FRANCIS LIEBER, INSTRUCTIONS FOR THE GOVERNMENT OF ARMIES OF THE UNITED STATES IN FIELD, by Order of the Secretary of War, General Order no.100 (1863), *reprinted in* 1 THE LAW OF WAR: A DOCUMENTARY HISTORY 27 (Leon Freedman ed., 1971).

[124] THE AIR FORCE MANUAL ON INTERNATIONAL LAW at 1-8.

devastation of a district," "maiming or wounding except in fight," and the "use of poison in any way."[125]

The manual goes on to state that the "mass annihilation of enemy people is neither humane, permissible, nor militarily necessary" and that "[d]estruction as an end in itself is a violation of international law, and there must be some reasonable connection between the destruction of property and the overcoming of enemy military forces."[126]

The Naval/Marine Commander's Handbook adds that this principle which is "declared in the Hague Regulations, article 23(e)" is now "confirmed in Additional Protocol I, article 35(2) [prohibiting] the employment of weapons, projectiles and materials and methods of warfare of a nature such as would cause superfluous injury or unnecessary suffering."[127]

Relevant Factual Considerations

In a helpful summary, *The Air Force Manual on International Law* recognizes four basic elements to the requirement of necessity:

> (i) that the force used is capable of being and is in fact regulated by the user;
> (ii) that the use of force is necessary to achieve as quickly as possible the partial or complete submission of the adversary;
> (iii) that the force used is no greater in effect on the enemy's personnel or property than needed to achieve his prompt submission (economy of force); and
> (iv) that the force used is not otherwise prohibited.[128]

From this statement of the law, it is evident that the lawfulness of the use of nuclear weapons under the rule of necessity will require consideration of such matters as the nature of the military objective in the given case; the level of force reasonably necessary to achieve that objective; the capabilities and likely effects of the nuclear and conventional weapons which might be used for that purpose; the controllability of the weapons effects; and the relative likelihood that such nuclear and conventional weapons would achieve the objective.

The Controllability Requirement

The requirement that the level of force implicit in the use of a weapon be controllable and controlled ("regulated") by the user is a

---

[125] *Id.* at 1-5, and 1-15 n.33.

[126] *Id.* at 5-9.

[127] THE NAVAL/MARINE COMMANDER'S HANDBOOK at 10-2.

[128] THE AIR FORCE MANUAL ON INTERNATIONAL LAW 1-6.

natural implication of the necessity requirement. If a State cannot control the level of destructiveness of a weapon, it cannot assure that the use of the weapon will involve only such a level of destructiveness as is necessary in the circumstances.

This requirement of controllability presents a central factual issue. The United States, as noted, argued before the ICJ that it was wrong to assume that there would be either widespread radiation or escalation. Ostensibly talking about unspecified tactical and other supposedly precision nuclear weapons, the U.S. lawyers stated that the effects of such weapons are controllable and would be controlled in the circumstances of actual use.

This raises factual questions we will address as to the nature of radiation and the means whereby it spreads and also as to the technical, political, doctrinal and other factors affecting the likelihood of escalation—all against the backdrop of my thesis that such considerations are quintessentially encompassed within the legality evaluation.

Requirement of Likely Net Military Advantage

It is clear from the above that, for the use of a nuclear weapon to satisfy the necessity principle, it has to be such as to lead or at least contribute to accomplishment of the military objective. If, instead, such use will likely cause more military harm than benefit to the using State, whether because of rebounding radiation or escalation of the conflict or the like, it will be unlawful.

Relative Capabilities of Conventional Weapons

It is also clear from the above that the principle of necessity requires that, before a State could use a nuclear weapon, it would have to determine that lesser weapons, and particularly conventional weapons, could not adequately do the job. This raises factual issues we will also address as to the respective capabilities and potential effects of nuclear versus conventional weapons.

Custom and Usage as Potentially Determining Necessity

The Air Force Manual on International Law gives as examples dum dum or exploding bullets and irregularly shaped bullets because of the types of injury and the inevitability of death.[129]

While numerous prohibitions of specific weapons have been memorialized in conventions, it is clear that the principle of necessity

---

[129] *Id.* at 6-3.

can proscribe the use of a particular weapon without such proscription having been so memorialized. The Army's *Law of Land Warfare*, in discussing the application of the prohibition of a combatant's using arms calculated to cause unnecessary suffering, states: "What weapons cause 'unnecessary injury' can only be determined in light of the practice of States in refraining from the use of a given weapon because it is believed to have that effect."[130]

The manual goes on to state:

> Usage has … established the illegality of the use of lances with barbed heads, irregular-shaped bullets, and projectiles filled with glass, the use of any substance on bullets that would tend unnecessarily to inflame a wound inflicted by them, and the scoring of the surface or the filing off of the ends of the hard cases of bullets.[131]

The Air Force Manual on International Law, addressing the issue from the perspective of criteria for formation of customary law, states: "Upon occasion, a prohibition is confirmed by the practice of states in refraining from the use of a weapon because of recognition of excessive injury or damage to civilians or civilian objects which will necessarily be caused by the weapon."[132]

The fact, of course, is that nuclear weapons were not used after Hiroshima and Nagasaki. On the other hand, each side to the Cold War on numerous occasions, as well as continuously through the policy of deterrence, threatened their use.

The Air Force Manual on International Law states that, while certain conventions have given "specific content to the [necessity] principle in the form of specific agreements to refrain from the use of particular weapons or methods or warfare, … usage and practice" have served to ban other weapons:

> Usage and practice has also determined that it is *per se* illegal to use projectiles filled with glass or other materials inherently difficult to detect medically, to use any substance on projectiles that tend unnecessarily to inflame the wound they cause, to use irregularly shaped bullets or to score the surface or to file off the ends of the hard cases of bullets which cause them to expand upon contact and thus aggravate the wound they cause. The rule against

---

[130] THE LAW OF LAND WARFARE at 18.

[131] *Id.* The manual states that "[t]he prohibition certainly does not extend to the use of explosives contained in artillery projectiles, mines, rockets, or hand grenades. *Id.* at 18.

[132] THE AIR FORCE MANUAL ON INTERNATIONAL LAW at 6-3.

unnecessary suffering applies also to the manner of use of a weapon or method of warfare against combatants or enemy military objectives. In this context, the prohibition precludes the infliction of suffering upon individuals for its own sake or mere indulgence in cruelty.[133]

As examples of weapons causing unnecessary suffering, *The Air Force Commander's Handbook* cites poisoned bullets and weapons using clear glass as the injuring mechanism.[134] As to poisoned bullets, the manual notes that "a person injured by modern military ammunition will ordinarily be placed out of the fighting by that alone; there is very little military advantage to be gained making sure of the death of wounded persons through poison since they will usually be out of the battle before the poison takes effect."[135] As to using glass in the explosive projectile or bomb, the manual notes that "glass is difficult for surgeons to detect in a wound and impedes treatment."[136]

Limitations on Necessity as a Permissive Principle

The rule of necessity, as we have discussed it so far, expresses a limitation on the level of force that a State may use. There is another sense in which the term has been used, to the effect that a State may use such a level of force as is militarily necessary—in effect, that it may do what it has to do.

With respect to this second usage of the term, the question arises of whether this authorization to use such force as is necessary is subject to —and itself limited by—the other rules of the law of war. The question in effect becomes: May a State use whatever force is necessary or only such necessary force as is in compliance with other applicable rules of law?

This is a big subject over which much ink has been spent. The Army's *Law of Land Warfare* sets forth the general position of the United States:

> The prohibitory effect of the law of war is not minimized by "military necessity" which has been defined as that principle which justifies those measures not forbidden by international law which are indispensable for securing the complete submission of the enemy as soon as possible. Military necessity has been generally rejected as a defense for acts forbidden by the customary and

---

[133] *Id.* at 6-2.
[134] THE AIR FORCE COMMANDER'S HANDBOOK at 6-1.
[135] *Id.*
[136] *Id.*

conventional laws of war inasmuch as the latter have been developed and framed with consideration for the concept of military necessity.[137]

The Naval/Marine Commander's Handbook states the same general rule, subject to the proviso that there are certain rules of customary and conventional international law that are subject to—in effect trumped by —military necessity:

> The customary rule of military necessity may be, and in many instances is, restricted in its application to the conduct of warfare by other customary or conventional rules. The opinion that all rules of warfare are subject to, and restricted by, the operation of the principle of military necessity has never been accepted by the majority of American and English authorities. Furthermore, this opinion has not been accepted by military tribunals. It has been held by military tribunals that the plea of military necessity cannot be considered as a defense for the violation of rules which lay down absolute prohibitions (*e.g.*, the rule prohibiting the killing of prisoners of war) and which provide no exception for those circumstances constituting military necessity. Thus, one United States Military Tribunal, in rejecting the argument that the rules of warfare are always subject to the operation of military necessity, stated:
>
> > It is an essence of war that one or the other side must lose and the experienced generals and statesmen knew this when they drafted the rules and customs of land warfare. In short, these rules and customs of warfare are designed specifically for all phases of war. They comprise the law for such emergency. To claim that they can be wantonly—and at the sole discretion of any one belligerent—disregarded when he considers his own situation to be critical, means nothing more or less than to abrogate the laws and customs of war entirely.[138]
>
> However, there are rules of customary and conventional law which normally prohibit certain acts, but which exceptionally allow a belligerent to commit these normally prohibited acts in circumstances of military necessity. In conventional rules, the precise formulation given to this exception varies. Some rules contain the clause that they shall be observed "as far as military necessity (military interests) permits." Examples include common article 8(3) (restricting activities of representatives or delegates of Protecting Powers); GWS, art. 33(2), GWS-Sea, art. 28 (use of

---

[137] THE LAW OF LAND WARFARE at 4.

[138] THE NAVAL/MARINE COMMANDER'S HANDBOOK at 5-4 to 5-7, citing *The Krupp Trial* (Trial of Alfred Felix Alwyn Krupp Von Bohlen und Halbach and Eleven Others), 10 LRTWC 139 (1949).

captured medical supplies); GWS, art. 32(2) (return of neutral persons); GPW, art. 30(1) (return of captured medical and religious personnel); GC, arts. 16(2) (facilitating search for wounded and sick), 55(3) (limiting verification of state of food and medical supplies in occupied territories), 108(2) (limitations on relief shipments); common article 42(4)/-/23(4)/18(4) (visibility of distinctive emblem). Other rules permit acts normally forbidden, if "required" or "demanded" by the necessities of war. Examples include HR, art. 23(g), GWS, art 34(2) ¶ GC, art. 53 (permitting destruction or seizure of property); common article 50/51/130/147 (grave breaches if not justified); GPW, art. 126(2) & GC, art. 143(3) (limiting visits of representatives and delegates of Protecting Powers); GC, arts. 49(2) (evacuation of protected persons from occupied territory), 49(5) (detention of protected persons in area exposed to dangers of war). Rules providing for the exceptional operation of military necessity require a careful consideration of the relevant circumstances to determine whether or not the performance of normally prohibited acts is rendered necessary in order to protect the safety of a belligerent's forces or to facilitate the success of its military operations. See also paragraph 6.2.3 regarding reprisals.[139]

Hence, the rule of necessity permits only such levels of force as are militarily necessary and in compliance with applicable requirements of the law of war. *The Naval/Marine Commander's Handbook* includes the point in its overall statement of the rule: "Only that degree and kind of force, not otherwise prohibited by the law of armed conflict, required for the partial or complete submission of the enemy with a minimum expenditure of time, life, and physical resources may be applied."[140]

The Air Force Manual on International Law similarly notes that the principle of necessity does not authorize actions otherwise prohibited.[141] The principle of military necessity thus is not the 19th Century German doctrine, *Kriegsraison*, potentially justifying any measures—even in violation of the laws of war—when the necessities of the situation purportedly demanded them.

Considerations Relevant to the Necessity Evaluation

In our review of the proportionality principle, we analyzed a number of considerations integral to understanding and applying that standard. Essentially the same discussion is applicable to the necessity

---

[139] THE NAVAL/MARINE COMMANDER'S HANDBOOK at 5-4 to 5-7.
[140] *Id.* at 5-4.
[141] THE AIR FORCE MANUAL ON INTERNATIONAL LAW at 1-6.

principle, including with respect to such matters as the following: (1)
the nature of the necessity test as one based on reason; (2) the objective
nature of the test as one based on the full range of information
reasonably available to the decision-maker; (3) the point that the test is
inherently one of evaluating probabilities since, by definition, it must
be applied in advance when all that can be known are estimates of
probabilities as to the likely contribution of the weapon to the achieving
of the military objective and the related costs of such use; (4) the point
that the decision to use nuclear weapons must be made at the highest
level of government; (5) questions as to how to value the relative
probabilities as to whether a particular use of force is "necessary"; (6)
questions as to the weight to be ascribed to the range of probabilities as
to the potential contribution of the weapon to the achievement of the
military objective and the related costs of such use; (7) the question of
the "burden of proof" applicable to the evaluation of these matters; and
(8) considerations as to the alternate likelihoods that conventional
weapons could achieve the military objective and the relative effects of
the use of such weapons.

Thus, it is evident that the rule of necessity, like that of
proportionality, involves the weighing of facts and probabilities.

The Naval/Marine Commander's Handbook notes the implicit
limitation that a military action may not be regarded as necessary that
causes more destruction than it is worth, *i.e.* which on a net basis does
not contribute to achieving the military objective:

> The opinion is occasionally expressed that these two principles,
> necessity and proportionality, contradict each other in the sense that
> they serve opposing ends. This is not the case. In allowing only
> that use of force necessary for the purpose of armed conflict, the
> principle of necessity implies the principle of proportionality which
> disallows any kind or degree of force not essential for the
> realization of this purpose; that is, force which needlessly or
> unnecessarily causes or aggravates both human suffering and
> physical destruction. Thus, the two principles may properly be
> described, not as opposing, but as complementing each other.[142]

Contemporary Applicability of the Necessity Principle

The contemporary viability and applicability of these rules of law
are unquestionable. The *Air Force Manual on International Law*

---

[142] THE NAVAL/MARINE COMMANDER'S HANDBOOK at 5-6 to 5-7 n.6. The
manual notes, "The real difficulty arises, not from the actual meaning of the
principles, but from their application in practice." *Id.* at 5-7 n.6.

recognizes the provisions of the Hague Regulations as currently binding "viable, active and enforceable standards" of international law[143] and characterizes the prohibition against the use of weapons causing unnecessary suffering or superfluous injury as "firmly established in international law," going back at least as far as the St. Petersburg Declaration of 1868.[144]

The manual states that the Hague Regulations "not only bind states which have agreed to them, such as the United States, but also reflect customary rules binding on all nations and all armed forces in international conflicts."[145]

In support of this importance of Hague IV and the Hague Regulations, the manual quotes the International Military Tribunal at Nuremberg: "[B]y 1939, these rules laid down in the Convention were recognized by all civilized nations, and were regarded as being declaratory of the Laws and Customs of War."[146] The manual further notes that "all of the major war criminals, including Herman Goering, the Air Minister, were convicted, among other crimes of the devastation of towns not justified by military necessity in violation of the law of war."[147]

Rule of Moderation

The law of war recognizes a general principle of moderation, expressed in the Hague Regulations by the maxim that "the right of belligerents to adopt means of injuring the enemy is not unlimited."[148] This principle is a basis of and generally overlaps with the principles of necessity and proportionality.[149]

The Naval/Marine Commander's Handbook refers to this principle as "an affirmation that the means of warfare are restricted by rules of conventional (*i.e.*, treaty) and customary international law."[150] The handbook states that this principle, which was memorialized in Article 22 of the Hague Regulations and Article 30 of the Lieber Code, is "viewed by the United States as customary international law."[151] The

---

[143] THE AIR FORCE MANUAL ON INTERNATIONAL LAW at 5-1.

[144] *Id.* at 6-2.

[145] *Id.* at 5-1.

[146] *Id.*

[147] *Id.* at 5-6.

[148] *See id.* at 5-1, 6-1 (citing Hague Reg., Art. 22).

[149] *See id.*

[150] THE NAVAL/MARINE COMMANDER'S HANDBOOK at 8-1 n.2.

[151] *Id.*

handbook adds that the further statement of the rule in Article 35(1) of Additional Protocol I is viewed by the United States as declarative of such customary law.[152]

Rule of Discrimination

The rule of discrimination prohibits the use of a weapon that cannot discriminate in its effects between military and civilian targets. This is a rule designed to protect civilian persons and objects. The law recognizes that the use of a particular weapon against a military target may cause unintended collateral or incidental damage to civilian persons and objects and permits such damage, subject to compliance with the other applicable rules of law, including the principle of proportionality. However, the weapon must have been intended for— and capable of being controlled and directed against—a military target, and the civilian damage must have been unintended and collateral or incidental.

Thus, if the weapon or its effects were not susceptible of being controlled and directed against a military target in the first place, the resultant damage to civilian persons and objects would not be unintended, collateral or incidental—and the use would be prohibited. Similarly, if the very purpose of the strike were to put pressure on the adversary through attacks on its population (the classic Cold War deterrence theory of "mutual assured destruction" or "MAD"), the strike would be unlawful.

The discrimination requirement is recognized by the United States. *The Air Force Commander's Handbook* states that a weapon is not unlawful "simply because its use may cause incidental casualties to civilians, as long as those casualties are not foreseeably excessive in light of the expected military advantage," but that weapons that are "incapable of being controlled enough to direct them against a military objective"[153] are unlawful. *The Air Force Manual on International Law* defines indiscriminate weapons as those "incapable of being controlled, through design or function," such that they "cannot, with any degree of certainty, be directed at military objectives."[154]

The *Naval/Marine Commander's Handbook* states that the law of war "is based largely on the distinction to be made between combatants

---

[152] *See id.*
[153] THE AIR FORCE COMMANDER'S HANDBOOK AT 6-1.
[154] THE AIR FORCE MANUAL ON INTERNATIONAL LAW at 6-3.

and noncombatants"[155] and hence prohibits making noncombatants the
"object of attack"[156] or targeting them "as such"[157] and requires that
civilians be safeguarded against "injury not incidental" to attacks
against military objectives.[158]

Two of the three "fundamental principles of the law of war"
identified by the handbook focus upon the requirement of
discrimination:

> 2. It is prohibited to launch attacks against the civilian
> population as such.
> 3. Distinctions must be made between combatants and
> noncombatants, to the effect that noncombatants be spared as much
> as possible.[159]

The handbook states that the foregoing points "2" and "3" were
customary rules of international law codified for the first time in
Additional Protocol I, articles 51(2) and 57(1), respectively.[160]

Discrimination as a Rule of Reason

The handbook—reflecting that this is a rule of reason—states that
customary international law "requires that all reasonable precautions
must be taken to ensure that only military objectives are targeted so that
civilians and civilian objects are spared as much as possible from the
ravages of war."[161]

Examples of Indiscriminate Weapons

As an example of an indiscriminate weapon, *The Air Force
Commander's Handbook* cites the use of unpowered and uncontrolled
balloons to carry bombs, since such weapons are "incapable of being
directed against a military objective."[162]

---

[155] THE NAVAL/MARINE COMMANDER'S HANDBOOK at 5-9. The handbook
defines "noncombatants" as "those individuals who do not form a part of the
armed forces and who otherwise refrain from the commission or direct support
of hostile acts." *See id.*

[156] *Id.* at 5-10.

[157] *Id.* at 8-1. *See also* THE LAW OF LAND WARFARE at 16.

[158] THE NAVAL/MARINE COMMANDER'S HANDBOOK at 5-10.

[159] *Id.* at 8-1 (citations omitted). Principle No. 1 identified by the handbook
is "The right of belligerents to adopt means of injuring the enemy is not
unlimited." *Id.* at 8-1.

[160] *Id.* at 8-1 n.3-4.

[161] *See id.* at 8-1.

[162] *See* THE AIR FORCE COMMANDER'S HANDBOOK at 6-1.

The Air Force Manual on International Law cites Germany's World War II V-1 rockets, with their "extremely primitive guidance systems" and Japanese incendiary balloons, without any guidance systems.[163] The manual states that the term "indiscriminate" refers to the "inherent characteristics of the weapon, when used, which renders *(sic)* it incapable of being directed at specific military objectives or of a nature to necessarily cause disproportionate injury to civilians or damage to civilian objects."[164]

Requirement of Controllability

On the question of the controllability of nuclear weapons, the issue becomes central as to whether the controllability element of the discrimination rule requires only that the attacking State be capable of delivering the weapon accurately to a particular military target, or whether it also requires that the State be able to control the weapon's effects, including radiation, upon delivery. Is it enough that the weapon can discriminate, in the sense of landing on the military target, or must the weapon's effects also be able to discriminate between military and civilian targets?

Controllability as Encompassing Inherent Effects of a Weapon

In its military manuals the United States has acknowledged that the scope of the law's prohibition extends to the effects of the use of a weapon. *The Air Force Manual on International Law* states that indiscriminate weapons include those which, while subject to being directed at military objectives, "may have otherwise uncontrollable effects so as to cause disproportionate civilian injuries or damage."[165] The manual elaborates that "uncontrollable" refers to effects "which escape in time or space from the control of the user as to necessarily create risks to civilian persons or objects excessive in relation to the military advantage anticipated."[166]

This statement of the rule potentially encompasses not only inaccurate or unreliable missiles but also the spread of radiation. Significantly, while imposing the requirement that the particular military action would "necessarily" cause certain effects, a requirement that itself merits scrutiny, the manual focused on the question of whether the action would necessarily cause excessive "risks" to

---

[163] *See* THE AIR FORCE MANUAL ON INTERNATIONAL LAW at 6-3.

[164] *See id.* at 6-9 n.7.

[165] *See id.* at 6-3.

[166] *See id.* at 6-3.

civilians. By the time the matter reached the ICJ, this became a requirement that the action would necessarily cause civilians excessive injury—a major distinction.

Examples of Uncontrollable Weapons

As a "universally agreed illustration of ... an indiscriminate weapon," *The Air Force Manual on International Law* cites biological weapons, noting that the uncontrollable effects from such weapons "may include injury to the civilian population of other states as well as injury to an enemy's civilian population."[167]   *The Naval/Marine Commander's Handbook* states that such weapons are "inherently indiscriminate and uncontrollable."[168]

The reference to biological weapons as "inherently" indiscriminate and uncontrollable raises the question of whether radiation is an inherent and natural effect of the use of nuclear weapons, and, if so, whether it is enough for the attacking nuclear power to say, "I am dropping this nuclear weapon to achieve the blast effects on the military target and have no intention to spread radiation." Or is the attacker charged with the fact, if established, that radiation is a natural and inevitable effect of the weapon and can be expected to be carried far and wide upon civilian and neutral persons and objects?

The Air Force Manual on International Law again addresses the controllability factor in its discussion of incendiary weapons. Noting that the use of such weapons have many legitimate applications in war, the manual adds the caveat that the potential of fire to spread beyond the immediate target area "has also raised concerns about uncontrollable or indiscriminate effects affecting the civilian population or civilian objects."[169] The manual notes that the capacity of fire to spread must also be considered in light of the rules protecting civilians and civilian objects, concluding that, "for example, incendiary weapons should be avoided in urban areas, to the extent that other weapons are available and as effective."[170]

The manual cites Hague VIII as illustrating the controllability issue:

---

[167] *See id.* at 6-3. The manual further states that the "wholly indiscriminate and uncontrollable nature of biological weapons has resulted in the condemnation of biological weapons by the international community, and the practice of states in refraining from their use in warfare has confirmed this rule." *Id.*

[168] THE NAVAL/MARINE COMMANDER'S HANDBOOK at 10-21.

[169] THE AIR FORCE MANUAL ON INTERNATIONAL LAW at 6-7.

[170] *Id.*

> Hague VIII ... sets forth the following prohibitions with respect to naval mines (1) to lay unanchored automatic contact mines, unless they be so constructed as to become harmless one hour at most after those who laid them have lost control over them; (2) to lay anchored automatic contact mines which do not become harmless as soon as they have broken loose from their moorings; (3) to use torpedoes which do not become harmless when they have missed their mark (Article 1); and (4) to lay automatic contact mines off the coasts and ports of the enemy, with the sole object of intercepting commercial navigation (Article 2).[171]

The Air Force Manual on International Law states that "the main legal problem" raised by mine warfare "is to make sure that civilian persons and property are not unnecessarily endangered, both during and after the conflict."[172] The types of post-hostility or post-battle cures of such risks—"warning civilians, using mines that self-destruct after a period of time and clearing minefields after the end of hostilities"[173]— possible with respect to mines are ostensibly not available with respect to the radiation effects of nuclear weapons.

The Meaning of "Collateral," "Incidental," and "Unintended"

The question emerges as to whether civilian injuries from radiation can be deemed incidental or collateral, or, for that matter, "unintended," if they represent the typical, inherent or inevitable effects of the weapon in question.

The related question also arises as to whether, semantically and legally, the requirement that injuries to civilians, in the course of a military strike, be limited to those which are "incidental" and "collateral" implies not only that such effects must be substantially less significant than the injury to the military target but also, that, objectively, they must be below some maximum threshold of seriousness. In other words, can cataclysmic injury to civilians be "collateral" or "incidental" in any sense?

The Intentionality/As Such Question

Similar issues are implicated by the traditional statement of the discrimination rule, reflected above, that the collateral or incidental injuries to civilians are unlawful if they were intended *"as such,"* ostensibly in the sense that the attacking State wanted this particular

---

[171] *Id.* at 6-11 n.21.
[172] *Id.* at 6-1.
[173] *Id.* at 6-1.

effect from the weapon as opposed to really just wanting to hit the military target in circumstances where the civilians happened to be in the line of fire.

We will address whether having such momentous matters turn on such metaphysical considerations has continuing legal validity under contemporary law in the nuclear era.

Discrimination as Requiring a Weighing Process

While certain elements of discrimination—such as controllability—may typically be questions of objective fact, it seems clear that the application of the discrimination rules, like the earlier rules we have examined, will often, and probably most typically, require a weighing process, generally of the same types of factors identified in our earlier discussion as to proportionality and necessity, including such matters as follows: (1) probabilities as to the likely effects of the strike in question upon military and civilian targets; (2) the corresponding probabilities as to the likely effects of alternate conventional strikes; and (3) questions as to how to value the various applicable probabilities.

Rule of Civilian Immunity

Occupying much the same ground as the rules of discrimination and proportionality is the rule of civilian immunity. The law of armed conflict prohibits the directing of attacks against civilians, making them immune from such attack. As *The Air Force Manual on International Law* expresses it, "The immunity of the civilian population or individual civilians not taking a direct part in hostilities has long been a cornerstone of the law of armed conflict and of conventions regulating hostilities."[174] The manual states, "The civilian population and individual civilians enjoy general protection against dangers arising from military operations."[175]

At the same time, as we have seen, the law recognizes that civilians will often be caught up in attacks directed against military targets, and accepts such reality as long as the attack in the first instant is one capable of discriminating between civilians and combatants and the civilian injury is unintended, collateral, incidental, and within the bounds of proportionality.

Hence, the "as such" rule: Civilians and civilian objects may not be targeted "as such," in the sense that the attack is intentionally directed

---

[174] *See id.* at 5-17 n.21.

[175] *Id.* at 5-7.

at them, but an attack is not necessarily unlawful simply because it may cause incidental injury to civilian persons and objects.

The Air Force Manual on International Law quotes the following articulation of the rule from Resolution 2444 (XXIII) unanimously adopted by the United Nations in January 1969 and recognized by the United States as "an accurate declaration of existing customary law:"

> (a) That the right of the parties to a conflict to adopt means of injuring the enemy is not unlimited;
> (b) That it is prohibited to launch attacks against the civilian population as such; and
> (c) That distinction must be made at all times between persons taking part in the hostilities and members of the civilian population to the effect that the civilians be spared as much as possible.[176]

The Air Force manual notes that the initial draft of Resolution 2444 contained a fourth principle "that the general principles of war apply to nuclear and similar weapons," and that, when the Soviets opposed this additional principle, the United States Representative, Mrs. Jean Picker, took the position that all four principles constituted a "reaffirmation of existing international law" and that such principles "apply as well to the use of nuclear and similar weapons."[177] The manual states that the fourth principle was dropped from the resolution based on the Soviet position, but that the resolution passed based on the understanding "that the remaining principles were applicable in all armed conflict regardless of their nature or the kinds of weapons used."[178]

The rule of civilian immunity prohibits attacks designed to terrorize the enemy population. *The Air Force Manual on International Law* states: "Acts or threats of violence which have the primary object of spreading terror among the civilian population are prohibited"[179] and further that "[a]ttacks primarily intended to terrorize the civilian population instead of destroying or neutralizing military objectives are also prohibited."[180]

---

[176] *Id.* at 5-7 (citing Rovine, *Contemporary Practice of the United States Relating to International Law*, 67 AM. J. INT'L L. 118, 122–125 (1973) (quoting DOD, General Counsel, Letter to the effect that Resolution 2444 is "declaratory of existing customary international law.")).

[177] *Id.* at 5-17 n.18.

[178] *Id.*

[179] *Id.* at 5-7.

[180] *Id.* at 5-8.

Limits on Target Area Bombing

The Air Force Manual on International Law noted that the Nuremberg Tribunal did not rule specifically on the limits of legal air warfare but that all of the major war criminals were convicted of the devastation of towns not justified by military necessity:

> After a comprehensive study of the reports of all military tribunals convened during World War II, the United Nations War Crimes Commission stated:
> "No record of trials in which allegations were made of the illegal conduct of aerial warfare had been brought to the notice of the United Nations War Crimes Commission, and since the indiscriminate bombing of allied cities by the German Air Force was not made the subject of a charge against any of the major German war criminals, the judgment of the Nuremberg International Military tribunal did not contain any ruling as to the limits of legal air warfare."
> However, all of the major war criminals including Herman Goering, the Air Minister, were convicted, among other crimes, of the devastation of towns not justified by military necessity in violation of the law of war.[181]

Noting that in World War II, the parties' "failure to separate effectively war industry and other vital targets from the population centers" necessitated "target area bombing" and that a substantial amount of such bombing took place and was not specifically prosecuted in the subsequent war crime trials, *The Air Force Manual on International Law* quotes Greenspan, identified as "a recognized legal scholar," for the proposition:

> Any legal justification of target-area bombing must be based on two factors. The first must be the fact that the area is so preponderantly used for war industry as to impress that character on the whole of the neighborhood, making it essentially an indivisible whole. The second factor must be that the area is so heavily defended from air attack that the selection of specific targets within the area is impracticable.[182]

On the question of the continued viability of the principle of discrimination in the light of the extensive bombing of cities by both sides during World War II, the manual concludes that much of the indiscriminate bombing resulted from two factors, inadvertence based

---

[181] *Id.* at 5-6 (citing 15 LAW REPORTS OF WAR CRIMINALS 110).

[182] *Id.* at 5-5 (citing GREENSPAN, THE MODERN LAW OF LAND WARFARE 336 (1959)).

on inaccuracy of bombing and reprisal/escalation based upon reaction to such inadvertent attacks. The manual notes that a 1940 study of Royal Air Force Bomber Command night operations revealed that two-thirds of all air crews were missing their targets by over 5 miles, and that this, in turn led to "enemy misconstruction of the attacker's intentions and to views that the attacker had engaged in indiscriminate bombing of civilians" and to an escalation of reprisals and counter reprisals.[183]

By way of example, the manual states that on August 24, 1940, the Germans unintentionally (based on a navigational error) bombed London, whereupon the British reprised by raids on Berlin, resulting in Hitler's launching the London blitz.[184] The manual concludes that this counter reprisal by Hitler materially backfired, in that the attacks on London replaced the previously ongoing attacks on RAF airfields, giving the RAF time to recover and regroup, "contributing significantly to British victory in the battle of Britain."[185]

Defining "aerial bombardment" as "includ[ing] dropping munitions, from manned or unmanned aircraft, strafing, and using missiles or rockets against enemy targets on land,"[186] the manual states that, subsequent to World War II, State practice, including in Korea, Vietnam, the various Middle East conflicts, the India-Pakistan and other conflicts, has reflected an "increased interest in avoiding civilian casualties from aerial bombardment."[187] The manual states that the "earlier emphasis by the United States on precision bombing of military objectives has been fully supported by other states,"[188] and that warring States have attempted, *inter alia*, "to assert distinct military advantages as the goal of specific aerial bombardments; to emphasize the limited nature and duration of the attacks; and to demonstrate the taking of all necessary precautions to avoid or minimize injury to the civilian population or damage to civilian objects."[189]

---

[183] *See id.* at 5-4.

[184] *See id.*

[185] *See id.* (citing Carnahan, *The Law of Air Bombardment in its Historical Context* 17 AFLR 39 (Summer 1975); 2 OPPENHEIM, INTERNATIONAL LAW 527 (Lauterpacht ed., 1952); HIGHAM, AIR POWER: A CONCISE HISTORY 104, 131 (1972); SPAIGHT, AIR POWER AND WAR RIGHTS 53 (1947); WHEATON, INTERNATIONAL LAW 351 vol.2 (7th ed. 1944)).

[186] *Id.* at 5-1.

[187] *Id.* at 5-6.

[188] *Id.*

[189] *Id.*

The manual states that "[s]ince World War II, increased emphasis upon protection of civilians, the civilian population, and civilian objects, coupled with advancements in bombing accuracy and technology, have led to reduced reliance upon target area bombing as a useful technique."[190]

The manual further states that the extent of the legal protection accorded civilians has been clarified. The four Geneva Conventions for the Protection of War Victims were adopted in 1949, in reaction to practices in World War II, providing humanitarian protections to civilians and others.[191] Similarly, the United Nations General Assembly in 1969 unanimously passed Resolution 2444 (XXIII) (discussed above) and other such resolutions reinforcing the rights of civilians and others.

Of course, given the nature of modern warfare, there is inherent ambiguity as to when a wide range of urban and other objects become military targets. *The Air Force Manual on International Law* notes that, while there is no question as to the combatant nature of such objects as an adversary's military encampments, armament, military aircraft, tanks, and the like:

> Controversy exists over whether, and the circumstances under which, other objects, such as civilian transportation and communications systems, dams and dikes can be classified properly as military objectives. The inherent nature of the object is not controlling since even a traditionally civilian object, such as a civilian house, can be a military objective when it is occupied and used by military forces during an armed engagement. A key factor in classification of objects as military objectives is whether they make an effective contribution to an adversary's military action so that their capture, destruction or neutralization offers a definite military advantage in the circumstances ruling at the time.[192]

The manual noted that in Vietnam, the United States regarded roads, railroads, petroleum facilities, barracks and supply depots in North Vietnam as legitimate targets and denied bombing hospitals, textile plants, fruit canning plants and dikes, while North Vietnam accused the United States of indiscriminately bombing hospitals, schools, road

---

[190] *Id.* at 5-15 n.9.
[191] *See id.* at 5-7.
[192] *Id.* at 5-8.

transport stations, markets, villages, fishing vessels, churches and pagodas.[193]

The manual concludes that, after consideration of the differences as to the facts, "[o]nly in the case of 'road transport stations' might there be a direct conflict between US and N. Vietnam as to legitimacy of targets."[194] The manual stated that the U.S. position as to the legitimacy of such targets is supported by the 1923 Draft Hague Rules and the Hague Convention on the Protection of Cultural Property in the Event of Armed Conflict.[195]

Principle of Neutrality

The principle of neutrality protects the territory of a neutral State from the effects of war being engaged in by other States. *The Naval/Marine Commander's Handbook* states that a neutral State is entitled to "inviolability"[196] and that, under customary international law, all acts of hostility are prohibited in "neutral territory, including neutral lands, neutral waters, and neutral airspace."[197]

The handbook elaborates that belligerents are forbidden to "move troops or war materials and supplies across neutral land territory"[198] and that, with limited exceptions related to self-defense and self-help, belligerents are obliged to "refrain from all acts of hostility in neutral territorial waters."[199]

The Air Force Manual on International Law similarly states that the territory and, hence, the airspace above the territory of neutrals is

---

[193] *See id.* at 5-18 n.23 (citing, for the two respective positions, 10 WHITEMAN, at 425–429 and Freymond, *Confronting Total War: A 'Global' Humanitarian Policy,* 67 AM. J. INT'L. L. 6782 (1973)).

[194] *Id.*

[195] *Id.* (stating that the 1923 Draft Hague Rules "fully recognized that lines of communications and transportation used for military purposes were military objectives" and that Article 8b of the Hague Convention on the Protection of Cultural Property in the Event of Armed Conflict, 14 May 1954, signed but not ratified by the United States, recognized as military targets such objects as "an aerodrome, broadcasting station, establishment engaged upon work of national defense, a port or railway station of relative importance or a mainline of communication").

[196] *See* THE NAVAL/MARINE COMMANDER'S HANDBOOK at 7-3.

[197] *See id.* at 7-16 (citing Hague V art. 1, Hague XIII art. 2).

[198] *See id.* at 7-11 (citing Hague V art. 2, U.S. Army Field Manual 27-10, THE LAW OF LAND WARFARE, 1956) ¶ 5-6-17).

[199] *See* THE NAVAL/MARINE COMMANDER'S HANDBOOK at 7-16.

inviolable[200] and that "therefore, belligerent aircraft may not enter the airspace of a neutral, even in hot pursuit (unless the neutral airspace is a sanctuary for the adversary)."[201]

The Air Force Commander's Handbook similarly states that, under the neutral's right of inviolability, a combatant may not "use, invade or pass through" a neutral's territory, including its airspace.[202] The handbook states, by way of illustration, that in World War II certain U.S. bombers bombed Swiss cities because of navigational errors and that, because of such violations, the United States compensated Switzerland after the war for resultant damages.[203]

The Naval/Marine Commander's Handbook states that, even in those exceptional circumstances where belligerents are permitted passage over a neutral nation's territory, the belligerents "must refrain from acts of hostility while in transit but may engage in activities that are consistent with their security and the security of accompanying surface and subsurface forces."[204]

The *Army's Law of Land Warfare*, citing the Hague Convention No. V Respecting the Rights and Duties of Neutral Powers and Persons in Case of War on Land, 18 October 1907, to which the United States is a signatory,[205] states that the inviolability of a neutral State's territory prohibits "any unauthorized entry" into the neutral's territory, including its territorial waters and airspace by "troops or instrumentalities of war."[206]

The question becomes, what is an "instrumentality of war"? Obviously, there is a potential for radioactive fallout resulting from the detonation of nuclear weapons in a war zone to be dispersed by the winds and other natural forces into neutral territory. Would that be an instrumentality of war?

In language that becomes relevant to the physical facts as to the spread of radiation resulting from the detonation of nuclear weapons, *The Air Force Manual on International Law* states, "The right of territorial integrity is coupled with a duty to avoid violations of that

---

[200] THE AIR FORCE MANUAL ON INTERNATIONAL LAW at 2-7 (citing, *inter alia*, Arts 1, 2, Hague V; US Navy, NWIP 10-2, LAW OF NAVAL WARFARE, § 444a (1955), *reprinted in* 11 WHITEMAN, DIGEST OF INTERNATIONAL LAW 203–04).

[201] *Id.* at 2-7.

[202] *See* THE AIR FORCE COMMANDER'S HANDBOOK at 7-1.

[203] *Id.* at 7-1.

[204] THE NAVAL/MARINE COMMANDER'S HANDBOOK at 7-22. *See also* 7-12.

[205] *See* THE LAW OF LAND WARFARE at 4, 185.

[206] *Id.* at 185.

neutrality by parties to a conflict including the expansion of the conflict into their territory or the use of their territory as a base of operations."[207]   Again, would the spread of radiation into the neutral space represent an expansion of the conflict into that space?

The manual also recognizes the applicability to neutrals of the principle of the illegality of the use of weapons whose effects cannot be controlled, noting that such uncontrollable effects "may include injury to the civilian population of other states as well as injury to an enemy's civilian population."[208]

As to the extent of the protection of neutrals, the manual further notes that enemy military aircraft or missiles may not be attacked in neutral airspace.[209]

As to the importance of the principle of neutrality, the manual states, "Failure to respect US maritime neutral rights prompted US entry in the War of 1812 and World War I and contributed to US entry in World War II.   Duties of neutrals caused extensive disputes between the US and Great Britain during the Civil War."[210]

I stated above that, to a striking extent, the United States and the opponents of the nuclear weapons regime agree on the content of the applicable rules of law and primarily disagree on the application of such law to the facts.   With the rule of neutrality, this is not so much the case.   As we shall see, the United States and the opponents of nuclear weapons disagree on the extent to which the rule of neutrality protects neutrals from the fallout of warring States' bellicose activities conducted in the war zone but with effects extending beyond it.

Prohibition of Chemical Weapons

The Air Force Manual on International Law notes that Article 23 of the Hague Regulations provides that it is "especially forbidden" to "employ poison or poisoned weapons."[211]   This prohibition on its face appears to prohibit both the use of poison itself and the use of weapons that have poison has a component or add-on.   The manual states that

---

[207] THE AIR FORCE MANUAL ON INTERNATIONAL LAW at 2-7.   Not only is the war not to be expanded into neutral territory, the neutral State has a duty to prevent that expansion if possible.   *Id.*

[208] *Id.* at 6-3.

[209] *Id.* at 4-1.

[210] *Id.* at 4-4.   *See also id*, at 1-8 (stating that the failure of Germany to respect the law of neutrality governing naval warfare has been cited as a principal basis for the U.S. entry into World War I on the side of the Allies).

[211] *Id.* at 5-1, 6-5.

the Hague Rule "reflected a customary rule noted in US Army, General Order No. 100, Instructions for the Government of Armies of the U.S. (1863), [Lieber Code] which stated in Article 70 'The use of poison in any manner, be it to poison wells, or food, or arms, is wholly excluded from modern warfare. He that uses it puts himself out of the pale of the law and usages of war.'"[212]

The manual defines poisons as "biological or chemical substances causing death or disability with permanent effects when, in even small quantities, they are ingested, enter the lungs or bloodstream, or touch the skin."[213] In further elaboration of the requirement of controllability of effects, the manual states, "The long-standing customary prohibition against poison is based on their uncontrolled character and the inevitability of death or permanent disability as well as on a traditional belief that it is treacherous to use poison."[214]

The manual goes on to elaborate that this prohibition from Article 23(a) of the Hague Regulations was included in the 1925 Geneva Gas Protocol, but only prohibits first use:

> The first use of lethal chemical weapons is now regarded as unlawful in armed conflicts. During World War II President Roosevelt, in response to reports that the enemy was seriously contemplating the use of gas warfare, stated: "Use of such weapons has been outlawed by the general opinion of civilized mankind .... We shall under no circumstances resort to the use of such weapons unless they are first used by our enemies." This United States position has been reaffirmed on many occasions by the United States as well as confirmed by resolutions in various international forums. On 11 August 1970, when the 1925 Geneva Protocol was resubmitted to the Senate for its advice and consent prior to United States ratification, President Nixon stated that the United States would ratify the Protocol with an appropriate reservation that "would permit the retaliatory use by the United States of chemical weapons and agents."[215]

The Air Force Manual on International Law also quotes the statement of the U.S. Representative to the United Nations, "The United States' position on this matter is quite clear and corresponds to

---

[212] *Id*. at 6-10 n.15.
[213] *Id*. at 6-5.
[214] *Id*.
[215] *Id*. at 6-4 (citations omitted).

the stated policy of almost all other governments.... The use of poison gases is clearly contrary to international law."[216]

The Air Force Commander's Handbook states that, "The international legal status of chemical and biological weapons is governed by a treaty, the 1925 Gas Protocol."[217] The handbook further states:

> The 1925 Geneva Gas Protocol prohibits using bacteriological or lethal chemical weapons in armed conflict. Most of the world's nations are parties to this treaty, including all NATO and Warsaw Pact members.[218]

As to the limited scope of the prohibition, the handbook further states:

> The United States, however, has reserved the right to use chemical weapons against " ... an enemy state if such state or any of its allies fails to respect the prohibitions of the Protocol." The USSR and the People's Republic of China have reserved similar rights.[219]

---

[216] *Id.* at 6-10 n.10 (citing 10 WHITEMAN, DIGEST OF INTERNATIONAL LAW 476 (1968)).

[217] THE AIR FORCE COMMANDER'S HANDBOOK at 6-3.

[218] *Id.*

[219] *Id.* In language that will become relevant to our analysis, THE NAVAL/MARINE COMMANDER'S HANDBOOK addresses the questions of whether the 1925 Gas Protocol's prohibition of use of chemical weapons has become part of customary international law and, if so, whether such weapons may still be used in retaliation or reprisal:

> There are different views as to the extent to which the prohibition of use of chemical weapons has become part of customary international law. At least three positions may be taken by nations on this question:
>
> 1) The 1925 Gas Protocol is not customary international law, and use of chemical weapons is not contrary, *per se*, to internationally accepted customary rules. The Protocol is a no-first-use agreement between the contracting parties.
>
> (2) The prohibition of first-use of chemical weapons as embodied in the 1925 Gas Protocol and relevant reservations thereto has become part of the customary international law and is, therefore, binding on all nations towards all the others, whether parties to it or not. This is the position of the United States.
>
> (3) Use of chemical weapons is contrary to customary international law. It is permitted only as a belligerent reprisal in response to a chemical attack.

***

The Air Force Manual on International Law similarly sets forth at length the Geneva Protocol's prohibition of the use of "asphyxiating, poisonous or other gases, and of all analogous liquids, materials or devices" and of the U.S. reservation of the right to use chemical weapons in response to an adversary's use of such weapons.[220]

The doctrine of reciprocity provides a basis for the legitimate use of chemical weapons. Under Article 60 of the Vienna Convention on the Law of Treaties, 8 INT'L LEG. MAT'LS 679 (1969), AFP 110-20, and the customary international law of reciprocity, a breach of a multilateral treaty, that is in violation of a provision essential to the accomplishment of the object of the treaty, can be invoked by the affected parties as a ground for suspending the operation of the treaty in their relations with the violating nation or nations. Therefore, all NATO nations, whether they ratified the Geneva Protocol with reservations or not, may invoke the customary rule stated in the Vienna Convention, as well as the application of the general principle of reciprocity, to justify a response with chemical weapons if attacked with such weapons by a Warsaw Pact country. Some nations, however, hold the view that Article 60 of the Vienna Convention does not apply to the 1925 Gas Protocol, since this protocol may be considered a treaty of humanitarian character (*see* Article 60, paragraph 5).

* * *

[I]f the view on the consolidation of the prohibition of chemical weapons into a rule of customary international law is accepted, then this right of retaliation is no longer applicable without limitations. According to this interpretation, since the prohibition of chemical weapons no longer stems from a multilateral treaty, but has become a rule of customary international law, the use of such weapons by an enemy does not confer on a nation the right to "suspend" the prohibition altogether, but only gives the nation the right to act in reprisal (including in-kind reprisal) against the violating nation, in accordance with international law.

As a consequence, and regardless of whether they ratified the 1925 Gas Protocol with reservations or not, nations which consider the general prohibition of chemical weapons as being part of the customary international law, may take the position that they are only allowed to act in reprisal, including in-kind reprisal where necessary, if attacked with chemical weapons. It is to be noted that the right to use chemical weapons in reprisal does not stem from reservations to the 1925 Gas Protocol, but from the law of reprisal.

Id. at 10-16, 10-17 n.21.

[220] THE AIR FORCE MANUAL ON INTERNATIONAL LAW at 6-3 (citing Geneva Protocol For the Prohibition Of The Use In War of Asphyxiating, Poisonous, or

Noting that the United States regards the prohibition of the first use of lethal and incapacitating[221] chemical weapons to be customary international law binding on non-signatories, *The Naval/Marine Commander's Handbook* states that the United States maintains such weapons only for deterrence and possible retaliatory purposes:

> Because the 1925 Gas Protocol effectively prohibits only first use of such weapons, the United States maintains a lethal and incapacitating chemical weapons capability for deterrence and possible retaliatory purposes only.[222]

As to the possible use of such weapons on a retaliatory basis, the handbook goes on to state:

> National Command Authorities (NCA) approval is required for retaliatory use of lethal or incapacitating chemical weapons by U.S. Forces. Retaliatory use of lethal or incapacitating chemical agents must be terminated as soon as the enemy use of such agents that prompted the retaliation has ceased and any tactical advantage

---

Other Gases, And of Bacteriological Methods of Warfare, 17 June 1925, 26 UST 571; TIAS 8061; 94 LNTS 65 (1975)), and quoting the U.S. reservation:
> That the said Protocol shall cease to be binding on the Government of the United States with respect to the use in war of asphyxiating, poisonous or other gases, and of all analogous liquids, materials, or devices, in regard to an enemy State if such State or any of its allies fails to respect the prohibitions laid down in the Protocol.

The manual notes that the 1925 Geneva Protocol came into force for the United States on April 10, 1975. *Id.* at 6-4.

THE AIR FORCE COMMANDER'S HANDBOOK similarly states:
> The 1925 Geneva Gas Protocol prohibits using bacteriological or lethal chemical weapons in armed conflict. Most of the world's nations are parties to this treaty, including all NATO and Warsaw Pact members.

Id. at 6-3.

THE AIR FORCE MANUAL ON INTERNATIONAL LAW similarly notes that the United States entered into this protocol subject to the reservation that it shall cease to be binding vis-a-vis enemies not observing same. *Id.* at 6-9 n.8.

[221] The United States distinguishes "lethal" and "incapacitating" chemical weapons from riot control and herbicidal agents, which it does not regard as subject to the prohibition of use of chemical weapons. THE NAVAL/MARINE COMMANDER'S HANDBOOK at 10-15.

[222] *Id.* at 10-17.

gained by the enemy through unlawful first use has been redressed.[223]

As we shall see, the United States contends and the ICJ concluded that the effects of nuclear weapons do not constitute "asphyxiating, poisonous or other gases, and ... analogous liquids, materials or devices" and hence are not within the prohibition of the 1925 Gas Protocol. Opponents of nuclear weapons contend that this prohibition encompasses such weapons.

The above summarizes the applicable law as set forth in the various military manuals. Subsequently, the prohibition on chemical weapons has extended to retaliatory use. Professor Richard K. Betts in a 1998 article has summarized the developments:

> In the past, the United States had a no-first-use policy for chemical weapons but reserved the right to strike back with them if an enemy used them first. The 1993 Chemical Weapons Convention (CWC), which entered into force last April, requires the United States to destroy its stockpile, thus ending this option.[224]

Prohibition of Bacteriological/Biological Agents

Comparable prohibitions apply to biological agents under the 1925 Gas Protocol and the 1972 Biological Weapons Convention. *The Air Force Manual on International Law* states:

> International law prohibits biological weapons or methods of warfare whether they are directed against persons, animals or plants. The wholly indiscriminate and uncontrollable nature of biological weapons has resulted in the condemnation of biological weapons by the international community, and the practice of states in refraining from their use in warfare has confirmed this rule.[225]

---

[223] *Id.* at 17-18. The handbook further cites various other federal statutes limiting activities by the U.S. military with respect to chemical weapons.

[224] Richard K. Betts, *The New Threat of Mass Destruction*, FOREIGN AFF., vol. 77, no. 1, January/February 1998, at 26, 30. Professor Betts goes on to note that the United States destroyed its biological weapons long ago, during the Nixon administration, and makes the interesting comment, vis-a-vis the interrelationship of U.S. policies towards the various weapons of mass destruction, "Eliminating its own [the U.S.] chemical and biological weapons practically precludes a no-first-use policy for nuclear weapons, since they become the only WMD [weapon of mass destruction] available for retaliation." *Id.* at 31.

[225] THE AIR FORCE MANUAL ON INTERNATIONAL LAW at 6-4 (citing Convention On the Prohibition of The Development, Production, And

Using similar language, *The Naval/Marine Commander's Handbook* states:

> International law prohibits all biological weapons or methods of warfare whether directed against persons, animals, or plant life. Biological weapons include microbial or other biological agents or toxins whatever their origin (*i.e.*, natural or artificial) or methods of production.[226]

In terms of the interplay of the 1925 Gas Protocol and the Biological Weapons Convention, the handbook states that the 1925 Gas Protocol "prohibits the use in armed conflict of biological weapons," and the Biological Weapons Convention "prohibits the production, testing and stockpiling of biological weapons."[227]

The handbook states that the Biological Weapons Convention "obligates nations that are a party thereto not to develop, produce, stockpile, or acquire biological agents or toxins 'of types and in quantities that have no justification for prophylactic, protective, or other peaceful purposes,' as well as 'weapons, equipment or means of delivery designed to use such agents or toxins for hostile purposes or in armed conflict.'"[228] The handbook further notes that all such weapons were to be destroyed by December 26, 1975.[229]

The handbook states that the United States accepted without reservation the 1925 Gas Protocol's prohibition of use of biological weapons, as contrasted with the reservation (discussed above) which it interposed with respect to the Protocol's prohibition of the use of chemical weapons.[230] The Army's *Law of Land Warfare* makes the same point: "The prohibition concerning bacteriological methods of warfare which the United States has accepted under the Protocol ... proscribes not only the initial but also any retaliatory use of bacteriological methods of warfare."[231]

Stockpiling of Bacteriological (Biological) And Toxin Weapons And On Their Destruction ("Biological Warfare Convention"), 26 UST 571; TIAS 8062, 1015 UNTS 163 (1972) and noting that the Biological Warfare Convention came into force for the United States on 26 March 1975).

[226] THE NAVAL/MARINE COMMANDER'S HANDBOOK at 10-21.

[227] *Id.*

[228] *Id.*

[229] *Id.*

[230] *Id.*

[231] Change No. 1, FM 27-10 C 13 (15 July 1976) to THE LAW OF LAND WARFARE.

As to the legal objections to biological weapons, *The Naval/Marine Commander's Handbook* states that such weapons "are inherently indiscriminate and uncontrollable and are universally condemned."[232] *The Air Force Manual on International Law* had similarly based the prohibition on the "wholly indiscriminate and uncontrollable nature" of biological weapons.[233]

The Naval/Marine Commander's Handbook further states that the United States "considers the prohibition against the use of biological weapons during armed conflict to be part of customary international law and thereby binding on all nations whether or not they are parties to the 1925 Gas Protocol or the 1972 Biological Weapons Convention" and that "the United States has, therefore, formally renounced the use of biological weapons under any circumstances."[234] The handbook states that, "Pursuant to its treaty obligations, the United States has destroyed all its biological and toxin weapons and restricts its research activities to development of defensive capabilities."[235]

As to the military effectiveness of such weapons, the handbook states:

> Any microorganism able to cause disease in man, animals, or plants, or cause the deterioration of materiel, is capable of being used as a biological agent. However due to difficulty in production, storage and dissemination, and to limited effectiveness, a large number of diseases would have little or no military utility. Even those capable of producing significant results would have a delayed effect due to the incubation period, and the results would be dependent on a variety of factors including weather, target characteristics, and countermeasures. Due to the delayed effectiveness, biological agents do not lend themselves to tactical, but rather to strategic employment to achieve long-term decrease in an enemy's warmaking capability.[236]

As to the distinction between chemical and biological weapons, the handbook states:

> Biological toxins are the toxic chemical by-products of biological organisms. They can be synthesized chemically and share many of the characteristics of chemical agents; however, they are considered

---

[232] THE NAVAL/MARINE COMMANDER'S HANDBOOK at 10-21 n.30.

[233] THE AIR FORCE MANUAL ON INTERNATIONAL LAW at 6-4.

[234] *Id.* at 10-22.

[235] *Id.* The handbook states that the U.S. research activities are devoted primarily to the development of vaccines.

[236] *Id.* at 10-21.

to be biologicals under the 1972 Biological Weapons Convention.
Toxins have advantages over organisms in storage, delivery, and
onset of effects. Some toxins are much more toxic than the most
powerful nerve agents.[237]

The Army's *Law of Land Warfare* similarly states that the United
States "considers bacteriological methods of warfare to include not
only biological weapons but also toxins, which, although not living
organisms and therefore susceptible of being characterized as chemical
agents, are generally produced from biological agents. All toxins ...
are regarded by the United States as bacteriological methods of warfare
within the meaning of the proscription of the Geneva Protocol of
1925."[238]

Principle of Environmental Protection

The Air Force Commander's Handbook states that weapons that
"may be expected to cause widespread, long-term, and severe damage
to the natural environment are prohibited,"[239] adding that this is a "new
principle" established by the 1977 Protocol I to the Geneva
Conventions, whose exact scope is not yet clear, but which the United
States does not regard as applying to nuclear weapons.[240]

The handbook adds, "It is not believed that any presently employed
conventional weapon would violate this rule."[241] This is an area, as we
shall see, as to which the United States and the opponents of the
nuclear weapons regime disagree.

Protection of Medical Facilities

The Air Force Manual on International Law quotes Article 27 of
the Hague Regulations as requiring combatants "to spare, as much as
possible, buildings dedicated to religion, art, science, or charitable
purposes, historical monuments, hospitals, and places where the sick
and wounded are collected, provided they are not being used at the time

---

[237] *Id.*

[238] Change No. 1, FM 27-10 C 13 at 3 (15 July 1976) to THE LAW OF LAND
WARFARE.

[239] *See* THE AIR FORCE COMMANDER'S HANDBOOK at 6-1.

[240] *See id.*

[241] *Id.* at 5-2.

for military purposes," and further requiring that such objects be identified as such.[242]

Prohibition of Genocide

As reflected in *The Navy/Marine Commander's Handbook*, the Genocide Convention ratified by the United States in 1986 made it a crime under international law to kill people with intent to destroy, in whole or in part, a national or other group.[243]

While the manuals do not address this Convention in detail, *The Air Force Manual on International Law* notes that in the Nuremberg trials one of the defendants charged with genocide for atrocities and murders of noncombatants argued in defense that shooting civilians under orders was no more culpable than an airman dropping bombs on a densely populated area, and that the Court rejected the argument on the basis that unlike the civilian shootings there were military purposes for bombing cities and the resultant killings were not individualized.[244] As military purposes for bombing the cities, the court cited destruction of communications, wrecking of railroads, and razing of factories for the purpose of impeding the military.[245]

The Martens Clause

If a particular use of a weapon is not covered by a convention or other specific rule of law, it nonetheless remains subject to the rule of law. *The Air Force Manual on International Law* sets forth this overriding principle famously expressed in the Martens Clause contained in the preamble to Hague IV:

> Until a more complete code of laws of war has been issued, the High Contracting Parties deem it expedient to declare that, in cases not included in the Regulations adopted by them, the inhabitants and belligerents remain under the protection and the rule of the principles of the law of nations, as they result from the usages

---

[242] THE AIR FORCE MANUAL ON INTERNATIONAL LAW at 5-2. The manual further cites Article 5 of Hague IX as restricting the bombing of such sites. *Id.* at 5-3.

[243] THE NAVAL/MARINE COMMANDER'S HANDBOOK at 10-2 (citing The Genocide Convention of 1948, 78 U.N.T.S. 277, AFP 110-20, at 5-56, with the Senate giving advice and consent to ratification on 19 February 1986, pursuant to SEN. EX. REP. NO. 99-5, 18 July 1985).

[244] THE AIR FORCE MANUAL ON INTERNATIONAL LAW at 5-6 and 5-16 n.13 (citing U.S. v. Ohlendorf, 4 US TRIALS BEFORE THE NUREMBERG MILITARY TRIBUNAL 466–467 (1948)).

[245] *Id.*

established among civilized peoples, from the laws of humanity, and from the dictates of the public conscience.[246]

The Army's *Law of Land Warfare* quotes the same provision of Hague IV, noting that Hague IV has "been held to be declaratory of the customary law of war, to which all States are subject."[247] The Army manual further notes that a "common article" of the Geneva Conventions of 1949 provides that the withdrawal from the conventions would not "impair the obligations which the Parties to the conflict shall remain bound to fulfill by virtue of the principles of the law of nations, as they result from the usages established among civilized peoples, from the laws of humanity and the dictates of the public conscience."[248]

Adopting a statement by Thomas Baty, *The Air Force Manual on International Law* recognizes international law as the "'last stronghold of true law' since its permanence is 'based on a general consciousness of stringent and permanent obligation.'"[249]

As discussed above, these principles were restated and reaffirmed in Article 1, paragraph 2, of Additional Protocol I of 1977. While broad and subject to interpretation, these principles ostensibly cover any potential gap in the reach of such rules as those of necessity, proportionality, moderation, discrimination, and neutrality.

Principle of Analogy

We saw above in the discussion of the necessity principle that the illegality of the use of particular weapons can be established not only from specific prohibitions embodied in international treaties but also from custom and usage.[250] We also saw in the immediately preceding discussion that, under such broad provisions as the Martens Clause and its progeny, the purposes and aspirations of international law are applicable to new threats to the international order as they emerge, based upon such considerations as the usages established among civilized peoples, the laws of humanity and the dictates of the public conscience.

---

[246] *Id.* at 1-7 (quoting Hague IV at 2-4). *See also id.* at 5-2.

[247] THE LAW OF LAND WARFARE at 6.

[248] *Id.* at 6.

[249] THE AIR FORCE MANUAL ON INTERNATIONAL LAW at 1-4 (citing Air Force News Release, Tuesday, November 4, 1975, Speech by The Honorable John L. McLucas, Secretary of the Air Force, citing THOMAS BATY, INTERNATIONAL LAW IN TWILIGHT).

[250] *See supra* notes 10, 133–135, & 225–226 and accompanying text.

The United States further recognizes "analogy" as a source of the law of armed conflict. *The Air Force Manual on International Law* states:

> The law of armed conflict affecting aerial operations is not entirely codified. Therefore, the law applicable to air warfare must be derived from general principles, extrapolated from the law affecting land or sea warfare, or derived from other sources including the practice of states reflected in a wide variety of sources. Yet the US is a party to numerous treaties which affect aerial operations either directly or by analogy.[251]

The manual further states:

> [A] new weapon or method of warfare may be illegal, *per se*, if it is restricted by international law including treaty or international custom. The issue is resolved, or attempted to be resolved, by analogy to weapons or methods previously determined to be lawful or unlawful.[252]

Principle of Humanity

As reflected in *The Air Force Manual on International Law*, the United States also recognizes an overriding principle of humanity:

> Complementing the principle of necessity and implicitly contained within it is the principle of humanity which forbids the infliction of suffering, injury or destruction not actually necessary for the accomplishment of legitimate military purposes. This principle of humanity results in a specific prohibition against unnecessary suffering, a requirement of proportionality, and a variety of more specific rules examined later. The principle of humanity also confirms the basic immunity of civilian populations and civilians from being objects of attack during armed conflict. This immunity of the civilian population does not preclude unavoidable incidental civilian casualties which may occur during the course of attacks against military objectives, and which are not excessive in relation to the concrete and direct military advantage anticipated.[253]

---

[251] THE AIR FORCE MANUAL ON INTERNATIONAL LAW at 1-7.
[252] *Id.* at 6-7.
[253] *Id.* at 1-6.

Principle of Reciprocity

The law of armed conflict recognizes a general principle of reciprocity, whereby many of a State's obligations are only binding as long as the adversary State complies, although this principle is not applicable to humanitarian rules of law that protect the victims of armed conflict.

The Naval/Marine Commander's Handbook states:

> 6.2.4 Reciprocity. Some obligations under the law of armed conflict are reciprocal in that they are binding on the parties only so long as both sides continue to comply with them. A major violation by one side will release the other from all further duty to abide by that obligation. The concept of reciprocity is not applicable to humanitarian rules of law that protect the victims of armed conflict, that is, those persons protected by the 1949 Geneva Conventions. The decision to consider the United States released from a particular obligation following major violation by the enemy will ordinarily be made by the NCA.[254]

The Air Force Manual on International Law states:

> Reciprocity. The most important relevant treaties, the 1949 Geneva Conventions for the Protection of War Victims, are not formally conditioned on reciprocity. Parties to each Convention "undertake to respect and to ensure respect for the present Convention in all circumstances" under Article 1 common to the Conventions. The Vienna Convention On the Law of Treaties, Article 60(5), also recognizes that the general law on material breaches, as a basis for suspending the operation of treaties, does not apply to provisions protecting persons in treaties of a humanitarian character. Yet reciprocity is an implied condition in other rules and obligations including generally the law of armed conflict. It is moreover a critical factor in the actual observance of the law of armed conflict.[255]

Reprisals

May a State respond with an unlawful use of force to an adversary's unlawful use of force?—That is the question posed by the notion of reprisals.

---

[254] THE NAVAL/MARINE COMMANDER'S HANDBOOK at 6-27 (citations omitted).

[255] THE AIR FORCE MANUAL ON INTERNATIONAL LAW at 10-1 (citations omitted).

Unlawful Acts Justified by Circumstances

The Naval/Marine Commander's Handbook defines reprisals as "act[s] which would otherwise be unlawful but which [are] justified as a response to the unlawful acts of an enemy."[256] *The Air Force Manual on International Law*, quoting a U.S. military tribunal, defines reprisals as acts which, "although illegal in themselves, may, under the specific circumstances of the given case, become justified because the guilty adversary has himself behaved illegally, and the action is taken in the last resort, in order to prevent the adversary from behaving illegally in the future."[257]

The manual states that "[r]eciprocity is ... explicitly the basis for the doctrine of reprisals."[258]

Issue as to Continuing Lawfulness of Reprisals

The United States has recognized that there is an issue as to the continuing legality of reprisals under the United Nations Charter. The Air Force manual quotes then–Acting Secretary of State Kenneth Rush:

> The United States has supported and supports the foregoing principle (referring to UN Resolution 2625 to the effect States have a duty to refrain from acts of reprisal involving the use of force). Of course, we recognize that the practice of states is not always consistent with this principle and that it may sometimes be difficult to distinguish the exercise of proportionate self-defense from an act of reprisal. Yet, essentially for reasons of the abuse to which the doctrine of reprisals particularly finds itself, we think it desirable to endeavor to maintain the distinction between acts of lawful self-defense and unlawful reprisals.[259]

Limitations on the Practice of Reprisals

The manual goes on to state the position that reprisals remain lawful for the purpose of seeking to attempt to compel the enemy to cease its violations of law, although not as an effort to redress the adversary's violations:

---

[256] THE NAVAL/MARINE COMMANDER'S HANDBOOK at 6-18.

[257] THE AIR FORCE MANUAL ON INTERNATIONAL LAW at 10-3; 10-6 n.12 (quoting US v. Ohlendorf, 4 TRIALS OF WAR CRIMINALS BEFORE THE NUREMBERG MILITARY TRIBUNALS 493 (1950)). *See also* THE AIR FORCE COMMANDER'S HANDBOOK at 8-1; THE LAW OF LAND WARFARE at 177.

[258] THE AIR FORCE MANUAL ON INTERNATIONAL LAW at 10-1.

[259] *Id.* at 10-6 to 10-7 n.13 (quoting 29 May 1974 statement of Acting Secretary of State Kenneth Rush, as reported at 68 AM. J. INT'L L. 736 (1974)).

For example, if an enemy employs illegal weapons against a state, the victim may resort to the use of weapons which would otherwise be unlawful in order to compel the enemy to cease its prior violation. Reprisals can be legally justified if they meet certain requirements of international law discussed in paragraph 10-7c.

A reprisal, in this context, does not refer to the use of force to redress violations of general international law. International law embodied in the UN Charter presently prohibits the use of armed force against the territorial integrity or political independence of another state except for collective or individual self-defiance.[260]

The United States recognizes severe constraints on the right of reprisal. *The Air Force Manual on International Law*, in the referred-to paragraph 10-7c, sets forth the following prerequisites to a legitimate reprisal:

(1) It must respond to grave and manifestly unlawful acts, committed by an adversary government, its military commanders or combatants for whom the adversary is responsible.

(2) It must be for the purpose of compelling the adversary to observe the law of armed conflict ... Above all, [reprisals] are justifiable only to force an adversary to stop its extra-legal activity. ...

(3) There must be reasonable notice that reprisals will be taken. ...

(4) Other reasonable means to secure compliance must be attempted. The victim of a violation in order to justify taking a reprisal must first exhaust other reasonable means of securing compliance ....

(5) A reprisal must be directed against the personnel or property of an adversary. ...

(6) A reprisal must be proportional to the original violation. Although a reprisal need not conform in kind to the same type of acts complained of (bombardment for bombardment, weapon for weapon) it may not significantly exceed the adversary's violation either in violence or effect. Effective but disproportionate reprisals cannot be justified by the argument that only an excessive response will forestall further transgressions.

(7) It must be publicized. ...

(8) It must be authorized by national authorities at the highest political level and entails full state responsibility.[261]

---

[260] *Id.* at 10-3 (citations omitted).
[261] *Id.* at 10-4 to 10-5. *See* the similar list set forth in THE NAVAL/MARINE COMMANDER'S HANDBOOK at 6-18 to 6-19 (citations omitted).

Proportionality Requirement as to Reprisals

The Naval/Marine Commander's Handbook states that a reprisal "must be proportional to the original violation."[262] It states that the requirement is not one of "strict proportionality," since a reprisal is usually "somewhat greater than the initial violation that gave rise to it,"[263] but that "care must be taken that the extent of the reprisal is measured by some degree of proportionality."[264] The handbook adds that "[t]he reprisal action taken may be quite different from the original act which justified it, but should not be excessive or exceed the degree of harm committed by the enemy."[265]

The handbook adds that "effective but disproportionate reprisals cannot be justified by the argument that only an excessive response will forestall a further transgression."[266] *The Air Force Manual on International Law* states that the German bombardments of London in the period September–November 1940 did not constitute lawful reprisals, notwithstanding German contentions to the contrary, since they were greatly disproportionate to the original alleged violation.[267]

Unlawful Nature of Many Purported Reprisals

The Air Force Manual on International Law states that "most attempted uses of reprisals" in past conflicts were unjustified, either because they were undertaken for an improper reason or were disproportionate.[268]

The Naval/Marine Commander's Handbook similarly states, "Many attempted uses of reprisals in past conflicts have been unjustified either because the reprisals were not undertaken to deter violations by an

---

[262] THE NAVAL/MARINE COMMANDER'S HANDBOOK at 6-19. *See also* THE AIR FORCE MANUAL ON INTERNATIONAL LAW at 10-5.

The Army's THE LAW OF LAND WARFARE states, "The acts resorted to by way of reprisal need not conform to those complained of by the injured party, but should not be excessive or exceed the degree of violence committed by the enemy." *Id.* at 177.

[263] THE NAVAL/MARINE COMMANDER'S HANDBOOK at 6-19.

[264] *See id.* at 6-19 n.38.

[265] *Id.*

[266] *Id. See also* THE AIR FORCE MANUAL ON INTERNATIONAL LAW, at 10-5.

[267] THE AIR FORCE MANUAL ON INTERNATIONAL LAW at 10-7 n.23 (citations omitted).

[268] *See id.* at 10-5. THE AIR FORCE MANUAL ON INTERNATIONAL LAW states that reprisals frequently backfire, hardening the enemy resolve and leading to escalation. *Id.*

adversary or were disproportionate to the preceding unlawful conduct."[269]

U.S. Stated Practice of Not Resorting to Reprisals

The Air Force Commander's Handbook similarly states, "In most twentieth century conflicts, the United States has, as a matter of national policy, chosen not to carry out reprisals against the enemy, both because of the potential for escalation and because it is generally in our national interest to follow the law even if the enemy does not."[270]

The Naval/Marine Commander's Handbook states, "Although reprisal is lawful when [the stated prerequisites] are met, there is always the risk that it will trigger retaliatory escalation (counter-reprisals) by the enemy. The United States has historically been reluctant to resort to reprisal for just this reason."[271]

The Air Force Manual on International Law notes that reprisals "will usually have an adverse impact on the attitudes of governments not participating in the conflict" and "may only strengthen enemy morale and will to resist."[272] *The Air Force Commander's Handbook* states that "as a practical matter, reprisals are often subject to abuse and merely result in escalation of a conflict."[273]

Targets Prohibited from Being Object of Reprisals

The Air Force Commander's Handbook states:

> Under the 1949 Geneva Conventions, reprisals may not be directed against hospitals, medical personnel, the sick and wounded, the shipwrecked, interned civilians, the inhabitants of occupied territory, and prisoners of war. (The reprisals against British prisoners of war that the US threatened during the Revolution would thus be illegal today, though at the time, reprisals against PWs were lawful.) A Protocol to the 1949 Geneva Conventions would expand this list to include all civilians and civilian property on land, a well as cultural property and the natural environment.

---

[269] THE NAVAL/MARINE COMMANDER'S HANDBOOK at 6-25 n.46.

[270] THE AIR FORCE COMMANDER'S HANDBOOK at 8-1.

[271] THE NAVAL/MARINE COMMANDER'S HANDBOOK at 6-25 (citations omitted).

[272] THE AIR FORCE MANUAL ON INTERNATIONAL LAW at 10-5.

[273] THE AIR FORCE COMMANDER'S HANDBOOK at 8-1.

The United States signed this Protocol in 1977, but has not yet ratified it.[274]

As to the referred-to Protocol, *The Naval/Marine Commander's Handbook* states that the United States "has found to be militarily objectionable the prohibition in Additional Protocol I, art. 51, of reprisal attacks against the civilian population because renunciation of the option of such attacks 'removes a significant deterrent that presently protects civilians and other war victims on all sides of a conflict.'"[275]

Thus, it is the U.S. position that reprisals against the enemy civilian population are lawful, although the United States recognizes that such attacks are "not appropriate:"

> Reprisals may lawfully be taken against enemy individuals who have not yet fallen into the hands of the forces making the reprisals. While the United States has always considered that civilian persons are not appropriate objects of attack in reprisal, members of the enemy civilian population are still legitimate objects of reprisals. However, since they are excluded from this category by the 1977 Protocol I Additional to the 1949 Geneva Conventions, for nations party thereto, enemy civilians and the enemy civilian population are prohibited objects of reprisal by their armed forces. The United States has found this new prohibition to be militarily unacceptable.[276]

As to permitted objects of reprisal, *The Naval/Marine Commander's Handbook* states:

> The following activities, prohibited under the law of armed conflict, are among those which may lawfully be taken in reprisal:
>
> 1. Restricted means and methods of warfare set forth in Hague Conventions (1907) (and Additional Protocol I for parties thereto, not including the Untied States ...) not specifically prohibited as a means of reprisal, such as:
>
> a. employing poison or poisoned weapons;

---

[274] *Id.* at 8-2. THE NAVAL/MARINE COMMANDER'S HANDBOOK adds the category of neutral parties' citizens. *Id.* at 6-22, Table ST6-1.

[275] THE NAVAL/MARINE COMMANDER'S HANDBOOK at 6-27 n.46 (quoting Sofaer, Remarks, contained in *The Sixth Annual American Red Cross-Washington College of Law Conference on International Humanitarian Law: A Workshop on Customary International Law and the 1977 Protocols Additional to the 1949 Geneva Conventions*, 2 AM. U.J. INT'L L. & POLICY 428, 469 (1987) and contrasting Hampson, *Belligerent Reprisals and the 1977 Protocols to the Geneva Conventions of 1949*, 37 INT'L & COMP. L.Q. 818 (1988)).

[276] THE NAVAL/MARINE COMMANDER'S HANDBOOK at 6-18 n.33.

***

e. employing weapons, projectiles, or material or methods of warfare of a nature to cause superfluous injury or unnecessary suffering;

***

g. use of unanchored submarine contact mines or mines and torpedoes which do not render themselves harmless within one hour after they have broken loose from their moorings or have been fired.

***

3. Military or other hostile use of environmental modification techniques prohibited by the 1977 Environmental Modification Convention.

4. For nations party thereto (not including the United States), the use of weapons the primary effect of which is to injure by fragments which in the human body escape detection by X-rays, in violation of Protocol I to the 1980 Conventional Weapons Convention.

5. For nations party thereto (not including the United States), the use of mines, booby traps and other devices, except against the civilian population or against individual civilians, in violation of Protocol II to the Conventional Weapons Convention.

6. For nations party thereto (not including the United States), the use of incendiary weapons in violation of Protocol III to the Conventional Weapons Convention.[277]

Mental State

The Air Force Manual on International Law states that the law of armed conflict "primarily emphasizes the behavior expected of nations and combatants—not the responsibility of individuals for its violation" —and that accordingly the law "often omits critical elements of individual criminal responsibility, such as intentional and deliberate acts."[278] Similarly, "[t]he law is not principally formulated with any

---

[277] *Id.* at 6-26 n.46. Subsequent to publication of the manual, the United States ratified the Convention on Prohibition or Restrictions on the Use of Certain Conventional Weapons Which May Be Deemed To Be Excessively Injurious or To Have Indiscriminate Effects, concluded at Geneva, 10 October 1980, entered into force, 2 December 1983, U.N. Doc. A/CONF. 95/15 (1980) and U.N. Doc. A/CONF. 95/15 Corr. 2; 1981 Misc. 23, Cmnd. 8370; *reprinted in* 19 I.L.M. 1523 (1980) & 2 Weston II.C.10., ratified, with qualification, by United States, 24 March, 1995, *cited in* SUPPLEMENT TO INTERNATIONAL LAW AND WORLD ORDER 262–71, 286 (Burns H. Weston et al. eds., 3rd ed. 1997).

[278] THE AIR FORCE MANUAL ON INTERNATIONAL LAW at 15-2.

view to individual criminal responsibility but rather to state responsibility."[279]

State Responsibility as Not Generally Requiring *Mens rea*

Accordingly, it would appear that, for purposes of State responsibility, the rules of law upon which we have focused—proportionality, necessity, discrimination, moderation, humanity, civilian immunity, and neutrality—do not contain a requirement of *mens rea* or guilty mind. Nor did the various statements of such rules by the military manuals contain any such element.

Explaining the general absence of a *mens rea* requirement for State, as opposed to individual, responsibility, the Air Force manual states that "if the law of armed conflict were couched in terms of intentional wrongs it would lose much of its efficacy; the issue then would be a State's intent, a troublesome concept to apply."[280]

The manual adds that from the "perspective of the victim—civilian, PW or other *hors de combat* personnel—the wrongful act has the same result whether done intentionally or inadvertently."[281] As a result, "[f]ailures to observe treaty rules or other international law rules may occur for which there may be general state responsibility without any individual criminal responsibility."[282]

Objective Reasonableness Standard for Main Applicable Rules

At the same time, we have seen that these are essentially rules of reason. Since the State does not act except through its representatives, State responsibility for violation of such rules must turn on the overall reasonableness of the actions of the applicable representatives of the State. The applicable standard is generally objective not subjective reasonableness.[283]

Mens Rea Required for "Grave Violations"

Quoting the applicable sections, the manual goes on to note that the element of willfulness is imposed with respect to many of the breaches defined as "grave" by the 1949 Geneva Conventions, with such element connoted through such words as "willful" and "wanton:"

GWS and GWS SEA

---

[279] *Id.* at 15-8 n.12.
[280] *Id.* at 15-2.
[281] *Id.*
[282] *Id.* at 15-3.
[283] *See supra* notes 84–90 and accompanying text.

Grave breaches to which the preceding Article relates shall be those involving any of the following acts, if committed against persons or property protected by the Convention: willful killing, torture or inhuman treatment, including biological experiments, willfully causing great suffering or serious injury to body or health, and extensive destruction and appropriation of property, not justified by military necessity and carried out unlawfully and wantonly. (Art. 50, GWS; Art 51, GWS-SEA).[284]

Individual Responsibility

The Air Force Manual on International Law goes on to state that *mens rea* or a guilty mind, at the level of purposeful behavior or intention or at least gross negligence, is required for individual, as opposed to State, criminal responsibility.[285]   The manual quotes Spaight's statement of the rule:

In international law, as in municipal law intention to break the law—*mens rea* or negligence so gross as to be the equivalent of criminal intent is the essence of the offense. A bombing pilot cannot be arraigned for an error of judgment ... it must be one which he or his superiors either knew to be wrong, or which was, *in se*, so palpably and unmistakenly a wrongful act that only gross negligence or deliberate blindness could explain their being unaware of its wrongness.[286]

The Air Force Commander's Handbook states that the 1949 Geneva Conventions "require" the trial of persons who have "intentionally committed 'grave breaches'" of the conventions."[287]   The handbook states that international law "allows a nation to try captured enemy personnel for deliberate, intentional violations of the law of armed conflict" and notes that after World War II the United States conducted or took part in over 800 such trials.[288]

Command Responsibility

A commander is responsible to maintain and prevent violations of the law of war by subordinates, and can be liable for breaches by subordinates.

---

[284] *Id.* at 15-1 to 15-2; 15-8 n.12. The manual quoted similar articles from other Geneva Conventions.

[285] *Id.* at 15-3; 15-8 n.13 (citing SPAIGHT, AIR POWER AND WAR RIGHTS 57, 58 (1947)).

[286] *Id.* at 15-8 n.13.

[287] THE AIR FORCE COMMANDER'S HANDBOOK at 8-1.

[288] *Id.*

The *Air Force Manual on International Law* states that "[c]ommand responsibility for acts committed by subordinates arises when the specific wrongful acts in question are knowingly ordered or encouraged."[289]　The manual states that the commander is also responsible "if he has actual knowledge, or should have had knowledge" that his subordinates "have or are about to commit criminal violations, and he culpably fails to take reasonably necessary steps to ensure compliance with the law and punish violators thereof."[290]

The *Naval/Marine Commander's Handbook* states, "A commander at any level is personally responsible for the criminal acts of warfare committed by a subordinate if the commander knew in advance of the breach about to be committed and had the ability to prevent it, but failed to take the appropriate action to do so."[291]　The handbook adds that "in determining the personal responsibility of the commander, the element of knowledge may be presumed if the commander had information which should have enabled him or her to conclude under the circumstances that such breach was to be expected."[292]　The handbook states that the applicable facts "will each be determined objectively."[293]

The handbook quotes the United States Military Tribunal's decision in *The Hostages Case* for the proposition that the commander is charged with available information even if not personally aware of same:

> Want of knowledge of the contents of reports made to him [*i.e.*, to the commander general] is not a defense. Reports to commanding generals are made for their special benefit. Any failure to acquaint

---

[289] THE AIR FORCE MANUAL ON INTERNATIONAL LAW at 15-3. *See also* 15-9 n.23 (citing Prosecution Statement, *International Military Tribunal Far East*, Apr. 1948); 11 WHITEMAN, DIGEST OF INTERNATIONAL LAW 993–994 (1968); MCDOUGAL & FELICIANO, LAW AND MINIMUM WORLD PUBLIC ORDER 331 (1961) ("[T]he most important target selection principle that emerged from the decisions in post World War II cases is that only individuals who ranked in the top policy formulating levels of authority and control structures of the violator state should be held liable to these deprivations"); GREENSPAN, LAW OF LAND WARFARE 449 (1959); CASTREN, PRESENT LAW OF WAR AND NEUTRALITY 84 (1954)).

[290] THE AIR FORCE MANUAL ON INTERNATIONAL LAW at 15-2 to 15-3. *See also* THE LAW OF LAND WARFARE at 178.

[291] THE NAVAL/MARINE COMMANDER'S HANDBOOK at 6-5 n.12.

[292] *Id.* at 6-5.

[293] *Id.*

themselves with the contents of such reports, or a failure to require additional reports where inadequacy appears on their face, constitutes a dereliction of duty which he cannot use in his behalf.[294]

The handbook states that the responsibility of a commanding officer "may be based solely upon inaction" and that it is "not always necessary to establish that a superior knew, or must be presumed to have known of the offense committed by his subordinates."[295] "While a commander may delegate some or all of his authority, he cannot delegate responsibility for the conduct of the forces he commands."[296]

Nuremberg Prosecutions Based on Command Responsibility

The Air Force Manual on International Law notes that the prosecutions for crimes against peace and against humanity following World War II were primarily against the principal political, military and industrial leaders responsible for the initiation of the war and related inhumane policies.[297] The manual states, "[A] soldier who merely performs his military duty cannot be said to have waged the war ... [O]nly the government, and those authorities who carry out governmental functions and are instrumental in formulating policy, wage the war."[298]

The Air Force Commander's Handbook states that the two International Military Tribunals following World War II punished "former cabinet ministers, and others of similar rank" in the Axis powers for planning and waging aggressive war.[299]

The Air Force Manual on International Law notes that States have "important customary and treaty obligations to follow the law not only as national policy but to ensure its implementation, observance and enforcement by its own combatant personnel."[300] The manual notes as examples that Article 1, Hague IV, requires parties to issue instructions in conformity with the Hague Regulations and that the 1949 Geneva Conventions require that the contracting states enact domestic

---

[294] *Id.* (citing United States v. Wilhelm List et al., 9 TWC 127 (1950)).

[295] *Id.* at 6-6 n.12.

[296] *Id.* at 6-5.

[297] *See* THE AIR FORCE MANUAL ON INTERNATIONAL LAW at 15-5.

[298] THE NAVAL/MARINE COMMANDER'S HANDBOOK at 15-9 n.23 (citing *Prosecution Statement, International Military Tribunal Far East, April 1948,* 11 WHITEMAN, DIGEST OF INTERNATIONAL LAW, at 993–994 (1968)).

[299] *See* THE AIR FORCE COMMANDER'S HANDBOOK at 1-2.

[300] THE AIR FORCE MANUAL ON INTERNATIONAL LAW at 15-1.

legislation providing penal sanctions for persons who commit or order any "grave breach" of said Conventions.[301]

War Crimes

The Army's *Law of Land Warfare* states that war crimes under international law are made up of:

> a. Crimes against peace;
> b. Crimes against humanity; and
> c. War crimes.[302]

Crimes against Peace

As noted in *The Naval/Marine Commander's Handbook*, the Charter of the International Military Tribunal at Nuremberg defined "crimes against the peace" as follows:

> planning, preparation, initiation, or waging of a war of aggression, or a war in violation of international treaties, agreements or assurances, or participation in a common plan or conspiracy for the accomplishment of any of the foregoing;[303]

The handbook cited the United Nations General Assembly's definition of aggression as "the use of armed force by a State against the sovereignty, territorial integrity or political independence of another State, or in any other manner inconsistent with the Charter of the

---

[301] *See id.* at 15-1 and 15-7 n.5 (citing Common Article found in Art. 49, GWS; Art. 50, GWS-SEA; Art. 129, GPW; Art. 146, GC; and noting that the principles of said Articles "declare customary law obligations to suppress violations of the law of armed conflict including particularly those committed by one's own armed forces;" and further citing FM 27-10, at 181; NWIP 10-2, at 3–5; and GREENSPAN, LAW OF LAND WARFARE 93 (1959)). *See also* THE LAW OF LAND WARFARE at 179.

[302] THE LAW OF LAND WARFARE at 178.

[303] THE NAVAL/MARINE COMMANDER'S HANDBOOK at 6-27 n.49 (quoting Charter of the International Military Tribunal at Nuremberg, U.S. Naval War College, INTERNATIONAL LAW DOCUMENTS 1944–45, at 254 (1945); Air Force Pamphlet 110-20, at 3-183).

United Nations,"[304] stating that such formulations accorded with the U.S. view of aggression.[305]

Crimes against Humanity

The Nuremberg Charter defined "crimes against humanity" as follows:

> murder, extermination, enslavement, deportation, and other inhumane acts committed against any civilian population, before or during the war, or persecutions on political, racial, or religious grounds in execution of or in connection with any crime within the jurisdiction of the Tribunal, whether or not in violation of the domestic law of the country where perpetuated.[306]

The Naval/Marine Commander's Handbook, noting that there is "certain difficulty in distinguishing war crimes from crimes against humanity," summarized judgments of various tribunals that have tried individuals for crimes against humanity as follows:

> 1. Certain acts constitute both war crimes and crimes against humanity and may be tried under either charge.
> 2. Generally, crimes against humanity are offenses against the human rights of individuals, carried on in a widespread and systematic manner. Thus, isolated offenses have not been considered as crimes against humanity, and courts have usually insisted upon proof that the acts alleged to be crimes against humanity resulted from systematic governmental action.
> 3. The possible victims of crimes against humanity constitute a wider class than those who are capable of being made the objects of war crimes and may include the nationals of the enemy state committing the offense as well as stateless persons.
> 4. Acts constituting crimes against humanity must be committed in execution of, or in connection with, crimes against peace, or war crimes.[307]

---

[304] THE NAVAL/MARINE COMMANDER'S HANDBOOK at 5-2 n.2 (quoting Resolution 3314 (XXIX), 29 U.N. GAOR, Supp. 31, v.1, U.N. Doc. A/9631, at 142 (1974); DEP'T ST. BULL., 3 Feb. 1975, at 158-60; AFP 110-20, at 5-78 & 5-79).

[305] THE NAVAL/MARINE COMMANDER'S HANDBOOK at 5-2 n.2 (citing DEP'T ST. BULL., 3 Feb. 1978, at 155–58).

[306] THE NAVAL/MARINE COMMANDER'S HANDBOOK at 6-27 n.49 (quoting Charter of the International Military Tribunal at Nuremberg, U.S. Naval War College, INTERNATIONAL LAW DOCUMENTS 1944–45, at 254 (1945); Air Force Pamphlet 110-20, at 3-183).

[307] *Id.* at 6-28, 6-28 n.49.

War Crimes

The Army's *Law of Land Warfare* defines the term "war crime" as "the technical expression for a violation of the law of war by any person or persons, military or civilian," adding that "[e]very violation of the law of war is a war crime."[308]

To the same effect, the Nuremberg Charter defined "war crimes" as follows:

> [V]iolations of the laws or customs of war. Such violations shall include, but not be limited to, murder, ill treatment, or deportation to slave labor or for any other purpose, of civilian population of or in occupied territory, murder or ill treatment of prisoners of war or persons on the seas, killing of hostages, plunder of public or private property, wanton destruction of cities, towns or villages, or devastation not justified by military necessity.[309]

Prohibitive Nature of Law of Armed Conflict

The law of armed conflict sets forth prohibitions of certain levels of force; it in no way authorizes levels of force. *The Air Force Manual on International Law* states, "The international law of armed conflict is generally characterized as prohibitive law forbidding certain manifestations of force rather than positive law authorizing other such manifestations."[310]

The manual further states:

> The law of armed conflict contains both affirmative obligations and prohibitions. Yet this body of law neither authorizes nor prohibits the basic decision to use force. That issue is related back to the concept of self defense–aggression .... The law of armed conflict represents "standards of civilization" which have been shaped by the concepts of military necessity, humanity and chivalry. ... For these reasons, the law of armed conflict cannot be argued to authorize the use of force since the legal regulation of that issue is by a separate and distinct legal regime. The law of armed conflict

---

[308] THE LAW OF LAND WARFARE at 178.

[309] THE NAVAL/MARINE COMMANDER'S HANDBOOK at 6-27 n.49 (quoting Charter of the International Military Tribunal at Nuremberg, U.S. Naval War College, INTERNATIONAL LAW DOCUMENTS 1944–45, at 254 (1945); Air Force Pamphlet 110-20, at 3-183).

[310] THE AIR FORCE MANUAL ON INTERNATIONAL LAW at 6-1.

> represents standards applicable whether or not the use of force was prohibited, permissible or unascertainable.[311]

The manual adds, "[T]he law of armed conflict does not authorize aggression—nor does it condemn aggression—it exists independently of the causes of the conflict and applies regardless of the causes." [312]

The Naval/Marine Commander's Handbook states:

> It is important to distinguish between resort to war, or armed conflict, and the conduct of armed conflict. "Whether or not resort to armed conflict in a particular circumstance is prohibited by the United Nations Charter (and therefore unlawful), the manner in which that armed conflict is conducted continues to be regulated by the law of armed conflict.[313]

Bases for *Per Se* Rule

The U.S. military manuals do not appear to define the bases for a *per se* rule, although they recognize that such rules can result from custom and from general principles as well as from treaties.

The Air Force Manual on International Law states that, "[u]sage and practice has also determined that it is *per se* illegal to use projectiles filled with glass or other materials inherently difficult to detect medically, to use any substance on projectiles that tend unnecessarily to inflame the wound they cause, to use irregularly shaped bullets or to score the surface or to file off the ends of the hard cases of bullets which cause them to expand upon contact and thus aggravate the wound they cause."[314]

The manual further states, "a new weapon or method of warfare may be illegal, *per se*, if it is restricted by international law including treaty or international custom. The issue is resolved, or attempted to be resolved, by analogy to weapons or methods previously determined to be lawful or unlawful."[315]

The U.S. view on the subject can, as we shall see, be gleaned from its ostensible view that, for the use of a weapon to be unlawful, it must be shown that the use of the weapon will "necessarily" cause unlawful effects.

---

[311] *Id.* at 1-15 n.30.

[312] *Id.* at 1-14 n.24.

[313] THE NAVAL/MARINE COMMANDER'S HANDBOOK at 5-1 to 5-2 (citations omitted).

[314] THE AIR FORCE MANUAL ON INTERNATIONAL LAW at 6-2.

[315] *Id.* at 6-7.

The Air Force Manual on International Law, addressing the criteria for formation of customary law, states, "Upon occasion, a prohibition is confirmed by the practice of states in refraining from the use of a weapon because of recognition of excessive injury or damage to civilians or civilian objects which will necessarily be caused by the weapon."[316]

The manual further states that the term "indiscriminate" refers to the "inherent characteristics of the weapon, when used, which renders *(sic)* it incapable of being directed at specific military objectives or of a nature to necessarily cause disproportionate injury to civilians or damage to civilian objects."[317]

Stating that indiscriminate weapons include those which, while subject to being directed at military objectives, "may have otherwise uncontrollable effects so as to cause disproportionate civilian injuries or damage," the manual elaborates that "uncontrollable" refers to effects "which escape in time or space from the control of the user as to necessarily create risks to civilian persons or objects excessive in relation to the military advantage anticipated."[318]

In comparing the military advantages to be secured by the use of a new weapon to the effects caused by the weapon, the manual notes the following questions, among others, as relevant, "(2) would its use necessarily result in excessive injury to civilians or damage to civilian objects, so as to be termed an "indiscriminate weapon" and "(4) would its use necessarily cause suffering excessive in relation to the military purpose which the weapon serves so as to violate that prohibition"?[319]

To the same effect, *The Naval/Marine Commander's Handbook*, addressing the lawfulness of the use of nuclear weapons, states, "It is not clear the use of nuclear weapons violates international law."[320]

---

[316] *Id.* at 6-3.

[317] *See id.* at 6-9 n.7.

[318] *See id.* at 6-3.

[319] *See id.* at 6-7.

[320] THE NAVAL/MARINE COMMANDER'S HANDBOOK at 10-2.

Chapter 2: The Law as Applied by the United States

In the preceding chapter we saw the rules of law which the United States recognizes as generally applicable to the lawfulness of the use of any weapon or level of force. We come now to how the United States views these rules as applying to nuclear weapons. For the U.S. position, I rely upon the United States' official oral and written statements to the ICJ and upon the U.S. military manuals.

With the applicable rules of law in large measure non-controversial, the question of how to apply these rules becomes the primary battleground between the proponents and opponents of the nuclear weapons regime. In describing the U.S. position, I identify the legal and factual issues it raises in an effort to set the stage for our overall evaluation of the matter.

Let me first summarize the position:

1) No *Per Se* Rule

There is no conventional or customary law specifically prohibiting the use of nuclear weapons.

As to conventional law, there is no international convention specifically prohibiting the general use of nuclear weapons "as such" because of their nature as nuclear. The prohibition by the Geneva Protocol of 1925 of the use of asphyxiating, poisonous or other gases, and of "all analogous liquids, materials or devices" does not apply to nuclear weapons.

As to customary law, there is no "custom" of nonuse, and hence no customary rule of law prohibiting such use. The fact that the nuclear powers have refrained from using such weapons since Hiroshima and Nagasaki does not mean that customary law recognizes that the use of such weapons would be unlawful, since a prerequisite for the creation of customary law—performance or restraint out of a "sense of obligation"—is lacking. The nuclear powers, both specifically and through the policy of deterrence, have regularly and continuously asserted the lawfulness of the use of nuclear weapons and expressed their readiness to use such weapons.

In addition, the nuclear and other powers have entered into a series of international agreements limiting, *inter alia*, the circumstances and extent to which nuclear weapons can be produced, maintained, tested, distributed and the like, thereby manifesting their belief that the use of such weapons is not generally prohibited.

The fact that the United States, along with the other nuclear powers and numerous other States, has espoused the general lawfulness of the use of nuclear weapons means that it cannot be said as a matter of law that the use of such weapons would be *per se* unlawful.

2) General Rule: Case by Case Determination

Nuclear weapons, like any other weapon, can be used lawfully or unlawfully, depending upon the circumstances of use. Nuclear weapons are no different from any other weapons. The lawfulness of any particular use must be determined in light of the circumstances.

Some uses of nuclear weapons would be lawful and others unlawful, depending upon the application to such use of the law of war, including the principles of proportionality, necessity, discrimination, moderation, civilian immunity, neutrality, humanity, and prohibition of genocide.

Many potential uses of nuclear weapons are capable of complying with such principles. The United States has low-yield precision nuclear weapons which it is capable of targeting and delivering with great accuracy against specific military targets, in the process limiting and controlling the effects, including radioactive fallout.

3) Right of Reprisal

If another State were to make an unlawful attack upon the United States, the United States would have a right of reprisal with nuclear weapons even if such use would otherwise have been unlawful. Such a reprisal would have to be proportional to the adversary's offending strike and otherwise satisfy prerequisites for lawful reprisal.

The foregoing reflects what appears to be the nuanced formal position of the United States. There is another less nuanced articulation of the position that is ostensibly implicit in U.S. educational, training, planning and operational practices and essentially assumes that the use of nuclear weapons is lawful. This can be seen, for instance, from *Joint Pub 3-12, Doctrine for Joint Nuclear Operations*, setting forth the operational planning of the military as of 1995 for the integrated use by

U.S. forces of nuclear weapons in conjunction with conventional weapons.[1]

This manual—which authoritatively establishes operational policy—states, without qualification:

> [T]here is no customary or conventional international law to prohibit nations from employing nuclear weapons in armed conflict. Therefore, the use of nuclear weapons against enemy combatants and other military objectives is lawful.[2]

The military's manual *Doctrine for Joint Theater Nuclear Operations* takes a somewhat more nuanced position:

> [The law of armed conflict] does not prohibit the use of nuclear weapons in armed conflict. However, any weapon must be considered a military necessity, and measures must be taken to avoid collateral damage and unnecessary suffering. Since nuclear weapons have greater destructive potential, in many instances they may be inappropriate.[3]

The manual states further:

---

[1] *See* JOINT CHIEFS OF STAFF, DOCTRINE FOR JOINT NUCLEAR OPERATIONS, Joint Pub 3-12, (Dec. 15, 1995), available at <http://www.dtic.mil/doctrine/jel/new_pubs/jp3_12.pdf> [hereinafter DOCTRINE FOR JOINT NUCLEAR OPERATIONS]. The 1995 manual "DOCTRINE FOR JOINT NUCLEAR OPERATIONS" was a reissue (with minor adjustments) to a 1993 manual of the same name and Joint Publication number. *See* JOINT CHIEFS OF STAFF, JOINT PUB. 3-12, DOCTRINE FOR JOINT OPERATIONS (April 29, 1993).

[2] DOCTRINE FOR JOINT NUCLEAR OPERATIONS, *supra* note 1, at II-1 (emphasis omitted). While the references to use of nuclear weapons against "enemy combatants and other military objectives" could be said to imply the more nuanced position, such a nuanced reading itself seems overly theoretical for this kind of operational document. The core of the policy, as communicated to the military by this authoritative document, appears that of the legality of the use of nuclear weapons. The manual provides: "If conflicts arise between the contents of this publication and the contents of Service publications [presumably, the publications of any one service], this publication will take precedence unless the Chairman of the Joint Chiefs of Staff, normally in consultation with other members of the Joint Chiefs of Staff, has provided more current and specific guidance." *Id.* at i.

[3] JOINT CHIEFS OF STAFF, JOINT PUB 3-12.1, DOCTRINE FOR JOINT THEATER NUCLEAR OPERATIONS v–vi (Feb. 9, 1996) (prepared under direction of the Chairman of the Joint Chiefs of Staff), as set forth at <http://www.dtic.mil/doctrine/jel/new_pubs/jp3_12_1.pdf> [hereinafter DOCTRINE FOR JOINT THEATER NUCLEAR OPERATIONS].

However, to comply with the law, a particular use of any weapon must satisfy the long-standing targeting rules of military necessity, proportionality, and avoidance of collateral damage and unnecessary suffering. Nuclear weapons are unique in this analysis only in their greater destructive potential (although they also differ from conventional weapons in that they produce radiation and electromagnetic effects and, potentially, radioactive fallout). In some circumstances, the use of a nuclear weapon may therefore be inappropriate. Treaties may impose additional restrictions on nuclear weapons.[4]

The foregoing statements seem carefully crafted in an effort at formal compliance with the legal requirements recognized by the United States (indeed, as expressed to the ICJ), while giving the message to the military that these weapons are within acceptable parameters. They are lawful, although, essentially as a bow to the technicalities, it is recognized that they may sometimes be inconsistent with "targeting rules" and hence, "in some circumstances" may be "inappropriate"—hardly a major legal issue for commanders to be concerned about.

That the potential effects of nuclear weapons are projected in real terms to the military as targeting and efficiency—not legality—considerations appears further from the manual's detailed discussion of "Relative Effectiveness:"

Relative Effectiveness. The relative effectiveness of nuclear and nonnuclear weapons must be weighed. The employment of nuclear weapons must offer a clearly significant advantage over nonnuclear munitions. When nuclear weapons will produce only a marginal gain in effectiveness over nonnuclear weapons, there may be no reason to use them since their employment is likely to have geopolitical and military implications beyond the immediate situation.[5]

Elaboration of the U.S. Formal Position

The United States, in its legal memoranda submitted to the ICJ, argued that there is no international agreement banning the use of nuclear weapons and hence that such use is not generally prohibited by

---

[4] *Id.* at I-1–2. (emphasis omitted). The manual further states: "Additional treaty information regarding nuclear weapons can be found in Joint Pub 3-12, "DOCTRINE FOR JOINT NUCLEAR OPERATIONS." *Id.* at I-2.

[5] *Id.* at III-1–2 (emphasis omitted).

conventional law but rather must be evaluated on a case to case basis.[6] As to customary law, the United States cited its long-standing assertion of the right to use such weapons, stating that "customary law could not be created over the objection of the nuclear-weapon states, which are the states whose interests are most specially affected."[7] The United States further argued that customary law could not be created by "abstaining from the use of nuclear weapons for humanitarian, political or military reasons, rather than from a belief that such abstention is required by law."[8]

That the U.S. commitment to the lawfulness of the use of the nuclear weapons is carried through to the operational level is clear from the United States' contemporary military manuals setting forth operational plans for the conducting of nuclear war.

The Joint Chief of Staff's *Doctrine for Joint Theater Nuclear Operations,* issued as recently as February 1996, states:

> Nuclear operations can be successful in achieving US military objectives if they are used in the appropriate situation and administered properly.[9]
>
> ***
>
> Nuclear weapons have many purposes, but should only be used after deterrence has failed.[10]

---

[6] *See* Conrad K. Harper (Legal Advisor, Department of State), Michael J. Matheson (Deputy Legal Advisor, Department of State), Bruce C. Rashkow (Assistant Legal Advisor, Department of State), and John H. McNeill (Senior Deputy General Counsel, Department of Defense), *Written Statement of the Government of the United States of America* (June 20, 1995), submitted to the International Court of Justice, The Hague, The Netherlands, in connection with the Request by the United Nations General Assembly for an Advisory Opinion on the Legality of the Threat or Use of Nuclear Weapons at 2, 8-14 ("U.S. ICJ Memorandum/GA App.") (citing U.S. Army Field Manual 27-10, Change No. 1, THE LAW OF LAND WARFARE at 4 ¶ 40(a)). *See also* Conrad K. Harper, Michael J. Matheson, & Bruce C. Rashkow, *Written Statement of the Government of the United States of America* (June 10, 1994), submitted to the International Court of Justice, The Hague, The Netherlands, in connection with the Request by the World Health Organization for an Advisory Opinion on the Question of the Legality Under International Law and the World Health Organization Constitution of the Use of Nuclear Weapons by a State in War or Other Armed Conflict at 2, 16-21 ("U.S. ICJ Memorandum/WHO App.").

[7] U.S. ICJ Memorandum/GA App. at 9

[8] *Id.* at 9.

[9] DOCTRINE FOR JOINT THEATER NUCLEAR OPERATIONS, *supra* note 3, at v (emphasis omitted).

[10] *Id.* at vi (emphasis omitted).

***

> The purpose of using nuclear weapons can range from
> producing a political decision to influencing an operation.[11]

The manual identifies types of situations where the use of nuclear
weapons may be "favored over a conventional attack" or otherwise
preferred:

> • Level of effort required for conventional targeting. If the
> target is heavily defended such that heavy losses are expected, a
> nuclear weapon may be favored over a conventional attack.
> • Length of time that a target must be kept out of action. A
> nuclear weapon attack will likely put a target out of action for a
> longer period of time than a conventional weapon attack.
> • Logistic support and anticipation of delays caused by the "fog
> and friction" of war. Such delays are unpredictable and may range
> from several hours to a number of days.[12]

The manual states:

> Should deterrence fail, our forces must be prepared to end the
> conflict on terms favorable to the United States, its interests, and
> its allies. Units capable of delivering nuclear weapons should be
> integrated with other forces in a combined arms, joint approach.
> When used, nuclear weapons should produce the results shown in
> Figure I-1.[13]

The referenced Figure I-1 states:

> Desired Results from the Use of Nuclear Weapons:
> Decisively change the perception of enemy leaders about their
> ability to win
> Demonstrate to enemy leaders that, should the conflict continue
> or escalate, the certain loss outweighs the potential gain
> Promptly resolve the conflict on terms favorable to the United
> States and our Allies
> Preclude the enemy from achieving its objectives
> Ensure the success of the effort by US and/or multinational
> forces
> Counter enemy weapons of mass destruction[14]

The manual identifies the following as National Command
Authority considerations as to whether to use nuclear weapons:

---

[11] *Id.*

[12] *Id.* at III-4 (emphasis omitted).

[13] *Id.* at I-2

[14] *Id.* fig. I-1.

5. NCA Considerations for Employment
a. Political
• Relationship to US vital interests, treaty commitments, diplomatic agreements, and area denial and escalation implications
• Perception of US will and resolve
• International reaction and geopolitical repercussions
b. Military
• Whether or not an alternative means exists to achieve the objective
• Geographical area for employment
• Type of delivery system
• Types of targets to be attacked
• Timing and duration of nuclear weapon employment
• Collateral damage constraints
• Target analysis
• The quantity, type, and yield of available weapons
c. Legal. Law of Armed Conflict
Along with the above considerations, additional factors may effect nuclear employment—supplementary guidance on these aspects can be found in the Nuclear Supplement to the JSCP.[15]

As to the purpose for using nuclear weapons, the manual states:

> The purpose of using nuclear weapons can range from producing a political decision at the strategic level of war to being used to influence an operation in some segment of the theater. Operations employing nuclear weapons will have a greater impact on a conflict than operations involving only conventional weapons.[16]

The manual identifies "enemy combat forces and facilities that may be likely targets for nuclear strikes:"

> • WMD ["weapons of mass destruction," including chemical, biological, and nuclear weapons] and their delivery systems, as well as associated command and control, production, and logistical support units
> • Ground combat units and their associated command and control and support units
> • Air defense facilities and support installations
> • Naval installations, combat vessels, and associated support facilities and command and control capabilities.
> • Nonstate actors (facilities and operation centers) that possess WMD

---

[15] *Id.* at III-7–8 (emphasis omitted).
[16] *Id.* at I-2 (emphasis omitted).

• Underground facilities[17]

The basic message is that the military has to be tough and decisive:

> The goals of nuclear execution must be clear to commanders and staff officers involved in the operation.
>
> Command guidance must be provided early in the planning process for use of nuclear weapons. Commanders and staff officers should understand effects, employment procedures, capabilities, and limitations of nuclear weapons systems. Command guidance may consist of a statement of desired results, circumstances leading to the request for nuclear execution, and the delivery systems available. It may also include the level of acceptable risk, restriction on fallout, and criteria for collateral damage, as well as criteria for intelligence collection and combat assessment.[18]

The U.S. military's training, planning and operational mindset is that the U.S. nuclear arsenal contains usable weapons:

> The US nuclear arsenal contains a wide range of systems that can be tailored to meet desired military and political objectives.[19]
>
> ***
>
> There are many nuclear support systems available for the geographic combatant commander.[20]

U.S. policy calls for warning to friendly forces of upcoming nuclear strikes:

> Strike warnings must be announced to the field immediately to ensure the safety of friendly forces.
>
> Friendly forces should receive advanced warning of nuclear strikes to ensure that they are not placed at unnecessary risk. Attacks are announced through a strike warning (STRIKEWARN) message. STRIKEWARN messages will be disseminated as rapidly as possible over secure networks, by the executing commander. When secure networks are not available, unit signal operation instructions will aid in disseminating the messages.[21]

The manual, while noting that the President has "sole authority for release of nuclear weapons,"[22] emphasizes the role of the place military commanders in nuclear targeting:

---

[17] *Id.* at III-6–7.

[18] *Id.* at ix (emphasis omitted).

[19] *Id.* at vi.

[20] *Id.* (emphasis omitted).

[21] *Id.* at x (emphasis omitted).

[22] *Id.* at vii.

The geographic combatant commander is responsible for promptly requesting nuclear support. Subordinate commanders responsible for target nominations submit requests to the geographic combatant commander.[23]

In discussing the dangers of degradation of command and control, the manual specifically notes that the "geographic combatant commander may exercise control for allocated nuclear weapons."[24]

Reinforcing the importance of the military mindset and basic contingency planning, the U.S. military in its manual *Doctrine for Joint Theater Nuclear Operations* identifies the need for advance planning as to the military aspects:

> Given an operation plan within an area of responsibility and/or joint operations area and a threat, it is advantageous to plan as many potential operations as possible in peacetime. The objective is to provide plans for nuclear operations that are ready to be used immediately should the need arise and yet are flexible enough to accommodate the dynamic environment that could develop as a conflict matures.[25]

Prerequisites for a *Per Se* Rule

The issue before the ICJ was whether the use or threatened use of nuclear weapons is *per se* unlawful. As to the prerequisites for such a rule, the United States argued to the Court, without citation of authority, that "scientific evidence could only justify a total prohibition on the use of nuclear weapons if such evidence covers the full range of variables and circumstances that might be involved in such uses."[26] For the use of nuclear weapons to be *per se* unlawful, all possible uses of nuclear weapons must be unlawful.

---

[23] *Id.* at vii. (emphasis omitted).

[24] *Id.* at II-2.

[25] *Id.* at IV-3 (emphasis omitted).

[26] Transcript of the November 15, 1995 public sitting of the ICJ in The Hague at the Peace Palace, President Bedjaoui presiding, in the case in Legality of the Use by a State of Nuclear Weapons in Armed Conflict (Request for Advisory Opinion Submitted by the World Health Organization) and in Legality of the Threat or Use of Nuclear Weapons (Request for Advisory Opinion Submitted by the General Assembly of the United States), Verbatim Record, at 90 [hereinafter ICJ Hearing, November 15, 1995].

General Applicability of the Rules of Law

The United States, in its oral and written presentations to the ICJ, acknowledged the general applicability to the use of nuclear weapons of the rules of proportionality, necessity, moderation, discrimination, civilian immunity, neutrality, and humanity, but argued that the use of nuclear weapons would not necessarily violate such rules.

Thus, in its memorandum to the ICJ on the General Assembly application, the United States stated:

> In the view of the United States, there is no general prohibition in conventional or customary international law on the threat or use of nuclear weapons. On the contrary, numerous agreements regulating the possession or use of nuclear weapons and other state practice demonstrate that their threat or use is not deemed to be generally unlawful.
>
> Moreover, nothing in the body of international humanitarian law of armed conflict indicates that nuclear weapons are prohibited *per se*. As in the use of other weapons, the legality of use depends on the conformity of the particular use with the rules applicable to such weapons. This would, in turn, depend on factors that can only be guessed at, including the characteristics of the particular weapon used and its effects, the military requirements for the destruction of the target in question and the magnitude of the risk to civilians. Judicial speculation about hypothetical future circumstances on a matter of such fundamental importance would, in our view, be inappropriate.[27]

This same position was set forth in *The Naval/Marine Commander's Handbook*, which stated that there are "no rules of customary or conventional international law" precluding nations from using nuclear weapons and hence that the use of such weapons "against enemy combatants and other military objectives" is not unlawful, subject to the following principles:

> (1) the right of the parties to the conflict to adopt means of injuring the enemy is not unlimited;
> (2) it is prohibited to launch attacks against the civilian population as such; and
> (3) the distinction must be made at all times between persons taking part in the hostilities and members of the civilian population to the effect that the latter be spared as much as possible.[28]

---

[27] U.S. ICJ Memorandum/GA App at 2. *See also* 7–47.

[28] UNITED STATES DEPARTMENT OF THE NAVY ANNOTATED SUPPLEMENT TO THE COMMANDER'S HANDBOOK ON THE LAW OF NAVAL OPERATIONS 10-1

The handbook described these rules as the "three fundamental principles" of the law of armed conflict.[29]

The Air Force Commander's Handbook states that the United States "takes the position" that the use of nuclear weapons is not unlawful, but that such use is "governed by existing principles of international law."[30]

The Air Force Manual on International Law states that "the use of explosive nuclear weapons, whether by air, sea or land forces, cannot be regarded as violative of existing international law in the absence of any international rule of law restricting their employment,"[31] but recognizes that such use is subject to the principles of the law of war generally.[32] The manual states that "[a]ny weapon may be used unlawfully, such as when it is directed at civilians and not at a military objective"[33] or "to inflict unnecessary suffering."[34]

The manual states that, in comparing the military advantages to be secured by the use of a new weapon to the effects caused by the weapon, the following questions are relevant:

(1) can the weapon be delivered accurately to the target;

(2) would its use necessarily result in excessive injury to civilians or damage to civilian objects, so as to be termed an "indiscriminate weapon;"

(Naval Warfare Publication 9, 1987) (With Revision A (5 October 1989), this handbook was adopted by the U.S. Marine Corps as FLEET MARINE FORCE MANUAL (FM FM) 1-10) [hereinafter THE NAVAL/MARINE COMMANDER'S HANDBOOK].

[29] *Id.* at 10-1.

[30] UNITED STATES DEPARTMENT OF THE AIR FORCE, COMMANDER'S HANDBOOK ON THE LAW OF ARMED CONFLICT 6-1 (Air Force Pamphlet 110-34, 25 July 1980) [hereinafter THE AIR FORCE COMMANDER'S HANDBOOK].

THE LAW OF LAND WARFARE states that, in the absence of a customary rule of law or international convention restricting the employment of atomic weapons, the use of such weapons cannot be deemed unlawful, although the manual appears to recognize the subjugation of the use of such weapons to the principles of moderation and necessity. UNITED STATES DEPARTMENT OF THE ARMY, THE LAW OF LAND WARFARE 18 (FM27-10/18 July 1956) with Change No. 1 (15 July 1976) [hereinafter THE LAW OF LAND WARFARE].

[31] THE UNITED STATES DEPARTMENT OF THE AIR FORCE, INTERNATIONAL LAW—THE CONDUCT OF ARMED CONFLICT AND AIR OPERATIONS 6-5 (Air Force Pamphlet 110-31, 19 November 1976) [hereinafter THE AIR FORCE MANUAL ON INTERNATIONAL LAW].

[32] *See id.* at 6-1 to 6-8.

[33] *Id.* at 6-1.

[34] *Id.* at 6-8.

(3) would its effects be uncontrollable or unpredictable in space or time as to cause disproportionate injury to civilians or damage to civilian objects; and

(4) would its use necessarily cause suffering excessive in relation to the military purpose which the weapon serves so as to violate that prohibition.[35]

The Army in its *International Law Manual* states that the provisions of international conventional and customary law that "may control the use of nuclear weapons" include:

(1) Article 23(a) of the Hague Regulations prohibiting poisons and poisoned weapons;

(2) the Geneva Protocol of 1925 which prohibits the use not only of poisonous and other gases but also of "analogous liquids, materials or devices;"

(3) Article 23(c) of the Hague Regulations which prohibits weapons calculated to cause unnecessary suffering; and

(4) the 1868 Declaration of St. Petersburg which lists as contrary to humanity those weapons which "needlessly aggravate the sufferings of disabled men or render their death inevitable."[36]

The acceptance by the United States of the applicability of these rules of international law is seminal. Nuclear weapons are subject to the law. The question becomes the scope and meaning of the law as applied to such weapons.

International Agreements on Nuclear Weapons

The Air Force Manual on International Law and *The Naval/Marine Commander's Handbook* note that the United States is a party to numerous international agreements regulating nuclear weapons in various respects but not prohibiting their use generally.[37] These include

---

[35] *Id.* at 6-7.

[36] United States, Department of the Army, *International Law*, vol. II, 27-161-2, at 42, Pamp. 27-161-2 (Oct. 1962), *quoted in* ELLIOTT L. MEYROWITZ, PROHIBITION OF NUCLEAR WEAPONS: THE RELEVANCE OF INTERNATIONAL LAW 223 (Transnational Publishers, Inc. 1990).

[37] *See* THE AIR FORCE MANUAL ON INTERNATIONAL LAW, *supra* note 31, at 6-6; 6-10 n.17:

• Treaty Banning Nuclear Weapon Tests in the Atmosphere, in Outer Space, and Under Water, 5 August 1963, 14 UST 1313; TIAS 5433; 480 UNTS 43 (1963);

• Treaty on the Non Proliferation of Nuclear Weapons, 1 July 1968, 21 UST 483; TIAS 6839 (1970);

• Additional Protocol II to the Treaty for Prohibition of Nuclear Weapons in Latin America, 14 February 1967, 22 UST 754; TIAS 7137; 634 UNTS 364 (1971) (Under this Protocol, the U.S., the U.S.S.R., China, France, and the U.K. agreed, *inter alia*, not to use nuclear weapons against Latin American nations party to the treaty. *See also* THE NAVAL/MARINE COMMANDER'S HANDBOOK at 10-5).
• Treaty on the Prohibition of the Emplacement of Nuclear Weapons and Other Weapons of Mass Destruction on the Seabed and the Ocean Floor and in the Subsoil Thereof, 11 February 1971, 23 UST 701; TIAS 7337 (1972);
• Treaty between the United States of America and the Union of Soviet Socialist Republics on the Limitation of Anti-Ballistic Missile Systems, 26 May 1972, 23 UST 3435; TIAS 7503 (1972);
• Interim Agreement between the Union of Soviet Socialist Republics and the United States of America on Certain Measures with Respect to the Limitation of Strategic Offensive Arms with Protocol, 26 May 1972, 23 UST 3462; TIAS 7504 (1972).

Id.

   See also THE NAVAL/MARINE COMMANDER'S HANDBOOK, *supra* note 28, listing the following additional such international agreements:
• Treaty on Principles Governing the Activities of States in the Exploration and Use of Outer Space, Including the Moon and Other Celestial Bodies, 27 January 1967, entered into force 10 October 1967, 18 U.S.T. 2410, T.I.A.S. No. 6347, AFP 110-20, (prohibiting the placement, installation, or stationing of nuclear or other weapons of mass destruction in earth orbit, on the moon or other celestial bodies);
• Antarctic Treaty, 23 June 1961, 12 U.S.T. 794, T.I.A.S. No. 4780, 402 U.N.T.S. 71, AFP 110-20, (prohibiting military measures, including nuclear explosions in Antarctica);
• Treaty for the Prohibition of Nuclear Weapons in Latin America (Treaty of Tlatelolco), Mexico City, 14 February 1967, entered into force 22 April 1968, AFP 110-20;
• Treaty Banning Nuclear Weapon Teats in the Atmosphere, in Outer Space, and Under Water, 14 U.S.T. 1313, T.I.A.S. No. 5433, 480 U.N.T.S. 43, AFP 110-20, (prohibiting the testing of nuclear weapons in the atmosphere, in outer space, and underwater);
• Memorandum of Understanding between the United States of America and the Union of Soviet Socialist Republics Regarding the Establishment of a Direct Communications Link, with Annex, 20 June 1963, 14 U.S.T. 825, T.I.A.S. No. 5362, 472 U.N.T.S. 163;
• Agreement Between the United States of America and the Union of Soviet Socialist Republics on Measures to Improve the USA-USSR Direct Communications Link, with Annex, 30 September 1971, 22 U.S.T. 1598, T.I.A.S. No. 7187, 806 U.N.T.S. 402, as

the many arms control agreements between the United States, the Soviet Union and other States. In its memorandum to the ICJ, the United States argued that the fact of these many conventions providing only partial limitation with respect to nuclear weapons evidences the overall legality of the use of such weapons.[38]

---

amended March 20 and April 29, 1975, 26 U.S.T. 564, T.I.A.S. No. 8059;

• Agreement on Measures to Reduce the Risk of Outbreak of Nuclear War Between the United States of America and the Union of Soviet Socialist Republics, 30 September 1971, 22 U.S.T. 1590, T.I.A.S. No. 7186, 807 U.N.T.S. 57;

• Agreement Between the United States of America and the Union of Soviet Socialist Republics on the Establishment of Nuclear Risk Reduction Centers, and two Protocols thereto, signed and entered into force, 15 September 1987, DEP'T ST. BULL., Nov. 1987, at 34, 27 INT'L LEG. MAT'LS 76 (1988);

• Agreement Between the United States of America and the Union of Soviet Socialist Republics on the Prevention of Nuclear War, 22 June 1973, 24 U.S.T. 1487, T.I.A.S. No. 7654;

• Treaty Between the United States of America and the Union of Soviet Socialist Republics on the Limitation of Underground Nuclear Weapon Tests and Protocol thereto, Moscow, 3 July 1974;

• Treaty Between the United States of America and the Union of Soviet Socialist Republics on Underground Nuclear Explosions for Peaceful Purposes and Protocol thereto, 28 May 1976, Sen. E. N. 94th Cong., 2d Sess.; SEN. EX REP. 100-1 ("the 1976 Treaty on Peaceful Nuclear Explosions");

• Interim Agreement Between the United States of America and the Union of Soviet Socialist Republics on Certain Measures with respect to the Limitation of Strategic Offensive Arms with associated Protocol, entered into force 3 October 1972, 23 U.S.T. 3462, T.I.A.S. No. 7504, AFP 110-20 ("SALT I");

• The Treaty Between the United States of America and the Union of Soviet Socialist Republics on the Elimination of Their Intermediate-Range and Shorter-Range Missiles, and associated documents, signed 8 December 1987; and

• Various military base agreements; for example, the U.S.–Philippines Military Bases Agreement, 17 October 1988, DEP'T ST. BULL., Dec. 1988, at 25.

Id. at 10-3 to 10-10.

[38] *See* U.S. ICJ Memorandum/GA App. at 2, 9-14 (citing U.S. Army Field Manual 27-10, Change No. 1, THE LAW OF LAND WARFARE at 4 ¶ 40(a)).

International Agreements on Other Weapons

The United States, in its memorandum to the ICJ, further noted the numerous prohibitions in international law of the use of other specific categories of weapons, concluding that the pattern of such prohibitions "implies that there is no such general prohibition on the use of nuclear weapons, which would otherwise have found expression in a similar international agreement."[39]

The United States repeated the point in oral argument:

> When the international community has decided to accept a prohibition on the use of a specific category of weapons, it has done so directly and expressly in the form of an international agreement. For example, international agreements expressly prohibit the use of chemical and biological weapons, as well as weapons with non-detectable fragments. Given the overriding significance of nuclear weapons, any general prohibition on their use would surely have found expression in such an international agreement, which would undoubtedly have included provisions for verification and other essential elements. The fact that such a

---

[39] U.S. ICJ Memorandum/GA App. at 10. As examples of such specific prohibitions, the memorandum cited:

• The use of biological and chemical weapons, per the 1925 Geneva Protocol, Protocol for the Prohibition of the Use in War of Asphyxiating, Poisonous or Other Gases, and of Bacteriological Methods of Warfare, 17 June 1925, 94 L.N.T.S. 65;

• the use of environmental modification techniques as weapons, per the 1977 Environmental Modification Convention, Convention on the Prohibition of Military or any other Hostile Use of Environmental Modification Techniques, 18 May 1977, 1125 U.N.T.S. 3;

• the use of exploding bullets, per the 1868 Declaration of St. Petersburg, Declaration Renouncing the Use, in Time of War, of Explosive projectiles under 400 Grammes Weight, 11 December 1868, *reprinted in* DOCUMENTS ON THE LAWS OF WAR 63 (A. Roberts & R. Guelff eds., 2nd. ed. 1989); and

• the use of weapons with non-detectable fragments, per the 1981 Convention on Specific Conventional Weapons, Convention on Prohibitions or Restrictions on the Use of Certain Conventional Weapons Which May be Deemed to be Excessively Injurious or to Have Indiscriminate Effects, 10 April 1981, *reprinted in* DOCUMENTS ON THE LAW OF WAR 471 (Roberts & Guelff eds., 2nd ed. 1989).

prohibition has not been so expressed indicates that, in fact, it does not exist.[40]

This position raises questions as to whether, as a general matter, the prohibition by convention of the use of a particular weapon in fact implies that, before the adoption of such prohibition, the use of that weapon was not already prohibited, whether by custom, by other conventional law or by the application of generally accepted principles of law.[41]

Sources of International Law

As discussed above, the United States recognizes that generally accepted principles of law are not only an independent source of law but also are sufficient in and of themselves to outlaw the use of a particular weapon or type of weapon. In its arguments before the ICJ, however, the United States retreated from this recognition, ostensibly recognizing only conventional and customary law as binding sources of international law, and indeed taking a narrow view of the scope of conventional law.

Conrad Harper, Legal Advisor of the United States Department of State, and chief U.S. lawyer before the ICJ, told the Court that its "starting point in examining the merits" should be "the fundamental principle of international law that restrictions on States cannot be presumed, but must be established by conventional law specifically accepted by them, or in customary law established by the conduct of the community of nations."[42]

---

[40] ICJ Hearing, November 15, 1995, at 76.

[41] As we have seen, the United States, in other contexts, has readily recognized that particular provisions set forth in conventions are expressive of pre-existing customary or other law. *See supra*, Chapter 1, at notes 10, 133–135, & 225–226 and accompanying text.

The attorney for Great Britain, in his oral argument to the ICJ, stated:

We fully accept ... that the use of nuclear weapons is subject to the principles of customary international law, and it is plain that some of the provisions of Additional Protocol I did no more than reaffirm and codify principles of the customary law of armed conflict which already existed and which apply to the use of all weapons, including nuclear weapons. But it is equally plain that other provisions of the Protocol, such as those on the environment and those on reprisals, were understood to be new rules.

ICJ Hearing, November 15, 1995, at 42 (Sir Nicholas Lyell, Attorney-General, arguing).

[42] *Id.* at 70.

Michael J. Matheson, the Principal Deputy Legal Advisor, in his presentation to the Court, made the same point: Restrictions upon States must "be found in conventional law specifically accepted by States, or in customary law generally accepted as such by the community of nations."[43] Matheson relied upon the Court's statement in the *Nicaragua* case that:

> "in international law there are no rules, other than such rules as may be accepted by the State concerned, by treaty or otherwise, whereby the level of armaments of a sovereign State can be limited."[44]

Matheson went on to argue that "an even higher standard" is applicable for "establishing the existence of peremptory norms of international law, which must be accepted and recognized by the international community as norms from which no derogation is permitted."[45]

Matheson further argued that, under the *North Sea Continental Shelf* case, States whose interests are "specially affected" by application of a putative norm must also subscribe to its legitimacy for it to attain customary status, and that, accordingly, "customary law prohibiting the use of nuclear weapons could not be created over the objection of States possessing such weapons or those relying upon them for their security."[46]

Hence, while the United States acknowledged in theory that the law of armed conflict applies to nuclear weapons, it seemed before the ICJ in effect to be staking out a narrower position: That it is not enough that the United States agree to a rule of such law, be it of conventional or customary law, or even, presumably, a generally recognized principle of law; the United States must also agree to any application of that rule for it to be applicable or binding in a particular case.[47] No rule of law

---

[43] *Id.* at 74–75. Matheson gave a restrictive interpretation to the "or otherwise" in the language from the *Nicaragua* decision.

[44] *Id.* (citing Nicaragua v. United States (1986 I.C.J. 135)).

[45] ICJ Hearing, November 15, 1995, at 75.

[46] *Id.* at 78 (citing *North Sea Continental Shelf,* I.C.J. Reports 3 at 42 (1969)).

[47] The attorney representing Great Britain before the ICJ stated:
But if the prohibition in Article 2, paragraph 4, extends to nuclear weapons, so too does the right of self-defense enshrined in Article 51. That is the most fundamental right of all, Mr. President, and it is preserved in terms which are general, not restrictive. It is impossible to argue that this fundamental, inherent right has been

can be applied against the United States in the absence of the United States' agreement to such application. Accordingly, the rules of armed conflict cannot be deemed to prohibit the use of nuclear weapons, since the United States does not agree to any such prohibition.

U.S. lawyer John McNeill took the argument even further:

> In their submissions to the Court a number of States have suggested that the law of armed conflict (sometimes referred to as the law of war or international humanitarian law) precludes the use of nuclear weapons. The United States has long shared the view that the law of armed conflict governs the use of nuclear weapons—just as it governs the use of conventional weapons. But it is contrary to the very nature and structure of the law of armed conflict to claim that it prohibits *per se* the use of nuclear weapons. Under the law of armed conflict, in the absence of an express prohibition, the legality of the use of any weapon, including nuclear weapons, is fundamentally dependent on the facts and circumstances of the use in question.[48]

U.S. lawyer Harper further argued:

> To be sure, principles of humanity circumscribe the conduct of armed conflict. But those principles only assume the force of customary international law when they satisfy criteria this Court has recognized as governing the establishment of legal norms. In this case, customary international law does not prohibit categorically the use of nuclear weapons.[49]

---

limited or abandoned on the basis of mere inferences drawn from other rules, whether conventional or customary. Moreover, the practice of those states vitally affected by such a rule shows that they entirely reject any such inference.
ICJ Hearing, November 15, 1995, at 37 (Sir Nicholas Lyell, arguing).

[48] ICJ Hearing, November 15, 1995, at 85.

[49] *Id.* at 99.

Similarly, the British attorney before the Court argued:

A new rule of customary law cannot, contrary to what has been claimed, be derived simply from general humanitarian principles. Nor can "general principles of humanity" be turned into rules of law by saying that they have been recognized by this Court in its previous decisions. General principles of humanity have indeed been referred to in two decisions by this Court, in the *Corfu Channel* case and in the *Military and Paramilitary Activities* case. But one cannot stop there, at the threshold, and refrain from looking at what the Court actually decided, and what it said. In both cases what the Court decided was that there was a legal

These statements raise the question whether nuclear weapons can be rendered *per se* unlawful by application of general provisions of a convention or pursuant to the general principles of law recognized by civilized nations.

The Martens Clause

The United States' minimization of the foregoing sources of international law, in this context, was further evidenced by its interpretation of the Martens Clause, which, it will be remembered, was the provision of the Hague Conventions, recently re-expressed in Additional Protocol I, to the effect that, in a situation not specifically covered by treaty, belligerents and others remain under the protection of the "rule of the principles of law of nations, as they result from the usages established among civilized peoples, from the laws of humanity, and the dictates of the public conscience."[50]

In its arguments before the ICJ, the United States portrayed the Martens Clause as simply "clarifying that customary international law may independently govern cases not explicitly addressed by the Conventions,"[51] stating, "This is what gives content and meaning to the Martens Clause."[52] The United States argued that "when as here,

---

obligation to notify, for the benefit of shipping, the existence of known minefields. In each case, an obligation to warn of a known danger. This is a far cry indeed from the proposed outlawing *per se* of a lawful weapon, still less a weapon of such importance in the strategic balance. In the *Corfu Channel* case the Court did not conjure up this obligation solely out of humanitarian considerations; it said explicitly that it was basing itself on several general and well-recognized principles, which included considerations of humanity, but also such principles of law as the freedom of maritime communication and the obligation of every State not knowingly to allow its territory to be used for acts contrary to the rights of other States. Similarly, in the *Military and Paramilitary Activities* case, the Court did not derive its conclusion solely from free-standing "principles of humanity," but analyzed them against the background of specific treaty provisions. *Id.* Statement of Sir. Nicholas Lyell, ICJ Hearing, November 15, 1995, at 55–56 (citing *Corfu Channel*, I.C.J. Reports 1949, p. 22; and *Military and Paramilitary Activities in and against Nicaragua* (Nicaragua v. United States of America), Merits, Judgment, I.C.J. Reports 1986, p. 14)).

[50] ICJ Hearing, November 15, 1995, at 98 (quoting Preamble, 1907 Hague IV). *See* discussion *supra,* Chapter 1, notes 246–251 and accompanying text.

[51] ICJ Hearing, November 15, 1995, at 98.

[52] *Id.*

customary international law does not categorically prohibit the use of nuclear weapons, the Martens Clause does not independently give rise to such a prohibition."[53]

Rule of Necessity

In its presentation to the ICJ, the United States applied the rule of necessity broadly:

> [The prohibition against unnecessary suffering] was intended to preclude weapons designed to increase the injury or suffering of the persons attacked beyond that necessary to accomplish the military objective. It does not prohibit weapons that may cause great injury or suffering if the use of the weapon is necessary to accomplish the military mission. For example, it does not prohibit the use of anti-tank munitions which must penetrate armor by kinetic-energy or incendiary effects, even though this may well cause severe and painful burn injuries to the tank crew. By the same token, it does not prohibit the use of nuclear weapons, even though such weapons can produce severe and painful injuries.[54]

The United States seems to be implying a requirement that a particular weapon be designed to add a particularly nasty and unnecessary effect before the use of the weapon will be deemed to violate the necessity rule. If the United States had specifically wanted to injure the enemy through radiation and purposefully added radiation as an effect, or "enhanced" the level of radiation, the use of such weapon might violate necessity, but, as long as radiation is merely a necessary albeit not specifically intended effect of the weapon, there is no problem.

McNeill stated the point specifically in oral argument, "The unnecessary suffering principle prohibits the use of weapons designed specifically to increase the suffering of persons attacked beyond that necessary to accomplish a particular military objective."[55]

The Naval/Marine Commander's Handbook articulated the U.S. position more fully:

---

[53] *Id.*

[54] U.S. ICJ Memorandum/GA App. at 28–29 (citing the Army's THE LAW OF LAND WARFARE, *supra* note 30, at 18). The memorandum noted that the prohibition against unnecessary suffering has been applied, for example, to lances with barbed tips and bullets that are irregularly shaped, scored or coated with a substance that would unnecessarily inflame a wound. U.S. ICJ Memorial/GA App., at 28 n.65.

[55] ICJ Hearing, November 15, 1995, at 91.

The Unnecessary Suffering Argument. Customary international law prohibits the use of weapons calculated to cause unnecessary suffering; the rule is declared in the Hague Regulations, article 23(e), and now confirmed in Additional Protocol I, article 35(2), which prohibits the employment of weapons, projectiles and materials and methods of warfare of a nature such as would cause superfluous injury or unnecessary suffering. However, these humanitarian considerations are offset by a due regard for the military interests at stake. The Declaration of St. Petersburg 1868 ... contrasts the two: on the one hand, the only legitimate object during a war is to weaken the military forces of the enemy. On the other, this object would be exceeded by the employment of arms which uselessly aggravate the sufferings of disabled men, or render their death inevitable. Nuclear weapons can be selectively directed against military targets. In the context of this balance, it is not clear the use of nuclear weapons necessarily violates international law.[56]

Premised on the factual assertion that nuclear weapons "can be selectively directed against military targets," the U.S. position purports to raise factual issues as to the controllability of such weapons and their effects, in the context of the comparable characteristics of conventional weapons, and legal and jurisprudential issues as to such matters as how the balance between military necessity and humanitarian law is to be struck and what level of likelihood of unlawful effects must be present for illegality to arise.

Controllability of the Effects of Nuclear Weapons

This point as to the controllability of the effects of nuclear weapons is raised in the application of virtually all of the rules of armed conflict. In his arguments before the ICJ on the point, McNeill stated:

Nuclear weapons, as is true of conventional weapons, can be used in a variety of ways: they can be deployed to achieve a wide range of military objectives of varying degrees of significance; they can be targeted in ways that either increase or decrease resulting incidental civilian injury or collateral damage; and their use may be lawful or not depending upon whether and to what extent such use was prompted by another belligerent's conduct and the nature of the conduct.[57]

Noting that it has been argued that nuclear weapons are inherently indiscriminate in their effect and cannot reliably be targeted at specific military objectives, McNeill stated:

---

[56] THE NAVAL/MARINE COMMANDER'S HANDBOOK, *supra* note 28, at 10-2.
[57] ICJ Hearing, November 15, 1995, at 87.

> This argument is simply contrary to fact. Modern nuclear weapon
> delivery systems are, indeed, capable of precisely engaging discrete
> military objectives.[58]

McNeill's language—"precisely engaging discrete military
objectives"—seems to suggest that the United States can control the
radioactive fallout from "modern delivery systems" or that such effects
are not relevant to the analysis. This is also suggested by McNeill's
statement that nuclear weapons "can be targeted in ways that either
increase or decrease resulting incidental civilian injury or collateral
damage."

In its memorandum to the ICJ, the United States, again in the
context of the discrimination rule, presented to the Court this same
picture that the effects of nuclear weapons—of which radioactive
fallout is obviously the most grave—are essentially controllable, and
not a real problem.   The United States stated that, through the
technological expertise of "modern weapon designers," it is now able to
control the effects of nuclear weapons—specifically, "to tailor the
effects of a nuclear weapon to deal with various types of military
objectives:"

> It has been argued that nuclear weapons are unlawful because
> they cannot be directed at a military objective. This argument
> ignores the ability of modern delivery systems to target specific
> military objectives with nuclear weapons, and the ability of modern
> weapons designers to tailor the effects of a nuclear weapon to deal
> with various types of military objectives. Since nuclear weapons
> can be directed at a military objective, they can be used in a
> discriminate manner and are not inherently indiscriminate.[59]

In support of his argument that each use of nuclear weapons would
have to be evaluated on an individual basis and not in "the abstract"
McNeill noted to the Court that the effects of nuclear weapons depend
on such factors as "the explosive yield and height of the burst of
individual weapons, on the character of their targets, as well as on
climatic and weather conditions,"[60] and on "the technology that
occasions how much radiation the weapon may release, where, in

---

[58] *Id.* at 88.

[59] U.S. ICJ Memorandum/GA App at 23 (citing the Army's THE LAW OF
LAND WARFARE, *supra* note 30, at 5).

[60] ICJ Hearing, November 15, 1995, at 87 (citing the Secretary-General's
1990 Report on nuclear weapons, p. 75, para. 290).

relation to the earth's surface it will be detonated, and the military objective at which it would be targeted."[61]

Addressing the subject of the many studies indicating that impermissible levels of damage would result from the use of nuclear weapons, McNeill objected that any given study "rests on static assumptions" as to such factors as the following: "the yield of a weapon, the technology that occasions how much radiation the weapon may release, where, in relation to the earth's surface it will be detonated, and the military objective at which it would be targeted."[62] Again, the United States appeared to be asserting the technological controllability of radiation effects of nuclear weapons.

The military's manual *Doctrine for Joint Theater Nuclear Operations* addresses potential collateral damage in pragmatic terms, identifying a number of factual considerations bearing on the likely extent of collateral damage:

> Nuclear Collateral Damage. Such damage includes dangers to friendly forces, civilians, and nonmilitary related facilities, creation of obstacles, and residual radiation contamination. Since the avoidance of casualties among friendly forces and civilians is a prime consideration when planning theater nuclear operations, preclusion limitation analysis must be performed to identify and limit the proximity of a nuclear strike to civilians and friendly forces. The amount of damage varies with the protective posture of civilians and friendly units, delivery system accuracy, weapon yield, and height of burst. Additionally, these operations may create obstacles that inhibit both friendly and enemy movement (*e.g.*, tree blow down, fires, area contamination, and rubble). Determining the possibility and extent of collateral damage is a joint force command level and USSTRATCOM responsibility. Joint Pub 3-12.2, "Nuclear Weapons Employment Effects Data," provides avoidance tables.[63]

The manual discusses in detail the following risk approaches for affecting collateral damage:

> Specific techniques for reducing collateral damage include:
> • Reducing Weapon Yield. Balance the size of the weapon needed to achieve the desired damage against the associated danger to areas surrounding the target.

---

[61] ICJ Hearing, November 15, 1995, at 89.

[62] *Id.* at 89.

[63] DOCTRINE FOR JOINT THEATER NUCLEAR OPERATIONS, *supra* note 3, at III-1–2 (Feb. 9, 1996) (emphasis omitted).

• Improving Accuracy. Accurate delivery systems are more likely to strike the desired aimpoint, reducing both the required yield and potential collateral damage.

• Employing Multiple Weapons. Collateral damage can be reduced by dividing a large target into several small ones and using smaller weapons rather than one large one.

• Adjusting the Height of Burst (HOB). HOB adjustments, including the use of subsurface detonations, are a major means of controlling collateral damage and fallout. The HOB has a significant influence on the radius of damage.

• Offsetting the Desired Ground Zero (DGZ). DGZ offset may achieve the desired weapon effects while avoiding collateral damage.[64]

Such statements raise many factual and legal issues, including:

1) What does it mean that a modern nuclear weapon delivery system is "capable of precisely engaging discrete military objectives?"

2) As to the environmental elements referred to by McNeill, such as climatic and weather conditions, and practical considerations, such as the height of the burst and the location, in relation to the earth's surface, at which the weapon will be detonated—to what extent are such factors predictable and controllable by the United States in the circumstances in which it might use a nuclear weapon? What is the legal effect of the extent to which such factors are not controllable? Would uncontrollability result in unlawfulness?

3) With what degree of reliability is the United States able to deliver nuclear warheads against designated targets, both statistically in the sense of likely reliability given a large number of launchings and more specifically vis-a-vis any one single launching?

4) Within the context of the level of reliability with which the particular warhead can be expected to be delivered against its target, with what degree of reliability can the effects of the resultant nuclear detonation be predicted and controlled? To what extent is the United States actually able to control the effects of the use of nuclear weapons? To what extent can radioactive fallout from a particular nuclear detonation be predicted and eliminated or controlled?

---

[64] *Id.* at III-2-3 (emphasis omitted).

5) How does the controllability of the effects of conventional weapons compare to that of nuclear weapons?

6) As a matter of law, is it enough that the nuclear weapon be accurately and controllably delivered to the military target, or is it also necessary that the resultant radiation be controlled and confined to the area of said target?

7) With respect to the statement that the lawfulness of the use may depend on the extent to which it was prompted by another belligerent's conduct and the nature of the conduct, what are the factual and legal prerequisites for the lawfulness of nuclear reprisals?

The U.S. position also raises issues as to the meaning and applicability of risk analysis. Noting the potential effect of such factors as those set forth above as to the height of the burst, character of the target hit, climatic and weather conditions, etc., McNeill argued that, "These differences, distinctions and variables cannot be ignored; they are critical to the appropriate legal analysis."[65]

Does this mean that it is necessary to wait and see, after the use, how the weather conditions and other variables worked out—or that, in advance, values must be placed on the various possibilities?   If the latter, how are such valuations and weightings to be made?

Issues as to Low-Yield Nuclear Weapons

Alluding to the assumptions made by the World Health Organization (WHO) in its 1987 study as to the effects of nuclear weapons, McNeill objected to the "four scenarios" depicted by the WHO as "highly selective" in that they addressed "civilian casualties expected to result from nuclear attacks involving significant numbers of large urban area targets or a substantial number of military targets."[66]

> But no reference is made in the report to the effects to be expected from other plausible scenarios, such as a small number of accurate attacks by low-yield weapons against an equally small number of military targets in non-urban areas.[67]

Reinforcing the point as to "other plausible [low-end use] scenarios," McNeill stated that such plausibility "follows from a fact noted in the WHO Report by Professor Rotblat: namely, that

---

[65] ICJ Hearing, November 15, 1995, at 87.
[66] *Id.* at 90.
[67] *Id.*

'remarkable improvements' in the performance of nuclear weapons in recent years have resulted in their 'much greater accuracy'"[68] stating that such scenarios "would not necessarily raise issues of proportionality or discrimination."[69]

While the United States in its presentations to the ICJ did not define what it meant by "low" yield nuclear weapons, the term is defined in the military's manual *Doctrine for Joint Theater Nuclear Operations*:

> Very low — less than 1 kiloton.
> Low — 1 kiloton to 10 kilotons.
> Medium — over 10 kilotons to 50 kilotons.
> High — over 50 kilotons to 500 kilotons.
> Very high — over 500 kilotons. (Joint Pub 1-02)[70]

The fact that the U.S. defense of the lawfulness of the use of nuclear weapons is premised on low-yield highly accurate nuclear weapons fired in non-urban areas raises factual questions as to such matters as the following:

> 1) How much of the United States' nuclear arsenal is made up of such accurate low-yield nuclear weapons?
> 2) To what extent has the United States withdrawn such weapons from its active nuclear arsenal?
> 3) How much of the nation's nuclear training and planning is premised on such weapons?
> 4) What are the potential military uses of such low-yield accurate nuclear weapons vis-a-vis conventional weapons? To what extent would conventional weapons be capable of accomplishing military missions for which low-yield nuclear weapons might be used?

---

[68] *Id.*

[69] *Id.*

[70] DOCTRINE FOR JOINT THEATER NUCLEAR OPERATIONS, *supra* note 3, at GL-3. The manual states: "This publication provides guidance for theater nuclear forces employment. It is written for those who provide strategic direction to, or employ, joint forces. This publication covers operational doctrine for theater nuclear operations, command responsibilities, staff procedures for theater nuclear operations, and guidance on target planning for theater nuclear operations." *Id.* at x.

The manual further states that the lead agent for the publication is the US Air Force and that the Joint Staff doctrine sponsor for the publication is the Director for Strategic Plans and Policy (J-5). *Id.* at B-1.

5) What are the likely effects of the use of such low-yield nuclear weapons, in the types of circumstances in which such use might actually take place?

6) What is the likelihood that the use of low-yield accurate nuclear weapons, in such circumstances, would lead to nuclear escalation? If there were to be such escalation, what would be the likely consequences?

7) What is the likelihood that the use of low-yield accurate nuclear weapons would lead to the adversary's use of other weapons of mass destruction, particularly chemical and bacteriological weapons? What would the likely consequences be of such escalatory use of the weapons of mass destruction?

8) Assuming, *arguendo*, that the use of even low level nuclear weapons could not be justified as a matter of law in circumstances where modern conventional weapons were available, what, if any, legal duty does a nation have to maintain an adequate conventional weapons capability so as not to be in a position of having only nuclear weapons to use? And could a State that put itself in such a position justify the use of nuclear weapons as militarily necessary because they were only ones available?

Significance of Probabilities as to Escalation

On the issue of whether even a small scale use of nuclear weapons would violate international humanitarian law because of the risk of resultant escalation, the United States argued in its memorandum to the ICJ that "[i]t seems to be assumed that any use of nuclear weapons would inevitably escalate into a massive strategic nuclear exchange, with the deliberate destruction of the population centers of the opposing sides."[71] The United States rejected this assumption as "speculative in the extreme."[72]

In its general dismissal of the risk of escalation, the United States is postulating that the relevant likelihood of such effect, before unlawfulness is triggered, is inevitability and that the relevant level of intentionality as to the resultant destruction is deliberateness. This implies that a use of nuclear weapons that was only likely or substantially likely to trigger escalation would not pose legal problems.

---

[71] U.S. ICJ Memorial/GA App. at 21.
[72] *Id.*

It ostensibly means that there is no legal jeopardy in the negligent or reckless destruction of population centers or the like.

McNeill in his oral argument stated:

> The argument that international law prohibits, in all cases, the use of nuclear weapons appears to be premised on the incorrect assumption that every use of every type of nuclear weapon will necessarily share certain characteristics which contravene the law of armed conflict. Specifically, it appears to be assumed that any use of nuclear weapons would inevitably escalate into a massive strategic nuclear exchange, resulting automatically in the deliberate destruction of the population centers of opposing sides.[73]

Repeatedly, the choice of language—"necessarily," "inevitably," "automatically," and "deliberate"—assumes that very high levels of certainty and intentionality as to adverse consequences must be present before a particular use of nuclear weapons would become unlawful, and hence, ostensibly, before a *per se* rule could arise.[74]

The question, of course, is whether such a high level of certainty as to unlawful effect is necessary before unlawfulness ensues. Legal systems throughout the world are regularly called upon to conduct probability analyses and to determine requisite levels of intentionality under both civil and criminal law. Certain widely accepted principles emerge which arguably are incorporated into international law and which we will review in analyzing the issue.

In addition, while the foregoing represents the formal position of the United States, the United States military at the operational level recognizes the potential uncontrollability of nuclear, chemical and biological weapons. This can be seen, for instance, from *Joint Pub 3-12, Doctrine for Joint Nuclear Operations*, setting forth the operational planning of the military as of 1995 for the integrated use by U.S. forces of nuclear weapons in conjunction with conventional weapons:[75]

> - Termination Strategy. The objective of termination strategy should be to end a conflict at the lowest level of destruction possible, consistent with national objectives. However, there can be no assurances that a conflict involving weapons of mass

---

[73] ICJ Hearing, November 15, 1995, at 85.

[74] The issue is only addressed in passing through the choice of language; the implicit legal point as to the applicable standard of probability as to effects and the requisite mental state as to level of intentionality does not appear to have been addressed directly by the United States or any other party before the ICJ or by the Court itself.

[75] *See* DOCTRINE FOR JOINT NUCLEAR OPERATIONS, *supra* note 1, at i.

destruction could be controllable or would be of short duration. Nor are negotiations opportunities and the capacity for enduring control over military forces clear.[76]

The manual further notes that the risks of using nuclear weapons could outweigh any conceivable advantage unless the facts were such that the use of such weapons could alter the operational situation favorably:

> In the event of a deteriorating military situation, employment of NSNF weapons must be capable of favorably altering the operational situation to the advantage of the user. Otherwise, the risks of using nuclear weapons might outweigh any conceivable advantage.[77]

The manual emphasizes the extremely short periods of time—often matters of minutes or even seconds—that would be available for crucial decision making in nuclear confrontations:

> - Decision Timelines. The decisionmaker may be required to review and select defensive and offensive actions within severely compressed timelines. Consideration must be given to procedures and equipment allowing informed decisions in this environment. Predelegated defensive engagement authority should be considered under certain conditions to permit efficient engagement of ballistic missile threats. The commander must evaluate the situation, weigh the options, and execute the optimum offense-defense force in a relatively short period of time. The time is limited because of the relatively short flight time of tactical missiles and potential increased uncertainty of mobile offensive force target locations. Deployment of air defenses should be accomplished early enough to send an unmistakable signal of NCA concern and resolve, thereby maximizing the deterrent potential of these forces.[78]

---

[76] *Id.* at I-6–7 (emphasis omitted). The manual further stated:
Terminating a global war involving the use of large numbers of WMD on both sides and the degradation and or destruction of their central means of control could be vastly more difficult than ending a theater or regional nuclear conflict involving the relatively constrained use of a limited number of nuclear weapons. In the latter case, war-termination strategies may more readily lead to a cessation of hostilities, assuming that the belligerents' interests in war termination are mutual.
Id. at I-6.

[77] *Id.* at III-2 (emphasis omitted).

[78] *Id.* at III-8 (emphasis omitted).

Noting that the joint force commander should have access to "near-real-time tradeoff analysis when considering the execution of any forces,"[79] the Nuclear Weapons Operations manual further states:

> Very short timelines impact decisions that must be made. In a matter of seconds for the defense, and minutes for the offense, critical decisions must be made in concert with discussions with NCA.[80]

The U.S. military in its manual *Doctrine for Joint Theater Nuclear Operations* further emphasizes the potential time constraints—and the need for quick ad hoc judgments as to targeting:

> Because preplanned theater nuclear options do not exist for every scenario, CINCs must have a capability to plan and execute nuclear options for nuclear forces generated on short notice during crisis and emergency situations. During crisis action planning, geographic combatant commanders evaluate their theater situation and propose courses of action or initiate a request for nuclear support.[81]

The *Nuclear Weapons Operations* manual notes the need for decisive strikes, once the decision to go nuclear has been made:

> - Responsiveness. Some targets must be struck quickly once a decision to employ nuclear weapons has been made. Just as important is the requirement to promptly strike high-priority, time-sensitive targets that emerge after the conflict begins. Because force employment requirements may evolve at irregular intervals, some surviving nuclear weapons must be capable of striking these targets within the brief time available. Responsiveness (measured as the interval between the decision to strike a specific target and

---

[79] *Id.* at III-8.

[80] *Id.* at III-8 (emphasis omitted).

[81] DOCTRINE FOR JOINT THEATER NUCLEAR OPERATIONS, *supra* note 3, at III-10 (emphasis omitted). The manual further states:

> USCINCSTRAT will coordinate and develop procedures, when required, for the storage, security, movement, deployment, and employment of nuclear weapons within the theater. The CJCS, in coordination with USCINCSTRAT and appropriate supporting CINCs, will initiate crisis action procedures contained in the Nuclear Supplement to the JSCP and the USSTRATCOM supporting plan to provide nuclear support to the supported geographic combatant commander.

Id.

detonation of a weapon over that target) is critical to ensure engaging some emerging targets.[82]

The manual also noted the potentially provocative nature of resorting to states of increased readiness:

> Alert posturing of nuclear delivery systems to dispersal locations can send a forceful message that demonstrates the national will to use nuclear weapons if necessary. For example, the generation of nuclear forces to higher alert levels during the October 1973 Mideast Crisis sent a strong signal. However, the danger also exists that the enemy may perceive either an exploitable vulnerability or the threat of imminent use.[83]

The manual also notes the interrelationship of operational readiness and escalation:

> - Escalation. Should a crisis become so severe as to prompt the United States to place all its nuclear forces at a high level of readiness, the United States must be prepared to posture its nuclear forces as quickly as possible. Nuclear forces should be generated and managed to ensure a sustained high level of readiness. Conventional forces and intelligence activities would have to be prudently managed to ensure avoidance of inadvertent escalation or mistaken warnings of nuclear attack.[84]

The manual further notes, on the issue of credibility, that, under the policy of deterrence, "[t]he potential aggressor must believe the United States could and would use nuclear weapons to attain its security objectives."[85]

In terms of the risks of escalation, the U.S. military has recognized the need for preemptive strikes against enemy delivery systems capable of delivering weapons of mass destruction. The U.S. military manual *Doctrine for Joint Theater Nuclear Operations* states:

> Operation planning should include the possibility that an enemy will use WMD. ... Operations must be planned and executed to destroy or eliminate enemy WMD delivery systems and supporting infrastructure before they can strike friendly forces.[86]

---

[82] DOCTRINE FOR JOINT NUCLEAR OPERATIONS, *supra* note 1, at II-3–4 (emphasis omitted).

[83] *Id.* at I-4 (emphasis omitted).

[84] *Id.* (emphasis omitted).

[85] *Id.* at I-3.

[86] DOCTRINE FOR JOINT THEATER NUCLEAR OPERATIONS, *supra* note 3, at ix (emphasis omitted).

Obviously, the potential for the United States' conducting such preemptive strikes is a risk factor as to the overall volatility of weapons of mass destruction in situations of acute crisis, imposing on the adversary the same "use 'em or lose 'em" mentality affecting the U.S. policy of preemptive strike in the first instance. A policy—or even the hint of a policy—of preemptive strike inherently breeds a counter policy of preemptive strike—with the potential for escalating levels of hair triggerism.

The *Nuclear Operations* manual specifically notes the risk of rapid escalation:

- Controlling Escalation. Nuclear weapons may influence the objectives and conduct of conventional warfare. Additionally, conventional warfare may result in attrition of nuclear forces and supporting systems (through antisubmarine warfare, conventional attacks in theater, sabotage, or antisatellite warfare), either unintended or deliberate, which could affect the forces available for nuclear employment. If this attrition results in a radical change in the strategic force posture by eliminating intermediate retaliatory steps, there may be a rapid escalation. The ability to precisely gauge the attrition of conventional and nuclear forces will directly effect calculations on the termination of war and the escalation to nuclear war.[87]

Proportionality

The U.S. memorandum stated and applied the proportionality test as follows:

> Whether an attack with nuclear weapons would be disproportionate depends entirely on the circumstances, including the nature of the enemy threat, the importance of destroying the objective, the character, size and likely effects of the device, and the magnitude of the risk to civilians. Nuclear weapons are not inherently disproportionate.[88]

This formulation—particularly its emphasis on the "likely" effects of the nuclear weapon and the "magnitude of the risk to civilians"— seems to presume the need for some form of probability analysis as to the consequences of using the nuclear weapon. Even more, it seems, if only implicitly, to recognize that what is relevant is the likelihood, not

---

[87] DOCTRINE FOR JOINT NUCLEAR OPERATIONS, *supra* note 1, at I-5–6 (emphasis omitted).

[88] U.S. ICJ Memorandum/GA App. at 23 (citing the Army's THE LAW OF LAND WARFARE at 5).

necessarily the certainty, of the various possible effects and the risks to civilians.

The U.S. formulation of the test is also instructive in its identification of factors to be weighed in the balance: (1) on the "utility" side, the value of the use of the weapon in light of the military objective and the threat posed by the enemy; and (2) on the "humanitarian" side, the likely effects of the use of the weapon and the magnitude of the risk to civilians. While this elaboration of the test answers some questions, it leaves much unanswered as to how such a probability analysis should be performed.

The U.S. memorandum further states that the lawfulness of a particular use of nuclear weapons would "depend on factors that can only be guessed at, including the characteristics of the particular weapon used and its effects, the military requirements for the destruction of the target in question and the magnitude of the risk to civilians."[89]

The foregoing represents the United States' formal declaratory position on the matter. Operational policy and planning—the entire military mindset—are an entirely different. There, reality is recognized that what we are threatening by the policy of deterrence is "unacceptable damage and disproportionate loss."[90] This can be seen from *Nuclear Weapons Operations* manual discussed above:

---

[89] *Id.* at 2.

The attorney for Great Britain argued to the ICJ:

Nor is it to be assumed that the use of a nuclear weapon against a military objective will inevitably cause disproportionate civilian casualties. Like the unnecessary suffering principle, this rule requires a balance to be struck between the concrete and direct military advantage anticipated and the level of collateral civilian casualties and damage foreseen. It is an inescapable feature of the legal principle itself that the greater the military advantage which can reasonably be expected to result from the use of a weapon in a particular case, the greater the risk of collateral civilian casualties which may have to be regarded as within the law. Where what is at stake is the difference between national survival and subjection to conquest, which may be of the most brutal and enslaving character, it is dangerously wrong to say that the use of a nuclear weapon could never meet the criterion of proportionality.

ICJ Hearing, November 15, 1985 at 48–49.

[90] DOCTRINE FOR JOINT NUCLEAR OPERATIONS, *supra* note 1, at I-2 (emphasis omitted).

US nuclear forces serve to deter the use of WMD across the spectrum of military operations. From a massive exchange of nuclear weapons to limited use on a regional battlefield, US nuclear capabilities must confront an enemy with risks of unacceptable damage and disproportionate loss should the enemy choose to introduce WMD into a conflict.[91]

----

[91] *Id.* (emphasis omitted).

As I discuss later in the book, while the old nuclear policy of mutual assured destruction, "MAD," specifically threatened massive civilian and societal destruction, and the modern more focused war-fighting theory of deterrence based on today's high tech accuracy and heightened controls theoretically threatens military targets in a more focused and controlled way, the reality is that these weapons are so destructive and the risks of escalation of WMD so great that there is little difference between MAD and war-fighting attacks.

Against that background, the military's recognition that today's deterrence threatens "unacceptable damage and disproportionate loss" becomes highly relevant in light in light of the established law that it is generally unlawful to threaten to do that which one is not legally permitted to do. *See* THE NAVAL/MARINE COMMANDER'S HANDBOOK at 6-4. *See also* Nuclear Weapons Advisory Opinion ¶¶ 47, 78, at 19, 28, 67, 35 I.L.M. at 823, 827, 913. *See infra* Chapter 3, note 142 and accompanying text.

A U.S. military study in the post Cold War era has focused on this point that the policy of deterrence needs to threaten the irrational use of nuclear weapons. A July 1995 report, the "Essentials of Post–Cold War Deterrence," issued by an advisory group subcommittee of U.S. Strategic Command ("STRATCOM") recommended that the United States project an "out of control" irrational and vindictive willingness to use nuclear weapons in certain circumstances. As described by Hans Kristensen:

> The review recommended a policy of ambiguity, using as an example President George Bush's warning to Saddam Hussein in January 1991 not to use chemical weapons. And the planners added another twist to the equation, warning that in threatening nuclear destruction, the United States should not appear too rational or cool-headed. If "some elements ... appear potentially 'out of control,'" it would create and reinforce fears and doubts within the minds of an adversary's decision-makers. "That the U.S. may become irrational and vindictive if its vital interests are attacked should be a part of the national persona we project."

Hans Kristensen, *Targets of Opportunity: How Nuclear Planners Found New Targets for Old Weapons*, BULL. OF ATOMIC SCIENTISTS, vol.55, no. 5, Sep./Oct. 1997, citing U.S. Strategic Command, *Essentials of Post–Cold War Deterrence,* [n.d., probably April 1995], at 3, 4 (partly declassified and released under the Freedom of Information Act).

Time Frame for Determining Lawfulness

In urging upon the Court the inappropriateness of determining the lawfulness of the use of nuclear weapons in the abstract, the U.S. attorney stated:

> [T]he request presents a very general and vague question that would of necessity involve complex legal, technical, political and practical considerations.
>
> These matters cannot usefully be addressed in the abstract without reference to the specific circumstances under which any use of nuclear weapons would be contemplated. The Court should not, on a matter of such fundamental importance, engage in speculation about unknown future situations.[92]

The report further reportedly suggested that the threat should include the "ultimate deterrent:"

> The penalty for using weapons of mass destruction should include not only military defeat, but "the threat of even worse consequences." On the other hand, it should not result in too many civilian casualties. Unless the United States itself were threatened, it "does not require the 'ultimate deterrent'—that a nation's citizens must pay with their lives for failure to stop their national leaders from undertaking aggression." Fear of "national extinction" should be enough.

Id. at 7.

[92] U.S. ICJ Memorandum/GA App. at 4.

The United States further stated that "[j]udicial speculation about hypothetical future circumstances on a matter of such fundamental importance would, in our view, be inappropriate." *Id.*

In his argument before the Court, Conrad Harper, the Legal Advisor of the U.S. Department of State, stated:

> The Court should not attempt to determine in advance whether hypothetical uses of nuclear weapons would violate international law. In our view, any attempt to do so would be inconsistent with this Court's responsibilities, for it would require the Court to engage in unrestrained speculation—to make assumptions of a distinctly non-judicial character regarding the facts and circumstances of possible future events.
>
> ***
>
> The nature of the question presented by the General Assembly is so hypothetical—so dependent upon facts not now ascertainable—that the Court could not, consistent with its judicial function, reasonably provide an answer that would afford guidance to the General Assembly.

ICJ Hearing, November 15, 1995, at 69–70.

While the U.S. point as to the complex legal, technical, political and practical considerations relevant to the issue recognizes the wide range of relevant considerations, the stated conclusion as to the impossibility of evaluating these questions in the abstract begs the question as to whether, in light of such considerations, any use of nuclear weapons could satisfy the applicable principles of law. The U.S. position also obviously raises issues as to the point in time when the lawfulness determination must be made.

Effects of Nuclear Versus Conventional Weapons

Beyond arguing that the effects of any particular use of a nuclear would depend on the particular circumstances, the United States minimized the differences between the effects of nuclear and conventional weapons. McNeill argued:

> It is true that the use of nuclear weapons would have an adverse collateral effect on human health and both the natural and physical environments. But so too can the use of conventional weapons. Obviously, World Wars I and II, as well as the 1990-1991 conflict resulting from Iraq's invasion of Kuwait, dramatically demonstrated that conventional war can inflict terrible collateral damage to the environment. The fact is that armed conflict of any kind can cause widespread, sustained destruction; the Court need not examine scientific evidence to take judicial notice of this evident truth.[93]

This raises fundamental factual questions as to the respective natures of nuclear and conventional weapons, and their respective effects. Are these two types of weapons qualitatively different, or is it just a matter of degree? McNeill's point that the Court could take judicial notice of the scientific evidence as to the effects of various forms of armed conflict opens the door for much of our factual analysis that will follow.

The U.S. military, in their military manual on the actual use of nuclear weapons, are more candid in recognizing the differences between nuclear and conventional weapons. They state, "Clearly, the use of nuclear weapons represents a significant escalation from conventional warfare and is caused by some action, event, or perceived threat."[94] The manual further states:

---

[93] ICJ Hearing, November 15, 1995, at 89.

[94] DOCTRINE FOR JOINT NUCLEAR OPERATIONS, *supra* note 1, at II-1.

The fundamental differences between a potential nuclear war and previous military conflicts involve the speed, scope, and degree of destruction inherent in nuclear weapons employment, as well as the uncertainty of negotiating opportunities and enduring control over military forces.[95]

In this same vein, the *Nuclear Weapons Operations* manual further states: "The immediate and prolonged effects of WMD—including blast, thermal radiation, prompt (gamma and neutron) and residual radiation—pose unprecedented physical and psychological problems for combat forces and noncombatant populations alike."[96]

The U.S. military also emphasizes the differences between conventional and nuclear weapons in its manual *Doctrine for Joint Theater Nuclear Operations*:

> Nuclear weapons are unique in this analysis [as to "the long-standing targeting rules" of military necessity, proportionality, and avoidance of collateral damage and unnecessary suffering] only in their greater destructive potential (although they also differ from conventional weapons in that they produce radiation and electromagnetic effects and, potentially, radioactive fallout).[97]
>
> ***
>
> The employment of nuclear weapons is restricted to situations where military gain is commensurate with political objectives and the law of armed conflict. Containment and a demonstrated will to employ additional nuclear weapons toward a specific goal are the desired methods of approach. The relative effectiveness of all weapons must be weighted and employed of nuclear weapons must offer a significant advantage. Preclusion limitation analysis must be performed to avoid casualties among friendly forces and civilians.[98]

The manual further recognizes that the employment of nuclear weapons "signifies an escalation of the war."[99]

The U.S. military in their manual *Doctrine for Joint Theater Nuclear Operations* specifically recognizes the need to consider information as to the potential effects of other weapons in deciding whether the use of nuclear would comply with the law of armed conflict:

---

[95] *Id.* at I-6 (emphasis omitted).

[96] *Id.* at II-7 (emphasis omitted).

[97] DOCTRINE FOR JOINT THEATER NUCLEAR OPERATIONS, *supra* note 3, at I-1 (emphasis omitted).

[98] *Id.* at vii–viii (emphasis omitted).

[99] *Id.* at III-1.

The relative effectiveness of all weapons must be weighted and employed of nuclear weapons must offer a significant advantage. Preclusion limitation analysis must be performed to avoid casualties among friendly forces and civilians.[100]

Discrimination/Civilian Immunity

As noted above, the United States argued to the ICJ that it can deliver the warheads with such accuracy and control the radiation and other effects with such certainty that nuclear weapons can readily discriminate between civilian and military targets.

As to civilian immunity, the United States relied on the position that collateral injury to the civilian population incidental to an attack on a military target is acceptable as long as the civilians were not targeted "as such."[101]   The United States argued that the rule of civilian immunity "would not be violated by the use of nuclear weapons to attack targets that constitute legitimate military objectives, and in any event is subject to the right of reprisal."[102]

Numerous questions are presented as to the meaning and implications of this "as such" test, including whether it is based on a subjective or objective standard of intent and whether foreseeability or inevitability is sufficient for unlawfulness.

The Law of Humanity; Prohibition of Genocide

The Naval/Marine Commander's Handbook states the U.S. position as follows:

> The Crime Argument. It has been argued that using nuclear weapons would constitute a crime against humanity, this being a violation of international law under the Agreement for the Prosecution and Punishment of the Major War Criminals of the European Axis ... . The definition of crimes against humanity in the Charter of the Nuremberg International Military Tribunal included murder committed against any civilian population, the object being to encompass acts of extermination of whole groups of civilians. The principles of international law recognized by the Charter of the Nuremberg Tribunal and by its Judgment were affirmed in Resolution 95(I) adopted unanimously by the UN General Assembly on 121 December 1946. ... This Resolution associated the General Assembly with the Nuremberg Judgment,

---

[100] *Id.* at viii (emphasis omitted).

[101] U.S. ICJ Memorandum/GA App. at 22 (citing the Army's THE LAW OF LAND WARFARE at 4).

[102] *Id.* at 22.

and also implied that judgment was consistent with international law. Similarly, the killing of people with intent to destroy, in whole or in part, a national or other group, is among conduct which the Genocide Convention ... makes a crime in international law. ... In neither case was nuclear warfare envisaged. The argument that would describe nuclear warfare as a crime against humanity or as genocide lacks legal and historical foundation.[103]

The manual nowhere sets forth a basis for its conclusion as to the absence of "legal" or "historical" foundation.

In its memorandum to the ICJ, the United States argued that the use of nuclear weapons would not generally be prohibited as constituting genocide, even where such use constituted the "deliberate killing of large numbers of people," unless the nuclear weapons were used "with intent to destroy, in whole or in part, a national, ethnic, racial or religious group, as such."[104] Specific subjective intent to destroy the group *qua* group is required.

The United States takes the position that this issue of specific intent is of great significance:

It has been claimed that the intent to engage in genocidal acts could be inferred from the failure of the party using nuclear weapons to appreciate fully the destructive consequences. In light of the atrocities and malevolence that the history of this century associates with genocide, the United States regrets that assertions of genocidal conduct have been so imprecisely made in this context.[105]

Implicit in this position is the premise that genocide and crimes against humanity cannot be based on negligent, grossly negligent or even reckless acts and that foreseeability and perhaps even inevitability are not legally sufficient for unlawfulness to arise, nor is objective intentionality.

Prohibition of Poisons

In its memorandum to the ICJ, the United States argued in effect that the radiation effects of nuclear weapons do not constitute prohibited poisons because such weapons also cause blast and heat effects, and those effects are potentially lawful:

---

[103] THE NAVAL/MARINE COMMANDER'S HANDBOOK, *supra* note 28, at 10-2 to 10-3.
[104] U.S. ICJ Memorandum/GA App. at 33–34 (citing Convention on the Prevention and Punishment of the Crime of Genocide, Dec. 9, 1948, UN G.A. Res. 260 A(III), 78 U.N.T.S. 277, Art. II).
[105] ICJ Hearing, November 15, 1995, at 96.

[The prohibition of the use of poison weapons] was established with particular reference to projectiles that carry poison into the body of the victim. It was not intended to apply, and has not been applied, to weapons that are designed to injure or cause destruction by other means, even though they also may create toxic byproducts.

For example, the prohibition on poison weapons does not prohibit conventional explosives or incendiaries, even though they may produce dangerous fumes. By the same token, it does not prohibit nuclear weapons, which are designed to injure or cause destruction by means other than poisoning the victim, even though nuclear explosions may also create toxic radioactive byproducts.[106]

The Poison Gas Analogy

The United States made essentially the same argument to the ICJ with respect to the application of the 1925 Geneva Protocol's prohibition of the first use in war of asphyxiating, poisonous or other gases and analogous liquids, materials and devices, contending, without citation of authority, that the Protocol was "not intended" to cover weapons that kill other than by the inhalation or other absorption into the body of poisonous gases or analogous substances[107] and that the prohibition of the use of poison weapons in the 1907 Hague Convention was only intended to cover the situation of projectiles which carry poison into the body of the victim.[108]

The United States further argued that the limitations on the scope of these agreements is reflected in the fact that they do not prohibit conventional explosives or incendiaries, even though such weapons "may produce dangerous fumes:"

This prohibition was intended to apply to weapons that are designed to kill or injure by the inhalation or other absorption into the body of poisonous gases or analogous substances.

This prohibition was not intended to apply, and has not been applied, to weapons that are designed to kill or injure by other means, even though they may create asphyxiating or poisonous byproducts. Once again, the Protocol does not prohibit conventional explosives or incendiary weapons, even though they

---

[106] U.S. ICJ Memorandum/GA App. at 23–23 (citing Hague Convention (IV) Respecting the Laws and Customs of War on Land, Annex, Art. 23(a) *reprinted in* ROBERTS & GUELFF, DOCUMENTS ON THE LAW OF WAR (2nd ed. 1989, p. 63)).

[107] *See* U.S. ICJ Memorandum/GA App. at 24–25 (citing F. Kalshoven, *Arms, Armaments and International Law*, 191 HAGUE ACADEMY OF INTERNATIONAL LAW, 283–84 (Recueil de Cours) (1985-II)).

[108] *See* U.S. ICJ Memorandum/GA App. at 24.

may produce asphyxiating or poisonous byproducts, and it likewise does not prohibit nuclear weapons.[109]

The Naval/Marine Commander's Handbook elaborates on the U.S. position:

> Poison Gas Analogy. It has been contended that nuclear radiation is sufficiently comparable to a poison gas to justify extending the 1925 Gas Protocol's prohibition to include the use of nuclear weapons. However, this ignores the explosive, heat and blast effects of a nuclear burst, and disregards the fact that fall-out is a by-product which is not the main or most characteristic feature of the weapon. The same riposte is available to meet an argument that the use of nuclear weapons would violate the prohibition on the use of poisoned weapons, set out in article 23(a) of the Hague Regulations.[110]

Thus, the U.S. position seems to be that the explosive, heat and blast effects of a nuclear weapon are the primary effects, against which radiation is only an incidental "by-product" which is not "the main or most characteristic feature" of the weapon, and that this secondary nature of radiation eliminates or diminishes its legal significance as an effect of the use of nuclear weapons.

This seems to be a variant of the "as such" rule of intentionality applicable to injury to civilians and civilian objects. The United States appears to be arguing that the radioactive injury resultant from the use of a nuclear weapon is permissible as long as it is "unintended" in the sense that the State firing the weapon is doing so for the weapon's explosive, heat and blast effects on the military target, and not for any radioactive effect it might have on the enemy or others. As long as the weapon has explosive, heat and blast effects and the attacking party is using the weapon for such effects and not specifically for the radioactive effects, such effects do not enter into the characterization of the weapon for purposes of its compliance with the 1925 Gas Protocol.

The U.S. position raises legal and factual questions as to the requirements of these conventions and rules of law and as to the extent to which the United States is actually able to limit and control the effects of nuclear weapons, including radioactive fallout.

---

[109] *Id.* at 24–25 (citing Protocol for the Prohibition of the Use in War of Asphyxiating, Poisonous, or Other Gases, and of Bacteriological Methods of Warfare, 17 June 1925, 94 L.N.T.S. 65; F. Kalshoven, *Arms, Armaments and International Law,* 191 HAGUE ACADEMY OF INTERNATIONAL LAW (RECUEIL DE COURTS) (1985-II), pp. 283–84).

[110] THE NAVAL/MARINE COMMANDER'S HANDBOOK, *supra* note 28, at 10-2.

Neutrality

Stating that the principle of neutrality is designed to preclude "military invasion or bombardment of neutral territory,"[111] the United States in its memorandum to the ICJ argued, without citation of authority, that neutral status is not a "broad guarantee to neutral States of immunity from the effects of war, whether economic or environmental"[112] and that the United States is "aware of no case in which a belligerent has been held responsible for collateral damage to neutral territory for lawful acts of war committed outside that territory."[113] What hedge, if any, was intended by the disclaimer of any guarantee of a "broad" nature was unclear.

The U.S. position, as originally stated, appeared to be that the neutrality principle provides little or no protection against collateral effects. The inviolability of the neutral's territory does not preclude warring parties from detonating nuclear weapons which will carry devastating radiation into neutral territory, whether by air, water or the like, as long as the use of the weapon is otherwise lawful. If India and Pakistan were to engage in a nuclear war, in a situation where the

---

[111] U.S. ICJ Memorandum/GA App. at 31 (citing GREENSPAN, THE MODERN LAW OF LAND WARFARE 356 (1959) and W. BISHOP, JR., INTERNATIONAL LAW CASES AND MATERIALS 1019–20 (1971)).

[112] *Id.* at 31–32.

[113] *See id.* The United States cited no precedent finding the imposition by belligerents of collateral damage upon neutrals to be lawful under the neutrality principle.

The attorney for Great Britain argued to the ICJ:

> The argument that the use of a nuclear weapon is *per se* unlawful because it would inevitably violate the territory of neutral States is equally unsound, Mr. President. The principle that neutral territory is inviolate means that the belligerent may not, save in rare and clearly defined circumstances, actually conduct military operations in the territory of a neutral State. It has never meant the neutral States can expect to be subject to none of the effects of war. The whole purpose of the law of neutrality has always been to achieve a balance between the interest of the neutral State and the needs of the belligerents. The needs of a State forced to fight for survival in the face of massive aggression must weigh very heavily in that balance. Moreover, whether any use of a nuclear weapon anywhere in the world would inevitably produce material effects on the territory of a neutral State is not a matter that can be approached by way of generalizations. Each case, once again, has to be judged in light of all the relevant circumstances.

ICJ Hearing, November 15, 1995, at 49.

United States was neutral, those States would be entitled to use their nuclear weapons against each other without consideration of the effects on the United States as a neutral State, and their using such weapons in such a way as to result in radioactive fallout over the United States and the death of millions or even tens or hundreds of millions of Americans would not be a violation of the United States' rights as a neutral, or otherwise ostensibly be an act of aggression, as long as the use of the weapons was otherwise in compliance with international law.

By the time of the oral argument, the United States seemed to have retreated somewhat from this position. McNeill argued: "[T]he principle of neutrality has never been understood to guarantee neutral States absolute immunity from the effects of armed conflict."[114] So there is protection from the effects of armed conflict, but it is not absolute. What limitation the qualification "absolute" was intended to encompass was nowhere specified, and ostensibly no one asked the question.

The United States did present arguments as to the required level of likelihood that the use of nuclear weapons would violate neutrality principles before unlawfulness would ensue. McNeill stated:

> [E]ven assuming arguendo that a belligerent's liability to a neutral could somehow be established in a particular case, the argument that unlawful damage would necessarily occur to neutral States whenever nuclear weapons are used cannot be maintained.[115]

The United States similarly stated in its memorandum to the Court that the argument that the principle of neutrality prohibits the use of nuclear weapons "is evidently based on the assertion that the use of such weapons would inevitably cause severe damage in the territory of neutral States,"[116] an assumption which the United States dismissed as "incorrect and in any event highly speculative."[117]

The validity of this proposition would ostensibly turn upon whether unlawfulness as to every imaginable use must be present before a *per se* rule prohibition could arise. The U.S. position overlooks the question of what weight should be ascribed to the various levels of probability in any given situation that a use of a nuclear weapon would lead to unlawful effects under the neutrality principle.

---

[114] ICJ Hearing, November 15, 1995, at 95–96.

[115] *Id.*

[116] U.S. ICJ Memorandum/GA App. at 32.

[117] *Id.* It is unclear what is intended by the reference to "severe damage." The neutral's inviolability has not generally been taken as limited to violations beyond any particular level of severity.

The argument similarly does not address the question of whether the application of the neutrality test requires a weighing process vis-a-vis neutrals as to the "likely effects" of the use of the weapon and the "magnitude of the risk," similar to the test described by the United States as applicable to the application of the proportionality principle.

The United States concluded in its memorandum: "Like any other weapons, nuclear weapons could be used to violate neutrality, but this in no way means that nuclear weapons are prohibited *per se* by neutrality principles."[118] McNeill expressed the same conclusion in his oral argument: "Whether or not the principles of neutrality might be violated once again clearly depends on the precise circumstances of a particular use of nuclear weapons."[119]

The U.S. position as to the extent to which neutrals are protected against the effects of war raises legal questions as to the nature of the inviolability of the neutral's persons and territory and factual questions as to the likelihood that the use of a nuclear weapon would cause effects upon neutrals. It also focuses attention again upon questions as to the controllability of the effects of nuclear weapons and as to the legal effect of different levels of probability of unlawful effects.

Most fundamentally, the U.S. position raises the question as to whether it can really be the law that it is unlawful to bombard a neutral State with a nuclear weapon, but lawful to drop the bomb against a military target right outside the border of the neutral, permitting the explosive, blast, heat and radiation effects to go across the border, knowing this would likely happen or that there was a likelihood it would happen.

Environmental Security

Additional Protocol I to the 1949 Geneva Conventions contains detailed provisions for the protection of the environment during war. In its presentations to the ICJ, the United States argued that such provisions were not intended to cover nuclear weapons, but rather are new rules not incorporated into customary law and not applicable to States, such as the United States,[120] that have not ratified the Protocol.[121]

---

[118] *Id.*

[119] ICJ Hearing, November 15, 1995, at 96.

[120] *See id.* at 92.

[121] *See* U.S. ICJ Memorial/GA App. at 25, 29–30 (citing Protocol Additional to the Geneva Conventions of 12 August 1949, and Relating to the

The United States further argued that Article I of the 1977 Environmental Modification Convention does not cover incidental effects of the use of particular weapons such as nuclear weapons, but rather only the "deliberate manipulation" of environmental forces, and hence cannot be said to constitute a general restriction on the use of nuclear weapons.[122] The United States argued that numerous other international agreements providing protection for the environment are not intended to apply and do not apply to acts of war.[123]

International Agreements on Human Rights

The United States in its memorandum to the ICJ argued that the numerous international agreements relating to the protection of human rights do not apply to the use of weapons in war and, in any event, are not inconsistent with the use of nuclear weapons in the exercise of legitimate self-defense.[124]

The Resolutions Argument

The Naval Marine Commander's Handbook states the U.S. position as to why the votes by the General Assembly declaring the unlawfulness of the use of nuclear weapons are not dispositive:

> The Resolutions Argument. In Resolution 1653(XVI) adopted on 24 November 1961, the UN General Assembly declared the use of nuclear weapons to be illegal, as being contrary to the UN Charter, the law of nations, and laws of humanity. However, an assumption that this resolution is legally binding may be countered first by the fact that the UN Charter confers no legislative power on

---

Protection of Victims of International Armed Conflicts ("Protocol I"), 12 December 1977, 1125 U.N.T.S. 3).

[122] *See id.* at 29–30 (citing Convention on the Prohibition of Military or any other Hostile Use of Environmental Modification Techniques, 18 May 1977, 1125 U.N.T.S. 3).

[123] *See id.* at 29 (referring to the 1985 Convention for the Protection of the Ozone Layer, 22 March 1985, the 1992 Convention on Climate Change, the 1992 Biodiversity Convention, 6 June 1992, as well as such International Environmental Declarations as the 1972 Stockholm Declaration on the Human Environment, 16 June 1972, and the 1992 Rio Declaration on Environment and Development, 13 June 1992).

[124] *See id.* at 42–46 (referring to the Universal Declaration of Human Rights, 10 December 1948, the International Covenant of Civil and Political Rights, 16 December 1966, the American Convention on Human Rights, 22 November 1969, and the European Convention on Human Rights, 4 November 1950).

the General Assembly, and second by examining the voting which took place in 1961. That resolution had a majority of only 35, 55 nations having voted for it and 20 against it (including the United States, the United Kingdom, and France), with 26 nations abstaining. ... The wording of the resolution is more appropriate to a condemnation in moral rather than in legal terms.[125]

The United States took the same position before the ICJ:

It is well established ... that aside from certain administrative matters, the General Assembly does not have the authority to "legislate" or create legally binding obligations on its members. Further, such General Assembly resolutions could only be declarative of the existence of principles of customary international law to the extent that such principles had been recognized by the international community, including the States most directly affected. In fact, there were a significant number of U.N. Member States that did not accept these resolutions: in particular, these resolutions were not accepted by a majority of the nuclear-weapon States.[126]

Reprisals

Acknowledging that reprisals must be taken with intent to cause the enemy to cease violations of the law of armed conflict and after all other means of securing compliance have been exhausted, and that they must be proportionate to the violations, the United States, in its memorandum to the ICJ, took the position that the legality of reprisals must be determined on a case-by-case basis.[127]

The United States further dismissed as inapplicable to nuclear weapons and as new provisions not assimilated into customary law the provisions of Additional Protocol I containing prohibitions on reprisals

---

[125] THE NAVAL/MARINE COMMANDER'S HANDBOOK, *supra* note 28, at 10-3.

[126] U.S. ICJ Memorandum/GA App. at 18–19 (citing Charter of the United Nations, Article 11(1); Voting Procedure on Questions Relating to Reports and Petitions Concerning the Territory of South West Africa, Advisory Opinion, I.CJ. Reports 1955, pp. 90, 116 (separate opinion of Judge Lauterpacht); S. Schwebel, 7 FORUM INTERNATIONALE (1985), pp. 11–12; Letter of U.S. State Department Deputy Legal Advisor Stephen Schwebel of 25 April 1975, 1975, DIGEST OF U.S. PRACTICE IN INTERNATIONAL LAW, p. 85; S. Schwebel, Lawmaking in the United Nations, 4 FEDERAL LAW REPORT (1970), pp. 115, 118).

[127] *See id.* at 30 (citing U.S. Army Field Manual 27-10, Change No. 1, THE LAW OF LAND WARFARE (1976), at 177, para. 497). *See also* ICJ Hearing, November 15, 1985 at 94–95.

against specific types of persons or objects, including the civilian population or individual civilians, civilian objects, cultural objects and places of worship, objects indispensable to the survival of the civilian population, the natural environment, and works and installations containing dangerous forces.[128]

The United States argued before the Court that, even if the use of nuclear weapons were deemed *per se* unlawful, such weapons could still be used in reprisal:

> Even if it were to be concluded—as we clearly have not—that the use of nuclear weapons would necessarily be unlawful, the customary law of reprisal permits a belligerent to respond to another party's violation of the law of armed conflict by itself resorting to what otherwise would be unlawful conduct.[129]

Deterrence

The United States took the position before the ICJ that nuclear deterrence "has contributed substantially during the past 50 years to the enhancement of strategic stability, the avoidance of global conflict and the maintenance of international peace and security,"[130] and that such success is, in effect, a basis for the lawfulness of the use of nuclear weapons.

U.S. lawyer Michael J. Matheson, in his oral argument to the Court, stated:

> [E]ach of the Permanent Members of the Security Council has made an immense commitment of human and material resources to acquire and maintain stocks of nuclear weapons and their delivery systems, and many other States have decided to rely for their security on these nuclear capabilities. If these weapons could not lawfully be used in individual or collective self-defense under any circumstances, there would be no credible threat of such use in response to aggression and deterrent policies would be futile and

---

[128] *See* U.S. ICJ Memorandum/GA App. at 31 (citing Additional Protocol I, arts. 51(6), 52(1), 53(c), 54(4), 55(2), and 56(4)).

[129] ICJ Hearing, November 15, 1995, at 95.

[130] *See id.* at 68. McNeill further argued:

Ours is in every sense a defensive strategy; and very frankly we believe the policy of nuclear deterrence has saved many millions of lives from the scourge of war during the past 50 years. In this special sense, nuclear weapons have been "used," defensively, every day for over half a century—to preserve the peace.

Id. at 86–87.

meaningless. In this sense, it is impossible to separate the policy of
deterrence from the legality of the use of the means of deterrence.
Accordingly, any affirmation of a general prohibition on the use of
nuclear weapons would be directly contrary to one of the
fundamental premises of the national security policy of each of
these many states.[131]

Nor was this a spontaneous or casual remark. The United States
stated in its memorandum to the ICJ:

> It is well known that the Permanent Members of the Security
> Council possess nuclear weapons and have developed and deployed
> systems for their use in armed conflict. These States would not
> have borne the expense and effort of acquiring and maintaining
> these weapons and delivery systems if they believed that the use of
> nuclear weapons was generally prohibited. On the contrary, the
> possible use of these weapons is an important factor in the structure
> of their military establishments, the development of their security
> doctrines and strategy, and their efforts to prevent aggression and
> provide an essential element of the exercise of their right of self-
> defense.[132]

McNeill in his oral argument to the Court stated, "The law of
reprisal does not and cannot ... be construed as prohibiting
categorically the use of nuclear weapons; indeed, if it were to be so
construed, the negative implications for strategic deterrence would be
obvious and dire."[133]

These are extraordinary statements, taking us back to the notion of
law as politics. The United States and other great nations have built
their national security policies upon the threat of use of nuclear
weapons to such an extent that their central policy—deterrence—
cannot be separated from the legality of the "use of the means of
deterrence," and hence the use of such weapons must be lawful. It is
politically necessary for it to be lawful so it must be lawful.

The statement is also extraordinary in that it answers the inevitable
"so what" question: What difference would it make if nuclear weapons
are unlawful, since they cannot be un-invented and hence will be used
if expedient. It would make a big difference. If these weapons are

---

[131] *Id.* at 78.

[132] U.S. ICJ Memorandum/GA App. at 14 (citing Report of the U.N.
Secretary-General on Nuclear Weapons, A/45/373, 18 September 1990, pp.
19–24).

[133] ICJ Hearing, November 15, 1995, at 95.

illegal, deterrence is dead since no one could credibly threaten their use.

McNeill urged the intra-war deterrence doctrine, that modulated levels of nuclear force could be used in war to deter and control the enemy's undesirable actions: "US deterrence strategy is designed to provide a range of options in response to armed aggression that will control escalation and terminate armed conflict as soon as possible."[134] McNeill stated that, under its policy of deterrence, the United States would only use nuclear weapons in self-defense.[135]

The United States' reliance on the doctrine of deterrence in justifying the potential use of nuclear weapons and the threat of such use highlights the significance of nuclear theory and policy (and related military training and contingency planning) to the legality analysis.

---

[134] *Id.* at 86.
[135] *See id.*

Chapter 3: The ICJ's Nuclear Weapons Advisory Opinion

The International Court of Justice ("ICJ") in its July 1996 advisory opinion set forth a delicate and ultimately ambiguous balancing of considerations bearing upon the legality issue, including the destructiveness of nuclear weapons, the restraints of humanitarian law, the right of self-defense, the practice of nuclear deterrence, the ongoing political process of restraining nuclear weapons, and the reality that the nuclear weapons States are the most powerful in the world. The Court concluded that, because of the potential effects, the use of nuclear weapons would generally violate the law of armed conflict, but that the Court did not have sufficient facts to determine whether, under existing international law, use would be lawful or unlawful in an extreme circumstance of self-defense when a State's very survival was at stake.[1]

---

[1] *Legality of the Threat or Use of Nuclear Weapons*, International Court of Justice, Advisory Opinion, General List at pt. VI, 35–36, No. 95 (July 8, 1996) [hereinafter Nuclear Weapons Advisory Opinion], available at <http://www.icj-cij.org/>. Also, all but five of the fifteen ICJ opinions are available at 35 I.L.M. 809 (1996). The remaining five, the declarations of Judges Bedjaoui, Herczegh and Bravo and the individual opinions of Judges Guillaume and Ranjeva, appear at 35 I.L.M. 1343 (1996). The opinions and various of the submissions to the Court are available at its own web site <http://www.icj-cij.org/> and also at <http://www.law.cornell.edu/world/>. Some of the same materials are also available in THE CASE AGAINST THE BOMB (Roger S. Clark & Madeleine Sanns eds., 1996). *See also* Roger S. Clark, *The Laws of Armed Conflict and the Use or Threat of Use of Nuclear Weapons*, 7 CRIM. L.F. 265, 266 (No. 2/1996).

As to the significance of the fact that its decision in the matter was of an advisory nature, the Court stated, "The purpose of the advisory function is not to settle—at least directly—disputes between States, but to offer legal advice to the organs and institutions requesting the opinion...." Nuclear Weapons Advisory Opinion ¶ 15, at 10–11, 35 I.L.M. at 818–819.

Judge Koroma stated, "[A]lthough the Advisory Opinions of the Court are not legally binding and impose no legal obligations either upon the requesting body or upon States, such Opinions are nonetheless not devoid of effect as they remain the law 'recognized by the United Nations.'" Dissenting opinion of Judge Koroma, at 12, 35 I.L.M. at 930 (citing case of *Admissibility of Hearings of Petitioners by the Committee on South West Africa*, I.C.J. Reports 1956, p. 23, Sep. Op., Judge Lauterpacht at 46).

Judge Bravo stated that an advisory opinion "is not a judgment of the Court." Declaration of Judge Bravo at 2, 35 I.L.M. at 1350.

The Court's decision had several overriding features:

> • strong proclamation of the general illegality of the threat or use of nuclear weapons;[2]
> • identification of factual issues as to the controllability of the effects of the use of a very small number of low-yield tactical nuclear weapons against remote targets;
> • heavy focus on the right of self-defense; and
> • language in which both the proponents and the opponents of the nuclear weapons regime may take solace.

The Court's factual uncertainty professedly centered around disputed questions as to whether low-yield tactical nuclear weapons could be targeted and used with such precision as to control their effects, including their radiation effects, and used in such a way as not to precipitate escalation to the use of high yield nuclear weapons or the multiple use of low-yield such weapons. In the absence of applicable evidence, the Court, professedly in part because of the advisory nature

---

The Court may have seen the advisory nature of its opinion as somehow limiting the extent to which it should reach out for the facts. In language we will discuss in another context, the Court stated:

> Certain States have however expressed the fear that the abstract nature of the question might lead the Court to make hypothetical or speculative declarations outside the scope of its judicial function. The Court does not consider that, in giving an advisory opinion in the present case, it would necessarily have to write "scenarios," to study various types of nuclear weapons and to evaluate highly complex and controversial technological, strategic and scientific information. The Court will simply address the issues arising in all their aspects by applying the legal rules relevant to the situation.

Id.

[2] Although I focus on the legality of the *use* of nuclear weapons, the Court also addressed the legality of the *threat* of such use, concluding in effect that the law as to threats is subsumed into the law as to use. Specifically, that a threat to use lawful force would be lawful, and to use unlawful force would be unlawful. Nuclear Weapons Advisory Opinion ¶ 47, at 19; ¶ 78, at 28, 35 I.L.M. at 823, 827 ("If an envisaged use of weapons would not meet the requirements of humanitarian law, a threat to engage in such use would also be contrary to that law.").

Judge Weeramantry in his dissenting opinion noted that Article 2(4) of the United Nations Charter outlawing the "threat or use of force ... draws no distinction between the use of force and the threat of force" and that "both equally lie outside the pale of action within the law." *Id.* at 67, 35 I.L.M. at 913.

of its role, declined to be drawn into an analysis of risk factors as to such matters.

The decision's central legal obscurities centered around the questions of whether the right of self-defense overrides humanitarian law, and, if so, whether it does so *in toto* or only as to low-yield tactical nuclear weapons.

The first ambiguity, one primarily of a legal nature, derived from the structure of the decision, whereby the Court first reviewed at length the requirements of the law of armed conflict, leading it to find general and potentially total unlawfulness, but then, as if tacking on conclusory language from an entirely different discussion, proceeded to set forth a broad statement of the right of self-defense in language arguably susceptible to being interpreted as signaling that such right is overriding, at least in extreme circumstances where a State's survival is at stake.

So too the second ambiguity, one hinging primarily on factual questions as to the effects of the use of nuclear weapons, derived from an ostensible incongruity between the Court's detailed general discussion in the body of the opinion and its conclusory language, whereby the Court first focused repeatedly on its factual uncertainty as to the effects of low-yield tactical nuclear weapons, ostensibly signaling that it was as to such weapons that there was an open question, and then stated broadly its conclusion as to possible legality in exceptional circumstances of self-defense, without expressly limiting such possibility to the limited use of low-yield tactical nuclear weapons.

In effect acknowledging such ambiguities and perhaps signaling the inevitable political process inherent in assembling its opinion, the Court, in the final paragraph before its conclusion, stated that all portions of the opinion have to be read in light of one another, so as to give effect to the totality of the opinion:

> At the end of the present Opinion, the Court emphasizes that its reply to the question put to it by the General Assembly rests on the totality of the legal grounds set forth by the Court above (paragraphs 20 to 103), each of which is to be read in the light of the others. Some of these grounds are not such as to form the object of formal conclusions in the final paragraph of the Opinion; they nevertheless retain, in the view of the Court, all of their importance.[3]

---

[3] Nuclear Weapons Advisory Opinion ¶ 104, at 35, 35 I.L.M. at 831.

With fourteen judges sitting,[4] the Court's overall conclusions were ostensibly reached on a seven to seven basis, with the tie being broken by the vote of Judge Bedjaoui, the President of the Court.[5] However, there were fifteen opinions in the case: the Court's opinion, five declarations (Judges Bedjaoui, Herczegh, Shi, Vereshchetin, and Bravo), three separate opinions (Judges Guillaume, Ranjeva, and Fleischhauer), and six dissents (Judges Schwebel, Oda, Shahabuddeen, Weeramantry, Koroma, and Higgins), together spanning the spectrum of opinion on the issue. The Court's opinion and those of the individual judges do not dispose of the issue, but they certainly lay the groundwork for further analysis and the continuing evolution of the law.

Upon parsing the various opinions, it becomes evident that the Court's conclusion of general illegality had greater support than at first appears. Three of the dissenting judges—Judges Shahabuddeen, Koroma and Weeramantry—did so on the basis that the Court's decision did not go far enough: They concluded that all uses or threatened uses of nuclear weapons would be *per se* unlawful.[6] This brings to ten the number of judges determining that the use of nuclear weapons would generally be unlawful, a substantial majority on this overriding point.

Of the seven judges joining in the Court's opinion, two—Judges Bedjaoui and Herczegh—shared the view of dissenting Judges Shahabuddeen, Koroma and Weeramantry that all uses of nuclear weapons would be *per se* unlawful. A third—Judge Bravo—came close to this position, concluding that the use of nuclear weapons is prohibited based upon the early recognition of such illegality in formative resolutions on a footing with the United Nations Charter but further concluding, somewhat equivocally, that the implementation of such unlawfulness was blunted by the emergence of the Cold War, with

---

[4] Judges Shahabuddeen (Guyana), Koroma (Sierra Leone), Weeramantry (Sri Lanka), Bedjaoui (Algeria), Herczegh (Hungary), Bravo (Italy), Ranjeva (Madagascar), Fleischhauer (Germany), Vereshchetin (Russia), Shi (China), Schwebel (U.S.), Higgins (U.K.), Guillaume (France), and Oda (Japan).

[5] Under Art. 31(2) of the I.C.J. Statute, the President of the Court has not only his own "deliberative" vote but also a second "casting" vote in the event of a tie, which had occurred in this instance because of a vacancy on the Court following the death of one of the judges.

[6] These three judges voted against the Court's conclusion that "[t]here is in neither customary nor conventional international law any comprehensive and universal prohibition of the threat or use of nuclear weapons as such." Nuclear Weapons Advisory Opinion ¶ 105 (2)(B), at 36, 35 I.L.M at 831.

the effect that the prohibition itself, albeit unimplemented, is still operative.

This gives six judges who generally support the *per se* illegality position. A seventh judge—Judge Ranjeva—concluded broadly that the use of nuclear weapons is generally unlawful and that the use of such weapons for self-defense is subject to the rules of law, indicating that the conclusion of "general" unlawfulness means "in the majority of cases and in doctrine."[7]

Of the remaining three judges who joined in the Court's opinion, Judge Fleischhauer supported the exception for self-defense, Judge Vereshchetin generally supported the existence of a *non liquet* whereby international law has not yet evolved to a comprehensive overall rule, and Judge Shi offered no elaboration. The four remaining judges— dissenters Schwebel, Higgins, Guillaume, and Oda—opposed the Court's decision as going too far. These judges concluded that the lawfulness of any threat or use would have to be made on a case-by-case basis, essentially supporting the overall U.S. position.

There is much the Court's opinion leaves unanswered, including:

> • Is the Court saying that only low-yield highly accurate, tactical nuclear weapons with only minor and controllable radiation effects, if such weapons exist, could potentially be lawful, or is it leaving open the possibility that the wide scale use of strategic nuclear weapons could be lawful?
> • What is the relationship between the general principles of the law of war (humanitarian law) and the law of self-defense? Is a State's right of self-defense subject to the humanitarian law or does it exist independently of or transcend such law?
> • What is meant by the category of "extreme circumstance of self-defense"?
> • What is the legal significance of the fact that the nuclear powers follow the policy of deterrence?
> • Is there a gap in the law of armed conflict—a "*non liquet*"—such that the law has not evolved to the point where it covers, or fully covers, nuclear weapons?
> • What is the legal significance of probabilities as to unlawful effects?

---

[7] Individual opinion of Judge Ranjeva to the Nuclear Weapons Advisory Opinion at 1, 35 I.L.M. at 1354 (No. 6 November 1996) [hereinafter Individual opinion of Judge Ranjeva].

It is unclear the extent to which the Court's decision reflects a potential limitation upon the use of nuclear weapons: Given that, under the United Nations Charter, a State, other than in an enforcement action, may only use force in individual or collective self-defense, a limitation that nuclear weapons could only be used in self-defense would not appear to be much of a limitation.[8] Of course, the Court referred to "an extreme circumstance of self-defense" when the state's "very survival [is] at stake"—and perhaps that is the limitation.

The further—and perhaps most important—limitation relates to the missing facts and their potential import. If those facts are found, and are inconsistent with lawful use, does that establish *per se* unlawfulness under the Court's approach?

The Issue Presented

The U.N. General Assembly, by resolution 49/75 K adopted on December 15, 1994, presented the following issue to the ICJ for advisory opinion: "Is the threat or use of nuclear weapons in any circumstance permitted under international law?"[9]

---

[8] Judge Shahabuddeen made this point in his dissenting opinion:
> [A]n "extreme circumstance of self-defense, in which the very survival of a State would be at stake" ... is the main circumstance in which the proponents of legality advance a claim to a right to use nuclear weapons. This is so for the reason that, assuming that the use of nuclear weapons is lawful, the nature of the weapons, combined with the limitations imposed by the requirements of necessity and proportionality which condition the exercise of the right of self-defense, will serve to confine their lawful right to that "extreme circumstance." It follows that to hold that humanitarian law does not apply to the use of nuclear weapons in the main circumstance in which a claim of a right of use is advanced is to uphold the substance of the thesis that humanitarian law does not apply at all to the use of nuclear weapons. That view has long been discarded; as the Court itself recalls, the NWS [nuclear weapons States] themselves do not advocate it. I am not persuaded that disfavored thesis can be brought back through an exception based on self-defense.

Dissenting opinion of Judge Shahabuddeen to the Nuclear Weapons Advisory Opinion at 35, 35 I.L.M. at 878 [hereinafter dissenting opinion of Judge Shahabuddeen].

[9] Nuclear Weapons Advisory Opinion ¶ 1, at 4, 35 I.L.M. at 811.
A similar but narrower issue had then recently been presented to the ICJ by the World Health Organization, asking for an advisory opinion on the question, "In view of the health and environmental effects, would the use of nuclear

The Court's Conclusion

The Court in its decretal paragraphs—the *"dispositif"*—stated that the threat or use of nuclear weapons "would generally be contrary to the rules of international law applicable in armed conflict, and in particular the principles and rules of humanitarian law," but that "in view of the current state of international law, and of the elements of fact at its disposal, the Court cannot conclude definitively whether the threat or use of nuclear weapons would be lawful or unlawful in an extreme circumstance of self-defense, in which the very survival of a State would be at stake."[10]

The Court's fuller statement of its conclusion in the body of its opinion is to similar effect.

> 95 ... [T]he principles and rules of law applicable in armed conflict—at the heart of which is the overriding consideration of humanity—make the conduct of armed hostilities subject to a number of strict requirements. Thus, methods and means of warfare, which would preclude any distinction between civilian and military targets, or which would result in unnecessary suffering to combatants, are prohibited. In view of the unique characteristics of nuclear weapons, to which the Court has referred above, the use of such weapons in fact seems scarcely reconcilable with respect for such requirements.[11]

---

weapons by a State in war or other armed conflict be a breach of its obligations under international law including the WHO Constitution?" *See* the Court's decision in *Legality of the Use by a State of Nuclear Weapons in Armed Conflict* (World Health Organization), 1996 I.C.J. 68 (July 8, 1996) [hereinafter the "WHO Advisory Opinion"].

Finding that the WHO request did not relate to a question arising within the scope of activities of the WHO, the Court found that it did not have jurisdiction to render the advisory opinion requested by that organization, and hence did not reach the substantive question presented on that request. WHO Advisory Opinion ¶ 31.

[10] Nuclear Weapons Advisory Opinion ¶ 105. E., at 36, 35 I.L.M. at 835.

Judges Weeramantry and Higgins in their dissenting opinions pointed to the ambiguity introduced by the Court's use of the word "generally." *See* dissenting opinion of Judge Weeramantry to the Nuclear Weapons Advisory Opinion at 2, 35 I.L.M. at 80; dissenting opinion of Judge Higgins to the Nuclear Weapons Advisory Opinion at 5, 35 I.L.M. at 936.

[11] Nuclear Weapons Advisory Opinion ¶ 95, at 32, 35 I.L.M. at 829. The Court's language—"scarcely reconcilable"—seems hedged, perhaps the product of drafting compromise. The Court went on to state:

Unique Characteristics of Nuclear Weapons

The "unique characteristics" of nuclear weapons to which the Court referred include the following:

> The Court ... notes that nuclear weapons are explosive devices whose energy results from the fusion or fission of the atom. By its very nature, that process, in nuclear weapons as they exist today, releases not only immense quantities of heat and energy, but also powerful and prolonged radiation. According to the material before the Court, the first two causes of damage are vastly more powerful than the damage caused by other weapons, while the phenomenon of radiation is said to be peculiar to nuclear weapons. These characteristics render the nuclear weapon potentially catastrophic. The destructive power of nuclear weapons cannot be contained in either space or time. They have the potential to destroy all civilization and the entire ecosystem of the planet.
>
> The radiation released by a nuclear explosion would affect health, agriculture, natural resources and demography over a very wide area. Further, the use of nuclear weapons would be a serious danger to future generations. Ionizing radiation has the potential to damage the future environment, food and marine ecosystem, and to cause genetic defects and illness in future generations.
>
> 36. In consequence ... it is imperative for the Court to take account of the unique characteristics of nuclear weapons, and in particular their destructive capacity, their capacity to cause untold human suffering, and their ability to cause damage to generations to come.[12]

> Nevertheless, the Court considers that it does not have sufficient elements to enable it to conclude with certainty that the use of nuclear weapons would necessarily be at variance with the principles and rules of law applicable in armed conflict in any circumstance.

Id.

[12] Nuclear Weapons Advisory Opinion ¶ 35, at 16–17, 35 I.L.M. at 821–22.

For further discussions of the effects of nuclear weapons, *see, e.g.*, dissenting opinion of Judge Weeramantry in connection with the WHO Advisory Opinion, 1996 I.C.J. 115–126; dissenting opinion of Judge Koroma in the same proceeding at 1996 ICJ 68, 173–180.

Judge Weeramantry in that proceeding further pointed out differences between the effects of conventional and nuclear weapons:

> The use of conventional weapons in war does not spread disease. It does not cause genetic deformities. It does not imperil crops. It does not cause intergenerational climatic effects which imperil the global food supply.

Judge Weeramantry in his dissenting opinion elaborated. He noted that before 1945, the most powerful conventional weapons had explosive effects of some 20 tons, whereas the "small" nuclear weapons exploded in Hiroshima and Nagasaki were approximately 15 and 12 kilotons respectively, *i.e.*, 15,000 and 12,000 tons of TNT (trinitrotoluene) respectively, and that many of today's nuclear weapons are in the megaton (million tons of TNT) and multimegaton range, some being in excess of 20 megatons (20 million tons of TNT).[13] He states that "[a] 5-megaton weapon would represent more explosive power than all of the bombs used in World War II and a twenty-megaton bomb more than all of the explosives used in all of the wars in the history of mankind."[14] He further noted that a one-megaton bomb would represent around 70 Hiroshimas and a 15-megaton bomb around 1000 Hiroshimas. In contrast, the Chernobyl explosion was at the level of some half-kiloton, about 1/25 of the Hiroshima bomb.[15]

WHO Advisory Opinion, dissenting opinion of Judge Weeramantry, 1996 I.C.J. 68, 147.

[13] Dissenting opinion of Judge Weeramantry at 15, 35 I.L.M. at 887 (citing NAGENDRA SINGH & EDWARD MCWHINNEY, NUCLEAR WEAPONS AND CONTEMPORARY INTERNATIONAL LAW 29 (1989)).

In his dissenting opinion in the WHO Advisory Decision proceeding, Judge Koroma stated that "in a conflict involving the use of a single nuclear weapon, such a weapon could have the destructive power of a million times that of the largest conventional weapon." The WHO Advisory Opinion, 1996 I.C.J. 68, 173.

[14] Dissenting opinion of Judge Weeramantry at 15, 35 I.L.M. at 887 (citing NAGENDRA SINGH & EDWARD MCWHINNEY, NUCLEAR WEAPONS AND CONTEMPORARY INTERNATIONAL LAW 29 (1989)).

[15] Dissenting opinion of Judge Weeramantry at 20, 35 ILM at 887 (citing Herbert Abrams, *Chernobyl and the Short-Term Medical Effects of Nuclear War, in* Proceedings of the International Physicians for the Prevention of Nuclear War, Cologne, 1986, *published in* MAINTAIN LIFE ON EARTH 154 (1987)).

Judge Weeramantry cited estimates that the bomb blasts in Hiroshima and Nagasaki produced temperatures of several million degrees centigrade and pressures of several hundred thousand atmospheres, and that the temperature at the center of the bright fireball of the nuclear explosion was the same as those at the center of the sun. Dissenting opinion of Judge Weeramantry at 21, 35 ILM at 887 (citing Don G. Bates, *The Medical and Ecological Effects of Nuclear War*, 28 MCGILL L.J. 717, 722 (1983)).

Judge Koroma in his dissenting opinion in the WHO Advisory Opinion proceeding stated that at least 9 million people are said to have been directly or indirectly affected by the Chernobyl event. He adds:

Judge Weeramantry noted the danger of nuclear winter, whereby fires from exploded nuclear weapons could release hundreds of millions of tons of soot in the atmosphere, causing huge clouds and debris blotting out the sun and destroying agriculture. He related the historical reports that in 1816 the eruption of the Indonesian volcano, Tambora, released so much smoke and dust into the atmosphere as to cause a worldwide crop failure and darkness for that year.[16]

The judge stated that the foregoing effects are measures only of the destructive effects of these weapons. Radiation is an additional effect, but one not containable in space or time and unique as a source of "continuing danger to human health, even long after its use," given the half-lives in the many thousands of years of the by-products of a nuclear explosion.[17]

Citing WHO estimates of 1 million to 1 billion deaths from various levels of nuclear weapons, with similar numbers of injured, Judge Weeramantry stated that the 140,000 deaths at Hiroshima and 74,000 at Nagasaki (with populations of 350,000 and 240,000 respectively) underestimated the potential effects of the detonation of a nuclear weapon in cities with densely-packed populations of millions, such as Tokyo, New York, Paris, London, or Moscow.[18]

> Morbidity rates are reported to be 30 per cent higher in one of the affected countries for those who lived in the contaminated region, and more than 50 per cent higher for those in the immediate area of the reactor. Thyroid cancer had increased 285-fold in one of the other affected countries, with children being mostly the victims while the general health conditions of the people in the area immediately affected continue to deteriorate....
>
> Even though the Chernobyl accident did not take place in a theatre of war, the analogy resulting from the use of nuclear weapons is appropriate, as the health and environmental effects are similar to those of nuclear weapons, except that in a nuclear war, such effects would be far worse and the consequences far more serious.

The WHO Advisory Opinion. 1996 I.C.J. 68, 199–200 (Koroma, J. dissenting).

[16] Dissenting opinion of Judge Weeramantry at 18 n.6, 35 I.L.M. at 870.

[17] *See id.* at 15, 35 I.L.M. at 868.

[18] *Id.* at 19, 35 I.L.M. at 870.

Judge Koroma in his dissenting opinion described the effects of the atomic bombs on Hiroshima and Nagasaki and of the 67 nuclear weapons tests on the Marshall Islands in the period June 30 to August 18, 1958. Dissenting opinion of Judge Koroma to the Nuclear Weapons Advisory Opinion at 10, 35 ILM at 939 [hereinafter dissenting opinion of Judge Koroma]. *See also* The WHO Advisory Opinion, 1996 I.C.J. 68, 177–78 (Koroma, J. dissenting).

Judge Weeramantry also noted the electromagnetic pulse as a further effect of the use of nuclear weapons, stating that this very sudden and intensive burst of energy throws all electronic devices out of action, including communications lines, such as nuclear command and control centers. The judge noted that the electromagnetic pulse caused by a nuclear explosion of some 400 km. altitude "can instantly put out of service the greater part of semiconductor electronic equipment in a large country, such as the United States, as well as a large part of its energy distribution networks, without other effects being felt on the ground."[19]

Judge Weeramantry discussed the long-term nature of the effects of radiation:

> The effects upon the eco-system extend, for practical purposes, beyond the limits of all foreseeable historical time. The half-life of one of the by-products of a nuclear explosion—plutonium 239—is over twenty thousand years. With a major nuclear exchange it would require several of these "half-life" periods before the residuary radioactivity becomes minimal. Half-life is "the period in which the rate of radioactive emission by a pure sample falls by a factor of two. ...
>
> The following table gives the half-lives of the principal radioactive elements that result from a nuclear test.

Nuclide	Half-life
Cesium 137	30.2 years
Strontium 90	28.6 years
Plutonium 239	24,100 years
Plutonium 240	6,570 years
Plutonium 241	14.4 years
Americium 241	432 years

> Theoretically, this could run to tens of thousands of years. At any level of discourse, it would be safe to pronounce that no one generation is entitled, for whatever purpose, to inflict such damage on succeeding generations.[20]

With respect to the argument that Hiroshima and Nagasaki show that nuclear war is survivable, Judge Weeramantry noted not only that the bombs used in Hiroshima and Nagasaki were of not more than 15 kilotons explosive power, but also that the use of those bombs ended the war and occurred in a context where the target country was not a

---

[19] Dissenting opinion of Judge Weeramantry at 25, 35 I.L.M. at 873 (citing DICTIONNAIRE ENCYCLOPEDIQUE D'ELECTRONIQUE).

[20] *Id.* at 16–17, 35 I.L.M. at 888 (citing RADIOECOLOGY (Holm ed., World Scientific Publishing Co. 1995)).

nuclear power and there were no other nuclear powers to come to Japan's assistance, all situations unlikely to characterize any future use of such weapons.[21]

Judge Koroma in his dissenting opinion stated:

> According to the material before the Court, it is estimated that more than 40,000 nuclear warheads exist in the world today with a total destructive capacity around a million times greater than that of the bomb which devastated Hiroshima. A single nuclear bomb detonated over a large city is said to be capable of killing more than 1 million people. These weapons, if used massively, could result in the annihilation of the human race and the extinction of human civilization. Nuclear weapons are thus not just another kind of weapon, they are considered the absolute weapon and are far more pervasive in terms of their destructive effects than any conventional weapon.[22]

---

[21] *Id.* at 30–31, 35 I.L.M. at 895.

[22] Dissenting opinion of Judge Koroma at 1, 35 I.L.M. at 934. Judge Koroma further stated:

Testimony was also given by the delegation of the Marshall Islands which was the site of 67 nuclear weapons tests from 30 June to 18 August 1958, during the period of the United Nations Pacific Islands territories trusteeship. The total yield of those weapons was said to be equivalent to more than 7,000 bombs of the size of that which destroyed Hiroshima. Those nuclear weapon tests were said to have caused extensive radiation, induced illnesses, death and birth defects. Further on in the testimony, it was disclosed that human suffering and damage to the environment occurred at great distances, both in time and geography, from the site of detonations even when an effort was made to avoid or mitigate harm. ...

The delegation further disclosed that birth defects and extraordinarily prolonged and painful illnesses caused by the radioactive fallout inevitably and profoundly affected the civilian population long after the nuclear weapons tests had been carried out. Such suffering had affected generations born long after the testings such weapons. It went on to say that, apart from the immediate damage at and under ground zero (where the detonation took place), the area experienced contamination of animals and plants and the poisoning of soil and water. As a consequence, some of the islands were still abandoned and in those that had recently been resettled, the presence of cesium in plants from radioactive fallout rendered them inedible. Women on some of the other atolls, the islands who had been assured that their atolls were not affected by radiation, were said to have given birth to "monster

Judge Koroma further noted, with respect to the atomic attacks on Hiroshima and Nagasaki:

> Over 320,000 people who survived but were affected by radiation still suffer from various malignant tumours caused by radiation, including leukaemia, thyroid cancer, breast cancer, lung cancer, gastric cancer, cataracts and a variety of other after-effects. More than half a century after the disaster, they are still said to be undergoing medical examinations and treatment.[23]

As to the legal significance of the effects of the use of nuclear weapons, Judge Koroma stated, "In my considered opinion, the unlawfulness of the use of nuclear weapons is not predicated on the circumstances in which the use takes place, but rather on the unique and established characteristics of those weapons which under any circumstance would violate international law by their use."[24]

Judge Shahabuddeen quoted Javier Perez de Cuellar, Secretary-General of the United Nations:

> "The world's stockpile of nuclear weapons today is equivalent to 16 billion tons of TNT. As against this, the entire devastation of the Second World War was caused by the expenditure of no more than 3 million tons of munitions. In other words, we possess a destructive capacity of more than a 5,000 times what caused 40 to 50 million deaths not too long ago. It should suffice to kill every man, woman and child 10 times over."[25]

As to the radiation effects of nuclear weapons, Judge Shahabuddeen stated:

> To classify these effects as being merely byproducts is not to the point; they can be just as extensive as, if not more so than, those immediately produced by blast and heat. They cause unspeakable sickness followed by painful death, affect the genetic code, damage the unborn, and can render the earth uninhabitable. These extended effects may not have military value for the user, but this does not

---

babies." A young girl on one of those atolls was said to have no knees, three toes on each foot and a missing arm; her mother had not been born by 1954 when the tests started but had been raised on a contaminated atoll.
Id. at 10–11, 35 I.L.M. at 929–930.

[23] *Id.* at 9, 35 I.L.M. at 929.

[24] *Id.* at 11, 35 I.L.M. at 930.

[25] Dissenting opinion of Judge Shahabuddeen at 5–6, 35 I.L.M. at 863–864 (quoting Javez Perez de Cuellar, *Statement at the University of Pennsylvania, 24 March 1983, in* DISARMAMENT, vol. VI, no. 1, 91).

lessen their gravity or the fact that they result from the use of nuclear weapons. This being the case, it is not relevant for present purposes to consider whether the injury produced is a byproduct or secondary effect of such use.

Nor is it always a case of the effects being immediately inflicted but manifesting their consequences in later ailments; nuclear fall-out may exert an impact on people long after the explosion, causing fresh injury to them in the course of time, including injury to future generations. The weapon continues to strike for years after the initial blow, thus presenting the disturbing and unique portrait of war being waged by a present generation on future ones—on future ones with which its successors could well be at peace.[26]

Judge Shahabuddeen further cited the preamble to the Treaty of Tlatelolco:

The preamble to the 1967 Treaty of Tlatelolco, Additional Protocol II of which was signed and ratified by the five [nuclear weapons states], declared that the Parties are convinced

"That the incalculable destructive power of nuclear weapons has made it imperative that the legal prohibition of war should be strictly observed in practice if the survival of civilization and of mankind itself is to be assured.

That nuclear weapons, whose terrible effects are suffered, indiscriminately and inexorably, by military forces and civilian population alike, constitute, through the persistence of the radioactivity they release, an attack on the integrity of the human species and ultimately may even render the whole earth uninhabitable."[27]

Finding of Insufficient Facts

Thus, the Court found the use of nuclear weapons to be "potentially catastrophic" and "scarcely reconcilable" with the rules of discrimination and necessity. The Court concluded, however, that it did not have "sufficient elements" to determine that all uses of nuclear weapons would be unlawful, particularly in light of considerations as to the right to self-defense for survival, the widespread practice at least in the past of deterrence, and practice of States reflecting a belief in the lawfulness of the use of nuclear weapons:

96. [T]he Court cannot lose sight of the fundamental right of every State to survival, and thus its right to resort to self-defense, in

---

[26] *Id.*
[27] *Id.*

accordance with Article 51 of the Charter, when its survival is at stake.

Nor can it ignore the practice referred to as "policy of deterrence," to which an appreciable section of the international community adhered for many years. The Court also notes the reservations which certain nuclear-weapon States have appended to the undertakings they have given, notably under the Protocols to the Treaties of Tlatelolco and Rarotonga, and also under declarations made by them in connection with the extension of the Treaty on the Non-Proliferation of Nuclear Weapons, not to resort to such weapons.

97. Accordingly, in view of the present state of international law viewed as a whole, as examined above by the Court, and of the elements of fact at its disposal, the Court is led to observe that it cannot reach a definitive conclusion as to the legality or illegality of the use of nuclear weapons by a State in an extreme circumstance of self-defense, in which its very survival would be at stake.[28]

The facts which the Court found to be missing ostensibly had to do with the likely effects of the use of low-yield tactical nuclear weapons and the risk of escalation. The Court first noted the view expressed by the United Kingdom in its written submission to the Court, and the United States in its oral argument:

> 91. ... The reality ... is that nuclear weapons might be used in a wide variety of circumstances with very different results in terms of

---

[28] Nuclear Weapons Advisory Opinion ¶ 96, at 33 I.L.M. at 830.

Judge Weeramantry in his dissenting opinion in the WHO Advisory Opinion proceeding noted that it is the Court's job to make findings as to disputed facts. Judge Weeramantry cited the Court's observation in the Advisory Opinion on *Namibia* that "to enable a court to pronounce on legal questions, it must also be acquainted with, take into account and, if necessary, make findings as to the relevant factual issues." WHO Advisory Opinion, 1996 ICJ 68, 161 (Weeramantry, J., dissenting) (citing I.C.J. Reports 1971 at 27).

Judge Weeramantry further noted the contentions made by Finland to the effect that:

> [T]he legality of the use of nuclear weapons can only be determined in respect of specific circumstances, for there can be a large number of potential situations—*e.g.*, first use, counter use, different practices of targeting, different types of nuclear weapons —and [that] the Court cannot hypothesize about all these possibilities.

WHO Advisory Opinion, 1996 I.C.J. 68, 161 (citing Written Statement of Finland at 4).

likely civilian casualties. In some cases, such as the use of a low yield nuclear weapon against warships on the High Seas or troops in sparsely populated areas, it is possible to envisage a nuclear attack which caused comparatively few civilian casualties. It is by no means the case that every use of nuclear weapons against a military objective would inevitably cause very great collateral civilian casualties.[29]

The Court then noted the contrasting view of other States:

92. ... [R]ecourse to nuclear weapons could never be compatible with the principles and rules of humanitarian law and is therefore prohibited. In the event of their use, nuclear weapons would in all circumstances be unable to draw any distinction between the civilian population and combatants, or between civilian objects and military objectives, and their effects, largely uncontrollable, could not be restricted, either in time or in space, to lawful military targets. Such weapons would kill and destroy in a necessarily indiscriminate manner, on account of the blast, heat and radiation occasioned by the nuclear explosion and the effects induced; and the number of casualties which would ensue would be enormous. The use of nuclear weapons would therefore be prohibited in any circumstance, notwithstanding the absence of any explicit conventional prohibition.[30]

While concluding that it was unable to resolve these polar factual positions, the Court noted that the proponents of legality had failed to substantiate their position as to the possibility of limited use, without escalation, of low level nuclear weapons or even of the potential utility of such use if it were possible:

95. ... [N]one of the States advocating the legality of the use of nuclear weapons under certain circumstances, including the "clean" use of smaller, low yield tactical nuclear weapons, has indicated what, supposing such limited use were feasible, would be the precise circumstances justifying such use; nor whether such limited use would not tend to escalate into the all-out use of high yield nuclear weapons. This being so, the Court does not consider that it has a sufficient basis for a determination of the validity of this view.[31]

---

[29] Nuclear Weapons Advisory Opinion ¶ 91 at 31, 35 I.L.M. at 829 (citing United Kingdom, Written Statement ¶ 3.70 at 53, and United States of America, Oral Statement, CR 95/34 at 89–90).

[30] Nuclear Weapons Advisory Opinion ¶ 92, at 32, 35 I.L.M. at 829.

[31] *Id.* ¶ 94 at 32.

Seemingly rejecting the notion of there being inadequate evidence before the Court, President Bedjaoui found that nuclear weapons are "blind," unable to discriminate between combatants and non-combatants.[32] Judge Guillaume in his individual opinion concluded that nuclear weapons are not necessarily blind, that they "obviously do not necessarily fall into this category."[33]

Judge Ranjeva concluded:

> [N]o evidence of the existence of a "clean nuclear weapon" was presented to the Court, and States merely argued that there was indeed a problem of compatibility between the legality of the use of nuclear weapons and the rules of humanitarian law.[34]

Judge Shahabuddeen in his dissenting opinion stated:

> It was said on the part of the proponents of legality that there are "tactical," "battlefield," "theatre," or "clean" nuclear weapons which are no more destructive than certain conventional weapons. Supposing that this is so, then *ex hypothesis* the use of nuclear weapons of this kind would be as lawful as the use of conventional weapons. It was in issue, however, whether the material before the Court justified that hypothesis, the argument of the proponents of illegality being that the use of any nuclear weapon, even if directed against a lone nuclear submarine at sea or against an isolated military target in the desert, results in the emission of radiation and nuclear fall-out and carries the risk of triggering a chain of events which could lead to the annihilation of the human species.[35]

Apparent Unlawfulness of High Yield Nuclear Weapons

The unavailable facts thus ostensibly had to do with whether the nuclear powers were able to limit the effects of nuclear weapons, and specifically whether small, clean, low-yield tactical nuclear weapons could be used in such circumstances on the High Seas or on troops in sparsely populated areas or the like in such a way as to discriminate

---

[32] Declaration of President Bedjaoui to the Nuclear Weapons Advisory Opinion ¶ 20, 35 I.L.M. at 1345 (No. 6 November 1996) [hereinafter declaration of President Bedjaoui].

[33] Individual opinion of Judge Guillaume to the Nuclear Weapons Advisory Opinion ¶ 5, 35 I.L.M. at 1352 (No. 6 November 1996) [hereinafter individual opinion of Judge Guillaume].

[34] Individual opinion of Judge Ranjeva to the Nuclear Weapons Advisory Opinion 35 I.L.M. at 1354 (No. 6, November 1996) [hereinafter individual opinion of Judge Ranjeva].

[35] Dissenting opinion of Judge Shahabuddeen at 5, 35 I.L.M. at 863.

between civilian and combatant persons and objects, limit civilian casualties and not tend to escalate into an out-out use of high yield nuclear weapons.

This suggests that the use of less clean, less small, higher yield tactical and all strategic nuclear weapons would be unlawful, although the Court does not actually say this. Indeed, the Court's conclusion is expressed not in terms of the possible lawfulness of the use of modern accurate low-yield nuclear weapons, but rather in terms of possible self-defensive use, without reference to the level of nuclear weapons that might be used.

Nonetheless, it is striking that the issue of self defense was joined in the context of possible low-level, limited, clean uses of tactical nuclear weapons. It does not appear that any State even suggested or that the Court considered the possible legality of the use of high yield nuclear weapons or of the wide scale use of even low-yield nuclear weapons.

Judge Shahabuddeen in his dissent confirmed the limited basis of the defense of nuclear weapons before the Court. As set forth above, he noted that the proponents of legality essentially based their argument on the putative effects of the use of "tactical," "theater," "battlefield," or "clean" nuclear weapons said to be no more destructive than certain conventional weapons.[36]

The Court's focus on small-scale nuclear weapons raises such factual questions as the following:

• How much of the U.S. nuclear arsenal is made up of such clean, low-yield tactical nuclear weapons?

• What role do such clean, low-yield tactical nuclear weapons have in U.S. military planning and training?

• To what extent are modern conventional weapons capable of performing the missions for which such clean, low-yield tactical nuclear weapons might be used?

Judge Schwebel, the U.S. judge on the Court, was most explicit in his analysis. At the one extreme he placed the use of strategic nuclear weapons "in quantities against enemy cities and industries."[37] Judge Schwebel found such "countervalue" strikes illegal on the basis that they could cause millions of deaths and render continents and perhaps the whole earth uninhabitable:

---

[36] *Id.*

[37] Dissenting opinion of Judge Schwebel to the Nuclear Weapons Advisory Opinion at 7, 35 I.L.M at 839 [hereinafter dissenting opinion of Judge Schwebel].

At one extreme is the use of strategic nuclear weapons in quantities against enemy cities and industries. This so-called "countervalue" use (as contrasted with "counterforce" uses directly only against enemy nuclear forces and installations) could cause an enormous number of deaths and injuries, running in some cases into the millions; and, in addition to those immediately affected by the heat and blast of those weapons, vast numbers could be affected, many fatally, by spreading radiation. Large-scale "exchanges" of such nuclear weaponry could destroy not only cities but countries and render continents, perhaps the whole of the earth, uninhabitable, if not at once then through longer-range effects of nuclear fallout. It cannot be accepted that the use of nuclear weapons on a scale which would—or could—result in the deaths of many millions in indiscriminate inferno and by far-reaching fallout, have profoundly pernicious effects in space and time, and render uninhabitable much or all of the earth, could be lawful.[38]

At the other extreme Judge Schwebel placed the use of "tactical nuclear weapons against discrete military or naval targets so situated that substantial civilian casualties would not ensue."[39] By way of example, he cited the use of a nuclear depth-charge to destroy a nuclear submarine that has fired or is about to fire nuclear missiles, arguing that such use might be lawful since it would not cause immediate civilian casualties, would be proportionate in the sense that it would cause much less damage than the destroyed submarine would have caused, and would be more likely than a conventional depth-charge to achieve the military objective. Such a strike, the judge concluded, would be lawful.

Judge Schwebel identified as an intermediate case the use of nuclear weapons to destroy an enemy army situated in the desert, saying that such a strike would in some instances be legal and in others illegal, depending on the circumstances and the application of such rules as those of discrimination and proportionality.[40]

Judge Schwebel ostensibly assumed that each use of a nuclear weapon is appropriately to be evaluated in isolation in the context of its direct effects without consideration of the other risk factors it poses, including the risks of retaliatory response and escalation, risks which loom high in the nuclear policy and military planning disciplines. He also appears to assume a static environment, where, for instance, the power whose nuclear submarine is taken out by a nuclear attack does

---

[38] *Id.*
[39] *Id.*
[40] *Id.*

not have other submarines or nuclear weapons of any kind with which to launch the attack it presumptively would otherwise have launched.

It is the invalidity of such static evaluations which underlie my central thesis that the legal evaluation of this lawfulness issue must be made in the light of the full range of applicable facts and risk factors as they would likely exist in the types of circumstances in which the weapons might actually be used.

Nuclear Weapons for Self-Defense

The Court's decision is equivocal as to the scope of a State's right to use nuclear weapons for self-defense. On the one hand, the Court says not once but several times that the question it is leaving open is that of the right of a state to use nuclear weapons in "an extreme circumstance of self-defense, in which [the State's] very survival would be at stake."[41] This sounds like a narrow reservation, as if the Court is saying that virtually all uses of nuclear weapons would be unlawful with the sole exception of a last-ditch effort at self-defense at the last barricade where not just defeat but extirpation was at hand, *i.e.*, that a State must take set-backs short of extirpation before resorting to nuclear weapons.[42]

On the other hand, the Court's decision could be read as leaving open a much broader area. As noted, the Court states that it "does not have sufficient elements to enable it to conclude with certainty that the use of nuclear weapons would necessarily be at variance with the principles and rules of law applicable in armed conflict in any circumstance"[43] and goes on to state that it "cannot lose sight of the fundamental right of every State to survival, and thus its right to resort to self-defense, in accordance with Article 51 of the Charter, when its survival is at stake."[44]

---

[41] Nuclear Weapons Advisory Opinion ¶ 97, at 33, 35 I.L.M. at 831. *See also id.* ¶ 105, at 36, 35 I.L.M. at 831.

[42] Justice Higgins in her dissenting opinion concluded that, given the effects of the use of nuclear weapons, "only the most extreme circumstances (defense against untold suffering or the obliteration of a State or peoples) could conceivably "balance" the equation between necessity and humanity." *Id.* at 4, 35 I.L.M. at 936.

[43] *See id.* ¶ 95, at 32, 35 I.L.M. at 829.

[44] *See id.* ¶ 96, at 33 35 I.L.M. at 830.

Great Britain's attorney had crystallized this position in oral argument to the ICJ:

> It was also said that no balance is possible between the suffering which would be caused by a use—any use—of a nuclear weapon

Perhaps, in the Court's view, the State does not have to be at that last barricade: it is only required, as a general matter, to be in a defensive posture under Article 51, and the Court is assuming that such posture by definition involves a State's "survival." The language seems susceptible to either reading.

It also bears noting that contemporary international law recognizes a right to self-defense in response to actions short of actual armed attack and recognizes a right of anticipatory self-defense. If the Court's decision is deemed to assume such an expanded notion of self-defense, the self-defense carve-out could potentially subsume the rule of general unlawfulness, depending on one's view as to the level of extremity that is required.

Judge Ranjeva quotes O. Schachter's "inventory of the cases in which, quite apart from any question of aggression, a State has claimed the privilege of self-defense:"

> 1. The use of force to rescue political hostages believed to face imminent danger of death or injury;
> 2. The use of force against officials or installations in a foreign State believed to support terrorist acts directed against nationals of the State claiming the right of defense;
> 3. The use of force against troops, planes, vessels, or installations believed to threaten imminent attack by a State with declared hostile intent;
> 4. The use of retaliatory force against a government or military force so as to deter renewed attacks on the State taking such action;
> 5. The use of force against a government that has provided arms or technical support to insurgents in a third State;
> 6. The use of force against a government that has allowed its territory to be used by military forces of a third State considered to be a threat to the State claiming self-defense;

---

and the military advantage which would be derived from that use. But such an abstract statement does not stand up to analysis. Let me take an example. A State or group of States is faced with invasion by overwhelming enemy forces. That State or group of States is certainly entitled to defend itself. If all the other means at their disposal are insufficient, then how can it be said that the use of a nuclear weapon must be disproportionate? Unless it is being suggested that there comes a point when the victim of aggression is no longer permitted to defend itself because of the degree of suffering which defensive measures will inflict. Such a suggestion is insupportable in logic and unsupported in practice.
ICJ Hearing, November 15, 1995, at 47.

7. The use of force in the name of collective defense (or counter intervention) against a government imposed by foreign forces and faced with large-scale military resistance by many of its people.[45]

The Court's focus on the "fundamental right" of self-defense could also be read to mean that the State's right to self-defense somehow transcends the normal limits of humanitarian and other law. President Bedjaoui, in his declaration summarized the issue:

22. A State's right to survival is also a fundamental law, similar in many respects to a "natural" law. However, self-defense—if exercised in extreme circumstances in which the very survival of a State is in question—cannot engender a situation in which a State would exonerate itself from compliance with the "intransgressible" norms of international humanitarian law. In certain circumstances, therefore, a relentless opposition can arise, a head-on collision of fundamental principles, neither one of which can be reduced to the other. The fact remains that the use of nuclear weapons by a State in circumstances in which its survival is at stake risks in its turn endangering the survival of all mankind, precisely because of the inextricable link between terror and escalation in the use of such weapons. It would thus be quite foolhardy unhesitatingly to set the survival of a State above all other considerations, in particular above the survival of mankind itself.[46]

Judge Guillaume identified the same problem:

The right of self-defense proclaimed by the Charter of the United Nations is characterized by the Charter as natural law. But Article 51 adds that nothing in the Charter shall impair this right. The same applies a fortiori to customary law or treaty law. This conclusion is easily explained, for no system of law, whatever it may be, could deprive one of its subjects of the right to defend its own existence and safeguard its vital interests. Accordingly, international law cannot deprive a State of the right to resort to nuclear weapons if such action constitutes the ultimate means by which it can guarantee its survival. In such a case the State enjoys

---

[45] Individual Opinion of Judge Guillaume, 35 I.L.M. at 1354 (No. 6 November 1996) (quoting O. Schachter, *Self-Defense over the Rule of Law,* A.J.I.L., 1989, p. 271).

[46] Declaration of President Bedjaoui ¶ 22, 35 I.L.M. at 1345 (No. 6, November 1996).

a kind of "ground for absolution" similar to the one which exists in all systems of criminal law.[47]

Judge Koroma in his dissenting opinion stated, in a far-reaching discussion of the law of self-defense, that the Court's "'non-finding' appears to have made serious inroads into the present legal restraints relating to the use of nuclear weapons, while throwing the regime of self-defense into doubt by creating a new category called the 'survival of the State,' seen as constituting an exception to Articles 2, paragraph 4, and 51 of the United Nations Charter and to the principles and rules of international law."[48]

Rejecting such a view, Judge Koroma stated:

> The right of self-defence is inherent and fundamental to all States. It exists within and not outside or above the law. To suggest that it exists outside or above the law is to render it probable that force may be used unilaterally by a State when it by itself considers its survival to be at stake. The right of self-defence is not a license to use force; it is regulated by law and was never intended to threaten the security of other states.[49]

Judge Ranjeva addressed this central element of the Court's decision:

> With regard to the substance of the law of armed conflict, the second clause of operative paragraph E introduces the possibility of an exception to the rules of the laws of armed conflict by introducing a notion hitherto unknown in this branch of international law: the "extreme circumstance of self-defense, in which the very survival of a State would be at stake" ... .
>
> The principal difficulty of the interpretation of clause 2 of paragraph E lies in the true nature of the exception of "extreme

---

[47] Individual opinion of Judge Guillaume ¶ 8, 35 I.L.M. at 1352 (No. 6, November 1996).

[48] Dissenting opinion of Judge Koroma at 3, 35 I.L.M. at 926.

Judge Higgins in her dissenting opinion makes a similar observation that the Court "does not restrict itself to the inadequacy of facts and argument concerning the so-called 'clean' and 'precise' weapons." Dissenting opinion of Judge Higgins at 6. She also adds, in light of the Court's recognition of the practice of deterrence, that it cannot be assumed that clean and precise weapons "perhaps to be used against submarines, or in deserts" can "suffice to represent for a nuclear weapon State all that is required for an effective policy of deterrence." Dissenting opinion of Judge Higgins, at 6, 35 I.L.M. at 937. Hence, the Court must be saying that the use even of the large-scale strategic dirty nuclear weapons may be lawful.

[49] Dissenting opinion of Judge Koroma at 4, 35 I.L.M. at 926.

circumstance of self-defense" to the application of humanitarian law and the law of armed conflict. Neither the legal precedents of the Court or of any other jurisdiction nor the doctrine offer any authority to confirm the existence of a distinction between the general case of application of the rules of the law of armed conflict and the exceptional case exempting a belligerent from fulfilling the obligations imposed by those rules.[50]

Judge Ranjeva went on to say that, if the drafters and parties to the various multinational instruments setting forth the humanitarian law and the laws of armed conflict had intended to except extreme circumstances of self-defense from such laws they would have so provided. The judge concludes that, instead:

> These principles were intended to be applied in all cases of conflict without any particular consideration of the status of the parties to the conflict—whether they were victims or aggressors. If an exceptional authorization had been envisaged, the authors of these instruments could have referred to it, for example by incorporating limits or exceptions to the universal application.[51]

Judge Ranjeva pointed out the major dilemma implicit in this potentially broad scope of self-defense:

> The question is to decide which category the case of an extreme circumstance of self-defense, in which the very survival of a State is at stake, must be placed in order to justify recourse to the ultimate weapon and the paralysis of the application of the rules of humanitarian law and the law applicable in armed conflict. This question must be answered with a negative assertion: the obligation of each belligerent to respect the rules of humanitarian law applicable in armed conflict is in no way limited to the case of self-defense; the obligation exists independently of the status of aggressor or victim.[52]

Judge Ranjeva further concluded that there was no basis in the record of the proceeding from which to conclude that there was a real possibility of potential compatibility between the use of nuclear weapons in self-defense and humanitarian law:

> Furthermore, no evidence of the existence of a "clean nuclear weapon" was presented to the Court, and States merely argued that there was indeed a problem of compatibility between the legality of the use of nuclear weapons and the rules of humanitarian law. In

---

[50] Individual opinion of Judge Ranjeva, 35 I.L.M. at 1354.

[51] *Id.*

[52] *Id.*

my view these criticisms strip the exception of "extreme circumstance of self-defense" of all logical and juridical foundation.[53]

Judge Ranjeva's solution is that the provisions of paragraph E as to "extreme circumstance of self-defense" must be read in light of paragraph C's provision that "[a] threat or use of force by means of nuclear weapons that is contrary to Article 2, paragraph 4, of the United Nations Charter and that fails to meet all the requirements of Article 51, is unlawful."[54] As a consequence, Judge Ranjeva concluded, "It must be acknowledged that in the final analysis the Court does affirm that the exercise of legitimate self-defense cannot be envisaged outside the framework of the rules of law."[55] He added, "The difficulty of the terms of the problem did not ... induce the Court to agree to assert the primacy of the requirements of the survival of a State over the obligation to respect the rules of international humanitarian law applicable in armed conflict."[56]

Judge Fleischhauer in his separate opinion identified a "dichotomy" between humanitarian law with which the use of nuclear weapons would seem "scarcely reconcilable" and the "inherent right of self-defense which every State possesses as a matter of sovereign equality," stating that that right would "be severely curtailed if for a State, victim of an attack with nuclear, chemical or bacteriological weapons or otherwise constituting a deadly menace for its very survival, nuclear weapons were totally ruled out as an ultimate legal option in collective or individual self-defense."[57]

Judge Fleischhauer concluded that to rule broadly that the use of nuclear weapons would violate humanitarian law would have the effect of depriving the victim State of its right of self-defense. It would have also have the effect, Judge Fleischhauer concluded, of giving humanitarian law precedence over the right of self-defense, contrary to the equivalence, the "equal ranking" of the rules and rights: "there is no

---

[53] *Id.*

[54] *Id.* Judge Herczegh, unconvinced of this interpretation, found it hard to reconcile the provisions of paragraphs C and E. Declaration of Judge Herczegh to the Nuclear Weapons Advisory Opinion 35 I.L.M. at 1348 (No. 6, November 1996) [hereinafter declaration of Judge Herczegh].

[55] Individual opinion of Judge Ranjeva, 35 I.L.M. at 1354 (No. 6, November 1996).

[56] *Id.*

[57] Separate opinion of Judge Fleischenauer to the Nuclear Weapons Advisory Opinion ¶ 1, at 834, 35 I.L.M. at 834 [hereinafter separate opinion of Judge Fleischhauer].

rule in international law according to which one of the conflicting principles would prevail over the other."[58]

As to this perceived "equal ranking" of humanitarian law and the right of self-defense, Judge Fleischhauer noted that "international law has so far not developed—neither in conventional nor in customary law —a norm on how these principles can be reconciled in the face of the nuclear weapon."[59] As a result, the judge concluded, it is necessary to find the "smallest common denominator" between these conflicting principles and rules.

Without explanation, he concluded that this means the use of nuclear weapons "could remain a justified legal option in an extreme situation of individual or collective self-defense in which the threat or use of nuclear weapons is the last resort against an attack with nuclear, chemical or bacteriological weapons or otherwise threatening the very existence of the victimized State."[60]

To the same effect, Judge Fleischhauer found the existence of a general principle of law recognized in all legal systems to the effect that no legal system is entitled to demand the self-abandonment, the suicide of one of its subjects, from which he seems to find an overriding right to use nuclear weapons in extreme circumstances of self-defense.[61]

Having gone through all of the foregoing analysis seemingly leading to a right of self-defense transcending the limits of humanitarian principles, Judge Fleischhauer seemingly took it all back:

> 6. For a recourse to nuclear weapons to be lawful, however, not only would the situation have to be an extreme one, but the conditions on which the lawfulness of the exercise of self-defense generally depends would also always have to be met. These conditions comprise, as the Opinion states *expressis verbis* (para. 41) that there must be proportionality. The need to comply with the proportionality principle must not *a priori* rule out recourse to nuclear weapons; as the Opinion states (para. 42): "The proportionality principle may thus not in itself exclude the use of nuclear weapons in all circumstances." The margin that exists for considering that a particular threat or use of nuclear weapons could be lawful is therefore extremely narrow.[62]

---

[58] *Id.* ¶ 3, at 2.
[59] *See id.* ¶ 5, at 3 35 I.L.M. at 835–36.
[60] *Id.*
[61] *Id.* ¶ 5, at 3–4, 35 I.L.M. at 835–36.
[62] *See id.* ¶ 6, at 4, 35 I.L.M. at 836.

Judge Fleischhauer's factual conclusions, when combined with this legal conclusion, would seem to require a finding of illegality:

> The nuclear weapon is, in many ways, the negation of the humanitarian considerations underlying the law applicable in armed conflict and of the principle of neutrality. The nuclear weapon cannot distinguish between civilian and military targets. It causes immeasurable suffering. The radiation released by it is unable to respect the territorial integrity of a neutral State.[63]

Ultimately, the reading of the Court's opinion as having the right of self-defense trump the principles of humanitarian law seems at odds with the totality of the opinion. The Court, after noting that a State's exercise of the right of self-defense must comply, *inter alia*, with the principle of proportionality, specifically stated that a "use of force that is proportionate under the law of self-defense, must in order to be lawful, also meet the requirements of the law applicable in armed conflict which comprise in particular the principles and rules of humanitarian law."[64]

The Court also quoted the statement on this point by the United Kingdom, a proponent of the potential lawfulness of the use of nuclear weapons, "Assuming that a State's use of nuclear weapons meets the requirements of self-defense, it must then be considered whether it conforms to the fundamental principles of the law of armed conflict regulating the conduct of hostilities."[65] The Court further emphasized in the final paragraph of its decision that the various grounds set forth in the Court's decision were to be read in the light of one another.[66]

---

[63] *See id.* ¶ 2, at 1, 35 I.L.M. at 834.

[64] Nuclear Weapons Advisory Opinion ¶ 42, at 18, 35 I.L.M. at 822. Judge Weeramantry in his dissenting opinion develops at length the case for the subjugation of the right of self-defense to the overall requirements of the law of armed conflict. Dissenting opinion of Judge Weeramantry at 58–63, 35 I.L.M. at 909–911.

[65] Nuclear Weapons Advisory Opinion ¶ 91, at 31, 35 I.L.M. at 829 (citing the written statement of the United Kingdom ¶ 3.44, at 40).

[66] The Court stated "that its reply to the question put to it by the General Assembly rests on the totality of the legal grounds set forth by the Court above (paragraphs 20 to 103), each of which is to be read in the light of the others. Some of these grounds are not such as to form the object of formal conclusions in the final paragraph of the Opinion; they nevertheless retain, in the view of the Court, all of their importance." Nuclear Weapons Advisory Opinion ¶ 104, at 35, 35 I.L.M. at 831.

The Court thus seemingly confirmed that all uses of force, including defensive ones of the most extreme sort, must comply with the law of armed conflict.

Several of the judges echoed this conclusion in their separate opinions. Judge Shahabuddeen stated in his dissenting opinion:

> Humanitarian law, it is said, must be read as being subject to an exception which allows a State to use nuclear weapons in self-defense when its survival is at stake, that is to say, even if such use would otherwise breach that law, and this for the reason that no system of law obliged those subject to it to commit suicide. That is the argument which underlies the second part of subparagraph E of paragraph (2) of the operative paragraph of the Court's Advisory Opinion.[67]

Judge Shahabuddeen concluded that there was no such self-defense exception to humanitarian law:

> [I]t is necessary to distinguish between the inherent right of self-defense and the means by which the right is exercisable. A State using force in self-defense is acting legally under the *ius ad bellum*. But, whether a State is acting legally or illegally under the *ius ad bellum*, if it is in fact using force it must always do so in the manner prescribed by the *ius in bello*. It is the *ius in bello* which lays down whether or not a particular means of warfare is permissible. Thus, where the use of a particular weapon is proscribed by the *ius in bello*, the denial of the use of that weapon is not a denial of the right of self-defense of the attacked State: the inherent right of self-defense spoken of in Article 51 of the Charter simply does not comprehend the use of the weapon in question.[68]

Judge Shahabuddeen added:

> The legal answer to the possible plight of the victim State is given by the principle, as enunciated by the United States military Tribunal at Nuremberg on 19 February 1948, that "the rules of international law must be followed even if it results in the loss of a battle or even a war. Expediency or necessity cannot warrant their violation."[69]

---

[67] Dissenting opinion of Judge Shahabuddeen at 34, referring to the Court's opinion ¶ 42, at 18. Judge Weeramantry in his dissenting opinion develops length the case for the subjugation of the right of self-defense to the overall requirements of the law of armed conflict. Dissenting opinion of Judge Weeramantry at 58–63, 35 I.L.M. at 909–911.

[68] Dissenting opinion of Judge Shahabuddeen at 30, 35 I.L.M. at 876.

[69] *Id.*

Judge Shahabuddeen saw the Court's failure to determine the legality of the use of nuclear weapons in extreme circumstances of self-defense as a failure to address the type of situation in which, if ever, the use of nuclear weapons could possibly be lawful, or to answer the central question presented for decision:

> Despite variations in formulation and references to the concept of "vital security interests," an "extreme circumstance of self-defence, in which the very survival of a state would be at stake," as defined by the Court, is the main circumstance in which the proponents of legality advance a claim to a right to use nuclear weapons. This is so for the reason that, assuming that the use of nuclear weapons is lawful, the nature of the weapons, combined with the limitations imposed by the requirements of necessity and proportionality which condition the exercise of the right of self-defence, will serve to confine their lawful use to that "extreme circumstance." It follows that to hold that humanitarian law does not apply to the use of nuclear weapon in the main circumstance in which a claim to a right of use is advanced is to uphold the substance of the thesis that humanitarian law does not apply at all to the use of nuclear weapons. That view has long been discarded; as the Court itself recalls, the NWS themselves do not advance it. I am not persuaded that that disfavoured thesis can be brought back through an exception based on self-defence.[70]

Judge Weeramantry made the same point:

> [M]uch of the argument of those opposing illegality seems to blur the distinction between *ius ad bellum* and the *ius in bello*. Whatever be the merits or otherwise of resorting to the use of force (the province of the *ius ad bellum*), when once the domain of force is entered, the governing law in that domain is the *ius in bello*. The humanitarian laws of war take over and govern all who participate, assailant and victim alike. The argument before the Court has proceeded as though, once the self-defense exception to the use of force comes into operation, the applicability of the *ius in bello* falls away. This supposition is juristically wrong and logically untenable. The reality, is, of course that while the *ius ad bellum* only opens the door to the use of force (in self-defense or by the Security Council), whoever enters that door must function subject to the *ius in bello*. The contention that the legality of the use of force justifies a breach of humanitarian law is thus a total non-sequitur.[71]

---

[70] *Id.* at 1–2, 35 I.L.M. at 861.
[71] Dissenting opinion of Judge Weeramantry at 63, 35 I.L.M. at 911.

So too Judge Schwebel concluded that the exercise of self-defense was subject to humanitarian law and indeed that generally accepted principles of law were included in the body of law to be applied by the Court, so there would always be available law, never a gap, a *non liquet*.[72]

UN Charter Provisions

Noting that under the UN Charter the threat or use of force is prohibited except in individual or collective self-defense in response to armed attack or in instances of military enforcement measures undertaken by the Security Council,[73] the Court stated that under customary international law the right of self-defense is subject to the conditions of necessity and proportionality. The Court quoted its decision in the *Nicaragua* case: "there is a specific rule whereby self-defense would warrant only measures which are proportional to the armed attack and necessary to respond to it, a rule well established in customary international law."[74]

Judge Weeramantry in his dissenting opinion stated that, while on first analysis it might appear that a nuclear response to a nuclear attack would satisfy the requirement of proportionality, on further analysis it appears that the levels of devastation caused by nuclear weapons are beyond measurement, making the proportionality requirement become "devoid of meaning," since one can only measure the measurable.[75] "If one speaks in terms of a nuclear response to a nuclear attack, that nuclear response will tend ... to be an all-out nuclear response which opens up all the scenarios of global Armageddon."[76]

Judge Weeramantry cited the risk factor of human error during the throes of war, noting that even in the "comparatively tranquil and leisured atmosphere of peace, error is possible, even to the extent of unleashing an unintentional nuclear attack."[77] He concluded that, in war, this risk factor would be heightened by the likely failure of

---

[72] Dissenting opinion of Judge Schwebel at 8, 35 I.L.M. at 84 (citing LAUETERPACHT, THE FUNCTION OF LAW IN THE INTERNATIONAL COMMUNITY (1933)).

[73] *See* Nuclear Weapons Advisory Opinion ¶ 38, at 17 35 I.L.M. at 822 (citing the U.N. CHARTER art. 51).

[74] Nuclear Weapons Advisory Opinion ¶ 41, at 18, 35 I.L.M. at 822 (citing the case *Concerning Military and Paramilitary Activities in and against Nicaragua* (Nicaragua v. United States of America 1986 I.C.J. Reports 94)).

[75] Dissenting opinion of Judge Weeramantry at 60, 35 I.L.M. at 910.

[76] *Id.*

[77] *Id.*

computer and other equipment.[78] Judge Weeramantry further stated, "No nation can be seen as entitled to risk the destruction of civilization for its own national benefit."[79]

Judge Higgins in her dissenting opinion stated that the Court's decision made it clear that "the concept of proportionality in self-defense limits a response to what is needed to reply to an attack" rather than imposing a "requirement of symmetry between the mode of the initial attack and the mode of response."[80]

Judge Guillaume in his individual opinion noted that the humanitarian law as to collateral damage implies comparisons: "The collateral damage caused to civilian populations must not be 'excessive' in relation to the 'military advantage anticipated'."[81]

Judge Schwebel in his dissenting opinion quoted the discussion in oral argument by the British Attorney General:

> If one is to speak of "disproportionality," the question arises: disproportionate to what? The answer must be "to the threat posed to the victim State." It is by reference to that threat that proportionality must be measured. So one has to look at all the circumstances, in particular the scale, kind and location of the threat. To assume that any defensive use of nuclear weapons must be disproportionate, no matter how serious the threat to the safety and the very survival of the State resorting to such use is wholly unfounded. Moreover, it suggests an overbearing assumption by the critics of nuclear weapons that they can determine in advance that no threat, including a nuclear, chemical or biological threat, is ever worth the use of any nuclear weapon. It cannot be right to say that if an aggressor hits hard enough, his victim loses the right to take the only measure by which he can defend himself and reverse the aggression. That would not be the rule of law. It would be an aggressor's charter.[82]

---

[78] *Id.*

[79] *Id.* at 61, 35 I.L.M. at 910.

[80] Dissenting opinion of Judge Higgins at 1, 35 I.L.M. at 934 (citing Professor Ago in the Addendum to his Eighth Report on State Responsibility, A/CN, 4/318/Adds. 5-7, ¶ 121, YBILC (1980), Vol. II, Part One, p. 69).

[81] Individual opinion of Judge Guillaume ¶ 5, 35 I.L.M. at 1352 (No. 6, November 1996).

[82] Dissenting opinion of Judge Schwebel at 7, 35 I.L.M. at 839 (citations omitted).

The Court's Refusal to Engage in Risk Analysis

The Court had warned at the outset of its opinion that, ostensibly based on the advisory nature of its task, it did not intend to descend into the nitty-gritty of the facts:

> The Court does not consider that, in giving an advisory opinion in the present case, it would necessarily have to write "scenarios," to study various types of nuclear weapons and to evaluate highly complex and controversial technological, strategic and scientific information. The Court will simply address the issues arising in all their aspects by applying the legal rules relevant to the situation.[83]

Similarly, in the above-quoted language as to proportionality, the Court stated that it did "not find it necessary to embark upon the quantification of [risk factors as to the use of nuclear weapons]" and did not "need to inquire into the question whether tactical nuclear weapons exist which are sufficiently precise to limit those risks."[84]

To the extent that the facts are available, this hands-off attitude of the Court, while perhaps understandable from a political perspective, may, from a judicial perspective, be the tragic flaw in the decision. The Court did, however, in the proportionality discussion recognize the relevance of the exigent risk factors as "considerations to be borne in mind by States believing they can exercise a nuclear response in self-defense in accordance with the requirements of proportionality."[85]

Judge Shahabuddeen in his dissenting opinion lamented the Court's approach:

> [O]nce it is shown that the use of a weapon could annihilate mankind, its repugnance to the conscience of the international community is not materially diminished by showing that it need not have that result in every case; it is not reasonable to expect that the conscience of the international community will, both strangely and impossibly, wait on the event to see if the result of any particular use is the destruction of the human species. The operative consideration is the risk of annihilation. That result may not ensue in all cases, but the risk that it can inheres in every case. The risk may be greater in some cases, less in others; but it is always present in sufficient measure to render the use of nuclear weapons unacceptable to the international community in all cases. In my

---

[83] Nuclear Weapons Advisory Opinion ¶ 15, at 11, 35 I.L.M. at 819.

[84] *Id.* ¶ 43, at 18, 35 I.L.M. at 822.

[85] *Id.*

view, the answer to the question of repugnance to the conscience of the international community governs throughout.[86]

Judge Shahabuddeen concluded that the Court has sufficient facts from which to conclude "that the international community as a whole considers that nuclear weapons are not merely weapons of mass destruction, but that there is a clear and palpable risk that their use could accomplish the destruction of mankind."[87]

Identification of Risk Factors

A number of the judges in their separate decisions focused on risks inherent in the use of nuclear weapons.

Judge Weeramantry addressed escalation as a risk factor, citing statements by Robert McNamara and others for the conclusion that "the state subjected to the first attack could be expected to respond in kind" and that "[a]fter the devastation caused by a first attack, especially if it be a nuclear attack, there will be a tendency to respond with any nuclear firepower that is available," and that "[w]ith such a response, the clock would accelerate towards global catastrophe, for a counter-response would be invited and, indeed, could be automatically be triggered off."[88]

In the quoted statement, McNamara stated:

> But under such circumstances, leaders on both sides would be under unimaginable pressure to avenge their losses and secure the interests being challenged. And each would fear that the opponent might launch a larger attack at any moment. Moreover, they would both be operating with only partial information because of the disruption to communications caused by the chaos on the battlefield (to say nothing of possible strikes against communication facilities). Under such conditions, it is highly likely that rather than surrender, each side would launch a larger attack, hoping that this step would bring the action to a halt by causing the opponent to capitulate.[89]

Judge Weeramantry stated that the target of a nuclear attack "will be so ravaged that it will not be able to make fine evaluation of the exact amount of retaliatory force required. In such event, the tendency to

---

[86] Dissenting opinion of Judge Shahabuddeen at 9, 35 I.L.M. at 865.
[87] *Id.*
[88] *Id.* at 59, 35 I.L.M. at 909.
[89] *Id.*

release as strong a retaliation as is available must enter into any realistic evaluation of the situation."[90]

Judge Weeramantry also identified the risk of human error:

> It is relevant also, in the context of nuclear weapons, not to lose sight of the possibility of human error. However carefully planned, a nuclear response to a nuclear attack cannot, in the confusion of the moment, be finely graded so as to assess the strength of the weapons of attack, and to respond in like measure. Even in the comparatively tranquil and leisured atmosphere of peace, error is possible, even to the extent of unleashing an unintentional nuclear attack. This has emerged from studies of unintentional nuclear war. The response, under the stress of nuclear attack, would be far more prone to accident.[91]

He continued:

> According to the Bulletin of the Atomic Scientists:
> "Top decision-makers as well as their subordinate information suppliers rely on computers and other equipment which have become even more complex and therefore more vulnerable to malfunction. Machine failures or human failures or a combination of the two could, had they not been discovered within minutes, have caused unintended nuclear war in a number of reported cases."[92]

Judge Weeramantry concluded that "[a] nuclear war will not end with the use of a nuclear weapon by a single power, as happened in the case of Japan. There will inevitably be a nuclear exchange, especially in a world in which nuclear weapons are triggered for instant and automatic reprisal in the event of a nuclear attack."[93]

Judge Weeramantry focused on the risks inherent in the contexts in which nuclear decision-making would have to be made in a nuclear war:

> A decision to use nuclear weapons would tend to be taken, if taken at all, in circumstances which do not admit of fine legal evaluations. It will in all probability be taken at a time when

---

[90] Dissenting opinion of Judge Weeramantry at 27, 35 I.L.M. at 893.

[91] *Id.* at 60, 35 I.L.M. at 910 (citing RISKS OF UNINTENTIONAL NUCLEAR WAR, (United Nations Institute of Disarmament Research (UNIDIR)); and *Risks of Unintentional Nuclear War,* BULL. OF THE ATOMIC SCIENTISTS, Vol. 38, June 1982, at 68).

[92] *Id.* (citing *Risks of Unintentional Nuclear War,* BULL. OF THE ATOMIC SCIENTISTS, Vol. 38, p. 68, June 1982).

[93] *Id.* at 67, 35 I.L.M. at 913.

passions run high, time is short and the facts are unclear. It will not be a carefully measured decision, taken after a detailed and detached evaluation of all relevant circumstances of fact. It would be taken under extreme pressure and stress. Legal matters requiring considered evaluation may have to be determined within minutes, perhaps even by military rather than legally trained personnel, when they are in fact so complex as to have engaged this Court's attention for months. The fate of humanity cannot fairly be made to depend on such a decision.[94]

He also addressed risk factors inherent in the use of "small," "clean," "low yield," or "tactical" nuclear weapons:

(i) no material has been placed before the Court demonstrating that there is in existence a nuclear weapon which does not emit radiation, does not have a deleterious effect upon the environment, and does not have adverse health effects upon this and succeeding generations. If there were indeed a weapon which does not have any of the singular qualities outlined earlier in this Opinion, it has not been explained why a conventional weapon would not be adequate for the purpose for which such a weapon is used. ...

(ii) the practicality of small nuclear weapons has been contested by high military and scientific authority;

(iii) reference has been made ... in the context of self-defence, to the political difficulties, stated by former American Secretaries of State, Robert McNamara and Dr. Kissinger, of keeping a response within the ambit of what has been described as a limited or minimal response. The assumption of escalation control seems unrealistic in the context of nuclear attack;

(iv) with the use of even "small" or "tactical" or "battlefield" nuclear weapons, one crosses the nuclear threshold. The state at the receiving end of such a nuclear response would not know that the response is a limited or tactical one involving a small weapon and it is not credible to posit that it will also be careful to respond in kind, *i.e.*, with a small weapon. The door would be opened and the threshold crossed for an all-out nuclear wear.

The scenario here under consideration is that of a limited nuclear response to a nuclear attack. Since, as stated above:

(a) the "controlled response" is unrealistic; and

(b) a "controlled response" by the nuclear power making the first attack to the "controlled response" to its first strike is even more unrealistic.

The scenario we are considering is one of all-out nuclear war, thus rendering the use of the controlled weapon illegitimate.

---

[94] *Id.* at 70, 35 I.L.M. at 915.

The assumption of a voluntary "brake" on the recipient's full-scale use of nuclear weapons is ... highly fanciful and speculative. Such fanciful speculations provide a very unsafe assumption on which to base the future of humanity.

***

(vii) The factor of accident must always be considered. Nuclear weapons have never been tried out on the battlefield. Their potential for limiting damage is untested and is as yet the subject of theoretical assurances of limitation. Having regard to the possibility of human error in high scientific operations—even to the extent of the accidental explosion of a space rocket with all its passengers aboard—one can never be sure that some error or accident in construction may deprive the weapon of its so-called "limited" quality. Indeed, apart from fine gradations regarding the size of the weapon to be used, the very use of any nuclear weapon under the stress of urgency is an area fraught with much potential for accident. ...

(viii) there is some doubt regarding the "smallness" of tactical nuclear weapons, and no precise details regarding these have been placed before the Court by any of the nuclear powers. Malaysia ... has referred the Court to a US law forbidding "research and development which could lead to the production ... of a low-yield nuclear weapon" ... which is defined as having a yield of less than five kilotons (Hiroshima and Nagasaki were 15 and 12 kilotons, respectively) [National Defense Authorization Act for Fiscal Year 1994, Pub Law, 103-160, 30 November 1993]. Weapons of this firepower may, in the absence of evidence to the contrary, be presumed to be fraught with all the dangers attendant on nuclear weapons....

(ix) It is claimed a weapon could be used which could be precisely aimed at a specific target. However, recent experience in the Gulf War has shown that even the most sophisticated or "small" weapons do not always strike its intended target with precision. If there should be such error in the case of nuclear weapon, the consequence would be of the gravest order.

(x) Having regard to WHO estimates of deaths ranging from one million to one billion in the event of a nuclear war which could well be triggered off by the use of the smallest nuclear weapon, one can only endorse the sentiment which Egypt placed before us when it observed that, having regard to such a level of casualties:

"even with the gravest miniaturization, such speculative margins of risk are totally abhorrent to the general principles of humanitarian law" (CR 95/23, p. 43).[95]

---

[95] *Id.* at 82–83, 35 I.L.M. at 921 (citing GENERAL COLIN POWELL, A SOLDIER'S WAY 324 ("No matter how small these nuclear payloads were,

Judge Weeramantry also identified the element of luck, in connection with the argument that deterrence during the Cold War prevented war:

> It is well documented that the use of nuclear weapons has been contemplated more than once during the past fifty years. Two of the best known examples are the Cuban Missile Crisis (1962) and the Berlin Crisis (1961). To these, many more could be added from well researched studies upon the subject. The world has on such occasions been hovering on the brink of nuclear catastrophe and has, so to speak, held its breath. In these confrontations, often a test of nerves between those who control the nuclear button, anything could have happened, and it is humanity's good fortune that a nuclear exchange has not resulted.[96]

Judge Oda, in contrast, saw there as being no real risk that nuclear weapons would be used:

> There is another point which should not be overlooked. As a matter of fact the nuclear-weapon States have tended to undertake not to use or threaten to use nuclear weapons against the States in some specific regions covered by the nuclear-free-zone treaties and these five nuclear-weapon States, early in 1995, gave security assurances through statements made in the Security Council in which they undertook not to use or threaten to use these weapons against the non-nuclear weapon States. In other words, if legal

---

would be crossing a threshold. Using nukes at this point would mark one of the most significant military decision since Hiroshima....I began rethinking the practicality of those small nuclear weapons."); BULL. OF THE ATOMIC SCIENTISTS, May 1985, at 35).

[96] *Id.* at 86, 35 I.L.M. at 922. Judge Weeramanatry added,

> [I]t is incorrect to speak of the nuclear weapon as having saved the world from wars, when well over 100 wars, resulting in 20 million deaths, have occurred since 1945. Some studies have shown that since the termination of World War II there have been armed conflicts around the globe every year, with the possible exception of 1968, while more detailed estimates show that in the 2,340 weeks between 1945 and 1990, the world enjoyed a grand total of only three that were truly war-free.

Id. (citing THE NUCLEAR PREDICAMENT, A SOURCEBOOK (D.V. Gregory ed., 1982); RUTH SIVARD, WORLD MILITARY AND SOCIAL EXPENDITURES, WORLD PRIORITIES 20 (1993) (counting 149 wars and 23 million deaths during this period); CHARLES ALLEN, THE SAVAGE WARS OF PEACE, SOLDIERS' VOICES, 1945–1989, (1989); ALVIN & HEIDI TOFFLER, WAR AND ANTI-WAR, SURVIVAL AT THE DAWN OF THE 21ST CENTURY 14 (1993)).

undertakings are respected, there is little risk of the use of nuclear weapons at present by the five declared nuclear-weapon States.[97]

The *Lotus*/Sovereignty Issue

The Court noted that various States had argued, based on dicta in the *Lotus* and *Nicaragua* cases, that international law is based on sovereignty and consent, such that States are permitted to do anything that is not precluded by treaty or conventional law.[98] The Court concluded that it did not have to reach this issue, since "the nuclear-weapon States appearing before it either accepted, or did not dispute, that their independence to act was indeed restricted by the principles and rules of international law, more particularly humanitarian law, as did the other States which took part in the proceedings."[99]

---

[97] Dissenting opinion of Judge Oda at 34, 35 I.L.M. at 859.

[98] Nuclear Weapons Advisory Opinion ¶ 21, at 12–13, 35 I.L.M. at 819–827 (citing *The Lotus Case*, P.C.I.J., Series A, No. 10, pp. 18 and 19). *See also Military and Paramilitary Activities in and against Nicaragua* (Nicaragua v. United States of America), 1986 I.C.J. Reports 94).

[99] Nuclear Weapons Advisory Opinion ¶ 22, at 13, 35 I.L.M. at 820. Judge Bedjaoui, the President of the Court, found the *Lotus* decision to be outmoded. *See infra* notes 267–270 and the accompanying text.

Judge Weeramantry in his dissenting opinion noted France's contrary position that the law of war and particularly the rule of proportionality does not preclude a State's using whatever weapon is militarily "appropriate" to withstand an attack. Dissenting Opinion of Judge Weeramantry at 12, 35 I.L.M. at 886.

Judge Weeramantry rejects this overall view—what he calls "extreme positivism"—as inconsistent not only with the specific provisions of the Martens clause but also with the very notion of general principles as an established source of international law. *Id.* at 43–45, 35 I.L.M. at 901–02.

Referring to the Court's statement in the Nicaraguan decision that "there are no rules, other than such rules as may be accepted by the State concerned, by treaty or otherwise, whereby the level of armaments of a sovereign State can be limited," Judge Weeramantry in his dissenting opinion in the WHO Advisory Opinion proceeding noted that language referred to possession not use. The WHO Advisory Opinion, 1996 I.C.J. 68, 166 (citations omitted). Judge Weeramantry went on to state, "it has never been argued that the rules relating to the laws of war or international humanitarian law, which in fact regulate the conduct of States, constitute an intrusion upon State sovereignty, or an interference in a State's military decisions." WHO Advisory Opinion, 1996 I.C.J. 68, 166.

Pattern of Specific Instruments

Noting that the "pattern until now has been for weapons of mass destruction to be declared illegal by specific instruments," the Court found that there was no such instrument prohibiting the use of nuclear weapons.[100]

The Court recognized that the absence of a specific convention prohibiting the use of nuclear weapons does not itself mean that there is no such legal prohibition, since conventions may reflect or codify pre-existing law.[101]

Covenant on Civil and Political Rights

The Court found that the right under this Covenant not to be arbitrarily deprived of life continues in time of war, but that whether there has been a violation of this right in time of war would have to be determined under the law of armed conflict.[102]

---

[100] Nuclear Weapons Advisory Opinion ¶ 57, at 21, 35 I.L.M. at 824 (citing the Convention of 10 April 1972 on the Prohibition of the Development, Production and Stockpiling of Bacteriological (Biological) and Toxin Weapons, prohibiting the possession of bacteriological and toxic weapons and reinforcing the prohibition of their use; and the Convention of 13 January 1993 on the Prohibition of the Development, Production, Stockpiling and Use of Chemical Weapons and on Their Destruction, prohibiting all use of chemical weapons and requiring the destruction of existing stocks).

[101] The Court recognized the Hague and Geneva Conventions as codifications, *Id.* ¶ 75, at 27, 35 I.L.M. at 827, and emphasized the applicability of the rules of humanitarian law to weapons of the future as well as to those of the present and the past, *Id.* ¶ 86, at 30, 35 I.L.M. at 828.

In addressing the applicability or not of Additional Protocol I of 1977 to nuclear weapons, the Court stated:

> [T]he Court recalls that all States are bound by those rules in Additional Protocol I which, when adopted, were merely the expression of the pre-existing customary law, such as the Martens Clause, reaffirmed in the first article of Additional Protocol I.

Id. ¶ 84, at 29, 35 I.L.M. at 828.

Similarly, the Court noted that the fundamental rules of humanitarian law "are to be observed by all States whether or not they have ratified the conventions that contain them, because they constitute intransgressible principles of international customary law." *Id.* ¶ 84, at 29, 35 I.L.M. at 828.

So also, the Court noted that the Nuremberg International Military Tribunal had found the humanitarian rules included in the Hague Regulations to be "recognized by all nations" and "declaratory of the laws and customs of war." *Id.* ¶ 80, at 28, 35 I.L.M. at 827.

[102] *Id.* ¶ 25, at 13–14, 35 I.L.M. at 820.

Genocide Convention

Noting that the Genocide Convention prohibits crimes involving "intent to destroy, in whole or in part, a national, ethical, racial or religious group," the Court concluded that such intent was a prerequisite to violation and would have to be determined on an individual case basis. The Court appeared to reject the arguments of anti-nuclear States that "the intention to destroy [the targeted groups] could be inferred from the fact that the user of the nuclear weapon would have omitted to take account of the well-known effects of the use of such weapons."[103]

By its language that the element of intent must be shown "towards a group as such,"[104] the Court ostensibly concluded that specific intent must be shown.[105]

Judge Weeramantry in his dissenting opinion rejected this focus on specific intentionality, concluding that it is enough that the State using the nuclear weapon "must know that it will have the effect of causing deaths on a scale so massive as to wipe out entire populations."[106] Rejecting the focus on the "as such" language of the convention, Judge Weeramantry stated, "[H]aving regard to the ability of nuclear weapons to wipe out blocks of population ranging from hundreds of thousands to millions, there can be no doubt that the weapon targets, in whole or in part, the national group of the State at which it is directed."[107] He added, "Nuremberg held that the extermination of the civilian population in whole or in part is a crime against humanity. This is precisely what a nuclear weapon achieves."[108]

Judge Weeramantry further stated, "Self defence, which will, as shown in the discussion on proportionality, result in all probability in all-out nuclear war, is even more likely to cause genocide than the act of launching an initial strike. If the killing of human beings, in numbers ranging from a million to a billion, does not fall within the definition of genocide, one may well ask what will."[109]

Judge Koroma in his dissenting opinion also rejected the Court's strict interpretation of the level of intent required by the Genocide

---

[103] *See id.* ¶ 26, at 14, 35 I.L.M. at 820.
[104] *See id.*
[105] *See id.*
[106] Dissenting opinion of Judge Weeramantry at 50, 35 I.L.M. at 905.
[107] *Id.*
[108] *Id.*
[109] *Id.* at 61, 35 I.L.M. at 910.

Convention, suggesting that it is enough that the "consequences of the act could have been foreseen."[110]

Protection of the Environment

The Court noted that various States have argued that legal constraints upon the use of nuclear weapons are imposed by international treaties and instruments relating to the protection of the environment, including:

> • Additional Protocol I of 1977 to the Geneva Conventions of 1949, Article 35, paragraph 3, prohibiting the employment of "methods or means of warfare which are intended, or may be expected, to cause widespread, long-term and severe damage to the natural environment";
> • the Convention of 18 May 1977 on the Prohibition of Military or Any Other Hostile Use of Environmental Modification Techniques, prohibiting the use of weapons which have "widespread, long-lasting or severe effects" on the environment (Art. 1);
> • Principle 21 of the Stockholm Declaration of 1972;
> • Principle 2 of the Rio Declaration of 1992, expressing the duty of the concerned States "to ensure that activities within their jurisdiction or control do not cause damage to the environment of other States or of areas beyond the limits of national jurisdiction."[111]

Determining that considerations as to environmental protection under such treaties could not have intended to deprive a State of the exercise of its right of self-defense under international law, the Court concluded that States' obligations as to protection of the environment must be considered in light of the law of armed conflict: "States must take environmental considerations into account when assessing what is necessary and proportionate in the pursuit of legitimate military objectives."[112]

---

[110] Dissenting opinion of Judge Koroma at 16, 35 I.L.M. at 932.

[111] Nuclear Weapons Advisory Opinion ¶ 27, at 14–15 35 I.L.M. at 820–21.

[112] *Id.* ¶ 30, at 15 35 I.L.M. at 821.

The Court took an expansive view of the importance of the environment:
> The Court also recognizes that the environment is not an abstraction but represents the living space, the quality of life and the very health of human beings, including generations unborn. The existence of the general obligation of States to ensure that

Thus, the environment is one of the interests protected by the principles of necessity and proportionality: "Respect for the environment is one of the elements that go to assessing whether an action is in conformity with the principles of necessity and proportionality."[113] The Court noted that "the use of nuclear weapons could constitute a catastrophe for the environment."[114]

The Court further concluded, as to the Rio Declaration (Principle 14) and Articles 35, paragraph 3, and 55 of Additional Protocol I:

> Taken together, these provisions embody a general obligation to protect the natural environment against widespread, long-term and severe environmental damage; the prohibition of methods and means of warfare which are intended, or may be expected, to cause such damage; and the prohibition of attacks against the natural environmental by way of reprisals.
>
> These are powerful constraints for all the States having subscribed to these provisions.[115]

As pointed by Judge Weeramantry in his dissenting opinion, it is noteworthy that this prohibition of environmental damage reaches not only effects that were intended but also those that the weapon "may be expected to cause."[116]

On the foregoing basis, the Court concluded that international law "indicates important environmental factors that are properly to be taken into account in the context of the implementation of the principles and rules of the law applicable in armed conflict."[117]

> activities within their jurisdiction and control respect the environment of other States or of areas beyond national control is now part of the corpus of international law relating to the environment.

Nuclear Weapons Advisory Opinion ¶ 29, at 15 35 I.L.M. at 821.

[113] *Id.* Judge Weeramantry in his dissenting opinion in the WHO Advisory Opinion proceedings reviewed relevant environmental law at some length. WHO Advisory Opinion. 1996 I.C.J. 68, 139–143.

[114] Nuclear Weapons Advisory Opinion ¶ 29, at 15, 35 I.L.M. at 821

[115] *Id.* ¶ 31, at 16, 35 I.L.M. at 821. The Court also referred to its recent Order in the Request for an Examination of the Situation in Accordance with Paragraph 63 of the Court's Judgment of 20 December 1974 in the *Nuclear Tests Case* (New Zealand v. France), where the Court stated that its conclusion was "without prejudice to the obligations of States to respect and protect the natural environment" (Order of 22 September 1995, I.C.R. Reports 1995 ¶ 64, at 306). Nuclear Weapons Advisory Opinion ¶ 32, at 16, 35 I.L.M. at 821.

[116] Dissenting opinion of Judge Weeramantry at 1, 35 I.L.M. at 880.

[117] Nuclear Weapons Advisory Opinion ¶ 33, at 16, 35 I.L.M. at 821.

As to the importance of the protection of the environment from the effects of nuclear war, Judge Weeramantry noted a comment that "the Earth's human population has a much greater vulnerability to the indirect effects of nuclear war, especially mediated through impacts on food productivity and food availability, than to the direct effects of nuclear war itself."[118]

Poisonous Weapons

The Court noted that opponents of nuclear weapons have urged the unlawfulness of such weapons under various conventions relating to poisonous weapons:

> (a) The Second Hague Declaration of 29 July 1899, which prohibits the "use of projectiles the object of which is the diffusion of asphyxiating or deleterious gases";
> (b) Article 23(a) of the Regulations respecting the laws and customs of war on land annexed to the Hague Convention IV of 18 October 1907, prohibiting the use of "poison or poisoned weapons"; and
> (c) the Geneva Protocol of 17 June 1925, which prohibits "the use in war of asphyxiating, poisonous or other gases, and of all analogous liquids, materials or devices."[119]

The Court concluded, without citation of authority, that these instruments did not specifically prohibit the use of nuclear weapons, since their provisions "have been understood, in the practice of States, in their ordinary sense as covering weapons whose prime, or even exclusive, effect is to poison or asphyxiate."[120]

In his dissenting opinion, Judge Shahabuddeen took issue with the characterization of radiation effects of nuclear weapons as secondary and the ascription of legal significance to such characterization:

> [N]uclear weapons are not just another type of explosive weapons, only occupying a higher position on the same scale: their destructive power is exponentially greater. Apart from blast and heat, the radiation effects over time are devastating. To classify these effects as being merely a byproduct is not to the point; they can be just as extensive as, if not more so than, those immediately

---

[118] Dissenting opinion of Judge Weeramantry at 27, 35 I.L.M. at 894 (citing ENVIRONMENTAL CONSEQUENCES OF NUCLEAR WAR, Scope publication 28, released at the Royal Society, London, on January 6, 1986, Vol. 1, p. 481).

[119] Nuclear Weapons Advisory Opinion ¶ 54, at 20–21, 35 I.L.M. at 823–24.

[120] *Id.* ¶ 55, at 21, 35 I.L.M. at 824.

produced by blast and heat. They cause unspeakable sickness followed by painful death, affect the genetic code, damage the unborn, and can render the earth uninhabitable. These extended effects may not have military value for the user, but this does not lessen their gravity or the fact that they result from the use of nuclear weapons. This being the case, it is not relevant for present purposes to consider whether the injury produced is a byproduct or secondary effect of such use.

... [N]uclear fall-out may exert an impact on people long after the explosion ... thus presenting the disturbing and unique portrait of war being waged by a present generation on future ones—on future ones with which its successors could well be at peace.[121]

Judge Weeramantry in his dissenting opinion concluded that, since radiation is not only a major by-product but also a "natural and foreseeable" effect and a "major consequence" of the use of nuclear weapons, it "cannot in law be taken to be unintended," notwithstanding any characterization as "collateral."[122] He stated that the U.S. argument that the absence of specific intent precludes culpability "involves the legally unacceptable contention that if an act involves both legal and illegal consequences, the former justify or excuse the latter."[123]

Judge Koroma in his dissenting opinion stated:

At the very least, the use of nuclear weapons would violate the prohibition of the use of poison weapons as embodied in Article 23(a) of the Hague Convention of 1899 and 1907 as well as the Geneva Gas Protocol of 1925 which prohibits the use of poison gas and/or bacteriological weapons. Because of its universal adherence, the Protocol is considered binding on the international community as a whole. Furthermore, the prohibition of the use of poison gas is now regarded as part of customary international law binding on all States, and the finding by the Court in Paragraph B cannot be sustained in the face of the Geneva Conventions of 1949 and 1977 Additional Protocols thereto either.[124]

Judge Koroma further noted that the Court had decided in the *Nicaragua* case that the Geneva Conventions of 1949 are now recognized as part of customary international law binding on all

---

[121] Dissenting opinion of Judge Shahabuddeen at 6, 35 I.L.M at 864.

[122] Dissenting opinion of Judge Weeramantry at 58, 35 I.L.M. at 908.

[123] *Id.* Judge Weeramantry goes through detailed analyses of the text of the 1925 Geneva Gas Protocol and Article 23(a) of the Hague Regulation, concluding that they preclude the use of nuclear weapons. *Id.*

[124] Dissenting opinion of Judge Koroma at 18, 35 I.L.M. at 933.

States.[125] The judge added that Additional Protocol I to the Geneva Conventions of 1949 "constitutes a restatement and a reaffirmation of customary law rules based on the earlier Geneva and Hague Conventions."[126]

Agreed Limitations on Use of Nuclear Weapons

Reviewing numerous treaties addressing the acquisition, manufacture, possession, deployment and testing of nuclear weapons without setting forth a general prohibition, the Court concluded that such treaties "certainly point to an increasing concern in the international community with these weapons" and that such treaties could be seen as "foreshadowing a future general prohibition of the use of such weapons" but not as "constitut[ing] such a prohibition by themselves."[127]

The Court further summarized circumstances in which States, including nuclear weapons States, have agreed not to use nuclear weapons:

> • Treaty of Tlatelolco of 14 February 1967 for the Prohibition of Nuclear Weapons in Latin America, creating a nuclear-weapons-free zone in Latin America and prohibiting the use of nuclear weapons by the Contracting Parties. This treaty also contains an Additional Protocol II open to nuclear-weapon States outside the region whereby the signatory parties agree "not to use or threaten to use nuclear weapons against the Contracting Parties." In ratifying the Protocol, the United States made a declaration stating that it was free to reconsider the extent to which it would be committed by the Protocol in the event of aggression by a Contracting Party in which that Party was supported by a nuclear-weapon State.[128]
> • Treaty of Rarotonga of 6 August 1985 establishing a South Pacific Nuclear Free Zone in which the Parties undertake not to manufacture, acquire or possess any nuclear explosive device. Protocol 2, which is open to the five nuclear-weapon States, provides that each Party undertakes not to use or threaten to use any nuclear explosive device against Parties to the Treaty or against

---

[125] *Id.* (citing 1986 I.C.J. Reports 114).

[126] *Id.*

[127] Nuclear Weapons Advisory Opinion ¶ 76, at 24, 35 I.L.M. at 825.

[128] Nuclear Weapons Advisory Opinion ¶ 59(a), at 22, 35 I.L.M. at 824. Other nuclear States imposed further limitations on their ratification of the Protocol. *Id.*

any territory within the South Pacific Nuclear Free Zone for which a State that has become a Party is internationally responsible.[129]

• Treaty on the Non-Proliferation of Nuclear Weapons, as extended in 1995, whereby the "five nuclear-weapon States gave their non-nuclear weapon partners, by means of separate unilateral statements ... , positive and negative security assurances against the use of such weapons," subject, other than in the case of China, to "an exception in the case of an invasion or any other attack against them, their territories, armed forces or allies, or on a State towards which they had a security commitment, carried out or sustained by a non-nuclear-weapon State party to the Non-Proliferation Treaty in association or alliance with a nuclear-weapon State."[130]

• The Antarctic Treaty of 1959 which prohibits the deployment of nuclear weapons in the Antarctic.[131]

• Treaty on the Southeast Asia Nuclear-Weapon-Free-Zone signed on 15 December 1995 at Bangkok;[132] and

• Treaty on the Creation of a Nuclear-Weapons-Free-Zone in Africa signed on 1 April 1996 at Cairo.[133]

The Court concluded that such treaties did not "[amount] to a comprehensive and universal conventional prohibition on the use, or the threat of use" of nuclear weapons.[134] The Court further noted that, even in the cases of the treaties of Tlatelolco and Rarotonga and their Protocols and the declarations made in connection with the indefinite extension of the Treaty on the Non-Proliferation of Nuclear Weapons, while restrictions on use were imposed, the nuclear-weapon States reserved the right to use nuclear weapons in certain circumstances and such reservations "met with no objection from the parties to the Tlatelolco or Rarotonga Treaties or from the Security Council."[135]

Judge Oda in his dissenting opinion went through a detailed review of efforts at the United Nations and among individual States over many

---

[129] *See id.* ¶ 59(b), at 22–23, 35 I.L.M. at 824–25. The Court notes that, while China and Russia ratified the Protocol subject to a number of limitations, the United States, France, and the United Kingdom had signed but not ratified the Protocol, and, in the case of France and the United Kingdom, had interposed limitations on their signing. *Id.*

[130] *Id.* ¶ 59(c), at 23, 35 I.L.M. at 825.

[131] *See id.* ¶ 60, at 24, 35 I.L.M. at 825.

[132] *See id.* ¶ 63, at 25, 35 I.L.M. at 826.

[133] *See id.*

[134] *Id.* ¶ 63, at 25, 35 I.L.M. at 826.

[135] *Id.* ¶ 62, at 24–25.

years to limit or ban nuclear weapons, arguing that the former efforts implied the legality of nuclear weapons and the latter efforts failed.

Judge Oda further recited the unsuccessful efforts over many years by States opposing nuclear weapons to achieve an international convention prohibiting the use or threat of use of such weapons, concluding that the perceived need for such a convention shows that such actions were not already illegal and that the failure to enact a convention shows that the international community was not ready to ban such actions.[136]   The judge further reviewed the various international efforts at disarmament in the Post World War II period, including particularly the Non-Proliferation Treaty and the creation of nuclear free zones, to the same effect.[137]

Laying particular emphasis upon the Non-Proliferation Treaty regime ("NPT regime") and particularly its distinction between the five nuclear-weapon States and the non-nuclear weapons States, whereby the former were permitted to have nuclear weapons and the latter were not, Judge Oda concluded, "The doctrine, or strategy, of nuclear deterrence, however it may be judged and criticized from different angles and in different ways, was made a basis for the NPT regime which has been legitimized by international law, both conventional and customary, during the past few decades."[138]

Focusing on the "titanic tension between State practice and legal principle" which this case presents, Judge Schwebel in his dissent similarly concluded that the practice of the nuclear States in having and threatening the use of nuclear weapons, in being ready, willing and able to use them, precludes a finding of international custom prohibiting such use. [139]

Practice of Non-Use

The Court noted that members of the international community "are profoundly divided on the matter of whether non-recourse to nuclear weapons over the past fifty years constitutes the expression of an *opinio juris*"—*i.e.*, whether non-use resulted from "existing or nascent custom" or "merely because circumstances that might justify ... use

---

[136] Dissenting opinion of Judge Oda to the Nuclear Weapons Advisory Opinion at 11–18, 35 I.L.M. at 848–851 [hereinafter dissenting opinion of Judge Oda].

[137] *See id.* at 23–29, 35 I.L.M. at 854–57.

[138] *See id.* at 33, 35 I.L.M. at 859.

[139] *See* dissenting opinion of Judge Schwebel at 12, 35 I.L.M. at 842.

have fortunately not arisen."[140]   The Court concluded that in such circumstances, it could not find that there is such an *opinio juris*.[141]

Deterrence

The Court noted, as a central part of its overall conclusion, that the non-use of nuclear weapons during the nuclear era must be juxtaposed against the policy of deterrence, further noting that that policy requires that the threat to use such weapons be credible and implies a belief in the lawfulness of such use.[142]   The Court stated that it did not intend to pronounce on the validity of the policy of deterrence.[143]

The Court, however, in its discussion of the law applicable to threats, noted that, since the policy of deterrence is based on a threat to use nuclear weapons, the legality of the policy is subject to the rule that it is unlawful to threaten to do that which is unlawful. Hence, the lawfulness of deterrence depends on the lawfulness of use, which brings us right back where we started.

Judge Higgins in her dissenting opinion suggested that the belief in the lawfulness of the use *in extremis* of nuclear weapons which is implicit in the practice of deterrence evidences significant international

---

[140]   *Id.* ¶ 66–67, at 25. The Court noted that some States argued the existence of a customary rule prohibiting the use of nuclear weapons, citing the "consistent practice of non-utilization of nuclear weapons by States since 1945," while other States pointed to the practice of deterrence, whereby States "reserved the right to use [nuclear] weapons in the exercise of the right of self-defense against an armed attack threatening their vital security interests," noting that such States contended that the non-use of nuclear weapons "is not on account of an existing or nascent custom but merely because circumstances that might justify their use have fortunately not arisen." *Id.*

[141]   *See id.* ¶ 67, at 25, 35 I.L.M. at 826.

[142]   *See id.* ¶ 95, at 33, ¶ 66, at 25, 35 I.L.M. at 823, 826.

As to the argument that possession of nuclear weapons "is itself an unlawful threat to use force," the Court stated, "Possession of nuclear weapons may indeed justify an inference of preparedness to use them. In order to be effective, the policy of deterrence, by which those States possessing or under the umbrella of nuclear weapons seek to discourage military aggression by demonstrating that it will serve no purpose, necessitates that the intention to use nuclear weapons be credible." *Id.* ¶ 48, at 19, 35 I.L.M. at 823.

The Court further stated, "[N]o State—whether or not it defended the policy of deterrence—suggested to the Court that it would be lawful to threaten to use force if the use of force contemplated would be illegal." *Id.*

[143]   *See id.* ¶ 67, at 25, 35 I.L.M. at 826.

practice "which is surely relevant not only to the law of self-defense but also to humanitarian law."[144]

So also Judge Fleischhauer in his separate opinion saw deterrence in a particularly positive light—as based on the right of individual or collective self-defense and "as expressive of state practice in the legal sense."[145] He saw deterrence as reflecting State practice not only of the nuclear powers but also of the non-nuclear States supporting or tolerating the policy.[146]

Judge Oda, too, in his dissenting opinion, was also supportive of the policy of deterrence, seeing it as a basis for the Non-Proliferation regime and hence as "legitimized by international law, both conventional and customary, during the past few decades."[147]

So too Judge Guillaume concluded that the Court "ought to have carried its reasoning to its conclusion and explicitly recognized the legality of deterrence for defense of the vital interests of States."[148] Tying together the practice of deterrence with the Court's central recognition of a broad right of self-defense, Judge Guillaume, in what may be a central insight as to the meaning of the decision, stated,

---

[144] Dissenting opinion of Judge Higgins at 7, 35 I.L.M at 957. In the same vein, she stated: "[S]uch weight as may be given to the State practice just referred to has a relevance for our understanding of the complex provisions of humanitarian law as much as for the provisions of the Charter law of self-defense." *Id.*

[145] Separate opinion of Judge Fleischhauer at 4, 35 I.L.M at 836. Yet one must ask to what extent this is the case. The policy of deterrence can certainly be seen as evidencing the absence of a belief on the part of the nations following the policy that the use of nuclear weapons would be unlawful and hence as countering the argument that the fact that nuclear states have not used nuclear weapons means that they have recognized that such use would be unlawful. But, under the very principles applied by the Court, it would not seem that the practice of deterrence could be deemed in a positive sense to establish the lawfulness of the use of such weapons, for the policy can hardly be seen as followed out of a sense of obligation or duty.

[146] Individual opinion of Judge Fleischhauer at 3, 35 I.L.M. at 836.

Judge Fleischhauer also noted that deterrence is directed not only against the use of nuclear but also chemical and bacteriological weapons. *Id.* As we shall see, the same point was made by Judge Schwebel in his focus on U.S. threats of using nuclear weapons as deterring Iraq from using chemical or bacteriological weapons during the Gulf War. Dissenting opinion of Judge Schwebel at 9–12, 35 I.L.M. at 865–67.

[147] Dissenting opinion of Judge Oda at 33, 35 I.L.M. at 859.

[148] Individual opinion of Judge Guillaume, 35 I.L.M. at 1352–53 (No. 6, November 1996).

"States can resort to 'the threat or use of nuclear weapons ... in an extreme circumstance of self-defense, in which the very survival of a State would be at stake'. This has always been the foundation of the policy of deterrence whose legality is thus recognized."[149]

As to the content of this policy, Judge Schwebel, Vice-President of the Court, stated in his dissenting opinion, "The policy of deterrence differs from that of the threat to use nuclear weapons by its generality. But if a threat of possible use did not inhere in deterrence, deterrence would not deter."[150]

In a very pragmatic approach, Judge Schwebel presented in detail reports that, in advance of the Desert Storm operation against Iraq for its attack on Kuwait, the United States threatened Iraq that, if it used chemical or biological weapons, the United States would retaliate with nuclear weapons, and argues that the perceived success of this threat in deterring Iraq proves the lawfulness of the U.S. threat since it prevented an acceleration of the violence.[151] Judge Schwebel concluded:

> Thus there is on record remarkable evidence indicating that an aggressor was or may have been deterred from using outlawed weapons of mass destruction against forces and countries arrayed against its aggression at the call of the United Nations by what the aggressor perceived to be a threat to use nuclear weapons against it should it first use weapons of mass destruction against the forces of the coalition. Can it seriously be maintained that Mr. Baker's calculated—and apparently successful—threat was unlawful?[152]

Judge Schwebel concluded that, rather than being an example of the ends justifying the means, this experience rather "demonstrates that, in some circumstances, the threat of the use of nuclear weapons—as long as they remain weapons unproscribed by international law—may be both lawful and rational."[153]

Judge Koroma in his dissenting opinion characterized as "injudicious" the Court's ostensible giving of legal recognition to the doctrine of deterrence, objecting that deterrence, if implemented, could result in "catastrophic consequences for the civilian population not only of the belligerent parties but those of States not involved in such a

---

[149] *Id.* 35 I.L.M. at 1353–54.
[150] Dissenting opinion of Judge Schwebel at 3, 35 I.L.M. at 835.
[151] *Id.* at 12, 35 I.L.M. at 842.
[152] *Id.*
[153] *Id.*

conflict, and could result in the violation of international law in general and humanitarian law in particular."[154]

Judge Shi in his declaration objected to the Court's treating the policy of deterrence espoused by the nuclear weapons States and those under their umbrella as evidence of conduct formative of international custom and hence of law. Noting that such pro nuclear States represented a small portion of the over 185 State members of the international community, Judge Shi concluded that the Court had it backwards: The law should regulate deterrence rather than deterrence regulating (constituting) the law:

> In my view, "nuclear deterrence" is an instrument of policy which certain nuclear weapon States use in their relations with other States and which is said to prevent the outbreak of a massive armed conflict or war, and to maintain peace and security among nations. Undoubtedly, this practice of certain nuclear States is within the realm of international politics, not that of law. It has no legal significance from the standpoint of the formation of a customary rule prohibiting the use of nuclear weapons as such. Rather, the policy of nuclear deterrence should be an object of regulation by law, not *vice versa*. The Court, when exercising its judicial function of determining a rule of existing law governing the use of nuclear weapons, simply cannot have regard to this policy practice of certain States as, if it were to do so, it would be making the law accord with the needs of the policy of deterrence. The Court would not only be confusing policy with law, but also take a legal position with respect to the policy of nuclear deterrence, thus involving itself in international politics—which would be hardly compatible with its judicial function.[155]

Focusing on the sovereign equality of all States, Judge Shi rejected the notion that the views of the nuclear powers should be given special weight because of their superpower status:

> Also, leaving aside the nature of the policy of deterrence, this "appreciable section of the international community" adhering to the policy of deterrence is composed of certain nuclear weapon States and those States that accept the protection of the "nuclear umbrella." No doubt, these States are important and powerful members of the international community and play an important role on the stage of international politics. However, the Court, as the principal judicial organ of the United Nations, cannot view this "appreciable section of the international community" in terms of

---

[154] Dissenting opinion of Judge Koroma at 17, 35 I.L.M. at 933.
[155] Declaration of Judge Shi at 1, 35 I.L.M. at 833.

material power. The Court can only have regard to it from the standpoint of States. The appreciable section of this community to which the Opinion refers by no means constitutes a large proportion of that membership, and the structure of the international community is built on the principle of sovereign equality. Therefore, any undue emphasis on the practice of this "appreciable section" would not only be contrary to the very principle of sovereign equality of States, but would also make it more difficult to give an accurate and proper view of the existence of a customary rule on the use of the weapon.[156]

Judge Weeramantry in his dissenting opinion noted that deterrence goes beyond mere possession in that it implies a readiness to act, so that deterrence is distinguishable from mere possession.[157] Emphasizing the "problem of credibility," whereby the nuclear power must convince the deterred State that "there is a real intention to use those weapons in the event of an attack," Judge Weeramantry concluded that the fine points of "minimum deterrence"[158] and modulated nuclear action are unrealistic:

> [I]n the split second response to an armed attack, the finely graded use of appropriate strategic nuclear missiles or "clean" weapons which cause minimal damage does not seem a credible possibility.[159]

Judge Weeramantry stated:

> The concept of deterrence goes a step further than mere possession. Deterrence is more than the mere accumulation of weapons in a storehouse. It means the possession of weapons in a state of readiness for actual use. This means the linkage of weapons ready for immediate take-off with a command and control system geared for immediate actin. It means that weapons are attached to delivery vehicles. It means that personnel are ready night and day to render them operational at a moment's notice. There is clearly a vast difference between weapons stocked in a warehouse and weapons so readied for immediate action. Mere possession and deterrence are thus concepts which are clearly distinguishable from each other.[160]

---

[156] *Id.*
[157] Dissenting opinion of Judge Weeramantry at 77–78, 35 I.L.M at 918–19.
[158] *Id.* at 77, 35 I.L.M. at 918
[159] *Id.* at 78, 35 I.L.M. at 919.
[160] *Id.*

As to minimum deterrence, Judge Weeramantry stated:

> Deterrence can be of various degrees, ranging from the concept of maximum deterrence, to what is described as a minimum or near-minimum deterrent strategy. Minimum nuclear deterrence has been described as:
> Nuclear strategy in which a nation (or nations) maintains the minimum number of nuclear weapons necessary to inflict unacceptable damage on its adversary even after it has suffered a nuclear attack.
>
> ***
>
> One of the problems with deterrence, even of a minimal character, is that actions perceived by one side as defensive can all too easily be perceived by the other side as threatening. Such a situation is the classic backdrop to the traditional arms race, whatever be the type of weapons involved. With nuclear arms it triggers off a nuclear arms race, thus raising a variety of legal concerns. Even minimum deterrence thus leads to counter-deterrence, and to an ever ascending spiral of nuclear armament testing and tension. If, therefore, there are legal objections to deterrence, those objections are not removed by that deterrence being minimal.[161]

As to the element of intent contained in the policy of deterrence, Judge Weeramantry stated:

> Deterrence needs to carry the conviction to other parties that there is a real intention to use those weapons in the event of an attack by that other party. A game of bluff does not convey that intention, for it is difficult to persuade another of one's intention unless one really has that intention. Deterrence thus consists of a real intention to use such weapons. If deterrence is to operate, it leaves the world of make-believe and enters the field of seriously-intended military threats.[162]

---

[161] *Id.* at 77 (citing SECURITY WITHOUT NUCLEAR WEAPONS? DIFFERENT PERSPECTIVE ON NON-NUCLEAR SECURITY 250 (R.C. Karp ed., 1992), citing HOLLINS, POWERS & SOMMER, THE CONQUEST OF WAR, ALTERNATIVE STRATEGIES FOR GLOBAL SECURITY 54–55 (1989)).

[162] *Id.* at 78, 35 I.L.M. at 919 (citing generally, JUST WAR, NONVIOLENCE AND NUCLEAR DETERRENCE 193–205, 207–219 (D.L. Cady & R. Werner eds., 1991); JOSEPH BOYLE & GERMAIN GRISEZ, NUCLEAR DETERRENCE, MORALITY AND REALISM (1987); ANTHONY KENNY, THE LOGIC OF DETERRENCE AND THE IVORY TOWER (1985); ROGER RUSTON, NUCLEAR DETERRENCE—RIGHT OR WRONG? (1981) and *Nuclear Deterrence and the Use of the Just War Doctrine, in* OBJECTIONS TO NUCLEAR DEFENSE (Blake & Pole eds., 1984)).

Judge Bravo in his declaration concluded that the concept of deterrence has "no legal force" and is "not able to create a legal practice which could serve as the basis for the creation of an international custom."[163] He stated:

> [I]t is thanks to the doctrine of deterrence that the revolutionary scope of Article 2, paragraph 4, of the Charter has been reduced, while at the same time the scope of Article 51, which ran counter to it according to a traditional logic, has been extended as a whole series of conventional constructions have taken shape around that norm, as can be seen from the two systems governing respectively the Atlantic Alliance on the one hand and on the other the Warsaw Pact, while it was in existence. These are systems which are doubtless governed by legal rules but which proceed from an idea derived essentially from the political—and hence not legal—finding according to which the Security Council cannot function in the face of a conflict as major as the type of warfare which is the subject of the present Advisory Opinion would probably be.
>
> In this way, the gulf separating Article 2, paragraph 4, from Article 51 may be compared to a river which has grown wider, thanks largely to the tremendous rock of deterrence which has been thrown into it ... .[164]

U.N. General Assembly Resolutions

Noting the annual resolutions of the General Assembly since 1961, by substantial majority votes, proclaiming the illegality of the use of nuclear weapons, the Court, while stating that such votes can have a normative value, concluded that the substantial negative votes and abstentions precluded the resolutions from establishing the existence of an *opinio juris* on the illegality of the use of such weapons.[165]

---

[163] Declaration of Judge Bravo at 3, 35 I.L.M. at 1349.

[164] *Id.* at 1349–50.

[165] Nuclear Weapons Advisory Opinion ¶ 70–73, at 26–27 35 I.L.M. at 826–27. Judge Oda in his dissenting opinion reviewed at length the history of General Assembly resolutions on the subject, concluding that there was a substantial divergence of opinion among States on the issue. Dissenting opinion of Judge Oda at 11–23, 35 I.L.M. at 848–851.

Judge Bravo in his declaration concluded that the resolutions beginning with resolution 1 (I) of 24 January 1946 and extending "at least" down to resolution 808 (IX), all of which were unanimously adopted, constituted "fundamental" documents in effect "on the same footing as the provisions of the Charter." Declaration of Judge Bravo at 2, 35 I.L.M. at 1349.

Judge Bravo saw such resolutions as "establish[ing] the existence of an actual undertaking of a solemn nature to eliminate all atomic weapons whose

International Humanitarian Law

The Court defined "international humanitarian law" as that body of laws and customs of war memorialized in the various Hague and Geneva Conventions and, most recently, in the Additional Protocols of 1977, which "give expression and attest to the unity and complexity of that law."[166]

The Court cited the Hague Regulations for the overall points that "the right of belligerents to adopt means of injuring the enemy is not unlimited" and for the prohibition of the use of "arms, projectiles, or material calculated to cause unnecessary suffering," the St. Petersburg Declaration for the prohibition against the use of weapons "which uselessly aggravate the suffering of disabled men or make their death inevitable."[167]

The Court stated:

> 78. The cardinal principles contained in the texts constituting the fabric of humanitarian law are the following. The first is aimed at the protection of the civilian population and civilian objects and establishes the distinction between combatants and non-combatants; States must never make civilians the object of attack

---

presence in military arsenals was considered illegal." *Id.* Judge Bravo added that it was the eruption of the Cold War that "prevented the development of that concept of illegality (which was subsequently abandoned by the United States which had been its promoter)." *Id.* at 1349. Judge Bravo concluded that, as a result of these political developments, a division of view developed in the 1960's on this issue between the nuclear weapon States (and their allies) on the one hand and the States threatened by the bomb on the other.

Judge Bravo concluded that the original recognition of the illegality of the use of nuclear weapons "has remained the same and still operates, at least at the level of the burden of proof, rendering it more difficult for the nuclear-weapon States to justify themselves by references to various applications of the theory of deterrence." *Id.* at 1349.

[166] Nuclear Weapons Advisory Opinion ¶ 7, at 27, 35 I.L.M. at 827.

Judge Weeramantry described the international law applicable generally to armed conflicts as *jus in bello* or "the humanitarian law of war," as contrasted with *jus ad bellum,* the law governing the right of states to go to war, stating that the latter is expressed in the United Nations Charter and related customary law. Dissenting opinion of Judge Weeramantry at 8. *See also* review of the principles of humanitarian law in Judge Koroma's dissenting opinion in the WHO Advisory Decision proceeding, 1996 I.C.J. 68, 182–85.

[167] Nuclear Weapons Advisory Opinion ¶ 77, at 28, 35 I.L.M. at 827 (citing Arts. 22 and 23 of the 1907 Hague Regulations relating to the laws and customs of war on land and The St. Petersburg Declaration).

and must consequently never use weapons that are incapable of distinguishing between civilian and military targets. According to the second principle, it is prohibited to cause unnecessary suffering to combatants: it is accordingly prohibited to use weapons causing them such harm or uselessly aggravating their suffering. In application of that second principle, States do not have unlimited freedom of choice of means in the weapons they use.[168]

The Court characterized the Martens Clause, first contained in the Hague Convention II with Respect to the Laws and Customs of War on Land of 1899, as "an effective means of addressing the rapid evolution of military technology."[169] The Court cited a "modern version" of that clause contained in Article 2, paragraph 2, of Additional Protocol I of 1977:

> In cases not covered by this Protocol or by other international agreements, civilians and combatants remain under the protection and authority of the principles of international law derived from established custom, from the principles of humanity and from the dictates of public conscience.[170]

The Court noted that the Nuremberg International Military Tribunal found in 1945 that the humanitarian rules included in the Hague Regulations "'were recognized by all civilized nations and were regarded as being declaratory of the laws and customs of war'."[171] The Court characterized the fundamental rules of international humanitarian law as "intransgressible principles of international customary law,

---

[168] Nuclear Weapons Advisory Opinion ¶ 78, at 28, 35 I.L.M. at 827.

[169] *Id.* Judge Weeramantry in his dissenting opinion noted that the Martens Clause is an established part of international law. He quoted the decision in the *Krupp Trial* (1948) as recognizing the clause as:

> a general clause, making the usages established among civilized nations, the laws of humanity and the dictates of the public conscience into the legal yardstick to be applied if and when the specific provisions of the Convention and the Regulations annexed to it do not cover specific case occurring in warfare, or concomitant to warfare.

Dissenting opinion of Judge Weeramantry at 39, 35 I.L.M. at 890.

The judge goes on to analyze at length the bases upon which he concludes that the dictates of the public conscience have rejected nuclear weapons. *Id.* at 39, 40–42, 35 I.L.M. at 900–01.

[170] Nuclear Weapons Advisory Opinion ¶ 78, at 28, 35 I.L.M. at 827.

[171] *Id.* ¶ 80 at 28, 35 I.L.M. at 827 (citing International Military Tribunal, Trial of the Major War Criminals, 14 November 1945–1 October 1946, Nuremberg, 1947, Vol. 1, p. 254).

which are to be observed by all States whether or not they have ratified the conventions that contain them."[172]

The Court emphasized that such principles apply to nuclear weapons even though the "evolution" of the principles pre-dated the invention and development of such weapons. The Court stated that the "intrinsically humanitarian character of the legal principles in question ... permeates the entire law of armed conflict and applies to all forms of warfare and to all kinds of weapons, those of the past, those of the present and those of the future."[173]

Judge Shahabuddeen stated in his dissenting opinion that if the principle of moderation "can apply to bar the use of some weapons, it is difficult to imagine how it could fail to bar the use of nuclear weapons."[174]

In a point that becomes integral to my analysis of the issue, Judge Shahabuddeen noted that the application of humanitarian law is not dependent upon the agreement of States with respect to the particular application:

> [W]hat is in issue is not the existence of the principle, but its application in a particular case. Its application does not require proof of the coming into being of an *opinio juris* prohibiting the use of the particular weapons; if that were so, one would be in the strange presence of a principle which could not be applied without proof of an *opinio juris* to support each application.[175]

Judge Weeramantry made a similar point:

> While no state today would repudiate any one of these principles [of customary international law], what seems to be in dispute is the application of those principles to the specific case of nuclear

---

[172] Nuclear Weapons Advisory Opinion ¶ 79, at 28, 35 I.L.M. at 827. The Court further noted:

> The extensive codification of humanitarian law and the extent of the accession to the resultant treaties, as well as the fact that the denunciation clauses that existed in the codification instruments have never been used, have provided the international community with a corpus of treaty rules the great majority of which had already become customary and which reflected the most universally recognized humanitarian principles. These rules indicate the normal conduct and behavior expected of States.

Id. ¶ 82, at 29, 35 I.L.M. at 828.

[173] *Id.* ¶ 86, at 30, 35 I.L.M. at 828.

[174] Dissenting opinion of Judge Shahabuddeen at 17, 35 I.L.M. at 869.

[175] *Id.*

weapons which, for some unarticulated reason, seem to be placed above and beyond the rules applicable to other weapons. If humanitarian law regulates the lesser weapons for fear that they may cause the excessive harm which those principles seek to prevent, it must a fortiori regulate the greater. The attempt to place nuclear weapons beyond the reach of these principles lacks the support not only of the considerations of humanity, but also of the considerations of logic.[176]

Judge Shahabuddeen further stated as to the meaning of the Martens Clause:

> In effect, the Martens Clause provided authority for treating the principles of humanity and the dictates of public conscience as principles of international law, leaving the precise content of the standard implied by these principles of international law to be ascertained in the light of changing conditions, inclusive of changes in the means and methods of warfare and the outlook and tolerance levels of the international community. The principles would remain constant, but their practical effect would vary from time to time: they could justify a method of warfare in one age and prohibit it in another. In this respect, M. Jean Pictet was right in emphasizing, according to Mr. Sean McBride, "that the Declarations in the *Hague Conventions* ... by virtue of the Martens Clause, imported into humanitarian law principles that went much further than the written convention: it thus gave them a dynamic dimension that was not limited by time."[177]

Judge Shahabuddeen concluded that the Martens Clause, rather than simply "supplying a humanitarian standard by which to interpret separately existing rules of conventional or customary international law on the subject of the conduct of hostilities," itself constituted an independent rule in its own right:

> Thus, the Martens Clause provided its own self-sufficient and conclusive authority for the proposition that there were already in existence principles of international law under which considerations of humanity could themselves exert legal force to govern military conduct in cases in which no relevant rule was provided by conventional law. Accordingly, it was not necessary

---

[176] Dissenting opinion of Judge Weeramantry at 40, 35 I.L.M. at 900.

[177] Dissenting opinion of Judge Shahabuddeen at 22, 35 I.L.M. at 872 (quoting Sean McBride, *The Legality of Weapons for Societal Destruction, in* STUDIES AND ESSAYS ON INTERNATIONAL HUMANITARIAN LAW AND RED CROSS PRINCIPLES IN HONOUR OF JEAN PICTET 402 (Christophe Swinarski ed., Geneva 1984)).

to locate elsewhere the independent existence of such principles of international law; the source of the principles lay in the Clause itself.[178]

Much of the law of war is made of broad principles, but this does not detract from its nature as law. Judge Weeramantry in his dissenting opinion stated, "As observed by the 1945 Nuremberg Tribunal, which dealt with undefined 'crimes against humanity' and other crimes, '[the law of war] is not static, but by continual adaptation follows the needs of a changing world.'"[179] He noted the question at hand called upon the Court to "scrutinize every available source of international law, quarrying deep, if necessary, into its very bedrock," noting that "[s]eams of untold strength and richness lie therein, waiting to be quarried."[180]

In response to the U.S. argument that the use of nuclear weapons cannot be deemed unlawful over the objection of the United States and other nuclear powers and their protégés espousing the practice of deterrence and the lawfulness of the use of such weapons since customary law cannot be created over the objection of the nuclear weapon States, Judge Weeramantry in his dissenting opinion pointed

---

[178] *Id.* at 23, 35 I.L.M. at 872. Judge Shahabuddeen further stated:

A similar view of the role of considerations of humanity appears in the *Corfu Channel* case. There Judge Alvarez stated that the "characteristics of an international delinquency are that it is an act contrary to the sentiments of humanity" ... and the Court itself said that Albania's "obligations are based, not on the Hague Convention of 1907, No. VIII, which is applicable in time of war, but on certain general and well-recognized principles namely: elementary considerations of humanity, even more exacting in peace than in war; ...." Thus, Albania's obligations were "based ... on ... elementary considerations of humanity ...," with the necessary implication that those considerations can themselves exert legal force. In 1986 the Court considered that "the conduct of the United States may be judged according to the fundamental general principles of humanitarian law"; and it expressed the view that certain rules stated in common Article 3 of the 1949 Geneva Conventions were "rules which, in the Court's opinion, reflect what the Court in 1949 called "elementary considerations of humanity...."

Id. at 22–23, 35 I.L.M. at 872.

[179] Dissenting opinion of Judge Weeramantry at 9, 35 I.L.M. at 884 (citing 22 Trial of the Major War Criminals before the International Military Tribunal, 1948 at 464).

[180] *Id.* at 5–6, 35 I.L.M. at 882–883.

out that the case for illegality (and the conclusion of illegality, as he finds it), is based on established general principles which preexist nuclear weapons: "The general principles of customary law applicable to [this issue] commanded the allegiance of the nuclear weapon States long before nuclear weapons were invented."[181] He added, "It is on those general principles that the illegality of nuclear weapons rests."[182]

As to the criteria for recognition of a rule of customary international law, Judge Weeramantry states the "widely accepted test" is that the rule be "so widely and generally accepted that it can hardly be supposed that any civilized State would repudiate it."[183]

Judge Weeramantry noted the characterization of the Martens Clause in the *Krupp Trial* as:

> a general clause, making the usages established among civilised nations, the laws of humanity and the dictates of the public conscience into the legal yardstick to be applied if and when the specific provisions of the Convention and the Regulations annexed to it do not cover specific cases occurring in warfare, or concomitant to warfare.[184]

Judge Schwebel identified the principles of proportionality, necessity, and discrimination as the primary principles of humanitarian law pre-dating the invention of nuclear weapons and applicable thereto.[185]

Jus Cogens

The term *jus cogens* is used to describe the most established and assimilated principles of international law. The Court in its decision declined to decide whether the principles and rules of humanitarian law applicable to the use of nuclear weapons have become part of the *jus cogens*, stating that the question presented to it for decision related to the application of such principles and rules to the use of nuclear weapons and not to "the character of [this] humanitarian law."[186]

---

[181] *Id.* at 40, 35 I.L.M. at 900.

[182] *Id.*

[183] *Id.* (citing West Rand Central Gold Mining Co., Ltd. v. R (1905), 2 KB, at 407).

[184] *Id.* at 39, 35 I.L.M. at 899.

[185] Dissenting opinion of Judge Schwebel, Vice-President of the Court, at 1, 35 I.LM. at 836.

[186] Nuclear Weapons Advisory Opinion ¶ 83, at 29, 35 I.L.M. at 828.

Judge Weeramantry in his dissenting opinion stated that the rules of humanitarian law are "fundamental rules of a humanitarian character, from

President Bedjaoui, in his separate declaration, found that "most of the principles and rules of humanitarian law and, in any event, the two principles, one of which prohibits the use of weapons with indiscriminate effects and the other use of arms causing unnecessary suffering, are a part of *jus cogens*."[187] President Bedjaoui noted that the Court had found that the fundamental rules of humanitarian law are "intransgressible principles of international customary law."[188]

Judge Koroma in his dissent criticized the Court's failure to recognize the status of the principles of humanitarian law as *jus cogens*, stating that there is "almost universal adherence to the fact that the Geneva Conventions of 1949 are declaratory of customary international law," and that in the *Reservations* case, the Court had recognized that the Genocide Convention had been adopted "for a purely humanitarian and civilizing purpose, 'to safeguard the very existence of certain human groups and ... to confirm and endorse the most elementary principles of humanity'."[189]

---

which no derogation is possible without negating the basic considerations of humanity which they are intended to protect," and have become part of the *jus cogens*. *Id.* at 46, 35 I.L.M. at 903 (citing Roberto Ago, RECUEIL DES COURS, at 324 n.37 (1971-III), and LAURI HANNIKAINEN, PEREMPTORY NORMS (JUS COGENS) IN INTERNATIONAL LAW 596–715 (1988)).

Judge Koroma in his dissenting opinion expressed the same conclusion, noting that there is "almost universal adherence to the fact that the Geneva Conventions of 1949 are declaratory of customary international law, and there is community interest and consensus in the observance of and respect for their provisions." Dissenting opinion of Judge Koroma at 13, 35 I.L.M. at 931.

Judge Higgins in her dissenting opinion states that the key elements of humanitarian law stem from a variety of "uncontested sources," such as the Petersburg Declaration of 11 December 1868, and the Regulations annexed to the Hague Convention IV, 1907, Articles 22 and 23(e), and that the Court had recognized that the Nuremberg Military Tribunal had found the Regulations annexed to Hague Convention IV to have become part of customary international law by 1939. Dissenting opinion of Judge Higgins at 2, 35 I.L.M. at 935. Judge Higgins defined "uncontested sources" as meaning ones not dependent on provisions of additional Protocol I nor upon any views as to the application of such provisions to nuclear weapons. *Id.*

[187] Declaration of President Bedjaoui ¶ 21, 35 I.L.M. at 1345 (No. 6 November 1996).

[188] *Id.* ¶ 21 at 1345, (No. 6, November 1996) (citing the Court's opinion ¶ 79 and the *Corfu Channel* case, I.C.J. Reports 1949, at 22 (9 April 1949)).

[189] Dissenting opinion of Judge Koroma at 13, 35 I.L.M. at 931 (citing the *Reservations* case, 1951 I.C.J. Reports 23). Judge Koroma further cited the Court's reference in the *Corfu Channel* case to "certain general and well-

Principle of Discrimination/Civilian Immunity

The Court recognized as the first of the "cardinal principles" of humanitarian law the protection of the civilian population and civilian objects and the distinction between combatants and non-combatants: "States must never make civilians the object of attack and must consequently never use weapons that are incapable of distinguishing between civilian and military targets."[190] Weapons that will have an "indiscriminate effect on combatants and civilians" are prohibited.[191]

As noted above, the application of this principle was a central focus of the Court's opinion, with the Court ultimately determining that the use of nuclear weapons seemed "scarcely reconcilable" with this principle or with the prohibition of unnecessary suffering, but that the Court did not have sufficient facts to determine the issue, particularly whether there existed smaller, low-yield tactical nuclear weapons capable of "clean" use.

President Bedjaoui stated in his declaration:

> 20. Nuclear weapons can be expected—in the present state of scientific development at least—to cause indiscriminate victims among combatants and non-combatants alike ... The very nature of this blind weapon therefore has a destabilizing effect on humanitarian law which regulates discernment in the type of weapon used. Nuclear weapons, the ultimate evil, destabilize humanitarian law which is the law of the lesser evil. The existence of nuclear weapons is therefore a challenge to the very existence of humanitarian law, not to mention their long-term effects of damage to the human environment, in respect to which the right to life can be exercised. Until scientists are able to develop a "clean" nuclear weapon which would distinguish between combatants and non-combatants, nuclear weapons will clearly have indiscriminate effects and constitute an absolute challenge to humanitarian law. Atomic warfare and humanitarian law therefore appear to be mutually exclusive: the existence of the one automatically implies the non-existence of the other.[192]

Judge Weeramantry in his dissenting opinion concluded that non-discrimination is built into the very nature of nuclear weapons: "A

---

recognized, namely, elementary considerations of humanity, even more exacting in peace than in war." *Id.* (citing I.C.J. Reports 1949, p. 223).

[190] Nuclear Weapons Advisory Opinion ¶ 78 at 28, 35 I.L.M. at 827.

[191] *Id.*

[192] Declaration of President Bedjaoui, 35 I.L.M. at 1349 ¶ 20 (No. 6 November 1996).

weapon that can flatten a city and achieve by itself the destruction caused by thousands of individual bombs, is not a weapon that discriminates."[193] Judge Koroma in his dissenting opinion concluded that, based on the "established facts," nuclear weapons are "unable to discriminate between combatants and non-combatants [and] cannot spare hospitals or prisoner-of-war camps."[194]

Judge Higgins in her dissent identified the major legal issues in this area that in her view the Court should have addressed:

> [D]oes the prohibition against civilians being the object of attack preclude attack upon a military target if it is realized that collateral civilian casualties will be unavoidable? And in the light of the answer to the above question, what then is meant by the requirements that a weapon must be able to discriminate between civilian and military targets and how will this apply to nuclear weapons?[195]

Judge Higgins also addressed an interesting question in this area: If the prohibition is only on strikes making civilians the "object" of attack, so that incidental or collateral injury to civilians is not prohibited, what, if any, limits are there on the extent of permitted civilian injuries? Judge Higgins' answer is that the principle of proportionality applies, with the effect that "even a legitimate target may not be attacked if the collateral civilian casualties would be disproportionate to the specific military gain from the attack."[196]

Judge Higgins then poses the ultimate question: "whether, if a target is legitimate and the use of a nuclear weapon is the only way of destroying that target, any need can ever be so necessary as to occasion massive collateral damage upon civilians."[197] Her answer is that in such circumstances the "military advantage" must be one "related to the very survival of a State or the avoidance of infliction (whether by

---

[193] Dissenting opinion of Judge Weeramantry at 48, 35 I.L.M. at 904.

An example is implicit in the judge's quoting the statement by the Mayor of Nagasaki that the bombing of Dresden by 773 British aircraft followed by attacks by an additional 450 American aircraft dropping 650,000 bombs resulted in some 135,000 deaths, a similar number to the dead in Hiroshima. *Id.* at 19, 35 I.L.M. 809, 889. Presumably there was at least the potential—in terms of the capability of the weapons involved—to make a good faith effort to limit the attacks to appropriate military targets.

[194] Dissenting opinion of Judge Koroma at 19, 35 I.L.M. at 889.

[195] Dissenting opinion of Judge Higgins at 4, 35 I.L.M. at 936.

[196] *Id.*

[197] *Id.*

nuclear or other weapons of mass destruction) of vast and severe suffering on its own population; and that no other method of eliminating this military target be available."[198]

Judge Higgins stated that the principle of discrimination flows from the "basic rule" that civilians may not be the target of attack. She stated that there is an unresolved debate as to whether the rule of discrimination (1) "refers to weapons which, because of the way they are commonly used, strike civilians and combatants indiscriminately" or (2) "refers to whether a weapon 'having regard to [its] effects in time and space' can 'be employed with sufficient or with predictable accuracy against the chosen target'."[199] The judge concluded: "For this concept to have a separate existence, distinct from that of collateral harm (with which it overlaps to an extent), and whichever interpretation of the term is chosen, it may be concluded that a weapon will be unlawful *per se* if it is incapable of being targeted at a military objective only, even if collateral harm occurs."[200]

Applying this requirement, Judge Higgins stated that nuclear weapons are not "monolithic" in all their effects, suggesting that the evaluation must be made in individual cases.[201]

Judge Fleischhauer in his separate opinion concluded that "The nuclear weapon cannot distinguish between civilian and military targets [and] causes immeasurable suffering."[202]

Judge Guillaume in his individual opinion regarded as the "one absolute prohibition" of customary humanitarian law the "prohibition of so-called 'blind' weapons which are incapable of distinguishing

---

[198] *Id.*

[199] *Id.* at 5, 35 I.L.M. at 936 (citing *Weapons that May Cause Unnecessary Suffering or have Indiscriminate Effects*, Report of the Work of Experts, published by the ICRC, 1973; Conference of Government Experts on the Use of Certain Conventional Weapons (Lucerne, 1974), Report published by the ICRC, 1975 at ¶ 31, 10–11; Kalshoven, *Arms, Armaments and Interpretation of Law*, RECUEIL DES COURS, at 236 (1985, II)).

[200] *Id.* For purposes of whether there is a *per se* rule, Judge Higgins appears to be adopting the second approach: For the strike to be unlawful *per se*, the weapon must be unable to hit the legitimate target, without regard to whether it will also, indiscriminately, hit civilians. If the strike can hit the target but will also hit civilians indiscriminately, Judge Higgins would apparently apply a proportionality evaluation on an ad hoc basis. *See id.* at 4.

[201] *Id.* at 5.

[202] Individual opinion of Judge Fleischhauer at 1, 35 I.L.M. at 834.

between civilian targets and military targets," concluding that nuclear weapons "obviously do not necessarily fall into this category."[203]

Principle of Necessity

The Court recognized as the second of the "cardinal principles" of humanitarian law the prohibition of causing unnecessary suffering to combatants and hence of using weapons causing such harm or uselessly aggravating their suffering. The Court stated that this is a limit on the weapons that a State may use, and defined unnecessary harm to combatants as harm "greater than that unavoidable to achieve legitimate military objectives."[204]

For this principle, the Court cited the St. Petersburg Declaration, condemning the use of weapons "which uselessly aggravate the suffering of disabled men or make their death inevitable" and the Hague Regulations which prohibit the use of "arms, projectiles, or material calculated to cause unnecessary suffering."[205]

President Bedjaoui, besides finding nuclear weapons to violate the principle of discrimination in the language quoted above, also found them to violate the principle of necessity, stating that nuclear weapons in their present state cause unnecessary suffering among combatants and non-combatants alike.[206] He further concluded that the prohibition of causing unnecessary or indiscriminate effects is part of the *jus cogens*.[207]

Judge Higgins in her dissenting opinion examined this principle at greater length, focusing the issue not on the extent of injury caused but rather the degree of military necessity. She described this rule as involving a balancing of necessity and humanity, stating that this is why certain extremely destructive weapons (such as incendiary projectiles, flame-throwers, napalm, high velocity weapons) are not specifically prohibited while other less destructive weapons (such as dum-dum bullets) are.[208]

Judge Higgins cited the Lucerne Conference of Governments' definition of "unnecessary" suffering as "some sort of equation

---

[203] Individual opinion of Judge Guillaume ¶ 5, 35 I.L.M. at 1352 (No. 6, November 1996).
[204] Nuclear Weapons Advisory Opinion ¶ 78, at 28, 35 I.L.M. at 827.
[205] *Id.* ¶ 77, at 28.
[206] *See* Declaration of President Bedjaoui ¶ 20, 35 I.L.M. at 1345 (No.6 November 1996).
[207] *See id.* at ¶ 21.
[208] Dissenting opinion of Judge Higgins at 3, 35 I.L.M. at 935.

between, on the one hand, the degree of injury or suffering inflicted (the humanitarian aspect) and, on the other, the degree of necessity underlying the choice of a particular weapon (the military aspect)."[209]

Judge Higgins indicated that the concept of military necessity entails a "'balancing' or 'equation' rather than a prohibition against a significant degree or even a vast amount of suffering."[210]   She summarized the rule:

> 17. The prohibition against unnecessary suffering and superfluous injury is a protection for the benefit of military personnel that is to be assessed by reference to the necessity of attacking the particular military target. The principle does not stipulate that a legitimate target is not to be attacked if it would cause great suffering.[211]

Judge Higgins went on to address what she described as the critical question: "what military necessity is so great that the sort of suffering that would be inflicted on military personnel by the use of nuclear weapons would ever be justified?"[212]

She first considered whether the use of tactical nuclear weapons could ever meet the test of necessity, concluding that the Court rightly concludes the evidence to be uncertain on that point. She went on to state: "If the suffering is of the sort traditionally associated with the use of nuclear weapons—blast, radiation, shock, together with risk of escalation, risk of spread through space and time—then only the most extreme circumstances (defense against untold suffering or the obliteration of a State or peoples) could conceivably "balance" the equation between necessity and humanity."[213]

Judge Koroma in his dissenting opinion concluded that the use of nuclear weapons "can cause suffering out of all proportion to military necessity leaving their victims to die as a result of burns after weeks of agony, or to be afflicted for life with painful infirmities."[214]

Judge Guillaume in his individual opinion noted that the application of the principle of necessity like that of proportionality implies a comparison: "The suffering caused to combatants must not be 'unnecessary', *i.e.*, it must not cause, in the words of the Court itself, 'a

---

[209] *Id.* (citing Conference Report, Lucerne Conference of Governmental Experts, published by ICRC, 1975, at ¶ 23).

[210] *Id.*

[211] *Id.*

[212] *Id.* at 4, 35 I.L.M. at 936.

[213] *Id.*

[214] Dissenting opinion of Judge Koroma at 19, 35 I.L.M. at 934.

harm greater than that unavoidable to achieve legitimate military objectives' (para. 78)."[215]

Judge Shahabuddeen elaborated on the content of the rule of necessity:

> [S]uffering is superfluous or unnecessary if it is materially in excess of the degree of suffering which is justified by the military advantage sought to be achieved. A mechanical or absolute test is excluded: a balance has to be struck between the degree of suffering inflicted and the military advantage in view. The greater the military advantage, the greater will be the willingness to tolerate higher levels of suffering.[216]

Judge Weeramantry in his dissenting opinion emphasized that military necessity cannot override humanitarian law, referring to "the collapse of that doctrine, if indeed it had ever existed."[217]

Principle of Neutrality

The Court recognizes the law of neutrality as a central part of the law of armed conflict, but fails in the decision to come to grips with the content and application of such law.

The Court sets the issue up by quoting from the Written Statement of one State (Nauru) to the effect that, "The principle of neutrality applies with equal force to transborder incursions of armed forces and to the transborder damage caused to a neutral State by the use of a weapon in a belligerent State."[218] The Court further notes that the principle of neutrality has been "considered by some to rule out the use of a weapon the effects of which simply cannot be contained within the territories of the contending States."[219]

---

[215] Individual opinion of Judge Guillaume ¶ 5, 35 I.L.M. at 1352 (No.6 November 1996).

[216] Dissenting opinion of Judge Shahabuddeen at 19, 35 I.L.M. at 870.

[217] Dissenting opinion of Judge Weeramantry at 82, 35 I.L.M. at 921 (citing the case of the *Peleus* (*War Crimes Reports*, 1-16 i (1946)) relating to submarine warfare, decided by a British military court; the *Milch* case (WAR CRIMES TRIALS 7, 44–65 (1948)), decided by the United States Military Tribunal at Nuremberg; and the *Krupp* case (WAR CRIMES TRIALS 10, 138 (1949)), addressing the question of grave economic necessity).

[218] Nuclear Weapons Advisory Opinion ¶ 88, at 31, 35 I.L.M. at 829 (citing Legality of the Use by a State of Nuclear Weapons in Armed Conflict, Nauru, Written Statement (I), at 35. IV E.).

[219] Nuclear Weapons Advisory Opinion ¶ 93, at 32, 35 I.L.M. at 829.

This, of course, is the issue: Does the right of neutrality preclude the use of nuclear weapons whose effects in terms of radiation or otherwise will enter the territory of a neutral State?

The Court does not apply the principle to the case at hand or define its parameters, but rather only states that the principle, "whatever its content," is a fundamental one applicable "(subject to the relevant provisions of the United Nations Charter), to all international armed conflict, whatever type of weapons might be used."[220]

Judge Shahabuddeen in his dissent adopted the position in Nauru's statement that the right of neutrality protected against transborder damage caused to a neutral State by the use of a weapon in a belligerent State.[221] While acknowledging the U.S. point that neutrality does not accord the neutral "absolute immunity," the judge concluded that the potential effects on neutrals of the use of nuclear weapons were too great not to be within the protection of neutrality:

> [R]adiation effects ... extend to the inhabitants of neutral States and causes damage to them, their off-spring, their natural resources, and possibly put them under the necessity to leave their traditional homelands. ... Whether direct or indirect ... [radiation effects] result from the use of nuclear weapons, for it is a property of such weapons that they emit radiation; their destructive effect on the enemy is largely due to their radiation effects. Such radiation has a high probability of transboundary penetration.[222]

Judge Shahabuddeen acknowledged the point (which had been made by the United States) that there was no precedent on this point, but concluded that radiation posed a new situation, a new danger to neutrals, and one which came within the protection of the inviolability of the neutral's territory.[223]

---

[220] *Id.* ¶ 89, at 31, 35 I.LM. at 829.

[221] Dissenting opinion of Judge Shahabuddeen at 9, 35 I.L.M. at 865.

[222] *Id.* Judge Shahabuddeen stated:

[T]he use of nuclear weapons could result, even in the case of neutral countries, in destruction of the living, in sickness and forced migration of survivors, and in injury to future generations to the point of causing serious illness, deformities and death, with the possible extinction of all life.

Id. at 24, 35 I.L.M. at 873.

[223] *Id.* at 9, 35 I.L.M. at 865. Judge Shahabuddeen stated:

To say that [radiation] and other transboundary effects of the use of nuclear weapons do not violate the neutrality of third States in the absence of belligerent incursion or transboundary bombardment is to cast too heavy a burden on the proposition that neutrality is not

Judge Weeramantry in his dissenting opinion cited Chernobyl as an example of the transboundary effects of radiation, noting that people were affected over large areas in many countries, including in Belarus, Russia, Ukraine, and Sweden, and that overall some nine million people have been affected in some way, since "the by-products of that nuclear reaction could not be contained."[224]

---

an absolute guarantee of immunity to third States against all possible effects of the conduct of hostilities. The Fifth Hague Convention of 1907 does not define inviolability; nor does it say that the territory of a neutral State is violated only by belligerent incursion or bombardment. Accepting nevertheless that the object of the architects of the provision was to preclude military incursion or bombardment of neutral territory, it seems to me that that purpose, which was related to the then state of warfare, does not conclude the question whether, in terms of the principle, "the territory of neutral powers" is violated where that territory and its inhabitants are physically harmed by the effects of the use elsewhere of nuclear weapons in the ways in which it is possible for such harm to occur. The causes of the consequential suffering and the suffering itself are the same as those occurring in the zone of battle.

Id. at 9–10, 35 I.L.M. at 865–866.

[224] Dissenting opinion of Judge Weeramantry at 23, 35 I.L.M. at 891. Judge Weeramantry stated:

The transboundary effects of radiation are illustrated by the nuclear meltdown in Chernobyl which had devastating effects over a vast area, as the by-products of that nuclear reaction could not be contained. Human health, agricultural and diary produce and the demography of thousands of square miles were affected in a manner never known before. On 30 November 1995, the United Nation's Under-Secretary-General for Humanitarian Affairs announced that thyroid cancers, many of them being diagnosed in children, are 285 times more prevalent in Belarus than before the accident, that about 375,000 people in Belarus, Russia and Ukraine remain displaced and often homeless—equivalent to numbers displaced in Rwanda by the fighting there—and that about 9 million people have been affected in some way. Ten years after Chernobyl, the tragedy still reverberates over large areas of territory, not merely in Russian alone, but also in other countries such as Sweden. Such results, stemming from a mere accident rather than a deliberate attempt to cause damage by nuclear weapons, followed without the heat or the blast injuries attendant on a nuclear weapon... .

Id.

The judge also noted the likelihood that electromagnetic pulses resultant of nuclear weapons would cross into neutral territories:

> [T]he electromagnetic pulse ... travels at immense speeds, so that the disruption of communication systems caused by the radioactive contamination immediately can spread beyond national boundaries and disrupt communication lines and essential services in neutral countries as well. Having regard to the dominance of electronic communication in the functioning of modern society at every level, this would be an unwarranted interference with such neutral states.[225]

Judge Weeramantry further concluded that irreparable injury to neutrals is a "natural and foreseeable consequence" of the use of nuclear weapons, since the "uncontainability of radiation extends it globally."[226] He added, "When wind currents scatter these effects further, it is well-established by the TTAPS and other studies that explosions in one hemisphere can spread their deleterious effects even to the other hemisphere. No portion of the globe—and therefore no country—could be free of these effects."[227]

Judge Weeramantry added that, once a strategy of self-defense "implies damage to a non-belligerent third-party, such a matter ceases to be one of purely internal jurisdiction."[228] He stated that the use of nuclear weapons would not be a situation of inadvertent and unintentional damage to neutrals.[229] Judge Weeramantry stated:

> The launching of a nuclear weapon is a deliberate act. Damage to neutrals is a natural, foreseeable and, indeed, inevitable consequence. International law cannot contain a rule of non-responsibility which is so opposed to the basic principles of universal jurisprudence.[230]

---

[225] *Id.* at 26, 35 I.L.M. at 893.

[226] *Id.* at 49, 35 I.L.M. at 904.

[227] *Id.* In his dissenting opinion in the WHO Advisory Opinion proceedings, Judge Weeramantry stated:

> The radiation victims of a nuclear attack would be a special group within the meaning of this clause. People far from the source of the explosion—hundreds or thousands of miles away—will be affected. Non-belligerent states, far distant from the scene, will need assistance.

WHO Advisory Opinion, 1996 I.C.J. 68, 95.

[228] Dissenting opinion of Judge Weeramantry at 61, 35 I.L.M. at 910.

[229] *See id.*

[230] *Id.* at 50, 35 I.L.M. at 905.

Judge Koroma in his dissenting opinion stated that the principle in Article 2, paragraph 1 of the Charter of the United Nations as to the sovereign equality of all members "is bound to be violated if nuclear weapons are used in a given conflict, because of their established and well-known characteristics."[231]   The judge added, "The use of such weapons would not only result in the violation of the territorial integrity of non-belligerent States by radioactive contamination, but would involve the death of thousands, if not millions, of the inhabitants of territories not parties to the conflict."[232]

Quoting Article 2, paragraph 1 of the Charter of the United Nations ("The Organization is based on the principle of sovereign equality of all of its Members"), Judge Koroma further stated:

> The principle of sovereign equality of States is of general application.   It presupposes respect for the sovereignty and territorial integrity of all States.   International law recognizes the sovereignty of each State over its territory as well as the physical integrity of the civilian population.   By virtue of this principle, a State is prohibited from inflicting injury or harm on another State. The principle is bound to be violated if nuclear weapons are used in a given conflict, because of their established and well-known characteristics.   The use of such weapons would not only result in the violation of the territorial integrity of non-belligerent States by radioactive contamination, but would involve the death of thousands, if not millions, of the inhabitants of territories not parties to the conflict.[233]

As noted above, Judge Koroma further concluded that the doctrine of deterrence, if implemented, could result in "catastrophic consequences for the civilian population not only of the belligerent parties but those of States not involved in such a conflict."[234]

Judge Fleischhauer in his separate opinion concluded that "The radiation released by [nuclear weapons] is unable to respect the territorial integrity of a neutral state."[235]

Judge Guillaume in his individual opinion found the protection of neutrality to be less open-ended:

> [O]n many occasions, it has been maintained or recognized that the legality of actions carried out by belligerents in neutral territory

---

[231] Dissenting opinion of Judge Koroma at 15, 35 I.L.M. at 932.
[232] *Id.*
[233] *Id.*
[234] *Id.* at 17, 35 I.L.M. at 933.
[235] Separate opinion of Judge Fleischhauer at 1, 35 I.L.M. at 834.

depends on the "military necessities," as the late Judge Ago noted in the light of a widespread practice described in the addendum to his eight report to the International Law Commission on the responsibility of States (para. 50 and note 101).[236]

Requirements for *Per Se* Rule

Nowhere does the Court specifically address the requirements for a *per se* rule, but, from its language, it ostensibly assumes that the use of nuclear weapons could be held *per se* unlawful only if all uses would be unlawful in all circumstances. This appears, for example, from the Court's conclusions that it does not have sufficient facts to determine that nuclear weapons would be unlawful "in any circumstance,"[237] that the proportionality principle may not in itself exclude the use of nuclear weapons in self-defense "in all circumstances,"[238] and that, for the threat to use nuclear weapons implicit in the policy of deterrence to be unlawful, it would have to be the case that such use would "necessarily violate the principles of necessity and proportionality."[239]

Judge Higgins in her dissenting opinion similarly assumed that 100% certainty must be present for there to be *per se* illegality: "I do not ... exclude the possibility that such a weapon could be unlawful by reference to the humanitarian law, if its use could never comply with its requirements—no matter what specific type within that class of weapon was being used and no matter where it might be used."[240]

In an approach which I will come back to when I examine the legal bases for the existence of a *per se* rule, Judge Shahabuddeen addressed this issue indirectly: "[I]n judging of the admissibility of a particular means of warfare, it is necessary, in my opinion, to consider what the means can do in the ordinary course of warfare, even if it may not do it in all circumstances."[241]

Judge Weeramantry, addressing the issue from the perspective of nuclear decision-making, concluded that nuclear weapons should be declared illegal in all circumstances, with the proviso that if such use

---

[236] Individual opinion of Judge Guillaume ¶ 6, 35 I.L.M. at 1352 (No. 6, November 1996).

[237] Nuclear Weapons Advisory Opinion ¶ 95, at 32, 35 I.L.M. at 829.

[238] *Id.* ¶ 42, at 18, 35 I.L.M. at 822.

[239] *Id.* ¶ 48, at 19, 35 I.L.M. at 823.

[240] Dissenting opinion of Judge Higgins at 5, 35 I.L.M. 809, 937. *See also* dissenting opinion of Judge Schwebel at 5, 8, and 13, 35 I.L.M. at 836, 840, and 842.

[241] Dissenting opinion of Judge Shahabuddeen at 17, 35 I.L.M. at 869.

would be lawful "in some circumstances, however improbable, those circumstances need to be specified."[242] Judge Weeramantry stated:

> A factor to be taken into account in determining the legality of the use of nuclear weapons, having regard to their enormous potential for global devastation, is the process of decision-making in regard to the use of nuclear weapons.
>
> A decision to use nuclear weapons would tend to be taken, if taken at all, in circumstances which do not admit of fine legal evaluations. It will, in all probability, be taken at a time when passions run high, time is short and the facts are unclear. It will not be a carefully measured decision taken after a detailed and detached evaluation of all relevant circumstances of fact. It would be taken under extreme pressure and stress. Legal matters requiring considered evaluation may have to be determined within minutes, perhaps even by military rather than legally trained personnel, when they are in fact so complex as to have engaged this Court's attention for months. The fate of humanity cannot fairly be made to depend on such a decision.
>
> Studies have indeed been made of the process of nuclear decision-making and they identify four characteristics of a nuclear crisis. These characteristics are:
>
> 1. The shortage of time for making crucial decisions. This is the fundamental aspect of all crises.
> 2. The high stakes involved and, in particular, the expectation of severe loss to the national interest.
> 3. The high uncertainty resulting from the inadequacy of clear information, *e.g.*, what is going on?, What is the intent of the enemy?; and
> 4. The leaders are often constrained by political considerations, restricting their options.[243]

Judge Weeramantry further concluded that even if there were a nuclear weapon which totally eliminated the dissemination of radiation and which was not a weapon of mass destruction, the Court, because of the technical difficulties involved, would not be able "to define those nuclear weapons which are lawful and those which are unlawful," and accordingly that the Court must "speak of legality in general terms."[244]

---

[242] Dissenting opinion of Judge Weeramantry at 70, 35 I.L.M. at 915.

[243] *Id.* (citing Conn Nugent, *How a Nuclear War Might Begin, in* PROCEEDINGS OF THE SIXTH WORLD CONGRESS OF THE INTERNATIONAL PHYSICIANS FOR THE PREVENTION OF NUCLEAR WAR 117).

[244] *Id.* at 84, 35 I.L.M. at 922. Judge Weeramantry added:

> The Court's authoritative pronouncement that all nuclear weapons are not illegal (*i.e.*, that every nuclear weapon is not

It is unclear whether Judge Koroma in his dissenting opinion, in concluding that the use of nuclear weapons would be unlawful "in any circumstance" was assuming that *per se* illegality required every possible use be unlawful.[245]

Legal Limitations on the Lawfulness of Reprisals

The Court noted that reprisals in time of peace "are considered to be unlawful" and that belligerent reprisals, like self-defense, are governed, *inter alia*, by the principle of proportionality.[246]

Judge Weeramantry in his dissenting opinion stated that reprisals are unlawful under international law, given the prohibition of the use of force by States except in self-defense, and that this unlawfulness is particularly so as to nuclear weapons: "The sole justification, if any, for the doctrine of reprisals is that it is a means of securing legitimate warfare. With the manifest impossibility of that objective in relation to nuclear weapons, the sole reason for this alleged exception vanishes."[247]

Judge Schwebel concluded that, if Iraq had employed chemical or biological weapons against coalition forces, that "would have been a wrong in international law giving rise to the right of belligerent reprisal." The judge then concluded that, even if the use of nuclear weapons following such a strike would have otherwise been unlawful, "their proportionate use by way of belligerent reprisal in order to deter further use of chemical or biological weapons would have been lawful," absent some specific prohibition.[248]

---

illegal) would then open the door to those desiring to use, or threaten to use, nuclear weapons to argue that any particular weapon they use or propose to use is within the rationale of the Court's decision. No one could police this. The door would be open to the use of whatever nuclear weapon a state may chose to use.

Id.

[245] *See* dissenting opinion of Judge Koroma at 1, 35 I.L.M. at 925.

[246] Nuclear Weapons Advisory Opinion ¶ 46, at 19, 35 I.L.M. at 823.

[247] Dissenting opinion of Judge Weeramantry at 80, 35 I.L.M. at 920 (citing D. Bowett, *Reprisals Involving Recourse to Armed Force,* 66 AMERICAN J. OF INTERNATIONAL LAW 1, (1972), *quoted in* Weston, Falk, D'Amato, INTERNATIONAL LAW AND WORLD ORDER 910 (1980)).

Judge Koroma in his dissenting opinion expressed a similar conclusion. Dissenting opinion of Judge Koroma at 14, 35 I.L.M. at 931.

[248] Dissenting opinion of Judge Schwebel at 12, 35 I.L.M. at 842. Interestingly, for the general lawfulness of reprisals, Judge Schwebel cites not

Judge Koroma concluded that belligerent reprisals with nuclear weapons "would grossly violate humanitarian law in any circumstance and international law in general," adding:

> More specifically the Geneva Conventions prohibit such reprisals against a range of protected persons and objects as reaffirmed in Additional Protocol I of 1977. According to the Protocol, all belligerent parties are prohibited from carrying out belligerent reprisals. If nuclear weapons were used and given the characteristics of those weapons, their inability to discriminate between civilians and combatants and between civilian and military objectives, together with the likelihood of violations of the prohibition of unnecessary suffering and superfluous injuries to belligerents, such reprisals would at a minimum be contrary to established humanitarian law and would therefore be unlawful.[249]

Whether the Court Found a *Non Liquet*

While the Court expressly found a gap in the evidence presented, such that it could not resolve certain key factual questions, the decision is open to interpretation as to whether the Court also found a gap in the law, a *non liquet.*

In a comment touching on this point, the Court stated, "The contention that the giving of an answer to the question posed would require the Court to legislate is based on a supposition that the present *corpus juris* is devoid of relevant rules in this matter. The Court could not accede to this argument; it states the existing law and does not legislate. This is so even if, in stating and applying the law, the Court necessarily has to specify its scope and sometimes note its general trend."[250]

The Court's reference to the "present state of international law" as one of the reasons it could not decide whether all uses of nuclear weapons would be unlawful supports the inference of a finding of *non liquet,*[251] but the reference could equally readily be read as meaning that, under the law as it does exist, the matter cannot be resolved without benefit of the missing facts.

Judge Koroma in his dissenting opinion, while concluding that the law is sufficiently developed to answer the question presented, stated

---

only customary and conventional law but also the military manuals of States issued in furtherance of such law. *Id.*

[249] Dissenting opinion of Judge Koroma at 14, 35 I.L.M. 931.

[250] Nuclear Weapons Advisory Opinion ¶ 18, at 12, 35 I.L.M. at 819.

[251] Dissenting opinion of Judge Higgins at 6, 35 I.L.M. at 937.

"the Court's findings could be construed as suggesting either that there is a gap, a lacuna, in the existing law or that the Court is unable to reach a definitive conclusion on the matter because the law is imprecise or its content insufficient or that it simply does not exist."[252]

Judge Higgins, in a detailed focus on the issue, concluded that the Court had found a *non liquet*:

> What the Court has done is reach a conclusion of "incompatibility in general" with humanitarian law; and then effectively pronounce a *non liquet* on whether a use of nuclear weapons in self-defense when the survival of a State is at issue might still be lawful, even were the particular use to be contrary to humanitarian law. Through this formula of non-pronouncement the Court necessarily leaves open the possibility that a use of nuclear weapons contrary to humanitarian law might nonetheless be lawful. This goes beyond anything that was claimed by the nuclear weapons States appearing before the Court, who fully accepted that any lawful or use of nuclear weapons would have to comply with both the *jus ad bellum* and the *jus in bello*.... [253]

Judge Vereshchetin in his declaration acknowledged that the Court's decision "admits the existence of a 'grey area' in the present

---

[252] Dissenting opinion of Judge Koroma at 2, 35 I.L.M. at 925. Judge Koroma added:

> It does not appear to me any new principles are needed for a determination of the matter to be made.
>
>   ***
>
> If the Court had applied the whole spectrum of the law, including international conventions, rules of customary international law, general principles of international law, judicial decisions, as well as resolutions of international organizations, there would have been no room for a purported finding of *non liquet*.

Id.

[253] Dissenting opinion of Judge Higgins at 6, 35 I.L.M. at 937. *See also* dissenting opinion of Judge Schwebel at 8, 35 I.L.M. at 846.

Judge Higgins developed at length her view of the legal resources available to the Court to avoid having to declare a *non liquet*, concluding that it is the Court's responsibility to find and apply the law. She stated:

> [H]umanitarian law ... is very well-developed. The fact that its principles are broadly stated and often raise further questions that require a response can be no ground for a *non liquet*. It is exactly the judicial function to take principles of general application, to elaborate their meaning and to apply them to specific situations.

Id. at 6.

regulation of the matter,"[254] and went on to defend the right of the Court to declare a *non liquet* when the law is not fully developed, particularly in the case of an advisory decision.[255]

Judge Vereshchetin was of the view that the law is simply not fully developed in this area. He stated, "[t]he Court could not but notice the fact that, in the past, all the existing prohibitions on the use of other weapons of mass destruction (biological, chemical), as well as special restrictions on nuclear weapons, had been established by way of specific international treaties or separate treaty provisions, which undoubtedly point to the course of action chosen by the international community as most appropriate for the total prohibition on the use and eventual elimination of weapons of mass destruction."[256]

Judge Herczegh, on the other hand, in his declaration concluded that, given the breadth of international law, particularly general principles of law, there can be no gap:

> In the fields where certain acts are not totally and universally prohibited "as such" the application of the general principles of law makes it possible to regulate the behaviour of subjects of the international legal order, obliging or authorizing them, as the case may be, to act or refrain from acting in one way or another.[257]

Judge Ranjeva reached this same conclusion, stating that, while the law of armed conflict is a matter of written law, the so-called Martens principle performs a residual function precluding the existence of lacunae in the law.[258]

Judge Shahabuddeen in his dissent concluded that there was no gap in the law, since, whatever position one took—that all that is not prohibited is permitted per *Lotus*, or that all that is not permitted is prohibited—there was an inherent rule if only by default:

> It follows that, so far as this case at any rate is concerned, the principle on which the Court acts, be it one of prohibition or one of authorization, leaves no room unoccupied by law and consequently

---

[254] Declaration of Judge Vereshchetin at 1, 35 I.L.M. at 833.

[255] *Id.*

[256] *Id.* at 2, 35 I.L.M. at 834.

[257] Declaration of Judge Herczegh, 35 I.L.M. at 1348 (No. 6, November 1996). Judge Herczegh went on to conclude, "The fundamental principles of international humanitarian law, rightly emphasized in the reasons of the advisory opinion, categorically and unequivocally prohibit the use of weapons of mass destruction, including nuclear weapons. International humanitarian law does not recognize any exceptions to these principles." *Id.*

[258] Individual opinion of Judge Ranjeva, 35 I.L.M. at 1356.

no space available to be filled by the *non liquet* doctrine or by arguments traceable to it.   The fact that these are advisory proceedings and not contentious ones makes no difference; the law to be applied is the same in both cases.[259]

So too Judge Schwebel, while ostensibly interpreted the Court as having found a *non liquet*, concluded that there was and could be no such lacuna in the law since in his view established law answered the issue.   Judge Schwebel stated that, based on the drafting history of Article 38 of the Statute of the Court, "the general principles of law recognized by civilized nations" were included as a source of international law precisely so that there would never be a *non liquet.*[260]

Legal Status in the Absence of Applicable Law

What if existent international law in the first instance does not directly or by implication provide an answer to the question of the legality of the use of nuclear weapons, *i.e.*, is devoid of either a prohibition or an authorization of such use?   What does international law contemplate in such a default situation?   Would the use of nuclear weapons thereby be lawful because not prohibited, prohibited because not lawful, or simply exist in some unregulated gray area?

The Court's conclusion in Paragraph 105(2)(E) of its opinion—that, given the "current state" of international law and the facts available to it, the Court cannot say whether use would be "lawful or unlawful in an extreme circumstance of self-defense"—provides no clear guidance on the point.[261]

It could be argued that the Court's finding that neither customary nor conventional international law provides any authorization of the use of nuclear weapons implies that, for legality, such an authorization would be necessary even in the absence of a prohibition,[262] yet this seems like a stretch.   The Court could as reasonably be seen as

---

[259] Dissenting opinion of Judge Shahabuddeen at 10–11, 35 I.L.M. at 866. *See also id.* at 35, 35 I L.M. at 878.

[260] Dissenting opinion of Judge Schwebel at 8–9, 35 I.L.M. at 840 (citing LAUTERPACHT, THE FUNCTION OF LAW IN THE INTERNATIONAL COMMUNITY 180 (1933); Permanent Court of International Justice, Advisory Committee of Jurists, PROCES-VERBAUX OF THE PROCEEDINGS OF THE COMMITTEE, June 16th–July 24th, 1920, The Hague, 1920, pp. 296, 307–320, 332, 336, 344).

[261] Nuclear Weapons Advisory Opinion ¶ 105, at 36 (2)(E), 35 I.L.M at 831.

[262] Individual opinion of Judge Guillaume, 35 I.L.M. at 1349 (No. 6 November 1996).

contextualizing its conclusion that international law provides neither an explicit authorization nor prohibition of the use of nuclear weapons. Indeed, at an earlier point in the opinion, the Court stated:

> 52. The Court notes by way of introduction that international customary and treaty law does not contain any specific prescription authorizing the threat or use of nuclear weapons or any other weapons in general or in certain circumstances, in particular those of the exercise of legitimate self-defense. Nor, however, is there any principle or rule of international law which would make the legality of the threat or use of nuclear weapons or of any other weapons dependent on a specific authorization. State practice shows that the illegality of the use of certain weapons as such does not result from an absence of authorization but, on the contrary, is formulated in terms of prohibition.[263]

Somewhat inconsistently, the Court, in discussing whether the question presented—whether the threat or use of nuclear weapons was "permitted"—was inconsistent with State sovereignty on the theory that States are permitted to do whatever is not prohibited, concluded that it need not reach the question because all States before it in the case, including the nuclear weapon States, had acknowledged the applicability of international law, including humanitarian law.[264]

President Bedjaoui, whose vote under Rule 55 of the Court's statute caused the adoption of Paragraph 105(2)(E) of the opinion,[265] addressed this question in his declaration, stating that the "operative" language of the decision "can in no manner be interpreted to mean that [the Court] is leaving the door ajar to recognition of the legality of the threat or use of nuclear weapons."[266] Limiting to its "judicial and temporal" context the language of the *Lotus* case to the effect that what is not prohibited to States is permitted, President Bedjaoui said that the law has developed from the "resolutely positivist, voluntarist approach of international law which still held sway at the beginning of the century."[267]

---

[263] Nuclear Weapons Advisory Opinion ¶ 52, at 20, 35 I.L.M. at 823. *See also* the Individual Opinion of Judge Guillaume ¶ 3, 35 I.L.M. at 1351 (No. 6 November 1996).

[264] Nuclear Weapons Advisory Opinion ¶¶ 21, 22, at 12–13, 35 I.L.M. at 819–820.

[265] Declaration of President Bedjaoui ¶ 1, 35 I.L.M. at 1345 (No. 6 November 1996).

[266] *Id.* ¶ 11 at 1353.

[267] *Id.* ¶ 13, quoting the Court's statement in the Lotus case, Judgment No. 9 of 17 September 1927, P.C.I.J., Series A, No. 10, at 18:

Noting that the Permanent Court in the *Lotus* case concluded that "behavior not expressly prohibited by international law was authorised by that fact alone,"[268] President Bedjaoui contrasted the ICJ's decision in the case at hand:

> In the present Opinion ... the Court does not find the threat or use of nuclear weapons to be either legal or illegal; from the uncertainties surrounding the law and the facts it does not infer any freedom to take a position. Nor does it suggest that such license could in any way whatever be deduced therefrom. Whereas the Permanent Court gave the green light of authorization, having found in international law no reason for giving the red light of prohibition, the present Court does not feel able to give a signal either way.
>
> 15. Thus, the Court, in this Opinion, is showing much more circumspection than its predecessor in the Lotus case in asserting today that what is not expressly prohibited by international law is not therefore authorized.[269]

Describing the changes in the international community which underlie this change in law, President Bedjaoui stated:

> 13. It scarcely needs to be said that the fact of contemporary international society is much altered [since the Lotus decision]. Despite the still limited emergence of "supra-nationalism," the progress made in terms of the institutionalization, not to say integration and "globalization," of international society cannot be denied. Witness the proliferation of international organizations, the gradual substitution of an international law of co-operation for the traditional international law of co-existence, the emergence of the concept of "international community" and its sometimes successful attempts at subjectivization. A testimony to all these developments is provided by the place which international law now accords to

---

> International law governs relations between independent States. The rules of law binding upon States therefore emanate from their own free will as expressed in conventions or by usages generally accepted as expressing principles of law and established in order to regulate the relations between these co-existing independent communities or with a view to the achievement of common aims.

Id.

[268] Declaration of President Bedjaoui ¶ 14, 35 I.L.M. at 1346 (No. 6 November 1996).

[269] *Id.* at ¶ 14–15.

concepts such as obligations erga omnes, rules of *jus cogens*, or the common heritage of mankind.[270]

Judge Guillaume in his individual opinion reached just the opposite conclusion that all that is not prohibited is permitted:

> 10. International law rests on the principle of the sovereignty of States and thus originates from their consent. In other words, in the excellent language of the Permanent Court, "international law governs relations between independent States. The rules of law binding upon States therefore emanate from their own free will." (Lotus, Judgment No. 9, 1927, C.P.J.I., series A, No. 10, p. 18).
>
> ***
>
> 11. The constant practice of States is along these lines as far as the *Jus in Bello* is concerned. All the treaties concerning certain types of weapons are formulated in terms of prohibition.[271]

Judge Shahabuddeen in his dissenting opinion stated:

> If the Court is in a position in which it cannot definitively say whether or not a prohibitory rule exists, the argument can be made that, on the basis of that case, the presumption is in favour of the right of States to act unrestrained by any such rule.[272]

Judge Shahabuddeen, however, rejected the argument, finding, to the contrary, that, in a matter of such shattering importance as the use of nuclear weapons, the absence of a rule would signify unlawfulness:

> [T]he test of prohibition does not suffice to determine whether there is a right to do an act with the magnitude of global implications which would be involved in [the threat or use of nuclear weapons].
>
> ***
>
> As to subparagraph A of paragraph (2) of the operative paragraph, I take the view, to some extent implicit in this subparagraph, that, at any rate in a case of this kind, the action of a State is unlawful unless it is authorized under international law; the mere absence of prohibition is not enough. In the case of nuclear

---

[270] *Id.* at ¶ 13.

[271] Individual opinion of Judge Guillaume ¶ 10, 35 I.L.M. at 1353, (No. 6 November 1996). Judge Guillaume quoted the language of The Tokyo District Court in its judgment of 7 December 1963: "Of course, it is right that the use of a weapon is legal as long as international law does not prohibit it," citing Japanese Annual of International Law, 1964, No. 8, at 235. *Id.* Judge Guillaume further stated, "[I]f the law is silent in this case, States remain free to act as they intend." *Id.* at 1353.

[272] Dissenting opinion of Judge Shahabuddeen at 35, 35 I.L.M. at 878.

weapons, there is no authorization, whether specific or otherwise.[273]

Given the Court's conclusion of general unlawfulness, Judge Ranjeva noted that what is at issue is a basis for the lawfulness of the use of nuclear weapons in the exceptional case:

> [N]o declaration of the legality of nuclear weapons in principle has been recorded; there is no need to emphasize the fact that it is in the form of a justification of an exception to a principle accepted as being established in law, in this case the illegality of the threat or use of nuclear weapons, that the nuclear-weapon States attempt to present the reasons for their attitude.[274]

Values Underlying International Law

The Court in its decision, while not focusing on the overall values underlying the law of armed conflict, emphasized the "respect of the human person" and the "elementary considerations of humanity" as basic values, "intransgressible principles."[275] The Court stated that "humanitarian law, at a very early stage, prohibited certain types of weapons either because of their indiscriminate effect on combatants and civilians or because of the unnecessary suffering caused to combatants, that is to say, a harm greater than that unavoidable to achieve legitimate objectives."[276]

A number of the individual opinions went further. President Bedjaoui, in his declaration, in addition to characterizing the important role of such concepts as obligations *erga omnes*, rules of *jus cogens*, and the "common heritage of mankind," went on to describe the current nature of international law as "an objective conception of international law more readily seen as the reflection of a collective juridical conscience and as a response to the social necessities of States organized as a community."[277]

---

[273] *Id.* at 2, 35 I.L.M. at 862.

[274] Individual opinion of Judge Ranjeva, at 2, 35 I.L.M. at 1355.

[275] Nuclear Weapons Advisory Opinion ¶ 79, at 28, 35 I.L.M. at 827.

[276] *Id.* ¶ 78, at 28, 35 I.L.M. at 827.

[277] Declaration of President Bedjaoui ¶ 13, 35 I.L.M. at 1345 (No. 6, November 1996).

The Court in its WHO Advisory Opinion relied on Article 31 of the 1969 Vienna Convention on the Law of Treaties for the proposition that the terms of a treaty must be interpreted "in their context and in the light of its object and purposes" and that there should be taken into account "any subsequent practice

Judge Shahabuddeen in his dissenting opinion stated that the law of armed conflict, "with roots reaching into the past of different civilizations," was premised on the notion "that weapons, however, destructive, would be limited in impact, both in space and in time."[278] Noting that the basis for international law will disappear if mankind in the broad is annihilated and States disappear, the judge stated that laws must be interpreted in light of the "purposes they are to serve" and that the ultimate purpose of a legal system is the preservation of the human species and of civilization.[279]

Judge Shahabuddeen further cited the first preambular paragraph of the U.N. Charter recording that "the Peoples of the United Nations" were "[d]etermined to save succeeding generations from the scourge of war, which twice in our lifetime has brought untold sorrow to mankind."[280] The judge concluded that the Court "was intended to serve a civilized society" and that such a society "is not one that

---

in the application of the treaty which establishes the agreement of the parties regarding its interpretation." WHO Advisory Opinion ¶ 19, 1996 I.C.J. 68, 75.

Judge Weeramantry in those proceedings noted, with respect to the interpretation of the WHO Constitution, a multinational treaty:

> In the interpretation of a multilateral convention of this type, particularly one which sets before itself certain sociological or humanitarian goals, the task of interpretation should be guided by the object and purpose which the Convention sets before itself. A literal interpretation, using strict methods of anchoring interpretation to the letter rather than the spirit of the Convention, would be inappropriate. Fitzmaurice observes of interpretation by reference to objects, principles and purposes (the teleological method) that:
>
> > "This is a method of interpretation more especially connected with the general multilateral convention of the 'normative', and, particularly, of the sociological or humanitarian type ... ."

1996 I.C.J. 68, 148 (citing 1 SIR GERALD FITZMAURICE, THE LAW AND PROCEDURE OF THE INTERNATIONAL COURT OF JUSTICE 341 (1986)).

Judge Koroma in his dissenting opinion in the WHO Advisory Decision proceeding notes that the Vienna Convention embodies the different approaches to treaty interpretation, the textual and teleological approaches and the intention of the parties. WHO Advisory Opinion, 1996 I.C.J. 68, 194.

[278] Dissenting opinion of Judge Shahabuddeen at 4, 35 I.L.M. at 863.

[279] *Id.* at 4–5 (quoting IBN KHALDUN, THE MUQADDIMAH, AN INTRODUCTION TO HISTORY 40 (tr. Franz Rosenthal, edited and abridged by N.J. Dawood, Princeton 1981)).

[280] Dissenting opinion Judge Shahabuddeen at 5, 35 I.L.M. at 863.

knowingly destroys itself, or knowingly allows itself to be destroyed."[281]

More broadly, Judge Shahabuddeen concluded that the preservation of mankind and of civilization is such a transcendent value that international law "could not authorize" a State to embark on a course of action that could result in destruction of such values.[282]

As to the distinction between nuclear and other weapons, the judge stated, "[I]f all the explosive devices used throughout the world since the invention of gunpowder were to detonate at the same time, they could not result in the destruction of civilization; this could happen if recourse were made to the use of nuclear weapons, and with many to spare."[283] He found the answer to the legal issue to be implicit in such facts:

> The principle limiting the right to choose means of warfare assumed that, whatever might be the means of warfare lawfully used, it would continue to be possible for war to be waged on a civilized basis in future. Thus, however free a State may be in its choice of means, that freedom encounters a limiting factor when the use of a particular type of weapon could ensue in the destruction of civilization.[284]

Judge Weeramantry in his dissenting opinion relied upon the underlying purposes of the United Nations, as expressed in the organization's Charter, as representing fundamental purposes underlying international law. As overriding values, he cited saving succeeding generations from the scourge of war, respect for human rights, the dignity and worth of the human person, and equal rights of nations large and small.[285]

Judge Weeramantry also relied upon the presumption of continued existence of the international order as implicit in the rule of law and as an ultimate value against which any use of force must be measured, finding that the use of nuclear weapons must be unlawful since it would be inconsistent with such continuation.[286] He cited the aims of war as

---

[281] *Id.*

[282] *Id.* at 16, 35 I.L.M at 869.

[283] *Id.* at 17.

[284] *Id.*

[285] Dissenting opinion of Judge Weeramantry at 2, 7, 35 I.L.M. at 881, 883.

[286] *Id.* at 64–66, 35 I.L.M. at 912–913 (citing H.L.A. HART, THE CONCEPT OF LAW 188 (1961); JOHN RAWLS, A THEORY OF JUSTICE (1972); B.S. Chimni, *Nuclear Weapons and International Law: Some Reflections, in* INTERNATIONAL LAW IN TRANSITION, ESSAYS IN MEMORY OF JUDGE NAGENDRA SINGH 142

an underlying value serving as a limit on the permissible levels of weapons that may lawfully be used. War, he concluded, is intended as a means, not an end in itself, and the end to which it is aimed is some form of restoration of the peace and continuation of international life.[287]

Judge Weeramantry stated:

> [A]ll the postulates of law presuppose that they contribute to and function within the premise of the continued existence of the community served by that law. Without the assumption of the continued existence, no rule of law and no legal system can have any claim to validity, however attractive the juristic reasoning on which it is based. That taint of invalidity affects not merely the particular rule. The legal system, which accommodates that rule, itself collapses upon its foundations, for legal systems are postulated upon the continued existence of society. Being part of society, they must themselves collapse with the greater entity of which they are a part.
>
> ***
>
> To approach the matter from another standpoint, the members of the international community have for the past three centuries been engaged in the task of formulating a set of rules and principles for the conduct of that society—the rules and principles we call international law. In so doing, they must ask themselves whether there is a place in that set of rules for a rule under which it would be legal, for whatever reason, to eliminate members of that community or, indeed, the entire community itself. Can the international community, which is governed by that rule, be considered to have given its acceptance to that rule, whatever be the approach of that community—positivist, natural law, or any other? Is the community of nations, to use Hart's expression a "suicide club?"[288]

Suggesting that international law, "which purports to be a legal system for the entire global community" cannot accommodate any principles that make possible the destruction of their community, Judge Weeramantry quoted B.S. Chimni:

> No legal system can confer on any members the right to annihilate the community which engenders it and whose activities it seeks to regulate. In other words, there cannot be a legal rule, which permits the threat or use of nuclear weapons. In sum,

---

(1992); NAGENDRA SINGH, NUCLEAR WEAPONS AND INTERNATIONAL LAW, 243 (1959)).
[287] *Id.* at 67, 35 I.L.M. at 913.
[288] *Id.* at 64, 35 I.L.M. at 912.

nuclear weapons are an unprecedented event which calls for rethinking the self-understanding of traditional international law. Such rethinking would reveal that the question is not whether one interpretation of existing laws of war prohibits the threat or use of nuclear weapons and another permits it. Rather, the issue is whether the debate can take place at all in the world of law. The question is in fact one which cannot be legitimately addressed by law at all since it cannot tolerate an interpretation which negates its very essence. The end of law is a rational order of things, with survival as its core, whereas nuclear weapons eliminate all hopes of realising it. In this sense, nuclear weapons are unlawful by definition.[289]

Applying Hart's approach that the proper end of human activity is survival, Judge Weeramantry further quoted Nagendra Singh, a former President of the Court:

"It would indeed be arrogant for any single nation to argue that to save humanity from bondage it was thought necessary to destroy humanity itself ... . No nation acting on its own has a right to destroy its kind, or even to destroy thousands of miles of land and its inhabitants in the vain hope that a crippled and suffering humanity—a certain result of nuclear warfare—was a more laudable objective than the loss of human dignity, an uncertain result which may or may not follow from the use of nuclear weapons."[290]

Judge Weeramantry further analyzed the issue under John Rawls' "veil of ignorance" approach:

If one is to devise a legal system under which one is prepared to live, this exposition posits as a test of fairness of that system that its members would be prepared to accept it if the decision had to be taken behind a veil of ignorance as to the future place of each constituent member within that legal system.

A nation considering its allegiance to such a system of international law, and now knowing whether it would fall within the group of nuclear nations or not, could scarcely be expected to subscribe to it if it contained a rule by which legality would be accorded to the use of a weapon by others which could annihilate it. Even less would it consent if it is denied even the right to possess

---

[289] *Id.* at 65, 35 I.L.M. at 912 (quoting B.S. Chimni, *Nuclear Weapons and International Law: Some Reflections, in* INTERNATIONAL LAW IN TRANSITION, ESSAYS IN MEMORY OF JUDGE NAGENDRA SINGH 142 (1992)).

[290] *Id.* at 65, 35 I.L.M. at 912 (quoting NAGENDRA SINGH, NUCLEAR WEAPONS AND INTERNATIONAL LAW 243 (1959)).

such a weapon and, least of all, if it could be annihilated or irreparable damaged in the quarrels of others to which it is not in any way a party.[291]

Judge Weeramantry further emphasized the classical theory, going back to Aristotle and the Indian epics, the *Ramayana* and the *Mahabharatha*, that the aim and purpose of war is to restore the peace, concluding that the use of nuclear weapons would go beyond and be inconsistent with such purpose:

> The nuclear exchanges of the future, should they ever take place, will occur in a world in which there is no monopoly of nuclear weapons. A nuclear war will not end with the use of a nuclear weapon by a single power, as happened in the case of Japan. There will inevitably be a nuclear exchange especially in a world in which nuclear weapons are triggered for instant and automatic reprisal in the event of a nuclear attack.
>
> Such a war is not one in which a nation, as we know it, can survive as a viable entity. The spirit that walks the nuclear wasteland will be a spirit of total despair, haunting victors (if there are any) and vanquished alike. We have a case here of methodology of warfare which goes beyond the purposes of war.[292]

Judge Ranjeva developed this point at some length in his individual opinion:

> But the characteristic consensualism of international law cannot be limited either to a technique of contractual or conventional engineering or to formalization by majority vote of the rules of international law. The law of nuclear weapons is one of the branches of international law which is inconceivable without a minimum of ethical requirements expressing the values to which the members of the international community as a whole subscribe. The survival of mankind and of civilization is one of these values. It is not a question of substituting a moral order for the legal order of positive law in the name of some higher or revealed order. The moral requirements are not direct and positive sources of prescriptions or obligations but they do represent a framework for the scrutiny and questioning of the techniques and rules of conventional and consensual engineering. On the great issues of mankind the requirements of positive law and of ethics make common cause, and nuclear weapons, because of their destructive

---

[291] *Id.* at 66, 35 I.L.M. at 913 (citing JOHN RAWLS, A THEORY OF JUSTICE (1972)).

[292] *Id.* at 67, 35 I.L.M. at 913 (citing ARISTOTLE, POETICS 212 (John Warrington trans., Herron Books 1934)).

effects, are one such issue. In these circumstances, is illegality a matter of *opinio juris*? To this question the Court gives an answer which some would consider dubiative, whereas an answer in the affirmative, in my view, cannot be questioned and prevails.[293]

So too Judge Bravo concluded as to the significance of emerging broad principles of law:

> Can one ... imagine that just as humanitarian law, an essential and increasingly significant part of the international law of warfare and (of late) of peace as well, is bringing into being a whole series of principles for the protection of the civilian population or the environment, that same international law should continue to accommodate the lawfulness of, for example, the use of the neutron bomb, which leaves the environment intact albeit ... with the slight drawback that the people living in it are wiped out! If that is the case, it matters little whether a rule specific to the neutron bomb can be found, since it becomes automatically unlawful, being quite out of keeping with the majority of the rules of international law.[294]

Judge Higgins stated that the "judicial lodestar, whether in difficult questions of interpretation of humanitarian law, or in resolving claimed tensions between competing norms, must be those values that international law seeks to promote and protect."[295] Judge Higgins saw the central such value to be "the physical survival of peoples."[296]

Sources of International Law

The Court in its opinion noted that the use of a weapon can be *per se* unlawful under treaty or custom, without making specific reference to such potential unlawfulness under generally recognized principles of law.[297] The Court, however, recognized the role and indeed confluence of conventional law, customary law, and generally accepted principles of law, alternately characterizing the principles of humanitarian law upon which it primarily relied, *inter alia*, as intransgressible principles, as the principles and rules of humanitarian law, as codifications of laws and customs of war, and as declaratory of the laws and customs of war.[298]

---

[293] Individual opinion of Judge Ranjeva, 35 I.L.M. at 1354.

[294] Declaration of Judge Bravo, 35 I.L.M. at 1349.

[295] Dissenting opinion of Judge Higgins at 8, 35 I.L.M. at 938.

[296] *Id.*

[297] Nuclear Weapons Advisory Opinion ¶ 39, at 18, 35 I.L.M. at 822.

[298] *Id.* ¶¶ 74–80, at 27–28, 35 I.L.M. at 827.

Judge Koroma in his dissenting opinion noted that the absence of a conventional or customary rule specifically authorizing or prohibiting the use of nuclear weapons does not mean that the use of such weapons is lawful since "it is generally recognized by States that customary international law embodies principles which are applicable to the use of such weapons."[299] The judge quoted the decision of the British-American Claims Arbitral Tribunal in the *Eastern Extension, Australia and China Telegraph Company* case:

> "International law, as well as domestic law, may not contain, and generally does not contain, express rules decisive of particular cases; but the function of jurisprudence is to resolve the conflict of opposing rights and interests by applying, in default of any specific provision of law, the corollaries of general principles, and so to find —exactly as in the mathematical sciences—the solution of the problem. This is the method of jurisprudence; it is the method by which the law has been gradually evolved in every country, resulting in the definition and settlement of legal relations as well as between States as between private individuals."[300]

Judge Schwebel saw the case as presenting "a titanic tension between State practice and legal principle," an "antinomy between practice and principle."[301] He addressed but did not resolve the issue of which, State practice or legal principle, should govern in the case of such a conflict, suggesting instead but without elaboration that the "chasm" between the two may be "bridged."[302]

As to the inappropriateness of disregarding State practice, he stated that "that is what those who maintain that the threat or use of nuclear weapons is unlawful in all circumstances do."[303] As to the inappropriateness of ignoring principles of international humanitarian

---

[299] Dissenting opinion of Judge Koroma at 14, 35 I.L.M. at 931.

Judge Weeramantry in the WHO Advisory Opinion proceeding stated:
[T]he law has always relied for its development on the ability of the judiciary to apply the general principle to the specific instance. Out of the resulting clarification comes further development.

If the law were all-embracing, self-evident and specifically tailored to cover every situation, the judicial function would be reduced to a merely mechanical application of rules.
The WHO Advisory Opinion 1996 I.C.J. 68, 164 (Weeramantry, J. dissenting).

[300] Dissenting opinion of Judge Koroma at 14, 35 I.L.M at 931 (citing United Nations Arbitral Reports, Vol. VI, at 114).

[301] Dissenting opinion of Judge Schwebel at 1, 35 I.L.M. at 836.

[302] *Id.*

[303] *Id.*

law, he stated that none of the States appearing in the proceeding, including even the nuclear States, disputed the applicability to nuclear weapons of such principles, particularly the principles of proportionality, discrimination and necessity.[304]

Judge Schwebel points the way to what may be the ultimate legal issue here: Can a contrary State practice temper or preclude the application of the established rules of humanitarian law? Put differently, Must humanitarian law be interpreted in light of State practice? If a use of nuclear weapons would be disproportionate or indiscriminate or unnecessary or violate some other principle of law, can it nonetheless be rendered legal by the fact that it is consistent with State practice?

As to relevant State practice, Judge Schwebel set forth numerous instances of such practice which he saw as precluding the "birth or survival of *opinio juris*" as to the illegality of the use of nuclear weapons, including not only the practice of deterrence and the reliance upon that practice by many non-nuclear as well as the nuclear powers, but also the Non-Proliferation Treaty and numerous other multinational treaties and Security Council resolutions—all of which he saw as impliedly recognizing the general lawfulness of the use of these weapons.[305] Judge Schwebel also pointed out the numerous votes against the General Assembly resolutions condemning nuclear weapons.[306]

As noted above, Judge Schwebel, in reviewing the drafting history of Article 38 of the Statute of the ICJ, concluded that the decision to include "the general principles of law recognized by civilized nations" as a source of international law was a studied one, precisely intended to increase the body of law available to the Court so it would never have to declare a *non liquet.* [307]

Judge Shahabuddeen emphasized the importance of general principles in the analysis:

> The circumstance that there is no "comprehensive and universal prohibition of the threat or use of nuclear weapons as such" in customary or conventional international law does not conclude the question whether the threat or use of such weapons is lawful; more general principles have to be consulted.[308]

---

[304] *Id.*

[305] *Id.* at 1–6, 35 I.L.M. at 836–39.

[306] *Id.* at 6, 35 I.L.M. at 834.

[307] *Id.* at 9, 35 I.L.M. at 840.

[308] Dissenting opinion of Judge Shahabuddeen at 2, 35 I.L.M. at 862.

Mental State

As noted, the Court, in its discussion of the intent requirement under the Genocide Convention, appeared to assume that specific intent was required, such that the requisite intent could not be inferred "from the fact that the user of the nuclear weapon would have omitted to take account of the well-known effects of the use of such weapons."[309] The Court did not focus more broadly on the requisite mental state generally required under the law of armed conflict for unlawfulness to arise.

Judge Weeramantry in his dissenting opinion rejected the notion that there is no State responsibility for the effects of nuclear weapons—"by-products" or "collateral damage"—that are not specifically intended:

> Such results are known to be the necessary consequences of the use of the weapon. The author of the act causing these consequences cannot in any coherent legal system avoid legal responsibility for causing them, any less than a man careering in a motor vehicle at a hundred and fifty kilometers per hour through a crowded market street can avoid responsibility for the resulting deaths on the ground that he did not intend to kill the particular person who died.[310]

Judge Weeramantry added: "The plethora of literature on the consequences of the nuclear weapon is so much part of common universal knowledge today that no disclaimer of such knowledge would be credible."[311]

To the argument that the rule of moderation—the prohibition of the use of arms "calculated to cause unnecessary suffering"—requires specific intent ("calculation"), Judge Weeramantry cited the "well-known legal principle that the doer of an act must be taken to have intended its natural and foreseeable consequences."[312] He also stated that reading into the requirement such a requirement of specific intent would not "take into account the spirit and underlying rationale of the provision—a method of interpretation particularly inappropriate to the construction of a humanitarian instrument."[313] He added that nuclear

---

[309] *See* Nuclear Weapons Advisory Opinion ¶ 26, at 14, 35 I.L.M. at 820. *See also* discussion *supra* note 103–110 and accompanying text.

[310] Dissenting opinion of Judge Weeramantry at 43, 35 I.L.M at 901.

[311] *Id.*

[312] *Id.* at 48, 35 I.L.M at 904.

[313] *Id.*

weapons "are indeed deployed 'in part with a view of utilizing the destructive effects of radiation and fall-out.'"[314]

As noted above, Judge Weeramantry made a similar argument with respect to the intentionality requirement as it applies to the rights of neutrals: "The launching of a nuclear weapon is a deliberate act. Damage to neutrals is a natural, foreseeable and, indeed, inevitable consequence."[315]

Judge Weeramantry also emphasized the element of intent contained in the policy of deterrence, as set forth above, in his statement that "Deterrence needs to carry the conviction to other parties that there is a real intention to use those weapons ... it leaves the world of make-believe and enters the field of seriously-intended military threats."[316]

Judge Weeramantry thus concluded that the policy of deterrence provides the element of intent:

> [D]eterrence becomes ... stockpiling with intent to use. If one intends to use them, all the consequences arise which attach to intention in law, whether domestic or international. One intends to cause the damage or devastation that will result. The intention to cause damage or devastation which results in total destruction of one's enemy, or which might indeed wipe it out completely, clearly goes beyond the purposes of war.[317]

Judge Weeramantry also makes the interesting point that the judgment today that the use of nuclear weapons would be unlawful does not necessarily mean that such use would have been unlawful at some point in the past, since vastly more information is available now. Judge Weeramantry states that "this additional information has a deep impact upon the question of legality now before the Court:"

---

[314] *Id.* (citing Ian Brownlie, *Some Legal Aspects of the Use of Nuclear Weapons*, 14 INT'L & COMP. L. Q. 445 (1965)).

[315] Dissenting opinion of Judge Weeramantry at 50, 35 I.L.M. at 905.

[316] *Id.* at 78, 35 I.L.M. at 919 (citing generally, JUST WAR, NONVIOLENCE AND NUCLEAR DETERRENCE 193–205, 207–219 (D.L. Cady & R. Werner eds., 1991); JOSEPH BOYLE & GERMAIN GRISEZ, NUCLEAR DETERRENCE, MORALITY AND REALISM (1987); ANTHONY KENNY, THE LOGIC OF DETERRENCE AND THE IVORY TOWER (1985); ROGER RUSTON, NUCLEAR DETERRENCE—RIGHT OR WRONG? (1981); and *Nuclear Deterrence and the Use of the Just War Doctrine, in* OBJECTIONS TO NUCLEAR DEFENSE (Blake & Pole eds., 1984)).

As noted, Judge Weeramantry thus concluded that mere possession of nuclear weapons goes further than mere possession in that it involves the intent and the actual readiness to use such weapons. *Id.*

[317] *Id.* at 78, 35 I.L.M. at 919.

Action with full knowledge of the consequences of one's act is totally different in law from the same action taken in ignorance of its consequences. Any nation using the nuclear weapon today cannot be heard to say that it does not know its consequences. It is only in the context of this knowledge that the question of legality of the use of nuclear weapons can be considered in 1996.[318]

Addressing the rules of civilian immunity and proportionality, Judge Higgins stated the issue, "does the prohibition against civilians being the object of attack preclude attack upon a military target if it is realized that collateral civilian casualties will be unavoidable?"[319] She noted two views: that legal responsibility is defined (1) by intent based on what one chooses to do, what one seeks to achieve through what one chooses to do; and (2) by foreseeability, such that one is assumed to intend the consequences of one's actions.[320]

As to the latter approach, Judge Higgins posed the question, "Does it follow that knowledge in concrete circumstances civilians will be killed by the use of a nuclear weapon is tantamount to an intention to attack civilians?"[321] Her answer appeared to be that specific intent is required. She stated, "Collateral injury in respect of these weapons has always been accepted as not constituting 'intent', provided always that the requirements of proportionality are met."[322]

---

[318] *Id.* at 30, 35 I.L.M. at 895.

[319] Dissenting opinion of Judge Higgins at 4, 35 I.L.M at 936.

[320] *Id.*

[321] *Id.*

[322] *Id.* Judge Higgins stated:

It is said that collateral damage to civilians, even if proportionate to the importance of the military target, must never be intended. "One's intent is defined by what one chooses to do, or seeks to achieve through what one chooses to do." (FINNIS, BOYLE & GRISEZ, NUCLEAR DETERRENCE, MORALITY AND IDEALISM 92–3 (1987)). This closely approximates to the legal doctrine of foreseeability, by which one is assumed to intend the consequences of one's actions. Does it follow that knowledge that in concrete circumstances civilians will be killed by the use of a nuclear weapon is tantamount to an intention to attack civilians? In law, any analysis must always be contextual and the philosophical question here put is no different for nuclear weapons than for other weapons. The duty not to attack civilians as such applies to conventional weapons also. Collateral injury in respect of these weapons has always been accepted as not constituting "intent," provided always that the requirements of proportionality are met.

Id.

Significance of a Finding of Illegality

Inevitably, the "so what" question arose in the course of the Court's consideration of this matter—the notion that nuclear weapons cannot be uninvented, so what significance would a finding of illegality have.

As noted above, the United States in its arguments to the Court acknowledged the significance of the legality issue:

> [E]ach of the Permanent Members of the Security Council has made an immense commitment of human and material resources to acquire and maintain stocks of nuclear weapons and their delivery systems, and many other States have decided to rely for their security on these nuclear capabilities. If these weapons could not lawfully be used in individual or collective self-defense under any circumstances, there would be no credible threat of such use in response to aggression and deterrent policies would be futile and meaningless. In this sense, it is impossible to separate the policy of deterrence from the legality of the use of the means of deterrence. Accordingly, any affirmation of a general prohibition on the use of nuclear weapons would be directly contrary to one of the fundamental premises of the national security policy of each of these many States.[323]

As noted, the United States went even further in its memorandum to the ICJ:

> It is well known that the Permanent Members of the Security Council possess nuclear weapons and have developed and deployed systems for their use in armed conflict. These States would not have borne the expense and effort of acquiring and maintaining these weapons and delivery systems if they believed that the use of nuclear weapons was generally prohibited.[324]

Judge Oda, in addressing what he saw as the low risk that nuclear weapons would ever be used, emphasized the potential significance of the extensive agreements in which States, including the nuclear

---

[323] Statement of Michael J. Matheson (Deputy Legal Advisor, Department of State) in oral argument to the Court, ICJ Hearing, November 15, 1995, at 78.

John H McNeill (Senior Deputy General Counsel, Department of Defense), in his oral argument to the Court, similarly asserted that, if the law of reprisals were to be construed as prohibiting categorically the use of nuclear weapons, "the negative implications for strategic deterrence would be obvious and dire." *See* ICJ Hearing, November 15, 1995, at 95.

[324] U.S. ICJ Memorandum/GA App. at 14, citing Report of the U.N. Secretary-General on Nuclear Weapons, A/45/373, 18 September 1990, pp. 19–24.

weapons States, have entered limiting their right to use nuclear weapons:

> [T]he nuclear-weapon States have tended to undertake not to use or threaten to use nuclear weapons against the States in some specific regions covered by the nuclear-free-zone treaties and these five nuclear-weapon States, early in 1995, gave security assurances through statements made in the Security Council in which they undertook not to use or threaten to use these weapons against the non-nuclear-weapon States. In other words, if legal undertakings are respected, there is little risk of the use of nuclear weapons at present by the five declared nuclear-weapon States.[325]

Obviously Judge Oda assumed that the perceived legal requirements as to nuclear weapons have practical significance.

Judge Weeramantry in his dissenting opinion in the WHO Advisory Opinion proceeding addressed the question of what the effect of States would be of a finding of illegality, concluding that such a decision could be a "building block in the realization of a world ruled by law."[326] Stressing the importance that the law be known, Judge Weeramantry stated, "Not for nothing were the XII Tables publicly posted in the Roman forum."[327]

Striking a note of caution as to the credibility of the Court, Judge Vereshchetin in his declaration stated that "the Court must be concerned about the authority and effectiveness of the 'deduced' general rule with respect to the matter on which the States are so fundamentally divided."[328]

Judge Higgins in her dissenting opinion concluded that a finding of *per se* illegality would not "best serve to protect mankind against that unimaginable suffering that we all fear."[329]

Characterization of the Court's Decision

Perhaps of necessity because of the range of conclusions expressed by the different judges, the Court's decision is not very satisfying. From a litigator's point of view, one—from either side of the issue—can find much language and expressed sentiment to quote and manipulate in arguing the issue in the next case, or in justification of

---

[325] Dissenting opinion of Judge Oda at 34, 35 I.L.M. at 859.

[326] Dissent of Judge Weeramantry in the WHO Advisory Opinion, 1996 I.C.J. 68, 159.

[327] *Id.*

[328] Declaration of Judge Vereshchetin at 2, 35 I.L.M. at 833.

[329] *Id.* at 8, 35 I.L.M. at 938.

policy decisions and contingency planning and military training and the like in the meantime.

For proponents of nuclear weapons, there is the wide-open barndoor of self-defense, and the basis to argue that, in virtually the only area in which the use of armed force is lawful—self-defense—nuclear weapons, like any other weapon, may be used, and, indeed, that arguably they may be used in extreme circumstances of self-defense regardless of the dictates of other provisions of international law.

For the opponents of nuclear weapons, there is the recognition of the "general" unlawfulness of nuclear weapons and the suggestion that all uses of nuclear weapons would be unlawful if the contention of the nuclear powers is disproved that they can deliver modern precision low-yield nuclear weapons precisely at a target, discriminating between military and nonmilitary targets and controlling collateral effects, particularly radiation.

Thus, on the one hand, the decision takes the great stride of bringing nuclear weapons within the confines of international law, and on the other hand, it has language arguably taking it all back.

Most fundamentally, the decision contains a grand and historic invitation: Show us the facts.

This may be the key. When viewed in light of the extraordinary fact discussed above that the United States defended the lawfulness only of the modern precision low-yield nuclear weapons, the Court's invitation becomes focused and real: Give us the facts as to the type of weapons whose legality is being defended and the putative circumstances of such lawful use, and the issue can be decided.

PART II

ADDITIONAL APPLICABLE PRINCIPLES OF LAW

Introduction

This section addresses a number of widely recognized principles of law ostensibly applicable to the issue at hand. I first analyze the prerequisites for a *per se* rule, particularly the level of certainty that must be present for such a rule to arise. I then analyze the rules applicable to the interpretation of international treaties and rules of law, focusing on the requirement that such law be interpreted in light of its purposes.

I then go into the principles of probability analysis, focusing particularly on the notion that under tort law the taking of even extremely low risks of very grave effects are generally deemed unreasonable and unlawful by the world's legal systems absent legally sufficient justification. I further address issues as to the requisite states of mind for criminal culpability, focusing particularly on concepts of recklessness and foreseeability.

In each instance—probability analysis and criminal state of mind— the purpose is to prepare the groundwork for analyzing the facts to be developed as to the escalation and other risks of the use of nuclear weapons.

I then analyze limitations on the right of private individuals and police officers to endanger or injure innocent third-parties in the course of what is otherwise a lawful use of force, whether of self-defense, law enforcement or otherwise.[1] Apropos of the option which the United States has of maintaining adequate conventional weapons to meet its military needs, I also review the significance under various legal systems of an actor's having brought about his own need to resort to extreme levels of force, even in self-defense.

In each of the above instances, I conduct my analysis under U.S. domestic law and then survey the treatment of the same issues by other legal systems. My treatment of these individual topics is necessarily of a broad nature. Each of them could be the topic of a separate book, indeed of many books, and the subject of far more extensive surveys.

The point in each instance is that the rules and approaches I am identifying appear to be so broadly recognized across the world's legal systems as to potentially constitute "general principles of law recognized by civilized nations." As such, they are, or become, binding

---

[1] I further analyze such matters under established principles of international law.

principles of international law fully as much as if formally subscribed in a multinational convention on the legality of the use of nuclear weapons.

The impact of these and similar principles on the issue at hand has not generally been recognized. My hope is to put these principles on the table, as it were. To demonstrate their relevance and foster further analysis of the scope of these rules and of their impact upon legality issues as to the use of nuclear weapons.

Even aside from the fact that such principles appear to be widely recognized by nations and legal systems throughout the world, it would seem likely that the United States would be deemed bound by these principles to the extent that they are recognized by the United States and, in some instances, central to its legal system and tradition.

I am hopeful that through the web site I have established, http://www.nuclearweaponslaw.org, we can foster the further development of the law in this area through continuing identification and analysis, with the participation of lawyers from legal systems throughout the world, of principles of the domestic law of nations potentially applicable to the issue at hand that are so widely accepted as to constitute binding principles of international law. I invite your participation in this effort.

Chapter 4: Prerequisites for a *Per Se* Rule

Perhaps most central to the analysis of the issue at hand is the question of the prerequisites for the existence of a *per se* rule. The United States, in defending the lawfulness of the use of nuclear weapons before the ICJ, argued that the use of nuclear weapons could only be found to be *per se* unlawful if all uses, over the full range of possible variables and circumstances, would be unlawful.[1]

From reviewing the transcripts of the arguments before the Court and the legal papers submitted by the parties, it does not appear that the appropriateness of this formulation of the requirements for a *per se* rule was developed for the Court or directly presented for decision. Ostensibly adopting the U.S. position, the Court determined that it could not find a *per se* rule on the record before it because it was unable to say there could be no circumstances in which use might be lawful.[2]

This question bears closer analysis. There is no specific rule of international law dictating that 100% or 80% or any particular level of applicability must be present before a *per se* rule can arise. We are in the realm of general principles of law. Under widely accepted practice across the world's legal systems, many circumstances are recognized in which *per se* rules arise on the basis that the conduct in question would be unlawful in the vast bulk of circumstances though not necessarily in all, particularly in circumstances where discrimination as between appropriate and inappropriate actions is difficult and it is believed that the prevention of the inappropriate action is so important as to merit also prohibiting actions that would otherwise have been tolerable or even desirable.

Professor Christopher Schroeder of Duke University, in his interesting article on "Rights versus Risks" identifies types of circumstances in which *per se* or "prophylactic" rules are deemed appropriate under U.S. practice:

> Prophylaxis.—Sometimes a rule is structured to ignore in its application facts acknowledged to be relevant to otherwise valid purposes. This may be justified if incorporating those further facts would severely impair attaining one or more of those purposes

---

[1] *See supra* Chapter 1, notes 314–320, Chapter 2, notes 26–27 and accompanying text.

[2] *See supra* Chapter 3 notes 237–245 and accompanying text.

thought to be paramount. Such a rule is called prophylactic: it prohibits a class of actions some of which do not by themselves merit prohibition in light of one's complete set of aims, in order to ensure that those actions whose prohibition is desired actually are prevented. In general prophylaxis is a plausible strategy whenever; (1) most, but not all, acts belonging to the class are wrong, and (2) attempts to pick right acts in the class from wrong ones are unreliable.[3]

As to the appropriateness of prophylactic rules based on the difficulty or impossibility of discriminating between right and wrong actions, Schroeder notes, "Such discrimination may require a precise knowledge of subtle characteristics which are frequently unascertainable by regulators, judges or juries."[4] In addition, individual actors may be unable to assess the risks: "Private individuals acting in good faith also may find it hard to distinguish right from wrong actions, so a prohibition is written in broad terms to foreclose the need to make fine distinctions."[5]

Prophylactic rules may also be appropriate based on a weighting of the potential detrimental effects of bad actions that might not have been perceived as such without the rule versus the loss of potentially acceptable actions that would have been deterred by the rule. Schroeder states: "[A] prophylactic argument may support some risk rules that apply without regard to case-by-case comparisons of adverse consequences and these rules may seem to ensure a certain categorical freedom from risk that ignores adverse consequences across a broad range of activities."[6] He gives as an example the development of U.S. environmental law relating to the discharge of pollutants into water. While the Congress started with an approach of "[correlating] discharge levels from specific polluters to water quality objections for the receiving water,"[7] the approach "floundered because of the complexity of establishing the causal relationships between polluters and water quality levels,"[8] leading to the prophylactic approach of requiring "all

---

[3] Christopher H. Schroeder, *Rights Against Risks*, at 503–506 (citing R. SARTORIUS, INDIVIDUAL CONDUCT AND SOCIAL NORMS 59–68 (1975)). This article originally appeared at 86 COLUM. L. REV. 495 (1986). Reprinted with permission.

[4] *Id.* at 523.

[5] *Id.*

[6] *Id.*

[7] *Id.*

[8] *Id.*

point sources [to] install the best practicable technology available for controlling water pollution."[9]

Schroeder notes that categorical rules are supported "by a conviction that efforts to assess adverse consequences and benefits at the level of specific cases are likely to produce larger errors than they cure."[10] He adds, "Moreover, the process of error comparison itself logically presupposes a commitment that adverse consequences matter, for the conviction that the categorical rule will encompass actions that are right despite the fact that they exhibit the same rule-relevant criteria as actions that are wrong presupposes that the omitted aspects of an action, the adverse consequences and the benefits, could make a decisive difference in some cases."[11]

Reinforcing the argument that uncertainty as to risk factors militates in favor of a prophylactic rule, Schroeder states:

> So long as precise information on risks and their effects remains unavailable or available only at substantial expense (in terms of both cost and regulatory delay), prophylactic rules will continue to be important regulatory tools, though the appropriate precision and detail of such rules for risks need further elucidation.[12]

Schroeder further notes that prophylactic rules are not necessarily as definitive as they sound, in that the overall approach leads to the need for a variance procedure and hence for exceptions.[13] Typically, *per se* rules are subject to various rules of interpretation, justification, excuse or other qualification rendering them less than absolute.

U.S. Law

The application of *per se* rules by U.S. courts can be seen in such areas as negligence *per se*, slander *per se*, the antitrust laws and State regulation of interstate commerce.

Thus, as to negligence *per se*, the majority of courts hold that the violation of a statute is conclusive proof of negligence.[14] However, the

---

[9] *Id.* (citing 33 U.S.C. § 1311(b)(1)(A) (1982)).

[10] *Id.*

[11] *Id.* at 523–24.

[12] *Id.* at 557.

[13] *See id.* at 523–24.

[14] *See, e.g.*, Martin v. Herzog, 228 N.Y. 164 (1920). *See* also KEETON ET AL., PROSSER & KEETON ON TORTS § 36 (5th ed. 1984). The Restatement of Torts § 288B states "[t]he unexcused violation of a legislative enactment or an administrative regulation which is adopted by the court as defining the standard of conduct of a reasonable man, is negligence in itself." RESTATEMENT OF

rule is subject to the qualification that it must be shown that the statute was enacted to protect the class of persons to which the plaintiff belongs and that the injury is the type of harm that was sought to be prevented.

Similarly, under the majority rule, slanderous statements imputing a crime or a loathsome disease or concerning a person's business, trade, profession or office, or accusing a woman of unchastity, are deemed to be actionable without proving special damages as otherwise required.[15] Yet this *per se* rule is far from absolute. Whether a statement falls within one of these categories is for the court to decide.[16] And, even if the statement is established to be slander *per se*, the defendant can avoid liability by showing either that the statement was true or that he had a privilege to utter it.[17]

Equally non-absolute is the *per se* rule applied by the Supreme Court to interstate commerce. The Constitution grants Congress the power to regulate interstate commerce.[18] In deciding a claim that a state statute is invalid for usurping Congress' authority under this provision, the federal courts first determine whether the statute on its face discriminates against out-of-state entities by giving an economic advantage to in-state entities.[19] If the statute does, it is deemed *per se* invalid, but may still be justified by the state's demonstration of a compelling interest, such as the protection of the health and safety of its citizens.[20] To overcome the *per se* invalidity, the state must show that

---

TORTS (SECOND) § 288B (1965). § 288B goes on to state an alternate formulation to the effect that such unexcused violation "may be relevant evidence bearing on the issue of negligent conduct," even when the courts have not adopted the statute or regulation as definitive of the standard of care exercised by the reasonable man. *Cf.* Zeni v. Anderson, 397 Mich. 117 (1976); RESTATEMENT OF TORTS (SECOND) § 288A (1965) (minority rule that the violation is only evidence of negligence).

[15] *See* KEETON ET AL., *supra* note 14, at § 112.

[16] *See* Meehan v. Amax Oil & Gas, Inc., 796 F. Supp. 461, 466 (D. Col. 1992).

[17] *See* KEETON ET AL., *supra* note 14, at § 114, 115.

[18] *See* U.S. CONST. art I, § 8, cl. 3.

[19] *See* Healy v. Beer Inst., 491 U.S. 324, 337 (1989); Amy M. Petragnani, *The Dormant Commerce Clause: On Its Last Leg*, 57 ALB. L. REV. 1215, 1217 (1994).

[20] *See* Healy, 491 U.S. at 337 (if the state regulation is not *per se* invalid, the court proceeds to balance the benefits of the regulation to local interests against the burdens on interstate commerce to determine the validity of the state regulation.) (citing Philadelphia v. New Jersey, 437 U.S. 617, 624 (1978)).

the compelling state interest could not be protected in a non-discriminatory manner.[21]

Even *per se* rules found in the realm of U.S. antitrust laws, while closer to being absolute, possess considerable flexibility. Section I of the Sherman Antitrust Act[22] permits courts to employ a *per se* rule of illegality when a contract or agreement is "manifestly anticompetitive."[23] The Supreme Court has determined that certain agreements or practices on their face, such as price fixing, division of markets, group boycotts, and tying arrangements, have such a detrimental effect on competition that they must be presumed "unreasonable and therefore illegal."[24] In such an instance, the Court dispenses with the detailed analysis otherwise required by the "rule of

---

See also Maine v. Taylor, 477 U.S. 131, 138 (1986); Oregon Waste Sys. v. Department of Envtl. Quality Comm'n, 511 U.S. 93, 100–01, 114 S. Ct. 1345, 1351 (1994):

> Because the Oregon surcharge is discriminatory, the virtually *per se* rule of invalidity provides the proper legal standard here, not the *Pike* balancing test. As a result, the surcharge must be invalidated unless respondents can "sho[w] that it advances a legitimate local purpose that cannot be adequately served by reasonable nondiscriminatory alternatives."

Id. (quoting New Energy Co. of Ind. v. Limbach, 486 U.S. 269, 278, 108 S.Ct. 1803, 1810 (1987)).

See also Allen v. State of Minnesota, 867 F.Supp. 853, 860 (D. Minn. 1994):

> If a state statute directly regulates or discriminates against interstate commerce or its effect is to favor in-state interests over out-of-state interests, it is "per se invalid" under the Commerce Clause and will be struck down ... and the burden falls upon the state to justify the economic regulation in terms of its benefits to the state and the lack of non-discriminatory alternatives that will accomplish the same goals.

Id.

Some courts have stated the test in terms a "virtually *per se* rule of invalidity." *See, e.g.*, Philadelphia, 417 U.S. at 623–24, 98 S.Ct. at 2535.

[21] *See* Petragnani, *supra* note 19, at 1217 (citing Maine v. Taylor, 477 U.S. 131, 138 (1986)).

[22] *See* 15 U.S.C. §1 (1982).

[23] *See* Troy Everett Peyton, Note, *Unraveling The Current Rule For Applying The Per Se Rule: Explanations, Solutions, And A Proposal,* 10 J. CORP. L. 1051, 1073 n.2 (1985).

[24] Northern Pac. Ry. v. United States, 356 U.S. 1, 5 (1958).

reason" approach to determine the precise harm allegedly caused by their use.[25]

The Supreme Court, in establishing such *per se* rules, has not required that the acts in question have such effects in all circumstances but rather that such effects seem likely in nearly all circumstances or in the most common, typical or important of circumstances.[26] As noted by Professor Easterbrook:

> The *per se* rule condemns whole categories of practices even though courts acknowledge that some practices in these categories are beneficial. The court permits such overbreadth because all rules are imprecise. One cannot have the savings of decision by rule without accepting the cost of occasional mistakes. We accept these mistakes because almost all of the practices covered by per se rules are anticompetitive, and an approach favoring case-by-case adjudication (to prevent condemnation of beneficial practices subsumed by the categories) would permit too may deleterious practices to escape condemnation.[27]

The Supreme Court in *Arizona v. Maricopa County Medical Society* stated:

> As in every rule of general application, the match between the presumed and the actual is imperfect. For the sake of business certainty and litigation efficiency, we have tolerated the invalidation of some agreements that a fullblown inquiry might have proved to be reasonable.[28]

In that case the Supreme Court held that the *per se* rule prohibiting price fixing was applicable even though the defendants asserted that the practices had procompetitive justifications.[29] The Court reasoned that "claims of enhanced competition are so unlikely to prove significant in any particular case that ... the rule of law ... is justified in its general application."[30]

In language analogous to the issue at hand, the Court in *Continental T.V. Inc. v. GTE Sylvania Inc.* stated:

---

[25] Thomas A. Piraino, *Reconciling The Per Se and Rule of Reason Approaches To Antitrust Analysis*, 64 S. CAL. L. REV. 685 (1991).

[26] *See e.g. id.* at 692–93.

[27] *See* Frank H. Easterbrook, *Vertical Arrangements and The Rule of Reason*, 53 ANTITRUST L.J. 135, 157 (1984).

[28] 457 U.S. 322, 344 (1982).

[29] *Id.* at 351.

[30] *Id.*

Per se rules thus require the Court to make broad generalizations about the social utility of particular commercial practices. The probability that anticompetitive consequences will result from a practice and the severity of those consequences must be balanced against its pro-competitive consequences. Cases that do not fit the generalization may arise, but a *per se* rule reflects the judgment that such cases are not sufficiently common or important to justify the time and expense necessary to identify them. Once established, *per se* rules tend to provide guidance to the business community and to minimize the burdens on litigants and the judicial system of the more complex rule-of-reason trials but those advantages are not sufficient in themselves to justify the creation of *per se* rules.[31]

In *FTC v. Superior Court Trial Lawyers Association*, the Supreme Court discussed the two types of analysis used in evaluating practices under the Sherman Antitrust Act.[32] The Court stated that administrative ease is only one justification for the use of a *per se* rule.[33] *Per se* rules "also reflect a longstanding judgment that the prohibited practices by their nature have 'a substantial potential for impact on competition.'"[34] The Court found that the *per se* rules were appropriate for those agreements "so plainly anticompetitive that no elaborate study of the industry is needed to establish their illegality."[35] Those agreements "whose competitive effect can only be evaluated by analyzing the facts peculiar to the business, the history of the restraint, and the reasons why it was imposed" invoke a reasonableness analysis.[36]

In explaining the nature of the *per se* rule the Court stated:

The *per se* rules in antitrust law serve purposes analogous to *per se* restrictions upon, for example, stunt flying in congested

---

[31] 433 U.S. 36, 50 n.16, 97 S.Ct. 2549, 2557 n.16 (1977). In this case the Court went on to find that a *per se* rule prohibiting restrictions in franchise agreements was not appropriate. Rather a rule of reason should be employed by the courts in evaluating the restrictions. *Id.* at 57. The Court stated that "*Per se* rules of illegality are appropriate only when they relate to conduct that is manifestly anticompetitive." *Id.* at 49–50 (citing Northern Pac. Ry. Co., 356 U.S. at 5). The Court went on to detail some of the pro-competitive advantages of vertical restrictions and found that the restrictions did not lack "any redeeming virtue" and, therefore, a *per se* prohibition was not appropriate. *Id.* at 50–57.

[32] *See* 493 U.S. 411, 431–435 (1990).

[33] *See id.* at 433.

[34] *See id.* (citation omitted)

[35] *See id.* (quoting Professional Engineers, 435 U.S. at 692).

[36] *See id.*

areas or speeding. Laws prohibiting stunt flying or setting speed limits are justified by the State's interest in protecting human life and property. Perhaps most violations of such rules actually cause no harm. No doubt many experienced drivers and pilots can operate much more safely, even at prohibited speeds, than the average citizen.[37]

The Court further noted:

In part, the justification for these *per se* rules is rooted in administrative convenience. They are also supported, however by the observation that every speeder and every stunt pilot poses some threat to the community. An unpredictable event may overwhelm the skills of the best driver or pilot, even if the proposed course of action was entirely prudent when initiated. A bad driver going slowly may be more dangerous than a good driver going quickly, but a good driver who obeys the law is safer still.[38]

In discussing why price fixing cartels are illegal *per se*, the Court stated:

The conceivable social benefits are few in principle, small in magnitude, speculative in occurrence, and always premised on the existence of price-fixing power which is likely to be exercised adversely to the public. Moreover, toleration implies a burden of continuous supervision for which the courts consider themselves ill-suited. And even if power is usually established while any defenses are not, litigation will be complicated, condemnation delayed, would be price-fixers encouraged to hope for escape, and criminal punishment less justified. Deterrence of a generally pernicious practice would be weakened. The key points are the first two. Without them, there is no justification for categorical condemnation.[39]

Similarly, in *NAACP v. Claiborne Hardware Co.*,[40] a group of white merchants challenged the legality of a boycott against their businesses organized as a protest by the NAACP. The Supreme Court held that boycotts in general are protected as an exercise of political free speech. Nevertheless, this was not an absolute protection but subject to certain limitations, such as a prohibition against violence.

---

[37] *Id.*

[38] *Id.* at 434.

[39] *Id.* at 435 (quoting 7 P. AREEDA, ANTITRUST LAW ¶ 1509, at 412–413 (1986)).

[40] *See* 458 U.S. 886, 102 S.Ct. 3409 (1982).

In addition, while the illegal *per se* categories preclude a determination of reasonableness, the court does have to determine whether the act or agreement actually falls into one of the prohibited categories and even if it does whether that act is "irredeemably anti-competitive."[41]

The use of *per se* rules in the antitrust context also demonstrates that such rules do not have to cover an entire field but may be limited to specific acts which are clearly violative of a law.[42] The use of a *per se* rule does not preclude the use of a parallel standard to cover situations not reached by the *per se* rule.

Prophylactic rules are often imposed by the courts in the constitutional area, including particularly in imposing limits on government authority and action.[43] An example is the U.S. Supreme Court's decision in *Miranda v. Arizona*,[44] requiring police to inform suspects in custody, prior to questioning, of their constitutional rights and prohibiting the admission into evidence of statements taken in violation of such requirement.[45]

The Miranda rule, as a prophylactic measure, went beyond the requirements of the Constitution. In subsequently applying Miranda, for example, in *Minnick v. Mississippi*, to bar police interrogation of a suspect who had requested and been provided counsel, the Court did not feel it necessary to justify its decision as required by the Fifth Amendment, instead explaining that the "gain in specificity" from a prophylactic rule barring questioning after a request for counsel "has been thought to outweigh the burdens ... impose[d] on law enforcement agencies and the courts by requiring the suppression of

---

[41] *See* Barry v. St. Paul Fire & Marine Ins. Co., 555 F.2d 3, 9 (1st Cir. 1977). *See also* Joseph E. Seagram & Sons v. Hawaiian Oke & Liquors, Ltd., 416 F.2d 71, 75 (9th Cir. 1969).

[42] *See, e.g.,* Nynex Corp. v. Discon, Inc. 525 U.S. 128, 119 S. Ct. 493, 142 L. Ed. 2d 510, 1998-2 Trade Cas. (CCH) ¶ 72,362 (1998).

[43] *See, e.g.,* Paul G. Cassell, *The Costs of the Miranda Mandate: A Lesson in the Dangers of Inflexible, "Prophylactic" Supreme Court Inventions,* 28 ARIZ. ST. L.J. 299 (Spring 1996); Nancy M. Kennelly, Note, *Davis v. United States: The Supreme Court Rejects a Third Layer of Prophylaxis,* LOY. U. CHI. L.J., Spring, 1995; David A. Strauss, *The Ubiquity of Prophylactic Rules,* 55 U.CHI.L.REV. 190 (Winter 1988); Joseph D. Grano, *Prophylactic Rules in Criminal Procedure: A Question of Article III Legitimacy,* 80 NW.U.L.REV. 100 (March 1985).

[44] Miranda v. Arizona, 384 U.S. 436, 86 S.Ct. 1602 (1966)

[45] *See* Cassell, *supra* note 43. *See also* Kennelly, *supra* note 43; Strauss, *supra* note 43; Grano, *supra* note 43.

trustworthy and highly probative evidence even though the confession might be voluntary under Fifth Amendment analysis."[46]

As Professor Cassell has summarized it,

> Today, with the benefit of nearly thirty years of subsequent interpretations we know the Miranda mandate is not a constitutional requirement. Rather, the Court has held specifically that Miranda rules are only "safeguards" whose purpose is to reduce the risk that police will violate the Constitution during custodial questioning. This means that the government can violate Miranda without actually violating the Fifth Amendment—without, that is, having compelled a defendant to become a witness against himself. As explained in Michigan v. Tucker, Miranda established a "series of recommended 'procedural safeguards' .... The [Miranda] Court recognized that these procedural safeguards were not themselves rights protected by the Constitution but were instead measures to insure that the right against compulsory self-incrimination was protected." Thus, in Tucker, the Court excused non-compliance with Miranda because failure to provide a full set of warnings "did not abridge respondent's constitutional privilege ... but departed only from the prophylactic standards later laid down by this Court in Miranda to safeguard that privilege." Quite simply, to violate any aspect of Miranda is not necessarily—or even usually—to violate the Constitution.[47]

The bases for *per se* rules can also be looked at in the context of the bases for injunctive relief. A *per se* rule is in a sense an injunction. Interestingly, Schroeder states that the traditional equity standard for enjoining tortious behavior is that the courts "may enjoin behavior that is virtually certain to harm an identifiable individual in the near

---

[46] Minnick v. Mississippi, 498 U.S. 146, 151 (1990). *See* discussion at Cassell, *supra* note 43, at 303. Professor Cassell notes that the Miranda decision, by the Court's own description in its later decision in Moran v. Burbine, 475 U.S. 412, 434 n.4 (1986), "embodied a carefully crafted balance designed to fully protect both the defendant's and society's interests," and hence that the Court was weighting "the costs and benefits, as it sees them, of extending the prophylactic requirements of the Miranda decision." Cassell, *supra* note 43, at 302.

[47] Cassell, *supra* note 43, at 301. (citations omitted). In 1999 The U.S. Supreme Court, in Dickerson v. United States, 99-5525, ostensibly agreed to decide whether the *Miranda* rule is in fact constitutionally mandated. *See Justices to Weigh Law's Limit on Landmark 'Miranda' Rule*, N.Y.L.J., Dec. 7, 1999 at 1.

future."[48] Absent the ability to make such a showing, the injured party generally must wait and sustain the injury and then sue for damages.[49]

On this basis, an extremely high level of likelihood of the proscribed harm would have to be shown before an injunction will issue. While the formulation "virtual certainty" may overstate the requirements of contemporary law, it is interesting that such a standard seems to approach the "inevitability" standard ostensibly applied by the United States in evaluating the lawfulness of a nuclear strike based on the likelihood of its escalating into a massive strategic nuclear exchange.[50]

Professor Schroeder recognizes that, even in the context of the traditional doctrine, it has widely been recognized that, where the harm threatened is particularly serious and the effects particularly irreparable, an injunction may issue based on a lower level of probability.[51] Schroeder summarizes this approach:

> If the harm anticipated is sufficiently great, why must one wait to stop the action until one is virtually certain the harm will occur? Unable to produce a satisfactory answer to this question, courts have modified the traditional doctrines, recognizing that the "magnitude of risk sufficient to justify regulation is inversely proportional to the harm to be avoided."[52]

Schroeder further notes that, while traditionally a high showing of probability of success had to be made, under the more modern rights approach recognizing some level of right not to be subjected to risk, a lesser showing is necessary:

> This probabilistic perspective [as to potential effects of risks] has been successful in dislodging the earlier unstinting devotion to freedom of action that supported the virtually-certain-to-occur standard. The earlier standard embodied a view of the individual liberty of risk creators that resisted restrictions until an offsetting rights violation could be conclusively presented. The virtually-certain standard was taken to mark the proper point of constraint that protected others and ensured a like liberty for all. Lately, the

---

[48] Schroeder, *supra* note 3, at 498 (citing Note, *Imminent Irreparable Injury: A Need for Reform,* 45 S. CAL. L. REV. 1025 (1972)).

[49] *See id.* at 499.

[50] *See supra* Chapter 1, notes 314–320, Chapter 2, notes 26, 74, and accompanying text.

[51] *See* Schroeder, *supra* note 3, at 508.

[52] *Id.* at 501 (citing Ethyl Corp. v. EPA, 541 F.2d 1, 19 (D.C.Cir), cert. denied, 426 U.S. 941 (1976)).

expansion of the technological risk has forced reappraisal of the substantial interests of the risk bearer. The norms for preventing risky action have been unmoored from the relatively well-defined, if extreme, virtually certain standard, and the appropriate accommodation between risk creator and risk bearer has swung decidedly towards increased protection of the risk bearers.[53]

That something less than virtual necessity will suffice for the issuance of injunctive relief is also clear from the practice under Rule 65 of the Federal Rules of Civil Procedure addressing injunctions in the federal courts.[54]

---

[53] *Id.* at 500–501.

[54] *See, e.g.*, 13 JAMES WM. MOORE, MOORE'S FEDERAL PRACTICE 3rd ed. § 65.02[2] at 65-13 (1997) ("In order to obtain injunctive relief, the movant must satisfy the court that there exists some cognizable danger of harm if the defendant is not enjoined from committing certain acts.") (citing United States v. W.T. Grant Co., 345 U.S. 629, 633, 73 S.Ct. 894, 97 L. Ed. 1303 (1953)). Moore also cites the decisions in Felter v. Cape Girardeau Sch. Dist., 810 F. Supp. 1062, 1070 (E.D. Mo. 1993) ("plaintiff must show that ... the threatened injury is real, not imagined") and in Baxter Int'l Inc. v. Morris, 976 F.2d 1189, 1194 (8th Cir. 1992) ("[a]lthough a former employer is not required to await actual harm before seeking relief ... injunctive relief must be based on a real apprehension that future acts are not just threatened but in all probability will be committed."). For examples of circumstances where injunctive relief might be appropriate notwithstanding an inability to show a high probability of success, *see, e.g.* Cox v. Brown, 498 F.Supp. 823 (D.C.D.C. 1980); Women's Health Care Services, P.A. v. Operation Rescue–National, 773 F.Supp. 258 (D. Kan. 1991); Jackson v. City of Markham, Ill, 773 F.Supp. 105; Productoso Carnic S.A. v. Central American Beef and Seafood Trading Co., C.A.Fla. 1980, 621 F.2d 683 (N.D.Ill. 1991). *See also* District 50, United Mine Workers of America v. International Union, United Mine Workers of America, 412 F.2d 165, 34 U.S.App.D.C. 34 (D.C. Cir. 1969).
The courts generally require that a plaintiff establish the following in order to qualify for a preliminary injunction:
  (1) a substantial likelihood that plaintiff will prevail on the merits;
  (2) a substantial threat that plaintiff will suffer irreparable injury if the injunction is not granted;
  (3) a showing that the threatened injury to plaintiff outweighs the threatened harm the injunction may cause to defendant; and
  (4) a showing that granting the preliminary injunction will not disserve the public interest.
See Canal Authority of the State of Fla. V. Callaway, 489 F.2d 567, 572–573 (5th Cir. 1974) (citing Giorgio v. Causey, 488 F.2d 527 (5th Cir. 1973) and Blackshear Residents Organization v. Romney, 472 F.2d 1197 (5th Cir 1973)).

In deciding whether to grant the injunction, the court is called upon to make an equitable weighting of such factors. It has been noted that "[t]he likelihood of success on the merits that a movant for injunctive relief must demonstrate varies with the quality and quantity of harm that it will suffer from the denial of an injunction," District 50, United Mine Workers of America v. Int'l Union, United Mine Workers of America, 412 F.2d 165, 168 (D.C. Cir. 1969), and that, for the granting of an injunction, there are "'two points on a sliding scale in which the degree of irreparable harm increases as the probability of success on the merits decreases.'" Vondran v. McLinn, 1995 U.S. Dist. LEXIS 21974 *7–8 (N. Cal. 1995), quoting Big Country Foods, Inc. v. Board of Educ. of the Anchorage School Dist., 868 F.2d 1085, 1088 (9th Cir. 1989).

The Seventh Circuit Court of Appeals expressed this point as to the offsetting balance between the necessary showing of likelihood of success and the potential level of harm:

> If Maxim's Limited is to win the preliminary injunction, therefore, it would have to impress the trial court with the amount by which the harm that threatens it (if there is no injunction) exceeds the harm threatening the defendant (if there is an injunction); for since the court determined that the chances of prevailing were slim, the balance of harms would have to lean rather obviously toward plaintiff's side to make a preliminary injunction appropriate. Specifically, the harm to the plaintiff, discounted by its chance of prevailing, must exceed the harm to the defendant discounted by his chance of prevailing.

Maxim's Ltd. v. Badonsky, 772 F.2d 388, 391–392 (7th Cir. 1985) (district court held not to have abused discretion in denying an injunction on use of the trade name Maxim's).

Activities endangering public health through nuisances have often been the subject of injunction, as illustrated by the *Reserve Mining* case discussed above:

> Such an inquiry [weighing the benefits and costs of the activity versus the injunction], however, must be weighed very heavily in favor of an injunction when the injury alleged is a type of public nuisance that endangers public health. In matters of public health, by their very nature, monetary damages are usually incapable of compensating those who are, or who will be, injured by the nuisance. In a situation where the scope of the health risk is great, therefore, the harm which would be caused by the issuance of an injunction abating the nuisance must be of an overwhelming magnitude [to prevent the issuance of the injunction

United States v. Reserve Mining Co., 380 F. Supp. 11, 55–56 (D. Minn. 1973), citing Board of Commissioners v. Elm Grove Mining Co., 122 W.Va. 442, 452, 9 S.E.2d 813, 817 (1940); 40 A.M.S.A. § 609.74.

Traditionally, the requisite showing, for purposes of obtaining injunctive relief, has been of the likelihood of the injury. If the underlying harm is conceptualized differently, however, and it becomes not the injury but the imposition of risk, the subjugation to risk, against which one is entitled to protection, the issue ostensibly becomes the likelihood of the risk.

The right not to be subjected to risk, traditionally protected, if only marginally or theoretically, by reckless endangerment statutes,[55] is becoming increasingly recognized. As Schroeder puts it, "Risks ... can be viewed as distinct concerns in and of themselves; whether or not harm eventually befalls someone, he may prefer to avoid the risk."[56] Similarly, "Avoidance of exposure to risk of serious harm or death can plausibly be considered a primary good."[57]

The same point can be seen from a California federal court case, where state prisoners obtained a preliminary injunction against alleged maltreatment. In granting the relief, the District Court stated:

> The conditions prohibited by this Court's preliminary injunction endanger not only the safety and sanity of prisoners; they endanger their custodians as well and, in the end, the citizenry at large. They are conditions which breed violence and dangerous disregard of human decency. Their constitutionality under the Eighth Amendment of the United States Constitution and Article I, section 17 of the California Constitution is in serious doubt. Existence of these conditions calls for the issuance of the preliminary injunction, both on federal constitutional grounds and, as well, on the basis of the Court's pendent jurisdiction of claims arising under state law.

Toussaint v. Rushen, 553 F. Supp. 1365, 1384 (N.D. Cal. 1983).

[55] *See, e.g.,* N.Y. Penal Law § 120.25, NY CLS Penal § 120.25 (1999). *See also* THE DANISH CRIMINAL CODE (Dr. Knud Waaben trans., 1958) (Chap. 22, Offenses Causing Danger to the Public).

[56] Schroeder, *supra* note 3, at 532. *See also id.* at 530–31. Schroeder also notes the contemporary focus on protection against "uncertainty costs"—"the fear and feeling of vulnerability associated with not knowing whether one will be injured in the future." *Id.* at 503.

[57] *Id.* at 538. Schroeder provides Charles Fried's answer as to what level of risk is permissible:

> What does Fried have to say about the standards applicable to prevention of risk-creating situations? He says only that adverse consequences must be taken into account in deciding what to prevent: "[I]t is wrong to expose the person or property of another to undue risk of harm, but what risk is undue is a function of the good to be attained and the likelihood and magnitude of the harm."

Id. at 529 (citing CHARLES FRIED, RIGHT AND WRONG 12 (1978)).

If such a right is recognized, the harm arises upon the imposition of the risk and ostensibly the risk bearer should potentially be entitled to injunctive relief at that time, rather than permitting the risk taker to proceed and only be subject to injunction if there appears to be a high probability of injury or to damages after the injury occurs.[58] Schroeder notes, "Statutory provisions authorizing agencies and courts to intervene to prevent the risk of harm rather than only the harm itself have accelerated the modern tendency beyond the pace set by the common law."[59]

Schroeder notes that while traditionally injunctions were granted, as in the context of proceedings against nuisance, where the action objected to was of a continuing nature, *i.e.*, in effect had already occurred, such that there were no real issues as to cause and effect, focus on "risk as the probabilistic anticipation of harm" introduces more complex variables: "In contrast, when we assess technological risk, causal links and accurate predictions of the harm that will eventually be caused become much more controversial and much less the province of common sense."[60] Whereas "[a] common method of proving a threat of a future tort is by proving a past tort under conditions that render its repetition or continuance probable," "injunctions of merely threatened harms are regarded as exceptional extensions of a general rule granting injunctions only against existing harms."[61]

He goes on to describe uncertainties that inevitably arise as to the evaluation of such risks:

> By their very nature, probabilistic estimates take relatively few variables as critical to prediction. They abstract from the highly particularized fact situations of injunction proceedings, thereby opening continuing debate on the propriety of ignoring the omitted variables. They also frequently rely on experimental data from

---

[58] *See id.* at 532.

[59] *Id.* at 501 (citing Ethyl Corp. v. EPA, 541 F.2d 1, 19 (D.C.Cir), cert. denied, 426 U.S. 941 (1976)). "Compare Village of Walsonville v. SCA Serv., Inc. ... (applying common law rule that an injunction against hazardous waste site is appropriate only if there exists a "dangerous probability' that the threatened injury will occur), with Reserve Mining Co. v. EPA ...(actual harm is not more likely than not, but Federal Water Pollution Control Act was intended to work in a 'precautionary or preventive sense, and, therefore, evidence of potential harm as well as actual harm comes within the purview of that term.')." *Id.*

[60] *Id.* at 502.

[61] *Id.* at 503 n.28.

animal studies for conclusions about human health effects, using only point estimates of dose-responses. These point estimates cannot be translated into estimates of risk at low exposures without making controversial and arbitrary assumptions.[62]

The relationship between injunctive relief and damages is a complex one. Injunctive relief precludes the actor from taking the action in question even if she would have chosen to have done so and paid any resultant damages if the threatened harm in fact eventualized. The enjoined action presumably never takes place, with the effects that the risk bearer is spared the risk while the risk taker is deprived of the potential benefits of the risk causing activity. Obviously, there are judgments to be made and balances to be struck as to what risks to prohibit entirely, what ones to permit and what ones to regulate.

Generally Accepted Principles of Law

Other legal systems have grappled with the issue of the requirements for a *per se* rule and have opted for a non-absolutist approach like that generally followed in the United States. Such legal systems recognize a broad basis in specific circumstances for a *per se* rule and then proceed to allow for a variety of outs.

This can be seen in the way other legal systems, following either an explicit *per se* rule or a cause of action for breach of statutory duty, treat what we call negligence *per se*. Throughout the world, civil liability is imposed under various rubrics for injuring a person or otherwise causing the person damages through the violation of a statute, often a criminal statute.[63] The injured person must generally establish breach of the duty and resultant damages, but even then, as under U.S. law, liability is subject to various defenses.[64]

Thus, in England, one breaches a statutory duty, subjecting himself to potential liability, when he violates a statute "that created a duty owed to the plaintiff."[65] However, the potential liability is not absolute:

---

[62] *Id.* at 502–03.

[63] *See, e.g.,* International Encyclopedia of Comparative Law, § 2-114 (Andre Tunc ed., Vol. XI, Part I) (1983). In some countries, negligence *per se* is known as a breach of statutory duty.

[64] *Id. See, e.g.* a defense, Cartwright v. G.K.N. Sankey LTD. [Court of Appeal (Civil Division)] 14 KIR 349, 27 February 1973; National Coal Board v. England. [House of Lords] [1954] AC 403, [1954] 1 All ER 546, [1954] 2 WLR 400, 25 February 1954 (rational limitations on defenses).

[65] *See, e.g.,* Anns and others v. London Borough of Merton, 1978 AC 728, [1977] All ER 492.

For the injured party to recover, he must further establish, as is generally required in the United States, that the statute was intended to prevent the damages that ensued from the statutory breach.[66]

Indian tort law, under the rubric of "statutory negligence," is to the same effect. For the injured party to recover, he must prove first that the defendant breached a statutory duty and caused the damage.[67] He must then establish that "the injury is of a kind ... within the ... scope of the [statute] creating such duty and not merely an accidental result of the breach."[68]

Negligence *per se* is used in a similar context in the Netherlands, Denmark, and Germany, all civil law countries. In the Netherlands, an injured party can recover civilly for a defendant's "act or omission contrary to a statutory duty or contrary to what according to unwritten law is due in society."[69] However, the claim is subject to defenses of justification, including the justifications set forth in the Netherlands Criminal Code, such as self-defense and necessity.[70]

In Denmark, one can be held liable in tort for not acting with the care displayed by the reasonable man. The standard of care can be established by the requirements of a statute, a "series of ... prohibitory acts."[71] Examples are statutes establishing safety measures to be taken in factories or measures to prevent pollution. But there are nuances of interpretation. It is not enough that the statute prohibits certain forms of conduct; "non-compliance with [the] acts will not automatically result in liability for any possible damage."[72] "[T]he particular

---

[66] *Id. See also* BRYAN M.E. MCMAHON, IRISH LAW OF TORTS 377–388 (2d ed., 1990) (Irish law, a common law system, has similar qualifications for the awarding of damages in the case of a statutory breach. The statute must be meant to benefit the class of person the plaintiff is in, the statute must be breached, there must be actual damages, and the accident must be of the kind the statute meant to prevent).

[67] RATANLAL RANCHHODDAS & DHIRAJLAL KESHAVAL THAKORE, LAW OF TORT 688 (22nd ed., 1992).

[68] *Id.*

[69] Elizabeth van Schilfgaarde, *Negligence Under The Netherlands Civil Code-An Economic Analysis*, 21 CAL. W.L.J. 265, 273 (1990/1991) (quoting Art. 6:162 sec. 2, NBW (New Civil Code)).

[70] *Id.* at 273.

[71] DANISH LAW: A GENERAL SURVEY 163 (Hans Gammeltoft-Hansen et al. eds., 1982) According to the editors, Danish law appears to require a criminal penalty to have been imposed on the defendant to establish his liability for civil damages. *Id.*

[72] *Id.*

prohibitory act [must] essentially establish a prudent conduct," that is, the statute must indicate what constitutes prudent care for its purposes.[73]

German law treats a breach of statutory duty in the same manner as English and Indian law. German judges must decide whether or not a statute was intended to prevent the damage caused by the defendant and whether the plaintiff is among the class of people the statute was intended to protect.[74]

A 1958 German case interprets these principles. A company violated a statute by not filing for bankruptcy in a timely fashion. A supplier to the company sued in a negligence action, claiming liability based upon its extension of credit to the company. The court first found that the plaintiff was within the class of people whom the statute was intended to protect. However, the court further found that the purpose of the statute was to ensure that if a company's debts exceeded its assets, the company would file for bankruptcy to protect its assets for the benefit of the company's creditors. Here, since the company's assets were secure, the plaintiff did not state a cognizable claim under the statute.[75]

Accordingly, a *per se* rule does not necessarily require absolute applicability. What, however, would be the point of recognizing the *per se* unlawfulness of the use of nuclear weapons if such unlawfulness was subject to elaborate potential defenses, justifications, qualifications and the like, such that not all such uses would necessarily be unlawful?

This is an important question which I will analyze further in the final chapters. The key, however, was found in the argument by the U.S. lawyer before the ICJ as to the importance of maintaining the legality of the practice of deterrence:

> If [nuclear] weapons could not lawfully be used in individual or collective self-defense under any circumstances, there would be no credible threat of such use in response to aggression and deterrent policies would be futile and meaningless. In this sense, it is impossible to separate the policy of deterrence from the legality of the use of the means of deterrence. Accordingly, any affirmation of a general prohibition on the use of nuclear weapons would be

---

[73] *Id.*

[74] B.S. MARKENSINIS, A COMPARATIVE INTRODUCTION TO THE GERMAN LAW OF TORTS 705 (3rd ed. 1994).

[75] *Id.* at 700–704.

directly contrary to one of the fundamental premises of the national security policy of each of these many States. [76]

---

[76] *See* ICJ Hearing, November 15, 1995, at 78.

Chapter 5: Interpreting International Law According to Its Purpose

Perhaps the most basic of all rules of construction is that a treaty is to be interpreted in such a way as to achieve, not frustrate, its purposes and the intent of the drafters. Article 31 of the Vienna Convention on the Law of Treaties provides: "A treaty shall be interpreted in good faith in accordance with the ordinary meaning to be given to the terms of the treaty in their context and in light of its object and purpose."[1]

---

[1] *See* Article 31 of the Vienna Convention on the Law of Treaties, May 23, 1969, 1155 U.N.T.S. 331, 8 I.L.M. 679. Article 31 provides:

1. A treaty shall be interpreted in good faith in accordance with the ordinary meaning to be given to the terms of the treaty in their context and in light of its object and purpose.

2. The context for the purpose of the interpretation of a treaty shall comprise, in addition to the text, including its preamble and annexes:

(a) any agreement relating to the treaty which was made between all the parties in connection with the conclusion of the treaty;

(b) any instrument which was made by one or more parties in connection with the conclusion of the treaty and accepted by the other parties as an instrument related to the treaty.

3. There shall be taken into account, together with the context:

(a) any subsequent agreement between the parties regarding the interpretation of the treaty or the application of its provisions;

(b) any subsequent practice in the application of the treaty which establishes the agreement of the parties regarding its interpretation;

(c) any relevant rules of international law applicable in the relation between the parties.

4. A special meaning shall be given to a term if it is established that the parties so intended.

There are several approaches to treaty interpretation: (1) textual, (2) subjective (intention of the parties), (3) teleological (the general object and purpose of the treaty), (4) contextual or inclusive, and (5) "interpretation in the spirit of equity that is accordance with good faith, common sense and reasonableness." *See* Blaine Sloan, *The United Nations Charter as a Constitution*, 1 PACE Y.B. INT'L L. 61, 95–98 (1989) (citing U.N. Conference on the Law of Treaties, Second Session Official Records, Vienna, 9 April–22 May 1969).

Historically, there was a strict approach to treaty interpretation. *Id.* The rules included: (1) the plain meaning of the words, (2) *ejusdem generis*, (3) *expressio unio*, (4) restrictive interpretation in favor of State sovereignty, and (5) principle of effectiveness. *Id.* at 97.

Article 31 further makes it clear that a treaty shall be interpreted in light of its overall context, including any other relevant rules of international law applicable in the relation between the parties.[2] Article 32 provides that resort may be had to supplementary means of interpretation, including the preparatory work of the treaty and the circumstances of its conclusion, to prevent an interpretation which would lead to a result which is "manifestly absurd or unreasonable."[3]

Similarly, rules of customary law and generally accepted principles of law are to be interpreted and applied in light of their purposes.[4]

Before the ILC Articles on Interpretation were adopted, the United States unsuccessfully urged that a broader contextual approach be adopted by proposing an amendment to combine the ILC Draft with the more contextual approach. *Id.*

The Comments to Article 31 indicates a reluctance to allow the use of materials used in the development and negotiation of the treaty as interpretative tools. *Id.* at 103–04 (citing RESTATEMENT (THIRD), FOREIGN RELATIONS LAW OF THE UNITED STATES 190, 196–98 (1987)). The Articles on Interpretation are not a road map to treaty interpretation but rather indicate the "relative weight to be given to various factors." *Id.* at 104 (citing I. SINCLAIR, THE VIENNA CONVENTION ON THE LAW OF TREATIES 116–17 (2d. ed. 1984)). *See also* Sloan, *supra*, at 91–94; U.N. Conference on the Law of Treaties, Second Session Official Records, Vienna, 9 April–22 May 1969.

[2] *See* Article 31 Vienna Convention on the Law of Treaties.

[3] Article 32 Vienna Convention on the Law of Treaties states:

Recourse may be had to supplementary means of interpretation, including the preparatory work of the treaty and the circumstances of its conclusion, in order to confirm the meaning resulting from the application of article 31, or to determine the meaning when the interpretation according to article 31: (a) leaves the meaning ambiguous or obscure; or (b) leads to a result which is manifestly absurd or unreasonable.

Sloan, *supra* note 1, at 102 (quoting Article 32 Vienna Convention on the Law of Treaties).

[4] *See supra* Chapter 1, notes 7–18 and accompanying text. *See, e.g.,* The Paquete Habana, 175 U.S. 677 (1899) (evaluating and interpreting customary law relating to the essential purposes of fishing and vessels); The A.M&S Case, 2 Common Market Law Reports 264 (1982) (where, in adjudicating an interpretation of general principles of recognized common law between States, the Court stated that its role was "to find the best solution in qualitative terms having regard to the spirit, orientation, and general tendency of the national laws," with the applicable principle of law being interpreted "in light of its wording, structure, aims, and having regard to the laws of the member-states."), as set forth in MARK W. JANIS & JOHN E. NOYES, INTERNATIONAL LAW: CASES AND COMMENTARY 101 (1997). *See also* Visuvanathan Rudrakumaran, *The*

These rules apply to the principles of proportionality, necessity, moderation, discrimination, civilian immunity, neutrality, and humanity and the prohibitions of genocide and war crimes, each of which has been subscribed to by the United States through international conventions.

"Requirement" of Plebiscite in Territorial Rapprochement, 12 HOUS. J. INT'L L. 23, 24 (1989).

Franck states:

> [C]oherence, and thus legitimacy, must be understood in part as defined by factors derived from a notion of community. Rules become coherent when they are applied so as to preclude capricious checkerboarding. They preclude caprice when they are applied consistently or, if inconsistently applied, when they make distinctions based on underlying general principles that connect with an ascertainable purpose of the rules and with similar distinctions made throughout the rule system.

Thomas M. Franck, *Legitimacy and the International System,* 82 AM. J. INT'L L. 705, 743 (1988).

See also J.L. BRIERLY, THE LAW OF NATIONS 67 (Sir Humphrey Waldock ed., Oxford 1963) (1928). Brierly quotes a passage in an award of the Claims Tribunal which was set up by agreement between the U.S. and Great Britain in 1910:

> Even assuming that there was ... no treaty and no specific rule of international law formulated as the expression of a universally recognized rule governing the case ..., it cannot be said that there is no principle of international applicable. International law, as well as domestic law, may not contain, and generally does not contain, express rules decisive of particular cases; but the function of jurisprudence is to resolve the conflict of opposing rights and interests by applying, in default of any specific provision of law, the corollaries of general principles, and so to find ... the solution of the problem. This is the method of jurisprudence; it is the method by which the law has been gradually evolved in every country resulting in the definition and settlement of legal relations as well between States as between private individuals.

Id. at 67.

Brierly further quotes Lord Mansfield: "The law of nations is founded on justice, equity, convenience, and the reason of the thing, and confirmed by long usage." *Id.* at 68 (emphasis omitted, citations omitted). *See also* CHARLES H. STOCKTON, OUTLINES OF INTERNATIONAL LAW 8 (Charles Scribner's Sons 1914) (discussing the Convention of the second Hague conference which has been ratified by the U.S.: "[I]t is provided that in the absence of treaty provisions this court shall apply the rules of international law. If no generally recognized rule exists, the court shall give judgement in accordance of the general principles of justice and equity.").

Applying these principles so as to achieve their purposes requires that the application be done before the weapons are used. Theoretical punishment after the fact, via war crimes prosecution or the like, would likely have no meaning after use of nuclear weapons in violation of such principles.

As noted, the U.S. military manuals also recognize the principle of analogy whereby the question of whether the use of a weapon would be unlawful *per se* may be determined pursuant to general principles or by analogy to weapons or methods previously determined to be unlawful.

Chapter 6: The Legal Significance of Probabilities as to the Potential Effects of the Use of Nuclear Weapons

I addressed above the legal bases for a *per se* rule, concluding that, under widely accepted principles of law, the use of nuclear weapons would not have to be unlawful in all cases for *per se* illegality to arise. I address now a related but different question: In evaluating the lawfulness of any particular use of nuclear weapons under the various rules of law upon which we have been focusing, such as those of proportionality, what level of likelihood of unlawful effects must be present for illegality to arise? This question in a sense precedes and anticipates the earlier question as to the bases for a *per se* rule in that it materially affects our evaluation of the potential lawfulness of various types of nuclear strikes.

Assume, for example, that the responsible military and civilian officials, analyzing the matter in advance, estimate that a particular nuclear strike would likely result in the collateral killing of some 5,000 non-combatants and that deaths up to that level would be justifiable in light of the value of the mission. Assume further that the officials estimate the following probabilities as to further possible effects:

Probability	Collateral Deaths
60%	5,000
12%	2,000
10%	8,000
9%	30,000
5%	100,000
3%	100,000,000
1%	900,000,000

The obvious question—although one that has not been much considered in addressing this matter—is how we should deal with such a range of probabilities. What is the tipping point from lawfulness into unlawfulness?

As we saw above, the United States at times has generally recognized that the lawfulness of the use of nuclear weapons under the proportionality rule depends on the effects of such use, particularly including the level of risk to civilians. In its arguments to the ICJ, the United States stated:

> Whether an attack with nuclear weapons would be disproportionate
> depends entirely on the circumstances, including the nature of the
> enemy threat, the importance of destroying the objective, the
> character, size and likely effects of the device, and the magnitude
> of the risk to civilians.[1]

However, in other formulations of the matter, the United States
ostensibly has taken the position, at least impliedly, that a particular use
should not be deemed unlawful unless it is certain to result in
impermissible effects. On the question of whether even a small scale
use of nuclear weapons would violate international humanitarian law
because of the risk of resultant escalation, the United States, as noted
above, objected that "[i]t seems to be assumed that any use of nuclear
weapons would inevitably escalate into a massive strategic nuclear
exchange, with the deliberate destruction of the population centers of
the opposing sides,"[2] and went on to reject this assumption as
"speculative in the extreme."[3]

Similarly, McNeill, one of lead U.S. lawyers before the ICJ, argued:

> The argument that international law prohibits, in all cases, the
> use of nuclear weapons appears to be premised on the incorrect
> assumption that every use of every type of nuclear weapon will
> necessarily share certain characteristics which contravene the law
> of armed conflict. Specifically, it appears to be assumed that any
> use of nuclear weapons would inevitably escalate into a massive
> strategic nuclear exchange, resulting automatically in the deliberate
> destruction of the population centers of opposing sides.[4]

To the same effect on the issue of the rights of neutrals, the United
States argued before the ICJ:

---

[1] *See* Conrad K. Harper (Legal Advisor, Department of State), Michael J.
Matheson (Deputy Legal Advisor, Department of State), Bruce C. Rashkow
(Assistant Legal Advisor, Department of State), & John H. McNeill (Senior
Deputy General Counsel, Department of Defense), *Written Statement of the
Government of the United States of America* (June 20, 1995), submitted to the
International Court of Justice, The Hague, The Netherlands, in connection with
the Request by the United Nations General Assembly for an Advisory Opinion
on the Legality of the Threat or Use of Nuclear Weapons ["U.S. ICJ
Memorial/GA App."] at 23. *See also id.* at 2, 7–8.

[2] *Id.* at 21.

[3] *See id.* at 21.

[4] *See* Statement of Michael J. Matheson (Deputy Legal Advisor,
Department of State) in oral argument to the Court, ICJ Hearing, Nov. 15,
1995, at 85.

However, even assuming arguendo that a belligerent's liability to a neutral could somehow be established in a particular case, the argument that unlawful damage would necessarily occur to neutral States whenever nuclear weapons are used cannot be maintained.[5]

Similarly, *The Naval/Marine Commander's Handbook*, in applying the necessity requirement, states:

> Nuclear weapons can be selectively directed against military targets. In the context of [the balance between humanitarian and military considerations], it is not clear the use of nuclear weapons necessarily violates international law.[6]

Thus, in terms of appraising the legal significance of the risk of large-scale escalation or other illegal effects, the United States appears to be suggesting or assuming that the relevant quantum of risk, for purposes of the legal significance of possible escalation, is inevitability and that the relevant intentionality as to the resultant destruction is deliberateness. Similarly, on the overall issue of the level of likelihood that a particular use of nuclear weapons would have unlawful effects before unlawfulness ensues, the U.S. lawyers' choice of such language as "necessarily" implies an extremely high standard of likelihood. So also with the issue of the necessary likelihood that a neutral's territory will be impermissibly violated by the use of nuclear weapons, the United States suggested that such repercussions have to be necessarily so before a violation would ensue.

Based upon a literal application of the standards suggested by the U.S. language, it would seem that the potential strike described above would pass muster. It offers a 72% probability of coming within or below the permissible number of non-combatant deaths, and indeed another 10% chance of an average of deaths of a relatively finite number. But what do we do with the 9% chance of 30,000 collateral deaths, the 5% chance of 100,000 deaths, the 3% chance of 100,000,000 deaths or the 1% chance of 900,000,000 deaths? What if it were a 0.05% chance of destroying substantially all life on earth?

The ICJ did not deal with the issue specifically although it appeared, in passing, basically to share the view expressed by the United States.

---

[5] *Id.* at 95–96.

[6] UNITED STATES DEPARTMENT OF THE NAVY ANNOTATED SUPPLEMENT TO THE COMMANDER'S HANDBOOK ON THE LAW OF NAVAL OPERATIONS 10-2 (Naval Warfare Publication 9, 1987) (With Revision A (5 October 1989), this handbook was adopted by the U.S. Marine Corps as FLEET MARINE FORCE MANUAL (FM FM) 1-10).

Thus, in applying the principles of necessity and proportionality, the Court stated that the question is whether the use of force would "necessarily" violate such principles.[7] On a more fundamental level, the Court ducked the matter, citing a lack of adequate facts:

> 43. Certain States ... contend that the very nature of nuclear weapons, and the high probability of an escalation of nuclear exchanges, mean that there is an extremely strong risk of devastation. The risk factor is said to negate the possibility of the condition of proportionality being complied with. The Court does not find it necessary to embark upon the quantification of such risks; nor does it need to enquire into the question whether tactical nuclear weapons exist which are sufficiently precise to limit those risks: it suffices for the Court to note that the very nature of all nuclear weapons and the profound risks associated therewith are further considerations to be borne in mind by States believing they can exercise a nuclear response in self-defense in accordance with the requirements of proportionality.[8]

It is perhaps understandable that the Court did not deal directly with this issue. Ostensibly no party did so.

There is a basis in international law to address this issue. Evaluation of responsibility, civil or criminal, in connection with risk taken of causing untoward injury to others is a familiar, indeed typical and inevitable, legal function. The United States and other States throughout the world regularly do so in their law, particularly in the fields of tort and criminal law. Certain widely accepted principles of law emerge, particularly the notion that even very low risks of grave results will generally be recognized as unlawful absent a high degree of justification.

---

[7] Nuclear Weapons Advisory Opinion ¶ 48, at 19, 35 I.L.M. at 823.

[8] *Id.* ¶ 43, 35 I.L.M. at 822. *See id.* ¶¶ 18, 32, 33, 36, 95, 97, at 18, 16, 17, 32, and 33, respectively.

U.S. Law

United States Court of Appeals Judge Learned Hand in the famous *Carroll Towing* case articulated a lasting formulation of a standard for evaluating risk in the tort law context.[9] In that case, Judge Hand addressed whether it constituted negligence for defendant barge company not to have had a caretaker on its barge when it broke loose from its mooring, allegedly resulting in injury to plaintiff.

Judge Hand concluded that whether the barge company was required to have a man aboard at the time of the accident was a "function of three variables: (1) The probability that she will break away; (2) the gravity of the resulting injury, if she does; (3) the burden of adequate precautions."[10] Judge Hand described the significance of these variables algebraically, concluding that the defendant would be negligent if $P \times L > B$, where P is the probability of injury, L is the gravity of the loss, and B is the burden which would be incurred in preventing the injury from occurring.[11]

In an earlier case, Judge Hand had defined the burden as "the interest which [the actor] must sacrifice to avoid the risk."[12] The "burden" element generally can be stated in terms of its interrelated positive or negative components. On the positive side, there is the actual benefit to the actor from taking the risk-taking action. On the negative side, there is the loss the actor would sustain in refraining from taking the action.

The latter includes the incremental cost to the actor of taking some other, presumably safer approach to achieve the same result, adjusted in light of the likelihood of some variation in the result. In the military context at hand, it is the anticipated military advantage to be derived from the use of the weapon adjusted in light of what could be accomplished through use of some other presumably safer weapon.

---

[9] *See* United States v. Carroll Towing, Co., 159 F.2d 169 (2d Cir. 1947).

[10] *See id.* at 173.

[11] *Id.*

[12] *See* Conway v. O'Brien 111 F.2d 611, 612 (2d Cir. 1940). Judge Hand's approach of determining tort liability based upon a balancing of such factors is followed in the tort law of other jurisdictions. *Id. See, e.g.,* Overseas Tankship (U.K.) Ltd. v. Miller Steamship Co. ("*Wagon Mound No. 2*"), 1 A.C. 617 Privy Council 1966 (1967) (stating "It does not follow that, no matter what the circumstances may be, it is justifiable to neglect a risk of … small magnitude. A reasonable man would only neglect such a risk if he has some valid reason for doing so, *e.g.*, that it would involve considerable expense to eliminate the risk. He would weigh the risk against the difficulty of eliminating it.").

Just as in the tort context one must weigh the likelihood that defendant's action will injure the plaintiff and the severity of such injury against the benefit to defendant of the conduct, so also, in our context, the military decision-maker must evaluate the likely extent of prohibited effects against the military utility of the strike.

The Hand type formulas are generally applied by the jury with appropriate legal instructions from the judge, and not necessarily by the actor in making the initial decision whether to go forward with the action. In contrast, the applicable decision-maker in our context is specifically called upon to perform this evaluation in the first instance before taking the action in question—and obviously before the actual effects can be known, highlighting the importance of developing an approach and overall protocol for performing this exercise, so the military commanders will have an informed and responsible basis upon which to proceed.

Some 32 years before Judge Hand's decision in *Carroll Towing*, Professor Harry Terry, in a seminal article, listed five factors to be applied in evaluating the reasonableness of a defendant's action in a negligence case:

> 1) the "principal object" (the value of the interest which might be harmed by the risk, essentially the plaintiff's interest);
> 2) the "magnitude of the risk" (the probability that the principal object might actually be harmed by the actor's risk);
> 3) the "collateral object" (the value of the interest which the actor seeks to advance by his risk);
> 4) the "utility of the risk" (the probability that the actor will obtain the collateral object by taking the risk); and
> 5) the "necessity of the risk" (the probability that the actor will obtain the collateral object if he does not take the risk).[13]

Some 60 years later, Professor Terry's factors were set forth in a formula defining negligence as arising under the following conditions:

$(P-P^1) B < P^2 L$, where
"B" = collateral object
"L" = principal object

---

[13] *See* Harry Terry, *Negligence*, 29 HARV. L. REV. 40 (1915).

"P" = probability of attaining the collateral object by taking the risk;

"P^1" = probability collateral object would have been attained without taking the risk;

"$P\text{-}P^1$" = the increase in the probability of attaining the collateral object which results from taking the risk (a positive number); and

"P^2" = the probability of injury to the principal object.[14]

Under this formulation, the defendant will be acting negligently when the goal he would be obtaining by his actions, multiplied by the increased likelihood he will obtain that goal through the action in question versus through other available means not threatening to the plaintiff, is less than the harm he may potentially inflict multiplied by a likelihood of his causing that harm.

Professor Keeton has described the basis of the negligence standard as follows:

> [T]he standard of conduct which is the basis of the law of negligence is usually determined upon a risk–benefit form of analysis: by balancing the risk, in the light of the social value of the interest threatened, and the probability and extent of the harm, against the value of the interest which the actor is seeking to protect, and the expedience of the course pursued.[15]

Integral to all these approaches is that the various likely effects, good and bad, of the action in question are being evaluated in light of their probability, and that, in the process, even a very low likelihood of a severe adverse consequence will weigh heavily in the balance.

While on their face these formulas seem to imply very precise calculations, it is obvious that such precision is not possible given the nature of the matters involved. Nor do the proponents of this overall approach, even in the tort context, suggest such possibility. Judge Hand himself indicated that the variables in question are "not

---

[14] *See* Note, *Origin of the Modern Standard of Due Care in Negligence*, 1976 WASH. U.L.Q. 447, 453–454.

[15] *See* W. PAGE KEETON ET AL., PROSSER & KEETON ON TORTS 173 (5th ed. 1984) (citing Terry, *Negligence*, 29 HARV. L. REV. 40, 42, (1915)). Professor Keeton further noted that "[t]he same balance between the threatened harm and the utility of the actor's conduct appears, of course, in the various privileges, such as self-defense, which are recognized as defenses to intentional torts." *Id.* at 173 n.48. *See also* RESTATEMENT (SECOND) OF TORTS §§291–293 (1965)

susceptible of any quantitative estimate," but that the formulaic approach is helpful in conceptualizing how finders of fact (in a civil context, generally juries) arrive at their decisions in negligence cases and how courts evaluate those decisions.[16]

Because of the inherent limits of quantitative analysis in these contexts, the courts in applying approaches such as those developed by Judge Hand, Professor Terry and the Washington University Law Quarterly article, often have resorted to gross categories such as "low," "moderate," and "high" risk.[17]

Cases applying these formulas in the tort context have focused expressly on the point of the increased duty of care imposed when there is even a low probability of an extremely adverse defect. A case in point is the decision by the Tenth Circuit in *Shute v. The Moon Elec. Assn., Inc.*[18]

This was a personal injury action against a utility company arising out of the crash of a helicopter after it flew into unmarked power lines strung by the defendant above the surface of a river in a wilderness area of the Rocky Mountains. The power lines had been strung behind trees on either bank of a river in such a way as to be difficult to see. Against the defendant's argument that the likelihood of a helicopter running into these lines was so low that precautionary measures on behalf of the defendant were not required, the plaintiff argued that, while the risk might be low, the repercussions of a possible crash of a helicopter were

---

[16] *See* Conway, 111 F.2d at 612; Moisan v. Loftus, 178 F.2d, 148, 149 (2d Cir. 1949) (stating "The injuries are always a variable within limits, which do not admit of even approximate ascertainment; and, although probability might theoretically be estimated if any statistics were available, they never are ....") (*quoted in* Washington v. Louisiana Power & Light, Co., 555 So. 2d 1350, 1355 n.2 (La. 1990)).

[17] McCarty v. Pheasant Run, Inc., 826 F.2d 1554, 1557 (7th Cir. 1987), is emblematic of the difficulty which often arises in quantifying Hand analysis. The McCarty court stated that

> Ordinarily ... the parties do not give the jury the information required to quantify the variables that the Hand Formula picks out as relevant ... . Conceptual as well as practical difficulties in monetizing personal injuries may continue to frustrate efforts to measure expected accident costs with the precision that is possible, in principle at least, in measuring the other side of the equation— the cost or burden of protection.

Id.

[18] *See* 899 F.2d 999, 1004 (10th Cir. 1990).

high, and that the cost to the defendant of having marked the wires would have been very low relative to the gravity of the risk.

The court stated:

> [T]he cost of marking lines ... is small compared to the gravity of the harm caused when a collision occurs. It is our judgment, therefore, that although the probability of this type of accident is low, the overall risk (*i.e.*, the probability multiplied by the gravity of harm) outweighs the limited burden imposed by our holding.[19]

In language particularly relevant to the issue at hand, Professors Prosser and Keeton stated the rule as follows:

> If the risk is an appreciable one and the possible consequences are serious, the question is not one of mathematical probability alone. The odds may be a thousand to one that no train will arrive at the very moment that an automobile is crossing a railroad track, but the risk of death is nevertheless sufficiently serious to require the driver to look for the train and the train to signal its approach. It may be highly improbable that lightening will strike at any given time or place; but the possibility is there, and it may require the precautions for the protection of inflammables. As the gravity of the possible harm increases, the apparent likelihood of its occurrence need be correspondingly less to generate a duty of precaution.[20]

The *Helling* case discussed by Professors Prosser and Keeton, involved the question of whether an ophthalmologist's failure to give a simple blood test for glaucoma to a patient under 40 years of age constituted negligence in a context where the risk of glaucoma to a person in that age range was one in 25,000. The court upheld the finding of negligence on the basis that the potential injury was so grave that even a low risk of such injury could not be justified.[21]

---

[19] *See id.*

[20] KEETON ET AL., *supra* note 15, at 171.

[21] *Id.* Similar approaches have been taken in other contexts. *See, e.g.,* Llaguno v. Mingey, 763 F.2d 1560, 1564 (7th Cir. 1985) (question of potential liability of Chicago police department under 42 U.S.C. § 1382 for search and seizure without a warrant). *See also* Villanova v. Abrams, 972 F.2d 792, 796 (7th Cir. 1992) (standard for civil commitment challenge under 42 U.S.C. § 1983). *See generally* United States v. Chalan, 812 F.2d 1302, 1314 (10th Cir. 1987) (intentional discrimination in jury selection). *See also* Camarra v. Municipal Court, 387 U.S. 523, 539–40 (1967) (probable cause for warrant for administrative searches); Reserve Mining Co. v. Environmental Protection Agency, 514 F.2d 492 (8th Cir. 1975) (standard for injunction relief under imminent hazard provision of the Federal Water Pollution Control Act).

It should be noted that the foregoing approach of balancing benefits and costs is essentially a utilitarian one flowing out of the tradition of Jeremy Bentham and John Stuart Mill, as opposed to the "rights" tradition expressed by John Locke and Immanuel Kant, and more recently by such scholars as John Rawls, Robert Nozick and Ronald Dworkin.[22] Ostensibly, the rights approach, which goes further in recognizing hard core rights not subject to such offsetting, is a basis for recognizing firmer prohibitions against invasions of the rights of protected persons:[23]

> In the rights tradition, the crucial criteria for assessing risks derive from the impact of those risks on risk victims, and the criteria are defined independently of the benefits flowing from risk creation. To be plausible, such a program cannot totally prohibit risk creation, but the ostensible advantage of this program over utilitarianism is that risk creation is circumscribed by criteria exclusively derived from considerations of the integrity of the individual, not from any balancing or weighing process. The root idea is that nonconsensual risks are violations of "individual entitlements to personal security and autonomy."[24]

In *Reserve Mining*, the court directly addressed the problem of scientific uncertainty, concluding that when proof with certainty is impossible, "concepts of potential harm, whether they be assessed as 'probabilities and consequences' or 'risk and harm' necessarily must apply." Reserve Mining, 514 F.2d at 520. *See* Nebraska Press Association v. Stuart, 427 U.S. 539, 562 (1976) (Constitutionality of a gag order restricting the press' ability to report details of a grisly rape and mass murder).

[22] *See* Christopher H. Schroeder, *Rights Against Risks*, at 503–506. This article originally appeared at 86 COLUM. L. REV. 495 (1986). Reprinted with permission (pointing out that the jurors in the Ford Pinto litigation were outraged when they learned that Ford had performed a cost–benefit analysis when deciding whether to move the Pinto's gas tank to a safer location and further noting that Congressional legislation in the environmental area has often rejected cost–benefit balancing in enacting environmental laws and instead recognized "inalienable rights" of citizens to a safe work-place and the like). Schroeder adds, "[A]cts of reckless endangerment that involve modern risks have begun to be the object of criminal punishment, as witnessed by the recent conviction of corporate executives of Film Recovery Systems Corporation after a worker had been wrongfully exposed to cyanide in a chemical reprocessing plant." *Id.* at 497 (citing *Murder in the Front Office*, NEWSWEEK, July 8, 1985, at 58).

[23] *See id.* at 509–510.

[24] *Id.*

As Duke Professor Christopher Schroeder expresses it, "The anxiety to preserve some fundamental place for the individual that cannot be overrun by larger social considerations underlies what H.L.A. Hart has aptly termed the 'distinctly modern criticism of utilitarianism,' the criticism that, despite its famous slogan, 'everyone [is] to count for one,' utilitarianism ultimately denies each individual a primary place in its system of values."[25]

Generally Accepted Principles of Law

Legal systems throughout the world recognize the general principle that a person who unjustifiably causes injury to another "is negligent, and therefore liable in tort, if the burden of precautions was less than the probability of harm times the gravity of injury."[26]   An actor's behavior is analyzed against that of the reasonable person in light of such factors as "the magnitude of the risk created, taking into account both the likelihood of harm, and its probable severity; the social utility of the defendant's conduct; [and] the possibility of guarding against [it]."[27]

If the potential harm is great, a high level of care is required, even though the likelihood of that harm be slight. So too, if the harm is less

---

[25] *Id.* at 509–510 (citing Hart, *Between Utility and Rights*, 79 COLUM. L.REV. 828, 829 (1979); J. MILL, *Utilitarianism, in* 10 COLLECTED WORKS OF JOHN STUART MILL 203 (1969); and J. BENTHAM, *Plan of Parliamentary Reform, in* 3 THE WORKS OF JEREMY BENTHAM 433, 459 (1843)).

[26] IZHAK ENGLARD, THE PHILOSOPHY OF TORT LAW 37–38 (1993) (stating "This book is concerned with the foundations of tortious liability in contemporary society. The focus is on Anglo-American law, but the basic theoretical issues are equally relevant for civil law systems."). *See also* XI INT'L ENCYCLOPEDIA OF COMPARATIVE LAW Part I, § 2-114 (Andre Tunc ed., 1983) ("Nowadays, the principal test of foreseeability of damages is giving way to a group of tests, which together spell out a 'risk concept.'") In the preface, the author mentions that he is analyzing the tort systems of industrialized countries.

[27] *See* INT'L ENCYCLOPEDIA OF COMPARATIVE LAW, *supra* note 26, at 2-113. *See also* RATANLAL RANCHHODDAS & DHIRAJLAL KESHAVAL THAKORE, THE LAW OF TORTS 408–409 (22nd ed., 1992). The authors state in the preface that this work is a treatise on the principles of English common law and Indian case law. *See also* Michael F. Rutter, *The Tort of Negligence: More Preference Than Principle* 5 SINGAPORE L. REV. 83 (1984). (Singapore, a common law country, takes the following factors into consideration when weighing negligent behavior: the seriousness of the potential injury, how expensive the cost of preventing such harm, the social utility of the actor's conduct, the knowledge of the probability of the harm occurring, etc.).

significant but its likelihood is great, a high level of care is required.[28] On the other hand, if the potential harm and its probability are slight, the degree of care required is correspondingly less. The reasonable man must take into consideration both the severity and the likelihood of the potential harm.

The working of the Hand type analysis can be seen in a hypothetical played out under Australian law.[29] Assume that plaintiff Smith, while purchasing coffee from defendant Mega Foods, suffered a third-degree burn when the coffee, which was extremely hot at some 180 degrees Fahrenheit, was spilled on him. Assume further that this kind of thing had happened before and indeed that Mega had been sued some 750 times in the past for similar injuries, and that Mega had not put up any signs warning consumers of the risk.

On these facts, Mega, under Australian law, would likely be found negligent on the basis that it owed Smith a duty of care with respect to this risk because the probability of harm was foreseeable, the potential harm was severe, and the costs of guarding against it through a warning would not have been burdensome.[30]

Canadian law also replicates the Hand factors in assessing fault in tort liability. Canadian judges recognize the premise that even taking a slight risk can be unlawful, if the potential harm is great.[31] In *Paris v Stepney Borough Council*, a man who only had vision in one eye was blinded in his other eye when a metal chip struck his eye while he was working on a machine. The man's employer was held liable for negligence because although the probability of the harm occurring was very low, the gravity of being blinded in the man's remaining good eye was grave. In addition, the cost of guarding against the harm, namely

---

[28] *See* RANCHHODDAS & THAKORE, *supra* note 27, at 408–09. *See also* INT'L ENCYCLOPEDIA OF COMPARATIVE LAW, *supra* note 26, at 2-114.

[29] Michael Tilbury & Harold Luntz, *Punitive Damages in Australian Law*, 17 LOY. L.A. INT'L & COMP. L.J. 769, 777 (1995). The authors discussed a hypothetical personal injury tort and have analyzed the situation under Australian tort law.

[30] *Id.* at 779.

[31] ALLEN M. LINDEN, CANADIAN TORT LAW 112 (1993):
When the potential loss is great, the creation of even a slight risk may give rise to liability ... . Dean Prosser summarized the position in this way: "[A]s the gravity of the possible harm increases, the apparent likelihood of its occurrence need be correspondingly less to generate a duty of precaution."
Id. (quoting PROSSER & KEETON ON THE LAW OF TORTS 171 (5th ed., 1984)).

providing employees with protective eyewear, was not especially onerous.[32]

Irish tort law applies these same factors[33] and recognizes that, "[w]here the potential injury is great, the creation of even a slight risk may constitute negligence."[34] Thus, in *Hughes v. Ballynahinch Gas Co.*, defendant gas company was found liable for negligence when gas it was transporting exploded, injuring several people. The court reasoned that although the risk of harm was small, the act of transporting poisonous gas was a "matter most dangerous to human life, and, therefore, the highest degree of reasonable care" was required of the defendant.[35]

Another example of the Hand type analysis at work can be seen in the West Indies case of *Mowser v. De Nobriga*. Here, a spectator at a horse race was injured when the horse ran off the track and into the crowd, at a point where the race track had no fence to prevent such an incident. The judge sustained liability on the basis that the risk of a horse's running into the crowd and trampling a spectator was foreseeable to the defendant, that the potential harm was substantial, and that the erecting a protective fence would not have been expensive.[36]

The Hand type approach has also been followed in civil law systems such as those of Germany and Japan.[37] In German law, for instance, the term *Verkehrssicherungspflicten* connotes that, if an actor creates a possible danger, the actor is legally responsible to protect others against it.[38] In applying this rule, the German courts have regularly utilized a Hand type analysis, focusing on the severity and probability of the potential harm in light of the social utility of the activity and the costs of refraining from the action or taking some alternate course.[39] The German tort system has imposed this tort duty on defendants on the

---

[32] Paris v. Stepney Borough Council, A.C. 367 (1951).

[33] BRYAN M. E. MCMAHON, IRISH LAW OF TORTS 110–111 (1990).

[34] *Id.* at 114.

[35] Hughes v. Ballynahinch Gas Co., 33 I.L.T.R. 74 (Palles C.B., 1898).

[36] Mowser v. De Nobriga, 15 W.I.R. 147 (1969) (discussed in GILBERT KODILINYE, THE LAW OF TORTS IN THE WEST INDIES, 66–70 (1992)).

[37] *See* B.S. MARKENSINIS, A COMPARATIVE INTRODUCTION TO THE GERMAN LAW OF TORTS 75 (3rd ed. 1994). *See also* HIROSHI ODA, JAPANESE LAW 213 (1992); INT'L ENCYCLOPEDIA OF COMPARATIVE LAW at 2-114, ENGLAND at 1.

[38] *See* MARKENSINIS, *supra* note 37, at 75.

[39] *Id.* at 69, 75.

basis that "[t]he need for such a duty is obvious in every civilized society."[40]

So also Japanese tort law recognizes that "[t]he unlawfulness of an act is decided by 'balancing' the nature of the interest which was violated and the mode of the tortious act."[41] Further, "[i]f the infringed interest is serious, even a slight contravention of law or breach of duty may result in liability ...."[42]

The Netherlands follows this same approach, including the balancing of "the probability that harm will result, the possible extent of the harm, and the extent of the defendant's objection to taking appropriate safety measures."[43] The Hoge Raad, the highest court of the country, applied this approach in a case where a worker of the Coca-Cola Bottling Company had left the door to the cellar of a bar open while he was making a delivery, and plaintiff bar patron fell down the open area, sustaining injury. The Court sustained liability because the risk of injury was both evident and potentially severe and the costs of avoidance, just setting up a barricade of chairs around the open hatch, would have been slight.[44]

So also under Dutch law a defendant is potentially liable in a traffic accident for not having checked the road for oncoming vehicles before turning even if it is assumed that the chances of there actually being an oncoming car are only 1%, since the severity of the potential harm is great and the costs of avoidance minimal.[45]

---

[40] *See id.* at 69.

[41] ODA, *supra* note 37, at 213.

[42] *Id.*

[43] Elizabeth van Schilfgaarde, *Negligence under the Netherlands Civil Code-An Economic Analysis*, 21 CAL. W. INT'L L.J. 265, 275 (quoting H.R. 5 Nov. 1965, N.J. 1996).

[44] *Id.* at 275–276.

[45] *Id.* at 278–79 (the author analyzes a hypothetical car accident under Dutch tort law, and uses a hypothetical point system to assess the damage).

Chapter 7: Probability Analysis under Generally Accepted Principles of Criminal Law—Rules as to Recklessness and Foreseeability

As we have seen, in tort law, negligence is often determined, at least conceptually, by the weighing of such factors as the utility of the conduct in question as against the probability of the injury threatened, the gravity of that injury and the burden of adequate precautions. Similar weightings can be found in the criminal law, where culpability is often made to turn upon such factors as the extent and utility of the risk the defendant took of causing the consequences for which he is now criminally charged and the level of the defendant's awareness of the risk created.[1]

Such rules of criminal law, like those discussed above relating to tort law, appear to be so widely recognized as to fall with "general principles of law recognized by civilized nations" as a binding source of international law.

U.S. Law

States of Mind

Criminal law typically defines crimes, at least in part, based upon the mental state of the actor. Thus, the Model Penal Code, adopted by many states,[2] defines four culpable mental states, "purposefully," "knowingly," "recklessly," and "negligently."[3] "Recklessly" is defined as follows:

> A person acts recklessly ... when he consciously disregards a substantial and unjustifiable risk that the ... element [of an offense] exists or will result from his conduct. The risk must be of such a nature and degree that ... its disregard involves a gross deviation

---

[1] *See* WAYNE R. LaFAVE & AUSTIN W. SCOTT, JR., CRIMINAL LAW, 2d ed. 232 (1986) [hereinafter LaFAVE & SCOTT] (citing RESTATEMENT, TORTS (SECOND) § 291 (1965)). *See also* W. PROSSER & W. KEETON, PROSSER & KEETON ON THE LAW OF TORTS § 31 at 182 et seq. (5th ed., W. Page Keeton ed., 1984) (knowledge and superior knowledge).

[2] *See* LaFAVE & SCOTT, *supra* note 1, at 618.

[3] *See* Model Penal Code §2.02(1) (A.L.I. 1985).

from the standard of conduct that a law-abiding person would observe in the actor's situation.[4]

Wharton points out the following as to the differences between acting "recklessly," "knowingly," and "negligently:"

> The difference between the terms "recklessly" and "negligently," as usually defined, is one of kind, rather than of degree. Each actor creates a risk of harm. The reckless actor is aware of the risk and disregards it; the negligent actor is not aware of the risk but should have been aware of it.
>
> A person who acts "recklessly" and one who acts "knowingly" share the common attribute of awareness; but the awareness is of mere risk (probability) in the former case and of practical certainty in the latter.[5]

Defining "depraved heart murder," Professors LaFave and Scott state:

> Extremely negligent conduct, which creates what a reasonable man would realize to be not only an unjustifiable but also a very high degree of risk of death or serious bodily injury to another or to others—though unaccompanied by any intent to kill or do serious bodily injury—and which actually causes the death of another, may constitute murder.[6]

The discussion of the element of recklessness in the Comments to Model Penal Code elaborates on the level of risk that must be present and the meaning of the requirement that the risk be unjustifiable:

> The risk of which the actor is aware must of course be substantial in order for the recklessness judgment to be made. The risk must also be unjustifiable. Even substantial risks, it is clear, may be created without recklessness when the actor is seeking to serve a proper purpose, as when a surgeon performs an operation that he knows is very likely to be fatal but reasonably thinks to be necessary because the patient has no other, safer chance.[7]

---

[4] Model Penal Code §2.02(c) (A.L.I. 1985) © 1985 by the American Law Institute. Reprinted with permission.

[5] WHARTON'S CRIMINAL LAW § 27, at 170 (Charles E. Torcia ed., 1993) (emphasis omitted).

[6] LaFAVE & SCOTT, *supra* note 1, § 7.4 at 199–200. Reprinted from CRIMINAL LAW, WAYNE LaFAVE & AUSTIN W. SCOTT, 2d ed., 1986, with permission of the West Group.

[7] MODEL PENAL CODE § 2.02 Comments ¶ 3 at 237 (A.L.I. 1985).

The Comments add that "less substantial risks might suffice for liability if there is no pretense of any justification for running the risk."[8]

Noting that describing the threshold levels of risk for liability as "substantial" and "unjustifiable" is "useful but not sufficient," the Comments conclude that "[t]here is no way to state this value judgment that does not beg the question in the last analysis," and hence that the jury must decide. The jury should "be asked to measure the substantiality and unjustifiability of the risk by asking whether its disregard, given the actor's perceptions, involved a gross deviation from the standard of conduct that a law-abiding person in the actor's situation would observe."[9] The Comments add, "It is, of course, impossible to prescribe in advance the precise balance in adjudging culpability between factors relating to the degree of the risk and factors going to its nature."[10]

The Comments further state:

> Ultimately, then, the jury is asked to perform two distinct functions. First, it is to examine the risk and the factors that are relevant to how substantial it was and to the justification for taking it. In each instance, the question is asked from the point of view of the actor's perceptions, *i.e.*, to what extent he was aware of risk, of factors relating to its substantiality and of factors relating to its unjustifiability. Second, the jury is to make the culpability judgment in terms of whether the defendant's conscious disregard of the risk justifies condemnation. Considering the nature and purpose of his conduct and the circumstances known to him, the question is whether the defendant's disregard of the risk involved a gross deviation from the standards of conduct that a law-abiding person would have observed in the actor's situation.[11]

The Comments make clear that the foregoing analysis applies regardless of whether the risk factors relate "to the nature of the actor's conduct, to the existence of the requisite attendant circumstances, or to the result that may ensue."[12]

The Model Penal Code also addresses this matter in the context of the requirements as to the necessary causative relationship between conduct and result for liability to arise. Section 2.03 provides that, for liability for recklessness, it is sufficient if the actual result is within the

---

[8] *Id.* § 2.02 Comments at 237 n.14.
[9] *Id.* § 2.02 Comments at 237.
[10] *Id.* § 2.02 Comments at 237 n14.
[11] *Id.* § 2.02 Comments at 238.
[12] *Id.* § 2.02 Comments at 236–237.

risk of which the actor was aware and would not have occurred but for the action in question.[13] Even the elements of "purposefully" or "knowingly" are potentially present in circumstances where the actual result, while not within the purpose or contemplation of the actor, "involves the same kind of injury or harm as that designed or contemplated and is not too remote or accidental in its occurrence to have a [just] bearing on the actor's liability or on the gravity of his offense" or where "the actual result differs from the probable result only in the respect that a different person or different property is injured or affected."[14]

As to the relevance of the breadth of the concept of recklessness, the Model Penal Code provides that, where the level of culpability required for a particular offense is not specifically provided, it is sufficient if the actor acted purposefully, knowingly, or recklessly.[15] The Explanatory Note states that there is "a rough correspondence between this provision and the common law requirement of 'general intent'"[16] and notes that this is generally the common law position.[17]

So also, Glanville Williams in his seminal treatise noted that recklessness is generally classed with intention for legal purposes and that "[t]he thing that usually matters is not desire of consequence but

---

[13] *See id.* § 2.03 Explanatory Note at 254–55.

[14] *Id.* § 2.03(2)(a) and (b). The Explanatory Note states, "The traditional language of proximate causation is replaced by language that focuses on the relationship between the purpose or contemplation of the actor and the actual result of his conduct." *Id.* § 2.03 Explanatory Note at 254.

[15] *See id.* § 2.02(3).

[16] *Id.* § 2.02(3) Explanatory Note at 228.

[17] *See id.* § 2.02(3) Comments ¶ 5 at 244. The Comments state, "When purpose or knowledge is required, it is conventional to be explicit. And since negligence is an exceptional basis of liability, it should be excluded as a basis unless explicitly prescribed." *Id.*

The Comments state, "No one has doubted that purpose, knowledge and recklessness are properly the basis for criminal liability, but some critics have opposed any penal consequences for negligent behavior." *Id.* § 2.02 Comments ¶ 4 (Negligence) at 243. Rejecting the arguments that there is no purpose or basis for criminalizing negligence and concluding that criminalization could foster higher levels of care, the Comments state, "Accordingly, negligence, as here defined, should not be wholly rejected as a ground of culpability that may suffice for purposes of penal law, though it should properly not generally be deemed sufficient in the definition of specific crimes and it should often be differentiated from conduct involving higher culpability for the purposes of sentence." *Id.* § 2.02 Comments (Negligence) ¶ 4 at 243–44 (citations omitted).

merely foresight of consequence, which is the factor common to intention and recklessness."[18] He concluded:

> It is this foresight of consequence that, it is submitted, constitutes *mens rea*. Consequently every crime requiring *mens rea*, if it does not positively require intention, requires either intention or recklessness.[19]

The distinction between recklessness and negligence marks the general boundary between criminal and civil liability, although some negligence (generally deemed to amount to "gross" negligence or the like) is deemed criminal.[20] An additional category of potential civil but

---

[18] GLANVILLE L. WILLIAMS, CRIMINAL LAW, THE GENERAL PART § 22 at 59 (Stevens & Sons Limited 1953). Williams further explains:

> In recklessness there is foresight of the possible consequence of conduct, whereas in inadvertent negligence there is no such foresight. For many, if not most, legal purposes recklessness is classed with intention. It is like intention in that the consequence is foreseen, but the difference is that whereas in intention the consequence is desired, or is foreseen as a certainty, in recklessness it is foreseen as possible or probable but not desired.

Id. § 19 at 49 (citations omitted).

Williams notes that while, recklessness "in its ordinary sense connotes a state of mind," *i.e.*, that "the consequence must have been foreseen," nonetheless "it seems that a person may be convicted of recklessness although it cannot be demonstrated that the consequence was foreseen, provided it can be inferred that he would still have acted as he did even if he had foreseen the consequences." *Id.* § 19 at 51.

[19] *Id.* § 22 at 59 (citations omitted).

[20] *See id.* §§ 29–31 at 88–100.

Wechsler and Michael described the boundaries of criminal and civil liability:

> The line dividing manslaughter from civil negligence is as shadowy as that dividing murder from manslaughter. For the most part, the negligence that is criminal is distinguished from the negligence that is not, only by the addition of an epithet such as "gross," "culpable," "wanton" or "reckless," as opposed to "ordinary" or "slight." What, if anything, these epithets mean remains for the most part undetermined. But the differences between two negligent acts that are significant for this purpose, must reside in the degree of the risk of injury they unjustifiably create, the character of the injury or the actor's awareness of the risk. There is authority for the view that the character and degree of risk distinguish criminal from non-criminal negligence, whereas awareness of the risk distinguishes murder from manslaughter. There is also authority

not criminal liability arises in the situation of conduct deemed justifiable under the criminal law. Model Penal Code Section 3.01(2) provides, "The fact that conduct is justifiable under this Article does not abolish or impair any remedy for such conduct that is available in any civil action."[21]

Herbert Wechsler and Jerome Michael in their seminal article on the rationale for the law of homicide described the jury's role in evaluating the culpability of risks taken by the defendant:

> The jury must still determine, first, whether the danger created was unduly great, *i.e.* whether the risk should be regarded as a normal and desirable, or as an abnormal, undesirable and, therefore, unjustifiable incident of an otherwise lawful activity; and, second, whether the unjustifiable risk was slight, great or very great. Since human beings can make only rough estimates of degrees of danger, the jury may be expected in many cases to do no more than ask itself whether the particular behavior should be punished.[22]

As to the appropriate framework for evaluating the risk of unintended consequences, Wechsler and Michael stated:

> Thus, the matter may be summarized as follows: when death is not intended, the desirability of preventing a particular act because it may result in death, turns upon the following factors: (1) the probability that death or serious injury will result; (2) the probability that the act will also have desirable results and the degree of their desirability, in the determination of which the actor's purposes are relevant; (3) if the act serves desirable ends, its efficacy as a means, as opposed to the efficacy of other and less dangerous means.[23]

Speaking of areas of risk creation not specifically regulated by statute, Wechsler and Michael stated:

> With respect to this vast residuum of behavior, the legislature can say no more, in effect, than (1) it is desirable if it is prudent and undesirable if it is not; (2) whether or not it is prudent in particular

---

> for the view that awareness of the risk is necessary for negligence to be criminal at all, and this, indeed, is what the epithets listed above are most likely to mean to a jury.

Herbert Wechsler & Jerome Michael, *A Rationale of the Law of Homicide*, 36 COLUM. L. REV. 701, 731 (1937).

[21] Model Penal Code § 3.01(2) (A.L.I. 1985) © 1985 by the American Law Institute. Reprinted with permission.

[22] Wechsler & Michael, *supra* note 20, at 731.

[23] *Id.* at 744 (citations omitted).

cases depends upon the desirability of the actor's ends, the efficacy and necessity of his means, and the probability that death or serious injury will result; and (3) in view of the rigor of the sanctions of the criminal law, the degree of imprudence should be substantial.[24]

The Model Penal Code's comments as to the significance of actual effects to the implementation of the criminal law highlight an important distinction between normal rules of criminal law where one can in effect wait to see how such results come out and the inquiry we are embarked upon as to the putative lawfulness or not of nuclear weapons:

> How far the penal law ought to attribute importance in the grading of offenses to the actual result of conduct, as opposed to results attempted or threatened, presents a significant and difficult issue. Distinctions of this sort are essential, at least when severe sanctions are involved, for it cannot be expected that jurors will lightly return verdicts leading to severe sentences in the absence of the resentment aroused by the infliction of serious injuries. Whatever abstract logic may suggest, a prudent legislator cannot disregard these facts in the enactment of a penal code.[25]

The definitions of crimes based upon such states of mind as "recklessness" and "depraved heart" become interesting for present purposes in terms of seeing what level of risk of the prohibited effects taken by the defendant give rise to criminal liability. Two cases discussed by Professors LaFave and Scott illustrate this point, *Banks v. State*[26] and *Commonwealth v. Ashburn*.[27]

In *Banks*, the defendant had fired two bullets into the caboose of a passing train, killing a brakeman.[28] LaFave and Scott note that the chances were much greater that the defendant would not kill than that he would kill, and that perhaps the chances of killing were no more than 5%, given the area of the side of the caboose in relation to the space taken up by the vital parts of its occupants. The authors note

---

[24] *Id.* at 746 (citations omitted).

[25] Model Penal Code § 2.03 Comments ¶ 1 at 257 (A.L.I. 1985).

Wechsler and Michael similarly concluded that the same basic principles apply to risk creating whether or not it results in death. *See* Wechsler & Michael, *supra* note 20, at 733.

[26] *See* Banks v. State, 85 Tex. Crim. 165, 211 S.W. 217 (1919). *See* LaFave & Scott, *supra* note 1, at 618–619.

[27] *See* Commonwealth v. Ashburn, 459 Pa. 625, 331 A.2d 167 (1975). *See also* LaFave & Scott, *supra* note 1, at 619.

[28] Banks, 85 Tex. Crim. at 167, 211 S.W. at 217–18.

that, in light of the lack of social utility in shooting into the side of the caboose, this small risk was held sufficient to constitute murder.[29]

Similarly, in *Ashburn*, the appellate court, upholding the trial judge's decision, rejected the assertion by defense counsel that, for the crime in question to be murder, death for the victim must have been at least 60% certain.[30] The court pointed out that depraved-heart murder "does not depend on any precise mathematical calculation of the probable consequences of the defendant's acts."[31]

Professors LaFave and Scott state the rule as follows:

> [I]t is what the defendant should realize to be the degree of risk, in the light of the surrounding circumstances which he knows, which is important, rather than the amount of risk as an abstract proposition as the mathematics of chance.[32]

Assume that there are 1,000 pistols on a table, only one of which is loaded. The defendant, knowing this, picks up one of the pistols at random and fires it at the victim, killing him. In this context, where the risk of killing the victim had been very low, (one-tenth of 1%), would defendant's conduct be a basis for criminal liability for manslaughter and possibly even for murder? LaFave and Scott believe that it would.[33]

Professors LaFave and Scott offer a further example:

> One may act recklessly if he drives fast through a thickly settled district though his chances of hitting anyone are far less than 90% or even 50%. Indeed, if there is no social utility, what he is doing might be reckless though the chances of harm are something less than 1%. Thus, while "knowledge" and the knowledge-type of "intention" require a consciousness of almost-certainty, recklessness requires a consciousness of something far less than certainty or even probability.[34]

---

[29] *See* LaFave & Scott, *supra* note 1, at 619. *See also* Banks, 85 Tex. Crim. at 166, 211 S.W. at 217.

[30] Ashburn, 459 Pa. at 632, 331 A.2d at 172.

[31] *Id* at 633, 331 A.2d at 172. *See also* LaFave & Scott, *supra* note 1, at 619.

[32] *Id.* at 619. Reprinted from Criminal Law, Wayne LaFave & Austin W. Scott, 2d ed., 1986, with permission of the West Group.

[33] *See id.* at 619 n.14.

[34] *Id.* at 239–240. *See also* Substantive Criminal Law Vol. II at 336–337.

Professors LaFave and Scott have identified other instances of conduct that have been held to involve the very high degree of unjustifiable homicidal danger necessary for depraved-heart murder:

> [F]iring a bullet into a room occupied, as the defendant knows, by several people; starting a fire at the front door of an occupied dwelling; shooting into the caboose of a passing train or into a moving automobile, necessarily occupied by human beings; throwing a beer glass at one who is carrying a lighted oil lamp; playing a game of "Russian roulette" with another person; shooting at a point near, but not aiming directly at, another person; driving a car at very high speeds along a main street; shaking an infant so long and so vigorously that it cannot breathe; selling "pure" (*i.e.*, undiluted) heroin. Other sorts of extremely risky conduct may be imagined; throwing stones from the roof of a tall building onto the busy street below; piloting a speedboat through a group of swimmers; swooping an airplane so low over a traveling automobile as to risk the decapitation of the motorist. In any such case, if death actually results to an endangered person and occurs in a foreseeable way, the defendant's conduct makes him an eligible candidate for a murder conviction.[35]

Glanville Williams provided an elaborate analysis of the rationale for the law in this area.[36] As to the scope of recklessness, he stated, "If the defendant foresaw the probability of the consequence he is regarded as reckless, even though he fervently desired and hoped for the exact opposite of the consequences, and even though he did his best (short of abandoning his main project) to avoid it."[37] He stated, "Recklessness is any determination to pursue conduct with knowledge of the risks involved though without a desire that they should eventuate."[38]

Addressing the subject of what level of likelihood of prohibited consequence is necessary for recklessness to arise, Williams concluded that knowledge of the mere possibility (as opposed to probability) of the consequence is enough since "a person is not generally at liberty to bring another causelessly even within slight danger of death."[39] He

---

[35] *See* LAFAVE & SCOTT, *supra* note 1, at 619–620 (citations omitted).

[36] *See* WILLIAMS, *supra* note 18.

[37] *Id.* § 19 at 49.

[38] *Id.*

[39] *Id.* § 21 at 53–54. Williams gave the following example:
Suppose that D possesses a number of pistols; he knows that all are unloaded save one, but does not know which one is loaded. He selects one at random and fires it at P, in order to obtain the excitement of putting P in peril. Here, the smaller the number of

went on to note, however, that "this does not mean that foresight of bare possibility is in every case tantamount to recklessness" since social utility will justify many risks (such as a person's driving a car or a surgeon's performing an operation).[40]

Williams concluded:

> The only rule that can be stated is that a risk may be run for reasonable cause; and whether the cause is reasonable may depend upon the magnitude of the risk undertaken, *i.e.*, the degree of probability of damage and the extent of the damage if it occurs.
>
> ***
>
> The conclusion is that knowledge of bare possibility is sufficient to convict of recklessness if the conduct has no social utility, but that the slightest social utility of the conduct will

---

> unloaded pistols, the greater is the probability that the pistol selected is the loaded one. Superficially one might think that the law ought to declare how many unloaded pistols to the single loaded one make a killing merely "possible" and how many make it "probable" or "likely."

Id.

Williams went on to adopt the position of an earlier Criminal Law Commission that:

> ...a killing with the loaded pistol is to be regarded as a killing with foresight of the probable consequence, however many unloaded pistols were with it when the choice was made. "The probability of a fatal result would be diminished as the number from which the selection was made was increased, but still there would be a willful risking of life attended with a fatal result, and as it seems a total absence of any intelligible principle of distinction for penal purposes." "Probable" here means what is usually called possible.

Id. (quoting 7th Rep. (1843), *Parl.Pap.* xix 28).

As to the meaning of these terms, Williams stated:

> On a determinist philosophy, the consequences of every act are physically certain; it is only knowledge of the consequences that is uncertain. For legal purposes such terms as possibility, probability and likelihood are to be construed as referring to this imperfect knowledge. A result is possible if it is reasonably conceivable; it is probable or likely if there is a somewhat high chance of its occurring, though how high this chance must be has not been authoritatively defined.

Id. § 21 at 53.

Williams added that in ordinary usage, "'likely' is a weaker term than 'probable.' ... Likely thus seems to be a strong possible and a weak probable."
Id. § 21 at 53 n.1.

[40] *Id.* § 21 at 54.

introduce an inquiry into a degree of probability of harm and a balancing of this hazard against its social utility. If this is the law, it would be useless to define probability in mathematical terms, because the degree of probability that is to constitute recklessness must vary in each instance with the magnitude of the harm foreseen and the degree of utility of the conduct.[41]

It is also clear that a *mens rea* of even less than overt intention can suffice for intentional murder.[42] Not only is there potentially liability for manslaughter for homicide committed recklessly, there is also potential liability for murder for some categories of unintentional murder.

Model Penal Code Section 210.2(1)(b) provides that an unintentional killing can be murder when "it is committed recklessly under circumstances manifesting extreme indifference to the value of human life."[43] At common law, under Blackstone's formulation, homicide constituted murder when "malice aforethought" was present, which could be found with or without intent when indicia were present of "a wicked, depraved, and malignant heart."[44]

Courts found such a depraved heart in the absence of intent based on such considerations as the following:
• the number of people put at risk;[45]
• the very great chance that a death would result from the act;[46] and
• the unnecessary brutality of the act.[47]

Under modern criminal law, four different approaches have been identified as dominating the modern treatment of unintended murder,

---

[41] *Id.* § 21 at 55. At another point, Williams stated, "Recklessness, as the term is used in this book, involves foresight of the possibility of a consequence." *Id.* at § 40 at 121.

[42] *See* Model Penal Code § 210.2(1)(b) (A.L.I. 1985). *See also* Note, *Defining Unintended Murder,* 85 COLUM. L. REV. 786 (May 1985).

[43] Model Penal Code § 210.2(1)(b) (A.L.I. 1985) © 1985 by the American Law Institute. Reprinted with permission.

[44] *See* Note, *Defining Unintended Murder,* 85 COLUM. L. REV. 786 (1985) (citing 4 W. Blackstone, Commentaries 198).

[45] *See id.* (citing Banks v. State, 85 Tex. Crim, 165, 166, 211 S.W. 217, 217u (1919) (man fires pistol into passing train, killing brakeman; court finds malice towards the group of persons necessarily on the train)).

[46] *See id.* (citing State v. Burris, 198 Iowa 1156, 198 N.W. 82 (1924) (intentional use of loaded pistol results in shooting death)).

[47] *See id.* (citing State v. John, 172 Mo. 220, 72 S.W. 525, 527 (1903) (dog catcher, after threatening a crowd gathered to watch him work, fatally strikes a bystander)).

each focusing on "a particular aspect of an actor's attitude or conduct in order to distinguish his crime from manslaughter and to justify its treatments as murder:"(1) the "Objective Circumstances" of the conduct in terms of its brutality and the like; (2) the "Degree of Risk" of the conduct in terms of the level of risk the actor took of causing death; (3) the "Multiple Victim" approach in terms of how many persons were endangered by the conduct; and (4) the "*Mens rea*" approach in terms of the culpability of the actor's state of mind.[48]

Without getting into the details of the different approaches, the overriding point for present purposes is that not only is recklessness sufficient for manslaughter but also that something less than actual intent can suffice for murder.

Thus, it is clear under domestic criminal law that, particularly where there is a risk of severe injury, far less than certainty is required for liability.

Generally Accepted Principles of Law

These principles of U.S. law to the effect that the taking of excessive risks of unlawful injury to others can give rise to criminal culpability are widely accepted in legal systems throughout the world. The concept of intent is recognized as elastic, extending beyond merely the state of mind of actually desiring a particular result and extending instead to the "foresight of probabilities" that a particular result could occur.[49] It is widely recognized in the world's legal systems that if an actor foresees the possibility that his conduct will cause a particular result and nonetheless proceeds with the conduct, he will be deemed to have intended that result if it eventuates, even if he did not actually desire it.[50]

This broad scope of intentionality is sometimes seen under the rubric of "constructive intention," a mental state akin to recklessness, which is implicated when the actor realizes that his conduct is creating a risk of injury, although he or she does not wish to bring about that

---

[48] *See id.* at 788–793.

[49] C.T. SISTARE, RESPONSIBILITY AND CRIMINAL LIABILITY 93 (1989).

[50] *See, e.g., id.* at 96 (stating that Austin and Bentham believed that "[e]ither purpose or foresight of possibility will suffice to establish [legal] intention, regardless of the agent's personal attitude or feelings about the consequences in question").

injury.[51] Australian law recognizes constructive intention as the "equivalent of actual intention."[52]

In a 1955 case in the Court of Criminal Appeal in New South Wales, the court held that "where a person applies their mind to the consequences of their act, and concludes 'that [it will] probably happen,' that is 'criminal intent'."[53] In addition, in a 1981 Queensland case, the judge stated that "'intentionality' is ... to be construed as including the mental state in which a result of D's conduct is foreseen as a 'likely consequence' of D's act, notwithstanding that he or she may not 'positively desire' this result."[54]

South Africa recognizes the concept of "legal intention," which is similar to the Australian constructive intention and to English and U.S. notions of recklessness. Under South African law, subject to a number of exceptions, "where a common law crime requires *mens rea* in the form of intention, actual intention is not necessary, legal intention will suffice for guilt."[55]

Such legal intention encompasses the situation where defendant had foresight that the consequence of his conduct was a possibility and was reckless as to whether the consequence would occur.[56] For such a state of mind, the accused must actually foresee the possibility of harm and act recklessly in relation to it. If he did not, but a reasonable person would have, he can be found guilty of negligence.[57]

South African law recognizes that the possibility of harm need not be great to warrant a finding of intentional behavior: "[L]egal intention is present if the accused 'foresees the possibility, however remote, of his act resulting in the death to another.'"[58]

Botswana, another common law country, recognizes that consequences are "intended" if the actor "fores[aw] that they [were] likely to come about."[59] So also Ethiopian law recognizes that "[c]riminal intention exists ... when the offender, being aware that his

---

[51] PETER GILLIES, CRIMINAL LAW 50 (1993).

[52] *Id.* at 49.

[53] *Id.* (discussing Stones, 56 S.R. (N.S.W.) 25 (1995)).

[54] *Id.* (discussing Lockwood, ex parte Attorney General, Qd. R. 209 (1981)).

[55] 1 E.M. BURCHELL & P.M.A. HUNT, SOUTH AFRICAN CRIMINAL LAW AND PROCEDURE 117 (1970).

[56] *Id.* at 117–19.

[57] *Id.* at 123.

[58] *Id.* at 124 (citing S. v. De Bruyn, 4 S.A. 498 (A.D.) (1968)).

[59] KWAME FRIMPONG & ALEXANDER MCCALL SMITH, THE CRIMINAL LAW OF BOTSWANA 19 (1992).

act may cause illegal and punishable consequences, commits the act regardless that such consequences may follow."[60]

Intention, with respect to the foresight of circumstances, can also be seen in civil law jurisdictions. Under Swiss law, "[a] person is deemed to have acted intentionally if he or she could have foreseen the criminal consequences of the behaviour and ha[ve] made allowance for them."[61] The probability of the consequences occurring must have "reached a sufficiently high degree."[62] In Ethiopia, "the offender must not only have taken seriously the possibility of producing a certain result, but in addition must have consented to its happening."[63]

Similarly, under Swedish law, intention exists "if the offender realized the possibility of the consequences and still undertook the act with the risk that the consequence might occur."[64] Under Greek law, intent can be found if the offender accepts a consequence as a necessary or even as a possible by-product of his intended act.[65] For example, if A places a bomb on a plane to kill B, A is thereby intending to kill the other passengers. Similarly, if a landlord burns down his own building to collect insurance money and in the process kills an invalid living in the building, he is deemed to have intended that killing.[66]

Similarly, the Soviet legal system recognized intent when an offender "foresees ... socially dangerous consequences, and ... consciously permits them to occur."[67] Similarly, Hungarian law during the Socialist era recognized intent when the accused "acquiesc[es] in [the] consequences [of his or her conduct]."[68]

Under German criminal law, direct intent is recognized when the actor desires a consequence to occur, regardless of the foreseeability of the consequence. In direct intent of the second degree, the actor knows that the consequence is certain to occur if he or she commits the act.

---

[60] STEVEN LOWENSTEIN, THE PENAL LAW OF ETHIOPIA 141 (1965).

[61] INTRODUCTION TO SWISS LAW 227 (F. Dessemontet & T. Ansay eds., 2nd ed., 1995). *See also id.* at 144.

[62] *Id.* at 227.

[63] LOWENSTEIN, *supra* note 60, at 144.

[64] MAJOR CRIMINAL JUSTICE SYSTEMS 115 (George F. Cole, Stanislaw J. Frankowski, & Marc G. Gertz eds., 1981).

[65] INTRODUCTION TO GREEK LAW 345 (Konstantinos D. Kerameus & Phaedon J. Kozyris eds., 2nd ed., 1993).

[66] *Id.*

[67] HAROLD J. BERMAN, SOVIET CRIMINAL LAW AND PROCEDURE 147 (1966).

[68] CRIMINAL CODE OF THE HUNGARIAN PEOPLE'S REPUBLIC 34 (Pal L'Amberg, trans., 1962).

Under *bedingter Vorsatz*, or conditional intent, the actor knows that his or her conduct may possibly result in harm and "approv[es] of the possible consequences of his conduct should they actually occur."[69] There is an additional state called "advertent negligence" under which "the actor is confident and has reason to believe that the result, though he foresees it as a possibility, will not occur while in the case of conditional intent this confidence is lacking."[70]

Under Norwegian criminal law, "intention exists first of all where purpose exists, that is, where the actor desires to cause the particular result by his act."[71] When the actor desires a particular result, the possibility of that result occurring is inconsequential. Intention will also exist if the actor believes that the consequences are "certain or predominantly probable" to occur.[72] In several decisions, Norwegian judges have held that intent can be recognized in cases where there is a lower degree of probability than the predominantly probable standard as long as the perpetrator "thought it more probable than not that the offensive result would occur."[73]

Dutch law similarly finds intent based on the actor's having foreseen the consequences without necessarily having desired them. Intent exists when the actor's "conduct is a manifestation of the actor's will."[74] Intent can be found when the actor foresees the consequences of his actions and also when there is a "high degree of probability."[75] This is called conditional intent, in which the actor "purposely or knowingly" creates the risk of an "in no way hypothetical chance."[76] The Dutch Supreme Court has stated that it can be assumed that one foresaw the results of his or her actions, if the results would have naturally or reasonably followed from the actor's conduct.[77]

Thus, not only is the concept of intent extremely broad, but also recklessness as a criminal state of mind is also widely recognized by legal systems throughout the world, as is the notion that the taking of

---

[69] INTRODUCTION TO GERMAN LAW at 388–389 (Werner F. Ebke & Matthew W. Finkin eds., 1996).

[70] *Id.* at 389.

[71] JOHANNES ANDENAES, THE GENERAL PART OF THE CRIMINAL LAW OF NORWAY 210 (1965) (emphasis omitted).

[72] *Id.* at 211 (emphasis omitted).

[73] *Id.* at 211–15 (emphasis omitted).

[74] INTRODUCTION TO DUTCH LAW FOR FOREIGN LAWYERS 338 (D.C. Fokkema, et al. eds., 1978).

[75] *Id.*

[76] *Id.*

[77] *Id.*

even a low level of risk of a severe danger may be criminal if not justified.[78]

Under Australian law, recklessness is defined as "advertent risk-producing conduct which conduct may or may not result in substantive harm. Where an offense requires proof of recklessness in this sense, it must be proven that D foresaw the occurrence of the specified harm."[79] So also, under South African law, the established meaning of recklessness in criminal law is that the accused "subjectively foresaw the probability or possibility of the harm that could result from his conduct ... but nevertheless persisted in such conduct."[80]

Similarly the Penal Codes of Uganda, Kenya, and Tanzania recognize the recklessness *mens rea*: "In recklessness the result is not the purpose of the conduct; it is merely incidental. Further, it is obvious that while in intention the conduct is aimed at resulting in certainty, in recklessness the mind adverts to a mere probability.

---

[78] BLACK'S LAW DICTIONARY 1271 (6th ed. 1990). Recklessness is "[t]he state of mind accompanying an act, which either pays no regard to its probably or possibly injurious consequences, or which, through foreseeing such consequences, persists in spite of such knowledge." *Id.*

[79] GILLIES, *supra* note 51, at 60.

In Australia, the 1995 Criminal Code Act attaches criminal liability to corporations. Under the statute, the removal by employees of safety guards or the disregarding of pollution controls in order to meet production deadlines could be seen as constituting reckless endangerment, if the "company culture" of the employer authorizes the "recklessly disregard[ing] [of a] substantial and unjustifiable risk of causing serious injury by removing equipment guards or ignoring the readings from pollution monitoring equipment." *See* Alan Rose, *Australian Criminal Code Act: Corporate Criminal Provisions*, 6 DEVELOPMENTS IN CRIMINAL LAW AND CRIMINAL JUSTICE 129, 136 (1995) ("This legislation does not merely punish a company because one of its officers committed an offense (vicarious responsibility). It also will allow the corporation to be held liable for criminal conduct if it can be proved that the practices or 'culture' of the company encouraged or at least did not prohibit the alleged offense.") *Id.* at 132.

[80] R.C. Williams, *Liability for Reckless Trading by Companies: The South African Experience*, 33 INT'L & COMP. L. Q. 684, 690–691 (1984) (The South African Companies Act of 1973 punishes any activity of a business which "is carried on recklessly or with intent to defraud creditors." The author notes that the term "recklessly," under the Act, is determined through an objective analysis.)

Finally, in intention the occurrence of the event is clearly desired; but in recklessness no such desire is necessary."[81]

Similarly, under Israeli law recklessness means that the actor is "aware of the nature of his conduct, of the circumstances appearing in the definition of the offense, and of the consequences of his conduct," and is indifferent to the results of his conduct or hopes they will not occur.[82]

German criminal law divides criminal mental states into intent and negligence. One can be prosecuted for acting with conscious negligence, meaning consciously taking a substantial and unjustifiable risk that causes another injury or death.[83] The 1974 crash of the Hersatt Bank provides an example. The bank's collapse, which was detrimental to the German economy, was ostensibly due in large measure to extremely risky foreign exchange transactions. The bank's officers were found to have acted recklessly and in violation of German criminal law.[84]

Sweden recognizes the concept of recklessness under the rubric of "oblique intent." "[One acts with] oblique intent if the offender realized the possibility of the consequences and still undertook the act with the risk that consequence might occur."[85]

The Philippine criminal law uses the term "imprudence" to connote the notion of recklessness: "If a person fails to take the necessary precaution to avoid injury to person or damage to property, there is imprudence."[86] Application of this concept can be seen in the instance of charges alleged against three officials in a Philippine mining company. In March 1996, between 2.4 and 4 million pounds of sediment were released into the Boac River when a drain plug broke,

---

[81] J. Byamugisha, *Criminal Responsibility Under the East African Penal Codes*, 3 & 4 ZAMBIA L. J. 76, 85 (1971/1972) (emphasis omitted).

[82] INTRODUCTION TO THE LAW OF ISRAEL 260 (Amos Shapiro & Keren C. DeWitt-Arar eds., 1995).

[83] MAJOR CRIMINAL JUSTICE SYSTEMS, *supra* note 64, at 155. In Germany, recklessness is equated to conscious negligence. "Offenders act with conscious negligence when they foresee that a certain consequence will possibly result from their conduct." *Id.*

[84] Maximilian Schiessl, *On the Road to a New German Reorganization Law —A Comparative Analysis of the Draft Proposed by the Insolvenzrechtskommission and Chap. 11 of the Bankruptcy Code*, 62 AM. BANKR. L. J. 233, 242.

[85] MAJOR CRIMINAL JUSTICE SYSTEMS, *supra* note 64, at 145.

[86] LUIS B. REYES, THE REVISED PHILIPPINE PENAL CODE 38–39 (8th ed. 1969).

endangering fish life and impairing the river's ability to serve as a source of potable water. Three high ranking officials of the mining company responsible for the damage were charged with reckless imprudence.[87]

Under Japanese law an actor can be criminally responsible for a number of offenses based upon the negligent creation of harm through a risk creating activity, regardless of whether the actor foresaw the harm.[88] Similarly, Norway has criminalized conscious negligence, defined as arising when one foresees a harmful result of his conduct, but nonetheless takes the chance that it will not occur.[89]

Through Article 28 of its Penal Code, Greece recognizes a similar type of criminal negligence when one, "foresaw th[e] consequence as possible but he trusted that it would not occur (negligence with realization of risk)."[90] Similarly, under Dutch penal law, "guilt is present when [the actor] consciously took unjustified risks which [he] should (could) have avoided."[91]

Similarly, under Swiss law, criminal liability can arise when the actor acted with advertent negligence or "luxuria," defined as the "form of guilt where the perpetrator is conscious of the danger that his or her activities might result in harmful consequences" of the behavior and "has made allowance for them."[92]

The former Soviet Union accepted the principle of recklessness, criminally sanctioning citizens for "anticipat[ing the possibility of] socially dangerous consequences ensuing from his or her action or omission, but recklessly rel[ying] on their being prevented ... ."[93] So

---

[87] *See id.*

[88] HIROSHI ODA, JAPANESE LAW 393 (1992).

[89] ANDENAES, *supra* note 71, at 213.

[90] INTRODUCTION TO GREEK LAW, *supra* note 65, at 308.

[91] INTRODUCTION TO DUTCH LAW FOR FOREIGN LAWYERS, *supra* note 74, at 338.

[92] INTRODUCTION TO SWISS LAW, *supra* note 61, at 227.

[93] MAJOR CRIMINAL JUSTICE SYSTEMS, *supra* note 64, at 198. *See also* BERMAN, *supra* note 67, at 147 ("A crime shall be deemed to be committed through negligence if the person who commits it foresees the possibility of the occurrence of the socially dangerous consequences of his actions ... but frivolously counts on their being prevented ... ."); Chris Osakwe, *Contemporary Soviet Criminal Law: An Analysis of the General Principles and Major Institutions of Post-1958 Soviet Criminal Law*, 6 GA. J. OF INT'L & COMP. L. 437, 451 (1976) (Under criminal negligence, "the individual is aware of the possible dangerous consequences of his contemplated act, however, he

also Hungarian law during the Socialist era provided that "[a] crime is due to negligence if the perpetrator foresees the consequences of his conduct but is recklessly confident that they will not ensue."[94]

The Polish Penal Code during the Socialist era specified the following *mens rea*: intent, recklessness, and inadvertent negligence. Recklessness was considered a nonintentional offense and under Polish law one could be punished for a nonintentional offense only when the law explicitly provided for such punishment.[95]

Thus, the sufficiency of recklessness as a criminal state of mind is widely recognized throughout the world's legal systems and has become a generally accepted principle of law. Legal systems throughout the world penalize actors for consciously taking risks that ultimately cause injury to others.

In addition, other legal systems, including those of England, Germany and the former Soviet Union have recognized extreme indifference as a potential *mens rea* element sufficient for murder:

> The criminal laws of many other countries, furthermore, have long recognized indifference as a *mens rea* element of murder. In England, the issue of murder versus manslaughter turns upon the actor's "willingness to kill".... In German and Soviet law, it is murder when the actor "reconciles himself" or "makes peace" with the death that will ensue from his actions.[96]

---

strongly believes that such danger could be averted and it turns out that his calculations ... proved to be wrong.").

[94] CRIMINAL CODE OF THE HUNGARIAN PEOPLE'S REPUBLIC *supra* note 68, at 34.

[95] Polish criminal law during the Socialist era also recognized recklessness as a basis of criminal liability. MAJOR CRIMINAL JUSTICE SYSTEMS, *supra* note 64, at 232. *See also* Phuong-Khanh T. Nguyen, *The Criminal Code of the Socialist Republic of Vietnam*, 13 REV. OF SOCIALIST L. 103, 124 (1987) (Article 10 of the Vietnamese Criminal Code states that, "[a] crime shall be deemed to be committed unintentionally ... [i]f the perpetrator realizes the possibility of the occurrence of the socially dangerous consequences of his act but believes that they will not occur or can be prevented."). *Id.*

[96] Note, *Defining Unintended Murder*, 85 COLUM. L. REV. 786, 805 n.106 (May 1985) (citing Gegan, *A Case of Depraved Mind Murder*, 49 ST. JOHN'S L. REV. 417 (1974) and G. FLETCHER, RETHINKING CRIMINAL LAW § 4.5.2 (1978)).

Chapter 8: Recklessness under Established Law of Armed Conflict

The broad adoption of recklessness as a potential basis for criminal liability in domestic law throughout the world is largely mirrored in established international law, where the potential for liability based on a mental state of less than full intentionality has been broadly recognized.

Potential liability can be evaluated in terms of the liability of States, of individuals and of commanders. Obviously States can act only through individuals. It is individuals, generally acting or purporting to act on behalf of States, who, in the first instance, commit war crimes— for which they are potentially liable under international law, as are the States on behalf of which they act.

Criminal Liability of States

As to States, we have seen that the United States, through its military manuals, generally recognizes, in effect, absolute liability for States, liability without regard to mental state.

The Air Force Manual on International Law states that the law of armed conflict "primarily emphasizes the behavior expected of nations and combatants—not the responsibility of individuals for its violation" —and that accordingly the law "often omits critical elements of individual criminal responsibility, such as intentional and deliberate acts."[1] Similarly, "[t]he law is not principally formulated with any view to individual criminal responsibility but rather to state responsibility."[2]

Explaining the general absence of a *mens rea* requirement for State, as opposed to individual, responsibility, the Air Force manual states that "if the law of armed conflict were couched in terms of intentional wrongs it would lose much of its efficacy; the issue then would be a State's intent, a troublesome concept to apply."[3]

---

[1] THE UNITED STATES DEPARTMENT OF THE AIR FORCE, INTERNATIONAL LAW—THE CONDUCT OF ARMED CONFLICT AND AIR OPERATIONS (Air Force Pamphlet 110-31, 19 November 1976), at 15-2 [hereinafter THE AIR FORCE MANUAL ON INTERNATIONAL LAW].

[2] *Id.* at 15-8 n.12.

[3] *Id.* at 15-2.

Other explanations have been given for the approach of not focusing on the *mens rea* of the State:

It is because of *mens rea* that international criminal law has
diverged from the classical international law rule of state
responsibility. As demonstrated by the Nuremberg Judgment,
international crime has traditionally emphasized the individual.
States might have been held responsible to pay penalties or make
reparation; but they were not perceived as having the *mens rea*
necessary for criminal accountability. As the ILC recognized at its
46th session, "collective punishment" of an entire nation also
violates the basic criminal law principle against punishing non-
actors.

Mark Allan Gray, *The International Crime of Ecocide*, 26 CAL. W. INT'L L.J.
215, 265 (1996) citing Geof Gilbert, *The Criminal Responsibility of States*, 39
INT'L & COMP. L.Q. 345, 357, 366 (1990), and Report of the Commission to the
General Assembly on the work of its forty-sixth session, U.N. GAOR, 49th
Sess., Supp. No. 10, U.N. Doc. A/49/10 (1994), at 348–49.

Gray goes on to say, "State responsibility for violation of *jus cogens*,
however, is well established; why should a state not be responsible for a serious
violation of *jus cogens* deemed an international crime?"

See also Gerry J. Simpson, *Conceptualizing Violence: Present and Future
Developments in International Law: Panel II: Adjudicating Violence: Problems
Confronting International Law and Policy on War Crimes and Crimes Against
Humanity: Didactic and Dissident Histories in War Crimes Trials*, 60 ALB. L.
REV. 801, 820 n.88 (1997) ("It is hard to imagine a state having the *mens rea*
necessary to carry out serious crime.").

Ian Brownlie, one of the sources cited by the United States in its military
manuals, states:

> State responsibility as a matter of law is, and in principle should be,
> limited to the obligation to make reparation, to compensate. The
> measures of security to which the aggressor is required to submit
> are hardly relevant to the present issue. The sources of
> international law indicate that the state is only liable for delicts, *i.e.*,
> to give compensation; the individual directly responsible for a
> crime against peace is liable to trial and punishment. The Charter
> of the Nuremberg Tribunal, the Draft Code of Offences, the
> Nuremberg Principles, recent peace treaties and state practice
> ignore the concept of state criminality. War guilt is simply an
> explanation, a moral justification for demanding reparation and for
> trying those individuals responsible for launching aggressive war.
> The imposition of collective sanctions would in any case violate
> general principles of justice and there is a strong presumption
> against vicarious responsibility in criminal law. The only effective
> sanction for crimes against peace is the punishment of the
> individuals and members of governments directly responsible, and
> the International Military Tribunal at Nuremberg expressed the
> matter clearly: 'Crimes against international law are committed by

The manual adds that from the "perspective of the victim—civilian, PW or other *hors de combat* personnel—the wrongful act has the same result whether done intentionally or inadvertently."[4] As a result, "[f]ailures to observe treaty rules or other international law rules may occur for which there may be general state responsibility without any individual criminal responsibility."[5]

Criminal Liability of Individuals

As we have also seen, the United States in its military manuals has recognized the potential criminal liability of individuals under the law of armed conflict for gross negligence as well as recklessness.

The Air Force Manual on International Law states that *mens rea* or a guilty mind, at the level of purposeful behavior or intention or at least gross negligence, is required for individual, as opposed to State, criminal responsibility.[6] The manual quotes Spaight's statement of the rule:

> In international law, as in municipal law, intention to break the law—*mens rea* or negligence so gross as to be the equivalent of criminal intent is the essence of the offense. A bombing pilot cannot be arraigned for an error of judgment ... it must be one which he or his superiors either knew to be wrong, or which was, *in se*, so palpably and unmistakenly a wrongful act that only gross negligence or deliberate blindness could explain their being unaware of its wrongness.[7]

---

men, not by abstract entities, and only by punishing individuals who commit such crimes can the provision of international law be enforced.'"
IAN BROWNIE, INTERNATIONAL LAW AND THE USE OF FORCE BY STATES 153–54 (Oxford University Press 1963) (quoting Judgment, H.M.S.O., Cmd. 6964, p. 41).
[4] THE AIR FORCE MANUAL ON INTERNATIONAL LAW, *supra* note 1, at 15-2.
[5] *Id.* at 15-3.
[6] *Id.* at 15-3; 15-8 n.13 (citing SPAIGHT, AIR POWER AND WAR RIGHTS 57, 58 (1947)).
[7] *Id.* at 15-2.
Another military manual states that the 1949 Geneva Conventions "require" the trial of persons who have "intentionally committed 'grave breaches'" of the conventions." UNITED STATES DEPARTMENT OF THE AIR FORCE, COMMANDER'S HANDBOOK ON THE LAW OF ARMED CONFLICT 8-3 (Air Force Pamphlet 110-34, 25 July 1980) [hereinafter THE AIR FORCE COMMANDER'S HANDBOOK]; Stating the test more restrictively, the manual states that international law "allows a nation to try captured enemy personnel for deliberate, intentional violations of

The Air Force Manual on International Law goes on to note that the element of willfulness is imposed with respect to many of the breaches defined as "grave" by the 1949 Geneva Conventions, with such element connoted through such words as "willful" and "wanton:"

> GWS and GWS SEA
> Grave breaches to which the preceding Article relates [which requires that the signatory nations "enact any legislation necessary to provide effective penal sanctions for ... grave breaches"] shall be those involving any of the following acts, if committed against persons or property protected by the Convention: willful killing, torture or inhuman treatment, including biological experiments, willfully causing great suffering or serious injury to body or health, and extensive destruction and appropriation of property, not justified by military necessity and carried out unlawfully and wantonly. (Art. 50, GWS; Art 51, GWS-SEA).[8]

The International Red Cross' Commentary to Article 85 of Protocol I (para. 3474) incorporating such provisions defines "willfully" as follows in this context:

> The accused must have acted consciously and with intent, *i.e.* with his mind on the act and its consequences, and willing them ('criminal intent' or 'malice aforethought'); this encompasses the concepts of 'wrongful intent' or 'recklessness', viz. the attitude of an agent who, without being certain of a particular result, accepts the possibility of it happening; on the other hand, ordinary negligence or lack of foresight is not covered, *i.e.*, when a man acts without having his mind on the act or its consequences (although failing to take the necessary precautions, particularly failing to seek precise information, constitutes culpable negligence punishable at least by disciplinary sanctions).[9]

---

the law of armed conflict" and notes that after World War II the United States conducted or took part in over 800 such trials. *Id.* at 8-3.

[8] THE AIR FORCE MANUAL ON INTERNATIONAL LAW, *supra* note 1, at 15-1 to 15-2; 15-8 n.12. The manual quoted similar articles from other Geneva Conventions. (GWS: "Geneva Convention for the Amelioration of the Condition of Wounded and Sick in Armed Forces in the Field;" GWS-SEA: "Geneva Convention for the Amelioration of the Condition of Wounded, Sick and Shipwrecked Members of the Armed Forces at Sea." The quoted articles appear in both these conventions).

[9] ICRC Commentary to Article 85 of Protocol I (para. 3474), *quoted in* Amnesty International—Report—IOR 40/10/98 May 1998 United Nations (UN) The International Criminal Court Making the Right Choices—Part V

Amnesty International, in a study of the then draft statute of the International Criminal Court ("ICC"), noted than "many of the grave breaches of the Geneva Conventions and Protocol I can be committed willfully—that is with intent or recklessly."[10] The report further

---

Recommendations to the Diplomatic Conference, <http://www.amnesty.org/ailib/aipub/1998/IOR/I4001098.htm> (citations omitted) (emphasis omitted).

[10] Amnesty International—Report—IOR 40/10/98 May 1998 United Nations (UN) The International Criminal Court Making the Right Choices—Part V Recommendations to the Diplomatic Conference, *supra* note 9.

The Statute of the recently established International Criminal Court ("ICC") defined the mental element necessary for war crimes restrictively so as to require "intent and knowledge." *See* The Rome Statute of the International Criminal Court, Adopted by the United Nations Diplomatic Conference of Plenipotentiaries on the Establishment of an International Criminal Court on 17 July 1998 (A/CONF.183/9 <http://www.un.org/icc/romestat.htm>), Part 3, General Principles of Criminal Law, Art. 30.

This Statute was adopted on Jul 17, 1999 by the United Nations Diplomatic Conference of Plenipotentiaries on the Establishment of an International Criminal Court. The Statute was opened for signature in Rome on July 17, 1998. It remained so in Rome until October 17, 1998, and then opened for signature in New York at the United Nations Headquarters. It is open for signature until December 31, 2000. As of October 20, 1999, it had been signed by eighty-nine States not including the United States, and ratified by four States. *See* <http://www.un.org/law/icc/statute/status.htm>.

A draft of the ICC statute contained a provision as to recklessness not included the final document:

Article 29

Mens rea (mental elements)

1. Unless otherwise provided, a person is only criminally responsible and liable for punishment for a crime under this Statute if the physical elements are committed with intent and knowledge.

2. For the purposes of this Statute and unless otherwise provided, a person has intent where:

(a) in relation to conduct, that person means to engage in the act [or omission];

(b) in relation to a consequence, that person means to cause that consequence or is aware that it will occur in the ordinary course of events.

3. For the purposes of this Statute and unless otherwise provided, "know", "knowingly" or "knowledge" means to be aware that a circumstance exists or a consequence will occur.

[4. For the purposes of this Statute and unless otherwise provided, where this Statute provides that a crime may be committed recklessly, a person is reckless with respect to a circumstance or a consequence if:

(a) the person is aware of a risk that the circumstance exists or that the consequence will occur;

(b) the person is aware that the risk is highly unreasonable to take; [and]

[(c) the person is indifferent to the possibility that the circumstance exists or that the consequence will occur.]]

N.B. The inclusion of the notion of recklessness should be re-examined in view of the definition of crimes.

United Nations Diplomatic Conference of Plenipotentiaries on the Establishment of an International Criminal Court Report of the Preparatory Committee on the Establishment of an International Criminal Court 55–56, Rome, Italy, 15 June–17 July 1998, Distr. General, A/CONF.183/2/Add.1 14 April 1998 Original: English. (emphasis omitted) (footnotes omitted).

This draft section of the ICC statute also contained a provision as to negligence in a footnote:

A view was expressed to the effect that there was no reason for rejecting the concept of commission of an offence also through negligence, in which case the offender shall be liable only when so prescribed by the Statute.

Id. at n.19.

The United States objected in a letter to the Secretary General of the United Nations to a further provision of a draft of the ICC statute establishing the mental element of willfully in connection with certain environmental offenses (which were later deleted from the document):

The term "willfully" is not defined, thereby creating considerable confusion concerning the precise volitional state needed for the imposition of criminal liability. The term "willfully" could simply mean that the defendant performed an act voluntarily, *i.e.*, without coercion, that had the unintended effect of causing harm ....
"Willfully" could also be construed to impose criminal liability only when the defendant acted for bad purpose, knowing and intending to cause serious harm .... As presently drafted the meaning of "willfully" is subject to a variety of interpretations.

Note from the U.S. Mission to the United Nations addressed to the Secretary-General (Feb. 1, 1993), Dept. of State File No. P93 0074-1851, No. P93 0071-0963/0970.

In support of the inclusion in the ICC statute of the elements of intention and knowledge (as ultimately happened in Article 30, quoted above), the United States argued that such elements are generally required in the United States for a crime punishable by incarceration:

A ... fundamental flaw that permeated the Code is its failure to specify the requisite knowledge of intent necessary to impose criminal liability on a potential defendant. In the U.S. system, criminal acts punishable by incarceration ordinarily must be committed knowingly or intentionally. The general failure of the

Code to address a defendant's knowledge and intent is further compounded because the article on environmental crimes—in contrast with the other articles—specifies that the crime must be committed "willfully." No other article has this provision, and the significance of the discrepancy is unclear.

Marian Nash (Leich), *Contemporary Practice of the United States Relating to International Law: International Criminal Justice: ILC Draft Code of Crimes*, 87 AM. J. INT'L L. 595, 607 (1993) (quoting Note from the U.S. Mission to the United Nations, *supra*).

In fact, U.S. criminal statutes regularly prescribe incarceration for crimes committed with recklessness and even criminal negligence. *See generally* Chapter 7 for discussion of liability for criminal recklessness and negligence.

In the course of the negotiation of the ICC statute, numerous states took the view that the statute should specify elements less restrictive than intention and knowledge. One report stated:

Acts of Omission, Negligence, and Conspiracy

Many participants in the Preparatory Committee stressed the need to ensure that the statute reconciles common law concepts, such as intention, gross negligence, and conspiracy, with their analogous civil law concepts, culpa, dolus eventualis, and complot. Such reconciliation would guarantee that omissions, negligence, and conspiracy that result in crimes falling within the jurisdiction of the proposed International Criminal Court would be punishable under its statute. Debate on the issue of whether causation should be a factor in international criminal liability, however, proved contentious. Some delegates felt that it was unnecessary to include provisions on causation and, in fact, that these might burden the statute: since criminal responsibility would exist only if traceable to a defendant, a provision on causation was unnecessary. In response to calls for a clear definition of intention, the Canadian delegation offered one that attempts to deal with civil and common law concepts of intent and implies that knowledge is a cornerstone of criminal liability. There were suggestions too that the statute provide for the prosecution of "willful blindness"—that is, cases in which a defendant's knowledge is clearly manifest but he or she has simply turned a blind eye. Switzerland argued that special intention must be determined in such cases as genocide but that a determination of intention may not be required when it comes to prosecuting other grave breaches of international law [U.N. press release L/2770, 3/29/96].

UNA–USA, The ILC, the International Criminal Court, and the Draft Code of Crimes, <http://www.unausa.org/programs/gaicc.htm>.

The United Nations, in describing the ICC's operations and the scope of the its jurisdiction, has characterized the restrictive nature of the crimes within its jurisdiction as a temporizing step designed to reflect broad consensus and foster wide accession to the convention establishing the court:

> Many reasons have been put forward for restricting the Court's jurisdiction to only 'the most serious crimes' of concern to the international community. Such reasons include the need to strengthen universal acceptance of the Court, which would pave the way for early ratification of the statute and establishment of the Court, and to avoid overburdening the Court and trivializing its role and function.

Background Information: Crimes within the Court's Jurisdiction, <http://www. un.org/icc/crimes.htm>.

Thus, the statute limits the court's jurisdiction to a curtailed list of war crimes, narrowly defined, with more restrictive *mens rea* elements than generally exists under international law. The list is limited not only to crimes deemed "based on well-established principles of international law," *id.,* but also to those for whose inclusion there was "broad support," *id.,* so that the establishment of the court could be effected. Background Information: Bringing Justice to the Victims, <http://www.un.org/icc/justice.htm>.

The statute of the court states that it does not intend to change or limit existing law. In the description of substantive crimes in Part 2, the statute (article 10) states: "Nothing in this Part shall be interpreted as limiting or prejudicing in any way existing or developing rules of international law for purposes other than this Statute." Rome Statute of the International Criminal Court, *supra*, Part 2, art. 10.

Some commentators have suggested that the restrictive nature of the *mens rea* requirements under the statute may be *de facto* broadened by providing relevant information to would-be actors as to the potential consequences of their actions, thereby laying the basis for the elements of willfulness and knowledge:

> Greater detail as to the intentions of the negotiating parties emerges from footnotes in the Draft Rome Statute. These footnotes reinforce the conclusion that a significant mental element is required to ground culpability. The negotiators "accept that it will be necessary to insert a provision ... which sets out the elements of knowledge and intent which must be found to have existed for an accused to be convicted of a war crime." An accused's actions are to be evaluated in light of the "relevant circumstances of, and information available to, the accused at the time." Given this defense, it will be important to educate military and political officials in both developing and developed nations as to the environmentally harmful effects of certain types of warfare and to disseminate the technologies to avoid reliance on such strategies in the first place.

Mark A. Drumbl, Essay: *Waging War Against the World: The Need to Move from War Crimes to Environmental Crimes*, 22 FORDHAM INT'L L.J. 122, referred to the term willfully as "encompass[ing] the concepts both of intent and recklessness, but exclud[ing] ordinary negligence."[11] The International Committee of the Red Cross, upon which the Amnesty International report relied, reached the same conclusion.[12]

130–131 (1998), quoting United Nations Conference on the Establishment of an International Criminal Court, (2 April 1998), § B(b) to the "War Crimes" section of Part 2, <http://www.un.org/icc/part2.htm>.

Another commentator has suggested that the potential expansion of "knowledge" to include what actors "should have known" and to the "natural consequences of one's actions" has the potential to broaden the scope of the court's jurisdiction. It has been noted that the mental state of knowledge can be inferred from the circumstances, including from evidence that the defendant was either directly conscious of the attendant circumstances, or was otherwise willfully blind to them. *See also* Beth Van Schaack, *The Definition of Crimes Against Humanity: Resolving the Incoherence,* 37 COLUM. J. TRANSNAT'L L. 787, 837, 837 n243 (1999), citing Paul H. Robinson et al., *Element Analysis in Defining Criminal Liability: The Model Penal Code and Beyond,* 35 STAN. L. REV. 681, 694–95 (1983). *See also* Model Penal Code 2.02(7) (providing that when knowledge of the existence of a particular fact is an element of an offense, such knowledge is established if a person is aware of a high probability of its existence, unless he actually believes that it does not exist); and United States v. Jewell, 532 F.2d 697 (9th Cir. 1976) ("deliberate ignorance and positive knowledge are equally culpable").

[11] Amnesty International—Report—IOR 40/10/98 May 1998 United Nations (UN) The International Criminal Court Making the Right Choices—Part V Recommendations to the Diplomatic Conference, <http://www.amnesty.org/ailib/aipub/1998/IOR/I4001098.htm> (emphasis omitted).

[12] The statement by the International Committee of the Red Cross is accompanied by the following footnotes:

> (13) We use the noun or the verb "act" below for the sake of clarity, but in the light of Art. 86 [of Protocol I] this should be understood to mean "conduct." That article deals with repression of failures to act when there is a duty to act;
>
> (14) On the various concepts which are not all defined identically by national law, cf. for example, G. Stefani, G. Levasseur, B. Bouloc, op. cit., pp. 213–234 (paras. 211–239). As regards recklessness, see also supra, p. 159, note 15 [that text is as follows: For a breach of these paragraphs to be considered a grave breach, it must fulfil the following conditions cumulatively: a) it must be a 'wilful' act or omission. Thus it is not possible to commit a grave breach through negligence, even though this may constitute a breach of paragraphs 1, 2 and 3, as we have seen. Moreover, the adjective "wilful" also excludes persons with an immature or greatly impaired intellectual capacity (children, mentally retarded persons etc.) or persons acting without knowing what they are

Article 85 paragraph 3 of Protocol I states that:

> 3. In addition to the grave breaches defined in Article 11, the following acts shall be regarded as grave breaches of this Protocol, when committed wilfully, in violation of the relevant provisions of this Protocol, and causing death or serious injury to body or health:
>
> (a) making the civilian population or individual civilians the object of attack;
>
> (b) launching an indiscriminate attack affecting the civilian population or civilian objects in the knowledge that such attack will cause excessive loss of life, injury to civilians or damage to civilian objects, as defined in Article 57, paragraph 2 (a)(iii);
>
> (c) launching an attack against works or installations containing dangerous forces in the knowledge that such attack will cause excessive loss of life, injury to civilians or damage to civilian objects, as defined in Article 57, paragraph 2 (a)(iii);

---

doing (*e.g.*, under the influence of drugs or medication). On the other hand, the concept of recklessness that may come into play— the person in question accepts the risk in full knowledge of what he is doing—must also be taken to be part and parcel of the concept of 'wilfulness'.[15] (n.15: In the French text of this commentary and of Art. 85 the term "intentionnel" is used. This is the legal term generally used, particularly in the context of penal law. The French text of Art. 11, para. 4, however, uses the term "volontaire", which is another translation of "wilful". As the latter term being used in the English text both in Art. 11, para. 4, and in Art. 85, paras. 3 and 4, it is clear that there is no difference of meaning. As to recklessness, the concept used in Civil Law systems "dol éventuel" can also be translated in English as "malice prepense.")] On failure to act and on negligence, cf. also commentary Art. 86, infra, p. 1005 [article 86 is devoted to wrongfully failing to act. The commentary cited noted that penalizing failure to fulfil a duty by failure to act is in parallel with the legal meaning of negligence];

(15) It should be noted that Austria when it ratified the Protocol made a reservation with regard to Articles 85 and 86: [French omitted] ("In order to judge any decision taken by military commanders, Articles 85 and 86 of Protocol I will be applied with military imperatives, the reasonable possibility of recognising them and information actually available at the time of the decision, being decisive." (Translated by the ICRC))

Commentary on Protocol Additional to the Geneva Conventions of 12 August 1949, and relating to the Protection of Victims of International Armed Conflicts (Protocol I), 8 June 1997, Part V: Execution of the conventions and of this protocol: Section II—Repression of breaches of the conventions and of this protocol, Art. 85—Repression of breaches of this Protocol, <http://www.icrc.org/ihl.nsf>.

(d) making non-defended localities and demilitarized zones the object of attack;

(e) making a person the object of attack in the knowledge that he is hors de combat;

(f) the perfidious use, in violation of Article 37, of the distinctive emblem of the red cross, red crescent or red lion and sun or of other protective signs recognized by the Conventions or this Protocol.[13]

In reviewing issues as to the mental state element to be included in the statute of the ICC, Jordan Paust reviewed numerous areas where treaties have recognized criminal liability under the law of armed conflict for states of mind less than intentionality:

> Sometimes the standard is "wilful," "wilfully," or "deliberate," as often used in article 147 of the 1949 Geneva Civilian Convention ..., but sometimes the standard includes "wanton" or "wantonly," as in article 147 of the Geneva Civilian Convention and certain crimes in the 1919 List. Both instruments are evidence that the two standards are different, that the drafters knew how to set higher or lower thresholds of criminal responsibility, and that they chose to do so in certain instances.
>
> More generally with respect to wanton or reckless disregard, it is informative that article 44 of the 1863 Lieber Code proscribed "all wanton violence" and article 16 addressed "wanton devastation." With respect to the post-World War II prosecutions of major German war criminals by the International Military Tribunal, the report of Justice Robert H. Jackson to the President of the United States identified "wanton destruction" as among the "atrocities and offenses against persons or property" to be addressed at Nuremberg. Similarly, United States v. List noted that "military necessity ... does not admit the wanton devastation of a district." Article 6(b) of the Charter of the International Military Tribunal at Nuremberg expressly recognized the crime of "wanton destruction of cities, towns or villages." Thereafter, the Principles of the Nuremberg Charter and Judgment, formulated by the International Law Commission and adopted by the UN General Assembly, affirmed that "violations of the laws or customs of war ... include, but are not limited to, ... wanton destruction of cities, towns, or villages." ....
>
> Article 51(5) of Protocol I to the Geneva Conventions   also provides a standard with perhaps a lower threshold when using the phrase "an attack which may be expected to cause incidental loss."

---

[13] Protocol Additional (No. I) to the Geneva Conventions of 12 August 1949, and relating to the Protection of Victims of International Armed Conflicts, 1977, 1125 U.N.T.S. 3, *reprinted in* 16 I.L.M. 1391, Art. 85(3).

Similarly, the phrase "intended, or may be expected, to cause," found in article 35(3) of Protocol I, includes a standard of responsibility far lower than "in the knowledge that such ... will cause." ... A contextually oriented word implicating a lower threshold than "in the knowledge that such attack will cause" can also be found in article 23(b) of the 1907 Hague Convention No. IV, Annex, assuring that it is "especially forbidden ... to kill or wound treacherously". Similarly, the phrase "unless such destruction ... be imperatively demanded," found in article 23(g), requires contextual inquiry concerning responsibility and can at least implicate wanton or reckless disregard. Even more generally, leader responsibility can be based on criminal negligence under the "knew or should have known" standard under customary international law.[14]

The statute of the International Criminal Tribunal for the Former Yugoslavia also recognizes willfulness and wantonness as bases for criminal liability, and, in some instances, including with respect to violations against the civilian population, ostensibly applies strict liability without requiring separate proof of *mens rea*. This is done in part through the statute's incorporation of the crimes spelt out in the

---

[14] Jordan J. Paust, *International Law Association—American Branch: Committee on a Permanent International Criminal Court: The Preparatory Committee's "Definition of Crimes"—War Crimes*, 8 Crim. L.F. 431, 438–441 (1997) (emphasis removed), citing JORDAN J. PAUST ET AL., INTERNATIONAL CRIMINAL LAW 22–23, 32–72 passim (1996); U.N. Doc. A/CONF.95/15 (1980), *reprinted in* 19 I.L.M. 1523; Jordan J. Paust, *Controlling Prohibited Weapons and the Illegal Use of Permitted Weapons*, 28 MCGILL L.J. 608, 617 & n.43 (1983); Report of the Secretary-General pursuant to Paragraph 2 of Security Council Resolution 808 (1993), U.N. Doc. S/25704 & Add. 1 (1993), Annex, arts. 2(d), 3(b); Prosecutor v. Karadzic, Case No. IT-95-5-I (Int'l Trib. for Former Yugo., Indictment, July 24, 1995), PP27, 41, 44; Report of the International Law Commission on Its Second Session, 5 June–29 July 1950, 5 U.N. GAOR, Supp. No. 12, at 11–14, P99, U.N. Doc. A/1316 (1950); 11 TRIALS OF WAR CRIMINALS 757 (1948); Report of Justice Robert H. Jackson to the President of the United States, released June 7, 1945, reprinted in Paust et al. at 1027; Instructions for the Government of Armies of the United States in the Field, General Orders No. 100, Apr. 24, 1863, arts. 16, 44, [Lieber Code]; Responsibilities Commission of the Paris Peace Conference, List of War Crimes (1919); Geneva Convention for the Amelioration of the Condition of the Wounded and Sick in Armed Forces in the Field, adopted Aug. 12, 1949, art. 50, 75 U.N.T.S. 31; Geneva Convention for the Amelioration of the Condition of Wounded, Sick, and Shipwrecked Members of Armed Forces at Sea, adopted Aug. 12, 1949, art. 51, 75 U.N.T.S. 85).

Geneva Conventions of 1949, which had defined as grave offenses certain act committed willfully:

International Criminal Tribunal for the Former Yugoslavia, Statute of the International Tribunal

Article 2

Grave breaches of the Geneva Conventions of 1949

The International Tribunal shall have the power to prosecute persons committing or ordering to be committed grave breaches of the Geneva Conventions of 12 August 1949, namely the following acts against persons or property protected under the provisions of the relevant Geneva Convention:

(a) wilful killing;

(b) torture or inhuman treatment, including biological experiments;

(c) wilfully causing great suffering or serious injury to body or health;

(d) extensive destruction and appropriation of property, not justified by military necessity and carried out unlawfully and wantonly;

(e) compelling a prisoner of war or a civilian to serve in the forces of a hostile power;

(f) wilfully depriving a prisoner of war or a civilian of the rights of fair and regular trial;

(g) unlawful deportation or transfer or unlawful confinement of a civilian;

(h) taking civilians as hostages.

Article 3

Violations of the laws or customs of war

The International Tribunal shall have the power to prosecute persons violating the laws or customs of war. Such violations shall include, but not be limited to:

(a) employment of poisonous weapons or other weapons calculated to cause unnecessary suffering;

(b) wanton destruction of cities, towns or villages, or devastation not justified by military necessity;

(c) attack, or bombardment, by whatever means, of undefended towns, villages, dwellings, or buildings;

(d) seizure of, destruction or wilful damage done to institutions dedicated to religion, charity and education, the arts and sciences, historic monuments and works of art and science;

(e) plunder of public or private property.

Article 5

Crimes against humanity

The International Tribunal shall have the power to prosecute persons responsible for the following crimes when committed in armed conflict, whether international or internal in character, and directed against any civilian population:

(a) murder;
(b) extermination;
(c) enslavement;
(d) deportation;
(e) imprisonment;
(f) torture;
(g) rape;
(h) persecutions on political, racial and religious grounds;
(i) other inhumane acts.[15]

The Air Force Manual on International Law notes that States have "important customary and treaty obligations to follow the law not only as national policy but to ensure its implementation, observance and enforcement by its own combatant personnel."[16] The manual notes as examples that Article 1, Hague IV, requires parties to issue instructions in conformity with the Hague Regulations and that the 1949 Geneva Conventions require that the contracting states enact domestic legislation providing penal sanctions for persons who commit or order any "grave breach" of said Conventions.[17]

---

[15] International Criminal Tribunal for the Former Yugoslavia, Statute of the International Tribunal (Adopted 25 May 1993) (as amended 13 May 1998) <http://www.un.org/icty/basic/statut/statute.htm>.

[16] THE AIR FORCE MANUAL ON INTERNATIONAL LAW, *supra* note 1, at 15-1.

[17] *See id.* at 15-1 and 15-7 n.5 (citing Common Article found in Art. 49, GWS; Art. 50, GWS-SEA; Art. 129, GPW; Art. 146, GC; and noting that the principles of said Articles "declare customary law obligations to suppress violations of the law of armed conflict including particularly those committed by one's own armed forces;" and further citing FM 27-10, at 181; NWIP 10-2, at 3-5; and GREENSPAN, LAW OF LAND WARFARE 93 (1959)). *See also* UNITED STATES DEPARTMENT OF THE ARMY, THE LAW OF LAND WARFARE 179 (FM27-10/18 July 1956) with Change No. 1 (15 July 1976) [hereinafter THE LAW OF LAND WARFARE].

Article 49 of the Geneva Conventions of 1949 reads as follows:

Article 49. The High Contracting Parties undertake to enact any legislation necessary to provide effective penal sanctions for persons committing, or ordering to be committed, any of the grave breaches of the present Convention defined in the following Article. ***

Article 50. Grave breaches to which the preceding Article relates shall be those involving any of the following acts, if committed against persons or property protected by the Convention: wilful killing, torture or inhuman treatment, including biological experiments, wilfully causing great suffering or serious injury to

In compliance with this requirement, the United States enacted war crimes legislation, largely incorporating by reference the requirements of the applicable regulations and conventions, including, ostensibly, the mental element of willfulness. In the one instance of a more recent treaty (covering landmines and the like), the United States specified the mental element of willfulness:

> § 2441. War crimes
>
> (a) Offense. Whoever, whether inside or outside the United States, commits a war crime, in any of the circumstances described in subsection (b), shall be fined under this title or imprisoned for life or any term of years, or both, and if death results to the victim, shall also be subject to the penalty of death.
>
> (b) Circumstances. The circumstances referred to in subsection (a) are that the person committing such war crime or the victim of such war crime is a member of the Armed Forces of the United States or a national of the United States (as defined in section 101 of the Immigration and Nationality Act [8 USCS § 1101]).
>
> (c) Definition. As used in this section the term "war crime" means any conduct—
>
> (1) defined as a grave breach   in any of the international conventions signed at Geneva 12 August 1949, or any protocol to such convention to which the United States is a party;
>
> (2) prohibited by Article 23, 25, 27, or 28 of the Annex to the Hague Convention IV, Respecting the Laws and Customs of War on Land, signed 18 October 1907;
>
> (3) which constitutes a violation of common Article 3 of the international conventions signed at Geneva, 12 August 1949, or any protocol to such convention to which the United States is a party and which deals with non-international armed conflict; or
>
> (4) of a person who, in relation to an armed conflict and contrary to the provisions of the Protocol on Prohibitions or Restrictions on the Use of Mines, Booby-Traps and Other Devices as amended at Geneva on 3 May 1996 (Protocol II as amended on 3

---

body or health, and extensive destruction and appropriating of property, not justified by military necessity and carried out unlawfully and wantonly.
Convention for the Amelioration of the Condition of the Wounded and Sick in Armed Forces in the Field. Done at Geneva, Aug. 12, 1949. Entered into force, Oct. 21, 1950; for the United States, Feb. 2, 1956. 6 U.S.T. 3114, T.I.A.S. No. 3362, 75 U.N.T.S. 31.

May 1996), when the United States is a party to such Protocol, willfully kills or causes serious injury to civilians.[18]

A recent Canadian decision, *Regina v. Finta,* has recognized the potential for individual criminal liability for violation of the law of armed conflict without a specific showing of *mens rea.*[19] In this case, the Canadian prosecutors proceeded against one Finta, formerly of the Hungarian Gendarmerie, for war crimes committed against Jews in Hungary during the Second World War, pursuant to the Nazi "final solution."

Finta was accused of forcing 8,617 Jews into boxcars that took them to concentration camps in June 1944, pursuant to manifestly illegal orders. Addressing the issue of *mens rea,* the court found that a mental state for each element of an international crime was not a prerequisite to a conviction: "Nobody ever really thought there was a need for individual *mens rea* that went beyond that required for the basic nature of the conduct, whether that be murder, assault, robbery or kidnapping."[20]

The court stated further, "The mental blameworthiness required for such crimes is already captured in the *mens rea* of the underlying offense [*i.e.* murder, manslaughter, persecution, robbery, etc.]"[21] In interpreting international law and war crimes, as incorporated by the Canadian Criminal Code's §§ 7(3.71) to (3.77), Canada's parallel to 18 U.S.C. § 2441, the court concluded, "all that is stated is that there be a behavior that constitutes an act or omission that is contrary to international law."[22]

Justice Cory stated, "Our domestic definition of the underlying offence will capture the requisite *mens rea* for war crimes and crimes

---

[18] Title 18. Crimes and Criminal Procedure, Part I. Crimes, Chap. 118. War Crimes: 18 USCS § 2441 (1999).

Willfulness is a broad concept susceptible to a broad range of meanings in the U.S. system. Cases have noted that willful is defined by dictionaries as meaning anything from malicious to "not accidental" to intentional, and that no one clear and plain meaning of the word exists. *See* McLaughlin v. Richland Shoe Co 486 U.S. 128, 137, 108 S. Ct. 1677, 1693. The U.S. Supreme Court has interpreted willfulness as encompassing "marked with a careless disregard" and "disregard." *See, e.g.* Trans World Airlines v. Thurston, 469 U.S. 111, 126, 105 S.Ct. 613, 624, quoting United States v. Murdock, 290 U.S. 389, 395, and United States v. Illinois Central R. Co., 303 U.S. 239, 242–243 (1938).

[19] Regina v. Finta, 1 S.C.R. 701 (1994).

[20] *Id.* at 754.

[21] *Id.*

[22] *Id.*

against humanity as well. Thus, the accused need not have known that his act, if it constitutes manslaughter or forcible confinement, amounted to an inhumane act either in the legal sense or moral sense. One who intentionally or knowingly commits manslaughter or kidnapping would have demonstrated the mental culpability required for an inhumane act. The normal *mens rea* for confinement, robbery, manslaughter, or kidnapping, whether it be intentional, knowledge, reckless or willful blindness, would be adequate."[23]

In evaluating the scope of war crimes and crimes against humanity under color of Canadian law, the court stated that "the essential quality of a war crime or a crime against humanity is that the accused must be aware of or willfully blind to the fact that he is inflicting untold misery on his victims."[24] "The mental element of a crime against humanity must involve an awareness of the facts or circumstances which would bring the acts within the definition of a crime against humanity. However, I emphasize it is not necessary to establish that the accused knew his actions were inhumane."[25] "Similarly for war crimes, the Crown would have to prove that the accused knew or was aware of the facts or circumstances ... were such that, viewed objectively, they would shock the conscience of all right thinking people."[26] "It would not be necessary to prove that the accused actually knew that his or her acts constituted war crimes."[27]

To the same effect, the International Criminal Tribunal for the Former Yugoslavia recently concluded, with respect to charges of aiding and abetting an international crime:

> With regard to *mens rea,* the Trial Chamber must determine whether it is necessary for the accomplice to share the *mens rea* of the principal or whether mere knowledge that his actions assist the perpetrator in the commission of the crime is sufficient to constitute *mens rea* in aiding and abetting the crime. The case law indicates that the latter will suffice.
>
> For example in the Einsatzgruppen case, knowledge, rather than intent, was held to be the requisite mental element.[28]

---

[23] *Id.* at 765.

[24] *Id.* at 816.

[25] *Id.* at 819.

[26] *Id.*

[27] *Id.* at 820. *See also* Attorney General of Israel v. Eichmann, 36 I.L.R. 277 (1962).

[28] International Criminal Tribunal for the Former Yugoslavia: Prosecutor v. Furundzija, 38 I.L.M. 317, 360 (1999), citing Trial of Otto Ohlendorf and

Foreseeability has been recognized as establishing the basis for criminal liability under international law. Article 2 of the Statute of the International Criminal Tribunal for the Former Yugoslavia entitled "Grave Breaches of the Geneva Conventions of 1949," lists "torture" as a grave breach.[29] The elements needed to establish torture are:

> Intentional and unlawful subjection to the infliction of severe physical or mental suffering by the accused.
> The pain or suffering was inflicted for any number of the following reasons: to obtain information or a confession from the victim or a third person, as punishment, for the purpose of intimidation or coercion, for any reason based on discrimination of any kind.[30]

Liability under this section based on acts of rape and other sexual assaults has been imposed on the theory that the proscribed acts of torture are the foreseeable consequences of such sexual attacks. As one author described it,

> "The requisite *mens rea* follows from the *actus reus* [forcible sexual penetration] regardless of whether the perpetrator committed the sexual assault with general or specific intent. It is inferred that a person acting with general intent intended the foreseeable consequences of that act. In the case of sexual assault, it is thus inferred that the severe physical and mental pain or suffering resulting from the act was a foreseeable consequence of the assault"[31]

Command Responsibility

A commander is responsible to maintain and prevent violations of the law of war by subordinates, and can be liable for breaches by subordinates. The scope of commander responsibility, and potential criminal liability, while not as broad as the strict liability to which the

---

Others (Einsatzgruppen), *in* Trials of War Criminals Before the Nuremberg Military Tribunals under Control Council Law No. 10, Vol. IV., at 568–573. *See generally* Regina v. Finta, 1 S.C.R. 701 (1994).

[29] Statute of the International Criminal Tribunal for the Former Yugoslavia, *supra* note 15, at § 2(b).

[30] *See* Patricia Viseur Sellers, Kaoru Okuizumi, *Intentional Prosecution of Sexual Assaults,* 7 TRANSNAT'L L. & CONTEMP. PROBS. 45, 61 (1997). § 5(g) of the Statute does expressly list rape as a crime against humanity. *See id.* at 57.

[31] Sellers & Okuizumi, *supra* note 30, at 61 (citing case 10.970, Inter-Am C.H.R. (Raquel Martin de Mejia Report No.5/96)).

State is potentially held, is extremely broad, potentially encompassing mere negligence and clearly not requiring strict intention.

The Air Force Manual on International Law states that "[c]ommand responsibility for acts committed by subordinates arises when the specific wrongful acts in question are knowingly ordered or encouraged."[32]   The manual states that the commander is also responsible "if he has actual knowledge, or should have had knowledge" that his subordinates "have or are about to commit criminal violations, and he culpably fails to take reasonably necessary steps to ensure compliance with the law and punish violators thereof."[33]

The Naval/Marine Commander's Handbook states, "A commander at any level is personally responsible for the criminal acts of warfare committed by a subordinate if the commander knew in advance of the breach about to be committed and had the ability to prevent it, but failed to take the appropriate action to do so."[34] The handbook adds that "in determining the personal responsibility of the commander, the element of knowledge may be presumed if the commander had information which should have enabled him or her to conclude under the circumstances that such breach was to be expected."[35]   The handbook states that the applicable facts "will each be determined objectively."[36]

The handbook quotes the United States Military Tribunal's decision in *The Hostages Case* for the proposition that the commander is

---

[32] THE AIR FORCE MANUAL ON INTERNATIONAL LAW, *supra* note 1, at 15-3. *See also id.* at 15-9 n.23 (citing Prosecution Statement, *International Military Tribunal Far East*, Apr. 1948); 11 WHITEMAN, DIGEST OF INTERNATIONAL LAW 993–994 (1968); MCDOUGAL & FELICIANO, LAW AND MINIMUM WORLD PUBLIC ORDER 331 (1961) ("[T]he most important target selection principle that emerged from the decisions in post World War II cases is that only individuals who ranked in the top policy formulating levels of authority and control structures of the violator state should be held liable to these deprivations"); GREENSPAN, LAW OF LAND WARFARE 449 (1959); CASTREN, PRESENT LAW OF WAR AND NEUTRALITY 84 (1954)).

[33] *Id.* at 15-2 to 15-3. *See also* THE LAW OF LAND WARFARE, *supra* note 17, at 178.

[34] UNITED STATES DEPARTMENT OF THE NAVY ANNOTATED SUPPLEMENT TO THE COMMANDER'S HANDBOOK ON THE LAW OF NAVAL OPERATIONS 6-5 n.12 (Naval Warfare Publication 9, 1987) (With Revision A (5 October 1989), this handbook was adopted by the U.S. Marine Corps as FLEET MARINE FORCE MANUAL (FM FM) 1-10) [hereinafter THE NAVAL/MARINE COMMANDER'S HANDBOOK].

[35] *Id.* at 6-5.

[36] *Id.*

charged with available information even if not personally aware of same:

> Want of knowledge of the contents of reports made to him [*i.e.*, to the commander general] is not a defense. Reports to commanding generals are made for their special benefit. Any failure to acquaint themselves with the contents of such reports, or a failure to require additional reports where inadequacy appears on their face, constitutes a dereliction of duty which he cannot use in his behalf.[37]

The handbook states that the responsibility of a commanding officer "may be based solely upon inaction" and that it is "not always necessary to establish that a superior knew, or must be presumed to have known of the offense committed by his subordinates."[38] "While a commander may delegate some or all of his authority, he cannot delegate responsibility for the conduct of the forces he commands."[39]

The Air Force Manual on International Law notes that the prosecutions for crimes against peace and against humanity following World War II were primarily against the principal political, military and industrial leaders responsible for the initiation of the war and related inhumane policies.[40] The manual states, "[A] soldier who

---

[37] *Id.* (citing United States v. Wilhelm List et al., 9 TWC 127 (1950)).

[38] *Id.* at 6-6 n.12.

[39] *Id.* at 6-5.

[40] *See* THE AIR FORCE MANUAL ON INTERNATIONAL LAW, *supra* note 1, at 15-5. Telford Taylor, U.S. Chief Counsel at Nuremberg, with the rank of brigadier general, stated that a "remarkable feature of the [Nuremberg] trials was that they brought about a great expansion of the principle that individuals may be held criminally liable under international law, even though their conduct was valid under, or even required by, domestic law." TELFORD TAYLOR, NUREMBERG AND VIETNAM: AN AMERICAN TRAGEDY 82 (Quadrangle 1970)

Noting that in the past the individuals against whom the laws of war had been enforced were "for the most part, ordinary soldiers or officers of middling or low rank," whereas at Nuremberg and Tokyo, nearly all the defendants "stood at or near the top of the military or civilian hierarchy," Professor Taylor stated, "In terms of substantive international law, and in the mind of the general public, the salient feature of the Nuremberg trials was the decision that individuals could be held guilty for participation in the planning and waging of 'a war of aggression.'" *Id.* at 83–4.

Professor Taylor noted that, unlike the case against German U-boat commander Karl Doenitz, whose conviction for waging aggressive war was based on his submarines being "prepared to wage war," a stricter standard, that of actual knowledge, was applied in the cases against the directors of the Krupp and I.G. Farben industries: "[E]ven if the defendants had reason to believe that

merely performs his military duty cannot be said to have waged the war ... [O]nly the government, and those authorities who carry out governmental functions and are instrumental in formulating policy, wage the war."[41]

The Air Force Commander's Handbook states that the two International Military Tribunals following World War II punished "former cabinet ministers, and others of similar rank" in the Axis powers for planning and waging aggressive war.[42]

A seminal decision in the law in this area was the war crime trial of Japanese General Tomoyuki Yamashita, following World War II[43] and

---

aggressive wars were in contemplation, they were not guilty because they were not privy to Hitler's personal plans and aims. In the case against high-ranking military leaders, even such privity did not suffice, because the accused did not have 'actual power to shape and influence the policy of their nation, prepare for or lead their country into or in an aggressive war.'" *Id.* at 88 (citing United States v. von Leeb, Case No. 12, vol. XI, TRIALS OF WAR CRIMINALS, at 489). Taylor noted that the Tokyo tribunal was "readier" to convict for joint participation by members of "powerful military ... and political cliques" in the formation of Japan's aggressive policies. *Id.* at 87.

Professor Taylor stated that the Nuremberg principles "reaffirm[ed] and enforce[d] in new spheres the principle that the laws of war, and some other rules of international law, are superior to domestic law, and that individuals may be held accountable to them." *Id.* at 83–4. Professor Taylor quoted the judgment of the International Tribunal at Nuremberg:

> ...individuals have international duties which transcend the national obligations of obedience imposed by the individual state. He who violates the laws of war cannot obtain immunity while acting in pursuance of the authority of the state if the state in authorizing action moves outside its competence under international law.

Id. at 83–4 (citing I TRIAL OF THE MAJOR WAR CRIMINALS BEFORE THE INTERNATIONAL MILITARY TRIBUNAL 223 (Nuremberg, 1947)).

[41] THE NAVAL/MARINE COMMANDER'S HANDBOOK, *supra* note 34, at 15-9 n.23 (citing *Prosecution Statement, International Military Tribunal Far East, April 1948,* 11 WHITEMAN, DIGEST OF INTERNATIONAL LAW, at 993–994 (1968)).

[42] *See* THE AIR FORCE COMMANDER'S HANDBOOK, *supra* note 7, at 1-2.

[43] *See* CHERIF BASSIOUNI & PETER MANIKAS, THE LAW OF THE INTERNATIONAL CRIMINAL TRIBUNAL FOR THE FORMER YUGOSLAVIA (1996); Timothy Wu & Jonathan Kang, *Criminal Liability for the Actions of Subordinates—the Doctrine of Command Responsibility and its Analogues in United States Law*, 38 HARV. INT'L L.J. 272 (1997); L.C Green, *Command Responsibility in International Humanitarian Law*, 5 TRANSNAT'L L. & CONTEMP. PROBS. 319 (1995); Major Bruce D. Landrum, *The Yamashita War*

the upholding of his conviction by the U.S. Supreme Court.[44] Charged with atrocities committed against the civilian population and American POWs in the Philippines by troops under his command, Yamashita was convicted based on his failure to supervise the troops and end the atrocities.

The military commission appointed to try Yamashita found that he "must have known" of the atrocities and that his inaction made him criminally liable for the acts of the subordinates.[45] The commission concluded "that the crimes of the subordinates were so 'extensive and widespread, both as to time and area, that they must have either have been willfully permitted by the accused, or secretly ordered by' the accused, and that where there is no effective attempt by a commander to discover and control the criminal acts, such a commander could be held responsible, even criminally liable, for the lawless acts of his troops."[46]

In upholding Yamashita's conviction, the U.S. Supreme Court ostensibly saw commander responsibility as a way of dealing with the risk of wanton acts by troops against protected persons:

> The question then is whether the law of war imposes on an army commander a duty to take such appropriate measures as are within his power to control the troops under his command for the prevention of the specified acts which are violations of the law of war and which are likely to attend the occupation of hostile territory by an uncontrolled soldiery, and whether he may be charged with personal responsibility for his failure to take such

---

Crimes Trial: Command Responsibility Then and Now, 149 Mil. L. Rev. 293 (1995).

[44] In re Yamashita, 327 U.S. 1 (1946).

[45] Wu & Kang, *supra* note 43, at 275; BASSIOUNI & MANIKAS, *supra* note 43, at 362.

[46] Wu & Kang, *supra* note 43, at 275 (quoting Yamashita at 34–35, 50). *See id.* at 275, and n.17 (noting that the case has been criticized as espousing a strict liability standard) and BASSIOUNI & MANIKAS, *supra* note 43, at 361 (noting that Yamashita espoused an "almost strict liability standard," based solely on the commander/subordinate relationship).

See also Wu & Kang, *supra* note 43, 277–278, n.30, commenting that in the Tribunal for the Former Yugoslavia, the charges of genocide against Radovan Karadzic and Ratko Mladic stem from their not preventing their subordinates from committing the intentional crime of genocide. (citing Richard J. Goldstone, Indictment, the International Criminal Tribunal For the Former Yugoslavia, The Prosecutor of the Tribunal Against Radovan Karadzic and Ratko Mladic, Par 32 (24 July, 1995)). *See also* Green *supra* note 43; Landrum, *supra* note 43.

measures when violations result. It is evident that the conduct of military operations by troops whose excesses are unrestrained by the orders of or efforts of their commanders would almost certainly result in violations which it is the purpose of the law of war to prevent.[47]

Another seminal decision was *The High Command Case*, a collection of 13 Nuremberg trials against high ranking German officers, where the tribunal raised the burden of knowledge of the commander from the "must have known" of *Yamashita* to the criminal negligence standard of "should have known."[48]

A commander is obligated to know what his troops are doing. "Criminality does not attach to every individual in this chain of command from that fact alone. There must be a personal dereliction that can occur only where the act is directly traceable to him or where his failure to properly supervise his subordinates constitutes criminal negligence on his part ... a personal neglect amounting to a wanton, immoral disregard of the actions of his subordinates amounting to acquiescence."[49]

The command responsibility doctrine can be viewed as establishing a prohibition, or the punishment of, risk taking. As stated by one of the judges of the Canadian Military Court in the *Abayye Ardenne* case: "An officer may be convicted of a war crime if he incites and counsels troops under his command to deny quarter, whether or not prisoners were killed thereof."[50]

The doctrine of command responsibility was codified in Protocol I to the Geneva Conventions of 1949, art. 86(2):

> 2. The fact that a breach of the Conventions or of this Protocol was committed by a subordinate does not absolve his superiors from penal or disciplinary responsibility, as the case may be, if they knew, or had information that should have enabled them to

---

[47] In re Yamashita, 327 U.S. 1, 15 (1946).

[48] *See* BASSIOUNI & MANIKAS, *supra* note 43, at 361, 362 (citing The High Command Case, 2 TRIALS OF WAR CRIMINALS BEFORE THE NUREMBERG MILITARY TRIBUNALS UNDER CONTROL COUNCIL LAW NO. 10 (1949) (a.k.a. United States v. Wilhelm von Leeb)).

[49] *See* 2 TRIALS OF WAR CRIMINALS BEFORE THE NUREMBERG MILITARY TRIBUNALS, *quoted in* BASSIOUNI & MANIKAS, *supra* note 43, at 362.

[50] *See* L.C Green, *Command Responsibility in International Humanitarian Law*, 5 TRANSNAT'L L. & CONTEMP. PROBS. 319, at 337 (1995) (citing Trial of S.S. Brigadefuhrer Kurt Meyer (Abbaye Ardenne Case) 4 UNITED NATIONS WAR CRIMES COMMISSION, LAW REPORTS OF CRIMES OF WAR CRIMINALS 97 (Canadian Military Court)).

conclude in the circumstances at the time, that he was committing or was going to commit such a breach and if they did not take all feasible measures within their power to prevent or repress the breach.[51]

The Statute of the International Criminal Tribunal for the Former Yugoslavia, Article 7(3) further incorporates this standard:

The fact that any of the acts referred to in articles 2 to 5 of the present Statute was committed by a subordinate does not relieve his superior of criminal responsibility if he knew or had reason to know that the subordinate was about to commit such acts or had done so and the superior failed to take the necessary and reasonable measures to prevent such acts and to punish the perpetrators thereof.[52]

The statute of the International Criminal Court similarly recognizes a broad scope of commander liability:

Article 28
Responsibility of commanders and other superiors
In addition to other grounds of criminal responsibility under this Statute for crimes within the jurisdiction of the Court:
1. A military commander or person effectively acting as a military commander shall be criminally responsible for crimes within the jurisdiction of the Court committed by forces under his or her effective command and control, or effective authority and control as the case may be, as a result of his or her failure to exercise control properly over such forces, where:
(a) That military commander or person either knew or, owing to the circumstances at the time, should have known that the forces were committing or about to commit such crimes; and
(b) That military commander or person failed to take all necessary and reasonable measures within his or her power to prevent or repress their commission or to submit the matter to the competent authorities for investigation and prosecution.
2. With respect to superior and subordinate relationships not described in paragraph 1, a superior shall be criminally responsible for crimes within the jurisdiction of the Court committed by subordinates under his or her effective authority and control, as a

---

[51] Wu & Kang, *supra* note 43, at 276 (quoting Protocol Additional to the Geneva Conventions of 12 August 1949, and relating to the Protection of Victims of International Armed Conflicts, 1977, 1125 U.N.T.S. 3, 42–43, reprinted in 16 I.L.M. 1391, 1428–29).

[52] S.C Res. 827, U.N.SCOR, 48th Sess., 3217th mtg., U.N Doc. S/RES/807 (1994), reprinted in 32 I.L.M. 1163 (1994).

result of his or her failure to exercise control properly over such subordinates, where:

(a) The superior either knew, or consciously disregarded information which clearly indicated, that the subordinates were committing or about to commit such crimes;

(b) The crimes concerned activities that were within the effective responsibility and control of the superior; and

(c) The superior failed to take all necessary and reasonable measures within his or her power to prevent or repress their commission or to submit the matter to the competent authorities for investigation and prosecution.[53]

---

[53] Rome Statute of the International Criminal Court, *supra* note 10, Art. 28.

Chapter 9: Application of Probability Analysis to Risks Associated with the Use of Nuclear Weapons

To probe the potential application of probability analysis to the determination of the lawfulness of the use of nuclear weapons, let us look at how such an approach might be integrated into the performance of the proportionality test.

As we have seen, proportionality is a rule of reason designed to prohibit and prevent in advance injury to combatant and noncombatant persons and objects which is disproportionate to the attendant military advantage. This requires the applicable decision-maker, in evaluating the lawfulness of the anticipated use of the nuclear weapon, to, at least metaphorically, get out the scales and place on either side (1) the value of the military objective sought to be achieved through the use of the weapon, the "benefits" side of the equation, and (2) the resultant injury to combatant and non-combatant persons and property likely to result from such use, the "cost" side of the equation.

This balancing might be visualized as follows:

Value of military objective likely to be achieved by the use of the nuclear weapon	Likely resultant injury to combatant and non-combatant persons and property

In the most idealized circumstances—with the decision-makers being persons of the highest judgment, experience and wisdom and possessing adequate factual information and ample time for contemplation—this weighing process is likely to be extraordinarily difficult, involving, as it does, the comparative evaluation of matters not only highly charged but also inherently subjective, veering on the imponderable.

How then do we determine the value of the military objective? Most fundamentally, our question becomes: How important is it to the acting State to take out this particular target, this bridge or plant or whatever? What will it yield in terms of winning the overall war or at least staving off defeat? It seems evident that the valuation of the objective must be fixed in light of its likely contribution to the overall war effort. The immediate objective must be specific—to take out this particular target—but the valuation of the objective can only be made within the context of the broader picture.

Although our focus is on the valuation of the military advantage secured by the use of the nuclear weapon, that valuation necessarily implies a comparison of the military effects of using the nuclear versus alternate conventional weapons. Namely, what are the incremental costs and benefits of using the nuclear weapon?

Further complexity arises from the fact that, since the acting State must make this evaluation in advance of the military action before its actual effects can be known, it will necessarily be evaluating probabilities not actualities. On the benefits side of the equation, it would be unreasonable, and far short of even that limited precision of which we are capable, to simply place a flat value on the prospective achievement of the military mission without adjustment for the attendant probabilities as to the likelihood that the mission will actually be successful and that such success will materially contribute to the overall war effort.

In view of such matters, the nuclear strike will obviously have a greater value if it seems certain to make a major contribution to the winning of the war than if it has a 10% chance of doing so. Similarly, the valuation placed on the benefits side of the equation will be greater if the use of the nuclear weapon reasonably appears to carry a 90% chance of achieving the objective versus a 5% chance.

Similar complexities inhere in valuing the resultant injuries to combatant and non-combatant persons and property, the "cost" side of the equation. Most fundamentally, how does one value such things even if one has certain knowledge as to the effects of the nuclear strike? But, of course, it is inherent in the matter that the most one is capable of "knowing" when performing the evaluation will be probabilities.

This balancing test—focusing on such additional considerations— might be conceptualized as follows:

$$(P-P^1) \bullet V \bullet (P^2-P^3) \bullet V^1 \qquad\qquad\qquad V^2-V^3$$

▲

where—
- "P" refers to the likelihood of achieving the short-term objective through the use of the nuclear weapon, *e.g.*, the likelihood of destroying the immediate target;

- "P^1" refers to the likelihood of achieving this same short-term objective through the use of conventional weapons;
- "V" refers to the concrete and direct military value of achieving the short-term objective;
- "P^2" refers to the likelihood that achieving the short-term military objective through the use of the nuclear weapon would materially contribute to the achievement of the overall military objective;
- "P^3" refers to the likelihood that achieving the short-term military objective through the use of conventional weapons would materially contribute to the achievement of the overall military objective;
- "V^1" refers to the value of the overall military objective;
- "V^2" refers to the likely effects upon combatant and non-combatant persons and property resultant from the use of the nuclear weapon; and
- "V^3" refers to the likely effects upon combatant and non-combatant persons and property resultant from the use of conventional weapons.

This formula represents a process for balancing the incremental benefits of using the nuclear weapon against the incremental costs. But it raises more questions than it answers, highlighting the complexity of the matter. Fixing a probability figure for any particular eventuality, difficult and subjective though it be, is possible. One ultimately exercises one's judgment in the light of the available information, and determines a number. Much more difficult, or at least nebulous, is the placing of reasonably objective "values" on the different probabilities, be it the success of the nuclear strike or its impact on the war or the value of the collateral deaths and other effects.

But even if all of these difficulties are passed, if one performs all these valuations, all one achieves is an overall balancing of the likely costs and benefits. From some formulations of the test, this might seem to be all that is required, indeed to be the essence of the test. But in a less literalistic sense, is it not readily apparent that the fundamental purpose of the proportionality test, at least as applied to nuclear weapons, requires that the acting State balance the likely military benefits not merely against the likely collateral effects but also against the whole range of possible collateral effects.

In a sense, such an approach is implicit in the more typical exercise in this area, when the analysis is performed after the damage has been done, and retrospective probabilities are applied to the various eventualities as they have in fact occurred, however improbable they may have seemed at the time of taking the action in question.

Returning to our example in Chapter 6,[1] is it not clear that the test must consider not only the fact that the strike is deemed 72% likely to cause collateral injuries within the range of those judged acceptable in the circumstances but also that it carries a 28% chance of causing excessive injuries, including a 3% chance of causing 100,000,000 deaths and a 1% chance of causing 900,000,000 deaths.

The question answers itself and makes obvious the need for a further test. If the likely collateral effects of the nuclear strike outweigh the likely military benefits, the strike flunks the proportionality test. But it is not enough that the strike passes this test, if there are also less likely but possible collateral effects of a catastrophic nature.

The incremental military benefit of using the nuclear weapon might be balanced against the risk of catastrophic collateral effects in the following way:

$$(P-P^1) \cdot V \cdot (P^2-P^3) \cdot V^1 \qquad\qquad (P^4-P^5) \cdot A$$

where—
- "P" refers to the likelihood of achieving the short-term objective through the use of the nuclear weapon, *e.g.*, the probability of destroying the bridge;
- "P^1" refers to the likelihood of achieving this same short-term objective through the use of conventional weapons;
- "V" refers to the concrete and direct military value of achieving the short-term objective;
- "P^2" refers to the likelihood that achieving the short-term military objective through the use of the nuclear weapon would materially contribute to the achievement of the overall military objective;
- "P^3" refers to the likelihood that achieving the short-term military objective through the use of conventional weapons would

---

[1] *See supra* Chapter 6, note 1 and accompanying text.

materially contribute to the achievement of the overall military objective;

- "V^1" refers to the value of the overall military objective;
- "P^4" refers to the likelihood that use of the nuclear weapon would result in catastrophic collateral effects upon combatant and non-combatant persons and objects;
- "P^5" refers to the likelihood that the use of conventional weapons would result in catastrophic collateral effects upon combatant and non-combatant persons and objects; and
- "A" refers to the valuation of catastrophic collateral effects.

Obviously, this test presents similar but even greater valuation challenges than the earlier one. How does one possibly place a value on such collateral effects? In a sense this test, once formulated, becomes metaphoric. Its value is in focusing us on the fundamental question: Can any military objective justify risking apocalyptic devastation?

The objection can further be made that this second test, balancing the likely military benefits not against the likely collateral effects but against the chance of extreme collateral effects, is too lenient. Certainly, if the strike risks such effects, it is or should be unlawful. But what of the case where the likely costs and benefits are in balance, yet there is some likelihood of impermissible but not catastrophic collateral effects?

Should not the strike be unlawful under the proportionality test unless the value of the likely military benefit outweighs the value of any probability that the strike will result in excessive and therefore unlawful collateral effects.

A test along these lines might go as follows:

$$(P-P^1) \bullet V \bullet (P^2-P^3) \bullet V^1 \qquad\qquad (P^6-P^7) \bullet C$$

$$\blacktriangle$$

where—
- "P" refers to the likelihood of achieving the short-term objective through the use of the nuclear weapon, *e.g.*, the probability of destroying the bridge;
- "P^1" refers to the likelihood of achieving the short-term objective through the use of conventional weapons;

- "V" refers to the concrete and direct military value of achieving short-term objective;
- "P^2" refers to the likelihood that achieving the short-term military objective through the use of the nuclear weapon would materially contribute to the achievement of the overall military objective;
- "P^3" refers to the likelihood that achieving the short-term military objective through the use of conventional weapons would materially contribute to the achievement of the overall military objective;
- "V^1" refers to the value of the overall military objective;
- "P^6" refers to the likelihood that use of the nuclear weapon would result in excessive and therefore unlawful collateral effects upon combatant and non-combatant persons and objects;
- "P^7" refers to the likelihood that the use of conventional weapons would result in excessive and therefore unlawful collateral effects upon combatant and non-combatant persons and objects; and
- "C" refers to the valuation of the unlawful collateral effects.

Putting all of this together, we might say that the use of a nuclear weapon could pass the balancing test inherent in the proportionality requirement only if $((P-P^1) \cdot V \times (P^2-P^3) \cdot V^1)$ is greater than each of:

1) (V^2-V^3);

2) $((P^4-P^5) \cdot A)$; and

3) $((P^6-P^7) \cdot C)$,

all as defined above.

On this basis we are saying that the likely incremental military benefit from the use of the weapon must outweigh the value not only of the likely collateral effects but also of the risk of catastrophic effects and, ultimately, of any unlawful effects.

It is obviously unrealistic to expect the applicable decision-makers, in the exigencies of war, to go through the kinds of complicated and intricate calculations described here. Indeed, even if the decision-makers in good faith wanted to go through such an exercise and had the requisite information, one must question the likelihood that the exigent circumstances would permit such a luxury.

The very complexities of these matters reinforce the need that they be rigorously analyzed in advance to the fullest extent humanly possible. If we expect the decision-makers to apply the proportionality test, we owe it to them to provide more guidance than is available from the simple statement of the rule.

Chapter 10: Limitations on the Extent to Which Innocent Third-Parties May Be Endangered in the Exercise of Otherwise Lawful Uses of Force

U.S. law and the law of States throughout the world recognize severe limitations on the extent to which a person may endanger innocent third-parties even in an otherwise lawful use of force, such as for self-defense. While sometimes expressed in terms of limits on the extent to which the right of self-defense can be used to justify or excuse injuries to innocent third-parties caused in the course of the self-defense, and other times viewed as implicit in the proportionality principle, and still other times in terms of the lesser evil (necessity) principle, the overriding point is that, while there are occasions in which injury to innocent third-parties may be excused in the otherwise lawful exercise of force, such occasions—and the extent of the permissible injury—are severely limited.

Here I focus on the limits on the rights of self-defense in terms of injuring innocent third-parties. In the next chapter I focus on the closely related necessity principle.

Model Penal Code Section 3.09(3) provides:

> When the actor is justified under Sections 3.03–3.08 in using force upon or toward the person of another but he recklessly or negligently injures or creates a risk of injury to innocent persons, the justification afforded by those Sections is unavailable in a prosecution for such recklessness or negligence towards innocent persons.[1]

The Comments to this Section state:

> Thus an actor who believed that deadly force was necessary in order to preserve his own life could be prosecuted for his reckless or negligent endangering of other lives during the course of saving his own. Similarly, an actor might be justified ... in using deadly force to prevent the consummation of a robbery in which the offender threatened the actor with deadly force, but could be prosecuted for recklessness or negligence if in the course of his conduct he exposed innocent persons to danger or actually inflicted

---

[1] MODEL PENAL CODE § 3.09(3) (A.L.I. 1985) © 1985 by the American Law Institute. Reprinted with permission. *See also* Ferdinand S. Tinio, Annotation, Unintentional Killing of or Injury to Third Person During Attempted Self Defense, 53 A.L.R. 3d 620 (1974).

injury upon them. The justifying incident, in other words, does not provide the occasion for reckless or negligent conduct towards innocent persons.[2]

The Comments further note, however, that the charge of recklessness or negligence must be evaluated in light of the potentially justifying circumstances:

> It should be added that in assessing such a charge of recklessness or negligence the actor's justifying purpose must, of course, be given weight in determining whether the risk to an innocent person was sufficient to establish a gross deviation from proper standards of conduct. The definitions of recklessness and negligence are explicit on this point, each involving a substantial and "unjustifiable" risk that a danger to innocent persons will result. Thus, if the only way to save one's life is to use deadly force that creates some risk of harm to others, that force might be justified. A similar use of force might not, however, be justified to stop a fleeing armed robber if there were danger to others. Although the risk to the life of the robber does not outweigh the benefits of preventing his escape, the risk to others might well do so.[3]

Professors LaFave and Scott elaborate:

> If A in proper self-defense aims at his adversary B but misses B and unintentionally strikes innocent bystander C, he is not liable for C's injury or death unless his conduct ... [u]nder all circumstances (including his need to defend himself) ... was reckless with regard to C. In such a case he would be liable for battery if he merely injures, involuntary manslaughter if he kills C.[4]

---

[2] MODEL PENAL CODE § 3.09(3) Comments ¶ 3 at 154 (A.L.I. 1985) (citations omitted).

[3] *Id.*

[4] LAFAVE & SCOTT, § 5.7(g). Reprinted from CRIMINAL LAW, WAYNE LAFAVE & AUSTIN W. SCOTT, 2d ed., 1986, with permission of the West Group. *See also* People v. Jackson, 212 N.W.2d 918, 919 (Mich. 1973) (citing to LAFAVE & SCOTT for support that unintentional murder of innocent bystander is not intentional murder); People v. Morris, 109 A.D.2d 415, 416 (4th Dept. 1985) (stating defendant justified in shooting aggressor is also justified in shooting innocent bystander but that justification does not preclude conviction based on negligence or recklessness as to bystander); People v. Adams, 9 Ill.App.3d 61, 63–64 (5th Dist. 1972) (holding defendant not guilty of murder where defendant was lawfully defending himself and did not act "wildly or carelessly"); State v. Green, 206 S.E. 2d 923, 926–927 (W. Va. 1974) (an emergency excusing the killing of aggressor will also excuse the unintentional killing of a bystander where the defendant is "free from fault").

This point, in the context of civil law, is addressed by Section 75 of the Restatement of Torts, Second:

> Liability to Third Person
> An act which is privileged for the purpose of protecting the actor from a harmful or offensive contact or other invasion of his interests of personality subjects the actor to liability to a third person for any harm unintentionally done to him only if the actor realizes or should realize that his act creates an unreasonable risk of causing such harm.[5]

The Comment to Section 75 states:

> This Section states the rule that one who unintentionally harms a third person by an act which is privileged as a self-defense against a real or supposed assailant is subject to liability if, but only if, his act is negligent toward such third person as creating an undue and so unreasonable risk of causing an invasion or impairment of some of the legally protected interests of the third person.[6]

The Comment to Section 75 also states:

> In determining whether the actor as a reasonable man should be aware that his act creates an unreasonable risk of causing an invasion of any of the third person's interests of personality, the factors which are to be considered are similar to those which determine the existence of negligence in many other situations. ... The exigency in which the actor is placed, though not due to the third person's conduct, with its attendant necessity of an almost instantaneous choice of a means of self-defense, is here a factor of great importance. So, too, is the comparison between the value of the respective interests of the actor and the third person, and the amount of harm likely to result to each if the actor adopts or refrains from adopting the particular means of self-defense which he employs.[7]

This issue also comes up in the context of questions as to the level of risk which law enforcement personnel may take of injuring innocent parties in dealing with criminal suspects. The Model Penal Code Section 3.07(2)(b) states:

> The use of deadly force is not justifiable under this Section unless:
> (i) the arrest is for a felony; and

---

[5] RESTATEMENT OF THE LAW OF TORTS SECOND § 75 (1965).
[6] *Id.* § 75 Comments at 128–29.
[7] *Id.* § 75 Comments at 129.

(ii) the person effecting the arrest is authorized to act as a peace officer or is assisting a person whom he believes to be authorized to act as a peace officer; and
(iii) the actor believes that the force employed creates no substantial risk of injury to innocent persons ... .[8]

The Comments to Model Penal Code Section 3.07 state that "[a]lthough some recently revised codes have followed the Model Code in barring any deadly force simply to effect an arrest if the actor realizes that such force risks injury to innocent persons, most codes and proposals fail to accord any special protection to innocent bystanders."[9] As to a more typical approach, the Comments cites the New York Penal Law, which potentially imposes liability on peace officers for reckless actions (reckless endangerment) against innocent persons:

> The fact that a peace officer is justified in using deadly physical force under circumstances prescribed [above] does not constitute justification for reckless conduct by such peace officer amounting to an offense against or with respect to innocent persons whom he is not seeking to arrest or retain in custody.[10]

The Comments note that this approach varies from the Model Penal Code approach in two respects: "First, where the peace officer is in fact reckless with respect to third persons under circumstances where he would otherwise be justified in using deadly force against the arrestee, he would not lose his justification with respect to the arrestee, although he might be liable for reckless endangerment as to such innocent persons. ... Second, under [the definition of "recklessly" in] N.Y. Section 15.05(3), for the peace officer to be found reckless with respect to third persons, he must be found to have disregarded a substantial and 'unjustifiable' risk of injury to third persons. Thus, the Section leaves open the possibility that the interest in making the arrest might outweigh the risk of injury to third persons."[11]

Analogously to the above principles of criminal liability, civil liability has regularly been imposed on States for the killing by police officers of innocent bystanders in self-defense in the course of attempting to apprehend criminal suspects. For example, *The New York Times* reported an incident in the summer of 1999 where a New

---

[8] MODEL PENAL CODE § 3.07(2)(b) (A.L.I. 1985).

[9] *Id.* § 3.07 Comments ¶ 3 at 119 (citations omitted).

[10] *Id.* § 3.07 Comments ¶ 3 at 119 n.30 (citing N.Y. Penal Code § 35.30(2) and noting numerous other states taking similar approach, some of them reaching negligence as well as recklessness).

[11] *Id.* § 3.07.

York jury awarded $5.7 million against New York City to the family of a woman killed by police officers who had fired 29 shots at an armed bank robber who had seized the woman as a human shield during a 1993 Upper West Side gun battle.[12]

While the police officers involved had been cleared of any wrongdoing by the Police Department, the jury found them negligent in shooting at the bank robber while he was holding the woman as a shield. The woman's family argued that the police could have saved the woman's life if they had negotiated with the bank robber, while the City contended that the officers had acted appropriately in a chaotic, fast-moving situation in which the bank robber had fired first and posed a threat to both the police and civilians.[13]

The *Times* reported that juries had awarded larger verdicts in shootings by the police in at least a half-dozen other cases, including a Brooklyn case in 1998 in which a victim of a wrongful shooting was awarded $76 million.[14]

Generally Accepted Principles of Law

Such limitations on the extent to which a person may endanger innocent third-parties even in the legitimate exercise of self-defense have recognized by other legal systems.

South African law is a case in point. Injury to third-parties is generally proscribed as beyond the scope of self-defense: "The right of private defense can only be exercised against the attacker, not against a third-party. Thus, if X, in defending himself against Y's attack, throws a stone at Y which misses him and hits Z, a passer-by, X cannot plead private defense to a charge of assaulting Z."[15]

This example is said to descend from Roman law. As a commentator on India's law of self defense has written, "The Roman lawyers held that a man who throws a stone in self-defense is not excused if the stone by misadventure strikes a person other than the assailant."[16]

---

[12] David Rohde, *Jury Awards $5.7 Million in Police Killing of a Hostage,* THE NEW YORK TIMES, July 21, 1999, at B1.

[13] *Id.*

[14] *Id.*

[15] E.M. BURCHELL & P.M.A. HUNT, SOUTH AFRICA CRIMINAL LAW AND PROCEDURE 276 (1970), citations omitted. The authors do say that South African law would potentially recognize the defenses of necessity and a lack of *mens rea.*

[16] ANUKUL CHANDRA MOITRA, THE LAW OF PRIVATE DEFENSE 398 (1930) (citations omitted).

Chapter 11: The Lesser Evil (Necessity) Principle

The limits on otherwise justifiable or excusable actions is also illustrated by the workings of the lesser evil or necessity principle. Under this principle, recognized by many legal systems throughout the world, otherwise illegal actions may in some instances be justified or excused on the ground of necessity when "the defendant was forced to break the law in order to protect [himself or herself] or someone else from the harm that is sought to be avoided."[1] In such circumstances, the defendant is deemed forced to choose between two evils, complying with the law or breaking the law to protect against the harm that will result from compliance. Necessity may be invoked to justify the choice of the lesser harm.

The question of which is the lesser of two harms is judged by an objective standard to protect against a misguided but well intentioned misperception of value, such as an actor's belief that his dog's life or the preservation of his property is more valuable than a stranger's life. Since the dog's life or the preservation of the property is objectively less valuable than the stranger's life, the actor would not be excused for killing the stranger.[2] Often it is obvious which is the lesser evil, but at times serious questions arise, as when one must choose one human life over another.[3]

Under one formulation of the lesser evil principle, otherwise unlawful conduct may be justified if:

> (1) any legally–protected interest is unjustifiably threatened, or an opportunity to further such an interest is presented; and
> (2) the actor engages in conduct, constituting the offense,
> > (a) when and to the extent necessary to protect or further the interest,

---

[1] *See* Danielle R. Dubin, *A Woman's Cry for Help: Why the United States Should Apply Germany's Model of Self-Defense For the Battered Woman*, 2 ILSA J. INT'L & COMP. L. 235, 249–250 (1995). *See* MODEL PENAL CODE § 3.02, Comments 6–7. *See also* Sanford H. Kadish, *Respect for Life and Regard for Rights in the Criminal Law*, 15 CAL. L. REV. 871, 885, 888–89 (July 1996).

[2] *Id.*

[3] R.A.A. MCCALL SMITH & DAVID SHELDON, SCOTS CRIMINAL LAW 136 (1992) ("The question of whether necessity justifies the taking of a life has long been a textbook problem").

(b) that avoids a harm or evil or furthers a legal interest greater
than the harm or evil caused by the actor's conduct.[4]

To illustrate such a balancing of evils, the Model Penal Code gives
as an example the situation where the actor breaks a dike, knowing it
will flood a farm and kill the inhabitants of the farmhouse, in
circumstances where so doing is the only way to save a whole town.[5]
The drafters of the Model Penal Code concluded that the actor, charged
with the homicide of the inhabitants of the farmhouse, has a defense of
necessity based on the net saving of innocent lives:

> The life of every individual must be taken in such a case to be of
> equal value and the numerical preponderance in the lives saved
> compared to those sacrificed should establish legal justification for
> the act.[6]

Model Penal Code Section 3.02 expresses the general rule as to
justification based on choice of evils by providing that "conduct that
the actor believes to be necessary to avoid a harm or evil to himself or
to another is justifiable, provided that the harm or evil sought to be
avoided by such conduct is greater than that sought to be prevented by
the law defining the offense charged...."[7]

Noting that "the necessity must arise from an attempt by the actor to
avoid an evil or harm that is greater than the evil or harm sought to be
avoided by the law defining the offense charged," the Comments to
Section 3.02 emphasize that "[a]n equal or a lesser harm will not
suffice."[8]

The Comments further state that an objective standard governs. It is
not enough that the actor genuinely believed that the interest he was
protecting outweighed the interest he sacrificed; the judge or jury must
decide the relative values.[9] "What is involved may be described as an
interpretation of the law of the offense, in light of the submission that
the special situation calls for an exception to the criminal prohibition

---

[4] *See* PAUL H. ROBINSON, CRIMINAL LAW DEFENSES § 124(a) (1984).
[5] *See* MODEL PENAL CODE § 3.02, Comments 3 at 14–15 (A.L.I. 1985).
[6] *Id.* at 15 (citing Wechsler & Michael, *A Rationale of the Law of Homicide,*
37 COLUM. L. REV. 701, 738–39 (1937)). © 1985 by the American Law
Institute. Reprinted with permission.
[7] Model Penal Code § 3.02 (A.L.I. 1985). § 3.02 further specifies certain
type of circumstance where the Model Penal Code or other applicable law or
evident legislative purpose would preclude such justification. *Id.* at §
3.02(1)(a) and (b).
[8] *Id.* § 3.02 Comments ¶ 2 at 12 (citations omitted).
[9] *See id.*

that the legislature could not reasonably have intended to exclude, given the competing values to be weighted."[10]

The Comments note that the Model Penal Code "does not resolve the question of how far the balancing of values should be determined by the court as a matter of law or submitted to the jury," noting that there was disagreement among the drafters and that it was decided "that this question was best remitted to the law that generally governs the respective functions of the court and jury."[11]

The Comments go on to note that this defense of justification does not apply to situations where a person sacrifices someone else's life to save his own:

> Nor would the defense be available to one who acted to save himself at the expense of another, as by seizing a raft when men are shipwrecked. But whatever may be thought of such cases as presenting a basis for excuse—and the problem must be faced at least in dealing with duress—they are not, in principle, cases of justification. In all ordinary circumstances lives in being must be assumed to be of equal value, equally deserving the protection of the law. If the values are equal, the case for a justification has not been made out.[12]

The Comments note that, while Roman Catholic moralists have generally taken the position (contrary to the thrust of Model Penal Code) that one should not cause effects that are directly evil even if they are thought to be a necessary means to a greater good, that, under the principle of double effect, such action potentially becomes permissible on the theory that the sacrificed life is only permitted, not intended, and is not itself a means to the desired end.[13] "Diverting a flood to destroy a farmhouse instead of a town would be acceptable since the destruction of the farmhouse is not intended and is not a means of saving the town."[14]

The Comments further note that the New York Penal Law, characterized as the second "primary model" for the law as to the necessity defense, is less permissive as to the scope of the defense,

---

[10] *Id.*

[11] *Id.* § 3.02 Comments ¶ 2 at 13 (citing ALI Proceedings 229–31 (1958)).

[12] *Id.* § 3.02 Comments ¶ 2 at 16.

[13] *See id.* § 3.02 Comments ¶ 3 at 15 n.15 (citing Ford, *The Morality of Obliteration Bombing,* in WAR AND MORALITY 15, 26–28 (R. Wasserstrom ed., 1970); D. CALLAHAN, ABORTION: LAW, CHOICE AND MORALITY 422–24 (1970)).

[14] Model Penal Code § 3.02 Comments ¶ 3 at 15 n.15 (A.L.I. 1985).

including in that it requires that the conduct be an "emergency measure to avoid an imminent injury," that the "desirability of avoiding the injury the actor has chosen to avoid 'clearly outweigh' the desirability of avoiding the injury sought to be prevented by the statute," and that the necessity for the action be occasioned or developed "through no fault of the actor."[15]

While this choice of evils defense is not everywheres available, its limits even where it is available are instructive. The killing of an innocent victim rarely outweighs the harm to be avoided.[16] In the classic case of *Regina v. Dudley*, the two defendants had killed a young cabin boy after the three of them and one other survivor had been forced from a yacht into a lifeboat and were starving to death.[17] The purported justification was based on the fact that the cabin boy was the weakest and, if defendants had not killed him, all three would have died.[18] Denying defendants a defense of justification, the English court concluded that a person could only be justified in killing an aggressor not an innocent person and that, to use necessity as a defense to killing an innocent person "would be at once dangerous, immoral, and opposed to all legal principles and analogy."[19]

A second British case illustrating the point is *R. v. Werner*, where the defendants had killed a fellow prisoner of war in compliance with orders from their superior officer. Rejecting the defendants' purported justification of the killing on the basis that they feared for their own lives if they did not comply, the court held that the necessity defense did not authorize one to take the life of an innocent person in the hopes of saving one's own.[20]

---

[15] *Id.* § 3.02 Comments ¶ 5 (discussing New York Penal Law § 35.05) (citations omitted).

[16] ROBINSON, *supra* note 4, at § 124(5)(g) (1984).

[17] R. v. Dudley & Stephens, 14 Q.B.D. 273, 281 (United Kingdom, 1884).

[18] *See id.*

[19] *See id.* Robinson points out that the Regina v. Dudley situation may be more difficult to apply to when the taking of innocent lives saves a greater number of other innocent lives. *See* ROBINSON, *supra* note 4, at § 124(5)(g).

[20] E.M. BURCHELL & P.M.A. HUNT, SOUTH AFRICAN CRIMINAL LAW AND PROCEDURE 289 (Vol. 1, 1970) (In Dudley, the judge stated that, "the broad proposition that a man may save his life by killing, if necessary an innocent and unoffending neighbour ... certainly is not law at the present day." In Werner, Watermeyer, C.J. stated, "the killing of an innocent person is never legally justifiable by compulsion or necessity"). *See also* GLANVILLE WILLIAMS, TEXTBOOK OF CRIMINAL LAW 559 (1978) ("It is very unlikely that anyone

In a South African case, *S v. Bradbury*, the accused was found guilty of murder based on his having helped a man kill the victim. The court rejected the defendant's purported necessity justification that he had only assisted in the killing out of fear for his own life. A commentator has said that this case "show[s] that [South African] law, like the English law, regards the intentional killing of an innocent victim as a greater evil than the death of the person threatened—no man is entitled to take the life of an innocent person simply to preserve his own [life]."[21]

The German Criminal Code delineates those circumstances in which necessity may serve as "a justification or excuse:"[22]

§34. Necessity as justification
Whoever commits an act in order to avert an imminent and otherwise unavoidable danger to the life, limb, liberty, honor, property or other legal interest of himself or of another does not act unlawfully if, taking into consideration all the conflicting interests, in particular the legal ones, and the degree of danger involved, the interest protected by him significantly outweighs the interest which he harms. This rule applies only if the act is an appropriate means to avert the danger.

§ 35. Necessity as excuse
Whoever commits an unlawful act in order to avert an imminent or otherwise unavoidable danger to his own life, limb, or liberty, or to that of a relative or person close to him, acts without guilt. This rule does not apply if under the prevailing circumstances the perpetrator could be expected to have assumed the risk, especially

---

would be held to be justified in killing for any purpose except the saving of other life, or perhaps the saving of great pain or distress").

[21] BURCHELL & HUNT, *supra* note 20, at 290 (The author does add that although it is not legal for one to take the life of an innocent person to save his or her own, the taking of X's life by Y to save Z could potentially be justifiable, as could X's taking Y's life to save the lives of several people, including his or her own.). *See also* TUDOR JACKSON, THE LAW OF KENYA 90 (1970) (Kenya, another common law country, follows the English rule, that it is not justifiable to kill an innocent person in order to protect one's self. The author states that in a hypothetical situation, a man who is mountain climbing cannot cut the rope to save himself and send others to their death. In a similar hypothetical, a man is guilty of murder if he pushes another man off a plank that is adrift in the middle of the ocean, so as to save his own life.).

[22] Penal Code of the Federal Republic of Germany, of May 15, 1871, as revised on Jan. 2, 1975, as amended as of Dec. 30, 1986, *as set forth in* THE PENAL CODE OF THE FEDERAL REPUBLIC OF GERMANY (Joseph J. Darby, trans., The American Series of Foreign Penal Codes, No. 28, London 1987).

because he was himself the cause of the danger or because he found himself in a special legal relationship. ...

If in committing the act, the perpetrator assumes the existence of circumstance which under subparagraph (1) would excuse his conduct, he shall be punished only if he could have avoided the error.[23]

The law of the Philippines, in language ostensibly limiting incursions on the rights of innocent third-parties as well as on attackers in the course of self-defense, provides as to necessity:

Art. 11. Justifying Circumstances.—The following do not incur any criminal liability:

***

4. Any person who, in order to avoid an evil or injury, does an act which causes damage to another, provided that the following requisites are present:
First. That the evil sought to be avoided actually exists;
Second. That the injury feared be greater than that done to avoid it;
Third. That there be no other practical and less harmful means of preventing it.[24]

Norway adopts the rule that self-serving actions taken out of necessity that endanger innocent third-parties are unlawful and unjustifiable yet "excusable"[25] and subjects such actions to the test of "reasonableness."[26] "The thing saved must be extremely significant in comparison to the damage done by the act ... strong reasons must exist before such a departure from general rules will be accepted."[27] Norwegian law further recognizes the limits on the doctrine of necessity by providing that "a person must generally pay damages for the harm that he caused by the act of necessity, whereas no such duty exists where self-defense is concerned."[28]

The Russian code similarly provides as to necessity:

Acts committed in necessary defence will not be regarded as criminal, provided they are not evidently out of proportion in view of the nature and dangerousness of the attack. Necessary defense

---

[23] *Id.*

[24] GUILLERMO B. GUEVARA, COMMENTARIES ON THE REVISED PENAL CODE OF THE PHILIPPINES 18–21, 27–28 (1957) (emphasis omitted).

[25] JOHANNES ANDENAES, THE GENERAL PART OF THE CRIMINAL LAW OF NORWAY 170 (1965).

[26] *Id.* at 163.

[27] *Id.* at 168.

[28] *Id.* at 165

concerns harm inflicted on the person engaging in criminal actions against the defender or other legitimate interests. Extreme necessity concerns harm inflicted to avert threats against legitimate interests. Violations of the criminal law committed in the course of extreme necessity will not be regarded as crimes, provided there was no other way to avert the harm threatened, and the harm inflicted is less significant than the harm averted.[29]

---

[29] F.J.M. FELDBRUDGE, RUSSIAN LAW: THE END OF THE SOVIET SYSTEM AND THE ROLE OF LAW 311 (1993).

The Statute of the former Czechoslovakia, in its provision on self-help, § 417(2), similarly provided: "if a citizen or his property is threatened and he tries to avert the threat he must do so in a commensurate manner."
T.H.J. VONDRACEK, COMMENTARY ON THE CZECHOSLOVAK CIVIL CODE 372 (1988) (citing Nove, 557, and Bicovsky, 463).

The Czechoslovak Civil code § 6 further provided, "If there is an imminent threat of an unjustifiable invasion of a right, the person so threatened may himself avert the invasion in a commensurate manner." *Id.* at 15–16.

The Commentary to § 6 stated:

Self-help in the sense of the present section may be effected only by way of rare exception and therefore several restrictive conditions are set: ... (2) the manner on which self-help is effected must be in reasonable proportion to the threat, meaning that no more intense violence may be exerted than warranted by the threat (if bodily force is sufficient to avert the threat, a gun may not be used) and no more damage may be caused than that which threatens to occur; ... (4) the imminent invasion must be genuinely unlawful, not merely so in the eye of the person threatened ....

Id. at 15–16 (citing Nove, 43, Svestka, 75).

Similarly, § 418 of the Czechoslovak Civil Code provided:

Section 418:

[1]Any person who has caused damage while averting directly impending danger which he has not caused himself, is not liable for such damage unless the danger could have been averted under the given circumstances in a different manner or if the result caused is obviously equally grave or even graver than would have been the result of the impending danger.

[2]Likewise, no one is liable for damage caused in necessary defense against an impending or continuous attack. There is no necessary defense if the act was obviously not commensurate with the nature and danger of the attack.

Subsection 1 refers to state of necessity *(stav nouze)* or extreme necessity *(krajni nouze)*, while subsection 2 refers to necessary defense *(nutna obrana),* including self-defense, defense of others, and defense of property. If the statutory conditions are met, both necessity and defense are justified, or in the words of the

Under Israeli law, the overall principle of necessity has been described as questionable and limited:

> The weighing of values in necessity ... is relatively easy when the interest to be saved relates to property: clearly, the value of such interest never justifies the taking of a man's life. Less clear is whether it allows one to save the life of one person by sacrificing the life of another. ... But what is the law when, in order to save a few lives, the sacrifice of many lives is necessary? Can a quantitative criterion be used to differentiate between the permitted and the forbidden? Regrettably, the Holocaust supplied a number of difficult examples in this connection. Even so, definitive answers have not been given to these questions in Israel, nor have they in England or the U.S.A.[30]

D.W. Bowett, in his leading treatise on the international law of self-defense, examines these matters in the context of the rights of neutrals under the principles of international law:

> In so far as self-preservation and necessity find a use as concepts justifying conduct which, though not lawful (and therefore distinct from self-defence) is yet excusable, their scope is necessarily limited. They cannot, in purporting to illustrate the maxim *'salus papuli suprema lex'*, excuse all *prima facie* unlawful conduct against states which are not in breach of any duty under international law.[31]

---

commentators, constitute "circumstances excluding unlawfulness of the act" *i.e.,* circumstances excluding liability for damage caused. Corresponding institutions are adopted by the Criminal Code, where necessity (section 14) and necessary defense (section 13) exclude criminal liability. *Id.* at 372–374 (citing Knapp-Plank, 414 *et seq.*; Matys, 91; Feldbrugge, 119; Nove, 558, Svestka, 79).

[30] Dan Bein, *Criminal Law, in* THE LAW OF ISRAEL: GENERAL SURVEYS 184 (Itzhak Zamir & Sylviane Colombo, eds., 1995) (citations omitted).

[31] D. W. BOWETT, SELF-DEFENCE IN INTERNATIONAL LAW 10 (1958). *See also* John-Alex Romano, Note, *Combating Terrorism and Weapons of Mass Destruction: Reviving the Doctrine of A State of Necessity,* 87 GEO. L.J. 1023 (April 1999).

Reviewing the law as to the obligation of States "'to protect within their territory the rights of other States, in particular their right to integrity and inviolability in peace and in war,'" Romano notes that the U.S. Supreme Court has recognized that international law imposes a duty of due diligence on states. Romano, *supra* at 1033 (citing RICHARD J. ERICKSON, LEGITIMATE USE OF MILITARY FORCE AGAINST STATE-SPONSORED INTERNATIONAL TERRORISM 96

Bowett concludes that the opposite view, to freely permit encroachments on third states, would be "destructive of the entire legal order."[32] Bowett notes that the excuse of unlawful acts based on necessity is narrower than the justification of self-defense (which renders the conduct in question lawful). The excuse based on necessity must inflict "relatively little harm:"

> The circumstances in which necessity may excuse the non-observance of the duties imposed by international law restricting the use of force are those in which, as an incidental to the exercise of the right of self-defence, the rights of an innocent state are infringed. The excusable character of this conduct towards an innocent state lies in the fact that, in order that a state may in self-defence protect its essential rights against a delinquent states, it may be necessary to disregard the rights of an innocent state which are thereby relatively little harmed in comparison to the harm which would have been suffered by the other state if denied the right to act out of necessity.[33]

(1989) (quoting Island of Palmas arbitral decision) and United States v. Arjona, 120 U.S. 479, 484 (1887) ("The law of nations requires every national government to use 'due diligence' to prevent a wrong being done within its own dominion to another nation with which it is at peace, or to the people thereof.")).

[32] BOWETT, *supra* note 31, at 10 (citing SCHWARZENBERGER, JUS PACIS AC BELLI? 344 (1943)).

[33] *Id.* at 10. The International Law Commission, in its 1980 report on the responsibility of states for internationally wrongful acts, set forth the conditions under which a State may invoke necessity:

> First, the act must be the sole means of protecting an essential interest of the state against a grave and imminent peril. In this regard, the Commission commented that an 'essential interest' will vary with the particulars of each case, and the 'peril must not have been escapable by any other means, even a more costly one.' Second, the act cannot 'seriously impair an essential interest of the State towards which the obligation existed.' The Commission clarified this point by requiring that the interests of the state acted against be less essential than those of the state taking the action. Third, the international obligation violated cannot be one which 'arises out of a peremptory norm of general international law.' Finally, a state cannot invoke a state of necessity if the international obligation violated is set forth in a treaty which, explicitly or implicitly, forecloses its invocation."

Romano, *supra* n. 31, at 1046–47 (quoting [1980] 2 Y.B. INT'L L. COMM'N 49–50, U.N. Doc. a/cn.4/Ser.A/1980/Add.1(Pt.2)).

Bowett states:

> [T]here may arise specific situations in which a belligerent violates
> neutral rights and justifies the violation by relying on the right of
> self-defence. *** Perhaps the strict answer to this situation is that
> the belligerent can only act against the neutral by virtue of a right
> of necessity, and not by right of self-defence.[34]

Bowett notes the argument that the encroachment on the rights of
the neutral may only be permissible when the neutral has somehow
itself failed in the performance of its legal duties:

> In international law it might be possible to argue for the limitation
> of the right of self-defence to cases where the violation of a state's
> rights is only justified as a reaction to a breach of duty by that
> state.[35]

Such a theory is based on the notion that "'[r]espect for the
inviolability of the territory of a State rests on the theory that it
possesses the power and the will to exercise control therein, and to a
degree sufficient to ensure the administration of justice in a broad
sense, throughout the national domain.'"[36] A neutral State's territory
can remain inviolate so long as the State controls its territory and the
actions taken therein. Failure to do so can lead to encroachment by
belligerents who need to protect their interests.[37]

On this basis, it is stated "that the right of territorial integrity is
never absolute, but conditional on the absence of any real threat to the
security of another state within the boundaries of the state claiming
integrity."[38] While "absolute inviolability" is not conferred by the U.N.
Charter,[39] integrity is the norm, and intrusions need to be justified: "The
traditional emphasis had been on the duty of any belligerent to respect
neutral rights."[40]

---

[34] *Id.* at 173. (citing WINFIELD, TORTS, 5TH ED. 53, 58–59; GLANVILLE
WILLIAMS, CRIMINAL LAW, THE GENERAL PART 573–4; Scott v. Sheperd 2
W.Bl., de Grey, C.J. at 900, and Gould, J. at 898 (1773); R. v. Dudley, 14
Q.B.D. 273; PROSSER, TORTS 129–39, 137; U.S. RESTATEMENT, TORTS Ch. 45
§890, p. 476; Bohlen, *Incomplete Privilege,* 39 H.L.R. 307–24).

[35] *Id.* at 173–174

[36] *Id.* at 39, quoting I HYDE, INTERNATIONAL LAW 646 (1945).

[37] *See id.* at 168, citing II RODICK, THE DOCTRINE OF NECESSITY IN
INTERNATIONAL LAW 698 (7th ed. 1928).

[38] *Id.* at 33.

[39] *Id.* at 34.

[40] *Id* at 167.

The primary example of a State's forfeiting its inviolability is where it permits or suffers combatant to use its territory, thereby subjecting itself to having the territory struck by the other combatant(s).[41]

A related example is the situation where a combatant strikes neutral territory or property to prevent an adversary from exploiting it, as in the case of the attack on the Danish fleet by the English in 1807, to preempt France from commandeering that fleet.[42]

A further example, also in a sense representing a failure by the neutral to exercise control over its territory, is where a combatant proceeds into neutral territory in "hot pursuit" of an enemy which has gone into that territory.[43]

Bowett notes that the emergency justification for affecting innocent territory can be over-pleaded, and struck down at law: The Nuremberg court rejected Germany's argument that its invasion of Norway had been a necessary encroachment on third-parties' territory to stop the attacks of the Allies, for example.[44]

---

[41] *See id.* at 167–174. Bowett recognizes the difficulties of imputing "fault" when the neutral has been unable to prevent occupation of its territory or violation of its rights by the other belligerent:

> The more difficult position arises where there cannot be found any breach of duty in the neutral to justify infringement of his rights by a belligerent acting in self-defence. This may arise in two ways; firstly, when the neutral despite due diligence has been unable to prevent occupation of its territory or other violation of its rights by one belligerent which brings about a situation in which the opposing belligerent is constrained to act in self-defence. Here if one rests the right of intervention by this opposing belligerent on the "fault" in the neutral, the dilemma is clearly apparent, for the belligerent cannot, in self-defence, violate the rights of the "innocent" neutral nor can he in reason be expected to tolerate the threat arising from his opponent's illegality.

Id. at 171.

[42] *See* IAN BROWNLIE, INTERNATIONAL LAW AND THE USE OF FORCE BY STATES 310 (Oxford University Press 1963).

[43] BOWETT, *supra* note 31, at 32–33.

[44] *See id.* at 173. Bowett noted:

> At Nuremberg the German contention was that the invasion of Norway was motivated solely by the desire to forestall an Allied invasion, and, as we have seen, the Tribunal rejected this argument on the facts; it is of interest to note that it did not reject, as a matter of law, the contention that a belligerent may invade neutral territory in order to forestall occupation by the opposing belligerent.

Id. (citation omitted).

The acceptance of this view that the taking of an innocent life may be justified brings up another issue: Which innocent lives should be sacrificed?   Robinson suggests four factors that should affect the determination of what innocent lives should be sacrificed in circumstances where justification may be available: (1) the non-aggressor's life should be protected; (2) the already endangered life

---

See also id. at 171, for the tension between respecting the rights of neutrals and the contrasting need of defense against wrongdoers.

Bowett discusses the peculiar problem in the traditional body of self-defense law that is posed by the vast destructiveness of nuclear weapons, and the suddenness by which a nation may now be overrun by nuclear arms. He holds out two solutions to enable the law to continue to conform to fact: to either deprive all nations of "the kind of armaments which, by their immediate destructive power, make the system unworkable; or ... [to move] towards a system of world federation in which competent states would be completely disarmed. ... [T]hese difficulties ... are not solved by distorting the concept of self-defence, individual or collective, out of all legal recognition." *Id.* at 247.

McDougal and Feliciano note the issue of nuclear weapons effects encroaching upon the territory of neutrals, and appurtenant fiscally oriented justice:

> The instrumentalities and techniques of coercion that the opposing belligerents employ against each other may pose particular problems and special dangers for non-participants. Most obvious and dramatic are the dangers and problems arising from the belligerent use of weapons whose physical effects are not always confined to the territorial domain of the target belligerent. Among these weapons are nuclear and thermonuclear explosives and chemical and bacteriological agents. ... People in nonparticipant states, whether contiguous to or remote from the nuclear target areas, would hence be exposed to the somatic and genetic effects of basic-energy weapons."

MYRES S. MCDOUGAL & FLORENTINO P. FELICIANO, LAW AND MINIMUM WORLD PUBLIC ORDER: THE LEGAL REGULATION OF INTERNATIONAL COERCION 388 (1961).

McDougal and Feliciano conclude as to this situation that instead of claims and counterclaims against warring states of economic warfare or wrongdoing, "[e]mphasis might shift to other kinds of controversies: for instance, controversies about compensation for damages suffered by nonparticipants from the effects of nuclear weapons exploding in adjoining territory." *Id.* at 393. Rather than hazard predictions for the economic justice policies after an atomic war, McDougal and Feliciano choose to constrain their study to situations of "'limited' wars between great powers who reciprocally refrain from invoking their strategic nuclear capabilities," or to war between non-nuclear states. *Id.* at 394, citing TUCKER, THE LAW OF WAR AND NEUTRALITY AT SEA 218 n.50 (1957).

may be sacrificed before the non-endangered life; (3) the taking of a short life to preserve a longer life may be justified; and (4) the innocent that has not contributed to the threat should be protected.[45]

Transnational Effects

As to the potential reach of the law, it is a widely established principle that a person is potentially subject to liability in a jurisdiction for causing effects in that jurisdiction, even if the underlying actions were performed outside the jurisdiction. This is the familiar basis of long-arm jurisdiction in U.S. constitutional practice.[46] The classic example is the person who fires a shot into New York City from across the Hudson River in New Jersey, leading to potential liability in New York.

The application of this point internationally can be seen from the Restatement (Revised), Foreign Relations Law of the United States:

> § 402. Bases of Jurisdiction to Prescribe
> Subject to § 403, a state has jurisdiction to prescribe law with respect to
> (1)(a) conduct all or a substantial part of which takes place within its territory;
> ***
> (c) conduct outside its territory which has or is intended to have substantial effect within its territory;
> ***
> (3) certain conduct outside its territory by persons not its nationals which is directed against the security of the state or a limited class of other state interests.
> § 403 (1) Even when one of the bases for jurisdiction under § 402 is present, a state may not exercise jurisdiction to prescribe law with respect to a person or activity having connections with another

---

[45] *See* ROBINSON, *supra* note 4, at §124(g)(A)–(D).

[46] *See* JACK H. FRIEDENTHAL, CIVIL PROCEDURE 142, §3.13 (2d Ed. 1993) (citing the Illinois interpretation *in* Gray v. American Radiator & Standard Sanitary Corporation, 22 Ill.2d 432, 176 N.E.2d 761 (1961); Scanlan v. Norma Projektil Fabrik, 345 F.Supp 292 (D.Mont. 1972); Coe & Payne Co. v. Wood-Mosaic Corp., 230 Ga. 58, 195 S.E. 399 (1973); Myers v. Brickwedel, 259 Or. 457, 486 P.2d 1286 (1971); Nixon v. Cohn, 62 Wn.2d 987, 385 P.2d 305 (1963)). *See also* Model Penal Code 10 U.L.A. 433 (1974), *quoted in* LOUIS HENKEN ET AL, INTERNATIONAL LAW, CASES AND MATERIALS 831–832 (1987).

state or states when the exercise of such jurisdiction is unreasonable.[47]

---

[47] RESTATEMENT (THIRD), FOREIGN RELATIONS LAW OF THE UNITED STATES §§ 402, 403 (1986).

Chapter 12: Legal Effect of Having Caused One's Own Need to Resort to Extreme Force

It is a generally recognized principle of law that an actor may not justify the use of a level of force when the actor himself created the necessity. Thus, the right of self-defense is generally limited in situations where the actor created the confrontation.[1]

In addition to withdrawing justifications from an actor, most jurisdictions also withdraw the right to assert an excuse when the actor placed himself in a situation where he caused the excusing conditions.[2] For example, jurisdictions generally withdraw the excuse of intoxication when the actor voluntarily becomes intoxicated.[3] Some

---

[1] PAUL H. ROBINSON, CRIMINAL LAW DEFENSES § 123(a) (1984). The use of a justification may be denied depending on the actor's culpability. *Id.*

There are three different approaches to determine whether or not an actor will lose the right to use a justification defense: (1) any causal contribution, (2) culpability in causing, and (3) distinguishing levels of culpability in causing. *Id.* at § 123(c)(1–3).

In the States adopting the "any causal contribution" approach, the justification is not allowed when the actor contributed in "any way, even faultlessly, to causing the threat of harm." *Id.* at §123(c)(1). These jurisdictions allow the use of justifications only when the actor's conduct contributed nothing to the circumstances causing the harm. *Id.*

In jurisdictions adopting the second approach, justifications are withdrawn only when the actor was at some level of fault for causing the justifying conditions. *Id.* at §123(c)(2). In these jurisdictions, even if the actor was at fault, he may be entitled to an "imperfect self defense" but will be denied a "perfect exoneration" for his actions *Id.* The difficulty in this approach is determining whether the level of fault needed (*i.e.* negligent, reckless, etc.) has been established. *Id.*

The third approach is the Model Penal Code approach and withdraws the justification only when the actor is being charged with an offense requiring a reckless or negligent culpability and was "reckless or negligent in bringing about the situation requiring a choice of harm or evils." *Id.* (citing MODEL PENAL CODE § 3.02(2)). The Model Penal Code withdraws the self defense justifications only when the "actor, with the purpose of causing death or serious bodily harm, provoked the use of force against himself in the same encounter." *Id.* (citing MODEL PENAL CODE § 3.04(2)(b)(i), 3.05(i)(a)).

[2] *See id.* at §162.

[3] *See id.* at § 162(b)(1).

jurisdictions withdraw the excuse of duress if the actor places himself in the situation that caused the duress.[4]

While the actor may be denied the use of the justification, the causal circumstances of his behavior may still be employed to mitigate the actor's culpable mental state.[5] For example, if an actor negligently gets drunk and then kills someone, he may only be vulnerable to prosecution for manslaughter or an equivalent homicide charge.[6]

In *United States v. Peterson*, the District of Columbia Circuit noted the limited availability of the justification of self defense:

> Hinged on the exigencies of self-preservation, the doctrine of homicidal self-defense emerges from the body of the criminal law as a limited though important exception to legal outlawry of the arena of self-help in the settlement of potentially fatal personal conflicts. So it is that necessity is the pervasive theme of the well defined conditions which the law imposes on the right to kill or maim in self-defense.[7]

The Court found that a claim of self-defense cannot be supported by "a self-generated necessity to kill" and that the right of self-defense is only granted to those "free from fault."[8] An aggressor may not use self-defense unless he has effectively withdrawn from the encounter and the other actor continues to use force.[9] An actor "must do everything in his power, consistent with his safety, to avoid the danger and avoid the necessity of taking life" before his right of self-defense arises.[10] The Court noted that, while a person does have the right to "deliberately arm himself for purposes of self defense against a pernicious assault which he has good reason to expect," the arming may be considered in connection with the other circumstances.[11]

In *United States v. Moore*, the Court of Military Appeals held that an actor does not lose the right to self-defense merely because he armed himself and sought out the victim.[12] The actor must "willingly and knowingly do some act ... reasonably calculated to lead to affray or

---

[4] *See id.* at §162(b)(3).
[5] *See id.* at §162(b)(2).
[6] *See id.*
[7] United States v. Peterson 483 F.2d 1222, 1229–31 (D.C. Cir. 1971) *cert. denied.*, 94 S. Ct. 367 (1973).
[8] *Id.* at 1231 (D.C. Cir. 1971).
[9] *See id.*
[10] *Id.*
[11] *Id.* (citing Thompson v. United States, 155 U.S. 271, 278 (1984)).
[12] *See* 35 C.M.R. 159, 166 (1964).

deadly conflict" before the right to self-defense is lost.[13] On this basis, an actor who commits a robbery armed with deadly force cannot assert the justification of self defense when the victim of the robbery responds with force.[14]

It is also clear that a level of force cannot be justified if the actor had the capability to take other action which would have obviated the force. Robinson states:

> Even if greater force might be reasonable in relation to the harm threatened, and even if most persons would find it necessary to use greater force, the force used is not justified if the individual actor could protect himself effectively with less. For instance, assume the actor is a karate expert who can, with no risk of harm to himself, dislodge an attacker's weapon with a high kick. While the average person might be justified in shooting an armed attacker, this actor, may only use karate to disarm, since any more harmful force, such as shooting, is not necessary to protect himself.[15]

These lines of thought would appear to be relevant to our inquiry. As a matter of reason, the requirement of necessity should be applied in the context of what a State which had time to act could reasonably have arranged during that time (such as the build-up of a conventional weapons capacity sufficient to deal with the State's reasonably anticipatable military needs). A State should not legally be permitted through inaction to create a situation where the use of nuclear weapons is "necessary" because of the State's purposeful choice not to establish a sufficient conventional weapons capability.

Testimony relevant to this point was given by Admiral Gayler in hearings before the House Committee on Foreign Affairs during the Cold War period:

> MR. SOLARZ. If the Soviet Union tomorrow offered to sign a verifiable treaty providing for the removal of all tactical nuclear weapons from Europe, East and West, would you think it was in our interest to agree to such a treaty?
>
> ADMIRAL GAYLER. Yes I would.
>
> MR. SOLARZ. Within the existing balance of conventional forces?

---

[13] *Id.* (quoting 26 AM. JUR. 2d, Homicide, sec. 131).

[14] *See* United States v. Thomas, 34 F.3d 44, 48 (2d Cir. 1994).

[15] ROBINSON, *supra* note 1, at § 121(a)(2)(A).

ADMIRAL GAYLER. Yes, I would, for two reasons. One, it might finally induce our European allies to pick up their socks and take the reasonable, not necessarily even very expensive means that are required to make a conventional defense of Europe practicable. There aren't even any antitank barriers or provisions for them along the borders of West Germany.

We are expected to start a nuclear war which will probably result in the destruction of Europe and of ourselves rather than take simple, straightforward measures. The supply of the NATO countries is based on who gets the business.

MR. SOLARZ. The second reason. The first was it might get our allies to spend more money on defense.

ADMIRAL GAYLER. The second reason is that if the capability for starting a nuclear war doesn't exist, the prospects of one starting are less likely.[16]

Generally Accepted Principles of Law

Throughout the world's legal systems it will often be the case that an accused who has put himself into a position of vulnerability will lose defenses of justification that might otherwise have been available. Examples can be seen as to the defenses of self-defense and intoxication. The accused will lose the privilege of self-defense if he was the aggressor or could have avoided the danger without resort to harm. Similarly, many legal systems will not allow a defendant an excuse of intoxication if he voluntarily became intoxicated.

Thus, in Scotland, as in many common law countries, voluntary intoxication is not a defense to a general or basic intent crime.[17] The court in the *Brennan* case of 1977 stated that "in crimes of basic 'intent' we understand the law of England to be at one with the law of

---

[16] Testimony of Adm. Noel Gayler, U.S. Navy (Retired), Former Commander in Chief, U.S. Forces in the Pacific, Former Director, National Security Agency, in Hearings on The Role of Arms Control in U.S. Defense Policy, before the Committee on Foreign Affairs, House of Representatives, Ninety-Eight Congress, Second Session, June 20, 21, 26, July 25, 1984 at 126. *See also* Statement of Ambassador Robert Blackwill, U.S. Representative to the Mutual and Balanced Force Reductions [MBFR] Negotiations, before the Committee on Foreign Affairs, House of Representatives, 98th Cong., 2nd Sess., June 20, 21, 26, July 25, 1984, at 4. *See* Chapter 17, notes 29–35, Chapter 18 note 5 and accompanying text.

[17] *See* R.A.A. McCall Smith & David Sheldon, Scots Criminal Law 110–11 (1992).

Scotland in refusing to admit self-induced intoxication as a defense of any kind."[18] The *Brennan* court refused to allow a defense of voluntary intoxication for crimes requiring a specific intent, that is what commentary on the case calls a "mental state required to form an intention in relation to that act's consequences."[19]

Israel, another common law jurisdiction, only allows a defense for voluntary partial intoxication. This defense, similar to the law in England and Scotland, is only recognized in crimes of specific intent.[20] The only time complete voluntary intoxication will be a defense to criminal liability is when the defendant "suffers from alcoholic psychosis."[21]

Several African common law countries also limit the defense of intoxication when the accused voluntarily becomes intoxicated. South Africa has followed the English rule that voluntary intoxication can only be a defense to a specific intent crime[22] and does not allow a defense for voluntary intoxication in crimes of basic intent. However, the defendant may be able to mitigate his sentence by indicating his ability to make conscious choices was limited by voluntary intoxication.[23]

Many other countries follow the common law lead by limiting the defense of intoxication when one becomes inebriated voluntarily. French criminal law provides that in a situation when one drinks in order to get the courage needed to commit the crime, not only will

---

[18] *Id.*

[19] *Id.* at 111–13.

[20] *See* THE LAW OF ISRAEL: GENERAL SURVEYS 178–179 (Itzak Zamir & Sylviane Colombo eds., 1995).

[21] *Id.* at 178.

[22] *See* E.M. BURCHELL & R.M.A. HUNT, SOUTH AFRICAN CRIMINAL LAW AND PROCEDURE 229 (Vol. 1, 1970).

[23] *See id.* at 231. *See also* CYPRIAN O. OKONKWO & MICHAEL E. NAISH, CRIMINAL LAW IN NIGERIA 149 (1965) ("In general, intoxication is not a defense to a criminal charge. But there may be a defense where intoxication is involuntary; and even voluntary intoxication may have some mitigating effect on criminal liability"); TUDOR JACKSON, THE LAW OF KENYA 89 (1970) ("Intoxication does not constitute a defense to any criminal charge unless the state of intoxication was such that 'he did not know that at such act or omission was wrong or did not know what he was doing'"); STEVEN LOWENSTEIN, THE PENAL LAW OF ETHIOPIA 181 (1965) "The provisions excluding or reducing liability to punishment shall not apply to the person who in order to commit an offense intentionally put himself into a condition of irresponsibility or of limited responsibility by means of alcohol or drugs or by any other means." *Id.* at art. 50(1).

drunkenness not be a defense, it will be treated as an aggravating circumstance.[24] French law is unclear as to the availability of a defense of voluntary intoxication when one commits a crime while intoxicated without forming the intent to commit the crime. However, "[i]n France, as in other countries, it seems increasingly necessary to punish one, who through his own fault becomes drunk, equally with the sober man."[25]

Under Norwegian law, "as long as it merely lowers the consciousness and thus weakens moral inhibitions, intoxication will never preclude criminal liability."[26]

Germanic law limits self-defense in both the Civil Code and the Criminal Code in circumstances where the actor brought on the need to use force:

> German Civil Code (B&B) Book I- General Part, Sixth Section, Exercise of Rights, Self-Defense, and Self-Help:
>
> § 228. [Self-defense against things] If a person damages or destroys a thing belonging to another in order to ward off from himself or from another a danger threatened by the thing, he does not act unlawfully, if such injury or destruction is necessary to ward off the danger, and the damage is not out of proportion to the danger. If the danger was caused by the fault of the person so acting, he is liable to make compensation.[27]

In the German criminal code, under "Defense and Necessity,"[28] the following limitations are set forth:

> § 35 Necessity as excuse
>
> Whoever commits an unlawful act in order to avert an imminent or otherwise unavoidable danger to his own life, limb, or liberty, or to that of a relative or person close to him, acts without

---

[24] *See* BOUZAT, DRUIT FENAL 252–54, *reprinted in* LOWENSTEIN, *supra* note 23, at 182.

[25] LOWENSTEIN, *supra* note 23, at 183.

[26] JOHANNES ANDENAES, THE GENERAL PART OF THE CRIMINAL LAW OF NORWAY 263 (1965).

[27] GEORGE BERMANN & HANS SMIT, MATERIALS ON COMPARATIVE LAW 465 (Columbia University School of Law, Spring 1982), quoting THE GERMAN CIVIL CODE 35–36, 41–48, 134–39 (trans. Forrester, Goren, & Ilgen) (1978).

[28] Penal Code of the Federal Republic of Germany, of May 15, 1871, as revised on Jan. 2, 1975, as amended as of Dec. 30, 1986, *as set forth in* THE PENAL CODE OF THE FEDERAL REPUBLIC OF GERMANY (Joseph J. Darby, trans., The American Series of Foreign Penal Codes, No, 28, London 1987).

guilt. This rule does not apply if under the prevailing circumstances the perpetrator could be expected to have assumed the risk, especially because he was himself the cause of the danger or because he found himself in a special legal relationship. ....

If in committing the act, the perpetrator assumes the existence of circumstance which under subparagraph (1) would excuse his conduct, he shall be punished only if he could have avoided the error.[29]

The former Czechoslovak civil code similarly limits the necessary defense to situations that the actor "has not caused himself."[30]

---

[29] *Id.*

[30] T.H.J. VONDRACEK, COMMENTARY ON THE CZECHOSLOVAK CIVIL CODE 372–374 (1988) (citing Knapp-Plank, 414 *et seq.*; Matys, 91; Feldbrugge, 119; Nove, 558, Svestka, 79).

PART III

Additional Legal History and Principles

Chapter 13: The Evolution of International Law as to Landmines

The indiscriminate and potentially disproportionate nature of the long term blast effects of antipersonnel land mines ("landmines") are in some respects analogous to the radiation effects of nuclear weapons. Just as radiation spreads out over an extended period in space and time, killing and injuring persons having nothing to do with the original conflict, so also do the hidden blast effects of landmines continue, at least in time, killing and maiming innocent persons long unborn as of the original conflict.

The extent of the landmine problem is considerable. There are estimated to be some 80 to 110 million landmines deployed throughout the world in some 62 different countries.[1] Each month landmines reportedly kill 800 people and maim 1200—a victim every twenty minutes.[2] According to the United Nations, mine clearance operations extracted some 80,000 landmines worldwide in 1993, but in the same year an additional 2.5 million landmines were deployed.[3]

The legality of the use of landmines has long been questioned and addressed, *inter alia*, in the context of the rules of discrimination, necessity and proportionality,[4] and of provisions of the 1907 Hague

---

[1] *See* BUREAU OF POLITICAL-MILITARY AFFAIRS, U.S. DEPARTMENT OF STATE: HIDDEN KILLERS: THE GLOBAL LANDMINE CRISIS 1 (1994) [hereinafter HIDDEN KILLERS]. *See also* American Red Cross & Gilles Laffon, *Landmines: The Incredible Cost to the World*, AGENCE FRANCE PRESS, Sept. 18, 1997.

[2] *See* American Red Cross & Laffon, *supra* note 1. *See also* Phillip Morrison & Kosta Tsipis, *New Hope in the Minefields*, 100 TECH. REV. 7 (1997); Kosta Tsipis, Editorial, *Act Now on Land Mines*, THE NEW YORK TIMES, Oct. 19, 1997, at 4-14.

[3] *See* HIDDEN KILLERS, *supra* note 1. Experts have concluded that not only does the rate at which landmines are being produced exceed the rate at which they are being dismantled, but also that there is a huge discrepancy as to clean-up costs. United Nations studies have found that while it might cost between three and twenty dollars to construct a mine, it costs many times more to disarm them. *See* James F. Dunnigan, HOW TO MAKE WAR (3rd ed. 1993). *See also* Kenneth Anderson & Monica Schurtman, *The United Nations Response to the Crisis of Landmines in the Developing World*, 36 HARV. INT'L L.J. 359 (1995).

[4] *See, e.g.*, STOCKHOLM PEACE INSTITUTE, THE LAW OF WAR AND DUBIOUS WEAPONS 73 (1976); Mary Ferrer, *Affirming Our Common Humanity: Regulating Landmines to Protect Civilians and Children in the Developing World*, 20 HASTINGS INT'L & COMP. L. REV. 135, 142 (1996); W.J. Fenrick, *New Developments in the Law Concerning the Use of Conventional Weapons*

Convention IV[5] and of Protocol II to the 1983 Convention on Prohibitions or Restrictions on the Use of Certain Weapons Which May be Deemed to be Excessively Injurious or to Have Indiscriminate Effects.[6]

A U.S. Department of State report concluded:

> Anyone who has seen the pictures of children with limbs mangled by landmines, or young men with no legs, or women torn and blinded by landmine explosions, will forever be haunted by the images. Mines are indiscriminate killers that can be lethal for decades.[7]

Former Secretary of State Cyrus Vance testified:

> The fact is that nothing short of a total ban on the production transfer and use of antipersonnel landmines will stop the killing and maiming of civilians ... because these weapons are indiscriminate by nature.[8]

Secretary Vance further testified:

---

in Armed Conflict, 19 CANADIAN Y.B. INT'L L AW. 229, 231 (1981); Memorandum for Members, Research, and Development Subcommittee, Military Procurement Subcommittee, and House National Security Committee, Fed. Clearing House Documents (Jan. 23, 1996) (statement of Chairman Curt Weldon of the Research and Development Subcommittee and Chairman Duncan Hunter of the Military Procurement Subcommittee). The widespread use of landmines by the "belligerent forces in marked and unmarked minefields and the indiscriminate scattering of individual mines, poses a number of challenges in landmine destruction and detection." *Id.*

[5] *See* Andrew C.S. Efaw, *The United States Refusal to Ban Landmines: An Intersection Between Tactics, Strategy, Policy and International Law*, 159 MIL. L. REV. 87, n.135 (1999). *See also* Burnham M. Carnahan, *The Law of Landmine Warfare: Protocol II to the United Nations Convention on Certain Conventional Weapons*, 105 MIL. L. REV. 73 (1984).

[6] *See* Carnahan, *supra* note 5; Convention on Prohibitions or Restrictions on the Use of Certain Conventional Weapons Which May be Deemed to Be Excessively Injurious or to Have Indiscriminate Effects, Oct. 10, 1980, 1342 U.N.T.S. 137, reprinted in 19 I.L.M. 1523 (1980) (entered into force Dec. 2, 1983). *See also* Protocol on Prohibitions or Restrictions on the Use of Mines, Booby-Traps and Other Devices, Oct. 10, 1980, 1342 U.N.T.S. 168, reprinted in 19 I.L.M. 1529 (1980).

[7] HIDDEN KILLERS, *supra* note 1, at 1.

[8] Cyrus R. Vance, Former Secretary of State, before the Foreign Operations Subcommittee of the Appropriations Committee of the U.S. Senate hearing on Global Mine Crisis, Fed. Doc. Clearing House, Pol. Transcripts, May 13, 1994.

[Landmines] may be the most toxic and wide spread pollution facing mankind. Their purpose is not just to maim and kill, but also to destroy the social and economic fabric of society by isolating whole communities, depopulating vast areas of territory, and preventing the return of refugees.[9]

Kenneth Anderson, Director of the Arms Project of Human Rights Watch, testified:

Human Rights Watch believes that customary international law … already requires that landmines *per se* violate the indiscriminateness and proportionality provisions of humanitarian law—that is, those that prohibit indiscriminate attacks on civilians and that require that the anticipated military utility of a weapon must exceed the expected humanitarian toll.[10]

The International Committee of the Red Cross (ICRC) concluded:

The ICRC observes, especially in non-international armed conflict, that the manner in which parties to a conflict use landmines is often in flagrant violation of some of the fundamental rules of this law. These rules, which are universally recognized as customary international law, clearly forbid the use of weapons that are by nature indiscriminate as well as the indiscriminate use of weapons in order to safeguard the fundamental principles of distinction between combatants and non-combatants.[11]

Elizabeth Dole, President of the American Red Cross, testified:

Beyond the immediate threat to the innocent people who must live out their lives in their midst, landmines also are a threat to the credibility and effectiveness of international humanitarian law. The

---

[9] *Id.*

[10] Foreign Operations Appropriations: Global Landmine Crisis Before the Senate Appropriations Subcommittee on Foreign Operations, Fed. Doc. Clearing House, Pol. Transcripts (May 13, 1994) [hereinafter Foreign Operations Appropriations] (Statement of Kenneth Anderson, Director of the Arms Project of Human Rights Watch). Anderson further stated: "Do the short term military benefits of landmines outweigh the long term human socioeconomic costs? I strongly believe that the answer is a resounding 'no.'" *Id.*

See also Mary Ferrer, *Affirming Our Common Humanity: Regulating Landmines to Protect Civilians and Children in the Developing World*, 20 HASTINGS INT'L & COMP. L. REV. 135 (1996) (citing RICHARD H. JOHNSON, WHY MINES? A MILITARY PERSPECTIVE (1995)).

[11] U.S. Landmine Policy: Hearings Before the U.S. Senate, Fed. Doc. Clearing House, Pol. Transcripts (1994) (written statement of the ICRC).

Geneva Convention of 1949 and their additional Protocols
expressly and unambiguously compel nations to protect civilians
from the ravages of war. They require governments to respect and
ensure respect for international humanitarian law. Clearly the
growing use of landmines threatens this commitment.[12]

Ms. Dole further stated: "The use of these weapons of terror is
prohibited by international humanitarian law and immediate
compliance must be demanded by all men and women of conscience."[13]

Secretary of State Warren Christopher concluded:

Anti-personnel landmines pose an enduring threat to post war
reconstruction around the world. These weapons continue to take
thousands of innocent lives every year, even in those countries
where the conflict has ceased.[14]

Congressman Lane Evans, in a statement before the House
Committee on Veteran Affairs, concluded:

It has also explicitly been recognized that landmines violate
other established principles of international law, namely
proportionality. The military benefit must outweigh the
humanitarian cost. Under international law, nations must weigh the
risks to civilians with the use of certain weapons in relation to their
military value. I believe the maiming and wholesale slaughter of
civilians by these weapons overwhelmingly outweighs any military
benefits. We must simply ask our military if these APL's are
essential in conducting their missions. I believe the answer is no.[15]

The Human Rights Watch concluded:

Landmines are blind weapons that cannot distinguish between the
footfall of a soldier and that of an old woman gathering firewood.
They recognize no cease-fire and, long after the fighting has

---

[12] 139 Cong. Rec. S7309-01 (1993) (statement of Elizabeth Dole, for the
Foreign Operations Appropriations Subcommittee Hearing on Landmines).

[13] *Id.*

[14] HIDDEN KILLERS, *supra* note 1.

[15] Foreign Operations Appropriations, *supra* note 10 (statement of the
Honorable Lane Evans, ranking Democratic Member House Committee on
Veteran's Affairs). *See also* Morrison & Tsipis, *supra* note 2 ("The damage
anti-personnel mines inflict—disabling victims for months or for life–is
economically worth orders of magnitude more than their cost of a few dollars a
piece.").

stopped, they can maim or kill the children and grandchildren of the soldiers who laid them.[16]

The Human Rights Watch and Physicians for Human Rights jointly concluded:

> [T]he presence of vast numbers of live mines also renders large areas of land inaccessible, prevents refugees and displace people from returning home, precludes farmers and shepherds from working their fields, hampers humanitarian aid and hinders development and rebuilding following the end of war.[17]

In its Annual Report of the Inter-American Commission on Human Rights, 1996, the Organization of the American States (OAS) recognized numerous humanitarian abuses in Columbia:

> The extremely difficult conditions caused by the various guerilla movements in Columbia continued in 1996. These groups committed numerous violent acts, many of which constitute violations of humanitarian law norms applicable to the internal armed conflict in Columbia. These acts included killing outside of armed conflict, indiscriminate use of land mines and oil pipeline bombings.[18]

Senator Leahy of Vermont concluded that landmines are "hideous, indiscriminate weapons that maim and kill the innocent and disrupt whole societies."[19]

The ICRC concluded:

> In the context of its mandate to work for faithful application and development of international humanitarian law applicable in armed conflicts, the ICRC observes that especially in non-international conflicts, the manner in which landmine are used by parties to a

---

[16] HUMAN RIGHTS WATCH PROJECT AND PHYSICIANS FOR HUMAN RIGHTS, LANDMINES: A DEADLY LEGACY (Kenneth Anderson et al., eds., 1993) [hereinafter LANDMINES].

[17] *Id.*

[18] ORGANIZATION OF AMERICAN STATES, 1996 IACHR ANN. REP. 647.

[19] Foreign Operations Subcommittee, *supra* note 10 (statement of Senator Leahy who was Chairman for the Foreign Appropriations Committee).

See also Statement of Steve Goose of the International Campaign to Ban Landmines: "Landmines have been used indiscriminately by most people who have in fact deployed landmines over the course of the past several decades. But, we further believe that landmines are inherently indiscriminate because of their time delay function. Because of that we think they should be considered illegal and inhumane weapons of war under customary international humanitarian law." 140 Cong. Rec. S10685-01, S10688.

conflict is often a flagrant violation of some of the fundamental rules of this law. These rules, which are universally recognized as part of customary international law, clearly forbid the use of such weapons that are by nature indiscriminate as well as the indiscriminate use of weapons in order to safeguard the fundamental principles of distinction between combatants and non-combatants. These basic rules, reaffirmed and developed in Protocol I of June 8, 1977 additional to the Geneva Convention of 1949, are binding even upon the large number of states that have not ratified the 1980 UN Weapons Convention.[20]

As to Protocol I, Senator Leahy stated:

> The goal should be nothing less than thorough revision of the Protocol. If we are to have a realistic chance to achieve this goal, I believe we must approach the conference with a presumption that anti-personnel landmines should be banned, because they have indiscriminate effects and cause unnecessary suffering.[21]

The ICJ in its decision in the *Nicaragua v. United States* recognized legal issues presented by mines (in that instance, sea mines), concluding that the United States' use of such mines as an embargo around Nicaragua was unlawful, particularly given the United States' nondisclosure of the whereabouts of the mines.[22] The Court stated:

---

[20] Foreign Operations Appropriations, *supra* note 10 (statement of ICRC).

[21] *Id.* (statement of Senator Leahy). Protocol II did not completely prohibit the use of landmines but sought to restrict how they were used and it proved to be an ineffective instrument. Since a total ban could not be achieved, a "core group of pro-ban states emerged at the beginning of 1996 to undertake a drive for a complete ban." Richard Price, *Reversing the Gun Sights: Transnational Civil Society Targets Landmines*, INT'L ORG., June 22, 1996. "The existing Protocol II is seen as far too weak as it fails to recognize the indiscriminate nature of antipersonnel landmines and as such, does not conform to existing customary international law." Peter Moszynski, *Mining Strike (landmines)*, NEW STATESMAN AND SOCIETY, Aug. 4, 1995. Writing before the signing of the Ottawa Treaty, Warren Strobel stated: "the only international accord governing landmines, Protocol II...has by general agreement been an abject failure." *Seeds of Terror: 85 Million Landmines Await Victims*, WASH. TIMES, Aug. 28, 1994, at A1.

[22] Nicaragua alleged that the United States, by laying unidentified sea mines in commercial ports, violated rules of customary international law. The court concluded that by failing to notify third-parties of the existence and placement of sea mines, the U.S. committed a "breach of the principles of humanitarian law underlying the specific provisions of Convention No. VIII (Hague Convention)." Nicaragua v. United States, 1986 I.C.J. 14, 112.

'Laying mines' is totally different, in that it is illegal in the absence of any justification recognized in International law ... a commercial treaty, can in no way be interpreted to justify a State party in derogating from this principle of general international law. I must add that this action did not meet the conditions of necessity and proportionality that may be required as a minimum in resort to the doctrine of self-defense under general and customary international law.[23]

Judge Sir Robert Jennings of the Court, in his dissenting opinion, stated:

There is of course, as already mentioned above, no question that the United States, by failing to make known the existence and location of the mines, has indeed acted in breach of its obligations under customary international law.[24]

Judge Jennings further stated, "the laying of unnotified mines is of itself an unlawful act!"[25]

The Court concluded that sea mines left after the conflict, especially those whose locations are both unknown and unidentified, violate general principles of international law under the Hague Convention because such mines could harm innocent civilian ships.[26]

Dr. Boutros Boutros-Ghalli of the United Nations concluded, "mines are prohibited under customary international law and we should build widespread support for an international agreement for their total ban."[27]

The widespread recognition of the legal problems associated with landmines led to an international effort to enact a convention banning the weapons, culminating in the Convention on the Prohibition of the Use, Stockpiling, Production, and Transfer of Anti-personnel Mines

---

[23] *Id.* at 252 (opinion of the court).

[24] *Id.* at 541 (dissenting opinion of Judge Sir Robert Jennings).

[25] *Id.* at 536.

[26] *Id.* at 112. The court stated: "[I]f a State lays mines in any waters whatever in which the vessels of another State have rights of access or passage, and fails to give any warning or notification whatsoever, in disregard of the security of peaceful shipping, it commits a breach of the principles of humanitarian law." *Id.*

[27] Foreign Operations Appropriations, *supra* note 10 (statement of Cyrus Vance quoting Dr. Boutros Boutros-Ghali).

and on Their Destruction (the "Ottawa Treaty") in 1999, broadly banning these weapons and calling for their destruction. [28]

Jody Williams, winner of the Nobel Peace Prize for her contribution to the landmine banning, stated: "The treaty represents 'civil society' which forces governments to recognize the 'moral imperative' that these landmines are illegal."[29] Advocates of the ban further stated:

> More that two-thirds of the world's nations have signed the international treaty banning antipersonnel landmines. These governments know, as do thousands of civilians maimed by landmines each year that this weapon should be considered illegal. The international community has overwhelmingly concluded that the horrendous humanitarian costs of anti-personnel mines far outweigh the limited military utility.[30]

The United States, while broadly recognizing the legal problems associated with landmines,[31] declined to enter into the Ottawa Treaty, ostensibly for two reasons, (1) that the United States needed to continue to use landmines in the Demilitarized Korean Zone and (2) that it the wording of the treaty would also ban U.S. tank mines deemed valuable against armored ground assaults.[32] During the negotiations, the United

---

[28] Convention on the Prohibition of the Use, Stockpiling, Production, and Transfer of Anti-personnel Mines and on Their Destruction, Sept. 18, 1997, 36 I.L.M. 1507 (entered into force Mar. 1, 1999).

As of April 1999, some 135 countries had signed the treaty, and 71 countries had either ratified or fully implemented it. *See* Stephen Laufer, *Anti-Landmine Pact Signatories Set to Meet*, BUS. DAY, Apr. 28, 1999; Holly Burkhalter, *Out of the Minefield: The U.S. Should Support the International Treaty*, LEGAL TIMES, vol. 21, Nov. 30, 1998, at 28.

However, a number of major countries, including the United States, Russia, China, India, Iraq, South Korea, and Pakistan, refused to sign. United Nations Landmine Ban Signatories <http://www.un.org/dept>.

[29] Marie O'Kalloran, *Two More Countries Needed to Make Mine Ban Stick; Landmine Conference Hopes International Treaty will Pressurize Governments to Halt Killings and Maimings*, THE IRISH TIMES, Sept. 16, 1998, at 7.

[30] *Mine Ban Campaign Criticizes NAM (non-aligned movement) Position International Campaign to Ban Landmines*, AFRICA NEWS SERVICES, Aug. 31, 1998.

[31] Secretary of State Madeleine Albright has stated, "Our premise is that the best way to protect civilians from landmines on the ground is to pull them out like the noxious weeds that they are." Madeleine Albright, Speech at the U.S. Agency for International Development Conference, Fed. Doc. Clearing House, Pol. Transcripts (1997).

[32] William J. Clinton, *Remarks by the President on Land-Mines*, 33 WEEKLY COMP. PRES. DOC. 1356–59 (Sept. 22, 1997). *See generally* Christian

States sought unsuccessfully to have included in the treaty an exception or exemption to the treaty for the Korean situation.[33]

Nonetheless, the United States appears to have substantially accepted the need to ban landmines. General Henry H. Shelton, Chairman of the Joint Chiefs of Staff, testified before the Congressional Appropriations Defense Subcommittee:

> The president has directed the Department of Defense to end the use of APL's outside Korea by 2003, to aggressively pursue and develop alternatives to APL's in Korea by 2006, and to search for alternatives to our mixed anti-tank systems. He also announced that we would sign the treaty by 2006, if we succeed in identifying these alternatives.[34]

Thus, there is an ongoing process in place that is not altogether unhopeful. Pressured by events, the United States ostensibly is responding and presumably will, in some finite amount of time, be able to find alternatives for the use of landmines in the Korea situation and adapt its antitank systems in a way conducive to acceptance of the ban of these weapons.

Accordingly, in terms of the areas of analogy between landmine and nuclear weapons effects, the landmine experience points in the direction of possible progress on the nuclear weapons issues. While the repercussions of landmines are appreciably less than those of nuclear

---

M. Capece, *The Ottawa Treaty and its Impact on U.S. Military Policy and Planning*, 25 BROOK. J. INT'L L. 183 (1999). The U.S. position has been that its troops have relied heavily on the use of landmines to protect the border zone and that removal of this capability would compromise many American soldiers. *Id., but see* Holly Burkhalter, *Landmines: Time to Back the Ban*, FULTON COUNTY DAILY REP., Dec. 1, 1998.

[33] "The president made it very clear that we could not sign the Ottawa Treaty, by virtue of the fact that there was no exception or exemption for protecting our forces in Korea." *Cohen Defends Decision to Opt Out of Global Landmine Ban*, AGENCE-FRANCE PRESSE, Mar. 1, 1999 (statement of U.S. Defense Secretary William Cohen). *See also* Senior Defense Department Officials Hold Background Briefing on Landmines, Fed. Doc. Clearing House, July 3, 1997.

[34] Before the Congressional Appropriations Defense Subcommittee, Fed. Doc. Clearing House, Pol. Transcripts (May 11, 1999) (statement of General Henry H. Shelton, USA Chairman of the Joint Chiefs of Staff). *See also* Philip Shenon, *Clinton Firmly Against Land-Mine Treaty*, THE NEW YORK TIMES, Oct. 11, 1997 at A6; Maya Kaneko, *Superpowers to Keep Mines Until Substitutes Available*, JAPAN ECONOMIC NEWSWIRE, Nov. 29, 1998.

weapons, the landmines ostensibly have the potential to be more useful militarily.

Nuclear weapons present even more of a controllability problem than landmines: Radiation and other nuclear weapons effects are uncontrollable, as opposed to the potential controllability, at least theoretically, of the delayed blast effects of landmines through recordkeeping and notification requirements.

Chapter 14: Limitations of the Principle of Double Effect

As we have seen, while noncombatants are protected persons who may not be made the object of attack, nonetheless attacks may be directed against military targets even in circumstances where it is known that noncombatants will be hit, so long as the injury to the noncombatants is unintended and not disproportionate to the military objective.[1] Conceptually, the purity of the intention in terms of its being directed against the military target immunizes the effects upon the protected persons. Since there was no intent to hit the innocent persons, we will forgive, accept or excuse it. Pragmatically, the approach reflects the reality that in war, as in life generally, legally and morally appropriate actions will often have unintended collateral evil effects.

This approach is based on the principle of double effect—a venerable medieval doctrine developed by St. Thomas Aquinas in his *Summa Theologica* in the 1200s and which ironically still largely directs the law of armed conflict in major respects in the year 2000.[2] St. Thomas stated:

> One act may have two effects only one of which is intended and the other outside of our intention. Moral acts are classified on the basis of what is intended, not on what happens outside of our intention since that is incidental to it, as explained above. The action of defending oneself may produce two effects—one, saving one's life, and the other, killing the attacker. Now an action of this kind intended to save one's own life cannot be characterized as illicit since it is natural for anyone to maintain himself in existence if he can. An act that is prompted by a good intention can become illicit if it is not proportionate to the end intended. This is why it is not allowed to use more force than necessary to defend one's life. ... It is not required for salvation that a man not carry out actions of proportionate self-defense in order to avoid killing another

---

[1] *See* Chapter 1, notes 149–195, 243–245 and accompanying text. *See also* Chapters 7–10.

[2] *See Biographical Note to Thomas Aquinas: I, Summa Theologica, appearing in* 19 GREAT BOOKS OF THE WESTERN WORLD v (Robert Maynard Hutchins, ed. in chief, 1952). *See also* AUSTIN FAGOTHEY, S.J., RIGHT AND REASON, ETHICS IN THEORY AND PRACTICE 113 n.1 (The C.V. Mosby Company 1963).

person, for a man is more obliged to provide for his own life than for that of another.[3]

Michael Walzer in his informative study, *Just and Unjust Wars*, summarizes the elements of the principle of double effect:

> 1. The act is good in itself or at least indifferent, which means, for our purposes, that it is a legitimate act of war.
> 2. The direct effect is morally acceptable—the destruction of military supplies, for example, or the killing of enemy soldiers.
> 3. The intention of the actor is good, that is, he aims only at the acceptable effect; the evil effect is not one of his ends, nor is it a means to his ends.
> 4. The good is sufficiently good to compensate for allowing the evil effect; it must be justifiable under Sidgwick's proportionality rule [proportionality between effects on permissible and impermissible targets].[4]

---

[3] AQUINAS, SUMMA THEOLOGIAE, I-II, Quest. 64, Art. 7, *quoted in* Stephen R. Latham, *Aquinas and Morphine: Notes on Double Effect at the End of Life,* 1 DEPAUL J. HEALTH CARE L. 625, 633 (also quoting ST. THOMAS AQUINAS ON POLITICS AND ETHICS 70–71 (Paul E. Sigmund, ed. & trans., 1988)). Dr. Latham presents an elaborate discussion of the meaning of Aquinas' statement in the context of his Treatise on Human Acts contained in the *Summa. See also* FAGOTHEY, *supra* note 2, at 113 n.1 (identifying the above discussion by St. Thomas of the principle of double effect as one of the first express uses of the principle of double effect); MICHAEL WALZER, JUST AND UNJUST WARS, A MORAL ARGUMENT WITH HISTORICAL ILLUSTRATIONS (New York 1968); Judith Jarvis Thomson, *Self-Defense,* 20 PHILOSOPHY & PUBLIC AFF. 283 (1991); Thomas Nagel, *War and Massacre,* 1 PHILOSOPHY & PUBLIC AFF. 123 (1972); Christopher H. Schroeder, *Rights Against Risks,* 86 COLUM. L. REV. 495 (April 1986).

[4] WALZER, *supra* note 3, at 153, 129 (citing DOUGHERTY, GENERAL ETHICS: AN INTRODUCTION TO THE BASIC PRINCIPLES OF THE MORAL LIFE ACCORDING TO ST. THOMAS AQUINAS 65–66 (Peekskill, N.Y. 1959); John C. Ford, S.J., *The Morality of Obliteration Bombing, in* WAR AND MORALITY, (Richard Wasserstrom, ed., 1970); HENRY SIDGWICK, ELEMENTS OF POLITICS 253–54 (London, 1891); R. B. Brandt, *Utilitarianism and the Rules of War,* 1 PHILOSOPHY AND PUBLIC AFF. 145–65 (1972)). As Walzer expresses it, "Double effect is a way of reconciling the absolute prohibition against attacking non-combatants with the legitimate conduct of military activity." *Id.* at 153.

Walzer suggests the need for a correction to the principle of double effect:

> Double effect is defensible, I want to argue, only when the two outcomes are the product of a double intention: first, that the "good" be achieved; second, that the foreseeable evil be reduced as

Austin Fagothey, S.J., provides a similar summary of the principle:

> 1. The act to be done must be good in itself or at least indifferent. ...
> 2. The good intended must not be obtained by means of the evil effect. ...
> 3. The evil effect must not be intended for itself but only permitted. ...
> 4. There must be a proportionately grave reason for permitting the evil. ...[5]

Walzer expresses the modern sense of dissatisfaction with the doctrine:

> The burden of the argument is carried by the third clause in the context of the law of war. The "good" and evil effects that come together, the killing of soldiers and nearby civilians, are to be defended only insofar as they are the product of a single intention, directed at the first and not the second. The argument suggests the great importance of taking aim in wartime, and it correctly restricts the targets at which one can aim. But we have to worry, I think, about all those unintended but foreseeable deaths, for their number can be large, and subject only to the proportionality rule—a weak constraint—double effect provides a blanket justification. The principle for that reason invites an angry or a cynical response: what difference does it make whether civilian deaths are a direct or an indirect effect of my actions? It can hardly matter to the dead civilians, and if I know in advance that I am likely to kills so many innocent people and go ahead anyhow, how can I be blameless?[6]

Noting the dilemma as to where to draw the line between permitting military operations to proceed and limiting effects on protected persons, Walzer states:

> Do civilians have a right not only not to be attacked but also not to be put at risk to such and such a degree, so that imposing a one-in-ten chance of death on them is justified, while imposing a three-in-

---

> far as possible. So the third of the conditions listed above can be restated:
> 3) The intention of the actor is good, that is, he aims narrowly at the acceptable effect; the evil effect is not one of his ends, nor is it a means to his ends, and, aware of the evil involved, he seeks to minimize it, accepting costs to himself.

Id. at 155.

[5] FAGOTHEY, *supra* note 2, at 107–108 (detailed discussion of each element omitted).

[6] WALZER, *supra* note 3, at 153.

ten chance is unjustified? In fact, the degree of risk that is permissible is going to vary with the nature of the target, the urgency of the moment, the available technology, and so on. It is best, I think, to say simply that civilians have a right that "due care" be taken.[7]

Walzer, however, in examining the extent of the care which the military have to take—specifically, the extent of the limitations they have to impose upon themselves—appears to see the limit as "fixed ... roughly at that point where any further risk-taking [by the military] would almost certainly doom the military venture or make it so costly that it could not be repeated."[8] In other words, in Walzer's view, killing the protected persons in the course of attacking the legitimate target is permissible if such a mode of hitting the target is militarily necessary.

Judith Jarvis Thomson in her discussion of the doctrine of double effect notes the implausibility of the principle as applied to the particular case of a pilot who has been told to bomb a munitions plan in the vicinity of a children's hospital comes and asks whether the strike is permissible:

> Suppose we make the following reply: "Well, it all depends on what your intentions would be in dropping the bombs. If you would be intending to destroy the munitions factory and thereby win the war, merely foreseeing, though not intending, the deaths of the children, then yes, you may drop the bombs. On the other hand, if you would be intending to destroy the children and thereby terrorize the Bads and thereby win the war, merely foreseeing, though not intending, the destruction of the munitions factory, then no, you may not drop the bombs." What a queer performance this would be! Can any one really think that the pilot should decide whether he may drop the bombs by looking inward for the intention with which he would be dropping them if he dropped them?[9]

---

[7] *Id.* at 156 (referencing Charles Fried, *Imposing Risks on Others, in* AN ANATOMY OF VALUES: PROBLEMS OF PERSONAL AND SOCIAL CHOICE Ch. XI (Cambridge, Mass. 1970)).

[8] *Id.* at 157.

[9] Thomson, *supra* note 3, at 283, 293 (citing Warren S. Quinn, *Actions, Intentions, and Consequences: The Doctrine of Double of Double Effect,* 18 PHILOSOPHY & PUBLIC AFF. 334–51 n.4 (Fall 1989); Jonathan Bennett's criticism of the Doctrine of Double Effect in *Morality and Consequences, in* THE TANNER LECTURES ON HUMAN VALUES III (Salt Lake City: University of Utah Press 1981)).

Schroeder in his study of *Rights against Risks* notes Charles Fried's formulation under the principle of double effect that "One intends a result if the result is chosen either as one's ultimate end or as one's means to that end."[10] One test: "[I]f the consequence under investigation could be prevented and the events were otherwise allowed to follow their expected course, would the actor still act as he did? If so, the consequence is unintended and therefore not within the ambit of any categorical prohibition."[11]

Schroeder then makes the same point as Walzer as to the heavy weight this medieval principle is caused to bear:

> This account of Fried's absolutist structure shows that the hunt for some absolute rule to guide technological risk decisions ends in a cul de sac. The device that makes his system of absolutes work, the principle of double effect, is highly dubious. Granted that there may be relevant differences between ends intended as conscious objects of an actor's design and those known or suspected to eventuate from carrying the action out, the distinction must bear enormous weight if absolute rules are to be maintained.[12]

Thomas Nagel argues that the principle of double effect does not even permit such bombing:

> [I]f one bombs, burns, or strafes a village containing a hundred people, twenty of whom one believes to be guerrillas, so that by killing most of them one will be statistically likely to kill most of the guerrillas, then isn't one's attack on the group of one hundred a means of destroying the guerrillas, pure and simple? If one makes no attempt to discriminate between guerrillas and civilians, as is impossible in a aerial attack on a small village, then one cannot regard as a mere side effect the deaths of those in the group that one would not have bothered to kill if more selective means had been available.

Nagel, *supra* note 3, at 123, 131.

Nagel goes on, however, to point out how slippery this ground is since the analysis is so heavily dependent upon the characterization of the act. If it is said that the air strike was conducted to take out the *area* used by the guerrillas, the entire analysis shifts and the strike arguably becomes permissible notwithstanding the effects upon the civilians. *Id.* at 131.

[10] Schroeder, *supra* note 3, at 527–28. (citing CHARLES FRIED, RIGHT AND WRONG 22 (1978)). This article originally appeared at 86 COLUM. L. REV. 495 (1986). Reprinted with permission.

[11] *Id.* at 528.

[12] *Id.* at 500 (citing J. MACKIE, ETHICS 166 (1977); Bennett, *Whatever the Consequences*, 26 ANALYSIS 83 (1966); Thomson, *Rights and Deaths*, 2 PHIL. & PUB. AFF. 146, 150 n.4 (1973)).

The United States goes so far as to apply the principle of double effect even to the physical effects of nuclear weapons, arguing that, since such weapons destroy through lawful effects, such as blast or heat, they are lawful, even though they also cause what may be deemed unlawful toxic effects through the operation of radiation. The radiation does not count because it is "a by-product," indeed "a by-product which is not the main or most characteristic feature of the weapon."[13]

One senses that the application of the principle of double effect to permit the "unintended" imposition of the effects of nuclear weapons upon civilians and other protected persons stretches it beyond any limit contemplated by its progenitors. Yes, intentionality is important. Yes, as the colloquialism has it, "'even a dog' knows the difference between being hit intentionally and unintentionally."

Nonetheless, beyond some threshold level of injury, it does not seem that it should matter what the actor intended if he knew or should have known of the risks of causing the "collateral" effect.[14] In addition, the principle of double effect seems inconsistent with the rules of proportionality, necessity and discrimination, prohibiting excessive effects. Those rules prohibit excessive effects even if they were only the anticipated but not the desired effects of the military strike in question. The principle of double effect would also seem inconsistent with the principle of potential liability for reckless and grossly negligent conduct.[15]

---

[13] *See supra* Chapter 2, notes 103–110 and accompanying text.

[14] As noted above, the drafters of the Model Penal Code ostensibly saw the principle of double effect as arising in the context of the working of the lesser evil/necessity principle, which, as we saw, is itself subject to a demanding proportionality standard. *See e.g. supra* Chapter 11, notes 7–14 and accompanying text.

Other than on a lesser evil/necessity theory, it would not appear that the principle of double effect could co-exist with the above analysis as to liability based in manslaughter, *see supra*, Chapter 7, notes 20, 42–43, 95 and accompanying text, or with the analysis based on the duty owed to innocent third-parties, *see supra*, Chapter 10.

[15] *See* Chapters 6–8.

PART IV

Risk Factors of The Nuclear Weapons Regime

Introduction

We have seen the U.S. position as to the lawfulness of the use of certain types of nuclear weapons and the ICJ's decision and related opinions on the subject. We have also reviewed certain additional applicable principles of law that appear to be generally recognized by civilized nations and hence binding under international law.

It is evident under this overall body of law that the ultimate conclusion as to lawfulness or unlawfulness turns largely upon probabilities as to the effects of the use of nuclear weapons, including probabilities as to the effects of the particular weapons in question and as to the escalation risks as to weapons that might be unleashed as a result of the first strike. Since, by definition, the legality evaluation is to be made before the weapons are used, it necessarily must be made before the actual effects can be known.

It is equally evident that this evaluation, involving the application of what are essentially rules of reason, requires a weighing of the probabilities as to all available facts and potential facts relating to these weapons and the circumstances in which they might be used.

I start with an examination of the weapons themselves, their capabilities, potential effects, and overall characteristics. I then examine that abstruse body of theory called "nuclear policy" that defines the circumstances in which these weapons might intentionally be used and the milieu in which an unintentional use occur. Because of the extent to which modern nuclear policy is affected by its Cold War origins, I start with an examination of those origins and then bring the analysis up to date.

I next focus on "operational policy," the integration of nuclear weapons into military training, weapons selection and contingency planning, and then upon the make-up of the U.S. nuclear arsenal, to bring into the analysis the potential impact upon decision-making of the nuclear capabilities and institutional mindset of the U.S. civilian and military leadership and operational personnel. I also examine the extent to which the U.S. arsenal is made up of the types of weapons whose legality the United States defended before the ICJ.

To ground the discussion, I next examine the times the United States has actually threatened the use of nuclear weapons (beyond the general threat inherent in the policy of deterrence), and, beyond that, the times the United States has actually considered such use.

I then come to the reliability of delivery issue (If the United States were actually to decide to use these weapons, what are the odds it would end up hitting the wrong targets?) and the overall risks inherent in the nuclear weapons regime, including not only the proliferation risks and related volatility but also the risks inherent in the laws of probability. In this latter connection, I examine the extent to which the improbable is likely to occur and regularly occurs in life, and hence, the extent to which one must assume that, in the fullness of time, possible but unlikely nuclear disasters will likely occur.

Since a U.S. decision to use nuclear weapons would presumably be made in relation to the actions of one or more other nuclear States, I next examine the nuclear capabilities of such States and the structure of their arsenals.

As we have seen, the defense of the nuclear weapons regime by the United States and other nuclear States before the ICJ largely focused upon such States' ability accurately to deliver tactical nuclear weapons, with limited and controllable radiation effects, against remote military targets where protected persons would not be affected. This position raises questions not only as to the likely effects of the particular weapons employed in such limited nuclear strikes but also of the escalation risks, which are my next major factual area of inquiry.

Because of the risk that the use of nuclear weapons would lead to the retaliatory use of chemical or biological weapons, and *vice versa*, I then examine the risk factors as to these other types of weapons of mass destruction.

Finally, I focus on the extent to which today's high tech conventional weapons, with their accuracy of delivery, obviate any possible need to use nuclear weapons.

Chapter 15: Risk Factors as to the Weapons Themselves

Are nuclear weapons just another, more powerful extension of conventional weapons? Or are they qualitatively as well as quantitatively different? What are their effects, and to what extent are such effects controllable?

On one level, the facts as to such matters would appear to be of an objective nature, such that one would expect them, this far into the nuclear era, to be beyond reasonable dispute. Yet, as we have seen from the U.S. presentation to the ICJ, the United States has asserted that nuclear weapons are not different in kind from conventional weapons, that their effects, including radiation effects, can be limited and are controllable and, indeed, that such weapons can be used in such a way that any resultant radiation can discriminate between combatant and non-combatant targets. The purpose of this chapter is to set forth what appear to be the objective facts on the issue.

Nuclear weapons include fission and fusion weapons.[1] The destructiveness of a weapon is generally measured by its "yield," the amount of nuclear energy released by its explosion, with the unit of measurement being the equivalent amount of energy released per metric tons of trinitrotoluene (TNT).[2] Conventional explosives

---

[1] *See* 1 THOMAS B. COCHRAN, ET AL., NUCLEAR WEAPONS DATABOOK, UNITED STATES NUCLEAR FORCES AND CAPABILITIES 32 (1984) [hereinafter NUCLEAR WEAPONS DATABOOK].

[2] *See* UNITED NATIONS DEPARTMENT FOR DISARMAMENT AFFAIRS, NUCLEAR WEAPONS: A COMPREHENSIVE STUDY 6 (1991) [hereinafter UNITED NATIONS DEPARTMENT]. *See also* THE NUCLEAR READER: STRATEGY, WEAPONS AND WAR (Charles W. Kegley et al. eds., 1985); WORLD HEALTH ORGANIZATION, EFFECTS OF NUCLEAR WAR ON HEALTH AND HEALTH SERVICES 7 (2d ed. 1987) [hereinafter 1987 WHO Study]. For a discussion of the physics of a nuclear bomb, *see* NATO HANDBOOK ON THE MEDICAL ASPECTS OF NBC DEFENSIVE OPERATIONS A MEDP-6(B) Part I, Chap. 1 (1996), adopted as Army Field Manual 8-9, Navy Medical Publication 5059, Air Force Joint Manual 44-151 [hereinafter NATO HANDBOOK ON THE MEDICAL ASPECTS].

Some nuclear weapons are based entirely on fission, while others also use fusion. In a fission weapon, uranium or plutonium nuclei are split into lighter fragments called fission products, which, at a certain volume (the "critical mass"), cause a chain reaction and explosion. In a fusion weapon, the nuclei of heavy hydrogen isotopes, deuterium and tritium, are fused together at very high temperatures through the trigger mechanism of a fission explosion, leading to a fusion explosion. *See* UNITED NATIONS DEPARTMENT, *supra,* at 6.

typically have destructive capability equivalent to the release of some number of tons of TNT.[3] Fission ("atomic") bombs of the type dropped on Hiroshima and Nagasaki have the destructiveness of some thousands of tons of TNT (kilotons, kt).[4] Fusion ("hydrogen" or "thermonuclear") bombs, have the destructiveness of up to some millions of tons of TNT (megatons, mt).[5]

Conventional weapons characteristically cause destruction through direct blast and heat resulting from their detonation. Though far-reaching climatic and environmental effects may in extreme cases result from the concentrated use of large numbers of conventional weapons, the physical effects of the use of conventional weapons, however devastating, are generally limited to life and property in the area of the blast and heat.[6]

The destruction caused by nuclear weapons is quantitatively different. Nuclear weapons also cause blast and heat damage, but their effects of this type are generally thousands of times greater than that caused by individual conventional weapons. The U.N. in its 1991 report found that "[n]uclear weapons represent a historically new form of weaponry with unparalleled destructive potential. A single large nuclear weapon could release explosive power comparable to all the energy released from the conventional weapons used in all past wars."[7]

Nuclear weapons are also qualitatively different from conventional weapons in that they release nuclear radiation which is extremely

---

[3] *See* UNITED NATIONS DEPARTMENT, *supra* note 2, at 6.

[4] *See* NUCLEAR WEAPONS DATABOOK, *supra* note 1, at 32 (noting that *Little Boy,* the fission bomb detonated over Hiroshima, had a yield of approximately 12–15 kilotons, and that *Fat Man*, the plutonium fission bomb detonated over Nagasaki, had an approximate yield of 22 kilotons).

[5] *See id.* at 26–27. *See also* UNITED NATIONS DEPARTMENT, *supra* note 2, at 8.

[6] *See, e.g.,* CARL SAGAN & RICHARD TURCO, A PATH WHERE NO MAN THOUGHT: NUCLEAR WAR AND THE END OF THE ARMS RACE 124 (1990).

[7] *See* 1987 WHO Study, *supra* note 2, at 7; discussion of the blast and thermal effects of nuclear weapons at NATO HANDBOOK ON THE MEDICAL ASPECTS, *supra* note 2, at Part I, Chap. 3, §§ II–III. The larger bombs destroy many square miles by their shock wave and heat effects. Windblown "missiles," that is, debris blown by the force of the bomb, are expected to take a heavy toll on human life. *See id.* at Part I, Chap. 3, § I-303, 304; §II-305–310, Chap. 6, § II. The blast from a one megaton bomb includes winds of 180 miles an hour four miles away from the center of the blast. *See* U.S. Congress, Office of Technology Assessment, *The Effects of Nuclear War* 16–17 NTIS order no. PB-296946 (Washington, DC: U.S. Government Printing Office, May 1979) [hereinafter The Effects of Nuclear War].

inimical to human and other forms of life.[8] Nuclear radiation wreaks its devastation both through the direct killing or injuring of those in the area of the detonation of the weapon and through radioactive fallout, the spread of radioactive materials biologically and environmentally.[9]

The effects of nuclear radiation are far-reaching, both in space, because the radiation-emitting debris that nuclear explosions produce can be carried great distances by the winds, the waters, the soil and otherwise, and in time, because the radioactive materials have an extraordinarily long life and their impacts on one generation can be carried on to the next, with resultant continuing effects on human and other forms of life potentially for thousands of years, as radiation damage is carried forward genetically through successive generations of human, animal and plant life, with such radiation effects also having the potential for the substantial destruction of the food chain and of the environmental pre-conditions to life, including water, soil, and air, and the overall destruction of the economic bases for modern society.[10]

In addition, nuclear weapons cause electromagnetic impulses which, while ostensibly not harmful to individuals, impair the functioning of electronic equipment.[11] This effect becomes important in assessing the potential overall effects of the use of a nuclear weapon, given the wild cards it introduces as to what will happen in terms of the enemy's and indeed one's own reactions, intentional and otherwise, to the loss of control of today's high tech weapons, command and control systems, and other technical accoutrements of modern life.[12]

---

[8] *See* The Effects of Nuclear War, *supra* note 7. *See also* SAGAN & TURCO, *supra* note 6, at 45–59.

[9] *See* SAGAN & TURCO, *supra* note 6, at 49–54; NATO HANDBOOK ON THE MEDICAL ASPECTS, *supra* note 2, at Part I, Chap 3 § I-303(c); also, § IV, § IV-320. A large nuclear attack on a State, such as the United States, would be expected to cause substantial numbers of deaths and other injuries outside the target State. *See* The Effects of Nuclear War, *supra* note 7, at 113 Table 14.

[10] *See* UNITED NATIONS DEPARTMENT, *supra* note 2, at 79–83. *See also* 8 CHARLES S. GRACE, NUCLEAR WEAPONS: PRINCIPLES, EFFECTS AND SURVIVABILITY 29–30 (Brassey's 1994); THE NUCLEAR READER: STRATEGY, WEAPONS AND WAR, *supra* note 2, at 320–26. It is estimated that only half of the suffering would be over as of the end of the war itself: "A failure to achieve [social and economic] viability would result in many additional deaths, and much additional economic, political, and social deterioration. This post war damage could be as devastating as the damage from the actual nuclear explosions." The Effects of Nuclear War, *supra* note 7, at 5.

[11] UNITED NATIONS DEPARTMENT, *supra* note 2, at 80.

[12] *See* ASHTON B. CARTER ET AL., MANAGING NUCLEAR OPERATIONS 273–81 (1987).

The destructiveness of nuclear weapons is exemplified by the fact that, during the height of the Cold War, just one American Poseidon submarine, with its approximately one hundred and sixty independently targetable nuclear warheads (each with a yield several times greater than the bombs dropped on Hiroshima and Nagasaki) had the capability of striking as many as one hundred and sixty Soviet cities, killing some thirty million people.[13]

A former CIA official has estimated that in World War II the total conventional bombs dropped by the U.S. Air Force amounted to only two megatons, the yield of one or two ordinary nuclear bombs today.[14]

At the same time, conventional weapons, as we will see in Chapter 28, have become extremely accurate and effective, particularly with the high tech revolution of recent decades, greatly reducing the amount of firepower that needs be directed at a particular target.

Even as of the Second World War, the disparity between the blast and heat effects of conventional and nuclear weapons could be compensated for by the use of a larger number of conventional weapons.[15] For example, on March 29, 1945, the United States firebombed Tokyo with conventional incendiary high explosives, killing and injuring 83,000 Japanese,[16] a number roughly comparable to

---

[13] *See* Spurgeon M. Keeny, Jr. & Wolfgang K. H. Panofsky, *MAD versus NUTS: Can Doctrine or Weaponry Remedy the Mutual Hostage Relationship of the Superpowers?*, 60 FOREIGN AFF. 287, 293 (Winter 1981–1982).

[14] *See* CENTER FOR DEFENSE INFORMATION, NUCLEAR WAR QUOTATIONS 39, [hereinafter NUCLEAR WAR QUOTATIONS] (quoting Ray S. Cline *in* WORLD POWER ASSESSMENT 58 (1975)).

[15] *See* John Mueller, *The Essential Irrelevance of Nuclear Weapons*, INT'L SECURITY, vol. 13, no. 2, Fall 1988, at 55, 57, 57 n.4 ("A nuclear war would certainly be vastly destructive, but for the most part nuclear weapons simply compound and dramatize a military reality that by 1945 had already become appalling. ... Even before the bomb had been perfected, world war had become spectacularly costly and destructive, killing some 50 million worldwide. ... [G]iven weapons advances, a full scale *conventional* World War III could be expected to be even more destructive than World War II."). *See also* MICHAEL MANDELBAUM, THE NUCLEAR REVOLUTION 21 (1981). The tanks and artillery of the Second World War, and especially the aircraft that reduced Dresden and Tokyo to rubble, might have been terrifying enough by themselves to keep the peace between the United States and the Soviet Union. *Id.*

[16] *See* LAWRENCE FREEDMAN, THE EVOLUTION OF NUCLEAR STRATEGY 17, 29 (1989). "After limited fire-bombing raids in January and February 1945, the Air Force embarked upon a remorseless campaign, beginning in March with an all-out attack on Tokyo that left nearly 300,000 buildings destroyed and over

the some 70,000 to 80,000 Japanese killed and wounded by the single nuclear bomb dropped on Hiroshima.[17]

Delivery Vehicles and Warheads

The distinction between the delivery vehicle and the nuclear warhead is relevant to the analysis of the risks inherent in the use of nuclear weapons. The delivery vehicle is the means of transporting the warhead,[18] the main U.S. launch vehicles being the "triad" of land-based ICBMs, submarines carrying missiles, and aircraft carrying missiles and bombs.[19] The warhead, in contrast, is the nuclear device itself, the actual explosive.[20] The combination of the launch vehicle and the nuclear device constitutes the "nuclear weapon."[21]

The U.S. military's 1996 *Joint Theater Nuclear Operations* manual describes types of nuclear weapons maintained by the United States:

> Weapons in the US Nuclear Arsenal:
> Gravity Bombs
> Tomahawk Land Attack Missiles (Nuclear)
> Cruise Missiles
> Submarine Launched Ballistic Missiles
> Intercontinental Ballistic Missiles[22]

The manual states:

> Weapons in the US nuclear arsenal ... include: gravity bombs deliverable by dual-capable aircraft (DCA) and long-range

---

80,000 dead." *Id.* General "Hap" Arnold calculated that the single atomic bomb on Hiroshima caused as "much damage as 300 planes would have done." *Id.*

[17] *See* Rufus E. Miles, Jr., *Hiroshima: The Strange Myth of Half a Million American Lives Saved,* INT'L SECURITY, vol. 10, no. 2, Fall 1985 121, 125.

[18] *See* NUCLEAR WEAPONS DATABOOK, *supra* note 1, at 100.

[19] *See* JOINT CHIEFS OF STAFF, JOINT PUB 3-12, DOCTRINE FOR JOINT NUCLEAR OPERATIONS II-2 (Dec. 15, 1995) (prepared under direction of the Chairman of the Joint Chiefs of Staff), as set forth at <http://www.dtic.mil/doctrine/jel/new_pubs/jp3_12.pdf> [hereinafter DOCTRINE FOR JOINT NUCLEAR OPERATIONS]. *See also* UNITED NATIONS DEPARTMENT, *supra* note 2, at 13–14. *See also* NUCLEAR WEAPONS DATABOOK, *supra* note 1, at 100–106.

[20] *See* UNITED NATIONS DEPARTMENT, *supra* note 2, at 6.

[21] *Id.*

[22] JOINT CHIEFS OF STAFF, JOINT PUB. 3-12.1, DOCTRINE FOR JOINT THEATER NUCLEAR OPERATIONS, I-3, fig. I-2 (Feb 9, 1996) (prepared under direction of the Chairman of the Joint Chiefs of Staff), as set forth at <http://www.dtic.mil/doctrine/jel/new_pubs/jp3_12_1.pdf> [hereinafter DOCTRINE FOR JOINT THEATER NUCLEAR OPERATIONS].

bombers; the Tomahawk Land Attack Missile/Nuclear (TLAM/N) deliverable by submarines; cruise missiles deliverable by long-range bombers; submarine-launched ballistic missiles (SLBM); and intercontinental ballistic missiles (ICBM). These systems provide the NCA and the geographic combatant commander with a wide range of options which can be tailored to meet desired military and political objectives.[23]

The different delivery systems, as noted, have different characteristics of importance to the analysis, including varying degrees of accuracy, reliability, speed, vulnerability to preemptive strike, susceptibility to defensive measures, overall tendency to promote stability or instability in crisis circumstances, and the like. For example, non-mobile land-based ICBMs are generally vulnerable and de-stabilizing, sitting fixedly in their silos open to a first strike.[24] To

---

[23] *Id* at I-3 (emphasis omitted).

[24] *See* UNITED NATIONS DEPARTMENT, *supra* note 2, at 11. *See also* NUCLEAR WEAPONS DATABOOK, *supra* note 1, at 100–103.

The DOCTRINE FOR JOINT THEATER NUCLEAR OPERATIONS, *supra* note 22, sets forth the following "advantages and disadvantages" of the different types of nuclear weapons maintained by the United States:

a. Gravity bombs deliverable by DCA [dual–capable aircraft] and long-range bombers.

• Advantages

•• Aircraft increases range (when properly supported by tankers) and provides flexibility and recall

•• Weapons may be employed against mobile targets

•• Various weapon yields available—from very high to very low

•• Aircraft can be launched from the continental United States

• Disadvantages

•• Crew at risk in high threat environment

•• Lead time required for planning and transit

•• Significant combat support and ground support infrastructure may be required, depending on scenario

•• Equipment may have to be released from other operation plan (OPLAN) tasking

b. TLAM/N. (Specifics can be found in NWP 28.)

• Advantages

•• Heavily defended areas may be penetrated without risk to crew

•• Highly mobile platforms in international waters may serve as launch sites

•• Weapons are highly accurate

•• Launching platform is recallable

•• Basing issues simplified; overflight of third party nations alleviated (depending on launch location)

•• Maximum stealth and surprise can be maintained prior to launch
• Disadvantages
•• Weapons not recallable in flight
•• Lead time required to generate and transit needed to desired launch point
•• System may be vulnerable to modern air defense systems
•• Terrain factors limit employment flexibility
•• Weapon yield may be too large for certain theater targets
•• Launch platform must receive updated data transfer device in order to update a mission plan
c. Cruise missiles launched from long-range bombers
• Advantages
•• Weapon can penetrate heavily defended area without risk to crew
•• Weapon can be launched from international airspace
•• Bomber aircraft range is significant
•• Weapon system is recallable prior to launch from bomber
• Disadvantages
•• Weapon yield may be too large for certain theater targets
•• System may have to be released from Single Integrated Operational Plan (SIOP) commitment
•• Missile is not recallable in flight
•• System may be vulnerable to modern air defense systems
•• Terrain factors limit employment flexibility
d. SLBMs
• Advantages
•• Weapon can penetrate heavily defended areas without risk to crew
•• Weapon can be launched in international waters
•• Weapon can be on target in minimal time
•• Maximum stealth and surprise can be maintained prior to launch
•• System provides flexible targeting capability
•• Weapon has multiple warheads
• Disadvantages
•• Weapon yield may be too large for certain theater targets
•• Multiple warheads present more planning challenges
•• Missile is not recallable in flight
•• System must be released from SIOP commitment
e. ICBMs
• Advantages
•• Weapon can penetrate heavily defended areas without risk to crew
•• Weapon can be on target in minimal time
•• Planning time is short
•• Weapon has multiple warheads
• Disadvantages

the extent that they are MIRVed, *i.e.* carrying multiple warheads, non-mobile ICBMs are particularly attractive targets, susceptible to being destroyed by appreciably fewer warheads than they are carrying.[25]

Submarines, in contrast, at least U.S. submarines,[26] are generally more secure, less susceptible to attack, since they are virtually undetectable at sea.[27] Aircraft, while generally vulnerable to detection like ICBMs, have the advantage, not possessed by either land or submarine launched missiles, of being subject to recall while en route, offering an extra margin of control.[28]

Categories of Nuclear Weapons

"Strategic" nuclear weapons are generally defined as those designed for attacking enemy territory from an intercontinental distance. Such weapons include intercontinental ballistic missiles, both land-based (ICBMs) and submarine-based (SLBMs); long-range bomber aircraft, with their bombs and air launched missiles; and long-range cruise missiles.[29]

While the terminology used to describe non-strategic nuclear weapons varies, such weapons generally include "tactical" or "battlefield" nuclear weapons, with an additional category of "theater" nuclear weapons sometimes being used. Tactical nuclear weapons are

---

•• Weapon yield may be too large for certain theater targets
•• System requires release from SIOP
•• Missile is not recallable
•• Booster may fall on US or Canadian territory
•• Multiple warheads present more planning challenges
Id. at I-3–5 (emphasis omitted).

[25] *See* Keeny & Panofsky, *supra* note 13, at 294 ("Simple arithmetic based on intelligence assessments of the accuracy and yields of the warheads on Soviet missiles and the estimated hardness of Minuteman silos does indeed show that a Soviet attack leaving only a relatively small number of surviving Minuteman ICBMs is mathematically possible in the near future."). *See generally,* Victor Utgoff, *In Defense of Counterforce*, INT'L SECURITY, vol. 6, no. 1, Spring 1982, 44–60 (arguing the merits of an American ICBM counterforce capability to destroy the Soviet ICBM force as promoting deterrence and crisis stability).

[26] *See* UNITED NATIONS DEPARTMENT, *supra* note 2, at 11–12. *See also* NUCLEAR WEAPONS DATABOOK, *supra* note 1, at 100–101.

[25] *Id.*

[28] *See* John F. McCarthy, Jr., *The Case for the B-1 Bomber*, INT'L SECURITY, vol. 1, no. 2, Fall 1976, 78, 84–5.

[29] *See* UNITED NATIONS DEPARTMENT, *supra* note 2, at 11–12. *See also* NUCLEAR WEAPONS DATABOOK, *supra* note 1, at 100–106.

short-range or battlefield weapons designed for local use in a particular battle and include nuclear bombs, short range missiles, nuclear artillery and atomic demolition munitions.[30] Theater nuclear weapons are generally those designed for use in an intermediate range, generally from about 1,500 to 3,000 nautical miles, and designated for use in regional confrontations, generally against targets such as bases and support facilities for the enemy military effort.[31] Typically, strategic nuclear weapons have been more destructive than the tactical or theater nuclear weapons.[32]

Radiation Effects of Nuclear Weapons

This, of course, goes to the heart of the issue. What are the likely effects of the use of a particular nuclear weapon, by itself and in the context of likely accompanying and escalatory nuclear strikes?

Radiation

Radiation, the release of energy in the form of alpha, beta, or gamma particles, ionizes atoms in cells through which it passes, stripping neutral atoms of an electron, leaving the atoms positively charged (ionized) and chemically unstable.[33] Molecules containing such unstable ions then react with other molecules to form new compounds, while the newly freed electrons similarly affect other atoms.[34] These molecular disruptions cause cellular and chromosomal injuries to human cells.[35] "[W]hen the molecules affected are essential for the normal functioning of a cell, the cell in turn suffers injury or dies."[36]

---

[30] *See* UNITED NATIONS DEPARTMENT, *supra* note 2, at 11–12.

[31] *See id.* at 12.

[32] *See id.* The larger strategic warheads also cause greater collateral loss of life than the tactical warheads. *See* The Effects of Nuclear War, *supra* note 7, at 6.

[33] *See* JACOB SHAPIRO, RADIATION PROTECTION: A GUIDE FOR SCIENTISTS AND PHYSICIANS 10 (1972). *See also* JOHN W. GOFMAN, RADIATION AND HUMAN HEALTH 62 (1983) (stating that the release of electrons by ionizing radiation causes cellular and chromosomal injuries); BIER V, HEALTH EFFECTS TO EXPOSURE TO LOW LEVELS OF IONIZING RADIATION 9 (1990).

[34] *See* James R. Cox, Comment, *Naturally Occurring Radioactive Materials in the Oil Field: Changing the Norm*, 67 TUL. L. REV. 1197, 1200–01 (1993); BIER V, *supra* note 33.

[35] *See* SHAPIRO, *supra* note 33, at 10; GOFMAN, *supra* note 33, at 62; BIER V, *supra* note 33.

[36] *See* SHAPIRO, *supra* note 33, at 9.

Radiation through this process of ionization has similar effects on all life it penetrates, including animal and plant life, and effects continue in such life forms genetically for generations to come. Radiation can also spread in the form of radioactive fallout through the dispersal of radioactive materials by water, air, soil, and other substances.

The unstablized nucleus in the radioactive atom relieves itself of this instability through losing energy in the form of radiation. The "half life" of a class of atom with an unstable, radiation-emitting nucleus (called a radionuclide, *e.g.* strontium-90), is defined as the amount of time it takes for one half of a mass of that type of radioactive atom to disintegrate into a more stable element and stop emitting radiation.[37]

Radiation is measured in roentgens, rads and rem. A roentgen (R) is a measure of radiation exposure in the air; a rad (r)[38] is a measure of radiation absorbed by living tissue; and a rem ("Roentgen Equivalent Man") is a measure of the radiation absorbed, weighted to account for the different types of radiation (alpha, beta or gamma).[39] For most external gamma radiation, the type most relevant, 1 R = 1 rad = 1 rem.[40]

---

[37] *See* Cox, *supra* note 34, at 1200–01. "Activity" is the measurement of the number of nuclei that disintegrate during a certain period of time. The standard measurement for activity is Curie, which is 37 billion disintegrations per second. A nuclide with a short half life would have high activity. BIER V, *supra* note 33, at 393. Hazards of radioactive substances are on life forms are calculated using "effective half-life" or "biological half-life" calculations, which take into account the time the radioactive substance remains in the body and emits its radiation directly against living tissue. *See* NATO HANDBOOK ON THE MEDICAL ASPECTS, *supra* note 2, at Part I, Chap. 5, § VI-529. *E.g.,* radioactive radium integrates itself into the bone and remains a long time; other radioactive substances get flushed out of the body quickly. *See infra* note 41.

[38] *See generally* Robert K. Temple, N., *Regulation of Nuclear Waste and Reactor Safety within the Commonwealth of Independent States: Toward a Workable Model*, 69 CHI-KENT L. REV. 1071, 1095 n.151 (1994). The amount of radioactivity in quantitative units (curies or becquerel) to produce a rad per organ (*i.e.*, thyroid) is different than the amount that produces a rad per whole body. *Id.*

[39] *See id.*

[40] *See* Medora Marisseau, Comment, *Seeing Through the Fallout: Radiation and the Discretionary Function Exception*, 22 ENVTL. L. 1509, 1538 note 142 (1992). *See also* NATO HANDBOOK ON THE MEDICAL ASPECTS, *supra* note 2, at Part I, Chap. 5 (particularly at § III, "Cellular effects of Ionizing Radiation" and § IV, Systemic Effects of Whole-Body Radiation," for

The effect of radiation on a life form depends upon the significance to the life form of the cells that have been injured or destroyed and the health of the individual victim's immune system.[41] The injury to human life caused by radiation manifests itself most typically as cancer and as fetal injury resulting in birth defects.[42]

---

discussion of cellular, organ, and organ system failure following radiation exposure).

Another unit of radioactive exposure is the Gray (GY). 1 gy = 100 rad. A whole body exposure of 1 Gy produces a mild radiation sickness and may reduce life expectancy 3 to 5 years.

A becquerel (Bq) is measurement of one radioactive disintegration per second. A curie (CI) = 3.7 X 10 to the 10th power Bq or 37 billion disintegrations per second. A radionuclide is a radioactive nuclide, a radioactive variety of a basic element, *e.g.* uranium or iodine.

One rem = 10 millisieverts, the dose received to produce the same biological effects as 1 rad of x-rays. In beta or gamma, 1 rem is almost the same as 1 rad, but with alpha much lower levels of radiation are needed to produce a rem. A Sievert (SV) is equal to 100 rem. *See id.*

[41] *See* Cox, *supra* note 34, at 1202. The biological effects of radiation vary primarily according to five factors: (1) the type of particles or photons released; (2) the energy of the particle; (3) the distance and duration of the exposure; (4) any shielding; and (5) the sensitivity of the tissue through which the particle passes. *See id.* at 1202.

Internal exposure requires consideration of additional factors, particularly 1) the manner in which the body processes the particular nuclides involved and its ability to expel them; 2) the importance of the organ and its sensitivity; and 3) the types and energies of the particle (alpha particles cause the most problems). While the skin can withstand significant bombardment of ionizing energy, internal tissues are far more sensitive. Certain radionuclides have a tendency to accumulate in specific areas of the body. Iodine gets deposited in the thyroid; radium in the bones; radon in the lungs. *See id.* at 1204–06.

[42] *See id.*

Levels of Radiation Necessary to Cause Injury

The following effects of radiation exposure levels have been noted:

.5-10 rem	undetectable increase of cancer incidence and statistically minor genetic effects
10-100 rem	detectable increase in cancer and genetic defects.
100-200 rem	radiation sickness syndrome
200-400 rem	acute radiation sickness syndrome
400-600 rem	lethal for bone marrow
600+ rem	lethal for intestine epithelium, other tissues[43]

According to another source, death is likely to occur within a period of a day to two weeks from a single dose of 100 rem or more.[44] According to a further source, hemorrhaging, radiation sickness, vomiting, nausea, and fever are likely effects for a person exposed to 200-400 rem and an exposure of 500 rem would kill half of the exposed population within a few weeks, and 1000 rem would kill everyone exposed within a few days to few weeks.[45]

According to an additional source, the "acute lethal dose" (individual doses) of ionizing radiation for an adult is 450 rads, although lower acute doses, combined with chronic doses from fallout and other sources and internal doses from food and water contamination, would also be lethal.[46] Because of the neoplastic diseases and genetic injuries caused by radiation, infants exposed to 100 rads as fetuses would suffer mental retardation and birth defects.

The threshold level at which radiation becomes harmful is not definitively known, with scientific opinions differing.[47] It is clear there

---

[43] *See* ZHORES A. MEDVEDEV, THE LEGACY OF CHERNOBYL 320 (1990). *See also* The Effects of Nuclear War, *supra* note 7, at 19–20; NATO HANDBOOK ON THE MEDICAL ASPECTS, *supra* note 2, at Part I, Chap. 5, §§ IV-520, "Median Lethal Dose (LD$_{50}$)," Part I, Chap. 5, fig. 5-1, "Typical Lethality as a Function of Dose."

With "[a]n outdoor radiation level of 60 rem per hour ... a person outdoors for 10 hours would almost certainly be killed by radiation." The Effects of Nuclear War, *supra* note 7, at 84.

[44] *See* Marisseau, *supra* note 40, at 1538 n.142.

[45] *See* NUCLEAR POWER: BOTH SIDES 28 (Michio Kaku & Jennifer Trainer eds., 1982). *See also* The Effects of Nuclear War, *supra* note 7, at 7.

[46] *See* Carl Sagan, *Nuclear War and Climatic Catastrophe: Some Policy Implications,* 62 FOREIGN AFF. 257, 273 (Winter 1983/1984).

[47] *See* IARC Study Group, *Direct Estimates of Cancer Mortality Due To Low Doses of Ionizing Radiation: An International Study,* 344 LANCET 1039 (1994).

is no level at which it is certain that radiation is harmless. It is also clear that the effects of radiation are cumulative, building up over time. The generally accepted theory has been that a greater dose of radiation causes a proportional increase in chromosome aberrations.[48] In recent years, some scientists have challenged this notion, arguing that the effects are supralinear, *i.e.* that the effect rises rapidly at low doses and levels off at high doses.[49]

Effects of low level radiation are insidious in that they are disguised, occurring not in a clearly visible way but as seemingly random incidences of cancer and other injuries. Based on a U.S. government assessment, each rem of radiation can be expected to result in .0004 fatal cancers among workers, or .0005 fatal cancers among the general population. Thus, out of every 500 workers who accumulate their permissible doses in one year, one can be expected to contract

---

[48] *See* BIER V, *supra* note 33, at 20–21. *See also* Cox, *supra* note 34, at 1203 n.29 ("Based on extensive but incomplete scientific evidence, it is prudent to assume that at low levels of exposure the risk of incurring either cancer or hereditary defects is linearly related to the dose received in the relevant tissue."); Jorge Contreras, Comment, *In the Village Square: Risk Misperception and Decision Making in the Regulation of Low-Level Radioactive Waste*, 19 ECOLOGY L.Q. 481, 492 (1992) (stating that the Nuclear Regulation Commission uses a "linear, no-threshold" model for estimating risks of low level radiation); GOFMAN, *supra* note 33, at 64 ("A very large body of information exists to show that the number of deletions produced is directly proportional to the dose of radiation delivered, in the low-dose range."); JAY M. GOULD & BENJAMIN A. GOLDMAN, DEADLY DECEIT: LOW LEVEL RADIATION AND COVER UP 16 (1990) (stating that most scientists accept the linear model and that the supralinear model probably overestimates the effects of low-level radiation). According to the linear model, an exposure of 100 rem would cause 1000 times the cancer risk of an exposure of 0.1 rem. *See* Contreras, *supra* at 490–92.

[49] *See* GOULD & GOLDMAN, *supra* note 48, at 16–17; Contreras, *supra* note 48, at 492 (citing John W. Gofman, *George Orwell Understated the Case, in* NUCLEAR POWER: BOTH SIDES (Michio Kaku & Jennifer Trainer eds., 1982)). Dr. Gofman's research on Hiroshima and Nagasaki is part of the basis for the supralinear theory. GOFMAN, *supra* note 33, at 66.

fatal cancer.[50] Under federal regulations, the radiation exposure limit for workers handling radioactive materials is set at 5 rem per year.[51]

In modern society people are exposed to radiation from many sources. It has been estimated that a round trip flight between Los Angeles and Paris can result in 4.8 mrems and that airline crew personnel receive one rem a year of radiation as an occupational hazard.[52]

---

[50] *See* Contreras, *supra* note 48, at 491; Cox, *supra* note 34, at 1204. Because genetic defects often accrue over the time period of generations, no authoritative study has established the risk of genetic damage due to radiation. *See* Contreras, *supra* note 48, at 491.

[51] *See* Elena Molodstova, *Nuclear Energy and Environmental Protection: Responses of International Law*, 12 PACE ENVTL. L. REV. 185, 208 n.132 (1994). The Nuclear Regulatory Commission has established standards for protection from ionizing radiation. *See* 10 C.F.R. § 20 (1995).

[52] *See* Contreras, *supra* note 48, at 497

The average annual radiation dose per person from all sources in the United States has been estimated at some 363 mrem,[53] occurring from the following sources:[54]

300 mrem	environmental factors;
53 mrem	X-rays;
5-13 mrem	consumer products (tobacco, television, computer terminals, luminous watch dials, smoke detectors, combustible fuel, etc.);
3 mrem	fallout from nuclear weapons testing and nuclear power facilities.[55]

---

[53] *See id.* A mrem = 1/1000 of a rem.

[54] Contreras, *supra* note 48, at 491 (citing NUCLEAR REGULATORY COMMISSION, BELOW REGULATORY CONCERN: POLICY STATEMENT 8 (1990) (reprinted at 55 Fed. Reg. 27522, 27525)). *See also* Cox, *supra* note 34, at 1204; Contreras, *supra* note 48, at 497, BIER V, *supra* note 33, at 18.

[55] The United States, the Soviet Union and the United Kingdom detonated plutonium nuclear weapons in the late 1940s, the 1950s and the early 1960s. GOFMAN, *supra* note 33, at 296. The United States is believed to have detonated 231 above ground detonations. China and France continued atmospheric testing after other nations stopped. *Id.*

As a result, it has been estimated that 320,000 curies of plutonium radionuclides were dispersed into the atmosphere, with the equivalent of about 40,000 Hiroshima bombs. GOFMAN, *supra* note 33, at 296; GOULD & GOLDMAN, *supra* note 48, at 92.

Almost all of the released plutonium through 1962 has returned to earth and is inhaled by humans. GOFMAN, *supra* note 33, at 297. The cumulative intake of plutonium through 1972 is estimated to be 42 picocuries or 6.85×10^{-4} micrograms per person. *See id.* at 5.

Dr. Gofman estimated that the plutonium fallout will cause a total of 104,460 lung cancer deaths in the United States, and 950,000 world wide. *Id.* at 299. Investigators have also concluded that the mortality rates during the 1950–1965 atomic testing period stopped getting better after decades of improvement. *Id.* When atomic testing was banned, the mortality rate improved once again. *Id.*

Epidemiological testing has detected excess cancer rates in areas affected by nuclear fallout from weapons testing in doses that would not have been expected to cause cancer. BIER V, *supra* note 33, at 373–77; GOULD & GOLDMAN, *supra* note 48, at 15 (stating that Chernobyl fallout in the U.S. during the summer months of 1986 caused a significant increase in the U.S. death rate).

One study has described the following results from the above ground testing and the subsequent cessation of such testing:

... By 1980, [the United States, the Soviet Union, the United Kingdom, France 1960, and China] had set off a total of 528 known nuclear explosions in the atmosphere. The lion's share of these tests—more than 80 percent—were conducted by the Soviet Union and the United States.

Much of the radioactive debris from these tests rained down in the vicinity of the explosions. However, significant amounts of radioactive particles were injected high enough into the atmosphere that air currents were able to disperse them globally before they precipitated back to Earth. At the peak of aboveground nuclear testing in 1962, the world's population was exposed to a level of radiation that was 7 percent higher than the naturally occurring background levels. ...

Aboveground testing of nuclear weapons was prohibited by the Limited Test Ban Treaty, which was concluded by the United States, the Soviet Union, and the United Kingdom in 1963. ... Underground tests were permitted so long as they did not cause radioactive debris to be deposited beyond the border of the country conducting them.

Marvin S. Soroos, *Preserving the Atmosphere as a Global Commons*, ENVIRONMENT, vol. 40., no. 2, Mar. 1998, at 6 (citing R.S. Noms and W. M. Arkin, *Known Nuclear Tests Worldwide, 1945-1993*, THE BULL. OF THE ATOMIC SCIENTISTS 52 (1996): 61; UNITED NATIONS SCIENTIFIC COMMITTEE ON THE EFFECTS OF ATOMIC RADIATION, IONIZING RADIATION: SOURCES AND BIOLOGICAL EFFECTS 19 (1982); Treaty Banning Nuclear Weapons Tests in the Atmosphere, in Outer Space, and under Water, Moscow, 1963, *in* 2 I.L.M. 889 (1963); NATIONAL ACADEMY OF SCIENCES, NUCLEAR ARMS CONTROL: BACKGROUND AND ISSUES 190–95 (1985); G. T. SEABORG, KENNEDY, KRUSHCHEV, AND THE TEST BAN (1981)).

Soroos states that, "By one more recent estimate, radioactive contamination from all the nuclear tests conducted between 1945 and 1980 and delivered to the world's people by 2000 will eventually result in 430,000 cancer deaths, mostly in the Northern Hemisphere. *See* International Physicians for the Prevention of Nuclear War and Institute for Energy and Environmental Research, Radioactive Heaven and Earth: The Health and Environmental Effects of Nuclear Weapons Testing In, On, and Above the Earth (New York: Apex Press, 1991), 42."

Soroos' ultimate statement of the result is that "Radiation levels from nuclear explosions fell from 7 percent of the natural level in 1963 to 2 percent by 1966 and 1 percent by 1970. *See* A. J. Damay, ed., Statistical Record of the Environment (Detroit, Mich.: Gale Research, Inc., 1992), 35–36."

Even underground testing spreads radiation, both at the time of the initial blast and thereafter. Underground testing places a supply of radioactive material in an arbitrary storage space for an indefinite period of time, giving rise to the risk of contamination through leakage over time.

Information regarding such risks has resulted from studies of the Moruroa atoll, where France performed underground testing:

Environmental Effects of Underground Testing at Moruroa

... At the time of the explosion, fracturing of the atoll surface triggers landslides, tsunamis (tidal waves), and earthquakes. There is also evidence that radionuclides have vented to the environment. Possible long-term effects include leakage of fission products to the biosphere and transfer of dissolved plutonium from the lagoon to the ocean and the food chain.

* Venting of Gaseous and Volatile Fission Products

Unusual concentrations of short-lived iodine 131 in marine organisms and krypton 85 and tritium in air or water indicate that venting has occurred.

The scientists of the Australia, New Zealand and Papua New Guinea Mission in 1983 were authorized to carry out a single experiment in situ at Moruroa. ... The measured tritium levels were 500 Becquerels per liter while the expected concentration due to atmospheric fallout should have been in the range of 0.2 Becquerels per liter. The report of this mission offers two explanations ... either venting of gaseous tritium directly from underground cavities or a faster ground water flow rate than admitted.

The venting explanation appears to be more likely, based on findings of Cousteau mission in 1987. Just days after a test, iodine 131 (half life of 8.05 days) was found in all sediment samples. The same mission measured radioactivity of plankton, which is an even better indicator of venting. In plankton, they found an iodine131 concentration of 22,000 picocuries per kilogram, by far the strongest radioactivity found during their mission. ***

* Medium and Long-term Leakage of Fission Products to the Biosphere

According to a model formulated by Hochstein and O'Sullivan, an underground nuclear explosion in rock saturated with seawater can set up an artificial geothermal system. ... The heated seawater dissolves the glassy materials, liberating the nuclear waste.

... [T]he heated seawater ... transfers the dissolved nuclear waste slowly upwards ... Under the assumptions of this model, radionuclides from a depth of around 500 meters would reach the cracks of the lagoon in less than 50 years instead of the 500 to 1,000 years assumed by the French authorities.

A first hint that the model ... might be correct was the discovery of cesium-134 by the Cousteau Mission in 1987. In December 1990, too, Greenpeace found cesium-134 in plankton collected outside the 12-mile exclusion zone around Moruroa. ... Global atmospheric fallout does not contain cesium134. ***

Effects of cumulative doses substantially below the potentially lethal levels discussed above are uncertain. Epidemiological testing has detected excess cancer rates among persons exposed to radiation from weapons testing, nuclear installations, high background radiation and the like, but the causative relationship appears to be a matter of debate.[56]

Scientists are also uncertain as to the significance of the way in which the low level radiation is received, whether through long term chronic radiation exposure or acute exposure, with at least some scientists believing that acute exposure causes more severe injury.[57]

Nuclear Weapons and Radiation

Radiation is a defining feature of nuclear weapons.[58] All existing nuclear weapons emit radiation when detonated.[59] The terms "clean"

> The 120 underground tests conducted at Moruroa have in effect turned it into a longterm waste dump. ... [S]ome may have found its way into the lagoons and ocean. ... Natural barriers play the most important role in the confinement of nuclear waste. Consequently, a planned storage site should meet very strict criteria including exclusion of water, lack of natural fractures or fissures, and a high absorption of radionuclides. ...
> ... Moruroa Atoll is a very poor site for storing nuclear waste of any type. ... The discovery of cesium-134 indicates only the beginning of longterm leakage from the underground "storage" sites.

International Physicians for the Prevention of Nuclear War and the Institute for Energy and Environmental Research, *Environmental Effects of French Nuclear Testing* (updated version of Chap. 9 from the book RADIOACTIVE HEAVEN AND EARTH: THE HEALTH AND ENVIRONMENTAL EFFECTS OF NUCLEAR WEAPONS TESTING, IN, ON, AND ABOVE THE EARTH. (1991)) <http://canterbury.cyberplace.org.nz/peace/nukenviro.html#under>.

[56] *See* BIER V, *supra* note 33, at 373–85;

[57] *See* Contreras, *supra* note 48, at 492. For example: (1) some researchers suggest that long term chronic radiation exposure is less severe than acute exposure; and (2) long latency periods for genetic defects and some cancers make it difficult to trace the radiation source of these effects. *Id.*

[58] *See* UNITED NATIONS DEPARTMENT, *supra* note 2, at 6; THE NUCLEAR READER: STRATEGY, WEAPONS AND WAR, *supra* note 2, at 4; 1987 WHO Study, *supra* note 2.

[59] *See* 1987 WHO Study, *supra* note 2, at 149. "Nuclear weapons represent a historically new form of weaponry with unparalleled destructive potential. A single large nuclear weapon could release explosive power comparable to all the energy released from the conventional weapons used in all past wars." *Id.* at 7.

and "dirty" nuclear weapons are sometimes used as a gross characterization of the levels of radiation likely to be released by a nuclear weapon,[60] but even the "cleanest" of nuclear weapons release radiation.[61]

Modern thermonuclear weapons release energy through a combination of nuclear fission and fusion.[62] A "primary" fission core device detonates to produce the radiation necessary to ignite a secondary fusion explosion.[63] The yield can be increased to create "boosted" nuclear weapons by surrounding the fusion weapon with a layer of U-238 as a third stage to produce a second fission explosion.[64] The radiation released by a thermonuclear weapon results from these two or three stages of detonation.[65] To obtain tailored radiation and yield effects, different ratios of fission-reactions to fusion-reactions may be designed, resulting in weapons that release more or less radiation.[66]

---

[60] *See* UNITED NATIONS DEPARTMENT, *supra* note 2, at 8. Nuclear fusion weapons typically are activated by a fission "trigger." "Extra fission energy can be supplied by surrounding the fusion weapons with a shell of uranium-238. The greater the proportion of fission energy released the 'dirtier' the thermonuclear weapon becomes. It is called 'dirty' because of the quantity of highly radioactive substances (*e.g.* strontium-90 and caesium-137) that are released into the atmosphere. 'Cleaner' weapons have a much smaller release of these substances." *Id.*

[61] *See id.*

[62] *See* Frank Barnaby, *Civil Science Could Drive Tomorrow's Nukes*, INT'L DEF. REV., Jan. 1, 1997:

Whereas in nuclear fission the nuclei of heavy isotopes (such as uranium or plutonium isotopes) are split into lighter ones, in nuclear fusion light nuclei (for example, hydrogen) are joined, or fused. The fusion process, like the fission process, is accompanied by the emission of energy which can be used to produce an explosion. Nuclear fusion is the process which gives the sun its energy, and extremely high temperatures and pressures—similar to those which occur in the sun—are required to produce it. Today's thermonuclear weapons consist of two separate stages: a nuclear-fission weapon which acts as a trigger for the second stage; the explosion of the fission trigger produces a high enough temperature and pressure to fuse nuclei of hydrogen contained in the second stage. The energy produces a large explosion."

Id.

[63] *See* NUCLEAR WEAPONS DATABOOK, *supra* note 1, at 27.

[64] *See id.* at 27–28.

[65] *See id.*

[66] *See id.* at 28.

All nuclear fission and fusion weapons release prompt and delayed radiation.[67] The nuclear fission of plutonium and uranium, which is at least the trigger of all nuclear explosives, releases unstable atomic nuclei.[68] These decay over hours or years, and release alpha, beta and gamma radiation.

The nuclear fusion involved in the explosion of thermonuclear weapons[69] results in a burst of immediate or prompt nuclear radiation, including neutron and gamma rays,[70] the most dangerous forms of nuclear radiation and capable of penetrating concrete, dirt and water.[71]

There are two sources of gamma radiation, prompt gamma rays resulting from the nuclear explosion and delayed gamma rays emitted by debris susceptible to being carried by winds hundreds or thousands of miles from ground zero before falling back to earth.[72] The intensity of the radiation declines tenfold for every sevenfold increase in time.[73] For example, "there's one-tenth as much radioactivity after a week as after a day; only one-tenth of that after 7 weeks; another 90% gone by $7 \times 7 = 49$ weeks, etc."[74] Radioactive fallout can be compounded by the targeting of strategic and tactical nuclear targets since their destruction would release additional nuclear materials into the atmosphere.[75]

A distinction must be made between "yield" and radiation. "Yield," as noted above, is the amount of energy released by the bomb's explosion, with the unit of measurement being the equivalent amount of energy released per metric ton of trinitrotoluene (TNT),[76] essentially expressing the destructiveness of the blast effect of the device. Radiation is the process of disruption of atomic and cellular structure.

The radiation released by nuclear weapons is generally measured in curies, roentgens, rads and rems.[77] This radiation results from both the

---

[67] *See id.*

[68] *See* SAGAN & TURCO, *supra* note 6, at 26.

[69] *See* NUCLEAR READER: STRATEGY, WEAPONS, AND WAR, *supra* note 2, at 26.

[70] *See id.*

[71] *See* SAGAN & TURCO, *supra* note 6, at 49.

[72] *See id.* at 52.

[73] *See id.*

[74] *Id.*

[75] *See, e.g., id.* at 54–55.

[76] *See* UNITED NATIONS DEPARTMENT, *supra* note 2, at 6. *See also* THE NUCLEAR READER: STRATEGY, WEAPONS AND WAR, *supra* note 2; 1987 WHO Study, *supra* note 2.

[77] *See generally* William Daugherty et al., *The Consequences of "Limited" Nuclear Attacks on the United States,* INT'L SECURITY vol. 10 no. 4 (1986), at

atomic/nuclear detonation devices used to set the bomb off and the nuclear materials in the bomb itself.[78] The resultant radioactive isotopes have half-lives ranging from seconds to millions of years.[79]

These radioactive nuclei are lifted by the rising clouds of a nuclear explosion and dispersed by prevailing winds. One hour after an explosion, the radioactivity released from a one megaton bomb is one hundred billion curies. Because nuclei return to a normal state by emitting energy, the fraction that remains radioactive steadily decreases in time. After one day, the radioactivity is down to one billion curies and after a month a bit below 100 million.[80]

The most important factor in determining the extent to which this radioactivity will affect the human population in distant areas is the height at which the nuclear bomb is detonated. If the fireball does not touch the ground, the radioactive debris is lifted into the upper atmosphere, becoming widely dispersed and descending very slowly. This type of explosion is believed to likely cause only a small increase in background radiation.[81]

However, if the nuclear weapon is exploded near the ground, the fireball carries large amounts of dirt into the atmosphere and radioactive nuclei attach to these particles. As the fireball cools, the particles descend back to the earth. But because these particles are

---

3–45; Frank N. von Hippel et al., *Civilian Casualties from Counterforce Attacks*, SCIENTIFIC AMERICAN vol. 259 no. 3, Sept. 1988, at 36–42; Barbara G. Levi et al., *Civilian Casualties from "Limited" Nuclear Attacks on the USSR*, INT'L SECURITY, vol. 12, no. 3, Winter 1987/1988, at 168–89. The yields, CEPs and other very precise technical information of American nuclear weapons are generally made public, but the amounts of radiation are not. Public information on released radiation is generally limited to estimates in civilian and academic sources. *See generally* Sagan, *supra* note 46.

[78] *See* UNDDA NUCLEAR WEAPONS, A COMPREHENSIVE STUDY 8 (1991).

The direct radiation likely to be released by typical tactical fission bombs with yields of some 10 kilotons is likely to be harmful up to some 100 miles and that of the most powerful strategic weapons to be in the range of 300 miles. THE NUCLEAR ALMANAC: CONFRONTING THE ATOM IN WAR AND PEACE 91, 94 (Jack Dennis ed., 1984) [hereinafter THE NUCLEAR ALMANAC]. The radioactivity from a one-megaton weapon is 100 billion curies, fatal to humans out to 1.7 miles immediately after an explosion. *Id.* at 85, 91.

[79] *Id.*

[80] *See id.* at 91.

[81] *See id.*

heavier than radioactive nuclei, they descend quicker and are not as widely dispersed.[82]

Little published data appears to be available as to the relationship between yield and radiation levels. The greater the extent to which fission detonation devices are used in a nuclear weapon, the "dirtier" the weapon becomes, the more radiation it releases. Also, the volume of the nuclear device itself must affect the radiation released. It is generally assumed that the higher yield devices release more radiation than the lower yield ones.[83]

Ted Postel, an MIT professor and former Pentagon nuclear war analyst, has stated that the Minuteman warhead, reported to have a yield of some 335 kt, could produce "a kills-everybody 3000 rads/per-hour dose over a 10-mile oval-shaped area one hour after a ground detonation."[84] Postel went on to state that the Minuteman would release a deadly dose of some 1000 rads/hour of radiation for up to another 10 miles and a possibly lethal dose of 300 rads for as far as 50 miles.[85]

The U.S. Army has estimated that a dose of 8000 rads will result in "immediate permanent incapacitation" of human beings.[86] This is known as the "radiation-kill radius."[87] At 650 rads, "personnel will become functionally impaired within 2 hours of exposure."[88] It has been estimated that a 10 kt fission weapon yields 8000 rads as far as 690 meters and 650 rads as far as 1100 meters.[89]

Non-Radiation Releasing Nuclear Weapons, An Oxymoron

As noted, there is no currently existing nuclear weapon that does not release radiation.[90] The neutron bomb is just the opposite: It releases

---

[82] *See id.* at 93–93. "Airbursts deliver a smaller radiation dose, over a longer period of time, to very large (global) populations; groundbursts deliver a heavy radiation exposure, rapidly, to a relatively smaller area and population." *Id.* at 104.

[83] *See* GRACE, *supra* note 10, at 22. Since high yield thermonuclear weapons are fission-fusion weapons, they are often considered "dirty weapons" because they produce a great deal of radioactivity. *Id.*

[84] *See* William M. Arkin, *Bring on the Radiation*, BULL. OF THE ATOMIC SCIENTISTS, Jan. 11, 1997, at 72.

[85] *See id.*

[86] *See* NUCLEAR WEAPONS DATABOOK, *supra* note 1, at 28 n.34

[87] *See id.*

[88] *See id.*

[89] *See id.*

[90] SAGAN & TURCO, *supra* note 6, at 49–53.

"enhanced" amounts of radiation with curtailed blast and heat effects.[91] While, as noted above, different ratios of fission-reactions to fusion-reactions may be designed to tailor the amount of radiation released, the release of radiation remains a defining feature of nuclear weapons.

As far back as 1957, nuclear scientist Edward Teller, the "Father of the H-Bomb," told President Eisenhower that the Lawrence Livermore laboratories were "within several years of perfecting a 'clean' nuclear device, one with little or no radioactive fallout, that would have myriad of peaceful uses. Such a bomb, argued Teller, also would lessen environmental damage from tests and reduce noncombatant casualties in a nuclear war."[92] However, for technical reasons "[p]lans for a 'clean bomb' were later abandoned and to this day scientists have not figured out a way to build one."[93]

Efforts to develop a clean nuclear weapon are still underway. According to Andre Gsponer, the director of the Independent Scientific Research Institute in Geneva, Switzerland, "compared with present-day nuclear arsenals, tomorrow's weapons will … offer significant military advantages, especially for tactical use, because most of them will produce no significant radioactivity."[94] He projects that "future thermonuclear weapons will probably not rely on a nuclear-fission trigger to provide the conditions needed for nuclear fusion. Instead they may use new types of very powerful conventional high explosives, arranged, for example, in a spherical shell around a capsule containing the hydrogen gases tritium and deuterium. When the explosives are detonated the capsule will be crushed inward and the gases rapidly heated to a suitably high temperature to allow the fusion of hydrogen nuclei to take place."[95]

Gsponer states that "new explosives are being developed which can produce energy concentrations much greater than those produced by today's high explosives, such as shock-sensitive HMX (Cyclotetramethylenetetranitramine). Pure-fusion weapons are likely to have explosive yields equivalent to those of up to 1,000 tons or so of TNT (trinitrotoluene). Delivered by precise navigating systems, such weapons would be sufficient to destroy virtually all military targets."[96]

---

[91] *See* THE NUCLEAR ALMANAC, *supra* note 78, at 185.
[92] *See "Teller's War" Offers Stinging Indictment of Star Wars*, NEW TECH. WK., vol. 6, no. 9, Mar. 2, 1992 (Reviewing *Teller's War*, by William Broad).
[93] *See id.*
[94] Barnaby, *supra* note 62, at 61–5.
[95] *Id.* at 62–3.
[96] *Id.* at 62–3.

Lawrence Livermore National Laboratory in California is also "researching nuclear isomers, such as the isotope hafnium-178, as nuclear explosives without radioactivity. Because nuclear isomers release energy electromagnetically, they produce no radioactivity. Research into nuclear isomers is underway mainly in France, Russia and the US."[97] In addition, "Congress has given scientists at the Lawrence Livermore Laboratory money to begin design of the NIF .... The results from the NIF could also help nuclear-weapon scientists to develop a laser-triggered pure-fusion bomb using miniaturized high-intensity lasers."[98] In this way, the radioactivity from the fission stage of a fusion bomb might be entirely eliminated.

Whether these efforts will be fruitful is unknowable. For present purposes, the radiation-producing effect of nuclear weapons remains such a defining feature of the weapons that any future radiationless nuclear weapons would have to be regarded as a qualitatively different kind of weapon.

Potential Effects of a Major Nuclear Exchange

The International Physicians for the Prevention of Nuclear War, in their 1992 projection of the effects of the use of nuclear weapons, concluded, *inter alia*, as follows:

> The following descriptions summarize only the immediate injuries resulting from a single explosion of a one-megaton warhead detonated on the ground—the equivalent of 1,000,000 tons of TNT, but less than 1/8000 of the destructive force that will remain after all current arms reduction plans are implemented. The immediate human casualties stem from three different sources of injury: the blast effects of the explosion itself; the burns resulting both from direct exposure to the intense heat generated by the explosion and from the resulting massive fires; and the radiation

---

[97] *Id.*

[98] *See id.* at 61–5:

The planned super-laser will cost significantly more than US$1 billion to construct, and will have a lifetime budget of more than US$4.5 billion. It will consist of 192 laser beams which together will produce a staggering 500 billion watts of power for three-billionths of a second. The beams will blast into a very small capsule of hydrogen, creating a sufficiently high temperature and pressure to cause the capsule to implode inward and the hydrogen atoms to fuse to form helium. The lasers will, in other words, produce small thermonuclear explosions.

Id.

released by a nuclear detonation, delivered in the form of fallout of radioactive material down wind from the explosion itself. The most important factor in predicting most of these injuries is the distance of human beings from the explosion itself, although other factors including the weather may be critical (on a rainy day the moist atmosphere will absorb more of the heat energy released by the explosion, and burn injuries may be reduced).

***

DISTANCE MEDICAL EFFECTS

Ground Zero:

At ground zero, the explosion creates a crater 92 meters deep and 367 meters in diameter. All life and structures are obliterated.

0-1.5 KM:

Within one second, the atmosphere itself in effect ignites into a fireball more than 1 km in diameter. The surface of the fireball (cooler than its center) radiates nearly three times the light and heat of a comparable area of the surface of the sun. The fireball rises to a height of six miles or more. All life below is extinguished in seconds.

1.5-5 KM:

The flash and heat from the explosion radiate outward at the speed of light, causing instantaneous severe burns. A blast wave of compressed air follows slightly more slowly, reaching a distance of 5 km in about 12 seconds. From the blast wave alone, most factories and commercial buildings collapse, and small frame and brick residences are destroyed. Debris carried by winds of 417 km/hour inflicts lethal injuries throughout this area. At least 50 percent of people die immediately, prior to any injuries from radiation or the developing firestorm.

5-10 KM:

The direct heat radiating from the explosion causes immediate third-degree burns to exposed skin, and the expanding blast wave destroys many small buildings. The combination of heat and blast causes fuel storage tanks to explode. A firestorm begins to develop, as winds and intense heat sweep individual fires together into a single raging conflagration. The firestorm consumes all nearby oxygen, sucking it out of any underground stations and asphyxiating the occupants. Shelters become ovens, and over the ensuing minutes to hours, fatalities are likely to approach 100 percent.

10-20 KM:

The shock wave reaches a distance of 15 km approximately 40 seconds after the initial explosion. People directly exposed to the electromagnetic radiation (in the form of intense light) generated by the exploding warhead suffer second-degree burns. Depending on the ability of protective structures to withstand blast and resist fire, total early casualties (killed and injured) may range from 5-50 percent.

Radiation Casualties

In the immediate proximity of the explosion (10 km or less) injuries resulting from radiation exposure have little significance, because most (perhaps all) susceptible individuals will have died from the more rapidly fatal burn and blast injuries. At greater distances, radioactive fallout becomes a major source of short-term and medium-term health problem. Accurate predictions about the location and extent of radiation injuries are much more difficult than for burn and blast injuries. The effects of radioactive fallout will depend on such factors as where the nuclear explosion takes place (an explosion in the air above a city will create much less radioactive debris and resulting fallout than an explosion at ground level), whether the local wind patterns that day are carrying fallout over heavily populated areas, and local weather conditions (on a rainy day, radioactive debris will be washed out of the air more rapidly, resulting in more intense fallout over a more localized area). Other important factors are whether individuals in the area of fallout are able to remain carefully sheltered, especially during the initial days of most intense radioactivity.

For those without effective shielding from fallout, a one-megaton nuclear explosion taking place near the ground will create a lethal radiation zone (450 rad doses in the first 48 hours) of approximately 1300 square kilometers. Serious radiation exposures, producing illness but not generally death, will occur over areas several times larger.

The most important medical problems resulting from acute radiation exposure include: central nervous system dysfunction (especially at very high doses); nausea, vomiting and diarrhea from damage to the gastrointestinal tract, leading to potentially fatal dehydration and nutritional problems; and destruction of the body's capacity to produce new blood cells, resulting in uncontrolled bleeding (because of the absence of platelets) and life-threatening infections (because of the absence of white blood cells). Many affected individuals will not be aware that they have received a potentially lethal radiation dose until days to weeks after the explosion, when the damage to their blood system becomes evident through bleeding from the gums or within their skin, or through uncontrolled infections or unhealing wounds.

Medical Care in the Aftermath of a Nuclear Explosion

Estimates of the ultimate casualties from a medical disaster often depend as much on the resources that are available to treat the victims as on the source of the original injuries themselves. In the case of nuclear explosion near human populations, the barriers to effective medical care will be enormous. The most important of these are the sheer numbers of casualties and the fact that the explosion itself will have destroyed hospitals and other medical facilities and killed or injured most medical personnel. The report of the U.S. Institute of Medicine estimated, for example, that in the United States burn injuries alone would require 142 times as many intensive care units as would be available.

Even for most of those with less severe injuries, however, effective medical care will likely be impossible. For example, many people in the aftermath of a nuclear explosion will have severe nausea and vomiting. Even if highly trained medical personnel are available, there will be no clear way for them to determine whether these symptoms are the result of lethal radiation exposure (in which case hospitalization with intravenous fluids and antibiotics is mandatory), or severe psychological stress with no significant radiation exposure at all (in which case emotional support alone is indicted). Effective use of the scarce medical resources that are available will simply not be realistic.[99]

---

[99] BRIEFING BOOK ON NUCLEAR WAR (1992) © INTERNATIONAL PHYSICIANS FOR THE PREVENTION OF NUCLEAR WAR, reprinted with permission, *quoted in* Peter Weiss, Burns H. Weston, Richard A. Falk, & Saul H. Mendlovitz, Draft Memorial in Support of the Application by the World Health Organization for an Advisory Opinion by the Court of International Justice of the Legality of the Use of Nuclear Weapons Under International Law, Including the W.H.O. Constitution, *reprinted in* 4 TRANSNAT'L L. & CONTEMP. PROBS. 721, 729–732 (1994).

It has been estimated that a 1 megaton bomb exploding at ground level would emit the following approximate fallout pattern, assuming a constant wind direction and speed of 20 mph and stable weather conditions:[100]

Fallout Arrival Time, hours	Downwind Distance, miles	Roentgens
1	25	3000
5	100	1000
8	160	300
12	240	100
16	320	30

A one megaton bomb exploding at ground level over Detroit, with winds from the southwest of a constant 15 mph, would deposit lethal fallout on Cleveland and hazardous fallout as far away as Pittsburgh, at such levels as the following over a seven day period: Detroit, 3000 rem; Cleveland, 900 rem; and Pittsburgh, 90 rem.[101]

It has been estimated that a twenty-megaton explosion over New York City would:

> [D]estroy all buildings not only in Manhattan but also in the Bronx, Brooklyn, and Queens, and in Hoboken and Jersey City as well. Exposed people would receive second-degree burns out to twenty-five miles from the detonation. There would be between five and ten million casualties.[102]

In the 1983 "World After Nuclear War" conference in Washington, D.C., leading scientists, including Carl Sagan, concluded that the long-term collateral consequences of a limited nuclear war could lead to a

---

[100] *See* THE NUCLEAR ALMANAC, *supra* note 78, at 94.

[101] *See id.* at 104–05. *See also* The Effects of Nuclear War, *supra* note 7, at 22–25, 81.

[102] *See* THE NUCLEAR ALMANAC, *supra* note 78, at 96. The NATO Medical Guide states "Total nuclear war with utilization of all available nuclear weapons could result in complete devastation of the involved nation's military combat and logistics systems as well as their supporting civilian social structures and economies. However, situations short of total nuclear war are possible in which nuclear weapons could be employed in limited numbers or for a limited time, along with conventional weapons. Under such circumstances, effective military operations could continue and would require the continuing support of an effective medical service." NATO HANDBOOK ON THE MEDICAL ASPECTS, *supra* note 2, at Part I, Chap. 1, §102(a). Thus this entire medical guide is hinged on the contingency of a limited use of nuclear weapons.

"nuclear winter" that could involve global climatic and biological catastrophe.[103]

Sagan stated: "There is a real danger of the extinction of humanity. A threshold exists at which the climatic catastrophe could be triggered ... [a] major first strike may be an act of national suicide, even if no retaliation occurs."[104] A major strategic nuclear exchange would cause up to 1.1 billion immediate casualties from direct consequences, including blast, prompt neutron and gamma radiation, and fire, while secondary consequences, such as severe social disruption, disease, and other casualties caused by the lack of electricity, fuel, transportation, food, supplies, communications, medical care and sanitation, could well cause an additional 1.1 billion casualties.[105]

The scientists further found additional long-term adverse environmental collateral consequences that could lead to profound global climatic and environmental disruption that "make the picture much more somber still."[106] These include obscuring smoke in the troposphere, obscuring dust in the stratosphere, the fallout of radioactive debris, and the partial damage to the ozone layer.[107]

Sagan concluded:

> The central point of the ... findings is that the long-term consequences of a nuclear war could constitute a global climatic catastrophe. The immediate consequences of a single thermonuclear weapon explosion are well known and well documented—fireball radiation, prompt neutrons and gamma rays, blast, and fires. ... No one knows, of course, how many warheads with what aggregate yield would be detonated in a nuclear war. ... [It] is generally accepted, even among most military planners, that a "small" nuclear war would be almost impossible to contain before it escalated to include much of the world arsenals. (Precipitating

---

[103] *See* Stanley L. Thompson & Stephen H. Schneider, *Nuclear War Reappraised,* 64 FOREIGN AFF. 981 (1986).

[104] Sagan, *supra* note 46, at 292.

[105] *See id.* at 262. In the U.S. alone, "[e]xecutive branch calculations show a range of U.S. deaths from 35 to 77 percent of the population (*i.e.*, from 70 million to 160 million dead)." The Effects of Nuclear War, *supra* note 7, at 8. For an extensive nuclear war, it is estimated that there would be cancer deaths and genetic damage in the millions. Because of the deaths from blasts, this would be "insignificant in the attacked areas, but quite significant elsewhere in the world." *Id.* at 10, Table 2. *See id.* at 94–106, for a extensively worked out model of political, governmental, social and economic consequences, as well as deaths and other health issues, arising from a full scale nuclear war.

[106] Sagan, *supra* note 46, at 262.

[107] *See id.* at 264.

factors include command and control malfunctions, communications failures, the necessity for instantaneous decisions on the fates of millions, fear, panic and other aspect of nuclear war fought by real people....) Many of the effects described ... , however, can be triggered by much smaller wars.[108]

Potential Effects of Limited Nuclear War

While the scientists focused on the effects of a major nuclear exchange, they found that even a relatively small exchange, involving some 500 warheads, could trigger "nuclear winter,"[109] resulting in global climatic and biological catastrophe.[110]

Others have noted the extreme effects of even lower level nuclear weapons:

> However, the collateral effects, on noncombatants and neutrals as well as on the environment, of an attack employing even a single 100 kiloton weapon would be extreme. Such an attack would likely destroy 50 to 100 armoured fighting vehicles (the equivalent of one regiment), and the direct effects would incinerate all people and structures within fifteen square miles, likely including, in the best case, villages and towns containing thousands of persons.[111]

During the resulting uncertainty and likely escalation from battlefield to the broader combat theatre, heavily populated areas would likely, by advertence or otherwise, become targets. In 1971, two former Pentagon aides described the effects of such a "limited" war in Europe as follows:

> Even under the most favourable assumptions, it appeared that between 2 and 20 million Europeans would be killed, even in a very limited nuclear attack, with widespread damage to the economy of the affected area and a high risk of 100 million dead if the war escalated to attacks on cities.[112]

---

[108] *Id.* at 259–261.

[109] *See id.* at 276–77.

[110] *Id. See also* Thompson & Schneider, *supra* note 103, at 985–87.

[111] *See* Daniel J. Arbess, *The International Law of Armed Conflict in Light of Contemporary Deterrence Strategies: Empty Promise or Meaningful Restraint,* 30 McGill L.J. 89, 118–19 (1984).

[112] *See id.* (citing A.C. Enthove & K.W. Smith, How Much Is Enough? 128 (1971)).

Another estimate concluded that a European tactical nuclear war "could kill nearly all the persons in the urban centers of Western Europe and subject those areas to near total destruction."[113]

Numerous major studies during the Cold War attempted to quantify the casualties that could be expected from limited nuclear attacks. Several found that civilian casualties from a Soviet counterforce strike on the U.S. would result in virtually as many deaths from radiation as from direct blast.[114] It was estimated that an attack on the 122 U.S. facilities designated as high priority military-industrial targets would result in casualties almost as high as an attack on city centers.[115]

It was further estimated that a Russian attack on 100 of the highest priority American nuclear targets, including 34 strategic nuclear bomber and aerial refueling tanker bases, 16 navy nuclear submarine bases, 9 major nuclear weapons depositories, and over 40 command and communication and early warning radar sites, would result in 3–11 million deaths and 10–16 million casualties.[116]

---

[113] *See id.* (citing M.T. Klare, *Conventional Arms, Military Doctrine and Nuclear War: The Vanishing Firebreak*, 59 THOUGHT 53 (1984); A.C. ENTHOVE & K.W. SMITH, HOW MUCH IS ENOUGH? 128 (1971)). *See also* United Nations, Comprehensive Study On Nuclear Weapons: Report of The Secretary General, 35 U.N. GAOR, Annex (Provisional Agenda Item 48(b) ch. 2, U.N. Doc. A/35/392 (1980) table 1 [hereinafter REPORT OF THE SECRETARY GENERAL].

[114] *See* Daugherty et al., *supra* note 77, at 35; von Hippel et al., *supra* note 77, at 42; Levi et al. *supra* note 77, at 168; Sagan, *supra* note 46.

[115] *See* Daugherty et al., *supra* note 77, at 25. This resulted, again, from co-location. Many U.S. military-industrial targets are located in major urban areas, such as Boston, Detroit, Los Angeles, Minneapolis, Philadelphia, Phoenix, Rochester, Sacramento, St. Louis, San Diego, Seattle, and Wichita. *Id.* Because of such co-location between American industrial targets and urban centers, deaths from a purely military-industrial attack during the Cold War were estimated to be only some 20–30% lower than those from an all-out attack on cities designed to maximize casualties. *Id.*

[116] *Id.* at 26.

There are Air National Guard refueling groups located at 4 major urban airports: O'Hare Airport outside Chicago, Mitchell Airport outside Milwaukee, Sky Harbor International Airport outside Phoenix and Salt Lake City International Airport. ... Four strategic bomber bases are near smaller cities, including Mather Air Force base outside of Sacramento, McConnell Air Force base outside Wichita, Carswell Air Force Base outside Fort Worth and Barksdale Air Force Base outside Shreveport, Louisiana. ... Two

Another Cold War limited nuclear war scenario was a Soviet major counterforce attack on all U.S. strategic nuclear targets, designed to take out the U.S. nuclear assets posing the greatest threat to the Russian forces.[117] According to U.S. Department of Defense estimates at the time, such a counterforce strike aimed at U.S. ICBM, bomber, and strategic nuclear missile submarine bases would likely result in 3.2 to 16.3 million deaths.[118]

The Daugherty-Levi-Hippel estimate,[119] which included a wider range of American targets, including national command and control posts, communications and early warning facilities, and radar sites, and took into consideration radiation fallout dispersal patterns and conflagration as well as overpressure and blast effects, projected between 13 and 34 million deaths, and 25 to 64 million total casualties.[120] Such a large scale comprehensive Russian attack was estimated to cover 1215 U.S. nuclear targets and to use some 3000 Soviet warheads with a total yield of 1340 megatons, representing some 1/3 of the then Soviet warheads and 1/4 of the Soviet megatonnage.[121]

According to these projections, the casualty figures would dramatically increase if the targets included likely bomber dispersal bases and also if they were calculated to include long-term estimates of deaths and illness from economic and social collapse that could be expected following an attack of such magnitude.[122]

Navy nuclear submarine bases are near urban areas, including Alameda in San Francisco Bay, and Long Beach near Los Angeles. *Id.*

Similarly, three major command targets are located in major cities, including the White House and the Pentagon in Washington, D.C., Strategic Air Command headquarters at Omaha, Nebraska and the North American Air Defense headquarters at Colorado Springs. *Id.*

[117] *Id.* at 29.

[118] *Id.*

[119] Levi et al, *supra* note 77, at 168.

[120] *See* Daugherty et al., *supra* note 77, at 29–30.

[121] *Id.* at 30. This major attack option would include attacks on 1016 ICBM silos, 34 strategic nuclear bomber bases, 16 Navy nuclear missile-firing submarine sites, 9 nuclear weapons storage bases, 100 missile command centers, 7 national command headquarters, 5 early warning radars, 10 Navy submarine transmitters, 9 bomber radio transmitters and 9 satellites. *Id.*

[122] *Id.*

The Daugherty-Levi-Hippel model projected similar results from a U.S. counterforce attack on the Soviet Union.[123] Other projections have made the same point:

> The mathematics of the various scenarios of "limited" nuclear war are quite straightforward, as Australian strategic analyst Desmond Ball has pointed out, and they do not support the notion that only a few people would be killed.
>
> ***
>
> In a comprehensive U.S. counterforce attack against the Soviet Union, the targets would include nearly 1,400 ICBM silos, 3 submarine bases (at Severomorsk, near Murmansk; Petropavlovsk on the Kamchatka Peninsula; and Vladivostok), 32 major air bases, and perhaps 700 other smaller missile sites, many of them in some of the most densely populated areas of the Soviet Union. Deaths from such an attack are estimated to range from 3.7 million to 27.7 million. Four of the ICBM fields are sufficiently close to Moscow that the capital would receive extensive fallout regardless of wind direction. Attacks on the political leadership would raise the civilian casualties even more, as Secretary Brown himself made clear: "Hardened command posts have been constructed near Moscow and other cities. For the some 100,000 people we define as the Soviet leadership, there are hardened underground shelters near places of work, and at relocation sites outside the cities. The relatively few leadership shelters we have identified would be vulnerable to direct attack."[124]

Kosta Tsipis has hypothesized a limited attack by the Soviet Union as of 1986 directed against U.S. energy supplies, particularly liquid hydrocarbons. By Dr. Tsipis' calculation, the Soviets, through the use of only some 239 nuclear warheads constituting less than 2 percent of their nuclear arsenal at the time, could have immobilized the U.S. economy, denying it transportation fuel, in effect cutting off access to existing fuel supplies in oil fields and coal mines, since fuel is needed to extract and transport fuel.[125] The attack, while designed to inflict the maximum economic damage while minimizing the attack size, would have killed some 20 million Americans immediately and injured

---

[123] Levi at al., *supra* note 77, at 168.

[124] PETER PRINGLE & WILLIAM ARKIN, S.I.O.P., THE SECRET U.S. PLAN FOR NUCLEAR WAR 192–93 (1983).

[125] *See* PHILIP MORRISON & KOSTA TSIPIS, REASON TO HOPE, AMERICA AND THE WORLD OF THE 21ST CENTURY 35–6 (M.I.T. PRESS 1998).

another 5 million, with casualties thus totaling 10 percent of the U.S. population.[126]

Dr. Tsipis states:

> As a consequence of the absence not of agricultural products themselves but of transportation for agricultural products, far more people would die of famine during the first two years after the attack (about 50%) than would be killed by the attack itself (about 10%). Urban starvation in the second and third years after the attack—evacuation of the cities would be arduous, especially in the Northeast—as a direct result of the lack of transportation would be unavoidable.
>
> Even if the improvisations and abrupt changes in citizen behavior—tight rationing, long refugee movements, and much more—make these broadly economic inferences uncertain, it is hard to see that the attack could do less than return many regions of our country to a state resembling the TV images of Somalia in 1991. At worst, a modest nuclear attack can induce a permanent collapse in the U.S. economy, even though no nuclear explosions occur in almost half of the fifty states! At the least it would induce stagnation and a much reduced standard of living for years for a major fraction of a pauperized nation, mourning more of our dead than in all the wars of this Republic.[127]

Human Side of the Effects of Nuclear Weapons

The above describes the effects of nuclear weapons in a scientific and statistical way. Such objectivized descriptions depict a reality so horrid as probably to be beyond human ability to take in. More comprehensible perhaps are descriptions by individual victims of their suffering at the hands of nuclear weapons.

Witnesses from the Marshall Islands, which were the object of some 67 nuclear weapons tests conducted while those islands were under UN trusteeship, including the 1954 "bravo" shot at Bikini Atoll, ostensibly the largest explosion in the history of humankind, testified before the ICJ that the effects upon human health of these nuclear detonations have stretched over several decades and thousands of miles from ground zero.

One witness, Lijon Eknilang, an indigenous woman and local council member from Rongelap Atoll, testified that all of the Rongelapese were excavated after bravo and when they returned their

---

[126] *Id.* Dr. Tsipis notes that fewer than 2 million American lives have been lost in all U.S. wars combined. *Id.*

[127] *Id.*

land had been poisoned. Mrs. Eknilang testifies that she has suffered 7 miscarriages and cannot have children and that such reproductive anomalies are common among her people. She said many women give birth to "monster babies" with transparent skin and no bones, and many die in childbirth.[128] Mrs. Eknilang further testified:

> [M]any of my friends keep quiet about the strange births they had in privacy. They give birth, not to children, as we like to think of them, but to things we can only described as 'octopuses,' 'apples,' 'turtles,' and other things in our experience. We do not have Marshallese words for these kinds of babies, because they were never born before the radiation came.[129]

The most common birth defect on Rongelap and nearby islands have been "jellyfish" babies.

> These are babies born with no bones in their bodies and with transparent skin. One can see the pulsating brains and hearts. The babies usually live for a day or two, before they stop breathing. Many women die from abnormal pregnancies, and those who survive give birth to what look like strands of purple grapes, which we quickly hide away and bury.[130]

Representatives of the Marshall Islands further stated:

> The Marshall Islands was the site of 67 nuclear weapons tests conducted by the administering authority (United States) from 30 June 1946 to 18 August 1958, during the period of United Nations Pacific Islands Territories Trusteeship. The total yield of those weapons was equivalent to more than 7,000 bombs the size of that which destroyed Hiroshima ....
> The Marshallese experience demonstrates that human suffering and damage to environment must occur at great distance, both in time and geography, from the site of the detonations, even when effort is made to avoid or mitigate harm... .

---

[128] *See* Testimony of Mrs. Lijon Eknilang, of the Marshall Islands, Council Member, Rongelap, 14 November 1995. It has been clinically noted that "if abnormalities are not severe enough to prevent fertilization, the developing embryos will not be viable in most instances. Only when the chromosome damage is very slight and there is no actual loss of genetic material will the offspring be viable and abnormalities be transferable to succeeding generations. ... Radiation increases the rate of these mutations and thus increases the abnormal genetic burden of future generations." NATO HANDBOOK ON THE MEDICAL ASPECTS, *supra* note 2, at Part I, Chap. 5, § IV-521(b).

[129] *See* Testimony of Mrs. Lijon Eknilang, *supra* note 128.

[130] *Id.*

From the Marshallese experience we conclude that birth defects and extraordinarily prolonged and painful illnesses caused by radioactive fallout must inevitably and profoundly affect civilians populations long after any nuclear strike has been carried out and the military operation has been concluded.[131]

Similarly, Dr. Najeeb Al-Nauimi, Minister of Justice of Quatar, presented testimony to the effect that nuclear weapons cause genetic disorders, and in particular, that the effect of such weapons on living organisms is similar to that of genotoxic poison and causes long-term genetic risk even for those who are not directly involved in the conflict, including the children of those who are directly exposed. He testified that this is an inherent characteristic of the use of nuclear weapons and would occur in any use, causing genetic risks for future generations.[132]

Mr. Iccho Itoh, Mayor of Nagasaki, testified as follows as to the American nuclear attack on Nagasaki:

Nagasaki became a city of death where not even the sound of insects could be heard. After a while, countless men, women and children began to gather for a drink of water at the banks of nearby Urakami River. Their hair and clothing scorched and their burnt skin hanging off in sheets like rags. Begging for help they died one after another in the water or in heaps on the banks. Then radiation began to take its toll, killing people like the scourge of death expanding in concentric circles from the hypocenter. Four months after the atomic bombing, 74,000 people were dead and 75,000 had suffered injuries, that is, two-thirds of the city population had fallen victim to this calamity that came upon Nagasaki like a preview of the Apocalypse.[133]

Mr. Itoh went on to talk about the 214,000 who perished in the atomic wastelands of Nagasaki and Hiroshima.[134]

Takashi Niraoka, Mayor of Hiroshima, testified as follows as to the American atomic attack on Hiroshima:

On that day there were approximately 350,000 people in Hiroshima. The city government presently estimates that some 140,000 had died by the end of December, 1945. However, in many cases, entire families were wiped out. The local community

---

[131] *See Week In Review*, THE NEW YORK TIMES, Jan. 14, 1996, at § 4, p. 7.

[132] Testimony of Dr. Jajeeb Al-Nauimi, Minister of Justice of Quatar, 10 November 1995 (174).

[133] Testimony of Mr. Iccho Itoh, Mayor of Nagasaki, 7 November 1995 (177).

[134] *Id.*

was in disarray. Records were lost in the fire. Nor was any thorough survey done at the time. Thus, even today, we have no truly accurate casualty figures.[135]

Mayor Niraoka further testified that approximately 330,000 people throughout Japan are still suffering 50 years later from delayed effects of the atomic bombs on Hiroshima and Nagasaki.

There was also testimony about increased cancer in the area of Semipalatinsk in Russia, an area of substantial Soviet nuclear testing.[136]

Hiroshima and Nagasaki

The long-term effects of the Hiroshima and Nagasaki nuclear bombings include bomb-related radiation deaths. On August 9, 1996, 2,691 new names were added to the list of Nagasaki victims, increasing the official death toll to 108,039,[137] with 74,000 people having been killed immediately in 1945. The Hiroshima bomb killed more than 197,045 people, including 5,030 who died recently,[138] with 140,000 having been killed immediately.[139]

Chernobyl

The April 26, 1986 Chernobyl accident provides a glimpse into the potential radioactive casualties that could result from a single nuclear detonation above ground. The accident took place during an experiment to see if the plant's turbine generator could power cooling pumps while in freewheeling motion after the steam had been cut off.[140]

---

[135] Testimony of Takashi Niraoka, Mayor of Hiroshima, 7 November 1995 (178).

[136] ICJ materials at 132.

[137] *See Nagasaki Mayor Ito Urges Northeast Asia Nuclear-Free Zone*, THE DAILY YOMIURI, Aug, 10, 1996, at 1.

[138] *See Japan Remembers 108,000 Victims of Nagasaki Atomic Bomb*, DEUTSCHE PRESSE-AGENT, Aug. 9, 1996.

[139] *See Listen to A-bomb Victims!*, MAINICHI DAILY NEWS, Aug. 7, 1996, at 2.

[140] RICHARD MOULD, CHERNOBYL, THE REAL STORY 8 (1988). The purpose was to see if the power requirement of reactor four could be maintained during a short power failure. *Id.* at 8. Because xenon builds up when a reactor is shut down, it is difficult to restart. Provisions were made to keep the reactor active at reduced power to repeat the test two or three times if necessary.

The reactor's emergency power systems to the cooling pumps were disconnected because the reduction in electrical supply would resemble a blackout causing the diesel generators to power the cooling systems (this would obstruct the experiment). MEDVEDEV, *supra* note 43, at 27. While reducing the

During the experiment, the emergency systems to the cooling pumps were detached.[141] The energy level to the reactor became insufficient to operate the cooling pumps and so the control rods were detracted.[142] To avoid a reactor shutdown, the staff blocked emergency signals.[143] Suddenly, the thermal power of the reactor began to rise sharply and the panic button was pressed, but the thermal energy level reached 100 times its normal amount before the rods could have any effect. The nuclear reaction continued and a thermal explosion occurred.[144]

---

reactor power, the control rods moved further down than expected and the power output of the reactor fell to below 30 MW (thermal) (almost to shutdown level). *Id.* at 28. The thermal power of the reactor was intended for 700–1000 MW during the experiment. MOULD, *supra,* at 9. This produced 10 MW of electrical energy from the slowly moving turbine, and it was insufficient to support the cooling pumps. MEDVEDEV, *supra* note 43, at 28.

At this point the reactor should have been shut down and the emergency generators used to operate the cooling pumps. *Id.* The test was probably not aborted because it might have taken another year before it could be attempted again. *Id.* The crew decided to increase reactor power to continue the experiment but this became difficult because xenon buildup occurred when the reactor's thermal energy was reduced 30 MW. The reactor power was raised to 200 MW thermal but this was insufficient for the experiment. *Id.* at 29.

To raise the power, the automatic control rods were manually moved. Other problems arose with the reactor because of an increased coolant flow, but to avoid an automatic mechanism from shutting down the system, the staff blocked the emergency signals. *Id.* at 29.

By this time the reactor was operating below the normal safety power of 700 MW (thermal) and an insufficient amount of control rods were in place (they were removed in an effort to compensate for the "negative reactivity" produced by the increased flow of the coolant). But the experiment continued. *Id.* The increased circulation of the coolant decreased the steam flow to the turbine; since the cooling pumps were being run off the turbine they began slowing down as well. *Id.* at 30.

Suddenly the thermal power of the reactor began to rise sharply. At that time the panic button inserting the control rods was pressed, but it is estimated that the thermal energy of the reactor reached 100 times its normal level before the rods had any effect. *Id.* at 31. The control rods stopped because a sharp increase in steam destroyed the fuel channels. The nuclear reaction continued and a thermal explosion occurred. *Id.*

[141] *See id.* at 28.
[142] *See id.* at 29.
[143] *See id.*
[144] *See id.* at 31.

Released Radiation

The release of radioactivity was extended over ten days, and a radioactive cloud rose high into the atmosphere and traveled far from the explosion.[145] It has been estimated that some 50 million curies of different radioactive isotopes were discharged from the reactor,[146] although some estimates were as high as 80 million curies.[147] While the explosion at Chernobyl was relatively small, reportedly some 1/25th the blast of the Hiroshima bomb,[148] the radiation released was appreciably more: Estimates have the radiation released as being some 50, 200, or more than 1,000[149] times the radiation released by the Hiroshima bomb.

---

[145] *See id.* at 76–77.

[146] *See id.* at 77.

[147] *See* Alina Tugend, *Victims of Silence*, PORTLAND OREGONIAN, June 21, 1993, at A3; Murray Feshbach, *A Nuclear Eco-Crisis,* SACRAMENTO BEE, July 18, 1993, at F1.

[148] Dissenting opinion of Judge Weeramantry at 20, 35 ILM at 887 (citing Herbert Abrams, *Chernobyl and the Short-Term Medical Effects of Nuclear War, in* Proceedings of the International Physicians for the Prevention of Nuclear War, Cologne, 1986, *published in* MAINTAIN LIFE ON EARTH 154 (1987)). *See* Chapter 3, note 15, and accompanying text.

[149] *See Effects of the Accident at the Chernobyl Power Plant*, 102nd Cong. 2nd sess. July 22, 1992, at 1; Harvey Wasserman, *In the Dead Zone: Aftermath of the Apocalypse; Chernobyl Ten Years After*, THE NATION, April 29, 1996, quoting Harvard professor Richard Wilson; Committee on International Environmental Law, *Preventing the Next Chernobyl: Recommendations to the International Community,* 49 THE RECORD OF THE ASSOC. OF THE BAR OF THE CITY OF NEW YORK 316, 317 (1994).

The Chernobyl explosion, as noted, was ostensibly a thermal or "steam explosion" caused by the sheer heat of the out-of-control reactor, not a nuclear explosion resulting from the release of the energy from the nuclei of atoms. *Russian Design Reactors; a Different View of Chernobyl*, NUCLEAR ENGINEERING INT'L, Jan. 31, 1999. As well there are a number of researchers who have concluded that a small nuclear explosion did occur. *See infra* note 150 and accompanying text. This "small" explosion resulted in so much radiation because it blew apart the containment cover and blew out the uranium and other radioactive material at the core of the power plant, spreading highly radioactive material by an aerial plume: (*see infra* notes 145–150 and accompanying text)

The scope of Chernobyl's tragic fallout stretches ever deeper into the unfathomable. Following the April 26, 1986, explosion, the reactor spewed out at least eight tons of radioactive poison, about 200 times more radioactivity than was released at Hiroshima and

Nagasaki. By some estimates, its fallout surpassed the total released by all nuclear weapons tests. Much of it was blasted into the jet stream through fuel tubes described by one Brookhaven National Laboratory scientist as "1,600 howitzers pointed at the sky." The radioactive shroud blanketed Ukraine and Belarus and Russia; blew deep into Scandinavia, Western Europe and Great Britain; and tripped radiation monitors from New England to Northern California.

Wasserman, *supra.* According to one source, "The explosion of Reactor Number Four [the Chernobyl site has several reactors] led to the largest recorded single-source release of radiation into the atmosphere, a level roughly equal to the explosion of 1,000 Hiroshima bombs." *Preventing the Next Chernobyl: Recommendations to the International Community, supra. See* Wasserman, *supra. See also* Alan Weisman, *Journey Through a Doomed Land: Exploring Chernobyl's Still-Deadly Ruins,* HARPER'S MAG., vol. 289, no. 1731, Aug. 1994, at 45.

This was an effect that could be achieved in a nuclear war (or other war activity, or indeed by terrorist acts) by targeting a nuclear power plant, missile silo, nuclear powered ship or other facility with a large stock of radioactive material subject to being dispersed. *See supra,* note 75 and accompanying text; Chapter 25, note 33 and accompanying text. The effect could also be achieved by a simple device that explosively spread radioactive materials, to maximize the poison effects of radiation without attempting the complex physics of fission or fusion. *See* Weisman, *supra.*

Such a weapon could be the tool of a militarily weak, poor nation or a group of extremists, as reported in the press:

> A more clear and present danger is lost or stolen uranium or plutonium, the heart of a bomb. Although terrorists couldn't fashion the stuff into a bomb, they could easily wrap it in old-fashioned TNT and touch it off.
>
> The TNT would cause only a bit of blast and fire damage. But the plutonium would drift and spread radioactivity. In a crowded city, this radiological bomb could kill whole blocks and put the area off-limits for decades.

Harry Levins, *How to Kill Lots and Lots and Lots of People; Weapons of Mass Destruction Come in Three Varieties; You'd be Surprised Who Has Them,* ST. LOUIS POST-DISPATCH, Nov. 23, 1997, at B1.

> The severity of damage in Oklahoma City could have been far worse had it involved stolen nuclear material—either radioactive substances dispersed by a chemical blast or a full-scale nuclear explosion.
>
> "Stick a source of plutonium in that car in Oklahoma and you've just magnified that mess by maybe—this is an arbitrary number—100," said Roxanne Dey, an official with the Energy Department in Las Vegas, Nev. "It would take a lot longer to clean up because of

"The heat from the reactor core would have made the radioactive plume rise, and the dry weather over Priyat was such that the cloud was reported to have risen to a height of 1200 meters on April 27, 1986."[150] Contamination from the radioactive cloud was first noticed at the Forsmark nuclear power station (100 kilometers north of Stockholm). The cloud "traveled over Finland and Sweden, becoming stagnant over the Ukraine and north-eastern Europe, with some rainfall over Scandinavia, and then spread widely, including passage over parts of the United Kingdom, France and neighboring countries."[151] Increased radiation was detected throughout Europe and low-level increases were detected as far as Japan and the United States.[152]

A Soviet report indicated that as much as 20 MCI of fission and transuranic (plutonium, neptunium, curium) isotopes may have been deposited within the 30 km radius that was evacuated. Other areas that were significantly contaminated in May and June included Bragin (about 60 km) and Elsk. Later studies in 1987 and 1988 also found significant contamination in several districts of the Mogilev and Gomel regions at a distance between 100 and 300 km from the Chernobyl plant.[153]

Most of the radiation occurred in the republics of Belarus, Ukraine and Russia, settling on 100,000 square kilometers of land.[154] More than 140,000 people had to abandon their homes due to high radiation levels[155] and 500,000 or more people continue to live among

---

the little tiny pieces of (radioactive particles) that you can't see or smell. The cleanup is just a nightmare."
Keay Davidson, *Blast Could Have Been Much Worse: Anti Nuclear Strike Force Tries to Head Off Atomic Terrorism*, DENVER ROCKY MOUNTAIN NEWS, April 25, 1995, at 24A. A Russian intelligence report, released by Sen. John Glenn, warned of the danger of "radiological bombs" as a sort of "poor man's bomb." Because of the extreme toxicity of plutonium, small amounts can contaminate large areas merely by being dispersed into the atmosphere. Jonathan Schell, *Bombing is Reminder of Persistent, Pernicious Threat Posed by Plutonium*, SUN-SENTINEL (Fort Lauderdale), March 11, 1993, 23A.

[150] *See* MOULD, *supra* note 140, at 122.

[151] *See id.* at 122–23.

[152] *See* CHERNOBYL: LAW AND COMMUNICATION 1 (Philippe Sands ed., 1988). *See also* Daniel M. Weintraub, *Traces of Chernobyl's Fallout Found in LA*, LOS ANGELES TIMES, May 15, 1986, at 1.

[153] *See id.*

[154] *See* Jay M. Gould, *Chernobyl—The Hidden Tragedy*, 256 NATION 331, 332–33 (March 15, 1993).

[155] *See* Jessica Mathews, *Full Chernobyl Story Still Far From Being Told*, HOUS. CHRON., Apr. 26, 1995, at 31; Lore Lawrence, *Ukrainian Town Still*

contaminated areas.[156]   The average level of ground contamination within 30 km (8–10 mCi/m^2) was high enough to cause ecological changes such as damage to rodent and plant populations. 400 hectares of pine trees around Chernobyl died.[157]   Ukrainian reports estimate that as much as one-half of Ukraine's territory was damaged by the radiation release.[158]

In Sweden, when a thousand reindeer were slaughtered in 1986, it was reported that 97% were found contaminated up to 10,000 Bq/kg (the Swedish limit then was 300 Bq/kg).[159]   However, in 1994, the Swedish Institute for Radiation Protection stated that the average level of contamination for reindeer in 1986–1987 consisted of 80,000 Bq/kg.[160]

Large quantities of milk were destroyed by radioiodine and radiocaesium in Poland, Hungary, Austria, and Sweden. At the end of April and May, vast amounts of green, leafy vegetable were destroyed in countries as far as Greece, Italy, and France.[161]   Low levels of iodine 131 were detected as far as Los Angeles due to Chernobyl fallout.[162]

Reports in 1994 reflected levels of cesium 137 two hours north of Stockholm as having not substantially declined since the accident.[163]   Radiation levels in reindeer were also still high, at 13,000 becquerells in animals then being killed.[164]   Some fish registered as high as 20,000 Bq/kg, while the limit is set at 1,500 Bq/kg.[165]   Levels of radioactive

---

Suffering From Chernobyl; Psychology Center Attempts to Aid, S.F. CHRON., July 28, 1995, at D2 (reporting the amount to be 160,000).

[156] *See* Mathews, *supra* note 155, at 31.

[157] *See* MEDVEDEV, *supra* note 43, at 89.

[158] *See* Mathews, *supra* note 155, at 31. *See also* Lawrence, *supra* note 155, at D2 (stating that 12% of Ukraine's farmland and 40% of its forests are contaminated).

[159] *See* MEDVEDEV, *supra* note 43, at 199; MOULD, *supra* note 140, at 123 (citing *The Last Round-up? A Cloud Hangs over the Lives of Lapps-Europe's Last Nomads,* SUNDAY TIMES, Nov. 30, 1986). In 1987, the Swedish National Food Board increased the maximum permissible content of cesium-137 for reindeer to 1,500 Bq/kg. NUCLEONICS WEEK, May 21, 1987.

[160] *See Swedish Experts Say Chernobyl Fallout No Risk to Consumers,* AGENCE FRANCE-PRESSE, Apr. 27, 1994.

[161] *See* MEDVEDEV, *supra* note 43, at 104.

[162] *See* Weintraub, *supra* note 152, at 1.

[163] *See Briefly Scandinavia: Chernobyl Anniversary,* NUCLEONICS WK., May 5, 1994.

[164] *See id.*

[165] *See Swedish Experts Say, supra* note 160.

cesium-137 in the water and soil of Sweden have remained the same since the accident.[166]

Human Injuries

There is no certain total of Chernobyl's casualties; estimates abound and, of course, the real number or even the order of magnitude may not be knowable for generations. Ukraine at one point estimated that roughly 3 million people, including 600,000 children, who were exposed to various degrees of radiation, face some risk[167] and that between 1,800 and 8,000 people have died as a result of radiation-related illnesses.[168] On April 26, 1995, Ukrainian Health Minister Andrei Serdyuk claimed that the Chernobyl accident caused as many as 125,000 deaths.[169]

In April 1995, officials in Belarus said that roughly 2 million people had suffered in some way from the accident. At a medical conference in Moscow, specialists said that the 1986 incident exposed more than 3

---

[166] *See id.*

[167] *See, e.g., Chernobyl's Legacy of Pain Only Began with Meltdown,* ST. LOUIS POST-DISPATCH, Sunday, August 13, 1995, at 13A. "The clearest link to Chernobyl has been drawn with thyroid cancer, which increased fivefold among Ukrainian children between 1986 and 1993. The increase reflected Chernobyl's pattern of contamination, with the most irradiated areas reporting as much as a 30-fold rise." *Id. See also* Ann MacLachlan, *Nearing 10th Anniversary Spurs Debate On Chernobyl Fatalities,* NUCLEONICS WK., Mar. 21, 1996.

[168] *See* MacLachlan, *supra* note 167; James Rupert, *Chernobyl Casualty Toll Still Climbing After 9 Yrs. After Blast,* CHICAGO SUN-TIMES, June 25, 1995, at 30. *See also* AGENCE FR.-PRESSE, Mar. 9, 1996 (stating that Chernobyl caused 180,000 deaths in Ukraine; a Ukrainian scientist told reporters in Rome that some death estimates were 230,000 in Ukraine and 120,000 in Belarus); WHO Executive Director Dr. Wilfried Kreisel described estimates that 100,000 people died as a fiction, insisting that the proven death toll was 40. EUR. ENERGY, Jan. 12, 1996; Lawrence, *supra* note 155, at D2 (stating "[i]t is impossible to know how many of the deaths could be credibly linked to Chernobyl ... .").

[169] *See* Mathews, *supra* note 155, at 31 (stating that a disproportionate number of deaths were among children, pregnant women, and rescue workers); Lawrence, *supra* note 155, at D2; FACTS ON FILE, Dec. 31, 1995; Chris Sincola, *Russia Imports Nuke Safety Ideas,* WORCESTER TELEGRAM AND GAZETTE, June 4, 1995, at B1. Some Soviet doctors expect oncological diseases to peak in the second decade after the accident.

million Russians to radiation.[170] About 370,000 Russians are believed to be at risk for radiation-induced illness.[171]

> ... Soviet physicians began quietly advising heavily exposed local women to have abortions. "How do you explain the thirty deformed babies in my village?" cried one woman brandishing photos at a public meeting in Minsk. "For us, everything is terrible," added Maria Sheluk of Nozdrishche, thirty-five kilometers from the explosion. "We can't drink the milk. We're afraid of the potatoes. Nothing could be worse."
>
> In 1995 the United Nations reported that in contaminated areas of Ukraine, illnesses of all kinds are up 38 percent above normal levels. In Gomel, over the Belarus border about 150 kilometers northeast of Chernobyl, government statistics show thyroid cancer rates among children to be fully 200 times higher than before the accident. Massive increases are also reported throughout Belarus and Ukraine as a whole. Writing in New Scientist, Dilwyn Williams, professor of histopathology at England's Cambridge University and president of the European Thyroid Association, predicts that thyroid cancer will ultimately strike more than 40 percent of the downwind children who were less than a year old when exposed. Williams says the irradiated babies are thirty times as likely to contract cancer as those who were 10 years old at the time of the accident. "I have done some sums" on future cancer deaths, he says, and "the answers terrify me." Adds Dr. John Gofman, who founded and directed a biomedical lab for the U.S. Atomic Energy Commission (predecessor to the Nuclear Regulatory Commission), "There is no way the children of the area could not have gotten a massive dose. The Soviets admitted they could not tell people living near the plant to stop drinking the milk in the first few days of the accident, when the radioactive iodine was concentrating in the grass being eaten by the cows there. The younger the children were, the heavier the doses."[172]

One reporter writes, "birth defects have doubled in the parts of Ukraine where, in 1986, the Chernobyl nuclear reactor exploded and the ensuing fire dumped most of its radioactive poisons. Miscarriages, cancers, heart disease and other illness also have risen sharply, according to reports in recent months by the Ukrainian government and the United Nations."[173]

---

[170] *See* Mathews, *supra* note 155, at 31.

[171] *See id.*

[172] Weisman, *supra* note 149.

[173] *See 9 Years After Chernobyl Fire, Radiation Defects Still Rising,* ATLANTA CONST., June 25, 1995.

Thirty-one fatalities were reported in a 1986 Soviet Newspaper.[174] Twenty-four people became disabled invalids.[175] Two hundred and thirty-eight people were diagnosed with acute radiation sickness (requiring 200 rem or higher);[176] 5,000 were diagnosed as having a milder form (requiring 100 to 200 rem).[177] About 50,000 people were exposed to levels of 50 rem.[178]

In a U.S. Congressional Hearing in 1992, experts reported a precipitous decline in the state of health of the Ukrainian population.[179] There were reports from the Soviet Union of increased incidents of thyroid cancer in children, leukemia, miscarriages and deaths of women during delivery, and genetic malformations in newborns.[180] Additionally, health experts do not expect the bulk of cancers and latent health effects to occur until 10 to 15 years after initial exposure, when the latency periods for strontium, cesium and other isotopes have tolled.[181]

Researchers have found an increased thyroid cancer rate among children in areas around Chernobyl due to fallout. In Gomel, a city in Belarus about 70 miles from Chernobyl, 143 cases of thyroid cancer were diagnosed between 1991 and 1994 in children under fifteen. That is a rate of 96.4 per million compared to the normal rate of .5 per million. The rate in Belarus was 30.6 per million with 330 cases being reported since 1986. The cancer is believed to be caused by contaminated milk.[182] The number of thyroid cancer cases among adults in Belarus and Ukraine is also abnormally high, with 2,309 registered in Belarus in 1994 (out of an estimated population of 10.5 million) and more than 3,000 in Ukraine (population: 53 million).[183]

---

[174] *See* MOULD, *supra* note 140, at 66.

[175] *See* MEDVEDEV, *supra* note 43, at 167.

[176] *Id.* at 320. *See also* KOSTA TSIPIS, MX MISSILE BASING 105 (1981) (stating that a 50% fatality level occurs at 450 rem and 90% at 600 rem); Cox *supra* note 34, at 1204–06.

[177] *See* MEDVEDEV, *supra note* 43, at 320.

[178] *See id.* at 169.

[179] *See Effects of the Accident, supra* note 149, at 5.

[180] *See id.* at 51–52 (indicating that, while the information is not completely reliable, it does show a declining state of health in Ukraine).

[181] *See id.* at 5.

[182] *See Cancer Rates Soar in Area of Chernobyl*, FORT WORTH STAR-TELEGRAM, Mar. 25, 1995, at 9.

[183] *See* WHO, *Increase in Thyroid Cancer Among Children After Chernobyl,* CANCER RESEARCHER WKLY., Jan. 3, 1994.

A statistical epidemiologist calculated the effects of Chernobyl fallout in the United States.[184]   Responses were determined by calculating the number of "excess deaths," the difference between the actual number of deaths at a time and place and the number of expected deaths based on national norms, when the difference is too great to be attributed to chance.

Research shows that radiation from Chernobyl reached the United States in May 1986.[185]   Almost immediately, excess deaths were observed, almost all in the spring and summer, especially in May; perhaps as much as 40,000 excess deaths occurred.[186] The acceleration of deaths particularly affected the very young, the very old, and those suffering from infectious diseases such as AIDS, suggesting that the ingestion of Chernobyl fission products had an immediate adverse impact on those with vulnerable immune systems.[187] Similar increases were seen in Germany.[188]

Dr. Robert Gal of the University of California at Los Angeles, a bone-marrow specialist and expert in radiological disease, estimated in

---

[184] *See* GOULD & GOLDMAN, *supra* note 48, at 14.

[185] On May 5th, nine days after the accident, a monitoring station in Washington found radioactive iodine-131 in the rainfall, peaking between May 12th and 19th. The first readings were in Richland and Olympia of 170 picocuries per liter (pCI/l). The highest levels were found in Spokane at 6,600 pCI/l and the EPA recorded low level radiation in milk at 50 stations. *See id.* at 14–15.

[186] Government statistics revealed a significant increase in deaths during the month of May (a 5.3% increase over the previous year, a probability of 1/1000 that it was due to chance).   States in the South Atlantic recorded a infant mortality increase of 28% in June over the previous year. In the U.S. as a whole, infant mortality jumped 12.3% over the previous June. *See id.* at 15. Records reveal significant increases in the number of deaths in May 1986 compared to May 1985 for two age groups (young adults aged 25–34 and persons over 65), and for three causes of death (infectious diseases, AIDS related diseases, and pneumonia). The probability that any of these changes is the result of chance is less than 1/1000, so the likelihood that all could be chance is less than one in a million. *See id.* at 15, 17.

[187] *See id.* at 2–3. An examination of the changes in total deaths among the nation's nine census regions for May-August 1986, compared with 1985 numbers, showed a high correlation with levels of radiation in pasteurized milk as reported by the EPA. Higher levels of radioactive iodine found in milk correlated to higher percentages of increased deaths. The Pacific region (California and Washington) had the highest levels of iodine in milk, 44pCi/l, and the highest increase in total deaths. *Id.* at 16.

[188] *See id.* at 19.

1986 that the accident would cause between 5,000 and 75,000 new cancers world wide.[189] Dr. John Gofman, a medical expert on the effects of radiation and professor emeritus at the University of California at Berkeley, estimated that the Chernobyl accident will cause as many as 500,000 cancer deaths.[190] Dr. Gofman predicted that more than half of the cancers would occur outside of the Soviet Union.[191]

The US Department of Energy predicted between 14,000 and 39,000 extra cancer related deaths in the next 50 years, but that number was subsequently lowered to 17,000.[192] Other estimates extended from 200–600 to 280,000 deaths.[193]

Yevgeny Velikohov, responsible for the clean-up of Chernobyl, stated, "What good was civil defense at Chernobyl, where we had to mobilize the entire country to clean up a relatively small nuclear mess? It is absolutely crazy to think that any kind of civil defense would have any significance in nuclear war."[194] The Chernobyl radiation "remains a threat to the environment and economy of Central and Eastern Europe."[195]

Injury Caused by Conventional Weapons

Conventional weapons can cause extreme damage, as illustrated by Iraqi attacks on Kuwait in 1990 and the U.S. attacks on Iraq in 1991, yet such attacks can be recovered from in a finite period of time, without ongoing effects of the type that would follow the use of nuclear weapons.

Iraq bombed oil refineries and wells in Kuwait, causing massive fires.[196] All told, 732 out of 950 active oil wells, twenty oil and gas

---

[189] *See* MEDVEDEV, *supra* note 43, at 165; Malcom W. Browne, *No Detectable Health Risk is Found Outside Chernobyl Vicinity,* THE NEW YORK TIMES, Dec. 27, 1988, at C4.

[190] *See US Expert Sees 500,000 Chernobyl Cancer Deaths,* WALL ST. J., September 10, 1986, at 15.

[191] *See id.*

[192] *See* MEDVEDEV, *supra* note 43, at 165 (citing Lyn R. Anspaugh et al., *The Global Impact of the Chernobyl Reactor Accident,* SCIENCE, Dec. 16, 1988, at 1513).

[193] *See* MEDVEDEV, *supra* note 43, at 165.

[194] *See* Sagan, *supra* note 46, at 166.

[195] *See The Lingering Nuclear Agenda,* CHI. TRIB., Apr. 21, 1996.

[196] Almost 110 million to 120 million pounds of explosives were dropped on targets in Kuwait and Iraq during the first five weeks of the Persian Gulf War. *Hundreds of Bombs Miss But Experts Say Accuracy Better than in Previous Wars,* THE WASH. POST, Feb. 24, 1991. Kuwait had had over "97.1

stations, four refineries, two natural gas gathering stations, and other downstream facilities were reportedly damaged or destroyed.[197] Of the oil wells hit by bomb attacks, 81% caught fire and 5.7% gushed oil, making the Gulf War what has been referred to as the first ever "environmental war."[198] Estimates as to the total damages varied, with some reaching as high as $100 billion.[199]

Within some seven years, Kuwait had completed the emergency phase of reconstruction. Basic infrastructure, including water, electricity, telephone, and transportation services, had been restored.[200] All 751 burning or damaged wells had been extinguished and/or capped. Kuwait had reinitiated oil exporting, reaching a level exceeding 900,000 barrels per day.[201] At least one major supermarket

---

billion barrels of crude oil and maintained one of the world's largest networks of pipelines, loading docks, and storage tanks—all in a country the size of New Jersey." Kyle Pope, *Prognosis Good for Oil Fields*, HOUS. CHRON., Feb. 23, 1991.

[197] *See* Note, *Environmental Liability Provisions under the U.N. Compensation Commission: Remarkable Achievement with Room for Improved Deterrence*, 11 GEO. INT'L ENVTL. L. REV. 209 (1998). *See* Pope, *supra* note 196; Kuwait: Pollution Control Equipment Market, Industry Sector Analysis, Dept. of State, 1998 (for samples of the Kuwaiti damage assessment). It was reported that the leaking and burning oil wells were costing Kuwait $1000 per second, or $40 million dollars a day. *See also* Deborah Blum, *Battle to Save Gulf's Ravaged Air, Land, Water*, THE SACRAMENTO BEE, Mar. 10, 1991; Sonni Efron, *Air Better, Fires Fewer as Kuwait Wars on Pollution Environment: Soon, Flames at Nearly One-fourth of the Emirates 600 Stricken Oil Wells Will Be Extinguished*, LOS ANGELES TIMES, June 7, 1991, at A1. Kuwait also lost approximately 6 million barrels of oil into the waters of the Gulf (24 times the amount of the Exxon Valdez spill) and 335 miles of beaches. *Id.*

[198] *See* Note, *Environmental Liability Provisions, supra* note 197. Kuwait reportedly lost 40 percent of its fresh water supply used for drinking, cleaning and bathing. Barry Shlachter & Seth Borenstein, *Reports of Airstrikes' Environmental Toll in Yugoslavia hard to Quantify*, THE FORT WORTH STAR-TELEGRAM, May 29, 1999. *See also* Blum, *supra* note 197.

[199] Jeffrey Fleishman, *Kuwaitis Repeat Gulf War Slogan: Go, Americans*, PORTLAND OREGONIAN, Feb. 22, 1998. A United Nations report declared that Iraq must pay $2.8 billion to compensate Kuwait for losses to its oil industry. *U.N. Panel Says Iraq to Pay Companies $2.8 billion in War Claims*, DOW JONES BUSINESS NEWS, July 12, 1999. 2.6 million war claims had been filed with the United Nations. *Kuwait Wants Quicker War Damage Payments from the U.N.*, DEUTSCHE PRESSE-AGENTUR, Sept. 28, 1998.

[200] Corey Wright, *Doing Business in Kuwait—An Update for American Exporters*, Business America (1992).

[201] *Id.*

and 22 cooperative markets were open and fully stocked, and major hotels were operational.[202] Overall, the environmental damages had mitigated very rapidly.[203] As quoted in the Seattle Times, "Kuwait has restored its ability to produce and export its sole natural resource after most of its wells and its three domestic refineries were destroyed or damaged during the six-week Gulf War."[204]

The United States responded to the Iraqi attack on Kuwait with Allied strategic bombing raids on Iraqi targets and troops. The Allied bombing campaign and the four-day ground war reportedly cost Iraq nearly 90 percent of its tanks and eighty percent of its artillery,[205] disrupted Iraqi chemical and biological weapons programs, and reduced to rubble large amounts of the Iraqi infrastructure and buildings.[206] Sources at the time said that "no matter how the Gulf War ends, Iraq is doomed to remain an economic cripple for years" and "rebuilding the country could cost up to $200 billion and take an entire generation."[207]

But Iraq also has made great strides in recovery. Despite the United Nations trade embargo, it continued to export oil to surrounding nations and its economy has shown signs of steady improvement.[208] Notwithstanding a loss of close to 75 percent of its oil industry infrastructure, Iraq is expected to return to full production as early as

---

[202] Compare *Kuwait's Hotels are Slow to Recover*, HOUS. CHRON., Aug. 4, 1991 with Wright, *supra* note 200 (discussing Kuwait's quick recovery).

[203] *See generally Bombs, Mines Help Kuwait's Desert Bloom*, ORLANDO SENTINEL, Jan. 24, 1993 (for an environmental impact assessment on vegetation and shoreline recovery).

[204] *News in Brief*, THE SEATTLE TIMES, Apr. 16, 1993.

[205] *Iraq Lost Most Tanks Sent South*, THE SAN FRANCISCO CHRON., Mar. 7, 1991. As of Feb. 23, 1991, only seven months after they had invaded Kuwait, Iraq had reported losing 135 planes, 6 helicopters, 73 ships, and over 1500 civilian lives in the bombings. *War Log*, USA TODAY, Feb. 23, 1991.

[206] Bernd Debusmann, *Iraq Will Need Years To Rebuild*, THE SACRAMENTO BEE, Feb. 26, 1991. Five weeks of allied bombing reportedly destroyed every power plant, telecommunications center and refinery in Iraq. Damage to oil and production and pumping facilities was thought to be extensive. *Id.* Before the war, Iraq had been the second largest exporter of oil, constituting some ninety percent of its gross national product. *Id.*

[207] *Id.*

[208] Leon Barkho, *Iraq Recovering Past Oil Production, Industry Up to Rate of 2.65 Million Barrels a Day in Production*, THE ATLANTA J., July 21, 1999.

the year 2000.[209]   Iraq has also reportedly reconstructed some 80 percent of its pre-war military manufacturing capability.[210]

---

[209] *Id.*

[210] Jim Wolf, *Hussein Mends War Machine*, CHICAGO SUN TIMES, June 30, 1993.

Chapter 16: Risk Factors Inherent in U.S. Declaratory Policy as to Nuclear Weapons in the Post World War II Era

Typically weapons are what they are. A conventional weapon has whatever characteristics and capabilities it has, and those characteristics become known through use in combat or on the test range. The weapons are themselves the reality.

It is different with nuclear weapons. Because their perceived military value inheres more in whatever ability they may have to deter hostile action by an enemy than in military advantage to be achieved through their use, there developed during the Cold War a very theoretical, conceptualistic body of "nuclear policy," consisting of complex, multi-layered hypotheses as to the probable effects of various possible nuclear thrusts and counter-thrusts by the United States and its enemies and potential enemies.[1]

With a bloodless conceptualism worthy of a medievalist addressing burning issues of theology, the nuclear strategist—manipulating such concepts as deterrence,[2] extended deterrence,[3] mutual assured destruction ("MAD"),[4] first-strike or first use,[5] second-strike

---

[1] *See generally* FRED KAPLAN, THE WIZARDS OF ARMAGEDDON (1989).

[2] *See* BERNARD BRODIE, THE ABSOLUTE WEAPON: ATOMIC POWER AND WORLD ORDER 70–77 (1946). In an early writing on the concept of nuclear deterrence, Brodie stated: "Thus far the chief purpose of our military establishment has been to win wars. From now on its chief purpose must be to avert them. It can have almost no other useful purpose." *Id.*
See also SECRETARY OF DEFENSE JAMES R. SCHLESINGER, 1975 DEPARTMENT OF DEFENSE ANNUAL REPORT, DETERRENCE, ASSURED DESTRUCTION, AND STRATEGIC OPTIONS 32–38 (U.S. Government Printing Office).

[3] *See* Secretary of Defense Robert McNamara, *Defense Arrangements of the North Atlantic Community* (DEPT. OF STATE BULL., 9 July 1962) *in* AMERICAN DEFENSE POLICY 295 (Schuyler et al. eds., 1990) (articulating the concept of "extended deterrence").

[4]*See* Secretary of Defense William Perry & General John Shalikashvili, Chairman, Joint Chiefs of Staff, *Defense Department Briefing,* COMPASS NEWSWIRE, Thursday, Sept. 22, 1994 (Secretary of Defense Perry stating, "I would liken MAD to two men holding revolvers and standing about 10 yards away and pointing their revolvers at each others' head, and the revolvers are loaded, cocked, their fingers are on the trigger, and then to make matters worse they're shouting insults at each other. And that characterized MAD, which was what we had to control this arms race—this nuclear terror during all the periods

of the Cold War.") [hereinafter *Department of Defense Briefing*]. *See* discussion *supra* Chapter 3, notes 160–164, and Chapter 15, notes 13, 99–108, and accompanying text. *See also* Brigid Schulte, *A Timeline of the Nuclear Age*, THE SEATTLE TIMES, August 9, 1995 (citing The Brookings Institution). In February 1964, Secretary of Defense Robert McNamara reflected the American policy of MAD: "A full-scale nuclear exchange between the United States and the USSR would kill 100 million Americans during the first hour. It would kill an even greater number of Russians, but I doubt that any sane person would call this 'victory.'" *Id.*

Ironically, to a certain extent MAD is still U.S. policy. The U.S. position is that it is entitled to target civilians in circumstances when reprisals are appropriate. U.S. Air Force Colonel Charles J. Dunlap, Jr., the Staff Judge Advocate, U.S. Strategic Command, Offutt Air Force Base, Nebraska, in a 1997 article, stated:

> Legal advisors should likewise be aware that while the U.S. does not target populations per se, it reserves the right to do so under the limited circumstances of belligerent reprisal. The U.S. (along with other declared nuclear powers) insists that Protocol I to the Geneva Conventions does not apply to nuclear weapons. Hence, prohibitions contained in Protocol I forbidding reprisals against civilians are not, in the U.S. view, applicable to nuclear operations.

Colonel Charles J. Dunlap, Jr., USAF, *Taming Shiva: Applying International Law to Nuclear Operations,* 42 A.F.L. REV. 157 (1997).

[5] *See* HERMAN KAHN, ON THERMONUCLEAR WAR 559–60 (1960). Kahn argued that American obligations to NATO required it to strike the Soviet Union first even if it had not been attacked itself. Calling for a "Credible First-Strike Capability," he argued that the U.S. should seek to prevail after an initial first-strike attack, contending that the U.S. would enhance deterrence with such a policy and posture. *Id.*

See LAWRENCE FREEDMAN, THE EVOLUTION OF NUCLEAR STRATEGY 135 (1989) ("A *first strike* was taken to refer to a strike that was not only the opening volley of a nuclear war, but was also directed against the nuclear capability of the enemy with the intention of crippling his means of retaliation.").

See BRODIE, *supra* note 2, (addressing the policy of first-strike: "Unless we can strike first and eliminate a threat before it is realized in action ... we are bound to perish under attack without even an opportunity to mobilize resistance.").

The United States has long had a first use policy whereby the United States is prepared to be the first State to use nuclear weapons in a confrontation. Of the five declared nuclear powers, it appears that only Russia and China officially adhere to a no-first-use policy. *See* Official Doctrinal Positions of the Nuclear-Weapon States, *in* NUCLEAR WEAPONS: A COMPREHENSIVE STUDY, Appendix 1 (U.N. Sales No. E.91.IX.101 1991); *Moscow Outlines "Doctrine" for Its Future Military use,* THE NEW YORK TIMES, November 3, 1993, at A11.

capability,[6] preemptive strike,[7] counter-force strike,[8] counter-value strike,[9] countervailing strategy[10]—creates a theoretical construct in

---

France and the United Kingdom also maintain a first use posture. *See* Peter Weiss, Burns H. Weston, Richard A. Falk, & Saul H. Mendlovitz, Draft Memorial in Support of the Application by the World Health Organization for an Advisory Opinion by the International Court of Justice on the Legality of the Use of Nuclear Weapons Under International Law, Including the WHO Constitution, [hereinafter World Court Memorial] *reprinted in* 4 TRANSNAT'L L. & CONTEMP. PROBS. 721 (1994).

[6] *See* FREEDMAN, *supra* note 5, at 135 ("A *second strike* was one capable of ensuring effective retaliation even after absorbing an enemy first strike. Whereas a first strike involved counter-force, a second strike need be no more than counter-value.")

[7] *See id.* at 126–27 (stating "[p]re-emptive war would be launched in all probability against an enemy of equivalent strength if slower in movement. The technical requirements would be exacting: a reliable intelligence system, to ensure adequate warning of attack, and an ability, including a capacity for quick movement, to abort this attack.").

[8] *See* Gray, *Nuclear Strategy: The Case for a Theory of Victory* (reprinted from INT'L SECURITY, vol. 4, no. 1 (1979), *in* AMERICAN DEFENSE POLICY 107 (Schuyler et al. eds., 1990)).

The U.S. military's Joint Pub 3-12, DOCTRINE FOR JOINT NUCLEAR OPERATIONS, states:

> Counterforce targeting is a strategy to employ forces to destroy, or render impotent, military capabilities of an enemy force. Typical counterforce targets include bomber bases, ballistic-missile submarine bases, ICBM silos, antiballistic and air defense installations, C2 centers, and WMD storage facilities.

JOINT CHIEFS OF STAFF, JOINT PUB 3-12, DOCTRINE FOR JOINT NUCLEAR OPERATIONS II-5 (Dec. 15, 1995), as set forth at <http://www.dtic.mil/doctrine/jel/new_pubs/jp3_12.pdf> [hereinafter DOCTRINE FOR JOINT THEATER NUCLEAR OPERATIONS] (emphasis omitted).

[9] *See* ROBERT JERVIS, THE ILLOGIC OF AMERICAN NUCLEAR STRATEGY (1984). During the Cold War, countervalue attacks were essentially directed at civilian targets. *Id.* "Defense now being impossible, the superpowers deter their adversaries not by threatening to defeat them, but by raising the cost of the conflict to unacceptably high levels—what is called deterrence by punishment." *Id.*

In the post Cold War era, countervalue attacks have been defined by the U.S. military as directed at "the destruction or neutralization of selected enemy military and military-related activities, such as industries, resources, and/or institutions that contribute to the enemy's ability to wage war." DOCTRINE FOR JOINT NUCLEAR OPERATIONS, *supra* note 8, at II-5 (emphasis omitted).

[10] *See* Secretary of Defense Harold Brown, *The Countervailing Strategy from Department of Defense Annual Report, FY 1982, in* AMERICAN DEFENSE

which every action an adversary might take is countered by a threat designed to deter such action or to punish for such action if taken, and then deter the next higher level of possible enemy action.[11] War is a modulated rational dispassionate calculation, composed of steps taken at the computer screen from the comfort of a posturepedic swivel chair.

POLICY 302 (Schuyler et al. eds., 1990). Secretary Brown stated that the United States has a "countervailing" strategy that seeks to deter Soviet aggression through flexible response and:

> a continuum of options, ranging from use of small numbers of strategic and/or theater nuclear weapons aimed at narrowly defined targets, to employment of large portions of our nuclear forces against a broad spectrum of targets. In addition to preplanned targeting options, we are developing an ability to design other employment plans, in particular, smaller scale plans, on short notice in response to changing circumstances. In theory, such flexibility also enhances the possibility of being able to control escalation of what begins as a limited nuclear exchange.

Id.

President Ronald Reagan on October 2, 1981 signed National Security Decision Directive–13 which called for a varied menu of nuclear war plans to choose from during a crisis. *Id.*

This is still the U.S. policy. On November 15, 1995, U.S. attorney John McNeill stated before the International Court of Justice, that "US deterrence strategy is designed to provide a range of options in response to armed aggression that will control escalation and terminate armed conflict as soon as possible." Statement of John McNeill, Senior Deputy General Counsel of the United States Department of Defense, in oral argument to the Court, ICJ Hearing, Nov. 15, 1995, at 86.

[11] *See generally* Gray, *supra* note 8, at 103. Counterforce and first-strike planning are conceptualized as serving the dual purposes of "intra–nuclear war" deterrence and making possible a U.S. victory in a limited nuclear exchange. *Id.*

This is still U.S. policy. U.S. attorney Matheson, in his argument to the ICJ in the Nuclear Weapons Advisory Opinion case, stated:

> US deterrent strategy is designed to provide a range of options in response to armed aggression that will control escalation and terminate armed conflict as soon as possible. *** [N]o reference is made in [the World Health Organization's] report to the effects to be expected from other plausible scenarios [in addition to scenarios of numerous nuclear attacks], such as a small number of accurate attacks by low-yield weapons against an equally small number of military targets....

Statement of Michael J. Matheson (Deputy Legal Advisor, Department of State) in oral argument to the Court, ICJ Hearing, Nov. 15, 1995, at 86, 90.

As long as both sides—or all sides in a multi-polar competition—religiously keep in step in this delicate tango, as indeed the United States and the Soviet Union and their allies did with such success during the Cold War, and as long as events do not lurch out of control and equipment does not malfunction in a terrible way—as long as rationality and technology prevail—this grand scheme, at least theoretically, has the potential to deter major direct superpower war or undue escalation in a confrontation that has already erupted.

U.S. nuclear policy is expressed in the following ways:

a) declaratory policy, purportedly defining the circumstances in which the United States would or might use nuclear weapons;[12]

b) operational policy, reflected in the training of military personnel, in weapons procurement, and in contingency planning for the use of such weapons;[13]

c) operational realities, reflected in the actual nuclear capabilities of the United States, including the number and characteristics of the weapons systems in its nuclear arsenal, the deployment and levels of readiness of such weapons, the controls over the potential use of such weapons, and the corresponding conventional weapons capability and readiness of the United States.

Declaratory Policy

During the Cold War, the United States' declaratory policy focused primarily upon the policy and practice of deterrence,[14] the threat that the United States would initiate a nuclear attack against the Soviet Union and its allies in the event of nuclear or serious conventional attack on the United States or its allies, or even the threat of imminent

---

[12] *See* Desmond Ball, *U.S. Strategic Forces: How Would They be Used?* INT'L SECURITY, vol. 7, no. 3, Winter 1982–1983, at 32.

[13] *Id.* at 33–4.

[14] *See* BRODIE, *supra* note 2; FREEDMAN, *supra* note 5; Aaron Friedberg, *The History of the U.S. Strategic "Doctrine," 1945–1980,* THE J. OF STRATEGIC STUDIES, Dec. 1980; Fred C. Ikle, *Nuclear Strategy: Can There be a Happy Ending?,* 63 FOREIGN AFF. 810–826 (Spring 1985); JERVIS, *supra* note 9; Michael McGwire, *Deterrence: The Problem, Not the Solution,* INT'L AFF., 1991; Spurgeon M. Keeny, Jr. & Wolfgang K. H. Panofsky, *MAD versus NUTS: Can Doctrine or Weaponry Remedy the Mutual Hostage Relationship of the Superpowers?* 60 FOREIGN AFF. 287 (Winter 1981–1982).

such attack. U.S. deterrence was expressly directed against potential Soviet conventional as well as nuclear attack.[15]

By definition, such deterrence depends upon the credibility of the threat that the United States, given sufficient provocation, would in fact initiate a nuclear attack. The threat is the policy.

U.S. declaratory policy as to the nature of the attack it would unleash under the rubric of deterrence varied from time to time during the Cold War. At one extreme, the original policy of mutual assured destruction (MAD), developed at the dawn of the era, threatened a wide scale U.S. attack upon the Soviet population: "Attack us and we will destroy you. You may destroy us, but you and your entire country will be destroyed as well."[16]

At the other extreme, the counterforce or war-fighting approach in theory threatened not massive attacks on population centers but precise surgical attacks upon specific military targets.[17] Strategists developed

---

[15] *See* Ball, *supra* note 12, at 32. SIOP, the official American nuclear war plan, has included massive preplanned attack options targeting Soviet strategic nuclear delivery forces, Soviet support forces, Soviet conventional forces, and Soviet command and control centers and systems. *Id. See also* Chapter 17, notes 29–35, Chapter 18, note 5, and accompanying text, regarding the U.S. and its allies falling into a need for nuclear weapons to counter greater Soviet conventional readiness.

[16] *See generally* Keeny & Panofsky, *supra* note 14, at 295. *See also* SECRETARY OF DEFENSE JAMES R. SCHLESINGER, 1975 DEPARTMENT OF DEFENSE ANNUAL REPORT, DETERRENCE, ASSURED DESTRUCTION, AND STRATEGIC OPTIONS 32–38 (U.S. Government Printing Office 1975).

[17] *See* WILLIAM LISCUM BORDEN, THERE WILL BE NO TIME: THE REVOLUTION IN STRATEGY (1946); Desmond Ball & Robert C. Toth, *Revising the SIOP: Taking War Fighting to Dangerous Extremes,* INT'L SECURITY, Spring, 1990, vol. 14, no. 4, 65, 66; PAUL BRACKEN, THE COMMAND AND CONTROL OF NUCLEAR FORCE (Yale University Press 1983); Gray, *supra* note 8; HERMAN KAHN ET AL., WAR TERMINATION ISSUES AND CONCEPTS, FINAL REPORT (1968); David Alan Rosenberg, *A Smoking Radiating Ruin at the End of Two Hours: Documents on American Plans for Nuclear War with the Soviet Union, 1954–55,* INT'L SECURITY, vol. 2, no. 3, Winter 1981–1982, at 3; David Alan Rosenberg, *The Origins of Overkill: Nuclear Weapons and American Strategy, 1945–1960,* INT'L SECURITY, vol. 7, no. 4, Spring 1993, at 3.

Generally, the war-fighting attack was also referred to as a counter-force attack, since it was an attack against the military capability of the adversary. Rosenberg, *supra.* "A counter-value attack" was defined as an attack against the target most valued by an adversary, at one point assumed to be the population centers in the Soviet Union, at other points assumed to the Communist leadership of the country, and at still others believed to be the military capability of the country. *Id.*

complex, multi-layered war-fighting scenarios based upon the premise of modulated "intra-war" deterrence, with provision for precise nuclear strikes at all levels of escalation.

The war-fighting approach was premised on the notions: (1) that such deterrence was more credible than one based on a MAD threat of attacks upon major population centers; and (2) that, should deterrence fail, the President would need modulated levels of nuclear attack to make negotiation possible before wide scale strategic attacks on urban centers were launched.[18]

The underlying premise was that limited nuclear war could be fought to achieve military and political goals, while remaining controlled and capable of being terminated before events careened out of control.[19] Secretary of Defense Harold Brown stated that the United States had a "countervailing" strategy that sought to deter Soviet aggression through flexible response and

> a continuum of options, ranging from use of small numbers of strategic and/or theater nuclear weapons aimed at narrowly defined targets, to employment of large portions of our nuclear forces against a broad spectrum of targets. In addition to preplanned targeting options, we are developing an ability to design other employment plans, in particular, smaller scale plans, on short notice in response to changing circumstances. In theory, such flexibility also enhances the possibility of being able to control escalation of what begins with a limited nuclear exchange.[20]

This approach led to the threat of first use, counter-military targeting and counterforce planning. A complex computer program of nuclear contingency planning—SIOP—was developed to give the U.S. President options to choose from in the event of a failure of deterrence, ranging from a single-warhead launch in a crisis to fighting a protracted nuclear war,[21] including first-strike, escalation control, damage

---

[18] *See* FREEDMAN, *supra* note 5; Friedberg, *supra* note 14; Ikle, *supra* note 14; JERVIS, *supra* note 9, at 109–11; McGwire, *supra* note 14; Keeny & Panofsky, *supra* note 14. *See also* Secretary of Defense Robert McNamara, *Defense Arrangements of the North Atlantic Community* (Dep't of State Bulletin, 9 July 1963) *reprinted in* AMERICAN DEFENSE POLICY 295 (Schuyler et al. eds., 1990).

[19] *See* Gray, *supra* note 8, at 72–73.

[20] *See* Secretary of Defense Harold Brown, *The Countervailing Strategy from Department of Defense Annual Report, FY 1982, in* AMERICAN DEFENSE POLICY 302 (Schuyler et al. eds., 1990).

[21] Ball, *supra* note 12, at 65. SIOP at the time covered four general types of targets: Russian nuclear forces; non-nuclear military forces, including

limitation, and war termination options in fighting an actual limited nuclear war "on terms favorable to the U.S."[22]

War-fighting theorists argued that a heavily counter-military SIOP (which avoids leadership targeting) ultimately served the goals of deterrence.[23] If a nuclear adversary had little prospect of winning either a limited or a general nuclear war, war might be averted.[24] Colin S. Gray argued that counter-force, or counter-military, targeting provided a:

> richer menu of attack options, small and large, [which] would provide a president with less-than-cataclysmic nuclear initiatives, should disaster threaten, or occur, in Europe or elsewhere. Selectivity of scale and kind of attack ... enhances deterrence because it promotes the vital quality of credibility ... . Selective nuclear options, even if of a very heavily counter-military character, make sense, and would have full deterrent value only if the Soviet Union discerned behind them an American ability and will to prosecute a war to the point of Soviet political defeat.[25]

Supporters of the war-fighting strategy further argued during the Cold War that counter-military targeting and planning was necessary because an adversary, Russia, China or some rogue State, would likely go beyond a MAD strategy to a warfighting approach.[26] Since there was always the possibility that the United States might slip into an acute crisis, the President needed to have options more sophisticated than full-scale nuclear suicide or surrender.[27]

---

stockpiles, bases, and installations; economic and industrial centers; and political and command and control centers. *Id.* at 66–8.

SIOP was further divided into four general categories of preplanned options for the employment of American nuclear forces: Major Attack Options (MAOs), Selected Attack Options (SAOs), Limited Nuclear Options (LNOs), and Regional Nuclear Options (RNOs). *Id.* at 69–72.

MAOs included large scale attacks; SAOs included smaller attack options, including first-strikes; LNOs included "selective destruction of fixed enemy military or industrial targets," and RNOs were intended to "destroy the leading elements of an attacking enemy [conventional] force." *Id.*

[22] *See* FREEDMAN, *supra* note 5. *See also* Friedberg, *supra* note 14; Gray, *supra* note 8.

[23] *See* Gray, *supra* note 8.

[24] *See id.*

[25] *See id.*

[26] *See* FREEDMAN, *supra* note 5; Gray, *supra* note 8.

[27] *See* KURT GOTTFRIED & BRUCE G. BLAIR, CRISIS STABILITY AND NUCLEAR WAR 159–212 (1988).

In the event of the failure of deterrence, the President would thus require realistic war plans to fight and win a limited nuclear exchange emerging with the "best outcome," while avoiding a full-scale general nuclear war.[28] This would require limited nuclear attack options that would discriminate between civilian and military targets, and would seek primarily to disarm the enemy without escalating to an all-out exchange.[29] Such war-fighting plans would include pre-emptive first-strikes and selective and full-scale counterforce nuclear strikes.[30] In theory, limited nuclear options on the theater level could also contain escalation to a limited geographic area during a conventional war in Western Europe.[31]

However, the theoretical distinction between MAD and war-fighting attacks floundered upon such realities as the following:

-     A substantial portion of the major Soviet military targets were located near major Soviet population centers, such as Moscow and Leningrad ("co-located"), so that the conceptualization of an attack upon such military targets as of a war-fighting nature would only be a euphemism for what was in reality a MAD attack;[32]

---

[28] *See* Gray, *supra* note 8.

[29] *See* Paul Bracken, *War Termination, in* MANAGING NUCLEAR OPERATIONS 197 (Ashton B. Carter et al. eds., 1987) [hereinafter War Termination].

[30] *See* KAHN ET AL., *supra* note 17, at 550–60; FREEDMAN, *supra* note 5, at 135.

[31] *See* KAHN ET AL., *supra* note 17, at 550–60; FREEDMAN, *supra* note 5, at 135.

[32] *See* Ball, *supra* note 12, at 40.

Major Soviet strategic military targets were frequently co-located near major urban areas. Moscow was surrounded by command and control centers, Leningrad was the headquarters of the Baltic Naval Fleet, Vladivostok was a major port for nuclear submarines and many ICBM fields and nuclear-bomber bases were close to densely populated regions in western Russia. It was estimated that a U.S. nuclear attack on 1,740 major Russian targets would result in 15 to 32 million civilian deaths from direct effects alone. *See* Levi et al., *Civilian Casualties,* INT'L SECURITY. vol.12, no. 3, Winter 87/88, at 183.

Likewise, many U.S. strategic nuclear and support targets were colocated near major urban areas, including tanker aircraft based at airports near Chicago, Milwaukee, Phoenix, and Salt Lake City; Navy bases for nuclear submarines based in San Francisco and Long Beach, near Los Angeles, and key command posts near Washington, D.C., Jacksonville, Sacramento, and San Diego. A Russian limited counterforce attack on 1,215 U.S. targets would result in 12 to 27 million deaths from direct effects alone. *Id.*

-     The sheer number of nuclear weapons held by the
United States eventually led to a search for more military
targets.[33]

"Tens of millions" of additional deaths might result from indirect effects, including radiation fallout, exposure, famine and disease. *See* von Hippel et al., *Civilian Casualties from Counterforce Attack,* SCIENTIFIC AMERICAN, vol. 259, no. 3, Sept. 1988, at 42.

Studies have shown clearly the enormous numbers of casualties that only one percent of the current Russian strategic arsenal could inflict on the U.S. even if the targets were counterforce rather than counterpopulation *per se. See* Daugherty et al., *The Consequences of "Limited" Nuclear Attacks on the United States,* INT'L SECURITY, vol.10, no. 4, 1986, at 4. *See also* Ball, *supra* note 12, at 42; Carl Sagan, *Nuclear War and Climatic Catastrophe: Some Policy Implications,* 62 FOREIGN AFF. 262 (Winter 1983–1984).

Pringle and Arkin have pointed out that, even if a U.S. attack against the Soviets had been such a "counterforce" attack directed against military targets, it was questionable whether the Soviets would perceive the attack as limited in that way. *See* PETER PRINGLE & WILLIAM ARKIN, S.I.O.P., THE SECRET U.S. PLAN FOR NUCLEAR WAR 193–94 (1983).

And, finally, how would the Russians have known a U.S. attack was supposed to be limited? Desmond Ball observed, "Given casualties of this magnitude and the particular Soviet difficulty of distinguishing a comprehensive counterforce attack from a more general military plus urban-industrial attack, the notion of limiting a nuclear exchange to supposedly surgical counterforce operations appears rather incredible." Ball, *supra* note 12, at 39–40.

This same point was raised in hearings before the House Committee on Foreign Affairs:

> CHAIRMAN FASCELL. ... It has been estimated ... it takes 400 nuclear warheads to wipe out the Soviet Union and the same for us, and we have many times more than that, but let's assume, for the purpose of this scenario that it takes 800 nuclear warheads of a given megatonnage to wipe out both countries effectively, including their military capability, their economic base, and their people.
>
> It has also been estimated ... that the fallout cloud, as a result of those explosions, would be so gigantic it would wipe out every human being, every animal in the world in a certain period of time.
>
> Now, whether or not you hit a city or a hard target, it seems to me doesn't make any difference ... .

Statement of Dante B. Fascell, Chairman of the House Committee on Foreign Affairs, in Hearings on The Role of Arms Control in U.S. Defense Policy, before the Committee on Foreign Affairs, House of Representatives, Ninety-Eighth Congress, Second Session, June 20, 21, 26, July 25, 1984, at 157.

[33] *See id.*

- The notion of a military target expanded, encompassing industries and persons supporting the war effort in even the most tangential of ways.[34]
- There remained a significant risk that, given the destructiveness of even the lower yield nuclear weapons, the Soviet Union, in the "fog of war," facing what was conceptualized by the United States as a very precise war-fighting strike, might perceive the attack as an all-out MAD attack and respond accordingly.[35]
- There was also the risk that the Soviets, while perceiving the intended nature of a war-fighting attack, might conclude that, since the nuclear threshold had been passed, they might as well launch a preemptive strike against whatever American nuclear capability they might be able to take out, such as the non-mobile, land-based ICBMs based in the continental United States, and whatever nuclear attack aircraft and submarine were visible in the U.S. storage and grouping or other assessable areas.
- Ironically, a significant risk also presented itself that the United States, having launched only a limited war-fighting attack, might then itself perceive, based on air surveillance or other intelligence, that the Soviets had interpreted the U.S. attack as a strategic one and were preparing a strategic response, and that the United States might accordingly

---

[34] *See* Ball, *supra* note 12, at 41.

[35] *See* Bracken, *supra* note 29, at 197; Levi et al., *supra* note 32, at 188. "Because the Soviet targets were spread over such a wide geographical area it would have been extremely difficult for the Soviet leadership to make an accurate 'attack assessment' of a U.S. strike; with command, control, and leadership targets clustered near the cities it would be hard to distinguish between a selective strike and an all-out attack." Ball, *supra* note 12, at 39–40. Chairman of the Joint Chief of Staff, Gen. Lyman Lemnitzer stated:

[T]here is considerable question that the [Russians] would be able to distinguish between a total attack and an attack on military targets only ... because of fallout from attack of military targets and colocation of many military targets with [cities], the casualties would be many million in number. Thus, limiting attack to military targets has little practical meaning as a humanitarian measure.

Id.

See von Hippel et al., *supra* note 32, at 7.

decide immediately to launch its own more expansive attack in anticipation of the upcoming Soviet nuclear response.[36]

- The development and deployment of a large number of war-fighting and other nuclear weapons created many attractive targets for attack by the enemy. The commander launching a war-fighting attack, using one or more of his precision nuclear weapons, would know that his remaining such weapons, sitting unlaunched and presumably highly visible to the enemy through modern satellite surveillance, had now become attractive and likely targets, and might accordingly decide that, rather than lose his nuclear weapons, he should use them right away—the "use 'em or lose 'em" syndrome. If the situation were dire enough to justify the use of any nuclear weapons, presumably it would be dire enough to justify the use of a number of such weapons, and maybe it made sense to take out as many of the enemy's weapons as possible, once the nuclear Rubicon has been passed.

- While deterrence based on war-fighting was ostensibly more credible and hence more effective than that based on MAD, it had the corresponding disadvantage of lowering the nuclear threshold.[37] The Rubicon type image of the nuclear threshold imbued any use of such weapons with portentous significance potentially of a self-fulfilling nature.[38]

---

[36] *See id.*

[37] *But see* Daugherty et al., *supra* note 32, at 3–45; von Hippel et al., *supra* note 32, at 36–42; Levi et al., *supra* note 32, at 168–189; Sagan, *supra* note 32, at 257, 273.

[38] *See* Secretary of Defense Harold Brown, *A Countervailing Strategic Strategy: Remarks from Speech to the Naval War College, August 20, 1980,* DEFENSE, Oct. 1980, vol. 80, at 2–9. In 1980, Secretary of Defense Harold Brown expressed skepticism about escalation control, "We are also not unaware of the immense uncertainties involved in any use of nuclear weapons." *Id.* at 9. "We know that what might start as a supposedly controlled, limited strike could well, in my view would very likely, escalate to full-scale nuclear war." *Id.*

See Keeny & Panofsky, *supra* note 14, at 290–91 "[I]t does not seem possible, even in the most specialized utilization of nuclear weapons, to envisage any situation where escalation to general nuclear war would not occur given the dynamics of the situation and the limits of the control mechanisms that could be made available to manage a limited nuclear war." *Id.* "We come back to the fundamental point that the only meaningful 'firebreak' in modern warfare, be it strategic or tactical, is between nuclear and conventional

The Military Principle of Concentration of Force

The foregoing dangers of the war-fighting approach were only heightened by the underlying reality of the military doctrine of concentration of force, whereby military commanders at least since the time of Caesar[39] have generally attempted, when possible, to address concentrated force against their enemy targets, including numerous strikes or bombs or the like instead of just one, to enhance the prospects of achieving the mission.[40]

Such redundant targeting—sometimes called "layering"—is part of the U.S. targeting planning for nuclear weapons. This can be seen from *Joint Pub 3-12, Doctrine for Joint Nuclear Operations*, setting forth the

---

weapons, not between self-proclaimed categories of nuclear weapons." *Id.* at 298.

See also Andrei Sakharov, *An Open Letter to Dr. Sidney Drell,* 61 FOREIGN AFF. 1001 (Summer 1983):

> I agree that if the "nuclear threshold" is crossed, *i.e.*, if any country uses a nuclear weapon even on a limited scale, the further course of events would be difficult to control and the most probable result would be swift escalation leading from a nuclear war initially limited in scale or by region to an all-out nuclear war, *i.e.*, to general suicide. It is relatively unimportant how the "nuclear threshold" is crossed—as a result of a preventive nuclear strike or in the course of a war fought with conventional weapons, when a country is threatened with defeat, or simply as result of an accident.

Id.

[39] *See* UNITED STATES GENERAL ACCOUNTING OFFICE, REPORT TO CONGRESS: OPERATION DESERT STORM: EVALUATION OF THE AIR WAR 11 (July 1996) ("Desert storm established a paradigm for asymmetrical post-cold war conflicts. The coalition possessed quantitative and qualitative superiority in aircraft, munitions, intelligence, personnel, support, and doctrine. It dictated when the conflict should start, where operations should be conducted, when the conflict should end, and how the terms of the peace should read." The classic paradigm of disproportionate conflict where the relative quantitative and technological advantages for the U.S. forces are multiples of enemy strength and capabilities and where the acceptable level of risk or attrition for the U.S. forces is low has been called the "Powell Doctrine.").

[40] *See* CARL VON CLAUSEWITZ, ON WAR 595–96 (Michael Howard & Peter Paret ed. & trans., 1976) (describing an offensive thrust at the adversary's "center of gravity" as a decisive principle in military warfare). *See generally* Alan Beyerchen, *Clausewitz, Nonlinearity, and the Unpredictability of War,* INT'L SECURITY, vol. 17, no. 3, Winter 1992–1993, at 59–90 (describing war as a "nonlinear phenomenon," that is "inherently unpredictable by analytical means").

operational planning of the military as of 1995 for the integrated use by U.S. forces of nuclear weapons in conjunction with conventional weapons:

> - Layering. Layering is a targeting methodology that plans employing more than one weapon against a target to increase the probability of its destruction or to improve the confidence that a weapon will arrive and detonate on that target and achieve a specified level of damage.[41]

Such redundant targeting is also accompanied by the use of different types of nuclear weapons and delivery vehicles:

> - Crosstargeting. At the same time it incorporates the concept of "layering," crosstargeting also uses different platforms for employment against one target to increase the probability of at least one weapon arriving at that target. Using different delivery platforms such as ICBMs, SLBMs, or aircraft-delivered weapons increases the probability of achieving the desired damage or target coverage.[42]

The *Joint Nuclear Operations* manual further emphasizes the need for the military to be able quickly to identify, target and strike additional "ad hoc" nuclear targets following a planned nuclear strike:

> - Emergent Targets and Adaptive Planning. Even after the initial laydown of nuclear weapons, there may be a residual requirement to strike additional (follow on and/or emerging) targets in support of retaliatory or war-termination objectives. Commanders must maintain the capability to rapidly strike previously unidentified or newly emerging targets. This capability includes planning for and being able to perform "ad hoc" planning on newly identified targets and maintaining a pool of forces specifically reserved for striking previously unidentified targets. It is important to recognize that success in engaging emerging targets depends heavily upon the speed with which they are identified, targeted, and attacked.[43]

Ironically, one of the factors rendering likely the use of multiple nuclear weapons, with the attendant risk factors, is the fact that the use of multiple smaller yield nuclear weapons is regarded by the military as more conservative—dividing the target up into sub targets for the smaller weapons—than the use of the higher yield more blunderbuss

---

[41] DOCTRINE FOR JOINT NUCLEAR OPERATIONS, *supra* note 8, at II-6 (emphasis omitted).

[42] *Id.* at II-6 (emphasis omitted).

[43] *Id.* at II-6 (emphasis omitted).

weapons capable of taking out all of the sub targets in one hit. The U.S. military in their manual *Doctrine for Joint Theater Nuclear Operations* recognized "employing multiple weapons" as one of the "[m]ethods for reducing collateral damage."[44]

On this basis, it would appear likely that, in any given situation, the military commander, rather than using just one or a few war-fighting nuclear weapons to achieve a particular objective, would use a number of them.[45] At the time of the U.S. atomic attacks on Hiroshima and Nagasaki, the United States, using aircraft to bring rare atomic bombs against essentially undefended targets, was not capable of such concentration.[46]

Reality as to the uncertainties of human and technological error with respect to the likely success of any particular nuclear strike further reinforce the likelihood that, were the situation dire enough to call for the use of nuclear weapons in the first place, multiple such weapons would be used.

Extended Deterrence

In the first instance, the U.S. policy of deterrence was designed to deter attack by the Soviets on the United States itself. But the United States had also undertaken extensive security obligations to Western Europe. As the destructiveness of nuclear weapons and the capabilities of the Soviet Bloc came to be appreciated in this area, the concern arose among the United States' European Allies: Would the United States actually use its strategic nuclear weapons to counter a nuclear attack on Western Europe?

The perceived unlikelihood that the United States would do so meant that deterrence was no longer adequate. Something else—what became known as "extended" deterrence—was necessary. The United States would place substantial numbers of intermediate and battlefield nuclear weapons in the hands of its forces in Western Europe at pivotal anticipated attack points where they would likely be quickly overrun by any Soviet attack.

This was the nuclear trip wire. In the event of a Soviet invasion, the United States would have to either use these weapons to defend Western Europe or see them totally overrun. With the hundreds of thousands of American military personnel placed as hostage to this policy, deterrence was again credible. Indeed, since many of these

---

[44] *Id.* at viii.

[45] *See* Rosenberg, *supra* note 17, at 3–39

[46] *See id.*

tactical nuclear weapons were capable of reaching the Soviet Union, the circle of deterrence seemed complete. The Soviets could not invade Western Europe because the United States would have to use nuclear weapons and also because of the likelihood that some of the weapons would reach the Soviet Union, resulting in a situation where the Soviet Union would likely feel that it had to respond against the United States, invoking total strategic nuclear war.

The Logic of Deterrence as Hinging Upon the Irrational

Deterrence during the Cold War, from the U.S. perspective, required a balance between making the Soviets believe that the United States meant what it said, *i.e.*, that it would use these weapons against Soviet aggression, while simultaneously reassuring the Soviets as to the United States' rationality and restraint, *i.e.* that it would not use the weapons.

Elaborate protocols of reassurance and procedures of communication were worked out.[47] By the end of the Cold War, the American and Soviet military had become essentially a conglomerate working together at maintaining and managing each side's counter-threats against the other and the attendant dangers.[48]

At the beginning of the nuclear era, before the destructive nature of these weapons had been able to sink into the mind set of the decision-makers, deterrence seemed only natural: These were simply another type of weapon, more powerful than previous ones, but not necessarily different. As the destructive power and sheer numbers of these weapons accelerated and the Soviets themselves developed comparable capabilities, the nature of deterrence changed in a discernable but largely unacknowledged way. The prospect of using these weapons became increasingly irrational, even as elaborate highly rational-sounding policy constructs were created one upon the other elaborating intricate scenarios of threat and counter-threat, real and perceived until the distinction between the two became substantially lost.

In a sense, the United States ended up with two levels of deterrence; the first was wholly rational: You dare not attack us or our allies because we will come back with a nuclear response. Because, however, of the incredibility of the policy, the second level of

---

[47] *See* KURT GOTTFRIED & BRUCE G. BLAIR, CRISIS STABILITY AND NUCLEAR WAR 159–212 (Oxford 1988).

[48] *See id.*

deterrence was necessary, the threat that "we just might be crazy enough to do it," the wild card of irrationality.[49]

To one not enmeshed in nuclear policy, the mad dog threat of irrationality seems perhaps not surprising, indeed seems to characterize the entire nuclear venture. From the perspective of the dominant nuclear policy, however, such irrationality represented a radical, if unacknowledged, departure strangely at variance with the rationalistic assumptions of nuclear policy with its nuanced layers of response and counter-response.

A U.S. military study in the post Cold War era has suggested that the policy of deterrence needs to threaten the irrational use of nuclear weapons. As discussed earlier, the July 1995 STRATCOM report "Essentials of Post-Cold War Deterrence" recommended that the United States project an "out of control," irrational, and vindictive willingness to use nuclear weapons in certain circumstances:

> If "some elements ... appear potentially 'out of control,'" it would create and reinforce fears and doubts within the minds of an adversary's decision-makers. "That the U.S. may become irrational and vindictive if its vital interests are attacked should be a part of the national persona we project."[50]

---

[49] *See, e.g.*, HENRY KISSINGER, WHITE HOUSE YEARS 215–220, 216 (Little, Brown 1979) ("The dilemma never resolved [by the doctrine of assured destruction] was psychological. It was all very well to threaten mutual suicide for purposes of deterrence, particularly in case of a direct threat to national survival. But no President could make such a threat credible except by constructing a diplomacy that suggested a high irrationality—and that in turn was precluded by our political system, which requires us to project an image of calculability and moderation").

[50] Hans Kristensen, *Targets of Opportunity: How Nuclear Planners Found New Targets for Old Weapons*, BULL. OF ATOMIC SCIENTISTS, vol.55, no. 5, Sep./Oct. 1997, quoting U.S. Strategic Command, *Essentials of Post–Cold War Deterrence,* [n.d., probably April 1995], at 3, 4 (partly declassified and released under the Freedom of Information Act).

Chapter 17: Risk Factors Inherent in U.S. Operational Policy as to Nuclear Weapons in the Post World War II Era

Given the situation that, pragmatically speaking, nuclear weapons are too risky—too suicidal—to use, but that, as long as the United States follows the policy of nuclear deterrence, it must project a readiness and willingness to use such weapons, the way out of the dilemma, at least conceptually, for the civilian and military leadership is to project to the world a readiness to use these weapons even as the leadership knows that the weapons cannot be used.

The problem with such a policy of bluff is that the first leg of the policy—projecting the readiness and willingness to use the weapons—itself requires that the second leg—the realization that the weapons cannot be used—be kept a secret, unacknowledged and indeed denied when its inconvenient reality is suggested, and that a completely inconsistent reality of potential usability be projected and indeed operationally implemented.

Not only must the United States maintain an arsenal of nuclear weapons sufficient to support deterrence, it must actively and credibly prepare for such use in terms of both personnel and equipment. Its military contingency plans, weapons procurement policies and decisions, weapons placement, educational and training processes for officers and troops alike, training exercises, and overall military and political posturing—all must coalesce to project a robust readiness and willingness to "go nuclear." And all this in a context of inevitable budgetary limitations and other limitations where the selection of a particular weapon and approach is generally the de-selection of other weapons and approaches.

While at the highest level, this projected readiness and willingness might be conceptualized as a ruse to back up a threat that is itself the policy (the oft repeated statements that the only use of nuclear weapons is deterrence), the troops cannot be permitted to know this and indeed the leadership must be prepared so broadly to deny it and to project the alternate reality that it too largely loses track of the original reality.

Even the most intelligent, educated and experienced of people are generally limited in the extent of their ability and willingness to integrate inconsistent realities. It seems to be human nature to try to simplify, and this tendency is perhaps heightened by the "sound bite" nature of so much of political dialogue. Nonetheless, great wisdom is required of the top decision-makers, particularly the President and whatever military personnel are in control, including physical control, of the weapons. To these persons falls the daunting task of avoiding and preventing the use of nuclear weapons in exigent circumstances, to the extent the system, at that point, is at all controllable.

Where the policy originally had two main elements, the ostensible intent to use the weapons and the realization of the suicidal nature of such use, now a third has been added, the practical impact of the operational integration of the ostensible intent to use the weapons. The effect of this third element tips the overall policy towards potential use.

The United States maintains a nuclear arsenal sufficient to destroy the planet, ongoing contingency plans for the use of such weapons and military personnel at the alert, trained and ready to implement such plans. Paradoxically, the real dangers of the U.S. operational policy probably outpace the theoretical dangers of its declaratory policy.

During the Cold War, U.S. nuclear forces were integrated with conventional weapons in American training and planning and, to some extent, in the actual placement of the weapons.[1] This integration was most salient in Western Europe, where American tactical nuclear weapons were placed along with conventional weapons in the hands of troops stationed in Western Europe to defend against a possible Soviet conventional attack.[2]

---

[1] *See The Evolution of American National Security Policy, in* AMERICAN NATIONAL SECURITY (Amos A. Jordan et al., 1989). "From Flexible Response, adopted in 1960, to current American defense policy, the United States has developed, trained and planned its nuclear and conventional forces to meet effectively a wide variety of threats." *Id.*

See generally WILLIAM J. PERRY, SECRETARY OF DEFENSE, 1996 ANNUAL REPORT TO THE PRESIDENT AND THE CONGRESS 11 (U.S. Government Printing Office).

> The United States' strategy of engagement and enlargement requires forces that are able, in concert with regional allies, to fight and win two major regional conflicts (MRCs) that occur nearly simultaneously ... including sustaining credible overseas presence, remaining prepared to conduct contingency operations, and maintaining strong nuclear deterrence as well as deterring and preventing the effective use of biological and chemical weapons.

Id.

[2] *See* William V. O'Brien, *Legitimate Military Necessity in Nuclear War, in* YEARBOOK OF WORLD POLICY 34, 35, 42 (quoting Admiral Arthur W. Radford, Chairman, Joint Chiefs of Staff, Testimony before Subcommittee of House Committee on Appropriations, U.S. Congress, January 17, 1957). *See also* General Nathan F. Twining, Air Force Chief of Staff (*quoted in* O'Brien, *supra*, at 35); Daniel J. Arbess, *The International Law of Armed Conflict in Light of*

As early as 1957, Admiral Author W. Radford, then Chairman of the Joint Chiefs of Staff, testified before Congress that the American military program was based on the contemplated use of atomic weapons:

> I want to reiterate ... that our whole military program is based on the use of atomic weapons in global war and in the use of atomic weapons in accordance with military necessity in situations short of global war.[3]

The same point was made by General Nathan F. Twining, the Air Force Chief of Staff:

> Our mind is made up that we are going to develop a new strategy built around the use of atomic weapons of war. The nuclear weapon is here to stay and they are going to be used in war. We know that. So let's build our forces around the new weapons.[4]

American military manuals have reflected the integration of nuclear weapons into military planning: Lt. Col. Jerry Sollinger, U.S. Army, in his 1983 study of American training and planning for the use of nuclear weapons, stated as follows:

> The [Army] Field manual 100-5 no longer confines nuclear guidelines to a single chapter, but instead intersperses them throughout the text, thus reinforcing the theme that planners must always consider nuclear weapons.[5]
>
> ***
>
> Swiftly massed field artillery, totally mobile tank and mechanized infantry battalions, air-mobile anti-armor weapons,

---

Contemporary Deterrent Strategies: Empty Promise or Meaningful Restraint?, 30 MCGILL L.J. 89, 127 (1984) (citing M.T. Klare, *Conventional Arms, Military Doctrine and Nuclear War: The Vanishing Firebreak* 59 THOUGHT 53 (1984)); Statement of General Bernard B. Rogers, Supreme Allied Commander of Europe in U.S. House of Representatives, Committee on Armed Services, Hearing On Department Of Defense Authorization Of Appropriations For Fiscal Year 1985 at 897 (Washington: Government Printing Office, 1984).

[3] *See* O'Brien, *supra* note 2, at 42 n.20 (citing Admiral Arthur W. Radford, then Chairman, Joint Chiefs of Staff, Testimony before Subcommittee of House Committee on Appropriations, U.S. Congress, Jan. 17, 1957).

[4] *See* O'Brien, *supra* note 2, at 80 n.28 (quoting General Nathan F. Twining, Air Force Chief of Staff).

[5] *See* LT. COL. JERRY M. SOLLINGER, IMPROVING US THEATER NUCLEAR DOCTRINE: A CRITICAL ANALYSIS 13 (Nat'l Defense University Press, Fort McNair 1983) (citing Army Field Manual 100-5 (July 1976) (emphasis omitted)).

attack helicopters, close air-support aircraft and, in some circumstances, tactical employment of nuclear weapons offer us the means to concentrate overwhelming combat power and to decisively alter force ratios when and where we choose.[6]

Sollinger further stated:

The Army's Field Manual 100-5 speaks of a "new phase" in operations brought about by the use of nuclear weapons and states that US first use would probably be defensive, thus implying an earlier phase. Field Manual 101-31-1 Nuclear Weapons Employment Doctrine and Procedures predicts an initial conventional phase followed by nuclear release once the situation turned sufficiently grave. Field Manual 6-20 Fire Support in Combat Operations outlines four indicators that might warrant nuclear weapons: sustained attack by superior forces, full commitment of friendly forces, inadequate support, and questionable survivability of the force... .[7]

Sollinger stated that the Army's assumption, as of that time, was that nuclear weapons would be used in the midst of conventional weapons and intermittently with conventional weapons:

The governing concept for Army employment of nuclear weapons is the Selective Employment Plan (SEP) ... which rests on the notion that this manner of use will "convey to the enemy that we are using nuclear weapons in a limited manner."[8]

***

---

[6] *Id.* (emphasis omitted).

[7] *Id.* at 7 (citing U.S., DEPARTMENT OF THE ARMY, COMBINED ARMS CENTER, COMBAT DEVELOPMENT STUDY PLAN: BATTLEFIELD NUCLEAR WARFARE LEVEL I MISSIONS AREA ANALYSIS 1 (Ft. Leavenworth, Kansas 18 August 1981)) (emphasis omitted).

[8] *See id.* at 8 (citing U.S., DEPARTMENT OF THE ARMY, FIELD MANUAL 6-20 FIRE SUPPORT IN COMBAT OPERATIONS 6-5 (Washington, D.C.: Government Printing Office, January 1980)).

Lt. Col. Sollinger goes on to state with respect to this notion of limited use of nuclear weapons:

To assume that the enemy will view a barrage of nuclear weapons as an indication of restraint appears risky if not stupid. It seems equally likely that he will interpret even limited use as an abandoning of restraint. These weapons could, after all, be the first of a series. Too much confusion reigns on the battlefield to allow for such refined reasoning. A return nuclear salvo would be a more logical expectation.

Id. at 8.

Current doctrinal writings, however, look for a cessation relatively soon after first use. Army Field Manual 101-31-1, for example, speaks of nuclear employment in terms of altering force ratios sufficiently to allow conventional means to control the battle "throughout a sufficient pause" to allow political channels to terminate the conflict. In discussing SEPs, Field Manual 6-20 states they should be planned prior to and refined during hostilities."[9]

***

The examples depict the SEPs as being "continually reviewed, revised, and exercised in corps and divisions FTXs [Field Training Exercises] and CPXs [Command Post Exercises]. Obviously, such meticulous preparation cannot occur during the fast-paced battles all expect in the next war.[10]

U.S. nuclear contingency planning, as discussed in the previous chapter, is expressed through SIOP, the Single Integrated Operating Plan constituting the United States' "highly secret blueprint for war that is still stored on three floors of mainframe computers at STRATCOM."[11] At the height of the Cold War, SIOP contained

---

[9] *See id.* at 5–6 (citing U.S., DEPARTMENT OF THE ARMY, COMBINED ARMS CENTER, COMBAT DEVELOPMENT STUDY PLAN: BATTLEFIELD NUCLEAR WARFARE LEVEL I MISSIONS AREA ANALYSIS 1 (Ft. Leavinworth, Kansas 18 August 1981)) (emphasis omitted).

[10] *See id.* at 8–9 (citing U.S. DEPARTMENT OF THE ARMY, FIELD MANUAL 101-31-1, STAFF'S OFFICERS FIELD MANUAL 5 (Washington, D.C.: Government Printing office, Mar. 1977) and U.S. DEPARTMENT OF THE ARMY FIELD MANUEL 6-20 FIRE SUPPORT IN COMBAT OPERATIONS 6-5 (Washington, D.C.: Government Printing Office, January 1980)).

[11] *See* R. Jeffrey Smith, *Ex-Commander of Nukes Wants to Scrap Them, A Believer No More,* THE SACRAMENTO BEE, Mar. 29, 1998; LAWRENCE FREEDMAN, THE EVOLUTION OF NUCLEAR STRATEGY (1989). *See also* Aaron L. Friedberg, *The History of the U.S. Strategic "Doctrine:" 1945–1980,* THE J. OF STRATEGIC STUDIES, Dec. 1980.
The Single Integrated Operating Plan ("SIOP") is the United States computer program for the use of nuclear weapons. *See* Patrick E. Tyler, *Air Force Reviews "Doomsday" Plan; Service Seeks Computer Capabilities for the 21st Century,* THE WASH. POST, July 11, 1990 at A1. "The SIOP presents the President with a range of options to respond to anything from single nuclear warhead strike by the [former] Soviet Union to all-out thermonuclear war" *Id. See also* David B. Otaway & Steve Coll, *Trying to Unplug the War Machine,* THE WASH. POST, Apr. 12, 1995, at A1; ROBERT S. NORRIS & WILLIAM M. ARKIN, NATURAL RESOURCES DEFENSE COUNCIL NUCLEAR NOTEBOOK; Desmond Ball & Robert C. Toth, *Revising the SIOP: Taking War Fighting to Dangerous Extremes,* INT'L SECURITY, Spring, 1990, vol. 14, no. 4, at 65, 66;

contingency plans for over 50,000 Soviet, Warsaw Pact, Chinese and other targets.[12]   By the end of the Cold War, SIOP contained some 12,500 Soviet targets.[13]   Secretary of Defense Cheney directed the reduction of the targets in SIOP from this peak to about 10,000 by 1991.[14]   By 1994, SIOP was reportedly down to some 2,500 targets in the former Soviet Union.[15]

In November 1997, President Clinton issued Presidential Decision Directive 60, characterized as the "first new national nuclear employment policy guidance since 1981,"[16] which reportedly set forth a "new formulation of nuclear deterrence that would permit warheads to be reduced to START III levels."[17]   The current SIOP—SIOP99, based on PDD 60, became effective on October 1, 1998, but reportedly is to be replaced by a "completely new plan,"—"a set of plans or options for using American nuclear forces, ranging from a demonstration attack with a single weapon to a half-hour spasm of more than 600 missile strikes, embracing almost 3,000 warheads."[18]

The modern SIOP, reportedly dubbed the "living SIOP" by the military, is intended to be more flexible and adaptable, maintained and revised on a daily basis, and ultimately less determined by pre-programming.[19]   Nonetheless, it still apparently demands what has been

---

Gray, *Nuclear Strategy: The Case for a Theory of Victory* (reprinted from INT'L SECURITY vol. 4, no. 1 (1979), *in* AMERICAN DEFENSE POLICY 107 (Schuyler et al. eds., 1990)).   Throughout the Cold War and continuously to the present day, SIOP contains the United States' elaborate contingency plans as to the circumstances and ways in which the United States might use nuclear weapons.

[12] *See* Ball & Toth, *supra* note 11, at 67.

[13] William M. Arkin & Hans Kristensen, *Dangerous Directions*, BULL. OF THE ATOMIC SCIENTISTS, vol. 54, no. 2, Mar. 1, 1998, at 28.

[14] *See* Desmond Ball, *U.S. Strategic Forces: How Would They be Used?* INT'L SECURITY, vol. 7, no. 3, Winter 1982–1983, 31–60, at 36; Otaway & Coll, *supra* note 11.

[15] *See* Ball, *supra* note 14.   Secretary of Defense Cheney's initiative to reduce the target database in the SIOP found an incredible amount of redundancy.   For example, nearly 40 weapons were assigned to attack Kiev, the capital of Ukraine.   *Id.*   General Butler, in charge of trimming the SIOP under President Bush, eliminated about 1,000 targets in newly liberated Eastern Europe, declaring "We do not target democracies." *Id.*

[16] Robert S. Norris & William M. Arkin, *U.S. Strategic Nuclear Forces End of 1998; Abstract,* BULL. OF THE ATOMIC SCIENTISTS, vol. 55, no. 1, Jan. 1999, at 78.

[17] Arkin & Kristensen, *supra* note 13, at 27.

[18] *Id.* at 28.

[19] *Id.*

characterized as "a grandiose guaranteed destruction of Russia's nuclear forces, command and control, industry, and conventional forces."[20] And, of course, other nuclear powers have similar computer programs and systems in place for their contingency plans as to the use of nuclear weapons.[21]

While U.S. nuclear weapons have ostensibly now been "detargeted" or pointed away from potential enemy targets, aimed instead at remote ocean areas,[22] the nuclear strike plans, however flexible, remain, and un-deployments can readily become re-deployments, as detargeting can become retargeting.

By his earlier Presidential Decision Directive, PDD-31, outlining U.S. strategic nuclear policy until the early 21st century, President Clinton had concluded that the United States continued to require a robust nuclear force for the foreseeable future and retained the nuclear triad.[23] Overall, as a hedge against resurgent Russian ultranationalism and a renewed Cold War, PDD-31 envisioned a 21st-century American nuclear force that resembled its Cold War predecessor, only smaller and on lower alert levels. Secretary of Defense William Perry planned to "hedge by maintaining [the United States'] ability to rebuild nuclear forces quickly and by keeping some of its nuclear missiles on Cold-War style alert."[24]

---

[20] *Id.* at 30

[21] *See* WILLIAM T. LEE & RICHARD F. STAAR, SOVIET MILITARY POLICY SINCE WORLD WAR II 23–26 (1986).

[22] *See also* Robert Norris & William Arkin, *U.S. Strategic Nuclear Forces, End of 1995,* BULL. OF ATOMIC SCIENTISTS, vol. 51, no. 1, Jan. 1995.

> Presidents Clinton and Yeltsin announced ... January [1994] that the United States and Russia would "detarget" their strategic missiles. For more than 30 years a variety of potential targets were stored in the U.S. weapon system computers according to the nuclear war plan known as the Single Integrated Operational Plan (SIOP). Detargeting involves changing the control setting so that, on a day-to-day basis, no country is targeted. This has been done with the MX, Trident I, and Trident II missiles. The older technology of the Minuteman IIIs requires that they be targeted at something, so they are pointed at ocean areas. The actions were complete by May 30. While this initiative was largely symbolic, since the missiles can be re-aimed back at the specific targets called for in the SIOP, the gesture nevertheless contributes to relaxing the readiness practices developed during the Cold War.

Id.

[23] PDD-31 was signed in April 1995.

[24] *See id.*

There is a perception in Washington and in the defense establishment generally that these contingency plans for the use of nuclear weapons are so complex and so specialized as essentially to be the domain of the military, and indeed of the small group within the military responsible for such matters, thereby largely excluding the President and other civilian leadership and even the military leadership itself from significant and intelligent participation.[25] Even more, there is the perception that the overall policy guidelines are so broad and the intricacies of the SIOP so arcane as to permit the military running the SIOP to do pretty much what they want without any significant oversight.[26]

As William Arkin and Hans Kristensen have expressed it in the *Bulletin of the Atomic Scientists:*

> Meanwhile, the [Clinton Administration] had begun to echo a perennial Washington complaint that strategic planners had effectively excluded both civilian and other military policy-makers from the details of nuclear war plans, and that they read into the national guidance whatever they chose, allowing them to retain never-changing first-strike options. ...
>
> But the problem went beyond a simple case of insubordination: The choreography of nuclear war-fighting was so complex that few outside STRATCOM's Omaha headquarters were in a position to challenge its claims about "required" readiness, synergy, or military capacity. And by staying firmly in control of all the analytic tools, STRATCOM [previously called "SAC"] could deflect any of Washington's changes.[27]

---

[25] Arkin & Kristensen, *supra* note 13, at 30.

[26] *Id.*

[27] *Id.* Arkin and Kristensen also describe the Nuclear Posture Review (NPR), *see* Chapter 18, as a process whereby the United States "failed to redefine the role of nuclear weapons after the Cold War" and characterize it as a success by the "war-planners" in avoiding change. Focusing on the acceptance by the NPR of the "hedge" whereby a supply of non-deployed warheads is maintained to supplement the agreed reductions, they state, "President Clinton's approval of the NPR in September 1994 confirmed the war-planners' views. They had avoided any significant post–Cold War change." *Id. See* Chapter 19, note 7 and accompanying text for a discussion of the hedge forces.

They state further:

> In the end, according to an internal STRATCOM report, the NPR "reaffirmed the benefits of ambiguity in existing nuclear weapon declaratory policy." In other words, any presidential de-targeting initiatives or other confidence building measures could be

Historically, conventional weapons have been far less destructive than nuclear weapons and ostensibly more expensive per unit of

---

> accommodated, because U.S. policy could say one thing and do another, and new systems increasingly allowed nearly instant shifts back to the core targeting that Washington had agreed was beyond change.

Arkin & Kristensen, *supra* note 13, at 30.

General George Lee Butler, who served as the Commander of the Strategic Air Command and hence as the Air Force general responsible for drafting the overall U.S. strategy for nuclear war, has reported being amazed "by how little high-level scrutiny [the U.S. nuclear war plan] had received over the years, and by how readily his military colleagues threw up their hands and rolled their eyes at the grim challenge of converting mathematical estimates of the destructiveness of nuclear arms and the resilience of Soviet structures into dry statistical formulas for nuclear war." R. Jeffrey Smith, *Ex-Commander of Nukes Wants to Scrap Them, A Believer No More*, THE SACRAMENTO BEE, Mar. 29, 1998. *See also* R. Jeffrey Smith, *The Dissenter*, THE WASHINGTON POST, Dec. 7, 1997, at Magazine, W18.

> "It was all Alice-in-Wonderland stuff," Butler says. The targeting data and other details of the war plan, which are written in an almost unfathomable million lines of computer software code, were typically reduced by military briefers to between 60 and 100 slides that could be presented in an hour or so to the handful of senior U.S. officials who were cleared to hear it. "Generally, no one at the briefings wanted to ask questions because they didn't want to embarrass themselves. It was about as unsatisfactory as could be imagined for that subject matter. The truth is that the president only had a superficial understanding" of what would happen in a nuclear war, Butler says. Congress knew even less because no lawmaker has ever had access to the war plan, and most academics could only make ill-informed guesses.

Id.

General Butler concluded that the plan had not been "tested against common sense" or military and scientific realities, concluding that the whole scheme could be chucked in favor of detonating warheads at even spaced intervals across Russian territory, and it would effectively produce the same catastrophic consequences for Russian society. *Id.*

General Butler further concluded that the plan depended on "heroic assumptions about the timing" of events, noting that the "President," warned of a Russian attack, would have some 10 minutes to decide how to respond. *Id.*

In terms of the level of communication of civilian policy and legal issues to the military, General Butler noted that, even as Commander of SAC, he had not been aware of the commitment the United States made years previously, in 1967, not to use nuclear arms first against nations that lacked them. *Id.*

destructiveness.[28] During the height of the Cold War, when the United States' nuclear weapons were clearly seen as the centerpiece of the United States' military posture, expenditures for nuclear weapons, at some $50 billion a year out of a total military budget of some $400 billion, represented a small portion of the United States' overall military budget.

In the wake of the World War II, as the Soviet Union came to be perceived as a serious and powerful antagonist, the United States had faced a central choice whether to maintain its mobilization and continue to build up its conventional weapons capability at great monetary cost, or, instead, to demobilize, modulate the conventional buildup, and rely upon the extraordinary fire power of nuclear weapons.

The decision was made to rely on nuclear weapons. The United States consciously permitted itself to fall into a position of conventional weapons inferiority vis-à-vis the Soviet Union, to the point where it was generally believed that the United States would not be able to defend itself and its allies against a Soviet conventional attack but rather would have to "go nuclear."[29]

Concomitantly with this growing reliance upon nuclear weapons, the United States strengthened and reinforced it commitment to the military defense of Western Europe against Soviet invasion. The crucial insight is that the United States specifically and consciously permitted itself, year after year, to fall into a position of convention weapons vulnerability vis-à-vis the Soviet Union and Western Europe, such that United States did not spend sufficient funds on conventional weapons, particularly anti-tank weapons, to stop a potential Soviet onslaught into Western Europe.[30] Instead, it placed some 6000–7000 tactical nuclear weapons in Western Europe.[31]

---

[28] *See* AMERICAN NATIONAL SECURITY: POLICY AND PROCESS 183–208 (Amos A. Jordon et al. eds., 1989).

[29] *See id.*

[30] *See* FREEDMAN, *supra* note 11, at 88. To reduce what was recognized as an over reliance on nuclear weapons, NATO at times attempted to match Soviet conventional capabilities. *Id.* The 1952 Lisbon force goals sought to match Soviet strength, calculated at about 170 divisions, with reserves doubling that. *Id.* The NATO forces were only able to reach 30 divisions, and tactical nuclear weapons were introduced to compensate for numerical inferiority. *Id.*

[31] *See* Spurgeon M. Keeny, Jr. & Wolfgang K. H. Panofsky, *MAD versus NUTS: Can Doctrine or Weaponry Remedy the Mutual Hostage Relationship of the Superpowers?* 60 FOREIGN AFF. 287, 296 (Winter 1981–1982). It is

Henry Kissinger has reflected upon the fact that the United States' failure to build up its conventional forces required it to rely upon nuclear weapons:

> It was a counsel of defeat to abjure both strategic and tactical nuclear forces, for no NATO country—including ours—was prepared to undertake the massive build-up of conventional forces that was the sole alternative. But what was "effective"? Given the political impossibility of raising adequate conventional forces, the Europeans saw nuclear weapons as the most effective deterrent.[32]

The extent to which the United States, and the West, generally permitted itself to be naked to Soviet aggression in Western Europe[33]

---

generally estimated that the United States possessed 20,000 tactical nuclear warheads in the early 1980s, with 6,000–7,000 deployed in Europe. *Id.*

See also LIMITED WAR: CONVENTIONAL AND NUCLEAR IN AMERICAN NATIONAL SECURITY (Amos A. Jordan et al. eds., 1989).

[32] *See* HENRY KISSINGER, WHITE HOUSE YEARS 218 (1979).

[33] *See, e.g.,* PAUL BRACKEN, THE COMMAND AND CONTROL OF NUCLEAR FORCES 9 (1983).

> Because of the large disparity in the ground forces of the Eastern and Western blocs in the late 1940s, all American war plans called for the immediate use of atomic weapons at the outbreak of another war. It was thought, reasonably enough, that the only way to halt an invasion of Western Europe was to destroy the Soviet armies before they could overrun the continent.

FREEDMAN, *supra* note 11, at 294.

British Secretary of State for Defense Duncan Sandys clearly stated Western strategy in 1958:

> The West, on the other hand, relies for its defense primarily upon the deterrent effect of its vast stockpile of nuclear weapons and its capacity to deliver them. The democratic Western nations will never start a war against Russia. But it must be well understood that, if Russia were to launch a major attack on them, even with conventional forces only, they would have to hit back with strategic nuclear weapons. In fact the strategy of NATO is based on the frank recognition that a full-scale Soviet attack could not be repelled without resort to a massive nuclear bombardment of the sources of power in Russia. In that event, the role of the allied defense forces in Europe would be to hold the front for the time needed to allow the effects of the nuclear counter-offensive to make themselves felt.

NSC-68, in AMERICAN DEFENSE POLICY 288 (Schuyler et al. eds., 1990). The classic American policy statement on the necessity of countering Soviet conventional superiority in Europe with American nuclear superiority is NSC-

was emphasized by retired American Admiral Gayler, former Director of the National Security Agency, in a hearing before the Congress in 1984, stating:

> We are expected to start a nuclear war which will probably result in the destruction of Europe and of ourselves rather than take simple, straightforward measures. The supply of the NATO countries is based on who gets the business.[34]

While the disparity in Central Europe between Western and Soviet conventional weapons capability differed over time and to some extent was a matter of debate at any particular time, its order of magnitude is indicated by the following statement of Ambassador Robert Blackwill, the U.S. representative to the Mutual and Balanced Force Reductions [MBFR] Negotiations:

> [T]here is the matter of the existing imbalance of conventional forces in Central Europe itself. According to Western estimates, the Warsaw Pact has over 200,000 more ground and air force personnel in the MGFR reductions area than does NATO. Achieving the Western goal of parity at lower manpower levels, which by definition requires that the East take significantly greater reductions than the West, runs into obvious difficulties, particularly

---

68, approved by President Truman in 1950 (no longer classified). The United States will not renounce the first-use of nuclear weapons given "our present situation of relative unpreparedness in conventional weapons." *Id.*

See Massive Retaliation, Address by Secretary of State John Foster Dulles to the Council on Foreign Relations, 12 Jan. 1954 (DEP'T ST. BULL., 25 Jan. 1954), *reprinted in* AMERICAN DEFENSE POLICY 294 (Schuyler et al. eds., 1990):

> Local defense will always be important. But there is no local defense which alone will contain the mighty land power of the Communist world. Local defenses must be reinforced by the further deterrent of massive retaliatory power. A potential aggressor must know that it cannot always prescribe battle conditions that suit it. Otherwise, for example, a potential aggressor, who is glutted with manpower, might be tempted to attack in confidence that resistance would be confined to manpower.

Id.

[34] Testimony of Adm. Noel Gayler, U.S. Navy (Retired), Former Commander in Chief, U.S. Forces in the Pacific, Former Director, National Security Agency, in Hearings on the Role of Arms Control in U.S. Defense Policy, before the Committee on Foreign Affairs, House of Representatives, Ninety-Eighth Congress, 2nd Sess., at 126 (June 20, 21, 26, July 25, 1984).

as the East claims that a balance of forces already exists in Central Europe.[35]

While the United States, as a result of the demise of the Soviet Union, the end of the Cold War and the consequent Nuclear Posture Review, has ostensibly de-emphasized nuclear weapons, the deterrent threat to use nuclear weapons—with its consequent need to maintain the nuclear equipment and personnel capability—continues, as I discuss in the next chapter.[36] So too does the nuclear training of American military personnel and the continued nuclear contingency planning as represented by SIOP.[37] The thinking may have changed or be in the process of changing at the top but for operational personnel, nuclear weapons remain operational equipment, and the overall process remains at best inchoate.[38]

The extent of the contemporary integration of nuclear weapons with conventional weapons can seen from not only from the high profile SIOP (which is at least ostensibly subject to Presidential oversight) but also from the U.S. military's own operational plans. An example is the *Joint Pub 3-12, Doctrine for Joint Nuclear Operations*, setting forth the

---

[35] Statement of Ambassador Robert Blackwill, U.S. Representative to the Mutual and Balanced Force Reductions [MBFR] Negotiations, before the Committee on Foreign Affairs, House of Representatives, 98th Cong., 2nd Sess., June 20, 21, 26, July 25, 1984, at 4.

[36] *See* Secretary of Defense William Perry & General John Shalikashvili, Chairman, Joint Chiefs of Staff, *Department of Defense Briefing.* After the 1994 Nuclear Posture Review, President Clinton signed Presidential Decision Directive, PDD-31, outlining U.S. strategic nuclear policy until the early 21st century. The directive concluded that the U.S. would maintain the nuclear triad for the foreseeable future, while ordering some reduction in alert levels and new safety features. Secretary of Defense Perry stated that the Nuclear Posture Review resulted in a new American nuclear policy and strategic nuclear posture: "[I]t is no longer based on Mutual Assured Destruction, no longer based on MAD. We have coined a new term for our new posture which we call Mutual Assured Safety, or MAS." *Id.* MAS is based on the twin goals of "leading" and "hedging:" The U.S. would lead in further reducing nuclear weapons, but hedge against a ultranationalist reversal of reform in Russia by maintaining its ability to rebuild and reconstitute nuclear forces quickly and by keeping some nuclear forces on Cold War–style alerts. In addition, MAS seeks to improve safety and security for the remaining nuclear forces inherent in the reduction of nuclear forces and in the improved technology in achieving safety and security. *See id.*

[37] *See* Ball & Toth, *supra* note 11, at 85–92.

[38] *See* WILLIAM J. PERRY, SECRETARY OF DEFENSE, 1996 ANNUAL REPORT TO THE PRESIDENT AND THE CONGRESS 213–15.

contemporary operational planning of the military for the integrated use by U.S. forces of nuclear weapons in conjunction with conventional weapons.[39]

Not a theoretical doctrine requiring further input from the White House or the Pentagon, or further authorization of any kind, this *Joint Nuclear Operations* manual "provides guidelines for the joint employment of forces in nuclear operations ... sets forth doctrine to govern the joint activities and performance of the Armed Forces of the United States in joint operations ... for the exercise of authority by combatant commander."[40] The manual also states that "[t]he guidance in this publication is authoritative; as such, this doctrine (or JTTP) will be followed except when, in the judgment of the commander, exceptional circumstances dictate otherwise"[41]—so that it is a living document reflecting the formulation of the mindset of the U.S. military as to the potential use of nuclear weapons.

As to the significance of this manual, the manual provides: "If conflicts arise between the contents of this publication and the contents of Service publications [presumably, the publications of any one service], this publication will take precedence unless the Chairman of the Joint Chiefs of Staff, normally in consultation with other members

---

[39] *See* JOINT CHIEFS OF STAFF, JOINT PUB 3-12, DOCTRINE FOR JOINT NUCLEAR OPERATIONS, (Dec. 15, 1995) <http://www.dtic.mil/doctrine/jel/new_pubs/jp3_12.pdf> [hereinafter DOCTRINE FOR JOINT NUCLEAR OPERATIONS].

[40] *Id.* at i, v–ix. The manual states that "[t]he decision to employ nuclear weapons at any level requires the explicit decision of the President." *Id.* at II-1 (emphasis omitted). The manual further notes the extensive authority of the combat commanders in the matter:

- Geographic combatant commanders are responsible for defining theater objectives, selecting targets, and developing plans required to support those objectives. Detailed mission planning, when required, is generally accomplished at the theater combatant commander level, with US Strategic Command assistance where appropriate. Combatant commanders may also be tasked to develop adaptively planned options to strike previously unidentified targets. Because the strike is meant to be decisive, it takes precedence over other missions.
- After conflicts occurs, combatant commanders may also be tasked to develop adaptively planned options to strike targets not previously identified. Nuclear weapons planning is continuous and is fully integrated with planning for conventional weapons.

Id. at III-4 (emphasis omitted).

[41] *Id.* at i.

of the Joint Chiefs of Staff, has provided more current and specific guidance."[42]

As to U.S. nuclear strategy, the manual broadly performs the usual dance that, while "nuclear forces have been developed, deployed, and maintained for the purpose of deterring large-scale aggression against the United States and its allies,"[43] such deterrence requires "creditable and capable nuclear forces."[44] While deterrence is founded in "real force capabilities" and requires the United States to maintain "military forces ... capable of achieving U.S. national objectives throughout the operational continuum," it also requires "the national determination to use those forces if necessary."[45]

Thus, these weapons are intended for actual use—and, indeed, for interim, low level use, the so-called "intra-war" deterrence: "[S]hould deterrence fail, forces of all types (both conventional and nuclear) must be structured, deployed, and ready to provide a variety of options."[46]

The manual clearly assumes the possible use of low level nuclear weapons, and assumes the potential operational viability of such an approach: "A selective capability of being able to use lower-yield weapons in retaliation, without destabilizing the conflict is a useful alternative for the US National Command Authorities (NCA)."[47] Nuclear "war-fighting" theory is alive and well in U.S. military planning.

Thus, the military's operational planning, training, and educational mindset ostensibly is that nuclear weapons are useable—and that it is their job to use them to win wars. As I discuss in the final chapters, this operational mindset and related operational planning are major risk factors affecting how events are likely to unfold in the time and adrenaline pressures of a major crisis. What a politician or a professor writes is perhaps interesting as to what U.S. policy should be; but these planning documents tell us what the military are planning—and hence are likely—to do.

The operational policy of the U.S. military is to "link" U.S. nuclear and conventional weapons:

> Nuclear forces deployed to or tasked to support theater nuclear requirements link conventional forces to the full nuclear capability

---

[42] *Id.*
[43] *Id.* at I-1 (emphasis omitted).
[44] *Id.* (emphasis omitted).
[45] *Id.* at I-2 (emphasis omitted).
[46] *Id.* (emphasis omitted).
[47] *Id.* at I-3 (emphasis omitted).

of the US. This linkage must be strong and visible to the extent of being capable of deterring a potential enemy from believing political and/or military advantage can be achieved by means of threats to employ nuclear, biological, or chemical weapons or by the threatened or actual execution of an all-out conventional offensive.[48]

The integration of nuclear with conventional weapons is also clear from the U.S. military's manual *Doctrine for Joint Theater Nuclear Operations*:

> For nuclear employment to be successful, advanced planning and integration are essential.[49]
>
> ***
>
> Units capable of delivering nuclear weapons should be integrated with other forces in a combined arms, joint approach.[50]
>
> ***
>
> Nuclear operations planning should be integrated into operations plans to maximize effects needed to achieve the CINC's desired objectives.[51]

The manual further makes it clear that the decision on which weapons to use—conventional or nuclear—is to be made in light of the "relative effectiveness"[52] of the two types of weapons, and individual weapons, subject to the requirement that the nuclear weapons, "offer a significant advantage:"[53]

> Advanced planning is critical to the successful use of nuclear weapons. Planners should consider the level of effort required for conventional targeting, the length of time that a target must be kept out of action, logistical support and anticipation of delays, the effect on all forces, and any national and theater level constraints.[54]

The manual identifies the following additional factors as ones the local commander should consider in deciding on targeting, defined as

---

[48] *Id.* at III-2 (emphasis omitted).

[49] JOINT CHIEFS OF STAFF, JOINT PUB 3-12.1, DOCTRINE FOR JOINT THEATER NUCLEAR OPERATIONS vii (Feb. 9, 1996) (prepared under direction of the Chairman of the Joint Chiefs of Staff) (emphasis omitted), set forth at <http://www.dtic.mil/doctrine/jel/new_pubs/jp3_12_1.pdf>.

[50] *Id.* at I-2 (emphasis omitted).

[51] *Id.* at III-1.

[52] *Id.* at viii.

[53] *Id.*

[54] *Id.* at viii (emphasis omitted).

the "process of selecting targets and matching the appropriate response to them:"[55]

> Geographic combatant commanders should consider the following factors in determining how to defeat the individual targets composing the overall threat: inability of friendly forces to destroy targets using conventional means, number and type of individual targets, vulnerability of targets, required level of damage for each target, optimum timing, enemy's ability to reconstitute, avoidance of collateral damage, and environmental conditions.[56]

The manual further states that "command guidance" should be provided early in the planning process as to such matters as "desired results [of use of nuclear weapons], circumstances leading to the request for nuclear execution, and the delivery systems available."[57]

This integration of nuclear weapons into the military mindset cannot fail materially to raise the likelihood of escalation on the American side[58]—and, of course, the other nuclear powers are subject to the same influences.[59]

---

[55] *Id.*

[56] *Id.*

[57] *Id.* at ix (emphasis omitted).

[58] *See* ROBERT JERVIS, THE ILLOGIC OF AMERICAN NUCLEAR STRATEGY at 158–59 (1984):

> Alert procedures, like the military organizations that produce them, are so large and complex that the details are beyond the comprehension and memory of any individual. It is unlikely that even well-informed generals and admirals, let alone the civilian decision makers, know exactly what the orders call for .... Thus when they recall the 1962 and 1973 alerts, key officials, even those who were close to the military activity, acknowledge that they knew only the general outlines of what their forces would do. ... As a result, it is quite likely that actions carried out in the name of the state during a nuclear crisis would be more provocative than those intended by the top leadership and the leaders would be unaware of what had happened. This may have been the case, for example, during the Cuban missile crisis, when Kennedy and his advisers apparently did not know of many of the navy's aggressive tactics.

Id.

[59] *See id.*

Chapter 18: Revised U.S. Strategic Policy in the Post Cold War Era: The Nuclear Posture Review—And Related Risk Factors

In 1994 the Pentagon completed the "Nuclear Posture Review," an overall review of American nuclear policy designed to determine the appropriate role of nuclear weapons in U.S. security in the post-Cold War era.[1] This Review, while supporting the continuing role of nuclear weapons for deterrence, concluded:

- that nuclear weapons are far less important to U.S. security than in the past; and
- that nuclear weapons have themselves become the primary enemy.[2]

As to the reduced role of nuclear weapons, the Nuclear Posture Review concluded that "nuclear weapons are playing a smaller role in U.S. security than at any other time in the nuclear age"[3] and that the United States "requires a much smaller nuclear arsenal under present circumstances."[4] In his description of the Nuclear Posture Review, Secretary of Defense Perry stated:

> U.S. nuclear weapons were for years justified by the potential for a massive conventional attack by the Warsaw Pact through the Fulda Gap which would overwhelm NATO conventional forces. The subsequent decision of the members of the Warsaw Pact to dissolve their alliance and the subsequent transformation of the Soviet Union into independent States removed this potential threat. No equivalent threat to American vital interests can be identified in the post-Cold War era, and for very few of the existing threats are nuclear weapons appropriate responses.[5]

---

[1] *See* WILLIAM J. PERRY, SECRETARY OF DEFENSE, 1995 ANNUAL REPORT TO THE PRESIDENT AND THE CONGRESS 83 (U.S. Government Printing Office) [hereinafter 1995 REPORT OF THE SECRETARY OF DEFENSE].

[2] *See id.* at 7, 10, 26, 32, 84–86, 163. The Nuclear Posture Review further suggested that, should deterrence fail, the United States' nuclear weapons might be used to respond to aggression. *Id.* at 86.

[3] *See id.* at 83.

[4] *See id.*

[5] *Id.* at 84–85. Secretary Perry further stated: "Although nuclear capabilities are now a far smaller part of the routine U.S. international presence, they remain an important element in the array of military capabilities that the United States can bring to bear, either independently or in concert with

Secretary Perry further stated that "[i]n contrast to World War II and the Cold War, most of the current and foreseeable threats to [U.S. interests] do not threaten the survival of the United States."[6]

Noting that more than 25 countries possess or are developing nuclear, chemical, or biological weapons and more than 15 countries have ballistic missiles, the Nuclear Posture Review concluded that "proliferation of nuclear weapons and other weapons of mass destruction, rather than the nuclear arsenal of a hostile superpower, poses the greatest security risk."[7]

The extent to which the weapons had become the enemy was evident from stated contemporary strategic concerns of the Pentagon: controlling and reducing nuclear weapons in Russia and dismantling and removing the nuclear weapons in Ukraine, Kazakhstan, and Belarus;[8] hedging against a renewed nuclear threat from Russia;[9] controlling the risk that nuclear materials, equipment and know-how could leak through the "porous" former Soviet Union borders to other nations;[10] hedging against an increased nuclear capability of China;[11] dealing with threats by potential adversaries to acquire or use nuclear and other weapons of mass destruction and their means of delivery;[12] and dealing with risks of loss or theft of fissile material or non deployed nuclear warheads.[13]

Secretary Perry reported that the United States now focused its planning on the simultaneous fighting of two major regional conflicts rather than on the Cold War model of global war with the Soviet Union centered on the defense of Western Europe.[14] He concluded there is a "high probability" that aggressors in such regional conflicts wars would "threaten, wield, or use" weapons of mass destruction (nuclear, biological, and chemical weapons): "Almost anywhere the United States is likely to deploy forces around the world—Northeast Asia, the Persian Gulf, the Middle East, and Europe—states are likely to have

---

allies to deter war, or should deterrence fail, to defeat aggression." *Id.* at 84. He made it clear that deterrence is still "central to the U.S. nuclear posture." *Id.*

   [6] *See id.* at 14.
   [7] *See id.* at 85.
   [8] *See id.* at 25.
   [9] *See id.* at 163.
   [10] *See id.* at 25.
   [11] *See id.* at 163.
   [12] *See id.*
   [13] *See id.* at 91.
   [14] *See id.* at 71.

[weapons of mass destruction]."[15] He emphasized the severity of the implications of the proliferation of nuclear and other weapons of mass destruction:

> The combination of WMD with theater ballistic missiles poses a unique threat to managing future regional crises. ... [W]ith WMD, even small-scale theater ballistic missile threats would raise dramatically the potential costs and risks of military operations, undermining conventional superiority and threatening the credibility of U.S. regional security strategy.[16]
>
> ***
>
> Weapons of mass destruction in the hands of a hostile regional power could threaten not only U.S. lives and U.S. interests but also the viability of its regional power projection strategy.[17]

It was evident from the results of the Nuclear Posture Review that the strategic interests of the United States as to nuclear weapons had shifted. During the Cold War, the United States had a conventional weapons inferiority vis-à-vis the Soviets and resorted to nuclear weapons to redress the balance.[18] Suddenly, the United States had conventional weapons superiority potentially and was itself facing the threat of nuclear weapons from nations otherwise militarily inferior.

Secretary Perry, in describing the Nuclear Posture Review, pointed out that since 1988 the United States had been engaged in a dramatic

---

[15] *Id.* at 71.

[16] *Id.* at 240.

[17] *Id.* at 25.

[18] *See NSC-68 in* AMERICAN DEFENSE POLICY 288 (Schuyler et al. eds., 1990). Per NSC-68, the classic American policy statement on the necessity of countering Soviet conventional superiority in Europe with American nuclear superiority approved by President Truman in 1950, the United States would not renounce the first-use of nuclear weapons given its "present situation of relative unpreparedness in conventional weapons." *Id.*

See also LAWRENCE FREEDMAN, THE EVOLUTION OF NUCLEAR STRATEGY 71 (1989). Under NSC-68, "[u]ntil conventional forces had been built up, the United States had no choice but to rely on its nuclear arsenal, and extend its breathing space by maintaining, for as long as possible, a clear superiority in nuclear capabilities over the Soviet Union. The imbalance in conventional capabilities meant that the United States was not even able to hold back nuclear weapons as a last resort." *Id. Cf.* Gaddis, John Lewis, and Paul Nitze, *NSC 68 and the Soviet Threat Reconsidered*, INT'L SECURITY, vol. 4, no. 4, Spring 1980, at 164–176.

Secretary of State John Foster Dulles, *Massive Retaliation* (Address to the Council on Foreign Relations, 12 Jan. 1954 (DEP'T ST. BULL., 25 Jan. 1954) *in* AMERICAN DEFENSE POLICY 294 (Schuyler et al. eds., 1990).

downsizing of its nuclear arsenal: Strategic warheads had been cut by 59% and non strategic forces by 90%.[19] The tactical nuclear posture the U.S. maintained in Western Europe and throughout the world during the Cold War had been sharply curtailed. Nuclear weapons had been taken from the custody of U.S. ground forces.[20] The Army and the Marines had been de-nuclearized: they no longer had any nuclear weapons.[21] The Navy no longer deployed non-strategic nuclear weapons and the Air Force had dramatically cut its tactical nuclear stockpile.[22] Nuclear weapons storage locations had been reduced by over 75%[23] and the number of personnel with access to nuclear weapons had been cut by 70%.[24] Some 15 nuclear weapons programs had been eliminated, truncated or never fielded[25] and no new strategic nuclear systems were either under development or planned.[26] Since the end of the Cold War, the United States professedly had reduced nuclear programs expenditures from $50 billion to some $15 billion per year.[27]

Quoting Albert Einstein's insight that we have changed everything except the way we think, Secretary Perry stated, "Now it's time to change the way we think about nuclear weapons, and the Nuclear Posture Review was conceived to do just that.[28]

The Secretary of Defense emphasized the Pentagon's increased efforts to develop conventional weapons to counter the potential use of nuclear or other weapons of mass destruction by an adversary:

---

[19] *See* 1995 REPORT OF THE SECRETARY OF DEFENSE, *supra* note 1, at 91. The strategic stockpile was expected to be reduced by 79% by 2003. *Id.* at 86.

[20] *See id.* at 86; Chart presented as part of Secretary of State Perry, Chairman, Joint Chiefs of Staff General John Shalikashvili, & Deputy Secretary of Defense Deutch, *Department of Defense Briefing*, FEDERAL NEWS SERVICE, Washington, September 22, 1994; Statement of Dr. Deutch.

[21] September 20, 1994 speech of Secretary of Defense William J. Perry at the Henry L. Stimson Center.

[22] *See id.*

[23] *See* 1995 REPORT OF THE SECRETARY OF DEFENSE, *supra* note 1, at 86.

[24] *See id.* at 86.

[25] *See id.* at 86.

[26] *See id.* at 87.

[27] *See id.* at 10. *See also* Secretary Perry stated, "I want to ... emphasize that there's been a 70 recent reduction in the amount of money we're spending on nuclear weapons, from the height of the Cold War to the program period we're talking about here, as well as a 70 percent reduction in the personnel who are concerned with nuclear weapons." *Department of Defense Briefing*, *supra* note 20.

[28] *See id.*

Moreover, the CPI [Counter Proliferation Initiative] has as its central tenet the creation and furtherance of conventional responses to the threat or use of weapons of mass destruction. Far from inventing new roles for nuclear weapons in countering WMD [weapons of mass destruction], the NPR supports the CPI, because in a potential case of WMD threat or use, senior political and military leaders must have a wide range of responses—especially non-nuclear—from which to choose. Having the conventional capability to respond to WMD threat or use further reduces U.S. dependence on nuclear weapons.[29]

Secretary Perry stated that the Nuclear Posture Review resulted in a new American nuclear policy and strategic nuclear posture: "[I]t is no longer based on Mutual Assured Destruction, no longer based on MAD. We have coined a new term for our new posture which we call Mutual Assured Safety, or MAS."[30] MAS is based on the twin goals of "leading" and "hedging."[31] According to Perry, under this policy, the U.S. will lead in further reducing nuclear weapons, but hedge against an ultranationalist reversal of reform in Russia by maintaining its ability to rebuild and reconstitute its nuclear forces quickly and by keeping some nuclear forces on Cold War-style alerts.[32] In addition, MAS seeks to improve safety and security for the remaining nuclear forces inherent in the reduction of nuclear forces and in the improved technology in achieving safety and security.[33]

In his March 1996 Annual Report to the President and Congress, Secretary Perry stated:

Although emphasis has shifted in the post-Cold War period from global, possibly nuclear war to regional conflicts, strategic nuclear deterrence remains a key U.S. military priority. The mission of U.S. strategic nuclear forces is to deter attacks on the United States or its allies and to convince potential adversaries that seeking nuclear advantage would be futile. To do this, the United States must maintain nuclear forces of sufficient size and capability to hold at risk a broad range of assets valued by potentially hostile foreign nations. The two basic requirements that guide U.S.

---

[29] 1995 REPORT OF THE SECRETARY OF DEFENSE, *supra* note 1, at 85. The United States' success in the Gulf War, as discussed *infra* Chapter 28, at notes 23, 30, and the accompanying text, have been taken as confirmation of the increased efficacy of today's conventional weapons.

[30] *See id.*

[31] *See id.*

[32] *See id.*

[33] *See id.*

planning for strategic nuclear forces therefore are: the need to provide an effective deterrent while conforming to treaty-imposed arms limitations, and the need to be able to reconstitute adequate additional forces in a timely manner if conditions require.[34]

This position was reiterated by Under Secretary Walter Slocombe in testimony before the International Security, Proliferation and Federal Services Subcommittee of the Senate Governmental Affairs Committee on February 12, 1997:

> For the foreseeable future, we will continue to need a reliable and flexible nuclear deterrent, survivable against the most aggressive attack, under highly confident constitutional command and control, and assured in its safety against both accidental and unauthorized use. We need such a force because nuclear deterrence, far from being made wholly obsolete, remains an essential, ultimate assurance against the gravest of threats. A key conclusion of the administration's national security strategy, released just a year ago, is that "The United States will retain a triad of strategic nuclear forces sufficient to deter any future hostile foreign leadership with access to strategic nuclear forces from acting against our vital interests, and to convince [it] that seeking a nuclear advantage would be futile. Therefore, we will continue to maintain nuclear forces of sufficient size and capability to hold at risk a broad range of assets valued by such political leaders."[35]

The Secretary of Defense's May 1997 report on the Nuclear Weapons Systems Sustainment Programs, updated in June 1998, designed to provide for the sustainment of U.S. efforts in the contemporary strategic environment of downsizing, stated that not only has testing been stopped but also no new nuclear weapons or new strategic delivery systems are in development.[36]

The report stated that, pursuant to the National Security Strategy of the United States, the President has defined the key tasks to be accomplished as follows:

---

[34] *See* WILLIAM J. PERRY, SECRETARY OF DEFENSE, 1996 ANNUAL REPORT TO THE PRESIDENT AND THE CONGRESS (U.S. Government Printing Office 1996), *quoted in* Office of the Secretary of Defense, NUCLEAR WEAPONS SYSTEMS SUSTAINMENT PROGRAMS (updated, 16 Jun 1998), <http://www.defenselink.mil/pubs/dswa/>).

[35] Statement of Under Secretary Walter Slocombe in testimony before the International Security, Proliferation and Federal Services Subcommittee of the Senate Governmental Affairs Committee on February 12, 1997, *quoted in* NUCLEAR WEAPONS SYSTEMS SUSTAINMENT PROGRAMS, *supra* note 34.

[36] *Id.*

• Maintain robust strategic nuclear forces.

• Retain the capability to respond forcefully and effectively and, where appropriate, overwhelmingly, against those who might contemplate the use of weapons of mass destruction so that the costs of such use will be seen as outweighing the gains.

• Develop improved defensive and offensive capabilities. To minimize the impact of proliferation of weapons of mass destruction on our interests, we will need the capability not only to deter their use against either ourselves or our allies and friends but also to successfully operate through WMD use and also, where necessary and feasible, to prevent it.[37]

The report further referred to the contemporary strategic environment as one in which "nuclear deterrent capabilities will continue to be important, but not receive the high level of emphasis prevalent during the Cold War."[38]

As recently as the summer of 1998, U.S. Secretary of Defense William S. Cohen, addressing environmental concerns, noted that the effort now is towards getting rid of systems designed during the Cold War to inflict horrific damage.[39]

Recent statements of U.S. policy have further confirmed the extent to which nuclear deterrence is today directed against a potential adversary's nuclear as opposed to conventional assets and aspirations. John M. Shalikashvili, Chairman of the Joint Chiefs of Staff, in his 1997 document titled "The National Military Strategy," defined the United States' deterrence policy as follows:

> The critical elements of deterrence are our conventional warfighting capabilities: forces and equipment strategically positioned, our capacity to rapidly project and concentrate military power worldwide; our ability to form and lead effective military coalitions; and our capacity to protect our homeland, forces, and critical infrastructure from the full range of potential threats. Our strategic nuclear forces complement our conventional capabilities by deterring any hostile foreign leadership with access to nuclear weapons from acting against our vital interests. Our nuclear forces may also serve to convince such leaders that attempting to seek a nuclear advantage would be futile.[40]

---

[37] *Id.*

[38] *Id.*

[39] Secretary William S. Cohen, *Speech to Coalition to Advance Sustainable Technology*, at Denver International Airport, Denver, Colo., June 26, 1998.

[40] JOHN M. SHALIKASHVILI, CJCS, NATIONAL MILITARY STRATEGY: SHAPE, RESPOND, PREPARE NOW—A MILITARY STRATEGY FOR A NEW ERA (1997),

As to the military purpose of nuclear weapons, President Clinton, in his 1998 legislatively mandated[41] annual National Security Strategy, reflected the assumption that such weapons are intended not for actual use in combat but rather to deter, and, specifically, to deter nuclear attack:

> Our nuclear deterrent posture is one of the most visible and important examples of how U.S. military capabilities can be used effectively to deter aggression and coercion, as reaffirmed in a Presidential Decision directive signed by President Clinton in November 1997. Nuclear weapons serve as a hedge against an uncertain future, a guarantee of our security commitments to allies and a disincentive to those who would contemplate developing or otherwise acquiring their own nuclear weapons. Our military planning for the possible employment of U.S. nuclear weapons is focused on deterring a nuclear war rather than attempting to fight

---

<http://www.dtic.mil/jcs/nms>. [hereinafter National Military Strategy, 1997]. The National Military Strategy states that it sets forth the advice of the Chairman of the Joint Chiefs in consultation with the Joint Chiefs of Staff and the Combatant Commanders on the strategic direction of the Armed Forces over the next three to five years, within the general parameters of the President's 1997 National Security Strategy and the Quadrennial Defense Review report prepared by the Secretary of Defense. *See id.*

The U.S. leadership (in a point that, as we shall see, is potentially controversial) has also at times characterized nuclear weapons as a hedge against the proliferation of biological and chemical as well as nuclear weapons. Secretary Cohen in his Report of the Quadrennial Defense Review in May 1997 stated:

> Our nuclear posture also contributes substantially to our ability to deter aggression in peacetime. The primary role of U.S. nuclear forces in the current and projected security environment is to deter aggression against the United States, its forces abroad, and its allies and friends. Although the prominence of nuclear weapons in our defense posture has diminished since the end of the Cold War, nuclear weapons remain important as a hedge against NBC proliferation and the uncertain futures of existing nuclear powers, and as a means of upholding our security commitments to allies.
>
> In this context, the United States must retain strategic nuclear forces sufficient to deter any hostile foreign leadership with access to nuclear weapons from acting against our vital interests and to convince such a leadership that seeking a nuclear advantage would be futile.

WILLIAM S. COHEN, REPORT OF THE QUADRENNIAL DEFENSE REVIEW, May 1997, § III, Defense Strategy, <http://www.fas.org/man/docsqdr/sec3.html>.

[41] *See* 50 U.S.C.S. §404(a) (1999).

and win a protracted nuclear exchange. We continue to emphasize the survivability of the nuclear systems and infrastructure necessary to endure a preemptive attack and still respond at overwhelming levels.[42]

Reflecting the focus on strategic rather than tactical weapons, President Clinton stated:

> The United States must continue to maintain a robust triad of strategic forces sufficient to deter any hostile foreign leadership with access to nuclear forces and to convince it that seeking a nuclear advantage would be futile.[43]

Secretary of Defense Cohen in his 1998 Report to Congress, in a restatement of U.S. nuclear deterrence doctrine, similarly reflected this emphasis on strategic rather than tactical weapons, although the statement ostensibly leaves room for tactical use:

> The new directive notes that nuclear weapons play a smaller role in the U.S. security posture today than they have at any point during the second half of the 20th century, but that nuclear weapons are still needed as a hedge against an uncertain future, as a guarantee of U.S. security commitments to allies, and as a disincentive to those who would contemplate developing or otherwise acquiring their own nuclear weapons. Accordingly, the United States will maintain survivable strategic nuclear forces of sufficient size and diversity to deter any hostile foreign leadership with access to nuclear weapons.
>
> The new directive provides a large measure of continuity with previous nuclear weapons employment guidance, including in particular the following three principles:
>
> • Deterrence is predicated on ensuring that potential adversaries accept that any use of nuclear weapons against the United States or its allies would not succeed.
>
> • A wide range of nuclear retaliatory options will continue to be planned to ensure the United States is not left with an all-or-nothing response.
>
> • The United States will not rely on a launch-on-warning nuclear retaliation strategy (although an adversary could never be sure the United States would not launch a counterattack before the adversary's nuclear weapons arrived).[44]

---

[42] PRESIDENT WILLIAM J. CLINTON, A NATIONAL SECURITY STRATEGY FOR A NEW CENTURY 12 (The White House, Oct. 1998).

[43] *Id.*

[44] WILLIAM S. COHEN, 1998 ANNUAL REPORT TO THE PRESIDENT AND CONGRESS, Chap. 5, Strategic Nuclear Forces, <http://www.dtic.mil/execsec/>

The Secretary of Defense's 1999 report further emphasized the point:

> Nuclear forces are an essential element of U.S. security that serve as a hedge against an uncertain future and as a guarantee of U.S. commitments to allies. Accordingly, the United States must maintain survivable strategic nuclear forces of sufficient size and diversity to deter potentially hostile foreign leaders with access to nuclear weapons.[45]

The 1999 report further stated:

> Strategic forces remain a critical element of the U.S. policy of deterrence. Although U.S. nuclear forces have been reduced substantially in size and the percentage of the defense budget devoted to them has been greatly reduced as well, strategic forces continue to provide a credible and a highly valuable deterrent.[46]

Although the policy of deterrence has not been abandoned, our national leadership has repeatedly recognized that nuclear weapons themselves, rather than any particular adversary or group of adversaries, today pose the greatest threat to our security. President Clinton is his 1998 National Security Strategy stated:

> • Spread of dangerous technologies: Weapons of mass destruction pose the greatest potential threat to global stability and security. Proliferation of advanced weapons and technologies threatens to provide rogue states, terrorists and international crime organizations the means to inflict terrible damage on the United States, its allies and U.S. citizens and troops abroad. We must continue to deter and be prepared to counter the use or threatened

---

[hereinafter 1998 ANNUAL REPORT OF THE SECRETARY OF DEFENSE]. "Launch-on-warning" is a strategic doctrine calling for the launch of missiles or the dispatching of bombers upon receipt of warning (generally from satellites or other early-detection systems) that a missile attack is underway; it calls for quick, potentially even knee jerk, response before sustaining the hit or even necessarily confirming that the attack is underway. *See* Louis Rene Beres, *After the "Peace Process;" Israel, Palestine, and Regional Nuclear War,* 15 DICK. J. INT'L L. 301, 302 (Winter 1997).

[45] WILLIAM S. COHEN, 1999 ANNUAL REPORT OF THE SECRETARY OF DEFENSE, at Chap. 6, Strategic Nuclear Forces and Missile Defenses, <http://www.dtic.mil/execsec/> [hereinafter 1999 ANNUAL REPORT OF THE SECRETARY OF DEFENSE].

[46] *Id.*

use of WMD, reduce the threat posed by existing arsenals of such weaponry and halt the smuggling of nuclear materials.[47]

In that same National Security Strategy, President Clinton further stated:

> Potential enemies, whether nations, terrorist groups or criminal organizations, are increasingly likely to attack U.S. territory and the American people in unconventional ways. Adversaries will be tempted to disrupt our critical infrastructures, impede continuity of government operations, use weapons of mass destruction against civilians in our cities, attack us when we gather at special events and prey on our citizens overseas.[48]

The limited value of nuclear weapons in deterring such unconventional attacks is evident. In his 1998 National Security Strategy, President Clinton stated:

> While our overall deterrence posture—nuclear and conventional— has been effective against most potential adversaries, a range of terrorist and criminal organization may not be deterred by traditional deterrent threats. For these actors to be deterred, they must believe that any type of attack against the United States or its citizens will be attributed to them and that we will respond effectively and decisively to protect our national interests and ensure that justice is done.[49]

Secretary of Defense Cohen has defined this new kind of "asymmetric" threat as one where an enemy does not seek to become more powerful than the United States, as had the Soviet Union, but rather uses unconventional means "to offset, rather than try to match America's military strengths. Asymmetric threats include threatened or actual use of nuclear, biological and chemical weapons; terrorism; and disruption."[50] "The proliferation of nuclear biological and chemical (NBC) weapons and the missiles that can deliver them pose a major threat to the security of the United States, its allies, and friendly nations."[51]

---

[47] PRESIDENT WILLIAM J. CLINTON, A NATIONAL SECURITY STRATEGY FOR A NEW CENTURY 6 (The White House, October 1998).

[48] *Id.* at 7.

[49] *Id.* at 12.

[50] *Prepared Statement of Secretary of Defense William S. Cohen to the Senate Armed Forces Committee,* Feb. 3, 1998 *set forth at* <http://www.dtic. mil/execsec/>.

[51] 1999 ANNUAL REPORT OF THE SECRETARY OF DEFENSE, *supra* note 45.

The December 1997 Report of the National Defense Panel made the point explicitly that traditional nuclear deterrence does not address today's dominant security threat:

> Traditional U.S. nuclear policies may not be sufficient to deter nuclear, chemical, or biological attacks by a rogue state against U.S. allies and coalition partners or forward bases and staging areas to which we seek access. It is unlikely, moreover, that our nuclear forces would deter nonstate actors (terrorists, criminals, or others) who seek to coerce or punish the United States or its allies.[52]

Explicitly making the point implicit in the repeated recognition by the U.S. senior civilian and military leadership that nuclear weapons have themselves become the primary security threat, the National Defense Panel in its 1997 report noted that the doctrine of deterrence as the United States' dominant nuclear policy is being supplanted by a new policy of preventing proliferation:

> Over time, the focus of our efforts to deter nuclear or conventional attacks against the United States, its allies, and interests may differ substantially from that of today. Deterrence of attack as the central focus of nuclear policy is already being supplanted by the need to manage—identify, account for, and safeguard against—the proliferation and possible use of nuclear and other weapons of mass destruction.[53]

The U.S. military, in its nuclear weapons planning, has specifically recognized that, while U.S. nuclear weapons are largely intended for deterrence, there is no assurance that deterrence will work and indeed a substantial risk that in the exigencies of confrontation, enemies specifically will not be subject to deterrence. The military have also recognized the fact that the effectiveness of deterrence depends upon "cultural" factors.

---

[52] NATIONAL DEFENSE PANEL, TRANSFORMING DEFENSE: NATIONAL SECURITY IN THE 21ST CENTURY 51 (Dec. 1997) (available at <http://www.dtic.mil/ndp/>).

No everyone agrees as to the extent to which rogue States are subject to deterrence. Jeane J. Kirkpatrick, the United States delegate to the United Nations under President Reagan, stated in October 1999, in the context of her opposition to the Comprehensive Test Ban Treaty, "[The U.S.] deterrent has never been as important to the security of Americans as it is today with rogue states developing the capacity to attack our cities and our population." Eric Schmitt, *50's Riddle Returns in Treaty Debate: Do Weapons Controls Erode or Enhance U.S. Deterrence?*, THE NEW YORK TIMES, Oct. 10, 1999, at A10.

[53] NATIONAL DEFENSE PANEL, *supra* note 52, at 50 (emphasis omitted).

This can be seen from *Joint Pub 3-12, Doctrine for Joint Nuclear Operations*, setting forth the operational planning of the military as of 1995 for the integrated use by U.S. forces of nuclear weapons in conjunction with conventional weapons:

> The political leadership of an opposing nation is the central object of deterrence, because that is where the ultimate decision to use military force lies. ... Deterrence of the employment of enemy WMD, whether it be nuclear, biological, or chemical, requires that the enemy leadership believes the United States has both the ability and will to respond promptly and with selective responses that are credible (commensurate with the scale or scope of enemy attacks and the nature of US interests at stake) and militarily effective. Any deterrence assumes an opposing nation's political leadership will act according to the logic of national self-interest, although this self-interest will be viewed through differing cultural perspectives and dictates of given situation.[54]

The manual further notes:

> Although nations possessing WMD have largely refrained from using them, their continuing proliferation and the means to deliver them increases the possibility that someday a nation may, through miscalculation or by deliberate choice, employ these weapons. This assumption does not rule out the possibility that an opponent may be willing to risk destruction or disproportionate loss in following a course of action based on perceived necessity, whether rational or not in a totally objective sense. In such cases deterrence, even based on the threat of massive destruction, may fail.[55]

The Nuclear Weapons Operations manual also notes the risk of misperception as fueling the possible failure of deterrence:

> The mix [of U.S. nuclear and conventional] forces must be capable of holding at risk those assets most valued by enemy leaders and providing a range of options in response to attack. It is possible, however, that an adversary may misperceive or purposefully ignore a credible threat. Therefore, should deterrence fail, forces of all types (both conventional and nuclear) must be structured, deployed, and ready to provide a variety of options designed to control

---

[54] JOINT CHIEFS OF STAFF, JOINT PUB 3-12, DOCTRINE FOR JOINT NUCLEAR OPERATIONS I-2 (Dec. 15, 1995) <http://www.dtic.mil/doctrine/jel/new_pubs/jp3_12.pdf> (prepared under direction of the Chairman of the Joint Chiefs of Staff) (emphasis omitted).
[55] *Id.* at I-2 (emphasis omitted).

escalation and terminate the conflict on terms favorable to the United States and its allies.[56]

General Henry H. Shelton, Chairman, Joint Chiefs of Staff, noting that the Soviet collapse created a marked reduction in strategic nuclear threat to the United States and the elimination of the Soviet conventional threat in Europe, testified before the Senate Armed Forces Committee in February 1998 that "while strategic nuclear deterrence remains vital, our strategy now seeks to counter the proliferation of weapons of mass destruction (WMD), while building trust among nations through arms control, transparency and confidence-building efforts."[57]

These then are today's greatest threats—nuclear weapons themselves, and particularly the threat of proliferation and potential use of such weapons by terrorist groups and rogue nations. These enemies are not subject to deterrence, which notably remains the United States dominant strategic defense policy.

Paradoxically, it is now Russia, itself inferior in conventional military capability, that, like the United States during the Cold War, has, at least in theory, an arguable need for a broad policy of nuclear deterrence against conventional attack. With the former Soviet Union having placed most of its most advanced conventional weaponry and military facilities at the outer edges of its controlled territories, Russia, after dissolution, found itself left with many nuclear weapons but a substantially reduced conventional capability.[58]

---

[56] *Id.* at I-2 (emphasis omitted).

[57] *Prepared Statement of Gen. Henry H. Shelton, chairman, Joint Chiefs of Staff, to the Senate Armed Forces Committee,* Feb. 3, 1998, set forth at <http://www.dtic.mil/execsec/>. *See also Thinking About Tomorrow During Today's Battles,* Defense Issues, vol. 13, no. 14 (Feb. 3, 1998) <http://www.defenselink.mil/speeches/1998/t19980203-shelton.html>.

[58] *See* Charles J. Dick, *Past Cruelties Hinder the Taming of the Bear,* JANE'S INTELLIGENCE REVIEW, vol. 10, no. 12, Dec. 1, 1998, at 5.
The New York Times reported in mid 1999:

> During Soviet times, Moscow and Washington piled up huge nuclear arsenals as they sought to best each other in the arms race.
> Still, Russia's conventional forces were enormous. In those years it was NATO, fearing that it was outnumbered, that openly threatened to initiate the use of nuclear weapons in response to a non-nuclear attack.
> Now that the Soviet Union has collapsed, however, the tables have turned. The West has become less dependent on nuclear weapons.

In a substantial variant on the policy of deterrence, Congress through the Nunn-Lugar Act or Cooperative Threat Reduction Act provided funding to enable nations from the former USSR to dismantle chemical and nuclear weapons.[59] Belarus, Kazakhstan and Ukraine became nuclear weapons free, as a result of this Nunn-Lugar funding program.[60] The Nunn-Lugar act "led Russia to willingly destroy 4,000 warheads that were all aimed at [the United States] ...."[61]

A similar policy of constructive funding was recently followed by the United States with North Korea when the United States "bought" inspections rights of some underground sites in North Korea suspected of being the site of a nuclear weapons reactor or other plants. Aid against the North Korean famine that may have claimed some three million casualties in recent years gave the United States its "deterrent" effect in this instance.[62]

The National Defense Panel in its recent report further made the ultimate point that today the United States' conventional superiority is such that the nation can deter nuclear as well as biological and chemical attack with conventional weapons. Our conventional

---

As the conflict with Yugoslavia showed, NATO fights its wars with laser-guided and satellite-guided non-nuclear bombs and missiles.
Michael R. Gordon, *Maneuvers Show Russian Reliance on Nuclear Arms,* THE NEW YORK TIMES, July 10, 1999, at 1.

In a recent widescale military exercise involving some 50,000 troops, the largest such exercise since the collapse of the Soviet Union in 1991, Russia found it quickly needed to resort to nuclear weapons to defend itself. *Id.* Russia's military spending is projected to be some $4 billion in 1999, as opposed to some $260 billion for the United States. *Id.* With the demonstration of NATO's huge lead in conventional military technology during NATO's bombing of Yugoslavia, President Boris N. Yeltsin, following meetings with his top national security advisers, reportedly approved a program for the development and use of non-strategic short range tactical nuclear weapons. *Id.*

[59] *Remarks by Secretary of Defense William S. Cohen to the Boston Chamber of Commerce*, Boston Marriott Copley Place, Boston (Sept. 17, 1998) <http://www.defenselink.mil/speeches/1998/s19980917secdef.htm>.

[60] *Id.*

[61] Dr. John J. Hamre, Deputy Secretary of Defense, *Remarks at the Defense Threat Reduction Agency Rollout Ceremony*, Dulles International Airport, Va. (Oct. 1, 1998) <http://www.defenselink.mil/speeches/1998/r19981102-depsecdef.html>.

[62] David E. Sanger, *N. Korea Consents to U.S. Inspection of a Suspect Site*, THE NEW YORK TIMES, Mar. 17, 1999, at A1.

firepower and ability to respond is so overwhelming as to enable us to threaten an unacceptable level of conventional retaliation:

> It is in the best interests of the United States, Russia, and the international community that the United States and Russia move as rapidly as possible to START II. We should also consider the potential of non-nuclear weapons to strengthen deterrence. Advancing military technologies that merge the capabilities of information systems with precision-guided weaponry and real-time targeting and other new weapons systems may provide a supplement or alternative to the nuclear arsenals of the Cold War.[63]

The report of the National Defense Panel further stated: "[W]e must provide a conventional non-nuclear deterrent capability against the use of weapons of mass destruction."[64]

> The United States is confident that it can maintain the deterrent called for in the new Presidential directive at the levels envisioned for a future Strategic Arms Reduction Treaty (START III) as agreed to in the March 1997 Helsinki Accords.[65]

The U.S. leadership has recognized that lower levels of nuclear weapons pose no risk to the nation's security. In his May 1997 Report of the Quadrennial Defense Review, Secretary Cohen stated:

> [F]or the foreseeable future, the United States will continue to need a reliable and flexible nuclear deterrent—survivable against the most aggressive attack, under highly confident, constitutional command and control, and safeguarded against both accidental and unauthorized use. We believe these goals can be achieved at lower force levels. Consistent with this, the United States remains committed to negotiating further reductions in U.S. and Russian strategic nuclear arsenals consistent with the agreed START III framework once Moscow ratifies the START II treaty.[66]

The 1997 Report of the National Defense Panel similarly recognized the lack of need for the current levels of nuclear weapons:

> Among the considerations critical to shaping future nuclear policy will be the need to take account of possible shifts in China's

---

[63] NATIONAL DEFENSE PANEL, *supra* note 52, at 51.

[64] *Id.* at 42.

[65] 1998 ANNUAL REPORT TO THE PRESIDENT AND CONGRESS, *supra* note 44, at Chap. 5, Strategic Nuclear Forces.

[66] WILLIAM S. COHEN, REPORT OF THE QUADRENNIAL DEFENSE REVIEW, May 1997, § III, Defense Strategy, <http://www.fas.org/man/docs/qdr/sec3.html>.

nuclear policy, the fate of the Russian nuclear arsenal, and the possibility that other states, including some hostile to the United States, may acquire nuclear weapons. Ensuring that there is a strategic equilibrium among Moscow, Beijing, and Washington will be important to our future security. That does not mean, however, that we will need large numbers of nuclear weapons. Effective deterrence of potential adversaries can be maintained at the reduced levels envisioned by START III and beyond. [67]

Secretary of Defense Cohen in his 1998 Report to Congress made this same point: "The United States is confident that it can maintain the deterrent called for in the new Presidential directive at the levels envisioned for a future Strategic Arms Reduction Treaty (START III) as agreed to in the March 1997 Helsinki Accords."[68]

The National Defense Panel in its 1997 report further stated: "Progress in U.S.–Russian arms control is currently stalled because the Russian Duma has not yet ratified START II. However, retaining nuclear arms at current levels for an extended period is not in the U.S. interest. Those levels will be expensive to maintain and do not facilitate the transformation process essential to respond to future threats."[69]

The Secretary of Defense made the same point in his 1999 report:

> The United States continues to work toward further agreed, stabilizing reductions in strategic nuclear arms, and is confident that on the Treaty on Further Reduction and Limitation of Strategic Offensive Arms (START II) has entered into force, it can maintain the required deterrent at the force levels envisioned in a future treaty (START III), as agreed to in the March 1997 Helsinki Accords.[70]

Ironically, the Pentagon has, for some years now, been pressing for reductions in the U.S. nuclear arsenal that have been blocked by Congress through legislation prohibiting unilateral reductions. In 1998 the Pentagon reportedly submitted a classified report to Congress outlining nine proposals for reducing the arsenal unilaterally, including through reducing the present arsenal of some 7,000 warheads to

---

[67] NATIONAL DEFENSE PANEL, *supra* note 52, at 50.

[68] 1998 ANNUAL REPORT TO THE PRESIDENT AND CONGRESS, *supra* note 44, at Chap. 5, Strategic Nuclear Forces.

[69] NATIONAL DEFENSE PANEL, *supra* note 52, at 50.

[70] 1999 ANNUAL REPORT TO THE PRESIDENT AND CONGRESS, *supra* note 45.

5,000–6,000, pending the Russian Parliament's approval of Start II, which provides for a reduction to some 3,000–3,500 warheads.[71]

---

[71] Steven Lee Myers, *Pentagon Ready to Shrink Arsenal of Nuclear Bombs*, NEW YORK TIMES, Nov. 23, 1998, at 1. The Pentagon recommendations were motivated by financial considerations as well as a sense of diminishing security threats and a belief that the recommended reductions would not diminish deterrence. *Id. See also About Defense Reform,* <http://www.defenselink.mil/dodreform/about_dod_reform.htm>, describing The Defense Reform Initiative (DRI), introduced by Secretary of Defense Cohen on November 10, 1997, to improve business practices in the Department of Defense, "to identify savings and migrate resources to support modernization accounts." *Id.*

In recent years, Republicans in Congress have included language in the Defense Department's budget bills explicitly prohibiting unilateral reductions below START I levels. Steven Lee Myers, *Pentagon Ready to Shrink Arsenal of Nuclear Bombs*, NEW YORK TIMES, Nov. 23, 1998, at 1.

The Pentagon has reportedly spent $95 million more during 1997 and 1998 than it would have if Start II had taken effect, with the incremental cost to reach $100 million in 1999 and $1 billion in 2000. *Id.*

Under START I, signed in 1991, the United States has drastically reduced its arsenal of strategic nuclear warheads, from more than 10,000 to about 7,000. With Start II calling for reductions to 3,000 to 3,500 warheads, Presidents Clinton and Yeltsin agreed in March 1997 that, once Russia's lower house approved START II, the United States and Russia would begin talks on further reductions to 2,000 to 2,500 warheads. *Id.*

Under the Pentagon proposals, the Navy reportedly would move ahead with its current plan to reduce its fleet of 18 Trident submarines by retiring the four oldest by 2003 and the Air Force would be able to reduce or eliminate the stockpile of 50 intercontinental ballistic missiles that it is now financing in its budget year to year. *Id.*

Chapter 19: U.S. Nuclear Force Structure and Related Risk Factors

As we have seen, the United States, in its arguments before the ICJ opposing the *per se* unlawfulness of the use of nuclear weapons, largely relied upon the allegedly limited, controllable and hence putatively lawful effects of tactical, low-yield, highly accurate nuclear weapons. This reliance raises questions as to the extent to which such weapons typify the U.S. nuclear arsenal. Specifically, what portion of the U.S. arsenal is made up of the types of weapons whose legality the United States actively defended?

As we saw, strategic weapons are essentially ones intended for broad use against the enemy from a distance to achieve overall objectives of the war and have characteristically been the larger yield weapons designed for major targets, whereas tactical weapons are smaller lower yield devices intended for potential use in the battlefield on more of an ad hoc basis. While tactical weapons have generally been deemed more controllable and accurate, and hence subject to surgical use, in recent years the anticipated accuracy—measured by the CEP—even of strategic weapons has greatly improved.

Strategic weapons consist of the triad of long-range bombers carrying bombs and cruise missiles, land based ballistic missiles such as the Minuteman III ICBMs, and submarine launched missiles such as Trident I and IIs capable of flying over 8,000 km to their targets.[1] Tactical weapons in contrast historically have included nuclear bombs, short range missiles, nuclear artillery and atomic demolition munitions either forwardly deployed in the war zone or carried by shorter range fighter-bombers and attack submarines capable of carrying the weapons such as tactical cruise missiles up to the coast or near naval targets.[2]

While the term "low-yield" in the context of nuclear weapons seems oxymoronic, there is actually a wide range of yields available across the nuclear spectrum, extending, as we shall see, from a sub-kiloton yield of a mere 300 tons to yields of well over a megaton.

---

[1] *See* Steven J. Zaloga, *The Thunder Inside Russia's 'Typhoons'*, 8 JANE'S INTELLIGENCE REV., no. 12, 533, Dec. 1, 1996; Robert S. Norris & William M. Arkin, *US Nuclear Stockpile, July 1998*, BULL. OF THE ATOMIC SCIENTISTS, vol. 54, no. 4, Jul. 1998, at 69.

[2] *See* Norris & Arkin, *US Nuclear Stockpile, July 1998, supra* note 1.

Looking at the make-up of the U.S. arsenal, it becomes evident that high yield strategic weapons predominate in numbers as well as destructive power.

The U.S. strategic arsenal, as of the end of 1998, was essentially as follows:

Strategic Weapon Basing	Number of Weapons	Number of Warheads
LAND: Land Based Intercontinental Ballistic Missiles (ICBM)	550[3]	2,000
SEA: Ballistic Missiles on Submarines (long-range missiles)	432[4]	3,456
AIR: Bombs on Long-range Bombers	950[5]	950
Cruise Missiles on Long-range Bombers	800[6]	800
TOTAL[7]:	2,732	7,206

---

[3] Robert S. Norris & William M. Arkin, *U.S. Strategic Nuclear Forces, End of 1998; Abstract,* BULL. OF THE ATOMIC SCIENTISTS, vol. 55, no. 1, Jan. 1999, at 78–79.

[4] *Id.*

[5] *Id.*

[6] *Id.*

[7] *See id.* The chart shows fewer "weapons" than "warheads," because many weapons are MIRV'ed, carrying multiple warheads ("Multiple Re-Entry Vehicles"). De-MIRVing of the ICBM force is a future possibility not yet in place: "If START II enters into force, the United States will modify all Minuteman missiles to carry only one warhead and will retire all Peacekeepers [aka the MX, which carries ten warheads per missile]." WILLIAM S. COHEN, 1999 ANNUAL REPORT TO THE PRESIDENT AND THE CONGRESS, Chap. 6, Strategic Nuclear Weapons and Missile Defenses (Department of Defense 1999).

The Strategic Arms Reduction Treaties (START I, II, and the yet to be negotiated START III) shape today's deployed arsenals.

Developments in the sizing of the U.S. strategic nuclear arsenal can been seen from the following chart published by the Secretary of Defense:

Weapons	FY 1990	FY 1999	START I (December 5, 2001)	START II (December 31, 2007)
Attributed Warheads on Ballistic Missiles [sea & land]	7,314 on ballistic missiles	5,456 on ballistic missiles	Not over 4,900 on ballistic missiles	Not over 2,250 on ballistic missiles
Heavy Bombers Available	282 primary mission, 324 total	115	97	97

See 1999 ANNUAL REPORT OF SECRETARY OF DEFENSE, *supra. See also* OFFICE OF THE SECRETARY OF DEFENSE, NUCLEAR WEAPONS SUSTAINMENT PROGRAMS, (dated 1997 and updated June 18, 1998) http://www.defenselink.mil/pubs/dswa/document.html>, table 1.

The above numbers go through START II. While START III has not been negotiated, sources within and without the government project it will entail additional reductions to some 2000–2500 warheads:

> Yeltsin said he will urge Russia's parliament to ratify START II, which the U.S. Senate already ratified. Once START II is ratified, Yeltsin said, negotiations will begin on START III. *** Clinton said START III will cap the number of strategic warheads each country retains at 2,000 to 2,500 by the year 2007. "This means that within a decade, we will have reduced both sides' strategic nuclear arsenal by 80 percent below their Cold War peak of just five years ago," he said.

Linda D. Kozaryn, *Clinton, Yeltsin Confer on NATO, Security Issues,* AMERICAN FORCES PRESS SERVICE, Jun. 17, 1998, <http://www.defenselink.mil/news/Mar1997/n03251997_9703251.html>. *See also* Norris & Arkin, *U.S. Strategic Nuclear Forces, End of 1998, supra* note 3, at 78–80; Secretary William Perry & General John Shalikashvili, Chairman, Joint Chiefs of Staff, *Department of Defense Briefing,* September 22, 1994; Robert S. Norris & William M. Arkin, *U.S. Strategic Nuclear Forces, End of 1994,* BULL. OF THE ATOMIC SCIENTIST, vol. 51, no. 1, Jan. 1, 1995, at 69; 1999 REPORT TO THE PRESIDENT AND CONGRESS, *supra.* "At the conclusion of their March 1997 meeting in Helsinki, President Clinton and Russian President Yeltsin issued a joint statement establishing parameters for future reductions in nuclear forces beyond START II. In this statement, they agreed to an overall limit of 2,000–2,500 deployed strategic warheads for a future START III treaty." Kozaryn, *supra.*

The foregoing numbers indicate progressive decreases in the size of the U.S. strategic nuclear arsenal in the post Cold War era. This apparent trend, while heartening, is misleading in terms of the nature and extent of the continuing risk posed by these weapons.

In a sense, there is a bit of a shell game being played. The numbers, such as those above, regularly provided by government and non-government sources alike as to the present and anticipated future arsenals under the START treaties refer to "attributed" or "accountable" weapons (including delivery vehicles and warheads per delivery vehicle), essentially deployed weapons. Such negotiated units of accountability permit weapons to be drawn down or held in reserve in such a way as not to be counted, with the result that realistically available weapons can be substantially greater than the published figures and charts indicate.

This situation results from the fact that the START treaties generally require the destruction not of warheads but of delivery vehicles and related equipment (the silos, submarine launch tubes, and the bombers), preferred items for destruction because their demolition can be readily verified by satellite. *See* Norris & Arkin, *US Nuclear Stockpile, July 1998, supra* note 1, at 69. Warheads retired from duty are removed in such a way as not to impede their reusability, particularly that of the internal fissile matter, the plutonium "pit." *See id.* When 10,000 active warheads were existent in the US possession in 1998, so too were an additional 5,000 "pits." *Id.*

Weapon not characterized as "accountable," and hence not counted, include "augmentation" or "hedge" forces, contingency stockpiles readily available for redeployment; "reliability replacement warheads" held in reserve to replace warheads in the operational arsenal that develop safety or reliability problems; weapons removed from duty but quickly redeployable; and other such categories of weapons readily subject to activation and use.

"[A]ugmentation warheads ... a contingency stockpile available for redeployment back onto missiles and aircraft," become particularly important as active forces are drawn down. It is projected that the current level of augmentation forces, some 2500 in 1999, will rise substantially as active forces are reduced to the some 5000 warheads projected for 2003. *See* Norris & Arkin, *US Nuclear Stockpile, July 1998, supra* note 1, at 70. The "formal decision" to maintain such hedge weapons was made in 1994 as part of the Nuclear Posture Review. *See id.*

An example of hedge creation can be seen from the Air Force's reductions in 1991 to bring its forces in compliance with START I. While the Air Force removed 1600 bombs and air launched cruise missiles from bomber deployment, retaining the best and most modern of its equipment, the withdrawn warheads "were moved to storage depots rather than dismantled." ARKIN ET AL., TAKING STOCK: WORLDWIDE NUCLEAR DEPLOYMENTS 1998 6 (NRDC 1998).

Beyond deployed warheads and the hedge force, it is estimated by Arkin and Norris that, in the future draw down of forces, an additional 3,000 warheads will be retained in a third category, "reliability replacement warheads." *See* Norris & Arkin, *US Nuclear Stockpile, July 1998, supra* note 1, at 71. Such remain available for deployment when presently deployed weapons develop safety or reliability problems. *See id.*

There are also substantial numbers of warheads simply awaiting dismantling. *See id* at 1–2. In a Russian case, one set of warheads slated to be scrapped has entered limbo, past their expiration date. *See id* at 10. Russia is hampered by "a lack of financing and the natural effects of aging." *Id.* at 11.

Under the START initiatives, of the 36,000 existing warheads worldwide as of 1998, 14,000 were awaiting dismantling or were being retired—and in the meantime remained in some state other than being deployed or demolished. *See* ARKIN ET AL. *supra* at 6. The "balance of almost 22,000 warheads are either active and operational, or are scheduled to be retained after all current reductions, retirements, and warhead dismantlement are completed." *Id.*

Thus, the numbers of realistically available weapons can be substantially larger than that indicated by the attributed/accountable figures, as they are in the case of the United States. They can also be substantially smaller in instances where weapons counted as "attributed" or "accountable" are in fact not operational. This is reportedly the case as to the Russian force. Of their nominal stockpile of 22,500 warheads as of 1998, it is thought that "only" 10,240 are operational. *Id.*

The grand total of U.S nuclear weapons overseas, at sea, and in the U.S. went from some 25,200 in 1985 to 18,970 in 1992 to 12,070 in 1998. *See id.* at 15. "The United States possesse[d] approximately 12,070 nuclear weapons as of the end of 1997, 8420 of which are operational, 2,300 are in long term storage, as part of a reserve, and 1,350 are awaiting dismantlement and disposal." *Id.* The number remaining more constant is the number deployed in the U.S, that being 14,600 in 1985, 16,200 in 1992, and 11,920 in 1998. *Id.* Morrison and Tsipis indicate world arsenals have halved, from 40–50 thousand to approximately 20 thousand. PHILIP MORRISON & KOSTA TSIPIS, REASON ENOUGH TO HOPE, AMERICA AND THE WORLD OF THE 21ST CENTURY 28 (M.I.T. Press 1998), citing William M. Arkin, *Nuclear Notebook*, BULL. OF THE ATOMIC SCIENTISTS, Jan./Feb. 1995, 69–71, William M. Arkin, *Nuclear Notebook*, BULL. OF THE ATOMIC SCIENTISTS, Mar./Apr., 1995, at 78–79.

If the future U.S. nuclear force is counted to include reserve and other non-"attributed" stockpiles, a realistic estimate of its strategic forces after full implementation of START I and II could be higher than 8,500 warheads: 3,500 in the active strategic forces, 3,000 drawn down into inactive reserve, and a continuation or expansion of the current 2,500 hedge. There would also be 1,000 tactical warheads and 500 spares. *See* Norris & Arkin, *US Nuclear Stockpile, July 1998, supra* note 1, at 69–70. It was predicted in 1999 that "over the next few years the actual number of intact [US] warheads of all categories will be approximately 10,000, given current policy directives." Norris & Arkin, *US. Strategic Nuclear Forces End of 1998, supra* note 3, at 78.

The U.S. active tactical nuclear arsenal, as of 1998, was essentially as follows:

Tactical Weapon Basing	Weapons	Warheads
AIR: Bombs on Fighter-Bomber Planes	750	750
SEA: Cruise Missiles on Submarines	320	320
TOTAL[8]:	1,070	1,070

Contrasted with the foregoing levels of forces are the appreciably lower levels believed by numerous experts to be necessary for traditional deterrence:

	Bush-Yeltsin for 2003	Morrison and Tsipis proposal for beyond
Land based ballistic missiles	500	300
Undersea ballistic missiles	1,728	240
Bombers	1,272	240
Total Strategic warheads	3,500	780
Tactical nuclear warheads	1,600	250

Set forth at MORRISON & TSIPIS, *supra*, at 41.

[8] Norris & Arkin, *US Nuclear Stockpile, July 1998, supra* note 1, at 70 The sea launched nuclear cruise missiles are not currently deployed at sea, but rather are stored ashore, allocated to submarines at sea. Called the Tomahawk Land Attack Missile/Nuclear, its CEP is variously reported at 30 meters (by Ian Curtis, *The Missile Tables,* DEFENSE & FOREIGN AFFAIRS' STRATEGIC POLICY, Mar. 1991), and at 100 meters (by Tamar A. Mehuron, *Characteristics for Nuclear Weapon Systems, Circa 2006,* AIR FORCE MAG., Mar. 1992, at 10).

Even greater accuracy may be in process. It has been stated: "Technologies involved in the cruise missile advanced guidance program are raising the possibility that both nuclear and non-nuclear weapons will be even more accurate and discriminate (down to zero circular error probable [CEP])." Andrew C. Goldberg, *A Postnuclear World? Offense and Defense in the Postnuclear System,* THE WASHINGTON QUARTERLY, vol. 57, no. 2, Spring, 1988, at 57).

Parallel to missile's CEP, it should be noted that bomber planes have a certain "success rate," whereby the military tracks the percentage of missions carried off with the bombs getting to where they were intended to go. Obviously on the other missions, the bombs go somewhere else. Reportedly the success rate of the United States' most advanced fighters falls below the 83% overall success rate that the Navy attained with its conventional BG-109 Tomahawk cruise missiles during the 1991 Gulf War. *See* David Fulghum, *Clashes with Iraq Continue After Heavy Air Strike,* AVIATION WEEK & SPACE TECH., Jan. 25, 1993, at 38.

Thus it is evident the U.S. maintains far more strategic than tactical nuclear weapons. The secondary nature of the tactical weapons is also evident from numerous other considerations.

Firstly, the United States, even while continuing to espouse the policy of nuclear deterrence, has essentially based that policy upon strategic nuclear weapons and broadly recognized the relative non-utility and even counter-productivity of tactical weapons for that purpose.

The point can perhaps best be seen from the contrast between our current deployment of tactical weapons and that during the Cold War. In that earlier period, substantial numbers of tactical nuclear weapons were widely dispersed in the hands of the Army, Navy, Air Force and Marines on land and sea throughout the world, including particularly in Western Europe and surrounding areas, for potential battlefield use.[9]

Now, as noted in our discussion of the Nuclear Posture Review, U.S. stockpiles of tactical nuclear weapons have been substantially reduced and only the Air Force deploys such weapons. Tactical nuclear weapons have been taken from the custody of U.S. ground forces; the Army and Marines have been de-nuclearized; and the Navy no longer deploys non-strategic nuclear weapons.[10]

---

[9] By 1975, the United States maintained 10,311 tactical nuclear weapons overseas. *See* ARKIN ET AL., TAKING STOCK, *supra* note 7, at 16. In the 1960s, when the number of warheads peaked at over 32,000, the U.S. forces consisted predominantly of tactical forces. COCHRAN, ARKIN & HOENIG, 1 NUCLEAR WEAPONS DATABOOK 3–4, 38 (NRDC 1984). By 1983, when the arsenal was at 26,000, the numbers of tactical and strategic weapons were about even, with tactical still outnumbering strategic weapons. *Id.* at 4, 15, 39, 102.

In Europe alone, stocks of U.S. nuclear weapons swelled to 7,920 warheads in eight countries by 1975. *See* ARKIN ET AL., TAKING STOCK, *supra* note 7, at 18. "Belgium, Greece, Italy, the Netherlands, Spain, Turkey, the United Kingdom and West Germany" were hosts. *Id.* Included at that time were the most direct battlefield weapons, including "mammoth Army 280mm nuclear artillery guns" and "atomic demolitions engineer units" known as nuclear landmines. *Id.* at 17–18.

In Asia, "nuclear warheads were deployed in Guam, the Philippines, South Korea, Taiwan, and Okinawa (under U.S. occupation)." *Id.* at 18. Marine and naval nuclear weapons based in Guam until the 1980s included battlefield use nuclear weapons, particularly nuclear depth charges and artillery. *See id.* Missile units and tactical air units also hosted nuclear warheads. *See id.* The 58th Tactical Missile Group operated out of Korea from 1959 to 1960, and tactical nuclear attack aircraft were deployed in the Philippines, Korea, and Taiwan. *See id.*

[10] *See* Chapter 18, notes 3–4, 19–27, and accompanying text.

In addition, Congress in 1994 banned research and development of nuclear weapons with yields of less than five kilotons.[11] Describing the

---

Professors Morrison and Tsipis have noted:

Tactical weapons, often of smaller energy yield, are meant for battlefield use against engaged combat forces or their forward support—the airfields, bases, and transportation nodes as far as a few hundred miles behind the lines. (They were not wholly wrong who coined the cynical definition that a tactical nuclear weapon was one intended to explode within Germany.) ...

In September 1991 President Bush wisely ordered the elimination of nearly all U.S. sea- or land-launched tactical nuclear weapons. At sea only the carrier-based attack bombers of longer range (mainly Grumman A-6 Intruders) remain afloat, fewer than 50 bombs on each active carrier, by our estimate 600 or 700 in total. Such shipboard capacity to initiate nuclear war against even nonnuclear states is hardly tolerable, and even dangerous. We recommend that all these weapons be set ashore and dismantled before the year 2000.

There is little military purpose for the nearly 1,000 nuclear gravity bombs we estimate the United States still deploys on offshore lands.

MORRISON & TSIPIS, *supra* note 7, at 38–39.

[11] § 3136 of P.L. 103-160, National Defense Authorization Act For Fiscal Year 1994, H.R. CONF. REP. 103-357:

SEC. 3136. PROHIBITION ON RESEARCH AND DEVELOPMENT OF LOW-YIELD NUCLEAR WEAPONS.

(a) United States Policy.—It shall be the policy of the United States not to conduct research and development which could lead to the production by the United States of a new low-yield nuclear weapon, including a precision low-yield warhead.

(b) Limitation.—The Secretary of Energy may not conduct, or provide for the conduct of, research and development which could lead to the production by the United States of a low-yield nuclear weapon which, as of the date of the enactment of this Act, has not entered production.

(c) Effect on Other Research and Development.—Nothing in this section shall prohibit the Secretary of Energy from conducting, or providing for the conduct of, research and development necessary

(1) to design a testing device that has a yield of less than five kilotons;

(2) to modify an existing weapon for the purpose of addressing safety and reliability concerns; or

(3) to address proliferation concerns.

rationale for the legislation, Congressman Spratt stated, "The United States has wisely decided to retire our tactical nuclear weapons."[12] The Congressman further stated, "A 5-kiloton yield nuclear weapon is a very small nuclear weapon that is surely tactical; it has virtually no strategic value."[13]

In a strategic environment where the United States is seen as potentially vulnerable to nuclear attack by far less powerful States or groups,[14] small nuclear bombs were seen as blurring the distinction between nuclear and conventional weapons, sending the wrong message "to a world we are trying to convince not to develop nuclear weapons."[15] As Congresswoman Furse stated, "we have no higher national security goal than to do everything possible to discourage the spread of nuclear weapons and to delegitimize their role. *** The reality is that we cannot contemplate ever using such weapons. Mini nukes would be a new generation of tactical nuclear weapons. ... Simply put, we are out of the business of developing tactical nuclear weapons in this country."[16]

By 2007, it is estimated that the United States' will commit merely some 20% of its operational arsenal to non-strategic purposes, and will have a concomitantly minor desire for bombs with low blast yields.[17]

Even the tactical weapons that do exist in the United States' active arsenal today are also strategic weapons.[18] This results from the "dial-

---

(d) Definition.—In this section, the term "low-yield nuclear weapon" means a nuclear weapon that has a yield of less than five kilotons.

Id. at 947–48. *See* 42 USCS § 2121 (1998) Prohibition on Research and Development of Low-Yield Nuclear Weapons, Act. Nov. 30, 1993, P.L. 103-160, Div C. Title XXX, Subtitle C § 3136, 107 Stat. 1946.

[12] *National Defense Authorization Act for Fiscal Year 1994*, 139 Cong. Rec. H. 7065, *H7083, 103rd Cong 1st Session, Sept. 28, 1993.

[13] Congressman Spratt, *National Defense Authorization Act for Fiscal Year 1994*, 139 Cong. Rec. H. 7065, *H7083, Sept. 28, 1993

[14] *See* 139 Cong. Rec. 7118, *H7122, 103rd Cong 1st Session, Sept 28, 1993.

[15] *Id.*

[16] *Id.*, quoting Les Aspin, former Chairman of the House Armed Services.

[17] *See* JOHN BURROUGHS, THE (IL)LEGALITY OF THREAT OR USE OF NUCLEAR WEAPONS 76 n.89 (1997). *See* ARKIN ET AL., TAKING STOCK, *supra* note 7, at 11.

[18] All available small yield tactical bombs in the U.S. arsenal today use one of several models of the B61 warhead. These warheads have adjustable yields. The chart *infra* indicates each weapon's range of possible yields. All models of the B61, and thus each tactical bomb weapon in the U.S. arsenal, can be

a-yield" feature of contemporary weapons, whereby the weapons have a range of potential yields which can be set before use, with the B61-3 bomb, for instance, having a potential range of yields from 300 tons to 170 kilotons.[19]

---

adjusted to medium or high yield explosions, by the definition of high yield in the DOCTRINE FOR NUCLEAR OPERATIONS. Likewise, the warheads on the cruise missiles adjust to two yields, one of which is a high yield. Therefore the U.S. armed forces today have no nuclear weapon solely capable of creating a low-yield blast. *See* BURROUGHS, *supra* note 17, at 76 n.89; Norris & Arkin, *US Nuclear Stockpile, July 1998, supra* note 1, at 70.

The U.S. military in its manual DOCTRINE FOR JOINT THEATER NUCLEAR OPERATIONS defines "dual capable unit," and characterizes yields:

> dual capable unit. A nuclear certified delivery unit capable of executing both conventional and nuclear missions. (Joint Pub 1-02)
>
> ***
>
Yields:
> Very low — less than 1 kiloton.
> Low — 1 kiloton to 10 kilotons.
> Medium — over 10 kilotons to 50 kilotons.
> High — over 50 kilotons to 500 kilotons.
> Very high — over 500 kilotons. (Joint Pub 1-02)

JOINT CHIEFS OF STAFF, JOINT PUB 3-12.1, DOCTRINE FOR JOINT THEATER NUCLEAR OPERATIONS GL-3 (Feb. 9, 1996) (prepared under direction of the Chairman of the Joint Chiefs of Staff) <http://www.dtic.mil/doctrine/jel/new_pubs/jp3_12_1.pdf> (emphasis omitted).

[19] *See* Norris & Arkin, *US Nuclear Stockpile, July 1998, supra* note 1, at 70. *See also* BURROUGHS, *supra* note 17, at 76 n.89:

> The bombs the U.S. dropped on Hiroshima and Nagasaki had yields in the range of 12 to 20 kilotons. A 300-ton warhead is an order of magnitude more powerful that the most powerful conventional explosives, and of course also releases radiation. While a 300-ton warhead may nonetheless be considered a "low yield" nuclear weapon on an absolute scale of destructive power as well as on a scale relative to nuclear weapons with yields in the hundreds of kilotons, it is hard to categorize a five-kiloton warhead as such.

BURROUGHS, *supra* note 17, at 76 n.89.

The range of potential yields of the weapons primarily making up the U.S. tactical nuclear weapons arsenal can be seen as follows:[20]

Tactical Warhead Type	Detonation Yield of Warhead
Bombs Carried By Fighter Bomber Aircraft[21]	
Model : B61-3[22]	Yield may be set to .3, 1.5, 60, and 170 Kt.
Model : B61-4[23]	Yield may be set to .3, 1.5, 10, and 45 Kt.
Model : B61-10[24]	Yield may be set to .3, 5, 10, and 80 Kt.
W80-1/ACM: Cruise Missiles Carried by Submarine[25]	Yield may be set at either 5 or 150 Kt.

---

[20] Norris & Arkin, *US Nuclear Stockpile, July 1998, supra* note 1, at 70.

[21] The U.S. fighter-bomber planes that carry tactical bombs include the F-117A stealth aircraft and the F-16C/D Falcon. *Taking the Pulse: Fighter-Bomber Aircraft,* <http://www.basicint.org> (website hosted by "BASIC," The British American Security Information Council, an independent research organization with offices in London and Washington, D.C.). The F-16 carries the several B61 bombs, including the B61-11 ground penetrating bomb now assigned to the strategic forces. *Id.*

Belgium, Germany, Greece, Italy, Netherlands, Turkey and England continue to host 150 U.S. tactical B61 bombs. *See* ARKIN ET AL., TAKING STOCK, *supra* note 7, at 16; *Taking the Pulse: Fighter-Bomber Aircraft,* <http://www.basicint.org>. "All non-strategic B61 nuclear weapons in the U.S. are thought to be based at Kirkland AFB in New Mexico and Nellis AFB in Nevada." *Id.*

[22] Norris & Arkin, *US Nuclear Stockpile, July 1998, supra* note 1, at 70.

[23] *Id.* Hans Kristensen has stated that, with the B61-11's "enhanced earth-penetrating capabilities and low yield," the B-2 with B61-11 bombs is the "likely weapon of choice for nuclear counterproliferation scenarios against rogue nations." Hans Kristensen, *Targets of Opportunity: How Nuclear Planners Found New Targets for Old Weapons,* BULL. OF ATOMIC SCIENTISTS, vol.55, no. 5, Sep./Oct. 1997.

[24] *Id.*

[25] Tactical cruise missiles are potentially to be carried by 25 Sturgeon-class, 62 Los Angeles-class and 3 Seawolf-class attack submarines, although, as noted, *supra* note 8, they are currently stored ashore. *Id.*

The United States' strategic nuclear weapons are characterized by yields ostensibly far beyond the levels actively defended by the United States before the ICJ:

Type and Basing	Yield	Weapons/ Warheads	CEP
Land based ICBMs			
Minuteman III Mk-12[1]	170 Kt.	200/600	120 m.
Minuteman III Mk-12A[2]	335 Kt.	300/900	200 m.
MX Peacekeeper[3]	300 Kt	50/500	100 m.
Sea based Missiles			
Surface vessels (none currently used)			
Ohio-Class Submarine's Ballistic Missiles[4]			
Trident I C4[5]	100 Kt	192 on 8 submarines/ 1,536 warheads	460 m.
Trident II D5[6]	100 Kt.	192 on 10 submarines/ 1,536 warheads	500 m.
Trident II D5[7]	475 Kt	48 on 10 submarines/ 384 warheads	500 m.
Air based, on B-52H, B-2s[8] long-range bombers			
Cruise missiles			
Air Launched Cruise Missile[9]	5 or 150 Kt	400 on 21 B-2 Stealth Bombers	100 m.
Advanced Cruise Missile[10]	5 or 150 Kt	400 on B-52Hs	not available

Type and Basing	Yield	Weapons/ Warheads	CEP
Bombs (on tactical and strategic bombers)			
B61-7[11]	Low- 350 Kt	300 on B-2s	N/A
B61-11 earth penetrating[12]	Low- 350 Kt	50 on B-2s	N/A
B83[13]	Low- 1,200Kt	480 on B-2s	N/A

---

[1] *See* Steven J. Zaloga, *The Thunder Inside Russia's 'Typhoons'*, 8 JANE'S INTELLIGENCE REV., no. 12, 533, Dec. 1, 1996; Robert S. Norris & William M. Arkin, *US Nuclear Stockpile, July 1998*, BULL. OF THE ATOMIC SCIENTISTS, vol. 54, no. 4, 69 Jul. 1998; Robert S. Norris & William M. Arkin, *U.S. Strategic Nuclear Forces End of 1998; Abstract*, BULL. OF THE ATOMIC SCIENTISTS, vol. 55, no. 1, Jan. 1999; Barbara Starr, *USAF, USN Duel Over Conventional Ballistics*, JANE'S DEFENCE WEEKLY, Vol. 22; No. 23, December 10, 1994, at pg. 8.

[2] Norris & Arkin, *U.S. Strategic Nuclear Forces End of 1998, supra* note 1. *See* Kosta Tsipis, *Cruise Missiles*, SCIENTIFIC AMERICAN, Feb. 1977, at 20-29.

[3] Norris & Arkin, *U.S. Strategic Nuclear Forces End of 1998, supra* note 1.

[4] The 18 submarines in a strategic posture are in Group 9 and Group 10. *See id.* Group 9 is at Naval Submarine Base, Bangor, Washington, consisting of one squadron with eight submarines, all armed with Trident Is. Group 10 is based at Kings Bay, Georgia, with two squadrons, Nos. 16 and 20, each consisting of five submarines all armed with Trident IIs. *See id.*

In 1998, some nine or ten nuclear armed submarines were maintained on patrol at any given time, a rate equal to that at the height of the Cold War. *See id.* Roughly half of those on patrol were being kept at hard alert, defined as within range of anticipated targets. *See id.*

[5] Zaloga, *supra* note 1; Norris & Arkin, *U.S. Strategic Nuclear Forces End of 1998, supra* note 1.

[6] Zaloga, *supra* note 1; Norris & Arkin, *U.S. Strategic Nuclear Forces End of 1998, supra* note 1.

[7] Zaloga, *supra* note 1; Norris & Arkin, *U.S. Strategic Nuclear Forces End of 1998, supra* note 1.

[8] The B-2 (stealth bomber) and the B-52H (stratofortress) long-range bombers are the U.S. aircraft that carry strategic nuclear weapons. B-2s are each individually fitted to carry a range of the nuclear bombs as well as air launched cruise missiles (ACLMs). *See* Norris & Arkin, *U.S. Strategic*

Nuclear Forces End of 1998, supra note 1. The B-52Hs carry the Advanced Cruise Missile (ACM). *Id.*

[9] Norris & Arkin, *U.S. Strategic Nuclear Forces End of 1998, supra* note 1. *See also* Kosta Tsipis, *Cruise Missiles*, SCIENTIFIC AMERICAN, Feb. 1977, 20-29; Ian Curtis, *Theatre Cruise Missiles*, DEFENSE & FOREIGN AFFAIRS' STRATEGIC POLICY, February, 1992.

[10] Norris and Arkin, *U.S. Strategic Nuclear Forces End of 1998, supra* note 1. The ACM's range and CEP are not known. *See* Ian Curtis, *Theatre Cruise Missiles.* Such information is conspicuously missing among the otherwise readily available information as to strategic missiles. *See, e.g.,* Strategic Missiles, <http://www.af.mil/news/airman/0199/missi.htm>.

The ACM is of presumptively greater range than the ALCM, as it has been given a larger fuel payload. Its forward swept wings and composite body make it a stealth cruise missile, an evader of radar. *See* Nick Cook, John Boatman, *USAF Lifts Veil on 'Secret' ACM*, 14 JANE'S DEFENSE WEEKLY 549, no. 13, September 29, 1990.

[11] Norris & Arkin, *US Nuclear Stockpile, July 1998, supra* note 1.

[12] *Id.*

[13] *Id.*

Chapter 20: Times the United States Threatened or Considered the Use of Nuclear Weapons

Beyond theory is practice. Given U.S. strategic theory and operational practice, what has the United States actually done? How close has it come to using nuclear weapons and what does this tell us as to the risk factors associated with such weapons?

In addition to the ongoing threat that is inherent in the policy of deterrence, the United States explicitly threatened to use nuclear weapons on at least five occasions[1] during the Cold War, including in Korea in 1950–53,[2] Suez in 1956,[3] Lebanon in 1958,[4] Cuba in 1962,[5]

---

[1] *See* WILLIAM A. SCHWARTZ ET AL., A NUCLEAR SEDUCTION, WHY THE ARMS RACE DOESN'T MATTER AND WHAT DOES 136 (1990) [hereinafter THE NUCLEAR SEDUCTION]; Desmond Ball, *U.S. Strategic Forces: How Would They Be Used?*, 7 INT'L SECURITY 31, 41–2 (1982).

[2] *See* MCGEORGE BUNDY, DANGER AND SURVIVAL: CHOICES ABOUT THE BOMB IN THE FIRST FIFTY YEARS 231 (1988); HARRY S. TRUMAN, MEMOIRS: THE YEARS OF TRIAL AND HOPE 1946–1952 450–51 (1965) (*quoted in* Daniel J. Arbess, *The International Law of Armed Conflict in Light of Contemporary Deterrent Strategies: Empty Promise or Meaningful Restraint?*, 30 MCGILL L.J. 89, 127 (1984)). *See also* Richard H. Kohn & Joseph P. Harahan, *U.S. Strategic Air Power, 1948–1962: Excerpts From An Interview With Generals Curtis E. LeMay, Leon W. Johnson, David A. Burchinal and Jack J. Cotton,* 12 INT'L SECURITY 82–83 (1988) (*cited in* THE NUCLEAR SEDUCTION, *supra* note 1, at 132); RICHARD K. BETTS, NUCLEAR BLACKMAIL AND NUCLEAR BALANCE 38 (Brookings Institution, Washington, D.C. 1987) (*cited in* THE NUCLEAR SEDUCTION, *supra* note 1, at 84); Daniel Ellsberg, *A Call to Mutiny, in* THE DEADLY CONNECTION: NUCLEAR WAR AND U.S. INTERVENTION 56–57 (Joseph Gerson ed., 1986); THE NUCLEAR SEDUCTION, *supra* note 1, at 88 (citing H.W. Brands, Jr. *Testing Massive Retaliation: Credibility and Crisis Management in the Taiwan Strait,* 12 INT'L SECURITY 124 (1988)).
Former Secretary of State William McNamara and McGeorge Bundy stated "In 1975 the Ford administration made public that the United States had stored nuclear weapons in Korea and had explicitly threatened to initiate the use of nuclear weapons, if necessary, to defend South Korea." Colman McCarthy, *Back to Brinkmanship*, WASH. POST, July 27, 1986, at H2.

[3] *See* THE NUCLEAR SEDUCTION, *supra* note 1, at 90 (citing BETTS, *supra* note 2, at 63, 65).

[4] *See* THE NUCLEAR SEDUCTION, *supra* note 1, at 90 (citing WILLIAM B. QUANDT, FORCE WITHOUT WARS 237, 256 (1978)) (Lebanon, 1958; Jordan, 1970.) Quandt concludes that nuclear capable howitzers were landed in Lebanon although others claim the nuclear ordnance remained aboard ship. *Id.,*

the Middle East in 1973,[6] and, after the Cold War, in Iraq during the Gulf War.[7]

---

citing QUANDT, *supra* at 256. Quandt further states that General Nathan D. Twining, the Chairman of the Joint Chiefs of Staff, was directed to be prepared to use nuclear weapons in Lebanon subject to Eisenhower's approval. *See id.* citing QUANDT, *supra* at 256.

[5] *See* THE NUCLEAR SEDUCTION, *supra* note 1, at 91 (citing ROBERT MCNAMARA, BLUNDERING INTO DISASTER 9 (1986)).

McNamara reports that the Soviets had 162 nuclear warheads in Cuba during the Cuban Missile Crisis and that, if the United States invaded Cuba at that time, there was a "high risk" that the "Soviet forces in Cuba would have decided to use their nuclear weapons rather than lose them." McNamara further reports that there were "many in the U.S. government, military and civilian alike," who were prepared to recommend that the United States conduct just such an invasion. ROBERT S. MCNAMARA, IN RETROSPECT: THE TRAGEDY AND LESSONS OF VIETNAM 341–342 (1995).

McNamara states that, "no one should believe that, had American troops been attacked with nuclear weapons, the United States would have refrained from a nuclear response." *Id* at 341.

> And where would it have ended? In utter disaster. Not only would our casualties in Cuba have been devastating, and the island destroyed, but there would have been a high risk of the nuclear exchange extending beyond Cuba as well.
>
> The point I wish to emphasize is this: human beings are fallible. We all make mistakes. In our daily lives, they are costly but we try to learn from them. In conventional war, they cost lives, sometimes thousands of lives. But if mistakes were to affect decisions relating to the use of nuclear forces, they would result in the destruction of whole societies. Thus, the indefinite combination of human fallibility and nuclear weapons carries a high risk of a potential catastrophe.
>
> Is there a military justification for continuing to accept that risk? The answer is no.

Id., at 341–342.

[6] *See* THE NUCLEAR SEDUCTION, *supra* note 1, at 91; FRED KAPLAN, THE WIZARDS OF ARMAGEDDON 370–71 (1983). *See also* ROBERT J. LIFTON & GREG MITCHELL, HIROSHIMA IN AMERICA, FIFTY YEARS OF DENIAL 221 (1995); RAYMOND L. GARTHOFF, DÉTENTE AND CONFRONTATION: AMERICAN–SOVIET RELATIONS FROM NIXON TO REAGAN 974 (1985); THE NUCLEAR SEDUCTION, *supra* note 1, at 137–138 (citing Ellsburg, *supra* note 2, at 37–39).

[7] There was talk of the possibility of using nuclear weapons in the Gulf War:

> Speaking for the use of tactical [nuclear] weapons was Congressman Dan Burton of Indiana, and against it the Republican whip, Newt Gingrich of Georgia. They spoke in January, with the

The Brookings Institution in a major study further counted some nineteen incidents between 1946–1973 in which "America's strategic nuclear forces were actively involved in a political incident 'in such a context that a nuclear signal of some type could be inferred.'"[8] Although the United States never used such weapons again after Hiroshima and Nagasaki, it demonstrated time and again its willingness to roll the "nuclear dice" in order to make its adversaries believe its threat to do so was a serious one.[9]

Desmond Ball, Head of the Strategic and Defense Studies Centre, Australian National University, Canberra, reported that there have been some twenty occasions during which "responsible officials of the United States government formally considered the use of nuclear weapons."[10] Such instances included: Vietnam in 1954;[11] Quemoy and

---

air war already begun and the ground war imminent. Congressman Burton's argument was simple—that if the alternative was bloody ground warfare, tactical nuclear weapons should be used to save American lives. Not so, said Congressman Gingrich, and he gave powerful general reasons for his view: if the United States should "establish a pattern out there that it is legitimate to use those kinds of weapons, our children and grandchildren are going to rue the day." On a more immediate note, he supplied: "We would not want to live in a world in which we had sent a signal to every country on the planet to get nuclear weapons as fast as we can." To top off his argument, Congressman Gingrich denied his colleague's premise that the conventional ground war was going to be bloody and protracted for Americans. "If you look at the quality of our weapons today, we can do an amazing amount of damage with a conventional weapon."

McGeorge Bundy, *Nuclear Weapons and the Gulf*, FOREIGN AFF., Fall 1991, at 83, 85–86.

It appears that there was a view in the Pentagon towards the use of nuclear weapons in the Gulf War sufficiently strong as to elicit a disclaimer from then President Bush's chief of staff, John Sununu, to the effect that there was no likelihood of the use of nuclear weapons.

See id. at 86.

[8] *See* THE NUCLEAR SEDUCTION, *supra* note 1, at 136 (citing BLECHMAN & STEVEN S. KAPLAN, FORCE WITHOUT WAR: U.S. ARMED FORCES AS A POLITICAL INSTRUMENT (1978)).

[9] *See id.*

[10] *See* Ball, *supra* note 1, at 41–42.

[11] *See* Ball, *supra* note 1, at 42; BETTS, *supra* note 2, at 38 (*cited in* NUCLEAR SEDUCTION, *supra* note 1, at 85). *See also* MCGEORGE BUNDY, DANGER AND SURVIVAL: CHOICES ABOUT THE BOMB IN THE FIRST FIFTY YEARS,

Matsu in 1954–1955, 1958;[12] Middle East in 1967;[13] Suez in 1970;[14] Jordan in 1970;[15] Cuba in 1970;[16] India and Pakistan in 1971;[17] Vietnam in 1968–1972;[18] and Lebanon in 1982–1983.[19]

266–667 (1988); Jim Calogero, *Conference at MIT Stresses Disarmament,* BOSTON GLOBE, Dec. 5, 1982.

> [W]hen the besieged French in Dien Bien Phu were desperate, French and U.S military leaders considered the possibility of relieving the fortress by using U.S. air strikes against the Vietnamese attackers. Within the U.S. military, discussion favored the use of low-yield nuclear weapons for that purpose. President Eisenhower later told his biographer that when these discussions were reported to him, he responded: "You boys must be crazy. We can't use those awful things against Asians for a second time in less than ten years. My God."

Carl Kaysen, Robert S. McNamara & George W. Rathjens, *Nuclear Weapons after the Cold War,* FOREIGN AFF. Fall 1991, at 95–110 (citing STEPHEN E. AMBROSE, EISENHOWER vol. 2, at 184 (1983)).

McNamara further reports that a Working Group which President Johnson established in 1964 under Assistant Secretary of State William Bundy to review U.S. options in the Vietnamese War concluded that the United States had to be ready to embark upon a Korean-scale ground action and possibly even the use of nuclear weapons at some point. McNamara states that the Joint Chiefs downplayed such risks, regarding them as acceptable, but that it was "precisely such risks" that President Johnson and he had been determined to avoid. MCNAMARA, IN RETROSPECT, *supra* note 5, at 160.

McNamara goes on to state:

> The president was shocked by the almost cavalier way in which the chiefs and their associates, on this and other occasions, referred to, and accepted the risk of, the possible use of nuclear weapons. Apart from the moral issues raised by nuclear strikes, initiating such action against a nuclear-equipped opponent is almost surely an act of suicide. I do not want to exaggerate the risks associated with the chiefs' views, but I believe that even a low risk of a catastrophic event must be avoided. That lesson had not been learned in 1964. I fear neither our nation nor the world has fully learned it to this day.

Id. at 160–61.

McNamara notes that the chiefs further recommended "that invasions of North Vietnam, Laos, and Cambodia might become necessary, involving …quite possibly, the use of nuclear weapons in southern China." McNamara states, "Their continued willingness to risk a nuclear confrontation appalled me." *Id.* at 275, 111.

[12] *See* Ball, *supra* note 1, at 42–43; THE NUCLEAR SEDUCTION, *supra* note 1, at 86, 88 (citing Gordon H. Chang, *To the Nuclear Brink: Eisenhower, Dulles, The Quemoy/Matsu Crisis,* 4 INT'L SECURITY 99 (1988)). *See also* Bundy,

Whether the United States would actually have followed through on its threats to use nuclear weapons is perhaps unknowable. From the after-the-fact ruminations of American decision-makers, it seems that they themselves are generally not certain.[20]

Heightening the ostensible danger that the United States might well have initiated nuclear war is the extent to which the U.S. threats exposed the decision-making process to the vagaries of chance, most particularly to the potential reactions and counter-threats of the other side, along with the dangers of miscommunication, misperception, irrationality, emotionality, fog of war, and the like.[21] Significantly, in

---

supra note 7, at 277–8; Telephone to General Twining, September 2, 1958, 8: 48 A.M., John Foster Dulles Paper, Box 9, DDE (*cited in* Bundy, *supra* note 7, at 279).

[13] *See* Ball, *supra* note 1, at 43; BETTS, *supra* note 2, at 128.

[14] *See* HENRY KISSINGER, THE WHITE HOUSE YEARS 570–71, 580–82 (1979).

[15] *See* RICHARD M. NIXON, R.N.: THE MEMOIRS OF RICHARD M. NIXON, 477, 483 (1978) [hereinafter NIXON]; THE NUCLEAR SEDUCTION, *supra* note 1, at 96 (citing SEYMOUR M. HERSCH, THE PRICE OF POWER: KISSINGER IN THE NIXON WHITEHOUSE 238 (1983)).

[16] *See* NIXON, *supra* note 15, at 486, 488, 528.

[17] *See* NIXON, *supra* note 15, at 528; NUCLEAR SEDUCTION, *supra* note 1, at 106 (citing MORTON H. HALPERIN, NUCLEAR FALLACY, DISPELLING THE MYTH OF NUCLEAR STRATEGISTS 41–42 (1987)).

[18] *See* KARL KAYSEN, ET. AL, 184; MCNAMARA, IN RETROSPECT, *supra* note 5, at 234 (1995); THE NUCLEAR SEDUCTION, *supra* note 1, at 107 (citing H. R. HALLDEMAN, MEMOIR, THE END OF POWER 82–83 (1978)); DANIEL ELLSBERG, A CALL TO MUTINY, THE DEADLY CONNECTION: NUCLEAR WAR AND US INTERVENTION 56–57 (Joseph Gerson ed., 1986); NIXON, *supra* note 15, at 481–482, 485 (*cited in* THE NUCLEAR SEDUCTION, *supra* note 1, at 133). *See also* BLECKMAN & STEPHENS KAPLAN, FORCE WITHOUT WAR: U.S. ARMS FORCES AS A POLITICAL INSTRUMENT 133 (1978).

[19] *See* THE NUCLEAR SEDUCTION, *supra* note 1, at 133 (citing BLECKMAN & KAPLAN, FORCE WITHOUT WAR; U.S. ARMED FORCES AS A POLITICAL INSTRUMENT (1978)).

[20] *See, e.g.,* MCNAMARA, IN RETROSPECT, *supra* note 5, at 160–161, 234.

[21] Robert McNamara has written recently of the results of meetings with former Russian officials highlighting how close we were to nuclear war with the Russians during the Cuban Missile Crisis. ROBERT S. MCNAMARA, JAMES G. BLIGHT, & ROBERT K. BRIGHAM, ARGUMENT WITHOUT END: IN SEARCH OF ANSWERS TO THE VIETNAM TRAGEDY 9–15 (1999). McNamara states, "By the conclusion of the third Cuban missile crisis conference, in Moscow in 1989, it had become clear that the decisions of each of the three nations before, during, and after the crisis had been distorted by misinformation, miscalculation, and

terms of the ability of the decision-makers in the above instances to
retain control of events, none of the instances reached the situation of a
threat of an actual attack upon the United States homeland.

---

misjudgment." *Id.* at 9. Among the misinformation was that the CIA had
concluded Russia had no tactical nuclear warheads on Cuba, whereas in fact it
had such warheads and bombs to be used in responding to any invasion of the
island by the United States, and that such warheads, with the written approval
of Khrushchev, had in the course of the conflict been moved from their storage
sites closer to their delivery vehicles in anticipation of a U.S. invasion. *Id.* at
9–10.

Chapter 21: Probabilities as to Accuracy of U.S. Targeting of Nuclear Weapons

Beyond nuclear policy and the fact of non-use is the question of what would happen if the United States actually launched a nuclear weapon. Since the lawfulness of a particular use of a nuclear weapon hinges in large measure on the probable effects of that use, it becomes important to ask such questions as the following:

> 1. With what level of accuracy is the United States able to deliver a nuclear weapon to its intended target?
> 2. With what level of reliability is the United States able to predict and control the level of destruction likely to be caused, directly or indirectly, by the use of a particular weapon?

Since no nuclear weapons were used in war after Hiroshima and Nagasaki, predicting the accuracy with which the United States could hit designated targets with nuclear weapons, and the likely destructiveness of such hits, is based upon technical calculations and assumptions and, to a lesser extent, upon actual testing.

The considerations relevant to the likely effects of the detonation of a nuclear weapon are legion, including such matters as the following: the characteristics and actual performance of the warhead and its delivery vehicle; characteristics of the earth and the earth's atmosphere, including gravitational force and the movement of stars (many missile guidance systems are based upon stellar movements); the topography and other physical conditions of the target area or of the area where the weapon actually hits; the weather; and the functioning of the computer components of the nuclear device itself and of the delivery mechanism.[1] Variations in any of these or a myriad of other factors could materially change the effects of a particular use of a nuclear weapons.

Data from actual testing is limited, both because of the dangers inherent in such testing, political factors, and the legal requirements of test ban treaties limiting the testing of nuclear weapons in the

---

[1] *See generally* Ashton B. Carter, *Sources of Error and Uncertainty, in* MANAGING NUCLEAR OPERATIONS 611–639 (Ashton B. Carter et al. eds., 1987).

atmosphere, under ground, under the sea, and in outer space, and, more recently, potentially banning all testing.[2]

---

[2]　*See* Norman Kempster & Jonathan Peterson, *Nuclear Powers Lead in Signing Atomic Test Ban,* LOS ANGELES TIMES, Wed., Sept. 25, 1996, at A1.

See also Alan Neidle, *Nuclear Test Bans: History and Future Prospects, in* U.S.–SOVIET SECURITY COOPERATION 175–181 (Alexander L. George et al. eds., 1988). After 235 atmospheric nuclear tests, the United States, the Soviet Union and Great Britain agreed to a treaty banning testing in the atmosphere, in outer space and under water under the Limited Test Ban Treaty (LTBT) of 1963. *Id.* The LTBT, which has been effective since 1963, now has over one hundred parties. *Id.* However, underground tests were not prohibited until the United States and the Soviet Union signed the Threshold Test Ban Treaty of 1974 (TTBT), which limited underground nuclear tests to explosions not more than 150 kilotons. *Id.* In 1976, the Peaceful Nuclear Explosions Treaty (PNET), a complementary bilateral treaty controlling underground nuclear tests for peaceful purposes, was signed. *Id.*

On September 25, 1996, the United States, Russia, China, the United Kingdom and France, and as many as 65 nations signed the Comprehensive Test Ban Treaty at the United Nations in New York. The CTBT effectively outlaws all nuclear testing and development of nuclear weapons. However, the treaty does not formally take effect until it is signed and ratified by all 44 nations that conduct nuclear research or have nuclear reactors, including India and Pakistan, which have refused to sign. *See* Barbara Crossette, *Defeat of a Treaty; The Shock Waves,* THE NEW YORK TIMES, Oct. 15, 1999, at A1. However, the other five declared nuclear powers had imposed voluntary moratoriums on nuclear testing, although questions have arisen as to whether China and Russia have complied with such moratoriums, and after their 1998 tests, India and Pakistan also declared moratoriums. *See* Kempster & Peterson, *supra,* citing Stockholm International Peace Research Institute; Chapter 23, note 6 and accompanying text. *See also Russian Nuke Tests,* WASH. TIMES, June 25, 1999, at A6.

On October 13, 1999, the U.S. Senate, in a partisan vote following the lead of Senator Jesse Helms, Chairman of the Foreign Relations Committee, rejected the CTBT. Eric Schmitt, *Senate Kills Test ban Treaty in Crushing Loss for Clinton; Evokes Versailles Pact Defeat,* THE NEW YORK TIMES, Oct. 14, 1999, at A1. *See also* James K. Wyerman, Gilbert Tucker & Paul Sedan, Letter to Editor, CHRISTIAN SCIENCE MONITOR, July 2, 1999, at 10.

The President, or a future president (Vice President Al Gore has vowed to do so if elected President), could resubmit the treaty to the Senate for ratification. *See* Scott Shepard, *CAMPAIGN 2000: Gore Attacks GOP's Test-Ban Stance in First TV Ad; Vice President Pens Campaign Spot While in Seattle Hotel,* THE ATLANTA JOURNAL & CONSTITUTION, Oct. 15, 1999, at 4C.

As of October 13, 1999, 26 of the 44 nations considered to have nuclear capability had approved the CTBT, including Britain, France and Japan, but

The testing which has taken place is subject to inherent limitations, decreasing the confidence level with which one may assume that the actual use of nuclear weapons would accord with the test results. Tests are generally conducted with more than adequate time for preparation, adjustments, special arrangements and the like, in contrast to the chaotic circumstances likely to prevail in circumstances of actual use in war. Tests of delivery vehicles are generally performed using available test facilities, targets and the like. In the process, variables peculiar to the testing circumstances may be adjusted for in ways perhaps skewering the test results, overstating reliability.

Thus, during the Cold War, the results of the United States' repeated testing of its ICBMs through firing them from the California coast at Vandenberg Air Force Base to a large enclosed lagoon, approximately 10 miles wide and 16 miles long, at the Kwajalein Atoll in the Marshall Island, bore an uncertain relationship to the likely results of firing the same ICBMs against variable real targets in circumstances of war.

M.I.T. Professor Kosta Tsipis has identified an extensive series of "known" and "unknown" factors affecting the accuracy with which nuclear weapons can be delivered to their targets. Known factors are basically categories of error known to arise. Unknown factors, correspondingly, are errors whose causes are unknown. This later category is more than just a contingency budget for the unexpected; it describes the reality that ballistic missile testing often results in misses and deviations that cannot be explained by known error sources.[3]

As to known errors, Dr. Tsipis has identified the following categories:

> 1. errors in specifying initial conditions, including such factors as the geographic location of the missile at launch, its velocity at take-off, and its alignment, as well as the physical condition of the equipment itself, including whether it has any technical deficiencies which will affect its performance;
> 2. errors caused by inertial guidance, involving issues as to the missile's velocity, position and orientation as measured by, and subject to the calibration of, the missile's guidance system, including its excelerometers, gyroscopes and other measuring instruments;

Russia and China had yet to ratify it and were expected to take their lead from the U.S. Senate. Eric Schmitt, *supra*, at A14;

[3] KOSTA TSIPIS, ARSENAL: UNDERSTANDING WEAPONS IN THE NUCLEAR AGE 68, 296 (1983).

3. errors in guidance formulation by the missile's computers, caused by faulty computations with respect to applicable known or assumed numbers;

4. errors in thrust termination, where, given the extraordinary speed of the missile, a millisecond error in the timing of terminating thrust can have an appreciable effect on accuracy;

5. errors due to gravitational anomalies, in a context where the gravitational forces of the earth play a major role in the trajectory of the missile in the early stages of flight so that, if the gravitational field is not known or is incorrectly measured, the missile will assume a different velocity and direction than intended, and where similar errors may be introduced once the powered flight is completed and the warhead floats toward a target under the influence of gravity in the vacuum of space, with its accuracy of delivery being subject to the accuracy of the mapping of the subject gravitational field;

6. targeting errors;

7. errors arising from re-entry, in a context where the warhead, cased in a re-entry vehicle (RV), will be subjected to strong aerodynamic forces, extreme heat and speed ablation, the burning away of the coating of the RV to, among other things, absorb the extraordinary heat created during re-entry, and the resultant dangers of equipment malfunction and loss of accuracy.[4]

As to the latter category of errors arising from re-entry, Dr. Tsipis has identified the following main sub-categories:

1. atmospheric variations/weather conditions in a context where the accuracy with which the warhead may be delivered to the target is affected by such weather conditions as wind, rain and the atmospheric density on the RV, none of which may be predicted with perfect accuracy, since, among other reasons, wind and air density in the many layers of atmosphere through which the RV will pass, change rapidly and unpredictably with the weather;

---

[4] *See id.* at 68–76, 114–115, 121–296. *See also* DONALD MCKENZIE, INVENTING ACCURACY: A HISTORICAL SOCIOLOGY OF NUCLEAR MISSILE GUIDANCE 349 (1990).

2. vehicle asymmetries,[5] in a context where microscopic "rough spots" on the RV can cause one part of the RV to weigh more than another, so that the RV, as it spins through the atmosphere, is overweighed on that one side, with the result that the accuracy of delivery can be significantly affected, based upon a combination of air pressure on the RV and the microscopic "rough spots"; and

3. warhead fusing or detonation, where, as is often the case, the warhead is designed for detonation above ground (*i.e.*, for air burst) and where the accuracy and reliably of the fusing device is key to the precision with which the warhead may be delivered to its intended target.[6]

The general precision with which a missile is likely to hit its designated target is defined by its circular error probability (CEP), which is essentially a prediction of the probability as to where the missile will hit.[7] A missile's CEP is measured through repeated firing of the missile against a target and a valuation of the distribution of the landing points around the target. The CEP is the radius of the circle drawn around the target in which, on average, half of the re-entry vehicles fired at the target will fall.[8]

------

[5] TSIPIS, *supra* note 3, at 72–75 (Vehicle asymmetries can also be created, *inter alia*, by ablation, which can have a significant effect on the accuracy of the weapon). Other atmospheric variations that an RV must pass through which can significantly effect the accuracy with which the warhead can be delivered are thick clouds, rain, snow and hail, as well as dust clouds raised by previous nuclear detonations, all of which can cause the erosion or the ablation of the RV's nose tip, contributing asymmetries affecting accuracy. *See id.* When a RV travels through a cloud, water droplets or dust particles erode the surface of the RV. Since the RV is traveling at several kilometers per second, the effect of such particles is akin to a sand blaster of extraordinary power. *See id.* at 77. The cloud cover is thick enough to erode away the nose tip of the RV completely, exposing the RV to the high temperatures of re-entry which may cause the RV to burn away completely. *See id.*

Such destruction of the RV during re-entry caused by dust clouds raised during previous nuclear explosions, is know as fratricide. *See id.* A half-megaton ground burst is like to raise some 200,000 tons of dust, which could destroy the accuracy of subsequent RVs which must pass through such dust. *See id.* at 78.

[6] *See id.* at 69–76.

[7] *See id.* at 139.

[8] *See id.*

CEPs of American's nuclear weapons are available in the public literature. Based upon such reports, the CEPs of the systems currently in place, including the ICBMs, SLBMs, and particularly the cruise missiles, reflect a high degree of accuracy.[9] The most extraordinary accuracy appears to be that of cruise missiles which are said to be so accurate they can be directed through the goal posts at both ends of a football field after a journey of several hundred miles.[10]

These CEP figures, while encouraging as to the probable accuracy of the United States' current delivery systems, in a sense answer only half of the story, and perhaps not the more important half. What about the other half of the missiles, the ones landing outside the CEP? Statistically, and operationally, where are they likely to fall? How many of the errant weapons will land at a considerable distance, perhaps many miles from the center of the subject, hitting targets of an entirely different character than that intended? If that happens, what will be the effects of such strikes?

And, of course, there is the issue of the error rate inherent in the calculation of the CEP as to any particular weapon, even with respect to the half of the weapons fired which are expected to strike within the CEP circle? Upon how many testings are these CEP calculations based? Under what conditions do these tests take place? What is the relationship of such test circumstances to the actual circumstances of war?

Several conclusions emerge from the data as to the reliability of the United State's contemporary delivery system. The good news is that it appears that, as a statistical matter, the United States is able to deliver nuclear weapons with a high degree of accuracy. Statistically, it can be expected that a fairly high percent of weapons launched will hit their intended target. The bad news is that, given the destructiveness of these weapons, the repercussions of the misdirection of even a small percentage of a nuclear weapons could be substantial.

Perhaps the best example was the United States' experience with its cruise missiles in the 1991 Gulf War. The Navy achieved a success

---

[9] *See* Kosta Tsipis, *Cruise Missiles*, SCIENTIFIC AMERICAN, Feb. 1977, at 20–29 (the CEP of the ALCM is 300 ft). *See also* charts at end of Chapter 19; Chapter 19, note 8 and accompanying text. *See also* 1 THOMAS B. COCHRAN ET AL., NUCLEAR WEAPONS DATABOOK, UNITED STATES NUCLEAR FORCES AND CAPABILITIES 118 (1984).

[10] *See* Stanley Kandebo, *Operation Desert Storm—Tomahawk Missiles Excel in First Wartime Use,* AVIATION WEEK & SPACE TECH., vol. 134, no. 3, Jan. 21, 1991, at 61.

rate of some 82% with its BG-109 cruise missile, the Tomahawk.[11] However, even this extraordinary success rate, which was higher than that for the United States' most advanced fighters,[12] was only an average. While some missions achieved a near perfect success rate,[13] one mission obtained a rate of only 67%.[14]

This was the June 26, 1991 effort by two U.S. Navy ships to launch 24 Tomahawk missiles against the Iraqi Central Intelligence Headquarters. Of the 24, one failed to launch, 16 hit their designated targets, 3 hit somewhere in the compound, 1 strike was ambiguous and 3 others crashed outside the compound in residential areas.[15]

If "one-target, one-bomb" efficiency could not be achieved in this war where there was little air defense or active enemy opposition on the level of sophisticated weaponry,[16] such efficiency seems unlikely of reliable attainment in the context of a "real war" between nuclear superpowers.

The cruise missile attacks of August 1998 confirm the risk that cruise missiles may stray widely from their intended targets. Two of the approximately 50 missiles intended for bin Laden's strongholds in Afghanistan and the Khartoum chemical factory in the Sudan reportedly ended up in Pakistan.[17]

---

[11] *See* David Fulghum, *Clashes with Iraq Continue After Heavy Air Strike*, AVIATION WEEK & SPACE TECH., Jan. 25, 1993, at 38.

[12] *See id.*

[13] *See* Kandebo, *supra* note 10, at 61.

[14] *See* Fulghum, *supra* note 11, at 38.

[15] *See id.* at 38–42.

[16] *See* United States General Accounting Office, Report To Congress: Operation Desert Storm: Evaluation of the Air War 5–7 (July 1996).

[17] *See* John Diamond, *US Strikes May Not Be The Last, Warns Pickering,* BIRMINGHAM POST, Aug. 22, 1998, at 8; Ian Mackinnon, *Pakistan Defuses US Cruise Missile,* THE SCOTSMAN, Aug. 25, 1998, at 8; *Pakistan—Cruise Missile Found Near Pakistan Nuclear Test Site,* FT ASIA INTELLIGENCE WIRE, Aug. 24, 1998; Louise Branson, *US Bombs "Terrorist Bases,"* THE STRAITS TIMES (Singapore), Aug. 22, 1998, at 1; *2nd Unexploded U.S. Missile Found In Pakistan,* THE COMMERCIAL APPEAL (Memphis, TN), Aug. 30, 1998, at A2.

According to a Pakistani foreign ministry spokesman, the two missiles ending up in Pakistan had been fired from U.S. ships 120 nautical miles off the coast of Pakistan, well within the country's territorial waters, and landed near the sites where Pakistan had tested nuclear weapons on May 28 and 30, 1998. Mackinnon, *supra,* at 8. Thus, the missiles that went astray had not even been sent a long distance.

A third unexploded warhead with its cruise missile delivery vehicle was reportedly found in Afghanistan. *See* BBC SUMMARY OF WORLD BROADCASTS,

Dr. Tsipis reported during the Cold War era that ballistic missiles were said to have a reliability rate "between 70% and 90%."[18] In 1978, Dr. Tsipis estimated that a Minuteman III missile launched against a Russian silo would have a 67% probability of a kill if two warheads were targeted against the silo, and a 44% if one warhead were so targeted.[19] Others estimated in the early 1980s that the reliability of U.S. missiles, in terms of the likelihood of their reaching their intended targets, varied between some 75% and 80%, with Soviet reliability being somewhere between 65% and 70%.[20]

While the various levels of probability cited here are offered more for illustrative purposes than for literal truth, the primary point seems ineluctable: that, with respect to any particular launch of a nuclear weapon, there is a not insignificant probability that the weapon will go afield, landing at some distance from its intended target. With conventional weapons, such a mishap could lead to unfortunate results; with nuclear weapons, the results could be catastrophic.

Sept. 7, 1998 (Taleban said ready to sell unexploded US cruise missile "to any country.").

All this in an operation where the United States apparently went to great lengths to achieve accuracy and precision, even to the point, in planning an attack on a chemical plant in Sudan, of modeling the "likely plume of [the] attack beforehand, using such factors as weather conditions, the building's structure and properties of the suspected chemicals inside." *See* John-Alex Romano, *Note, Combating Terrorism and Weapons of Mass Destruction: Reviving the Doctrine of a State of Necessity,* 87 GEO. L.J. 1023 (April 1999) (quoting Eugene Robinson & Dana Priest, *Reports of U.S. Strikes' Destruction Vary; Afghanistan Damage 'Moderate to Heavy'; Sudan Plant Leveled,* WASH. POST, Aug. 22, 1998, at A1).

It also emerged after these strikes that the intelligence upon which they had been based, including as to the nature of the intended targets, had been questionable, as had the communications of the available intelligence between the applicable military and political officials, including the President and his closest advisors. *See* James Risen, *Question of Evidence, A Special Report.; To Bomb Sudan Plant, or Not: A Year Later, Debates Rankle,* NEW YORK TIMES, October 27, 1999, at A1.

[18] TSIPIS, ARSENAL: UNDERSTANDING WEAPONS IN THE NUCLEAR AGE, *supra* note 3, at 114.

[19] *See* KOSTA TSIPIS, NUCLEAR EXPLOSION EFFECTS ON MISSILE SILOS 83–87 (1978).

[20] *See* ROBERT C. ALDRIDGE, FIRST STRIKE! THE PENTAGON'S STRATEGY FOR NUCLEAR WAR 56 (1983); HELEN CALDICOTT, MISSILE ENVY—THE ARMS RACE AND NUCLEAR WAR 121 (1984). *See also* THE BOSTON STUDY GROUP, THE PRICE OF DEFENSE—A NEW STRATEGY FOR MILITARY SPENDING 83 (1979).

Once the weapon reaches its target, if it does, the second question set forth above is raised, as to the predictability and controllability of the effects of the detonation.

As to the blast and heat effects, this largely depends upon the nature, particularly the yield of the weapon, and the nature of the target area.[21] As to the radiation effects, many of the same climatic effects affecting accuracy of delivery similarly affect the potential dispersal of radiation, including such proverbially uncontrollable variables as the weather.

As the United States, through its attorney McNeill, argued to the ICJ, the effects of nuclear weapons depend on such factors as "the explosive yield and height of the burst of individual weapons, on the characteristics of their targets, as well as on climatic and weather conditions,"[22] and on "the technology that occasions how much radiation the weapon may release, where, in relations to the earth's surface it will be detonated, and the military objective at which it would be targeted."[23] As to the potential effects of such factors, McNeill argued that, "These differences, distinctions and variables cannot be ignored; they are critical to the appropriate legal analysis."[24]

As we have seen, the question of whether the weapon detonates in the air or on the ground is of major significance in terms of the likely dispersal of radiation.[25] Obviously there is a major risk factor in terms of our ability to predict and control this matter.

Nor are the risks of hitting the wrong target limited to the technological and human risks inherent in the effort to deliver any particular payload to a particular location. As the United States' mistaken bombing of the Chinese embassy in Belgrade in May 1999 during the Kosovo operation illustrated, misdelivery of warheads can occur for other reasons, such as failures of intelligence.

In that instance, the United States, using JDAM guided bomb munitions delivered by a B-2 stealth bomber, while targeting a Serbian armament agency, mistakenly hit the Chinese embassy, killing at least three people, including two Chinese reporters and the wife of one, setting off an international incident characterized by anger, suspicion,

---

[21] *See* Chapter 15, notes 99–127 and accompanying text.

[22] ICJ Hearing, November 15, 1995, at 87 (citing the Secretary-General's 1990 Report of Nuclear Weapons, p. 75, para. 290).

[23] ICJ Hearing, November 15, 1995, at 89.

[24] ICJ Hearing, November 15, 1995, at 87.

[25] *See* Chapter 15, 81–82, 100; THE NUCLEAR ALMANAC: CONFRONTING THE ATOM IN WAR AND PEACE 91, 94 (Jack Dennis ed., 1984).

mistrust and, arguably, manipulative jingoism on the part of China.[26] The Chinese reaction apparently arose not only out of the incident itself, but also out of skepticism as to the accidental nature of the strike.[27]

While the Chinese reaction was only verbal and arguably of a "propagandistic" nature, one can readily imagine how, if bellicose antagonism had existed between the two nations at the time or had seemed opportune to either side, more serious repercussions might have ensued.

The mishap apparently resulted from faulty intelligence, itself possibly resulting at least in part from budgetary constraints, leading to the use of a 1992 map, updated in 1997 and then again in 1998, that listed the embassy building as the Serbian armament agency actually located a block away.[28] It turned out that the embassy had been built in the location three years previously, but U.S. intelligence maps and "multiple no-strike databases" had not been updated to reflect its presence.[29]

The incident highlighted the obvious reality, beyond even the ever-present statistical and other risks of misdirection discussed above, that the most high tech of equipment capable of the most precise of targeting does not confer immunity from hitting the wrong target.[30]

Nor was the Chinese embassy mishap the only mistargeting event of the Kosovo operation. There were numerous other incidents of hitting the wrong target or of collateral damage being inflicted upon noncombatant targets.

Examples: Albanian refugees were bombed by NATO forces on a road in southern Kosovo; Aleksinac, a town miles from a military target was similarly hit by mistake, resulting in six civilians dead and fifty badly injured; civilian homes in Merdare were hit with

---

[26] *See* Rowan Scarborough, *What's Left*; *Kosovo Agreement*, THE WASH. TIMES, June 11, 1999, at A12. *See* Rowan Scarborough, *As Strikes Mount, So Do Errors*, THE WASH. TIMES, May 11, 1999, at A1. *See* Joyce Price, *Pentagon Regrets "Embassy Error,"* THE WASH. TIMES, May 9, 1999, at C10.

[27] *See* Andrew Cain, *U.S. Says Embassy Was Not a Target*, THE WASH. TIMES, May 25, 1999, at A14.

[28] *See* Scarborough, *As Strikes Mount, supra* note 26. *See also* Price, *Crisis in Kosovo*, THE WASH. TIMES, May 10, 1999, at A11.

[29] Bill Gertz & Rowan Scarborough, *Inside the Ring*, THE WASH. TIMES, May 14, 1999, at A9 (quoting a senior intelligence official). *See also* Price, *Pentagon Regrets, supra* note 26).

[30] *See* Helle Bering, *Commentary Op-Ed, War of the Worlds*, THE WASH. TIMES, May 19, 1999, at A19.

antipersonnel bombs; rockets hit a passenger train crossing a targeted bridge in Belgrade.[31]   There were also many incidents with cluster bombs used by NATO forces, reportedly resulting in "unprecedented amputations in Kosovo hospitals ....   These bombs have hundreds of shrapnellike fragments that enter the body and cannot easily be removed, causing unbearable pain.   Serb children have picked up unexploded bombs and been mutilated."[32]   On May 7, 1999 a cluster bomb went off course spraying bomblets on a hospital and an open-air market.[33]

---

[31] Howard Zinn, *Their Atrocities—And Ours*, THE PROGRESSIVE, vol. 63, issue 7, July 1, 1999, at 20.

[32] *See* Zinn, *supra* note 31, at 20–21.

[33] *See* Scarborough, *As Strikes Mount, supra* note 26.

Chapter 22: Risk Factors Inherent in the Practice of Nuclear Deterrence

As we have seen, the practice of deterrence requires the availability of equipment and personnel sufficient to deter potential adversaries. Obviously, the maintenance of such a practice and of the related equipment and personnel entails many risks, including the following:

-   The Danger of Precipitating a Nuclear War: Both the policy and the weapons are provocative and in a crisis could readily precipitate actual use.
-   The Fostering of an Arms Race: Mankind and its societies are inherently competitive, particularly where self-image, self-interest, patriotism, and potential survival are at stake. There is also a strong human and societal instinct to build things, including particularly weapons, bigger and "better." States can be expected to want to have weapons comparable to, and indeed more powerful than, those possessed by their potential enemies.
-   The Fostering of Nuclear Proliferation: While the major powers can be expected to engage in an arms race with one another, "lesser" States can be expected to want to acquire at least some nuclear weapons to secure the power, prestige and ostensible security such weapons confer. The desire to wield extremely powerful weapons, particularly when potential enemies have or may acquire them, seems central to human nature and societies.
-   The Risks of Terrorism: As quintessential terror weapons, nuclear weapons are obviously potentially attractive to terrorist groups and individuals. With the broad availability of technical information as to nuclear weapons and indeed potential availability of the weapons themselves, the risks of a terrorist group or individual getting ahold of such weapons and wreaking mayhem on urban society is very real, only heightened by the fact such weapons have gotten much smaller to the point of now truly being deliverable in a "suitcase" or "pickup truck."
-   The Risks of Human and Equipment Failure: The normal proclivity of humans and their equipment to mistake and error is rendered exponentially more significant when the potential effects of nuclear weapons are involved.

-   Risks of Testing, Production, Storage and Disposal of Nuclear Weapons Materials: While at the outset of the Cold War it had appeared that nuclear weapons, with their ostensible "bigger bang for the buck," offered substantial economies per unit of destruction, time has revealed extraordinary environmental and epidemiological costs associated with the production, storage and disposal of nuclear weapons materials, a kind of economic "fallout" imposing costs potentially in the billions and even trillions of dollars for generations to come and with health costs and human pain and suffering beyond calculation.

-   The Risk of the Degradation of Conventional Weapons Capability: As demonstrated by the U.S. experience during the Cold War and presently by the Russian situation in the post Cold War era, the possession of nuclear weapons can become a substitute for a State's maintenance of a conventional weapons capability sufficient for its self-defense, providing a ready excuse for not expending the funds necessary to maintain such a conventional capability—leading to the situation where the State, in a crisis situation, may have no option other than to surrender or use nuclear weapons.

-   Jeopardy to Rule of Law: However one comes out as to the niceties of international law, the nature of nuclear weapons seems so inconsistent with the rule of law that it becomes difficult on a macro basis to accept that a system that accepted the legality of such weapons could be based on the rule of law. Nuclear weapons seem to be the very antithesis of the sense of restraint underlying the rule of law, and the milieu they foster even has the potential to undermine domestic law.

-   Overriding Risk Factors as to the Likelihood that the Unlikely Will Occur: I have discussed throughout this book bases for concluding that the current nuclear weapons regime makes the use of nuclear weapons likely over some period of time, whether intentionally or by inadvertence. Even if it is assumed, however, that that risk is small or remote, some risk remains. Yet even extremely improbable events occur with great regularity, reinforcing our intuitive sense that the obvious risks of the nuclear weapons regime will likely eventuate at some point in time unless we radically alter our current policies, practices, arsenals and overall course of action.

Referring to the overall dangers, retired Air Force Gen. Lee Butler, who commanded thousands of strategic nuclear weapons as head of the United States Strategic Command, stated, "Despite all the evidence, we have yet to fully grasp the monstrous effect of these weapons, that the consequences of their use defy reason, transcending time and space, poisoning the Earth and deforming its inhabitants."[1] Nuclear weapons are "inherently dangerous, hugely expensive and militarily inefficient."[2]

General Butler stated that "accepting nuclear weapons as the ultimate arbiter of conflict condemns the world to live under a dark cloud of perpetual anxiety. Worse, it codifies mankind's most murderous instincts as an acceptable resort when other options for resolving conflict fail."[3] He added, "I have spent years studying nuclear weapons effects ... have investigated a distressing array of accidents and incidents involving strategic weapons and forces .... I came away from that experience deeply troubled by what I see as the burden of building and maintaining nuclear arsenals ... the grotesquely destructive war plans, the daily operational risks, and the constant prospect of a crisis that would hold the fate of entire societies at risk."[4]

In a joint statement with Retired Army Gen. Andrew J. Goodpaster, a former Supreme Commander of NATO forces who had commanded thousands of tactical nuclear weapons based in Europe, General Butler stated, "With the end of the Cold War, these weapons are of sharply reduced utility and there is much now to be gained by substantially reducing their numbers and lowering their alert status, meanwhile exploring the feasibility of their ultimate complete elimination."[5]

The Danger of Precipitating a Nuclear War

Train military personnel to use nuclear weapons; conduct regular exercises reinforcing the training; put the weapons and controls in the hands of the military personnel; provide them with contingency plans as to the circumstances in which they are to use the weapons; instill them with a sense of mission as to the lawful and significant purposes of such weapons in upholding the national defense and honor; make them part of an elite corps; have them stand at the ready for decades at

---

[1] Otto Kreisher, *Retired Generals Urge End to Nuclear Arsenal*, THE SAN DIEGO UNION-TRIB., Dec. 5, 1996, at A-1.

[2] *Id.*

[3] *Id.*

[4] *Id.*

[5] *Id.*

a time waiting for the call; instill firm military discipline; make the weapons a publicly advertised centerpiece of the nation's military strategy; locate the weapons so as to leave them vulnerable to pre-emptive attack; villanize the enemy as godless and evil or as a rogue and terrorist nation; convey to military personnel that the weapons will be a major target of enemy attack and that it may be necessary to use them quickly before they can be destroyed; warn the enemy that, in the event of attack, the weapons may or will be used; inculcate in military personnel the notion of intra-war deterrence whereby nuclear weapons may need to be used following an enemy attack to deter further escalating attacks, give the military insufficient alternate conventional capacity to defeat the enemy attack; cut numerous nuclear weapons bearing units and control centers off from each other and from contact with higher authorities; create a situation of hopelessness where the whole society is about to be destroyed, at least unless these weapons can be gotten off fast to destroy and restrain the enemy; give the President and other upper level command authorities only an imperfect understanding of the options and repercussions and accord them only 5 to 10 minutes, or even a matter of seconds, to decide, against the background of SIOP based computer and other plans decades in the making and ostensibly reflecting a broad historical consensus as to approach—do any number of these things, and the stage is set for the actual use of the nuclear weapons.

Threats and the brandishing of the means of implementing them are inherently provocative and likely to evoke escalating counter-threats. The vulnerability of the weapons themselves contributes to the problem. At the extreme is the policy of "launch on warning," whereby a State organizes its equipment to launch when it believes it is under attack, without waiting to confirm the facts. Nonetheless, given the small amounts of time that would be available in any event, the difference between a launch on warning and a simple preemptive strike would appear to be more theoretical than real.

The "use 'em or lose 'em" dilemma also heightens the prospect of use. This very dilemma was the motivating force behind the development of the policy of extended deterrence and the placement of thousands of tactical nuclear weapons in Western Europe during the Cold War, but the risk transcends the tactical nuclear weapons situation. Many types of strategic nuclear weapons, particularly those placed on non-mobile ICBMs, are inviting first strike targets, as are aircraft and submarines while at base.

Even if the decision-makers at the top of the command chain understood that the weapons were only intended for deterrence and not use, the personnel down the line might well have taken their training and instructions and the war plans seriously.[6] And they will likely be exercising control of the weapons.[7] In any event, in the "fog of war," the ability to make careful reasoned decisions in the light of the facts and a calm appraisal of options and ramifications is likely to be impaired.

Given the genetic and environmental effects of nuclear weapons and the extent to which the applicable legal tests, such as the rule of proportionality, turn on the numbers of people killed and injured, it is relevant to consider the number of people potentially living in the future who could be affected by the use of nuclear weapons today.

The U.S. Census Bureau estimates the number of people living in the world as of September 6, 1999 to be 6,010,449,025.[8] The Bureau estimates there were 2,556,000,053 people in 1950, and 4,086,291,229 in 1975.[9]

The Population Division of the United Nations estimates that the world population will stabilize at 11,600,000,000 just after 2200.[10]

---

[6] *See* PAUL BRACKEN, THE COMMAND AND CONTROL OF NUCLEAR FORCES 198 (1983). ("In September 1957 a former commander of NORAD, General Earle E. Partridge stated in an interview that he had been given emergency authority to use certain nuclear weapons. Apparently the reason behind these measures was the fear that there might be no president surviving to send out the necessary orders if the United States absorbed the first blow in a nuclear war. In 1964, General Lauris Norstad, then a former commander of American forces in Europe, broadly hinted in an interview that he too was given such power by President Kennedy. In 1977, Daniel Ellsberg [a high-level nuclear policy-maker] asserted that such predelegated authority had been given to the military by presidents Eisenhower, Kennedy and Johnson .... He stated that the authority had been given to the 'six or seven three-and four-star generals. These generals must have corresponded to the unified and specified commanders.'").

[7] *Id. See generally* HERMAN KAHN ET AL., WAR TERMINATION ISSUES AND CONCEPTS, FINAL REPORT 197–214 (1968).

[8] World POPClock Projection, Source: U.S. Census Bureau, International Data Base, <http://www.census.gov/cgi-bin/ipc/popclockw>, data updated 12/28/98.

[9] Total Midyear Population for the World: 1950–2050, Source: U.S. Census Bureau, International Data Base, <http://www.census.gov/ipc/www/worldpop. html>, data updated 12/28/98.

[10] United Nations, World Population Growth From Year 0 to Stabilization, Data from the Population Division Department of Economic and Social Information and Policy Analysis, <gopher://gopher.undp.org:70/00/ungophers/ popin/wdtrends/histor>, citing J.D. Durand, Historical Estimates of World

Scholars estimate there were between 170,000,000 and 400,000,000 people in year 1 A.D., and between 1,000,000 and 10,000,000 in year 10,000 B.C.[11]

The dynamic of population changes over units of time have been estimated as follows:

WORLD VITAL EVENTS PER TIME UNIT: 1999[12]
(Figures may not add to totals due to rounding)

Time Unit	Births	Natural Deaths	Increase
Year	131,468,233	54,147,021	77,321,212
Month	10,955,686	4,512,252	6,443,434
Day	360,187	148,348	211,839
Hour	15,008	6,181	8,827
Minute	250	103	147
Second	4.2	1.7	2.5

Given the potential effects of nuclear weapons upon noncombatant and neutral States and the assumption of the equality of States, it is also relevant to note the number of States existing in the world.

Population: An Evaluation (1974), mimeo; UNITED NATIONS, THE DETERMINANTS AND CONSEQUENCES OF POPULATION TRENDS, VOL. 1 (1973); UNITED NATIONS, WORLD POPULATION PROSPECTS AS ASSESSED IN 1963 (1966); UNITED NATIONS, WORLD POPULATION PROSPECTS: THE 1994 REVISION (1993); UNITED NATIONS, LONG-RANGE WORLD POPULATION PROJECTION: TW O CENTURIES OF POPULATION GROWTH, 1950–2150 (1992).

[11] Historical Estimates of World Population, <http://www.census.gov/ipc/www/worldhis.html> (citing Jean-Noel Biraben, An Essay Concerning Mankind's Evolution, Population, *in* Selected Papers, December, table 2 (1980); J.D. Durand, *Historical Estimates of World Population: An Evaluation,* U. OF PENN. POPULATION CENTER ANALYTICAL AND TECHNICAL REPORTS, No. 10, 1974, at table 2; Carl Haub, *How Many People Have Ever Lived on Earth?,* POPULATION TODAY, Feb 1995, at 5; McEvedy et al., *Atlas of World Population History,* FACTS ON FILE 1978 at 342–351; RALPH THOMLINSON, DEMOGRAPHIC PROBLEMS, CONTROVERSY OVER POPULATION CONTROL Table 1 (2d ed., 1975); United Nations, The Determination and Consequences of Population Trends, Population Studies, no. 50, 1973, at 10; United Nations, World Population Growth From Year 0 to Stabilization (1996) <gopher://gopher.undp.org:70/00/ungophers/popin/wdtrends/histor>; Total Midyear Population for the World: 1950–2050, data updated 2-28-96 <http://www.census.gov/ipc/www/worldpop.html>).

[12] U.S. Bureau of the Census, World Vital Events, <http://www.census.gov/cgi-bin/ipc/pcwe>.

As of December 2, 1998, the U.S. State Department identified a total of 190 independent States[13] and 62 "Dependencies and Areas of Special Sovereignty," such as Hong Kong, Puerto Rico, and the Isle of Man.[14]

The Fostering of an Arms Race

Whether policy drives technology, or technology, policy, the only certainty is the resultant arms race.[15] Year after year, the United States and the Soviet Union added to their respective nuclear arsenals, far beyond the point of any military need or utility.[16] By 1980, the two countries possessed a total of some 25,000 strategic nuclear weapons, while each side recognized that a tenth would be sufficient to destroy the other.[17] Once set in motion, the machine keeps developing further weapons (eventually setting off a desperate search for targets) until some curtailing incident happens, such as the economic and political

---

[13] U.S. State Department, Independent States of the World, as released by the Office of the Geographer and Global Issues, December 2, 1998, <http://www.state.gov/www/regions/independent_states.html>.

[14] U.S. State Department, Dependencies and Areas of Special Sovereignty, as released by the Office of the Geographer and Global Issues, June 3, 1999, <http://www.state.gov/www/regions/dependencies.html>.

[15] *See* Desmond Ball, *U.S. Strategic Forces: How Would They be Used?* INT'L SECURITY, vol. 7, no. 3, Winter 1982–1983, at 31–60; David B. Otaway & Steve Coll, *Trying to Unplug the War Machine Series: Rethinking the Bomb*, THE WASH. POST, Apr. 12, 1995, at A1.

[16] *See* William Daugherty et al., *The Consequences of "Limited" Nuclear Attacks on the United States*, INT'L SECURITY, vol. 10, no. 4, Spring 1986, at 3; Frank N. von Hippel et al., *Civilian casualties from counterforce attacks*, SCIENTIFIC AMERICAN, vol. 281 no. 3, Sept. 1988, at 36, 37; Barbara G. Levi et al., *Civilian Casualties from "Limited" Nuclear Attacks on the USSR*, INT'L SECURITY, vol. 12, no. 3, Winter 1987/1988, 168–189; Carl Sagan, *Nuclear War and Climatic Catastrophe: Some Policy Implications*, 62 FOREIGN AFF. 257 (Winter 1983–1984).

[17] *See* Sagan, *supra* note 16, at 260. (Sagan states here that by 1983–1984, the U.S. and the U.S.S.R., together, had a total of about 36,000 strategic nuclear weapons. The number of all nuclear weapons, including tactical nuclear weapons, would have been substantially higher.); Daugherty et al., *supra* note 16, at 3; von Hippel et al., *supra* note 16; Levi et al., *supra* note 16. One study found that 100 high yield weapons could potentially devastate each superpower. Levi et al., *supra* note 16. *See also* CARL SAGAN & RICHARD TURCO, A PATH WHERE NO MAN THOUGHT: NUCLEAR WAR AND THE END OF THE ARMS RACE 7 (1990).

collapse of the Soviet Union, although even with an event of that magnitude curtailment is difficult.

The Fostering of Nuclear Proliferation

The continued reliance by the nuclear nations upon nuclear weapons means almost inevitably that additional nations will want to possess such weapons. The theoretical premise of the Non-Proliferation Treaty,[18] renewed in 1995, was that the nuclear powers would negotiate to abandon nuclear weapons and that no additional nations would develop a nuclear weapons capability.[19] The Treaty was successful neither in galvanizing the nuclear powers to negotiate nuclear disarmament nor in preventing additional proliferation, although it ostensibly contributed to limiting such proliferation.[20]

At the negotiations of the renewal of the treaty in 1995, the disenchantment of the non-nuclear powers with the fact that the nuclear powers were not engaging in serious negotiations towards denuclearization, while the non-nuclear powers were expected to abstain from such weapons, was evident. The continued maintenance

---

[18] *See* UNITED STATES ARMS CONTROL AND DISARMAMENT AGENCY, THREAT CONTROL THROUGH ARMS CONTROL: 1995 ANNUAL REPORT TO CONGRESS 1. The Treaty on Non-Proliferation of Nuclear Weapons (NPT) was originally negotiated in 1968 and entered into force in 1970. At one point, over 181 nations were signatories to the NPT. *Id.*

See Brigid Schulte, *A Timeline of the Nuclear Age*, THE SEATTLE TIMES, August 9, 1995 (citing The Brookings Institution). On May 1995, 170 nations, including the United States and Russia, voted to extend the Non-Proliferation Treaty. *Id.*

[19] *See id.*

[20] *See id.* (citing The Brookings Institution). An excellent example is that when the Non-Proliferation Treaty was extended, "U.S. officials [sought to call] attempts by Mexico and Japan to push for disarmament a 'clear and present danger' to U.S. security. [The] Move is quashed." *Id.*

See Davis S. Yost, *France, in* DOUGLAS J. MURRAY & PAUL R. VIOTTI, THE DEFENSE POLICIES OF NATIONS: A COMPARATIVE STUDY 233, 234 (Johns Hopkins Press 1994). In addition, the NPT/International Atomic Energy Agency (IAEA) regime has been questioned as to its ability to prevent additional proliferation. *See id.* Iraq's success in developing a secret uranium processing program, discovered by the United Nations Special Commission after the Gulf War, has been partly blamed on the policy of the IAEA to inspect only declared sites and monitor only declared nuclear materials. *See id.*

of a nuclear weapons capability by the nuclear powers can only be expected to lead in time to increasing proliferation.[21]

During the Cold War, the United States and the Soviet Union came to understand the perils of nuclear war and developed attitudes of restraint and modes of dealing with each other. While the two countries came to the brink in Cuba in 1962,[22] by the end of the Cold War both sides appeared to have concluded that nuclear weapons were essentially unusable except to deter. An obvious danger of continued proliferation is that additional countries developing nuclear capability may blunder into use before they have mastered the learning curve.[23]

The Risks of Terrorism

The vulnerability of nuclear weapons to terrorist attack is increased by the dispersal by States of their nuclear assets so as to reduce

---

[21] *See* Schulte, *supra* note 18. The Brookings Institution estimates that 47 tons of plutonium remain in nuclear weapons. *See id.* In July 1995, the National Academy of Science called surplus plutonium a "clear and present danger" to U.S. Security. *See id.* According to this source, four kilograms of plutonium are estimated to be sufficient to make a nuclear device. *See id.*

[22] *See* BRACKEN, *supra* note 6, at 9 ("Never has there been a Soviet–American confrontation during this modern period … The Cuban missile crisis of 1962 was the highest level alert ever declared by the United States"). At the height of the crisis, the U.S. nuclear alert level was raised to Defense Condition 2, one stage before full thermonuclear war. *Id.* Strategic Air Command authorized nuclear-armed B-52 bombers to fly past their fail-safe points to preplanned targets in the Soviet Union before being recalled. *See id.*

[23] *See, e.g.,* Steven E. Miller, *The Case Against a Ukrainian Nuclear Deterrent,* FOREIGN AFF., vol. 72 no. 3, Summer 1993, at 67, 73. This perception that other nations, particularly third-world nations, are not as capable as the United States and others of the traditional nuclear powers to handle nuclear weapons can be challenged as culturally arrogant and self-serving. *See id.* At the same time, however, one does sense that, as with other complex technologies, there must be a learning curve. *See id.* The United States and the Soviet Union with their respective allies certainly had front-line time and experience during the Cold War passing through that learning curve and did so successfully, whether because of wisdom and good judgment or simply good luck. *See id.* One wonders how long and over how many nations' learning-curves such wisdom or luck can hold out, given the world's experience as to human aggressiveness and fallibility. *See id.* For the case, specifically as to Ukraine, that that country has the technical, intellectual and political wherewithal to be trusted with nuclear weapons, *i.e.,* that its elite are "likely to grasp the essentials of national security policy" and the "nuances of nuclear deterrence theory," *see* John F. Mearsheimer, *The Case for Ukrainian Nuclear Deterrent,* FOREIGN AFF., Summer 1993, at 61–63.

exposure to a first strike. While security in an overall sense may be generally possible, the defendability of any particular point in an overall system seems inherently limited, assuming a determined and well-planned attack by expert and committed individuals, particularly ones willing to die for the cause.

There have repeated alerts as to terrorist groups seeking to gain nuclear capability.[24] These risks have been exacerbated by the demise

---

[24] *See GAO Says Soviet Nuclear Materials "Highly Attractive to Theft,"* THE ASSOCIATED PRESS, Mar. 12, 1996.

> Nuclear materials stored in the former Soviet Union are "highly attractive to theft" because inventory records are incomplete and antiquated safeguards can't detect missing materials quickly, congressional auditors said in a report Tuesday. The report from the General Accounting Office was released on the eve of Senate hearings into the threat that nuclear materials at nuclear reactors and storage facilities in the former Soviet Union pose to U.S. national security. The former Soviet Union has stockpiled about 1,400 metric tons of plutonium and highly enriched uranium. Those stores, in Russia and the newly independent states, are growing as missiles are dismantled.
>
> "Much of this material is outside of nuclear weapons, is highly attractive to theft, and the newly independent states may not have accurate and complete inventories of the material they inherited," the report said. The report said the former Soviet nuclear facilities "rely on antiquated accounting systems that cannot quickly detect" the loss of nuclear materials and lack modern equipment to safeguard them. Although there is no evidence of a black market for weapons-grade nuclear materials, the GAO said the seizure of nuclear materials in Russia and Europe has "heightened concerns about theft."

Id.

See also David Hughes, When Terrorists Go Nuclear: The Ingredients and Information Have Never Been More Available, POPULAR MECHANICS, Jan. 1, 1996. This source stated:

> It will take Russia years to properly account for all the material it has—much less determine if any is missing. That raises concern now, because it takes only 30 to 50 pounds of highly enriched uranium or 10 to 20 pounds of plutonium to make a bomb. According to physicist David Albright, president of the Institute for Science and International Security in Washington, D.C., there are more than 1700 tons of highly enriched uranium and 1100 tons of plutonium in the world. Only 22% of the plutonium is under military control ....

Id.

of the Soviet Union, the growth of international organized crime and the loose controls ostensibly exercised over some of the former Soviet nuclear assets.[25]

The Risks of Human and Equipment Failure

It is a truism that humans are fallible; we are constantly making mistakes, even when we are most careful, well-informed and well-intentioned. Equipment is as fallible as the humans who create, maintain and operate it. This is why the U.S. space program, notwithstanding the greatest of care, has experienced major disasters, and why nuclear power plants blow up.[26] During the fog of war, the occurrence of such failures is even more likely, with potentially catastrophic effects if nuclear weapons are involved.

Many of the technical challenges faced by U.S. space program and the nuclear weapons delivery program are similar. The overall challenges inherent in the nature of technology, its vulnerability down to the reliability of the smallest washer or valve, are identical. NASA and the space program were based organizationally on the U.S. Air Force ICBM program.[27] Far more time and opportunity for testing,

---

[25] *See* Jessica Eve Stern, *Moscow Meltdown: Can Russia Survive?* INT'L SECURITY, vol. 18, no. 4, Spring 1994, at 40 (citing The Office of Threat Assessment, "The Russian Mafia" (Washington, D.C.: Department of Energy, Nov. 1, 1993)) ("A U.S. government report concludes that 'the infrastructure of transborder smuggling and extortion rings has been put in place,' paving the way for potential proliferation of special nuclear materials by corrupt military personnel or other criminal elements.").

[26] *See* HOWARD E. MCCURDY, INSIDE NASA: HIGH TECHNOLOGY AND ORGANIZATIONAL CHANGE IN THE U.S. SPACE PROGRAM 1 (The Johns Hopkins University Press 1993). *See also* Ashton B. Carter, *Sources of Error and Uncertainty, in* MANAGING NUCLEAR OPERATIONS 611–12, 625 (Ashton B. Carter et al. eds., 1987):

> Even people without military experience easily draw an analogy between the vast organizations and technical apparatus belonging to the two superpowers that together constitute the "deterrent system" and the nuclear power plants, air traffic control systems and chemical plants of everyday life that suffer infrequent but disturbingly unexpected failures.
>
> Undoubtedly surprises of comparable magnitude lie undiscovered. Such "unknown unknowns" do not show up in any analysis, however attentive to uncertainty, because they are unsuspected.

Id.

[27] *See* MCCURDY, *supra* note 26.

planning and revision were present for the space program. The stakes were high in each instance. The best technical minds were attracted. Money was no real problem. Yet we ended up with the Challenger Space Shuttle explosion and other high profile malfunctions.

It has been noted that NASA's early success resulted from "extensive testing, in-house technical capability, hands-on experience, exceptional people, acceptance of risk and failure and an R&D organizational culture."[28] By way of explanation as to how the errors and oversights could have followed, permitting disaster to take over, it has been noted that the performance of high-technology agencies such as NASA inherently tends to decline over time because of increasing bureaucracy, normal organizational aging process, reduced budgets, fading public and political support, lack of testing, and change of personnel.[29]

Because these same elements have their parallels in the U.S. nuclear weapons program, it seems reasonable to anticipate that the U.S. nuclear forces may in practice be as vulnerable to catastrophic technical failure as the Challenger and other such programs.[30] The technical and organizational success of individual warheads and delivery systems would be far from assured.

There were many instances during the Cold War when serious nuclear mishaps occurred in the U.S. nuclear weapons program because of human or equipment failure. In 1968, a B-52 crashed in Greenland, spreading plutonium and uranium in the area of the crash. Later in the same year, another B-52 collided with its refueling tanker off Palomares on the coast of Spain, with the two planes crashing into the sea. Only three of the nuclear weapons carried by the B-52 were recovered.[31]

There was the infamous incident when American intelligence perceived a flock of geese as an incoming Soviet nuclear attack and almost retaliated preemptively.[32] In another incident several B-52s loaded with nuclear bombs skidded off the runway in New York.[33]

---

[28] *Id.* at 1.

[29] *See id.*

[30] *See id.*

[31] *See* PETER PRINGLE & WILLIAM ARKIN, S.I.O.P.— THE SECRET U.S. PLAN FOR NUCLEAR WAR (1983).

[32] *See* UNITED NATIONS DEPARTMENT FOR DISARMAMENT AFF., NUCLEAR WEAPONS: A COMPREHENSIVE STUDY 116 (1991) [hereinafter UNITED NATIONS DEPARTMENT].

[33] R. Jeffrey Smith, *Ex-Commander of Nukes Wants to Scrap Them, A Believer No More*, THE SACRAMENTO BEE, Mar. 29, 1998, at Forum.

Another B-52 crashed in California, causing the death of all 10 crew members.[34] In 1980 a Titan missile exploded in its silo in Damascus, Ark., killing one Air Force specialist, injuring 21 others and ejecting a crudely designed warhead packed with plutonium onto nearby farmland.[35]

In yet another incident, a 64-cent computer chip at the military's Colorado Springs warning center failed, causing bomber pilots to leap into their planes and start their engines and launch crews to ready themselves to receive launch codes.[36] Major studies have identified over 200 accidents involving nuclear weapons.[37]

The Risks of Testing

The testing of nuclear weapons carries with it extreme environmental hazards. It has been estimated that over one thousand

---

[34] *Id.*

[35] *Id.*

[36] *Id.*

[37] *See* SHAUN GREGORY, THE HIDDEN COST OF DETERRENCE: NUCLEAR WEAPONS ACCIDENTS (1990). A major study in 1977 identified over 130 nuclear weapons accidents between 1950 and 1976. From 1976 to 1987, another 77 nuclear accidents have been identified. *Id. See also* SHAUN GREGORY & ALISTAIR EDWARDS, A HANDBOOK OF NUCLEAR WEAPONS ACCIDENTS (1988).

The accidents at nuclear power plants, like the inadvertent chain reaction at the uranium processing plant in Tokaimura, Japan, in October 1999, further highlight the dangers of human and equipment failure. In that incident, workers had apparently been mixing too much uranium in a small vessel. This led to such a high density of the uranium that the neutrons did not get absorbed by the other material around, leading to the out-of-control reaction. THE NEW YORK TIMES, Oct. 1, 1999, at A-1.

Dr. Arjun Makhijani, president of the Institute for Energy and Environmental Research in Washington, said at the time that the Tokaimura plant had had other accidents in recent years and should be shut down for a thorough, independent investigation. *Id.* at A10. Later reports concluded that the plant had cut corners on safety, "routinely skipping critical safety steps for years in order to increase the production of uranium fuel." Howard W. French, *Atom Plant Cut Corners On Safety, Japan Is Told*, THE NEW YORK TIMES, Oct. 4, 1999, at A8.

Similar criticality accidents have occurred in fuel processing plants in the United States, including one at a plant in Charlestown, Rhode Island in 1964, one at Los Alamos, New Mexico during the Manhattan project, and one in Wilmington, North Carolina in 1991. THE NEW YORK TIMES, Oct. 1, 1999, at A10.

tests of nuclear materials were conducted by the United States,[38] and extensive tests have also been conducted by Russia, Britain, France and China.[39] As noted above, the effects of radiation are cumulative. Worldwide, it has been estimated that over 2,000 nuclear weapons have been tested during the nuclear era, releasing substantial amounts of radiation throughout the world.[40]

---

[38] *See* Kosta Tsipis, Editorial, *1000 Tests, 1,000 Poisoned Craters*, THE NEW YORK TIMES, Oct. 3, 1994, at A-3; UNITED NATIONS DEPARTMENT, *supra* note 32, at 62. From 1945 to 1989, the United States has tested 921 nuclear weapons, primarily at its test site in Nevada. *Id.* The Soviet Union from 1949 to 1989 tested a total of 642 nuclear weapons, primarily at the Semipalatinsk/Novaya Zemlya test facility. *Id.* From 1952 to 1989, the United Kingdom tested a total of 42 nuclear weapons, primarily in Nevada. *Id.* From 1960 to 1989, France tested 180 nuclear weapons, primarily at its Mururoa/Fangataufa test site. *Id.* From 1964 to 1989, China tested 34 nuclear devices, primarily at Lop Nor and Sinkiang. *Id.* Between 1945 and 1989, 1,819 internationally recorded nuclear tests occurred, with a total yield of "many hundred megatons." *Id. See also* Chapter 15, note 2 and accompanying text; Norman Kempster & Jonathan Peterson, *Nuclear Powers Lead in Signing Atomic Test Ban*, LOS ANGELES TIMES, Sept. 25, 1996 (citing Stockholm International Peace Research Institute). From 1945 to 1996, the United States reportedly tested a total of 1,030 nuclear weapons, the Soviet Union 715, France 210, Britain 45 and China 45. *Id.*

The United States imposed a moratorium on underground testing in 1992, and, as of 1999, employed a $4.5 billion annual program of computer models and non-nuclear tests assertedly to maintain the safety and reliability of its nuclear arsenal. Questions have been raised as to the United States' success in this effort. John Diamond, *US Nuclear Experts Question Reliability of Aging Weapons*, CHI TRIB., Oct. 8, 1999 at 15; Eric Schmitt, *Senate Kills Test Ban Treaty in Crushing Loss for Clinton; Evokes Versailles Pact Defeat*, THE NEW YORK TIMES, Oct. 14, 1999, at A1.

[39] *See* Scott Kraft, *France Ends Nuclear Tests, To Press for Ban*, THE LOS ANGELES TIMES, Jan. 30, 1996, at A1. "After completing six of eight planned nuclear-weapon tests in the South Pacific, French President Jacques Chirac announced Monday night a "definitive end" to the detonations, and he raced to mend fences with other nations by vowing to lead the drive to ban such tests worldwide." *Id.* The last test, at the Fangataufa atoll, yielded 120 kilotons. *Id.*

India and Pakistan conducted underground tests in 1998. *Russian Nuke Tests*, WASH. TIMES, June 25, 1999, at A6. Intelligence reports in the summer of 1999 indicated that China may have set off a small nuclear explosion in violation of its announced ban on underground testing. *Id.* The same reports indicated that Russia had conducted as many as 18 nuclear tests in 1998 and 1999. *Id.*

[40] *See* Kempster & Peterson, *supra* note 38 (citing Stockholm International Peace Research Institute); UNITED NATIONS DEPARTMENT, *supra* note 32, at 72.

The Risks of Production, Storage and Disposal

The production, storage and disposal of nuclear weapons also carry with them extraordinary risks of the release of radioactivity into the environment and costs of managing such risk.[41] Not only are defense industry workers and military personnel regularly exposed to substantial dosages of radiation, in addition small amounts of radiation are regularly released into the environment and occasional catastrophic releases occur.[42] The environment problems in the United States in a number of areas around nuclear weapons facilities have become extreme.[43]

And, of course, other countries, including the former Soviet Union have been appreciably less careful than the United States with respect to preventing and controlling releases of radioactive material from military weapon programs—with severe potential effects throughout the world, given the ease with which radioactive materials can be transmitted environmentally through such means as the air, the water, the soil and the food chain and the human genetic process.

The Office of Technological Assessment estimated that 126 underground tests in Nevada from 1970 to 1989 released about 54,000 curies of radiation, constituting small releases compared to atmospheric testing. *Id.*

[41] *See* UNITED NATIONS DEPARTMENT, *supra* note 32, at 61.

[42] *Id.* at 67. "Accidental releases of radioactive substances and chemicals during ongoing processes or by effluents, transports and so on resulting from mismanagement of waste may cause environmental damage." *Id.*

The Federal Government acknowledged in the summer of 1999 that thousands of workers on nuclear weapons during the Cold War had suffered injuries as a result of exposure to beryllium, asbestos, mercury, uranium and other materials. Matthew L. Wald, *Work on Weapons Affected Health, Government Admits*, THE NEW YORK TIMES, July 15, 1999, at A12. "I am reversing a policy of denial of compensation," said Secretary of Energy Bill Richardson in announcing the government's decision to provide compensation for victims of beryllium disease and to study providing compensation to workers exposed to asbestos and radioactive materials. *Id.* Beryllium is used almost exclusively by weapons program, while workers could have been exposed to asbestos and other radioactive materials elsewhere. *Id.*

[43] *See* UNITED NATIONS DEPARTMENT, *supra* note 32, at 61. The U.S. nuclear production industry includes 17 major production facilities in 13 states. *Id.* Ed Rampell, *The Military's Mess: Johnston Atoll, the Army's "Model" Chemical Disposal Facility, is an Environmental Disaster*, EARTH ACTION NETWORK, INC., vol. 7, no. 1, Jan. 11, 1996. The U.S. Army maintains a $240 million facility to destroy a mere 6.6% percent of the total U.S. chemical weapons stockpile, which includes over 400,000 weapons. *See id.* Recently, it requested an additional $650 million to complete this task. *See id.*

Overall Cost Factors

Historically, nuclear weapons were seen as cheaper than conventional weapons, as a way for the United States to contain the Soviet threat without spending the money necessary for a conventional capability comparable to the Soviet's. Today, that economy appears to have been illusory. The direct costs turn out to have been much higher than realized and substantial indirect costs have become recognized, including the ongoing costs of storing and disposing of associated toxic and radioactive wastes and the costs of dismantling nuclear weapons systems and disposing of surplus nuclear materials.[44]

---

[44] *See* Stephen I. Schwartz, *Introduction, in* ATOMIC AUDIT 4 (Stephen I. Schwartz ed., 1998). In the period from 1940 through 1996, the United States, according to recent estimates published by the Brookings Institution, expended some $5.5 trillion (in constant 1996 dollars) on nuclear weapons and weapons-related programs, not including an estimated additional $320 billion in future-year costs for storing and disposing of more than five decades' worth of accumulated toxic and radioactive wastes and $20 billion for dismantling nuclear weapons systems and disposing of surplus nuclear materials, for total costs exceeding some $5.8 trillion, with the $5.5 trillion spent through 1996 representing some 29% of the United States' overall expenditures of $18.7 trillion on national defense and some 11% of all governmental expenditures during the period and averaging some $98 billion per year. *Id.* at 3.

This $5.5 trillion is estimated to have been made up of some $405 billion for building "the bomb," $3,241 billion for deploying the bomb, $831 billion for targeting and controlling the bomb, $937 billion for defending against the bomb, $11 billion for dismantling the bomb, $45 billion for nuclear waste management and environmental remediation, $2 billion for victims of the bomb, $3 billion for costs and consequences of nuclear secrecy, and $1 billion for Congressional oversight of the bomb. *Id.* at 4.

On an ongoing basis the United States expends some $35 billion a year (in 1998 dollars) on nuclear weapons, some 14% of all defense spending, with about $25 billion going towards operating and maintaining the arsenal and the remainder allocated to environmental remediation and waste management, arms reduction measures, and the storage and disposition of excess fissile material. *Id.* at 31.

See also Schulte, *supra* note 18 (citing an estimate by the Brookings Institution in 1995 that the U.S. had spent $4 trillion on its strategic and tactical nuclear weapons program in the 50 years since World War II (in 1995 dollars)).

See also UNITED NATIONS DEPARTMENT, *supra* note 32, at 65, setting forth the estimate that the total amount of weapons-grade uranium produced by all the nuclear powers since 1945 has been some 1,000–2,000 tons and the total amount of weapons-grade plutonium some 100 to 200 tons. *Id. See also*

Jeopardy to Rule of Law

In the summer of 1999 the Congress' House Appropriations Committee issued a detailed report concluding that the Pentagon had defied the law and the Constitution by spending hundreds of millions of dollars on military projects that had either been shut down or never approved at all, including millions of dollars on a "Star Wars" missile defense program, the Medium Altitude Air Defense program, that had been cancelled by Congress.[45] While the expenditures were defended by the Pentagon as honest errors and also misunderstandings and disagreements as to what is required, the incident illustrated the danger of a run-away military establishment that is perhaps fostered by the minimalization of law inherent in the United States' current official position as to the lawfulness of the use of nuclear weapons.

Catastrophe Theory

Statistically extremely rare events occur routinely in daily life. Common experience by its very nature consists of confluences of millions of individually unlikely events.[46] For example, it is unlikely, beyond normal turns of phrase, that any three or four words will appear next to each other in their exact sequence. Quite likely most particular sequences of four occur only once within this book. Nevertheless, the unlikely confluence of each group of four words occurs continually across hundreds of pages.

The placing of each object in a room is another example. That each object looks as it does, and sits where it does in its exact relationship to each other object, is the result of numerous remote chances that have coincided. Yet it is not merely in the realm of probability that such rare events occur. They are the essence of much of human reality.

As events nearly random draw a pattern over time, and the infinite number of events fit themselves into a finite space, if that finite set of all events, however improbable, could never include the accidental or intentional recourse to nuclear weapons, the present inquiry might not be necessary. Yet reality is obviously to the contrary. With massive arsenals held by hot blooded as well as often misguided and accident prone humans, and with more States and groups gaining access to such weapons and the means of delivery, the absence of disaster to date

---

Schulte, *supra* note 18 (citing the estimate by The Brookings Institution that the amount of plutonium still contained in weapons in 1995 was some 47 tons).

[45] *See* Tim Weiner, *Pentagon Misused Millions in Funds, House Panel Says*, NEW YORK TIMES, July 22, 1999, at A1.

[46] *See* JAMES GLEICK, CHAOS 83–86 (1988).

reflects and has perhaps been as much dependent on luck as on human wisdom, skill, good intentions or the like.

If the catastrophic use of nuclear weapons is possible, the question becomes, will or must such possibility come to pass?

"Catastrophe theory" mathematics, aptly named for present purposes, study the occurrence of unlikely events, resulting from whatever combination of gradual progression or sudden change (a "jump"). The theory addresses the matter of when one straw can break the camel's back.[47] "A catastrophe" can be seen as the mathematical determination and resolution of all the varied possibilities, such as the geometric forms that arise as a ball rolls along a landscape and settles into some particular configuration vis-à-vis everything else.[48]

It has been observed that the rolling of a ball on a three dimensional sheet reveals numerous patterns of the development of events, and hence patterns for predicting the future, including the phenomena of the jump, of hysteresis, of divergence and of multiple paths, just some of the many ways of conceptualizing the capriciousness of the occurrence of events and ultimately of catastrophes.

Probabilities and possibilities we may believe we can assess and control (*e.g.*, through the arcane theology of deterrence theory and SIOP contingency planning in the context of projected reciprocal calculations of advantage and the like) are also subject to the sudden consequences of nasty turns of events. A certain series of probable events may find a much shorter way of getting from one point to another—they may jump rather than take slower more orderly routes.[49]

Events may lurch irreversibly out of control. Thus, if as events unfold, a particular jump is sought to be reversed by a second jump, the mechanisms of the reversal may, pursuant to the phenomenon of hysteresis, result in a far different end picture than the mere withdrawal of the first action as though it had never happened. The attempted reversal of activities, to go back up the path one just jumped or otherwise traversed, may be impossible due to the intricacies of the cause and effect world underlying one's actions and results. "You can't go home again," or at least you cannot necessarily get back by merely reversing your known footprints.

Pursuant to the phenomenon of divergence, even slight differences in path, in the context of the exact same future possibilities, may, as the

---

[47] *See* TIM POSTON & IAN STEWART, CATASTROPHE THEORY AND ITS APPLICATIONS 1 (1996).

[48] *Id.* at 2.

[49] *Id.* at 84.

result of smooth progression, result in wildly different final consequences, even without any jumps. Under the phenomenon of multiple paths, events may be navigated in a variety of ways from one point to another, in whatever combination of logical progression, meandering moves, jumps, and the effects of hysteresis and divergence.[50]

Under catastrophe theory, a potential nuclear incident might be conceptualized as a giant wave at sea resulting from the build-up of many small waves, like the "tidal waves" in the Agulhas current off the coast of Africa. Minor waves, each a probability in itself, when aroused by heavy weather, funnel and become funneled by the current, and resolve into a giant wall capable of crushing power.[51]

The application of catastrophe theory to social modeling of prison riots indicates that the riot may be a case of a "jump" from order to disorder, as if from one place to another, along a complex curve. The smooth and predictable surface of this curve has been conceptualized as mapping levels of disorder from peace to violence, against the level of tension and alienation amongst prisoners.[52] Sticking to the smooth predictable surface of the curve requires remaining within a certain ratio of tension to alienation, in a context where alienation was taken to connote social distance among prisoners leading to inability to take organized or concerted action, and tension was taken to be a galvanizing force capable at some point of enabling prisoners to overcome alienation. Failing to maintain the correct ratio by having too much tension, and too little alienation—or far too much tension, and no matter how much alienation—will push events off the surface of the curve, by a catastrophic jump and not a smooth transition, into the riot part of the curve.[53]

Riots then might be avoided and kept on predictable smooth footing achieved by peaceable transitions, if necessary ratios are maintained between the tension and alienation of the potential rioters—obviously by means other than math.[54] Just so, military and social confrontations could, at some point on a curve now unmapped, entail a "jump" to the use of nuclear weapons. We cannot know at what point this is, when we cross the line from controlled confrontation to nuclear disaster.

---

[50] *See id.* at 86.

[51] *See id.* at 281–283.

[52] *See id.* at 416–418 (modeling the factors of alienation and tension at Gartree prison during 1972).

[53] *See id.* at 416–418, fig. 17.7 at 418.

[54] *See id.*

It is noted that catastrophe theory, by use of quite complex calculus, "gives numbers."[55] It is not merely qualitative. If the data can be made into a chart, the numerical answers of when a nuclear strike will occur perhaps could be churned out. That events have their breaking point, and that human input can potentially adjust the place of that breaking point, seems evident from the prison riots study. In that context, changes in institutional philosophy ostensibly can change the placement of the cusp on the catastrophe model for riots.[56] "Changing the institutional philosophy" of nuclear weapons, by denying them a legal place in war planning, might have a similar effect on the catastrophe chart on which potential jumps to nuclear disaster might be plotted.

It is noteworthy, in light of the frequency of international conflict involving States possessing weapons of mass destruction, that the frequency with which a risk is taken affects its likelihood. Duke University Professor Schroeder summarizes the matter:

> An increasingly sophisticated understanding of the probabilistic consequences of risky actions threatens to collapse the distinction between cocking a fist [overt threats] and driving a car [risky actions]. Once the probability of harm associated with a risky action can be gauged, an axiom of statistical theory holds that a sufficient number of repetitions of that action practically guarantees that the harm actually will occur. When a risky action—say, exposing someone to a known carcinogen—is repeated often enough, whether through repetitions on that same individual or by increasing the size of the exposed population, the entire set of actions becomes, probabilistically, virtually certain to produce the feared harm.[57]

---

[55] *See id.* at 427 (emphasis omitted).

[56] *See id.* at 418.

[57] Christopher H. Schroeder, *Rights Against Risks*, at 500. This article originally appeared at 86 COLUM. L. REV. 495 (1986). Reprinted with permission. Talking in the context of the appropriateness of injunctive relief, Schroeder notes the basis for concluding that, giving the synchronicity of effect, the imposition of generalized risk should be treated similarly to the direct imposition of specific injury:

> By generalizing from the discrete action to the class of actions, the situation takes the shape of an enjoinable offense because, taken collectively, the group of actions is as likely to cause harm as the cocked fist. If it is appropriate to stop the cocked fist, is it not then appropriate to stop the group of actions that will cause as certain a harm, even if the probabilities of any single or discrete action—an

Schroeder elaborates:

> One definition of probability states that the probability of an outcome occurring is the limit of its relative frequency. That is, it is the ratio of the number of times that outcome occurs to the number of times a test is performed that might have that outcome, as the number of tests approaches infinity:
>
> $Pr(e) = \lim [n(e) / n]$
>
> Where $Pr(e)$ is the probability of outcome e, $n(e)$ equals the number of times e is the outcome, and n equals the number of times the test is performed. ... Given this definition, the occurrence of any outcome with a nonzero probability will approximate its probability as n increases. For a relatively small n, the chances of the adverse outcome not occurring can be significant. For instance, if the chance of contracting cancer from an exposure is 1 in 100, the chance that none of one hundred people exposed will contract cancer is 37%. The probability of no harm decreases as n increases: if 200 people are exposed, the no harm probability falls to 13%.[58]

The risks of a nuclear accident at the Chernobyl plant had been estimated at one chance in 10,000 reactor years, yet the disaster occurred.[59] Even aside from the quirkiness of statistical probabilities, the multiplication of the numbers of nuclear weapons compounds the danger, as do the other surrounding circumstances, particularly the military mindset and predisposition fostered by nuclear training, policy and planning and the limits on the testability of the possible uses scenarios.

The question becomes, how much time will history allow before precipitating, permitting or suffering some powerful Agulhas type current to funnel the smaller waves of common international confrontation into nuclear catastrophe?

---

isolated carcinogen exposure—causing harm are vanishingly small?

Id. See also Chapter 4, notes 48–62 and accompanying text (addressing the injunctions point).

[58] *Id.* (citing T. WONNACOTT & R. WONNACOTT, INTRODUCTORY STATISTICS 32 (2d ed. 1972)).

[59] *See* Peter Weiss, Burns H. Weston, Richard A. Falk, & Saul H. Mendlovitz, Draft Memorial in Support of the Application of the World Health Organization for an Advisory Opinion by the International Court of Justice on the Legality of the Use of Nuclear Weapons Under International Law, Including the W.H.O. Constitution, *reprinted in* 4 TRANSNAT'L L. & CONTEMP. PROBS. 721, 732 (1994), quoting INTERNATIONAL PHYSICIANS FOR THE PREVENTION OF NUCLEAR WAR, BRIEFING BOOK ON NUCLEAR WAR (1992).

Chapter 23: States Possessing Nuclear Weapons Capability

Analysis of the risks attendant upon the international nuclear weapons regime, including the risks that such weapons will be used intentionally or in error and the risks of escalation, requires consideration of the nature and structure of the nuclear weapons possessed by the various nuclear powers.[1] In this chapter I survey the basic facts as to such matters.

The United States, Russia,[2] China,[3] France,[4] Great Britain,[5] India and Pakistan[6] are acknowledged nuclear powers. There are also a

---

[1] A recent report provided the following summary as to the nuclear arsenals of the major powers as of 1998:

	Warheads Total*	Warheads Operational	Silos
United States	12,070	8,425	550
Russia	22,500	10,240	350
Britain	280	260	0
France	500	450	0
China	450	400	7
Total	~36,000	19,775	907

*including the U.S. hedge force and those awaiting dismantling.
WILLIAM M. ARKIN, ROBERT S. NORRIS, JOSHUA HANDLER, TAKING STOCK, WORLDWIDE NUCLEAR DEPLOYMENTS 1998 1 (NRDC 1998).
[2] Robert S. Norris & William Arkin, *Estimated Russian Stockpile, September 1996*, NRDC NUCLEAR NOTEBOOK; BULL. OF ATOMIC SCIENTISTS, vol. 63, Aug. 13, 1996, at 62–63. (The estimated Russia nuclear stockpile in September 1996 included 727 ICBMs (3,750 nuclear warheads), 440 SLBMs (2,350 warheads), and 69 bombers (1,400 bombs). In addition, Russia was estimated to have 425 land-based "non-strategic" bombers and fighters (1,600 bombs), 1,200 strategic defense warheads (ABMs and SAMs), and 1,600 naval based nonstrategic weapons (attack bombers, SLCMs and ASWs). *Id. See also* Norman Kempster & Jonathan Peterson, *Nuclear Powers Lead in Signing Atomic Test Ban*, LOS ANGELES TIMES, Sept. 25, 1996 (citing Stockholm International Peace Research Institute), estimating Russia to possess 7,000+ nuclear weapons in 1996. *Id.*

Under START II, by the year 2003 (extended to 2007) Russia's strategic nuclear arsenal is expected to include 525 ICBMs, each with one warhead (340 SS-25s, 40 SS-13s, 40 SS-17 and 105 SS-19), 264 SLBMs (SS-N-18, SS-N-20, SS-N-23) with a total of 1,744 warheads and 128 bombers (Tu-95H16, Tu-95H6, Tu-95B/G) carrying a total of 892 ALCMs and bombs, for a total of 3,161 warheads. Russia is likely to end up with 400 single warhead ICBMs-SS-19s, SS-25s and SS-27s, mobile and silo-based, by the year 2003. It is also thought that Russia will come under the START II 1750 warhead limit by retiring older weapons, even though they have not yet ratified START II. *See* ARKIN ET AL., *supra* note 1, at 12. Russia's situation is "unclear." *Id.*

During the 1999 warfare in Kosovo, "the Russian National Security Council approved modernization of all nuclear warheads, including new low yield tactical warheads." *Editorial, Showdown in Pristina,* THE NATION, July 5, 1999, at 3–4. Apropos of the vagaries to which military developments are subject, the editorial went on to state: "The derailing of nuclear arms control is one of the gravest long-term costs of the Kosovo war. ... NATO's war may have the perverse effect of subduing a conventionally armed Milosevic in Belgrade but ushering in a Milosevic-like nationalist in a nuclear-armed Russia." *Id. See also* Perry & General John Shalikashvili, Chairman, Joint Chiefs of Staff, *Department of Defense Briefing as set forth at* FED. NEWS SERVICE, Wash., Sept. 22, 1994. Secretary of Defense Perry stated that "[as of 1994] Russia has between six [6,000] and 13,000 non-strategic nuclear weapons ... ."

[3] Varying estimates have been given as to the size of China's nuclear arsenal. As noted above, one source shows China as having 450 total warheads, 400 of them operational, as of 1998. ARKIN ET AL., TAKING STOCK, *supra* note 1, at 1.

See also The NRDC Nuclear Program, Nuclear Data Table of Chinese Nuclear Forces, End of 1996, <http://www.nrdc.org/nrdcpro/nudb/datab17. html>.

Such weapons included 113 of the older Dong Feng ("East Wind") land based missiles, including seven 13,000 km range Dong Feng 5A/CSS-4 missiles. *See* ARKIN ET AL., TAKING STOCK, *supra* note 1, at 45. Two new classes of Dong Feng missiles with ranges of 8,000km and 12,000 km were described as slated to come out in the late 1990s and by 2010 respectively. *See id.* In 1998 China also fielded 150 older nuclear capable aircraft, including 30 MiG-19 based planes and 120 longer range (3,100km) bomber aircraft. *See id.* However, this bomber force "is antiquated." *Id.* at 48. China also had deployed one submarine with twelve Julang-1 ("Giant Wave") submarine based missiles with a 1,700km range and had a much improved 8,000km range missile slated to come out by the late 1990s. *See id.* "It seems unlikely a future fleet will number more than four to six submarines." *Id.* By 1996, China had fielded an unknown number of low kiloton tactical weapons. *See* Nuclear Data Table of Chinese Nuclear Forces, *supra.* By 1998, the number was estimated to be 120. *See* ARKIN ET AL., TAKING STOCK, *supra* note 1, at 45.

As of 1993, China reportedly deployed 14 single warhead ICBMs, 60 single warhead IRBM and 12 SLBMs; in addition, it fielded up to 120 strategic and medium range nuclear bombers each capable of carrying up to two nuclear bombs, for a total of approximately 326 nuclear devices. THE INT'L INSTITUTE FOR STRATEGIC STUDIES, THE MILITARY BALANCE, 1993–1994 244 (1993) [hereinafter THE MILITARY BALANCE]. In September 1988, China reportedly began to deploy 2 submarines carrying a total of 12 SLBMS (CSS-N-3). *See* UNITED NATIONS DEPARTMENT FOR DISARMAMENT AFFAIRS, NUCLEAR

WEAPONS: A COMPREHENSIVE STUDY 16 (1991) [hereinafter UNITED NATIONS DEPARTMENT].

Limitations of the Chinese nuclear production system have been noted: "One feature of all Chinese weapons programs is that it takes a long time for a missile, submarine or bomber to enter service. From initial research through development and testing to deployment can take a decade or two, by which time it is largely obsolete." ARKIN ET AL., TAKING STOCK, *supra* note 1, at 45. The appropriation through espionage of research and development advancements from United States' laboratories may speed up this process. *See infra* note 27.

The above estimates as to the Chinese nuclear arsenal generally focus on deployed weapons. But China may have many weapons hidden in tunnels and under forests, circumventing satellite surveillance. *See* PHILIP MORRISON & KOSTA TSIPIS, REASON ENOUGH TO HOPE, AMERICA AND THE WORLD OF THE 21ST CENTURY 45 (M.I.T. Press 1998). *See also* Yang Zheng, *China's Nuclear Arsenal*, Mar. 16, 1996, <http://www.kimsoft.com/korea/ch-war.htm>. ("An anonymous poster ... sent an internal document of the Chinese Defense Ministry to the Hong Kong magazine The Trend (Dong Xiang). This document reveals that China at present has a total of 2,350 nuclear warheads. ... 550 tactical ... and 1800 strategic"). Some sources have described the Chinese arsenal as containing about 2,000 warheads. *See* China, Nuclear Weapons, <http://www.fas.org/nuke/guide/china/nuke/index.html>. It is noted that "[i]nformation on Chinese tactical nuclear weapons is limited and contradictory, and there is no confirmation from official sources of their existence. China's initial interest in such weapons may have been spurred by worsening relations with the Soviet Union in the 1960s and 1970s." ARKIN ET AL., TAKING STOCK, *supra* note 1, at 45.

Morrison & Tsipis have noted that China has maintained such secrecy around its nuclear programs and been subject to so little scrutiny that the public information as to its weapons program is less reliable or complete. *See* MORRISON & TSIPIS, REASON ENOUGH TO HOPE, *supra,* at 45.

China pursued "minimum deterrence" until about 1987, as opposed to the Soviet Union and the United States, which pursed "maximum deterrence." Federation of American Scientists, Web Site, Doctrine—China Nuclear Forces, <http://www.fas.org/nuke/guide/china/doctrine/index.html>. Since then China has expanded into a medium theory, including warfighting deterrence and possible engagement against Soviet aggression. *See id.*

"In January 1996 meetings with top Chinese military officials, ... [a former Clinton administration assistant secretary of defense who had served as President Nixon's interpreter in Beijing in 1972] was told by Lt. Gen. Xiong Guangkai, deputy chief of China's general staff, 'In the 1950s, you three times threatened nuclear strikes on China, and you could do that because we couldn't hit back. Now we can. So you are not going threaten us again because, in the end, you care a lot more about Los Angeles than Taipei.'" Doctrine—China Nuclear Forces, *supra.*

Nonetheless, there have been some indications that China does not intend a substantial expansion of its nuclear capability. "'A more rapid or large-scale military build-up is seen by the Chinese leadership as unnecessary and detrimental to continued economic growth.'" ARKIN ET AL., TAKING STOCK, *supra* note 1, at 2 (citing DOD, SELECTED MILITARY CAPABILITIES OF THE PEOPLE'S REPUBLIC OF CHINA, Apr. 1997, p.1 (a report from the Pentagon to Congress)).

China became a member of the Non-Proliferation Treaty Exports Committee in 1997. *See* Doctrine—China Nuclear Forces, *supra.* After 1998, "China has also decided not to engage in new nuclear cooperation with Iran (even under safeguards), and will complete existing cooperation, which is not of proliferation concern, within a relatively short period." *Id.*

[4] By 1998, France had some 450 warheads deployed. *See* ARKIN ET AL., TAKING STOCK, *supra* note 1, at 42. The French "historical peak" was 538 warheads in 1991–1992. *Id.* In 1996, French President Chirac announced dramatic reforms of the French military to span 1997–2002, including withdrawal of obsolete nuclear weapons systems, dismantling of some ICBM silos, and also the dismantling of the Hades short range missile, but in such a way that it could be stored for redeployment "if need be." *See id.*

"The center piece of France's current and future nuclear force is the ballistic missile submarine fleet." *Id.* at 43. Four submarines are afloat, with three more planned for deployment through 2005. *See id.* New warheads continue to be produced. *See id* at 44. France had fewer nuclear ready aircraft in 1998 then she had fielded in the Cold War. *See id.*

As of 1993–1994, France fielded 18 IRBMs (SSBS S-3D) with single warheads, 5 nuclear submarines carrying 80 SLBMs, each with six warheads, for a total of 498 nuclear warheads. In addition, France possessed 15 short-range *Hades* nuclear missiles in storage, and 98 tactical nuclear bombs aboard nuclear fighter-bombers (not including 32 in storage). *See* THE MILITARY BALANCE, *supra* note 3, at 238.

See also Alad Ned Sabrosky, *"France,"* in THE DEFENSE POLICIES OF NATIONS: A COMPARATIVE STUDY, 3D. 206, 248–49 (Douglas J. Murary & Paul R. Viotti eds., 1994). In May 1992, Defense Minister Pierre Joxe stated that "In addition to having arms capable of massive distant strikes against predetermined targets, we should perhaps develop more flexible weapons systems that promote deterrence more through the precision with which they strike than through the threat of a general nuclear exchange." *Id.*

See Defense Doctrine of France, in UNITED NATIONS DEPARTMENT, *supra* note 3, at 155 (1991):

> Deterrence means preventing any possible aggressor from meddling with our vital interests because of the risk he would run. French deterrence has another component, the final warning, which is an integral part of it. The final warning, delivered against a military target—by pre-strategic weapons in the first instance, even if the final warning is not solely a matter of short range weapons—

is to indicate to the aggressor that the vital interests of France are at
stake and that continued aggression will result in strategic weapons
being used.

Id.

5 "According to [the United Kingdom's] July 1998 Strategic Defense
Review [SDR], in current circumstance, nuclear forces continue to make a
unique contribution to ensuring stability and preventing crisis escalation. They
also help guard against any possible re-emergence of a strategic scale threat to
British security. The Review confirmed that in a changing and uncertain world,
Britain continues to require a credible and effective minimum nuclear deterrent
based on the Trident submarine force." Doctrine and Policy—United Kingdom
Nuclear Forces, <http//www.fas.org/nuke/guide/uk/doctrine>. Britain has
withdrawn all other nuclear weapons systems, most recently withdrawing the
Royal Air Force's free-fall nuclear bombs. *See id.* "[The] Trident force
provides ... strategic and sub-strategic nuclear capacity in support of NATO's
strategy of war prevention and as the ultimate guarantee of British national
security." *Id.*

By 1998 the number of nuclear devices in Britain's stockpile had reportedly
been reduced to some 260 deployed warheads, following the retiring of
numerous weapons, but still counting some 100 warheads then deployed on
aircraft. *See* TAKING STOCK, *supra* note 1, at 39.

While Great Britain has never fielded a triad, it has at different times
deployed land based missiles, submarine based missiles and bombers. *See*
UNITED NATIONS DEPARTMENT, *supra* note 3, at 15. *See also* THE MILITARY
BALANCE, *supra* note 3, at 244.

As of 1993–1994, Great Britain fielded 3 Polaris nuclear submarines, each
carrying up to 16 SLBMs with 3 warheads each, for a total of 128 strategic
nuclear warheads, and fielded 60 tactical nuclear bombs aboard nuclear fighter-
bombers, not including 4 in storage. *See* UNITED NATIONS DEPARTMENT, *supra*
note 3, at 50. As of 1998, Great Britain floated two nuclear submarines, each
carrying U.S. Trident II missiles said to be interchangeable with Britain's own
missiles. *See* TAKING STOCK, *supra* note 1, at 40.

There appears to be a substantial integration of at least part of Britain's
nuclear program with that of the United States. Britain reportedly has "title" to
submarine ballistic missiles at a Georgia, USA base, "but does not own them
outright." *Id.* The British submarines can sail into Kings Bay, Georgia, arm
themselves with the American Trident missiles, and take them back to Britain
to be mated there with British nuclear warheads. *Id.* at 40–41. An extended
sub-strategic, smaller, shorter range role is planned for the British submarines,
as of 1998. *See id.* at 41. *See also* NRDC's Nuclear Data—Table of British
Nuclear Forces, end 1996, <http://www.nrdc.org/nrdcpro/nudb/datab18.html>.

For the British position during the Cold War, *see United Kingdom Nuclear
Doctrine: Deterrence After The INF Treaty, in* UNITED NATIONS DEPARTMENT,
supra note 3 at 158–9:

number of States which, while not acknowledging nuclear status, are known to have such weapons, such as Israel,[7] or to have an imminent capability to have such weapons, such as Brazil and Argentina.[8]

> Flexible response is the only strategic concept that makes sense for a defensive alliance in the nuclear age. Military victory in the classical sense is not feasible; the use of force at any level, but especially the nuclear level, can have no other aim than to deny an aggressor swift success and to show him that he has underrated the defender's resolve and must for his own survival, back off. The circumstances in which this task would arise could vary greatly; the defense must therefore have a wide range of options, enabling it to react to any military situation promptly and with the least force needed for the basic political aim of ending the war.
>
> ***
>
> For flexible response, NATO has to maintain an effective nuclear armoury at several levels."

Id.

[6] India and Pakistan both detonated nuclear weapons in May 1998. India detonated five bombs on May 11 and 13, 1998, at a test site close to the Pakistani border, and Pakistan carried out six nuclear tests two weeks later. *Pakistan Announces Test Halt*, CHICAGO TRIB., June 11, 1998, NEWS, at 1.

On May 28, 1998, Pakistan announced that five nuclear tests were complete. Pakistan Nuclear Weapons, <http://www.fas.org/nuke/guide/pakistan/nuke/index.html>. The largest explosion was said to have a blast of 40 Kt. *See id.* Pakistan announced that three of its putative five blasts were in the sub-kiloton range. *See id.* One more warhead was tested on May 30, 1998, with a stated yield of 12 KT. India disputed the number and power of Pakistan's blasts. *See id.*

In April 1998, Pakistan had tested a medium range missile delivery system, capable of penetrating 900 miles into India. *World In Brief: Pakistan: Mid-Range Missile Successfully Tested,* TIME WIRE REPORTS, Apr. 7, 1998, at A12. Both nations mentioned repeatedly the contested areas of Jammu and Kashmir, over which they have shed blood, in discussing both the tests and the moratoriums following the tests.

India's long-range missile is the Agni, with a range of 1,600 miles and capable of carrying a payload of 2,200 lbs. *See Raising the Stakes in South Asia: Ground Zero*, LOS ANGELES TIMES, May 29, 1998, at A20.

In May of 1998, Pakistan had the material resources to build about ten nuclear weapons, and India, about twenty-five weapons. Joie Chen & Jamie McIntyre, *India and Pakistan's Arms Build-up*, CNN WORLD TODAY, May 14, 1998, 8:13pm Eastern Time, CNN Correspondent Jamie McIntyre speaking from the Pentagon (based on the estimated production ability of weapons grade plutonium and uranium in those two countries). *Id.*

[7] *See* KURT GOTTFRIED & BRUCE G. BLAIR, CRISIS STABILITY AND NUCLEAR WAR 244 (1988). Detailed reports put Israel's nuclear arsenal at 100–200

sophisticated warheads with "appreciable" yields. *Id. See also* THE MILITARY BALANCE, *supra* note 3, at 231 ("[I]t is widely recognized that Israel has nuclear [arms] ...."); LEONARD S. SPECTOR, NUCLEAR AMBITIONS: THE SPREAD OF NUCLEAR WEAPONS 1989–1990, 16 (Westview Press 1990) [hereinafter NUCLEAR AMBITIONS]; NUCLEAR PROLIFERATION HANDBOOK: PREPARED FOR THE COMMITTEE ON GOVERNMENTAL AFFAIRS, UNITED STATES SENATE 677 (Washington, D.C.: GPO 1995).

Threats made by Israel during the 1991 Gulf War were taken to imply a readiness to use nuclear arms that were at Israel's disposal. *See* CAREY SUBLETTE, NUCLEAR WEAPONS FREQUENTLY ASKED QUESTIONS Version 2.19 20 February 1999 § 7.3.3 Nuclear Weapon Nations and Arsenals, Suspected States, Israel <http://www.fas.org/nuke/hew/Nwfaq/Nfaq7.html>. The Federation of American Scientists suggests the arsenal could be about 100 devices. *See id.* Others have stated 300. *Israeli Nuclear 'Debate' Explosive,* CHIAGO TRIBUNE, Feb. 2, 2000 at 6. As recently as February 2000, Israeli officials attempted to preserve the policy of ambiguity. *See id.. See also* Deborah Sontag, *Israel Eases Secrecy Over Nuclear Whistleblower's Trial,* N. Y. TIMES, Nov. 25, 1999 at A3.

Israel has apparently preferred the neutron bomb, potentially effective against the massed armor formations along its borders, and, for a delivery system, has primarily relied on the Jericho II, with an estimated range of 5,000 km. *See* Avner Cohen, *And Then There Was One, Israel is the Last Nuclear "Threshold State,"* BULL. OF ATOMIC SCIENTISTS, vol. 54, no. 5, 51 (Sept. 1, 1998).

[8] *See* NUCLEAR AMBITIONS, *supra* note 7, at 6.

The Comprehensive Nuclear Test Ban Treaty listed 44 nations as nuclear capable, based on their possession of nuclear reactors. All such States were required to sign before the treaty would enter into force: Algeria, Argentina, Australia, Austria, Bangladesh, Belgium, Brazil, Bulgaria, Canada, Chile, China, Colombia, Democratic People's Republic of Korea, Egypt, Finland, France, Germany, Hungary, India, Indonesia, Iran (Islamic Republic of), Israel, Italy, Japan, Mexico, Netherlands, Norway, Pakistan, Peru, Poland, Romania, Republic of Korea, Russian Federation, Slovakia, South Africa, Spain, Sweden, Switzerland, Turkey, Ukraine, United Kingdom of Great Britain and Northern Ireland, United States, Viet Nam, and Zaire (based on a List of States members of the Conference on Disarmament of 18 June 1996 which formally participated in the work of the 1996 session of the Conference and which appear in Table 1 of the International Atomic Energy Agency's April 1996 edition of "Nuclear Power Reactors in the World," and of States members of the Conference on Disarmament of 18 June 1996 which formally participated in the work of the 1996 session of the Conference and which appear in Table 1 of the International Atomic Energy Agency's December 1995 edition of "Nuclear Research Reactors in the World."). *See* The Comprehensive Nuclear Test–Ban Treaty, annex 2, <http://www.acda.gov/treaties/ramaker.htm>

South Africa, which had acknowledged having nuclear weapons, has professedly dismantled them.[9] North Korea, which is believed to

---

(hosted by the Arms Control and Disarmament Agency of the U.S. Department of State).

[9] It appears that in 1971 South Africa commenced nuclear explosives research, completing its first fully assembled nuclear device in 1979 and thereafter deciding to manufacture six additional nuclear devices. *See generally* J.W. de Villiers et al., *Why South Africa Gave Up the Bomb*, FOREIGN AFF., Nov./Dec. 1993, at 98.

By 1989 six of the seven nuclear devices had been fully assembled, each using an estimated 50 to 60 kilograms of highly enriched uranium and having a yield of 10 to 18 kilotons. *See id.* at 99–103.

Ostensibly, the motivation for the South African build-up was twofold: (1) fear of Soviet expansion in southern Africa; and (2) a growing sense in South Africa of the country's isolation and the fact that, in the face of a military crisis, it would have to fend for itself; no one would come to its aid. Specific concerns included the build-up of Cuban forces in Angola starting in 1975 and the imminent independence of neighboring Zimbabwe under an actively anti-apartheid regime. *See id.* at 100–101.

In 1989 South Africa decided to terminate and completely dismantle its nuclear weapons program—and proceeded to do so by early July 1991. *See id.* at 103–104. This was ostensibly based on political reform in the country and a sensitivity to the collapse of the Soviet Union, the independence of Namibia, the cessation of hostilities in Angola, and the withdrawal from that country of 50,000 Cuban troops, such that South Africa determined it no longer needed a nuclear deterrent. *See id.* at 102–103. *See also* THE MILITARY BALANCE, *supra* note 3, at 231 (On March 24, 1993, President de Klerk of South Africa admitted that his country had built six nuclear warheads between 1974 and 1990. He claimed that all six were destroyed between 1990 and 1991); NUCLEAR PROLIFERATION HANDBOOK, *supra* note 7, at 675.

One author concludes:

> [T]he story of South Africa's acquisition and subsequent dismantlement of its nuclear arsenal holds vital lessons. Pretoria's action establishes the precedent of nuclear rollback for other threshold nuclear states. Moreover, the careful and responsible manner in which South Africa dismantled its weapons, joined the NPT, cooperated fully with the IAEA and accepted comprehensive safeguards on its nuclear facilities may serve as a useful future model. Finally, Pretoria's gradual realization that its nuclear weapons were not only superfluous but actually counterproductive to achieving South Africa's political, military and economic objectives may be the most important lesson of all.

Villiers, et al., *supra* at 109.

have possessed sufficient fissile material to create a nuclear weapon,[10] agreed to dismantle its nuclear weapons program, although its compliance is uncertain.[11] Other States which have had nuclear

---

[10] *See* THE MILITARY BALANCE, *supra* note 3, at 232; NUCLEAR PROLIFERATION HANDBOOK, *supra* note 7, at 678. *See also* WILLIAM J. PERRY, SECRETARY OF DEFENSE, 1995 ANNUAL REPORT TO THE PRESIDENT AND THE CONGRESS 271 [hereinafter 1995 REPORT OF THE SECRETARY OF DEFENSE].

[11] Since 1950 North Korea has pursued nuclear power and arms. Nuclear Weapons Program—North Korea, <http://www.fas.org/nuke/guide/dprk/nuke/index.html>. Ties with the Soviet Union led to North Korea's obtaining a Soviet research reactor in 1965. *See id.* Independently, North Korean scientists modernized it in 1974, and simultaneously commenced construction of a second reactor. *See id.* In 1977 an agreement was reached between North Korean and the International Atomic Energy Agency ("IAEA") for inspection of the second reactor. *See id.* A large reactor and the reprocessing plant necessary for weaponry were constructed in the 1980s. *See id.* In 1985, the United States announced that an additional secret reactor was under construction near Yongbyon, *see id.,* a site still of interest today. *See id.* Also in 1985, North Korea acceded to the Treaty on the Non-Proliferation of Nuclear Weapons. *See id.*

In 1994, the United States and North Korea signed an energy agreement entailing the installation of new "proliferation–resistant" nuclear power reactors and oil burning energy plants in return for a stop and reversal of the North Korean nuclear project. *Id.* As part of this arrangement, the Korean Peninsula Energy Development Organization (KEDO), whose leading members are the United States, Japan, and South Korea, entered into an agreement to provide two light water reactors by 2003. *See id.*

The United States as of that time believed that North Korea had enough plutonium to make a bomb. *See id.* (quoting Department of Defense spokesman Kenneth Bacon, April 22, 1997). Following the agreement, the IAEA found North Korea had extracted 24 kilograms of plutonium—enough fissile material to form the core of three twenty kiloton bombs. *See id.*

In the summer of 1998, reports were made of a secret underground nuclear site 25 miles from North Korea's known reactor site at Yongbyon. Towards the end of 1998, North Korea had still not reported the existence of this site to the International Atomic Energy Agency, the global nuclear agency. *See Clinton's North Korean Headache,* JANE'S INFO. GROUP FOREIGN REPORT, Dec. 17, 1998; *Remarks by Secretary of Defense William S. Cohen to the Boston Chamber of Commerce, Boston Marriott,* Sept. 17, 1998, <http://www.defenselink.mil/speeches/1998/s19980917-secdef.html>. In his November 1998 trip to Japan, Korea and Guam, President Clinton mentioned the parallel between fears of a North Korean bomb and Iranian ambitions. In late 1998, the Clinton Administration urgently sought to inspect a vast construction site in North Korea, believing it may be the beginnings of a nuclear weapons plant.

See James Bennet, *Clinton Appeals to North Korea for Closer Ties*, THE NEW YORK TIMES, Nov. 22, 1998, at 1.

The United States Congress responded with conditions to be placed on the Clinton Administration, in relation to the $35 million appropriated for KEDO for 1999 related to the implementation of the denuclearization Agreement. *See Remarks by Secretary of Defense William S. Cohen to the Boston Chamber of Commerce, supra.*

Under the Congressional restrictions, before KEDO could receive the first $15 million, slated for March 1, 1999, the Clinton Administration had to certify to Congress that:
- That the North and South are taking "demonstrable steps" to implement the 1991 denuclearization agreement, which calls for a joint inspection regime;
- That North Korea is cooperating in the safe storage of the spent fuel at Yongbyon that contains enough plutonium for four to five nuclear bombs; and
- That the dialog between the two nations is progressing.

See id.

Prior to the remaining $20 million (slated for June 1, 1999) being dispersed to KEDO, the Clinton Administration was further required to certify to Congress that agreement had been reached between the United States and North Korea regarding "suspect underground construction" and that the Administration was making progress towards reducing the North Korean ballistic missile threat, especially including exports from North Korea. *See id.*

Certifications to the foregoing effect were filed by the President with Congress, as required. *See* House of Representatives Committee on International Relations, Survey of Activities, Committee Business Scheduled Week of March 15, 1999, June 21, 1999; *US Official Comments on Planned Fuel Shipments to DPRK*, WORLD REPORTER WORLD NEWS CONNECTION, May 15, 1999 (referring to completion of the March certification, enabling release of the year's first allotment of financing).

It is widely recognized that North Korea has "several types of short range land and sea launched anti-ship cruise missiles" and "a variety of fighters, bombers, helicopters, artillery, rockets, mortars, and sprayers available as potential means of delivering for NBC [Nuclear Chemical Biological] weapons." In August 1998, North Korea launched a three-stage rocket over Japan in a threatening display of delivery system capacities. *See* WILLIAM S. COHEN, PROLIFERATION: THREAT AND RESPONSE, Section I, *Northeast Asia*, (Nov. 1997) <http://www.defenselink.mil/pubs/prolif97/ne_asia.html>. *See also Clinton's North Korean Headache, supra.* That same year, a panel led by former Defense Secretary Donald H. Rumsfield warned that North Korea and Iran could strike American territory with "little or no warning," and a follow-up report gave "ominous scenarios of what potential enemies could do against the United States in the next 15 years." Jane Perlez, *A Nuclear Safety Valve Is Shut*

weapons programs at one time or another include Iraq,[12] Iran,[13] Libya,[14] and Taiwan.[15]

Off, but U.S. Maintains Other Safeguards, THE NEW YORK TIMES, Oct. 14, 1999, at A12.

The economic support to North Korea in exchange for its curtailing its nuclear weapons program represents one of various "carrots and sticks" used by the United States to combat proliferation and curb nuclear arsenals, including "arms control accords with the old Soviet Union; economic and political incentives to persuade non-nuclear weapons nations not to build the bomb, and the threat of political and economic isolation against those who do." *Id.* at A12.

Following the 1998 nuclear tests by India and Pakistan, the United States imposed a series of economic sanctions against the two countries and led the effort to curb lending by international financial institutions, and then eased the sanctions as an incentive to induce the countries to sign the Comprehensive Test Ban Treaty. While these efforts worked, with both nations agreeing to sign the treaty, such agreements were jeopardized by the U.S. Senate's rejection of the treaty in October 1999. *Id.*

Professedly because of the failure of nonproliferation measures against States like Iran and Iraq, the United States has been seeking to negotiate a modification of the Antiballistic Missile Treaty of 1972 with Russia, to allow the United States to build a limited missile defense system as a shield against the weapons of emerging nuclear states. *Id.*

[12] *See* Iraqi Nuclear Weapons—Iraq Special Weapons, <http://www.fas.org/nuke/guide/iraq/nuke/program.html>. The Iraqi nuclear program, which is under observation by the IAEA, has apparently been dismantled pursuant to agreements resulting from the 1991 Gulf War, but the danger of present or future circumvention of such agreements and break-out remains. The IAEA is conducting an ongoing investigation of the Iraqi nuclear program, to determine what steps had been taken by Iraq and what became of the products of the Iraqi nuclear efforts. *See id.*

It appears that in or about 1975 Iraq started a substantial program to develop domestic technology and facilities to build indigenous material into a nuclear device. *See id.* This program was then set back by Israel's 1981 bombing of Iraq's Osirak nuclear reactor at Tuwaith. *Id.* Iraq then made the political decision to rebuild its nuclear program underground, and on a wholly self-sufficient basis. *See id.*

By 1990, Iraq was apparently so close to success that it appeared that, if it had given up its policy of indigenous self-reliance and turned to international sources for materials, it could have produced a nuclear bomb in a period of some six months to two years. *See id.* Delivery systems sufficient to carry a heavy nuclear weapon were also in process but needed additional work. *See id.* The Al Abid satellite launcher was scheduled to receive modifications to enable it to deliver a 1 ton warhead almost 1,200 km., work having begun on this modification in April 1989 and was planned for completion in 1993. *See id.* As an option, the Al Hussein missile could launch a 1 ton warhead 300 km, and a modified Al Hussein/Al Abbas missile could have been made by a crash program to reach 650 km. *See id.*

Bombing in January 1991 in the course of the Gulf War destroyed "technical tools at the nuclear research center at Tuwaith for processing the highly enriched uranium" needed for continuing the work. *See id.* Following defeat in this war, Iraq was forced to agree to dismantle its nuclear program, although its compliance thereafter became an issue. *See* THE MILITARY BALANCE, *supra* note 3, at 231 (The 1993 report by the IAEA to the UN on Iraq's compliance with the requirement that it dismantle its program found evidence of efforts at circumvention by Iraq but concluded that Iraq did not possess the capability to produce nuclear weapons). The IAEA worked intensively on the Iraq nuclear programs, removing equipment and material from Iraq, and finding no more than a few grams of "weapon-usable nuclear material." IAEA and Iraqi Nuclear Weapons, Iraq Special Weapons, <http://www.fas.org/nuke/guide/iraq/nuke/iaea.htm>. *See also* 1995 REPORT OF THE SECRETARY OF DEFENSE, *supra* note 10, at 71; NUCLEAR PROLIFERATION HANDBOOK, *supra* note 7, at 676.

Equipment was removed to IAEA's Vienna headquarters from 1991 to 1994. IAEA and Iraqi Nuclear weapons—Iraq Special Weapons, *supra.* Monitoring and verification continued to be carried out by the IAEA. In September 1996 Iraq released a "Full Final and Complete Disclosure" that was consistent with the IAEA's then understanding of Iraq's program. *See id.* In 1997 Iraq made a further disclosure via a "Declaration" describing activities at sites once involved in its nuclear program. *See id.* Then in 1998 Iraq filed further disclosures describing its "clandestine nuclear programme," again providing information basically consistent with the detailed findings of the IAEA. *See id.*

[13] *See* Nuclear Weapons—Iran, <http://www.fas.org/nuke/guide/iran/nuke/index.html>. Iran, with a nuclear development program well in progress, is ostensibly within a small number of years of achieving a nuclear capability. *See id.*

Iranian President Ali Akbar Rajsanjani stated in 1989 that Iran could not ignore the nuclear nature of the rest of the world, and since then Iran has ostensibly applied itself to developing nuclear and missile technology, receiving aid from a variety of countries, including Russia, China, Pakistan, South Africa, and India. Al. J. Venter, *Iran's Nuclear Ambition: Innocuous Illusion or Ominous Truth?*, INT'L DEFENSE REV., vol. 30, no. 9, 29, Sept. 1, 1997. *See also Witnesses, Senate Foreign Relations Committee, Near Eastern and South Asian Affairs Subcommittee, Hearing Regarding United States Policy toward Iran*, May 14, 1998, Chaired by Sen. Sam Brownback (R-KS).

There have also been reports of Iran's recruiting nuclear scientists and engineers from the former Soviet Union and purchasing potential delivery systems, such as long-range aircraft and missiles. *See* THE MILITARY BALANCE, *supra* note 3, at 233. It has been reported that North Korea, Russia and China sell Iran ballistic missiles and submarines. *See* Nuclear Weapons—Iran, *supra.*

While the IAEA has made visits to Iran and found no evidence of a military nuclear program, Iran is strongly suspected of developing a nuclear weapons program based on its purchase of a 300-megawatt reactor from China and two 440-megawatt reactors from Russia (considering that Iran is a major exporter of oil and gas, it seems unlikely that Iran is purchasing nuclear reactors purely to provide energy). *Id.* Iran reportedly complies with the NPT apparently by means that will allow, in exigent circumstance, Iran's application of peacetime energy nuclear knowledge to nuclear weapons production. *See id.*

"Israel and the United States believed in 1992 that Iran would attain a military capability within eight to 10 years. ... As of 1998 the estimate of the US Central Command was that Iranian efforts could result in the development of a nuclear device by the middle of the next decade, that is, by the year 2005." *Id*

[14] *See* NUCLEAR AMBITIONS, *supra* note 7, at 175. Libya has over the years apparently attempted to acquire a nuclear weapons capability, but ostensibly has not yet succeeded. *See id. See also* NUCLEAR PROLIFERATION HANDBOOK, *supra* note 7, at 677; Libya Special Weapons, <http://www.fas.org/nuke/guide/libya/index.html>.

Apparently hoping for nuclear arms in return, Libya in 1977 provided Pakistan with financial assistance and uranium originating from Niger. *See* Libya Special Weapons, <http://www.fas.org/nuke/guide/libya/index.html>. Qahdafi denied this in 1986, stating to an Indian newspaper that Libya would never help Pakistan obtain a bomb, and that nuclear weapons were "'a great mistake against humanity.'" *Id.* (quoting an Indian newspaper of March, 1986).

The Soviet Union supplied a research reactor to Libya in 1979. *See id.* Libyans studied nuclear technology abroad, with 200 in the United States until the United States proscribed training Libyans in nuclear science in early 1983. *See id.* Libya planned to buy a nuclear power station from the Soviet Union, but was unsatisfied with the Soviet offer and instead turned to a Belgian firm. *See id.* In 1984, Belgium decided to refuse the billion dollar contract, under pressure from the United States. *See id.* Thereafter the Soviet Union and Libya agreed to construct a plant, for US$4 billion. *See id.* These plans apparently never came to fruition. Libya is still reported to have only the original Soviet research reactor "that is subject to IAEA safeguards." SUBLETTE, *supra* note 7.

Libya apparently still pursues a bomb ready made, as it once had from Pakistan. "It was reported in the September 1997 *Jane's Defence Review* that Judith Miller, formerly head of the *New York Times* bureau in Cairo, was told by a senior presidential aide in Libya that the country had offered China and India US$15 billion each for a single atomic bomb." *Id.*

Libya's delivery capacity includes short range FROG and Scud missiles, and missiles fired from medium range Tu-22 bombers. *See id.* The Scud-B system was acquired from the Soviet Union in the 1970s. The international community has made efforts to restrain Libya from obtaining longer range

In addition, Ukraine, Belarus and Kazakhstan, former Soviet Republics which at the time still possessed nuclear weapons, agreed, pursuant to the Trilateral Accord of January 1994, to relinquish to Russia the nuclear weapons they inherited from the Soviet Union, and apparently have complied.[16] More broadly, many nuclear weapons "were moved from Eastern Europe and the 14 former non-Russian Soviet republics to storage sites in Russia."[17]

Egypt has announced that, if necessary, it will acquire nuclear weapons to counter an Israeli military build-up.[18] Egypt's reactor at

---

weapons, but Libya continues to seek to develop or purchase such a capability. *See* THE PROLIFERATION CHALLENGE, <http://www.defenselink.mil/pubs/prolif/>.

[15] *See* Tim Zimmermann & Susan V. Lawrence, *Will Taiwan Succumb to the Nuclear Temptation? Feeling the Heat*, U.S. NEWS & WORLD REP., vol. 120, no. 6, Feb. 12,1996 ("During the 1970s and 1980s, Taiwan pursued a secret nuclear weapons program, abandoned in March 1988 under pressure from the United States."). *See also* Laura Tyson, *Taiwan to Study Nuclear Arms Options*, THE FINANCIAL TIMES, July 29, 1995 ("Taiwan's President Lee Teng-hui yesterday hinted that his government might consider reviving its long-dormant nuclear weapons development programme, in comments likely to alarm governments across Asia. Mr. Lee's remarks come at a time of escalating tension between Taiwan [and mainland China]. While the island was still under martial law in the 1980s, a military defector revealed that Taiwan was conducting nuclear weapons research."); *Taiwan Will Not Revive Nuclear Weapons Program*, AGENCE FRANCE-PRESSE, July 31, 1995 ("Taiwan President Lee Teng-hui Monday denied the nationalist island would revive its nuclear weapons program, saying remarks he made earlier were misinterpreted by some of the foreign press. 'The Republic of China (Taiwan) has the power to make a nuclear arsenal, but we definitely will not develop nuclear weapons,' Lee told the National Assembly which began a one-month session July 21."); NUCLEAR AMBITIONS, *supra* note 7, at 60 (stating that Taiwan had pursued a nuclear weapons program in the 1970s and the 1980s, but ostensibly dismantled the program under intense U.S. pressure).

[16] *See* 1995 REPORT OF THE SECRETARY OF DEFENSE, *supra* note 10, at 25. *See also* Robert S. Norris & William M. Arkin, *Russian (C.I.S.) Strategic Nuclear Forces: End of 1995*, BULL. OF THE ATOMIC SCIENTISTS, Mar. 13, 1996 (In 1995, 1,000 strategic warheads formerly deployed in Ukraine, Kazakhstan and Belarus were transferred to Russia. The remaining warheads were scheduled to be removed from Ukraine in 1996). They were apparently so removed. ARKIN ET AL., TAKING STOCK, *supra* note 1, at 2.

[17] *See* ARKIN ET AL., TAKING STOCK, *supra* note 1, at 2.

[18] Ed Blanche, *Egypt "Can Easily Go Nuclear" If the Necessity Arises*, JANE'S DEFENCE WEEKLY, vol. 30, no. 15, Oct. 14, 1998.

Inshas research center north of Cairo has features built-in features enabling it to be converted to making weapons grade plutonium.[19]

Nor is nuclear technology esoteric. The information as to how to manufacture a nuclear device is readily available to the public on a non-classified basis, as evidenced by the various reports in the press as to individuals who, using publicly available sources, have figured out the requirements for manufacturing a nuclear weapon.[20]

Nor is the obtaining of the materials, including fissile materials, necessary for the production of nuclear weapons an insurmountable obstacle, given sufficient time and money. The dismantling of the Soviet Union and resultant political, economic, and military dislocations have created a situation where substantial amounts of such materials are potentially available.[21] Secretary of Defense Perry noted the danger that the materials, equipment, and know-how needed to make nuclear weapons could leak through "porous former Soviet Union

---

[19] *Id.*

[20] *See* David Hughes, *When Terrorists go Nuclear: The Ingredients and Information Have Never Been More Available,* POPULAR MECHANICS, vol. 173, no. 1, Jan. 1, 1996, at 56:

If you were planning to build a nuclear bomb, you would probably want to visit your local library to read such classics as Los Alamos Primer: First Lectures on How to Build an Atomic Bomb. Saddam Hussein's bomb development team had a copy in its library, and you can obtain one for $27.50 by calling the University of California Press.

Id.

[21] *See Weapons of Mass Destruction: Remarks by Defense Secretary William Perry at Georgetown University,* FED. NEWS SERVICE, Apr. 18, 1996; Frans Berkhout et al., *A Cutoff in the Production of Fissile Material,* INT'L SECURITY, vol. 19, No. 3, Winter 1994–1995, at 168; Jessica Eve Stern, *Moscow Meltdown: Can Russia Survive?,* INT'L SECURITY, Spring 1994, vol. 18, No. 4, at 41 (citing Office of Threat Assessment, *The Russian Mafia,* November 1, 1993); Brigid Schulte, *A Timeline of the Nuclear Age,* THE SEATTLE TIMES, August 9, 1995 (citing The Brookings Institution). In 1994, German police investigated 267 cases of suspected trading in radioactive material, seizing smuggled plutonium on three occasions. In one instance, scientists were arrested in Prague with 7 pounds of weapons-grade uranium. *Id.* In another, in August 1994, German authorities at Munich found over 500 grams of plutonium smuggled out of Russia targeted for sale on the black market in the baggage from a Lufthansa flight from Moscow. Nesha Starcevic, *Biggest Find Yet of Bomb-Quality Plutonium in Germany,* ASSOCIATED PRESS, August 13, 1994.

borders to other nations."[22] More recently, Secretary of Defense Cohen stated, "Integral ... is U.S. support of efforts to secure and stem the export of any former-Soviet NBC [nuclear biological or chemical] weapons, weapons material, and associated delivery systems and to eliminate any Soviet nuclear-capable systems remaining in the other New Independent States."[23]

Indeed, one need not look solely to the former Soviet Union for such exposure. Security with respect to American nuclear weapons and materials has ostensibly been lax or at least ineffective, as perhaps is not a surprise, given such a large program and an open society. Numerous instances of losses of fissile materials from American stockpiles have been reported and the threat is always present.[24] The reports are legion that Israel was facilitated in the development of its nuclear weapons program through nuclear materials diverted from the United States.[25] A number of terrorist groups have made and are likely continuing to make efforts to obtain control of nuclear weapons.[26]

---

[22] 1995 ANNUAL REPORT TO THE PRESIDENT AND THE CONGRESS, *supra* note 10, at 25.

[23] WILLIAM S. COHEN, 1999 ANNUAL REPORT TO THE PRESIDENT AND THE CONGRESS Chap. 1, p. 13.

[24] *See* Schulte, *A Timeline of the Nuclear Age, supra* note 21 (citing Brookings Institution estimates that eleven U.S. nuclear bombs were lost in accidents and never recovered).

[25] *See, e.g.,* Federation of American Scientists: "Up to 100 kilograms of enriched uranium missing from a facility at Apollo, Pennsylvania, are believed to have been taken to Israel. And in 1968 200 tons of ore disappeared from a ship in the Mediterranean Sea and were probably diverted to Israel." Dimona— Israel Special Weapons Facilities, <http://www.fas.org/>; "Hersch relates extensive (and highly successful) efforts by Israel to obtain targeting data from U.S. intelligence." SUBLETTE, *supra* note 7.

[26] John Deutch, then the Director of the Central Intelligence Agency, stated, "The ability for our country or, I might say, any other country in the developed world to protect their infrastructure from a terrorist attack based on nuclear, chemical or biological weapons is very, very small, indeed." *See Nuclear Safety and Security in Russia*, NATIONAL PUBLIC RADIO, Apr. 17, 1996. Robert Blitzer, Federal Bureau of Investigation stated, "The growing strength of international organized crime, especially within the former Soviet republics, has raised the specter of an underground market for these materials. International organized-crime groups are capable of providing weapons of mass-destruction materials to terrorist groups and to rogue nations." *Id.*

Referring to the Tokyo subway gas attack, the World Trade Center bombing and the Oklahoma City bombing, Senators Richard Lugar and Sam Nunn have called the transition into a new era of radiological terrorism our

Most recently, there have been extensive revelations as to widespread espionage by China in the United States over many decades, whereby China apparently gained access to substantial information as to major U.S. nuclear weapons systems.[27]

---

greatest national security threat. Richard Benedetto, *Don't Cloud Over the Nuclear Threat*, USA TODAY, Apr. 22, 1996, at A6. Lugar stated, "A single act of nuclear terrorism perpetrated against an American city could be more deadly and destructive to the vitality and confidence of our nation than almost any other conceivable event." *Id.*

Gordon Oehler, Director of the CIA's Nonproliferation Center and a CIA official, warned Congress that the threat of nuclear chemical or biological attacks by extremists has never been greater:

> The chilling reality is that nuclear materials and technologies are more accessible now than at any other time in history—due primarily to the dissolution for the former Soviet Union and the region's worsening economic conditions. Extremist groups worldwide are increasing learning how to manufacture chemical and biological agents and the potential for additional chemical and biological attacks by such groups continues to grow.

Reuters, *CIA Warns of Nuclear Threat by Extremists*, THE SAN DIEGO UNION TRIB., Mar. 28, 1996, at A2 (citing the 1995 Tokyo subway attack by Aum Shinri Kyo, the Japanese cult).

It has been stated that a "crude, low-yield bomb of half a kiloton placed on the front steps could knock the Twin Towers into the Hudson River. It would take only a dozen kilos of plutonium-oxide powder, some high explosives and some items from a hardware store to kill 50,000 people." David Hughes, *When Terrorists Go Nuclear: The Ingredients and Information Have Never Been More Available*, POPULAR MECHANICS, Jan. 1, 1996.

"Saddam Hussein has obtained some of Britain's most closely guarded nuclear secrets. According to the authoritative U.S. magazine Nucleonics Week, Iraq has the blueprints of the latest uranium-enrichment centrifuge, code-named TC-11. It is alleged that a German scientist who previously worked with Urenco, a British-German-Dutch consortium involved in the enrichment of uranium to grades suitable for atomic weapons, stole the secret designs and sold them to Iraq before 1991." Alan George, *Iraq Obtains Nuclear Secrets From Consortium,* MONTREAL GAZETTE, Jan. 26, 1996, at B11.

[27] Recent news reports and the 1999 Congressional Cox Report resulting from a widescale Congressional investigation indicate that, starting in the late 1970s and 1980s, China through espionage obtained substantial nuclear weapons secrets, including the designs of the W-70 warhead and of the highly advanced, miniature W-88 thermonuclear strategic warhead deployed on the MiRVing [multiple re-entry vehicle] submarine launched Trident ballistic missiles, as well as the designs of many of the United States' thermonuclear fusion bombs. THE COX REPORT, REPORT OF THE UNITED STATES HOUSE OF REPRESENTATIVES SELECT COMMITTEE ON U.S. NATIONAL SECURITY AND

MILITARY/ COMMERCIAL CONCERNS WITH THE PEOPLE'S REPUBLIC OF CHINA 68, (Jan. 1999) <http://hillsource.house.gov/CoxReport/report>. (This is the unclassified, redacted version of the FINAL REPORT OF THE SELECT COMMITTEE ON U.S. NATIONAL SECURITY AND MILITARY/COMMERCIAL CONCERNS WITH THE PEOPLES REPUBLIC OF CHINA, issued on January 3, 1999) (hereinafter THE COX REPORT).

The W-70 "can be used as a strategic thermonuclear warhead or an enhanced radiation ("neutron bomb") warhead." *Id.* Neutron bombs were never deployed by the United States, but were tested by China in 1988. *See id.* The W-88 miniature warhead is prized for posing less a burden on ballistic launch missile and having so small a footprint as to permit MiRVing. *See id.* at 73.

China obtained the information apparently from Department of Energy sites devoted to the production of nuclear weapons. The technology taken enabled China to make a smaller warhead more quickly than they could have were they to pursue independent research. The miniaturization information obtained by China is valuable because miniature warheads make launch vehicles more capable and mobile. *See id.*

That the Chinese have the plans of the W-88 warhead is clear. A "walk-in" uninvited informant, came to the U.S. Central Intelligence Agency in 1995 and displayed:

> an official PRC [People's Republic of China] document classified "Secret" that contained design information on the W-88 Trident D-5 warhead, the most modern in the U.S. arsenal, as well as technical information concerning other thermonuclear warheads. *** The CIA later determined that the "walk-in" was directed by the PRC intelligence services. *** There is speculation as to the PRC's motives for advertising to the United States the state of its nuclear weapons development.

Id. at 83–84.

"A series of PRC nuclear weapons test explosions from 1992 to 1996 [had begun] a debate in the U.S. government about whether the PRC's designs for its new generation of nuclear warheads were in fact based on stolen U.S. classified information." *Id.* at 63.

The Department of Energy also reports that China has acquired some United States software relevant to nuclear war, including that used to calculated dose penetration in humans and the survivability of systems to electronic penetration. *See id.* at 85.

Strict attempts are being made to heighten the Department of Energy's security, along with increasing its counter intelligence budget from the $7.6 million in fiscal year 1998 to $15.6 million in fiscal year 1999. *Id.* at 92. The Cox Report's "Select Committee judges that the new counter-intelligence program at the Department of Energy will not be even minimally effective until at least the year 2000." *Id.* at 64.

The Cox report attempts to soften the leak to China by noting the test numbers. While the Soviet Union has had 715 tests, the United States 1,030,

There has also been a substantial proliferation of delivery systems, including, most disturbingly, long-range missiles, that are increasingly available to States and groups.[28] In addition, many of today's nuclear weapons are extremely small and readily susceptible to being smuggled into target areas. For example, the submarine launched Trident missiles and the land based Minuteman III missiles bear a thermonuclear warhead only one-half the size of an adult.[29]

As of 1998, the United States, China, Russia, Britain and France have very long-range ballistic missiles, at the following approximate ranges: the United States: "more than 6,000 miles,"[30] China: 8000 miles, Britain: 7,750 miles, Russia: 6,800 miles, and France: 3700 miles (submarine launched).[31] In addition, some 20 or 30 other States reportedly have ongoing ballistic missile programs, with the programs of Iran, Iraq and North Korea, with ranges of some 800, 300 and 900

---

and France, 210, China has carried out 45 tests. *See id.* at 76. China signed the Comprehensive Test Ban Treaty in 1996, thus agreeing to no further tests. *See id.* at 84–85. The report states that China would need high performance computers and sophisticated code to simulate testing by means of computer models. *See id.* at 85.

China nonetheless has speeded up its weapons development by obtaining designs from the United States, saving time and mistakes. *See id.* at 73. Still, "Completing the development of its next-generation warhead poses challenges for the PRC. The PRC may not be able to match precisely the exact explosive power and other features of U.S. weapons. Nonetheless, the PRC may be working towards this goal, and the difficulties it faces are surmountable. Work-arounds exist ...." *Id.* at 72.

In connection with the leaks to China, a nuclear weapons engineer was indicted on charges of "illegally removing the highly classified design, construction and testing data from the Los Alamos weapons laboratory where he was employed." David Johnson and James Risen, *Nuclear Weapons Engineer Indicted in Removal of Data,* NEW YORK TIMES, Dec. 11, 1999, at A1.

[28] Lisbeth Gronlund & David Wright, *What They Didn't Do,* BULL. OF THE ATOMIC SCIENTISTS, Nov./Dec. 1998, at 48.

[29] THE COX REPORT, *supra* note 27, at 76.

[30] Strategic Missiles, <http://www.af.mil/news/airman/0199/missi.html>. Ballistic missiles are extraordinarily fast:

The Air Force said it recently completed two successful unarmed Minuteman III intercontinental ballistic missile launches from Vandenberg AFB, Calif. ... [E]ach ICBM covered 4,200 miles in 30 minutes, hitting predetermined targets at the Kwajalein Missile Range in the western Marshall Islands.

Sarah Hood, *News Notes,* AIR FORCE MAG., Aug., 1997 at 15.

[31] Gronlund & Wright, *supra* note 28, at 48.

miles respectively, being of particular concern to the United States.[32] The North Koreans are working on a "Taepo Dong" missile that reportedly could have a range of 6,200 miles.[33]

While the missiles possessed by Iran, Iraq and North Korea are reportedly not very accurate, accuracy is not necessarily important (indeed, very much the opposite may be the case) to a State willing to threaten and even inflict indiscriminate destruction through the use of nuclear, chemical or biological weapons.[34] This could be seen through the Cold War policy of MAD, which, as a matter of policy, threatened blunderbuss indiscriminate effects. Some of the smaller missiles of Iran, Iraq and North Korea which are not capable of carrying a heavy nuclear warhead could carry biological or chemical devices.[35]

Nor is the threat of delivery by smuggling limited to terrorist groups. The Israelis "reportedly attempted to deter the Soviet Union from supporting an Arab attack on Israel by quietly informing Soviet leaders that they could not prevent Israel from smuggling a nuclear bomb into the Soviet Union." The threat was apparently taken seriously.[36]

---

[32] *Id.* at 47.

[33] *See id.*

[34] *See id.* at 46.

[35] *See id.* at 47.

[36] *Id.* at 49 (citing SEYMOUR HERSCH, THE SAMSON OPTION (1991)).

Chapter 24: U.S. Recognition That The Use of Nuclear Weapons Would Serve No Military Purpose

Throughout the nuclear era, even while the United States was professedly following war-fighting policies of limited nuclear war and intra-war deterrence as well as full blown nuclear deterrence, it was widely espoused within the political and military leadership of the country that nuclear weapons could not rationally be used. Statements to such effect are particularly credible because they were so contrary to the stated policy that such weapons could and would be used.

Following is a sampling of such statements.

Statements by U.S. Political Leadership

Secretary of State Jimmy Byrnes during the Truman Administration stated, "[b]ut from the day the first bomb fell on Hiroshima one thing has been clear to all of us. The civilized world cannot survive an atomic war."[1]

President Eisenhower, in the early days of the hydrogen bomb, stated: "We're rapidly getting to the point that no war can be won."[2] Eisenhower noted that the outlook of a nuclear war is "'destruction of the enemy and suicide.'"[3]

President Kennedy stated:

> [I]f someone thinks we should have a nuclear war in order to win, I can inform them that there will be no winners in the next nuclear war, if there is one, and this country and other countries will suffer very heavy blows. So that we have to proceed with responsibility

---

[1] Sec. of State, Jimmy Byrnes, World Cooperation Address (Nov. 16, 1945) (delivered at Charleston, S.C., in connection with the "Jimmy Byrnes Homecoming Day" and broadcast over the network of the Nat'l Broadcasting Company), *in* DEP'T ST. BULL. XIII, Nov. 1945, at 34.

[2] *The Consequences of Nuclear War on the Global Environment, Hearing Before the Subcommittee on Investigations and Oversight of the Committee on Science and Technology*, 97th Cong., 2d Sess. (1982) (statement of Dr. Sidney D. Drell, Stanford Linear Accelerator Center Stanford University, quoting President Eisenhower in 1956).

[3] *Id.*

and with care in an age where the human race can obliterate itself
....[4]

In February 1964, Secretary of Defense Robert McNamara stated of the American policy of Mutually Assured Destruction ("MAD"):

> A full-scale nuclear exchange between the United States and the USSR would kill 100 million Americans during the first hour. It would kill an even greater number of Russian, but I doubt that any sane person would call this "victory."[5]

McNamara later stated:

> In 1991, a committee of the U.S. National Academy of Sciences, in a report signed by retired Joint Chiefs of Staff Chairman Gen. David C. Jones, stated: "Nuclear weapons should serve no purpose beyond the deterrence of ... nuclear attack by others."[6]

McNamara disclosed:

> In the early 1960s, I had reached conclusions similar to these. In long private conversations, first with President Kennedy and then with President Johnson, I had recommended, without qualification, that they never, under any circumstances, initiate the use of nuclear weapons. I believe they accepted my recommendations. But neither they nor I could discuss our position publicly because it was contrary to established NATO policy.[7]

Secretary McNamara more recently stated that he had long concluded that the use of nuclear weapons, "is no longer—if it ever was —justifiable on military grounds."[8]

Secretary of State Dean Rusk of the Johnson Administration stated:

> "I believe it is widely understood that a thermonuclear aggression would not be a rational act."[9]

---

[4] HAROLD W. CHASE & ALLEN H. LERMAN, KENNEDY AND THE PRESS: THE NEWS CONFERENCES 186 (1965) (statement of John F. Kennedy, Feb. 14, 1962).

[5] Brigid Schulte, *A Timeline of the Nuclear Age*, THE SEATTLE TIMES, Aug. 9, 1995 (citing The Brookings Institution).

[6] ROBERT S. MCNAMARA, IN RETROSPECT, THE TRAGEDY AND LESSONS OF VIETNAM 344 (1995) [hereinafter IN RETROSPECT].

[7] *Id.* at 345.

[8] *Id.* at 338.

[9] Organizing the Peace for Man's Survival, Address before the Council on Foreign Relations (May 24, 1966), *reprinted in* DEPT OF ST. BULL., JUNE 1966, at 1407.

Former President Richard Nixon, addressing the U.S. and Soviet positions on whether a nuclear war would be winnable, stated:

> For years the prevailing U.S. concept has been that nuclear war could and would not bring any meaningful form of victory, either military or political....[10]

President Nixon further quoted with approval Harvard historian Richard Pipes' statement of U.S. policy:

> The prevalent U.S. doctrine holds that an all-out-war between countries in possession of sizable nuclear arsenals would be so destructive as to leave no winner....[11]

Melvin Laird, Secretary of Defense in the Nixon Administration, stated with respect to nuclear weapons:

> These weapons are useless for military purposes.[12]

Secretary Laird further stated:

> A worldwide zero nuclear option with adequate verification should now be our goal. ... These weapons ... are useless for military purposes.[13]

Henry Kissinger, President Nixon's National Security Advisor and Secretary of State, speaking in Brussels in 1979, reportedly questioned whether the United States would ever initiate a nuclear strike against the Soviet Union based upon a Soviet attack on Western Europe:

> Our European allies, he said, should not keep asking us to multiply strategic assurances that we cannot possibly mean or if we do mean, we would not execute because if we execute we risk the destruction of civilization.[14]

Secretary Kissinger further stated:

> I have also mentioned the transformation of the nature of power wrought by nuclear weapons. Because nuclear weapons are so

---

[10] RICHARD NIXON, THE REAL WAR 163 (1980).

[11] *Id.* at 163–64.

[12] ROBERT S. MCNAMARA, OUT OF THE COLD, NEW THINKING FOR AMERICAN FOREIGN AND DEFENSE POLICY IN THE 21ST CENTURY 175–76 (1989) [hereinafter NEW THINKING].

[13] IN RETROSPECT, *supra* note 6, at 345.

[14] *Id.* at 344–45.

cataclysmic, they are hardly relevant to a whole gamut of challenges: probes, guerrilla wars, local crises.[15]

Stating that there was little enthusiasm for NATO's proclaimed strategy of "flexible response," whereby the United States would use tactical nuclear weapons against a Soviet attack on western Europe, Kissinger noted that a NATO study on military options was "unable to find any use for nuclear weapons in NATO even though our stockpile there numbered in the thousands."[16] Kissinger stated that NATO concluded that the primary role of American nuclear forces in Europe was to "raise the Soviet estimate of the expended costs of aggression and add great uncertainty in their calculations."[17]

Edmund S. Muskie, Secretary of State during the Carter Administration, stated in testimony before the Senate Foreign Relations Committee:

> [N]uclear conflict cannot be an instrument for achieving national policy goals, either for us or for the Soviet Union; there surely can be no victor in a nuclear war.[18]

The following extraordinary exchange took place in Congressional hearings in 1980 between Secretary of Defense Harold Brown and Senators John Glenn and Frank Church:

> Secretary Brown: We [the United States] don't think we can win a nuclear war... .
> Senator Glenn: I don't think so either, but still I don't understand why we telegraph our punches on this. I want the Soviets to think we have every option.
> Honorable Frank Church (Chairman of the Committee on Foreign Relations): I am wondering if, as we move toward a greater and greater flexibility, if we are not engaging in the same sort of exercise and moving toward a place and a time when we will think that it is possible to wage some kind of limited war, confine it in some way that would permit us to use [nuclear] weapons? Is not that danger very real on both sides?
> Secretary of Defense, Harold Brown: As a hypothetical situation, I think it is; but I have never seen anything that a U.S. Chairman of the Joint Chiefs of Staff has written that says that. You know and your colleagues know that I have testified on this now for years. I

---

[15] HENRY KISSINGER, WHITE HOUSE YEARS 115 (1979).

[16] *Id.* at 218.

[17] *Id.*

[18] Hearing before the Committee on Foreign Relations, United States Senate, 96th Cong. (1980).

would not rule out the possibility that some lower-ranking U.S. general or flag officer would say, Yes, if we do things right we can win a nuclear war. I can't point to such a case.

I am really quite well informed on the views of all the senior U.S. military, and none of them would write anything like this. What civilians outside might write, who consider 40-kiloton weapons to be nuclear confetti, I don't know; but that has never been the position of anybody in a position of responsibility within the United States, at a high level within the administration, or any U.S. administration.[19]

President Reagan stated:

A nuclear war cannot be won and must never be fought. The only value in possessing nuclear weapons is to make sure they will never be used.[20]

James Woolsey, then Delegate-at-Large to the US. delegation for Strategic Arms Reduction Talks in 1984, stated:

[Nuclear weapons] are not usable weapons militarily in any theater in any context.[21]

The American/Soviet communiqué of November 1985, following a summit meeting, stated:

---

[19] *Id.*

[20] President Reagan, State of the Union Address (Jan. 25, 1984).
President Reagan further stated:
No one could "win" a nuclear war. Yet as long as nuclear weapons were in existence, there would always be risks they would be used, and once the first nuclear weapon was unleashed, who knew where it would end?
My dream, then, became a world free of nuclear weapons....
HENRY KISSINGER, DIPLOMACY 781 (1994), quoting RONALD REAGAN, AN AMERICAN LIFE 550 (1990).
President Reagan further stated:
I can't believe that this world can go on beyond our generation and on down to succeeding generations with this kind of weapon on both sides poised at each other without someday some fool or some maniac or some accident triggering the kind of war that is the end of the line for all of us.
Id., quoting Ronald Reagan, Remarks at a White House Briefing for Chief Executive Officers of Trade Associations and Corporations on Deployment of the MX Missile, May 16, 1983, in *Reagan Papers,* 1983 vol., bk. 1, p.715.
[21] *Hearings on The Role of Arms Control in U.S. Defense Policy Before the Committee on Foreign Affairs, House of Representatives,* 98th Cong. 2nd Sess., at 82 (June 20, 21, 26, July 25, 1984) (Strategic Arms Reduction Talks).

> [T]he sides have agreed that a nuclear war cannot be won and can never be fought. Recognizing that any conflict between the U.S.S.R. and the United States could have catastrophic consequences, they emphasize the importance of preventing any war between them, whether nuclear or conventional."[22]

In 1994, Secretary of Defense William Perry stated:

> I would liken MAD to two men holding revolvers and standing about 10 yards away and pointing their revolvers at each others' head, and the revolvers are loaded, cocked, their fingers are on the trigger, and then to make matters worse they're shouting insults at each other. And that characterized MAD, which was what we had to control this arms race—this nuclear terror during all the periods of the Cold War.[23]

Statements by U.S. Military Leadership:

In November 1984 retired Air Force Lt. Col. Edward A. Walsh, who had served ten of his twenty-five year in Air Force intelligence, stated:

> The very nature, mutuality, and magnitude of nuclear devastation has made nuclear war obsolete as an instrument of national policy, except as a deterrent force, which cancels it out as a weapon of offense. Nuclear was not only unthinkable psychologically, it is unfeasible and untenable technically.[24]

General David Jones, former Chairman of the Joint Chiefs of Staff, stated:

> I don't know any American officer, or any Soviet officer, who really believes either superpower can achieve a true first-strike capability, that one side could ever so disarm the other as to leave it

---

[22] DANIEL J. ARBESS & SIMEON A. SAHAYEACHNY, NUCLEAR DETERRENCE AND INTERNATIONAL LAW: SOME STEPS TOWARDS OBSERVATION, ALTERNATIVES XII 83–111 (1987).

[23] Secretary of Defense William Perry & General John Shalikashvili, Chairman, Joint Chiefs of Staff, *Dep't of Defense Briefing, in* FED. NEWS SERVICE, Wash. (Sept. 22, 1994).

[24] Edward A. Walsh, *Armageddon Is Not Around the Corner, reprinted from* U.S.A TODAY, Nov. 1984, *quoted in* NUCLEAR WAR OPPOSING VIEWPOINTS 47–48 (David Bender & Bruno Leone, eds., 1985) [hereinafter OPPOSING VIEWPOINTS].

without the ability to retaliate.... . [B]oth strongly agree that neither side can win a nuclear war in any meaningful sense.[25]

Admiral Noel Gayler, former Commander-in-Chief of the U.S. Forces in the Pacific and the Director of the National Security Agency, testified before the House Committee on Foreign Affairs:

> No one believes the nine new strategic nuclear weapons systems or the 17,000 new weapons now in our program or the corresponding Soviet buildup have any military usefulness.[26]

Admiral Gayler went on to quote George Kennan's "profoundly sensible words:"

> [T]here is no issue at stake in our political relations with the Soviet Union—no hope, no fear, nothing in which we aspire, nothing we would like to avoid—which would conceivably be worth a nuclear war....[27]

In a subsequent hearing, Admiral Gayler testified further as to the potential military uses of nuclear weapons, stating that such weapons "have no sensible military use."[28] He further stated:

> There is no sensible military use of any of our nuclear forces. The only reasonable use is to deter our opponents from using his nuclear forces.[29]

General Larry Welch, former United States Air Force Chief of Staff and Commander of the Strategic Air Command, expressed the same thought, as follows:

---

[25] WILLIAM A. SCHWARTZ ET AL., THE NUCLEAR SEDUCTION: WHY THE ARMS RACE DOESN'T MATTER—AND WHAT DOES 45 (University of California Press 1990) [hereinafter THE NUCLEAR SEDUCTION]. *See also* CENTER FOR DEFENSE INFORMATION NUCLEAR WAR QUOTATIONS at 48.

[26] *Hearings on The Role of Arms Control in U.S. Defense Policy, before the Committee on Foreign Affairs, House of Representatives*, 98th Cong. 2nd Sess., (June 20, 21, 26, July 25, 1984) at 82 (statement of Adm. Noel Gayler, U.S. Navy (Retired), Former Commander in Chief, U.S. Forces in the Pacific, Former Director, National Security Agency).

[27] *Id.* at 82.

[28] *Hearings before the Special Panel on Arms Control and Disarmament of the Procurement and Military Nuclear Systems Subcommittee of the Committee on Armed Services of the House of Representatives*, 98th Cong. 280–83 (1995) (statement of Adm. Noel Gayler, U.S.N (retired), American Committee on East–West Accord).

[29] IN RETROSPECT, *supra* note 6, at 345.

Nuclear deterrence depended on someone believing that you would commit an act totally irrational if done.[30]

General Charles A. Horner, Chief of Staff of the United States Space Command, stated:

The nuclear weapon is obsolete. I want to get rid of them all.[31]

Lt. General Arthur S. Collins, Deputy Commander-in-Chief, U.S. Army, Europe, 1971–74 stated:

Having fought in two wars, I still have not seen anything comparable to what I saw in Hiroshima in October 1945. I spent a day looking around the city over which the first, small, primitive atomic bomb had been exploded two months earlier. It was hard to believe that one bomb could devastate such a large area, or that it could kill so many people and create such a variety of casualties. I tried to relate it to other battle areas I had seen and other towns which troops had fought through and liberated. There was no correlation. Since then, as a soldier, I have never considered nuclear war to be a rational form of warfare or a rational instrument of policy.[32]

Statements by Foreign Leaders

Soviet leader Nikita Khrushev, in announcing the cut-back in the production of some missiles, stated that rockets:

are not cucumbers, you know—you don't eat them—and more than a certain number are not required to repel aggression. Nuclear war is stupid, stupid, stupid! If you reach for the button, you reach for suicide.[33]

By 1982, five of the seven retired chiefs of the British Defense Staff had reached the conclusion that "initiating the use of nuclear weapons, in accordance with the then NATO policy, would lead to disaster."[34] Lord Louis Mountbatten, Chief of the British Defense Staff from 1959 to 1965, stated in 1979, "As a military man I can see no use for any nuclear weapons."[35] And Field Marshall Lord Carver, Chief of British

---

[30] *Id.*

[31] *Id.*

[32] NUCLEAR WAR QUOTATIONS at 48 (quoting *Current NATO Strategy: A Recipe for Disaster, in* THE NUCLEAR CRISIS READER 48 (1984)).

[33] THE NUCLEAR SEDUCTION, *supra* note 25, at 53.

[34] IN RETROSPECT, *supra* note 6, at 344.

[35] *Id.*

Defense Staff from 1973 to 1976, wrote in 1982 that he was totally opposed to NATO ever initiating the use of nuclear weapons.

Field Marshal Lord Carver further stated:

> At the theater or tactical level any nuclear exchange, however limited it might be, is bound to leave NATO worse off in comparison to the Warsaw Pact, in terms of military and civilian casualties and destruction.[36]

Helmut Schmidt, former Chancellor of the Federal Republic of Germany, stated in 1987:

> Flexible response [NATO's strategy calling for the use of nuclear weapons] is nonsense. Not out of date but nonsense, because it puts at risk the lives of sixty million Germans and some fifteen million Dutch and I don't know how many million Belgian people and others who live on continental European soil. The Western idea—which was created in the 1950s—that we should be willing to use nuclear weapons first, in order to make up for our so-called conventional deficiency, has never convinced me. I can assure you that after the use of nuclear weapons on German soil, the war would be over as far as the Germans go, because they would just throw up their hands. To fight on after nuclear destruction of your own nation has started is a very unlikely scenario, and you need to be a mathematician or a military brain to believe such nonsense.[37]

Statements by Defense Experts

John J. Gilligan, Director of the Institute for International Peace Studies, University of Notre Dame and former Governor of Ohio, stated:

> The fact is that we have amassed these enormous arsenals of nuclear weapons, quite capable of obliterating human existence on this planet, and both sides now recognize the fundamental fact that these instruments of destruction are not weapons, as we normally use the term, because we dare not use them. We dare not use them against each other for fear of massive retaliation. This situation is referred to as the balance of terror and declared to be a state of peace. Cold War is not peace, it is war .... The further fact is that nations possessing nuclear weapons have been unable, or unwilling, to use them even against adversaries who lacked them .... And still, while we have conclusively demonstrated the utter

---

[36] NEW THINKING, *supra* note 12, at 175–76.
[37] IN RETROSPECT, *supra* note 6, at 345. *See* NEW THINKING, *supra* note 12, at 175–76.

uselessness of nuclear weapons against any foe, weak or strong, we continue to build more. No wonder we frighten our children ....[38]

M.I.T. Professor Kosta Tsipis concluded that nuclear weapons ultimately are not even weapons:

> Today, neither the United States nor its chief adversary, the Soviet Union, could win a war against the other with the 25,000 nuclear explosives each has amassed .... If these explosives can never lead to winning then they are not weapons .... Deterrence, however, is a state of mind. It has to do with how opponents perceive one another. ... We have been amassing nuclear explosives in order to effect a state of mind, lest we be perceived as irresolute or weak .... The Soviets, in turn, have mirrored our fears, accumulating over the years an equal number of nuclear explosives, so that they will not be perceived as weak or militarily incompetent. ... We both know that nuclear explosives are not weapons since their use cannot bring victory. We both know that using even a small number would spell the doom of both nations and more. We even know that even a small fraction of our arsenals suffices to intimidate the other nation .... Yet, neither nation dares stop accumulating these militarily useless explosives.[39]

Dr. Tsipis elaborated, with respect to each side's increasing modernization of their forces:

> So, we are trading in fears here. We are not trading in actual military realities .... We cannot use these objects to win. We cannot. The Soviet Union cannot use it to defeat us because they will also be destroyed.[40]

The continued recognition by U.S. government officials and experts of a lack of usefulness of these weapons in actual warfighting is evidenced by the United States' substantial withdrawal of tactical nuclear weapons from its active forces.[41]

---

[38] John J. Gilligan, *Law, the Path to Justice; Justice, the Road to Peace,* 19 DEN. J. INT'L L. & POL'Y 77, 80 (1990).

[39] *Hearings Before the Special Panel on Arms Control and Disarmament of the Procurement and Military Nuclear Systems Subcommittee of the Committee on Armed Services of the House of Representatives,* 98th Cong. 416 (1985).

[40] *Id.* at 423.

[41] *See* Chapter 19, notes 9–25 and accompanying text.

Chapter 25: U.S. Recognition That Even a Limited Use of Nuclear Weapons Would Likely Escalate Into a Widescale Nuclear Exchange

But what of the war-fighting theory, the notion that tactical nuclear weapons could be used not cataclysmally against enemy population centers but in a surgical way against significant military targets, such as hardened command centers and weapons of mass destruction? It has been recognized by the political and military leadership of the United States and other defense experts and commentators that even such a limited use of nuclear weapons would likely lead to escalation and massive nuclear exchanges.

As noted above, the U.S. military, in today's strategic environment, specifically recognizes numerous factors fostering escalation. The overriding factor is the uncontrollability of the situation once nuclear, chemical or biological weapons are used. As reflected in *Joint Pub 3-12, Doctrine for Joint Nuclear Operations*, "There can be no assurances that a conflict involving weapons of mass destruction could be controllable or would be of short duration."[1]

The U.S. military's recognition of the potential need for preemptive strikes against enemy delivery systems highlights the risks of escalation. As reflected in the *Doctrine for Joint Theater Nuclear Operations*, "Operations must be planned and executed to destroy or eliminate enemy WMD delivery systems and supporting infrastructure before they can strike friendly forces."[2] The potential for such preemptive strikes fosters the potential for the enemy's corresponding preemptive strikes.

The *Joint Nuclear Operations* manual notes that "there may be a rapid escalation" once strikes against nuclear assets begin to affect "the forces available for nuclear employment."[3]

---

[1] *See* JOINT CHIEFS OF STAFF, JOINT PUB 3-12, DOCTRINE FOR JOINT NUCLEAR OPERATIONS i (Dec. 15, 1995) <http://www.dtic.mil/doctrine/jel/new_pubs/jp3_12.pdf> [hereinafter DOCTRINE FOR JOINT NUCLEAR OPERATIONS]. *See also id.* at I-6–7.

[2] JOINT CHIEFS OF STAFF, JOINT PUB 3-12.1, DOCTRINE FOR JOINT THEATER NUCLEAR OPERATIONS ix (Feb. 9, 1996) (prepared under direction of the Chairman of the Joint Chiefs of Staff), as set forth at <http://www.dtic.mil/doctrine/jel/new_pubs/jp3_12_1.pdf> (emphasis omitted).

[3] DOCTRINE FOR JOINT NUCLEAR OPERATIONS, *supra* note 1, at I-5–6.

The military's policies of concentration of force and redundant targeting, including "layering"[4] and "cross-targeting,"[5] potentially involving the use of multiple nuclear weapons, are inherently escalatory, as are the extreme time pressures involved—potentially "seconds for the defense, and minutes for the offense."[6] The time is limited because of such factors as "the relatively short flight time of theater missiles and potential increased uncertainty of mobile offensive force target locations."[7]

Also inherently of an escalatory nature is the U.S. nuclear targeting doctrine of decapitation, as reflected in the *Joint Nuclear Operations* manual, whereby the political leadership of an opposing nation is the "central object of deterrence" on the theory that "that is where the ultimate decision to use military force lies."[8]

The potential for escalation is also fostered by the risks of miscalculation and irrationality:

> "[S]omeday a nation may, through miscalculation or by deliberate choice, employ these weapons. ... [A]n opponent may be willing to risk destruction or disproportionate loss in following a course of action based on perceived necessity, whether rational or not in a totally objective sense. In such cases deterrence, even based on the threat of massive destruction, may fail.[9]

The *Joint Nuclear Operations* manual also notes the risk of misperception and non-susceptibility to deterrence, "It is possible ... that an adversary may misperceive or purposefully ignore a credible threat."[10]

There have been many statements by the leadership of the United States over the years as to the unlikelihood that a low level use of nuclear weapons would stay at that level.

Statements by the Political Leadership

Robert McNamara, Secretary of Defense during the Kennedy Administration, stated:

> It is inconceivable to me, as it has been to others who have studied the matter, that "limited" nuclear wars would remain limited—any

---

[4] *Id.* at II-6.

[5] *Id.* at II-6.

[6] *Id.* at III-8.

[7] *Id.* at III-8.

[8] *Id.* at I-2.

[9] *Id.* at I-2 (emphasis omitted).

[10] *Id.* at I-2.

decision to use nuclear weapons would imply a high probability of the same cataclysmic consequences as a total nuclear exchange. In sum, I know of no plan which gives reasonable assurance that nuclear weapons can be used beneficially in NATO's defense.[11]

Mr. McNamara, along with McGeorge Bundy and George F. Kennan, further concluded:

It is time to recognize that no one has ever succeeded in advancing any persuasive reason to believe that any use of nuclear weapons, even on the smallest scale, could reliably be expected to remain limited.[12]

Harold Brown, Secretary of Defense during the Carter Administration stated:

None of this potential flexibility changes my view that a full-scale thermonuclear exchange would be an unprecedented disaster for the Soviet Union as well as for the United States. Nor is it at all clear that an initial use of nuclear weapons—however selectively they might be targeted—could be kept from escalating to a full-scale thermonuclear exchange. Whether weapons were used against tactical or strategic targets, that control would be lost on both sides and the exchange would become unconstrained.[13]

Secretary Brown further testified before the House Appropriations Committee, as follows:

My own judgment is that once one starts to use nuclear weapons, even in a tactical way, it is quite likely that it will escalate, that there is a kind of powder train and even if both sides do not want it to happen—the compression of the time for decision, the lack of information that would be available on both sides, the expected great advantage that a military commander might think would come from being the first to get in his blow, all push for rapid escalation.[14]

Secretary Brown further stated:

---

[11] Robert S. McNamara, *The Military Role of Nuclear Weapons: Perceptions and Misperceptions, in* THE NUCLEAR CONTROVERSY, A FOREIGN AFFAIRS READER 90 (1985).

[12] Bundy et al., *Nuclear Weapons and the Atlantic Alliance,* 60 FOREIGN AFF. 753 (1982).

[13] HAROLD BROWN, 1976 DEPARTMENT OF DEFENSE ANNUAL REPORT.

[14] CENTER FOR DEFENSE INFORMATION, NUCLEAR WAR QUOTATIONS 43 (Center for Defense Information, Washington D.C.).

We are also not unaware of the immense uncertainties involved in any use of nuclear weapons. We know that what might start as a supposedly controlled, limited strike could well, in my view would very likely, escalate to full-scale nuclear war."[15]

Representative Robert S. Walker, in hearings before the Congress, stated:

Reasonable men have all agreed that a nuclear exchange is unthinkable, and that there could be no such thing as a "limited" nuclear exchange.[16]

Donald A. Quarles, then Secretary of the Air Force in the Eisenhower Administration, stated (February 2, 1957):

No matter what their original intent may have been, I cannot believe that any atomic power would accept defeat while withholding its best weapon. If, in desperation, the losing side resorted to atomic weapons, the winning side would also be forced to use them or face defeat. So eventually, even though it starts out to be nonatomic war, war between atomic powers, it seems to be it will inevitably be atomic war.[17]

Statements by the Military Leadership

Chairman of the Joint Chiefs of Staff Lyman Lemnitzer reported to President Kennedy:

---

[15] A Countervailing Strategic Strategy, Remarks from Speech to the Naval War College, August 20, 1980, *as set forth at* DEFENSE, Oct. 1980, at 2–9. *See also* Spurgeon M. Keeny, Jr. & Wolfgang K. H. Panofsky, *MAD Versus NUTS*, 60 FOREIGN AFF., 287, 290–91, 298 (Winter 1981–82):

[I]t does not seem possible, even in the most specialized utilization of nuclear weapons, to envisage any situation where escalation to general nuclear war would not occur given the dynamics of the situation and the limits of the control mechanisms that could be made available to manage a limited nuclear war. We come back to the fundamental point that the only meaningful "firebreak" in modern warfare, be it strategic or tactical, is between nuclear and conventional weapons, not between self-proclaimed categories of nuclear weapons.

Id.

[16] *The Consequences of Nuclear War on the Global Environment: Hearing Before the Subcommittee on Investigations and Oversight of the Committee on Science and Technology*, 97th Cong. (1982) (statement by Representative Robert S. Walker).

[17] CENTER FOR DEFENSE INFORMATION NUCLEAR WAR QUOTATIONS at 40.

There is considerable question that the Soviets would be able to distinguish between a total attack and an attack of military targets only ... . [B]ecause of fallout from attack of military targets and co-location of many military targets with military-industrial targets, the casualties would be many millions in number. Thus, limited attack to military targets has little practical meaning as a humanitarian measure.[18]

General David C. Jones, former Chairman of the Joint Chiefs of Staff, states, "I don't see much of a chance of nuclear war being limited or protracted."[19]

Admiral Noel A. Gayler, former Commander in Chief of U.S. Ground, Air and Sea Forces in the Pacific, wrote, "There is no sensible military use of any of our nuclear forces."[20]

Admiral Gayler further testified:

Either the first use or tactical use and counterforce are dangerous and inherently destabilizing. Control of a protracted nuclear war is both illusion and threat. ... In my judgment, there is no prospect whatever of effective control by our national command authority, or by the corresponding Soviet entities, of what goes on after any kind of a nuclear war is started. It will play itself out of control....[21]

On the use of tactical nuclear weapons in Western Europe and the danger of escalation, Admiral Gayler testified:

If we were to attempt to defend Europe by the first use of nuclear weapons, the first thing that would happen would be that a great many noncombatants, in the millions, mostly women and children, would be killed, probably mostly German. That would fractionate the alliance.... The second that would happen would be an almost certain escalation. Certainly, the Soviet doctrine would be coming back with more. Whether the escalation went up to a final total

---

[18] Scott D. Sagan, *SIOP-62: The Nuclear War Plan Briefing to President Kennedy,* INT'L SECURITY, vol. 12, no. 1, Summer 1987, at 50–51.

[19] WILLIAM A. SCHWARTZ ET AL., THE NUCLEAR SEDUCTION: WHY THE ARMS RACE DOESN'T MATTER—AND WHAT DOES 38 (University of California Press 1990) [hereinafter THE NUCLEAR SEDUCTION].

[20] ROBERT S. MCNAMARA, OUT OF THE COLD, NEW THINKING FOR AMERICAN FOREIGN AND DEFENSE POLICY IN THE 21ST CENTURY 175–76 (1989).

[21] *Hearings before the Special Panel on Arms Control and Disarmament of the Procurement and Military Nuclear Systems Subcommittee of the Committee on Armed Services of the House of Representatives,* 98th Cong. 282 (1985) (statement of Adm. Noel Gayler, U.S.N (Retired), American Committee on East-West Accord).

conflict in one step or two steps or three steps wouldn't make much difference.[22]

General A. S. Collins, Jr., former Deputy Commander-in-Chief of the United States Army in Europe has stated:

> From my experience in combat there is no way that [nuclear escalation] ... can be controlled because of the lack of information, the pressure of time and the deadly results that [would be] taking place on both sides of the battle line.[23]

General Bernard W. Rogers, U.S. Army Supreme Commander, Allied Forces Europe, in testimony before the House Armed Services Committee on March 10, 1983, stated:

> We are not going to contain a nuclear war in Western Europe. A nuclear war in Western Europe is going to escalate to a strategic exchange. I feel the war would escalate quickly.[24]

Admiral Charles R. Brown, U.S. Navy, stated,

> I have no faith in the so-called controlled use of atomic weapons. There is no dependable distinction between tactical and strategic situations. I would not recommend the use of any atomic weapon, no matter how small, when both sides have the power to destroy the world.[25]

The role of command and control in preventing escalation and the problems with sustaining such communications in the context of what starts out as a limited nuclear detonation was addressed by Lt. General Brent Scowcroft, National Security Advisor to President Ford (October 1981):

> There's a real dilemma here that we haven't sorted out. The kinds of controlled nuclear options to which we're moving presume communication with the Soviet Union; and yet, from a military point of view, one of the most efficient kinds of attack is against leadership and command and control systems.[26]

---

[22] *Id.* at 280.

[23] General A. S. Collins, Jr., *Theater Nuclear Warfare: The Battlefield, in* AMERICAN DEFENSE POLICY 359–60 (J.F. Reichart & S. R. Stern 5th ed. 1982).

[24] CENTER FOR DEFENSE INFORMATION NUCLEAR WAR QUOTATIONS at 43.

[25] *Id.* at 42.

[26] CENTER FOR DEFENSE INFORMATION, NUCLEAR WAR QUOTATIONS at 44.

Statements by Defense Experts

Advocates and developers of the war-fighting approach, such as Herman Kahn and Colin Gray, while suggesting that a nuclear conflict might be modulated, have recognized that such modulation is neither guaranteed nor even likely.[27]

The war-fighting advocates further recognize that the target of a nuclear strike is likely not to perceive the purported limited nature of the strike, given the extraordinary destructiveness of even low level nuclear weapons, the co-location of many nuclear targets with MAD targets and other such factors.[28] War-fighting advocates have also acknowledged the extreme dangers inherent in destruction of a nuclear adversary's leadership and command and control, particularly the risks of resultant inadvertent or un-thought-out escalation.

Dr. Sidney Drell of the Stanford Linear Accelerator Center of Stanford University, testified before a Congressional Committee:

> [A]ny use of nuclear weapons, including use in so-called limited wars, would very likely escalate to general nuclear war; and science

---

[27] *See* HERMAN KAHN, ON THERMONUCLEAR WAR 559–60 (1960); Colin S. Gray, *Nuclear Strategy: The Case for a Theory of Victory* (*reprinted* from INT'L SECURITY 4, no. 1, 1979, at 54–87) *in* AMERICAN DEFENSE POLICY 107 (Schuyler et al. eds., 1990).

[28] *See generally* William Daugherty et al., *The Consequences of "Limited" Nuclear Attacks on the United States*, INT'L SECURITY, vol. 10, no. 4, Spring 1986, at 3; Frank N. von Hippel et al., *Civilian Casualties from Counterforce Attacks*, SCIENTIFIC AMERICAN, vol. 281 no. 3, Sept. 1988, at 36, 37; Barbara G. Levi, Frank N. von Hippel, & William Daugherty, *Civilian Casualties from "Limited Nuclear Attacks" on the USSR*, INT'L SECURITY, vol. 12, no. 3, Winter 1987/1988, at 168–189.

Carl Sagan stated:

> It is generally accepted, even among most military planners, that a "small" nuclear war would be almost impossible to contain before it escalated to include much of the world arsenals. Precipitating factors include command and control malfunctions, communications failures, the necessity for instantaneous decisions on the fates of millions, fear, panic and other aspects of nuclear war fought by real people ... .

Carl Sagan, *Nuclear War and Climatic Catastrophe: Some Policy Implications*, FOREIGN AFF., vol. 62 no. 2, Winter 1983/1984, at 28–29.

offers no prospect of effective defense against nuclear war and mutual destruction.[29]

He further testified:

Once the nuclear threshold is crossed, there will inevitably be a broad delegation down the line of authority for nuclear release. This will be required by the very short missile flight times and by the potential vulnerabilities of any conceivable worldwide command and control and communication system from a national command center to the broadly dispersed military units with thousands of nuclear weapons. For these reasons, both human and technical, a limited nuclear war seems a most improbable event....
Neither past experience and precedent nor war-gaming gives cause for much hope that the nuclear exchange and resulting devastation would remain limited and aimed exclusively at counterforce and direct military targets. In addition there is no technical basis for any confidence that it will be possible to control the escalation of a limited nuclear conflict.[30]

The National Academy of Sciences in Washington D.C. in its Resolution on Nuclear War and Arms Control explicitly concluded, "[A]ny use of nuclear weapons, including use in so-called 'limited wars,' would very likely escalate to general nuclear war."[31]

The escalatory ladder has been described as follows in the context of the Cold War:

[A] limited Soviet attack on the U.S. is unrealistic because even if U.S. retaliation were also limited it could still be more severe. In that case hostilities would not be likely to end there. If the response inflicted greater damage the Soviets would undoubtedly feel it necessary to even things up. This escalation could develop into a total war which would devastate both sides. It is highly improbable that a potential belligerent would discount such a risk and gamble on a limited exchange. The hypothetical set of circumstances used to justify the targeting doctrine of selectivity and flexibility cannot stand close scrutiny.[32]

---

[29] *The Consequences of Nuclear War on the Global Environment, Hearing Before the Subcommittee on Investigations and Oversight of the Committee on Science and Technology*, 97th Cong. (1982).

[30] *Id.*

[31] *Id.* (Resolution of April 27, 1982, statement of Dr. Sidney D. Drell). *See also* NUCLEAR WAR OPPOSING VIEWPOINTS 21 (David Bender & Bruno Leone, eds., 1985).

[32] OPPOSING VIEWPOINTS, *supra* note 31, at 21.

Howard S. Levie, Professor of Law at St. Louis University Law School, stated as follows with respect to a nuclear exchange at sea:

> [S]hould a war reach the nuclear stage, it is a virtual certainty that any naval engagement would include the use of nuclear weapons against the opposing enemy fleets. When this occurs the extent of the contamination of the oceans and of the atmosphere is incalculable as nuclear explosions would be taking place both in the atmosphere and in the water and nuclear-powered ships would be sunk with their reactors in operation.[33]

Peter Weiss, Esq., Professor Burns H. Weston, Professor Richard A. Falk, and Professor Saul H. Mendlovitz, in their memorandum in support of the Application by the World Health Organization for an Advisory Opinion by the International Court of Justice on the Legality of the Use of Nuclear Weapons Under International Law, stated:

> Any use of even the tiniest nuclear weapon is likely to escalate into a nuclear exchange of increasing magnitude, and thus the country initiating such use would bear the gravest responsibility for its consequences and would, at the very least, be in violation of the principle of proportionality.[34]

The authors quoted Professor Weston:

> [N]ot withstanding voguish theories of 'intra-war   ' bargaining, "intra-war deterrence," and controlled escalation, it is highly improbable that the opposing sides would or could restrict themselves to fighting a "limited" rather than "total" nuclear war.[35]

Weston further stated:

> [O]nce unleashed, the probability that tactical nuclear warfare could be kept at theater or battlefield level would be small. A crisis escalating to the first use of even relatively small nuclear weapons

---

[33] Howard S. Levie, *Nuclear, Chemical, and Biological Weapons in Handbook on the Law of Naval Operations,* NAVAL WARFARE PUBLICATION 9 (NWP 9) 334 (1987).

[34] Peter Weiss, Burns H. Weston, Richard A. Falk, & Saul H. Mendlovitz, Draft Memorial in Support of the Application by the World Health Organization for an Advisory Opinion by the International Court of Justice on the Legality of the Use of Nuclear Weapons Under International Law, Including the WHO Constitution, *reprinted in* 4 TRANSNAT'L L. & CONTEMP. PROBS. 721 (1994).

[35] *Id.* at 784 n.226 (citing Burns H. Weston, *Nuclear Weapons Versus International Law: A Contextual Reassessment,* 28 McGILL L.J. 542, 581 (1983)).

would bring us dangerously close to the ultimate stage, a "strategic exchange" particularly if one of the two sides was itself at a disadvantage in a drawn out "tactical exchange."[36]

Yale Professor Bruce Russett presented one scenario, in the Cold War context, as to how this could happen:

> In practice, a Soviet invasion of West Germany might very well trigger an all-out nuclear war whether or not the American government wished it to do so. American nuclear weapons would be widely dispersed, to low-level commanders who would very likely have operational control over the weapons. (The PAL [Permissive Action Link] codes that prevent unauthorized use in peacetime very likely would be released to low-level commanders in a time of high crisis in Europe.) One of those commanders, in the "fog of war" with his troops under siege, might very well use the weapons. Or the Soviet Union, fearing they would be used, might stage a preemptive attack on them. Use of a few tactical or theater nuclear weapons would be very likely to escalate into a strategic exchange between the American and Soviet homelands....[37]

Professor Russett further described the risk of escalation:

> One problem is therefore the illusion that any large-scale nuclear exchange could in any real sense be "limited" in its consequences. The other problem is with the expectation that nuclear war could be fought in some precise fashion of strike and counterstrike, that in any substantial nuclear exchange the war could be restricted to a limited number of strictly military targets. There are people in the government who imagine it could be done, with acceptable consequences. The majority of analysts, however, consider the likelihood of such limitation, under wartime conditions of anger, confusion, ignorance, and loss of control, to be extremely small. One cannot definitely rule out the possibility, but neither should one bet the future of civilization on it. Probably the two most knowledgeable experts on this matter are Desmond Ball and John Steinbruner, who offer nearly identical skeptical views. In Steinbruner's words: "Once the use of as many as 10 or more nuclear weapons directly against the U.S.S.R. is seriously contemplated, U.S. strategic commanders will likely insist on attacking the full array of Soviet military targets .... If national commanders seriously attempted to implement this strategy (controlled response) in a war with existing and currently projected

---

[36] *Id.*

[37] Bruce M. Russett, *The Doctrine of Deterrence, in* CATHOLICS AND NUCLEAR WAR 149, 161 (Philip J. Murnion ed., 1983).

U.S. forces, the result would not be a finely controlled strategic campaign. The more likely result would be the collapse of U.S. forces into isolated units undertaking retaliation on their own initiative against a wide variety of targets at unpredictable moments."[38]

Pringle and Arkin point out that, even if a U.S. attack against the Soviets had been intended as a "counterforce" attack directed against military targets, it is unlikely that the Soviets would have perceived it as such.

[H]ow might the Russians know a U.S. attack was supposed to be limited? Desmond Ball observes, "Given casualties of this magnitude and the particular Soviet difficulty of distinguishing a comprehensive counterforce attack from a more general military plus urban-industrial attack, the notion of limiting a nuclear exchange to supposedly surgical counterforce operations appears rather incredible." What he means is that, because the Soviet targets are spread over such a wide geographical area it would be extremely difficult for the Soviet leadership to make an accurate "attack assessment" of a U.S. strike; with command, control, and leadership targets clustered near the cities it would be hard to distinguish between a selective strike and an all-out attack. [39]

Of course, the escalation would not necessarily be intentional:

But the conventional conflict in a nuclear environment raises the risk not only of intentional nuclear escalation, which leaders will have incentives to avoid, but also of inadvertent nuclear escalation, which leaders may not be able to avoid even if they want. A conventional war could jeopardize nuclear deterrent capabilities directly or degrade other important capabilities, such as warning systems, thus increasing the possibility of successful nuclear preemption. The most extensive analysis of this question concludes that the problem of inadvertent escalation will "loom especially large for small and medium-sized nuclear powers, since they will have the most difficult time building nuclear forces that can survive."[40]

Similarly, religious leaders who have investigated the matter have recognized the likelihood of the escalation of the limited nuclear

---

[38] *Id.* at 159–60.

[39] PETER PRINGLE & WILLIAM ARKIN, S.I.O.P., THE SECRET U.S. PLAN FOR NUCLEAR WAR 193–94 (1983).

[40] Steven E. Miller, *The Case Against a Ukrainian Nuclear Deterrent,* FOREIGN AFF., vol. 72, no. 3, Summer 1993, at 67, 71.

release into a general conflagration. The National Conference of Catholic Bishops in its study concluded:

> The technical literature and other personal testimony of public officials who have been closely associated with U.S. nuclear strategy have both convinced us of the overwhelming probability that major nuclear exchange would have no limits.[41]

The Bishops further concluded:

> Whether under conditions of war in Europe, parts of Asia or the Middle East, or the exchange of strategic weapons directly between the United States and the Soviet Union, the difficulties of limiting the use of nuclear weapons are immense. A number of expert witnesses advise us that commanders operating under conditions of battle probably would not be able to exercise strict control; the number of weapons used would rapidly increase, the targets would be expanded beyond the military, and the level of civilian casualties would rise enormously. No one can be certain that this escalation would not occur, even in the face of political efforts to keep such an exchange "limited." The chances of keeping use [of nuclear weapons] limited seem remote, and the consequences of escalation to mass destruction would be appalling. Former public officials have testified that it is improbable that any nuclear war could actually be kept limited. Their testimony and the consequences involved in this problem lead us to conclude that the danger of escalation is so great that it would be morally unjustifiable to initiate nuclear war in any form.[42]

The Bishops, in their study, identified such concerns as the following with respect to whether a "limited" nuclear war would remain limited:

> - Would leaders have sufficient information to know what is happening in a nuclear exchange?
> - Would they be able under the conditions of stress, time pressures, and fragmentary information to make the extraordinarily precise decision needed to keep the exchange limited if this were technically possible?
> - Would military commanders be able, in the midst of the destruction and confusion of a nuclear exchange, to maintain a policy of discriminate targeting? Can this be done in modern warfare, waged across great distances by aircraft and missiles?

---

[41] Pastoral Letter on War and Peace, The Challenge of Peace: God's Promise and Our Response (May 3, 1983), at 45.

[42] *Id.* at 48.

- Given the accidents we know about in peacetime conditions, what assurances are there that computer errors could be avoided in the midst of a nuclear exchange?
- Would not the casualties, even in a war defined as limited by strategists, still run in the millions?
- How 'limited' would be the long-term effects of radiation, famine, social fragmentation, and economic dislocation?[43]

In their testimony before the House Committee on Foreign Affairs, Cardinal Joseph L. Bernardin, Archbishop of Chicago, and Archbishop John J. O'Connor, Archbishop of New York, summarized the Bishops' conclusions as follows:

[T]he majority of experts consulted by the drafting committee of the bishops thought that once nuclear war had begun, it would be difficult if not impossible to prevent escalation to unacceptable levels of destruction.[44]

Cardinal O'Connor further noted:

[W]hile it seems technically probable that you could fire some tactical nuclear weapons at sea, for example, where they might be so highly sophisticated and contained and selective that you would not have the immediate danger of fallout and particularly of devastating civilian populations, nevertheless the psychological volatility of the world is such, that the first nuclear weapon that is fired of any yield, any capacity, brings with it the very grave risk of such escalation that this commonly called holocaust could be assured.[45]

Chairman Dante B. Fascell of the House Committee on Foreign Affairs responded to Archbishop O'Connor:

I know we have all struggled with the problem of nuclear weapons and their utility. I finally came to the conclusion that I could not visualize, I couldn't make myself accept the proposition that in a nuclear exchange, tactical or otherwise, that the losing side would suddenly say, "Oh, we are losing, and therefore, we cannot use the rest of our nuclear weapons... ." I find that very hard to assimilate. I don't believe it, and therefore, I was compelled to the conclusion,

---

[43] *Id.* at 49–50.

[44] *Hearings on The Role of Arms Control in U.S. Defense Policy, before the Committee on Foreign Affairs, House of Representatives*, 98th Cong. 2nd Sess. (June 20, 21, 26; July 25, 1984), at 143.

[45] *Id.* at 158.

that if you fire one, you better look out, because the rest are coming right behind....[46]

---

[46] *Id.*

Chapter 26: Risks of Use of Nuclear Weapons in the Post Cold War Era

The above examination of the risks of escalation focused on the Cold War context of the U.S.–Soviet standoff. The escalation risks, as well as the overall risks that these weapons will be used in the first place, seem, if anything, even greater in the post Cold War era.

Where the United States and the Soviet Union recognized the need for self-restraint,[1] the players and potential players and the nature of the play in the modern multi-polar world seem more volatile and unpredictable. What is the basis to believe that, in the event of crisis today, North Korea, Pakistan, India, Iran, Iraq, Libya or even China,[2] not to speak of some terrorist group or individual obtaining a nuclear capability, would exercise comparable restraint, or even that the modern Russia would—or could—do so?

Competitive and at times confrontational as the U.S.–Soviet relationship was, its very bi-polarity, combined with each nation's dominance of its respective portions of the world, served to restrain the

---

[1] *See* Alexander George, *Soviet Approaches to Super Power Securities Relations*, *in* U.S. SOVIET SECURITY COOPERATION: ACHIEVEMENTS, FAILURES, LESSONS 601–605 (George et al. eds., 1988) (describing the Soviet approach to superpower relations as changing over time to accept "mutual hostage posture" and engage in arms control negotiations). *See also* THE MAKING OF AMERICA'S SOVIET POLICY (Joseph S. Nye, Jr. ed., 1984).

One analyst described the Soviet approach in 1985:

> Official Soviet attitudes toward nuclear war have varied; there still is no fixed view. But the military seems to be moving closer to the political view—that victory is impossible. That there will be no victors in a nuclear war is now commonplace in public statements by Soviet scientists, commentators, politicians, and military men.

Stephen Shenfield, *Soviet Thinking About the Unthinkable*, THE BULL. OF THE ATOMIC SCIENTIST, vol. 41 no. 2, Feb. 1985, at 23.

See also Desmond Ball, *U.S. Strategic Forces: How Would They be Used?*, INT'L SECURITY, vol. 7, no. 3, Winter 1982–1983, 31–60 at 41.

[2] *See, e.g.*, THE DEFENSE POLICIES OF NATIONS: A COMPARATIVE STUDY, 3D. 526–7 (Douglas J. Murary & Paul R. Viotti eds., 1994):

> [Under] crisis conditions Israel's initial move might be to state publicly that it has, and is prepared to use, nuclear weapons to defend itself. ... If such moves aimed at deterring a perceived genocidal invasion failed, nuclear weapons might be used to inflict devastating losses on any aggressor poised to overrun Israel.

Id.

bellicose tendencies of States throughout the world, as appears evident
from subsequent events such as those in the former Yugoslavia. The
Soviet Union's nuclear policies essentially mirrored those of the United
States,[3] and the leadership of both nations ostensibly understood the
need to manage the risks of the nuclear standoff.

Whether resulting from the long decades of experience of the two
adversaries in developing the relationship, or from the Soviets' having
been less interested in precipitating a hot war than the United States
believed,[4] or from the ironic absence of antipathy between the two
peoples,[5] the Soviet restraint is ostensibly not something one can count
on recurring in a different strategic environment. Indeed, even the post
Cold War Russia, greatly weakened as a military power, appears far
more likely to resort to nuclear weapons in crisis than its predecessor.[6]

However one analyzes such matters, it must be assumed that the
risks will likely only become greater as multiple nuclear and chem-bio
actors and terrorist groups face one another without the organizing
constraints of the American-Soviet hegemony or of the U.S./Soviet

---

[3] *See* WILLIAM T. LEE & RICHARD F. STAAR, SOVIET MILITARY POLICY
SINCE WORLD WAR II (1986) (discussing the Soviet Union's concept of
"deterrence" as essentially the same as that of the United States, but noting that
Soviet concepts of nuclear war-fighting continued to provide options for use of
nuclear weapons in case of deterrence failure). *See also* RAYMOND L.
GARTHOFF, DETERRENCE AND THE REVOLUTION IN SOVIET MILITARY DOCTRINE
(Brookings 1990).

[4] *See* Stephen Shenfield, *Soviet Thinking About the Unthinkable*, THE BULL.
OF THE ATOMIC SCIENTIST, vol. 41 no. 2, Feb. 1985, at 23.

[5] *See Richard Nixon, U.S. Foreign Policy for the 1970's: A New Strategy
for Peace, a Report to the Congress*, Feb. 18, 1970, at 133. The
American–Soviet rivalry was often characterized as a Cold War between
competing States, rather than between two peoples. *See* John Steinbruner, *U.S.
and Soviet Security Perspectives*, BULL. OF THE ATOMIC SCIENTISTS, Aug. 1985,
at 89–93; George W. Downs et al., *Arms Races and Cooperation*, WORLD
POLITICS, vol. 37, no. 1, Oct. 1985, at 118–146; and John Lewis Gaddis, *The
Long Peace: Elements of Stability in the Postwar International System,* INT'L
SECURITY, vol. 10, no. 4, Spring 1986, at 99–100.

[6] *See supra* Chapter 18, note 58 and accompanying text. *See also See*
Charles J. Dick, *Past Cruelties Hinder the Taming of the Bear*, JANE'S
INTELLIGENCE REVIEW, vol. 10, no. 12, Dec. 1, 1998, at 5; Michael R. Gordon,
Maneuvers Show Russian Reliance on Nuclear Arms, THE NEW YORK TIMES,
July 10, 1999, at 1; THE INT'L INSTITUTE FOR STRATEGIC STUDIES, THE
MILITARY BALANCE, 1993–1994 232 (London 1993); NUCLEAR PROLIFERATION
HANDBOOK, at 678; 1995 REPORT OF THE SECRETARY OF DEFENSE at 271.

learning curves in managing such weapons[7] and perhaps without the benefit of the stable political situations that largely characterized the United States and the Soviet Union during the Cold War.[8]

There are obviously traps of cultural arrogance in assuming that other nations and peoples may have lower levels of respect for human life and welfare,[9] but there is no denying the significance in ordinary human and societal experience of progressing through learning curves or of developing layers of understanding and potentially of some form of trust even in the most contentious of relationships. There is also no avoiding the reality that with every new nuclear power the risk of a reckless act or reaction potentially increases.[10]

Stephen Miller addressed the issue in the context of the nuclear weapons on the territory of Ukraine after the break-up of the Soviet Union:

> The risks of "instant" proliferation. If Ukraine does succeed in obtaining custody of some or all of the nuclear weapons on its territory, it will have become, in effect, an "instant" nuclear power. Unlike other nuclear states, it will not have experienced a protracted, multi-year nuclear development program during which appropriate organizations and procedures can be created, personnel can be trained and thinking can be adjusted. While Ukraine has undoubtedly inherited some military personnel who have expertise derived from their involvement in the Soviet nuclear program, its government will inevitably be inexperienced in nuclear weapons

---

[7] *See* ALEXANDER GEORGE ET AL., U.S. SOVIET SECURITY COOPERATION: ACHIEVEMENTS, FAILURES, LESSONS 606–646 (1990) (discussing the lessons the Soviet Union and the United States learned through success and failure during the Cold War).

[8] *See generally* JAMES N. ROSENAU, TURBULENCE IN WORLD POLITICS: A THEORY OF CHANGE AND CONTINUITY (Princeton 1990).

[9] *See generally* ROBERT S. JERVIS, PERCEPTION AND MISPERCEPTION IN INTERNATIONAL POLITICS (Columbia 1983).

[10] *See Weapons of Mass Destruction: Remarks by Defense Secretary William Perry at Georgetown University,* FED. NEWS SERVICE, Apr. 18, 1996. Secretary of Defense Perry stated:

> There are still tens of thousands of nuclear weapons in the world, and there are many nations trying to acquire these weapons, as well as other weapons of mass destruction. So this is not a brave new world; this is a grave new world. During the Cold War, we knew who the enemy was, what weapons he had, where he might attack and why. But today anybody can shop the global market for the components to make weapons of mass destruction.

Id.

matters and in the immediate future will lack a coherent nuclear establishment.[11]

The U.S. military in their manual on *Doctrine for Joint Theater Nuclear Operations* state:

> The threat of nuclear exchange by regional powers and the proliferation of WMD have grown following the end of the Cold War.[12]
>
> ***
>
> The dissolution of the Soviet Union has greatly reduced the possibility of a large scale nuclear exchange. However, the loss of the stability inherent in a clearly bipolar world has increased the likelihood of a nuclear exchange by regional powers. In addition, the threat to the United States, its allies, and its deployed forces due to the proliferation of WMD has grown following the end of the Cold War. The flow of advanced technology to potential or actual hostile nations has led to a proliferation of systems (missiles and aircraft) capable of delivering WMD. The possibility of a WMD exchange in a regional conflict has risen dramatically, threatening our forward-deployed forces and challenging our long-range power projection capabilities.[13]

The manual identifies the threat further:

> b. The current threat in theater consists primarily of short-, medium-, and intermediate-range missiles capable of carrying nuclear, biological, or chemical warheads. Future threat systems may exhibit greater capabilities, such as increased accuracy, range, and destructive power. Additionally, aircraft systems and cruise missiles capable of delivering WMD will also pose a threat.[14]

The manual further recognizes that this is a threat that increases with proliferation:

---

[11] *See* Steven E. Miller, *The Case Against a Ukrainian Nuclear Deterrent*, FOREIGN AFF., Summer 1993, at 67, 73. For the case that Ukraine had the technical, intellectual and political wherewithal to be trusted with nuclear weapons, *i.e.*, that its elites were "likely to grasp the essentials of national security policy" and the "nuances of nuclear deterrence theory," *see* John F. Mearsheimer, *The Case for a Ukrainian Nuclear Deterrent*, FOREIGN AFF., Summer 1993, at 50, 61–63.

[12] JOINT CHIEFS OF STAFF, JOINT PUB 3-12.1, DOCTRINE FOR JOINT THEATER NUCLEAR OPERATIONS vi (Feb. 9, 1996) (prepared under direction of the Chairman of the Joint Chiefs of Staff), as set forth at http://www.dtic.mil/doctrine/jel/new_pubs/jp3_12_1.pdf (emphasis omitted).

[13] *Id.* at I-2 (emphasis omitted).

[14] *Id.* at I-2–3 (emphasis omitted).

c. As nations continue to develop and obtain WMD and viable delivery systems, the potential for US operations in such a lethal environment increases. In addition to proliferation of WMD among rogue states, proliferation may also expand to include nonstate actors as well.[15]

The potential for use of these weapons in a situation of acute crisis is also heightened by the U.S. military's in-place plan to in fact use them. As noted above, the military has concluded, "Nuclear operations can be successful in achieving US military objectives if they are used in the appropriate situation and administered properly."[16]

As noted, the U.S. military have identified types of situations where the use of nuclear weapons may be "favored over a conventional attack" or otherwise preferred:

> • Level of effort required for conventional targeting. If the target is heavily defended such that heavy losses are expected, a nuclear weapon may be favored over a conventional attack.
> • Length of time that a target must be kept out of action. A nuclear weapon attack will likely put a target out of action for a longer period of time than a conventional weapon attack.
> • Logistic support and anticipation of delays caused by the "fog and friction" of war. Such delays are unpredictable and may range from several hours to a number of days.[17]

The military have also identified the following "enemy combat forces and facilities that may be likely targets for nuclear strikes:"

> • WMD and their delivery systems, as well as associated command and control, production, and logistical support units
> • Ground combat units and their associated command and control and support units
> • Air defense facilities and support installations
> • Naval installations, combat vessels, and associated support facilities and command and control capabilities
> • Nonstate actors (facilities and operation centers) that possess WMD
> • Underground facilities.[18]

---

[15] *Id.* at I-3 (emphasis omitted).
[16] *Id.* at v (emphasis omitted).
[17] *Id.* at III-4 (emphasis omitted).
[18] *Id.* at III-6–7.

Chapter 27: Risks That Even a Limited Use of Nuclear Weapons Would Precipitate Use of Chemical and Biological Weapons, and *Vice Versa*

Chemical and biological weapons are central to the analysis of the risks of the policy of nuclear deterrence and of the potential use of nuclear weapons, since the threat or use of such weapons could lead to a chemical or biological weapons response, and vice versa.[1]   To a

---

[1] *See* U.S. Congress, Office of Technology Assessment, *Proliferation of Weapons of Mass Destruction: Assessing the Risks,* OTA-ISC-559, at 100 (Washington, DC: U.S. Government Printing Office, August 1993) (report prepared at request of Congress "to assist Congress in its efforts to strengthen and broaden U.S. policies to control the proliferation of weapons of mass destruction").

Chemical weapons are chemicals manufactured into weapons form. Biological weapons, commonly bacteria but also some of a fungal or viral nature, are living organisms that cause diseases in nature, refined and harnessed to perform as weapons. Toxins—nonliving products, such as spider or snake venom, originally produced by living things—are an intermediate category bridging chemical and biological weapons. *See id.* at 3. *See also* Bill Gertz, *Horror Weapons*, AIR FORCE MAGAZINE, Jan. 1996 at p. 44.

The U.S. military's DOCTRINE FOR JOINT THEATER NUCLEAR OPERATIONS describes the relative effects of nuclear, chemical and biological weapons:

> Nuclear weapons can cause casualties or damage through blast, overpressure, thermal radiation, proximity to initial nuclear radiation, fallout radiation, and EMP. Biological and chemical weapons cause serious injury or death through their toxic properties.   WMD can also produce casualties from the psychological effect of their use. More specific guidance can be found in Joint Pub 3-11, "Joint Doctrine for Nuclear, Biological, and Chemical (NBC) Defense."

JOINT CHIEFS OF STAFF, JOINT PUB 3-12.1, DOCTRINE FOR JOINT THEATER NUCLEAR OPERATIONS III-8 (Feb. 9, 1996) (prepared under direction of the Chairman of the Joint Chiefs of Staff), as set forth at <http://www.dtic.mil/doctrine/jel/new_pubs/jp3_12_1.pdf> (emphasis omitted) [hereinafter DOCTRINE FOR JOINT THEATER NUCLEAR OPERATIONS].

The U.S. military's DOCTRINE FOR JOINT THEATER NUCLEAR OPERATIONS defines "weapons of mass destruction:"

> In arms control usage, weapons that are capable of a high order of destruction and/or of being used in such a manner as to destroy large numbers of people. Can be nuclear, chemical, biological, and radiological weapons, but excludes the means of transporting or

considerable extent, the risk factors as to the various categories of weapons of mass destruction—"NBC" or nuclear, biological and chemical weapons—are interconnected and overlapping.

Threats exchanged between the United States, Israel and Iraq at the time of the 1990–91 Gulf War illustrate the connection. Saddam Hussein threatened that if any nation used nuclear weapons against Iraq, Iraq would respond with chemical weapons.[2] He reportedly stated, "Whoever threatens us with the atomic bomb, we will annihilate him with the binary chemical ... we will make the fire eat up half of Israel if it tries to do anything against Iraq."[3] Similarly, the United

---

propelling the weapon where such means is a separable and divisible part of the weapon. (Joint Pub 1-02)
DOCTRINE FOR JOINT THEATER NUCLEAR OPERATIONS, *supra,* at GL-4.

Since the Cold War, the United States has seemed administratively to treat nuclear weapons jointly with chemical and biological weapons. This has included ending the separate status of the Defense Nuclear Agency (DNA), which had had long been the administrative group with overall responsibility for the United States' nuclear weapons programs, under a far-ranging charter extending from decisions as to what nuclear weapons to develop and purchase, to creating designs and plans for dealing with irradiated dust on vehicles in the battlefield.

In 1995 these functions were rolled into the Defense Special Weapons Agency (DSWA), which had had the charter of handling information and policy on the larger range of weapons of mass destruction. In 1998 administrative responsibility for nuclear programs was folded into the Defense Threat Reduction Agency (DTRA), an agency responsible for a broad line of terrorist and weapons of mass destruction attacks, be they chemical, biological and nuclear. *See The Pen Changes of May 23, 1998 to the DoD Department of Defense Directive Number 5105.31, June 14, 1995,* tasking the "Defense Special Weapons Agency" with the duties previously assigned the Defense Nuclear Agency, *e.g.* "9. Support the DoD Components, and other organizations, as appropriate, through technical support, guidance, operational support, studies, and joint programs dealing with nuclear weapons effects, nuclear force operability, operation survivability, and other matters assigned to the DNA." *Id.* For further details as to how the DTRA supplants the DNA [and the DSWA], *see* <http://www.dtra.mil/>.

[2] *See Proliferation of Weapons of Mass Destruction: Assessing the Risks, supra* note 1, at 100, citing Saddam Hussein, Apr. 2, 1990, Baghdad INA, translation in FBIS-NEW-90-064, Apr. 3, 1990, at 36.

[3] *Id.* Saddam's reference was ostensibly to the binary sarin nerve gas artillery that Iraq had developed. U.S. DEPARTMENT OF DEFENSE, PROLIFERATION: THREAT AND RESPONSE *Middle East and North Africa* 10 (1997), *set forth at* <http://www.defenselink.mil/pubs/prolif97/>. This was the same gas ostensibly used by the Japanese terrorist group Aum Shinrikyo in the

States reportedly threatened Iraq with the use of nuclear weapons if Iraq used chemical weapons.[4]

U.S. officials have expressed the matter broadly: "[I]f some nation were to attack the United States with chemical weapons then they would have to fear the consequences of a response from any weapon in our inventory .... And I would not think that any nation should feel that they can use a chemical weapon against us without receiving a devastating response. ... That is, we could make a devastating response without the use of nuclear weapons, but we would not forswear that possibility."[5]

Risks of Chemical and Biological Weapons

In a major study the U.S. government recently identified the following risks of nuclear weapons proliferation, finding them to be ostensibly applicable to chemical and biological weapons and characterizing such risks as uncontrollable:[6]

- Existing nuclear powers might use force to prevent others from getting nuclear weapons (as Israel tried against Iraq);
- New nuclear powers might only be able to afford nuclear forces vulnerable to destruction by preemptive first strikes, leading to instabilities;
- Those controlling nuclear weapons might believe they could fight and win nuclear wars; and

---

1995 Tokyo subway attack. Robert Taylor, *The Bio-Terrorist Threat; Potential for Use of Biological Weapons by Terrorist Groups*, WORLD PRESS REVIEW, Sept. 1996, reprinted from NEW SCIENTIST, May 11, 1996.

[4] *See Legality of the Threat or Use of Nuclear Weapons*, International Court of Justice, Advisory Opinion, General List at pt. VI, 35–36, No. 95 (July 8, 1996), dissenting opinion of Judge Schwebel at 3, 35 I.L.M 842. *See supra* Chapter 3, notes 151–153 and accompanying text.

[5] PROLIFERATION: THREAT AND RESPONSE, *supra* note 3, at *Middle East and North Africa* 14, quoting Secretary of Defense William J Perry, Statement on Libyan Chemical Warfare Facility at Tarhunah, Air War College Conference on Nuclear Proliferation Issues, Maxwell Air Force Base, Alabama (April 26, 1996).

[6] *Proliferation of Weapons of Mass Destruction: Assessing the Risks, supra* note 1, at 70, citing John Mearscheimer, *Back to the Future: Instability in Europe After the Cold War*, INT'L SECURITY, vol. 15, no. 1, Sum. 1990, at 37–38.

- Increasing the number of fingers on the nuclear trigger would increase the probability that someone would use them accidentally or irrationally, or that terrorists would steal them.[7]

As to such risks, the report concluded:

> The same principles would probably apply, in varying degrees, to chemical and biological weapons. The predominant view amongst scholars—and national governments—is that these dangers are not controllable and that proliferation should be avoided, not accepted.[8]

Legal Regime as to Chemical and Biological Weapons

The legal regime as to chemical and biological weapons is clearer than that as to nuclear weapons since the former types of weapons have been banned by a series of conventions explicitly prohibiting both their use and possession.[9] The United States and other signatory nations

---

[7] *Id.*

[8] *Id.*

[9] The Hague Gas Declarations in the 1899 and 1907 Hague Conferences, *in* Convention (No. II) Respecting the Laws and Customs of War on Land, Done at the Hague, July 29, 1899, 32 Stat. 1803, 187 Parry's T.S. 429 (Fr. Text) and Convention (No. IV) Respecting the Laws and Customs of War on Land, Done at the Hague, Oct. 18, 1907, 36 Stat. 2277, 205 Parry's T.S. 216 (Fr. Text), reprinted in THE LAWS OF ARMED CONFLICTS, 63–68 (D. Schindler & J. Toman eds., 1973) (establishing complex, incomplete regulations as to the use of chemical weapons); The Protocol for the Prohibition of the Use in War of Asphyxiating, Poisonous or Other Gases, and of Bacteriological Methods of Warfare, June 17, 1925, T.I.A.S. No. 8061, 26 U.S.T. 571 (prohibiting categories of use but not stockpiling or production of biological and chemical weapons); The Convention on the Prohibition of the Development, Production and Stockpiling of Bacteriological (Biological) and Toxin Weapons and on Their Destruction, Apr. 10, 1972, T.I.A.S. No. 8062, 26 U.S.T. 583 (requiring the destruction of stocks of biological weapons); The Convention on the Prohibition of the Development, Production, Stockpiling and Use of Chemical Weapons and On Their Destruction, January 13, 1993, 31 I.L.M. 800, 2 Weston II.C.39 (requiring the destruction of stocks of chemical weapons by 2007).

See also JOINT CHIEFS OF STAFF, JOINT PUB. 3-11, DOCTRINE FOR NUCLEAR, BIOLOGICAL, AND CHEMICAL (NBC) DEFENSE Appendix A-A-1, (July 10, 1995) <http://www.dtic.mil/doctrine/jel/new_pubs/>, for an extensive listing of United States and international conventions and bi-lateral agreements; David B. Merkin, *The Efficacy of Chemical-Arms Treaties in the Aftermath of the Iran-Iraq War,* 9 B.U. INT'L L.J. 175, 177–178, (1991); 1997 US DEPARTMENT OF DEFENSE NUCLEAR BIOLOGICAL CHEMICAL DEFENSE ANNUAL REPORT TO CONGRESS 6-3, as set forth at <http://www.acq.osd.mil/cp/nbc97.htm>; Chemical Weapons, United States, <http://www.fas.org/nuke/guide/usa/cbw/

have destroyed their biological weapons and are in the process of destroying their chemical stockpiles.[10]

---

cw.htm>; Richard K. Betts, *The New Threat of Mass Destruction,* FOREIGN AFF., vol. 77, no. 1, January/February 1998, at 26, 30–31; Chemical Weapons Convention, Summary, Talking Points and Legislative Situation, Council for a Livable World, <http://www.clw.org/clw/cwcpoint.html>; William R. Youngblood, *Managing Non-Proliferation Regimes in the 1990s: Power, Politics, and Policies,* 9 EMORY INT'L L. REV. 329, 333 (1995).

[10] When the 1972 Biological Weapons Convention entered into effect, the United States and other signatories became required to destroy their stockpiles of such weapons. The United States reportedly completed this process in 1969 during the Nixon Administration. *See* Betts, *supra* note 9, at 26, 30–31. *See also Proliferation of Weapons of Mass Destruction: Assessing the Risks, supra* note 1, at 106.

When the Chemical Weapons Convention entered into effect in 1993, the United States and other signatories became required to destroy their stockpiles of chemical weapons by April 29, 2007. *See* 1997 US DEPARTMENT OF DEFENSE NUCLEAR BIOLOGICAL CHEMICAL DEFENSE ANNUAL REPORT TO CONGRESS *supra* note 9, at 6-3; Chemical Weapons, United States, *supra* note 9; Betts, *supra* note 9, at 30–31; Chemical Weapons Convention, Summary, Talking Points and Legislative Situation, *supra* note 9.

As of July 11, 1997, the United States maintained a large quantity of chemical weapons in several sites: *e.g.,* 90,231 8-inch artillery projectiles containing the nerve agent GB were at the Pine Bluff Chemical Activity site in Arkansas, and 258,912 155mm artillery projectiles containing the blister agent Mustard Gas were at the Anniston Chemical Activity site in Alabama. *See* Chemical Weapons, United States, *supra* note 9.

The United States reportedly has commenced destruction of chemical weapons. *See* Office of Assistant Secretary of Defense (Public Affairs), U.S. Chemical Weapons Stockpile Information Declassified, News Release, Ref. No. 024-96, Jan. 22, 1996, <http://www.defenselink.mil:80/news/Jan1996 /b012496_bt024-96.html>. *See also* Office of Assistant Secretary of Defense (Public Affairs), Interim Assessment of Chemical Demilitarization Program, News Release, Ref. No. 256–96, May 3, 1996, <http://www.defenselink. mil:80/news/May1996/b50396_bt256-96.html>; Office of Assistant Secretary of Defense (Public Affairs), National Conference on Chemical Weapons Stockpile, Destruction Environmental Issues, News Release, Ref. No. 526-96, Jul. 10, 1996, <http://www.defenselink.mil:80/news/Jul1996/b071296_bt426-96.html>.

Apropos of the risk of non-compliance and break-out, the Chemical Weapons Convention, unlike the Biological Weapons Convention, contains verification and enforcement provisions designed to support compliance. *See Prepared Statement of Gen. Henry H. Shelton, Chairman, Joint Chiefs of Staff, to the Senate Armed Services Committee,* Feb. 3 1998, *reprinted in* DEFENSE ISSUES, vol. 13, no. 14 (1998), *as set forth at* AMERICAN FORCES INFORMATION

Vast Destructiveness of Chemical and Biological Weapons

Chemical and biological weapons are extremely destructive, having the potential to kill millions of people and destroy whole urban areas and environmental systems. A small amount of a virus or toxin could poison substantial portions of the population of any U.S. city through only a few droplets placed in the water supply or through aerosol sprayed into the air.[11]

The U.S. Government's Office of Technology Assessment (OTA) in a 1993 study concluded that chemical weapons can be lethal when vaporized and inhaled in amounts as small as a few milligrams and that biological weapons are even more destructive.[12] The study stated, "Biological weapons are so potent that under conditions favorable to the attacker, they can kill as many people as comparably sized nuclear weapons, potentially making them extremely dangerous as a strategic or terrorist weapon against dense population centers."[13]

SERVICE DEFENSE VIEWPOINT, <http://www.defenselink.mil/speeches/1998/t19980203-shelton.html>.

Following the Russian admission that the Soviet Union had violated the Biological Weapons Convention, the United States, the United Kingdom, and Russia agreed on a program to inspect each other's biological facilities. *See Proliferation of Weapons of Mass Destruction: Assessing the Risks, supra* note 1 at 19, citing Joint U.S./U.K./Russian Statement on Biological Weapons, Sept. 14, 1992, *reproduced at* 11 THE ARMS CONTROL REPORTER 701, D.1. (Institute for Defense and Disarmament Studies, Cambridge, Mass. 1992). Japan, France, Germany, Britain and South Africa have also worked on a verification inspection system for biological weapons, to put teeth into the 1972 treaty. *See Gains Made on Biological Weapons Ban,* THE DESERET NEWS (SALT LAKE CITY), Jan. 23, 1999, at A04.

[11] *See* Daryn Kagan & Eileen O'Connor, *President Clinton to Announce Plan to Counter Biological Weapons Threat,* CNN MORNING NEWS, May 22, 1998, 9:20 Eastern Time (statement of John Boatman of Janes Information Group). The delivery through aerosol of "[l]ess than ten pounds of anthrax" could have the effect of destroying "a city the size of Albuquerque." Anne Boyle, *Biological Weapons Still Pose a Serious Threat, Sandia Labs Researcher Says,* ALBUQUERQUE TRIBUNE, Aug. 7, 1997, at A6.

[12] *See Proliferation of Weapons of Mass Destruction: Assessing the Risks, supra* note 1, at 54, fig. 2.2. The report found that 100 kg (100,000 grams) of anthrax spores (a form of disease-inducing bacteria) could produce one thousand times as many casualties as a ton (one million grams) of sarin nerve agent. *Id.*

[13] *Id.* at 3, 8. The report stated, "Like nuclear weapons, [biological weapons] have the potential in modest amounts (*e.g.* a few kilograms of an

While the 200,000 people killed in the Dresden firebombings in World War II required an extensive infrastructure of personnel and equipment to support some 1400 aircraft sorties over two days and the 100,000 killed in the Tokyo firebombings required similar levels of backup,[14] an isolated 100 kg. biological attack could be carried out by a light airplane, causing more devastation than the World War II firebombings and even more than a substantial nuclear strike.[15]

The U.S. Government's 1993 report stated that a single light plane flying over Washington, D.C. could disperse 100 kg. of anthrax spores by an "aerosol device" such as a crop sprayer, killing one to three million people,[16] an effect potentially greater than the estimated 570,000 to 1,900,000 deaths in the same area from the blast and shock effects of a 1.0 megaton hydrogen bomb.[17]

The report further stated, "A biological weapons attack with a non-contagious agent such as anthrax could go undetected for days—a sleeper catastrophe detectable only after victims exhibited symptoms that local physicians correctly diagnose *** A contagious viral agent, such as chicken pox, could be easily spread nationwide by unsuspecting victims before discovery. *** 'One of the most chilling aspects (of an attack) is that we may not know that an attack had occurred until several days later,' Stephan Sharro, acting director of the Federal Emergency Management Agency (FEMA) said."[18]

While vaccines are possible against some biological threats, stockpiling sufficient numbers is a large and expensive task, and the difficulties of administering hundreds of thousands, even millions, of doses daunting,[19] particularly in light of the time requirements as to

---

agent), properly dispersed, to kill and disable many thousands of urban residents and to seriously impair war-supporting activities." *Id.* at 3, 62.

[14] *See id.* at 2, 46.

[15] *See id.* at 54, fig. 2-1, 2-2.

[16] *Id.* at 54, fig. 2-2.

[17] *See id.* at 53, fig. 2-1. Note that, for purposes of this estimate, the hydrogen bomb effects are essentially limited to blast destruction: "The atomic weapons (fission and fusion) are assumed to be ah [*sic*—an air?] burst for optimum blast and radiation effects, producing little lethal fallout. The lethal area is assumed to be that receiving 5lb/in^2 of overpressure—enough to level wood or unreinforced brick houses." *Id.* at 53. *See also The Effects of Nuclear War*, NTIS order #PB-296946 at 37, Ch. II-A (May 1979).

[18] *Biological Weapons Pose Danger to U.S., Experts Say*, Deutsche Presse-Agentur, April 27, 1998. *See also Proliferation of Weapons of Mass Destruction: Assessing the Risks, supra* note 1, at 61, 62.

[19] *See* Kagan & O'Connor, *supra* note 11.

how quickly vaccines generally need to be administered to potentially
be effective.[20] The *Quadrennial Defense Review*, a major U.S.
government study completed in 1997, found the United States to be
vulnerable to potential chemical and biological weapons attack by
terrorists or other nations.[21]

Biological weapons are potentially more destructive than chemical:
"The importance of the different types among them has also shifted.
Biological weapons should now be the most serious concern, with
nuclear weapons second and chemical weapons a distant third."[22] By
way of example of biological weapon's potency, "[e]xperts have
reported that botulinum toxin [is] 100,000 times more deadly than sarin
nerve gas, the type allegedly released by religious fanatics in Japan's
Tokyo subway."[23]

John Holum stated in his confirmation hearing, as he became Under
Secretary of State for Arms Control and International Security:

> I'm concerned about the biological weapons threat. In particular,
> it's very often practiced to group chemical and biological weapons
> together as a CBW, as one category. They're actually very
> different. Chemical weapons I think are more suitable—they
> certainly have been prepared for and used in war, but I think they're
> more suitable for terrorist activity. They aren't—and they're on the
> margins of being a weapon of mass destruction. Biological agents
> are different. I think they're better classed closer to nuclear
> weapons in terms of their destructive potential. A very small
> quantity of anthrax or botulinum could infect a huge population
> sprayed out of a single airplane. If someone perfects the ability to
> use smallpox or some other virus that is contagious, you can
> imagine the consequences of infecting a large number and them not
> knowing they had it, and then getting on airplanes and traveling
> around the country or around the world. It could just be
> devastating. So I think biological weapons are a very major
> concern.[24]

---

[20] *See id.* ("A program at the Pentagon already approved to develop and
stockpile vaccines for U.S. troops carries an estimated price tag of $320 million
over five years. A civilian program could cost billions.").

[21] *See Biological Weapons Pose Danger to U.S., Experts Say, supra* note
18; SECRETARY OF DEFENSE WILLIAM COHEN, THE QUADRENNIAL DEFENSE
REVIEW § II (1997), *see infra* notes 60–61.

[22] Betts, *supra* note 9.

[23] Gertz, *supra* note 1.

[24] *Hearing of the Senate Foreign Relations Committee, Nomination of John
David Holum to be Undersecretary of State for Arms Control and International*

Chemical and Biological Weapons States

Yet many States maintain these weapons or programs to develop them. In a leading study in 1993, the United States identified twenty-nine States suspected as having chemical weapons programs,[25] and fifteen States as suspected as having biological weapons programs.[26] The Federation of American Scientists[27] has identified twenty-five to twenty-nine States as having chemical weapons and nineteen States as having biological weapons as of October 16, 1997.[28]

John Holum was quoted in 1998 as stating that "25 nations were believed to have the capability to produce biological weapons, which ... were far deadlier than chemical weapons and more comparable to nuclear arms."[29] The United States anticipates an increase in the number of States possessing these weapons and in the destructiveness of the weapons. John Holum warned, "They are incredibly lethal ... .

Security, Chaired by Senator Charles Hagel (R-NE), FEDERAL NEWS SERVICE, June 28, 1999.

[25] *See Proliferation of Weapons of Mass Destruction: Assessing the Risks*, *supra* note 1, at 80, Appendix 2-A, Table 2-A-1. The study emphasized that it was based on published sources and did not purport to be authoritative or comprehensive. *Id.* at 79.

[26] *See id.* at 80, Appendix 2-A, Table 2-B-1. The report noted, "The states seeking these weapons today are generally pursuing them covertly, attesting to the reluctance states have to admit to such developments." *Id.* at 2.

[27] The Federation of American Scientists (FAS) describes itself as "engaged in analysis and advocacy on science, technology and public policy for global security. A privately-funded non-profit policy organization whose Board of Sponsors includes over 55 American Nobel Laureates, FAS was founded as the Federation of Atomic Scientists in 1945 by members of the Manhattan Project who produced the first atomic bomb." <http://www.fas.org>.

[28] *See* Federation of American Scientists, States Possessing Weapons of Mass Destruction, <http://www.fas.org/irp/threat/wmd_state.htm>, citing Leonard A. Cole, *The Specter of Biological Weapons*, SCIENTIFIC AMERICAN Dec. 1996; DEFENSE NUCLEAR AGENCY, BIOLOGICAL WEAPONS PROLIFERATION 46 (Ft. Detrick, Md.: US Army Medical Research Institute of Infectious Diseases, Apr. 1994); *Proliferation of Weapons of Mass Destruction: Assessing the Risks*, *supra* note 1. The FAS describes its lists as encompassing "all states with nuclear, chemical or biological weapons, and missile delivery systems," that is, all states possessing weapons of mass destruction, as opposed to being mere suspects. *See* States Possessing Weapons of Mass Destruction, *supra*.

[29] Erik Kirschbaum, *US Urges Tighter Controls on Biological Weapons*, AAP NEWSFEED, Feb. 12, 1998.

They are also not that difficult to make, so I think we have to anticipate a very high risk of these being more widely available."[30]

Subject to the available information,[31] it appears that the States continuing to maintain chemical and biological weapons programs include North Korea,[32] China,[33] India,[34] Pakistan,[35] Iran,[36] Iraq,[37] Libya,[38]

---

[30] Gertz, *supra* note 1 (quoting John Holum).

[31] Chemical and biological weapons programs are less subject to detection than nuclear programs and hence the available information is less reliable. *See Proliferation of Weapons of Mass Destruction: Assessing the Risks, supra* note 1, at 7.

[32] *See* PROLIFERATION THREAT AND RESPONSE, *supra* note 3, at *Northeast Asia* 1. North Korea is believed to have "a sizable stockpile of chemical weapons" and to have "achieved the capability to manufacture large quantities of nerve, blister, choking, and blood agents," such that "chemical weapons may have become an integral part of North Korea's warfighting strategy." *Id.* North Korea has also reportedly developed a capacity to deliver chemical agents, including through "domestically produced artillery, multiple rocket launchers, mortars, aerial bombs, and ballistic missiles." *Id.* North Korea has not signed the Chemical Weapon Convention and is not likely to be likely to do so in the near future, given the Convention's intrusive inspections and verification provisions. *Id.* at *Northeast Asia* 4.

North Korea has pursued biological warfare capacity for many years and is believed to have, at a minimum, "a biotechnical infrastructure ... sufficient to support production of limited quantities of infectious biological warfare agents, toxins, and possibly crude biological weapons." *Id.* at *Northeast Asia* 5. North Korea has signed the Biological Weapons Convention. *See id.* at *Northeast Asia* 3, 4.

North Korea is believed likely to use chemical weapons in a conflict with South Korea. *See id.* North Korea provides ballistic missiles to countries in the Middle East. *See id.* at *Northeast Asia* 2. Despite recent economic hardship, "Pyongyang [North Korea] continues to invest scarce resources in developing and maintaining its military forces, including its chemical and biological warfare and missile programs." *Id.*

[33] *See id.* at *Northeast Asia* 6. "China's current inventory of chemical agents includes the full range of traditional agents, and China is conducting research into more advanced agents. It has a wide variety of delivery systems for chemical agents, including tube artillery, rockets, mortars, landmines, aerial bombs, sprayers, and SRBMs." *See id.* at *Northeast Asia* 8. China "[l]ikely has maintained an offensive biological warfare program since acceding to the Biological and Toxin Weapons Convention in 1984." *Id.* at *Northeast Asia* 7. China also supplies NBC and ballistic weapons technology to the countries of Pakistan, Iran, and Syria. *See id.* at *Northeast Asia* 11. It has signed the Chemical Weapons Convention and ratified it shortly after the United States. *See id.*

[34] *See id.* at *South Asia.* "India has a sizable chemical industry and recently [acknowledged] its chemical warfare program, as called for under the CWC." *Id.* at *South Asia* 2. "India has research and development facilities geared to biological warfare defense." *See id.* at *South Asia* 2. India has exported microorganisms and equipment "to several countries of proliferation concern in the Middle East." *Id.*

[35] *See id.* at *South Asia.* "Pakistan has imported a number of chemicals that can be used to make chemical agents and is moving slowly towards a commercial chemical industry capable of producing all precursor chemicals needed to support a chemical weapons stockpile. Pakistan has ... ratified the CWC." *Id.* at *South Asia* 3.

Pakistan may have the capacity to support a limited biological weapons program. *See id.* at *South Asia* 2–4. "Pakistan has a capable ... biotechnology infrastructure and may be seeking to upgrade hardware for selected biotechnology facilities. ... Pakistan is believed to have the resources and the capabilities to support a limited biological warfare research and development effort." *Id.* at *South Asia* 3–4. It has ratified the Biological Weapons Convention of 1972. *Id.* at *South Asia* 3–4.

[36] *See id.* at *Middle East and North Africa* at 2–7. Iran maintains a limited capacity to produce chemical weapons, relying on Chinese assistance. *See id.* "Therefore, Chinese supply policies will be key to whether Tehran attains its long-term goal of independent production for these weapons." *See id.* at *Middle East and North Africa* 5. "Iran manufactures weapons for blister, blood, and choking agents; it is also believed to be conducting research on nerve agents. Iran has a stockpile of these weapons, including artillery shells and bombs, which could be used in another conflict in the region." *See id.* at *Middle East and North Africa* 5.

"Since the early 1990s, [Iran] has put a high priority on its chemical weapons program because of its inability to respond in kind to Iraq's chemical attacks and the discovery of substantial Iraqi efforts with advanced agents, such as the highly persistent nerve agent VX. Iran ratified the CWC, under which it will be obligated to eliminate its chemical program over a number of years. Nevertheless, it continues to upgrade and expand its chemical warfare production infrastructure and munitions arsenal." *Id.* Iran used chemical weapons in the Iran–Iraq War. *See id.* at *Middle East and North Africa* 3.

Iran possesses expertise and infrastructure for a biological warfare program, may have some agents available and may seek more, even though it has ratified the Biological Weapons Convention. *See id.* at *Middle East and North Africa* 3. "Iran's biological warfare program began during the Iran–Iraq war. The pace of the program probably has increased because of the 1995 revelations about the scale of Iraqi efforts prior to the Gulf War. ... Although this program is in the research and development phase, the Iranians have considerable expertise .... [W]ithin 10 years, Iran's military forces may be able to deliver biological agents effectively." *See id.* at *Middle East and North Africa* 5.

[37] *See id.* at *Middle East and North Africa* 7–12.

Iraq suffered grave hits to it program in the NATO bombings of the 1990s, but could restart: As to chemical weapons, it is reported that Iraq "[c]ould restart agent production and have a small usable stockpile in several months, if sanctions and monitoring were lifted or substantially reduced." *See id.* at *Middle East and North Africa* 8. As to biological weapons, it is similarly reported that Iraq "[c]ould restart some limited agent production quickly, if sanctions and monitoring were lifted or substantially reduced."

Iraq ratified the Biological Weapons Convention of 1972, but has not signed the Chemical Weapons Convention. *See id.* In addition to the treaties, "UN Security Council Resolution (UNSCR) 687, in force since 1991, calls for Iraq to eliminate its NBC weapons and missiles and forbids it from developing, producing, or possessing any NBC weapons or missiles with ranges greater than 150 kilometers. However, Saddam Hussein's government endeavors to conceal and protect these weapons and related equipment, technology or documentation from UN Special Commission on Iraq (UNSCOM) inspections and monitoring." *See id.* at *Middle East and North Africa* 7.

In 1995 Iraq released a cache of documents whose existence had previously been denied. These documents indicated a program to develop the advanced chemical agents including nerve agent VX, and "a very sizable biological agent production and weaponization program." *See id.* at *Middle East and North Africa* 8.

Iraqi biological agents included 19,000 liters of botulinum toxin, causing weakness and gastro-intestinal distress, leading to respiratory failure and death if untreated; 8,500 liters of anthrax, causing a flu-like respiratory distress and fever and also leading to respiratory failure and death; 2,400 liters of aflatoxin, causing headache, jaundice, gastro-intestinal distress, leading to liver disease, internal bleeding and death. *See id.* at *Middle East and North Africa* 10, 11.

"During the 1980s, Iraq developed the largest and most advanced biological warfare program in the Middle East. A variety of biological agents were studied .... Anthrax, botulinum, and aflatoxin were declared to be weaponized." *Id.* It is reported Iraq had "[b]iological weapons deployed to operational delivery sites in December 1990." *See id.* at *Middle East and North Africa* 12.

The 1991 Coalition bombing damaged biological warfare facilities, but the critical materials had already been moved to Al Hakam and agents were buried to escape bombing. *See id.* at *Middle East and North Africa* 11. In 1996, biological equipment at Al Hakam and Daura were destroyed, and Al Hakam razed. *See id.*

"Iraq had a wide variety of chemical warfare agents available before the Gulf War, including blister (mustard) and nerve (tabun and sarin) agents, as well as several means of delivery, including artillery, rockets, mortars, spray tanks, aerial bombs and SCUD-type missiles." *See id.* at *Middle East and North Africa* 10. It could have generated 400 tons of the sophisticated VX toxin every year. *See id.* Its stockpiles of nerve agent sarin filled artillery rounds were considerable. *See id.*

Syria,[39] and Russia.[40] Non-national entities and groups also are a threat,[41] such as the Aum Shinrikyo in Japan and the Aryan Nations in the United States.[42]

---

[38] *See id.* at *Middle East and North Africa* 12–16.

Libya developed a chemical warfare program in the 1980s, producing up to 100 tons of blister and nerve agent at its Rabta facility. *See id.* at *Middle East and North Africa* 14. While the Rabta facility was thereafter closed in 1990 and ostensibly reopened in 1995 as a pharmaceutical facility, Libya constructed a suspected weapons facility at Tarhunah. *See id.* at *Middle East and North Africa* 13. *See also supra,* note 5; Chapter 28, notes 56–57, 68–71 and accompanying text. Libya used chemical weapons against Chadian troops in 1987 and has not signed the Chemical Weapons Convention. *See id.* at *Middle East and North Africa* 13.

Libya reportedly lacks the science and the technology for biological weapons, remaining at the R&D phase. It has ratified the Biological and Toxin Weapons Convention. *See id.* at *Middle East and North Africa* 13.

[39] *See id.* at *Middle East and North Africa* 1.

Syria pursues chemical weapons development to become independent of supplier nations and has not signed the Chemical Weapons Convention. *See id.* at *Middle East and North Africa* 17. "Syria has a stockpile of the nerve agent sarin and may be trying to develop advanced nerve agents as well. In future years, Syria will likely try to improve the infrastructure for producing and storing chemical agents. At this point, it probably has weaponized sarin into aerial bombs and SCUD missile warheads, which gives Syria the capability to employ chemical agents against targets in Israel." *See id.* at *Middle East and North Africa* 18.

"Syria possesses a substantial force of ballistic missiles capable of reaching targets throughout Israel .... Syria views Israel as its primary external threat and sees its chemical weapons and ballistic missiles as a means to counter Israel's conventional superiority." *Id.* at *Middle East and North Africa* 1.

"Syria is pursuing the development of biological weapons. Syria probably has adequate biotechnical infrastructure to support a small biological warfare program, although the Syrians are not believed to have begun any major weaponization or testing related to biological warfare." *See id.* at *Middle East and North Africa* 18. Syria has signed the Biological Weapons Program. *Id.* at 18.

[40] *See id.* at *Russia, Ukraine, Kazakhstan, and Belarus.* Russia, which ratified the Chemical Weapons Convention, reportedly maintains the world's largest chemical weapons arsenal, some 40,000 metric tons, and may be creating a new generation of chemical weapons. *See id.* at *Russia, Ukraine, Kazakhstan, and Belarus* 2. Key components of the Soviet biological weapons program remain in Russia, and Russia may be continuing research into biological warfare. *See id.* at *Russia, Ukraine, Kazakhstan, and Belarus* 2.

The Soviet Union reportedly had had the largest and most advanced chemical and biological weapons programs in the world. Its collapse led to substantial concern as to the spread of information, technology and expertise as to such weapons to additional States as to well as terrorist individuals and groups. *See* PROLIFERATION: THREAT AND RESPONSE, *supra* note 3, at *Former Soviet Union.* "Key components of the former Soviet program remain largely intact and may support a possible future mobilization capability for the production of biological agents and delivery systems. *** Despite official statements by the governments of Russia, Ukraine, Kazakhstan, and Belarus that they are opposed to proliferation of NBC weapons and missiles, some sales have and are taking place. Whether these are officially sanctioned or efforts by local entities to ignore or circumvent controls is unclear. ... Some officials may turn a blind eye to such activities because of the critical need for revenues." *Id.* at *Former Soviet Union* 6, 7. "There are indications that Moscow is not fully capable of controlling personnel and institutions involved in chemical warfare. If this situation continues, Russian entities could become a major source for advanced chemical warfare–related material and technology. There is similar evidence that Russian technologies and expertise related to biological warfare may be reaching countries of proliferation concern." *Id.* at *Former Soviet Union* 6. "The United States remains concerned at the threat of proliferations, both of biological warfare expertise and related hardware, from Russia. Russian scientists, many of whom either are unemployed or have not been paid for an extended period, may be vulnerable to recruitment by states trying to establish biological warfare programs." *Id.*

On this migration of weapons expertise, John Holum told the U.S. Senate. "We're pursuing that issue on just about every front you can conceive of from trying to find alternative employment and opportunities for the former weapons scientists, some 30,000 not just nuclear but all weapons-of-mass-destruction scientists in the former Soviet Union are being—are involved in various kinds of training and entrepreneurial efforts that would take them out of the nuclear field, make them less interested in traveling to willing employers in Iraq or North Korea or elsewhere." *Hearing of the Senate Foreign Relations Committee, Nomination of John David Holum to be Undersecretary of State for Arms Control and International Security, supra* note 24.

[41] *See* Taylor, *supra* note 3. *See also* PROLIFERATION, THREAT AND RESPONSE, *supra* note 3, at *The Transnational Threat* 2–3.

[42] *See* PROLIFERATION: THREAT AND RESPONSE, *supra* note 3, at *The Transnational Threat* 2. *See also* Taylor, *supra* note 3. In March 1995, Aum Shinrikyo, a Japanese cult group, launched the most notorious chemical weapons attack by a non-national entity, releasing a poisonous chemical, ostensibly sarin nerve gas, in a Japanese subway. *See* PROLIFERATION: THREAT AND RESPONSE, *supra* note 3, at *The Transnational Threat* 2. *See also* Taylor, *supra* note 3. Prior to that attack, the group had reportedly conducted chemical weapons tests on sheep at a ranch owned by a group member in Western Australia, and had purchased Russian helicopters as well two remotely piloted vehicles which could have delivered a large chemical attack. *See*

States reportedly having biological weapons programs include a number of signatories to the 1972 Biological Weapons Convention barring such programs, such as Iraq, Iran, Libya and possibly Russia.[43] Some nations, China for example,[44] have signed the Chemical Weapons Convention requiring all such weapons to be destroyed by 2007, yet appear to be actively pursuing additional and newer chemical weapons. Signatories of the 1925 Protocol banning the use of chemical arms in warfare nonetheless have used them, including the former Soviet Union, Iraq, and Iran.[45]

It appears that that Soviet Union had maintained an extensive biological weapons program, including a largescale germ warfare program known as "Biopreparat" concentrating on a variety of bioarms, including bacteria capable of causing a "superplague" to wipe out entire cities.[46] While Russia purportedly terminated this program, some doubts remain.[47]

Proliferation Risks as to Chemical and Biological Weapons

I made the point earlier as to the ease of access to nuclear weapons, given such factors as the public availability of the requisite technical information and of the major ingredients, including the necessary nuclear materials such as plutonium and highly enriched weapons grade uranium, and also of risk factors as to the availability of the weapons

---

PROLIFERATION: THREAT AND RESPONSE, *supra* note 3, at *The Transnational Threat* 2. *See also* Taylor, *supra* note 3.

In that same year, a member of the U.S. Aryan Nations white supremacist group successfully obtained a sample of the organism that causes bubonic plague. *See* Taylor, *supra* note 3. "In March, 1995, Larry Harris, a microbiologist and a member of the Aryan Nations white supremacist group, used a forged letter head and his professional credentials to order samples of Yersinia pestis, the organism that causes bubonic plague, from the American Type Culture Collection, a clearinghouse for microbiological sample in Rockville, Maryland. ... [T]he ATCC mailed the samples, but the staff became suspicious .... The vials were recovered unopened. Harris is now being prosecuted for mail fraud. Owning plague is not illegal in the U.S." *Id.*

[43] *See Proliferation of Weapons of Mass Destruction: Assessing the Risks*, *supra* note 1, at 80–82, Table 2-A-1 and 2-B-1. *See Gains Made on Biological Weapons Ban*, *supra* note 10.

[44] *See supra* note 33.

[45] *See infra* notes 88, 92–93. *See also* S. H. AMIN, LEGAL SYSTEM OF IRAQ 52–53 (1989).

[46] Gertz, *supra* note 1.

[47] *See Proliferation of Weapons of Mass Destruction: Assessing the Risks*, *supra* note 1, at 65.

themselves, through black market and other criminal sources, including nuclear assets of the former Soviet Union.[48]   Yet chemical and biological weapons—both the technology and the weapons themselves —are generally far more accessible than nuclear weapons.

The underlying technical information as to chemical and biological weapons—including as to their ingredients and as to the technology for production—is much less complex than that for nuclear weapons and even more readily available publicly.[49] The underlying materials, many of which have other perfectly innocent applications, are likewise generally far more readily available[50] and the prerequisites for acquiring, implementing and setting up the necessary production facilities and processes less daunting.[51]

Chemical and biological weapons programs are also less expensive,[52] smaller,[53] less technically intensive,[54] and easier to

---

[48] *See supra* Chapter 22, notes 24–25 and accompanying text. *See also Proliferation of Weapons of Mass Destruction, Assessing the Risk, supra* note 1, at 15.

[49] *See* Gertz, *supra* note 1. "Highly advanced communications are putting such weapons know-how in the hands of anyone with a computer and modem. 'The ingredients for sarin and other chemical weapons are easily accessible over the Internet,' said Sen. Sam Nunn (D. Ga.), the senior Democrat on the Senate Armed Services Committee, 'as is information about biological weapons and even instructions on how to make a nuclear device.'" *Id.*

[50] *See Proliferation of Weapons of Mass Destruction, Assessing the Risk, supra* note 1, at 6. "Virtually all the equipment underlying production of biological and toxin agents has civil applications and has become widely available as fermentation technology, and the pharmaceutical and biotechnology industries more generally, have spread worldwide." *Id.*

[51] *See id.* at 1. "Barring a shortcut, such as the direct acquisition of nuclear materials usable in weapons, the infrastructure required to produce nuclear weapons is considerably more difficult and expensive than for either biological or chemical weapons. Mass production of lethal chemicals requires a greater investment than that of biological weapons, but is not nearly as expensive or challenging as production of nuclear materials." *Id.*

Similarly, "A nuclear bomb in the hands of a deranged person has long been the stuff of nightmares, but the materials needed to make such a device are hard to obtain and exceedingly tricky to assemble. Biological weapons are not nearly so difficult to manufacture." Taylor, *supra* note 3.

[52] It is often said that chemical and biological weapons are a poor man's nuclear weapons, because they are appreciably cheaper, more accessible and substantially easier to deliver. *See* Boyle, *supra* note 11. *See also* Thomas Graham, *Conventional Response; Nuclear Stance Could Worsen Chem-Bio Threat,* DEFENSE NEWS, Feb. 23, 1998/Mar. 1, 1998, at 31; JOINT DOCTRINE FOR NUCLEAR, BIOLOGICAL, AND CHEMICAL (NBC) DEFENSE, *supra* note 9;

disguise.[55] Because of such factors and also the greater proliferation that has already occurred, as well as the nature of a number of the States possessing such weapons, the risks of chemical and biological weapons proliferation are substantial, both from States and the black market and other criminal sources.[56] Because they are lighter and smaller, chemical and bacteriological weapons are also easier to deliver.[57]

Biological Weapons Pose Danger to U.S., Experts Say, *supra* note 18; 1997 US DOD NUCLEAR BIOLOGICAL CHEMICAL DEFENSE ANNUAL REPORT TO CONGRESS, *supra* note 9; PROLIFERATION THREAT AND RESPONSE, *supra* note 3.

[53] *See* David Rohde, *Standoff With Iraq: The Inspections*, THE NEW YORK TIMES, Feb. 12, 1998, at A6. ("In a 1996 report on biological weapons, the Center for Strategic and International Studies, a public policy research institution in Washington, D.C., warned that it was easy for a would-be terrorist to assemble biological weapons—using commercial equipment with a capacity of 130 gallons."). Chemical weapons generally require somewhat larger production facilities that would be visible from the air. *See* Boyle, *supra* note 11.

[54] *See* Boyle, *supra* note 11 ("'Anybody who has taken Microbiology 202 can make a biological weapon' .... Sophisticated lab equipment and exotic materials are not needed. 'You can brew up a biological weapon in a small brewer—like one you'd use for homemade beer,'" quoting Alan Zelicoff of Sandia National Laboratories.).

[55] *See* Gertz, *supra* note 1. A nation or group gains tremendous flexibility if it chooses a biological weapons program: "Unlike chemical weapons programs, which require the use of large scale industrial equipment and possession of precursor chemicals, BW weapons do not need to be stockpiled. Nations can keep small quantities or even sample cultures on hand in freeze-dried form. Cultures can be mass produced at any time." *Id.* With biological weapons, "the threat resists taming because the weapon are easy to make and their production is hard for international monitors to detect." Boyle, *supra* note 11.

[56] *See* Gertz, *supra* note 1. "Samples of deadly viruses needed for starting BW programs can be obtained on the international black market. US counterproliferation officials are especially concerned that BW starter cultures could be smuggled out of the territory of the old Soviet Union by scientists looking to make money." *Id.* "The number of nations capable of developing and possessing WMD is steadily increasing. Developing nations are receiving these weapons or means to develop them through technology transfer, overt or covert direct transfer, or support to belligerent groups or governments." JOINT DOCTRINE FOR NUCLEAR, BIOLOGICAL AND CHEMICAL (NBC) DEFENSE, *supra* note 9, at I-1.

[57] "Crude dissemination of biological agents can be performed with commercially available equipment, such as an agricultural sprayer mounted on

Chemical and Biological Weapons as a Major Security Threat

The United States in recent years has repeatedly recognized the potential use of chemical and biological weapons by adversaries as one of our major security risks.[58]

The Department of Defense concluded in its 1997 Quadrennial Defense Review ("QDR"), the Department's "strategy and the plan [to] give us the military capability and forces we need throughout the 1997–2015 time frame and beyond ... dealing with the threats of 2015,"[59] that the spread of biological and chemical as well as nuclear weapons and their means of delivery is of "primary concern."[60]

---

a truck, ship, or airplane." *Proliferation of Weapons of Mass Destruction, Assessing the Risk, supra* note 1 at 6. "For at least the next decade, few if any [States actively working to develop weapons of mass destruction] will be able to deliver such weapons more than a thousand kilometers or so in a reliable and timely manner. ... Despite there current limitations in long-range military delivery systems, however, proliferant states—at least in principle—can threaten any country on earth using unconventional means (*e.g.*, covert or disguised delivery systems such as a ship or truck)." *Id.* at 4. A chemical or biological weapon can be delivered by "even a suitcase." *Id.* at 3. "[A] given quantity of certain lethal microorganisms would probably kill even more people if spread effectively by human agents than if by a missile." *Id.* at 3.

In addition, the proliferation of ballistic missiles, such as the Soviet-made SCUD systems, has increased the risks of the potential use of chemical or biological weapons. *See* JOINT DOCTRINE FOR NUCLEAR, BIOLOGICAL, AND CHEMICAL (NBC) DEFENSE, *supra* note 9, at I-3. "Ballistic missiles offer potential proliferators several advantages in delivering NBC weapons. *** The potential for coercion is, perhaps, the long-range ballistic missile's greatest value to proliferators ... [to] threaten[] distant cities and ... distract and tie up military resources." 1997 COUNTERPROLIFERATION PROGRAM REVIEW COMMITTEE REPORT TO CONGRESS 3–8 (1997).

[58] *See* THE QUADRENNIAL DEFENSE REVIEW, *supra* note 21; *Proliferation of Weapons of Mass Destruction: Assessing the Risks, supra* note 1, at 100; PROLIFERATION: THREAT AND RESPONSE, *supra* note 3; JOINT DOCTRINE FOR NUCLEAR, BIOLOGICAL AND CHEMICAL (NBC) DEFENSE, *supra* note 9, at I-1; JOINT CHIEFS OF STAFF, JOINT PUB 3-12, DOCTRINE FOR JOINT NUCLEAR OPERATIONS, April 23, 1993, *set forth at* <http://www.fas.org/nuke/guide/usa/doctrine/dod/jp3_12.htm>, updated as JOINT CHIEFS OF STAFF, JOINT PUB 3-12, DOCTRINE FOR JOINT NUCLEAR OPERATIONS, (Dec. 15, 1995), <http://www.dtic.mil/doctrine/jel/new_pubs/jp3_12.pdf>.

[59] THE QUADRENNIAL DEFENSE REVIEW, *supra* note 21, at The Secretary's Message p. 7.

[60] *Id.* § II, at 1.

The OTA study emphasized the risks of these weapons, and "According to the commander of the recently created U.S. Army Chemical and Biological Defense Agency (CBDA) *** 'the biological threat has been recently singled out as the one major threat that still poses the ability for catastrophic effects on a theater-deployed force. Desert Storm solidified the perception in our country—in the congress and among our military leadership—that [biological warfare] was something that third-world nations considered a potential equalizer.'"[61]

In one U.S. response to the rising probability of meeting a chemical or biological attack even outside of a nuclear confrontation, the Marines have made a new unit, the Chemical/Biological Incident Response Force, to "perform consequence management in chemically and biologically contaminated environments."[62]

Secretary of Defense Cohen said:

> I believe the proliferation of weapons of mass destruction presents the greatest threat that the world has ever known. We are finding more and more countries who are acquiring technology—not only missile technology—and are developing chemical weapons and biological weapons capabilities to be used in theater and also on a long-range basis. So I think that is perhaps the greatest threat that any of us will face in the coming years.[63]

Major U.S. Government sources have further stated that biological and chemical weapons, like nuclear weapons "give small states or subnational groups the ability to inflict damage that is wholly disproportionate to their conventional military capabilities or to the nature of the conflict in which they are used."[64] Addressing the risks of weapons of mass destruction from terrorist groups, Gen. Henry H. Shelton, Chairman of the Chiefs of Staff, recently stated, "In the near future, these organizations could attempt to employ weapons of mass

---

[61] *Proliferation of Weapons of Mass Destruction, Assessing the Risks, supra* note 1, at 61, quoting Brig. Gen. George Friel, commanding General, U.S. Army CBDA, *quoted in* John G. Roos, *Chem-Bio Defense Agency Will Tackle 'Last Major Threat to a Deployed Force'*, ARMED FORCES J. INT'L, Dec. 1992, at 10.

[62] THE QUADRENNIAL DEFENSE REVIEW, *supra* note 21, § VII at 11.

[63] PROLIFERATION: THREAT AND RESPONSE, *supra* note 3, at 1 (quoting Secretary Cohen's confirmation hearing of January 1997.)

[64] *Proliferation of Weapons of Mass Destruction: Assessing the Risks, supra* note 1, at 2.

destruction, such as chemical or biological agents, or even small nuclear devices, to achieve their ends."[65]

The United States has recognized that "with NBC [nuclear, chemical or biological] weapons, even small-scale theater missile threats would raise dramatically the potential costs and risks of military operations, undermine conventional superiority, and jeopardize the credibility of U.S. regional security strategies."[66]

Secretary Cohen stated, "Because of U.S. conventional military dominance, adversaries who might challenge the United States are likely to do so using unconventional means, including NBC weapons."[67]

Interrelation of NBC Threats

The interrelationship of the risks attendant on nuclear weapons with those presented by chemical and biological weapons has been widely recognized by the United States. These overall categories of weapons are particularly similar in their destructiveness and the uncontrollability of their effects, as well as in the proliferation risks.[68] The Department of Defense in the Quadrennial Defense Review repeatedly addressed nuclear, biological and chemical weapons as part of the same overall problem of weapons of mass destruction.[69] The Department stated that "nuclear weapons remain important as a hedge against NBC proliferation."[70] The recent OTA study concluded, "[T]he reduced

---

[65] *Prepared Statement of Gen. Henry H. Shelton, supra* note 10.

[66] SEC. OF DEFENSE WILLIAM S. COHEN, 1998 ANNUAL REPORT TO THE PRESIDENT AND CONGRESS Chap. 6, p. 1.

[67] PROLIFERATION: THREAT AND RESPONSE, *supra* note 3, at Department of Defense Response 1.

[68] *See generally Proliferation of Weapons of Mass Destruction, Assessing the Risks, supra* note 1.

[69] *See, e.g.,* THE QUADRENNIAL DEFENSE REVIEW, *supra* note 21, § II at 1–2, 3, 5.

Issues as to chemical, biological and nuclear attack are addressed by the U.S. Defense Department jointly, including under the leadership of an Assistant to the Secretary of Defense for Nuclear, Chemical and Biological Weapons. *See* Dr. John J. Hamre, Deputy Secretary of Defense, at Dulles International Airport, Va., Edited Remarks at the Ceremony Marking the Establishment of the Defense Threat Reduction Agency, Which was Established as a Part of the Defense Reform Initiative, Oct. 1, 1998, *as set forth at* AMERICAN FORCES INFORMATION SERVICE DEFENSE VIEWPOINT, <http://www.defenselink.mil/speeches/1998/r19981102-depsecdef.html>.

[70] THE QUADRENNIAL DEFENSE REVIEW, *supra* note 21, § III at 4.

military threat from the former Soviet Union has increased the relative importance of lesser powers, especially if armed with weapons of mass destruction."[71]

President Clinton, addressing the subject of dangers from criminals of the future, stated, "We have to defend our future from these predators of the 21st century. They feed on the free flow of information and technology. They actually take advantage of the freer movement of people, information, and ideas. And they will be all the more lethal if we allow them to build arsenals of nuclear, chemical, and biological weapons, and the missiles to deliver them."[72]

So too, the Congress in its 1997–1998 hearings of the Senate Foreign Relations Committee regarding Iranian weapons of mass destruction, focused on the overlap of the threat posed by Iran's chemical, nuclear, and biological programs.[73]

The U.S. military in its manual *Doctrine for Joint Theater Nuclear Operations* states:

---

[71] *Proliferation of Weapons of Mass Destruction: Assessing the Risks, supra* note 1 at 1.

[72] The White House, Office of the Press Secretary, Remarks by the President on Iraq to Pentagon Personnel, The Pentagon, February 17, 1998, as set forth at <http://www.defenselink.mil/topstory/prezoniraq.html>.

[73] *See, e.g., Prepared Testimony of Leonard S. Spector, Director, Nuclear Non-Proliferation Project, Carnegie Endowment for International Peace, Before the Senate Foreign Relations Committee, Near Eastern and South Asian Affairs Subcommittee, U.S. Efforts to Halt Weapons of Mass Destruction and Missile Programs in Iran,* FED. NEWS SERVICE, Apr. 17, 1997. ("Based on the open record, Iran can be thought of as pursuing WMD and missile programs along at least eleven distinct paths, including: 1. Nuclear Weapons (…production of weapons material) … 4. Biological Weapons (domestic production, with some outside assistance) 5. Basic chemical weapons … 6. Advanced chemical weapons … [7–11, missile programs: purchasing and building Scud missiles, building ballistic missiles, and purchasing Chinese cruise missiles.] *See also Senate Foreign Relations Committee, Near Eastern and South Asian Affairs Subcommittee, Hearing Regarding United States Policy Toward Iran, Witnesses: Panel I: Martin Indyk, Ass. Sec. Of State for Near Eastern Affairs, Panel II: Richard Murphy, Senior Fellow, Council on Foreign Relations, Michael Eisenstadt, Senior Fellow, Washington Institute for Near East Policy, Chaired by Sen. Brownback (R-KS),* FED. NEWS SERVICE, May 14, 1998. "The Iranian regime still seeks to protect its regional influence through a conventional military buildup and through the development of weapons of mass destruction and advanced missile systems. Iran continues to pursue nuclear technologies, chemical and biological weapons components, and production materials." *Id.*

When formulating courses of action, operation planning should address the possibility that an enemy will use WMD. Planning should also evaluate nuclear, biological and chemical (NBC) defensive measures. Joint Pub 3-11, "Joint Doctrine for Nuclear, Biological and Chemical (NBC) Defense," and the appropriate Joint Pub 3-01 series provide additional guidance. In theater, the combatant commander must consider the enemy's NBC weapon and delivery system capability when considering courses of action. If the enemy threat capability assessment indicates an NBC potential, the campaign plan should address active and passive defense measures necessary to counter the potential use of such weapons and provide for guidance in defending against such a threat.[74]

Chemical and Biological Weapons in the World's Hot Spots

The U.S. Government's 1993 study of risk factors inherent in proliferation of weapons of mass destruction emphasized that the proliferation that has occurred to date has largely been in hot spots of the world, major trip wire points such as the Koreas, India–Pakistan, and the Middle East, exacerbating the risks.[75]

A further risk factor as to the use of nuclear weapons is the interconnectedness of States, whereby even a State that might appear to be a safe target for nuclear weapons—*e.g.*, a Libya because of a problem like the threatening underground chemical weapons program at Tarhunah which might be taken out by a preemptive nuclear strike —may be allied by treaty, national, geographic or religious affiliation with other States having access to weapons of mass destruction.

The risks factors are exacerbated because weapons of mass destruction "will be weapons of the weak—states or groups that militarily are at best second-class."[76] Chemical and biological weapons attacks are anticipated as an asymmetrical attack, whereby a small enemy would use such a device to react to "overwhelming U.S. conventional dominance."[77]

The materially weakened Russia also raises the risk levels as to the use of weapons of mass destruction. So recently the world's major military power essentially co-equal with the United States and having

---

[74] DOCTRINE FOR JOINT THEATER NUCLEAR OPERATIONS, *supra* note 1, at III-8 (emphasis omitted).

[75] *See Proliferation of Weapons of Mass Destruction: Assessing the Risks*, *supra* note 1, at 66.

[76] Betts, *supra* note 9.

[77] THE QUADRENNIAL DEFENSE REVIEW, *supra* note 21, at § III 6–7.

the world's most substantial conventional weapons capability, Russia in a few short decades has become a secondary military power dependant on nuclear weapons for its defense and other projections of military power.[78]

Nuclear Deterrence as against Chemical and Biological Weapons

While there has been debate as to the wisdom of using the threatened use of nuclear weapons to deter the use of chemical or biological weapons,[79] it appears that, at least implicitly and at times overtly, the United States has embraced such deterrence[80]—and indeed

---

[78] *See supra* Chapter 18, note 58 and accompanying text.

[79] Thomas Graham, the U.S. special representative for arms control, nonproliferation and disarmament from 1994–97, has expressed the view that "the United States should ... maintain the longstanding firebreak between nuclear weapons and chemical and biological weapons" and hence should not employ nuclear deterrence against chemical and biological weapons. Graham, *supra* note 52. *See also* Betts, *supra* note 9. ("[D]eterrence now covers fewer of the threats the United States faces than it did during the Cold War. *** deterrence is clearest when the issue is preventing unprovoked and unambiguous aggression .... Deterrence is less reliable when both sides in a conflict see the other as the aggressor.... Such situations are ripe for miscalculation.") *Id.*

[80] *See* John Diamond, *U.S. May Use Nuclear Arms Against Chemicals: Rogue States Pose a Growing Threat,* THE RECORD (Bergen County, N.J.), Dec. 8, 1997, at A08, quoting John Pike of the Federation of American Scientists.

Note that this policy ostensibly violates the United States' pledge, made by the Carter Administration in 1978 at the first U.N. Special Session on Disarmament, not to use or threaten to use a nuclear weapon against a non-nuclear weapon State or its allies, if that State was a party to the Non Proliferation Treaty ("NPT"). *See* Graham, *supra* note 52. The pledge contained no reservation for use or threatened use of nuclear weapons against chemical or biological weapons threats or use. *See id.* Many states joined the NPT immediately after the United States made this pledge. Repudiation by the United States of this pledge could trigger further nuclear proliferation. *See id.*

The United States, along with Britain, China, Russia, and France repeated this pledge in 1995. *See* Diamond, *supra.*

Just two months after the Clinton Administration reaffirmed this pledge in 1995, a STRATCOM advisory group subcommittee issued its review "Essentials of Post–Cold War Deterrence" criticizing the Presidential policy and warning that U.S. deterrence has to be directed against threats of use of chemical and biological as well as nuclear weapons, and then, in February 1996, the Joint Chiefs of Staff issued JOINT PUB. 3-12.1, DOCTRINE FOR JOINT THEATER NUCLEAR OPERATIONS, implementing this policy operationally by directing that the targets of deterrence were to be short-, medium-, and

that the practice of such a policy is fostered by the United States' agreement not to use or possess chemical or biological weapons.[81]

It seems clear that, at the operational level, the U.S. military contemplates the potential use of nuclear weapons in response to chemical or biological attack. The Joint Chiefs of Staff, in their 1995 *Doctrine for Joint Nuclear Operations* manual, stated that nuclear weapons are designed "to deter the use of weapons of mass destruction (WMD), particularly nuclear weapons, and to serve as a hedge against the emergence of an overwhelming conventional threat."[82] Further, "US nuclear forces serve to deter the use of WMD across the spectrum of potential conflict. From a massive exchange of nuclear weapons to limited use on a regional battlefield, US nuclear capabilities must confront an enemy with risks of unacceptable damage and disproportionate loss should the enemy choose to introduce WMD in a conflict."[83]

---

intermediate-range missiles capable of carrying nuclear, biological, or chemical weapons. *See* Hans Kristensen, *Targets of Opportunity: How Nuclear Planners Found New Targets for Old Weapons*, BULL. OF ATOMIC SCIENTISTS, vol.55, no. 5, Sep./Oct. 1997 (citing U.S. Strategic Command, *Essentials of Post–Cold War Deterrence,* [n.d., probably April 1995], at 3, 4 (partly declassified and released under the Freedom of Information Act); U.S. Strategic Command, *Minutes of the Fifty-Third United States Strategic Command Strategic Advisory Group Meeting (U), 2–21 April 1995, Offutt afb, Nebraska,* Secret/noforn/nd. July 21, 1995, at 4, 15 (partly declassified and released under the Freedom of Information Act); JOINT CHIEFS OF STAFF, DOCTRINE FOR JOINT NUCLEAR OPERATIONS, *supra* note 58).

[81] *See* Betts, *supra* note 9.

[82] DOCTRINE FOR JOINT NUCLEAR OPERATIONS, *supra* note 58, at I-1.

[83] *Id.*

It appears that, with the end of the Cold War, the military focused on the application of nuclear weapons to the mission of "counterproliferation" of weapons of mass destruction, including chemical and biological weapons, and on the continued integration of nuclear forces with conventional ones, as reflected in JOINT PUB 3-12, DOCTRINE FOR JOINT NUCLEAR OPERATIONS and JOINT PUB 3-12.1, DOCTRINE FOR JOINT THEATER NUCLEAR OPERATIONS.

Following the 1989 reduction of the SIOP target base from 10,000 to around 2,500 in 1989, *see* Kristensen, *supra* note 80, the Joint Chief's "Military Net Assessment" in March 1990 cited "increasingly capable Third World Threats" to justify additional targeting of nuclear weapons. *Id.* In June 1990, appearing before the Senate Appropriations Committee, Defense Secretary Dick Cheney testified that the proliferation of weapons of mass destruction was a rationale for keeping U.S. nuclear weapons. *Id.*

Following the Gulf War and the disclosure of Iraq's nuclear weapons program, Secretary Cheney reportedly issued a classified "Nuclear Weapons

As noted above in the discussion of the ICJ decision in the 1996 ICJ Nuclear Weapons case, Judge Schwebel, the U.S. judge on the ICJ, in his dissent, presented in detail reports that, in advance of the Desert Storm operation against Iraq for its attack on Kuwait, the United States threatened Iraq that, if it used chemical or biological weapons, the United States would retaliate with nuclear weapons.[84]

A similar threat was made during the Clinton Administration:

> The Joint Chief of Staff in 1993 during the Clinton Administration asserted a willingness to use nuclear weapons in response to attacks of weapons of mass destruction. This willingness to use nuclear endangerment in response to the chemical threat has been characterized as the White House "bowing to strategies already set by the military ... 'the colonels and lieutenant colonels figured out what they wanted to do, and you've just got the White House catching up with that.'"[85]

Employment Policy" directing the military to plan nuclear operations against potential proliferators. *Id* (citing William M. Arkin, *Agnosticism When Real Values are Needed: Nuclear Policy in the Clinton Administration*, FEDERATION OF AM. SCIENTISTS PUB. INTEREST REPORT, Sept./Oct. 1994, at 7). By 1991, the "Joint Military Net Assessment' reportedly suggested that non-strategic nuclear weapons "could assume a broader role globally in response to the proliferation of nuclear capability among Third World nations." *Id.*

Then, in 1993, General George Butler told *The New York Times* that "our focus now is not just the former Soviet Union, but any potentially hostile country that has or is seeking weapons of mass destruction." *Id.*

With the less centralized threat, the military began to foster the more spontaneous, less pre-planned use of nuclear weapons: "General Butler described the new concept in a May 11, 1993 interview with Jane's Defence Weekly: 'Adaptive planning' was designed to respond to 'spontaneous threats which are more likely to emerge in a new international environment unconstrained by the Super Power stand-off.' The plans would use 'generic targets, rather than identifying specific scenarios and specific enemies.' Adaptive planning would offer 'unique solutions, tailored to generic regional dangers involving weapons of mass destruction.'" *Id.* (quoting General George Butler). *See discussion supra* Chapter 17, notes 19–21 and accompanying text.

[84] *See* Chapter 3, notes 151–153 and accompanying text. *See also* Nuclear Weapons Advisory Opinion, at 35–36; dissenting opinion of Judge Schwebel at 3, 12, 35 I.L.M 842.

[85] Diamond, *supra* note 80, quoting John Pike of the Federation of American Scientists.

Prior Use of Chemical Weapons as a Risk Factor

Chemical weapons have been used extensively,[86] exacerbating the risks of future use. The taboo that exists as to nuclear weapons does not exist as to them.

Examples include extensive use by seven countries including Germany and England during World War I,[87] use by Italy in Ethiopia in 1935,[88] by the Soviet Union against internal rebels throughout its history,[89] by Japan against China just prior to World War II,[90] by the United Arab Republic in the Yemen Civil War,[91] by the United States

---

[86] *See, e.g.,* 1997 COUNTERPROLIFERATION PROGRAM REVIEW COMMITTEE ANNUAL REPORT, *supra* note 57.

[87] *See* Merkin, *supra* note 9, quoting Kaplow, *Long Arms and Chemical Arms: Extraterritoriality and the Draft Chemical Weapons Convention,* 15 YALE J. INT'L L. 1, 8 (1990). "During World War I '[s]even different countries used a total of 113,000 tons of [chemical weapons] between 1915 and 1918, on virtually all fronts of the war, producing some 1.3 million casualties, including almost 100,000 deaths' *** chemical weapons had become an omnipotent weapon—much like nuclear weapons today." *Id.*

The United States harbored chemical weapons in World War II professedly for potential retaliation in kind, if necessary. However, stemming from this practice, "[o]ver 600 military casualties and an unknown number of civilian casualties resulted from the 1943 German bombing in Bari Harbor, Italy, of the John Harvey, an American ship loaded with two thousand 1200-pound mustard bombs." *See* Chemical Weapons, United States, *supra* note 9.

[88] *See* Merkin, *supra* note 9, at 181. Italy reportedly used some 700 tons of chemical weapons in its invasions of Ethiopia in 1935, causing some 15,000 casualties. *See id.*

[89] *See id.* at 181, citing Note, *Establishing Violations of International Law: "Yellow Rain" and the Treaties Regulating Chemical and Biological Warfare,* 35 STAN. L. REV. 259, 264 (1983).

In 1989, a Georgian nationalist demonstration was reportedly put down with the use of chemical weapons. *See id.* at 182, citing *Party Chief in Soviet Georgia Admits Some Died From Gas,* THE NEW YORK TIMES, Apr. 25, 1989, at A8. The Soviet Union admitted to use of a form of tear gas. *See* Merkin, *supra* note 9, at 182. American doctors also found traces of chloropicrin, a gas used in WW I. *See id.* 182. Tear gas is arguably unlawful under the English translations of the Geneva Protocol banning asphyxiating and poisonous gases but certainly unlawful under the French translation outlawing "toxic gases." *Id.* 182–183, 179–180. Other accusations were made of Soviet use of chemical weapons, including of "yellow rain" in satellite nations against rebels, but apparently were never proven. *See id.* at 181, 182.

[90] *See* Chemical Weapons, United States, *supra* note 9.

[91] *See* Merkin, *supra* note 9, at 183.

in Viet Nam,[92] by Iran and Iraq in the Iran–Iraq War starting in 1980,[93] by Iraq on internal dissidents after the Iran–Iraq War,[94] and by the Aum Shinrikyo terrorist group in its sarin nerve gas attack on a Japanese subway in 1995.[95] Biological weapons were reportedly used by Japan against China in World War II.[96]

The United Arab Republic was accused of use of chemical weapons in the Yemen Civil War, with reports first surfacing in 1963, and The International Committee of the Red Cross in fact found evidence of use of chemical weapons. *See id.* at 183–84, citing Note, *Chemical and Biological Weapons— Recent Legal Developments May Prove to be a Turning Point in Arms Control,* 12 BROOK. J. INT'L LAW 95, 102 (1986).

[92] *See id.* at 183. The United States used irritants and defoliants in the Vietnam War. *See id.* While the United Nations General Assembly condemned this use as "prohibited," the United States disputed the illegality. Issues were raised as to the different language of the English and French versions of the 1925 Protocol. *See id.* at 183 The United States did not feel it was restrained from use of such weapons. *See id.* at 183

[93] *See id.* at 184. "Iran used chemical weapons during the 1980–1988 war with Iran, resulting in some 50,000 Iranian casualties, with Iran belatedly retaliating in kind." *Proliferation of Weapons of Mass Destruction: Assessing the Risks, supra* note 1, at 10. U.N. inspectors subsequently generated voluminous reports confirming the "substantial uses of chemical arms," although Iran and Iraq denied any such use. *Id.* at 184.

[94] *See id.* at 185. Following the Iran–Iraq War, Iraqi forces reportedly continued to use the weapons against dissenters within its borders, particularly the Kurdish minority. *See also Proliferation of Weapons of Mass Destruction: Assessing the Risks, supra* note 1, at 10.

In July 1995, the Iraqi authorities admitted producing anthrax spores and botulinum toxin at Al Hakam in late 1990, but denied that the agents had been put into bombs or missile warheads. The United Nations razed the entire Al Hakam complex in June 1996. *See* Rohde, *supra* note 53. A United Nations team thereafter found fermentation, production, aerosol testing equipment and storage at the Salmon Pak site southeast of Baghdad, although it appeared that much equipment had been removed before the inspectors had arrived. *See id.*

[95] *See supra* note 42 and accompanying text.

[96] *See Proliferation of Weapons of Mass Destruction: Assessing the Risks, supra* note 1, at 58, 10 n.5, 60 n.23 (citing *Japan's Germ Warfare: The U.S. Cover-Up of a War Crime,* BULL. OF CONCERNED ASIAN SCHOLARS, vol. 12, Oct.–Dec 1980, at 2–17; John W. Powell, *A Hidden Chapter in History,* BULL. OF THE ATOMIC SCIENTISTS, vol. 37, No. 8, Oct. 1981, at 44–52; and PETER WILLIAMS & DAVID WALLACE, UNIT 73J: JAPAN'S SECRET BIOLOGICAL WARFARE IN WORLD WAR II (New York N.Y.: Free Press, 1989)). ("In World War II, Japan used biological agents including bubonic plague on an experimental basis in occupied China, reportedly killing some hundreds of Chinese civilians but also causing thousands of illnesses among its own troops.

Impact of Chem/Bio Illegality on Nuclear Weapons Use

By agreeing to the bans on chemical and biological weapons, the United States put itself in the position where nuclear weapons are the only weapons of mass destruction it can threaten or ostensibly use to counter other States' use of chemical and biological weapons, thereby lowering the threshold for use of nuclear weapons, a lowering whose riskiness is heightened by the widespread and ongoing proliferation of chemical and biological weapons and the nature of some of the States possessing such weapons.

By espousing the lawfulness of nuclear weapons, the United States further fosters the overall legitimacy and validity of the use of weapons of mass destruction, thereby lowering the threshold for use and increasing the likelihood of further proliferation of all such weapons.[97]

While, as discussed earlier, the United States ostensibly has a conventional weapons capability sufficient to address virtually all military challenges it faces, the combination of ongoing legitimization and proliferation of weapons of mass destruction in the world's hotspots obviously raises many risk factors.

Biological weapons were not used in any other theater of the war.") *Id.* at 10 n.5.

[97] Hans Kristensen has noted:

The expansion of the nuclear role was probably aided by the U.S. decision to eliminate its own chemical and biological weapons. In the cynical logic of deterrence, removing these weapons from the U.S. arsenal meant that if rogue nations were to use them, the United States no longer had a tit-for-tat response. The only "big stick" left in the U.S. arsenal—apart from overwhelming conventional superiority—was nuclear weapons.

Kristensen, *supra* note 80.

It has further been pointed out that the United States, by eliminating its own chemical and biological weapons "practically precludes a no-first-use policy for nuclear weapons, since they become the only WMD available for retaliation." Betts, *supra* note 9, at 26, 30, 31.

Chapter 28: The High Tech Conventional Weapons Alternative

Obviously, conventional weapons generally have much less destructive capability than nuclear weapons, by many orders of magnitude. Nonetheless, in achieving a particular mission, such lesser destructiveness can be compensated for in a number of ways, including by mere numbers of conventional weapons used, the accuracy with which such weapons are delivered, and the capabilities, particularly the modern computer-assisted capabilities, of the particular weapons. Recent decades have witnessed a sea change in the capabilities of conventional weapons, as well as in the international strategic environment, to the point that conventional weapons are now ostensibly sufficient not only to meet virtually all reasonably foreseeable military needs of the United States but also to deter virtually all reasonably deterrable threats the United States faces.

If the objective of a particular military strike is terror—as with the Cold War doctrine of mutual assured destruction (MAD)—then the more firepower the better and the precision of delivery does not necessarily make that much difference. If, however, the objective is the destruction of some particular target or targets, then there is a clear trade off between fire power and accuracy. With surgical precision of delivery, the level of firepower needed goes down exponentially. Hence the extent to which today's modern high tech conventional weapons (given a sufficient supply of them) literally remove virtually any need that ever existed for nuclear weapons.

The Allied carpet bombings of Germany and Japan, with their massive wind-driven fire storms enveloping entire square miles of the target cities, illustrated the extreme levels of destructiveness of which conventional weapons, used in volume, were capable, even as of the 1940's.[1] The Allied conventional bombing of Tokyo, involving the use

---

[1] SAMUEL B. PAYNE, THE CONDUCT OF WAR 8 (1989); ROBERT JAY LIFTON & GREG MITCHELL, HIROSHIMA IN AMERICA 35 (1995) ("Americans did not learn that as many as 100,000 had been killed in the March 9, 1945 firebombing of Tokyo until three weeks after Hiroshima, when a witness ... described the attack over ABC radio.").

A 1991 United Nations study of nuclear weapons highlighted the relationship of missile accuracy and the level of destructiveness needed for a particular mission:

   Missile accuracy is usually given in terms of the circular error
   probable (CEP), defined as the distance from an aiming point

of hundreds of bombers, wrought destruction comparable to that of the single atomic attack on Hiroshima.

While nuclear weapons obviated such extensive and drawn out conventional attacks upon Hiroshima and Nagasaki, today the technological revolution in conventional weaponry obviates the potential use of nuclear weapons, to the extent they are often unwanted even by the military.[2] Smart weapons, missiles and shells with computers in their noses, and cruise missiles guided by satellite oversight can now achieve missions that in the 1940's could be accomplished only by massive air superiority or nuclear weapons.[3]

---

within which, on the average, half the shots aimed at this point will fall. Using this concept, assessments of the efficiency of various missile systems can be illustrated. For example, a 1 Mt nuclear warhead may be needed in order to destroy a particular hardened structure if the CEP of that nuclear weapon is 1 km. The same effect could result from a 125 kt warhead with a 0.5 km CEP accuracy, or a 40 kt warhead with a 0.33 km CEP. Thus, increased accuracy meant that smaller yield warheads could replace high yield warheads as a threat to these types of targets.

UNITED NATIONS DEPARTMENT FOR DISARMAMENT AFFAIRS, NUCLEAR WEAPONS, A COMPREHENSIVE STUDY 30 (United Nations 1991).

[2] *See* Steven Lee Myers, *Pentagon Ready to Shrink Arsenal of Nuclear Bombs*, THE NEW YORK TIMES, Nov. 23, 1998, at A1.

[3] *See* Chris Bellamy, *Soviet Artillery and Missile Force Challenge*, INT'L DEF. REV., vol. 21, no. 4, Apr. 1, 1988, at 347.

Other nations have similarly developed modern computer based conventional weapons. As Sweden and Italy's navies have similar requirements, Italy's Alenia-Difeesa and Sweden's Saab Dynamics joined to develop maritime missiles with stealth capacity, radar seeker and imaging infrared guidance, and navigational computers. *See Missile Programs Pursue Collaboration*, INT'L DEFENSE DIGEST, vol. 31, no. 12, Nov. 28, 1998, at 5. These missiles may be used on sea, littoral, and land targets. *See id.*

On land, Israel has unveiled a long-range guided tank round, which can steer to its target after leaving the tank's barrel, also using imaging infrared guidance. *See LAHAT Long-Range Tank Rounds Unveiled*, INT'L DEFENSE REVIEW, vol. 31, no. 12, Nov. 28, 1998, at 17. The Israeli producer promotes the missile for use by the Egyptian and US Army tank fleets. *See id.*

In the air, the new laser guided bombs now can steer in towards targets, as can laser and imaging infrared missiles, and now there are even weapons guided by satellite communication. *See* Luca Peruzzi, *Italy's Avionics Plans For AMX*, JANE'S DEFENCE UPGRADES, vol. 2, no. 20, Oct. 16, 1998, at 6.

An example might be the use of a single laser-guided bomb to take out a bridge.[4] In 1944, in order to achieve such a mission, an overflight of many B-17 bombers dropping hundreds of bombs might have been needed. During the Cold War, an attack with tactical nuclear weapons might have been contemplated. During the Desert Storm operation, highly accurate conventional weapons were used. In the 1999 Kosovo conflict, "smart" computer driven conventional weapons dominated.

Newt Gingrich, in addressing the needlessness of resorting to nuclear weapons against Iraq in Desert Storm, noted that the modern conventional weapons of the United States military are good enough to defeat and deter any current and foreseeable enemy.[5] Gone are the days of a superior Soviet tank force, whose onslaught against Europe could only be stopped by tactical or strategic nuclear response.

Defense Secretary Cohen announced that the Clinton Administration inherited the defense posture which won the Cold War and Desert Storm and intended to leave a legacy of a "defense strategy, military forces and support structure" that meets the challenges of a new era.[6] Bringing business-style practices into the military, using monies saved by his Defense Reform initiatives and base closures, he would modernize and transform the United States' military capabilities.[7] Noting a coming "Revolution in Military Affairs,"[8] he sought a general strategy of preventative care, of engaging other nations in peacetime so they would friends and not enemies in the future.[9] This "revolution promises to enable our forces to attack enemy weaknesses directly and with great precision—and therefore fewer munitions, less logistics and less collateral damage."[10]

Emphasizing the modern capability of "precision engagement," Secretary Cohen stated:

---

[4] *See* Bellamy, *supra* note 3. Even as of 1988, such a mission could be carried out by a "single" smart missile (with a computer in its nose) launched from a helicopter, flying into its target with laser guidance. *Id.* A computer sits in the nose of this expensive missile.

[5] *See* McGeorge Bundy, *Nuclear Weapons and the Gulf*, FOREIGN AFF., Fall 1991, at 83, 85–86.

[6] *Prepared Statement of Secretary of Defense William S. Cohen to the Senate Armed Forces Committee, Feb. 3, 1998; New Defense Strategy: Shape, Respond, Prepare*, DEFENSE ISSUES, vol. 13, no. 13, <http://www.defenselink.mil/speeches/1998/t19980203-secdef.html>.

[7] *See id.*

[8] *Id.*

[9] *See id.*

[10] *Id.*

The precision engagement concept transcends the notion of firepower. It encompasses achieving precise effects in cyberspace, as well as accurate and timely deliveries of humanitarian relief supplies or medical treatment to population, and directed psychological operations for greatest influences. Precise, nonlethal weapons are currently under development for use in operations in which an important goal is to minimize fatalities and collateral damage. Precision engagement enables joint force commanders to develop revolutionary strategies, operational ideas, and schemes of maneuver. Working together, the Services and DoD combat support agencies are striving to increase battlespace situational awareness and the effectiveness of precision munitions and to ensure that equipment provided to U.S. forces is fully integrated into the advanced systems that support precision engagement.[11]

For decades, numerous types of conventional weapons have had destructive power comparable to the direct effects of small yield (two to three kiloton) tactical nuclear weapons.[12] Developments in microelectronics and computers for communications, command, control and intelligence, defense suppression and precision guidance—many of them showcased for the first time in the Desert Storm operation, in the second Gulf War starting in 1998, and in the Kosovo operation in 1999—have created what is widely regarded as a "revolutionary new military technology" affording a "force multiplier" enhancing the efficacy of conventional forces.

In 1991 William Perry, soon to become U.S. Secretary of Defense, stated:

> This new conventional military capability adds a powerful dimension to the ability of the United States to deter war ... It should also strengthen the already high level of deterrence of a major war in Europe or Korea. The United States can now be confident that the defeat of a conventional armored assault in those regions could be achieved by conventional military forces, which

---

[11] WILLIAM S. COHEN, 1999 ANNUAL REPORT TO THE PRESIDENT AND THE CONGRESS Chap. 10, p. 5, The Revolution in Military Affairs, and Joint Vision 2010, *as set forth at* <http://www.dtic.mil/execsec/adr1999/>.

[12] *See* Senator Sam S. Nunn, *NATO: Can the Alliance Be Saved?, in* U S SENATE, REPORT OF THE COMMITTEE ON ARMED SERVICES 16 (Washington: Government Printing Office, 1982); Michael Klare, *Near-Nukes: the Conventional Weapons Fallacy,* NATION, 9 Apr. 1983, at 438; Michael Klare, *NATO's Improved Conventional Weapons,* TECH. REV., vol. 88, no 4, May/June 1985, at 34.

could enable the United States to limit the role of its nuclear forces to the deterrence of nuclear attack.[13]

Eliot Cohen has written:

> In the view of some, [the Persian Gulf War] represented the opening shot of a fundamental transformation in the nature of warfare, a "military-technical revolution" as the Russians have termed it for more than a decade. Thus the Russian military sadly read the outcome of a war that vindicated their predictions even as it sealed their profound sense of inferiority vis-a-vis the United States. Secretary of Defense Richard Cheney agreed: "This war demonstrated dramatically the new possibilities of what has been called the 'military-technological revolution in warfare.'" Others, outside the Bush administration, expressed this view no less enthusiastically.[14]

Further examples of modern technological breakthroughs in weaponry are Advanced Imaging Infra Red (IIR) and laser sensor en-route navigational and terminal guidance systems.[15] Such systems—given the trade-off between accuracy and destructiveness—enable conventional weapons, with their far smaller yields, to be placed so precisely as to accomplish the same types of task as only the large blasts of a nuclear weapon or of a large number of conventional weapons could formerly have accomplished.

The Hellfire missile, for example, incorporates a laser seeker, and may be fired from helicopters or airplanes.[16] Another example is the radar seeker weapon Hughes Inc. was reportedly developing in the early 1990s that would allow a missile to find high value targets after being launched to a specified position and heading.[17] Such technology,

---

[13] William J. Perry, *Desert Storm and Deterrence*, FOREIGN AFF., vol. 70 no. 4, Fall 1991, at 66 (reviewing the revolutionary effectiveness of these advancements in the Gulf War, contributing to extraordinary low level of coalition losses, roughly a thousand to one, *id.* at 67).

[14] Elliot A. Cohen, *The Mystique of U.S. Air Power*, FOREIGN AFF., January/February 1994, at 109–110. Later reports have called into question whether the results in the Gulf War of the use of the high-tech weapons were as revolutionary as they at first seemed. *See infra* note 69 and accompanying text. Whether the initial characterizations were exaggerated or not, the fundamental reality that conventional weapons have greatly increased in effectiveness is beyond question.

[15] *ASMs Increased Accuracy at Lower Cost*, INT'L DEFENSE REVIEW, vol. 23, no. 11, Nov. 1, 1990.

[16] *See ASMs Increased Accuracy, supra* note 15.

[17] *See Bellamy, supra* note 3.

with enormous computing power packed into small spaces, typifies the new conventional weaponry.[18]

Modernization efforts of recent times have also included such extraordinary conventional weapons as the Army's Bradley fighting vehicle, Abram's tank, and Apache Longbow helicopter.[19]   These weapons, with the like of the Longbow's Hellfire self-guiding smart missiles, can perform pinpoint hits against hard targets, thereby creating the military results that once might have required a nuclear blast. Precision, again, is the word:

> The new budget supports the [Quadrennial Defense Reviews']
> emphasis on munitions of superior precision. Substantial funding
> is provided for ATACMS/BAT [Army Tactical Missile/Brilliant
> Anti-Armor], Longbow Hellfire [missile], SADARM [Sense and
> Destroy Armor artillery round] and Javelin for the Army; Sensor-
> Fuzed Weapon for the Air Force; and JSOW [Joint Standoff
> Weapon], JDAM [Joint Direct Attack Munition] and AMRAAM
> [Advanced Medium Range, Air-to-Air Missile] for both the Air
> Force and Navy. The Navy will continue to improve its inventory
> of Tomahawk missiles and convert anti-ship Harpoon missiles to
> SLAM–ER [Stand-Off Land Attack Missile–Expanded Response]
> land-attack missiles.[20]

Unmanned aerial vehicles also sharpen the conventional weapons arsenal, enabling over-the-horizon targeting.[21]   Datalinks become part of payloads, as computers link unmanned aerial vehicles to launchers and weapons.[22]   Battleship and unmanned aerial vehicle partnerships were active in the 1991 Gulf War, heightening the effectiveness of the conventional weapons used.[23]

Effectiveness increases as technology shrinks the CEP or Circular Error Probable, the circle in which the steered missile is likely to hit, while the area that a conventional weapon can devastate increases.[24]   A cruder launch system of enormous artillery also exists and is in development, with 203 millimeter shells being tested in the United States' SADARM (Search and Destroy Armor) program for firing off

---

[18] *See id.*

[19] *See id.*

[20] *Id.*

[21] *See* Rupert Pengelley, *Shipborne UAVs Await Take-Off,* JANE'S NAVY INT'L, vol. 103, no. 1, Jan. 1, 1998, at 37.

[22] *See id.*

[23] *See id.*

[24] Bellamy, *supra* note 3.

smart weapons, designed to be fired and then steered in flight.[25] Conventional missile development also includes work on shaped charges, penetration/blast fragmentation warheads, and selective fuzing capabilities such that the fuse goes off only after the projectile goes through a mass of earth and a selected number of concrete floors, to defeat target hardening.[26]

Even during the Cold War, the increasing sophistication, accuracy and lethality of non-nuclear arms led the Union of Concerned Scientists and the European Security Study to find that improved conventional weapons were a credible substitute for nuclear forces in many situations.[27] West German Defense Minister Manfred Woerner and U.S. Senator Sam Nunn reached similar conclusions.[28] Deep-strike, "near-nuclear" conventional offensive weapons deployed on the Lance, Pershing II, Tomahawk and Trident missiles were seen as approximating "the destructive potential of the smallest nuclear weapons in the one-to-three kiloton range:"[29]

> The conventional Tomahawks used in the Gulf War against Iraqi "hard targets" were the BM-109C, a land attack version (LAM-C) armed with a 1,000 lb. conventional warhead. Over 240 of these 700-mile range weapons were fired during the Gulf War, often in multiples of two or three at a target to assure destruction. These missiles were credited with successfully attacking the Iraqi presidential palace, ministry of defense and a central communications center in Baghdad.[30]

---

[25] *See id.* The army contracted for the production of 600 155mm SADARM projectiles in 1997, a low rate of production, to be completed by Jan 31, 1998. Contract No. 054-97, News Release, Office of Assistant Secretary of Defense, Feb. 4, 1997.

[26] *See ASMs Increased Accuracy, supra* note 15.

[27] *See* Michael Klare, *NATO's Improved Conventional Weapons*, TECH. REV., vol. 88, no 4, May/June 1985, at 34.

[28] *See id.*

[29] *Id.*

[30] Stanley Kandebo, *Operation Desert Storm—Tomahawk Missiles Excel in First Wartime Use*, AVIATION WEEK & TECH., Jan. 21, 1991, vol. 134, no. 3, at 61. The range of strategic targets hit in Iraq during the Gulf War included command, control and communication facilities (C3), electrical facilities (ELE), ground forces (GOB), government centers (GVC), lines of communication (LOC), military industrial base facilities (MIB), naval facilities (NAV), nuclear, biological and chemical facilities (NBC), offensive counterair installations (OCA), oil refining, storage, and distribution facilities (OIL), surface-to-air missile installations (SAM) and Scud missile facilities (SCU).

In 1984, Marshall Ogarkov of the former USSR said that "Highly accurate, terminally guided weapon systems, unmanned aircraft and ... new electronic control systems ... make it possible to increase sharply (by at least an order of magnitude) the destructive power of conventional weapons, bringing them closer to weapons of mass destruction in terms of effectiveness."[31]

The United States and the Soviets had also created advanced fuel air explosives capable of creating an aerosol cloud spread over a large area, followed by a blast. Peak over-pressure figures for the fuel air blasts compare in military significance to those of a "miniature nuclear 'fireball:'"[32]

> With current technology, the peak overpressure (i. e. , over and above atmospheric pressure) of a 500kg methane-based FAE detonation is 0.9kp/cm2, 100m from the edge of the aerosol cloud. At just under 200m, over-pressures of 0.42kp/cm2 are achieved. In the context of a nuclear explosion, over-pressures of 0.366kp/cm2 are considered "severe blast" and 0.19kp/cm2, "moderate blast." These figures indicate that FAEs are clearly comparable with nuclear weapons in their ability to create militarily significant blast effects well outside the aerosol cloud, which could be equated to a miniature nuclear "fireball." Further in, the overpressures are very much greater: the American 225kg CBU-55 FAE (a 1960s-vintage weapon) can create an over-pressure of nearly 29kp/cm2, at a distance of 15m from the detonation point. This level of over-pressure is capable of demolishing reinforced concrete structures.
>
> Open source material in the mid-1970s showed that the Soviet scientists S.M. Kogarko and others were working on second generation, methane-based FAEs. Their results indicated that the Soviets were not yet achieving the same degree of effectiveness as the American, but also showed that the full potential of a developed FAE was well understood. Perhaps this is what Marshall Ogarkov was referring to when he talked of increases in lethality "of an order of magnitude," which corresponds exactly with the predicted ten-fold increase in efficiency of FAEs over TNT. This would make large FAE warheads equivalent to small sub-kiloton nuclear warheads. The immense destructive force and visual impact of a

---

Twelve Strategic Target Categories in the Desert Storm Air Campaign, United States General Accounting Office, Report to Congress: Operation Desert Storm: Evaluation of the Air War at 17 (July 1996).

In all, 862 strategic targets were compiled in the U.S. Air Force's missions database, including the Iraqi Air Force headquarters in Baghdad. *See id.*

[31] Bellamy, *supra* note 3.

[32] *Id.*

large FAE explosion might create a traumatic psychological effect close to that of a real nuclear weapon. This brings an attendant risk that FAEs may be mistaken for nuclear weapons by the enemy, who then responds with his nuclear systems. However, FAEs are available now for [improved conventional missile] use, whereas terminal guidance is still under development."[33]

The Desert Storm operation provides a contemporary example of the efficacy of conventional weapons, both in volume and accuracy.[34] The U.S. air campaign involved 40,000 air-to-ground and 50,000 support sorties, dropping every day, often with very high hit rates, the equivalent of 85% of the average daily bombs dropped by the U.S. on Germany and Japan in World War II.[35] With the BG-109 Tomahawk cruise missile, for example, average success rates of some 82% were reached, rates higher than that for the United States' most advanced fighters.[36]

While smart weapons debuted in the last days of the Vietnam War,[37] and great advances have been made, this technology is very much still unfolding. Less than 10% of the bombs dropped in the 1991 Operation Desert Storm bombing campaigns were smart weapons,[38] but by the time of the 1999 Kosovo operation, less than a decade later, smart weapons dominated.[39]

---

[33] *Id.*

[34] *See* UNITED STATES GENERAL ACCOUNTING OFFICE, REPORT TO CONGRESS: OPERATION DESERT STORM: EVALUATION OF THE AIR WAR (July 1996).

[35] *See id.* at 2. The U.S. relied heavily on a multi-tiered mix of high-technology, conventional air campaign systems, mixing conventional Tomahawk Land-Attack cruise missiles (TLAMs); high-payload heavy strategic bombers such as the B-52 and F-111F; stealth bombers capable of dropping laser-guided bombs, Maverick missiles and other precision guided munitions, such as the F-117A; and high-sortie attack fighters, such as F-15E, F-16, F/A-18, A-6E and A-10 attack fighters. *See id.* at 5–7. The 43-day air campaign by the United States and its allies against Iraq between January 17, 1991 and February 28, 1991 occupied 90% of the war; the main ground campaign occurred only during the final 100 hours of the war. *See id.*

[36] *See* David Fulghum, *Clashes with Iraq Continue After Heavy Air Strike*, AVIATION WEEK & SPACE TECH., Jan. 25, 1993, at 38.

[37] *See* David Learmount, *Smart Bombs in Demand,* FLIGHT INT'L, June 9, 1999.

[38] *See id.*

[39] *See id. See also* Paul Richter, *Crisis in Yugoslavia, Almost All U.S. Airstrikes Involve 'Smart' Bombs,* L.A. TIMES, Apr. 13, 1999, at A19. In pursuit of adequate stocks of smart weapons, the Air Force has contracted to

The 1999 NATO air strikes in the 1999 Kosovo operation particularly highlighted the revolutionary effectiveness of modern high technology conventional weapons.[40] High tech operations included 15 launches of a new launch-and-leave, air-to-air missile, 190 launches of Maverick air-to-ground missiles guided through infra red and laser systems with the aid of TV cameras on the missiles, 370 launches of HARM anti-radar missiles, along with the use of thousands of high tech guided gravity bombs.[41]   Some 3,585 laser guided bombs were dropped, along with 600 global positioning satellite guided bombs, the JDAM, and 8,860 unguided 500 lb. and 2000 lb. bombs.[42]

Among the most interesting new munitions used were the JDAMs, dropped by B-2 stealth bombers, billion dollar planes designed for radar penetration and nuclear war.[43] The JDAM, or Joint Direct Attack Munition, is a strap on guidance system attached to a gravity bomb. Capable of delivering its bomb within twenty feet of the target from 15 miles away through guidance from satellite global positioning technology,[44] the JDAM overcomes the susceptibility of laser guided systems to being diverted by smoke (often present in battle conditions) and by clouds in the sky.[45]

---

convert its remaining 325 older-style Air Launched Cruise Missiles (ALCMs) from nuclear to conventional payloads (CALCMs) but with global positioning technology. This interest arose as less than 100 CALCMs remained to launch from the Air Force's B-52s. *See* Learmount, *Smart Bombs in Demand, supra* note 37.

[40] *See, e.g.,* Rowan Scarborough, *What's Left After Kosovo,* WASH. TIMES, June 13, 1999, at C1.

[41] *See id.*

[42] *See id.*

[43] *See* James Wallace, *Boeing—Built System Used on Bombs in Yugoslavia,* SEATTLE POST-INTELLIGENCER, Mar. 27, 1999, at A5; Scarborough, *What's Left, supra* note 40, at C1.

[44] *See* Wallace, *Boeing—Built System, supra* note 43, at A5, Scarborough, *What's Left, supra* note 40, at C1.

[45] *See* Scarborough, *What's Left, supra* note 40, at C1. Laser-guided weapons are "'fair weather friends'," in the words of John Pike, military analyst at the Federation of American Scientists. Paul Richter, *Crisis in Yugoslavia, Almost All U.S. Airstrikes Involve 'Smart' Bombs,* LOS ANGELES TIMES, Apr. 13, 1999, at A19. "'This will be the last war, hopefully, that we will use laser guided rather [than] GPS-guided munitions,' Pike said." *U.S. Reliance on Precision-Guided Munitions Grows Dramatically,* AEROSPACE DAILY, Apr. 19, 1999. A highlight of the Belgrade precision bombing was the blasting of the Yugoslav security police bureau headquarters, while a hospital a block away was virtually untouched. *See* Richter, *supra* note 39, at A19.

The B-2s delivering the JDAMs to the area flew directly out of Whiteman AFB in Missouri, to the Balkans, and back again. "As of Mid-May [1999], six B-2 stealth bombers operation flew almost daily from Whiteman AFB, Missouri, dropping more than 454,000 kg of JDAMs on Serbian targets with no civilian casualties, according to USAF Brig Gen. Leroy Barnidge, commander of the 509th Bomber Wing."[46]

As discussed above, the United States in the Post Cold War era has recognized that a major impact of the technological revolution in the means of warfare is that conventional weapons are now sufficient to maintain deterrence. This point bears repeating, for it is quite startling in its contrast to the traditional Cold War thinking and perhaps correspondingly difficult to take seriously and integrate into our thinking: Modern conventional weapons are so accurate and powerful as to be able to threaten such a substantial and certain retaliation upon an enemy as to deter virtually any hostile action that is deterrable. If the threat of overwhelming retaliation is sufficient to deter an enemy, conventional weapons are sufficient to deliver that threat, and, indeed to deliver it more credibly, given the inherent restraints on the use of nuclear weapons.

In language noted earlier, the National Defense Panel made the point in its recent report:

> It is in the best interests of the United States, Russia, and the international community that the United States and Russia move as rapidly as possible to START II. We should also consider the potential of non-nuclear weapons to strengthen deterrence. Advancing military technologies that merge the capabilities of information systems with precision-guided weaponry and real-time targeting and other new weapons systems may provide a supplement or alternative to the nuclear arsenals of the Cold War.[47]

The satellite global position technology of JDAM is also cheaper than laser guidance, costing some $23,000 a kit, including production and support. *See* James Wallace, *Boeing Plans to Speed Up Production of Bomb Kits*, SEATTLE POST-INTELLIGENCER, Apr. 2, 1999, at A4. This compares favorably to the $50,000 price of the laser guided kits *See* Paul Richter, *Crisis in Yugoslavia, Almost All U.S. Airstrikes Involve 'Smart' Bombs*, L.A. TIMES, Apr. 13, 1999 at A19. The Airforce contracted to buy 62,000 JDAM kits from Boeing, and the Navy, 25,000. *See* Wallace, *Boeing-Built System, supra* note 43, at C1.

[46] David Learmount, *Smart Bombs in Demand, supra* note 37.

[47] NATIONAL DEFENSE PANEL, TRANSFORMING DEFENSE: NATIONAL SECURITY IN THE 21ST CENTURY 51 (Dec. 1997).

This reality, taken as true, implies an answer to the question of what difference it would make if the use of nuclear weapons were recognized as unlawful. So long as nuclear weapons are seen as a backup, there is no reason to spend the money to maintain an adequate arsenal of conventional weapons, even today's most modern high tech weapons. If, however, the unlawfulness of the use of nuclear weapons were recognized, the whole decision-making matrix as to contingency planning—and hence as to spending and training—changes.

If the legalities were then to be observed, an effort would have to be made to provide for adequate supplies of conventional weapons. "'Smart' munitions dropped from high altitudes with pinpoint accuracy offer a 'cheap,' antiseptic alternative to a prolonged and costly ground war...[reducing] the risk of casualties—both in terms of pilots and civilians on the ground"[48]—but only as long as supplies hold out.

Even in the relatively short Kosovo operation, under current supply policy, the United States quickly ran short in its supply of modern conventional weapons, including the JDAMS and Maverick cruise missiles,[49] nearly encountering a "winchester" situation, Air Force code language for being out of ammunition, and quickly had to step up Boeing's production schedule.[50] The Air Force experienced shortages of "stand-off" weapons, those fired from afar. "'Many of our air forces ... have to fly more or less over the target, which is the most stupid thing you can do because you expose yourself to the enemy's air defenses.'"[51]   Deficiencies in transport capability were also

---

[48] John D. Morrocco, *Kosovo Conflict Highlights Limits of Airpower and Capability Gaps*, AVIATION WEEK & SPACE TECH., May 17, 1999, at 31.

[49] *See* Bryan Bender, *JDAM Stocks Running Very Low, Says USA*, JANE'S DEFENCE WEEKLY, May 5, 1999. "Not surprisingly, the newest weapons were in short supply. The JDAM guided non-stand off weapon ran into this situation —"Gen. Hawley said USAF and US Navy aircraft participating in 'Allied Force' could expend JDAM stocks. 'We didn't have a robust inventory,' he said, because of the recent fielding of the Global Positioning System (GPS)-guided munition." *Id.*

"Obviously, development of high tech weapons continues apace. Networking between unmanned aerial vehicles and various munitions, for example, is being actively worked on, and so are their production runs and trial forays." Nick Cook, *Serb Air War Changes Gear*, JANE'S DEFENCE WEEKLY HEADLINES, Mar. 4, 1999.

[50] *JDAM Inventory 'Touch and Go' Over Kosovo*, ARMED FORCES NEWS, Apr. 30, 1999. *See also* Bender, *JDAM Stocks, supra* note 49.

[51] Morrocco, *supra* note 48, at 31 (citing Gen. Klaus Naumann of Germany, the head of NATO Military Committee for three years up to 1999).

experienced. Forces bearing the smart weapons deployed "'deplorably'"[52] slowly in transporting Army helicopters into service from other sites in Europe.

Limits on the Capabilities of Conventional Weapons

The question remains: Are there some military jobs for which only nuclear weapons could be used, objectives which could not be achieved without the use of nuclear weapons?

One possible area of such need has been "superhardened" or "hard" targets. Many of the prime military facilities of the superpowers, including nuclear, biological and chemical ("NBC") production and storage facilities, airbuses, missile bases and major command and control centers, are buried in super hardened underground shelters or protected by steel and concrete hangars.[53]

Some non-nuclear powers also possess such hardened facilities, some of which may pose challenges to conventional air attack.[54] A prime example is the Libyan chemical weapons production facility in Tarhunah,[55] buried deep into a mountain and covered by 100 feet of sandstone and reinforced concrete.[56]

---

[52] *Id.* (citing Gen. Klaus Naumann).

[53] *See* Clifford Beal, Mark Hewish & Leland Ness, *Hard Target Attack: Forging a Better Hammer*, INT'L DEFENSE REV., July 1996, at 32.

[54] *See id.*

[55] *See id.*

[56] *See id.* at 32; Robert Waller, *Libyan Chemical Warfare Raises the Issue of Pre-emption*, JANE'S INTELLIGENCE REV., November 1, 1996. North Korea has been suspected of constructing nuclear weapons in such underground tunnels. *See* Dr. Joshua Sinai, *Ghadaffi's Libya: The Patient Proliferator*, JANE'S INTELLIGENCE REV., vol. 10, no. 12, Dec. 1, 1998, at 27.

Former U.S. Central Intelligence Agency director John Deutch called Tarhunah the world's largest underground chemical weapons plant. Reportedly, Tarhunah already stores most of Libya's 100-ton stockpile of poison gas weapons previously produced at Rabta and, once operational, it is expected to produce the ingredients for an estimated 2,500 tons of poison agents each year. *See id.* U.S. suspicions about the Tarhunah and Rabta facilities contributed to the United States' remaining at a stand-off with Libya when the United Nations lifted their sanctions on Libya in April 1999:

Washington suspects Libya is trying to develop chemical and biological weapons and questions its claim that a huge underground facility in Tarhunah, 40 miles south of Tripoli, is part of the nation's irrigation system.

"As far as we are concerned, we are maintaining our sanctions against Libya, and we are still concerned with weapons of mass

Starting in April 1996, Secretary of Defense William Perry and thereafter numerous other senior U.S. officials announced that the United States would not permit Tarhunah to open and refused to rule out a U.S. preemptive nuclear attack on the facility.[57] U.S. officials noted that a relatively low-yield nuclear warhead, such as the B-61, could be used to destroy the plant.[58]

There was considerable discussion, over a period of months, in the U.S. civilian and military leadership as to whether Tarhunah was vulnerable to conventional attack.[59] The U.S. threats of possible nuclear preemption were controversial for many reasons, including an apparent U.S. policy against nuclear preemption,[60] the sense of the portentousness of crossing the nuclear threshold,[61] the inconsistency of

---

destruction," a State Department official said. "We are sticking to our policies, sticking to a tough line. What other countries do is their business."

Richard Engel, *Libya Re-Engages After Seven Years of U.N. Sanctions*, THE WASH. TIMES, Apr. 22, 1999.

Libya has contended that the facility at Rabta is a pharmaceutical plant and that the one at Tarhunah is part of the country's Great Man-Made River irrigation project. *See* Gregory Koblenz, *Countering Dual-Use Facilities: Lessons from Iraq and Sudan*, JANE'S INTELLIGENCE REV., Mar.1, 1999, at 48 (citing JIR, December 1998, 27–30).

[57] *See* Waller, *supra* note 56, at 526; Micheal Klare, *Nuking Libya: U.S. Consider Preemptive Nuclear Strike against Libya*, THE NATION, vol. 263, No. 2, July 8, 1996, at 5–6:

For the first time in many years, Pentagon officials are talking openly about using nuclear weapons in a pre-emptive strike against a nonnuclear power. The intended target is Libya, which is reported by U.S. intelligence to be completing work on an underground chemical weapons production facility at Tarhunah, some forty miles south of Tripoli. Defense Secretary William declared in early April that the United States will not allow Libya to open the plant, and Assistant Secretary of Defense Kenneth Bacon said later that month that the United States was considering a number of options for destroying the chemical weapons plant, including the use of nuclear weapons.

Id.

[58] *See* Waller, *supra* note 56, at 560.

[59] *See id.*

[60] *See id.* at 522.

[61] *See id.* at 560. *See also* discussion *supra* Chapter 16, note 38 and accompanying text.

such use with the United States' stated counter-proliferation policy,[62] the sense that use of nuclear weapons would be very unpopular internationally,[63] U.S. pledges not to use nuclear forces against an African State except to respond to a NBC attack,[64] and legal issues including concerns as to proportionality.[65]

Ultimately, the United States withdrew the threat of use of nuclear weapons against the facility,[66] with assurances from some officials, including General Shalikashvili, Chairman of the Joint Chief of Staff, that the United States has the capability with conventional weapons to destroy the facility.[67]

Whether such targets are in fact subject to conventional bombing today, the development of such a capability seems on the horizon.[68]

---

[62] *See id.* at 522 (quoting Assistant Secretary of Defense Ashton Carter, "Our counter-proliferation capabilities are being devised for winning MRCs [major regional conflicts], not for pre-emptive attack on proliferators.").

As noted above, the Nuclear Posture Review concluded that "proliferation of nuclear weapons and other weapons of mass destruction [to rogue Third World nations], rather than the nuclear arsenal of a hostile superpower, poses the greatest security risk" to the United States. WILLIAM J. PERRY, SECRETARY OF DEFENSE, 1995 ANNUAL REPORT TO THE PRESIDENT AND THE CONGRESS 85 (U.S. Government Printing Office 1995). *See generally* WILLIAM J. PERRY, SECRETARY OF DEFENSE, 1996 ANNUAL REPORT TO THE PRESIDENT AND THE CONGRESS 11 (U.S. Government Printing Office).

In June 1993, the U.S. Department of Defense outlined a new policy, the "Counter-proliferation Initiative" (CPI), to prevent, deter and prepare U.S. forces for the spread and potential use of nuclear, biological and chemical (NBC) weapons by Third World adversaries. Waller, *supra* note 56, at 522.

[63] *See id.*

[64] *See id.* at 560. Similar pledges have been made with respect to other potential target areas. *See supra* Chapter 3, notes 27–28 and accompanying text.

[65] *See id.* at 523.

[66] *See id.*

[67] *See id.* at 522–23.

[68] *See id.* at 561; Beal et al., *supra* note 53. *See also Use of Nuclear Arms Still Viable in Some Cases, Says US Agency*, JANE'S DEFENCE WEEKLY, vol. 28, no. 8, Aug. 27, 1997, at 3.

While "it may be several years before the United States has conventional ordnance capable of destroying Tarhunah in a single air strike," the military is highly confident Tarhunah can be destroyed by conventional weapons in the near future. Waller, *supra* note 56, at 529, 561.

Focusing on such underground targets, the U.S. Department of Defense's Defense Special Weapons Agency (DSWA) in 1997 publicly advertised that it considered nuclear weapons as still a viable option for attacking certain high

The Pentagon, the U.S. Congress and the U.S. military services have made this a major objective and have focused initiatives underway to achieve it.[69] Similar efforts have been underway in Great Britain and France.[70]

---

value targets. Publishing a request for proposals seeking a comprehensive automated target-planning process to potentially use nuclear and conventional weapons to attack deep underground tunnels, the DSWA detailed a plan to also use advanced weapons including new high explosives and novel incendiaries. *See Use of Nuclear Arms Still Viable in Some Cases, Says US Agency*, JANE'S DEFENCE WEEKLY, vol. 28, no. 8, Aug. 27, 1997, at 3. The B-61 (Mod 11) is reportedly the newest nuclear munition in the US inventory designed for attacking deep targets.

[69] During the 1990–91 Gulf War, the "allied air offensive eliminated fewer hardened targets than initially thought." Waller, *supra* note 56, at 529. After the war, the U.S. Air Force began a crash program to develop a new deep-penetrating bomb to attack deeply buried, super hardened Iraqi command and control bases with non-nuclear warheads, resulting in the GBU-28/B which incorporates a reworked artillery barrel as the penetrator. The GBU-28/B weighs 2,135 kg and could penetrate more than 25–30 meters of earth or 6 meters of concrete, far short of that needed to defeat Tarhunah. *Id.* The FY 1997 DOD budget included $18.4 million to purchase 161 rounds. A rocket-boosted version of the GBU-28 is being considered that can punch a warhead into as much as 90 meters of soil, close to the penetration necessary to defeat Tarhunah. *Id.*

Concerned with the proliferation of WMD in the rogue States like Libya, Iraq, Iran and North Korea, Congress provided $108 million in FY 1996 to jumpstart the United States Department of Defense's counter-proliferation efforts. *Id.* at 525. In July 1996, Colonel Ghadaffi announced "There is no longer any logic between us (Libya and the U.S), no common denominator or rationality. We are looking for ways to frighten America so that it retreats." *Id.* In response, the DOD initiated the "Hard and Deeply Buried Target Defeat Capability" program to design a new generation of non-nuclear kinetic and chemical energy weapons capable of defeating the vast majority of hardened NBC targets. *Id.*

One approach has been to use the kinetic energy of an intercontinental ballistic missile or a non-nuclear hypervelocity air-to-ground missile with a steel-cased, armored, penetrating warhead to drive a long-rod penetrator or explosive device deep into an underground NBC complex. McDonnell Douglas was awarded a $6 million contract to develop the "Small Smart Bomb" by the year 2005 that combines recently developed high-explosives technology with highly-accurate inertial guidance and second-generation smart fuzing to produce a miniaturized smart bomb that can be carried in large numbers on bombers, allowing multiple "kills" per pass. The Small Smart Bomb weighs 113kg, but is capable of destroying targets that only a bomb nine times its size previously was capable. Beal et al., *supra* note 53, at 37.

An ongoing project to develop a conventional weapon to penetrate six meters of ground and then detonate is the "Hard, Deeply Buried, and Tunnel Target Defeat Programme."[71] Successful completion of this and similar developmental efforts would appear to represent essentially the last step in rendering conventional weapons capable of

---

In parallel, the Air Force is developing a larger "high-payoff" deep-penetrating bomb to destroy targets against which the Small Smart Bomb will be ineffective. *Id.* Under the three year "Dense Metal Case Penetrating Weapon" (DMCPW) program, funded by the DOD and Great Britain, the USAF is developing technologies that could lead to significant improvements in attacking hardened targets.   These include advanced earth-penetrating missiles that are miniaturized (to maximize the number that may be carried by a single bomber on a single attack run), armed with multiple "tandem" warheads (secondary "precursor" warheads are used to clear earth debris in front of the primary warhead which detonates within the actual NBC facility), propelled with additional boosters that optimize the attack angle, guided by "terra dynamic" steering that allows the bomb to maneuver inside the earth, and hard target "smart fuses" that count layers to allow detonation in precise stages (to ensure that the explosion occurs well within the complex and not uselessly on the outside in front-end clutter, target soil overlays or in non-essential void layers). *Id.* The Air Force is additionally developing "Agent Defeat Warhead Technology," or non-nuclear explosive agents that are specifically designed to destroy the physical target and neutralize any chemical or biological agents that are expelled. *See id.* at 38. The French Air Force has developed armored steel encased missiles that impacts at a speed of Mach 1.4, kinetically tripling the effect of the explosive charge. *See id.* at 34.

A second approach would use unconventional weapons to destroy the site and neutralize chemical and biological agents stored inside the complex. Candidates being examined include solid and gas fuel air explosives, magneto-hydrodynamic warheads, corrosive acids and electronic weapons. *Id.* at 34. While chemical agents dissipate quickly and are lethal only up to one kilometer, biological agents can be lethal up to 100 km away. The U.S. DOD was scheduled to spend $4 million in FY 1996 to develop munitions capable of neutralizing chemical and biological fallout. Waller, *supra* note 56, at 561.

[70] *See id.*

[71] *USA Seeks More Protection Against WMD*, JANE'S DEFENCE WEEKLY, vol. 29, no. 21, p. 13, May 27, 1998. In May of 1998, officials expected to decide by Oct. 1998 which one of sixty proposals to fund, deciding amongst "direct attack munitions, cruise and ballistic missile" proposals. By 1999, proposals being considered included bombs that could disable the poisons without causing a violent blast and deep penetrating bombs simulating an earthquake. Thomas E. Ricks, *U.S. Seeks to Build A Bomb That Kills Weapons, Not People, Bleach and Foam Might Ruin Chemical Arms Stockpiles; 'Fred Flintstone' Solution*, THE WALL STREET J. EUROPE July 5, 1999 at 1.

accomplishing virtually any lawful mission for which nuclear weapons might have been used.

And, of course, bombing, conventional or nuclear, is not the only way to take out such a hardened target. Special forces could in some circumstances be used, as could aggressive intelligence operations and infiltration efforts. Other options would obviously include coercive diplomacy, the use of sanctions and embargoes, and the tight enforcement of the prohibition against the international smuggling of NBC technology and equipment into Libya.[72]

---

[72] *See* Waller, *supra* note 56, at 560.

PART V

APPLICATION OF THE LAW TO THE FACTS

Chapter 29: Unlawfulness of Use of Nuclear Weapons under Rules of International Law Recognized by the United States

In this chapter I set forth my analysis as to the application of the law of armed conflict as recognized by the United States to the facts developed above as to the risks inherent in the use of nuclear weapons. Then, in the next and final chapter, I factor into the analysis the widely recognized rules of law discussed in Part II as to the taking of even minor risks of causing severe injury to innocent or protected persons and as to the prerequisites for a *per se* rule.

I take as a given the ICJ's determination, not actively disputed by the United States before the Court,[1] that the use of nuclear weapons, and particularly of high yield strategic and multiple tactical weapons,

---

[1] While, as noted, there was an ambiguity in the Court's decision as to the potential lawfulness of the widescale use of nuclear weapons in extreme circumstances of self-defense, it was striking that the United States only argued the possible lawfulness of the limited use of a small number of low-yield nuclear weapons in non-urban areas. As to the Court's decision, *see Legality of the Threat of Use of Nuclear Weapons,* Advisory Opinion ¶¶ 104, 105.E, (2)(B), 35 I.L.M. 809, 823, 827, 831 (July 8, 1996); Chapter 3, notes 1–8, 36–40, and accompanying text. As to the U.S. position, *see* ICJ Hearing November 15, 1995, at 85–91; Conrad K. Harper (Legal Advisor, Department of State), Michael J. Matheson (Deputy Legal Advisor, Department of State), Bruce C. Rashkow (Assistant Legal Advisor, Department of State), and John H. McNeill (Senior Deputy General Counsel, Department of Defense), *Written Statement of the Government of the United States of America* (June 20, 1995), submitted to the International Court of Justice, The Hague, The Netherlands, in connection with the Request by the United Nations General Assembly for an Advisory Opinion on the Legality of the Threat or Use of Nuclear Weapons at 23, *reprinted as Written Observations on the Request by the General Assembly for an Advisory Opinion,* 7 CRIM. L.F. 401 (1996) (citing the Army's THE LAW OF LAND WARFARE at 5); Chapter 2, notes 57–73 and accompanying text.

The question of the lawfulness of the limited use of low-yield nuclear weapons is more challenging since, if such an attack is assumed to be of the nature hypothesized by the United States (*e.g.*, as involving limited and controlled radiation and other effects, limited injury to protected persons and other interests, no retaliation or escalation with nuclear, chemical or biological weapons, and major military significance), the argument of potential legality seems appealing. The question becomes whether the U.S. assumptions are realistic and how one should deal with various levels of probability of more serious effects.

would generally be unlawful[2]—and therefore address the more challenging question of whether the use of a small number of highly accurate low-yield (generally tactical) nuclear weapons in remote areas in extreme circumstances of self-defense could ever be lawful.[3] If my analysis as to the more limited use is correct, the broader question is not reached.

Per Se Rules under General Principles of Law

Issue is joined at the most basic point, the nature and limits of the consensual basis of international law.

The United States position, as expressed before the ICJ, is that there is no *per se* rule banning the use of nuclear weapons because the United States has not consented to any such rule, and hence that each contemplated use of such weapons must be evaluated on an *ad hoc* basis.

The United States argues that it is only bound by conventional law specifically agreed to by the United States and customary law established by the practice of the community of nations, including the nations specially involved (here, the nuclear powers), out of a sense of obligation. The United States concludes that, since it has not agreed to a convention specifically prohibiting the use of nuclear weapons and has not refrained from their use out of a sense of obligation, such use cannot be *per se* unlawful.

Conrad K. Harper, Legal Advisor of the United States Department of State, told the Court that its "starting point in examining the merits" should be "the fundamental principle of international law that restrictions on States cannot be presumed, but must be established by conventional law specifically accepted by them, or in customary law established by the conduct of the community of nations."[4]

Michael J. Matheson, the Deputy Legal Advisor, Department of State, in his presentation to the Court, made the same point: Restrictions upon States must "be found in conventional law specifically accepted by States, or in customary law generally accepted

---

[2] *See* Nuclear Weapons Advisory Opinion ¶ 105.E, 35 I.L.M. at 829 (July 8, 1996); Chapter 3, opening sections and notes 10–11, 36–40, and accompanying text.

[3] *See* Chapter 3, opening section and notes 28–35, 41–72, and accompanying text.

[4] ICJ Hearing, November 15, 1995, at 70. *See* Chapter 2, notes 42–49 and accompanying text.

as such by the community of nations."[5]   Matheson relied upon the Court's statement in the *Nicaragua* case that:

> "in international law there are no rules, other than such rules as may be accepted by the State concerned, by treaty or otherwise, whereby the level of armaments of a sovereign State can be limited."[6]

The U.S. position on this point, as presented to the ICJ, overlooks the existence of other sources of international law, including general principles of law.   It ignores the fact that the United States has recognized that the broad rules of the law of armed conflict—such as the rules of proportionality, necessity, discrimination, and neutrality— apply to nuclear weapons[7] and that *per se* rules can arise from them.[8]

Once the applicability of such rules is acknowledged, the United States is bound by their application regardless of whether it agrees with the particular application.   Neither the consensual basis of international law nor the principle of sovereignty limits the application of established rules of law.   If the use of nuclear weapons is *per se* unlawful under those principles, the United States is subject to such unlawfulness fully as much as if it had signed a convention or purposefully joined in the formation of custom to that effect.

The Air Force Manual on International Law states that the use of a weapon may be unlawful based not only on "expressed prohibitions contained in specific rules of custom and convention," but also on

---

[5] *Id.* at 74–75. *See* Chapter 2, notes 43–45 and accompanying text.

[6] *Id.* (citing Nicaragua v. United States (1986 I.C.J. 135)). *See* Chapter 2, note 44 and accompanying text.

[7] The United States has recognized these rules as arising under customary and treaty law and general principles of law. *See* Chapter 2, notes 77, 88–91 (proportionality), 54–56 (necessity), 57–65 (moderation; discrimination), 111–119 (neutrality), and accompanying text.

The United States has recognized these rules as customary and generally accepted rules of law and as embodied in conventions. *See, e.g.,* Chapter 1, notes 246–252 and accompanying text.

[8] *See infra* notes 10–15 and accompanying text. In its arguments before the ICJ, the United States acknowledged that scientific evidence could justify a total prohibition of nuclear weapons if it demonstrated the unlawfulness of all such uses: "[S]cientific evidence could only justify a total prohibition on the use of nuclear weapons if such evidence covers the full range of variables and circumstances that might be involved in such uses." ICJ Hearing, November 15, 1995, at 90.

"those prohibitions laid down in the general principles of the law of war."[9]

Similarly, in discussing how the lawfulness of new weapons and methods of warfare is determined, the manual states that such determination is made based on international treaty or custom, upon "analogy to weapons or methods previously determined to be lawful or unlawful," and upon the evaluation of the compliance of such new weapons or methods with established principles of law, such as the rules of necessity, discrimination and proportionality.[10]

The manual notes that the International Military Tribunal at Nuremberg in the case of the *Major War Criminals* found that international law is contained not only in treaties and custom but also in the "general principles of justice applied by jurists and practiced by military courts."[11]

The Air Force Manual on International Law further states that the practice of States "does not modify" the legal obligation to comply with treaty obligations since such obligations are "contractual in nature."[12]

The Army's *Law of Land Warfare* states "[t]he conduct of armed hostilities on land is regulated by the law of land warfare which is both written and unwritten."[13]

The United States recognizes "analogy" as well as "general principles" as sources of the law of armed conflict. *The Air Force Manual on International Law* states:

> The law of armed conflict affecting aerial operations is not entirely codified. Therefore, the law applicable to air warfare must be derived from general principles, extrapolated from the law affecting land or sea warfare, or derived from other sources including the practice of states reflected in a wide variety of

---

[9] THE UNITED STATES DEPARTMENT OF THE AIR FORCE, INTERNATIONAL LAW—THE CONDUCT OF ARMED CONFLICT AND AIR OPERATIONS 6-1, 6-9 n.3 (Air Force Pamphlet 110-31, 19 November 1976) [hereinafter THE AIR FORCE MANUAL ON INTERNATIONAL LAW]. *See* Chapter 1, notes 14–18, 24, Chapter 2, notes 42–49, and accompanying text.

[10] *See id.* at 6-7; Chapter 1, note 25 and accompanying text.

[11] *Id.* at 1-6. *See* Chapter 1, note 26 and accompanying text.

[12] *Id.* at 1-15 n.35. *See* Chapter 1, note 27 and accompanying text.

[13] UNITED STATES DEPARTMENT OF THE ARMY, THE LAW OF LAND WARFARE 3 (FM27-10/18 July 1956) with Change No. 1 (15 July 1976) [hereinafter THE LAW OF LAND WARFARE]. *See* Chapter 1, note 3 and accompanying text.

sources. Yet the US is a party to numerous treaties which affect aerial operations either directly or by analogy.[14]

The manual notes that *per se* unlawfulness is not limited to prohibitions established in treaties or customary law:

> [A] new weapon or method of warfare may be illegal, *per se*, if it is restricted by international law including treaty or international custom. The issue is resolved, or attempted to be resolved, by analogy to weapons or methods previously determined to be lawful or unlawful.[15]

Based on the foregoing, it seems clear that the use of nuclear weapons can be unlawful *per se* regardless of whether there is a treaty or custom establishing such unlawfulness.

Uncontrollability as Connoting Unlawfulness

The United States has recognized that the rules of discrimination, necessity, and proportionality prohibit the use of weapons whose effects cannot be controlled by the user.

Uncontrollability under Rule of Discrimination

The Air Force Commander's Handbook states that weapons that are "incapable of being controlled enough to direct them against a military objective" are unlawful.[16] *The Air Force Manual on International Law* defines indiscriminate weapons as those "incapable of being controlled, through design or function," such that they "cannot, with any degree of certainty, be directed at military objectives."[17]

In its military manuals the United States has acknowledged that the scope of this prohibition extends to the *effects* of the use of a weapon. *The Air Force Manual on International Law* states that indiscriminate weapons include those which, while subject to being directed at military objectives, "may have otherwise uncontrollable effects so as to

---

[14] THE AIR FORCE MANUAL ON INTERNATIONAL LAW, *supra* note 9, at 1-7. *See* Chapter 1, note 251 and accompanying text.

[15] *Id.* at 6-7. *See* Chapter 1, note 252 and accompanying text.

[16] *See* UNITED STATES DEPARTMENT OF THE AIR FORCE, COMMANDER'S HANDBOOK ON THE LAW OF ARMED CONFLICT 6-1 (Air Force Pamphlet 110-34, 25 July 1980) [hereinafter THE AIR FORCE COMMANDER'S HANDBOOK]. *See* Chapter 1, note 153 and accompanying text.

[17] THE AIR FORCE MANUAL ON INTERNATIONAL LAW, *supra* note 9, at 6-3. *See* Chapter 1, note 154 and accompanying text.

cause disproportionate civilian injuries or damage."[18]   The manual states that "uncontrollable" refers to effects "which escape in time or space from the control of the user as to necessarily create risks to civilian persons or objects excessive in relation to the military advantage anticipated."[19]   It is noteworthy that this prohibition encompasses the causing of risks, not just injury.

As a "universally agreed illustration of ... an indiscriminate weapon," *The Air Force Manual on International Law* cites biological weapons, noting that the uncontrollable effects from such weapons "may include injury to the civilian population of other states as well as injury to an enemy's civilian population."[20]   *The Naval/Marine Commander's Handbook* states that such weapons are "inherently indiscriminate and uncontrollable."[21]

The Air Force Manual on International Law further cites Germany's World War II V-1 rockets, with their "extremely primitive guidance systems" and Japanese incendiary balloons, without any guidance systems.[22]   The manual states that the term "indiscriminate" refers to the "inherent characteristics of the weapon, when used, which renders *(sic)* it incapable of being directed at specific military objectives or of a nature to necessarily cause disproportionate injury to civilians or damage to civilian objects."[23]

As an example of an indiscriminate weapon, *The Air Force Commander's Handbook* similarly cites the use of unpowered and uncontrolled balloons to carry bombs, since such weapons are "incapable of being directed against a military objective."[24]

---

[18] *See id.*; Chapter 1, note 165 and accompanying text.

[19] *Id. See* Chapter 1, note 166 and accompanying text.

[20] *Id. See* Chapter 1, note 167 and accompanying text.

[21] UNITED STATES DEPARTMENT OF THE NAVY ANNOTATED SUPPLEMENT TO THE COMMANDER'S HANDBOOK ON THE LAW OF NAVAL OPERATIONS 10-21 (Naval Warfare Publication 9, 1987) (With Revision A (5 October 1989), this handbook was adopted by the U.S. Marine Corps as FLEET MARINE FORCE MANUAL (FM FM) 1-10) [hereinafter THE NAVAL/MARINE COMMANDER'S HANDBOOK]. *See* Chapter 1, note 168 and accompanying text.

[22] THE AIR FORCE MANUAL ON INTERNATIONAL LAW, *supra* note 9, at 6-3. *See* Chapter 1, note 163 and accompanying text.

[23] *Id.* at 6-9 n.7. *See* Chapter 1, note 164 and accompanying text.

[24] THE AIR FORCE COMMANDER'S HANDBOOK, *supra* note 16, at 6-1. *See* Chapter 1, note 162 and accompanying text.

Uncontrollability under Rule of Necessity

The requirement that the level of force implicit in the use of a weapon be controllable and controlled by the user is a natural implication of the necessity requirement. If a State cannot control the level of destructiveness of a weapon, it cannot assure that the use of the weapon will involve only such a level of destructiveness as is necessary in the circumstances.

The Air Force Manual on International Law recognizes as a basic requirement of necessity "that the force used is capable of being and is in fact regulated by the user."[25]

Uncontrollability under Rule of Proportionality

So also, if the State using a weapon is unable to control the effects of the weapon, it is unable to evaluate whether the effects would satisfy the requirement of being proportionate to the concrete and direct military advantage anticipated from the attack or to assure such limitation of effects.

The Air Force Manual on International Law notes that the requirement of proportionality prohibits "uncontrollable effects against one's own combatants, civilians or property."[26]

U.S. Position as to Controllability

At the ICJ, the United States did not retrench on the applicability of the controllability requirement, but rather argued the matter on a factual level, asserting that nuclear weapons—or at least the type of nuclear weapons whose legality the United States defended—are controllable.

Without arguing the lawfulness of the use of strategic nuclear weapons or even of a substantial number of tactical weapons or of a small number of such weapons in urban areas, the United States asserted the possible lawfulness of the use of a small number of highly accurate low-yield nuclear weapons (ostensibly tactical weapons) directed against non-urban targets, arguing that the effects of such attacks could be so limited and controlled as to be lawful.

Ostensibly as to such weapons and usages, the United States argued:

---

[25] THE AIR FORCE MANUAL ON INTERNATIONAL LAW, *supra* note 9, at 1-6. *See* Chapter 1, note 128 and accompanying text.

[26] *Id.* at 6-2. *See also id.* at 5-10. *See* Chapter 1, note 80 and accompanying text.

(1) That it is capable of using nuclear weapons in such a way as to control their effects and keep them within appropriate legal bounds; and

(2) That the use of such weapons would have adverse collateral effect on human health and the natural and physical environments generally comparable to those that would result from conventional weapons—that armed conflict of any kind can cause widespread, sustained destruction and it does not much matter whether nuclear or conventional weapons are used.

John H. McNeill, the U.S. Senior Deputy General Counsel, Department of Defense, told the Court:

> The argument that international law prohibits, in all cases, the use of nuclear weapons appears to be premised on the incorrect assumption that every use of every type of nuclear weapon will necessarily share certain characteristics which contravene the law of armed conflict. Specifically, it appears to be assumed that any use of nuclear weapons would inevitably escalate into a massive strategic nuclear exchange, resulting automatically in the deliberate destruction of the population centers of opposing sides.[27]
>
> ***
>
> Nuclear weapons, as is true of conventional weapons, can be used in a variety of ways: they can be deployed to achieve a wide range of military objectives of varying degrees of significance; they can be targeted in ways that either increase or decrease resulting incidental civilian injury or collateral damage; and their use may be lawful or not depending upon whether and to what extent such use was prompted by another belligerent's conduct and the nature of the conduct.[28]

Noting that it has been argued that nuclear weapons are inherently indiscriminate in their effect and cannot reliably be targeted at specific military objectives, McNeill stated:

> This argument is simply contrary to fact. Modern nuclear weapon delivery systems are, indeed, capable of precisely engaging discrete military objectives.[29]

---

[27] ICJ Hearing, November 15, 1995, at 85 (John H. McNeill, arguing). *See* Chapter 2, note 73 and accompanying text.

[28] *Id.* at 87. *See* Chapter 2, note 57 and accompanying text.

[29] *Id.* at 88. *See* Chapter 2, note 58 and accompanying text.

Alluding to the assumptions made by the World Health Organization (WHO) in its 1987 study as to the effects of nuclear weapons, McNeill objected to the "four scenarios" depicted by the WHO as "highly selective" in that they addressed "civilian casualties expected to result from nuclear attacks involving significant numbers of large urban area targets or a substantial number of military targets."[30]

> But no reference is made in the report to the effects to be expected from other plausible scenarios, such as a small number of accurate attacks by low-yield weapons against an equally small number of military targets in non-urban areas.[31]

Reinforcing the point as to "other plausible [low-end use] scenarios," McNeill stated that such plausibility "follows from a fact noted in the WHO Report by Professor Rotblat: namely, that 'remarkable improvements' in the performance of nuclear weapons in recent years have resulted in their 'much greater accuracy,'"[32] stating that such scenarios "would not necessarily raise issues of proportionality or discrimination."[33]

In its memorandum to the ICJ, the United States stated that, through the technological expertise of "modern weapon designers," it is now able to control the effects of nuclear weapons—specifically, "to tailor the effects of a nuclear weapon to deal with various types of military objectives:"

> It has been argued that nuclear weapons are unlawful because they cannot be directed at a military objective. This argument ignores the ability of modern delivery systems to target specific military objectives with nuclear weapons, and the ability of modern weapons designers to tailor the effects of a nuclear weapon to deal with various types of military objectives. Since nuclear weapons can be directed at a military objective, they can be used in a discriminate manner and are not inherently indiscriminate.[34]

Beyond arguing that the effects of any particular use of a nuclear would depend on the particular circumstances, the United States

---

[30] *Id.* at 90. *See* Chapter 2, note 66 and accompanying text.

[31] *Id. See* Chapter 2, note 67, Chapter 3, notes 31–40, and accompanying text.

[32] *Id. See* Chapter 2, note 68 and accompanying text.

[33] *Id. See* Chapter 2, note 69 and accompanying text.

[34] U.S. ICJ Memorandum/GA App at 23. *See* Chapter 2, note 59 and accompanying text.

minimized the differences between the effects of nuclear and conventional weapons. McNeill argued:

> It is true that the use of nuclear weapons would have an adverse collateral effect on human health and both the natural and physical environments. But so too can the use of conventional weapons. Obviously, World Wars I and II, as well as the 1990-1991 conflict resulting from Iraq's invasion of Kuwait, dramatically demonstrated that conventional war can inflict terrible collateral damage to the environment. The fact is that armed conflict of any kind can cause widespread, sustained destruction; the Court need not examine scientific evidence to take judicial notice of this evident truth.[35]

The U.S. position seems to come down to the following factual contentions:

- That any use by the United States of nuclear weapons would be of a small number of highly accurate low-yield weapons in a non-urban area;
- that the United States could deliver such weapons accurately to their designated targets;
- that the damage caused by such weapons upon reaching their targets would be limited and controllable;
- that such damages would essentially be in line with those caused by conventional weapons, with no greater collateral damage—no greater injuries to non-combatants and neutrals; and
- that such limited use of low-yield weapons would not lead to escalation or the use of chemical or biological weapons.

U.S. Acknowledgment of Uncontrollability

The U.S. position appears to be inconsistent with the nature of nuclear weapons and their effects; the make-up of the U.S. nuclear force structure; the circumstances, if any, in which the United States would likely resort to nuclear weapons; the types of nuclear weapons it would likely use in such circumstances; the accuracy with which it

---

[35] ICJ Hearing, November 15, 1995, at 89. *See* Chapter 2, note 93 and accompanying text.

While the damage caused by the Iraqi attack on Kuwait caused extensive environmental damage, within less than ten years such effects have largely been dissipated. *See* Chapter 15, notes 196–204 and accompanying text.

could deliver the weapons; and the likely responses of targeted States and their allies.

Outside the courtroom, the United States recognizes the potential uncontrollability of the effects of nuclear weapons. This can be seen from the Chairman of the Joint Chief's *Joint Pub 3-12, Doctrine for Joint Nuclear Operations*, setting forth the current operational planning for the integrated use by U.S. forces of nuclear weapons in conjunction with conventional weapons:[36]

> [T]here can be no assurances that a conflict involving weapons of mass destruction could be controllable or would be of short duration. Nor are negotiations opportunities and the capacity for enduring control over military forces clear.[37]

As noted by Judge Shahabuddeen in his dissent in the Nuclear Weapons Advisory Decision, the United States, in ratifying the Treaty of Tlatelolco, subscribed to the following statement of preamble as to the indiscriminate and excessive injury caused by nuclear weapons:

> The preamble to the 1967 Treaty of Tlatelolco, Additional Protocol II of which was signed and ratified by the five [nuclear weapons states, including the United States], declared that the Parties are convinced
>
> "That the incalculable destructive power of nuclear weapons has made it imperative that the legal prohibition of war should be strictly observed in practice if the survival of civilization and of mankind itself is to be assured.
>
> That nuclear weapons, whose terrible effects are suffered, indiscriminately and inexorably, by military forces and civilian population alike, constitute, through the persistence of the radioactivity they release, an attack on the integrity of the human species and ultimately may even render the whole earth uninhabitable."[38]

---

[36] JOINT CHIEFS OF STAFF, JOINT PUB 3-12, DOCTRINE FOR JOINT NUCLEAR OPERATIONS i, (Dec. 15, 1995), available at <http://www.dtic.mil/doctrine/jel/new_pubs/jp3_12.pdf>. *See* Chapters 26, 27; Chapter 2, note 75, Chapter 17, notes 38–53, Chapter 18, note 56, and accompanying text.

[37] *Id.* at i, I-6, I-6–7 (emphasis omitted). *See* Chapter 2, note 76 and accompanying text.

[38] Treaty for the Prohibition of Nuclear Weapons in Latin America (Treaty of Tlatelolco), Feb. 14, 1967, 22 U.S.T. 762, 634 U.N.T.S. 762, *quoted in* dissenting opinion of Judge Shahabuddeen at 5–6, 35 I.L.M. at 863–864. *See* Chapter 3, note 27 and accompanying text.

The extreme and disproportionate effects threatened by nuclear weapons are acknowledged by the U.S. military in their operational policy, training, and planning. The *Nuclear Weapons Joint Operations* manual states:

> US nuclear forces serve to deter the use of WMD ["weapons of mass destruction," including chemical, biological, and nuclear weapons] across the spectrum of military operations. From a massive exchange of nuclear weapons to limited use on a regional battlefield, US nuclear capabilities must confront an enemy with risks of unacceptable damage and disproportionate loss should the enemy choose to introduce WMD into a conflict.[39]

Similarly:

> [S]omeday a nation may, through miscalculation or by deliberate choice, employ these weapons. ... [A]n opponent may be willing to risk destruction or disproportionate loss in following a course of action based on perceived necessity, whether rational or not in a totally objective sense. In such cases deterrence, even based on the threat of massive destruction, may fail.[40]

The Fact of Uncontrollability

Contrary to the U.S. position, if the United States were ever to use nuclear weapons, it would likely be multiple strategic weapons, and any use of nuclear weapons, in the circumstances in which such use would likely take place, would likely result in escalation and other uncontrollable effects.

The U.S. Nuclear Force Structure

The type of nuclear strikes the United States defended before the ICJ—the use of highly accurate low-yield tactical nuclear weapons with controllable radiation effects—does not typify the U.S. nuclear force structure. The United States was defending an arsenal other than its own.

The U.S. nuclear force structure is comprised predominantly of high kilotonnage strategic nuclear weapons threatening devastating effects. In its active arsenal, United States currently has some 7206 strategic versus 1070 tactical warheads,[41] and, of those tactical warheads, none

---

[39] DOCTRINE FOR JOINT NUCLEAR OPERATIONS, *supra* note 36, at I-2 (emphasis omitted). *See* Chapter 2, note 91, Chapter 27, note 83, and accompanying text.

[40] *Id.* (emphasis omitted). *See* Chapter 18, note 55 and accompanying text.

[41] *See* Chapter 19, notes 7–8 and accompanying text and charts.

are limited to 10 kilotons or less, the military's outer limit for "low" yield nuclear weapons.[42]

The United States has professedly de-emphasized nuclear weapons, particularly tactical nuclear weapons.[43] The Army and Marines have been de-nuclearized.[44] The Navy no longer deploys non-strategic nuclear weapons[45] and the Air Force has dramatically cut its tactical nuclear stockpile.[46] The United States has also passed legislation outlawing research and development that could lead to production of a

---

[42] *See* Chapter 19, notes 20–25 and accompanying text and yield chart. *See also* JOINT CHIEFS OF STAFF, JOINT PUB 3-12.1, DOCTRINE FOR JOINT THEATER NUCLEAR OPERATIONS GL-3 (Feb. 9, 1996) (prepared under direction of the Chairman of the Joint Chiefs of Staff), as set forth at <http://www.dtic.mil/doctrine/jel/new_pubs/jp3_12_1.pdf>; JOHN BURROUGHS, THE (IL)LEGALITY OF THREAT OR USE OF NUCLEAR WEAPONS 76 n.89 (1997).

[43] *See* Chapters 18, 19; Chapter 3, note 95, Chapter 18, notes 19–27, Chapter 19, notes 7–16, and accompanying text; WILLIAM J. PERRY, SECRETARY OF DEFENSE, 1995 ANNUAL REPORT TO THE PRESIDENT AND THE CONGRESS 10, 86–87; Secretary William S. Cohen, *Speech to Coalition to Advance Sustainable Technology,* at Denver International Airport, Denver, Colo., June 26, 1998.

In the 1960s, when the number of warheads peaked at over 32,000, the U.S. forces consisted predominantly of tactical forces. By 1975, the United States maintained 10,311 tactical nuclear weapons overseas. *See* ARKIN ET AL., TAKING STOCK: WORLDWIDE NUCLEAR DEPLOYMENTS 1998 16 (NRDC 1998); COCHRAN, ARKIN & HOENIG, 1 NUCLEAR WEAPONS DATABOOK 3–4, 38 (NRDC 1984). By 1983, when the U.S. arsenal was at 26,000, the numbers of tactical and strategic weapons were about even, with tactical still slightly outnumbering strategic weapons. COCHRAN ET AL., *supra,* at 4, 15, 39, 102.

[44] *See* Chapter 18, notes 19–27, Chapter 19, notes 7–10, 25, and accompanying text and charts. *See also* ARKIN ET AL., TAKING STOCK: WORLDWIDE NUCLEAR DEPLOYMENTS 1998 (NRDC 1998); PHILIP MORRISON & KOSTA TSIPIS, REASON ENOUGH TO HOPE, AMERICA AND THE WORLD OF THE 21ST CENTURY (M.I.T. Press 1998); COCHRAN, ARKIN & HOENIG, 1 NUCLEAR WEAPONS DATABOOK 3–4, 38 (NRDC 1984); WILLIAM J. PERRY, SECRETARY OF DEFENSE, 1995 ANNUAL REPORT TO THE PRESIDENT AND THE CONGRESS 83.

[45] *See* Chapter 18, notes 22–23, Chapter 19 notes 8–10, 25, and accompanying text and charts. *See also* Robert S. Norris & William M. Arkin, *US Nuclear Stockpile, July 1998*; PHILIP MORRISON & KOSTA TSIPIS, REASON ENOUGH TO HOPE; WILLIAM J. PERRY, SECRETARY OF DEFENSE, 1995 ANNUAL REPORT TO THE PRESIDENT AND THE CONGRESS 83.

[46] *See* Chapter 18, notes 22–23, Chapter 19, notes 8–10, and accompanying text. *See also* ARKIN ET AL., TAKING STOCK: WORLDWIDE NUCLEAR DEPLOYMENTS 1998 (NRDC 1998); WILLIAM J. PERRY, SECRETARY OF DEFENSE, 1995 ANNUAL REPORT TO THE PRESIDENT AND THE CONGRESS 83.

low-yield nuclear weapon, defined for that purpose as one with a yield of less than five kilotons.[47]

Volatile and Extreme Circumstances of Any Possible Use

The United States recognizes the extreme risks inherent in the use of nuclear weapons. Its essential policy is one of deterrence, based on the hope that the threat of the use of such weapons will preclude the need ever to use them. The United States would ostensibly only intentionally resort to nuclear weapons, if at all, in the most serious and extreme of military situations threatening the most fundamental interests of the United States or possibly its allies, circumstances that would by their nature be extremely volatile, pressured, and threatening to all concerned.[48]

Such a situation would ostensibly only arise in the context of an adversary capable of inflicting severe injury on the United States or possibly its allies and with a perceived determination to do so.[49] If the situation were deemed imperative enough to require nuclear weapons, it would likely be deemed to require the greater destructive capability of strategic nuclear weapons.

Particularly given the vagaries of targeting just one or a small number of missiles, the limitations of experience with the use of nuclear weapons and their delivery mechanisms, and the inherent volatility of the situation that by definition would exist, the United States, if it were to resort to nuclear weapons at all, would almost certainly do so in a way conducive to having maximum impact on the

---

[47] *See* National Defense Authorization Act for Fiscal Year 1994, Pub Law, 103-160, 30 November 1993; § 3136 of P.L. 103-160; 42 USCS § 2121 (1998) Prohibition on Research and Development of Low-Yield Nuclear Weapons, Act. Nov. 30, 1993, P.L. 103-160, Div C. Title XXX, Subtitle C § 3136, 107 Stat. 1946; Chapter 3, notes 48, 95, Chapter 19, notes 11–16, and accompanying text.

[48] *See* Chapter 2, notes 78–85, Chapter 3, notes 88–94, 96, Chapter 17, notes 5–10, 25–27, Chapter 18, notes 34–35, 37, and accompanying text. *See also* NUCLEAR WEAPONS SYSTEMS SUSTAINMENT PROGRAMS (updated, 16 Jun 1998) <http://www.defenselink.mil/pubs/dswa/>; DOCTRINE FOR JOINT NUCLEAR OPERATIONS, *supra* note 36, at I-4, III-8; dissenting opinion of Judge Weeramantry at 27, 35 I.L.M. at 893–915.

[49] *See* Chapter 2, note 91; Chapter 3, note 213, Chapter 16, notes 14–15, Chapter 27, notes 79–83, and accompanying text. *See also* dissenting opinion of Judge Higgins at 3, 35 I.L.M. at 936; *The History of the U.S. Strategic "Doctrine," 1945–1980,* THE J. OF STRATEGIC STUDIES, Dec. 1980; DOCTRINE FOR JOINT NUCLEAR OPERATIONS, *supra* note 36, at I-1.

enemy, and hence would likely strike with multiple nuclear weapons.[50] Any one weapon could fail or miss its target.

The pressure on a nuclear State to "use 'em or lose 'em" in a major nuclear confrontation,[51] given the attractiveness of nuclear assets as targets and the inevitable escalation risks, as well as the risk that an adversary might be in a "launch on warning mode,"[52] would foster the early use of multiple nuclear weapons, particularly fixed base "sitting duck" nuclear weapons and other vulnerable such weapons.[53]

The circumstances in which the United States might actually resort to nuclear weapons would be unlikely in the end to be logical or controlled, and the likely bias would be towards over-use. Threat would have led to counter-threat and events, even technology, would have taken on a life of their own, contrary probably to either side's desires or expectations. The enemy's response and the circumstances of the fog of war, misperception, failure of command and control, and human and equipment failure would likely be driving events. Rationality, even self-preservation, would have been left behind.[54]

---

[50] *See* Chapter 16, notes 15–18, 39–46, Chapter 27, note 83, and accompanying text. *See also* DOCTRINE FOR JOINT NUCLEAR OPERATIONS, *supra* note 36, at II-6; David Alan Rosenberg, *A Smoking Radiating Ruin at the End of Two Hours: Documents on American Plans for Nuclear War with the Soviet Union, 1954–55*, INT'L SECURITY, vol. 2, no. 3, Winter 1981–1982, at 3; David Alan Rosenberg, *The Origins of Overkill: Nuclear Weapons and American Strategy, 1945–1960*, INT'L SECURITY, vol. 7, no. 4, Spring 1993, at 3.

[51] *See* Chapter 2, notes 86–87, Chapter 16, notes 29–30, 86–87, Chapter 22, notes 5–6, and accompanying text. *See also* DOCTRINE FOR JOINT THEATER NUCLEAR OPERATIONS, *supra* note 42, at ix, I-5–6.

[52] *See* Chapter 15, notes 24–25, Chapter 22, notes 5–6, and accompanying text.

[53] *See* Chapter 15, notes 24–25, 121, Chapter 16, note 8, Chapter 22, notes 5–6, and accompanying text. *See also* Spurgeon M. Keeny, Jr. & Wolfgang K. H. Panofsky, *MAD versus NUTS: Can Doctrine or Weaponry Remedy the Mutual Hostage Relationship of the Superpowers?*, 60 FOREIGN AFF. 287, 294 (Winter 1981–1982); Victor Utgoff, *In Defense of Counterforce*, INT'L SECURITY, vol. 6, no. 1, Spring 1982, 44–60.

[54] *See* Chapter 15, note 24; Chapter 18, notes 54–55, Chapter 20, note 21, Chapter 22, notes 6–7, Chapter 25, notes 9–10, and accompanying text. *See also* Paul Bracken, *War Termination, in* MANAGING NUCLEAR OPERATIONS 197 (Ashton B. Carter et al. eds., 1987); PAUL BRACKEN, THE COMMAND AND CONTROL OF NUCLEAR FORCES 198 (1983); HERMAN KAHN ET AL., WAR TERMINATION ISSUES AND CONCEPTS, FINAL REPORT 197–214 (1968); ROBERT S. MCNAMARA, JAMES G. BLIGHT, & ROBERT K. BRIGHAM, ARGUMENT

Use of Tactical Nuclear Weapons Unlikely

As noted, the United States, in defending the lawfulness of the use of nuclear weapons before the ICJ, argued that the use of a limited number of low-yield nuclear weapons could be used lawfully in non-urban areas. Such hypothetical low-yield surgical strikes at remote targets not precipitating escalation do not appear to be realistic in light of the full range of relevant facts.

While a very limited low-yield tactical nuclear strike against, say, a hardened underground WMD facility, such as Libya's chemical weapons production facility at Tarhunah,[55] might seem plausible, the United States either has or could develop a conventional capability to deal with such targets, and hence such use could not be deemed militarily or legally necessary.[56]

The same is true of virtually any imaginable threat by a "rogue nation" to use nuclear, chemical or biological weapons. With the modern high technology revolution, our conventional weapons are sufficient not only to deter any threat but also to address virtually any military need, including virtually any threat that might otherwise have been the basis of using tactical nuclear weapons.[57]

WITHOUT END: IN SEARCH OF ANSWERS TO THE VIETNAM TRAGEDY 9–15 (1999); DOCTRINE FOR JOINT OPERATIONS, *supra* note 36, at I-2.

[55] *See* Chapter 27, notes 75–77, Chapter 28, notes 54–72, and accompanying text. *See also Use of Nuclear Arms Still Viable in Some Cases, Says US Agency*, JANE'S DEFENCE WEEKLY, vol. 28, no. 8, Aug. 27, 1997, at 3. *USA Seeks More Protection Against WMD*, JANE'S DEFENCE WEEKLY, vol. 29, no. 21, p. 13, May 27, 1998; Robert Waller, *Libyan Chemical Warfare Raises the Issue of Pre-emption*, JANE'S INTELLIGENCE REV., November 1, 1996.

[56] *See* Chapter 12, notes 15–16; Chapter 18, notes 28–29, Chapter 28, notes 5, 13, 47, 68–70, and accompanying text. *See also* National Defense Panel, Transforming Defense: National Security in the 21st Century 51 (Dec. 1997); WILLIAM J. PERRY, SECRETARY OF DEFENSE, 1995 ANNUAL REPORT TO THE PRESIDENT AND THE CONGRESS 85.

[57] *See* Chapter 18, notes 38–40, 50–52, 63–64, Chapter 28, notes 47, 53–72, and accompanying text. *See also Prepared Statement of Secretary of Defense William S. Cohen to the Senate Armed Forces Committee, Feb. 3, 1998; New Defense Strategy: Shape, Respond, Prepare*, DEFENSE ISSUES, vol. 13, no. 13, <http://www.defenselink.mil/speeches/1998/t19980203-secdef.html>; William J. Perry, *Desert Storm and Deterrence*, FOREIGN AFF., vol. 70 no. 4, Fall 1991, at 66; NATIONAL DEFENSE PANEL, TRANSFORMING DEFENSE: NATIONAL SECURITY IN THE 21ST CENTURY 51 (Dec. 1997).

Recent statements of U.S. policy have further confirmed the extent to which nuclear deterrence is today directed against a potential adversary's nuclear as opposed to conventional assets and aspirations. *See* JOHN M. SHALIKASHVILI,

In any event, even the most limited of uses of the smallest of tactical nuclear weapons, in the circumstances in which such use would likely take place, would likely precipitate escalatory nuclear, chemical or biological attacks from the target state or one of its allies or some other adversary of the United States,[58] whether because the enemy or some other State:[59]

- perceived the strike as a major strategic attack or anticipated such a strike;[60]
- saw the crossing of the nuclear threshold as the abandonment of restraint;[61]

CJCS, NATIONAL MILITARY STRATEGY: SHAPE, RESPOND, PREPARE NOW—A MILITARY STRATEGY FOR A NEW ERA (1997), <http://www.dtic.mil/jcs/nms>; WILLIAM S. COHEN, REPORT OF THE QUADRENNIAL DEFENSE REVIEW, MAY 1997, § III, Defense Strategy, <http://www.fas.org/man/docsqdr/sec3.html>.

[58] *See* Chapter 25; Chapter 1, notes 183, 270–273; Chapter 2, notes 14–15, 71–87; Chapter 3, notes 31, 46, 89–90; Chapter 4, note 50; Chapter 15, note 22, and accompanying text. *See also* THE AIR FORCE COMMANDER'S HANDBOOK, *supra* note 16, at 8-1; DOCTRINE FOR JOINT NUCLEAR OPERATIONS, *supra* note 36, at I-3–6; DOCTRINE FOR JOINT THEATER NUCLEAR OPERATIONS, *supra* note 42, at ix, III-7–8; Nuclear Weapons Advisory Opinion ¶ 94 at 32; declaration of President Bedjaoui ¶ 22, 35 I.L.M. at 1345; dissenting opinion of Judge Weeramantry at 27, 59, 35 I.L.M. at 909, 893.

[59] *See* Chapter 3, notes 151–153, Chapter 27, notes 2–5, 61, 68–85, and accompanying text. *See also* U.S. Congress, Office of Technology Assessment, *Proliferation of Weapons of Mass Destruction, Assessing the Risks* 61, 100 (1993) (report prepared at request of Congress "to assist Congress in its efforts to strengthen and broaden U.S. policies to control the proliferation of weapons of mass destruction"); dissenting opinion of Judge Schwebel at 3, 12, 35 I.L.M 842; U.S. DEPARTMENT OF DEFENSE, PROLIFERATION: THREAT AND RESPONSE *Middle East and North Africa* 10 (1997).

For a review of statements of civilian, military and policy leaders of the United States throughout the nuclear era as to the lack of military usefulness of nuclear weapons, *see* Chapter 24. For similar statements as to the likelihood that even the most limited use of nuclear weapons would lead to escalation to higher levels of such use, *see* Chapter 25. For a discussion of the risks of escalation inherent in the proliferation of chemical and biological weapons, *see* Chapter 27.

[60] *See* Chapter 20; Chapter 2, notes 83–84, Chapter 3, notes 88–90, Chapter 16, notes 35–36, Chapter 18, note 56, Chapter 25, notes 18, 39, and accompanying text. *See also* DOCTRINE FOR JOINT NUCLEAR OPERATIONS, *supra* note 36, at I-5–6; dissenting opinion of Judge Weeramantry, 35 I.L.M. at 909; Paul Bracken, *War Termination, in* MANAGING NUCLEAR OPERATIONS 197 (1987); PETER PRINGLE & WILLIAM ARKIN, S.I.O.P., THE SECRET U.S. PLAN FOR NUCLEAR WAR 193–94 (1983).

- felt the need to demonstrate its own resolve and national standing or to warn the United States against further escalation;[62]
- felt the need to use its own nuclear weapons before they were destroyed by a further U.S. strike;[63]
- resolved to destroy U.S. nuclear weapons before more could be launched;[64]
- felt it could control escalation, going only one step up the escalatory ladder; [65] or

---

[61] *See* Chapter 1, note 34, Chapter 3, note 95, Chapter 16, notes 36–38, Chapter 22, note 22, Chapter 25, notes 34, 45, Chapter 26, note 1, and accompanying text.

[62] *See* Chapter 2, notes 15, 78, 83, Chapter 23, note 5, Chapter 25, note 9, and accompanying text. *See also* DOCTRINE FOR JOINT THEATER NUCLEAR OPERATIONS, *supra* note 42, at III-7–8; *United Kingdom Nuclear Doctrine: Deterrence After The INF Treaty, in* UNITED NATIONS DEPARTMENT FOR DISARMAMENT AFFAIRS, NUCLEAR WEAPONS: A COMPREHENSIVE STUDY 158–9 (1991).

[63] *See* Chapter 2, notes 86–87, Chapter 15, notes 24–25, Chapter 18, note 55, Chapter 22, note 32, Chapter 25, notes 1–3, 37, 40, Chapter 27, note 7, and accompanying text. *See also* UNITED NATIONS DEPARTMENT FOR DISARMAMENT AFFAIRS, NUCLEAR WEAPONS: A COMPREHENSIVE STUDY 116 (1991); DOCTRINE FOR JOINT OPERATIONS, *supra* note 36, at ix; Bruce M. Russett, *The Doctrine of Deterrence, in* CATHOLICS AND NUCLEAR WAR 149, 161 (1983); Steven E. Miller, *The Case Against a Ukrainian Nuclear Deterrent,* FOREIGN AFF., vol. 72, no. 3, Summer 1993, at 67, 71.

[64] *See* Chapter 2, notes 78–82, Chapter 15, notes 24, 25, and accompanying text. *See also* DOCTRINE FOR JOINT NUCLEAR OPERATIONS, *supra* note 36, at III-8.

[65] *See* Chapter 2, notes 87, 134, Chapter 16, notes 1–11, 30, Chapter 17, notes 47–59, Chapter 25, notes 21–25, 45, and accompanying text. *See also* ICJ Hearing, November 15, 1995, at 86; BERNARD BRODIE, THE ABSOLUTE WEAPON: ATOMIC POWER AND WORLD ORDER 70–77 (1946); SECRETARY OF DEFENSE JAMES R. SCHLESINGER, 1975 DEPARTMENT OF DEFENSE ANNUAL REPORT, DETERRENCE, ASSURED DESTRUCTION, AND STRATEGIC OPTIONS 32–38; Secretary of Defense Robert McNamara, *Defense Arrangements of the North Atlantic Community* (Department of State Bulletin, 9 July 1962) *in* AMERICAN DEFENSE POLICY 295 (1990); DOCTRINE FOR JOINT NUCLEAR OPERATIONS, *supra* note 36, at i, I-1–2; *Hearings before the Special Panel on Arms Control and Disarmament of the Procurement and Military Nuclear Systems Subcommittee of the Committee on Armed Services of the House of Representatives,* 98th Cong. 282 (1985) (statement of Adm. Noel Gayler, U.S.N (Retired), American Committee on East-West Accord); *Hearings on The Role of Arms Control in U.S. Defense Policy, before the Committee on Foreign*

- was driven by bloodlust or suicidal vengefulness or human or equipment failure or cultural factors or the like.[66]

The nuclear response by the adversary, or even the likelihood of such a response, would likely lead to escalating nuclear strikes by the United States for the same types of reasons that would have driven the enemy's actions.[67]

Given the fog of war and the inherent uncertainties as to the enemy's perception of the attack and reaction thereto, a low level nuclear attack would have all the disadvantages of crossing the nuclear Rubicon, including substantially the same risks of precipitating

---

Affairs, House of Representatives, 98th Cong. 2nd Sess. (June 20, 21, 26; July 25, 1984), at 158; Robert S. McNamara, *The Military Role of Nuclear Weapons: Perceptions and Misperceptions, in* THE NUCLEAR CONTROVERSY, A FOREIGN AFFAIRS READER 90 (1985); HAROLD BROWN, 1976 DEPARTMENT OF DEFENSE ANNUAL REPORT TO THE PRESIDENT AND CONGRESS; General A. S. Collins, Jr., *Theater Nuclear Warfare: The Battlefield, in* AMERICAN DEFENSE POLICY 359–60 (J.F. Reichart & S. R. Stern 5th ed. 1982); CENTER FOR DEFENSE INFORMATION, NUCLEAR WAR QUOTATIONS at 42.

[66] *See* Chapter 3, notes 77–78, 92, Chapter 15, note 108, Chapter 18, notes 47–52, Chapter 22, notes 26–37, Chapter 25, note 9, Chapter 27, note 7, Chapter 16, notes 48–50, and accompanying text. *See also* dissenting opinion of Judge Weeramantry at 60, 35 I.L.M. at 910 (citing *Risks of Unintentional Nuclear War,* BULL. OF THE ATOMIC SCIENTISTS, Vol. 38, p. 68, June 1982); Carl Sagan, *Nuclear War and Climatic Catastrophe: Some Policy Implications,* 62 FOREIGN AFF. 257, 259–261 (Winter 1983/1984); Ashton B. Carter, *Sources of Error and Uncertainty, in* MANAGING NUCLEAR OPERATIONS 611–12, 625 (1987); UNITED NATIONS DEPARTMENT FOR DISARMAMENT AFFAIRS, NUCLEAR WEAPONS: A COMPREHENSIVE STUDY 116 (1991); *Proliferation of Weapons of Mass Destruction: Assessing the Risks, supra* note 59, at 70; DOCTRINE FOR JOINT NUCLEAR OPERATIONS, *supra* note 36, at I-2; ROBERT S. MCNAMARA, JAMES G. BLIGHT, & ROBERT K. BRIGHAM, ARGUMENT WITHOUT END: IN SEARCH OF ANSWERS TO THE VIETNAM TRAGEDY 9–15 (1999); Pastoral Letter on War and Peace, The Challenge of Peace: God's Promise and Our Response (May 3, 1983), at 48; *The Consequences of Nuclear War on the Global Environment, Hearing Before the Subcommittee on Investigations and Oversight of the Committee on Science and Technology,* 97th Cong. (1982) (Resolution of April 27, 1982, statement of Dr. Sidney D. Drell).

[67] *See supra* notes 58–66 and accompanying text; Chapter 17, notes 1–21, Chapter 27, notes 1–5, and accompanying text. *See also* LT. COL. JERRY M. SOLLINGER, IMPROVING US THEATER NUCLEAR DOCTRINE: A CRITICAL ANALYSIS (1983); PROLIFERATION: THREAT AND RESPONSE, *supra* note 59, at *Middle East and North Africa* 14, quoting Secretary of Defense William J. Perry; William M. Arkin & Hans Kristensen, *Dangerous Directions,* BULL. OF THE ATOMIC SCIENTISTS, vol. 54, no. 2, Mar. 1, 1998.

escalation, without delivering the potential firepower of a strategic attack and without knocking out some of the enemy's WMD capability.

Thus, if the strike was going to be perceived as a major nuclear attack, eliciting a response as if it were such an attack, it might as well be such an attack.

Uncontrollability of Risks as to Likely Escalation

The U.S. military's recognition of the potential need for preemptive strikes against enemy delivery systems highlights the risks of escalation. As reflected in the *Doctrine for Joint Theater Nuclear Operations*, "Operations must be planned and executed to destroy or eliminate enemy WMD delivery systems and supporting infrastructure before they can strike friendly forces."[68]

Also inherently of an escalatory nature is the U.S. nuclear targeting doctrine of decapitation, as reflected in the *Joint Theater Nuclear Operations* manual, whereby the command and control centers of an opposing nation are "facilities that may be likely targets for nuclear strikes:"

> Enemy combat forces and facilities that may be likely targets for nuclear strikes are:
> • WMD and their delivery systems, as well as associated command and control, production, and logistical support units;
> • Ground combat units and their associated command and control and support units.[69]

The *Joint Theater Nuclear Operations* manual notes that "there may be a rapid escalation" once strikes against nuclear assets begin to affect "the forces available for nuclear employment."[70]

---

[68] DOCTRINE FOR JOINT THEATER NUCLEAR OPERATIONS, *supra* note 42, at ix (emphasis omitted). *See* Chapter 3, notes 86–87 and accompanying text. *See also* Chapter 26, notes 12–15 and accompanying text, for discussion of the new post–Cold War asymmetric risks of a weaker power using a WMD, including a nuclear weapon, against the United States.

[69] *Id.* at III-6–7. *See also* Eric Schmitt, *50's Riddle Returns in Treaty Debate: Do Weapons Controls Erode or Enhance U.S. Deterrence*, THE NEW YORK TIMES, Oct. 10, 1999, at A10; NATIONAL DEFENSE PANEL, TRANSFORMING DEFENSE: NATIONAL SECURITY IN THE 21ST CENTURY 51 (Dec. 1997). *See* Chapter 2, note 17, Chapter 18, notes 52–55, Chapter 25, note 26, Chapter 26, notes 16–18, and accompanying text.

[70] DOCTRINE FOR JOINT THEATER NUCLEAR OPERATIONS, *supra* note 42, at I-5–6. *See* Chapter 25, notes 1–3 and accompanying text.

The military's policies of concentration of force and redundant targeting, including "layering"[71] and "cross-targeting,"[72] potentially involving the use of multiple nuclear weapons, are inherently escalatory.

The quality of decisions being made will be affected by the severe time constraints caused by such factors as "the relatively short flight time of tactical missiles and potential increased uncertainty of mobile offensive force target locations."[73]

Noting that the joint force commander should have access to "near-real-time tradeoff analysis when considering the execution of any forces,"[74] the *Joint Theater Nuclear Operations* manual states:

> Very short timelines impact decisions that must be made. In a matter of seconds for the defense, and minutes for the offense, critical decisions must be made in concert with discussions with NCA.[75]

The *Joint Nuclear Operations* manual also notes the risk of misperception and non-susceptibility to deterrence, "It is possible ... that an adversary may misperceive or purposefully ignore a credible threat."[76]

Uncontrollatility as to Delivery of Nuclear Weapons

The U.S. position before the ICJ that it is capable of delivering nuclear weapons accurately and directly upon discrete military targets, precisely engaging such targets, overlooks central facts as to the accuracy and controllability of available delivery devices.

---

[71] *Id.* at II-6. *See* Chapter 16, notes 41–44, Chapter 25, note 4, and accompanying text.

[72] *Id.* at II-6. *See* Chapter 16, note 42, Chapter 25, note 5, and accompanying text.

[73] *Id.* at III-8. *See* Chapter 25, notes 6–7 and accompanying text.

[74] *Id. See* Chapter 2, notes 79–82 and accompanying text.

[75] *Id.* (emphasis omitted). *See* Chapter 2, notes 80–81, Chapter 23, note 30, and accompanying text. Ballistic missiles are extraordinarily fast:

> The Air Force said it recently completed two successful unarmed Minuteman III intercontinental ballistic missile launches from Vandenberg AFB, Calif. ... [E]ach ICBM covered 4,200 miles in 30 minutes, hitting predetermined targets at the Kwajalein Missile Range in the western Marshall Islands.

Sarah Hood, *News Notes*, AIR FORCE MAG., Aug., 1997 at 15.

[76] DOCTRINE FOR JOINT NUCLEAR OPERATIONS, *supra* note 36, at I-2. *See* Chapter 18, notes 55–56 and accompanying text.

U.S. nuclear weapons would typically be delivered to their targets by missiles based on either land, submarine, surface vessel or aircraft, or dropped by bombers.[77]

Statistically, modern U.S. missiles are generally capable of extreme accuracy.[78] A high percentage of missiles launched can be expected to strike within a close distance of their intended targets.[79]

However, this tells only part of the story. The accuracy of any particular missile is uncertain and no one can know where it might end up.[80]

Variables affecting this matter are legion, including the weather; gravitational effects; the accuracy of test or computational assumptions as to how the missile will perform and as to the location and nature of the target; the extent to which the launch was programmed and implemented correctly to reach the target; the extent to which the mechanical and electronic equipment in the missile functions as intended; the effect of the detonation of other nuclear or other weapons on performance; and the height at which the warhead detonates.[81]

---

[77] *See* Chapter 19; Chapter 15, notes 18–28 and accompanying text; DOCTRINE FOR JOINT NUCLEAR OPERATIONS, *supra* note 36, at II-2; DOCTRINE FOR JOINT THEATER NUCLEAR OPERATIONS, *supra* note 42, at I-3–5.

[78] *See* Chapter 21, notes 8–10, Chapter 19, note 8, endnotes, and accompanying text and charts. *See also* Kosta Tsipis, *Cruise Missiles*, SCIENTIFIC AMERICAN, Feb. 1977, 20–29; 1 THOMAS B. COCHRAN ET AL., NUCLEAR WEAPONS DATABOOK, UNITED STATES NUCLEAR FORCES AND CAPABILITIES 118, 146 (1984); Nick Cook, John Boatman, *USAF Lifts Veil on 'Secret' ACM*, 14 JANE'S DEFENSE WEEKLY 549, no. 13, September 29, 1990; Strategic Missiles, <http://www.af.mil/news/airman/0199/missi.htm>; Robert S. Norris & William M. Arkin, *U.S. Strategic Nuclear Forces End of 1998; Abstract,* BULL. OF THE ATOMIC SCIENTISTS, vol. 55, no. 1, Jan. 1999.

[79] *See* Chapter 21, note 11, Chapter 19, note 8, endnotes, and accompanying text and charts. *See also* David Fulghum, *Clashes with Iraq Continue After Heavy Air Strike*, AVIATION WEEK & SPACE TECH., Jan. 25, 1993, at 38.

[80] *See* Chapter 21, notes 5, 7–17, Chapter 28, notes 42–46, and accompanying text. *See also* United States General Accounting Office, Report To Congress: Operation Desert Storm: Evaluation of the Air War 5–7 (July 1996); BBC SUMMARY OF WORLD BROADCASTS, Sept. 7, 1998; *Pakistan— Cruise Missile Found Near Pakistan Nuclear Test Site,* FT ASIA INTELLIGENCE WIRE, Aug. 24, 1998.

[81] *See* Chapter 2, notes 60–62, Chapter 21 notes 1, 5–6, and accompanying text. *See also* ICJ Hearing, November 15, 1995, at 87, 89 (citing the Secretary-General's 1990 Report on nuclear weapons, p. 75, para. 290); KOSTA TSIPIS, ARSENAL: UNDERSTANDING WEAPONS IN THE NUCLEAR AGE 72–75 (1983);

The United States reportedly achieved an overall accuracy level of some 82% in the Gulf War with its BG-109 Tomahawk cruise missiles, but that was only an average, with some missions achieving a near perfect success rate and one mission obtaining a rate of only 67%.[82]

With the U.S. attacks on terrorist bases in Afghanistan and Sudan in 1998, some missiles reportedly ended up in the wrong country (Pakistan).[83]

Ashton B. Carter, *Sources of Error and Uncertainty, in* MANAGING NUCLEAR OPERATIONS 611–639 (1987).

As the United States, through its attorney McNeill, argued to the ICJ, the effects of nuclear weapons depend on such factors as "the explosive yield and height of the burst of individual weapons, on the characteristics of their targets, as well as on climatic and weather conditions," ICJ Hearing, November 15, 1995, at 87 (citing the Secretary-General's 1990 Report of Nuclear Weapons, p. 75, para. 290), and on "the technology that occasions how much radiation the weapon may release, where, in relation to the earth's surface it will be detonated, and the military objective at which it would be targeted." *Id.* at 89. As to the significance of such factors, McNeill argued, "These differences, distinctions and variables cannot be ignored; they are critical to the appropriate legal analysis." *Id.* at 87.

[82] *See* David Fulghum, *Clashes with Iraq Continue After Heavy Air Strike,* AVIATION WEEK & SPACE TECH., Jan. 25, 1993, at 38; Stanley Kandebo, *Operation Desert Storm—Tomahawk Missiles Excel in First Wartime Use,* AVIATION WEEK & SPACE TECH., vol. 134, no. 3, Jan. 21, 1991, at 61; Chapter 21, notes 11–14 and accompanying text.

[83] *See* BBC SUMMARY OF WORLD BROADCASTS, Sept. 7, 1998; *2nd Unexploded U.S. Missile Found In Pakistan,* THE COMMERCIAL APPEAL (Memphis, TN), Aug. 30, 1998, at A2; Chapter 21, note 17 and accompanying text.

See also John Diamond, *US Strikes May Not Be The Last, Warns Pickering,* BIRMINGHAM POST, Aug. 22, 1998, at 8; Ian Mackinnon, *Pakistan Defuses US Cruise Missile,* THE SCOTSMAN, Aug. 25, 1998, at 8; *Pakistan—Cruise Missile Found Near Pakistan Nuclear Test Site,* FT ASIA INTELLIGENCE WIRE, Aug. 24, 1998; Louise Branson, *US Bombs "Terrorist Bases,"* THE STRAITS TIMES (Singapore), Aug. 22, 1998, at 1.

According to a Pakistani foreign ministry spokesman, the two missiles ending up in Pakistan had been fired from U.S. ships 120 nautical miles off the coast of Pakistan, purportedly within the country's territorial waters, and landed near the sites where Pakistan had tested nuclear weapons on May 28 and 30, 1998. Mackinnon, *supra,* at 8. Thus, the missiles that went astray had not even been sent a long distance.

A third unexploded warhead with its cruise missile delivery vehicle was reportedly found in Afghanistan. *See* BBC SUMMARY OF WORLD BROADCASTS,

Similarly, in the 1999 Kosovo operation, there were numerous missile strikes that ended up at the wrong targets, both because of weapons and human error, including intelligence error.[84]

Delivery of nuclear weapons by bomber, while having the advantage that a bomber may generally be recalled before releasing its weapons, is subject to equipment, pilot and situational error.[85]

While certain of the more modern U.S. aircraft are extraordinarily fast and ostensibly have the capability of eluding radar detection, aircraft are inherently subject to pursuit, radar and human error—and hence to substantial risk factors as to accuracy of delivery.[86]

These limitations on accuracy of delivery obviously impose limitations on nuclear operations not present as to conventional

---

Sept. 7, 1998 (Taleban said ready to sell unexploded US cruise missile "to any country.").

It is sobering that these deviations from targeting could occur in an operation where the United States apparently went to great lengths to achieve accuracy and precision, even to the point, in planning an attack on a chemical plant in Sudan, of modeling the "likely plume of [the] attack beforehand, using such factors as weather conditions, the building's structure and properties of the suspected chemicals inside." *See* John-Alex Romano, *Note, Combating Terrorism and Weapons of Mass Destruction: Reviving the Doctrine of a State of Necessity,* 87 GEO. L.J. 1023 (April 1999) (quoting Eugene Robinson & Dana Priest, *Reports of U.S. Strikes' Destruction Vary; Afghanistan Damage 'Moderate to Heavy'; Sudan Plant Leveled,* WASH. POST, Aug. 22, 1998, at A1).

[84] *See* Chapter 21, notes 21–28 and accompanying text. *See also As Strikes Mount, So Do Errors,* THE WASH. TIMES, May 11, 1999, at A1; Joyce Price, *Pentagon Regrets "Embassy Error,"* THE WASH. TIMES, May 9, 1999, at C10; Bill Gertz & Rowan Scarborough, *Inside the Ring,* THE WASH. TIMES, May 14, 1999, at A9.

[85] *See* Chapter 15, notes 22, 24, 28; Chapter 22, note 22, and accompanying text. *See also* THE DOCTRINE FOR JOINT THEATER NUCLEAR OPERATIONS, *supra* note 42, at I-3–5.

[86] *See* Chapter 14, note 24, Chapter 19, note 8, Chapter 21, note 26, and accompanying text. *See also* KOSTA TSIPIS, ARSENAL: UNDERSTANDING WEAPONS IN THE NUCLEAR AGE, at 68–76, 114–115, 121–296; THE DOCTRINE FOR JOINT THEATER NUCLEAR OPERATIONS, *supra* note 42, at I-3–5.

Reportedly the "success level of the United States' most advanced fighters" is less than the 83% overall success rate that the Navy attained with its BG-109 Tomahawk cruise missiles (conventional) during the 1991 Gulf War. *See* David Fulghum, *Clashes with Iraq Continue After Heavy Air Strike,* AVIATION WEEK & SPACE TECH., Jan. 25, 1993, at 38.

weapons where the implications of weapons going astray are much less serious.[87]

Even if the warhead is delivered accurately at the target, its performance is subject to its correct functioning.[88]

Uncontrollability of Radiation Effects if Weapons Reach Targets

As to the controllability of the radiation effects of nuclear weapons, the United States argued the following proposition to the Court, either directly or by implication:

- The characteristic and primary effects of nuclear weapons are the explosive, heat and blast effects.[89]
- Radiation is only an incidental, unintended, collateral and secondary by-product of nuclear weapons, not the main or most characteristic feature of such weapons.[90]
- Just as conventional weapons may produce dangerous fumes, so also nuclear weapons may cause radiation.[91]

---

[87] *See* Chapter 15, notes 99–102, Chapter 21, notes 3–20, 26–28 and accompanying text. *See also* KOSTA TSIPIS, ARSENAL: UNDERSTANDING WEAPONS IN THE NUCLEAR AGE, at 68–76, 114–115, 121–296; INTERNATIONAL PHYSICIANS FOR THE PREVENTION OF NUCLEAR WAR, BRIEFING BOOK ON NUCLEAR WAR (1992), *quoted in* Peter Weiss, Burns H. Weston, Richard A. Falk, & Saul H. Mendlovitz, Draft Memorial in Support of the Application by the World Health Organization for an Advisory Opinion by the Court of International Justice of the Legality of the Use of Nuclear Weapons Under International Law, Including the W.H.O. Constitution, *reprinted at* 4 TRANSNAT'L L. & CONTEMP. PROBS. 721, 729–732 (1994).

[88] *See* Chapter 21, notes 4–6, and accompanying text; KOSTA TSIPIS, ARSENAL: UNDERSTANDING WEAPONS IN THE NUCLEAR AGE 68–76 (1983).

[89] *See* U.S. ICJ Memorandum/GA App. at 23–25; THE NAVAL/MARINE COMMANDER'S HANDBOOK, *supra* note 21, at 10-2; Chapter 2, notes 106, 109–110, and accompanying text.

[90] *See* U.S. ICJ Memorandum/GA App. at 23–25; Chapter 2, notes 106–109 and accompanying text.

Ironically, the United States further argued the contrary provision that because radiation is a natural characteristic of the explosion of nuclear weapons, and not some added element to increase the victim's suffering, the radiation effects do not render the use of nuclear weapons unlawful. McNeill told the ICJ, "The unnecessary suffering principle prohibits the use of weapons designed specifically to increase the suffering of persons attacked beyond that necessary to accomplish a particular military objective." ICJ Hearing, November 15, 1995, at 91. *See also* Chapter 2, note 55 and accompanying text.

[91] *See* U.S. ICJ Memorandum/GA App. at 23–25 (citing Hague Convention (IV) Respecting the Laws and Customs of War on Land, Annex, Art. 23(a)

- Through modern weapons technology, the United States is capable of limiting and controlling the amount of radiation a nuclear weapon would release.[92]
- The United States is capable of controlling the radioactive fallout from the detonation of nuclear weapons upon military targets.[93]
- There is no reason to believe that the use of nuclear weapons would cause extensive or significant radiation or extreme effects upon noncombatants or neutrals.[94]

The United States' minimization of the significance of the radiation effects of nuclear weapons does not seem tenable, in light of such ostensibly incontrovertible facts as the following:

- Radiation is a defining feature of nuclear weapons. All nuclear weapons emit radiation when detonated.[95]
- Radiation is inimical to life and cumulative in its buildup and effects, surviving in the environment and genetically in human and other life forms typically for many years (as to some elements, for thousands of years).[96]

---

reprinted in ROBERTS & GUELFF, DOCUMENTS ON THE LAW OF WAR (2nd ed. 1989, p. 63)); Chapter 2, notes 106–109 and accompanying text.

[92] See ICJ Hearing, November 15, 1995, at 88; U.S. ICJ Memorandum/GA App at 23 (citing the Army's THE LAW OF LAND WARFARE, supra note 13, at 5); Chapter 2, notes 58–59 and accompanying text.

[93] See id. (citing the Secretary-General's 1990 Report on nuclear weapons, p. 75, para. 290); Chapter 2, notes 60–61 and accompanying text.

[94] See id. at 87, 90; U.S. ICJ Memorandum/GA App. at 32; Chapter 2, notes 57, 68–69, 117, and accompanying text.

[95] See Chapter 2, note 4, Chapter 3, notes 12, 222, Chapter 15, notes 58–98 and accompanying text; NATO HANDBOOK ON THE MEDICAL ASPECTS OF NBC DEFENSIVE OPERATIONS Part I, Chap. 1 (A MedP-6(B) 1996), adopted as Army Field Manual 8-9, Navy Medical Publication 5059, Air Force Joint Manual 44-151; DOCTRINE FOR JOINT THEATER NUCLEAR OPERATIONS, supra note 42, at I-1–2; Nuclear Weapons Advisory Opinion ¶ 35, at 16–17, 35 I.L.M. at 821–22; dissenting opinion of Judge Shahabuddeen at 9, 35 I.L.M. at 865; UNITED NATIONS DEPARTMENT FOR DISARMAMENT AFFAIRS, NUCLEAR WEAPONS: A COMPREHENSIVE STUDY 6–8 (1991).

[96] See Chapter 3, notes 19–20, Chapter 15, notes 99, 114, 128–136, and accompanying text; NATO HANDBOOK ON THE MEDICAL ASPECTS OF NBC DEFENSIVE OPERATIONS, supra note 95, at Part I, Chap. 1; dissenting opinion of Judge Weeramantry at 16–17, 35 I.L.M. at 888 (citing RADIOECOLOGY (1995)); Testimony of Mrs. Lijon Eknilang, of the Marshall Islands, Council Member, Rongelap, I.C.J. materials, 14 November 1995; INTERNATIONAL PHYSICIANS

-    The spread of radiation from the detonation of nuclear
weapons could not be controlled or predicted since radiation
is dispersed in the environment by forces such as the winds,
the waters, the soil, animals, plants, and genetic effects, as
well as vagaries as to the point of delivery of the weapon in
relation to the surface and applicable environmental
factors.[97]

-    Radiation cannot discriminate between friend and foe,
combatant and noncombatant, adversary and neutral, one's
own population and forces and those of the enemy.[98]

FOR THE PREVENTION OF NUCLEAR WAR, BRIEFING BOOK ON NUCLEAR WAR
(1992). Numerous major studies during the Cold War attempted to quantify the
casualties that could be expected from limited nuclear attacks. Several found
that civilian casualties from a Soviet counterforce strike on the U.S. would
result in virtually as many deaths from radiation as from direct blast. *See*
William Daugherty et al., *The Consequences of "Limited" Nuclear Attacks on
the United States,* INT'L SECURITY vol. 10 no. 4 (1986), at 35; Frank N. von
Hippel et al., *Civilian Casualties from Counterforce Attacks,* SCIENTIFIC
AMERICAN vol. 259 no. 3, Sept. 1988, at 42; Barbara G. Levi et al., *Civilian
Casualties from "Limited" Nuclear Attacks on the USSR,* INT'L SECURITY, vol.
12, no. 3, Winter 1987/1988, at 168.

[97] *See* Chapter 2, notes 63–64, Chapter 3, notes 12, 228–231, Chapter 15,
note 9, Chapter 21, notes 3–6, and accompanying text; DOCTRINE FOR JOINT
THEATER NUCLEAR OPERATIONS, *supra* note 42, at III-2–3; THE NUCLEAR
READER: STRATEGY, WEAPONS AND WAR 320–26 (1985); NATO HANDBOOK
ON THE MEDICAL ASPECTS OF NBC DEFENSIVE OPERATIONS, *supra* note 95, at
Part I, Chap. 1, Chap 3, §§ I-303(c), IV-320; U.S. Congress, Office of
Technology Assessment, *The Effects of Nuclear War,* NTIS order no. PB-
296946 (Washington, DC: U.S. Government Printing Office, May 1979), at
113 Table 14; 8 CHARLES S. GRACE, NUCLEAR WEAPONS: PRINCIPLES, EFFECTS
AND SURVIVABILITY 29–30 (Brassey's 1994); KOSTA TSIPIS, ARSENAL:
UNDERSTANDING WEAPONS IN THE NUCLEAR AGE 68–76, 114–115, 121–296
(1983).

[98] *See* Chapter 2, note 96, Chapter 3, notes 3, 11, 32, 37, 192–193, 228–235,
249, and accompanying text; DOCTRINE FOR JOINT THEATER NUCLEAR
OPERATIONS, *supra* note 42, at II-7; Nuclear Weapons Advisory Opinion ¶ 95,
at 32 35 I.L.M. at 829; dissenting opinion of Judge Shahabuddeen at 5–6, 35
I.L.M. at 863–864 (quoting Javez Perez de Cuellar, *Statement at the University
of Pennsylvania, 24 March 1983, in* DISARMAMENT, vol. VI, no. 1, 91);
declaration of President Bedjaoui ¶ 20, 35 I.L.M. at 1345, 1349 (No. 6
November 1996); dissenting opinion of Judge Schwebel at 7, 35 I.L.M at 839;
dissenting opinion of Judge Weeramantry at 48, 35 I.L.M. at 904; dissenting
opinion of Judge Koroma at 14, 35 I.L.M. 931.

-    Radiation from the Hiroshima and Nagasaki bombs, from atomic testing, and from the Chernobyl releases have caused and continue to cause substantial and widespread injury to human health and other life and may be expected to continue to do so for generations to come.[99]

-    With escalation, the levels of radiation will increase.[100]

Uncontrollability of Overall Effects of Nuclear Weapons

Also unfounded is the U.S. position before the Court that effects of nuclear weapons are essentially comparable to those of conventional weapons.

The ICJ described the "unique characteristics" of nuclear weapons:

> The Court ... notes that nuclear weapons are explosive devices whose energy results from the fusion or fission of the atom. By its very nature, that process, in nuclear weapons as they exist today, releases not only immense quantities of heat and energy, but also powerful and prolonged radiation. According to the material before the Court, the first two causes of damage are vastly more powerful than the damage caused by other weapons, while the phenomenon of radiation is said to be peculiar to nuclear weapons. These characteristics render the nuclear weapon potentially catastrophic. The destructive power of nuclear weapons cannot be contained in either space or time. They have the potential to destroy all civilization and the entire ecosystem of the planet.
>
> The radiation released by a nuclear explosion would affect health, agriculture, natural resources and demography over a very wide area. Further, the use of nuclear weapons would be a serious danger to future generations. Ionizing radiation has the potential to damage the future environment, food and marine ecosystem, and to cause genetic defects and illness in future generations.
>
> 36. In consequence ... it is imperative for the Court to take account of the unique characteristics of nuclear weapons, and in particular their destructive capacity, their capacity to cause untold

---

[99] *See* Chapter 3, notes 12, 121, Chapter 15, notes 9, 10, 55, 137–195, and accompanying text; Nuclear Weapons Advisory Opinion ¶ 35, at 16–17, 35 I.L.M. at 821–22; dissenting opinion of Judge Shahabuddeen at 6, 35 I.L.M at 864, UNITED NATIONS DEPARTMENT FOR DISARMAMENT AFFAIRS, NUCLEAR WEAPONS: A COMPREHENSIVE STUDY 79–83 (1991).

[100] *See* Chapter 3, notes 17–18, Chapter 15, notes 101–102, and accompanying text; *The Effects of Nuclear War, supra* note 97, at 22–25, 81; dissenting opinion of Judge Weeramantry, at 19, 35 I.L.M. at 870.

human suffering, and their ability to cause damage to generations to come.[101]

The effects of nuclear weapons were described further in dissenting opinions of individual judges of the ICJ. Judge Weeramantry stated that "[a] 5-megaton weapon would represent more explosive power than all of the bombs used in World War II and a twenty-megaton bomb more than all of the explosives used in all of the wars in the history of mankind."[102]

Judge Koroma stated:

> According to the material before the Court, it is estimated that more than 40,000 nuclear warheads exist in the world today with a total destructive capacity around a million times greater than that of the bomb which devastated Hiroshima. A single nuclear bomb detonated over a large city is said to be capable of killing more than 1 million people. These weapons, if used massively, could result in the annihilation of the human race and the extinction of human civilization. Nuclear weapons are thus not just another kind of weapon, they are considered the absolute weapon and are far more pervasive in terms of their destructive effects than any conventional weapon.[103]

Judge Shahabuddeen quoted Javier Perez de Cuellar, Secretary-General of the United Nations, to similar effect:

> "The world's stockpile of nuclear weapons today is equivalent to 16 billion tons of TNT. As against this, the entire devastation of

---

[101] Nuclear Weapons Advisory Opinion ¶ 35, at 16–17, 35 I.L.M. at 821–22. *See* Chapter 3, note 11 and accompanying text. *See also* Chapter 15, notes 1–14, 33–43, 58–89, 99, 102–108 and accompanying text; NATO HANDBOOK ON THE MEDICAL ASPECTS OF NBC DEFENSIVE OPERATIONS, *supra* note 95, at Part I, Chap. 1, §102(a); INTERNATIONAL PHYSICIANS FOR THE PREVENTION OF NUCLEAR WAR, BRIEFING BOOK ON NUCLEAR WAR (1992); Carl Sagan, *Nuclear War and Climatic Catastrophe: Some Policy Implications,* 62 FOREIGN AFF. 257, 273 (Winter 1983/1984). *See generally The Effects of Nuclear War, supra* note 97, at 16–17 (It is estimated that only half of the suffering would be over as of the end of the war itself: "A failure to achieve [social and economic] viability would result in many additional deaths, and much additional economic, political, and social deterioration. This post war damage could be as devastating as the damage from the actual nuclear explosions." *Id.* at 5).

[102] Dissenting opinion of Judge Weeramantry at 15, 35 I.L.M. at 887. *See* Chapter 3, note 13 and accompanying text.

[103] Dissenting opinion of Judge Koroma at 1, 35 I.L.M. at 934. *See* Chapter 3, note 22 and accompanying text.

the Second World War was caused by the expenditure of no more than 3 million tons of munitions. In other words, we possess a destructive capacity of more than a 5,000 times what caused 40 to 50 million deaths not too long ago. It should suffice to kill every man, woman and child 10 times over."[104]

The U.S. Joint Chief of Staff's *Joint Nuclear Operations* manual recognizes that "the use of nuclear weapons represents a significant escalation from conventional warfare."[105] The manual states:

> The fundamental differences between a potential nuclear war and previous military conflicts involve the speed, scope, and degree of destruction inherent in nuclear weapons employment, as well as the uncertainty of negotiating opportunities and enduring control over military forces.[106]
>
> ***
>
> Since nuclear weapons have greater destructive potential, in many instances they may be inappropriate.[107]
>
> ***
>
> The immediate and prolonged effects of WMD—including blast, thermal radiation, prompt (gamma and neutron) and residual radiation—pose unprecedented physical and psychological problems for combat forces and noncombatant populations alike.[108]

The U.S. Joint Chief of Staff's *Joint Theater Nuclear Operations* manual similarly states:

> Nuclear weapons are unique in this analysis [as to "the long-standing targeting rules of military necessity, proportionality, and avoidance of collateral damage and unnecessary suffering] only in their greater destructive potential (although they also different from conventional weapons in that they produce radiation and electromagnetic effects and, potentially, radioactive fallout).[109]

---

[104] Dissenting opinion of Judge Shahabuddeen at 5–6, 35 I.L.M. at 863–864 (quoting Javez Perez de Cuellar, Statement at the University of Pennsylvania, in DISARMAMENT, Vol. VI, No. 1, March, 24 1983, at p. 91). *See* Chapter 3, note 25 and accompanying text.

[105] DOCTRINE FOR JOINT NUCLEAR OPERATIONS, *supra* note 36, at II-1. *See* Chapter 2, notes 95–97 and accompanying text.

[106] *Id.* at I-6. *See* Chapter 2, notes 76, 95, and accompanying text.

[107] DOCTRINE FOR JOINT THEATER NUCLEAR OPERATIONS, *supra* note 42, at v–vi. *See* Chapter 2, notes 3, 4, and accompanying text.

[108] DOCTRINE FOR JOINT NUCLEAR OPERATIONS, *supra* note 36, at II-7. *See* Chapter 2, note 96 and accompanying text.

[109] DOCTRINE FOR JOINT THEATER NUCLEAR OPERATIONS, *supra* note 42, at I-1. *See* Chapter 2, note 97 and accompanying text (emphasis omitted).

The manual further recognizes that the employment of nuclear weapons "signifies an escalation of the war."[110]

Uncontrollability of Chemical and Biological Weapons Effects

The same risk factors as to uncontrollability of potential effects pertain to chemical and biological weapons, and the risk factors as to each of these three types of weapons of mass destruction are interrelated because the use of any one type could readily lead to use of the other types.

In a major study the U.S. government identified the following risks of nuclear weapons proliferation, finding them to be ostensibly applicable to chemical and biological weapons and characterizing such risks as uncontrollable:[111]

> • Existing nuclear powers might use force to prevent others from getting nuclear weapons (as Israel tried against Iraq);
> • New nuclear powers might only be able to afford nuclear forces vulnerable to destruction by preemptive first strikes, leading to instabilities;

---

[110] *Id.* at III-1. *See* Chapter 2, note 99, Chapter 16, note 38 and accompanying text; Secretary of Defense Harold Brown, *A Countervailing Strategic Strategy: Remarks from Speech to the Naval War College, August 20, 1980,* DEFENSE, Oct. 1980, vol. 80, at 2–9. In 1980, Secretary of Defense Harold Brown expressed skepticism about escalation control: "We are also not unaware of the immense uncertainties involved in any use of nuclear weapons." *Id.* at 9. "We know that what might start as a supposedly controlled, limited strike could well, in my view would very likely, escalate to full-scale nuclear war." *Id.*

See also Andrei Sakharov, *An Open Letter to Dr. Sidney Drell,* 61 FOREIGN AFF. 1001 (Summer 1983):

> I agree that if the "nuclear threshold" is crossed, *i.e.*, if any country uses a nuclear weapon even on a limited scale, the further course of events would be difficult to control and the most probable result would be swift escalation leading from a nuclear war initially limited in scale or by region to an all-out nuclear war, *i.e.*, to general suicide. It is relatively unimportant how the "nuclear threshold" is crossed—as a result of a preventive nuclear strike or in the course of a war fought with conventional weapons, when a country is threatened with defeat, or simply as result of an accident.

Id.

[111] *Proliferation of Weapons of Mass Destruction: Assessing the Risks, supra* note 59, at 70, citing John Mearscheimer, *Back to the Future: Instability in Europe After the Cold War,* INT'L SECURITY, vol. 15, no. 1, Sum. 1990, at 37–38. *See* Chapter 27, notes 6–8 and accompanying text.

• Those controlling nuclear weapons might believe they could fight and win nuclear wars; and

• Increasing the number of fingers on the nuclear trigger would increase the probability that someone would use them accidentally or irrationally, or that terrorists would steal them.[112]

As to such risks, the report concluded:

> The same principles would probably apply, in varying degrees, to chemical and biological weapons. The predominant view amongst scholars—and national governments—is that these dangers are not controllable and that proliferation should be avoided, not accepted.[113]

The destructiveness of chemical and biological weapons rivals that of nuclear weapons. Some biological weapons are capable of destruction potentially exceeding that of nuclear weapons.[114] Secretary of Defense Cohen has stated:

> I believe the proliferation of weapons of mass destruction presents the greatest threat that the world has ever known. We are finding more and more countries who are acquiring technology—not only missile technology—and are developing chemical weapons and biological weapons capabilities to be used in theater and also on a long-range basis. So I think that is perhaps the greatest threat that any of us will face in the coming years.[115]

The risks factors are exacerbated because weapons of mass destruction "will be weapons of the weak—states or groups that militarily are at best second-class."[116] Chemical and biological

---

[112] *Id.*

[113] *Id.*

[114] *See* Chapter 27, notes 11–13, 16–24, and accompanying text. *See also Proliferation of Weapons of Mass Destruction: Assessing the Risks, supra* note 59, at 2, 3, 8, 46, 53–54, 53, fig. 2-1, 54, fig. 2-1, 2-2, 61, 62; *Hearing of the Senate Foreign Relations Committee, Nomination of John David Holum to be Undersecretary of State for Arms Control and International Security, Chaired by Senator Charles Hagel (R-NE),* FEDERAL NEWS SERVICE, June 28, 1999; SECRETARY OF DEFENSE WILLIAM COHEN, THE QUADRENNIAL DEFENSE REVIEW § II (1997).

[115] PROLIFERATION: THREAT AND RESPONSE, *supra* note 59, at 1 (quoting Secretary Cohen's confirmation hearing of January 1997). *See* Chapter 27, notes 4–5, 24 and accompanying text. *See also Nomination of John David Holum, supra* note 114.

[116] Betts, *supra* note 125. *See* Chapter 27, notes 75–78 and accompanying text.

weapons attacks are anticipated as an asymmetrical attack, whereby a small enemy would use such a device to react to "overwhelming U.S. conventional dominance."[117]

There are presently some twenty-five–twenty-nine States having chemical and biological weapons programs, including North Korea, China, India, Pakistan, Iran, Iraq, Libya, Syria, and Russia.[118] Non-national groups that have obtained such weapons at various times include the Aum Shinrikyo in Japan and the Aryan Nations in the United States.[119]

The potential risks of chemical and biological weapons are only exacerbated by the fact that their proliferation has been concentrated in the hot spots of the world, major trip wire points such as the Koreas, India–Pakistan, and the Middle East.[120]

Threats exchanged between the United States, Israel and Iraq at the time of the 1990–91 Gulf War illustrate the inter-relatedness of the potential use of nuclear, chemical and biological weapons. Saddam Hussein reportedly threatened that if any nation used nuclear weapons against Iraq, Iraq would respond with chemical weapons:[121] "Whoever threatens us with the atomic bomb, we will annihilate him with the binary chemical ... we will make the fire eat up half of Israel if it tries to do anything against Iraq."[122] Similarly, the United States reportedly

---

[117] THE QUADRENNIAL DEFENSE REVIEW, *supra* note 114, at § III 6–7. *See* Chapter 27, notes 75–78 and accompanying text.

[118] *See* Chapter 27, notes 32–40 and accompanying text. *See also* PROLIFERATION: THREAT AND RESPONSE, *supra* note 59; *Nomination of John David Holum, supra* note 114.

[119] *See* Chapter 27, notes 41–42 and accompanying text. *See also* PROLIFERATION: THREAT AND RESPONSE, *supra* note 59, at The Transnational Threat; Robert Taylor, *The Bio-Terrorist Threat; Potential for Use of Biological Weapons by Terrorist Groups*, WORLD PRESS REVIEW, Sept. 1996, reprinted from NEW SCIENTIST, May 11, 1996.

[120] *See Proliferation of Weapons of Mass Destruction: Assessing the Risks, supra* note 59, at 66; Chapter 27, notes 75–78 and accompanying text.

[121] *See* Chapter 27, notes 1–5 and accompanying text. *See also Proliferation of Weapons of Mass Destruction: Assessing the Risks, supra* note 59, at 100, citing Saddam Hussein, Apr. 2, 1990, Baghdad INA, translation in FBIS-NEW-90-064, Apr. 3, 1990, at 36.

[122] *Id.* Saddam's reference was ostensibly to the binary sarin nerve gas artillery that Iraq had developed. *See,* PROLIFERATION: THREAT AND RESPONSE, *supra* note 59, at *Middle East and North Africa* 10. This was the same gas ostensibly used by the Japanese terrorist group Aum Shinrikyo in the 1995 Tokyo subway attack. *See* Taylor, *supra* note 119; Chapter 27, notes 3, 42 and accompanying text.

threatened Iraq with the use of nuclear weapons if Iraq used chemical weapons.[123]

U.S. officials have expressed the matter broadly: "[I]f some nation were to attack the United States with chemical weapons then they would have to fear the consequences of a response from any weapon in our inventory .... And I would not think that any nation should feel that they can use a chemical weapon against us without receiving a devastating response. ... That is, we could make a devastating response without the use of nuclear weapons, but we would not forswear that possibility."[124]

Conclusion as to Uncontrollability

Based on the foregoing, the uncontrollability of the effects of nuclear weapons, including of the escalation, radiation and other destructive effects, seems clear, causing the use of such weapons to be unlawful under the rules of discrimination, necessity, and proportionality.

Further Bases of Unlawfulness

Even beyond the element of uncontrollability, the use of nuclear weapons would violate the law of armed conflict.

Rule of Proportionality

If my statements of the facts and law are correct, it would seem clear that virtually any use of nuclear weapons, in the types of circumstances in which such use would likely take place, would violate the test of proportionality.

If any use would likely involve the multiple use of strategic nuclear weapons and subsequent escalation; or if even the most limited of nuclear strikes would likely precipitate escalation to broader use of nuclear, chemical and/or biological weapons; or if the effects, including particularly the radiation effects, of the weapon would be

---

[123] *See* Nuclear Weapons Advisory Opinion, at 35–36; dissenting opinion of Judge Schwebel at 3, 35 I.L.M 842; Chapter 3, notes 151–153, Chapter 27, notes 4–5, and accompanying text.

[124] PROLIFERATION: THREAT AND RESPONSE, *supra* note 59, at *Middle East and North Africa* 14, quoting Secretary of Defense William J Perry, Statement on Libyan Chemical Warfare Facility at Tarhunah, Air War College Conference on Nuclear Proliferation Issues, Maxwell Air Force Base, Alabama (April 26, 1996). *See* Chapter 27, notes 4–5, 79–85, and accompanying text; DOCTRINE FOR JOINT NUCLEAR OPERATIONS, *supra* note 36, at I-1. *See also* DOCTRINE FOR JOINT THEATER NUCLEAR OPERATIONS, *supra* note 42.

uncontrollable and would threaten ongoing injury potentially to millions of people unlimited in time or space, it would seem the potential risks would virtually always outweigh the potential military benefits.

Valuation Issues

But what of the valuation issues: What of the State that says, "The chance of saving my country justifies risking substantial injury to the rest of the world!"

This valuation question, in a world of sovereign nations, is, of course, a difficult one. But there is an answer. Indeed, several answers.

First of all, the proportionality, necessity, and discrimination rules, as we have seen, are rules of reason subject to an objective standard.[125]

Thus, *The Naval/Marine Commander's Handbook*, addressing how the proportionality determination is to be made, states that the commander "must determine whether incidental injuries and collateral damage would be excessive, on the basis of an honest and reasonable estimate of the facts available to him."[126] "[T]he commander must decide, in light of all the facts known or reasonably available to him ... whether to adopt an alternate method of attack, if reasonably available, to reduce civilian casualties and damage."[127]

Secondly, the rules of interpretation would appear to offer a principled basis for resolving any stalemate, particularly the rule that the law is to be interpreted in light of its purpose.

Nature and Purposes of the Law of Armed Conflict

The United States has recognized numerous fundamental purposes of the law of armed conflict that would ostensibly preclude actions precipitating the extreme effects that could result from the use of nuclear weapons:

- to provide common ground of rationality between enemies;

[125] *See* Chapter 1; Chapter 1, notes 84–94, 161, Chapter 5, notes 3–4, Chapter 6, notes 26–27, and accompanying text. *See also* Vienna Convention on the Law of Treaties Article 32, May 23, 1969, 1155 U.N.T.S. 331, 8 I.L.M. 679; J.L. BRIERLY, THE LAW OF NATIONS 67 (1963) (1928); XI INT'L ENCYCLOPEDIA OF COMPARATIVE LAW § 2-114 (1983).

[126] THE NAVAL/MARINE COMMANDER'S HANDBOOK, *supra* note 21, at 8-5. *See* Chapter 1, notes 84–90 and accompanying text.

[127] *Id.* at 8-5 to 8-6. *See* Chapter 1, notes 85–90 and accompanying text.

- to represent minimum standards of civilization;
- to preclude purposeless, unnecessary destruction of life and property;
- to ensure that violence is used only to defeat the enemy's military forces;
- to safeguard fundamental human rights of persons falling into the hands of the enemy, particularly prisoners of war, the wounded and sick, and civilians;
- to facilitate the restoration of peace and friendly relations; and
- to assure the survival of civilization and of the human species.

The Naval/Marine Commander's Handbook states that the "essential" purpose of the law of war is to provide "common ground of rationality between enemies," adding, "The law of armed conflict is intended to preclude purposeless, unnecessary destruction of life and property and to ensure that violence is used only to defeat the enemy's military forces."[128]

The handbook further describes the objective of the law of armed conflict:

> If followed by all participants, the law of armed conflict will inhibit warfare from needlessly affecting persons or things of little military value. By preventing needless cruelty, the bitterness and hatred arising from armed conflict is lessened, and thus it is easier to restore an enduring peace. The legal and military experts who attempted to codify the laws of war more than a hundred years ago reflected this reality when they declared that the final object of an armed conflict is the "re-establishment of good relations and a more solid and lasting peace between the belligerent States."[129]

The Air Force Manual on International Law states that the law of armed conflict is "inspired by the humanitarian desire of civilized nations to diminish the effects of conflicts" and represents an attempt to prevent "degeneration of conflicts into savagery and brutality, thereby

---

[128] *Id.* at 5-7 n.7. *See* Chapter 1, note 28 and accompanying text. *See also* Chapter 3, notes 275–296 for the discussion by the ICJ and the individual judges of the court of the underlying purposes of the law of armed conflict and the significance of such matter to the issue of the lawfulness of the use of nuclear weapons.

[129] *Id.* at 5-7 n.7 (citing Final Protocol of the Brussels Conference of 27 August 1874, Schindler & Toman 26). *See* Chapter 1, note 29 and accompanying text.

facilitating the restoration of peace and the friendly relations which must, at some point, inevitably accompany or follow the conclusion of hostilities."[130]

The manual adds that the law of armed conflict "has been said to represent in some measure minimum standards of civilization."[131] Noting that the law of armed conflict developed from "an amalgam of social, political and military considerations," the manual states, "The primary basis for the law, and the principal reason for its respect, is that it generally serves the self-interest of everyone subject to its commands."[132] The manual further notes the principle set forth in the "Lieber Code" that military necessity does not justify "any act of hostility which makes the return to peace unnecessarily difficult."[133]

To the objection that a particular limitation of the law of armed conflict might affect the ability of a combatant to win a particular battle or even the war itself, the answer—startling though it may be at first— is that this is implicit in the fact that this body of law imposes restraints. As the United States has recognized, "It is an essence of war that one or the other side must lose and the experienced generals and statesmen knew this when they drafted the rules and customs of land warfare."[134]

Admiral Noel Gayler, former Commander-in-Chief of the U.S. Forces in the Pacific and the Director of the National Security Agency, testified before the House Committee on Foreign Affairs:

> No one believes the nine new strategic nuclear weapons systems or the 17,000 new weapons now in our program or the corresponding Soviet buildup have any military usefulness. ..[135]

---

[130] THE AIR FORCE MANUAL ON INTERNATIONAL LAW, *supra* note 9, at 1-5. *See* Chapter 1, notes 28–36 and accompanying text.

[131] *Id.* at 1-5, 1-15 n.30. *See* Chapter 1, notes 30–31 and accompanying text.

[132] *Id.* at 1-11. *See* Chapter 1, notes 32–35 and accompanying text.

[133] *Id.* at 1-15 n.33. *See* Chapter 1, notes 33, 36, and accompanying text.

[134] THE NAVAL/MARINE COMMANDER'S HANDBOOK, *supra* note 21, at 5-6, citing The Krupp Trial (Trial of Alfred Felix Alwyn Krupp Von Bohlen und Halbach and Eleven Others), 10 LRTWC 139 (1949). *See* Chapter 1, notes 30, 36, and accompanying text.

[135] *Hearings on The Role of Arms Control in U.S. Defense Policy, before the Committee on Foreign Affairs, House of Representatives*, 98th Cong. 2nd Sess., (June 20, 21, 26, July 25, 1984) at 82 (statement of Adm. Noel Gayler, U.S. Navy (Retired), Former Commander in Chief, U.S. Forces in the Pacific,

Admiral Gayler went on to quote George Kennan's "profoundly sensible words:"

> [T]here is no issue at stake in our political relations with the Soviet Union—no hope, no fear, nothing in which we aspire, nothing we would like to avoid—which would conceivably be worth a nuclear war....[136]

Emphasizing the broad scope of international law, *The Air Force Manual on International Law* adopts Whiteman's comment that international law is evidenced by the "general norms of civilization."[137]

It is also in the nature of the law of war that it be dynamic, evolving out of human experience and necessity and advancing with the progress of civilization. *The Air Force Manual on International Law* recognizes, as one of "the most descriptive definitions of international law," Hackworth's statement:

> International law ... is a system of jurisprudence which, for the most part, has evolved out of the experiences and the necessities of situations that have arisen from time to time. It has developed with the progress of civilization with the increasing realization by nations that their relations *inter se*, if not their existence, must be governed by and dependent upon rules of law fairly certain and generally reasonable ....[138]

The manual similarly relies upon Whiteman's definition, which also emphasizes the dynamic nature of international law:

> International law is the standard of conduct, at a given time, for states and other entities subject thereto. It comprises the rights, privileges, powers, and immunities of states and entities invoking its provisions, as well as the correlative fundamental duties, absence of rights, liabilities and disabilities. International law is, more or less, in a continual state of change and development.[139]

Former Director, National Security Agency). *See* Chapter 24, notes 26–27 and accompanying text.

[136] *Id.*

[137] THE AIR FORCE MANUAL ON INTERNATIONAL LAW, *supra* note 9, at 1-3 (quoting 1 WHITEMAN, DIGEST OF INTERNATIONAL LAW 1-2); Chapter 1, notes 37–39 and accompanying text.

[138] *Id.* at 1-2; 1-13 nn.5–6 (quoting 1 HACKWORTH, DIGEST OF INTERNATIONAL LAW at 1, 7 vols. (1940–43)).

[139] *Id.* at 1-2; 1-13 nn.6–7 (quoting 1 WHITEMAN, DIGEST OF INTERNATIONAL LAW 1, 15 vols. with index (1963–1973)).

Such considerations as to the purpose of the law of armed conflict would appear to be available to resolve potential valuation issues in the balancing of the advantage to a particular State of using nuclear weapons versus the risks of unlawful effects, imposing restraint on the use of such weapons.

The ICJ in its decision recognized such fundamental values as substantive law, identifying the "respect of the human person" and the "elementary considerations of humanity" as basic values, "intransgressible principles."[140] The Court stated that "humanitarian law, at a very early stage, prohibited certain types of weapons either because of their indiscriminate effect on combatants and civilians or because of the unnecessary suffering caused to combatants, that is to say, a harm greater than that unavoidable to achieve legitimate objectives."[141]

President Bedjaoui, in his declaration, in addition to characterizing the important role of such concepts as obligations *erga omnes*, rules of *jus cogens*, and the "common heritage of mankind," went on to describe the current nature of international law as "an objective conception of international law more readily seen as the reflection of a collective juridical conscience and as a response to the social necessities of States organized as a community."[142]

Judge Higgins stated that the "judicial lodestar, whether in difficult questions of interpretation of humanitarian law, or in resolving claimed tensions between competing norms, must be those values that international law seeks to promote and protect."[143] Judge Higgins saw the central such value to be "the physical survival of peoples."[144]

Judge Shahabuddeen concluded that the preservation of mankind and of civilization is such a transcendent value that international law "could not authorize" a State to embark on a course of action that could result in destruction of such values.[145]

---

[140] Nuclear Weapons Advisory Opinion ¶¶ 79, 84, at 28, 29, 35 I.L.M. 827, 828. *See* Chapter 1, note 60, Chapter 3, notes 101, 172, 188–189, 275, 298 and accompanying text.

[141] *Id.* ¶ 78, at 28, 35 I.L.M. at 827. *See* Chapter 3, note 276 and accompanying text.

[142] Declaration of President Bedjaoui, 35 I.L.M., ¶ 13 at 1345. *See* Chapter 3, note 277 and accompanying text.

[143] Dissenting opinion of Judge Higgins at 8, 35 I.L.M. at 938. *See* Chapter 3, note 295 and accompanying text.

[144] *Id. See* Chapter 3, note 296 and accompanying text.

[145] Dissenting opinion Judge Shahabuddeen at 16, 35 I.L.M at 869. *See* Chapter 3, note 282 and accompanying text.

As to the distinction between nuclear and other weapons, the judge stated, "[I]f all the explosive devices used throughout the world since the invention of gunpowder were to detonate at the same time, they could not result in the destruction of civilization; this could happen if recourse were made to the use of nuclear weapons, and with many to spare."[146] He found the answer to the legal issue to be implicit in such facts:

> The principle limiting the right to choose means of warfare assumed that, whatever might be the means of warfare lawfully used, it would continue to be possible for war to be waged on a civilized basis in future. Thus, however free a State may be in its choice of means, that freedom encounters a limiting factor when the use of a particular type of weapon could ensue in the destruction of civilization.[147]

Judge Weeramantry stated:

> [A]ll the postulates of law presuppose that they contribute to and function within the premise of the continued existence of the community served by that law. Without the assumption of the continued existence, no rule of law and no legal system can have any claim to validity, however attractive the juristic reasoning on which it is based. That taint of invalidity affects not merely the particular rule. The legal system, which accommodates that rule, itself collapses upon its foundations, for legal systems are postulated upon the continued existence of society. Being part of society, they must themselves collapse with the greater entity of which they are a part.
>
> ***
>
> To approach the matter from another standpoint, the members of the international community have for the past three centuries been engaged in the task of formulating a set of rules and principles for the conduct of that society—the rules and principles we call international law. In so doing, they must ask themselves whether there is a place in that set of rules for a rule under which it would be legal, for whatever reason, to eliminate members of that community or, indeed, the entire community itself. Can the international community, which is governed by that rule, be considered to have given its acceptance to that rule, whatever be the approach of that community—positivist, natural law, or any

---

[146] *Id.* at 17, 35 I.L.M at 869. *See* Chapter 3, note 283 and accompanying text.

[147] *Id. See* Chapter 3, note 284 and accompanying text.

other? Is the community of nations, to use Hart's expression a "suicide club?"[148]

Sovereign Equality of Individual States

Also relevant to the proportionality analysis is the principle of the equality under international law of the over 190 independent States that exist in the world today.[149]

Quoting Article 2, paragraph 1 of the Charter of the United Nations ("The Organization is based on the principle of sovereign equality of all of its Members"), Judge Koroma, in his dissenting opinion in the Nuclear Weapons Advisory Decision, stated:

> The principle of sovereign equality of States is of general application. It presupposes respect for the sovereignty and territorial integrity of all States. International law recognizes the sovereignty of each State over its territory as well as the physical integrity of the civilian population. By virtue of this principle, a State is prohibited from inflicting injury or harm on another State. The principle is bound to be violated if nuclear weapons are used in a given conflict, because of their established and well-known characteristics. The use of such weapons would not only result in the violation of the territorial integrity of non-belligerent States by radioactive contamination, but would involve the death of thousands, if not millions, of the inhabitants of territories not parties to the conflict.[150]

Numbers of People Potentially at Risk

Given the genetic and environmental effects of nuclear weapons and the extent to which the applicable legal tests turn on the number of protected persons killed and injured, it is relevant to consider the number of people living in the world and potentially living in the future who could be affected by the use of nuclear weapons today.

---

[148] Dissenting opinion of Judge Weeramantry at 64, 35 I.L.M. at 912. *See* Chapter 3, note 288 and accompanying text.

[149] *See* Chapter 22, notes 13–14 and accompanying text; U.S. State Department, Independent States of the World, as released by the Office of the Geographer and Global Issues, December 2, 1998, <http://www.state.gov/www/regions/independent_states.html>.

[150] Dissenting opinion of Judge Koroma at 15, 35 I.L.M. at 932. *See* Chapter 1, notes 196–210, Chapter 2, notes 111–119, Chapter 3, notes 218–236, and accompanying text.

The U.S. Census Bureau estimates the number of people living in the world as of September 6, 1999 to be 6,010,449,025[151] and the Population Division of the United Nations projects the world population as stabilize at 11,600,000,000 just after 2200.[152]

The High Tech Conventional Weapons Alternative

Also of central relevance to the proportionality analysis is the question of the extent to which the particular mission could be carried out with conventional weapons.

The Air Force Commander's Handbook states that, in making the proportionality determination, the commander must decide, "in the light of all the facts known ... whether to adopt any alternative method of attack to further reduce civilian casualties and damage."[153]

The Air Force Manual on International Law states that application of the proportionality test requires consideration "whether some alternative form of attack would lessen collateral damage and casualties."[154] The manual adds that "those who plan or decide upon an attack" must "[t]ake all feasible precautions in the choice of means and methods of attack with a view to avoiding, and in any event to minimizing, incidental loss of civilian life, injury to civilians, and damage to civilian objects."[155]

---

[151] *See* World POPClock Projection, Source: U.S. Census Bureau, International Data Base <http://www.census.gov/cgi-bin/ipc/popclockw>, data updated 12/28/98; Chapter 22, note 8 and accompanying text.

[152] *See* United Nations, World Population Growth From Year 0 to Stabilization, Data from the Population Division Department of Economic and Social Information and Policy Analysis, <gopher://gopher.undp.org:70/00/ungophers/popin/wdtrends/histor> (citing J.D. Durand, Historical Estimates of World Population: An Evaluation (1974), mimeo; UNITED NATIONS, THE DETERMINANTS AND CONSEQUENCES OF POPULATION TRENDS, VOL. 1 (1973); UNITED NATIONS, WORLD POPULATION PROSPECTS AS ASSESSED IN 1963 (1966); UNITED NATIONS, WORLD POPULATION PROSPECTS: THE 1994 REVISION (1993); UNITED NATIONS, LONG-RANGE WORLD POPULATION PROJECTION: TW O CENTURIES OF POPULATION GROWTH, 1950–2150 (1992)); Chapter 22, note 8 and accompanying text.

[153] THE AIR FORCE COMMANDER'S HANDBOOK, *supra* note 16, at 3-3. *See* Chapter 1, notes 106–108, Chapter 2, notes 95, 97–100, and accompanying text.

[154] THE AIR FORCE MANUAL ON INTERNATIONAL LAW, *supra* note 9, at 5-9. *See* Chapter 1, notes 106–108, Chapter 2, notes 95, 97–100, and accompanying text.

[155] *Id.*

Thus, the determination of proportionality with respect to the use of nuclear weapons includes a comparison of the probable results of using conventional as opposed to nuclear weapons.[156]

During the Cold War the United States had permitted a strategic situation to develop whereby the Soviet Union had a superior conventional weapons capacity to the United States, to the extent that the Soviet Union was potentially able to overrun Western Europe with such weapons.[157]

While the United States and Western Europe had had the financial means of developing a conventional weapons capability sufficient to meet the Soviet threat, they had chosen not to do so, relying instead on nuclear weapons and the policy of nuclear deterrence.[158]

This choice was based on many factors, including perhaps a failure in the beginning to grasp the significance and implications of these weapons and the related risk factors.

Historically, nuclear weapons were seen as cheaper than conventional weapons and hence as a way for the United States to contain the Soviet threat without spending the money necessary for a conventional capability comparable to that maintained by the Soviet Union and, as a result, to have more funds for civilian pursuits.[159]

That economy has turned out to have been illusory. The direct costs of nuclear weapons have been much higher than anticipated and substantial indirect costs have become apparent, including the ongoing

---

[156] *See* Chapter 9; Chapter 2, notes 95, 97–100, Chapter 17, notes 27–36, and accompanying text. *See also* DOCTRINE FOR JOINT THEATER NUCLEAR OPERATIONS, *supra* note 42, at vii–viii, I-1, II-7, III-1.

[157] *See* Chapter 15, notes 14–15, Chapter 17, notes 29–35, and accompanying text. *See also* WILLIAM J. PERRY, SECRETARY OF DEFENSE, 1995 ANNUAL REPORT TO THE PRESIDENT AND THE CONGRESS, at 84–85; HENRY KISSINGER, WHITE HOUSE YEARS 218 (1979).

[158] *See* Chapter 17, notes 30, 32–35, and accompanying text. *See also* WILLIAM J. PERRY, SECRETARY OF DEFENSE, 1995 ANNUAL REPORT TO THE PRESIDENT AND THE CONGRESS, at 84–85; Testimony of Adm. Noel Gayler, U.S. Navy (Retired), Former Commander in Chief, U.S. Forces in the Pacific, Former Director, National Security Agency, in Hearings on the Role of Arms Control in U.S. Defense Policy, before the Committee on Foreign Affairs, House of Representatives, Ninety-Eighth Congress, 2nd Sess., at 126 (June 20, 21, 26, July 25, 1984); LAWRENCE FREEDMAN, THE EVOLUTION OF NUCLEAR STRATEGY 88 (1989); *NSC-68, in* AMERICAN DEFENSE POLICY 288 (Schuyler et al. eds., 1990).

[159] *See* Chapter 17, notes 30, 32, Chapter 22, note 44, and accompanying text. *See also* HENRY KISSINGER, WHITE HOUSE YEARS 218 (1979); Stephen I. Schwartz, *Introduction, in* ATOMIC AUDIT 3–4 (1998).

costs of storing and disposing of radioactive and other toxic wastes and of dismantling nuclear weapons systems and disposing of surplus nuclear materials, as well as compensating workers and family members of workers whose health has been impaired by nuclear materials.[160]

While, during the Cold War, the United States depended upon the threat of use of nuclear weapons to compensate for conventional weapons inferiority, today the tables have turned. The United States is the preeminent conventional power in the world and is now itself threatened by the nuclear weapons possessed or potentially possessed by weaker States and groups.[161]

In ironic contrast, Russia is now substantially weakened and heavily dependent on nuclear weapons, far more so than the United States ever was.[162]

Like nuclear weapons, conventional weapons destroy through blast and heat, but conventional weapons do not generally emit radiation. Their effects are generally limited to the blast and heat.[163]

---

[160] *See* Chapter 22, note 44 and accompanying text. *See generally* ATOMIC AUDIT (Stephen I. Schwartz ed., 1998); Arjun Makhjani & Stephen I. Schwartz, *Victims of the Bomb, in* ATOMIC AUDIT 395–431 (1998).

[161] *See* Chapters 23, 26; Chapter 18, notes 7–13, Chapter 22, notes 18–25, Chapter 27, note 76, and accompanying text. *See also* WILLIAM S. COHEN, PROLIFERATION: THREAT AND RESPONSE, (Nov. 1997) <http://www.defenselink.mil/pubs/prolif97/ne_asia.html>; WILLIAM J. PERRY, SECRETARY OF DEFENSE, 1995 ANNUAL REPORT TO THE PRESIDENT AND THE CONGRESS, at 85; JOINT CHIEFS OF STAFF, JOINT PUB. 3-11, DOCTRINE FOR NUCLEAR, BIOLOGICAL, AND CHEMICAL (NBC) DEFENSE (July 10, 1995), Richard K. Betts, *The New Threat of Mass Destruction,* FOREIGN AFF., vol. 77, no. 1, January/February 1998, at 26, 30–31; Jessica Eve Stern, *Moscow Meltdown: Can Russia Survive?* INT'L SECURITY, vol. 18, no. 4, Spring 1994, at 40.

[162] *See* Chapter 18, note 58, Chapter 23, note 2, and accompanying text. *See also* WILLIAM J. PERRY, SECRETARY OF DEFENSE, 1995 ANNUAL REPORT TO THE PRESIDENT AND THE CONGRESS, at 84–85; Robert S. Norris & William Arkin, *Estimated Russian Stockpile, September 1996,* NRDC NUCLEAR NOTEBOOK; BULL. OF ATOMIC SCIENTISTS, vol. 63, Aug. 13, 1996, at 62–63; Charles J. Dick, *Past Cruelties Hinder the Taming of the Bear,* JANE'S INTELLIGENCE REVIEW, vol. 10, no. 12, Dec. 1, 1998, at 5; Michael R. Gordon, *Maneuvers Show Russian Reliance on Nuclear Arms,* THE NEW YORK TIMES, July 10, 1999, at 1; *Editorial, Showdown in Pristina,* THE NATION, July 5, 1999, at 3–4.

[163] *See* Chapter 2, note 97, Chapter 15, notes 6–12, 15–16, Chapter 28, note 1, and accompanying text. *See, e.g.,* DOCTRINE FOR JOINT THEATER NUCLEAR OPERATIONS, *supra* note 42, at I-1.

Modern computer technology, with the tradeoff between accuracy and firepower, has led to a revolution in conventional weaponry, as demonstrated in the 1999 Kosovo operation, to the extent that the United States could now likely achieve with conventional weapons most if not all missions for which it might have used strategic or tactical nuclear weapons.[164]

The key is twofold (1) the number of weapons used; and (2) the relationship between necessary blast and accuracy of delivery.

While even the most powerful conventional weapons do not have the destructive power of nuclear weapons, such lesser destructiveness can generally be compensated for when necessary by using a greater number of conventional weapons, particularly given the substantial increase in the accuracy with which such weapons can be delivered.[165]

It has always been the case that a combatant could achieve with multiple conventional weapons levels of immediate destruction comparable to those achievable with nuclear weapons. The Allied conventional bombing of Tokyo, involving the use of hundreds of bombers, wrought destruction comparable to that of the single atomic attack on Hiroshima.[166]

We saw further examples from the 1991 United Nations analysis to the trade-off between missile accuracy and the level of destructiveness needed for a particular mission:

> Missile accuracy is usually given in terms of the circular error probable (CEP), defined as the distance from an aiming point within which, on the average, half the shots aimed at this point will fall. Using this concept, assessments of the efficiency of various missile systems can be illustrated. For example, a 1 Mt nuclear warhead may be needed in order to destroy a particular hardened

---

[164] *See* Chapter 28, *see* Chapter 15, notes 15–17, Chapter 28 notes 1, 13–14, 37–52, and accompanying text. *See also* NATIONAL DEFENSE PANEL, TRANSFORMING DEFENSE: NATIONAL SECURITY IN THE 21ST CENTURY 51 (Dec. 1997); David Learmount, *Smart Bombs in Demand,* FLIGHT INT'L, June 9, 1999; William J. Perry, *Desert Storm and Deterrence,* FOREIGN AFF., vol. 70 no. 4, Fall 1991, at 66.

[165] *See* Chapter 28, Chapter 28, note 11 and accompanying text. *See also* WILLIAM S. COHEN, 1999 ANNUAL REPORT TO THE PRESIDENT AND THE CONGRESS Chap. 10, p. 5, The Revolution in Military Affairs, and Joint Vision 2010, *as set forth at* <http://www.dtic.mil/execsec/adr1999/>.

[166] *See* LAWRENCE FREEDMAN, THE EVOLUTION OF NUCLEAR STRATEGY 17, 29 (1989), Rufus E. Miles Jr., *Hiroshima: The Strange Myth of Half a Million American Lives Saved,* INT'L SECURITY, vol. 10, no. 2, Fall 1985 121, 125; Chapter 15, notes 15–17 and accompanying text.

structure if the CEP of that nuclear weapon is 1 km. The same effect could result from a 125 kt warhead with a 0.5 km CEP accuracy, or a 40 kt warhead with a 0.33 km CEP. Thus, increased accuracy meant that smaller yield warheads could replace high yield warheads as a threat to these types of targets.[167]

If, instead even of a 0.33 km CEP, the target can be hit directly on the head, even less firepower, whether delivered by conventional or nuclear weapon, would be necessary.[168]

The National Defense Panel in its 1997 report stated:

> We should also consider the potential of non-nuclear weapons to strengthen deterrence. Advancing military technologies that merge the capabilities of information systems with precision-guided weaponry and real-time targeting and other new weapons systems may provide a supplement or alternative to the nuclear arsenals of the Cold War.[169]

---

[167] UNITED NATIONS DEPARTMENT FOR DISARMAMENT AFFAIRS, NUCLEAR WEAPONS, A COMPREHENSIVE STUDY 30 (United Nations 1991). *See* Chapter 21, notes 9–10, Chapter 28, note 1, and accompanying text.

[168] *See* Chapter 19, note 8 and accompanying text. The main U.S. tactical nuclear weapon delivery vehicle carried by submarine is the Sea Launched Cruise Missile, called the Tomahawk Land Attack Missile/Nuclear. This missile can carry either nuclear or non-nuclear warheads, and launch off of ships or submarines. Its CEP is reported as being 30 meters by a collector of data on missiles worldwide (*see* Ian Curtis, *The Missile Tables,* DEFENSE & FOREIGN AFFAIRS' STRATEGIC POLICY, Mar. 1991), and as 100 meters by a writer in a military publication (*see* Tamar A. Mehuron, *Characteristics for Nuclear Weapon Systems, Circa 2006,* AIR FORCE MAG., Mar. 1992, at 10).

The JDAM, or Joint Direct Attack Munition, a strap-on guidance system attached to a gravity bomb, is also extremely accurate. It is reportedly capable of delivering its bomb within twenty feet of the target from 15 miles away through guidance from satellite global positioning technology. *See* James Wallace, *Boeing—Built System Used on Bombs in Yugoslavia,* SEATTLE POST-INTELLIGENCER, Mar. 27, 1999, at A5; Rowan Scarborough, *What's Left After Kosovo,* WASH. TIMES, June 13, 1999, at C1; Stanley Kandebo, *Operation Desert Storm—Tomahawk Missiles Excel in First Wartime Use,* AVIATION WEEK & SPACE TECH., vol. 134, no. 3, Jan. 21, 1991, at 61. *See* Chapter 19, note 8, Chapter 21, note 10, Chapter 28, note 44, and accompanying text.

[169] NATIONAL DEFENSE PANEL, TRANSFORMING DEFENSE: NATIONAL SECURITY IN THE 21ST CENTURY 51 (Dec. 1997). *See* Chapter 18, note 63, Chapter 20, note 7, and accompanying text.

Conclusion as to Proportionality Rule

Based on the foregoing, it would seem that virtually any realistically likely use of nuclear weapons would violate the proportionality rule.

Rules of Discrimination and Neutrality

Given the facts discussed above, it would seem equally clear that virtually any realistically likely use of nuclear weapons would violate the rules of discrimination and neutrality. The effects are too big, too broad and too blunderbuss. Even the radiation from a single limited use of nuclear weapons would be potentially so uncontrollable and unlimited as to violate these rules, but that would only be the beginning, given the unrealistic nature of the assumption that that is the way nuclear weapons would be used, if they were ever used, and the likelihood of escalation.

On a more general level as to the rule of neutrality, we saw that the issue, in light of the United States' position, focuses on the question of the extent to which a neutral is protected from the effects of war between the combatants.

Stating that the principle of neutrality is designed to preclude "military invasion or bombardment of neutral territory,"[170] the United States in its memorandum to the ICJ argued, without citation of authority, that neutral status is not a "broad guarantee to neutral States of immunity from the effects of war, whether economic or environmental"[171] and that the United States is "aware of no case in which a belligerent has been held responsible for collateral damage to neutral territory for lawful acts of war committed outside that territory."[172]

By the time of the oral argument, the United States seemed to have retreated somewhat from this position. McNeill argued, "[T]he principle of neutrality has never been understood to guarantee neutral States absolute immunity from the effects of armed conflict."[173] So there is protection from the effects of armed conflict, but it is not absolute.

Without defining the scope of potential protection extended to the neutral, McNeill stated:

---

[170] U.S. ICJ Memorandum/GA App. at 31. *See* Chapter 3, note 111 and accompanying text.

[171] *Id.* at 31–32. *See* Chapter 3, note 112 and accompanying text.

[172] *Id. See* Chapter 3, note 113 and accompanying text.

[173] ICJ Hearing, November 15, 1995, at 95–96. *See* Chapter 3, note 114 and accompanying text.

> [E]ven assuming arguendo that a belligerent's liability to a neutral could somehow be established in a particular case, the argument that unlawful damage would necessarily occur to neutral States whenever nuclear weapons are used cannot be maintained.[174]

The United States stated in its memorandum to the Court that the argument that the principle of neutrality prohibits the use of nuclear weapons "is evidently based on the assertion that the use of such weapons would inevitably cause severe damage in the territory of neutral States,"[175] an assumption which the United States dismissed as "incorrect and in any event highly speculative."[176]

The United States concluded in its memorandum: "Like any other weapons, nuclear weapons could be used to violate neutrality, but this in no way means that nuclear weapons are prohibited *per se* by neutrality principles."[177] McNeill expressed the same conclusion in his oral argument: "Whether or not the principles of neutrality might be violated once again clearly depends on the precise circumstances of a particular use of nuclear weapons."[178]

The United States has otherwise recognized a broad scope of protection of neutrals. *The Naval/Marine Commander's Handbook* states that a neutral State is entitled to "inviolability"[179] and that, under customary international law, all acts of hostility are prohibited in "neutral territory, including neutral lands, neutral waters, and neutral airspace."[180]

The Air Force Commander's Handbook states that, under the neutral's right of inviolability, a combatant may not "use, invade or pass through" a neutral's territory, including its airspace.[181]

The *Army's Law of Land Warfare*, citing the Hague Convention No. V Respecting the Rights and Duties of Neutral Powers and Persons in Case of War on Land, 18 October 1907, to which the United States is a

---

[174] *Id. See also* Chapter 3, note 115 and accompanying text.

[175] U.S. ICJ Memorandum/GA App., at 32. *See also* Chapter 3, note 116 and accompanying text.

[176] *Id.* at 32. *See also* Chapter 3, note 117 and accompanying text.

[177] *Id. See* Chapter 3, note 118 and accompanying text.

[178] ICJ Hearing, November 15, 1995, at 96. *See* Chapter 3, note 117 and accompanying text.

[179] THE NAVAL/MARINE COMMANDER'S HANDBOOK, *supra* note 21, at 7-3. *See* Chapter 1, notes 196–210 and accompanying text.

[180] *Id.* at 7-16. *See* Chapter 1, notes 196–210 and accompanying text.

[181] THE AIR FORCE COMMANDER'S HANDBOOK, *supra* note 16, at 7-1; Chapter 1, note 202 and accompanying text.

signatory,[182] states that the inviolability of a neutral State's territory prohibits "any unauthorized entry" into the neutral's territory, including its territorial waters and airspace by "troops or instrumentalities of war."[183]

The Air Force Manual on International Law, as noted above, also recognizes the applicability to neutrals of the principle of the illegality of the use of weapons whose effects cannot be controlled, noting that such uncontrollable effects "may include injury to the civilian population of other states as well as injury to an enemy's civilian population."[184]

The ICJ in its decision set the issue up by quoting from the Written Statement of one State (Nauru): "The principle of neutrality applies with equal force to transborder incursions of armed forces and to the transborder damage caused to a neutral State by the use of a weapon in a belligerent State."[185] The Court further noted that the principle of neutrality has been "considered by some to rule out the use of a weapon the effects of which simply cannot be contained within the territories of the contending States."[186]

The Court, however, did not go on to decide the issue or define the scope of the right of neutrality or its application to the case in point, but rather limited itself to stating that the principle, "whatever its content," is a fundamental one applicable "(subject to the relevant provisions of the United Nations Charter), to all international armed conflict, whatever type of weapons might be used."[187]

Judge Shahabuddeen in his dissent adopted the position in Nauru's statement that the right of neutrality protected against transborder damage caused to a neutral State by the use of a weapon in a belligerent

---

[182] *See* THE LAW OF LAND WARFARE, *supra* note 13, at 4, 185; Chapter 1, note 205 and accompanying text.

[183] *Id.* at 185. *See* Chapter 1, note 206 and accompanying text.

[184] THE AIR FORCE MANUAL ON INTERNATIONAL LAW, *supra* note 9, at 6-3. *See* Chapter 1, note 206 and accompanying text.

[185] Nuclear Weapons Advisory Opinion ¶ 88, at 31, 35 I.L.M. at 829 (citing Legality of the Use by a State of Nuclear Weapons in Armed Conflict, Nauru, Written Statement (I), at 35. IV E). *See* Chapter 3, notes 218–236 and accompanying text.

[186] *Id.* ¶ 93, at 32, 35 I.L.M. at 829. *See* Chapter 3, note 219 and accompanying text.

[187] *Id.* ¶ 89, at 31, 35 I.LM. at 829. *See* Chapter 3, note 220 and accompanying text. *See also* Chapter 10, notes 31–44 and accompanying text.

State.[188] While acknowledging the U.S. point that neutrality does not accord the neutral "absolute immunity," the judge concluded that the potential effects on neutrals of the use of nuclear weapons were too great not to be within the protection of neutrality:

> [R]adiation effects ... extend to the inhabitants of neutral States and causes damage to them, their off-spring, their natural resources, and possibly put them under the necessity to leave their traditional homelands. ... Whether direct or indirect ... [radiation effects] result from the use of nuclear weapons, for it is a property of such weapons that they emit radiation; their destructive effect on the enemy is largely due to their radiation effects. Such radiation has a high probability of transboundary penetration.[189]

Judge Shahabuddeen acknowledged the point made by the United States that there was no precedent on the point, but concluded that radiation posed a new situation, a new danger to neutrals, and one which came within the protection of the inviolability of the neutral's territory.[190]

Judge Weeramantry in his dissenting opinion cited Chernobyl as an example of the transboundary effects of radiation, noting that people were affected over large areas in many countries, including in Belarus, Russia, Ukraine, and Sweden, and that overall some nine million people have been affected in some way, since "the by-products of that nuclear reaction could not be contained."[191]

The judge also noted the likelihood that electromagnetic pulses resultant of nuclear weapons would cross into neutral territories:

> [T]he electromagnetic pulse ... travels at immense speeds, so that the disruption of communication systems caused by the radioactive contamination immediately can spread beyond national boundaries and disrupt communication lines and essential services in neutral countries as well. Having regard to the dominance of electronic communication in the functioning of modern society at every level, this would be an unwarranted interference with such neutral states.[192]

---

[188] *See* dissenting opinion of Judge Shahabuddeen at 9, 35 I.L.M. at 865; Chapter 3, notes 221–223 and accompanying text.

[189] *Id. See* Chapter 3, note 222 and accompanying text.

[190] *See id.*; Chapter 3, note 223 and accompanying text.

[191] Dissenting opinion of Judge Weeramantry at 23, 35 I.L.M. at 891. *See* Chapter 3, note 224 and accompanying text.

[192] *Id.* at 26, 35 I.L.M. at 893. *See* Chapter 3, note 225 and accompanying text.

Judge Weeramantry further concluded that irreparable injury to neutrals is a "natural and foreseeable consequence" of the use of nuclear weapons, since the "uncontainability of radiation extends it globally."[193] He added, "When wind currents scatter these effects further, it is well-established by the TTAPS and other studies that explosions in one hemisphere can spread their deleterious effects even to the other hemisphere. No portion of the globe—and therefore no country—could be free of these effects."[194]

Judge Weeramantry added that, once a strategy of self-defense "implies damage to a non-belligerent third-party, such a matter ceases to be one of purely internal jurisdiction."[195] Noting that the use of nuclear weapons would not be a situation of inadvertent and unintentional damage to neutrals,[196] Judge Weeramantry stated:

> The launching of a nuclear weapon is a deliberate act. Damage to neutrals is a natural, foreseeable and, indeed, inevitable consequence. International law cannot contain a rule of non-responsibility which is so opposed to the basic principles of universal jurisprudence.[197]

Judge Koroma in his dissenting opinion stated that the principle in Article 2, paragraph 1 of the Charter of the United Nations as to the sovereign equality of all members "is bound to be violated if nuclear weapons are used in a given conflict, because of their established and well-known characteristics."[198] The judge added, "The use of such weapons would not only result in the violation of the territorial integrity of non-belligerent States by radioactive contamination, but would involve the death of thousands, if not millions, of the inhabitants of territories not parties to the conflict."[199]

Quoting Article 2, paragraph 1 of the Charter of the United Nations ("The Organization is based on the principle of sovereign equality of all of its Members"), Judge Koroma, as noted, further stated:

---

[193] *Id.* at 49, 35. I.L.M. at 904. *See* Chapter 3, note 226 and accompanying text.

[194] *Id. See* Chapter 3, note 227 and accompanying text.

[195] *Id.* at 61, 35 I.L.M. at 910. *See* Chapter 3, note 228 and accompanying text.

[196] *See id.*; Chapter 3, note 229 and accompanying text.

[197] *Id.* at 50, 35 I.L.M. at 905. *See* Chapter 3, note 230 and accompanying text.

[198] Dissenting opinion of Judge Koroma at 15, 35 I.L.M. at 932. *See* Chapter 3, note 231 and accompanying text.

[199] *Id. See* Chapter 3, note 232 and accompanying text.

> International law recognizes the sovereignty of each State over its territory as well as the physical integrity of the civilian population. By virtue of this principle, a State is prohibited from inflicting injury or harm on another State. The principle is bound to be violated if nuclear weapons are used in a given conflict, because of their established and well-known characteristics.[200]

As further noted, Judge Koroma concluded that the doctrine of deterrence, if implemented, could result in "catastrophic consequences for the civilian population not only of the belligerent parties but those of States not involved in such a conflict."[201]

Judge Fleischhauer in his separate opinion concluded that "The radiation released by [nuclear weapons] is unable to respect the territorial integrity of a neutral state."[202]

Judge Guillaume in his individual opinion found the protection of neutrality to be less open-ended:

> [O]n many occasions, it has been maintained or recognized that the legality of actions carried out by belligerents in neutral territory depends on the "military necessities," as the late Judge Ago noted in the light of a widespread practice described in the addendum to his eight report to the International Law Commission on the responsibility of States (para. 50 and note 101).[203]

It would seem implicit in the United States' ultimate position before the Court on the point and in the law of neutrality that some level of protection must be extended to neutrals from effects of other States' wars—presumably at least a level of protection generally commensurate with that extended to noncombatants through the rules of proportionality and discrimination, and arguably, as reflected in the U.S. statements referenced above, a protection against severe effects. On this basis, it would appear that virtually any use of nuclear weapons would be unlawful under the law of neutrality, given such risks as those of uncontrollability and escalation.

As we saw, Bowett noted that the excuse of unlawful acts based on necessity is narrower than the justification of self-defense (which

---

[200] *Id. See* Chapter 3, note 233 and accompanying text.

[201] *Id.* at 17, 35 I.L.M. at 933. *See* Chapter 3, note 234 and accompanying text.

[202] Separate opinion of Judge Fleischhauer at 1, 35 I.L.M. at 834. *See* Chapter 3, note 235 and accompanying text.

[203] Individual opinion of Judge Guillaume, ¶ 6, 35 I.L.M. at 1352 (No. 6, November 1996). *See* Chapter 3, note 236 and accompanying text.

renders the conduct in question lawful). The excuse based on necessity must inflict "relatively little harm:"

> The circumstances in which necessity may excuse the non-observance of the duties imposed by international law restricting the use of force are those in which, as an incidental to the exercise of the right of self-defence, the rights of an innocent state are infringed. The excusable character of this conduct towards an innocent state lies in the fact that, in order that a state may in self-defence protect its essential rights against a delinquent states, it may be necessary to disregard the rights of an innocent state which are thereby relatively little harmed in comparison to the harm which would have been suffered by the other state if denied the right to act out of necessity.[204]

Rule of Necessity

Obviously, the requirement of necessity is not met in circumstances where the mission could be handled by conventional weapons. But there is an additional point that has not been much focused on: The rule of necessity requires that the strike appear likely to yield a concrete military benefit.[205]

Accordingly, a strike that is likely to boomerang, resulting, whether because of escalation or miscalculation or mistake or the operation of the winds and waters or the like, in a net detriment to the acting State, would not satisfy the necessity test.

The United States has further acknowledged that military necessity does not override the law of armed conflict. The Army's *Law of Land Warfare* states:

> The prohibitory effect of the law of war is not minimized by "military necessity" which has been defined as that principle which justifies those measures not forbidden by international law which are indispensable for securing the complete submission of the enemy as soon as possible. Military necessity has been generally rejected as a defense for acts forbidden by the customary and

---

[204] D. W. BOWETT, SELF-DEFENCE IN INTERNATIONAL LAW 10 (1958). For a discussion of broadly recognized principles of law applicable to the extent to which an actor may put innocent third-parties at risk, *see* Chapter 10; Chapter 11, note 33, and accompanying text.

[205] *See* Chapter 1, notes 109–128, 142, Chapter 2, notes 56–59, 98 and accompanying text. *See also* DOCTRINE FOR JOINT THEATER NUCLEAR OPERATIONS, *supra* note 42, at vii–viii; THE NAVAL/MARINE COMMANDER'S HANDBOOK, *supra* note 21, at 8-2, 10-2; THE AIR FORCE MANUAL ON INTERNATIONAL LAW, *supra* note 9, at 5-9.

conventional laws of war inasmuch as the latter have been developed and framed with consideration for the concept of military necessity.[206]

The Naval/Marine Commander's Handbook states the same general rule:

> The customary rule of military necessity may be, and in many instances is, restricted in its application to the conduct of warfare by other customary or conventional rules. The opinion that all rules of warfare are subject to, and restricted by, the operation of the principle of military necessity has never been accepted by the majority of American and English authorities. Furthermore, this opinion has not been accepted by military tribunals. It has been held by military tribunals that the plea of military necessity cannot be considered as a defense for the violation of rules which lay down absolute prohibitions (*e.g.*, the rule prohibiting the killing of prisoners of war) and which provide no exception for those circumstances constituting military necessity. Thus, one United States Military Tribunal, in rejecting the argument that the rules of warfare are always subject to the operation of military necessity, stated:
>
> > It is an essence of war that one or the other side must lose and the experienced generals and statesmen knew this when they drafted the rules and customs of land warfare. In short, these rules and customs of warfare are designed specifically for all phases of war. They comprise the law for such emergency. To claim that they can be wantonly—and at the sole discretion of any one belligerent—disregarded when he considers his own situation to be critical, means nothing more or less than to abrogate the laws and customs of war entirely.[207]

Hence, the rule of necessity permits only such levels of force as are militarily necessary and in compliance with other requirements of the law of war. *The Naval/Marine Commander's Handbook* includes the point in its overall statement of the rule: "Only that degree and kind of force, not otherwise prohibited by the law of armed conflict, required

---

[206] THE LAW OF LAND WARFARE, *supra* note 13, at 4. *See* Chapter 1, notes 137–141 and accompanying text. *See also* Chapter 1, note 138 and accompanying text for a discussion of the U.S. position of what rules of armed conflict are potentially trumped by military necessity.

[207] THE NAVAL/MARINE COMMANDER'S HANDBOOK, *supra* note 21, at 5-4 to 5-7 (quoting The Krupp Trial (Trial of Alfred Felix Alwyn Krupp Von Bohlen und Halbach and Eleven Others), 10 LRTWC 139 (1949)). *See* Chapter 1, notes 138–141 and accompanying text.

for the partial or complete submission of the enemy with a minimum expenditure of time, life, and physical resources may be applied."[208]

The Air Force Manual on International Law similarly notes that the principle of necessity does not authorize actions otherwise prohibited.[209]

Rule of Moderation

The law of war recognizes a general principle of moderation, expressed in the Hague Regulations by the maxim that "the right of belligerents to adopt means of injuring the enemy is not unlimited."[210] This principle is a basis of and generally overlaps with the principles of necessity and proportionality.[211] Nuclear weapons seem inconsistent with the notion of limited effects.

Principle of Humanity

As reflected in *The Air Force Manual on International Law*, the United States also recognizes an overriding principle of humanity:

> Complementing the principle of necessity and implicitly contained within it is the principle of humanity which forbids the infliction of suffering, injury or destruction not actually necessary for the accomplishment of legitimate military purposes. This principle of humanity results in a specific prohibition against unnecessary suffering, a requirement of proportionality, and a variety of more specific rules examined later. The principle of humanity also confirms the basic immunity of civilian populations and civilians from being objects of attack during armed conflict.

---

[208] *Id.* at 5-4. *See* Chapter 1, note 140 and accompanying text.

[209] THE AIR FORCE MANUAL ON INTERNATIONAL LAW, *supra* note 9, at 1-6 (citing *inter alia* Carnegie Endowment for Int'l Peace, *Report of the Conference on Contemporary Problems, the Law of Armed Conflicts,* 1970, at 352; Note, *Military Necessity in War Crimes Trials,* 29 BRIT. Y. B. INT'L L. 442 (1953)). *See* Chapter 1, note 141 and accompanying text.

[210] *Id.* at 5-1, 6-1 (citing Hague Reg., Art. 22). *See also* T HE NAVAL/MARINE COMMANDER'S HANDBOOK, *supra* note 21, at 8-1 n.2; Nuclear Weapons Advisory Opinion ¶ 77, at 28, 35 I.L.M. at 827 (citing Arts. 22 and 23 of the 1907 Hague Regulations relating to the laws and customs of war on land and The St. Petersburg Declaration). *See* Chapter 1, notes 148–152, Chapter 2, notes 88–91, Chapter 3, note 167, and accompanying text.

[211] *See* THE AIR FORCE MANUAL ON INTERNATIONAL LAW, *supra* note 9, at 5-1, 6-1 (citing Hague Reg., Art. 22); Nuclear Weapons Advisory Opinion ¶ 38, at 17, 35 I.L.M. at 822 (citing the U.N. CHARTER art. 51); Chapter 1, notes 148–152, Chapter 2, notes 88–91, Chapter 3, notes 73–82; and accompanying text.

> This immunity of the civilian population does not preclude
> unavoidable incidental civilian casualties which may occur during
> the course of attacks against military objectives, and which are not
> excessive in relation to the concrete and direct military advantage
> anticipated.[212]

If my conclusions above as to the legal status of the use of nuclear
weapons under the rules of proportionality, discrimination, necessity
and neutrality are correct, then ostensibly the same conclusions would
be required under the rules of moderation and humanity.

Prohibition of Poisons and Poison Gas and Analogous Materials

In its memorandum to the ICJ, the United States argued in effect
that the radiation effects of nuclear weapons do not constitute
prohibited poisons because such weapons also cause blast and heat
effects, and those effects are potentially lawful:

> [The prohibition of the use of poison weapons] was established
> with particular reference to projectiles that carry poison into the
> body of the victim. It was not intended to apply, and has not been
> applied, to weapons that are designed to injure or cause destruction
> by other means, even though they also may create toxic byproducts.
>
> For example, the prohibition on poison weapons does not
> prohibit conventional explosives or incendiaries, even though they
> may produce dangerous fumes. By the same token, it does not
> prohibit nuclear weapons, which are designed to injure or cause
> destruction by means other than poisoning the victim, even though
> nuclear explosions may also create toxic radioactive byproducts.[213]

The United States made essentially the same argument with respect
to the application of the 1925 Geneva Protocol's prohibition of the first
use in war of "asphyxiating, poisonous or other gases and of all
analogous liquids, materials or devices," contending that the Protocol
was "not intended" to cover weapons that kill other than by the
inhalation or other absorption into the body of poisonous gases or
analogous substances[214] and that the prohibition of the use of poison

---

[212] THE AIR FORCE MANUAL ON INTERNATIONAL LAW, *supra* note 9, at 1–6.
See Chapter 1, notes 247–249, 253, Chapter 3 notes 166–185, and
accompanying text.

[213] U.S. ICJ Memorandum/GA App. at 23–23 (citations omitted). *See*
Chapter 2, note 106 and accompanying text.

[214] *Id.* at 24–25. *See also* Nuclear Weapons Advisory Opinion ¶ 54, at
20–21, 35 I.L.M. at 823–24. *See* Chapter 2, note 106–110, Chapter 3, notes
119–126, and accompanying text.

weapons in the 1907 Hague Convention was only intended to cover the situation of projectiles which carry poison into the body of the victim.[215]

The United States further argued that the limitations on the scope of these agreements is reflected in the fact that they do not prohibit conventional explosives or incendiaries, even though such weapons "may produce dangerous fumes:"

> This prohibition was intended to apply to weapons that are designed to kill or injure by the inhalation or other absorption into the body of poisonous gases or analogous substances.
>
> This prohibition was not intended to apply, and has not been applied, to weapons that are designed to kill or injure by other means, even though they may create asphyxiating or poisonous byproducts. Once again, the Protocol does not prohibit conventional explosives or incendiary weapons, even though they may produce asphyxiating or poisonous byproducts, and it likewise does not prohibit nuclear weapons.[216]

The Naval/Marine Commander's Handbook elaborates on the U.S. position:

> Poison Gas Analogy. It has been contended that nuclear radiation is sufficiently comparable to a poison gas to justify extending the 1925 Gas Protocol's prohibition to include the use of nuclear weapons. However, this ignores the explosive, heat and blast effects of a nuclear burst, and disregards the fact that fall-out is a by-product which is not the main or most characteristic feature of the weapon. The same riposte is available to meet an argument that the use of nuclear weapons would violate the prohibition on the use of poisoned weapons, set out in article 23(a) of the Hague Regulations.[217]

The ICJ noted that opponents of nuclear weapons have urged the unlawfulness of such weapons under various conventions relating to poisonous weapons:

---

[215] *See* U.S. ICJ Memorandum/GA App. at 24; Nuclear Weapons Advisory Opinion ¶ 54, at 20–21, 35 I.L.M. at 823–24; Chapter 2, notes 106–110, Chapter 3, notes 119–126, and accompanying text.

[216] U.S. ICJ Memorandum/GA App. at 24–25 (citations omitted). *See also* Nuclear Weapons Advisory Opinion ¶ 54, at 20–21, 35 I.L.M. at 823–24. *See* Chapter 2, notes 106–110, Chapter 3, notes 119–126, and accompanying text.

[217] THE NAVAL/MARINE COMMANDER'S HANDBOOK, *supra* note 21, at 10-2. *See* Chapter 2, note 110 and accompanying text.

(a) The Second Hague Declaration of 29 July 1899, which prohibits the "use of projectiles the object of which is the diffusion of asphyxiating or deleterious gases;"

(b) Article 23(a) of the Regulations respecting the laws and customs of war on land annexed to the Hague Convention IV of 18 October 1907, prohibiting the use of "poison or poisoned weapons;" and

(c) the Geneva Protocol of 17 June 1925, which prohibits "the use in war of asphyxiating, poisonous or other gases, and of all analogous liquids, materials or devices."[218]

Accepting the U.S. position, the Court concluded, without citation of authority, that these instruments did not specifically prohibit the use of nuclear weapons, since their provisions "have been understood, in the practice of States, in their ordinary sense as covering weapons whose prime, or even exclusive, effect is to poison or asphyxiate."[219]

In his dissenting opinion, Judge Shahabuddeen took issue with the characterization of radiation effects of nuclear weapons as secondary and the ascription of legal significance to such characterization:

[N]uclear weapons are not just another type of explosive weapons, only occupying a higher position on the same scale: their destructive power is exponentially greater. Apart from blast and heat, the radiation effects over time are devastating. To classify these effects as being merely a byproduct is not to the point; they can be just as extensive as, if not more so than, those immediately produced by blast and heat. They cause unspeakable sickness followed by painful death, affect the genetic code, damage the unborn, and can render the earth uninhabitable. These extended effects may not have military value for the user, but this does not lessen their gravity or the fact that they result from the use of nuclear weapons. This being the case, it is not relevant for present purposes to consider whether the injury produced is a byproduct or secondary effect of such use.

… [N]uclear fall-out may exert an impact on people long after the explosion … thus presenting the disturbing and unique portrait of war being waged by a present generation on future ones—on future ones with which its successors could well be at peace.[220]

---

[218] Nuclear Weapons Advisory Opinion ¶ 54, at 20–21, 35 I.L.M. at 823–24. *See* Chapter 3, notes 119–126 and accompanying text.

[219] *Id.* ¶ 55, at 21, 35 I.L.M. at 824; Chapter 3, note 120 and accompanying text.

[220] Dissenting opinion of Judge Shahabuddeen at 6, 35 I.L.M at 864. *See* Chapter 3, note 121 and accompanying text.

Judge Weeramantry in his dissenting opinion concluded that, since radiation is not only a major by-product but also a "natural and foreseeable" effect and a "major consequence" of the use of nuclear weapons, it "cannot in law be taken to be unintended," notwithstanding any characterization as "collateral."[221] He stated that the U.S. argument that the absence of specific intent precludes culpability "involves the legally unacceptable contention that if an act involves both legal and illegal consequences, the former justify or excuse the latter."[222]

Judge Koroma in his dissenting opinion stated:

> At the very least, the use of nuclear weapons would violate the prohibition of the use of poison weapons as embodied in Article 23(a) of the Hague Convention of 1899 and 1907 as well as the Geneva Gas Protocol of 1925 which prohibits the use of poison gas and/or bacteriological weapons. Because of its universal adherence, the Protocol is considered binding on the international community as a whole. Furthermore, the prohibition of the use of poison gas is now regarded as part of customary international law binding on all States, and the finding by the Court in Paragraph B cannot be sustained in the face of the Geneva Conventions of 1949 and 1977 Additional Protocols thereto either.[223]

Judge Koroma further noted that the Court had decided in the *Nicaragua* case that the Geneva Conventions of 1949 are now recognized as part of customary international law binding on all States.[224] The judge added that Additional Protocol I to the Geneva Conventions of 1949 "constitutes a restatement and a reaffirmation of customary law rules based on the earlier Geneva and Hague Conventions."[225]

It is interesting to recall that the Army in its *International Law Manual* stated that the provisions of international conventional and customary law that "may control the use of nuclear weapons" include:

---

[221] Dissenting opinion of Judge Weeramantry at 58, 35 I.L.M. at 908. *See* Chapter 3, note 122 and accompanying text.

[222] *Id.* Judge Weeramantry goes through detailed analyses of the text of the 1925 Geneva Gas Protocol and Article 23(a) of the Hague Regulation, concluding that they preclude the use of nuclear weapons. *See* Chapter 3, note 123 and accompanying text.

[223] Dissenting opinion of Judge Koroma at 18, 35 I.L.M. at 933. *See* Chapter 3, note 124 and accompanying text.

[224] *See id.*; Chapter 3, note 125 and accompanying text.

[225] *Id. See* Chapter 3, note 126 and accompanying text.

(1) Article 23(a) of the Hague Regulations prohibiting poisons and poisoned weapons;
(2) the Geneva Protocol of 1925 which prohibits the use not only of poisonous and other gases but also of "analogous liquids, materials or devices;" ....[226]

The United States' restrictive interpretation of these conventions—particularly of the 1925 Geneva Protocol's prohibition of the first use in war of asphyxiating, poisonous or other gases and analogous liquids, materials and devices—seems out of line with open-ended nature of the treaty language and ostensible purpose. Of course, if my broader conclusions as to unlawfulness under the rules of proportionality, discrimination, and necessity are valid, the questions as to the application of the poisons conventions to nuclear weapons need not be reached.

Reprisals

The United States argued before the Court that, even if the use of nuclear weapons were deemed *per se* unlawful, such weapons could still be used in reprisal:

> Even if it were to be concluded—as we clearly have not—that the use of nuclear weapons would necessarily be unlawful, the customary law of reprisal permits a belligerent to respond to another party's violation of the law of armed conflict by itself resorting to what otherwise would be unlawful conduct.[227]

---

[226] United States, Department of the Army, *International Law*, vol. II, 27-161-2, at 42, Pamp. 27-161-2 (Oct. 1962), *quoted in* ELLIOTT L. MEYROWITZ, PROHIBITION OF NUCLEAR WEAPONS: THE RELEVANCE OF INTERNATIONAL LAW 223 (Transnational Publishers, Inc. 1990) (emphasis supplied). *See* Chapter 2, note 36 and accompanying text.

[227] ICJ Hearing, November 15, 1995, at 95. *See* Chapter 1, notes 257–277, Chapter 2, notes 127–129, Chapter 16, note 4, and accompanying text.

Ironically, to an extent MAD is still U.S. policy. The U.S. position is that it is entitled to target civilians in circumstances when reprisals are appropriate. U.S. Air Force Colonel Charles J. Dunlap, Jr., the Staff Judge Advocate, U.S. Strategic Command, Offutt Air Force Base, Nebraska, in a 1997 article, stated:

> Legal advisors should likewise be aware that while the U.S. does not target populations per se, it reserves the right to do so under the limited circumstances of belligerent reprisal. The U.S. (along with other declared nuclear powers) insists that Protocol I to the Geneva Conventions does not apply to nuclear weapons. Hence, prohibitions contained in Protocol I forbidding reprisals against civilians are not, in the U.S. view, applicable to nuclear operations.

The United States acknowledged, however, before the Court that reprisals must be proportionate to the violation.[228] *The Air Force Manual on International Law* describes this requirement:

> (6) A reprisal must be proportional to the original violation. Although a reprisal need not conform in kind to the same type of acts complained of (bombardment for bombardment, weapon for weapon) it may not significantly exceed the adversary's violation either in violence or effect. Effective but disproportionate reprisals cannot be justified by the argument that only an excessive response will forestall further transgressions.[229]

The Naval/Marine Commander's Handbook states that a reprisal "must be proportional to the original violation."[230] It states that the requirement is not one of "strict proportionality," since a reprisal is usually "somewhat greater than the initial violation that gave rise to

---

Colonel Charles J. Dunlap, Jr., USAF, *Taming Shiva: Applying International Law to Nuclear Operations,* 42 A.F.L. REV. 157 (1997).

Secretary of Defense Perry described MAD: "I would liken MAD to two men holding revolvers and standing about 10 yards away and pointing their revolvers at each others' head, and the revolvers are loaded, cocked, their fingers are on the trigger, and then to make matters worse they're shouting insults at each other. And that characterized MAD, which was what we had to control this arms race—this nuclear terror during all the periods of the Cold War." Secretary of Defense William Perry & General John Shalikashvili, Chairman, Joint Chiefs of Staff, *Defense Department Briefing,* COMPASS NEWSWIRE, Thursday, Sept. 22, 1994. *See* Chapter 3, notes 160–164, Chapter 15, notes 13, 99–108, and accompanying text; Brigid Schulte, *A Timeline of the Nuclear Age,* THE SEATTLE TIMES, August 9, 1995 (citing The Brookings Institution).

For a discussion of circumstances in which the United States contends that a right of reprisal trumps otherwise applicable rules of the law of armed conflict, *see* Chapter 1, notes 138, 246–277, Chapter 2, notes 127–129 and accompanying text.

[228] *See* U.S. ICJ Memorandum/GA App. at 30.   *See also* ICJ Hearing, November 15, 1985 at 94–95; Chapter 2, notes 127–129 and accompanying text.

[229] THE AIR FORCE MANUAL ON INTERNATIONAL LAW, *supra* note 9, at 10-4 to 10-5; *see* the similar list set forth in THE NAVAL/MARINE COMMANDER'S HANDBOOK, *supra* note 21, at 6-18 to 6-19. *See* Chapter 1, note 261 and accompanying text.

[230] THE NAVAL/MARINE COMMANDER'S HANDBOOK, *supra* note 21, at 6-19. *See also* THE AIR FORCE MANUAL ON INTERNATIONAL LAW, *supra* note 9, at 10-5. *See* Chapter 1, note 262 and accompanying text.

it,"[231] but that "care must be taken that the extent of the reprisal is measured by some degree of proportionality."[232] The handbook adds that "[t]he reprisal action taken may be quite different from the original act which justified it, but should not be excessive or exceed the degree of harm committed by the enemy."[233]

Given such a requirement, it would seem clear that a nuclear reprisal could never be justified in response to a conventional attack. It would further seem that a nuclear reprisal could generally not be justified in response to a nuclear attack, since it would likely represent such a step of escalation as to precipitate further escalation and nuclear exchange.

The United States has also recognized that there is an issue as to the continuing legality of reprisals under the United Nations Charter. The Air Force manual quotes then–Acting Secretary of State Kenneth Rush:

> The United States has supported and supports the foregoing principle (referring to UN Resolution 2625 to the effect States have a duty to refrain from acts of reprisal involving the use of force). Of course, we recognize that the practice of states is not always consistent with this principle and that it may sometimes be difficult to distinguish the exercise of proportionate self-defense from an act of reprisal. Yet, essentially for reasons of the abuse to which the doctrine of reprisals particularly finds itself, we think it desirable to endeavor to maintain the distinction between acts of lawful self-defense and unlawful reprisals.[234]

In addition, the United States recognizes severe constraints on the scope and effectiveness of reprisals. *The Air Force Manual on International Law* concludes that "most attempted uses of reprisals" in past conflicts were unjustified, either because they were undertaken for an improper reason or were disproportionate.[235]

The Naval/Marine Commander's Handbook similarly states, "Many attempted uses of reprisals in past conflicts have been unjustified either because the reprisals were not undertaken to deter violations by an

---

[231] THE NAVAL/MARINE COMMANDER'S HANDBOOK, *supra* note 21, at 6-19. *See* Chapter 1, note 263 and accompanying text.

[232] *Id.* at 6-19 n.38. *See* Chapter 1, note 264 and accompanying text.

[233] *Id. See* Chapter 1, note 265 and accompanying text.

[234] THE AIR FORCE MANUAL ON INTERNATIONAL LAW, *supra* note 9, at 10-6 to 10-7 n.13 (quoting 29 May 1974 statement of Acting Secretary of State Kenneth Rush, as reported at 68 AM. J. INT'L L. 736 (1974)). *See* Chapter 1, note 259 and accompanying text.

[235] *Id.* at 10-5. *See* Chapter 1, note 268 and accompanying text.

adversary or were disproportionate to the preceding unlawful conduct."[236] The handbook adds that "effective but disproportionate reprisals cannot be justified by the argument that only an excessive response will forestall a further transgression."[237] *The Air Force Manual on International Law* states that the German bombardments of London in the period September–November 1940 did not constitute lawful reprisals, notwithstanding German contentions to the contrary, since they were greatly disproportionate to the original alleged violation.[238]

The Air Force Commander's Handbook similarly states, "In most twentieth century conflicts, the United States has, as a matter of national policy, chosen not to carry out reprisals against the enemy, both because of the potential for escalation and because it is generally in our national interest to follow the law even if the enemy does not."[239]

The Naval/Marine Commander's Handbook states, "Although reprisal is lawful when [the stated prerequisites] are met, there is always the risk that it will trigger retaliatory escalation (counter-reprisals) by the enemy. The United States has historically been reluctant to resort to reprisal for just this reason."[240]

The Air Force Manual on International Law notes that reprisals "will usually have an adverse impact on the attitudes of governments not participating in the conflict" and "may only strengthen enemy morale and will to resist."[241] *The Air Force Commander's Handbook* states that "as a practical matter, reprisals are often subject to abuse and merely result in escalation of a conflict."[242]

It is also noteworthy that, even if it were assumed that some uses of nuclear weapons in reprisal might be lawful notwithstanding the unlawfulness of the initial use of nuclear weapons, considerable

---

[236] THE NAVAL/MARINE COMMANDER'S HANDBOOK, *supra* note 21, at 6-25 n.46. *See* Chapter 1, note 269 and accompanying text.

[237] *Id.* at 6-19 n.38. *See also* THE AIR FORCE MANUAL ON INTERNATIONAL LAW, *supra* note 9, at 10-5. *See* Chapter 1, note 266 and accompanying text.

[238] *See* THE AIR FORCE MANUAL ON INTERNATIONAL LAW, *supra* note 9, at 10-7 n.23 (citations omitted); Chapter 1, note 267 and accompanying text.

[239] THE AIR FORCE COMMANDER'S HANDBOOK, *supra* note 16, at 8-1. *See* Chapter 1, note 270 and accompanying text.

[240] THE NAVAL/MARINE COMMANDER'S HANDBOOK, *supra* note 21, at 6-25 (citations omitted). *See* Chapter 1, note 271 and accompanying text.

[241] THE AIR FORCE MANUAL ON INTERNATIONAL LAW, *supra* note 9, at 10-5. *See* Chapter 1, note 272 and accompanying text.

[242] THE AIR FORCE COMMANDER'S HANDBOOK, *supra* note 16, at 8-1. *See* Chapter 1, note 273 and accompanying text.

progress would have been made in de-legitimizing these weapons, progress which would ostensibly have a substantial effect on military training, planning and weapons procurement, as well as on the international attitude towards such weapons, and hence potentially on the evolution of events in circumstances of extreme confrontation.

The Martens Clause

In its arguments before the ICJ, the United States portrayed the Martens Clause as simply "clarifying that customary international law may independently govern cases not explicitly addressed by the Conventions,"[243] stating, "This is what gives content and meaning to the Martens Clause."[244] The United States argued that "when as here, customary international law does not categorically prohibit the use of nuclear weapons, the Martens Clause does not independently give rise to such a prohibition."[245]

This position seems inconsistent with the language of the Martens Clause. *The Air Force Manual on International Law* sets forth the clause as contained in the preamble to Hague IV:

> Until a more complete code of laws of war has been issued, the High Contracting Parties deem it expedient to declare that, in cases not included in the Regulations adopted by them, the inhabitants and belligerents remain under the protection and the rule of the principles of the law of nations, as they result from the usages established among civilized peoples, from the laws of humanity, and from the dictates of the public conscience.[246]

The Army's *Law of Land Warfare* quotes the same provision of Hague IV, noting that Hague IV has "been held to be declaratory of the customary law of war, to which all States are subject."[247] The manual notes that a "common article" of the Geneva Conventions of 1949 provides that the withdrawal from the conventions would not "impair the obligations which the Parties to the conflict shall remain bound to fulfill by virtue of the principles of the law of nations, as they result

---

[243] ICJ Hearing, November 15, 1995, at 98. *See* Chapter 1, notes 246–249, Chapter 2, notes 50–53, Chapter 3, notes 166–185, and accompanying text.

[244] *Id. See* Chapter 2, note 52 and accompanying text.

[245] *Id. See* Chapter 2, note 53 and accompanying text.

[246] THE AIR FORCE MANUAL ON INTERNATIONAL LAW, *supra* note 9, at 1-7. *See* Chapter 1, note 246 and accompanying text.

[247] THE LAW OF LAND WARFARE, *supra* note 13, at 6. *See* Chapter 1, note 247 and accompanying text.

from the usages established among civilized peoples, from the laws of humanity and the dictates of the public conscience."[248]

The ICJ in its Nuclear Weapons Advisory Decision characterized the Martens Clause as "an effective means of addressing the rapid evolution of military technology."[249] The Court quoted a "modern version" of that clause contained in Article 2, paragraph 2, of Additional Protocol I of 1977:

> "In cases not covered by this Protocol or by other international agreements, civilians and combatants remain under the protection and authority of the principles of international law derived from established custom, from the principles of humanity and from the dictates of public conscience."[250]

The Tribunal at Nuremberg enforced such rules and there seems no reason to believe they would not be enforced in a future war crimes trial following a nuclear war, if there were to be any trials after such an event.

Self-Defense as Subject to Law of Armed Conflict

Great Britain's attorney before the ICJ argued that the right of self-defense trumps the requirements of humanitarian law:

> It was also said that no balance is possible between the suffering which would be caused by a use—any use—of a nuclear weapon and the military advantage which would be derived from that use. But such an abstract statement does not stand up to analysis. Let me take an example. A State or group of States is faced with invasion by overwhelming enemy forces. That State or group of States is certainly entitled to defend itself. If all the other means at their disposal are insufficient, then how can it be said that the use of a nuclear weapon must be disproportionate? Unless it is being suggested that there comes a point when the victim of aggression is no longer permitted to defend itself because of the degree of suffering which defensive measures will inflict. Such a suggestion is insupportable in logic and unsupported in practice.[251]

---

[248] *Id. See* Chapter 1, note 248 and accompanying text.

[249] Nuclear Weapons Advisory Opinion ¶ 78, at 28, 35 I.L.M. at 827. *See also* dissenting opinion of Judge Weeramantry. at 39, 40–42, 35 I.L.M. at 900–01. *See* Chapter 3, note 169 and accompanying text.

[250] Nuclear Weapons Advisory Opinion ¶ 78, at 28, 35 I.L.M. at 827. *See* Chapter 3, note 170 and accompanying text.

[251] ICJ Hearing, November 15, 1995, at 46–47. *See* Chapter 3, note 44 and accompanying text.

Great Britain further argued:

> But if the prohibition in Article 2, paragraph 4, extends to nuclear weapons, so too does the right of self-defense enshrined in Article 51. That is the most fundamental right of all, Mr. President, and it is preserved in terms which are general, not restrictive. It is impossible to argue that this fundamental, inherent right has been limited or abandoned on the basis of mere inferences drawn from other rules, whether conventional or customary. Moreover, the practice of those states vitally affected by such a rule shows that they entirely reject any such inference.[252]

Judge Guillaume in his individual opinion appeared to adopt the British position:

> The right of self-defense proclaimed by the Charter of the United Nations is characterized by the Charter as natural law. But Article 51 adds that nothing in the Charter shall impair this right. The same applies a fortiori to customary law or treaty law. This conclusion is easily explained, for no system of law, whatever it may be, could deprive one of its subjects of the right to defend its own existence and safeguard its vital interests. Accordingly, international law cannot deprive a State of the right to resort to nuclear weapons if such action constitutes the ultimate means by which it can guarantee its survival. In such a case the State enjoys a kind of "ground for absolution" similar to the one which exists in all systems of criminal law.[253]

So also France argued that the law of war and particularly the rule of proportionality does not preclude a State's using whatever weapon is militarily "appropriate" to withstand an attack.[254]

President Bedjaoui, in his declaration, rejected this broad scope of the right of self-defense:

> 22. A State's right to survival is also a fundamental law, similar in many respects to a "natural" law. However, self-defense —if exercised in extreme circumstances in which the very survival of a State is in question—cannot engender a situation in which a State would exonerate itself from compliance with the "intransgressible" norms of international humanitarian law. In

---

[252] *Id.* at 37 (Sir Nicholas Lyell, arguing). *See* Chapter 3, note 47 and accompanying text.

[253] Individual opinion of Judge Guillaume, 35 I.L.M. ¶ 8, at 1352 (No. 6, November 1996). *See* Chapter 3, note 47 and accompanying text.

[254] Dissenting Opinion of Judge Weeramantry at 12, 35 I.L.M. at 886. *See* Chapter 3, note 99 and accompanying text.

certain circumstances, therefore, a relentless opposition can arise, a head-on collision of fundamental principles, neither one of which can be reduced to the other. The fact remains that the use of nuclear weapons by a State in circumstances in which its survival is at stake risks in its turn endangering the survival of all mankind, precisely because of the inextricable link between terror and escalation in the use of such weapons. It would thus be quite foolhardy unhesitatingly to set the survival of a State above all other considerations, in particular above the survival of mankind itself.[255]

The United States, in its oral and written presentations to the ICJ, contrary to asserting such broad notions of the rights of self-defense and sovereignty, acknowledged, as noted, the general applicability to the use of nuclear weapons of the rules of proportionality, necessity, moderation, discrimination, civilian immunity, neutrality, and humanity.[256]

Thus, in its memorandum to the ICJ on the General Assembly application, the United States stated, "As in the use of other weapons, the legality of use depends on the conformity of the particular use with the rules applicable to such weapons."[257] U.S. lawyer John McNeill similarly stated, "The United States has long shared the view that the law of armed conflict governs the use of nuclear weapons—just as it governs the use of conventional weapons."[258]

The U.S. memorandum formulated the proportionality test as follows:

> Whether an attack with nuclear weapons would be disproportionate depends entirely on the circumstances, including the nature of the

---

[255] Declaration of President Bedjaoui, 35 I.L.M. ¶ 22, at 1345 (No. 6, November 1996). *See* Chapter 3, note 46 and accompanying text.

[256] *See* Chapter 2, notes 6–8, 27–88, 101–135, and accompanying text. *See also* U.S. ICJ Memorandum/GA App. at 2, 8–14; Conrad K. Harper, Michael J. Matheson, & Bruce C. Rashkow, *Written Statement of the Government of the United States of America* (June 10, 1994), submitted to the International Court of Justice, The Hague, The Netherlands, in connection with the Request by the World Health Organization for an Advisory Opinion on the Question of the Legality Under International Law and the World Health Organization Constitution of the Use of Nuclear Weapons by a State in War or Other Armed Conflict at 2, 16–21.

[257] U.S. ICJ Memorandum/GA App. at 2. *See also id.* 7–47. *See* Chapter 2, note 27 and accompanying text.

[258] ICJ Hearing, November 15, 1995, at 85. *See* Chapter 2, note 48 and accompanying text.

enemy threat, the importance of destroying the objective, the
character, size and likely effects of the device, and the magnitude
of the risk to civilians.[259]

The Naval/Marine Commander's Handbook similarly states that the
lawfulness of the use of nuclear weapons is subject to the following
principles:

> (1) the right of the parties to the conflict to adopt means of
> injuring the enemy is not unlimited;
> (2) it is prohibited to launch attacks against the civilian
> population as such; and
> (3) the distinction must be made at all times between persons
> taking part in the hostilities and members of the civilian population
> to the effect that the latter be spared as much as possible.[260]

The Air Force Manual on International Law states that "[a]ny
weapon may be used unlawfully, such as when it is directed at civilians
and not at a military objective"[261] or "to inflict unnecessary
suffering."[262]   The manual states that, in comparing the military
advantages to be secured by the use of a new weapon to the effects
caused by the weapon, the following questions are relevant:

> (1) can the weapon be delivered accurately to the target;
> (2) would its use necessarily result in excessive injury to
> civilians or damage to civilian objects, so as to be termed an
> "indiscriminate weapon";
> (3) would its effects be uncontrollable or unpredictable in space
> or time as to cause disproportionate injury to civilians or damage to
> civilian objects; and
> (4) would its use necessarily cause suffering excessive in
> relation to the military purpose which the weapon serves so as to
> violate that prohibition.[263]

Addressing this same question from a different perspective, the
I.C.J. noted that various States had argued, based on dicta in the *Lotus*
and *Nicaragua* cases, that international law is based on sovereignty and
consent, such that States are permitted to do anything that is not

---

[259] U.S. ICJ Memorandum/GA App. at 23 (citing the Army's THE LAW OF
LAND WARFARE at 5). *See* Chapter 2, note 88 and accompanying text.

[260] THE NAVAL/MARINE COMMANDER'S HANDBOOK, *supra* note 21, at 10-1.
See Chapter 2, note 28 and accompanying text.

[261] THE AIR FORCE MANUAL ON INTERNATIONAL LAW, *supra* note 9, at 6-1.
See Chapter 2, note 33 and accompanying text.

[262] *Id.* at 6-8. *See* Chapter 2, note 34 and accompanying text.

[263] *Id.* at 6-7. *See* Chapter 2, note 35 and accompanying text.

precluded by treaty or conventional law.[264] The Court concluded that it did not have to reach this issue, since "the nuclear-weapon States appearing before it either accepted, or did not dispute, that their independence to act was indeed restricted by the principles and rules of international law, more particularly humanitarian law, as did the other States which took part in the proceedings."[265]

War Crimes

The Army's *Law of Land Warfare* defines the term "war crime" as "the technical expression for a violation of the law of war by any person or persons, military or civilian," and states that "[e]very violation of the law of war is a war crime."[266] The manual describes war crimes as encompassing crimes against peace and crimes against humanity.[267]

To the same effect, the Nuremberg Charter defined "war crimes" as follows:

> [V]iolations of the laws or customs of war. Such violations shall include, but not be limited to, murder, ill treatment, or deportation to slave labor or for any other purpose, of civilian population of or in occupied territory, murder or ill treatment of prisoners of war or persons on the seas, killing of hostages, plunder of public or private property, wanton destruction of cities, towns or villages, or devastation not justified by military necessity.[268]

As noted in *The Naval/Marine Commander's Handbook*, the Charter of the International Military Tribunal at Nuremberg defined "crimes against the peace" as follows:

> planning, preparation, initiation, or waging of a war of aggression, or a war in violation of international treaties, agreements or

---

[264] *See* Nuclear Weapons Advisory Opinion ¶¶ 21–80, at 12–13, 35 I.L.M. at 819–827; Chapter 3, notes 98–99 and accompanying text.

[265] *Id.* ¶ 22, at 13, 35 I.L.M. at 820. *See* Chapter 3, notes 98–99, 262–270, and accompanying text.

[266] THE LAW OF LAND WARFARE, *supra* note 13, at 178. *See* Chapter 1, note 308 and accompanying text.

[267] *See id.*; Chapter 1, note 302 and accompanying text.

[268] THE NAVAL/MARINE COMMANDER'S HANDBOOK, *supra* note 21, at 6-27 n.49 (quoting Charter of the International Military Tribunal at Nuremberg, U.S. Naval War College, INTERNATIONAL LAW DOCUMENTS 1944–45, at 254 (1945); Air Force Pamphlet 110-20, at 3-183). *See* Chapter 1, note 309 and accompanying text.

assurances, or participation in a common plan or conspiracy for the accomplishment of any of the foregoing.[269]

The Nuremberg Charter defined "crimes against humanity" as follows:

> murder, extermination, enslavement, deportation, and other inhumane acts committed against any civilian population, before or during the war, or persecutions on political, racial, or religious grounds in execution of or in connection with any crime within the jurisdiction of the Tribunal, whether or not in violation of the domestic law of the country where perpetuated.[270]

Thus, any violation of the law of armed conflict—including the use of nuclear weapons if my analysis is correct—would constitute a war crime.

Mental State

Often overlooked is the mental state required for unlawfulness. Both the State and individuals associated with it, generally its governmental, military and industrial leadership and in some instances working personnel, are subject to criminal liability for commission of war crimes. The State obviously can only act through individuals, and it is now well-established that, for purposes of the law of armed conflict, such individuals—every bit as much as States and indeed even more so—are subject to potential liability for war crimes.

Indeed, as the Nuremberg proceedings exemplified, individuals, not States, are potentially put in prison or executed.[271] States can, and historically have been, subject to damages and reparations, but, in contemporary international law, the focus of war crimes trials is on the responsible individuals.[272]

---

[269] *Id. See* Chapter 1, note 303 and accompanying text.

[270] *Id. See* Chapter 1, note 306 and accompanying text.

[271] *See* Chapter 8, note 3 and accompanying text. *See generally* Chapter 8; IAN BROWNIE, INTERNATIONAL LAW AND THE USE OF FORCE BY STATES 150–171 (1963), Matthew Lippman, *Crimes Against Humanity*, 17 B.C. THIRD WORLD L.J. 171 (1997) (International Law and Human Rights Edition); Mark Allan Gray, *The International Crime of Ecocide*, 26 CAL. W. INT'L L.J. 215, 265 (1996), citing Geof Gilbert, *The Criminal Responsibility of States,* 39 INT'L & COMP. L.Q. 345, 357, 366 (1990), and Report of the Commission to the General Assembly on the work of its forty-sixth session, U.N. GAOR, 49th Sess., Supp. No. 10, U.N. Doc. A/49/10 (1994), at 348–49.

[272] *See* Chapter 8, notes 1–7, 40, and accompanying text. *See generally* Chapter 8; IAN BROWNIE, INTERNATIONAL LAW AND THE USE OF FORCE BY

The United States has recognized a very broad range of potential criminal liability of individuals for war crimes, including not only for activity of an intentional nature, but also for reckless, grossly negligent, and even negligent conduct.

The Air Force Manual on International Law states, focusing on the potential liability of States, notes that the law of armed conflict "often omits critical elements of individual criminal responsibility, such as intentional and deliberate acts."[273]

Explaining the general absence of a *mens rea* requirement for State, as opposed to individual, responsibility, the Air Force manual states that "if the law of armed conflict were couched in terms of intentional wrongs it would lose much of its efficacy; the issue then would be a State's intent, a troublesome concept to apply."[274]

The manual adds that from the "perspective of the victim-civilian, PW or other *hors de combat* personnel—the wrongful act has the same result whether done intentionally or inadvertently."[275] As a result, "[f]ailures to observe treaty rules or other international law rules may occur for which there may be general state responsibility without any individual criminal responsibility."[276]

Quoting the applicable sections, the manual goes on to note that the element of willfulness is imposed with respect to many of the breaches defined as "grave" by the 1949 Geneva Conventions, with such element connoted through such words as "willful" and "wanton:"

> GWS and GWS SEA
> Grave breaches to which the preceding Article relates shall be those involving any of the following acts, if committed against persons or property protected by the Convention: willful killing, torture or inhuman treatment, including biological experiments, willfully causing great suffering or serious injury to body or health, and extensive destruction and appropriation of property, not justified by military necessity and carried out unlawfully and wantonly. (Art. 50, GWS; Art 51, GWS-SEA).[277]

STATES 133–149 (1963); TELFORD TAYLOR, NUREMBERG AND VIETNAM: AN AMERICAN TRAGEDY 82–88 (Quadrangle 1970).

[273] THE AIR FORCE MANUAL ON INTERNATIONAL LAW, *supra* note 9, at 15-2. *See* Chapter 1, notes 278–282 and accompanying text.

[274] *Id. See* Chapter 1, note 280 and accompanying text.

[275] *Id. See* Chapter 1, note 281 and accompanying text.

[276] *Id. See* Chapter 1, note 282 and accompanying text.

[277] *Id.* at 15-1 to 15-2; 15-8 n.12. The manual quoted similar articles from other Geneva Conventions. *See* Chapter 1, note 284 and accompanying text.

The Air Force Manual on International Law goes on to state that *mens rea* or a guilty mind, at the level of purposeful behavior or intention or at least gross negligence, is required for individual, as opposed to State, criminal responsibility.[278]   The manual quotes Spaight's statement of the rule:

> In international law, as in municipal law intention to break the law—*mens rea* or negligence so gross as to be the equivalent of criminal intent is the essence of the offense. A bombing pilot cannot be arraigned for an error of judgment ... it must be one which he or his superiors either knew to be wrong, or which was, *in se*, so palpably and unmistakenly a wrongful act that only gross negligence or deliberate blindness could explain their being unaware of its wrongness.[279]

The Air Force Commander's Handbook states that the 1949 Geneva Conventions "require" the trial of persons who have "intentionally committed 'grave breaches'" of the conventions."[280]   The handbook states that international law "allows a nation to try captured enemy personnel for deliberate, intentional violations of the law of armed conflict" and notes that after World War II the United States conducted or took part in over 800 such trials.[281]

As to commander liability, a commander is responsible to maintain and prevent violations of the law of war by subordinates and can be liable based on such violations.

The Air Force Manual on International Law states that "[c]ommand responsibility for acts committed by subordinates arises when the specific wrongful acts in question are knowingly ordered or encouraged."[282]   The manual states that the commander is also responsible "if he has actual knowledge, or should have had knowledge" that his subordinates "have or are about to commit criminal violations, and he culpably fails to take reasonably necessary

---

See also Chapter 8 for a discussion of *mens rea* requirements for war crimes under established international law.

[278] *Id.* at 15-3; 15-8 n.13 (citing SPAIGHT, AIR POWER AND WAR RIGHTS 57, 58 (1947)). *See* Chapter 1, note 285 and accompanying text.

[279] *Id.* at 15-8 n.13. *See* Chapter 1, note 286 and accompanying text.

[280] THE AIR FORCE COMMANDER'S HANDBOOK, *supra* note 16, at 8-1. *See generally* Chapter 8. *See* Chapter 1, note 287, Chapter 8, note 18, and accompanying text.

[281] *Id.* at 8-1. *See* Chapter 1, note 288 and accompanying text.

[282] THE AIR FORCE MANUAL ON INTERNATIONAL LAW, *supra* note 9, at 15-3. *See also id.* at 15-9 n.23 (citations omitted). *See* Chapter 1, note 289 and accompanying text.

steps to ensure compliance with the law and punish violators thereof."[283]

The Naval/Marine Commander's Handbook states, "A commander at any level is personally responsible for the criminal acts of warfare committed by a subordinate if the commander knew in advance of the breach about to be committed and had the ability to prevent it, but failed to take the appropriate action to do so."[284] The handbook adds that "in determining the personal responsibility of the commander, the element of knowledge may be presumed if the commander had information which should have enabled him or her to conclude under the circumstances that such breach was to be expected."[285] The handbook states that the applicable facts "will each be determined objectively."[286]

The handbook quotes the United States Military Tribunal's decision in *The Hostages Case* for the proposition that the commander is charged with available information even if not personally aware of same:

> Want of knowledge of the contents of reports made to him [*i.e.*, to the commander general] is not a defense. Reports to commanding generals are made for their special benefit. Any failure to acquaint themselves with the contents of such reports, or a failure to require additional reports where inadequacy appears on their face, constitutes a dereliction of duty which he cannot use in his behalf.[287]

The handbook states that the responsibility of a commanding officer "may be based solely upon inaction" and that it is "not always necessary to establish that a superior knew, or must be presumed to have known of the offense committed by his subordinates."[288] "While a commander may delegate some or all of his authority, he cannot delegate responsibility for the conduct of the forces he commands."[289]

The Air Force Manual on International Law notes that the prosecutions for crimes against peace and against humanity following

---

[283] *Id.* at 15-2 to 15-3. *See also* THE LAW OF LAND WARFARE, *supra* note 13, at 178. *See* Chapter 1, note 290 and accompanying text.

[284] THE NAVAL/MARINE COMMANDER'S HANDBOOK, *supra* note 21, at 6-5 n.12. *See* Chapter 1, note 291 and accompanying text.

[285] *Id.* at 6-5. *See* Chapter 1, note 292 and accompanying text.

[286] *Id. See* Chapter 1, notes 293 and accompanying text.

[287] *Id.* (quoting United States v. Wilhelm List et al., 9 TWC 127 (1950)).

[288] *Id.* at 6-6 n.12. *See* Chapter 1, note 295 and accompanying text.

[289] *Id.* at 6-5. *See* Chapter 1, note 296 and accompanying text.

World War II were primarily against the principal political, military and industrial leaders responsible for the initiation of the war and related inhumane policies.[290]

The Air Force Commander's Handbook states that the two International Military Tribunals following World War II punished "former cabinet ministers, and others of similar rank" in the Axis powers for planning and waging aggressive war.[291]

Conclusion

The conclusion that the use of nuclear weapons would be unlawful based on uncontrollability seems compelling. The U.S. acknowledgement in its military manuals of the unlawfulness under the discrimination, necessity, and proportionality principles of the use of weapons that cannot be controlled is unequivocal and the rules themselves are clear to the same effect. Similarly, the facts as to the uncontrollable nature of the effects of nuclear weapons, including particularly the radiation effects, seem beyond reasonable dispute.

The conclusion as to unlawfulness on this basis is in no way subject to any assumptions as to the actual effects of the use of the weapons or to any arguments as to the extension of the law or the broadening of the notion of the prerequisites for a *per se* rule.

The arguments as to unlawfulness based more broadly on the likelihood that virtually any use of nuclear weapons, in the circumstances in which such use would likely take place, would lead to large scale use of nuclear, chemical or biological weapons and resultant impermissible effects obviously involve judgments as to matters that by definition cannot be known with certainty.

However, based upon the totality of the facts, including U.S. declaratory and operational nuclear policy and statements by leading members of the civilian and military leadership of the country as to the likelihood of escalation once the nuclear threshold is crossed,[292] unlawfulness seems evident on this basis as well.

The lack of seriousness of the arguments marshaled by the United States before the ICJ—particularly the contention that the effects of nuclear weapons can be controlled and will likely be no greater than those of conventional weapons—lays bare the unreality of our current

---

[290] THE AIR FORCE MANUAL ON INTERNATIONAL LAW, *supra* note 9, at 15-5; *See* Chapter 1, note 297 and accompanying text.

[291] THE AIR FORCE COMMANDER'S HANDBOOK, *supra* note 16, at 1-2. *See* Chapter 1, note 299 and accompanying text.

[292] *See* Chapter 25.

policy, as the nation's civilian and military leaders and its attorneys struggle to justify the anachronistic historical legacy that nuclear deterrence has become.

There is a telling interplay between the rules of necessity and proportionality. If the military objective is, in a relative sense, not all that challenging, such as ostensibly the recent enforcement type operations against the Iraqis and Serbians, the use of nuclear weapons even of a low-yield tactical nature would not generally be necessary— conventional weapons would easily suffice, or certainly could potentially suffice, given adequate planning. So, even if one assumed a high value to the military objective in terms of winning the particular engagement and further assumed a totally static riskless environment, where there would be no nuclear, chemical or biological weapons response to the strike and no escalation, the strike would still be unlawful under the necessity rule even though potentially lawful under the proportionality rule.

On the other hand, if ones assumes an extremely challenging military situation, such as a nuclear confrontation between the United States and Russia or a nuclearized rogue nation with long-range missiles, obviously the risk factors increase exponentially, ostensibly precluding proportionality, even if it were assumed the use of nuclear weapons was militarily necessary.

Chapter 30: Unlawfulness of Nuclear Weapons under Additional Generally Recognized Principles of Law

Generally recognized principles of law are a primary source of international law. *The Naval/Marine Commander's Handbook* states, "In recent years there has been a marked tendency to include among the sources of the rules of warfare certain principles of law adopted by many nations in their domestic legislation."[1] The handbook quotes the decision of the United States Military Tribunal in *The Hostage Case*:

> The tendency has been to apply the term "customs and practices accepted by civilized nations generally" as it is used in international law, to the laws of war only. But the principle has no such restricted meaning. It applies as well to fundamental principles of justice which have been accepted and adopted by civilized nations generally. In determining whether such a fundamental rule of justice is entitled to be declared a principle of international law, an examination of the municipal laws of states in the family of nations will reveal the answer. If it is found to have been accepted generally as a fundamental rule of justice by most nations in their municipal law, its declaration as a rule of international law would seem to be fully justified.[2]

Risk Analysis

In the preceding chapter, I set forth my conclusions to the effect that the use of nuclear weapons, in the circumstances in which such use would likely take place, would likely cause impermissible effects and hence would be unlawful. In this chapter I explore the further question: What if it is assumed that the use of the nuclear weapons is not necessarily *likely* to lead to impermissible effects but *may* result in such

---

[1] UNITED STATES DEPARTMENT OF THE NAVY ANNOTATED SUPPLEMENT TO THE COMMANDER'S HANDBOOK ON THE LAW OF NAVAL OPERATIONS 5-11 (Naval Warfare Publication 9, 1987) (With Revision A (5 October 1989), this handbook was adopted by the U.S. Marine Corps as FLEET MARINE FORCE MANUAL (FM FM) 1-10) [hereinafter THE NAVAL/MARINE COMMANDER'S HANDBOOK]. *See* Chapter 1, notes 14–15 and accompanying text. *See also* Chapter 1, notes 3–5, 14–18, 24–26, Chapter 2, notes 47–50, and accompanying text; Article 38 of The Statute of the International Court of Justice (Annex to UN Charter), 59 Stat 1031; USTS 993.

[2] *Id.* at 5-11 to 5-12. *See* Chapter 1, notes 14–15 and accompanying text.

effects? What if there is a risk, even an extremely small one, that such use will result in apocalyptic effects?

The question becomes: To what extent may any one State put protected persons and indeed the whole human venture at risk in an attempt to further the State's own military objectives, even its survival?

Presumably, absent some political or military aberration or mistake (obviously themselves risk factors),[3] the United States would not resort to use of nuclear weapons except in the most extreme of circumstances. Yet, as noted, such circumstances[4] would by definition be volatile and highly pressured, with little time for rational or careful decision-making.[5]

In any such circumstance in which these weapons might be used, whether intentionally or by mistake, is it not ineluctably the case that there would be some risk of the occurrence of extreme effects, given the potential destructiveness of the weapons, the inherent uncontrollability of radiation,[6] and the overall potential for escalation, misperception, and loss of command and control?[7]

---

[3] *See* Chapter 22, notes 32–37 and accompanying text. *See also* Chapter 22, notes 38–40 and accompanying text; SHAUN GREGORY, THE HIDDEN COST OF DETERRENCE: NUCLEAR WEAPONS ACCIDENTS (1990).

[4] As noted, I have written this book from the perspective of the United States. *See* Introduction before Part I. The question arises, to what extent is this a limitation? Could the use of nuclear weapons be unlawful for the United States, but lawful for some other State?

I think not. Such rules of law as those of proportionality, necessity, discrimination, and neutrality are equally applicable to all States. While my focus, in developing the facts and law based on statements by the United States, heightens the extent to which such matters have been "admitted" by the United States, these matters are not controversial. The U.S. admissions are not esoteric or idiosyncratic, but rather essentially acknowledge the incontrovertible.

While it is true, in terms of the legal issue of the implications of bringing upon oneself the need to use extreme force, that the United States, as such a wealthy country, might be regarded as particularly culpable in bringing upon itself a dependency upon nuclear weapons, as it did during the Cold War, nonetheless, the prohibitions of the applicable rules of law override even severe military necessity. *See* Introduction before Part I; Chapter 29, notes 128–136, 205–209, and accompanying text.

[5] *See* Chapter 17, note 33, Chapter 29, notes 48–54, and accompanying text.

[6] *See* Chapter 29, notes 41–124 and accompanying text.

[7] *See* Chapters 15, 25, 26; Chapter 2, notes 63–87, Chapter 15, notes 1–14, 33–43, 58–89, 99, 102–108, Chapter 16, notes 32–38, and accompanying text; NATO HANDBOOK ON THE MEDICAL ASPECTS OF NBC DEFENSIVE OPERATIONS, Part I, Chap. 1, §102(a) (A MedP-6(B) 1996), adopted as Army Field Manual

This is clear even from the types of examples that have been given by proponents of legality. As we saw, for instance, Judge Schwebel, at the time the U.S. judge on the ICJ and now the President of the Court, after finding unlawful the use of strategic nuclear weapons "in quantities against enemy cities and industries,"[8] found to be lawful the use of "tactical nuclear weapons against discrete military or naval targets so situated that substantial civilian casualties would not ensue."[9]

By way of example, he hypothesized the use of a nuclear depth-charge to destroy a nuclear submarine that has fired or is about to fire nuclear missiles, arguing that such use might be lawful since it would not cause substantial civilian casualties, would be proportionate in the sense that it would cause much less damage than the destroyed submarine would have caused, and would be more likely than a conventional depth-charge to achieve the military objective.[10]

Judge Schwebel identified as an intermediate case the use of nuclear weapons to destroy an enemy army situated in the desert, concluding that such a strike would in some instances be legal and in others illegal, depending on the circumstances and the application of such rules as those of discrimination and proportionality.[11]

As we saw, the ICJ in its decision referenced similar arguments the United States and Great Britain had made:

> 91. ... The reality ... is that nuclear weapons might be used in a wide variety of circumstances with very different results in terms of likely civilian casualties. In some cases, such as the use of a low yield nuclear weapon against warships on the High Seas or troops

---

8-9, Navy Medical Publication 5059, Air Force Joint Manual 44-151; INTERNATIONAL PHYSICIANS FOR THE PREVENTION OF NUCLEAR WAR, BRIEFING BOOK ON NUCLEAR WAR (1992); Carl Sagan, *Nuclear War and Climatic Catastrophe: Some Policy Implications,* 62 FOREIGN AFF. 257, 273 (Winter 1983/1984); U.S. Congress, Office of Technology Assessment, *The Effects of Nuclear War* 16–17 NTIS order no. PB-296946 (Washington, DC: U.S. Government Printing Office, May 1979). *See also* Chapters 7–9, on weighing risks and the legal relevance of risks.

The escalation risk is particularly extreme, as has been recognized by the civilian and military leadership of the United States and by defense experts throughout the nuclear era. *See* Chapters 24, 25.

[8] Dissenting opinion of Judge Schwebel to the Nuclear Weapons Advisory Opinion at 7, 35 I.L.M at 839. *See* Chapter 3, notes 37–40 and accompanying text.

[9] *Id.*

[10] *See id.*

[11] *See id.*

in sparsely populated areas, it is possible to envisage a nuclear attack which caused comparatively few civilian casualties. It is by no means the case that every use of nuclear weapons against a military objective would inevitably cause very great collateral civilian casualties.[12]

These examples, and the ones used by the United States and Great Britain before the ICJ, appear to assume one of two things:

- that the submarine in the ocean and the army in the desert or other such remote targets would exist independently of the rest of the world, rather than being affiliated with a State that either itself or with its allies has nuclear, chemical or biological weapons that it is likely to use in response to nuclear attack, and that the State using the nuclear weapons has no other enemies that might find the attack provocative and retaliate; or
- that the potential escalation by the attacked State or other party is not relevant to the analysis.

Neither assumption seems reasonable. As the United States has recognized, the legality evaluation is to be made in light of all available facts as to potential risk factors.[13] Although it may be possible that there could be a scenario where the submarine or the army in the desert and the related conflict existed independently of the rest of the world,

---

[12] Nuclear Weapons Advisory Opinion ¶ 91 at 31, 35 I.L.M. at 829 (citing United Kingdom, Written Statement ¶ 3.70 at 53, and United States of America, Oral Statement, CR 95/34 at 89–90). *See* Chapter 1, note 29 and accompanying text.

[13] *See* Chapter 1, notes 84–93, 109–120, 161, Chapter 5, notes 3–4, Chapter 6, notes 26–27, Chapter 29, notes 125–127, and accompanying text; THE UNITED STATES DEPARTMENT OF THE AIR FORCE, INTERNATIONAL LAW—THE CONDUCT OF ARMED CONFLICT AND AIR OPERATIONS 1-8 to 1-9 (citing SPAIGHT, AIR POWER AND WAR RIGHTS 57, 58 (1947)) (Air Force Pamphlet 110-31, 19 November 1976) [hereinafter THE AIR FORCE MANUAL ON INTERNATIONAL LAW]; THE NAVAL/MARINE COMMANDER'S HANDBOOK, *supra* note 1, at 8-5 to 8-6; UNITED STATES DEPARTMENT OF THE AIR FORCE, COMMANDER'S HANDBOOK ON THE LAW OF ARMED CONFLICT 3-3, 6-1 (Air Force Pamphlet 110-34, 25 July 1980) [hereinafter THE AIR FORCE COMMANDER'S HANDBOOK]; UNITED STATES DEPARTMENT OF THE ARMY, THE LAW OF LAND WARFARE 23–24 (FM27-10/18 July 1956) with Change No. 1 (15 July 1976) [hereinafter THE LAW OF LAND WARFARE]. *See also* Vienna Convention on the Law of Treaties Article 32, May 23, 1969, 1155 U.N.T.S. 331, 8 I.L.M. 679; J.L. BRIERLY, THE LAW OF NATIONS 67 (1963) (1928); XI INT'L ENCYCLOPEDIA OF COMPARATIVE LAW § 2-114 (1983).

such a prospect seems so remote as to preclude its constituting the basis, on any rational level, for the overall lawfulness of the use of nuclear weapons.

Interestingly, Judge Schwebel recognized the legal point that if a use of nuclear weapons could cause severe effects, it would be unlawful:

> At one extreme is the use of strategic nuclear weapons in quantities against enemy cities and industries. This so-called "countervalue" use (as contrasted with "counterforce" uses directly only against enemy nuclear forces and installations) could cause an enormous number of deaths and injuries, running in some cases into the millions; and, in addition to those immediately affected by the heat and blast of those weapons, vast numbers could be affected, many fatally, by spreading radiation. Large-scale "exchanges" of such nuclear weaponry could destroy not only cities but countries and render continents, perhaps the whole of the earth, uninhabitable, if not at once then through longer-range effects of nuclear fallout. It cannot be accepted that the use of nuclear weapons on a scale which would—or *could*—result in the deaths of many millions in indiscriminate inferno and by far-reaching fallout, have profoundly pernicious effects in space and time, and render uninhabitable much or all of the earth, could be lawful.[14]

The ICJ, as we have seen, concluded that it had not been given sufficient facts to resolve the issue:

> 95. ... [N]one of the States advocating the legality of the use of nuclear weapons under certain circumstances, including the "clean" use of smaller, low yield tactical nuclear weapons, has indicated what, supposing such limited use were feasible, would be the precise circumstances justifying such use; nor whether such limited use would not tend to escalate into the all-out use of high yield nuclear weapons. This being so, the Court does not consider that it has a sufficient basis for a determination of the validity of this view.[15]

The Court declined to engage in risk analysis:

> 43. Certain States ... contend that the very nature of nuclear weapons, and the high probability of an escalation of nuclear

---

[14] Dissenting opinion of Judge Schwebel to the Nuclear Weapons Advisory Opinion at 7, 35 I.L.M at 839 (emphasis added). *See* Chapter 1, note 38 and accompanying text.

[15] Nuclear Weapons Advisory Opinion ¶ 94 at 32. *See* Chapter 3, note 31 and accompanying text.

exchanges, mean that there is an extremely strong risk of devastation. The risk factor is said to negate the possibility of the condition of proportionality being complied with. The Court does not find it necessary to embark upon the quantification of such risks; nor does it need to enquire into the question whether tactical nuclear weapons exist which are sufficiently precise to limit those risks: it suffices for the Court to note that the very nature of all nuclear weapons and the profound risks associated therewith are further considerations to be borne in mind by States believing they can exercise a nuclear response in self-defense in accordance with the requirements of proportionality.[16]

This issue of risk analysis would appear to be the heart of the matter. In a milieu in which the dominant policy of nuclear deterrence is inherently provocative, the question of the extent to which any State may subject the rest of the world, or any appreciable portion of it, to the risk of severe, even apocalyptic, effects would appear to be one that must be addressed if the law in this area is to be meaningful.

The applicability of risk analysis would seem to be recognized by the U.S. statement of the proportionality test to the ICJ:

Whether an attack with nuclear weapons would be disproportionate depends entirely on the circumstances, including the nature of the enemy threat, the importance of destroying the objective, the character, size and likely effects of the device, and the magnitude of the risk to civilians.[17]

Applicable Risk Factors

As we have seen, the U.S. military recognize the presence of such risk factors. The Joint Chief of Staff's *Joint Nuclear Operations* manual, for example, states that "there can be no assurances that a conflict involving weapons of mass destruction could be controllable or would be of short duration."[18] The manual further notes that "US forces must be able to survive a first strike and endure conventional and

---

[16] Nuclear Weapons Advisory Opinion ¶ 43, 35 I.L.M. at 822. *See* Chapter 6, note 8 and accompanying text. *See also* Nuclear Weapons Advisory Opinion ¶¶ 18, 32, 33, 36, 95, 97, at 18, 16, 17, 32, and 33, respectively.

[17] U.S. ICJ Memorandum/GA App. at 23 (citing the Army's THE LAW OF LAND WARFARE at 5). *See* Chapter 1, notes 75–108, Chapter 2, notes 88–91, and accompanying text.

[18] JOINT CHIEFS OF STAFF, JOINT PUB 3-12, DOCTRINE FOR JOINT NUCLEAR OPERATIONS i, (Dec. 15, 1995), available at <http://www.dtic.mil/doctrine/jel/new_pubs/jp3_12.pdf> at I-6–7 (emphasis omitted); Chapter 2, note 76, Chapter 16, notes 22, 41–46, and accompanying text.

escalatory attrition with sufficient retaliatory strength to inflict unacceptable damage on the enemy in a counterstrike."[19] To the same effect, the manual states, "From a massive exchange of nuclear weapons to limited use on a regional battlefield, US nuclear capabilities must confront an enemy with risks of unacceptable damage and disproportionate loss should the enemy choose to introduce WMD into a conflict."[20]

The *Joint Theater Nuclear Operations* manual further notes that the risks of using nuclear weapons depend upon such matters as delivery system accuracy and height of burst, certainly themselves prime risk factors.[21] Discussing "Nuclear Collateral Damage," the manual states, "The amount of damage varies with the protective posture of civilians and friendly units, delivery system accuracy, weapon yield, and height of burst."[22] In its arguments before the ICJ, the United States acknowledged the significance of "climatic and weather conditions," certainly risk factors of a notoriously unpredictable nature, as well as the "character of the targets," also a major variable, particularly given accuracy of delivery and escalation risks.[23]

The *Joint Nuclear Operations* manual, as noted, also emphasizes the extremely compressed time frames in which decisions as to use of nuclear weapons will have to be made, certainly another major risk factor: "In a matter of seconds for the defense, and minutes for the offense, critical decisions must be made in concert with discussions with NCA."[24]

The U.S. military's *Joint Theater Nuclear Operations* and the *Joint Nuclear Operations* manuals note the flexibility of target selection the

---

[19] *Id.* at I-3.

[20] *Id.* at I-2 (emphasis omitted). *See* Chapter 2, note 91, Chapter 27, note 83, and accompanying text.

[21] DOCTRINE FOR JOINT THEATER NUCLEAR OPERATIONS III-1–2 (Feb. 9, 1996) (prepared under direction of the Chairman of the Joint Chiefs of Staff), *as set forth at* <http://www.dtic.mil/doctrine/jel/new_pubs/jp3_12_1.pdf> (emphasis omitted). *See* Chapter 22, notes 4–6 and accompanying text; KOSTA TSIPIS, ARSENAL: UNDERSTANDING WEAPONS IN THE NUCLEAR AGE 69–76 (1983).

[22] DOCTRINE FOR JOINT THEATER NUCLEAR OPERATIONS, *supra* note 21, at III 1–2. *See* Chapter 2, note 63 and accompanying text.

[23] ICJ Hearing, November 15, 1995, at 87 (citing the Secretary-General's 1990 Report on nuclear weapons, p. 75, para. 290). *See* Chapter 2, notes 60–62 and accompanying text.

[24] DOCTRINE FOR JOINT NUCLEAR OPERATIONS, *supra* note 18, at III-8 (emphasis omitted). *See also* Chapter 2, note 80 and accompanying text.

combat commanders must have in such compressed time frames and the need for ad hoc judgments:

> Because preplanned theater nuclear options do not exist for every scenario, CINCs must have a capability to plan and execute nuclear options for nuclear forces generated on short notice during crisis and emergency situations. During crisis action planning, geographic combatant commanders evaluate their theater situation and propose courses of action or initiate a request for nuclear support.[25]

> Emergent Targets and Adaptive Planning. Even after the initial laydown of nuclear weapons, there may be a residual requirement to strike additional (follow on and/or emerging) targets in support of retaliatory or war-termination objectives. Commanders must maintain the capability to rapidly strike previously unidentified or newly emerging targets. This capability includes planning for and being able to perform "ad hoc" planning on newly identified targets and maintaining a pool of forces specifically reserved for striking previously unidentified targets. It is important to recognize that success in engaging emerging targets depends heavily upon the speed with which they are identified, targeted, and attacked.[26]

The *Nuclear Weapons Operations* manual further notes the need for decisive strikes, once the decision to go nuclear has been made:

> Some targets must be struck quickly once a decision to employ nuclear weapons has been made. Just as important is the requirement to promptly strike high-priority, time-sensitive targets that emerge after the conflict begins. Because force employment requirements may evolve at irregular intervals, some surviving nuclear weapons must be capable of striking these targets within the brief time available. Responsiveness (measured as the interval between the decision to strike a specific target and detonation of a weapon over that target) is critical to ensure engaging some emerging targets.[27]

The manual also notes the potentially provocative nature of resorting to states of increased readiness:

---

[25] DOCTRINE FOR JOINT THEATER NUCLEAR OPERATIONS, *supra* note 21, at III-10 (emphasis omitted). *See* Chapter 16, note 43 and accompanying text.

[26] DOCTRINE FOR JOINT NUCLEAR OPERATIONS, *supra* note 18, at II-6 (emphasis omitted). *See* Chapter 16, note 43 and accompanying text.

[27] *Id.* at II-3–4 (emphasis omitted). *See* Chapter 2, note 83 and accompanying text.

Alert posturing of nuclear delivery systems to dispersal locations can send a forceful message that demonstrates the national will to use nuclear weapons if necessary. For example, the generation of nuclear forces to higher alert levels during the October 1973 Mideast Crisis sent a strong signal. However, the danger also exists that the enemy may perceive either an exploitable vulnerability or the threat of imminent use.[28]

The manual further notes, on the issue of credibility, that, under the policy of deterrence, "[t]he potential aggressor must believe the United States could and would use nuclear weapons to attain its security objectives."[29] The manual notes the interrelationship of operational readiness and escalation:

- Escalation. Should a crisis become so severe as to prompt the United States to place all its nuclear forces at a high level of readiness, the United States must be prepared to posture its nuclear forces as quickly as possible. Nuclear forces should be generated and managed to ensure a sustained high level of readiness. Conventional forces and intelligence activities would have to be prudently managed to ensure avoidance of inadvertent escalation or mistaken warnings of nuclear attack.[30]

In terms of the risks of escalation, the U.S. military has recognized the need for preemptive strikes against enemy delivery systems capable of delivering weapons of mass destruction. The *Joint Theater Nuclear Operations* manual states:

Operation planning should include the possibility that an enemy will use WMD. ... Operations must be planned and executed to destroy or eliminate enemy WMD delivery systems and supporting infrastructure before they can strike friendly forces.[31]

Obviously, the potential for the United States' conducting such preemptive strikes is a risk factor as to the overall volatility of weapons of mass destruction in situations of acute crisis, imposing on the adversary the same "use 'em or lose 'em" mentality affecting the U.S. policy of preemptive strike in the first instance. A policy—or even the hint of a policy—of preemptive strike inherently breeds a counter

---

[28] *Id.* at I-4 (emphasis omitted). *See* Chapter 2, notes 86–87 and accompanying text.

[29] *Id.* at I-3. *See* Chapter 2, note 85 and accompanying text.

[30] *Id.* at I-4 (emphasis omitted). *See* Chapter 2, notes 86–87 and accompanying text.

[31] DOCTRINE FOR JOINT THEATER NUCLEAR OPERATIONS, *supra* note 21, at ix (emphasis omitted). *See* Chapter 2, notes 86–87 and accompanying text.

policy of preemptive strike—with the potential for escalating levels of hair triggerism.

The *Joint Nuclear Operations* manual notes the risk of rapid escalation if conventional warfare leads to an attrition of nuclear forces and supporting systems, "If this attrition results in a radical change in the strategic force posture by eliminating intermediate retaliatory steps, there may be a rapid escalation."[32]

The manual further notes how the loss of intelligence as to the level of attrition of nuclear and other forces "will directly effect calculations on the termination of war and the escalation to nuclear war:"[33]

> - Controlling Escalation. Nuclear weapons may influence the objectives and conduct of conventional warfare. Additionally, conventional warfare may result in attrition of nuclear forces and supporting systems (through antisubmarine warfare, conventional attacks in theater, sabotage, or antisatellite warfare), either unintended or deliberate, which could affect the forces available for nuclear employment. If this attrition results in a radical change in the strategic force posture by eliminating intermediate retaliatory steps, there may be a rapid escalation. The ability to precisely gauge the attrition of conventional and nuclear forces will directly effect calculations on the termination of war and the escalation to nuclear war.[34]

Another risk factor is the likely use of multiple nuclear weapons, were any such weapons to be used. The U.S. military in their manual *Doctrine for Joint Theater Nuclear Operations* characterize "employing multiple weapons" as one of the "[m]ethods for reducing collateral damage."[35] Redundant targeting—sometimes called "layering"—is part of the U.S. targeting planning for nuclear weapons, as reflected in the *Joint Nuclear Operations* manual:

> - Layering. Layering is a targeting methodology that plans employing more than one weapon against a target to increase the probability of its destruction or to improve the confidence that a

---

[32] DOCTRINE FOR JOINT NUCLEAR OPERATIONS, *supra* note 18, at I-5–6 (emphasis omitted). *See* Chapter 2, note 87 and accompanying text.

[33] *Id.*

[34] *Id.*

[35] DOCTRINE FOR JOINT THEATER NUCLEAR OPERATIONS, *supra* note 21, at viii. *See* Chapter 16, note 44 and accompanying text.

weapon will arrive and detonate on that target and achieve a specified level of damage.[36]

Redundant targeting is also accompanied by the use of different types of nuclear weapons and delivery vehicles:

> - Crosstargeting. At the same time it incorporates the concept of "layering," crosstargeting also uses different platforms for employment against one target to increase the probability of at least one weapon arriving at that target. Using different delivery platforms such as ICBMs, SLBMs, or aircraft-delivered weapons increases the probability of achieving the desired damage or target coverage.[37]

The potential for events lurching out of control, causing warfare never intended or desired by combatant States or groups and their leaders, has become a truism. Barbara W. Tuchman in *The March of Folly* traced the vagaries involved in the precipitation of such conflicts as the Trojan War, the Protestant Succession against the Renaissance Popes, the American Revolution, and the Vietnam War.[38] So also, in *The Guns of August*, Tuchman described steps whereby World War I broke out against the desires and expectations of participants.[39]

The recent revelations as to the misinformation leading to the U.S. cruise missile attacks against the pharmaceutical plant at Al Shifa in Sudan in 1998 further illustrate the vagaries of such decision making even in the absence of great military pressure.[40] Serious disagreement existed within various organs of the U.S. government as to whether the target plant was in fact a chemical weapons facility, and it appears that the evidence to that effect was limited[41] and seriously doubted by senior intelligence officials.[42] It further appears that questions and uncertainties as to the legitimacy of the venture were suppressed for purposes of avoiding rocking the boat.[43]

---

[36] DOCTRINE FOR JOINT NUCLEAR OPERATIONS, *supra* note 18, at II-6 (emphasis omitted). *See* Chapter 16, note 39–42 and accompanying text.

[37] *Id.* (emphasis omitted).

[38] *See* BARBARA W. TUCHMAN, THE MARCH OF FOLLY: FROM TROY TO VIETNAM (1984).

[39] *See* BARBARA W. TUCHMAN, GUNS OF AUGUST (1994).

[40] *See* James Risen, *Question of Evidence, A Special Report; To Bomb Sudan Plant, or Not: A Year Later, Debates Rankle*, NEW YORK TIMES, October 27, 1999, at A1. *See also* Chapter 21, notes 17, 21, and accompanying text.

[41] *See id.*

[42] *See id.*

[43] *See id.*

Former Secretary of Defense Robert S. McNamara has similarly noted the extraordinary extent of the misinformation under which the United States and the Soviets were laboring during the Cuban missile crisis—and how close the parties came to nuclear war that neither wanted.[44] Secretary McNamara has also described, based on recent exchanges among former leaders of both sides of the Vietnam war, how poor each side's intelligence was about the other, how profound the cultural misunderstandings were, and how mistaken the assessments of each other's intentions and motivations.[45]

Yet none of these were situations where the United States or any other State had found it necessary to use nuclear weapons, circumstances in which the volatility would obviously have become exponentially greater.[46]

Although the policy of deterrence has not been abandoned, the United States has repeatedly recognized that nuclear weapons themselves, rather than any particular adversary or group of adversaries, today pose the greatest threat to our security. President Clinton in his 1998 National Security Strategy stated:

> Weapons of mass destruction pose the greatest potential threat to global stability and security. Proliferation of advanced weapons and technologies threatens to provide rogue states, terrorists and international crime organizations the means to inflict terrible damage on the United States, its allies and U.S. citizens and troops abroad. We must continue to deter and be prepared to counter the use or threatened use of WMD, reduce the threat posed by existing arsenals of such weaponry and halt the smuggling of nuclear materials.[47]

---

[44] *See* ROBERT S. MCNAMARA, IN RETROSPECT: THE TRAGEDY AND LESSONS OF VIETNAM 341–342 (1995); Chapter 20, note 5 and accompanying text.

[45] *See id.* at 210–215. *See also* Desmond Ball, *U.S. Strategic Forces: How Would They Be Used?*, 7 INT'L SECURITY 31, 42 (1982); RICHARD K. BETTS, NUCLEAR BLACKMAIL AND NUCLEAR BALANCE 38 (Brookings Institution, Washington, D.C. 1987) (*cited in* WILLIAM A. SCHWARTZ ET AL., A NUCLEAR SEDUCTION, WHY THE ARMS RACE DOESN'T MATTER AND WHAT DOES 85 (1990)); MCGEORGE BUNDY, DANGER AND SURVIVAL: CHOICES ABOUT THE BOMB IN THE FIRST FIFTY YEARS, 266–667, 536–541 (1988); Chapter 20, note 11 and accompanying text.

[46] *See* Chapter 20; Chapter 2, notes 78–87 and accompanying text.

[47] PRESIDENT WILLIAM J. CLINTON, A NATIONAL SECURITY STRATEGY FOR A NEW CENTURY 6 (The White House, October 1998). *See* Chapter 18, note 47 and accompanying text.

In that same National Security Strategy, President Clinton further stated:

> Potential enemies, whether nations, terrorist groups or criminal organizations, are increasingly likely to attack U.S. territory and the American people in unconventional ways. Adversaries will be tempted to disrupt our critical infrastructures, impede continuity of government operations, use weapons of mass destruction against civilians in our cities, attack us when we gather at special events and prey on our citizens overseas.[48]

The Nuclear Posture Review, while supporting the continuing role of nuclear weapons for deterrence, concluded:

> • that nuclear weapons are far less important to U.S. security than in the past; and
> • that nuclear weapons have themselves become the primary enemy.[49]

The extent to which the weapons have become the enemy was evident from stated contemporary strategic concerns of the Pentagon during the Nuclear Posture Review: controlling and reducing nuclear weapons in Russia and dismantling and removing the nuclear weapons in Ukraine, Kazakhstan, and Belarus;[50] hedging against a renewed nuclear threat from Russia;[51] controlling the risk that nuclear materials, equipment and know-how could leak through the "porous" former Soviet Union borders to other nations;[52] hedging against an increased nuclear capability of China;[53] dealing with threats by potential adversaries to acquire or use nuclear and other weapons of mass destruction and their means of delivery;[54] and dealing with risks of loss or theft of fissile material or non deployed nuclear warheads.[55]

Paradoxically, as noted, it is now Russia, itself inferior in conventional military capability, that, like the United States during the Cold War, has, at least in theory, an arguable need for a broad policy of

---

[48] *Id.* at 7. *See* Chapter 18, notes 47–52 and accompanying text.

[49] *See* 1995 REPORT OF THE SECRETARY OF DEFENSE at 7, 10, 26, 32, 84–86, 163; Chapter 18, note 2 and accompanying text.

[50] *See id.* at 25; Chapter 18, notes 5–17, Chapter 26, notes 1–11, and accompanying text.

[51] *See id.* at 163.

[52] *See id.* at 25.

[53] *See id.* at 163.

[54] *See id.*

[55] *See id.* at 91.

nuclear deterrence against conventional attack. With the former Soviet Union having placed much of its most advanced conventional weaponry and military facilities at the outer edges of its controlled territories, Russia, after dissolution, found itself left with many nuclear weapons but a substantially reduced conventional capability, and, in addition, after the break-up, Russia was unable to keep up with the expenses of the technological revolution in conventional warfare.[56]

Secretary Perry stated there is a "high probability" that aggressors in regional conflicts wars would "threaten, wield, or use" weapons of mass destruction (nuclear, biological, and chemical weapons). He stated, "Almost anywhere the United States is likely to deploy forces around the world—Northeast Asia, the Persian Gulf, the Middle East, and Europe—states are likely to have [weapons of mass destruction]."[57] He emphasized the severity of the implications of the proliferation of nuclear and other weapons of mass destruction:

> The combination of WMD with theater ballistic missiles poses a unique threat to managing future regional crises. ... [W]ith WMD, even small-scale theater ballistic missile threats would raise dramatically the potential costs and risks of military operations, undermining conventional superiority and threatening the credibility of U.S. regional security strategy.[58]
> ***
> Weapons of mass destruction in the hands of a hostile regional power could threaten not only U.S. lives and U.S. interests but also the viability of its regional power projection strategy.[59]

Secretary of Defense Cohen has defined this new kind of "asymmetric" threat as one where an enemy does not seek to become more powerful than the United States, as had the Soviet Union, but rather uses unconventional means, such as nuclear, chemical or

---

[56] *See* Charles J. Dick, *Past Cruelties Hinder the Taming of the Bear*, JANE'S INTELLIGENCE REVIEW, vol. 10, no. 12, Dec. 1, 1998, at 5; Michael R. Gordon, *Maneuvers Show Russian Reliance on Nuclear Arms,* THE NEW YORK TIMES, July 10, 1999, at 1; Chapter 18, note 58, Chapter 28, and accompanying text.

[57] WILLIAM J. PERRY, SECRETARY OF DEFENSE, 1995 ANNUAL REPORT TO THE PRESIDENT AND THE CONGRESS 71. *See* Chapter 18, notes 14–17 and accompanying text.

[58] *Id.* at 240.

[59] *Id.* at 25.

biological weapons, "to offset, rather than try to match America's military strengths."[60]

The reality of the risks of use of nuclear or other weapons of mass destruction can be seen from the numerous instances during the Cold War in which the United States considered, threatened or took preparatory steps for the use of nuclear weapons.[61] In addition to the ongoing threat that is inherent in the policy of deterrence, the United States explicitly threatened to use nuclear weapons on at least five occasions during the Cold War, including in Korea in 1950–53, Suez in 1956, Lebanon in 1958, Cuba in 1962, the Middle East in 1973, and, after the Cold War, in Iraq during the Gulf War.[62]

Analysts have noted additional times when "responsible officials of the United States government formally considered the use of nuclear weapons,"[63] including Vietnam in 1954; Quemoy and Matsu in 1954–1955, 1958; Middle East in 1967; Suez in 1970; Jordan in 1970; Cuba in 1970; India and Pakistan in 1971; Vietnam in 1968–1972; and Lebanon in 1982–1983.[64]

And that is just the United States. Each of the other nuclear, chemical and biological weapons States poses its own risk factors, assuring the presence of considerable potential volatility in any significant international crisis.

The extent of the proliferation of these weapons also constitutes a risk factor. Declared nuclear powers are the United States, Russia, Britain, France, China, India, and Pakistan.[65] Israel also has nuclear weapons[66] and Brazil and Argentina have an imminent capacity to have

---

[60] *Prepared Statement of Secretary of Defense William S. Cohen to the Senate Armed Forces Committee*, Feb. 3, 1998 *set forth at* <http://www.dtic.mil/execsec/>. *See* Chapter 18, notes 47–52 and accompanying text; WILLIAM S. COHEN, 1999 ANNUAL REPORT TO THE PRESIDENT AND THE CONGRESS *as set forth at* <http://www.dtic.mil/execsec/adr1999/>.

[61] *See generally* Chapter 20.

[62] *See* Chapter 20, notes 1–7 and accompanying text.

[63] *See* Desmond Ball, *U.S. Strategic Forces: How Would They Be Used?*, 7 INT'L SECURITY 31, 41–2 (1982); Chapter 20, notes 10–19 and accompanying text.

[64] *Id.*

[65] *See* Chapter 23, notes 2–6 and accompanying text.

[66] *See* Chapter 23, note 7 and accompanying text. As recently as November 1999, Israel affirmed its policy of ambiguity as to its known nuclear status. *See* Deborah Sontag, *Israel Eases Secrecy Over Nuclear Whistleblower's Trial*, THE NEW YORK TIMES, Nov. 25, 1999 at A3.

such weapons.[67] South Africa, North Korea, Iraq, Iran, Libya, Taiwan, Ukraine, Belarus and Kazakhstan[68] have all had nuclear weapons programs at one time or another and Egypt has declared its determination to acquire nuclear weapons if necessary for its security.[69]

More than twenty-five nations possess biological or chemical weapons capability, including North Korea, China, India, Pakistan, Iran, Iraq, Libya, Syria, and Russia, along with such non-national entities and groups as the Aum Shinrikyo in Japan and the Aryan Nations in the United States at various times.[70] Numerous States have long-range missile capabilities, including China, India, Iran, Israel, Libya, North Korea, Syria, and Russia.[71]

As another risk factor, former Secretary of Defense Robert McNamara has noted the "cavalier" attitude at times the U.S. military has had to the use of nuclear weapons, including towards the potential use of nuclear weapons in the Vietnam war.[72] He cited the Joint Chief's willingness potentially to use nuclear weapons in Vietnam even at the risk of nuclear confrontation with China and the Soviet Union "in Southeast Asia or elsewhere"[73] and their willingness potentially to use nuclear weapons even in "southern China" in early 1964.[74]

The military and at times the White House appear to have abnegated the pledge made by several Presidents not to use nuclear weapons against non-nuclear adversaries, such pledge being made by the United States first as a matter of policy and then by way of security assurance to non-nuclear States as an inducement to them to extend the Treaty on the Non-Proliferation of Nuclear Weapons.[75]

It further appears that the military have pressed in the post Cold War era to extend deterrence to widescale targeting of chemical and

---

[67] *See* Chapter 23, notes 7–8 and accompanying text.

[68] *See* Chapter 23, notes 9–17 and accompanying text.

[69] *See* Chapter 23, note 18 and accompanying text.

[70] *See* Chapter 27; Chapter 18, note 7, Chapter 27, notes 31–42 and accompanying text.

[71] *See* Chapter 23, notes 2–7, 12–14, 30–35, Chapter 28, note 23, and accompanying text.

[72] ROBERT S. MCNAMARA, IN RETROSPECT: THE TRAGEDIES AND LESSONS OF VIETNAM 160–61 (1995). *See* Chapter 20, note 11 and accompanying text.

[73] *Id.* at 234.

[74] *Id.* at 275.

[75] *See* Nuclear Weapons Advisory Opinion ¶ 59(c), at 23, 35 I.L.M. at 825; R. Jeffrey Smith, *Ex-Commander of Nukes Wants to Scrap Them, A Believer No More*, THE SACRAMENTO BEE, Mar. 29, 1998; Chapter 3, notes 127–133, Chapter 17, notes 24–27, Chapter 27, note 80, and accompanying text.

biological targets, and that the White House has acceded and at times participated.[76]

As noted above, Judge Schwebel, the U.S. judge on the ICJ, in his dissent in the Nuclear Weapons Advisory Opinion, related in detail reports that, in advance of the Desert Storm operation against Iraq for its attack on Kuwait, the United States threatened Iraq that, if it used chemical or biological weapons, the United States would retaliate with nuclear weapons.[77]

A similar threat was reportedly made during the Clinton Administration:

> The Joint Chief of Staff in 1993 during the Clinton Administration asserted a willingness to use nuclear weapons in response to attacks of weapons of mass destruction. This willingness to use nuclear endangerment in response to the chemical threat has been characterized as the White House "bowing to strategies already set by the military ... 'the colonels and lieutenant colonels figured out what they wanted to do, and you've just got the White House catching up with that.'"[78]

The heavily technical nature of these matters only accentuates the risks of military nullification during the fog of war.[79]

General George Lee Butler, who served as the Commander of the Strategic Air Command and hence as the Air Force general responsible for drafting the overall U.S. strategy for nuclear war, has reported how amazed he was "by how little high-level scrutiny [the U.S. nuclear war plan] had received over the years, and by how readily his military colleagues threw up their hands and rolled their eyes at the grim challenge of converting mathematical estimates of the destructiveness

---

[76] *See* Chapter 27, notes 79–85 and accompanying text; Hans Kristensen, *Targets of Opportunity: How Nuclear Planners Found New Targets for Old Weapons*, BULL. OF ATOMIC SCIENTISTS, vol.55, no. 5, Sep./Oct. 1997; Chapter 27, notes 80–97 and accompanying text.

[77] *See* Chapter 3, notes 151–153, Chapter 27, notes 83–85, and accompanying text. *See also* Nuclear Weapons Advisory Opinion, at 35–36; dissenting opinion of Judge Schwebel at 3, 12, 35 I.L.M 842.

[78] John Diamond, *U.S. May Use Nuclear Arms Against Chemicals: Rogue States Pose a Growing Threat*, THE RECORD (Bergen County, N.J.), Dec. 8, 1997, at A08, quoting John Pike of the Federation of American Scientists. *See* Chapter 27, notes 80–85 and accompanying text.

[79] *See* Chapter 27, notes 80–85 and accompanying text.

of nuclear arms and the resilience of Soviet structures into dry statistical formulas for nuclear war."[80]

> "It was all Alice-in-Wonderland stuff," Butler says. The targeting data and other details of the war plan, which are written in an almost unfathomable million lines of computer software code, were typically reduced by military briefers to between 60 and 100 slides that could be presented in an hour or so to the handful of senior U.S. officials who were cleared to hear it:
>
> "Generally, no one at the briefings wanted to ask questions because they didn't want to embarrass themselves. It was about as unsatisfactory as could be imagined for that subject matter. The truth is that the president only had a superficial understanding" of what would happen in a nuclear war, Butler says. "Congress knew even less because no lawmaker has ever had access to the war plan, and most academics could only make ill-informed guesses."[81]

There is a perception in Washington and in the defense establishment generally that the contingency plans for the use of nuclear weapons are so complex and specialized as essentially to be the domain of the military, and indeed of the small group within the military responsible for such matters, thereby largely excluding the President and other civilian leadership and even the military leadership itself from significant and intelligent participation.[82] Even more, there is the perception that the overall policy guidelines are so broad and the intricacies of the SIOP so arcane as to permit the military running the SIOP to do pretty much what they want without any significant oversight.[83]

As William Arkin and Hans Kristensen expressed it in the *Bulletin of the Atomic Scientists:*

> Meanwhile, the [Clinton Administration] had begun to echo a perennial Washington complaint that strategic planners had effectively excluded both civilian and other military policy-makers from the details of nuclear war plans, and that they read into the national guidance whatever they chose, allowing them to retain never-changing first-strike options. ...

---

[80] R. Jeffrey Smith, *Ex-Commander of Nukes Wants to Scrap Them, A Believer No More*, THE SACRAMENTO BEE, Mar. 29, 1998, (quoting Gen. Butler). *See* Chapter 27, notes 80–85 and accompanying text.

[81] *Id.*

[82] *See* William M. Arkin & Hans Kristensen, *Dangerous Directions*, BULL. OF THE ATOMIC SCIENTISTS, vol. 54, no. 2, Mar. 1, 1998, at 30; Chapter 27, note 80 and accompanying text.

[83] *See id.*

But the problem went beyond a simple case of insubordination: The choreography of nuclear war-fighting was so complex that few outside STRATCOM's Omaha headquarters were in a position to challenge its claims about "required" readiness, synergy, or military capacity. And by staying firmly in control of all the analytic tools, STRATCOM [previously called "SAC"] could deflect any of Washington's changes.[84]

Notwithstanding the doctrine that only the President can authorize the use of nuclear weapons, there is evidence that this authority has at times been delegated to the military. Paul Bracken has reported:

In September 1957 a former commander of NORAD, General Earle E. Partridge stated in an interview that he had been given emergency authority to use certain nuclear weapons. Apparently the reason behind these measures was the fear that there might be no president surviving to send out the necessary orders if the United States absorbed the first blow in a nuclear war. In 1964, General Lauris Norstad, then a former commander of American forces in Europe, broadly hinted in an interview that he too was given such power by President Kennedy. In 1977, Daniel Ellsberg [who had served as a nuclear policy-maker] asserted that such predelegated authority had been given to the military by presidents Eisenhower, Kennedy and Johnson .... He stated that the authority had been given to the 'six or seven three-and four-star generals. These generals must have corresponded to the unified and specified commanders.'[85]

Arkin and Kristensen describe the Nuclear Posture Review (NPR) as a process whereby the United States "failed to redefine the role of nuclear weapons after the Cold War" and characterize it as a success by the "war-planners" in avoiding change. Focusing on the acceptance by the NPR of the "hedge," whereby a supply of non-deployed warheads is maintained to supplement the agreed reductions,[86] they state, "President Clinton's approval of the NPR in September 1994 confirmed the war-planners' views. They had avoided any significant post–Cold War change."[87]

Worse is the possibility that the military (and even the civilian) leadership seem to address the limitations of law and policy in this area

---

[84] *Id. See* Chapter 17, notes 25–27 and accompanying text.

[85] PAUL BRACKEN, THE COMMAND AND CONTROL OF NUCLEAR FORCES 198 (1983). *See* Chapter 22, note 6 and accompanying text.

[86] *See* Arkin & Kristensen, *supra* note 82. *See also* Chapter 19, note 7 and accompanying text.

[87] *Id. See* Chapter 17, note 27, Chapter 19, note 7, and accompanying text.

as merely window dressing. We saw this in the statement of the law in the *Doctrine for Joint Nuclear Operations* manual: This manual—which authoritatively establishes U.S. operational military policy—states, without qualification:

> [T]here is no customary or conventional international law to prohibit nations from employing nuclear weapons in armed conflict. Therefore, the use of nuclear weapons against enemy combatants and other military objectives is lawful.[88]

The military's manual *Doctrine for Joint Theater Nuclear Operations* takes a somewhat more nuanced position:

> [The law of armed conflict] does not prohibit the use of nuclear weapons in armed conflict. However, any weapon must be considered a military necessity, and measures must be taken to avoid collateral damage and unnecessary suffering. Since nuclear weapons have greater destructive potential, in many instances they may be inappropriate.[89]

The manual further states:

> However, to comply with the law, a particular use of any weapon must satisfy the long-standing targeting rules of military necessity, proportionality, and avoidance of collateral damage and unnecessary suffering. Nuclear weapons are unique in this analysis only in their greater destructive potential (although they also differ from conventional weapons in that they produce radiation and electromagnetic effects and, potentially, radioactive fallout). In some circumstances, the use of a nuclear weapon may therefore be inappropriate. Treaties may impose additional restrictions on nuclear weapons.[90]

The latter statements seem carefully crafted in an effort at formal compliance with the legal requirements recognized by the United States (indeed, as expressed to the ICJ), while giving the message to the military that these weapons are within acceptable parameters. They are lawful, although, essentially as a bow to the technicalities, it is

---

[88] DOCTRINE FOR JOINT NUCLEAR OPERATIONS, *supra* note 18, at II-1 (emphasis omitted).

[89] DOCTRINE FOR JOINT THEATER NUCLEAR OPERATIONS, *supra* note 21, at v–vi. *See* Chapter 2, notes 2–4 and accompanying text.

[90] *Id.* at I-1–2. (emphasis omitted). The manual further states: "Additional treaty information regarding nuclear weapons can be found in Joint Pub 3-12, "DOCTRINE FOR JOINT NUCLEAR OPERATIONS." *Id.* at I-2. *See* Chapter 2, notes 2–4 and accompanying text.

recognized that they may sometimes be inconsistent with "targeting rules," and hence, "in some circumstances" may be "inappropriate"— hardly a major legal issue for commanders to be concerned about.

Similarly, in terms of the level of communication of civilian policy and legal issues to the military, General Butler noted that, even as Commander of SAC, he had not been aware of the commitment the United States made years previously, in 1967, not to use nuclear arms first against nations that lacked them.[91]

The United States' continuing legitimization of nuclear weapons, while purportedly delegitimizing the more accessible but comparably dangerous chemical and biological weapons,[92] ostensibly undermines the rule of law—in effect legitimizing the philosophies, threats and, potentially, the appeal, of the rogue nations, groups and individuals the United States most needs to delegitimize and marginalize.[93]

Even if it one assumes that I am wrong and the risks I am describing as substantial are in fact quite small, that does not remove the prospect of substantial risk as to such items. Not only would they be nonetheless risks of extreme effects, in addition the improbable occurs all the time—to the extent that, paradoxically, one can state that even the improbable is probable—particularly over the type of ongoing repetition implicit in the practice of deterrence.[94]

Duke University Professor Christopher Schroeder summarizes the matter, "When a risky action—say, exposing someone to a known carcinogen—is repeated often enough, whether through repetitions on that same individual or by increasing the size of the exposed

---

[91] *See* R. Jeffrey Smith, *Ex-Commander of Nukes Wants to Scrap Them, A Believer No More*, THE SACRAMENTO BEE, Mar. 29, 1998 (quoting Gen. Butler); Chapter 17, note 27 and accompanying text.

[92] *See* Chapter 27; Chapter 27, notes 9–10, 97, and accompanying text. *See also* DOCTRINE FOR NUCLEAR, BIOLOGICAL, AND CHEMICAL (NBC) DEFENSE; Hans Kristensen, *Targets of Opportunity: How Nuclear Planners Found New Targets for Old Weapons*, BULL. OF ATOMIC SCIENTISTS, vol.55, no. 5, Sep./Oct. 1997.

[93] *See* Chapter 27, note 97 and accompanying text.

[94] *See* Chapter 22, notes 1–5, 46–59, and accompanying text, Otto Kreisher, *Retired Generals Urge End to Nuclear Arsenal*, THE SAN DIEGO UNION-TRIB., Dec. 5, 1996, at A-1. *See generally* TIM POSTON & IAN STEWART, CATASTROPHE THEORY AND ITS APPLICATIONS (1996).

population, the entire set of actions becomes, probabilistically, virtually certain to produce the feared harm."[95]

While in a sense the world seems safer from the perspective of the United States following the demise of the Soviet Union and the end of the Cold War, paradoxically that is not necessarily the case. Extreme as the competition between the U.S. and Soviet blocs seemed at times, with hindsight it obviously served as a unifying force, whereby each of the two leader nations, stalemated by the nuclear confrontation, controlled its respective allies. Today's multi-polar world offers quite a contrast, with the potential for situations that would have been controlled or prevented by the United States or the Soviet Union to now careen out of control.

It is for such reasons that the U.S. military has recognized that in many respects the threats from nuclear, chemical and biological weapons are greater today. The Joint Chief's *Doctrine for Joint Theater Nuclear Operations* states:

> The threat of nuclear exchange by regional powers and the proliferation of WMD have grown following the end of the Cold War.[96]
>
> ***
>
> The dissolution of the Soviet Union has greatly reduced the possibility of a large scale nuclear exchange. However, the loss of the stability inherent in a clearly bipolar world has increased the likelihood of a nuclear exchange by regional powers. In addition, the threat to the United States, its allies, and its deployed forces due to the proliferation of WMD has grown following the end of the Cold War. The flow of advanced technology to potential or actual hostile nations has led to a proliferation of systems (missiles and aircraft) capable of delivering WMD. The possibility of a WMD exchange in a regional conflict has risen dramatically, threatening our forward-deployed forces and challenging our long-range power projection capabilities.[97]

The manual identifies the threat further:

> The current threat in theater consists primarily of short-, medium-, and intermediate-range missiles capable of carrying nuclear, biological, or chemical warheads. Future threat systems may

---

[95] Christopher H. Schroeder, *Rights Against Risks*, at 500. This article originally appeared at 86 COLUM. L. REV. 495 (1986). Reprinted with permission. Chapter 22, notes 55–59 and accompanying text.

[96] DOCTRINE FOR JOINT THEATER NUCLEAR OPERATIONS, *supra* note 21, at vi. *See* Chapter 26, notes 12–15 and accompanying text.

[97] *Id.* at I-2 (emphasis omitted).

exhibit greater capabilities, such as increased accuracy, range, and destructive power. Additionally, aircraft systems and cruise missiles capable of delivering WMD will also pose a threat.[98]

The manual further recognizes that this is a threat that increases with proliferation:

> c. As nations continue to develop and obtain WMD and viable delivery systems, the potential for US operations in such a lethal environment increases. In addition to proliferation of WMD among rogue states, proliferation may also expand to include nonstate actors as well.[99]

If the United States has purportedly determined that nuclear weapons are useable, and that is the basis of its training of its personnel, why should we believe that some other State might not actually use them? The potential for use of these weapons in a situation of acute crisis is heightened by the U.S. military's in-place plan to in fact use them, and no doubt the comparable plans of other States. As noted, the military has concluded, "Nuclear operations can be successful in achieving US military objectives if they are used in the appropriate situation and administered properly."[100]

The U.S. military have identified types of situations where the use of nuclear weapons may be "favored over a conventional attack" or otherwise preferred:

> • Level of effort required for conventional targeting. If the target is heavily defended such that heavy losses are expected, a nuclear weapon may be favored over a conventional attack.
> • Length of time that a target must be kept out of action. A nuclear weapon attack will likely put a target out of action for a longer period of time than a conventional weapon attack.
> • Logistic support and anticipation of delays caused by the "fog and friction" of war. Such delays are unpredictable and may range from several hours to a number of days.[101]

The military have also identified the following "enemy combat forces and facilities that may be likely targets for nuclear strikes:"

---

[98] *Id.* at I-2–3 (emphasis omitted).
[99] *Id.* at I-3 (emphasis omitted).
[100] *Id.* at v (emphasis omitted). *See* Chapter 26, notes 16–18 and accompanying text.
[101] *Id.* at III-4 (emphasis omitted).

• WMD and their delivery systems, as well as associated command and control, production, and logistical support units
• Ground combat units and their associated command and control and support units
• Air defense facilities and support installations
• Naval installations, combat vessels, and associated support facilities and command and control capabilities.
• Nonstate actors (facilities and operation centers) that possess WMD
• Underground facilities.[102]

The U.S. planning and professed intentions to this effect are open and notorious—findable on the internet by even a computer duffer like myself within a five minute search.[103]

As to the applicability of risk analysis to nuclear weapons, Robert McNamara, reacting to the potential willingness of the United States' military leaders to use nuclear weapons in Vietnam, objected that "even a low risk of a catastrophic event must be avoided."[104]

Henry Kissinger, speaking in Brussels in 1979, reportedly questioned whether the United States would ever initiate a nuclear strike against the Soviet Union based upon a Soviet attack on Western Europe, given the attendant risk factors:

> Our European allies, he said, should not keep asking us to multiply strategic assurances that we cannot possibly mean or if we do mean, we would not execute because if we execute we risk the destruction of civilization.[105]

Law as to Risk Creation

As we have seen, legal systems throughout the world recognize civil and criminal liability for taking even minor risks of extremely severe effects, absent sufficient justification.[106] This is reflected in tort law

---

[102] *Id.* at III-6–7.

[103] As noted, the JOINT NUCLEAR OPERATIONS and JOINT THEATER OPERATIONS manuals are available at <http://www.dtic.mil/doctrine/jel/new_pubs/jp3_12.pdf> and <http://www.dtic.mil/doctrine/jel/new_pubs/jp3_12_1.pdf>, respectively.

[104] *See* ROBERT S. MCNAMARA, IN RETROSPECT: THE TRAGEDY AND LESSONS OF VIETNAM 160–61 (1995); Chapter 20, note 11 and accompanying text.

[105] *Id.* at 344–45. *See generally* Chapter 24.

[106] *See* Chapters 6–11; Chapter 6, notes 8–10, 17–21, 26–44, Chapter 7, notes 6, 22–24, 28–96, Chapter 10, note 18, Chapter 11, note 24, and

under principles such as the Hand formula[107] and in criminal law by the imposition of culpability based on the reckless and grossly negligent taking of unjustified risks.[108]

The element of justification would appear to be inherently limited by the purposes of the law of armed conflict, as reviewed in the preceding chapter, and the principle of interpreting law in light of its purposes.[109] Destruction beyond the limits of the purposes of armed conflict cannot be the basis of legal justification.

The principles of sovereign equality and neutrality and legal restrictions on injuring third-parties would also appear to impose limitations on permissible justification: No one State can justify risking the destruction of other innocent States or of humankind even to save itself.[110]

Relation of Risk Factors to Mental State

As noted, the United States argued in its memorandum to the ICJ, "It seems to be assumed that any use of nuclear weapons would inevitably escalate into a massive strategic nuclear exchange, with the deliberate destruction of the population centers of the opposing sides."[111]

U.S. lawyer McNeill in his oral argument stated:

> The argument that international law prohibits, in all cases, the use of nuclear weapons appears to be premised on the incorrect assumption that every use of every type of nuclear weapons will necessarily share certain characteristics which contravene the law of armed conflict. Specifically, it appears to be assumed that any

---

accompanying text; United States v. Carroll Towing, Co., 159 F.2d 169, 173 (2d Cir. 1947); Herbert Wechsler & Jerome Michael, *A Rationale of the Law of Homicide*, 36 COLUM. L. REV. 701, 731 (1937) GLANVILLE L. WILLIAMS, CRIMINAL LAW, THE GENERAL PART § 21 at 53–54 (1953); Model Penal Code § 210.2(1)(b) (A.L.I. 1985).

[107] *See* Chapter 6, notes 9–25 and accompanying text; United States v. Carroll Towing, Co., 159 F.2d 169 (2d Cir. 1947).

[108] *See* Chapter 1, notes 285–296, Chapters 7–12, 14; Chapter 7, notes 4–11, 27–31, 49–96, Chapter 8, notes 6–53, Chapter 10, notes 2–11, and accompanying text.

[109] *See* Chapter 29, notes 128–149 and accompanying text. *See also* Chapter 5.

[110] *See* Chapter 29, notes 149–150, 170–204, and accompanying text. *See also* Chapters 10, 11.

[111] U.S. ICJ Memorial/GA App. at 21. *See* Chapter 2, notes 71–74, Chapter 29, notes 259–291, and accompanying text.

use of nuclear weapons would inevitably escalate into a massive strategic nuclear exchange, resulting automatically in the deliberate destruction of the population centers of the opposing sides.[112]

While the language quoted may have been focused upon the U.S. position that 100% unlawfulness is necessary for *per se* unlawfulness, the underlying point seems the same: that a high level of certainty is necessary before unlawfulness incepts. This seems inconsistent with rules of law recognized by the United States, whereby States are subject to war crimes culpability without regard to mental state, individuals are subject to culpability based not only on recklessness but also on gross negligence, and commanders are subject to culpability based on mere negligence or something approaching it.[113]

In upholding the defendant's conviction in the *Yamashita* case, the U.S. Supreme Court ostensibly saw commander responsibility as a way of dealing with the risk of wanton acts by troops against protected persons:

> The question then is whether the law of war imposes on an army commander a duty to take such appropriate measures as are within his power to control the troops under his command for the prevention of the specified acts which are violations of the law of war and which are likely to attend the occupation of hostile territory by an uncontrolled soldiery, and whether he may be charged with personal responsibility for his failure to take such measures when violations result. It is evident that the conduct of military operations by troops whose excesses are unrestrained by the orders of or efforts of their commanders would almost certainly

---

[112] ICJ Hearing, November 15, 1995, at 85. *See* Chapter 2, notes 71–87 and accompanying text.

[113] *See generally* Chapters 8, 29. *See* Chapter 1, notes 278–301, Chapter 8, notes 45–49, Chapter 29, notes 277–289, and accompanying text. *See also* THE AIR FORCE MANUAL ON INTERNATIONAL LAW, *supra* note 13, at 15-2, 15-3, 15-8 n.13 (citing SPAIGHT, AIR POWER AND WAR RIGHTS 57, 58 (1947)); THE AIR FORCE COMMANDER'S HANDBOOK, *supra* note 13, at 8-1; THE NAVAL/MARINE COMMANDER'S HANDBOOK, *supra* note 1 at 6-5, 6-5 n.12, 6-6 n.12 (citing United States v. Wilhelm List et al., 9 TWC 127 (1950)); THE LAW OF LAND WARFARE, *supra* note 13, at 178; CHERIF BASSIOUNI & PETER MANIKAS, THE LAW OF THE INTERNATIONAL CRIMINAL TRIBUNAL FOR THE FORMER YUGOSLAVIA 361, 362 (1996) (citing The High Command Case, 2 TRIALS OF WAR CRIMINALS BEFORE THE NUREMBERG MILITARY TRIBUNALS UNDER CONTROL COUNCIL LAW NO. 10 (1949) (aka United States v. Wilhelm von Leeb)).

result in violations which it is the purpose of the law of war to prevent.[114]

Established Law of Armed Conflict as to Requisite Mental State

It is also clear that the law of armed conflict generally recognizes recklessness and other mental states less than strict intentionality as a basis for war crimes liability.[115] The Geneva conventions extensively provide for criminal culpability for violations committed wilfully,[116] a state of mind broadly recognized as encompassing recklessness.[117] The law of armed conflict similarly recognizes criminal culpability for acts of wantonness and of wanton destruction, acts also not reaching the level of strict intentionality.[118]

---

[114] In re Yamashita, 327 U.S. 1, 15 (1946). *See* Chapter 8, notes 45–49 and accompanying text.

[115] *See* Chapter 8 notes 6–15 and accompanying text. *See generally* Chapter 8.

[116] *See* Chapter 8, notes 8–14 and accompanying text; THE AIR FORCE MANUAL ON INTERNATIONAL LAW, *supra* note 13, at 15-1 to 15-2; 15-8 n.12 (quoting Geneva Convention for the Amelioration of the Condition of the Wounded and Sick in Armed Forces in the Field, adopted Aug. 12, 1949, 75 U.N.T.S. 31; Geneva Convention for the Amelioration of the Condition of Wounded, Sick, and Shipwrecked Members of Armed Forces at Sea, adopted Aug. 12, 1949, 75 U.N.T.S. 85, and other Geneva Conventions).

[117] *See* Chapter 8, notes 6–18 and accompanying text. *See generally* Chapter 8. *See also* GLANVILLE WILLIAMS, CRIMINAL LAW, THE GENERAL PART § 22, 59–62 (1953); ICRC Commentary to Article 85 of Protocol I (para. 3474), *quoted in* Amnesty International—Report—IOR 40/10/98 May 1998 United Nations (UN), The International Criminal Court Making the Right Choices—Part V Recommendations to the Diplomatic Conference, <http://www.amnesty.org/ailib/aipub/1998/IOR/I4001098.htm>; Commentary on Protocol Additional (No. I) to the Geneva Conventions of 12 August 1949, and Relating to the Protection of Victims of International Armed Conflicts (Protocol I), concluded at Geneva 8 June 1997, Part V: Execution of the conventions and of this protocol: Section II—Repression of breaches of the conventions and of this protocol, Art. 85—Repression of breaches of this Protocol, <http://www.icrc.org/ihl.nsf>.

[118] *See* Art. 3(b), International Criminal Tribunal for the Former Yugoslavia, Statute of the International Tribunal (Adopted 25 May 1993) (as amended 13 May 1998) <http://www.un.org/icty/basic/statut/statute.htm>; Jordan J. Paust, *International Law Association—American Branch: Committee on a Permanent International Criminal Court: The Preparatory Committee's "Definition of Crimes"—War Crimes*, 8 CRIM. L.F. 431, 438–441 (1997) (emphasis removed) (citing, *inter alia*, U.N. Doc. A/CONF. 95/15 (1980),

Similarly, in imposing war crimes culpability for "an attack which may be expected to cause" certain impermissible effects, as prescribed, for example, in Protocol I to the Geneva Conventions, Article 51(5), or for acts that are "intended, or may be expected, to cause" certain impermissible effects, as prescribed, in Protocol I, Article 35(3), the law again recognizes potential culpability for war crimes committed with a mental element of less than strict intentionality.[119]

So also, as discussed above, the law of armed conflict recognizes an extremely scope of potential commander culpability for war crimes based on what the commander "knew or should have known."[120]

While the ICJ did not focus on the question of the general *mens rea* requirements under the law of armed conflict, a number of the judges made the point that information as to the potential effects of nuclear weapons is so widely known and available as to provide a basis for war crimes based on the use of such weapons.

Judge Weeramantry in his dissenting opinion stated:

> ["By-products" or "collateral damage"] are known to be the necessary consequences of the use of the weapon. The author of the act causing these consequences cannot in any coherent legal system avoid legal responsibility for causing them, any less than a man careering in a motor vehicle at a hundred and fifty kilometers

---

reprinted in 19 I.L.M. 1523; Report of the Secretary-General pursuant to Paragraph 2 of Security Council Resolution 808 (1993), U.N. Doc. S/25704 & Add. 1 (1993), Annex, arts. 2(d), 3(b); Prosecutor v. Karadzic, Case No. IT-95-5-I (Int'l Trib. for Former Yugo., Indictment, July 24, 1995), PP27, 41, 44; Report of the International Law Commission on Its Second Session, 5 June–29 July 1950, 5 U.N. GAOR, Supp. No. 12, at 11–14, P99, U.N. Doc. A/1316 (1950); 11 TRIALS OF WAR CRIMINALS 757 (1948); Report of Justice Robert H. Jackson to the President of the United States, released June 7, 1945, reprinted in PAUST ET AL. INTERNATIONAL CRIMINAL LAW at 1027; Instructions for the Government of Armies of the United States in the Field, General Orders No. 100, Apr. 24, 1863, arts. 16, 44, [Lieber Code]; Responsibilities Commission of the Paris Peace Conference, List of War Crimes (1919); Geneva Convention for the Amelioration of the Condition of the Wounded and Sick in Armed Forces in the Field, adopted Aug. 12, 1949, art. 50, 75 U.N.T.S. 31; Geneva Convention for the Amelioration of the Condition of Wounded, Sick, and Shipwrecked Members of Armed Forces at Sea, adopted Aug. 12, 1949, art. 51, 75 U.N.T.S. 85). *See also* Chapter 8, note 13–15 and accompanying text.

[119] Paust, *supra* note 118, at 438–441 (emphasis omitted) (citations omitted). *See* Chapter 8, note 13 and accompanying text.

[120] *Id.* at 438–441 (emphasis omitted) (citing, *inter alia*, 11 TRIALS OF WAR CRIMINALS 757 (1948)). *See* Chapter 8, note 13, Chapter 29, notes 281–289, and accompanying text.

per hour through a crowded market street can avoid responsibility for the resulting deaths on the ground that he did not intend to kill the particular person who died.[121]

Judge Weeramantry added, "The plethora of literature on the consequences of the nuclear weapon is so much part of common universal knowledge today that no disclaimer of such knowledge would be credible."[122]

To the argument that the rule of moderation—the prohibition of the use of arms "calculated to cause unnecessary suffering"—requires specific intent, Judge Weeramantry cited the "well-known legal principle that the doer of an act must be taken to have intended its natural and foreseeable consequences."[123] He also stated that reading into the law a requirement of specific intent would not "take into account the spirit and underlying rationale of the provision—a method of interpretation particularly inappropriate to the construction of a humanitarian instrument."[124]

Making a point that, as we saw above,[125] is confirmed by the United States' military manuals, Judge Weeramantry added that nuclear weapons "are indeed deployed 'in part with a view of utilizing the destructive effects of radiation and fall-out.'"[126]

As noted above, Judge Weeramantry reached a similar conclusion with respect to the rights of neutrals: "The launching of a nuclear weapon is a deliberate act. Damage to neutrals is a natural, foreseeable and, indeed, inevitable consequence."[127]

---

[121] Dissenting opinion of Judge Weeramantry at 43, 35 I.L.M at 901. *See* Chapter 3, note 310 and accompanying text.

[122] *Id.* at 43, 35 I.L.M at 901. *See* Chapter 3, note 311 and accompanying text.

[123] *Id.* at 48, 35 I.L.M at 904. *See* Chapter 3, note 312 and accompanying text.

[124] *See* Chapter 3, note 313 and accompanying text.

[125] *See supra* notes 14–22; Chapter 29, notes 38–40, and accompanying text.

[126] Dissenting opinion of Judge Weeramantry at 48, 35 I.L.M at 904 (citing Ian Brownlie, *Some Legal Aspects of the Use of Nuclear Weapons*, 14 INT'L & COMP. L. Q. 445 (1965)). *See also* MICHAEL WALZER, JUST AND UNJUST WARS, A MORAL ARGUMENT WITH HISTORICAL ILLUSTRATIONS 273–283 (New York 1968); DOCTRINE FOR JOINT NUCLEAR OPERATIONS, *supra* note 18, at I-2; Chapter 2, notes 90–91, Chapter 3, note 314, Chapter 18, note 55, and accompanying text.

[127] Dissenting opinion of Judge Weeramantry at 50, 35 I.L.M. at 905. *See* Chapter 3, note 315 and accompanying text.

Judge Weeramantry also emphasized the element of intent contained in the policy of deterrence: "Deterrence needs to carry the conviction to other parties that there is a real intention to use those weapons ... it leaves the world of make-believe and enters the field of seriously-intended military threats."[128]

Judge Weeramantry concluded that the policy of deterrence provides the element of intent:

> [D]eterrence becomes ... stockpiling with intent to use. If one intends to use them, all the consequences arise which attach to intention in law, whether domestic or international. One intends to cause the damage or devastation that will result. The intention to cause damage or devastation which results in total destruction of one's enemy, or which might indeed wipe it out completely, clearly goes beyond the purposes of war.[129]

While a stricter view of the necessary intentionality was presented by Judge Higgins,[130] the British judge on the Court, this view is interesting for its contrast with the position generally taken by the United States, as set forth above, to the effect that far less than intentionality is necessary for war crimes liability.

Judge Weeramantry makes the interesting point that the judgment today that the use of nuclear weapons would be unlawful does not necessarily mean that such use would have been unlawful at some point in the past, since vastly more information is available now. Judge Weeramantry states that "this additional information has a deep impact upon the question of legality now before the Court:"

> Action with full knowledge of the consequences of one's act is totally different in law from the same action taken in ignorance of its consequences. Any nation using the nuclear weapon today cannot be heard to say that it does not know its consequences. It is

---

[128] *Id.* at 78, 35 I.L.M. at 919 (citations omitted). *See* Chapter 3, note 316 and accompanying text.

[129] *Id. See* Chapter 3, note 316 and accompanying text.

[130] *See* dissenting opinion of Judge Higgins at 4, 35 I.L.M at 936. Judge Higgins posed the question, "Does it follow that knowledge in concrete circumstances civilians will be killed by the use of a nuclear weapon is tantamount to an intention to attack civilians?" Her answer appeared to be that specific intent is required: "Collateral injury in respect of these weapons has always been accepted as not constituting 'intent', provided always that the requirements of proportionality are met." *See also* Chapter 3, notes 319–322 and accompanying text.

only in the context of this knowledge that the question of legality of the use of nuclear weapons can be considered in 1996.[131]

The challenging aspect of the evaluation of the lawfulness of the use of nuclear weapons is the fact that—unlike the legal determinations made at Nuremberg or in war crime trials generally—with nuclear weapons it is obviously not a prudently available strategy to wait until after the weapons are used to make the evaluation. While war crimes charges seem to have rarely been brought based on risk taking that did not result in illicit effects, nuclear weapons pose a threat that requires full and effective advance evaluation and compliance if the applicable law is to be given effect.[132]

That is perhaps the best way to conceptualize the nuclear threat: that the rules of the law of war applicable to nuclear weapons will be frustrated—in effect nullified—if they are not applied in advance. The eggs of Armageddon could not be unscrambled.

The Invalidity of the "As Such" Rule

Occupying much the same ground as the rules of discrimination and proportionality is the rule of civilian immunity. The law of armed conflict prohibits the directing of attacks against civilians, making them immune from such attack.[133]

At the same time, as we have seen, the law recognizes that civilians will often be caught up in attacks directed against military targets, and accepts such reality as long as the attack in the first instance is one capable of discriminating between civilians and combatants, and the civilian injury is unintended, collateral, incidental, and within the bounds of proportionality.[134]

Hence, the "as such" rule: Civilians and civilian objects may not be targeted "as such," in the sense that the attack is intentionally directed

---

[131] Dissenting opinion of Judge Weeramantry at 30, 35 I.L.M. at 895. *See* Chapter 3, note 318 and accompanying text.

[132] The need for prudence in planning in this area goes also to the need for adequate procurement of conventional weapons, so the United States will not find itself in a position of needing to use nuclear weapons. *See* Chapter 1, notes 91–101, Chapter 17, notes 29–36, 45–50, Chapter 18, note 5, and accompanying text.

[133] *See* Chapter 1, notes 174–185 and accompanying text. *See also* THE AIR FORCE MANUAL ON INTERNATIONAL LAW, *supra* note 13, at 5-7, 5-17 n.21.

[134] *See* Chapter 14; Chapter 1, notes 75–81, 105–108, 174–195, Chapter 2, note 101, Chapter 3, notes 190–203, and accompanying text. *See also* THE AIR FORCE MANUAL ON INTERNATIONAL LAW, *supra* note 13, at 5-10, 6-2.

at them, but an attack is not necessarily unlawful simply because it may cause incidental injury to civilian persons and objects.[135]

The Air Force Manual on International Law quotes the articulation of this rule—"that it is prohibited to launch attacks against the civilian population *as such*"[136]—from United Nations Resolution 2444 (XXIII), recognized by the United States as "an accurate declaration of existing customary law."[137]

As discussed in Chapter 14, this "as such" principle is based on the medieval doctrine of double effect, whereby necessary and foreseen but unintended evil effects of an otherwise good action are accepted on the ground that they were not intended.[138]

This doctrine, useful as it may be as a philosophical matter for distinguishing between various kinds of actions, seems fatally anachronistic when made to bear the weight of the lawfulness of nuclear weapons use. Destruction as extreme as that likely to result from nuclear weapons ostensibly has a legal and moral content transcending the niceties of intentionality. In any event, to the extent intentionality is relevant, the principles of commander and other individual liability would seem to trump this medieval doctrine.

This over-used and poorly understood doctrine even by its own terms does not appear to justify the use of nuclear weapons. One of the elements of the doctrine is that the actor not use the evil effect as an end or as a means to an end.[139] Yet the United States, like other nuclear

---

[135] *See* Chapter 14; Chapter 1, notes 176–180, Chapter 2, notes 28, 101, 110, Chapter 29, notes 23, 26, 259–263, and accompanying text. *See also* THE AIR FORCE MANUAL ON INTERNATIONAL LAW, *supra* note 13, at 6-9 n.7; THE NAVAL/MARINE COMMANDER'S HANDBOOK, *supra* note 1, at 10-1.

[136] THE AIR FORCE MANUAL ON INTERNATIONAL LAW, *supra* note 13, at 5-7. *See* Chapter 1, note 176 and accompanying text.

[137] *Id.* (citing Rovine, *Contemporary Practice of the United States Relating to International Law*, 67 AM. J. INT'L L. 118, 122–125 (1973) (quoting DOD, General Counsel, Letter to the effect that Resolution 2444 is "declaratory of existing customary international law")). *See* Chapter 1, note 176 and accompanying text.

[138] *See* Chapters 11, 14; Chapter 11 notes 43–45, Chapter 14, notes 2–3, and accompanying text. *See also* AQUINAS, SUMMA THEOLOGIAE, I–II, Quest. 64, Art. 7, *quoted in* Stephen R. Latham, *Aquinas and Morphine: Notes on Double Effect at the End of Life*, 1 DEPAUL J. HEALTH CARE L. 625, 633 (also quoting ST. THOMAS AQUINAS ON POLITICS AND ETHICS 70–71 (Paul E. Sigmund, ed. & trans., 1988)); D. W. BOWETT, SELF-DEFENCE IN INTERNATIONAL LAW 10 (1958).

[139] *See* Chapter 14, notes 3–5 and accompanying text; AUSTIN FAGOTHEY, S.J., RIGHT AND REASON, ETHICS IN THEORY AND PRACTICE 107–108 (The C.V.

nations, is not only threatening, but also, in the case of use, would be using, the "evil effect," the excessive and indiscriminate injury to the enemy's non-combatants and other protected persons and objects, since the doctrine of deterrence by its terms threatens such excessive and disproportionate effects.[140]

As we saw, the Joint Chief of Staff's *Joint Nuclear Operations* manual states that "the US nuclear capabilities must confront an enemy with risks of unacceptable damage and disproportionate loss should the enemy choose to introduce WMD into a conflict"[141] and that the adversary is in the position of "risk[ing] destruction or disproportionate loss."[142]

The principle of double effect also includes a requirement of proportionality between the evil effect and the direct effect, here the achieving of the military objective.[143] Accordingly, if my analysis as to proportionality is correct, the principle of double effect, on this basis as well, would be unavailable to provide a legal justification for the effects of the use of nuclear weapons.

Hence, the "as such" rule, based not only upon its terms but also upon its underlying rationale and the developments in weapons and law since the Middle Ages, is ostensibly not applicable to nuclear or other weapons of mass destruction. The established substantive rules of law, with their requirements as to mental state, govern. It is time for international law to recognize that a State cannot justify the killing of millions of civilians or neutrals on the theory it was not aiming at them "as such."

Mosby Company 1963); WALZER, *supra* note 124, at 153, 129 (citing DOUGHERTY, GENERAL ETHICS: AN INTRODUCTION TO THE BASIC PRINCIPLES OF THE MORAL LIFE ACCORDING TO ST. THOMAS AQUINAS 65–66 (Peekskill, N.Y. 1959); John C. Ford, S.J., *The Morality of Obliteration Bombing, in* WAR AND MORALITY, (Richard Wasserstrom, ed., 1970)).

[140] *See* Chapter 2, note 91, Chapter 14, notes 3–8, Chapter 18, note 55, Chapter 27, note 83, and accompanying text. *See also* DOCTRINE FOR JOINT NUCLEAR OPERATIONS, *supra* note 18, at I-1, I-2; WALZER, *supra* note 124, at 153, 273–283 (1968); FAGOTHEY, *supra* note 139, at 113 n.1.

[141] DOCTRINE FOR JOINT NUCLEAR OPERATIONS, *supra* note 18, at I-1 (emphasis omitted). *See* Chapter 2, note 91, Chapter 26, note 83, and accompanying text.

[142] *Id. See* Chapter 18, note 55, Chapter 25, note 9, and accompanying text.

[143] *See* Chapter 11; Chapter 11, notes 16–45 and accompanying text. *See also* MODEL PENAL CODE § 3.02, Comments 3, at 14–15 (A.L.I. 1985).

Prerequisites for a *Per Se* Rule

The United States contended,[144] in a position that the ICJ ostensibly accepted *sub silentio*,[145] that 100% illegality—the unlawfulness of all uses of nuclear weapons—would be necessary before a rule of *per se* illegality could arise. To the extent one concludes, as I have, that all or "virtually all" uses of nuclear weapons would be unlawful, either because the resultant effects, particularly radiation and escalation, would be uncontrollable, or because any such use would be likely to precipitate impermissible effects, or would involve the risk of precipitating extreme impermissible effects, the issue of whether unlawfulness in 100% or virtually 100% of cases is required is not reached.

If one concludes, however, that the U.S. position—that some uses could potentially be lawful—has merit, one reaches the question of the prerequisites for a *per se* rule.

The ICJ ostensibly assumed that the use of nuclear weapons could be held *per se* unlawful only if all uses would be unlawful in all circumstances. This appears, for example, from the Court's conclusions that it does not have sufficient facts to determine that nuclear weapons would be unlawful "in any circumstance,"[146] that the proportionality principle may not in itself exclude the use of nuclear weapons in self-defense "in all circumstances,"[147] and that, for the threat to use nuclear weapons implicit in the policy of deterrence to be unlawful, it would have to be the case that such use would "necessarily violate the principles of necessity and proportionality."[148] However, the Court's approach may have been affected by the wording of the question referred to it by the General Assembly: "Is the threat or use of

---

[144] *See* Chapter 1, notes 314–320, Chapter 2, note 26, and accompanying text; THE AIR FORCE MANUAL ON INTERNATIONAL LAW, *supra* note 13, at 6-3; THE NAVAL/MARINE COMMANDER'S HANDBOOK, *supra* note 1, at 10-2; ICJ Hearing, November 15, 1995, at 90.

[145] *See* Chapter 3, notes 237–245 and accompanying text; Nuclear Weapons Advisory Opinion ¶¶ 42, 48, 95, at 32, 35 I.L.M. at 822, 823, 829; dissenting opinion of Judge Higgins at 5, 35 I.L.M. 809, 937; dissenting opinion of Judge Weeramantry at 70, 35 I.L.M. at 915.

[146] Nuclear Weapons Advisory Opinion ¶ 95, at 32, 35 I.L.M. at 829. *See* Chapter 3, notes 9, 30, 43, 237, 245, 249, and accompanying text.

[147] *Id.* ¶ 42, at 18, 35 I.L.M. at 822. *See* Chapter 3, notes 30, 62, 237–242, 303 and accompanying text.

[148] *Id.* ¶ 48, at 19, 35 I.L.M. at 823. *See* Chapter 3, note 239 and accompanying text.

nuclear weapons in any circumstance permitted under international law?"[149]

Judge Higgins in her dissenting opinion assumed that 100% certainty must be present for there to be *per se* illegality: "I do not ... exclude the possibility that such a weapon could be unlawful by reference to the humanitarian law, if its use could never comply with its requirements—no matter what specific type within that class of weapon was being used and no matter where it might be used."[150]

This issue deserves more attention. I have described in Chapter 4 numerous bases for inferring that, under widely accepted principles of law, a *per se* rule can arise under circumstances of less than 100% applicability,[151] and that this is particularly appropriate where unlawfulness would exist in the vast majority of cases and the potential benefits of avoiding the repercussions of unlawful uses exceed the benefits of using such weapons in instances of putative lawfulness.[152] A number of the judges of the ICJ, in their individual opinions, addressed the issue. Judge Shahabuddeen stated, "[I]n judging of the admissibility of a particular means of warfare, it is necessary, in my

---

[149] *Id.* ¶ 1, at 4, 35 I.L.M. at 811 (question presented to the Court by U.N. General Assembly resolution 49/75 K, adopted on December 15, 1994). *See* Chapter 3, note 9 and accompanying text.

[150] Dissenting opinion of Judge Higgins at 5, 35 I.L.M. 809, 937. *See also* dissenting opinion of Judge Schwebel at 5, 8, and 13, 35 I.L.M. at 836, 840, and 842. *See* Chapter 3, notes 237–243 and accompanying text.

[151] *See* Chapter 4, notes 3–13 and accompanying text. *See, e.g.,* International Encyclopedia of Comparative Law, § 2-114 (Andre Tunc ed., Vol. XI, Part I) (1983); B.S. MARKENSINIS, A COMPARATIVE INTRODUCTION TO THE GERMAN LAW OF TORTS 700–705 (3rd ed. 1994); Christopher H. Schroeder, *Rights Against Risks*, 86 COLUM. L. REV. 495, 500–506, 523–524 (April 1986) (citing R. SARTORIUS, INDIVIDUAL CONDUCT AND SOCIAL NORMS 59–68, 530–532 (1975)); Frank H. Easterbrook, *Vertical Arrangements and The Rule of Reason*, 53 ANTITRUST L.J. 135, 157 (1984); Continental T.V. Inc. v. GTE Sylvania Inc., 457 U.S. 322, 344, 102 S.Ct. 2466 (1982).

[152] *See* Christopher H. Schroeder, *Rights Against Risks*, at 503–506 (citing R. SARTORIUS, INDIVIDUAL CONDUCT AND SOCIAL NORMS 59–68 (1975)) ("In general prophylaxis is a plausible strategy whenever; (1) most, but not all, acts belonging to the class are wrong, and (2) attempts to pick right acts in the class from wrong ones are unreliable."). This article originally appeared at 86 COLUM. L. REV. 495 (1986). Reprinted with permission. *See also* Chapter 4, notes 3–5, 10, 25–31, 37–39, and accompanying text.

opinion, to consider what the means can do in the ordinary course of warfare, even if it may not do it in all circumstances."[153]

Judge Weeramantry, addressing the issue from the perspective of nuclear decision-making, concluded that nuclear weapons should be declared illegal in all circumstances, with the proviso that if such use would be lawful "in some circumstances, however improbable, those circumstances need to be specified."[154] Judge Weeramantry stated:

> A factor to be taken into account in determining the legality of the use of nuclear weapons, having regard to their enormous potential for global devastation, is the process of decision-making in regard to the use of nuclear weapons.
>
> A decision to use nuclear weapons would tend to be taken, if taken at all, in circumstances which do not admit of fine legal evaluations. It will, in all probability, be taken at a time when passions run high, time is short and the facts are unclear. It will not be a carefully measured decision taken after a detailed and detached evaluation of all relevant circumstances of fact. It would be taken under extreme pressure and stress. Legal matters requiring considered evaluation may have to be determined within minutes, perhaps even by military rather than legally trained personnel, when they are in fact so complex as to have engaged this Court's attention for months. The fate of humanity cannot fairly be made to depend on such a decision.
>
> Studies have indeed been made of the process of nuclear decision-making and they identify four characteristics of a nuclear crisis. These characteristics are:
>
> 1. The shortage of time for making crucial decisions. This is the fundamental aspect of all crises.
>
> 2. The high stakes involved and, in particular, the expectation of severe loss to the national interest.
>
> 3. The high uncertainty resulting from the inadequacy of clear information, *e.g.*, what is going on?, What is the intent of the enemy?; and
>
> 4. The leaders are often constrained by political considerations, restricting their options.[155]

---

[153] Dissenting opinion of Judge Shahabuddeen at 17, 35 I.L.M. at 869. *See* Chapter 3, note 241 and accompanying text.

[154] Dissenting opinion of Judge Weeramantry at 70, 35 I.L.M. at 915. *See* Chapter 3, note 242 and accompanying text.

[155] *Id.* (citing Conn Nugent, *How a Nuclear War Might Begin*, in PROCEEDINGS OF THE SIXTH WORLD CONGRESS OF THE INTERNATIONAL PHYSICIANS FOR THE PREVENTION OF NUCLEAR WAR 117). *See* Chapter 3, note 243 and accompanying text.

Judge Weeramantry further concluded that, even if there were a nuclear weapon that totally eliminated the dissemination of radiation and was not a weapon of mass destruction, the Court, because of the technical difficulties involved, would not be able "to define those nuclear weapons which are lawful and those which are unlawful," and accordingly that the Court must "speak of legality in general terms."[156]

Even using the U.S. formulation of requiring 100% unanimity, there is room for "sub-classes" of *per se* unlawfulness. Based on the Court's decision, there is a basis for concluding that the use of strategic nuclear weapons and the wide scale use of tactical nuclear weapons or their use in urban areas, would be *per se* unlawful.[157] As far as equipment is concerned, this would ostensibly render unlawful the use of something on the order of 80% of the nuclear weapons in the United States' active arsenal. As far as circumstances are concerned, this would ostensibly render unlawful a very large portion of the instances in which the United States might use such weapons.

To the objection that such piecemeal illegalization would be incomplete or unworkable, the answer is that we already have something analogous in practice and that, in any event, social and political evolution, like chance in catastrophe theory,[158] work in sequential steps as well as jumps. Incrementalism in the right direction is not necessary bad, and can be infinitely better than nothing, particularly if it is the most that is available at a particular point in time.

As to the workability of partial limitations, the United States has already undertaken numerous such limitations. In addition to the pledge not to use nuclear weapons against non-nuclear adversaries,[159] the United States has agreed not to use nuclear weapons, subject to certain conditions:

---

[156] *Id.* at 84, 35 I.L.M. at 922. *See* Chapter 3, note 244 and accompanying text.

It is unclear whether Judge Koroma in his dissenting opinion, in concluding that the use of nuclear weapons would be unlawful "in any circumstance," was assuming that *per se* illegality required every possible use be unlawful. *See* dissenting opinion of Judge Koroma at 1, 35 I.L.M. at 925. *See* Chapter 3, note 245 and accompanying text.

[157] *See* Chapter 3, notes 10–11 and accompanying text. *See, e.g.,* Nuclear Weapons Advisory Opinion ¶¶ 95, 105. E., at 36, 35 I.L.M. at 829, 835.

[158] *See* Chapter 22, notes 46–59 and accompanying text.

[159] *See supra* note 75 and accompanying text.

- in Latin America, pursuant to the Treaty of Tlatelolco of February 14, 1967;[160]
in the South Pacific, pursuant to the Treaty of Rarotonga of August 6, 1985;[161]
- in Southeast Asia, pursuant to the Southeast Asia Nuclear-Weapon-Free Zone Convention of December 15, 1995;[162]
- in Africa, pursuant to the nuclear weapons free zone convention signed on April 1, 1996;[163] and
- in the Antarctic, pursuant to the Antarctic Treaty of 1959.[164]

So also, the United States, in its appearance before the ICJ in the Nuclear Weapons Advisory case, strongly reassured the Court that the U.S. doctrine of nuclear deterrence is purely of a defensive nature, such that the United States would never use such other weapons other than in a defensive mode.[165]

It could be said that this issue I have raised as to the prerequisites for a *per se* rule are semantic, since *per se* rules I have identified, as arising under circumstances of less than 100%, are themselves generally subject to exceptions and qualifications.[166] Nonetheless, on the assumption that law matters, it seems clear that, were the United States to recognize the *per se* unlawfulness of the use of nuclear weapons, in whole or in part, even if there were qualifications and footnotes to the recognition, a powerful first step would have been taken, with positive implications for training, planning, and weapons procurement programs, inevitably affecting the actions and potential actions of the United States and potentially other States in a crisis situation.

---

[160] *See* Nuclear Weapons Advisory Opinion ¶ 59(a), at 22, 35 I.L.M. at 824. Other nuclear States imposed further limitations on their ratification of the Protocol. *See* Chapter 3, notes 127–133 and accompanying text.

[161] *See id.* ¶ 59(b), at 22–23, 35 I.L.M. at 824–25.

[162] *See id.* ¶ 63, at 25, 35 I.L.M. at 826.

[163] *See id.*

[164] *See id.* ¶ 60, at 24, 35 I.L.M. at 825.

[165] *See* ICJ Hearing, November 15, 1995, at 86. *See also* Chapter 2, notes 130–135 and accompanying text.

[166] *See* Chapter 4; Chapter 4, notes 3–5, 10–13, 16–30, 41–42, and accompanying text. *See also supra* note 151 and accompanying text.

Deterrence, the Naked and Toothless Emperor

The United States objected to the ICJ that the outlawing of the use of nuclear weapons would undermine nuclear deterrence, characterized as the mainstay of U.S. and Western defense policy throughout the nuclear era. But nuclear deterrence, long the naked emperor, is now also largely the toothless emperor.

During the Cold War it was recognized that these weapons were so destructive and the likelihood of escalation so high that they could not be used;[167] the threat of deterrence was recognized by the main protagonists to be essentially an idle one,[168] subject to the ever present possibility of irrational action in a confrontation.

Now we have a strategic environment where the major types of enemies the United States faces—terrorist nations, groups and individuals—are largely not subject to deterrence,[169] and in a sense the

---

[167] *See* Chapter 24; and Chapter 24, notes 2–4, 9–10, 44–45, and accompanying text. *See also* H AROLD W. CHASE & ALLEN H. LERMAN, KENNEDY AND THE PRESS: THE NEWS CONFERENCES 186 (1965) (statement of John F. Kennedy, Feb. 14, 1962); Cardinal O'Connor, *Hearings on The Role of Arms Control in U.S. Defense Policy, before the Committee on Foreign Affairs, House of Representatives*, 98th Cong. 2nd Sess. (June 20, 21, 26; July 25, 1984), at 143; RICHARD NIXON, THE REAL WAR 163 (1980); Secretary of State Dean Rusk, Organizing the Peace for Man's Survival, Address before the Council on Foreign Relations (May 24, 1966), *reprinted in* DEPT OF ST. BULL., JUNE 1966, at 1407.

[168] *See* Chapter 23, notes 34–36, Chapter 24, note 46, Chapter 25, notes 1–3, 12–46, and accompanying text. *See generally* Chapter 25. *See also* DOCTRINE FOR JOINT NUCLEAR OPERATIONS, *supra* note 18, at i, ix (Dec. 15, 1995); Chairman Dante B. Fascell of the House Committee on Foreign Affairs, *Hearings on The Role of Arms Control in U.S. Defense Policy, before the Committee on Foreign Affairs, House of Representatives*, 98th Cong. 2nd Sess., (June 20, 21, 26; July 25, 1984) at 158; Bundy et al., *Nuclear Weapons and the Atlantic Alliance*, 60 FOREIGN AFF. 753 (1982).

[169] *See* Chapter 18, notes 48–62, Chapter 26, note 15, Chapter 27, notes 6–8, and accompanying text. *See generally* Chapter 27. *See also* DOCTRINE FOR JOINT THEATER NUCLEAR OPERATIONS, *supra* note 21, at I-3; *Proliferation of Weapons of Mass Destruction: Assessing the Risks, supra* note 59, at 70 (citing John Mearscheimer, *Back to the Future: Instability in Europe After the Cold War*, INT'L SECURITY, vol. 15, no. 1, Sum. 1990, at 37–38); PRESIDENT WILLIAM J. CLINTON, A NATIONAL SECURITY STRATEGY FOR A NEW CENTURY 6 (The White House, October 1998) at 7.

President Clinton, in his 1998 National Security Strategy, stated:
While our overall deterrence posture—nuclear and conventional—has been effective against most potential adversaries, a range of

threat of use of nuclear weapons, as suggested above, only legitimizes the kinds of force they threaten.

Secretary Kissinger has stated:

> I have also mentioned the transformation of the nature of power wrought by nuclear weapons. Because nuclear weapons are so cataclysmic, they are hardly relevant to a whole gamut of challenges: probes, guerrilla wars, local crises.[170]

The December 1997 Report of the National Defense Panel made the point explicitly as to the insufficiency of nuclear deterrence against today's threats:

> Traditional U.S. nuclear policies may not be sufficient to deter nuclear, chemical, or biological attacks by a rogue state against U.S. allies and coalition partners or forward bases and staging areas to which we seek access. It is unlikely, moreover, that our nuclear forces would deter nonstate actors (terrorists, criminals, or others) who seek to coerce or punish the United States or its allies.[171]

In addition, our conventional capabilities now are so overwhelming that we are capable of delivering a devastating response through conventional weapons to virtually any action an enemy might take against us or our allies[172]—and the potential efficacy of such weapons would only be enhanced by the additional resources that could be committed to them following the delegitimization of nuclear weapons.

Even if it were assumed that this situation could end up having us engaged in conflicts that might have been deterred by nuclear weapons,

---

> terrorist and criminal organization may not be deterred by traditional deterrent threats. For these actors to be deterred, they must believe that any type of attack against the United States or its citizens will be attributed to them and that we will respond effectively and decisively to protect our national interests and ensure that justice is done.

Id. at 12.

[170] HENRY KISSINGER, WHITE HOUSE YEARS 115 (1979). *See* Chapter 24, note 15 and accompanying text.

[171] NATIONAL DEFENSE PANEL, TRANSFORMING DEFENSE: NATIONAL SECURITY IN THE 21ST CENTURY 51 (Dec. 1997) (available at <http://www.dtic.mil/ndp/>). *See* Chapter 18, notes 47–52 and accompanying text.

[172] *See* Chapter 28; Chapter 27, note 5, Chapter 29, notes 55–57, 124, 153–169, 208, and accompanying text. *See also* WILLIAM S. COHEN, 1999 ANNUAL REPORT TO THE PRESIDENT AND THE CONGRESS Chap. 10, p. 5, The Revolution in Military Affairs, and Joint Vision 2010.

there would be potentially be an inestimable net saving in light of the likely catastrophic effects of a failure of nuclear deterrence.

Recognition of the unlawfulness of nuclear weapons use would be an act not of do-good-ism but of supreme self-interest. While paradoxically such a recognition might leave us, at least in the short run, spending more for weapons, we would then be acquiring potentially usable conventional weapons.[173] We would also in time reap the benefits of fostering the observance of law.[174]

As to such benefits, *The Air Force Manual on International Law* quotes the Chairman of the Joint Chiefs of Staff:

> The Armed Forces of the United States have benefited from, and highly value, the humanitarianism encompassed by the laws of war. Many are alive today only because of the mutual restraint imposed by these rules, notwithstanding the fact that the rules have been applied imperfectly.[175]

Even in the relatively short Kosovo operation, under current supply policy, the United States quickly ran short in its supply of modern conventional weapons, including the JDAMS and Maverick cruise missiles,[176] nearly encountering a "'winchester'" situation, Air Force code language for being out of ammunition.[177] The Air Force experienced shortages of "stand-off" weapons, those fired from afar.

---

[173] *See* Chapter 18, notes 40–42 and accompanying text.

[174] *See* Chapter 22, notes 1–5 and accompanying text.

[175] THE AIR FORCE MANUAL ON INTERNATIONAL LAW, *supra* note 13, at 1-9 (citing Address by General George S. Brown, Chairman of the Joint Chiefs of Staff, DOD News Release No. 479-74 (10 Oct 1974)). *See* Chapter 1, note 34 and accompanying text.

[176] *See* Paul Richter, *Crisis in Yugoslavia, Almost All U.S. Airstrikes Involve 'Smart' Bombs*, LOS ANGELES TIMES, Apr. 13, 1999, at A19; David Learmount, *Smart Bombs in Demand,* FLIGHT INT'L, June 9, 1999; Chapter 28, notes 43–46 and accompanying text.

[177] Bryan Bender, *JDAM Stocks Running Very Low, Says USA,* JANE'S DEFENCE WEEKLY, May 5, 1999. *See also* James Wallace, *Boeing Plans to Speed Up Production of Bomb Kits,* SEATTLE POST-INTELLIGENCER, Apr. 2, 1999, at A4; Chapter 28, notes 49–51 and accompanying text.

Obviously, development of high tech weapons continues apace. Networking between unmanned aerial vehicles and various munitions, for example, is being actively worked on, and so are their production runs and trial forays. *See* Cook, *Serb Air War Changes Gear,* JANE'S DEFENCE WEEKLY HEADLINES, Mar. 4, 1999; *JDAM Inventory 'Touch and Go' Over Kosovo,* ARMED FORCES NEWS, Apr. 30, 1999; Chapter 28, notes 49–50 and accompanying text.

"'Many of our air forces ... have to fly more or less over the target, which is the most stupid thing you can do because you expose yourself to the enemy's air defenses.'"[178] Deficiencies in transport capability were also experienced. Forces bearing the smart weapons deployed "'deplorably'"[179] slowly in transporting Army helicopters into service from other sites in Europe.

A potential result of the shift in focus implicit in delegitimizing nuclear weapons would be the instigation of practices designed to avoid such winchester situations, certainly so early in a relatively minor conflict.

In addition, as discussed in Chapter 22, the policy of deterrence itself introduces significant risk factors, including:

- The Danger of Precipitating a Nuclear War;
- The Fostering of an Arms Race;
- The Fostering of Nuclear Proliferation;
- The Risks of Terrorism;
- The Risks of Human and Equipment Failure;
- Risks of Testing, Production, Storage and Disposal of Nuclear Weapons Materials;
- The Risk of the Degradation of Conventional Weapons Capability;
- Jeopardy to Rule of Law; and
- Overriding Risk Factors as to the Likelihood that the Unlikely Will Occur.

If my overall conclusions are correct, the policy of nuclear deterrence is also vulnerable under the established principle of law accepted by the United States[180] and confirmed by the ICJ in the Nuclear Weapons Advisory Opinion,[181] to the effect that it is unlawful

---

[178] John D. Morrocco, *Kosovo Conflict Highlights Limits of Airpower and Capability Gaps*, AVIATION WEEK & SPACE TECH., May 17, 1999, at 31 (citing Gen. Klaus Naumann of Germany, the head of NATO Military Committee for three years up to 1999). *See* Chapter 28, note 51 and accompanying text.

[179] *Id.* (citing Gen. Klaus Naumann). *See* Chapter 28, note 52 and accompanying text.

[180] *See* THE NAVAL/MARINE COMMANDER'S HANDBOOK, *supra* note 1, at 6-4; THE AIR FORCE MANUAL ON INTERNATIONAL LAW, *supra* note 13, at 5-7; Nuclear Weapons Advisory Opinion ¶ 48, at 19, 35 I.L.M. at 823; Chapter 1, notes 95–97, 179, Chapter 2, notes 91, 131–132, Chapter 3, notes 2, 142–164, and accompanying text.

[181] *See* Chapter 3, notes 2, 142–164, and accompanying text. The Court stated, "[N]o State—whether or not it defended the policy of deterrence—

to threaten to do that which it is unlawful to do. This vulnerability is highlighted by the statements noted above in the U.S. military manuals, whereby the military acknowledge that deterrence threatens disproportionate and indiscriminate injury.[182]

The Federalist Papers and Denuclearization

The U.S. constitutional structure of separation of powers and federalism is based on a skeptical view of human nature no less realistic today. Justifying the separation of powers, James Madison in No. 51 of the Federalist Papers stated:

> The provision for defense must in this, as in all other cases, be made commensurate to the danger of attack. Ambition must be made to counteract ambition. The interest of the man must be connected with the constitutional rights of the place. It may be a reflection on human nature that such devices should be necessary to control the abuses of government. But what is government itself but the greatest of all reflections on human nature? If men were angels, no government would be necessary. If angels were to govern men, neither external nor internal controls on government would be necessary. In framing a government which is to be administered by men over men, the great difficulty lies in this: you must first enable the government to control the governed; and in the next place oblige it to control itself. A dependence on the people is, no doubt, the primary control on the government; but experience has taught mankind the necessity of auxiliary precautions.[183]

The same human nature, indeed in the even less bridled form of the international relations of sovereign nations, is at play on the issue of nuclear weapons. Ordinary prudence on the part of the United States would seem to point to the wisdom of delegitimizing nuclear weapons.

The fact that these weapons cannot be uninvented and that a convention acknowledging their unlawfulness may not be politically achievable at this time does not mean there is no point in recognizing

---

suggested to the Court that it would be lawful to threaten to use force if the use of force contemplated would be illegal," and "[i]f an envisaged use of weapons would not meet the requirements of humanitarian law, a threat to engage in such use would also be contrary to that law." Nuclear Weapons Advisory Opinion ¶ 48, at 19, 35 I.L.M. at 823. *See also id.* ¶¶ 47, 78 at 19, 28, 35 I.L.M. at 823, 827, 913.

[182] *See* Chapter 29, notes 37, 39–40, and accompanying text.

[183] THE FEDERALIST NO. 51, at 319–320 (James Madison) (Isaac Kramnick ed., Penguin Classics 1987).

their unlawfulness.[184] Kenneth Adelman in 1984 in the early days of the Reagan Administration wrote a then provocative article in *Foreign Affairs* on arms control without agreements through a process of independent reductions potentially evolving into what might be called conscious parallelism.[185] I contemplate something similar through the U.S. recognition of the unlawfulness of the use of nuclear weapons.

Of course, the U.S. recognition of the unlawfulness of the use of nuclear weapons and jettisoning of the policy of nuclear deterrence would no more mean that nuclear weapons would never be used than that they would be uninvented. Unlawfulness of actual and threatened use does not necessarily mean the unlawfulness of possession, and, pending further developments, nations would remain in possession.

Which means that implicit or virtual deterrence would continue, but, in the meantime, presumably military training and planning—indeed, the entire military mindset, as reflected in documents such as the Joint Chief of Staff's *Joint Nuclear Operations*[186] and *Joint Theater Nuclear Operations*[187] manuals—would ostensibly shift to conventional

---

[184] The International Physicians for the Prevention of Nuclear War, The International Association of Lawyers Against Nuclear Arms, and The International Network of Engineers and Scientists Against Proliferation have proposed a Model Nuclear Weapons Convention banning the use and possession of nuclear weapons. *See* The Model Convention on the Prohibition of the Development, Testing, Production, Stockpiling, Transfer, Use and Threat of Use of Nuclear Weapons and on Their Elimination, *reprinted in* SECURITY AND SURVIVAL: THE CASE FOR A NUCLEAR WEAPONS CONVENTION (1999), available at <http://www.ippnw.org>.

However, in a political environment where the Comprehensive Test Ban Treaty cannot be passed in the U.S. Senate, *see* Eric Schmitt, *Senate Kills Test ban Treaty in Crushing Loss for Clinton; Evokes Versailles Pact Defeat*, THE NEW YORK TIMES, Oct. 14, 1999, at A1; *See also,* James K. Wyerman, Gilbert Tucker & Paul Sedan, Letter to Editor, CHRISTIAN SCIENCE MONITOR, July 2, 1999, at 10; Chapter 21, note 2 and accompanying text, nor START II in the Russian Duma, *see* Linda D. Kozaryn, *Clinton, Yeltsin Confer on NATO, Security Issues,* AMERICAN FORCES PRESS SERVICE, Jun. 17, 1998, <http://www.defenselink.mil/news/Mar1997/03251997_9703251.html>; Chapter 19, note 7 and accompanying text, the reaching of such a convention banning use of nuclear weapons seems unlikely pending political changes. Hence, in the interim, my suggestion of the Ken Adelman type approach.

[185] *See* Kenneth L. Adelman, *Arms Control With and Without Agreements*, FOREIGN AFF., 1984/1985 Winter, at 240.

[186] DOCTRINE FOR JOINT NUCLEAR OPERATIONS, *supra* note 18.

[187] DOCTRINE FOR JOINT THEATER NUCLEAR OPERATIONS, *supra* note 21.

weapons. As the United States argued before the Court, in language I have pointed to repeatedly:

> [E]ach of the Permanent Members of the Security Council has made an immense commitment of human and material resources to acquire and maintain stocks of nuclear weapons and their delivery systems, and many other States have decided to rely for their security on these nuclear capabilities. If these weapons could not lawfully be used in individual or collective self-defense under any circumstances, there would be no credible threat of such use in response to aggression and deterrent policies would be futile and meaningless.[188]

As noted, the United States went even further in its memorandum to the ICJ, in suggesting that the United States could not continue to maintain nuclear weapons if they were unlawful:

> It is well known that the Permanent Members of the Security Council possess nuclear weapons and have developed and deployed systems for their use in armed conflict. These States would not have borne the expense and effort of acquiring and maintaining these weapons and delivery systems if they believed that the use of nuclear weapons was generally prohibited.[189]

As Judge Weeramantry concluded, a recognition of illegality could be a "building block in the realization of a world ruled by law."[190] Stressing the importance that the law be known, Judge Weeramantry— drawing on a deep insight of our legal systems—stated, "Not for nothing were the XII Tables publicly posted in the Roman forum."[191]

---

[188] Statement of Michael J. Matheson (Deputy Legal Advisor, Department of State) in oral argument to the Court, ICJ Hearing, November 15, 1995, at 78.

John H McNeill (Senior Deputy General Counsel, Department of Defense), in his oral argument to the Court, similarly asserted that, if the law of reprisals were to be construed as prohibiting categorically the use of nuclear weapons, "the negative implications for strategic deterrence would be obvious and dire." *See* ICJ Hearing, November 15, 1995, at 95. *See* Chapter 2, note 131, Chapter 3, note 323, and accompanying text

[189] U.S. ICJ Memorandum/GA App. at 14, citing Report of the U.N. Secretary-General on Nuclear Weapons, A/45/373, 18 September 1990, pp. 19–24. *See* Chapter 2, note 132, Chapter 3, note 324, and accompanying text.

[190] Dissent of Judge Weeramantry in the WHO Advisory Opinion, 1996 I.C.J. 68, 159. *See* Chapter 3, note 326 and accompanying text.

[191] *Id. See* Chapter 3, note 327 and accompanying text.

Denial and the Nature of Evil

No one can pretend nuclear issues are easy to deal with. Carl Sagan pointed out the psychological element of denial that has the potential of closing our minds to these matters:

> Understanding the long-term consequences of nuclear war is not a problem amenable to experimental verification—at least not more than once. Another part of the resistance is psychological. Most people—recognizing nuclear war as a grave and terrifying prospect, and nuclear policy as immersed in technical complexities, official secrecy and bureaucratic inertia—tend to practice what psychiatrists call denial: putting the agonizing problem out of our heads, since there seems nothing we can do about it. Even policy makers must feel this temptation from time to time. But for policymakers there is another concern: if it turns out that nuclear war could end our civilization or our species, such a finding might be considered a retroactive rebuke to those responsible, actively or passively, in the past on in the present, for the global nuclear arms race.[192]

There is a further element, the routine nature these extraordinary matters can assume over time. Hannah Arendt's comments upon observing the Eichmann trial are worth remembering. Noting that our literary, theological and philosophic traditions of thought have conceptualized evil as "something demonic" incarnated in Satan and based on some wicked vice, Arendt stated:

> [W]hat I was confronted with was utterly different and still undeniably factual. I was struck by a manifest shallowness in the doer that made it impossible to trace the uncontestable evil of his deeds to any deeper level of roots or motives. The deeds were monstrous, but the doer—at least the very effective one now on trial—was quite ordinary, commonplace, and neither demonic nor monstrous. There was no sign in him of firm ideological convictions or of specific evil motives, and the only notable characteristic one could detect in his past behavior as well as in his behavior during the trial and throughout the pre-trial police examination was something entirely negative: it was not stupidity but thoughtlessness.[193]

---

[192] Carl Sagan, *Nuclear War and Climatic Catastrophe: Some Policy Implications, in* THE NUCLEAR CONTROVERSY, A FOREIGN AFFAIRS READER 117 (1985).

[193] HANNAH ARENDT, THE LIFE OF THE MIND 3–4 (1978).

We know far more about these weapons than was known when President Truman approved the bombings of Hiroshima and Nagasaki and cannot escape the burden of such knowledge.

It is not as if there is no historical model for delegitimizing nuclear weapons. In addition to the numerous limitations on nuclear weapons agreed to by the superpowers during the Cold War,[194] the various security assurances extended by the United States as to the use of these weapons, the geographical limitations on areas of possible use already accepted by the United States,[195] and the analogous conventions banning chemical and biological weapons,[196] there are also a number of nations that have developed or inherited nuclear weapons programs and then stepped back.

By 1998, South Africa had fully assembled six nuclear devices, each with an estimated 50 to 60 kilograms of highly enriched uranium and having yields of 10 to 18 kilotons.[197] When the security developments that had ostensibly motivated South Africa's nuclear program receded,[198] South Africa made a radical change. It dismantled its nuclear weapons program:

> [T]he story of South Africa's acquisition and subsequent dismantlement of its nuclear arsenal holds vital lessons. Pretoria's action establishes the precedent of nuclear rollback for other threshold nuclear states. Moreover, the careful and responsible manner in which South Africa dismantled its weapons, joined the NPT, cooperated fully with the IAEA and accepted comprehensive safeguards on its nuclear facilities may serve as a useful future model. Finally, Pretoria's gradual realization that its nuclear weapons were not only superfluous but actually counterproductive to achieving South Africa's political, military and economic objectives may be the most important lesson of all.[199]

---

[194] *See* Chapter 2, note 37, Chapter 3, notes 100–139, and accompanying text. *See also* THE AIR FORCE MANUAL ON INTERNATIONAL LAW, *supra* note 13, at 6-6; 6-10 n.17.

[195] *See supra* note 75. *See also* THE NAVAL/MARINE COMMANDER'S HANDBOOK, *supra* note 1, at 10-3 to 10-10.

[196] *See* Chapter 27, note 9 and accompanying text. *See also* DOCTRINE FOR NUCLEAR, BIOLOGICAL, AND CHEMICAL (NBC) DEFENSE Appendix, *supra* note 92, at A-A-1.

[197] *See* Chapter 23, note 9 and accompanying text. *See also* J.W. de Villiers et al., *Why South Africa Gave Up the Bomb*, FOREIGN AFF., Nov./Dec. 1993, at 98.

[198] *See id.*

[199] *Id.* at 109.

Similarly, following the break-up of the Soviet Union, Belarus, Kazakhstan and Ukraine gave up their nuclear weapons, as a result of the Nunn-Lugar funding program,[200] whereby Congress provided funding to enable nations from the former USSR to dismantle chemical, biological and nuclear weapons.[201] The Nunn-Lugar act "led Russia to willingly destroy 4,000 warheads that were all aimed at [the United States]."[202]

So also with North Korea, although not in as completed a fashion. The United States, through constructive funding, essentially "bought" inspections rights to some underground sites in North Korea suspected of containing a nuclear weapons reactor or other plants.[203] Similarly, Taiwan had pursued a nuclear weapons program in the 1970s and 1980s, but abandoned it in 1988 under pressure from the United States.[204]

Unlawfulness of Second Use

The above analysis as to applicable law and risk factors applies to second as well as first uses of nuclear weapons, whether viewed from

---

[200] *See* Chapter 18, notes 59–61, Chapter 23, note 16, and accompanying text. The Nunn-Lugar Act or Cooperative Threat Reduction Act provided funding to enable nations from the former USSR to dismantle and account for chemical, biological and nuclear weapons. *See Remarks by Secretary of Defense William S. Cohen to the Boston Chamber of Commerce*, Boston Marriott Copley Place, Boston (Sept. 17, 1998) <http://www.defenselink.mil/speeches/1998/s19980917secdef.htm>; Robert S. Norris & William M. Arkin, *Russian (C.I.S.) Strategic Nuclear Forces: End of 1995*, BULL. OF THE ATOMIC SCIENTISTS, Mar. 13, 1996.

[201] *See* Chapter 18, note 59, and accompanying text; *Remarks by Secretary of Defense William S. Cohen to the Boston Chamber of Commerce*, *supra* note 200.

[202] Dr. John J. Hamre, Deputy Secretary of Defense, *Remarks at the Defense Threat Reduction Agency Rollout Ceremony*, Dulles International Airport, Va. (Oct. 1, 1998) <http://www.defenselink.mil/speeches/1998/r19981102-depsecdef.html>. *See* Chapter 18, note 61 and accompanying text.

[203] *See* Chapter 18, note 62, Chapter 23, note 11, and accompanying text; Nuclear Weapons Program—North Korea, <http://www.fas.org/nuke/guide/dprk/nuke/index.html>; *Clinton's North Korean Headache*, JANE'S INFO. GROUP FOREIGN REPORT, Dec. 17, 1998; *Remarks by Secretary of Defense William S. Cohen to the Boston Chamber of Commerce, Boston Marriott, supra* note 200; David E. Sanger, *N. Korea Consents to U.S. Inspection of a Suspect Site*, THE NEW YORK TIMES, Mar. 17, 1999, at A1.

[204] *See* Sanger, *supra* note 203; Chapter 18, note 62 and accompanying text.

the perspective of general unlawfulness under the rules discussed above or the limitations on lawful reprisal.

Obviously, if my conclusion is correct that the use of nuclear weapons is *per se* unlawful, second use, absent justification as a reprisal, would be as unlawful as first use. Even if the U.S. position is correct that a limited use of low-yield nuclear weapons in a remote area could be lawful, I would argue that the second use would nonetheless be unlawful because of the heightened risks attendant such further use.

Specifically, even assuming the first use could be conducted in such a limited fashion as not to threaten impermissible effects, the second use—constituting the fact of a mutual willingness to engage in nuclear war and the heightened likelihood of precipitating major escalation—would involve the risk of such severe and uncontrollable effects as to trigger unlawfulness under the analysis set forth above and in Chapter 29.

Moreover, thinking about the matter in such artificial bites—the lawfulness of the first versus that of the second use—is artificial since the whole process of strike and counter-strike is interrelated, and the unlawfulness of the second use implies the unlawfulness of the first use. Presumably, one of the very reasons the first use would have been unlawful would be that it foreseeably would have set in motion a chain of events potentially leading to the second use. Since the rules of necessity, proportionality, and discrimination are rules of reason, they must be applied in light of all the reasonably available facts, making it inappropriate to evaluate the lawfulness of any particular use based on just that use without reference to the totality of the inter-related possible uses and risks.

And, of course, just as the legality of the first use must be evaluated in light of its likelihood of precipitating the second use and other potential effects, the second use must be evaluated in light of the full range of *its* potential effects.

Nor could a second use be justified under the law of reprisal. As we saw, the United States recognizes as a requirement for lawful reprisal that the strike be limited to that necessary to force the adversary to cease its unlawful actions.[205] If my factual conclusions are correct, a second use would not be susceptible of being so limited.

First of all, the effects of the second use would be uncontrollable, as discussed in Chapter 29. Uncontrollable actions by definition cannot be limited and could not be constrained within the requirements for

---

[205] *See* discussion of the application of the law of reprisal to nuclear weapons in Chapter 29, notes 227–242 and accompanying text.

lawful reprisal. Similarly, if my factual conclusions as to the capabilities of modern high tech conventional weapons are well-founded, the legitimate objective of reprisal could be achieved through conventional weapons.

Look at the potential effects of the second use: the sheer destructiveness of the nuclear weapon(s) used; the electromagnetic effects; the radiation effects; the risks of hitting the wrong target; the risks of precipitating escalation to higher levels of nuclear warfare; the risks of precipitating the enemy's or even one's own further preemptive strikes; the long-term effects of radioactive fallout; the risks of precipitating chemical or biological weapons use. Any one of these effects would likely exceed the level of action necessary to convince the other side to constrain itself to lawful warfare and be so provocative as to have the opposite effect of precipitating total violence. Taken together, these effects would appear to be of a radically different nature and order than that contemplated by the law of reprisal.[206]

The very premise of the attempted justification of the second use as a reprisal (the assumption that the first strike was unlawful for failure to comply with such rules as those of necessity, proportionality, discrimination, civilian immunity and neutrality) portends the unlawfulness of the second use. Just as the likely effects of the first use were impermissibly excessive and far-reaching, so too would be the likely effects of the second use.

The point I have make throughout—that under applicable law the evaluation of the lawfulness of the use of nuclear weapons must be made in light of the types of circumstances that would likely be present in situations in which nuclear weapons might intentionally be resorted to—again becomes important. While one can hypothesize anything, including the most remote of possibilities, and doing so is a central part of the lawyer's analytic approach, it is unlikely in the extreme that the United States or any nuclear power, having sustained a nuclear hit, would even try to limit its nuclear response, if it made one, to a level of force necessary to compel the adversary to comply with law.

---

[206] For the same reasons, a second use would likely fail to meet the requirement of proportionality recognized by the United States as an element of lawful reprisal. *See* Chapter 29, notes 228–233 and accompanying text. The risks of a second strike, particularly the radiation effects in time and space, are inherently disproportionate to the likelihood that the strike would cause the enemy to revert to lawful conducting of the war and the benefit of that likelihood.

While one can conjure up reprisals comparable to the limited strikes at remote sea or desert targets that were the basis of the U.S. defense of nuclear weapons before the ICJ, such legalistic exercises are unrealistic in the real world context of the types of circumstances in which these weapons might be used and their potential effects, and cannot reasonably serve as the basis for the evaluation of lawfulness.

The probabilities are overwhelming that the second use would be designed to punish the enemy and, not incidentally, in the case of a substantial nuclear adversary, to use one's own nuclear assets before they could be preemptively struck by the adversary, and to attempt to preemptively strike the adversary's nuclear assets (many of which would likely be "co-located" with civilian targets) before they could be used. Even assuming adequate command and control, crucial decisions would have to be made within a very short time and would likely be dictated largely by existing war plans contemplating nuclear weapons use. The notion of a second strike as limited to the legitimate objectives of reprisal seems oxymoronic.

In addition, the United States, while it disputes the applicability to nuclear weapons of the limitations upon reprisals imposed by Protocol I,[207] recognizes that the law of armed conflict, including that as to reprisals, is subject to the limitations inherent in the purposes of the law of armed conflict, such as preserving civilization and the possibility of the restoration of the peace, purposes that would likely be exceeded by the use of nuclear weapons.

Even if it were assumed that certain second uses of nuclear weapons, although otherwise unlawful, might be legitimized as reprisals, such legitimization—like the lawfulness of the limited use of a small number low-yield nuclear weapons in remote areas asserted by the United States before the ICJ—would only affect a small portion of the potential uses for nuclear weapons contemplated by U.S. policy and planning. It would leave unaffected the unlawfulness of the vast bulk of potential uses and virtually the totality of *likely* possible uses, including first uses against conventional, chemical and biological weapons targets, second uses intended to defeat and destroy the enemy, disproportionate second uses, and other high-megatonnage nuclear strikes with likely extreme effects.

The purported justification of the lawfulness of nuclear weapons based on the putative lawfulness of a second strike as a reprisal would

---

[207] *See* Chapter 1, notes 274–277 and accompanying text; Chapter 2, notes 127–129 and accompanying text. *See also* Chapter 3, notes 246–249 and accompanying text.

also be artificial in light of the fact that the United States, as a matter of policy, assertedly has generally not resorted to reprisals, based on their propensity to be excessive and counter-productive.[208] Even aside from the obvious potential for escalation as a result of a nuclear strike, the United States has particularly recognized that reprisals present "the potential for escalation"[209] and that "it is generally in our national interest to follow the law even if the enemy does not."[210]

Conclusion

Based on the above risk factors, their open and notorious nature, and the fact that a mental state of recklessness or less suffices for war crimes liability, it seems evident that virtually any use, and certainly the vast majority of uses, of nuclear weapons, in the types of circumstances in which such use would likely take place, would be unlawful, and hence that the use of such weapons is *per se* unlawful.

Whatever the best model for addressing such unlawfulness, we are capable of figuring it out. But we must first take the imaginative leap of integrating the insights that we no longer need these weapons and that they have themselves become the enemy and of accepting the implications of the applicable rules of law.

It was evident from the results of the Nuclear Posture Review that the strategic interests of the United States as to nuclear weapons legitimacy have shifted. The time has come to deal with this issue.

This late in the book, perhaps I might be forgiven a personal reference. The nuclear weapons program sent me to college. My father was an attorney, director of legal affairs, at what was then Thiokol Chemical Corporation, in charge of negotiating that company's contracts with the Pentagon for such programs as the Minuteman ICBM (If I recall correctly, Thiokol provided the solid fuel component and my father negotiated the contracts). He was also an old military man. Having never gotten over the fact that a medical problem had prevented his being sent overseas during the Second World War, he spent most of his life in the Army reserves, reaching the rank of Colonel. I remember how difficult it was for him when he joined the Washington D.C. Anti–Vietnam War Peace March with my sister Mona and me in the winter of 1969. If he could make that kind of leap, so can all the rest of us and so can the country.

---

[208] *See* discussion at Chapter 29, notes 234–242 and accompanying text.
[209] THE AIR FORCE COMMANDER'S HANDBOOK, *supra* note 13, at 8-1.
[210] *Id.*

I propose that the United States recognize the unlawfulness of nuclear weapons and start immediately acting accordingly in its personnel training, weapons development and placement, and contingency planning—and that, in this new millennium, we strive to lead the world into a non-nuclear weapons future. I cannot predict whether we will be successful, but it seems evident that, absent a serious effort, we will continue to leave our children hostage to some apocalyptic blunder. If even the improbable becomes likely over an extended period of time, the danger is that the merely likely at some point becomes the virtually inevitable.

Index

Note: Some entries that appear throughout the book, like United States and International Court of Justice, are not listed in the Index.

Author Biographical Sketch

Charles J. Moxley, Jr. is a practicing attorney who has served on the faculty of St. John's University School of Law and the adjunct faculty of New York Law School.

He received his law degree from Columbia University School of Law, where he concentrated in international law and was managing editor of the Columbia Journal of Transnational Law. He received an M.A. in Russian Area Studies and B.A. in political science from Fordham University.

Moxley has served on the board of the Lawyers Alliance for World Security, the Committee of International Arms Control and Security Affairs of the Association of the Bar of the City of New York, and the International Law Committee of the New York County Lawyers' Association.

Moxley is in private practice in New York City, specializing in the litigation and arbitration of complex disputes. He has served as an arbitrator, hearing and deciding many complex matters before the American Arbitration Association, and as a Special Master in Supreme Court, New York County.